THE ANNOTATED®
Shakespeare

THE ANNOTATED®
Shakespeare

VOLUME I

The Comedies

Edited, with Introductions, Notes,
a Biography and Bibliography by

A. L. ROWSE

Clarkson N. Potter, Inc./Publishers New York
DISTRIBUTED BY CROWN PUBLISHERS, INC.

Annotated, illustrated and designed by
Octavian Books Limited
Copyright © 1978 Orbis Publishing Limited

Published simultaneously in Great Britain by
Orbis Publishing Limited, 20–22 Bedfordbury,
London WC2

Printed in the U.S.A.

Library of Congress Cataloging in Publication Data
Shakespeare, William, 1564–1616.
    The annotated Shakespeare
    Bibliography: p.
    CONTENTS: v. 1. Comedies.—v. 2. Histories—
v. 3. I. Tragedies and romances.
        I. Rowse, Alfred Leslie 1903–   II. Title.
PR2754.R67   822.3′3   78-12271
ISBN 0-517-535092   ISBN 0-517-535068 (v. 1.)

Annotation and introduction text composed by
SX Composing Ltd., Rayleigh, Essex

The Shakespeare text used in this edition is that of the
Globe Edition (edited by William George Clark and
William Aldis Wright), Macmillan, 1900
10   9   8   7   6   5   4   3

CONTENTS

William Shakespeare

1564-1616

MORE IS KNOWN about William Shakespeare than any other of the Elizabethan dramatists, with the single exception of Ben Jonson. Even here we know far less about Ben's early life—more about the later, for he was ten years younger and lived right on into the reign of Charles I, when more information was available about everybody.

The reason for our fuller knowledge of Shakespeare's earlier life is that his father was a prominent townsman at Stratford-upon-Avon, where he rose to become alderman and bailiff (i.e. mayor) of the busy market-town. It was conveniently placed between the woodland country of Arden and the rich arable of South Warwickshire; to the south, the Cotswolds for sheep and shepherds and country sports; to the west, down river to Worcester and the cattle routes to Wales; not far from Watling Street, the direct route to London, or over Clopton's fine bridge (still there!) to Oxford and thence to London.

John Shakespeare and Mary Arden came into Stratford on marriage, both from Arden country. He set up business as a glover, in the two houses in Henley Street which he owned. Mary Arden was socially superior, almost certainly a sprig of the Arden gentlefolk of north Warwickshire; for her father's house out at Wilmcote was rather grander than an ordinary farmer's, with arras hangings on the walls, and she inherited some land. When William, upon success in London, bought the best house in Stratford and took out a coat-of-arms in his father's name—so that *he* should be a gentleman born—he later proposed quartering his Spear *(Non sans droict!)* with the arms of the Ardens. He is constantly referred to as 'gentle', which in Elizabethan English meant 'gentlemanly'—and such was always his bearing, in contrast to many of the theatre-folk. His granddaughter, Elizabeth, ended up as a lady of title, Lady Barnard.

The borough archives at Stratford are full of the municipal activities of the alderman, as the parish registers are liberally sprinkled with the baptisms and burials of the family. William, the eldest son, was baptised in Holy Trinity on 26 April 1564, when he would have been a few days old. In the end most of his own immediate family were gathered together in the chancel, where they all lie with him, before the altar, his monument, the familiar bust, looking down upon them there.

Opposite: *William Shakespeare. This engraving by Martin Droeshout is the only authentic likeness of Shakespeare*

7

⚜ Mr William Shakespear.

was borne at Stratford vpon Avon in the County of Warwick.
his father was a Butcher, & I have been told heretofore by some
of the neighbours, that when he was a boy he exercised his fathers
Trade, but when he kill'd a Calfe, he would doe it in a high style, &
make a Speech. There was at that time another Butchers son in
this Towne, that was held not at all inferior to him for a naturall
witt, his acquaintance & coëtanean, but dyed young. This Wm
being inclined naturally to Poetry and acting, came to London
I guesse about 18: and was an Actor at one of the Play-houses
and did act exceedingly well: now B. Johnson was never a
good Actor, but an excellent Instructor. He began early to
make essayes at Dramatiq Poetry, wch at that time was very
lowe; and his Playes tooke well: He was a handsome well
shap't man very good company, and of a very readie and
pleasant smooth Witt. The Humor of . . . . the Constable
in a Midsomernights Dreame, he happened to take at
*Grendon in Bucks wch is the roade from London to Stratford
and there was living that Constable about 1642 when I
first came to Oxon. Mr Jos: Howe is of yt parish and knew him.
Ben Johnson and he did gather Humours of men dayly
where euer they came. One time as he was at the Tavern
at Stratford supr Avon, one Combes an old rich Vsurer
was to be buryed, he makes there this extemporay Epitaph
      Ten in the hundred the Devill allowes
But Combes will have twelve, he sweares & vowes:
If any one askes who lies in this Tombe:
Hoh! quoth the Devill, 'Tis my John o'Combe.

He was wont to goe to his native Country once a yeare
I thinke I have been told that he left 2 or 300li per annum there
and thereabout: to a sister. I have heard Sr Wm Dave
nant and Mr Thomas Shadwell (who is counted the best Co-
mœdian we have now) say, that he had a most prodigious Witt,
and did admire his naturall parts beyond all other Dramaticall
writers. He *was wont to say, That he never blotted out a line
in his life: sayd Ben: Johnson, I wish he had blotted out a thousand. His Comedies will remaine witt, as long as the English
tongue is understood; for that he handles mores hominum: now
our present writers reflect so much upon particular persons, &
coxcombeities, that 20 yeares hence, they will not be understood.
Though as Ben Johnson sayes of him, that he had but little Latine and
lesse Greek: He understood Latine pretty well: for he had been in his younger
yeares a Schoolmaster in the Countrey.

* I thinke it was Mid-
son night that he
happened to lye there —

v. his Epitaph
in Dugdales Warw —

B. Johnsons Vnder-
wood —

from Mr . . . Beeston —

Nothing is more remarkable than the continuous and close association he managed to keep with his native town, in the pressures of so strenuous and exacting a career. Where other actors like Heming and Condell, or Edward Alleyn, invested their savings in London or near London, Shakespeare invested his in Stratford. He was determined to make a figure as an independent gentleman in his native town; he is referred to as 'gentleman' and 'Master' Shakespeare from the years of success in London.

One notices a contrast with his father, who was easy-going about business and devoted too much of his time to the town's affairs, so that from 1577 he lost money and had to sell off some of his wife's inheritance. When William at last, belatedly, achieved success he was more careful. He had, however, a 'merry' disposition in common with his father—he refers to his own 'sportive blood'; and, at eighteen, can hardly have helped himself by getting a neighbour's daughter, Anne Hathaway, with child. Gentlemanly as ever, he married the woman, eight and a half years older—which meant much more in those days of early maturing and early deaths—and in May 1583 his first child, the clever girl Susanna, was born. Twenty months later, in 1585, twins were born, Hamnet and Judith, named after nearby neighbours. Judith was the stupid member of the family; the boy did not live to carry on the name, dying at eleven in 1596. No more children were born. But, in 1585, what was a young parent of twenty-one to do, with a wife and three children to support, his father's affairs having gone downhill? He is recorded once more in Stratford, in 1587, before he achieved public acclaim and success with his *Henry VI* plays in 1590–1.

In the interval, we have the information going right back to Beeston of the Globe Company, that he was a schoolmaster in the country. Everything corroborates this. All of his early plays are full of school-material, and he is an adept at making the most of it. Elizabethan grammar-school education was entirely based on Latin, with some logic and more rhetoric; then there were Prayer Book and Bible. The allusions and references that well up naturally in Shakespeare's mind are always these: they bespeak his *bildung*. It was not different from Marlowe's, though he was a university man, or

Above: *Shakespeare's birthplace, Stratford-upon-Avon*

Opposite: *John Aubrey's Brief Life of Shakespeare, 1681. Aubrey notes the source of his information in the margin*

Above: *Robert Greene, the pamphleteer. Title-page of a pamphlet 'Greene in Conceipte', 1598*

Above right: *Henry Wriothesley, 3rd Earl of Southampton, and Shakespeare's patron. From an oil painting by John de Critz the Elder c.1601–3*

Jonson's, who was not.

John Aubrey tells us, in only the next generation, that Shakespeare lived in Shoreditch; this would be early on, near the first theatres, the Theatre and Curtain, where he acted. Here too lived other theatre and writing folk, Marlowe, Watson, Greene, and the foreign musicians of the Queen, notably the prolific Bassanos. Aubrey added, 'the more to be admired q(uia) he was not a company keeper . . . wouldn't be debauched.' This is convincing—a reason why we do not hear of him, bumbling about the town, drinking and whoring like notorious Robert Greene, or, perhaps worse, like Marlowe. The newcomer was busy and ambitious, with his way to make, playing, touring in the country, with a respectable wife and three children to maintain at Stratford. There they remained: no evidence of them ever in London, though we find Shakespeare lodging at various times in Bishopsgate, in Silver Street, and in Southwark, all convenient to the theatres. His permanent home was always Stratford; Aubrey says that he was 'wont to go into Warwickshire once a year.'

By 1591 the touring actor who had taken to writing plays, in some association with Kyd and Marlowe—since they all wrote partly for Pembroke's—had broken through to success. We have an unfriendly glimpse of him through the eyes of Robert Greene, jealous of the player, an 'upstart crow' (actually Shakespeare was more of a magpie for picking up bits everywhere). 'A player!' says Greene, 'I took you rather for a gentleman of great living; for, if by outward habit men should be censured, you would be taken for a substantial man.' 'So I am, where I dwell . . . What though the world once went hard with me, when I was fain to carry my playing-fardel a footback? *Tempora mutantur* . . . it is otherwise now, for my very share in playing apparel will not be sold for £200.' 'Truly,' said Greene, 'it is strange that you should so prosper in that vain practice for that it seems to me your voice is nothing gracious.' No doubt he had a West Midlands accent. The gentleman-like player, nothing abashed, replied: 'I was a country author, passing at a moral . . . and for seven years was absolute interpreter of the puppets.' Now seven years from 1592 takes us back to 1585 and the addition of twins to his family at twenty-one, when he would need to look about.

The encounter ends with Greene, employed by the player, having to pen plays— needs must—as we know Greene did, no actor himself. And from his death-bed he indited his famous attack on the players, warning against them his fellow-writers, to whom they were so beholden, in particular, against the player who was now rivalling them at their job, thinking himself as good as any of them, if not better, a 'perfect Johannes Factotum'. Hostile as this was, there is a great deal that is revealing in the picture.

Success was longer in coming to the player, the family man, than it had to the unattached Marlowe with *Tamburlaine* or Kyd with *The Spanish Tragedy*. But it won for him the patronage of the young Earl of Southampton and experience which was of crucial importance in the life of the man and the development of the artist. For it meant the introduction to a cultivated, aristocratic circle to which his nature ardently responded; and it opened up chances and vistas hitherto glimpsed only from afar. The sonnets of the poet to the youthful patron began, formally enough, in persuasion of him to marry and do his duty by the family, but they soon developed into a warm, if always deferential, friendship. Shakespeare was attracted by a dark and musical, but also equivocal, lady; in the usual Elizabethan manner the poet got his lord to write to her on his behalf. The lady seized the opportunity to entangle the youth, for whom Shakespeare felt a quasi-tutorial responsibility and a more than parental affection. We now know that the lady was Emilia Lanier, natural daughter of Baptista Bassano, one of the Queen's Italian musicians, and the discarded mistress of Lord Chamberlain Hunsdon. She had been married off to another royal musician, Alfonso Lanier, with whom she was unhappy and discontented.

Another complication in Shakespeare's exceptional experience of friendship was his patron's taking up Marlowe briefly, just before his tavern-death in May 1593. These tensions strained, but deepened and enriched, the complex psychological experience recorded in the sonnets. Highly sexed and heterosexual, Shakespeare fell helplessly under the spell of his temperamental, tormenting mistress, who led him a frightful dance, driving him 'frantic-mad'. In the end, she gave him his dismissal; the affair was broken off, with the poet repairing to Bath for cure of love's distemper.

Nevertheless, the friendship with Southampton remained unbroken, though subjected to these strains. For the poet owed, as he expressed, eternal gratitude to the generous young patron for support during the critical years 1592 and 1593, when the theatres were closed owing to the recurrence of plague. Plague two years running imposed a fearful burden upon the theatre-folk, broke some of the touring companies, necessitated kaleidoscopic chops and changes, killed off actors' families, besides the mortality from other causes to the poets: Greene, Marlowe's friend Watson, Marlowe himself, and shortly after Kyd; not long after, Peele.

That Shakespeare came through the crisis unscathed he owed largely to Southampton; no less important was the inspiration he derived from these passionate emotional experiences. There were also his opportunities and alternatives so fortunately provided during the closure of the theatres. The actor-dramatist was free to challenge fame as a poet with the long narrative poems he dedicated to his patron, *Venus and Adonis* (1593) and, with exceptional warmth and gratitude, *The Rape of Lucrece* (1594). Contemporaneously with these he was writing the sonnets, private offerings of a poet to a patron, never published by him (indeed, some of them were much too near the bone, so intimate an autobiography they record).

At the same time, there were private theatrical opportunities. *Love's Labour's Lost* (1593) was a skit on the young patron's abnegation of marriage, with a self-portrait of the dramatist as Berowne and of his dark mistress as Rosaline. The marriage of South-ampton's mother to Sir Thomas Heneage, Vice-Chamberlain to the Queen—who did not approve of it—provided the occasion for *A Midsummer Night's Dream* (which ends with Mayday rejoicings) at the private wedding of this elderly couple on 2 May 1594.

In that year, the plague over, the ground was clear for a new start. The initiative was taken by James Burbage, who had built the first Theatre, properly so called, in 1576. He had always been Lord Chamberlain Hunsdon's man. His son, Richard Burbage, was to become the star of the Company, famous in the role of Richard III, London's leading actor after Alleyn's retirement. He and Shakespeare were the Castor and Pollux of the Company. Aubrey tells us that Shakespeare 'did act exceedingly well', as we might have guessed from the leading place he is given in the lists of actors. 'Now Ben Jonson was never a good actor, but an excellent instructor'—that also we might have guessed. More important, Shakespeare brought to the new combination more than half-a-dozen plays he had already written, his experience in producing, his not inconsiderable business capacity and self-confidence; above all, his abundant creative-ness.

It is likely that Augustine Phillips, Heming, Pope and the leading comic actor, Will Kemp, went back to the beginning. This group, except for Kemp who left in 1599, held together for the rest of their lives. They shortly overtook the Admiral's Company, which had enjoyed a lead with Alleyn to act and Marlowe to write for it; by the end of the reign the Chamberlain's Men were performing twice as often as all the rest at Court. In 1599 they constructed their permanent home on the South Bank with the Globe—the great 'round O' of the Prologue to *Henry V*—in which Shakespeare had a part share. It is fairly certain that his patron bought him this original share in the Company. On James I's accession he took on their patronage and they became the King's Men; their remuneration for performances at Court was doubled, their status enhanced by being formally enrolled as Grooms of the Chamber.

All this registered the ascent to social respectability of a profession which had been disconsidered earlier: 'strolling players' were equated with vagrants. William Shake-speare had indeed hitched his players' wagon to a star; several of his colleagues became armigerous gentlemen too, laughed at for it by Ben. Nevertheless, it was they who gave Jonson his chance by putting on in 1598 his *Every Man in his Humour*, in which Shakespeare acted, as also later in *Sejanus*.

The formation of the Chamberlain's Company provided the stable foundation for the actor-dramatist's career, by which he made his money, after a long uphill struggle. From that he never looked back—indeed he never had done so, except in a nostalgic sense; for he was a backward-looking, historically-minded man, conservative and traditionalist, who found inspiration in the past, not in any doctrinaire vision of the future. Hence the magnificent role of the historical plays—more than one-third of his output was historical in one shape or another.

Here we must confine ourselves to the external marks of his career. By 1602, in possession of New Place and a coat-of-arms, he invested his growing profits in 107 acres of the best land in Old Stratford. Three years later he made a larger investment in one-half of all the tithes on and around the town, which had belonged to the former canons of Holy Trinity, in whose chancel he was to be buried as a kind of lay-rector

Far left:
Richard Burbage,
Shakespeare's
chief actor. His
father built the
Globe Theatre in
1599. Oil painting
probably by
Burbage himself

Left: *The Globe*
Theatre : detail
from Visscher's
'View of London',
1616

of the parish. He was indeed its gentleman now, quite a leading figure, consulted by his cousin the town-clerk over the town's affairs, improvement of highways, enclosures. He was too busy to take a hand in them—when he bought his land, his bachelor brother, Gilbert, had to take possession for him during his absence.

We have a close-up of him in London at the turn of the century, from a fascinating legal case a dozen years later. In 1612 'William Shakespeare of Stratford-upon-Avon, gentleman, of the age of 48 years or thereabouts' (quite correct) gave evidence concerning the betrothal of the daughter of the Montjoies, the French household in Silver Street, where he had been lodging ten years or so before. He had indeed effected the betrothal to an apprentice of these wig-makers, moved thereto by Madame Montjoie, with whom he was evidently on terms of some confidence. We do not know how long he lodged there, but it takes us back to the French background of *All's Well* and perhaps to the French scenes of *Henry V*.

From 1599 we have a description of a performance of *Julius Caesar* at the Globe by a young Swiss tourist, Thomas Platter, who was highly impressed. By this time the theatres, though disapproved of by the growing number of pious Puritans, had graduated into being among the leading attractions of London, especially to foreign visitors. Plays regularly punctuated occasions at Court—so that Shakespeare had every opportunity of surveying the scene and hearing the gossip, from a privileged position; similarly with performances at the Inns of Court[1] or at the universities, while touring was not completely given up. As the years went on Shakespeare acted less and was more at Stratford.

Unlike Jonson, he had never written for the Boys' companies, and, unlike Marlowe, he was not interested in boys, except as actors. But from 1596 to 1608 the Burbages had leased the hall within Blackfriars to the Boys' companies, where they put on a successful run of largely satirical comedies, in rivalry with the men's companies. They provided

[1] Inns of Court were residential colleges for the study of law located along the north bank of the Thames

13

a draw for a more select, sophisticated, upper-class audience, willing to pay more for something new, within doors, out of the elements. After much thought Shakespeare's Company decided to enter this new field, with its promise for the future, while continuing at the Globe with its larger, more mixed public. This move provided a new challenge to the powers of the dramatist, always popular with the wider public, and partly accounts for the new direction observable in his last plays. There had been provision for masques in some of his earlier plays, now they took on an added importance, with more music and scenery. We are on the way to his collaboration with John Fletcher, being trained up as Shakespeare's successor as dramatist-in-chief to the Company, preparatory to retirement to Stratford.

The country's most popular dramatist was fair game to the not well organised and not wholly respectable trade of publishing. For it must be remembered that an author had not modern copyright in his works, unless he published them first—and it was not to the interest of a dramatist or his Company to publish his plays, at 6d a time: it was performance that brought in the money. Thus Shakespeare, whose interests were entirely in the theatre and its prosperity, did not wish his plays to be published. They were, however, so popular as to be often pirated; sometimes the Company took action to 'stay' publication, even then not always effective, and sometimes a better version of a play was put forth to correct the travesty of it which had been reconstructed (usually by actors) from memory from the theatre. It was not at all the thing for professional dramatists to publish their plays, and not in their interest to do so.[1] Ben Jonson was the first to collect, edit and publish his plays as his *Works*, in the year of Shakespeare's death, and was laughed at for doing so. But then he was not really a professional: he thought of himself as something better than a playwright—a Poet.

Shakespeare's poems also were got hold of and published without his consent, the popularity of his name taken advantage of on the title page. In 1599 William Jaggard published *The Passionate Pilgrim*, as 'by W. Shakespeare'. It contains some half-a-dozen of his poems, three from *Love's Labour's Lost* and a couple of his sonnets which had got into circulation. Thomas Heywood, who *was* a professional dramatist, tells us how Shakespeare reacted: 'so the Author I know much offended with Mr. Jaggard that—altogether unknown to him—presumed to make so bold with his name.' It was like the publication of Greene's attack on him years before, for which Chettle had so handsomely apologised: 'because myself have seen his demeanour no less civil than he excellent in the quality he professes', i.e. as an actor. 'Besides, divers of worship have reported his uprightness of dealing, which argues his honesty [Elizabethan for honourableness], and his facetious grace in writing, that approves his Art'.

What a noble tribute it is!—the most generous apology I know of in the age. We may place it beside the critical Jonson's no less revealing characterisation: 'he was indeed honest, and of an open and free nature'. And this even apart from his genius as a writer: 'an excellent fancy, brave notions and gentle (i.e. gentlemanly) expressions', his flowing wit and prolific 'facility'. His patron had stood by him at the critical time of Greene's attack on him in 1592.

> Your love and pity doth the impression fill,
> Which vulgar scandal stamped upon my brow;
> For what care I who calls me well or ill,
> So you *o'er-greene* my bad, my good allow.

[1] cf. G. E. Bentley's authoritative *The Profession of Dramatist in Shakespeare's Age.*

Now, in 1609, there came out the most important of all works for Shakespeare's biography, his *Sonnets*, the most intimately autobiographical and revealing ever written

—as we should expect of one whose nature was open and free, utterly candid. It does not seem that Shakespeare had a hand in their publication, they are too revealing and moreover are badly proof-read, as were not the two poems he himself had dedicated to Southampton years before. There turned up with the Sonnets a longish poem, *A Lover's Complaint,* rather like *Venus and Adonis;* in it the young patron is again recognisable—evidently a diploma-piece on the threshold of being taken into his favour. For all those early works, poems and sonnets alike, were for him:

> all alike my songs and praises be
> To one, of one, still such, and ever so.

And again:

> Why write I still all one, ever the same . . .
> That every word doth almost tell my name?

The answer was:

> O, know, sweet love, I always write of you.

What he was writing in those years belonged to the patron, which points to *A Lover's Complaint* and the Sonnets together coming out of the Southampton *cache.* They were published now by Thomas Thorp, the publisher, with a typically flowery dedication which has given trouble to generations who do not know Elizabethan social usage. For he dedicated the work to 'Mr. W. H.', when it was quite regular to refer to a knight as Mr. (i.e. Master), though never a Lord. Indeed Southampton's mother always referred to her second husband, Sir Thomas Heneage as Master Heneage. Her third husband was a young man, Sir William Hervey, to whom she left all her household goods and chattels in 1607. In 1608 he married a young wife: this is why in 1609 Thorp is wishing him 'all happiness and that eternity promised by our everlasting poet', i.e. the eternity of having children and carrying on the family to posterity, which the poet had promised his young patron if only he would marry. Thus 'the only begetter' was not the patron, the young Lord of the Sonnets, but his step-father, the only person who had got the manuscript of them. Thorp was fulsome in his gratitude; we have reason to be even more so.

One person had no reason to be grateful, for the indelible, unforgettable portrait of her that has come down to posterity in the Sonnets—at the opposite pole to the ideal Delias and Celias of conventional sonnet-sequences. Emilia Lanier had every reason to resent the delineation of her, though written years before and not put into circulation (the patron had the title to his poet's work). In the interval she had undergone a religious conversion—no improbable rebound from such a life for such a temperament. She immediately announced the publication of her own long religious poem, *Salve Deus Rex Judaeorum,* which appeared in 1611, and inserted in the volume a furious riposte to those men who demean women. The temperament is still recognisable in her tirade against 'evil disposed men who forgetting that they were born of women, nourished of women, and that if it were not by the means of women they would be quite extinguished out of the world and a final end to them all—do, like Vipers, deface the wombs wherein they were bred.'[1] No reply was possible to that: indeed silence was the best policy, and the little volume was completely overlooked till our time.

At Stratford his father had died in 1601, his mother, Mary Arden in 1608. The year before, in 1607, his elder daughter Susanna married a well qualified physician, a

[1] c.f. my edition of *The Poems of Shakespeare's Dark Lady,* with Introduction covering her biography.

15

Above: *Plan of Stratford c. 1768 by Samuel Winter. The town was not so very different from the one Shakespeare knew*

Above right: *South-east prospect of Stratford-upon-Avon, 1746*

Cambridge man, Dr. John Hall, who had a successful practice in the county round about. Among those he treated was Shakespeare's friend, the poet Drayton, and his own daughter Elizabeth, who did not enjoy good health—and she had no children. With her Shakespeare's own progeny came to an end. In her will she left money to her poor relations, the Hathaways. She had moved to her husband's house, Sir John Barnard's near Northampton; when he died he left instructions for the lumber and books in the old house at Stratford to be destroyed. Alas!

Shakespeare's affairs were looked after by his lawyer cousin, Thomas Greene, the town clerk. When he was in London in November 1614 with his son-in-law, Greene notes in his diary, 'at my cousin Shakespeare coming yesterday to town I went to see him how he did', and they discussed the enclosures out at Welcombe and how it would affect the property there. He had never been able to get back his mother's land, which had been mortgaged to the Lamberts, his uncle and aunt.

In 1613 he purchased a house within Blackfriars, very convenient for the theatre in which he had invested. A witness to the transaction was the host of the 'Mermaid'— another corroboration of what has traditionally come down to us. In that same year we find him designing the *impresa*, emblem and motto, for the Earl of Rutland's shield for the tilt, and Burbage, who was a good amateur painter, making and painting it. Rutland had belonged to the Essex-Southampton party, and the family had connexions with the Burbages through owning the land where the original Theatre had been built. Shakespeare's youngest brother, Edmund, also an actor, died in Southwark in December 1607, where he was given a good funeral in the big church, 'with a forenoon knell of the great bell'. We may guess who paid for this.

His own time came somewhat unexpectedly, for when he made his will in March 1616, he was 'in perfect health and memory, God be praised'. It gives us a corroborative picture of the man, it is so full of neighbourly bequests to relatives, friends and their children. His religious belief was, as all his work shows, that of a conforming churchman of the time: 'I commend my soul into the hands of God my Creator, hoping and assuredly believing through the only merits of Jesus Christ my Saviour to be made partaker of life everlasting.' The bulk of his property in Stratford and London went to Susanna, who had for some time run the household; by a kindly thought he reserved the second best bed for his widow—Susanna and her husband would need the best big one. His 'Fellows' of the Company were remembered: 'John Heming, Richard Burbage, and Henry Condell, 26s 8d apiece, to buy them rings'; the house in Black-

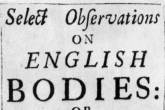

Select Observations
ON
ENGLISH
BODIES:
OR,
Cures both Empericall and Hiftoricall, performed up-
on very eminent Per-
fons in defperate
Difeafes.

First, written in Latine
by Mr. *John Hall* Phyfician,
living at *Stratford* upon *Avon*
in *Warwick-fhire,* where he
was very famous, as alfo in
the Counties adjacent, as ap-
peares by thefe Obfervations
drawn out of feverall hun-
dreds of his, as choyfeft.

Now put into Englifh for com-
mon benefit by *James Cooke*
Practitioner in *Phyfick* and
Chirurgery.

London, Printed for *John Sherley*, at the
Golden Pellican, in *Little-Britain.* 1657

Far left: *The case-book of Dr John Hall, husband of Shakespeare's daughter, Susanna*

Left: *This portrait is thought to represent Elizabeth Hall, Shakespeare's granddaughter, with her first husband Thomas Nash*

friars went with the rest of the property to Susanna. It is the will of a Stratford man who had made his money in the theatre in London, but whose loyalties and family pride were in his native town. Here he died on 23 April 1616.

The whole world knows what he looked like, even from the inadequate representations of him that have come down to us. Few men have equalled the grand St. Paul's dome of that cranium; other features also speak to us, the rather sensual nose, the mobile, hairless cheeks of an actor, the sensitive, sensuous nostril and small mouth, the large and luminous eyes full of intelligence and observation.

A fair monument, from a Southwark workshop, was shortly erected to him in the familiar church; and the county historian, Sir William Dugdale, almost immediately claimed distinction for Stratford-upon-Avon in that 'it gave birth and sepulture to our late famous poet, William Shakespeare'.

His real monument, however, was the great Folio volume of his plays which came out in 1623. This was an enormous and complicated undertaking, unprecedented except for the tribute Ben Jonson paid to himself by publishing his *Works* in 1616. Now he lent a hand to the much bigger undertaking of assembling all the plays of the Master from the playbooks of the Company, comparing them with printed versions that had appeared, etc. What an undertaking it was! It necessitated the co-operation of several printers and publishers, under the direction of Shakespeare's Fellows, Heming and Condell. For it was an enterprise of the Company, a quite exceptional tribute, 'only to keep the memory of so worthy a friend and Fellow alive as was our Shakespeare'.

And what reason the world has to be grateful to all those who took part in the joint undertaking; for, without it, we should have only half of his plays, some of them in very unsatisfactory shape. It was left to Ben Jonson, who knew best, to say that 'he was for all time'.

T. D. SCOTT.

G. GREATBACH

Shakespeare's Comedies

Dr. Johnson, greatest of Shakespearean critics—for there we have a mind on a level with the author he is criticising—observed that comedy was what first came naturally to Shakespeare. Comedy was instinctive with him; he had to work, the deepening experience of life aiding, towards tragedy. 'In his comic scenes, he seems to produce without labour what no labour can improve.'

This was, of course, in keeping with his nature, as Robert Greene and John Aubrey observed, and as he described himself in the character of Berowne:

> but a merrier man . . .
> I never spent an hour's talk withal.
> His eye begets occasion for his wit;
> For every object that the one doth catch
> The other turns to a mirth-moving jest.

His earlier comedies are full of merriment and give an impression of a happy nature. They are running over with high spirits, one sees it in the wit-combats, the verbal quibbles and endless punning which appealed so much to Elizabethans. This aspect of his genius helped him to gain popularity with them—the 'facetious grace' to which Chettle paid tribute. It is the one aspect that has dated most and appeals least to us.

What, then, was the nature of his contribution to comedy, what was its character, and how did it differ from others? It is not easy to state briefly, for this author was above all so Protean, so various and diverse, as well as diverting.

We may diagnose that his first essential contribution to Elizabethan comedy was to shape it up, give it shapely dramatic form. Hitherto comedies, rather rustic and rude, however lively, were apt to be wanting in form—indeed much of the traditional drama in every kind was apt to be shapeless. This was not true of the courtly comedy of Lyly, from whom Shakespeare learned. In observing his development we must pay attention to what Ben Jonson tells us, who knew him so well:

> how far thou didst our Lyly outshine,
> Or sporting Kyd, or Marlowe's mighty line.

Opposite:
Frontispiece to Comedies volume, The Complete Works of Shakespeare *edited by J. O. Halliwell, 1853*

ANNO DNI   ÆTATIS SVÆ 21
1585

VOD ME NVTRIT
E DESTRVIT

For his comedy he learned much from Lyly, chiefly from *Endimion*: the banter of Sir
Tophas and his page gave the model for that of Armado and Moth; the constables of
the watch gave a hint for Dogberry and Verges, as the fairies pinching Corsites black
and blue for that of Falstaff in *The Merry Wives*.

Lyly, Kid and Marlowe were the dominant influences upon his early work; but more
important was the discipline of the theatre itself. No writer was ever more a man of the
theatre—not even Molière—and he owed his skill in construction, his technique, the
sense of the scene, the nucleus from which he worked, to his life's experience as an
actor. His poetic power grew with the demands of the theatre for expression.

Even more important was his sense of character. Others had that too, notably
Jonson; but none of the world's writers has ever had so penetrating or so various a sense
of character—from the simplest, most foolish and light-hearted to the most tragic and
profound; no writer has created such a gallery of living, memorable characters with
such instinctive sympathy and understanding as he. Here is his supreme achievement.

Then all is expressed with marvellous virtuosity as to language. He was very lordly
about language. The actor's profession doubled his literary facility—one notices the
astonishing increase of command from the Sonnets, say, to *Troilus and Cressida* or
Antony and Cleopatra. His vocabulary was twice that of the normal educated Englishman; but his actor's memory picked up words and phrases from everywhere, as his
eye and ear noted 'humours' and characters.

So his third specific contribution is style, in the widest sense of the term, expressing the mimetic personality of an actor, though with greater literary ambition than he has been credited with. For he was determined to stake his claim as an educated poet, to challenge fame with others, and was recognised as such even by Cambridge dons like Gabriel Harvey.

His earliest comedy, like his earliest tragedy, came out of his schooling; Elizabethan scholars took their standard of comedy from Plautus *(The Comedy of Errors)*, and of tragedy partly from Seneca *(Titus Andronicus)*. From the first his creations expressed his own personality; it is not only that he added elements, invented new characters, but suffused the whole with his own atmosphere. We may call it romantic, for it is compounded of emotion and poetry. With Jonson's comedy the appeal is to the intellect, and he saved his poetry for his poetry and tragedy. His comedies are essentially prose works, where in Shakespeare even the prose is poetic.

They differ too in the effect of their comedy. Jonson laughs at, and bids us laugh at, his creatures. Shakespeare is subtler and more ambivalent: we both laugh at and with his creations. What we owe to his laughter has been well put by an American critic. 'Not only does he laugh as all England laughed, but he believes as all England believes; and no more of the critical spirit is there in him than must needs be in one so well-balanced and sane. And not a single ideal, ethical judgment, or custom of his time does he question. . . . By choice he accepted life.' The result is that his imagination is the more embracing. He had quite as much wit as Jonson or Molière, but the appeal to intellect is narrowing and inhibiting: Shakespeare kept both paths, indeed all possibilities, open. He gives us as searing a portrait of a Pandarus, as complete an exposure of a Parolles or a Lucio, as any intellectual satire could provide. There is plenty to disapprove of in Falstaff, but we are left with the feeling that the old rogue is irresistible. Shakespeare's humour inclines to the kindly. He knew quite as well as Swift the depths and universality of human folly, but, unlike Swift, he gives humanity the benefit of the doubt.

In short, Shakespeare's comedy provides a catharsis no less effective than his tragedy: laughter is a release from tensions, a warming of the heart, gives one a feeling of good fellowship with our fellow-men, quite apart from reducing pride and showing us a mirror of our less noble selves.

It seems certain that justice has never been done—the Victorians could not face it— to the enormously bawdy aspect, and content, of Shakespeare. Yet the salty humour has been a preservative through the centuries, one of the forces that have kept him alive. For sex is a force, indeed the life-force; and Shakespeare is the sexiest, bawdiest of all great writers. Nothing snooping and prurient, just the normal, highly-sexed heterosexual's enjoyment of 'the facts of life'. The more one knows of Elizabethan language the more one appreciates not only the direct fun and frolics, but the constant innuendos and puns with their physical suggestions, laughable, rueful, rollicking. Some of it, no doubt, was for the groundlings and helped his never-dying appeal to his audience; but it is a mistake to put it down merely to the audience, as Robert Bridges did, who as a Victorian aesthete of the purest water, was shocked by it. Silly: such is the nature of life —and without it there would not be life as we know it on the planet. It is absolutely part of the nature of the man, a nature as comprehensive (and comprehending) as any in literature.

This is a part of the completeness of his characters: he suggests them to us in the round, instead of restricting them to one humour as in *Volpone* or *Le Misanthrope*. These are in consequence less interesting, where Shakespeare's characters are open-ended, leave more to our minds; he followed his intuition and his extraordinary observation of human nature, unlimited by theory, for theorising is always restrictive and often inhibiting.

Hence the enormous variety of his creations, the many permutations and combinations that exfoliated from a few basic patterns. The elemental situations in life are perhaps few enough, and the emotions involved not many; and so we watch Shakespeare repeating the situations, or the plot, refining upon them, improving, usually elaborating with his own additions to the story, until the prentice-mark of *The Two Gentlemen of Verona* becomes the masterpiece that is *Twelfth Night*.

The dominant theme is that of love: another reason for regarding his work as 'romantic', going back to traditional romance; love in various aspects and forms, un-requited or requited, frustrated or fulfilled, mistaken or misjudged, competitive, crossed by mischance or magic, rivalled by the power and claims of friendship. Again, as with any real writer, this reflected the man and his experience. Ben Jonson was not interested in love, and he was not successful in marriage.

A perceptive critic has written of the progress marked from *The Two Gentlemen* to *Love's Labour's Lost*: 'Valentine's adoration of Silvia was . . . a shade "literary", since it was probably due to the dramatist's inexperience at that date of the way gentlemen and ladies actually made love. When he wrote *Love's Labour's Lost* he had become more intimate with "divers of worship" who stood by him in 1592 . . . and after Berowne there was no return to Valentine.' It was very rapid progress that he made from 1592 to 1593: something inspiring, and immediately maturing, had supervened. 'Might there not be something personal behind it after all? About the time the dramatist was composing his *Two Gentlemen* the poet was beginning to address Sonnet-letters to his friend who, when introduced to the poet's lady, plays the traitor as Proteus does and is freely forgiven as Valentine forgives Proteus. But we "ask and ask".'

But we do not need to ask and ask, as Matthew Arnold did; we know: he did not. We turn again to Dr. Johnson for enlightening common sense: 'I am always inclined to believe that Shakespeare has more allusions to particular facts and persons than his readers commonly suppose.' But, of course—as with any real writer; and after two centuries of intensive research into the Elizabethan age we are in a much better position to know. William Shakespeare did not need to read up friendship in Cicero's *De Amicitia*.

Love's Labour's Lost is altogether more sophisticated because of the personal experience that had supervened the introduction into a cultivated aristocratic circle to which Shakespeare's genius responded with alacrity and which gave him inspiration. He also tells us, in Berowne's famous speech, what he meant by love and why he attached such importance to it: as an enhancement of life, a sharpening of all the senses, of eye, ear, touch, taste; as inspiration, doubling the powers to achieve, leading men on to conquer new realms of experience. Women's eyes:

> They are the books, the arts, the academes,
> That show, contain, and nourish all the world.

Such faith is, of course, liable to disenchantment; nor did it fail to appear in the sequel —and that experience again goes into the work.

All is grist to the dramatist's mill, all his experience is in his work. Hence his knowledge of the human heart, and the force of his expression of it—even when he is at play, as in *The Taming of the Shrew,* which no one is likely to forget, as they might forget the first two comedies. The *Shrew* is a very original exercise on the theme of how to tame a woman. There is a stronger element of realism in this play than we usually realise, for the theme was a traditional one in his day, and the actuality is reinforced by the Stratford background of the Induction. Shortly came something totally different, a magical play, *A Midsummer Night's Dream*. Though this swims in the usual element of love—in this case doubly crossed and led astray, in both human couples and in the Fairy King and Queen—perhaps most memorable are the fairy tale of Beauty and the Beast, transformed into Titania and Bottom, and the recognisable realism of Bottom and his fellows for all that they are caricatured.

We perceive that we have to add to the other major elements in Shakespeare's genius the astonishing realism with which he drew lower-class life, for all the caricature, the malapropisms and lapses which he observed in it or with which he endowed it. There is a kind of poetic surrealism in the doubled reality of Lance and his Dog, Bottom the Weaver and his rude mechanicals, Dogberry and Verges, Elbow and Pompey.

All this came out of the native tradition—no-one was closer to the heart of it, or had it more at heart, than this Warwickshireman, from the heart of England. The mixture, still more the bordering of the comic with the tragic, was condemned by Philip Sidney, to whose purely literary impulse Shakespeare owed much. Sidney's pre-judgment was based on the classics; he did not live long enough to see the triumphs of the native tradition in the 1590's. Again, with the dramatist's instinctive respect for tradition—and what a harvest he reaped from it!—he carried forward and developed the role of the Fool, clown or jester. This came not only from the earlier forms of drama but from the actual life of great houses—one more realistic stroke. It enabled him to counterpoint the behaviour of the clown's betters with occasional sharp commentary.

He distinguishes between the professional clown and the 'country clown', the ordinary rustic simpleton. They are all part of a common humanity: 'Shakespeare was too wise not to know that for most of the purposes of human life stupidity is a most valuable element. He had nothing of the impatience which sharp logical minds habitually feel when they come across those who do not apprehend their quick and precise deductions.'[1] Few things are more remarkable than Shakespeare's patience in this direction—such a contrast with Swift at the opposite pole! It belongs to the dramatist's realm of 'negative capability'; like Burke, he appreciated the adhesive uses of simplicity, prejudice, stupidity, ordinary human foolishness. A society of rationalist intellectuals (never so rational as they suppose) could never stick together for long.

And what could be more kindly and humane, after the fiasco of Bottom's play, than the comment: 'the best in this kind are but shadows, and the worst are no worse, if imagination amend them.' There, behind the compassionate imagination, is the double-minded suggestiveness of the man, for it is an epigraph, which holds universally, on his profession.

The farcical enters largely into the early comedies. It is usual to disconsider farce, as drama concerned *only* to excite laughter; but it is absurd to do so, when we have a better appreciation of the cathartic, indeed therapeutic, function of laughter. And William Shakespeare—with a proper combination of innate modesty and satisfaction in his achievement—would be the last person to do so. *The Comedy of Errors* (except for the original framework into which it is put) is pure farce, as it was enacted that farcical night at Gray's Inn at Christmas 1594. *The Taming of the Shrew* is farce, for all that its ending with its moral is serious; not to appreciate that is anachronistic, for it is in keeping with what Elizabethans thought, as usual with Shakespeare. Again, towards the end of this period, *The Merry Wives of Windsor,* is farce, though again how different: middle-class, bourgeois farce, featuring the townsfolk he knew so well at Stratford, the Fords and Pages as it might be the Quineys and Sadlers—with consequences that might be expected from having Sir John Falstaff plumped down in the middle of them.

[1] Thus Walter Bagehot, himself a sharp logical mind.

23

For all this, the potentiality of tragedy is implicit in the comedy, as one can see in *The Rape of Lucrece* alongside of the high spirits and comedy of *Venus and Adonis* (the tragic ending of which has to be taken with a grain of salt: it was intended as a moral for Southampton). *The Merchant of Venice* and *Much Ado* may well be regarded as tragi-comedies, something again different. For a considerable part of the action *The Merchant* borders on tragedy; and, though the cruder Elizabethans saw Shylock as a comic figure, there is a tragic element in him too—Shakespeare's attitude is ambivalent, as so often. He does not close down on us, as the domineering Ben did: he leaves the matter open, like the enigmatic in Leonardo.

As You Like It is different again—nothing tragic in that: it is a romantic pastoral play, for which the dramatist took the hint from Lodge's pastoral novel, *Rosalynde*. But Shakespeare filled it with his own feeling for the woodland, his own Forest of Arden (rather than Ardennes), and there are more than the usual personal or auto-biographical flecks in it. We must point out that, though the stories sometimes come from Italian sources and the plays are often given an appealing Italian colouring in places and names, they are all indefeasibly English. It is Elizabethan England, town or country, that is portrayed—never more so than in *The Merchant of Venice*. To anyone who knows the ways of the port of London at the time, the merchants and their shipping, their argosies and the risks they took, it is all there. Even the character of Shylock has its contemporary starting point at home in Marlowe's Barabas and Dr. Lopez.

We observe the development to the last of the romantic comedies in *Twelfth Night*, filled with music and melancholy. Something of the situation is repeated from *The Two Gentlemen*, but with what deeper echoes in human nature and fuller, rounder characterisation. Once more there is the typical Shakespearean mixture: the serious and complex theme of love, taking different forms and at cross-purposes, frustration, misconception, what not—all mitigated by the realism, if caricatured, of Sir Toby Belch and his cronies, and the ambivalent character of Malvolio. (Once more Shakespeare leaves us to think what we will about *him*—there is no doubt about the others.)

In this play Violà appears as a boy for most of the time she is on stage, as again was the heroine of *As You Like It*. We must never forget how dominant an importance casting had for this most practical of dramatists, an actor himself, who lived in and by the theatre. Disguising female characters as boys, in the intrigue of the plot, was a most convenient ploy when the women's parts were taken by boys—and how talented, precocious and well-trained Elizabethan boy-actors were! The actor-dramatist worked with the materials he had at hand, not in the vacuum of the critic. One effect may be seen in the transformation of the rôle of the Fool with the departure of the rumbustious extrovert Will Kemp, and the arrival of the introvert, reflective Armin, for whom the parts of Feste, Lavache and the philosophic Fool in *Lear* were written.

Everyone notices the melancholy with which the theme of love is endued in *Twelfth Night*; we have the sense that something is ending, as indeed his romantic comedy ends with it. After the War of the Theatres of 1600–2, and the horrid experiences in the background that was yet close to Shakespeare—Southampton condemned to death, in the Tower, Essex executed—things were never the same. Shakespearean comedy was over, the future lay with Jonson's.

We can see something of the influence of the younger master upon the older, always willing to learn from anybody—as he had from Lyly, Kyd, Marlowe. *Troilus and Cressida* is an extraordinary play by all counts—no wonder 'criticism' has been foiled by it; it is a disturbing, as it is a disturbed, play, by an author whose nerves and temper are on edge. Nothing of the 'happy', genial Shakespeare in this. Yet, perhaps by the very fact of his being so disturbed, it contains some of his most brilliant writing and profound reflections on society. It also contains some of his most savage—and that is unlike the nature of the man we know: he did not go this way again until he wrote *Timon*, and, significantly, he left that unfinished.

With *All's Well* and *Measure for Measure* we have something different again: they are hardly comedies, though they are brought to happy endings. Again, though they go together, they are quite different. *All's Well* is a kind of morality; perhaps Shakespeare is harking back to the morality-plays of his youth. At the same time it has a considerable element, which has gone unnoticed, of the autobiographical: close observation and his own experience have gone into it—perhaps too close for aesthetic comfort (for creation, one needs a certain distance).

We may regard the play as experimental, something new; if so, the experiment was justified in the masterly, and more moving, *Measure for Measure* that followed. This play, for most of its action, borders on the tragic: we are already in the world of the great tragedies.

Far left: *William Kemp, the comedian, who left Shakespeare's company in 1599 and danced his way from London to Norwich; and* (left) *Robert Armin, his replacement, a more subtle comedian*

The Comedy of Errors

1591-2

Background. This is the earliest of Shakespeare's comedies, and it is significant that it was based partly on Plautus, from whom with Terence Elizabethans learned their Latin comedy at school—and grammar school education was largely in Latin. In writing the play Shakespeare was recalling and revivifying what he had learned at school, and had probably used when he taught briefly in a country school. Moreover there is a caricature of a schoolmaster, one of several in his work, in Doctor Pinch.

He based his play on the *Menaechmi (The Two Men Called Menaechmus)* of Plautus, and adapted another scene from Plautus' *Amphitruo*. With characteristic ingenuity he doubled the chief characters, and added more, to add to the confusions of mistaken identity upon which the play pivots.

Gray's Inn Hall, where The Comedy of Errors *was performed in December 1594*

Even so, the play is the shortest of all the plays, and would have been briefer still in the continuous performance, unbroken by divisions into Acts and Scenes, which Elizabethan plays received. So it was particularly suited to be followed by a jig—dancing with gesture and song—as was frequent on the stage, or to provide an item in a sequence of revels, at Christmas time or some festive occasion.

We happen to know that it was performed at a Grand Night at Gray's Inn on 28 December 1594, amid much rowdy junketing that added more confusion to that presented in the play. We learn that 'after such sports a Comedy of Errors—like to Plautus' *Menaechmi*—was played by the players. So that night was begun and continued to the end in nothing but confusion and errors; whereupon it was ever afterwards called "the Night of Errors".

It would seem that there had been an afternoon performance that same Innocents' day before the Queen at Greenwich—we may imagine the barge-ful of players coming up-river with the tide to perform again at night, and appreciate how hard-worked the Chamberlain's men were. Shakespeare would have been among them, and at this time Francis Bacon was an active member of the Inn, who took a hand in its entertainments—though he could hardly have been a greater contrast to the actor-dramatist, as a son of a Lord Keeper, a known homosexual, a genius in prose, law and science.

Date. The play had been written more than a couple of years earlier, following upon Shakespeare's first popular success with his *Henry VI* plays. There are contemporary touches that relate it firmly to those early 1590's, when England had to come to the aid of the Protestant Henry of Navarre fighting for his legitimate right to succeed Henri III, assassinated in 1589, on the throne of France.

In a comic passage comparing England and her neighbours to different parts of the body, a character sees France as 'armed and reverted, making war against her heir'. Henry of Navarre was the heir to the throne, whom the country as a whole did not accept till 1594, with the surrender of Paris. The use of the word 'heir' is perfectly understandable, if loosely used: there is no point in arguing about it. Shakespeare was not writing a piece of historical research and never bothered about that kind of thing. The reference was perfectly clear to the audience. America and the Indies are named for the treasure of which Elizabethans were so envious, 'declining their rich aspect to the hot breath of Spain, who sent whole armadas of carracks'. Here is a reference to the quite recent Armada of 1588, very fresh in everybody's memory.

Greenwich Palace where Queen Elizabeth may have witnessed an afternoon performance of The Comedy of Errors *on 28th December 1594. Drawing by Anthony van Wyndgaerde*

Ephesus, the setting for The Comedy of Errors. *This 19th century engraving shows the remains of the Amphitheatre*

The passage is underscored—a kind of double talk—by suggestions off-colour or rather bawdy. 'In what part of her body stands Ireland?' 'Marry, sir, in her buttocks—I found it out by the bogs.' Ireland was good for a joke, or rather more than a joke, to the Elizabethans, as today. Scotland is characterised by her barrenness, 'hard in the palm of the hand': the country was poor, and therefore penurious. 'Where stood Belgia, the Netherlands?' 'O, sir, I did not look so low!'—with appropriate gestures. It is Shakespeare all over, even thus early.

Moreover, behind Ephesus and Syracuse, the top-dressing or colouring of the play, we find as usual the contemporary scene familiar to the audience. The action is set going by the trade dispute between Ephesus and Syracuse, placing an embargo on all traffic between them; an old merchant has been caught in the conflict, in the enemy town, and condemned to death.

> The enmity and discord which of late
> Sprung from the rancorous outrage of your Duke
> To merchants, our well-dealing countrymen,
> Who, wanting guilders to redeem their lives,
> Have sealed his rigorous statutes with their bloods.

In the circumstances of the long-continuing war with Spain Elizabethans were all too familiar with trade-embargoes and their consequences. The old trade with Spain was disrupted; there had been a prolonged embargo on trade between England and her chief market abroad, the Netherlands, when the Duke of Alva ruled there—and that this was at the back of Shakespeare's mind shows itself in the word 'guilders'.

Contemporary touches. The *real* life of the age is revealed in many touches, obvious to those instructed in it. The foreign merchant visiting the city tells his man that till dinner-time

> I'll view the manners of the town,
> Peruse the traders, gaze upon the buildings,
> And then return and sleep within mine inn.

We are reminded of the visit of Navarre's follower, the Duc de Biron, in 1600 when Sir Walter Ralegh conducted him round the sights of London, and to Westminster to view the tombs in the Abbey, etc.

Far more important is the atmosphere of witchery in which the characters think themselves caught, so great is the confusion between their crossed identities and cross-purposes: they are driven almost to doubt their own identity.

> They say this town is full of cozenage:
> As, nimble jugglers that deceive the eye,
> Dark-working sorcerers that change the mind,
> Soul-killing witches that deform the body,
> Disguised cheaters, prating mountebanks,
> And many such-like liberties of sin.

This is recognisably Elizabethan London—as we see it revealed nakedly, for example, in 'Dr.' Forman's Case-Books. And we must always remember that witchery and being bewitched were ever-present and ready to Elizabethan minds, increasing the impact and probabilism of a play so improbable in its action to us. We do not have to go, with some literary commentators, to St. Paul's Epistle to the Ephesians when we know the facts of life in Elizabethan London.

Even the reference to Lapland sorcerers—

> Sure, these are but imaginary wiles,
> And Lapland sorcerers inhabit here—

is a commonplace of the voyagers to Russia by the Northern sea-route, reported in Hakluyt's *Principal Navigations* recently printed, which Shakespeare—like the rapid reader and writer he was—looked into, as we know.

The Play. We do not need to waste time discussing what kind of label to attach to this play—Shakespeare set no store by such pedantry, as he takes the trouble to inform us later in *Hamlet*. And, of course, in his work he constantly transcended the bounds, and transgressed against the rules, beloved by critics, of dull categories. This, however, is the only play to which the label 'Comedy' is attached, but a great deal of the action is farcical; there is much knock-about, slapstick beating to appeal to the groundlings, and not only to them.

But Shakespeare has given a romantic setting in the story of the aged merchant, Aegeon, the threat to his life, and the resolution into all's well at the end. As Quiller-Couch,[1] a creative writer himself, well understood: 'in this early play Shakespeare already discloses his propensity for infusing romance into each or every "form" of drama: that unique propensity which in his later work makes him so magical and so hard to define.' Exactly, that is the point, and 'Q' drives it home: 'there is no line of demarcation—all such lines, or attempts at them, are a professional humbug of

[1] Sir Arthur Quiller-Couch, co-editor of the Cambridge Shakespeare

Final scene of
The Comedy of
Errors, *Royal
Shakespeare
Company
production,
Stratford-upon-
Avon, 1962*

criticism.' If this appears too scathing, from a good critic to lesser ones, we may compromise and say simply that categories, rough as they are, are conveniences, to be held as such.

The play is by no means empty of content, as people may be misled into thinking with so much farce about. There is the real theme of the strains of marriage, in the discussion between the two sisters, Luciana and Adriana. Whatever it expresses in the strains of Shakespeare's own married life, with himself so much away from home, living a double life in London, there is always sympathy for the woman's point of view (unlike Marlowe or Ben Jonson):

> Alas, poor women! make us but believe,
> Being compact of credit, that you love us—
> Though others have the arm, show us the sleeve,
> We in your motion turn, and you may move us.

The sympathy shines through the smile of irony. And there is the theme of men's mastery shortly to provide the stuff of *The Taming of the Shrew :*

> Why, headstrong liberty is lashed with woe . . .
> Men—

this is Luciana speaking—

> Are masters to their females, and their lords.

Personal Touches. Many revealing flecks bring the personality of the author home to us. Several references to hunting the deer and the hounds bring this out-of-doors countryman before us, and corroborate what we know of him externally. We recognise the man speaking in so characteristic a thought as

> The pleasing punishment that women bear;

or the grandiloquence that annoyed Robert Greene in such a phrase as we have already quoted, '*peruse* the traders' for simply look them over. A mere line—

What needs all that, and a pair of stocks in the town?

—brings the country town of the time vividly before us. Dr. Pinch, the schoolmaster, is also a conjurer: he can exorcise, deliver the poor mixed-up characters out of the confusion in which they are caught. Quite so: for he is a clerk, if not in holy orders yet a reading man. He is described in terms that make one think his part was taken by the lean and skinny Sinkler, who seems to have come along with Shakespeare via Strange's and Pembroke's men to the Lord Chamberlain's Company:

> a hungry, lean-faced villain,
> A mere anatomy, a mountebank,
> A threadbare juggler, and a fortune-teller,
> A needy, hollow-eyed, sharp-looking wretch,
> A living-dead man. This pernicious slave . . .

Elizabethans enjoyed that kind of baiting.

At the end the complicated confusions of the play are straightened out and all made plain in recognition and reconciliation at the neighbouring abbey. Outside the walls is

> the melancholy vale,
> The place of death and sorry execution,
> Behind the ditches of the abbey here.

James Burbage, Lord Chamberlain Hunsdon's man, had built the Theatre—first of London's theatres in the fields by Holywell Priory out beyond Bishopsgate, where Shakespeare lodged later. Here in the melancholy vale were gibbets where hangings took place. All very neighbourly and recognisable to the audience which saw the play there. Oddly enough, the Abbess, who turns out to be Aegeon's long-lost wife, is called Aemilia, the spelling which Shakespeare's Dark Lady affected for herself in publishing her poems years later. He knew her in this crucial year 1592.

Style. The style corroborates what we may call the school character of the play—so much of it is built up on the regular usages in the teaching of rhetoric. Much use is made of *inventio*, i.e. the logical elaboration of an idea, or a conceit, step by step into the structure; and of stichomathia, i.e. dialogue alternating fixedly line by line. Then there is endless punning, which the Elizabethans could not have enough of—and we easily too much. Shakespeare was a dab at this, an adept at word-play like no other—as he describes himself, in *Love's Labour Lost,* 'conceit's expositor'. Difficult to put into modern English, this means that he was a virtuoso at word-play, at expressing ideas, notions, conceits. There is much rhyme, as in all the early plays: it came easily to him.

Text. The text is a good one, from the First Folio of 1623, fairly certainly from a manuscript of the author, for the speech-prefixes prefer descriptive characters to personal names. This tendency of Shakespeare's points to his thinking practically in terms of characters as they fitted his available cast. There are various small inconsistencies which need not detain us, since they did not bother Shakespeare.

THE COMEDY OF ERRORS.

DRAMATIS PERSONÆ.

SOLINUS, duke of Ephesus.
ÆGEON, a merchant of Syracuse.
ANTIPHOLUS of Ephesus,
ANTIPHOLUS of Syracuse, } twin brothers, and sons to Ægeon and Æmilia.
DROMIO of Ephesus,
DROMIO of Syracuse, } twin brothers, and attendants on the two Antipholuses.
BALTHAZAR, a merchant.
ANGELO, a goldsmith.
First Merchant, friend to Antipholus of Syracuse.

Second Merchant, to whom Angelo is a debtor.
PINCH, a schoolmaster.

ÆMILIA, wife to Ægeon, an abbess at Ephesus.
ADRIANA, wife to Antipholus of Ephesus.
LUCIANA, her sister.
LUCE, servant to Adriana.
A Courtezan.

Gaoler, Officers, and other Attendants.

SCENE: *Ephesus.*

● *A bullet beside a text line indicates an annotation in the opposite column*

ACT I.

SCENE I. *A hall in the* DUKE'S *palace.*

Enter DUKE, ÆGEON, Gaoler, Officers, *and other* Attendants.

Æge. Proceed, Solinus, to procure my fall
And by the doom of death end woes and all.
  Duke. Merchant of Syracusa, plead no more ;
I am not partial to infringe our laws :
The enmity and discord which of late
Sprung from the rancorous outrage of your duke
To merchants, our well-dealing countrymen,
●Who wanting guilders to redeem their lives
Have seal'd his rigorous statutes with their bloods,
Excludes all pity from our threatening looks. 10
●For, since the mortal and intestine jars
'Twixt thy seditious countrymen and us,
It hath in solemn synods been decreed,
Both by the Syracusians and ourselves,
To admit no traffic to our adverse towns :
Nay, more,
If any born at Ephesus be seen
At any Syracusian marts and fairs ;
Again : if any Syracusian born

Ephesus. Engraving from Charles Knight's *Pictorial Edition of the Works of William Shakspere,* 1839–43

8 *guilders.* The guilder was a Dutch and German silver coin worth about one shilling and eight pence. Such foreign currency was often in circulation in Elizabethan England.

11 *intestine jars.* Internal quarrels.

Opposite: The Resolution Scene. Engraving by H. Gravelot from Theobald's edition of Shakespeare's works, 1740

Aegeon, Solinus and attendants. William Poel's production at Gray's Inn Hall, London, 1895

22 *marks.* Worth thirteen shillings and four pence in Shakespeare's day.

28 *evening sun.* This reference defines the play's time-span.

38-39 *happy . . . our hap been bad.* This can be paraphrased: 'happy except in me; and who would have been happy in me, too, had we not had a misfortune'.

42 *Epidamnum.* The setting of *Menaechmi* was in this town on the Adriatic in what is now Albania. *factor's.* The factor was a commercial agent.

43 *at random.* Untended.

59 *not meanly.* Not a little.

75 *delays.* i.e. from death.

77 *our boat.* The ship's boat.

Come to the bay of Ephesus, he dies,   20
His goods confiscate to the duke's dispose,
● Unless a thousand marks be levied,
To quit the penalty and to ransom him.
Thy substance, valued at the highest rate,
Cannot amount unto a hundred marks ;
Therefore by law thou art condemn'd to die.
Æge.   Yet this my comfort : when your words are done,
● My woes end likewise with the evening sun.
Duke.   Well, Syracusian, say in brief the cause
Why thou departed'st from thy native home   30
And for what cause thou camest to Ephesus.
Æge.   A heavier task could not have been imposed
Than I to speak my griefs unspeakable :
Yet, that the world may witness that my end
Was wrought by nature, not by vile offence,
I'll utter what my sorrow gives me leave.
In Syracusa was I born, and wed
● Unto a woman, happy but for me,
And by me, had not our hap been bad.

With her I lived in joy ; our wealth increased   40
By prosperous voyages I often made
● To Epidamnum ; till my factor's death
● And the great care of goods at random left
Drew me from kind embracements of my spouse :
From whom my absence was not six months old
Before herself, almost at fainting under
The pleasing punishment that women bear,
Had made provision for her following me
And soon and safe arrived where I was.
There had she not been long but she became   50
A joyful mother of two goodly sons ;
And, which was strange, the one so like the other
As could not be distinguish'd but by names.
That very hour and in the self-same inn
A meaner woman was delivered
Of such a burden, male twins, both alike :
Those, for their parents were exceeding poor,
I bought and brought up to attend my sons.
● My wife, not meanly proud of two such boys,
Made daily motions for our home return :   60
Unwilling I agreed ; alas ! too soon
We came aboard.
A league from Epidamnum had we sail'd,
Before the always wind-obeying deep
Gave any tragic instance of our harm :
But longer did we not retain much hope ;
For what obscured light the heavens did grant
Did but convey unto our fearful minds
A doubtful warrant of immediate death ;
Which though myself would gladly have embraced,
Yet the incessant weepings of my wife,   71
Weeping before for what she saw must come,
And piteous plainings of the pretty babes,
That mourn'd for fashion, ignorant what to fear,
● Forced me to seek delays for them and me.
And this it was, for other means was none :
● The sailors sought for safety by our boat,
And left the ship, then sinking-ripe, to us :
My wife, more careful for the latter-born,
Had fasten'd him unto a small spare mast,   80
Such as seafaring men provide for storms ;
To him one of the other twins was bound,
Whilst I had been like heedful of the other :
The children thus disposed, my wife and I,
Fixing our eyes on whom our care was fix'd,
Fasten'd ourselves at either end the mast ;

And floating straight, obedient to the stream,
Was carried towards Corinth, as we thought.
At length the sun, gazing upon the earth,
Dispersed those vapours that offended us ;   90
And, by the benefit of his wished light,
The seas wax'd calm, and we discovered
Two ships from far making amain to us,
Of Corinth that, of Epidaurus this :
But ere they came,—O, let me say no more !
Gather the sequel by that went before.
    Duke.   Nay, forward, old man ; do not break
      off so ;
For we may pity, though not pardon thee.
    Æge.   O, had the gods done so, I had not now
Worthily term'd them merciless to us !   100
For, ere the ships could meet by twice five leagues,
We were encounter'd by a mighty rock ;
Which being violently borne upon,
Our helpful ship was splitted in the midst ;
So that, in this unjust divorce of us,
Fortune had left to both of us alike
What to delight in, what to sorrow for.
Her part, poor soul ! seeming as burdened
With lesser weight but not with lesser woe,
Was carried with more speed before the wind ;   110
And in our sight they three were taken up
By fishermen of Corinth, as we thought.
At length, another ship had seized on us ;
And, knowing whom it was their hap to save,
Gave healthful welcome to their shipwreck'd
    guests ;
And would have reft the fishers of their prey,
Had not their bark been very slow of sail ;
And therefore homeward did they bend their
    course.
Thus have you heard me sever'd from my bliss,
That by misfortunes was my life prolong'd,   120
To tell sad stories of my own mishaps.
    Duke.   And, for the sake of them thou sorrow-
      est for,
●Do me the favour to dilate at full
What hath befall'n of them and thee till now.
●   *Æge.*   My youngest boy, and yet my eldest
    care,
At eighteen years became inquisitive
After his brother : and importuned me
That his attendant—so his case was like,
Reft of his brother, but retain'd his name—
Might bear him company in the quest of him :
●Whom whilst I labour'd of a love to see,   131
I hazarded the loss of whom I loved.
Five summers have I spent in furthest Greece,
Roaming clean through the bounds of Asia,
And, coasting homeward, came to Ephesus ;
Hopeless to find, yet loath to leave unsought
Or that or any place that harbours men.
But here must end the story of my life ;
And happy were I in my timely death,
Could all my travels warrant me they live.   140
    Duke.   Hapless Ægeon, whom the fates have
      mark'd
To bear the extremity of dire mishap !
Now, trust me, were it not against our laws,
Against my crown, my oath, my dignity,
Which princes, would they, may not disannul,
My soul should sue as advocate for thee.
But, though thou art adjudged to the death
And passed sentence may not be recall'd
But to our honour's great disparagement,

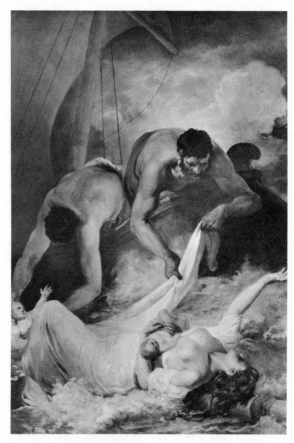

The Rescue of Aemilia from the Shipwreck. Painting by
Francis Wheatley (1747–1801)

123 *dilate.* Describe.

125 *youngest boy.* According to an earlier line the
mother took the younger boy. Such inconsistencies,
however, would not be noticed on stage.

131-132 *Whom whilst . . . I loved.* This can be ex-
plained : 'while he strove to see the lost twin out of love
for him, he hazarded the loss of the other, whom he also
loved'.

SD *Enter . . .* DROMIO. This is the name of a servant in John Lyly's *Mother Bombie*, printed in 1594, but acted probably some years before. Shakespeare may have borrowed the name from this play, although 'Dromo' is the name given to a slave in several of Terence's comedies.

An English merchant. Engraving from F. Modius' *Gynaeceum*, 1586

---

9 *host.* Lodge.

11 *dinner-time.* Between 11 am and 12 noon.

18 *mean.* Opportunity.

32 *commend you to your own content.* i.e. wish you all you wish for yourself.

Yet I will favour thee in what I can.   150
Therefore, merchant, I'll limit thee this day
To seek thy life by beneficial help:
Try all the friends thou hast in Ephesus;
Beg thou, or borrow, to make up the sum,
And live; if no, then thou art doom'd to die.
Gaoler, take him to thy custody.
    Gaol. I will, my lord.
    Æge. Hopeless and helpless doth Ægeon
        wend,
But to procrastinate his lifeless end.   [*Exeunt.*

SCENE II.   *The Mart.*

Enter ANTIPHOLUS *of Syracuse,* DROMIO *of Syracuse, and* First Merchant.

    First Mer.   Therefore give out you are of
        Epidamnum,
Lest that your goods too soon be confiscate.
This very day a Syracusian merchant
Is apprehended for arrival here;
And not being able to buy out his life
According to the statute of the town
Dies ere the weary sun set in the west.
There is your money that I had to keep.
    Ant. S.   Go bear it to the Centaur, where we
        host,
And stay there, Dromio, till I come to thee.   10
Within this hour it will be dinner-time:
Till that, I'll view the manners of the town,
Peruse the traders, gaze upon the buildings
And then return and sleep within mine inn,
For with long travel I am stiff and weary.
Get thee away.
    Dro. S.   Many a man would take you at your
        word,
And go indeed, having so good a mean.   [*Exit.*
    Ant. S.   A trusty villain, sir, that very oft,
When I am dull with care and melancholy,   20
Lightens my humour with his merry jests.
What, will you walk with me about the town,
And then go to my inn and dine with me?
    First Mer.   I am invited, sir, to certain mer-
        chants,
Of whom I hope to make much benefit;
I crave your pardon.   Soon at five o'clock,
Please you, I'll meet with you upon the mart
And afterward consort you till bed-time:
My present business calls me from you now.
    Ant. S.   Farewell till then: I will go lose my-
        self   30
And wander up and down to view the city.
    First Mer.   Sir, I commend you to your own
        content.   [*Exit.*
    Ant. S.   He that commends me to mine own
        content
Commends me to the thing I cannot get.
I to the world am like a drop of water
That in the ocean seeks another drop,
Who, falling there to find his fellow forth,
Unseen, inquisitive, confounds himself:
So I, to find a mother and a brother,
In quest of them, unhappy, lose myself.   40

Enter DROMIO *of Ephesus.*

Here comes the almanac of my true date.
What now? how chance thou art return'd so soon?
    Dro. E.   Return'd so soon! rather approach'd
        too late:

The capon burns, the pig falls from the spit,
The clock hath strucken twelve upon the bell;
My mistress made it one upon my cheek:
She is so hot because the meat is cold;
The meat is cold because you come not home;
You come not home because you have no stomach;
You have no stomach having broke your fast;
But we that know what 'tis to fast and pray   51
Are penitent for your default to-day.
   Ant. S.   Stop in your wind, sir: tell me this,
    I pray:
Where have you left the money that I gave you?
   Dro. E.   O,—sixpence, that I had o' Wednes-
    day last
•To pay the saddler for my mistress' crupper?
The saddler had it, sir; I kept it not.
   Ant. S.   I am not in a sportive humour now:
Tell me, and dally not, where is the money?
We being strangers here, how darest thou trust
So great a charge from thine own custody?   61
   Dro. E.   I pray you, jest, sir, as you sit at
    dinner:
•I from my mistress come to you in post;
If I return, I shall be post indeed,
For she will score your fault upon my pate.
•Methinks your maw, like mine, should be your
    clock
And strike you home without a messenger.
   Ant. S.   Come, Dromio, come, these jests are
    out of season;
Reserve them till a merrier hour than this.

Where is the gold I gave in charge to thee?   70
   Dro. E.   To me, sir? why, you gave no gold
    to me.
   Ant. S.   Come on, sir knave, have done your
    foolishness
And tell me how thou hast disposed thy charge.
   Dro. E.   My charge was but to fetch you from
    the mart
•Home to your house, the Phœnix, sir, to dinner:
My mistress and her sister stays for you.
   Ant. S.   Now, as I am a Christian, answer me
In what safe place you have bestow'd my money,
Or I shall break that merry sconce of yours
That stands on tricks when I am undisposed: 80
Where is the thousand marks thou hadst of me?
   Dro. E.   I have some marks of yours upon my
    pate,
Some of my mistress' marks upon my shoulders,
But not a thousand marks between you both.
If I should pay your worship those again,
Perchance you will not bear them patiently.
   Ant. S.   Thy mistress' marks? what mistress,
    slave, hast thou?
   Dro. E.   Your worship's wife, my mistress at
    the Phœnix:
She that doth fast till you come home to dinner
And prays that you will hie you home to dinner.
   Ant. S.   What, wilt thou flout me thus unto
    my face,   91
Being forbid?   There, take you that, sir knave.
   Dro. E.   What mean you, sir? for God's sake,
    hold your hands!
Nay, an you will not, sir, I'll take my heels.
                      [*Exit.*
   Ant. S.   Upon my life, by some device or other
The villain is o'er-raught of all my money.
•They say this town is full of cozenage,
As, nimble jugglers that deceive the eye,

56   *crupper*. Leather strap securing a horse's saddle.

63-64   *in post . . . post*. 'In post' means in haste; the 'post' was the door post on which tavern reckonings were scored (scratched).

66   *maw*. Belly.

75   *the Phœnix*. The house and also the shop of the merchant, Antipholus of Ephesus, identified by the sign of the phoenix.

The sign of the phoenix. Woodcut from *Libellus Natura Animalium*, 15th century bestiary

97   *cozenage*. Cheating.

97-105   *They say this town . . . is not safe*. This passage owes something to *Acts* xix where the magical practices of Ephesus are mentioned.

Mrs Herbert Morris as Adriana in William Poel's
production at Gray's Inn Hall, London, 1895

---

3 *two o'clock*. It was 12 noon in the previous scene.

16-24 *There's nothing . . . their lords*. These lines are
derived from certain biblical passages.

Mrs Charles Wyllie as Luciana in William Poel's
production, Gray's Inn Hall, London, 1895

Dark-working sorcerers that change the mind,
Soul-killing witches that deform the body,   100
Disguised cheaters, prating mountebanks,
And many such-like liberties of sin:
If it prove so, I will be gone the sooner.
I'll to the Centaur, to go seek this slave:
I greatly fear my money is not safe.   [*Exit*.

ACT II.

SCENE I. *The house of* ANTIPHOLUS *of Ephesus*.

Enter ADRIANA *and* LUCIANA.

Adr. Neither my husband nor the slave re-
turn'd,
That in such haste I sent to seek his master!
● Sure, Luciana, it is two o'clock.
   Luc. Perhaps some merchant hath invited him
And from the mart he's somewhere gone to
dinner.
Good sister, let us dine and never fret:
A man is master of his liberty:
Time is their master, and when they see time
They'll go or come: if so, be patient, sister.
   Adr. Why should their liberty than ours be
more?   10
   Luc. Because their business still lies out o'
door.
   Adr. Look, when I serve him so, he takes it
ill.
   Luc. O, know he is the bridle of your will.
   Adr. There's none but asses will be bridled so.
   Luc. Why, headstrong liberty is lash'd with
woe.
● There's nothing situate under heaven's eye
But hath his bound, in earth, in sea, in sky:
The beasts, the fishes and the winged fowls
Are their males' subjects and at their controls:
Men, more divine, the masters of all these,   20
Lords of the wide world and wild watery seas,
Indued with intellectual sense and souls,
Of more pre-eminence than fish and fowls,
Are masters to their females, and their lords:
Then let your will attend on their accords.
   Adr. This servitude makes you to keep unwed.
   Luc. Not this, but troubles of the marriage-bed.
   Adr. But, were you wedded, you would bear
some sway.
   Luc. Ere I learn love, I'll practise to obey.
   Adr. How if your husband start some other
where?   30
   Luc. Till he come home again, I would for-
bear.
   Adr. Patience unmoved! no marvel though
she pause;
They can be meek that have no other cause.
A wretched soul, bruised with adversity,
We bid be quiet when we hear it cry;
But were we burden'd with like weight of pain,
As much or more we should ourselves complain:
So thou, that hast no unkind mate to grieve thee,
With urging helpless patience wouldst relieve me;
But, if thou live to see like right bereft,   40
This fool-begg'd patience in thee will be left.
   Luc. Well, I will marry one day, but to try.
Here comes your man; now is your husband nigh.

Enter DROMIO *of Ephesus*.

   Adr. Say, is your tardy master now at hand?

Dro. E. Nay, he's at two hands with me, and that my two ears can witness.

Adr. Say, didst thou speak with him? know'st thou his mind?

Dro. E. Ay, ay, he told his mind upon mine ear:
Beshrew his hand, I scarce could understand it.

Luc. Spake he so doubtfully, thou couldst not feel his meaning? 51

Dro. E. Nay, he struck so plainly, I could too well feel his blows; and withal so doubtfully that I could scarce understand them.

Adr. But say, I prithee, is he coming home?
It seems he hath great care to please his wife.

● *Dro. E.* Why, mistress, sure my master is horn-mad.

Adr. Horn-mad, thou villain!

Dro. E.   I mean not cuckold-mad;
But, sure, he is stark mad.
When I desired him to come home to dinner, 60
He ask'd me for a thousand marks in gold:
''Tis dinner-time,' quoth I; 'My gold!' quoth he:
'Your meat doth burn,' quoth I; 'My gold!' quoth he:
'Will you come home?' quoth I; 'My gold!' quoth he,
'Where is the thousand marks I gave thee, villain?'
'The pig,' quoth I, 'is burn'd;' 'My gold!' quoth he:
'My mistress, sir,' quoth I; 'Hang up thy mistress!
I know not thy mistress; out on thy mistress!'

Luc. Quoth who?

Dro. E. Quoth my master: 70
'I know,' quoth he, 'no house, no wife, no mistress.'
● So that my errand, due unto my tongue,
I thank him, I bare home upon my shoulders;
For, in conclusion, he did beat me there.

Adr. Go back again, thou slave, and fetch him home.

Dro. E. Go back again, and be new beaten home?
For God's sake, send some other messenger.

Adr. Back, slave, or I will break thy pate across.

Dro. E. And he will bless that cross with other beating:
Between you I shall have a holy head. 80

Adr. Hence, prating peasant! fetch thy master home.

Dro. E. Am I so round with you as you with me,
That like a football you do spurn me thus?
You spurn me hence, and he will spurn me hither:
If I last in this service, you must case me in leather. [*Exit.*

Luc. Fie, how impatience loureth in your face!

● *Adr.* His company must do his minions grace,
Whilst I at home starve for a merry look.
Hath homely age the alluring beauty took
From my poor cheek? then he hath wasted it: 90
Are my discourses dull? barren my wit?
If voluble and sharp discourse be marr'd,
Unkindness blunts it more than marble hard:
Do their gay vestments his affections bait?
That's not my fault: he's master of my state:

Costume design for Adriana by J. Gower Parks, Regent's Park Open Air Theatre, London, 1934

57 *horn-mad.* Mad with rage (as of animals ready to attack with their horns); but the phrase quibbles on the anger of a cuckold.

72-73 *my errand . . . upon my shoulders.* i.e. I carried back on my shoulders (as a beating) the message (errand) that should have been given to me to deliver by word.

87 *minions.* Mistresses, paramours.

98 *fair.* Beauty.

100 *pale.* Fence.

101 *stale.* Plaything.

107 *alone, alone.* The general sense is either 'I would not mind if he kept the chain' or 'I wish that he would keep his love to himself'.

109-115 *I see . . . and weeping die.* As 'jewel' refers to Antipholus, Adriana seems to say that although he wastes his outward attractions with other women, his true value as a husband cannot be affected by falsehood or corruption.

2-5 *the heedful slave . . . at first.* Antipholus seems to be saying that he cannot find Dromio, who has not stayed at the inn, working out where he might be on the host's advice.

Dromio of Syracuse being beaten by Antipholus of Syracuse. Engraving by Kenny Meadows from Barry Cornwall's *The Works of Shakspere*, 1846

What ruins are in me that can be found,
By him not ruin'd? then is he the ground
● Of my defeatures. My decayed fair
A sunny look of his would soon repair:
● But, too unruly deer, he breaks the pale   100
● And feeds from home; poor I am but his stale.
    Luc. Self-harming jealousy! fie, beat it hence!
    Adr. Unfeeling fools can with such wrongs dispense.
I know his eye doth homage otherwhere;
Or else what lets it but he would be here?
Sister, you know he promised me a chain;
● Would that alone, alone he would detain,
So he would keep fair quarter with his bed!
● I see the jewel best enamelled
Will lose his beauty; yet the gold bides still,   110
That others touch, and often touching will
† Wear gold: and no man that hath a name,
By falsehood and corruption doth it shame.
Since that my beauty cannot please his eye,
I'll weep what's left away, and weeping die.
    Luc. How many fond fools serve mad jealousy!
                                 [Exeunt.

SCENE II. *A public place.*

Enter ANTIPHOLUS *of Syracuse.*

    Ant. S. The gold I gave to Dromio is laid up
● Safe at the Centaur; and the heedful slave
Is wander'd forth, in care to seek me out
By computation and mine host's report.
I could not speak with Dromio since at first
I sent him from the mart. See, here he comes.

Enter DROMIO *of Syracuse.*

How now, sir! is your merry humour alter'd?
As you love strokes, so jest with me again.
You know no Centaur? you received no gold?
Your mistress sent to have me home to dinner?   10
My house was at the Phœnix? Wast thou mad,
That thus so madly thou didst answer me?
    Dro. S. What answer, sir? when spake I such a word?
    Ant. S. Even now, even here, not half an hour since.
    Dro. S. I did not see you since you sent me hence,
Home to the Centaur, with the gold you gave me.
    Ant. S. Villain, thou didst deny the gold's receipt
And told'st me of a mistress and a dinner;
For which, I hope, thou felt'st I was displeased.
    Dro. S. I am glad to see you in this merry vein: 20
What means this jest? I pray you, master, tell me.
    Ant. S. Yea, dost thou jeer and flout me in the teeth?
Think'st thou I jest? Hold, take thou that, and that.   *[Beating him.*
    Dro. S. Hold, sir, for God's sake! now your jest is earnest:
Upon what bargain do you give it me?
    Ant. S. Because that I familiarly sometimes
Do use you for my fool and chat with you,
Your sauciness will jest upon my love
And make a common of my serious hours.
When the sun shines let foolish gnats make sport,   30
But creep in crannies when he hides his beams.

• If you will jest with me, know my aspect
And fashion your demeanour to my looks,
• Or I will beat this method in your sconce.
    Dro. S. Sconce call you it? so you would leave
battering, I had rather have it a head: an you
use these blows long, I must get a sconce for my
head and insconce it too; or else I shall seek my
wit in my shoulders.   But, I pray, sir, why am I
beaten?   40
    Ant. S. Dost thou not know?
    Dro. S. Nothing, sir, but that I am beaten.
    Ant. S. Shall I tell you why?
    Dro. S. Ay, sir, and wherefore; for they say
every why hath a wherefore.
    Ant. S. Why, first,—for flouting me; and
    then, wherefore,—
For urging it the second time to me.
    Dro. S. Was there ever any man thus beaten
    out of season,
When in the why and the wherefore is neither
    rhyme nor reason?
Well, sir, I thank you.   50
    Ant. S. Thank me, sir! for what?
    Dro. S. Marry, sir, for this something that
you gave me for nothing.
    Ant. S. I'll make you amends next, to give
you nothing for something   But say, sir, is it
dinner-time?
    Dro. S. No, sir: I think the meat wants that
I have.
    Ant. S. In good time, sir; what's that?
•   *Dro. S.* Basting.
    Ant. S. Well, sir, then 'twill be dry.   60
    Dro. S. If it be, sir, I pray you, eat none of it.
    Ant. S. Your reason?
    Dro. S. Lest it make you choleric and pur-
chase me another dry basting.
    Ant. S. Well, sir, learn to jest in good time:
there's a time for all things.
    Dro. S. I durst have denied that, before you
were so choleric.
    Ant. S. By what rule, sir?
    Dro. S. Marry, sir, by a rule as plain as the
plain bald pate of father Time himself.   71
    Ant. S. Let's hear it.
    Dro. S. There's no time for a man to recover
his hair that grows bald by nature.
    Ant. S. May he not do it by fine and recovery?
    Dro. S. Yes, to pay a fine for a periwig and
recover the lost hair of another man.
    Ant. S. Why is Time such a niggard of hair,
being, as it is, so plentiful an excrement?   79
    Dro. S. Because it is a blessing that he be-
stows on beasts; and what he hath scanted men
in hair he hath given them in wit.
    Ant. S. Why, but there's many a man hath
more hair than wit.
•   *Dro. S.* Not a man of those but he hath the
wit to lose his hair.
    Ant. S. Why, thou didst conclude hairy men
plain dealers without wit.
    Dro. S. The plainer dealer, the sooner lost:
• yet he loseth it in a kind of jollity.   90
    Ant. S. For what reason?
    Dro. S. For two; and sound ones too.
    Ant. S. Nay, not sound, I pray you.
    Dro. S. Sure ones then.
    Ant. S. Nay, not sure, in a thing falsing.
    Dro. S. Certain ones then.

32 *aspect.* In astrology, the relative positions of the planets (their aspects) were thought to influence an individual's behaviour.

34 *sconce.* This word meant 1) a head, 2) a small fort (subject to battering), 3) a screen or shelter.

59 *Basting.* Beating (used punningly).

85-86 *he hath the wit to lose his hair.* This is probably an allusion to the consequences of syphilis. Dr. Johnson noted: 'those who have more hair than wit are easily entrapped by loose women, and suffer the consequences of lewdness, one of which, in the first appearance of the disease in Europe, was the loss of hair'.

90 *jollity.* i.e. through sexual pleasure.

99 *tiring*. Dressing his hair. *they*. i.e. his hair.

100 *porridge*. Soup.

110 *bald*. Trivial, foolish.

125 *better part*. This could refer either to a man's soul or to his best qualities, possibly both.

138 *stain'd skin*. The brow proverbially indicated character, especially shame or guilt.

149 *Plead you to me, fair dame?* A memorable production of the play at Stratford-upon-Avon, 1962, directed by Clifford Williams, was full of new stresses—especially when Alec McCowen (Antipholus of Syracuse), after listening to thirty-seven lines of fervent blank verse by Adriana, said in bewilderment: 'Plead you to *me*, fair dame?'

Antipholus of Syracuse: 'Plead you to me . . .' Engraving by H. Fuseli from George Steevens' *The Plays of William Shakspeare*, 1805

Ant. S. Name them.

Dro. S. The one, to save the money that he
● spends in tiring; the other that at dinner they
● should not drop in his porridge.   100

Ant. S. You would all this time have proved there is no time for all things.

Dro. S. Marry, and did, sir; namely, no time to recover hair lost by nature.

Ant. S. But your reason was not substantial, why there is no time to recover.

Dro. S. Thus I mend it: Time himself is bald and therefore to the world's end will have bald followers.

● *Ant. S.* I knew 'twould be a bald conclusion:
But, soft! who wafts us yonder?   111

Enter ADRIANA *and* LUCIANA.

Adr. Ay, ay, Antipholus, look strange and frown:
Some other mistress hath thy sweet aspects;
I am not Adriana nor thy wife.
The time was once when thou unurged wouldst vow
That never words were music to thine ear,
That never object pleasing in thine eye,
That never touch well welcome to thy hand,
That never meat sweet-savour'd in thy taste,
Unless I spake, or look'd, or touch'd, or carved to thee.   120
How comes it now, my husband, O, how comes it,
That thou art thus estranged from thyself?
Thyself I call it, being strange to me,
That, undividable, incorporate,
● Am better than thy dear self's better part.
Ah, do not tear away thyself from me!
For know, my love, as easy mayst thou fall
A drop of water in the breaking gulf
And take unmingled thence that drop again,
Without addition or diminishing,   130
As take from me thyself and not me too.
How dearly would it touch thee to the quick,
Shouldst thou but hear I were licentious
And that this body, consecrate to thee,
By ruffian lust should be contaminate!
Wouldst thou not spit at me and spurn at me
And hurl the name of husband in my face
● And tear the stain'd skin off my harlot-brow
And from my false hand cut the wedding-ring
And break it with a deep-divorcing vow?   140
I know thou canst; and therefore see thou do it.
I am possess'd with an adulterate blot;
My blood is mingled with the crime of lust:
For if we two be one and thou play false,
I do digest the poison of thy flesh,
Being strumpeted by thy contagion.
Keep then fair league and truce with thy true bed;
I live unstain'd, thou undishonoured.
● *Ant. S.* Plead you to me, fair dame? I know you not:
In Ephesus I am but two hours old,   150
As strange unto your town as to your talk;
Who, every word by all my wit being scann'd,
Want wit in all one word to understand.

Luc. Fie, brother! how the world is changed with you!
When were you wont to use my sister thus?
She sent for you by Dromio home to dinner.

Ant. S. By Dromio?

Dro. S. By me?

Adr.   By thee; and this thou didst return
      from him,
That he did buffet thee and in his blows   160
Denied my house for his, me for his wife.
    Ant. S.   Did you converse, sir, with this gen-
      tlewoman?
● What is the course and drift of your compact?
    Dro. S.   I, sir? I never saw her till this time.
    Ant. S.   Villain, thou liest; for even her very
      words
Didst thou deliver to me on the mart.
    Dro. S.   I never spake with her in all my life.
    Ant. S.   How can she thus then call us by
      our names?
Unless it be by inspiration.
    Adr.   How ill agrees it with your gravity   170
To counterfeit thus grossly with your slave,
Abetting him to thwart me in my mood!
Be it my wrong you are from me exempt,
But wrong not that wrong with a more contempt.
● Come, I will fasten on this sleeve of thine:
● Thou art an elm, my husband, I a vine,
Whose weakness married to thy stronger state
Makes me with thy strength to communicate:
If aught possess thee from me, it is dross,
Usurping ivy, brier, or idle moss;   180
Who, all for want of pruning, with intrusion
Infect thy sap and live on thy confusion.
    Ant. S.   To me she speaks; she moves me for
      her theme:
What, was I married to her in my dream?
Or sleep I now and think I hear all this?
What error drives our eyes and ears amiss?
Until I know this sure uncertainty,
I'll entertain the offer'd fallacy.

    Luc.   Dromio, go bid the servants spread for
      dinner.
    Dro. S.   O, for my beads! I cross me for a
      sinner.   190
This is the fairy land: O spite of spites!
We talk with goblins, owls and sprites:
If we obey them not, this will ensue,
They'll suck our breath or pinch us black and
      blue.
    Luc.   Why pratest thou to thyself and an-
      swer'st not?
Dromio, thou drone, thou snail, thou slug, thou
      sot!
    Dro. S.   I am transformed, master, am I not?
    Ant. S.   I think thou art in mind, and so am I.
    Dro. S.   Nay, master, both in mind and in my
      shape.
    Ant. S.   Thou hast thine own form.
    Dro. S.   No, I am an ape.   200
    Luc.   If thou art changed to aught, 'tis to an
      ass.
● *Dro. S.*   'Tis true; she rides me and I long
      for grass.
'Tis so, I am an ass; else it could never be
But I should know her as well as she knows me.
    Adr.   Come, come, no longer will I be a fool,
To put the finger in the eye and weep,
Whilst man and master laugh my woes to scorn.
Come, sir, to dinner. Dromio, keep the gate
Husband, I'll dine above with you to-day
● And shrive you of a thousand idle pranks.   210
Sirrah, if any ask you for your master,
Say he dines forth and let no creature enter.
Come, sister. Dromio, play the porter well.

163 *course and drift*. These two words have the same
meaning 'gist'. *compact*. Agreement.

175 *sleeve*. This seems more appropriate to the doublet
of Shakespeare's time than to a Roman garment.

176-182 *Thou art an elm . . . thy confusion*. References
to the training of vines on elm trees are found in the
Bible, in proverbs and in Ovid's *Metamorphoses*. The
last was Shakespeare's likely source since here the image
occurs in a passage dealing with marriage.

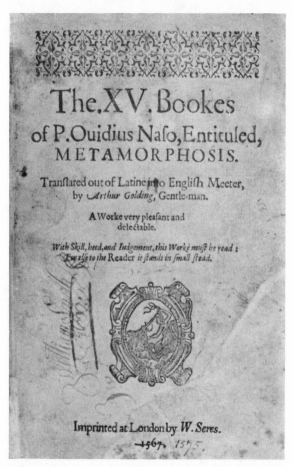

Title page of the XV book of Ovid's *Metamorphoses*
translated by Arthur Golding, 1575

202 *for grass*. For freedom.

210 *shrive you*. Forgive you.

Costume design for the Dromios by J. Gower Parks,
Regent's Park Open Air Theatre, London, 1934

---

4 *carcanet*. Necklace set with jewels.

28 *cates*. Delicacies.

Ant. S. Am I in earth, in heaven, or in hell?
Sleeping or waking? mad or well-advised?
Known unto these, and to myself disguised!
I'll say as they say and persever so
And in this mist at all adventures go.
    Dro. S. Master, shall I be porter at the gate?
    Adr. Ay; and let none enter, lest I break your
    pate.   220
    Luc. Come, come, Antipholus, we dine too
    late.   [*Exeunt.*

ACT III.

SCENE I. *Before the house of* ANTIPHOLUS *of*
Ephesus.

Enter ANTIPHOLUS *of* Ephesus, DROMIO *of*
Ephesus, ANGELO, *and* BALTHAZAR.

    Ant. E. Good Signior Angelo, you must ex-
    cuse us all;
My wife is shrewish when I keep not hours:
Say that I linger'd with you at your shop
• To see the making of her carcanet
And that to-morrow you will bring it home.
But here's a villain that would face me down
He met me on the mart and that I beat him
And charged him with a thousand marks in gold
And that I did deny my wife and house.
Thou drunkard, thou, what didst thou mean by
    this?   10
Dro. E. Say what you will, sir, but I know what
    I know;
That you beat me at the mart, I have your hand
    to show:
If the skin were parchment and the blows you
    gave were ink,
Your own handwriting would tell you what I think.
    Ant. E. I think thou art an ass.
    Dro. E.   Marry, so it doth appear
By the wrongs I suffer and the blows I bear.
I should kick, being kick'd; and, being at that
    pass,
You would keep from my heels and beware of
    an ass.
    Ant. E. You're sad, Signior Balthazar: pray
    God our cheer
May answer my good will and your good wel-
    come here.   20
    Bal. I hold your dainties cheap, sir, and your
    welcome dear.
    Ant. E. O, Signior Balthazar, either at flesh
    or fish,
A table full of welcome makes scarce one dainty
    dish.
    Bal. Good meat, sir, is common; that every
    churl affords.
    Ant. E. And welcome more common; for
    that's nothing but words.
    Bal. Small cheer and great welcome makes a
    merry feast.
    Ant. E. Ay to a niggardly host and more
    sparing guest:
• But though my cates be mean, take them in good
    part;
Better cheer may you have, but not with better
    heart.
But, soft! my door is lock'd. Go bid them let
    us in.   30

Dro. E. Maud, Bridget, Marian, Cicely, Gillian, Ginn!

● *Dro. S.* [*Within*] Mome, malt-horse, capon, coxcomb, idiot, patch!
Either get thee from the door or sit down at the hatch.
Dost thou conjure for wenches, that thou call'st for such store,
When one is one too many? Go get thee from the door.

Dro. E. What patch is made our porter? My master stays in the street.

● *Dro. S.* [*Within*] Let him walk from whence he came, lest he catch cold on's feet.

Ant. E. Who talks within there? ho, open the door!

Dro. S. [*Within*] Right, sir; I'll tell you when, an you'll tell me wherefore.

Ant. E. Wherefore? for my dinner: I have not dined to-day. 40

Dro. S. [*Within*] Nor to-day here you must not; come again when you may.

Ant. E. What art thou that keepest me out from the house I owe?

Dro. S. [*Within*] The porter for this time, sir, and my name is Dromio.

Dro. E. O villain! thou hast stolen both mine office and my name.

● The one ne'er got me credit, the other mickle blame.
If thou hadst been Dromio to-day in my place,

● Thou wouldst have changed thy face for a name or thy name for an ass.

Luce. [*Within*] What a coil is there, Dromio? who are those at the gate?

Dro. E. Let my master in, Luce.

Luce. [*Within*] Faith, no; he comes too late;
And so tell your master.

Dro. E.   O Lord, I must laugh!

● Have at you with a proverb—Shall I set in my staff?

Luce. [*Within*] Have at you with another; that's—When? can you tell?

Dro. S. [*Within*] If thy name be call'd Luce,— Luce, thou hast answer'd him well.

● *Ant. E.* Do you hear, you minion? you'll let us in, I hope?

● *Luce.* [*Within*] I thought to have ask'd you.

Dro. S.   [*Within*] And you said no.

Dro. E. So, come, help: well struck! there was blow for blow.

Ant. E. Thou baggage, let me in.

Luce. [*Within*] Can you tell for whose sake?

Dro. E. Master, knock the door hard.

Luce.   [*Within*] Let him knock till it ache.

Ant. E. You'll cry for this, minion, if I beat the door down.

Luce. [*Within*] What needs all that, and a pair of stocks in the town? 60

Adr. [*Within*] Who is that at the door that keeps all this noise?

● *Dro. S.* [*Within*] By my troth, your town is troubled with unruly boys.

Ant. E. Are you there, wife? you might have come before.

Adr. [*Within*] Your wife, sir knave! go get you from the door.

● *Dro. E.* If you went in pain, master, this 'knave' would go sore.

Ang. Here is neither cheer, sir, nor welcome: we would fain have either.

32 *Mome, malt-horse, capon . . . patch. Mome*: blockhead; *malt-horse*: a heavy dray horse, hence a stupid person; *capon*: gelded cockerel, therefore, a eunuch; *patch*: a fool.

37 *catch cold on's feet.* The Italian proverb 'to have a cold at the feet' meant 'to be forced to sell cheap'.

45 *mickle.* Great.

47 *Thou wouldst . . . an ass.* This line could mean either 'You would have been willing to exchange your *face* (identity) for someone else's *name* (so as to avoid blame)', or 'your *name* for that of an *ass* (as an acknowledgement of the situation)'.

51 *Shall I set in my staff?* i.e. shall I make myself at home here?

54 *minion.* Hussy.

55 *I thought to have ask'd you.* A mocking retort. Lyly uses the same expression in *Mother Bombie*.

Dromio of Ephesus: 'Master, Knock the door hard . . .'
Engraving by Kenny Meadows from Barry Cornwall's *The Works of Shakspere*, 1846

62 *boys.* Fellows (used contemptuously).

65 *If you went . . . go sore.* Dromio could be saying to his master 'You are the knave she means'; or perhaps 'If you are beaten, I, who am properly a knave (servant), will suffer even more'.

The structure shown in the rear of this woodcut of a
Terence play suggests how the Elizabethans might have
staged a 'within' and 'without' scene. Illustration from
The Comedies of Terence, published by Johann Trechsel,
1493

---

68 *They*. i.e. Angelo and Balthasar. Dromio is having
a jest at his master's expense, since none of them can get
in.

71 *Your cake there*. Probably an allusion to Adriana.
'Cake' when used with reference to a woman means 'a
delicacy'.

77 *hind*. Countryman, rustic.

83 *pluck a crow together*. A proverbial expression meaning 'settle our quarrel'.

102 *ungalled*. Unsullied.

115 *chain*. i.e. the necklace (carcanet).

Bal. In debating which was best, we shall
 part with neither.
• *Dro. E.* They stand at the door, master; bid
 them welcome hither.
Ant. E. There is something in the wind, that
 we cannot get in.
Dro. E. You would say so, master, if your
 garments were thin. 70
• Your cake there is warm within; you stand here
 in the cold:
It would make a man mad as a buck, to be so
 bought and sold.
Ant. E. Go fetch me something: I'll break
 ope the gate.
Dro. S. [*Within*] Break any breaking here,
 and I'll break your knave's pate.
Dro. E. A man may break a word with you,
 sir, and words are but wind,
Ay, and break it in your face, so he break it not
 behind.
• *Dro. S.* [*Within*] It seems thou want'st
 breaking: out upon thee, hind!
Dro. E. Here's too much 'out upon thee!' I
 pray thee, let me in.
Dro. S. [*Within*] Ay, when fowls have no
 feathers and fish have no fin.
Ant. E. Well, I'll break in: go borrow me a
 crow. 80
Dro. E. A crow without feather? Master,
 mean you so?
For a fish without a fin, there's a fowl without a
 feather:
• If a crow help us in, sirrah, we'll pluck a crow
 together.
Ant. E. Go get thee gone; fetch me an iron
 crow.
Bal. Have patience, sir; O, let it not be so!
Herein you war against your reputation
And draw within the compass of suspect
The unviolated honour of your wife.
Once this,—your long experience of her wisdom,
Her sober virtue, years and modesty, 90
Plead on her part some cause to you unknown;
And doubt not, sir, but she will well excuse
Why at this time the doors are made against you.
Be ruled by me: depart in patience,
And let us to the Tiger all to dinner,
And about evening come yourself alone
To know the reason of this strange restraint.
If by strong hand you offer to break in
Now in the stirring passage of the day,
A vulgar comment will be made of it, 100
And that supposed by the common rout
• Against your yet ungalled estimation
That may with foul intrusion enter in
And dwell upon your grave when you are dead;
For slander lives upon succession,
For ever housed where it gets possession.
Ant. E. You have prevail'd: I will depart
 in quiet,
And, in despite of mirth, mean to be merry.
I know a wench of excellent discourse,
Pretty and witty, wild and yet, too, gentle: 110
There will we dine.   This woman that I mean,
My wife—but, I protest, without desert—
Hath oftentimes upbraided me withal:
To her will we to dinner. [*To Ang.*] Get you
 home
• And fetch the chain; by this I know 'tis made:

Bring it, I pray you, to the Porpentine;
For there's the house: that chain will I bestow—
Be it for nothing but to spite my wife—
Upon mine hostess there: good sir, make haste.
Since mine own doors refuse to entertain me, 120
I'll knock elsewhere, to see if they'll disdain me.
    Ang. I'll meet you at that place some hour
    hence.
    Ant. E. Do so. This jest shall cost me some
    expense.   [*Exeunt.*

SCENE II. *The same.*

Enter LUCIANA *and* ANTIPHOLUS *of Syracuse.*

    Luc. And may it be that you have quite
    forgot
A husband's office? shall, Antipholus,
Even in the spring of love, thy love-springs rot?
    Shall love, in building, grow so ruinous?
If you did wed my sister for her wealth,
    Then for her wealth's sake use her with more
    kindness:
Or if you like elsewhere, do it by stealth;
    Muffle your false love with some show of
    blindness:
Let not my sister read it in your eye;
    Be not thy tongue thy own shame's orator; 10
Look sweet, speak fair, become disloyalty;
    Apparel vice like virtue's harbinger:
Bear a fair presence, though your heart be
    tainted;
    Teach sin the carriage of a holy saint;
Be secret-false: what need she be acquainted?
•   What simple thief brags of his own attaint?
'Tis double wrong, to truant with your bed
•   And let her read it in thy looks at board:
Shame hath a bastard fame, well managed;
    Ill deeds are doubled with an evil word.   20
Alas, poor women! make us but believe,
•   Being compact of credit, that you love us;
Though others have the arm, show us the sleeve;
    We in your motion turn and you may move us.
Then, gentle brother, get you in again;
    Comfort my sister, cheer her, call her wife:
•'Tis holy sport to be a little vain,
    When the sweet breath of flattery conquers
    strife.
    Ant. S. Sweet mistress,—what your name is
    else, I know not,
•   Nor by what wonder you do hit of mine,— 30
Less in your knowledge and your grace you
    show not
    Than our earth's wonder, more than earth
    divine.
Teach me, dear creature, how to think and
    speak;
    Lay open to my earthy-gross conceit,
Smother'd in errors, feeble, shallow, weak,
    The folded meaning of your words' deceit.
Against my soul's pure truth why labour you
    To make it wander in an unknown field?
Are you a god? would you create me new?
    Transform me then, and to your power I'll
    yield.   40
But if that I am I, then well I know
    Your weeping sister is no wife of mine,
Nor to her bed no homage do I owe:
    Far more, far more to you do I decline.
O, train me not, sweet mermaid, with thy note,

16 *attaint.* Disgrace.

18 *at board.* At table.

22 *compact of credit.* Credulous.

27 *to be . . . vain.* To utter false words.

30 *hit of.* Guess at.

Antipholus of Syracuse (Roger Reese) and Luciana
(Francesca Annis). Royal Shakespeare Co, 1976

Antipholus of Syracuse: 'Sing, siren . . .' Engraving from Charles Knight's *Pictorial Edition of the Works of William Shakspere*, 1839–43

51 *to die*. This was commonly used in reference to an orgasm.

54 *mated*. Quibbling on the word meaning both 'confounded' and 'partnered (wedded)'.

66 *I am thee*. i.e. call yourself 'sister' if you wish: it is in you that I have lost my identity.

93 *'Sir-reverence'*. A corruption of 'save-your-reverence', and used as an apology for saying something offensive.

97 *grease*. Punning on 'grace', since both words had a similar pronunciation.

To drown me in thy sister's flood of tears:
Sing, siren, for thyself and I will dote:
  Spread o'er the silver waves thy golden hairs,
And as a bed I'll take them and there lie,
And in that glorious supposition think   50
He gains by death that hath such means to die:
  Let Love, being light, be drowned if she sink!
   Luc. What, are you mad, that you do reason so?
   Ant. S. Not mad, but mated; how, I do not know.
   Luc. It is a fault that springeth from your eye.
   Ant. S. For gazing on your beams, fair sun, being by.
   Luc. Gaze where you should, and that will clear your sight.
   Ant. S. As good to wink, sweet love, as look on night.
   Luc. Why call you me love? call my sister so.
   Ant. S. Thy sister's sister.
   Luc.   That's my sister.
   Ant. S.   No;   60
It is thyself, mine own self's better part,
Mine eye's clear eye, my dear heart's dearer heart,
My food, my fortune and my sweet hope's aim,
My sole earth's heaven and my heaven's claim.
   Luc. All this my sister is, or else should be.
   Ant. S. Call thyself sister, sweet, for I am thee.
Thee will I love and with thee lead my life:
Thou hast no husband yet nor I no wife.
Give me thy hand.
   Luc.   O, soft, sir! hold you still:
I'll fetch my sister, to get her good will. [*Exit.* 70

    Enter DROMIO of Syracuse.

   Ant. S. Why, how now, Dromio! where runn'st thou so fast?
   Dro. S. Do you know me, sir? am I Dromio? am I your man? am I myself?
   Ant. S. Thou art Dromio, thou art my man, thou art thyself.
   Dro. S. I am an ass, I am a woman's man and besides myself.
   Ant. S. What woman's man? and how besides thyself?   80
   Dro. S. Marry, sir, besides myself, I am due to a woman; one that claims me, one that haunts me, one that will have me.
   Ant. S. What claim lays she to thee?
   Dro. S. Marry, sir, such claim as you would lay to your horse; and she would have me as a beast: not that, I being a beast, she would have me; but that she, being a very beastly creature, lays claim to me.
   Ant. S. What is she?   90
   Dro. S. A very reverent body; ay, such a one as a man may not speak of without he say 'Sir-reverence.' I have but lean luck in the match, and yet is she a wondrous fat marriage.
   Ant. S. How dost thou mean a fat marriage?
   Dro. S. Marry, sir, she's the kitchen wench and all grease; and I know not what use to put her to but to make a lamp of her and run from her by her own light. I warrant, her rags and the tallow in them will burn a Poland winter: if she lives till doomsday, she'll burn a week longer than the whole world.

Ant. S.   What complexion is she of?

Dro. S.   Swart, like my shoe, but her face nothing like so clean kept: for why, she sweats; a man may go over shoes in the grime of it.

Ant. S.   That's a fault that water will mend.

Dro. S.   No, sir, 'tis in grain; Noah's flood could not do it.

Ant. S.   What's her name?   110

Dro. S.   Nell, sir; but her name and three quarters, that's an ell and three quarters, will not measure her from hip to hip.

Ant. S.   Then she bears some breadth?

Dro. S.   No longer from head to foot than from hip to hip: she is spherical, like a globe; I could find out countries in her.

Ant. S.   In what part of her body stands Ireland?

Dro. S.   Marry, sir, in her buttocks: I found it out by the bogs.   121

Ant. S.   Where Scotland?

Dro. S.   I found it by the barrenness; hard in the palm of the hand.

Ant. S.   Where France?

Dro. S.   In her forehead; armed and reverted, making war against her heir.

Ant. S.   Where England?

Dro. S.   I looked for the chalky cliffs, but I could find no whiteness in them; but I guess it stood in her chin, by the salt rheum that ran between France and it.

Ant. S.   Where Spain?

Dro. S.   Faith, I saw it not; but I felt it hot in her breath.

Ant. S.   Where America, the Indies?

Dro. S.   Oh, sir, upon her nose, all o'er embellished with rubies, carbuncles, sapphires, declining their rich aspect to the hot breath of Spain; who sent whole armadoes of caracks to be ballast at her nose.   141

Ant. S.   Where stood Belgia, the Netherlands?

Dro. S.   Oh, sir, I did not look so low. To conclude, this drudge, or diviner, laid claim to me; called me Dromio; swore I was assured to her; told me what privy marks I had about me, as, the mark of my shoulder, the mole in my neck, the great wart on my left arm, that I amazed ran from her as a witch:
And, I think, if my breast had not been made of
    faith and my heart of steel,   150
She had transform'd me to a curtal dog and made
    me turn i' the wheel.

Ant. S.   Go hie thee presently, post to the road.
An if the wind blow any way from shore,
I will not harbour in this town to-night:
If any bark put forth, come to the mart,
Where I will walk till thou return to me.
If every one knows us and we know none,
'Tis time, I think, to trudge, pack and be gone.

Dro. S.   As from a bear a man would run for life,
So fly I from her that would be my wife. [*Exit.*

Ant. S.   There's none but witches do inhabit
    here;   161
And therefore 'tis high time that I were hence.
She that doth call me husband, even my soul
Doth for a wife abhor.   But her fair sister,
Possess'd with such a gentle sovereign grace,
Of such enchanting presence and discourse,
Hath almost made me traitor to myself:
But, lest myself be guilty to self-wrong,

104 *Swart.* Dark, swarthy.

111 *Nell.* This character is clearly the same person as Luce. Shakespeare altered her name for the sake of the pun on *ell* and to avoid confusion with Luciana.

112 *ell.* A measure indicating 1¼ yards.

126-127 *armed . . . her heir.* This is a reference to the civil war (in France) between Henry IV and the (Catholic) League. Dr. Johnson also saw an allusion here to the consequences of venereal disease: 'By a forehead "armed", he means covered with encrusted eruptions; by "reverted", he means having the hair turning backward'.

Henry IV of France. Engraving from a painting by Frans Pourbus (1569–1622)

140 *armadoes of caracks.* Fleets of merchant ships.

141 *ballast.* i.e. loaded.

151 *curtal dog.* Household dog with its tail cut short. *turn i' the wheel.* Tread, as dogs often did, a wheel which turned a roasting spit.

185 *vain.* Foolish.

187 *shifts.* Tricks.

Costume design for the Antipholuses by J. Gower Parks. Regent's Park Open Air Theatre, London, 1934

22 *holp up.* Helped.

I'll stop mine ears against the mermaid's song.

Enter ANGELO *with the chain.*

Ang.   Master Antipholus,—
Ant. S.   Ay, that's my name.   170
Ang.   I know it well, sir: lo, here is the chain.
I thought to have ta'en you at the Porpentine:
The chain unfinish'd made me stay thus long.
Ant. S.   What is your will that I shall do with
   this?
Ang.   What please yourself, sir: I have made
   it for you.
Ant. S.   Made it for me, sir! I bespoke it not.
Ang.   Not once, nor twice, but twenty times
   you have.
Go home with it and please your wife withal;
And soon at supper-time I'll visit you
And then receive my money for the chain.   180
Ant. S.   I pray you, sir, receive the money now,
For fear you ne'er see chain nor money more.
Ang.   You are a merry man, sir: fare you well.
                                          [*Exit.*

Ant. S.   What I should think of this, I cannot
   tell:
• But this I think, there's no man is so vain
   That would refuse so fair an offer'd chain.
• I see a man here needs not live by shifts,
   When in the streets he meets such golden gifts.
   I'll to the mart and there for Dromio stay:
   If any ship put out, then straight away.   [*Exit.*

ACT IV.

SCENE I.   *A public place.*

Enter Second Merchant, ANGELO, *and an*
Officer.

Sec. Mer.   You know since Pentecost the sum
   is due,
And since I have not much importuned you;
Nor now I had not, but that I am bound
To Persia and want guilders for my voyage:
Therefore make present satisfaction,
Or I'll attach you by this officer.
Ang.   Even just the sum that I do owe to you
Is growing to me by Antipholus,
And in the instant that I met with you
He had of me a chain: at five o'clock   10
I shall receive the money for the same.
Pleaseth you walk with me down to his house,
I will discharge my bond and thank you too.

Enter ANTIPHOLUS of Ephesus *and* DROMIO
of Ephesus *from the courtezan's.*

Off.   That labour may you save: see where he
   comes.
Ant. E.   While I go to the goldsmith's house,
   go thou
And buy a rope's end: that will I bestow
Among my wife and her confederates,
For locking me out of my doors by day.
But, soft! I see the goldsmith.   Get thee gone;
Buy thou a rope and bring it home to me.   20
Dro. E.   I buy a thousand pound a year: I
   buy a rope.   [*Exit.*
• *Ant. E.*   A man is well holp up that trusts to
   you:
I promised your presence and the chain;
But neither chain nor goldsmith came to me.

Belike you thought our love would last too long,
If it were chain'd together, and therefore came
   not.
   Ang.   Saving your merry humour, here's the
      note
How much your chain weighs to the utmost carat,
●The fineness of the gold and chargeful fashion,
●Which doth amount to three odd ducats more 30
Than I stand debted to this gentleman:
I pray you, see him presently discharged,
For he is bound to sea and stays but for it.
   Ant. E.   I am not furnish'd with the present
      money;
Besides, I have some business in the town.
Good signior, take the stranger to my house
And with you take the chain and bid my wife
Disburse the sum on the receipt thereof:
Perchance I will be there as soon as you.
   Ang.   Then you will bring the chain to her
      yourself?   40
   Ant. E.   No; bear it with you, lest I come
      not time enough.
   Ang.   Well, sir, I will.   Have you the chain
      about you?
   Ant. E.   An if I have not, sir, I hope you
      have;
Or else you may return without your money.
   Ang.   Nay, come, I pray you, sir, give me
      the chain:
Both wind and tide stays for this gentleman,
And I, to blame, have held him here too long.
   Ant. E.   Good Lord! you use this dalliance
      to excuse
Your breach of promise to the Porpentine.
I should have chid you for not bringing it,   50
But, like a shrew, you first begin to brawl.
   Sec. Mer.   The hour steals on; I pray you,
      sir, dispatch.
   Ang.   You hear how he importunes me;—the
      chain!
   Ant. E.   Why, give it to my wife and fetch
      your money.
   Ang.   Come, come, you know I gave it you
      even now.
Either send the chain or send me by some token.
   Ant. E.   Fie, now you run this humour out of
      breath,
Come, where's the chain?   I pray you, let me
      see it.
   Sec. Mer.   My business cannot brook this dalli-
      ance.
Good sir, say whether you'll answer me or no: 60
If not, I'll leave him to the officer.
   Ant. E.   I answer you! what should I answer
      you?
   Ang.   The money that you owe me for the
      chain.
   Ant. E.   I owe you none till I receive the
      chain.
   Ang.   You know I gave it you half an hour
      since.
   Ant. E.   You gave me none: you wrong me
      much to say so.
   Ang.   You wrong me more, sir, in denying it:
Consider how it stands upon my credit.
   Sec. Mer.   Well, officer, arrest him at my suit.
   Off.   I do; and charge you in the duke's name
      to obey me.   70
   Ang.   This touches me in reputation.

29   *chargeful.* Costly.

30   *ducats.* Gold coins of several European countries.

Costume design for Angelo by J. Gower Parks, Regent's
Park Open Air Theatre, London, 1934

78 *apparently*. Openly.

87 *fraughtage*. Baggage.

89 *balsamum and aqua-vitæ*. Balm, aromatic resin: aqua-vitae, spirits.

Compounding a balsam. Woodcut from a broadside in the collection of the Society of Antiquaries

95 *waftage*. Passage.

110 *Dowsabel*. From French *Douce et belle,* (i.e. sweet and beautiful, applied ironically to Nell).

Either consent to pay this sum for me
Or I attach you by this officer.
  Ant. E.   Consent to pay thee that I never
    had!
Arrest me, foolish fellow, if thou darest.
  Ang.   Here is thy fee; arrest him, officer.
I would not spare my brother in this case,
• If he should scorn me so apparently.
  Off.   I do arrest you, sir: you hear the suit.
  Ant. E.   I do obey thee till I give thee bail.
But, sirrah, you shall buy this sport as dear   81
As all the metal in your shop will answer.
  Ang.   Sir, sir, I shall have law in Ephesus,
To your notorious shame; I doubt it not.

Enter DROMIO *of Syracuse, from the bay.*

  Dro. S.   Master, there is a bark of Epidamnum
That stays but till her owner comes aboard
• And then, sir, she bears away.   Our fraughtage,
    sir,
I have convey'd aboard and I have bought
• The oil, the balsamum and aqua-vitæ.
The ship is in her trim; the merry wind   90
Blows fair from land: they stay for nought at all
But for their owner, master, and yourself.
  Ant. E.   How now! a madman!   Why, thou
    peevish sheep,
What ship of Epidamnum stays for me?
•   *Dro. S.*   A ship you sent me to, to hire waftage.
  Ant. E.   Thou drunken slave, I sent thee for
    a rope
And told thee to what purpose and what end.
  Dro. S.   You sent me for a rope's end as soon:
You sent me to the bay, sir, for a bark.
  Ant. E.   I will debate this matter at more
    leisure   100
And teach your ears to list me with more heed.
To Adriana, villain, hie thee straight:
Give her this key, and tell her, in the desk
That's cover'd o'er with Turkish tapestry
There is a purse of ducats; let her send it:
Tell her I am arrested in the street
And that shall bail me: hie thee, slave, be gone!
On, officer, to prison till it come.
    [*Exeunt Sec. Merchant, Angelo,*
        Officer, and Ant. E.
  Dro. S.   To Adriana! that is where we dined,
• Where Dowsabel did claim me for her husband:
She is too big, I hope, for me to compass.   111
Thither I must, although against my will,
For servants must their masters' minds fulfil.
        [*Exit.*

SCENE II.   *The house of* ANTIPHOLUS *of*
    Ephesus.

Enter ADRIANA *and* LUCIANA.

  Adr.   Ah, Luciana, did he tempt thee so?
Mightst thou perceive austerely in his eye
That he did plead in earnest? yea or no?
  Look'd he or red or pale, or sad or merrily?
What observation madest thou in this case
Of his heart's meteors tilting in his face?
  Luc.   First he denied you had in him no right.
  Adr.   He meant he did me none; the more
    my spite.
  Luc.   Then swore he that he was a stranger
    here.

Adr. And true he swore, though yet forsworn he were. 10
Luc. Then pleaded I for you.
Adr.   And what said he?
Luc. That love I begg'd for you he begg'd of me.
Adr. With what persuasion did he tempt thy love?
Luc. With words that in an honest suit might move.
First he did praise my beauty, then my speech.
● *Adr.* Didst speak him fair?
Luc.   Have patience, I beseech.
Adr. I cannot, nor I will not, hold me still;
My tongue, though not my heart, shall have his will.
● He is deformed, crooked, old and sere,
Ill-faced, worse bodied, shapeless everywhere; 20
Vicious, ungentle, foolish, blunt, unkind,
● Stigmatical in making, worse in mind.
Luc. Who would be jealous then of such a one?
No evil lost is wail'd when it is gone.
Adr. Ah, but I think him better than I say,
And yet would herein others' eyes were worse.
Far from her nest the lapwing cries away:
My heart prays for him, though my tongue do curse.

Enter DROMIO of Syracuse.

Dro. S. Here! go; the desk, the purse! sweet, now, make haste.
Luc. How hast thou lost thy breath?
Dro. S.   By running fast. 30
Adr. Where is thy master, Dromio? is he well?
● *Dro. S.* No, he's in Tartar limbo, worse than hell.
● † A devil in an everlasting garment hath him;
One whose hard heart is button'd up with steel;
A fiend, a fury, pitiless and rough;
A wolf, nay, worse, a fellow all in buff;
● A back-friend, a shoulder-clapper, one that countermands
The passages of alleys, creeks and narrow lands;
● A hound that runs counter and yet draws dry-foot well;
One that before the judgement carries poor souls to hell. 40
Adr. Why, man, what is the matter?
Dro. S. I do not know the matter: he is 'rested on the case.
Adr. What, is he arrested? Tell me at whose suit.
Dro. S. I know not at whose suit he is arrested well;
But he's in a suit of buff which 'rested him, that can I tell.
Will you send him, mistress, redemption, the money in his desk?
Adr. Go fetch it, sister. [*Exit Luciana.*]
This I wonder at,
That he, unknown to me, should be in debt.
● Tell me, was he arrested on a band?
Dro. S. Not on a band, but on a stronger thing; 50
A chain, a chain! Do you not hear it ring?
Adr. What, the chain?
Dro. S. No, no, the bell: 'tis time that I were gone:

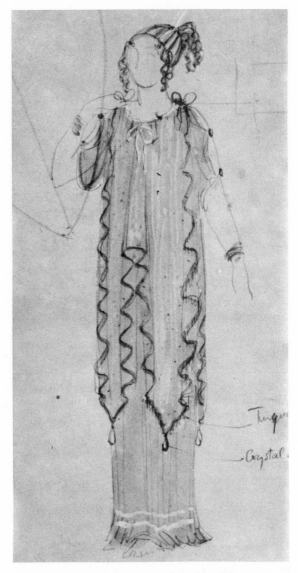

Costume design for Luciana by J. Gower Parks, Regent's Park Open Air Theatre, London, 1934

16 *speak him fair?* i.e. you speak kindly to him?

19 *sere.* Withered.

22 *Stigmatical in making.* Deformed in appearance.

32 *Tartar limbo.* i.e. worse than Christian hell.

33 *everlasting garment.* Everlasting was the name of the material used for the dress of prison officers.

37 *back-friend, shoulder-clapper.* A back friend is a false friend; the reference is to the police officer's clapping a person on the back as he arrests him.

39 *draws dry-foot.* To hunt by the mere scent of the foot.

49 *band.* Bond.

58 *Time . . . owes more than he's worth to season.* This cryptic line is usually taken to mean 'there is never time to do all that occasion offers'.

65 *conceit.* Thought, or fancy.

11 *Lapland sorcerers.* Lapland was noted for sorcery.

Map of Europe showing Lapland. From Ortelius' *Epitome to the Theatre of the World*, 1598

13-14 *What . . . new-apparelled.* The general sense of this could be 'Have you managed to get the sergeant, who resembled old Adam in wearing buff, into another "suit"?'

18-19 *calf's skin . . . Prodigal.* An allusion to the fatted calf that was killed for the prodigal son. Dromio also refers to the sergeant's leather coat.

25 *sob.* A rest given to a horse to allow it to recover its wind.

27 *sets up his rest.* Is determined.

28 *morris-pike.* Moorish pike.

It was two ere I left him, and now the clock
    strikes one.
Adr. The hours come back ! that did I never
    hear.
Dro. S. O, yes; if any hour meet a sergeant,
    a' turns back for very fear.
Adr. As if Time were in debt ! how fondly
    dost thou reason !
● *Dro. S.* Time is a very bankrupt and owes
    more than he's worth to season.
Nay, he's a thief too : have you not heard men say,
That Time comes stealing on by night and day ? 60
If Time be in debt and theft, and a sergeant in
    the way,
Hath he not reason to turn back an hour in a day ?

Re-enter LUCIANA *with a purse.*

Adr. Go, Dromio ; there's the money, bear it
    straight,
And bring thy master home immediately.
●Come, sister : I am press'd down with conceit—
Conceit, my comfort and my injury. [*Exeunt.*

SCENE III.   *A public place.*

Enter ANTIPHOLUS *of Syracuse.*

Ant. S. There's not a man I meet but doth
    salute me
As if I were their well-acquainted friend ;
And every one doth call me by my name.
Some tender money to me ; some invite me ;
Some other give me thanks for kindnesses ;
Some offer me commodities to buy :
Even now a tailor call'd me in his shop
And show'd me silks that he had bought for me
And therewithal took measure of my body.
Sure, these are but imaginary wiles   10
●And Lapland sorcerers inhabit here.

Enter DROMIO *of Syracuse.*

Dro. S. Master, here's the gold you sent me
●for.   What, have you got the picture of old Adam
new-apparelled ?
Ant. S. What gold is this ? what Adam dost
    thou mean ?
Dro. S. Not that Adam that kept the Paradise, but that Adam that keeps the prison : he
●that goes in the calf's skin that was killed for the
Prodigal ; he that came behind you, sir, like an
evil angel, and bid you forsake your liberty.   20
Ant. S. I understand thee not.
Dro. S. No ? why, 'tis a plain case : he that
went, like a bass-viol, in a case of leather ; the
man, sir, that, when gentlemen are tired, gives
●them a sob and 'rests them ; he, sir, that takes
pity on decayed men and gives them suits of
●durance ; he that sets up his rest to do more ex-
●ploits with his mace than a morris-pike.
Ant. S. What, thou meanest an officer ?
Dro. S. Ay, sir, the sergeant of the band ; he
that brings any man to answer it that breaks his
band ; one that thinks a man always going to bed
and says 'God give you good rest !'
Ant. S. Well, sir, there rest in your foolery.
Is there any ship puts forth to-night ? may we be
gone ?
Dro. S. Why, sir, I brought you word an
hour since that the bark Expedition put forth
to-night ; and then were you hindered by the

sergeant, to tarry for the hoy Delay.   Here
are the angels that you sent for to deliver you.
    Ant. S.   The fellow is distract, and so am I ;
And here we wander in illusions :
Some blessed power deliver us from hence !

            Enter a Courtezan.
    Cour.   Well met, well met, Master Anti-
    pholus.
I see, sir, you have found the goldsmith now :
Is that the chain you promised me to-day ?
    Ant. S.   Satan, avoid ! I charge thee, tempt
    me not.
    Dro. S.   Master, is this Mistress Satan ?
    Ant. S.   It is the devil.   50
    Dro. S.   Nay, she is worse, she is the devil's
dam ; and here she comes in the habit of a light
wench : and thereof comes that the wenches say
'God damn me ;' that's as much to say 'God
make me a light wench.'   It is written, they
appear to men like angels of light : light is an
effect of fire, and fire will burn ; ergo, light
wenches will burn.   Come not near her.
    Cour.   Your man and you are marvellous
    merry, sir.
Will you go with me ?   We'll mend our dinner
    here ?   60
    Dro. S.   Master, if you do, expect spoon-
meat ; or bespeak a long spoon.
    Ant. S.   Why, Dromio ?
    Dro. S.   Marry, he must have a long spoon
that must eat with the devil.
    Ant. S.   Avoid then, fiend ! what tell'st thou
    me of supping ?
Thou art, as you are all, a sorceress :
I conjure thee to leave me and be gone.
    Cour.   Give me the ring of mine you had at
    dinner,
Or, for my diamond, the chain you promised, 70
And I'll be gone, sir, and not trouble you.
    Dro. S.   Some devils ask but the parings of
    one's nail,
A rush, a hair, a drop of blood, a pin,
A nut, a cherry-stone ;
But she, more covetous, would have a chain.
Master, be wise : an if you give it her,
The devil will shake her chain and fright us
    with it.
    Cour.   I pray you, sir, my ring, or else the
    chain :
I hope you do not mean to cheat me so.
    Ant. S.   Avaunt, thou witch !   Come, Dromio,
    let us go.   80
    Dro. S.   'Fly pride,' says the peacock : mis-
tress, that you know.
              [*Exeunt Ant. S. and Dro. S.*
    Cour.   Now, out of doubt Antipholus is mad,
Else would he never so demean himself.
A ring he hath of mine worth forty ducats,
And for the same he promised me a chain :
Both one and other he denies me now.
The reason that I gather he is mad,
Besides this present instance of his rage,
Is a mad tale he told to-day at dinner,
Of his own doors being shut against his entrance.
Belike his wife, acquainted with his fits,   91
On purpose shut the doors against his way.
My way is now to hie home to his house,
And tell his wife that, being lunatic,

40 *hoy*. A small coasting vessel.

41 *angels*. Gold coins worth up to ten shillings, here
having a punning reference.

Courtezan (Vivienne Bennett), Antipholus of Syracuse
(John Van Eyssen) and Dromio of Syracuse (John
Garley), Royal Court Theatre, London, 1952

56-57 *light . . . will burn*. i.e. will infect with venereal
disease.

72-74 *parings . . . cherry-stone*. These are objects used
in witchcraft.

80 *Avaunt*. Be off !

John Dunstal, 18th century English actor, as Dromio of Ephesus, Covent Garden Theatre, London, 1762

40 *wont*. Is accustomed to.

44-46 *'respice finem'* . . . *rope's end'*. There are two jokes here. One is a pun on *respice finem* i.e. think of your end, and *respice funem* i.e. a rope for hanging. Parrots were taught to cry 'rope'.

He rush'd into my house and took perforce
My ring away.   This course I fittest choose;
For forty ducats is too much to lose.   [*Exit.*

SCENE IV.   *A street.*

Enter ANTIPHOLUS of Ephesus *and the* Officer.

Ant. E.   Fear me not, man; I will not break
          away:
I'll give thee, ere I leave thee, so much money,
To warrant thee, as I am 'rested for.
My wife is in a wayward mood to-day,
And will not lightly trust the messenger.
That I should be attach'd in Ephesus,
I tell you, 'twill sound harshly in her ears.

Enter DROMIO of Ephesus *with a rope's-end.*

Here comes my man; I think he brings the
          money.
How now, sir! have you that I sent you for?
  Dro. E.   Here's that, I warrant you, will pay
          them all.   10
  Ant. E.   But where's the money?
  Dro. E.   Why, sir, I gave the money for
the rope.
  Ant. E.   Five hundred ducats, villain, for
a rope?
  Dro. E.   I'll serve you, sir, five hundred at
the rate.
  Ant. E.   To what end did I bid thee hie thee
home?
  Dro. E.   To a rope's-end, sir; and to that end
am I returned.
  Ant. E.   And to that end, sir, I will welcome
you.   [*Beating him.*
  Off.   Good sir, be patient.
  Dro. E.   Nay, 'tis for me to be patient; I am
in adversity.   21
  Off.   Good now, hold thy tongue.
  Dro. E.   Nay, rather persuade him to hold
his hands.
  Ant. E.   Thou whoreson, senseless villain!
  Dro. E.   I would I were senseless, sir, that I
might not feel your blows.
  Ant. E.   Thou art sensible in nothing but
blows, and so is an ass.
  Dro. E.   I am an ass, indeed; you may prove
it by my long ears.   I have served him from the
hour of my nativity to this instant, and have
nothing at his hands for my service but blows.
When I am cold, he heats me with beating;
when I am warm, he cools me with beating:
I am waked with it when I sleep; raised with
it when I sit; driven out of doors with it when I
go from home; welcomed home with it when I
return: nay, I bear it on my shoulders, as a
beggar wont her brat; and, I think, when he
hath lamed me, I shall beg with it from door to
door.
  Ant. E.   Come, go along; my wife is coming
yonder.

Enter ADRIANA, LUCIANA, *the* Courtezan,
and PINCH.

  Dro. E.   Mistress, 'respice finem,' respect
your end; or rather, †the prophecy like the
parrot, 'beware the rope's-end.'
  Ant. E.   Wilt thou still talk? [*Beating him.*

56

Cour. How say you now? is not your husband mad?

Adr. His incivility confirms no less.
● Good Doctor Pinch, you are a conjurer;   50
Establish him in his true sense again,
And I will please you what you will demand.

Luc. Alas, how fiery and how sharp he looks!

Cour. Mark how he trembles in his ecstasy!

Pinch. Give me your hand and let me feel
your pulse.

Ant. E. There is my hand, and let it feel
your ear.   [*Striking him.*

Pinch. I charge thee, Satan, housed within
this man,
To yield possession to my holy prayers
And to thy state of darkness hie thee straight:
I conjure thee by all the saints in heaven!   60

Ant. E. Peace, doting wizard, peace! I am
not mad.

Adr. O, that thou wert not, poor distressed
soul!

Ant. E. You minion, you, are these your
customers?
Did this companion with the saffron face
Revel and feast it at my house to-day,
Whilst upon me the guilty doors were shut
And I denied to enter in my house?

Adr. O husband, God doth know you dined
at home;
Where would you had remain'd until this time,
Free from these slanders and this open shame!

Ant. E. Dined at home! Thou villain, what
sayest thou?   71

Dro. E. Sir, sooth to say, you did not dine at
home.

Ant. E. Were not my doors lock'd up and I
shut out?
● *Dro. E.* Perdie, your doors were lock'd and
you shut out.

Ant. E. And did not she herself revile me
there?

Dro. E. Sans fable she herself reviled you
there.

Ant. E. Did not her kitchen-maid rail, taunt
and scorn me?

Dro. E. Certes, she did; the kitchen-vestal
scorn'd you.

Ant. E. And did not I in rage depart from
thence?

Dro. E. In verity you did; my bones bear
witness,   80
That since have felt the vigour of his rage.

Adr. Is't good to soothe him in these con-
traries?

Pinch. It is no shame: the fellow finds his vein
And yielding to him humours well his frenzy.

Ant. E. Thou hast suborn'd the goldsmith to
arrest me.

Adr. Alas, I sent you money to redeem you,
By Dromio here, who came in haste for it.

Dro. E. Money by me! heart and good-will
you might;
● But surely, master, not a rag of money.

Ant. E. Went'st not thou to her for a purse
of ducats?   90

Adr. He came to me and I deliver'd it.

Luc. And I am witness with her that she did.

Dro. E. God and the rope-maker bear me
witness

50 *Doctor Pinch.* Pinch, played by Robert Helpmann, stole the show in the Old Vic production of 1957. Kenneth Tynan in the *Observer* called his 'a riveting intervention . . . acting all by himself in the left-hand corner of the stage, and got up like one of the less inhibited members of the Chinese Classical Theatre'.

Robert Helpmann as Dr Pinch, Old Vic, 1957

74 *Perdie.* i.e. per dieu (assuredly).

89 *rag of money.* A farthing.

97 *bound and laid in some dark room.* This was the accepted treatment for lunacy.

The binding of Antipholus of Ephesus. Engraving from a design by F. Hayman for Hanmer's edition, 1744

124 *knowing how the debt grows.* i.e. knowing the reason for the debt.

132 *idly.* Foolishly.

That I was sent for nothing but a rope!
Pinch.   Mistress, both man and master is possess'd;
I know it by their pale and deadly looks:
●They must be bound and laid in some dark room.
Ant. E.   Say, wherefore didst thou lock me
    forth to-day?
And why dost thou deny the bag of gold?
Adr.   I did not, gentle husband, lock thee
    forth.   100
Dro. E.   And, gentle master, I received no
    gold;
But I confess, sir, that we were lock'd out.
Adr.   Dissembling villain, thou speak'st false
    in both.
Ant. E.   Dissembling harlot, thou art false in all
And art confederate with a damned pack
To make a loathsome abject scorn of me:
But with these nails I'll pluck out these false eyes
That would behold in me this shameful sport.

*Enter three or four, and offer to bind him.   He
    strives.*

Adr.   O, bind him, bind him! let him not
    come near me.
Pinch.   More company!   The fiend is strong
    within him.   110
Luc.   Ay me, poor man, how pale and wan he
    looks!
Ant. E.   What, will you murder me?   Thou
    gaoler, thou,
I am thy prisoner: wilt thou suffer them
To make a rescue?
Off.   Masters, let him go:
He is my prisoner, and you shall not have him.
Pinch.   Go bind this man, for he is frantic too.
    [*They offer to bind Dro. E.*
Adr.   What wilt thou do, thou peevish officer?
Hast thou delight to see a wretched man
Do outrage and displeasure to himself?
Off.   He is my prisoner: if I let him go,   120
The debt he owes will be required of me.
Adr.   I will discharge thee ere I go from thee:
Bear me forthwith unto his creditor
●And, knowing how the debt grows, I will pay it.
Good master doctor, see him safe convey'd
Home to my house.   O most unhappy day!
Ant. E.   O most unhappy strumpet!
Dro. E.   Master, I am here enter'd in bond
    for you.
Ant. E.   Out on thee, villain! wherefore dost
    thou mad me?
Dro. E.   Will you be bound for nothing? be
mad, good master: cry 'The devil!'   131
● *Luc.*   God help, poor souls, how idly do they
    talk!
Adr.   Go bear him hence.   Sister, go you with
    me.   [*Exeunt all but Adriana, Luciana,
                    Officer and Courtezan.*]
Say now, whose suit is he arrested at?
Off.   One Angelo, a goldsmith: do you know
    him?
Adr.   I know the man.   What is the sum he
    owes?
Off.   Two hundred ducats.
Adr.   Say, how grows it due?
Off.   Due for a chain your husband had of him.
Adr.   He did bespeak a chain for me, but had
    it not.

Cour. When as your husband all in rage to-day
Came to my house and took away my ring— 141
The ring I saw upon his finger now—
Straight after did I meet him with a chain.
　Adr. It may be so, but I did never see it.
Come, gaoler, bring me where the goldsmith is :
I long to know the truth hereof at large.

Enter ANTIPHOLUS of Syracuse *with his rapier
drawn, and* DROMIO *of Syracuse.*

　Luc. God, for thy mercy ! they are loose again.
　Adr. And come with naked swords.
Let's call more help to have them bound again.
　Off. Away ! they'll kill us.　　　　150
　　[*Exeunt all but Ant. S. and Dro. S.*
　Ant. S. I see these witches are afraid of
swords.
　Dro. S. She that would be your wife now ran
from you.
　Ant. S. Come to the Centaur ; fetch our stuff
from thence :
I long that we were safe and sound aboard.
　Dro. S. Faith, stay here this night ; they will
surely do us no harm : you saw they speak us
fair, give us gold : methinks they are such a
gentle nation that, but for the mountain of mad
flesh that claims marriage of me, I could find in
my heart to stay here still and turn witch.　160
　Ant. S. I will not stay to-night for all the
town ;
Therefore away, to get our stuff aboard.
　　　　　　　　　　　　　　[*Exeunt.*

ACT V.

SCENE I.　*A street before a Priory.*

Enter Second Merchant *and* ANGELO.

　Ang. I am sorry, sir, that I have hinder'd you ;
But, I protest, he had the chain of me,
Though most dishonestly he doth deny it.
　Sec. Mer. How is the man esteem'd here in
　　the city ?
　Ang. Of very reverend reputation, sir,
Of credit infinite, highly beloved,
Second to none that lives here in the city :
● His word might bear my wealth at any time.
　Sec. Mer. Speak softly : yonder, as I think,
　　he walks.

Enter ANTIPHOLUS of Syracuse *and* DROMIO
of Syracuse.

　Ang. 'Tis so ; and that self chain about his
　　neck　　　　　　　　　　　　10
Which he forswore most monstrously to have.
Good sir, draw near to me, I'll speak to him.
Signior Antipholus, I wonder much
That you would put me to this shame and trouble ;
And, not without some scandal to yourself,
With circumstance and oaths so to deny
This chain which now you wear so openly :
Beside the charge, the shame, imprisonment,
You have done wrong to this my honest friend,
Who, but for staying on our controversy,　20
Had hoisted sail and put to sea to-day :
This chain you had of me ; can you deny it ?
　Ant. S. I think I had ; I never did deny it.
　Sec. Mer. Yes, that you did, sir, and forswore
　　it too.

Design for Courtezan's costume by J. Gower Parks,
Regent's Park Open Air Theatre, London, 1934

8 *His word might bear my wealth at any time.* i.e. he might
borrow so much on his word alone.

Second Merchant: 'I dare and do defy thee . . .' William
Poel's production, Gray's Inn Hall, London, 1895

Elizabeth Inchbald, 18th century actress, as Lady
Abbess. Engraved from a design by R. Ramberg, 1781

Ant. S. Who heard me to deny it or forswear it?
Sec. Mer.   These ears of mine, thou know'st,
    did hear thee.
Fie on thee, wretch! 'tis pity that thou livest
To walk where any honest men resort.
    Ant. S. Thou art a villain to impeach me thus:
I'll prove mine honour and mine honesty   30
Against thee presently, if thou darest stand.
    Sec. Mer. I dare, and do defy thee for a villain.
                             [*They draw.*

Enter ADRIANA, LUCIANA, *the* Courtezan, *and
            others.*

    Adr. Hold, hurt him not, for God's sake! he
    is mad.
Some get within him, take his sword away:
Bind Dromio too, and bear them to my house.
    Dro. S. Run, master, run; for God's sake,
    take a house!
This is some priory.   In, or we are spoil'd!
    [*Exeunt Ant. S. and Dro. S. to the Priory.*

        Enter the Lady Abbess.
    Abb. Be quiet, people.   Wherefore throng you
    hither?
    Adr. To fetch my poor distracted husband
    hence.
Let us come in, that we may bind him fast   40
And bear him home for his recovery.
    Ang. I knew he was not in his perfect wits.
    Sec. Mer. I am sorry now that I did draw on
    him.
    Abb. How long hath this possession held the
    man?
    Adr. This week he hath been heavy, sour, sad,
And much different from the man he was;
But till this afternoon his passion
Ne'er brake into extremity of rage.
    Abb. Hath he not lost much wealth by wreck
    of sea?
Buried some dear friend?   Hath not else his eye
Stray'd his affection in unlawful love?   51
A sin prevailing much in youthful men,
Who give their eyes the liberty of gazing.
Which of these sorrows is he subject to?
    Adr. To none of these, except it be the last;
Namely, some love that drew him oft from home.
    Abb. You should for that have reprehended him.
    Adr. Why, so I did.
    Abb.   Ay, but not rough enough.
    Adr. As roughly as my modesty would let me.
    Abb. Haply, in private.
    Adr.   And in assemblies too.
    Abb. Ay, but not enough.   61
    Adr. It was the copy of our conference:
In bed he slept not for my urging it;
At board he fed not for my urging it;
Alone, it was the subject of my theme;
In company I often glanced it;
Still did I tell him it was vile and bad.
    Abb. And thereof came it that the man was
    mad:
The venom clamours of a jealous woman
Poisons more deadly than a mad dog's tooth.   70
It seems his sleeps were hinder'd by thy railing,
And thereof comes it that his head is light.
Thou say'st his meat was sauced with thy up-
    braidings:
Unquiet meals make ill digestions;

Thereof the raging fire of fever bred ;
And what's a fever but a fit of madness ?
Thou say'st his sports were hinder'd by thy brawls :
Sweet recreation barr'd, what doth ensue
But moody and dull melancholy,
Kinsman to grim and comfortless despair,   80
And at her heels a huge infectious troop
Of pale distemperatures and foes to life ?
In food, in sport and life-preserving rest
To be disturb'd, would mad or man or beast :
The consequence is then thy jealous fits
Have scared thy husband from the use of wits.
   Luc.   She never reprehended him but mildly,
When he demean'd himself rough, rude and wildly.
Why bear you these rebukes and answer not ?
●   *Adr.*   She did betray me to my own reproof. 90
Good people, enter and lay hold on him.
   Abb.   No, not a creature enters in my house.
   Adr.   Then let your servants bring my husband
    forth.
   Abb.   Neither : he took this place for sanctuary,
And it shall privilege him from your hands
Till I have brought him to his wits again,
Or lose my labour in assaying it.
   Adr.   I will attend my husband, be his nurse,
Diet his sickness, for it is my office,
And will have no attorney but myself ;   100
And therefore let me have him home with me.
   Abb.   Be patient ; for I will not let him stir
Till I have used the approved means I have,
With wholesome syrups, drugs and holy prayers,
To make of him a formal man again :
It is a branch and parcel of mine oath,
A charitable duty of my order.
Therefore depart and leave him here with me.
   Adr.   I will not hence and leave my husband
    here :
And ill it doth beseem your holiness   110
To separate the husband and the wife.
   Abb.   Be quiet and depart : thou shalt not have
    him.   [*Exit.*
   Luc.   Complain unto the duke of this indignity.
   Adr.   Come, go : I will fall prostrate at his feet
And never rise until my tears and prayers
Have won his grace to come in person hither
And take perforce my husband from the abbess.
   Sec. Mer.   By this, I think, the dial points at
    five :
Anon, I'm sure, the duke himself in person
Comes this way to the melancholy vale,   120
The place of death and sorry execution,
Behind the ditches of the abbey here.
   Ang.   Upon what cause ?
   Sec. Mer.   To see a reverend Syracusian
    merchant,
Who put unluckily into this bay
Against the laws and statutes of this town,
Beheaded publicly for his offence.
   Ang.   See where they come : we will behold
    his death.
   Luc.   Kneel to the duke before he pass the
    abbey.

Enter DUKE, *attended* ; ÆGEON *bareheaded* ;
   with the Headsman *and other* Officers.

   Duke.   Yet once again proclaim it publicly, 130
If any friend will pay the sum for him,
He shall not die ; so much we tender him.

90 *She did betray me to my own reproof.* i.e. trick me into
testifying against myself.

Solinus, Duke of Ephesus (Dennis Hoey), Regent's
Park Open Air Theatre, London, 1934

138 *important*. Importunate.

175 *nicks him like a fool*. Cuts his hair to make him look like a professional fool.

185 *halberds*. Long spears with a small axe at top.

Costume design for the guards of Solinus by J. Gower Parks, Regent's Park Open Air Theatre, London, 1934

Adr.   Justice, most sacred duke, against the abbess!
Duke.   She is a virtuous and a reverend lady:
It cannot be that she hath done thee wrong.
Adr.   May it please your grace, Antipholus my husband,
Whom I made lord of me and all I had,
• At your important letters,—this ill day
A most outrageous fit of madness took him;
That desperately he hurried through the street,—
With him his bondman, all as mad as he,—   141
Doing displeasure to the citizens
By rushing in their houses, bearing thence
Rings, jewels, any thing his rage did like.
Once did I get him bound and sent him home,
Whilst to take order for the wrongs I went
That here and there his fury had committed.
Anon, I wot not by what strong escape,
He broke from those that had the guard of him;
And with his mad attendant and himself,   150
Each one with ireful passion, with drawn swords,
Met us again and madly bent on us
Chased us away, till raising of more aid
We came again to bind them.   Then they fled
Into this abbey, whither we pursued them:
And here the abbess shuts the gates on us
And will not suffer us to fetch him out,
Nor send him forth that we may bear him hence.
Therefore, most gracious duke, with thy command
Let him be brought forth and borne hence for help.
Duke.   Long since thy husband served me in my wars,   161
And I to thee engaged a prince's word,
When thou didst make him master of thy bed,
To do him all the grace and good I could.
Go, some of you, knock at the abbey-gate
And bid the lady abbess come to me.
I will determine this before I stir.

Enter a Servant.

Serv.   O mistress, mistress, shift and save yourself!
My master and his man are both broke loose,
Beaten the maids a-row and bound the doctor,   170
Whose beard they have singed off with brands of fire;
And ever, as it blazed, they threw on him
Great pails of puddled mire to quench the hair:
My master preaches patience to him and the while
• His man with scissors nicks him like a fool,
And sure, unless you send some present help,
Between them they will kill the conjurer.
Adr.   Peace, fool! thy master and his man are here,
And that is false thou dost report to us.
Serv.   Mistress, upon my life, I tell you true;
I have not breathed almost since I did see it.   181
He cries for you and vows, if he can take you,
To scorch your face and to disfigure you.
[*Cry within.*
Hark, hark! I hear him, mistress: fly, be gone!
Duke.   Come, stand by me; fear nothing.
Guard with halberds!
Adr.   Ay me, it is my husband!   Witness you,
That he is borne about invisible:
Even now we housed him in the abbey here;
And now he's there, past thought of human reason.

Enter ANTIPHOLUS *of Ephesus and* DROMIO *of Ephesus.*

   Ant. E. Justice, most gracious duke, O, grant
     me justice !   190
Even for the service that long since I did thee,
•When I bestrid thee in the wars and took
Deep scars to save thy life ; even for the blood
That then I lost for thee, now grant me justice.
   Æge. Unless the fear of death doth make me
     dote,
I see my son Antipholus and Dromio.
   Ant. E. Justice, sweet prince, against that
     woman there !
She whom thou gavest to me to be my wife,
That hath abused and dishonour'd me
Even in the strength and height of injury !   200
Beyond imagination is the wrong
That she this day hath shameless thrown on me.
• *Duke.* Discover how, and thou shalt find me
     just.
   Ant. E. This day, great duke, she shut the
     doors upon me,
•While she with harlots feasted in my house.
   Duke. A grievous fault ! Say, woman, didst
     thou so ?
   Adr. No, my good lord : myself, he and my
     sister
To-day did dine together. So befall my soul
As this is false he burdens me withal !

   Luc. Ne'er may I look on day, nor sleep on
     night,   210
But she tells to your highness simple truth !
   Ang. O perjured woman ! They are both
     forsworn :
In this the madman justly chargeth them.
   Ant. E. My liege, I am advised what I say,
Neither disturbed with the effect of wine,
Nor heady-rash, provoked with raging ire,
Albeit my wrongs might make one wiser mad.
This woman lock'd me out this day from dinner :
That goldsmith there, were he not pack'd with her,
Could witness it, for he was with me then ; 220
Who parted with me to go fetch a chain,
Promising to bring it to the Porpentine,
Where Balthazar and I did dine together.
Our dinner done, and he not coming thither,
I went to seek him : in the street I met him
And in his company that gentleman.
There did this perjured goldsmith swear me down
That I this day of him received the chain,
Which, God he knows, I saw not : for the which
He did arrest me with an officer.   230
I did obey, and sent my peasant home
For certain ducats : he with none return'd.
Then fairly I bespoke the officer
To go in person with me to my house.
By the way we met
My wife, her sister, and a rabble more
Of vile confederates. Along with them
They brought one Pinch, a hungry lean-faced
     villain,
A mere anatomy, a mountebank,
A threadbare juggler and a fortune-teller,
A needy, hollow-eyed, sharp-looking wretch, 240
A living-dead man : this pernicious slave,
Forsooth, took on him as a conjurer,
And, gazing in mine eyes, feeling my pulse,
And with no face, as 'twere, outfacing me,

192 *bestrid thee.* i.e. stood over you (in your defence).

203 *Discover how.* Reveal how.

205 *harlots.* Low company.

Antipholus of Ephesus : 'They brought one Pinch . . . a mountebank . . .' Seventeenth century engraving of a mountebank

Circe bewitching a man. Illustration from a Greek vase
painting

270 *Circe's cup.* The sorceress Circe's poisoned cup
turned men into swine.

281 *mated.* Confounded.

Cries out, I was possess'd. Then all together
They fell upon me, bound me, bore me thence
And in a dark and dankish vault at home
There left me and my man, both bound together;
Till, gnawing with my teeth my bonds in sunder,
I gain'd my freedom and immediately   250
Ran hither to your grace; whom I beseech
To give me ample satisfaction
For these deep shames and great indignities.
  Ang. My lord, in truth, thus far I witness with
    him,
That he dined not at home, but was lock'd out.
  Duke. But had he such a chain of thee or no?
  Ang. He had, my lord: and when he ran in
    here,
These people saw the chain about his neck.
  Sec. Mer. Besides, I will be sworn these ears
    of mine
Heard you confess you had the chain of him 260
After you first forswore it on the mart:
And thereupon I drew my sword on you;
And then you fled into this abbey here,
From whence, I think, you are come by miracle.
  Ant. E. I never came within these abbey-
    walls,
Nor ever didst thou draw thy sword on me:
I never saw the chain, so help me Heaven!
And this is false you burden me withal.
  Duke. Why, what an intricate impeach is
    this!
● I think you all have drunk of Circe's cup.   270
If here you housed him, here he would have
    been;
If he were mad, he would not plead so coldly:
You say he dined at home; the goldsmith here
Denies that saying. Sirrah, what say you?
  Dro. E. Sir, he dined with her there, at the
    Porpentine.
  Cour. He did, and from my finger snatch'd
    that ring.
  Ant. E. 'Tis true, my liege; this ring I had
    of her.
  Duke. Saw'st thou him enter at the abbey
    here?
  Cour. As sure, my liege, as I do see your
    grace.
  Duke. Why, this is strange. Go call the
    abbess hither.   280
● I think you are all mated or stark mad.
                    [*Exit one to the Abbess.*
  Æge. Most mighty duke, vouchsafe me speak
    a word:
Haply I see a friend will save my life
And pay the sum that may deliver me.
  Duke. Speak freely, Syracusian, what thou
    wilt.
  Æge. Is not your name, sir, call'd Anti-
    pholus?
And is not that your bondman, Dromio?
  Dro. E. Within this hour I was his bondman,
    sir,
But he, I thank him, gnaw'd in two my cords:
Now am I Dromio and his man unbound.   290
  Æge. I am sure you both of you remember
    me.
  Dro. E. Ourselves we do remember, sir, by
    you;
For lately we were bound, as you are now.
You are not Pinch's patient, are you, sir?

Æge. Why look you strange on me? you
    know me well.
Ant. E. I never saw you in my life till now.
Æge. O, grief hath changed me since you
        saw me last,
And careful hours with time's deformed hand
Have written strange defeatures in my face:
But tell me yet, dost thou not know my voice?
    Ant. E. Neither.   301
Æge. Dromio, nor thou?
Dro. E.   No, trust me, sir, nor I.
Æge. I am sure thou dost.
Dro. E. Ay, sir, but I am sure I do not; and
whatsoever a man denies, you are now bound to
believe him.
    Æge. Not know my voice! O time's extre-
        mity,
Hast thou so crack'd and splitted my poor tongue
In seven short years, that here my only son
Knows not my feeble key of untuned cares?   310
Though now this grained face of mine be hid
● In sap-consuming winter's drizzled snow
And all the conduits of my blood froze up,
Yet hath my night of life some memory,
● My wasting lamps some fading glimmer left,
My dull deaf ears a little use to hear:
All these old witnesses—I cannot err—
Tell me thou art my son Antipholus.
    Ant. E. I never saw my father in my life.
    Æge. But seven years since, in Syracusa,
        boy,   320
Thou know'st we parted: but perhaps, my son,
Thou shamest to acknowledge me in misery.
    Ant. E. The duke and all that know me in
        the city
Can witness with me that it is not so:
I ne'er saw Syracusa in my life.
    Duke. I tell thee, Syracusian, twenty years
Have I been patron to Antipholus,
During which time he ne'er saw Syracusa:
I see thy age and dangers make thee dote.

Re-enter Abbess, *with* ANTIPHOLUS *of Syracuse
    and* DROMIO *of Syracuse.*

    Abb. Most mighty duke, behold a man much
        wrong'd.   [*All gather to see them.* 330
    Adr. I see two husbands, or mine eyes de-
        ceive me.
●   *Duke.* One of these men is Genius to the
        other;
And so of these.   Which is the natural man,
And which the spirit? who deciphers them?
    Dro. S. I, sir, am Dromio: command him
        away.
    Dro. E. I, sir, am Dromio: pray, let me
        stay.
    Ant. S. Ægeon art thou not? or else his
        ghost?
    Dro. S. O, my old master! who hath bound
        him here?
    Abb. Whoever bound him, I will loose his
        bonds
And gain a husband by his liberty.   340
Speak, old Ægeon, if thou be'st the man
That hadst a wife once call'd Æmilia
● That bore thee at a burden two fair sons:
O, if thou be'st the same Ægeon, speak,
And speak unto the same Æmilia!

312 *sap-consuming winter's drizzled snow.* i.e. his beard.

315 *lamps.* Eyes.

Abbess: '. . . behold a man much wrong'd'. Engraving
from a painting by John Francis Rigaud (1742–1810)

332 *Genius.* The spirit that governs one.

343 *burden.* Birth.

Charles and Henry Webb as the two Dromios. Princess's
Theatre, London, 1864

John Henry and Maria Ann Johnston as Aegeon and
Aemilia. Illustration by W. Hamilton (1751–1801)

397 *sympathized.* Shared by all.

Æge. If I dream not, thou art Æmilia:
If thou art she, tell me where is that son
That floated with thee on the fatal raft?
   Abb. By men of Epidamnum he and I
And the twin Dromio all were taken up;   350
But by and by rude fishermen of Corinth
By force took Dromio and my son from them
And me they left with those of Epidamnum.
What then became of them I cannot tell;
I to this fortune that you see me in.
   Duke. Why, here begins his morning story
     right:
These two Antipholuses, these two so like,
And these two Dromios, one in semblance,—
Besides her urging of her wreck at sea,—
These are the parents to these children,   360
Which accidentally are met together.
Antipholus, thou camest from Corinth first?
   Ant. S. No, sir, not I; I came from Syracuse.
   Duke. Stay, stand apart; I know not which
     is which.
   Ant. E. I came from Corinth, my most gra-
     cious lord,—
   Dro. E. And I with him.
   Ant. E. Brought to this town by that most
     famous warrior,
Duke Menaphon, your most renowned uncle.
   Adr. Which of you two did dine with me to-
     day?
   Ant. S. I, gentle mistress.
   Adr.   And are not you my husband?
   Ant. E. No; I say nay to that.   371
   Ant. S. And so do I; yet did she call me so:
And this fair gentlewoman, her sister here,
Did call me brother. [*To Luc.*] What I told
     you then,
I hope I shall have leisure to make good;
If this be not a dream I see and hear.
   Ang. That is the chain, sir, which you had
     of me.
   Ant. S. I think it be, sir; I deny it not.
   Ant. E. And you, sir, for this chain arrest-
     ed me.   380
   Ang. I think I did, sir; I deny it not.
   Adr. I sent you money, sir, to be your bail,
By Dromio; but I think he brought it not.
   Dro. E. No, none by me.
   Ant. S. This purse of ducats I received from
     you
And Dromio my man did bring them me.
I see we still did meet each other's man,
And I was ta'en for him, and he for me,
And thereupon these ERRORS are arose.
   Ant. E. These ducats pawn I for my father
     here.
   Duke. It shall not need; thy father hath his
     life.   390
   Cour. Sir, I must have that diamond from
     you.
   Ant. E. There, take it; and much thanks for
     my good cheer.
   Abb. Renowned duke, vouchsafe to take the
     pains
To go with us into the abbey here
And hear at large discoursed all our fortunes:
And all that are assembled in this place,
● That by this sympathized one day's error
Have suffer'd wrong, go keep us company,
And we shall make full satisfaction.

Thirty-three years have I but gone in travail 400
Of you, my sons ; and till this present hour
My heavy burthen ne'er delivered.
The duke, my husband and my children both,
● And you the calendars of their nativity,
● Go to a gossips' feast, and go with me ;
After so long grief, such festivity !
 Duke.   With all my heart, I'll gossip at this
 feast. [*Exeunt all but Ant. S., Ant. E.,*
      Dro. S., and Dro. E.
 Dro. S.   Master, shall I fetch your stuff from
 shipboard ?
 Ant. E.   Dromio, what stuff of mine hast thou
 embark'd ?
 Dro. S.   Your goods that lay at host, sir, in
 the Centaur. 410
 Ant. S.   He speaks to me.   I am your master,
 Dromio :
Come, go with us ; we'll look to that anon :
Embrace thy brother there ; rejoice with him.
     [*Exeunt Ant. S. and Ant. E.*
 Dro. S.   There is a fat friend at your master's
 house,
● That kitchen'd me for you to-day at dinner :
She now shall be my sister, not my wife.
 Dro. E.   Methinks you are my glass, and not
 my brother :
I see by you I am a sweet-faced youth.
● Will you walk in to see their gossiping ?
 Dro. S.   Not I, sir ; you are my elder. 420
 Dro. E.   That's a question : how shall we
 try it ?
 Dro. S.   We'll draw cuts for the senior : till
 then lead thou first.
 Dro. E.   Nay, then, thus :
We came into the world like brother and brother ;
And now let's go hand in hand, not one before
 another. [*Exeunt.*

404 *calendars.* i.e. the Dromios.

405 *gossips' feast.* A baptismal feast at which all the characters will be re-named.

415 *kitchen'd me.* Entertained in the kitchen.

419 *gossiping.* Merrymaking.

The two Dromios meet. Illustration by Alexander Stuart Boyd, 1916

The Two Gentlemen of Verona

1592

THE ESSENTIAL THING about this play is that it is experimental: it is Shakespeare's first offering of a romantic comedy, with its promise of more mature works in the same *genre* to come. Aspects of character and situation, dramatic strokes of plot, are repeated in subsequent plays more satisfactorily in fuller, rounded development. Here they are rather sketched—evidently, too, somewhat hurriedly: the end is quickly ravelled up, and there may have been a few cuts. Since there is no record of early performances, it was possibly written for private production—for Southampton and his friends. It has the character of artificial comedy, with an Italian colouring, appropriate to an aristocratic circle.

Right: *A street in Verona. Painting (1837) by James Holland R.A.*

Far right: *Ada Rehan as Julia in Augustin Daly's production of* The Two Gentlemen of Verona, *London 1895*

Background. But the background is recognisably Elizabethan London. The play starts with a send-off of a young gentleman, Valentine, by his friend Proteus, on a tour abroad which was the regular thing for a young gentleman to undertake:

> To see the wonders of the world abroad;

his friend bids him to look out for

> Some rare noteworthy object in thy travel.

This was especially a time, the late 1580's and early 1590's, when young men set out—

> Some to the wars to try their fortunes there,
> Some to discover islands far away—

(like Sir Walter Ralegh and Sir Richard Grenville)—

> Some to the studious universities.

Proteus later follows his friend; his man Launce is late in getting aboard ship; a fellow-servant hurries him up:

> Thy master is shipped, and thou art to post after with oars. . . . You'll lose the tide if you tarry any longer.

It is, of course, the tidal Thames, where it was important to catch the tide if one was to 'shoot' London Bridge—to go down river to ship for a sea-voyage. It does not much matter that Shakespeare leaves the places somewhat mixed up in the play—too busy to bother about details of that sort.

Date. There is no difficulty about dating from internal evidence. There are two specific references to the theme of Hero and Leander, each of them extending to several lines. The subject would be to the fore in Shakespeare's mind in 1592, when Marlowe was writing his *Hero and Leander* in rivalry with *Venus and Adonis* for the favour of the young patron, Southampton.

Others have noticed that there are flecks of the Sonnets being written contemporaneously—the imagery of the canker in the rose, the poet's favourite flower; or:

> O, how this spring of love resembleth
> The uncertain glory of an April day,
> Which now shows all the beauty of the sun,
> And by and by a cloud takes all away!

This is a clear parallel to the fuller descriptions in Sonnets 33 and 34 of the uncertain spring days of friendship, with their early morning sun overtaken and overcast by clouds. It is all early 1592.

Theme. Far more important, the theme of the play is that of the Sonnets: the conflicting claims of love and friendship. Here, as there, Shakespeare comes down on the side of friendship. We do not need to think in pedantic terms that this was a traditional literary option: it was the option that Shakespeare made in his own life, and the play—as with any writer—bears traces of his own experience.

For, in the play, as in life, the situation presented worse than awkwardness: it led to a real strain, the resolution of which all commentators have regarded as the most unsatisfactory feature of the action, the unconvincing *dénouement* when Valentine abnegates his love for Silvia in favour of his friend Proteus, who has seriously offended but is now penitent:

> By penitence the Eternal's wrath's appeased;
> And, that my love may appear plain and free,
> All that was mine in Silvia I give thee.

Everybody has been shocked by this casual handing-over of his love to his friend, and there is no explaining it away by academic doctrine as to the rewards of penitence. Nor is there any need to; for it is precisely what happened between Shakespeare and his young friend over his mistress, Emilia Lanier.

In the Sonnets Shakespeare reproaches his young patron for taking his place with her:

> Ay me! but yet thou mightst my seat forbear . . .

And in the very sonnets which describe the clouding over of their friendship like an uncertain spring day, and the 'canker in the sweetest bud', Shakespeare excuses the young man:

> No more be grieved at that which thou hast done.

And yet, though the young friend has shed tears for his offence and repented,

> Though thou repent, yet I have still the loss.

Then, in a generous outburst, whether convincing or not:

> Take all my loves, my love, yea, take them all.

This is precisely what Valentine does in the play: he yields up his love, Silvia, to his friend.

It is very unsatisfactory, as everybody has thought: an academic critic, a lady—citing Cervantes and Francis Bacon and Richard Edwardes and John Lyly—sagely concludes that in the play 'the love and friendship motifs proved less easy to reconcile'. No more did they in real life, the experience that goes into a real writer's writing. Sonnet 40 continues ruefully:

> I do forgive thy robbery, gentle thief,
> Although thou steal thee all my poverty.

Needs must, when the thief—'gentle' in Elizabethan English means 'gentlemanly'—was the noble patron.

The theme of the play, then, is the conflict between friendship and love—dominating Shakespeare's mind in 1592—the offender's repentance, the too generous, rather unconvincing forgiveness and yielding up the girl.

And yet no-one has ever observed the close parallel between *The Two Gentlemen of Verona* and the contemporary Sonnets that record the conflict, 33 to 36 and 40 to 42.

Personal Touches. Various descriptive flecks in passing make the thing more real to us. Valentine—the one who was to give up his girl—describes his friend:

> His years but young, but his experience old;
> His head unmellowed, but his judgment ripe . . .
> He is complete in feature and in mind
> With all good grace to grace a gentleman.

Shakespeare, very gentlemanly himself, is always ready with a courtly compliment. The Duke says of the young friend, Proteus:

> if he make this good
> He is as worthy for an empress' love
> As meet to be an emperor's counsellor.

We can all recognise what this compliment means and what it implies: young Southampton was intelligent, well-educated, ambitious and always anxious to obtain the Queen's favour, though he did not go the right way about it and, in the event, failed to obtain it.

Interchangeably, Valentine does penance for 'contemning love', and is now so subject to it that

> Love hath chased sleep from my enthrallèd eyes . . .
> Nor to his service no such joy on earth,
> Now no discourse, except it be of Love;
> Now can I break my fast, dine, sup, and sleep,
> Upon the very naked name of Love.

This was the susceptible actor-dramatist's case; we can see something of him in Valentine, still more—as has been generally recognised—in Berowne in *Love's Labour's Lost*.

The mercurial about-turns in the play—when Proteus drops his love Julia for Valentine's Silvia, and Valentine as suddenly yields up Silvia—were less surprising to Elizabethans, so mercurial and changeable themselves, than they are to us. In any case, with them they did not seek the 'probable'; they looked out for the dramatic and preferred the surprises, the sensational.

It has been observed, too, that it is the women who come out best against the not altogether satisfactory Valentine and the distasteful Proteus, whose name explains but does not excuse him, in the battledore and shuttlecock between them to which the ladies are subjected. A woman critic notes of this, Shakespeare's first romantic comedy: 'his tendency to hand over most of the initiative and just judgment to the women in his cast of characters was already marked.'

We may add that Julia, in assuming the guise of a page to follow Proteus, provides a first example of what the practising actor-dramatist was to employ so much later. Since women's parts were played by boys, it was very practical and convincing to dress these boy actors as boys.

We have a recognisable reminiscence from Shakespeare's own boyhood, when

Julia says:

> at Pentecost,
> When all our pageants of delight were played,
> Our youth got me to play the woman's part,
> And I was trimmed in Madam Julia's gown.

It reminds one of the Whitsun pastorals which were performed at Stratford and in so many places all over the country in that dramatising age. The part she played was a classical one, Ariadne lamenting Theseus' perjury and flight—to remind us that the dramatist's schooling was in the classics.

Realism. Most appealing of all to us today are the scenes that bring the life of the time realistically before us. Notably in the characters of Launce, and no less his dog Crab, and his fellow-servant Speed: they are drawn authentically from life below stairs, and have their just comment to offer on their betters and what goes on above. In the talk between these two we have Shakespeare's sharp ear for the speech and idiom of the people—like Scott, or Hardy; and absolute virtuosity in Launce addressing his dog, which never fails to bring the house down:

> He thrusts me himself into the company of three or four gentleman-like dogs under the Duke's table. He had not been there—bless the mark—a pissing-while but all the chamber smelt him. 'Out with the dog,' says one. 'What cur is that?' says another. 'Whip him out,' says the third. 'Hang him up,' says the Duke. I, having been acquainted with the smell before, knew it was Crab, and goes me to the fellow that whips the dogs. 'Friend,' quoth I, 'you mean to whip the dog?' 'Ay, marry, do I,' quoth he. 'You do him the more wrong,' quoth I, ' 'twas I did the thing you wot of.' He makes me no more ado, but whips me out of the chamber. How many masters would do this for his servant?'

Anyone who knows the strict regulations governing great households of the time, conduct in hall, cleanliness in courtyards, etc. will appreciate the authentic note of this. And then, a final reproach: 'Nay, I remember the trick you served me when I took my leave of Madam Silvia. Did not I bid thee still mark me and do as I do? When didst thou see me heave up my leg and make water against a gentlewoman's farthingale? Didst thou ever see me do such a trick?'

There are the usual bawdy exchanges between these good fellows—on the love-affairs of the gentry, for example:

> Speed: Why, then, how stands the matter with them?
> Launce: Marry, thus: when it stands well with him, it stands well with her.

There follows a good deal of bawdy talk and punning about standing: the same joke as Shakespeare applies to himself in regard to his mistress, 'rising at thy name', in Sonnet 151.

We find punning everywhere—the Elizabethan weakness for which was noted with disapprobation by the august taste of the 18th century, expressed by Dr. Johnson. On the other hand, we have the overriding love of the age for music: this comedy initiates the use of music which was to expand so notably in the plays. We have a reference to a well known contemporary ballad, 'Light o'Love'—to proliferate innumerably later; and the first of the charming songs that decorate the plays like jewels:

Launce and his dog. Illustration by Walter Crane, 1894

"LAUNCE:— He is a stone, a very pebble stone, and has no more pity in him than a dog" Act IV.

Who is Silvia? What is she,
That all our swains commend her?

Text. The text which we have is a good one, from the First Folio, probably from the Company's prompt-book based on Shakespeare's manuscript.

He derived the hint for his plot from the story in Montemayor's romance, *Diana*. All that is most valuable he added himself, from his own experience, with the character Valentine and the complications of his relationship with his young patron; most of all, with Launce and his dog, who remain in the mind when the rest are but shadows.

THE
TWO GENTLEMEN OF VERONA.

DRAMATIS PERSONÆ.

DUKE OF MILAN, Father to Silvia.
VALENTINE, ⎫ the two Gentlemen.
PROTEUS, ⎭
ANTONIO, Father to Proteus.
THURIO, a foolish rival to Valentine.
EGLAMOUR, Agent for Silvia in her escape.
HOST, where Julia lodges.
OUTLAWS, with Valentine.
SPEED, a clownish servant to Valentine.

LAUNCE, the like to Proteus.
PANTHINO, Servant to Antonio.

JULIA, beloved of Proteus.
SILVIA, beloved of Valentine.
LUCETTA, waiting-woman to Julia.

Servants, Musicians.

SCENE, *Verona; Milan; the frontiers of Mantua.*

● *A bullet beside a text line indicates an annotation in the opposite column*

Verona. An open place. Engraving from Charles Knight's *Pictorial Edition of the Works of William Shakspere*, 1839–43

SD *Enter* . . . PROTEUS. In Greek mythology Proteus escaped from questioners by assuming different shapes.

The mythological Proteus. From a Greek vase painting

18 *beadsman.* One who was engaged to pray (i.e. tell his beads) for another.

Opposite: Valentine rescues Silvia from Proteus. Engraving from a painting by Angelica Kauffmann (1741–1807)

ACT I.

SCENE I. *Verona. An open place.*

Enter VALENTINE *and* PROTEUS.

Val. Cease to persuade, my loving Proteus:
Home-keeping youth have ever homely wits.
Were't not affection chains thy tender days
To the sweet glances of thy honour'd love,
I rather would entreat thy company
To see the wonders of the world abroad
Than, living dully sluggardized at home,
Wear out thy youth with shapeless idleness.
But since thou lovest, love still and thrive therein,
Even as I would when I to love begin.   10
    Pro. Wilt thou be gone? Sweet Valentine, adieu!
Think on thy Proteus, when thou haply seest
Some rare note-worthy object in thy travel:
Wish me partaker in thy happiness
When thou dost meet good hap; and in thy danger,
If ever danger do environ thee,
Commend thy grievance to my holy prayers,
●For I will be thy beadsman, Valentine.

22 *Leander cross'd the Hellespont.* In classical mythology Leander swam the Hellespont each night to visit his love Hero.

24-25 *over shoes . . . over boots.* Literally, wet above the shoes or boots. Both phrases express 'reckless continuance in a course already begun'.

27 *give me not the boots.* A proverbial expression which meant 'don't make a laughing stock of me'.

36-37 *circumstance . . . circumstance.* 'Argument', and 'condition'.

44 *wits.* Minds, intellects.

49 *verdure.* Freshness.

52 *votary.* Devotee.

Proteus and Valentine. Illustration by Walter Crane, 1894

73 *sheep.* This is a quibble on 'ship' which was similarly pronounced in Shakespeare's time.

Val. And on a love-book pray for my success?
Pro. Upon some book I love I'll pray for thee.
Val. That's on some shallow story of deep love: 21
• How young Leander cross'd the Hellespont.
Pro. That's a deep story of a deeper love;
• For he was more than over shoes in love.
Val. 'Tis true; for you are over boots in love,
And yet you never swum the Hellespont.
• *Pro.* Over the boots? nay, give me not the boots.
Val. No, I will not, for it boots thee not.
Pro.   What?
Val. To be in love, where scorn is bought with groans;
Coy looks with heart-sore sighs; one fading moment's mirth   30
With twenty watchful, weary, tedious nights:
If haply won, perhaps a hapless gain;
If lost, why then a grievous labour won;
However, but a folly bought with wit,
Or else a wit by folly vanquished.
• *Pro.* So, by your circumstance, you call me fool.
Val. So, by your circumstance, I fear you'll prove.
Pro. 'Tis love you cavil at: I am not Love.
Val. Love is your master, for he masters you:
And he that is so yoked by a fool,   40
Methinks, should not be chronicled for wise.
Pro. Yet writers say, as in the sweetest bud
The eating canker dwells, so eating love
• Inhabits in the finest wits of all.
Val. And writers say, as the most forward bud
Is eaten by the canker ere it blow,
Even so by love the young and tender wit
Is turn'd to folly, blasting in the bud,
• Losing his verdure even in the prime
And all the fair effects of future hopes.   50
But wherefore waste I time to counsel thee
• That art a votary to fond desire?
Once more adieu! my father at the road
Expects my coming, there to see me shipp'd.
Pro. And thither will I bring thee, Valentine.
Val. Sweet Proteus, no; now let us take our leave.
To Milan let me hear from thee by letters
Of thy success in love and what news else
Betideth here in absence of thy friend;
And I likewise will visit thee with mine.   60
Pro. All happiness bechance to thee in Milan!
Val. As much to you at home! and so, farewell.   [*Exit.*
Pro. He after honour hunts, I after love:
He leaves his friends to dignify them more;
I leave myself, my friends and all, for love.
Thou, Julia, thou hast metamorphosed me,
Made me neglect my studies, lose my time,
War with good counsel, set the world at nought;
Made wit with musing weak, heart sick with thought.

Enter SPEED.

Speed. Sir Proteus, save you! Saw you my master?   70
Pro. But now he parted hence, to embark for Milan.
Speed. Twenty to one then he is shipp'd already,
• And I have play'd the sheep in losing him.
Pro. Indeed, a sheep doth very often stray,

An if the shepherd be a while away.

Speed. You conclude that my master is a shepherd then and I a sheep?

Pro. I do.

● *Speed.* Why then, my horns are his horns, whether I wake or sleep. 80

Pro. A silly answer and fitting well a sheep.

Speed. This proves me still a sheep.

Pro. True; and thy master a shepherd.

Speed. Nay, that I can deny by a circumstance.

Pro. It shall go hard but I'll prove it by another.

Speed. The shepherd seeks the sheep, and not the sheep the shepherd; but I seek my master, and my master seeks not me: therefore I am no sheep. 91

Pro. The sheep for fodder follow the shepherd; the shepherd for food follows not the sheep: thou for wages followest thy master; thy master for wages follows not thee: therefore thou art a sheep.

Speed. Such another proof will make me cry 'baa.'

Pro. But, dost thou hear? gavest thou my letter to Julia? 100

● *Speed.* Ay, sir: I, a lost mutton, gave your letter to her, a laced mutton, and she, a laced mutton, gave me, a lost mutton, nothing for my labour.

Pro. Here's too small a pasture for such store of muttons.

● *Speed.* If the ground be overcharged, you were best stick her.

Pro. Nay: in that you are astray, 'twere best pound you. 110

Speed. Nay, sir, less than a pound shall serve me for carrying your letter.

Pro. You mistake; I mean the pound,—a ● pinfold.

Speed. From a pound to a pin? fold it over and over,
'Tis threefold too little for carrying a letter to your lover.

Pro. But what said she?

Speed. [*First nodding*] Ay.

Pro. Nod—Ay—why, that's noddy.

Speed. You mistook, sir; I say, she did nod: and you ask me if she did nod; and I say, 'Ay.'

Pro. And that set together is noddy. 122

Speed. Now you have taken the pains to set it together, take it for your pains.

Pro. No, no; you shall have it for bearing the letter.

● *Speed.* Well, I perceive I must be fain to bear with you.

Pro. Why, sir, how do you bear with me?

Speed. Marry, sir, the letter, very orderly; having nothing but the word 'noddy' for my pains.

Pro. Beshrew me, but you have a quick wit.

Speed. And yet it cannot overtake your slow purse.

Pro. Come, come, open the matter in brief: what said she?

Speed. Open your purse, that the money and the matter may be both at once delivered.

Pro. Well, sir, here is for your pains. What said she? 140

Speed. Truly, sir, I think you'll hardly win her.

Proteus and Speed. Engraving by Kenny Meadows from Barry Cornwall's *Works of Shakspere*, 1846

---

80 *my horns are his horns.* A cuckold's horns, commonest and stalest of Elizabethan jokes.

102 *laced mutton.* Frequently used for a prostitute.

107-108 *ground . . . stick her.* i.e. if the ground be overstocked it would be best to slaughter her (with a bawdy innuendo).

114 *pinfold.* Enclosure for stray animals.

127-128 *fain to bear with you.* i.e. pleased to put up with you.

148 *in telling your mind.* i.e. when you tell her in person.

153 *testerned.* The tester was an Elizabethan sixpence.

158 *destined to a drier death on shore.* A reference to the proverb 'he that is born to be hanged shall never be drowned'.

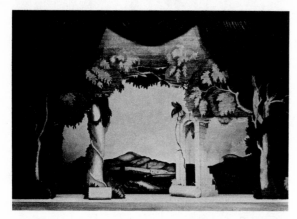

Set design for garden of Julia's house by J. Gower Parks, Stratford-upon-Avon, 1938

9 *Sir Eglamour.* A pseudo-romantic name for a carpet-knight.

Pro. Why, couldst thou perceive so much from her?

Speed. Sir, I could perceive nothing at all from her; no, not so much as a ducat for delivering your letter: and being so hard to me that brought your mind, I fear she'll prove as hard to you in telling your mind. Give her no token but stones; for she's as hard as steel.

Pro. What said she? nothing?   150

Speed. No, not so much as 'Take this for thy pains.' To testify your bounty, I thank you, you have testerned me; in requital whereof, henceforth carry your letters yourself: and so, sir, I'll commend you to my master.

Pro. Go, go, be gone, to save your ship from wreck,
Which cannot perish having thee aboard,
Being destined to a drier death on shore.
                              [*Exit Speed.*
I must go send some better messenger:
I fear my Julia would not deign my lines,   160
Receiving them from such a worthless post. [*Exit.*

SCENE II. *The same. Garden of* JULIA'S *house.*

Enter JULIA *and* LUCETTA.

Jul. But say, Lucetta, now we are alone,
Wouldst thou then counsel me to fall in love?

Luc. Ay, madam, so you stumble not unheedfully.

Jul. Of all the fair resort of gentlemen
That every day with parle encounter me,
In thy opinion which is worthiest love?

Luc. Please you repeat their names, I'll show my mind
According to my shallow simple skill.

Jul. What think'st thou of the fair Sir Eglamour?

Luc. As of a knight well-spoken, neat and fine;
But, were I you, he never should be mine.   11

Jul. What think'st thou of the rich Mercatio?

Luc. Well of his wealth; but of himself, so so.

Jul. What think'st thou of the gentle Proteus?

Luc. Lord, Lord! to see what folly reigns in us!

Jul. How now! what means this passion at his name?

Luc. Pardon, dear madam: tis a passing shame
That I, unworthy body as I am,
Should censure thus on lovely gentlemen.

Jul. Why not on Proteus, as of all the rest?

Luc. Then thus: of many good I think him best.

Jul. Your reason?

Luc. I have no other but a woman's reason;
think him so because I think him so.

Jul. And wouldst thou have me cast my love on him?

Luc. Ay, if you thought your love not cast away.

Jul. Why he, of all the rest, hath never moved me.

Luc. Yet he, of all the rest, I think, best loves ye.

Jul. His little speaking shows his love but small.   29

Luc. Fire that's closest kept burns most of all.

Jul. They do not love that do not show their love.

Luc. O, they love least that let men know their love.

Jul. I would I knew his mind.
Luc. Peruse this paper, madam.
Jul. 'To Julia.' Say, from whom?
Luc. That the contents will show.
Jul. Say, say, who gave it thee?
Luc. Sir Valentine's page; and sent, I think,
from Proteus.
He would have given it you; but I, being in the
way,
Did in your name receive it: pardon the fault, I
pray.   40
Jul. Now, by my modesty, a goodly broker!
Dare you presume to harbour wanton lines?
To whisper and conspire against my youth?
Now, trust me, 'tis an office of great worth
And you an officer fit for the place.
There, take the paper: see it be return'd;
Or else return no more into my sight.
Luc. To plead for love deserves more fee than
hate.
Jul. Will ye be gone?
Luc.   That you may ruminate.
                                        [*Exit.*
Jul. And yet I would I had o'erlooked the
letter: 50
It were a shame to call her back again
And pray her to a fault for which I chid her.
What a fool is she, that knows I am a maid,
And would not force the letter to my view!
Since maids, in modesty, say 'no' to that
Which they would have the profferer construe 'ay.'
Fie, fie, how wayward is this foolish love
That, like a testy babe, will scratch the nurse
And presently all humbled kiss the rod!
How churlishly I chid Lucetta hence,   60
When willingly I would have had her here!
How angerly I taught my brow to frown,
When inward joy enforced my heart to smile!
My penance is to call Lucetta back
And ask remission for my folly past.
What ho! Lucetta!

Re-enter LUCETTA.

Luc.   What would your ladyship?
Jul. Is't near dinner-time?
Luc.   I would it were,
● That you might kill your stomach on your meat
And not upon your maid.
Jul. What is't that you took up so gingerly?
Luc. Nothing.   71
Jul. Why didst thou stoop, then?
Luc. To take a paper up that I let fall.
Jul. And is that paper nothing?
Luc. Nothing concerning me.
Jul. Then let it lie for those that it concerns.
Luc. Madam, it will not lie where it concerns,
Unless it have a false interpreter.
Jul. Some love of yours hath writ to you in
rhyme.
● *Luc.* That I might sing it, madam, to a tune.
● Give me a note: your ladyship can set.   81
Jul. As little by such toys as may be possible.
● Best sing it to the tune of 'Light o' love.'
Luc. It is too heavy for so light a tune.
● *Jul.* Heavy! belike it hath some burden
then?
Luc. Ay, and melodious were it, would you
sing it.

Julia and Lucetta. Illustration by Walter Crane, 1894

68 *stomach.* A play on the word meaning both 'appetite' and 'anger'. *meat.* Pronounced 'mate'. There is an obvious quibble with 'maid'.

80-96 *That I might sing it . . . unruly bass.* All the quibbles here are based on the musical terminology of the time.

81 *note.* The two meanings are 'letter' and 'musical note'. *set.* 'write' and 'set to music'.

83 *'Light o' love.'* A popular tune.

85 *burden.* The two meanings are 'load' and 'musical refrain'.

87 *I cannot reach so high.* The two meanings are 'it is beyond the range of my voice' and 'he is of too high a rank for me'.

94 *descant.* Refers to the variations upon a tune and to Julia's variations of mood.

95 *mean.* Tenor.

96 *bass.* A quibble on 'base' (low conduct).

97 *bid the base.* A phrase from the game of prisoner's base.

99 *coil with protestation.* Fuss over a protestation of love.

102 *makes it strange.* Pretends to be indifferent.

104 *would I were so anger'd with the same!* Julia is referring to the letter she has just torn up.

Julia: 'O hateful hands to tear such loving words'. Drawing by H. J. Richter (1772–1857)

137 *month's mind.* Desire. Originally a 'month's mind' referred to a mass said for a deceased person one month after his death. Later it came to mean the desire for food fancied by women in the last month of pregnancy.

139 *wink.* Close my eyes (to them).

Jul. And why not you?
Luc.   I cannot reach so high.
Jul. Let's see your song.   How now, minion!
Luc. Keep tune there still, so you will sing
  it out:
And yet methinks I do not like this tune.   90
Jul. You do not?
Luc.   No, madam; it is too sharp.
Jul. You, minion, are too saucy.
Luc. Nay, now you are too flat
And mar the concord with too harsh a descant:
There wanteth but a mean to fill your song.
Jul. The mean is drown'd with your unruly
  bass.
Luc. Indeed, I bid the base for Proteus.
Jul. This babble shall not henceforth trouble
  me.
Here is a coil with protestation! [*Tears the letter.*
Go get you gone, and let the papers lie: 100
You would be fingering them, to anger me.
Luc. She makes it strange; but she would be
  best pleased
To be so anger'd with another letter.   [*Exit.*
Jul. Nay, would I were so anger'd with the
  same!
O hateful hands, to tear such loving words!
Injurious wasps, to feed on such sweet honey
And kill the bees that yield it with your stings!
I'll kiss each several paper for amends.
Look, here is writ 'kind Julia.'   Unkind Julia!
As in revenge of thy ingratitude,   110
I throw thy name against the bruising stones,
Trampling contemptuously on thy disdain.
And here is writ 'love-wounded Proteus.'
Poor wounded name! my bosom as a bed
Shall lodge thee till thy wound be throughly
  heal'd;
And thus I search it with a sovereign kiss.
But twice or thrice was ' Proteus' written down.
Be calm, good wind, blow not a word away
Till I have found each letter in the letter,
Except mine own name: that some whirlwind bear
Unto a ragged fearful-hanging rock   121
And throw it thence into the raging sea!
Lo, here in one line is his name twice writ,
' Poor forlorn Proteus, passionate Proteus,
To the sweet Julia:' that I'll tear away.
And yet I will not, sith so prettily
He couples it to his complaining names.
Thus will I fold them one upon another:
Now kiss, embrace, contend, do what you will.

Re-enter LUCETTA.

Luc. Madam,   130
Dinner is ready, and your father stays.
Jul. Well, let us go.
Luc. What, shall these papers lie like tell-
  tales here?
Jul. If you respect them, best to take them up.
Luc. Nay, I was taken up for laying them
  down:
Yet here they shall not lie, for catching cold.
Jul. I see you have a month's mind to them.
Luc. Ay, madam, you may say what sights
  you see;
I see things too, although you judge I wink.
Jul. Come, come; will't please you go?   140
      [*Exeunt.*

SCENE III. *The same.* ANTONIO'S *house.*

Enter ANTONIO *and* PANTHINO.

● *Ant.* Tell me, Panthino, what sad talk was
    that
Wherewith my brother held you in the cloister?
    Pan. 'Twas of his nephew Proteus, your son.
    Ant. Why, what of him?
    Pan.   He wonder'd that your lordship
Would suffer him to spend his youth at home,
While other men, of slender reputation,
Put forth their sons to seek preferment out:
Some to the wars, to try their fortune there;
Some to discover islands far away;
Some to the studious universities.   10
For any or for all these exercises
● He said that Proteus your son was meet,
And did request me to importune you
To let him spend his time no more at home,
Which would be great impeachment to his age,
In having known no travel in his youth.
    Ant. Nor need'st thou much importune me
    to that
● Whereon this month I have been hammering.
I have consider'd well his loss of time
And how he cannot be a perfect man,   20
Not being tried and tutor'd in the world:
Experience is by industry achieved
And perfected by the swift course of time.
Then tell me, whither were I best to send him?
    Pan. I think your lordship is not ignorant
How his companion, youthful Valentine,
Attends the emperor in his royal court.
    Ant. I know it well.
    Pan. 'Twere good, I think, your lordship
    sent him thither:
● There shall he practise tilts and tournaments, 30
Hear sweet discourse, converse with noblemen,
And be in eye of every exercise
Worthy his youth and nobleness of birth.
    Ant. I like thy counsel; well hast thou ad-
    vised:
And that thou mayst perceive how well I like it
The execution of it shall make known.
Even with the speediest expedition
I will dispatch him to the emperor's court.
    Pan. To-morrow, may it please you, Don
    Alphonso
With other gentlemen of good esteem   40
Are journeying to salute the emperor
And to commend their service to his will.
    Ant. Good company; with them shall Pro-
    teus go:
● And, in good time! now will we break with him.

Enter PROTEUS.

    Pro. Sweet love! sweet lines! sweet life!
Here is her hand, the agent of her heart;
Here is her oath for love, her honour's pawn.
O, that our fathers would applaud our loves,
To seal our happiness with their consents!
O heavenly Julia!   50
    Ant. How now! what letter are you reading
    there?
    Pro. May't please your lordship, 'tis a word
    or two
Of commendations sent from Valentine,
Deliver'd by a friend that came from him.
    Ant. Lend me the letter; let me see what news.

1 *sad.* Serious.

12 *meet.* Fitted.

18 *hammering.* Pondering.

30 *tilts and tournaments.* A tilt was a mock contest between two parties of knights.

Tilting match in the 14th century. Engraving from *Old England*, 1854

Preparations for a tournament, 13th century. From J. Strutt's *The Sports and Pastimes of the People of England*, 1810

44 *break with him.* Tell him what we have in mind.

Costume design for Proteus by J. Gower Parks, Stratford-upon-Avon, 1938

69 *Like exhibition.* Allowance of money.

81 *take exceptions.* Object to.

Pro. There is no news, my lord, but that he writes
How happily he lives, how well beloved
And daily graced by the emperor;
Wishing me with him, partner of his fortune.
　Ant. And how stand you affected to his wish?
　Pro. As one relying on your lordship's will 61
And not depending on his friendly wish.
　Ant. My will is something sorted with his wish.
Muse not that I thus suddenly proceed;
For what I will, I will, and there an end.
I am resolved that thou shalt spend some time
With Valentinus in the emperor's court:
What maintenance he from his friends receives,
Like exhibition thou shalt have from me.
To-morrow be in readiness to go: 70
Excuse it not, for I am peremptory.
　Pro. My lord, I cannot be so soon provided:
Please you, deliberate a day or two.
　Ant. Look, what thou want'st shall be sent after thee:
No more of stay! to-morrow thou must go.
Come on, Panthino: you shall be employ'd
To hasten on his expedition.
　　　　　　　[Exeunt Ant. and Pan.
　Pro. Thus have I shunn'd the fire for fear of burning,
And drench'd me in the sea, where I am drown'd.
I fear'd to show my father Julia's letter, 80
Lest he should take exceptions to my love;
And with the vantage of mine own excuse
Hath he excepted most against my love.
O, how this spring of love resembleth
　The uncertain glory of an April day,
Which now shows all the beauty of the sun,
　And by and by a cloud takes all away!

　　　　　Re-enter PANTHINO.

Pan. Sir Proteus, your father calls for you:
　He is in haste; therefore, I pray you, go. 89
Pro. Why, this it is: my heart accords thereto,
And yet a thousand times it answers 'no.'
　　　　　　　　　　　[Exeunt.

ACT II.

SCENE I. *Milan.   The* DUKE'S *palace.*

Enter VALENTINE *and* SPEED.

Speed. Sir, your glove.
Val. 　　　　　Not mine; my gloves are on.
Speed. Why, then, this may be yours, for this is but one.
Val. Ha! let me see: ay, give it me, it's mine:
Sweet ornament that decks a thing divine!
Ah, Silvia, Silvia!
　Speed. Madam Silvia! Madam Silvia!
　Val. How now, sirrah?
　Speed. She is not within hearing, sir.
　Val. Why, sir, who bade you call her?
　Speed. Your worship, sir; or else I mistook. 10
　Val. Well, you'll still be too forward.
　Speed. And yet I was last chidden for being too slow.
　Val. Go to, sir: tell me, do you know Madam Silvia?
　Speed. She that your worship loves?
　Val. Why, how know you that I am in love?
　Speed. Marry, by these special marks: first,

you have learned, like Sir Proteus, to wreathe your arms, like a malecontent; to relish a love-song, like a robin-redbreast; to walk alone, like one that had the pestilence; to sigh, like a school-boy that had lost his A B C; to weep, like a young wench that had buried her grandam; to fast, like one that takes diet; to watch, like one
• that fears robbing; to speak puling, like a beggar at Hallowmas.   You were wont, when you laughed, to crow like a cock; when you walked, to
• walk like one of the lions; when you fasted, it was presently after dinner; when you looked sadly, it was for want of money: and now you are metamorphosed with a mistress, that, when I look on you, I can hardly think you my master.
     Val.   Are all these things perceived in me?
• *Speed.*   They are all perceived without ye.
     Val.   Without me? they cannot.
• *Speed.*   Without you? nay, that's certain, for, without you were so simple, none else would: but you are so without these follies, that these follies are within you and shine through you like
• the water in an urinal, that not an eye that sees you but is a physician to comment on your ma-lady.

     Val.   But tell me, dost thou know my lady Silvia?
     Speed.   She that you gaze on so as she sits at supper?
     Val.   Hast thou observed that? even she, I mean.
     Speed.   Why, sir, I know her not.   50
     Val.   Dost thou know her by my gazing on her, and yet knowest her not?
• *Speed.*   Is she not hard-favoured, sir?
• *Val.*   Not so fair, boy, as well-favoured.
     Speed.   Sir, I know that well enough.
     Val.   What dost thou know?
     Speed.   That she is not so fair as, of you, well favoured.
     Val.   I mean that her beauty is exquisite, but her favour infinite.   60
     Speed.   That's because the one is painted and the other out of all count.
     Val.   ·How painted? and how out of count?
     Speed.   Marry, sir, so painted, to make he fair, that no man counts of her beauty.
     Val.   How esteemest thou me? I account of her beauty.
     Speed.   You never saw her since she was de-formed.
     Val.   How long hath she been deformed?   70
     Speed.   Ever since you loved her.
     Val.   I have loved her ever since I saw her; and still I see her beautiful.
     Speed.   If you love her, you cannot see her.
     Val.   Why?
     Speed.   Because Love is blind.   O, that you had mine eyes; or your own eyes had the lights they were wont to have when you chid at Sir Proteus for going ungartered!
     Val.   What should I see then?   80
     Speed.   Your own present folly and her passing deformity: for he, being in love, could not see to garter his hose, and you, being in love, cannot see to put on your hose.
     Val.   Belike, boy, then, you are in love; for last morning you could not see to wipe my shoes.
     Speed.   True, sir; I was in love with my bed:

26-27 *beggar at Hallowmass.* The feast of All Hallows (November 1) was a day when paupers received special alms.

29 *one of the lions.* This is probably a reference to the lions in the Tower of London or to the lions on the royal standard which would have been displayed in theatres.

35 *without ye.* i.e. outside of you.

Gyles Isham as Valentine, Stratford-upon-Avon, 1938

37-38 *Without you? . . . without.* Playing on the senses 'outside' and 'unless'. *none·else would.* Dr. Johnson ex-plains this as 'none else would be so simple'.

41 *urinal.* Transparent glass vessel for testing urine.

53 *hard-favoured.* Ugly.

54 *Not so fair, boy, as well-favoured.* i.e. Silvia's beauty is exceeded by her charm.

88 *swinged.* Beat, thrashed.

91 *set.* Seated. There is also a bawdy pun here where Speed takes 'stand' to mean the male erection.

100 *motion.* A 'motion' was a puppet-show. Speed means that Silvia is a puppet because she has not been able to speak of her love for Valentine, but has had to employ him as an interpreter.

106 *servant.* Swain.

Valentine, Silvia and Speed. Painting by H. P. Briggs (1791?–1844)

115 *came hardly off.* Was difficult to write.

119 *stead.* Benefit.

122 *period.* A pause.

128 *quaintly.* Ingeniously.

● I thank you, you swinged me for my love, which makes me the bolder to chide you for yours.
   Val. In conclusion, I stand affected to her. 90
● *Speed.* I would you were set, so your affection would cease.
   Val. Last night she enjoined me to write some lines to one she loves.
   Speed. And have you?
   Val. I have.
   Speed. Are they not lamely writ?
   Val. No, boy, but as well as I can do them. Peace! here she comes.
● *Speed.* [*Aside*] O excellent motion! O exceeding puppet! Now will he interpret to her.

Enter SILVIA.

   Val. Madam and mistress, a thousand good-morrows.
   Speed. [*Aside*] O, give ye good even! here's a million of manners.
● *Sil.* Sir Valentine and servant, to you two thousand.
   Speed. [*Aside*] He should give her interest, and she gives it him.
   Val. As you enjoin'd me, I have writ your letter
Unto the secret nameless friend of yours;
Which I was much unwilling to proceed in
But for my duty to your ladyship.
   Sil. I thank you, gentle servant: 'tis very clerkly done.
● *Val.* Now trust me, madam, it came hardly off;
For being ignorant to whom it goes
I writ at random, very doubtfully.
   Sil. Perchance you think too much of so much pains?
● *Val.* No, madam; so it stead you, I will write,
Please you command, a thousand times as much;
And yet—
● *Sil.* A pretty period! Well, I guess the sequel;
And yet I will not name it; and yet I care not;
And yet take this again; and yet I thank you,
Meaning henceforth to trouble you no more.
   Speed. [*Aside*] And yet you will; and yet another 'yet.'
   Val. What means your ladyship? do you not like it?
● *Sil.* Yes, yes: the lines are very quaintly writ;
But since unwillingly, take them again.
Nay, take them.   130
   Val. Madam, they are for you.
   Sil. Ay, ay: you writ them, sir, at my request;
But I will none of them; they are for you;
I would have had them writ more movingly.
   Val. Please you, I'll write your ladyship another.
   Sil. And when it's writ, for my sake read it over,
And if it please you, so; if not, why, so.
   Val. If it please me, madam, what then?
   Sil. Why, if it please you, take it for your labour:
And so, good morrow, servant.   [*Exit.* 140
   Speed. O jest unseen, inscrutable, invisible,
As a nose on a man's face, or a weathercock on a steeple!
My master sues to her, and she hath taught her suitor,

He being her pupil, to become her tutor.
O excellent device! was there ever heard a better,
That my master, being scribe, to himself should
    write the letter?
  Val.   How now, sir? what are you reasoning
with yourself?
  Speed.   Nay, I was rhyming: 'tis you that have
the reason.   150
  Val.   To do what?
  Speed.   To be a spokesman from Madam Silvia.
  Val.   To whom?
  Speed.   To yourself: why, she wooes you by a
    figure.
  Val.   What figure?
  Speed.   By a letter, I should say.
  Val.   Why, she hath not writ to me?
  Speed.   What need she, when she hath made
you write to yourself? Why, do you not perceive
the jest?   160
  Val.   No, believe me.
  Speed.   No believing you, indeed, sir. But
did you perceive her earnest?
  Val.   She gave me none, except an angry word.
  Speed.   Why, she hath given you a letter.
  Val.   That's the letter I writ to her friend.
  Speed.   And that letter hath she delivered, and
there an end.
  Val.   I would it were no worse.
  Speed.   I'll warrant you, 'tis as well: 170
For often have you writ to her, and she, in
    modesty,
Or else for want of idle time, could not again
    reply;
Or fearing else some messenger that might her
    mind discover,
Herself hath taught her love himself to write unto
    her lover.
All this I speak in print, for in print I found it.
Why muse you, sir? 'tis dinner-time.
  Val.   I have dined.
  Speed.   Ay, but hearken, sir; though the cha-
meleon Love can feed on the air, I am one that
am nourished by my victuals and would fain have
meat. O, be not like your mistress; be moved,
be moved.   [*Exeunt.*

SCENE II.   *Verona.*   JULIA'S *house.*

Enter PROTEUS *and* JULIA.

  Pro.   Have patience, gentle Julia.
  Jul.   I must, where is no remedy.
  Pro.   When possibly I can, I will return.
  Jul.   If you turn not, you will return the
    sooner.
Keep this remembrance for thy Julia's sake.
                    [*Giving a ring.*
  Pro.   Why, then, we'll make exchange; here,
    take you this.
  Jul.   And seal the bargain with a holy kiss.
  Pro.   Here is my hand for my true constancy;
And when that hour o'erslips me in the day
Wherein I sigh not, Julia, for thy sake,   10
The next ensuing hour some foul mischance
Torment me for my love's forgetfulness!
My father stays my coming; answer not;
The tide is now: nay, not thy tide of tears;
That tide will stay me longer than I should.
Julia, farewell!   [*Exit Julia.*
    What, gone without a word?

154 *by a figure.* Indirectly. The phrase refers to a device used in rhetoric.

175 *in print,* i.e. 'with exactness' and 'in a printed book'.

177 *I have dined.* Valentine implies that the sight of Silvia has satisfied his appetite.

178-179 *chameleon Love.* It was commonly believed that the chameleon fed on air. Love was described as chameleon because of the changeability of those in love.

4 *turn not.* Do not prove unfaithful.

Proteus: 'Here is my hand for my true constancy'.
Engraving by W. Hopwood (active early 19th century)

Launce and his dog. Frontispiece by W. Cruikshank to Cumberland edition, *The Two Gentlemen of Verona*, 1822

19-20 *worser sole . . . my mother.* It was a common debating point whether a woman's soul was inferior to a man's. There is also here a bawdy reference to the female sex organ.

30-31 *wood woman.* i.e. mad woman.

32 *up and down.* i.e. exactly.

53-54 *tongue . . . tale.* This is another bawdy pun, repeated in *The Taming of the Shrew*, II, i, 218–219.

Ay, so true love should do: it cannot speak;
For truth hath better deeds than words to grace it.

Enter PANTHINO.

Pan.   Sir Proteus, you are stay'd for.
Pro.   Go; I come, I come.   **20**
Alas! this parting strikes poor lovers dumb.

[*Exeunt.*

SCENE III.   *The same.   A street.*

Enter LAUNCE, *leading a dog.*

Launce.   Nay, 'twill be this hour ere I have done weeping; all the kind of the Launces have this very fault. I have received my proportion, like the prodigious son, and am going with Sir Proteus to the Imperial's court. I think Crab my dog be the sourest-natured dog that lives: my mother weeping, my father wailing, my sister crying, our maid howling, our cat wringing her hands, and all our house in a great perplexity, yet did not this cruel-hearted cur shed one tear: he is a stone, a very pebble stone, and has no more pity in him than a dog: a Jew would have wept to have seen our parting; why, my grandam, having no eyes, look you, wept herself blind at my parting. Nay, I'll show you the manner of it. This shoe is my father: no, this left shoe is my father: no, no, this left shoe is my mother: nay, that cannot be so neither: yes, it is so, it is
● so, it hath the worser sole. This shoe, with the hole in it, is my mother, and this my father; a vengeance on't! there 'tis: now, sir, this staff is my sister, for, look you, she is as white as a lily and as small as a wand: this hat is Nan, our maid: I am the dog: no, the dog is himself, and I am the dog—Oh! the dog is me, and I am myself; ay, so, so. Now come I to my father; Father, your blessing: now should not the shoe speak a word for weeping: now should I kiss my father; well, he weeps on. Now come I to my
● mother: O, that she could speak now like a wood woman! Well, I kiss her; why, there 'tis; here's my mother's breath up and down. Now come I to my sister; mark the moan she makes. Now the dog all this while sheds not a tear nor speaks a word; but see how I lay the dust with my tears.

Enter PANTHINO.

Pan.   Launce, away, away, aboard! thy master is shipped and thou art to post after with oars. What's the matter? why weepest thou, man? Away, ass! you'll lose the tide, if you tarry any longer.
Launce.   It is no matter if the tied were lost; for it is the unkindest tied that ever any man tied.
Pan.   What's the unkindest tide?
Launce.   Why, he that's tied here, Crab, my dog.
Pan.   Tut, man, I mean thou'lt lose the flood, and, in losing the flood, lose thy voyage, and, in losing thy voyage, lose thy master, and, in losing thy master, lose thy service, and, in losing thy service,—Why dost thou stop my mouth?   **51**
Launce.   For fear thou shouldst lose thy tongue.
● *Pan.*   Where should I lose my tongue?
Launce.   In thy tale.
Pan.   In thy tail!

Launce. Lose the tide, and the voyage, and the master, and the service, and the tied! Why, man, if the river were dry, I am able to fill it with my tears; if the wind were down, I could drive the boat with my sighs.   60
Pan. Come, come away, man; I was sent to call thee.
Launce. Sir, call me what thou darest.
Pan. Wilt thou go?
Launce. Well, I will go.   [*Exeunt.*

Scene IV. *Milan.   The* Duke's *palace.*

Enter Silvia, Valentine, Thurio, *and* Speed.

Sil. Servant!
Val. Mistress?
Speed. Master, Sir Thurio frowns on you.
Val. Ay, boy, it's for love.
Speed. Not of you.
Val. Of my mistress, then.
Speed. 'Twere good you knocked him. [*Exit.*
Sil. Servant, you are sad.
Val. Indeed, madam, I seem so.
Thu. Seem you that you are not?   10
Val. Haply I do.
Thu. So do counterfeits.
Val. So do you.
Thu. What seem I that I am not?
Val. Wise.
Thu. What instance of the contrary?
Val. Your folly.
Thu. And how quote you my folly?
● *Val.* I quote it in your jerkin.
Thu. My jerkin is a doublet.   20
Val. Well, then, I'll double your folly.
Thu. How?
Sil. What, angry, Sir Thurio! do you change colour?
Val. Give him leave, madam; he is a kind of chameleon.
Thu. That hath more mind to feed on your blood than live in your air.
Val. You have said, sir.
Thu. Ay, sir, and done too, for this time.   30
Val. I know it well, sir; you always end ere you begin
Sil. A fine volley of words, gentlemen, and quickly shot off.
● *Val.* 'Tis indeed, madam; we thank the giver.
Sil. Who is that, servant?
Val. Yourself, sweet lady; for you gave the fire. Sir Thurio borrows his wit from your ladyship's looks, and spends what he borrows kindly in your company.   40
Thu. Sir, if you spend word for word with me, I shall make your wit bankrupt.
Val. I know it well, sir; you have an exchequer of words, and, I think, no other treasure to give your followers, for it appears, by their bare liveries, that they live by your bare words.
Sil. No more, gentlemen, no more: here comes my father.

Enter Duke.

● *Duke.* Now, daughter Silvia, you are hard beset.
Sir Valentine, your father's in good health: 50
What say you to a letter from your friends
Of much good news?

Peggy Livesey as Silvia, Stratford-upon-Avon, 1938

19-20 *jerkin . . . doublet.* The jerkin was a long jacket worn over or in place of a doublet, which was shorter.

35 *giver.* 'Direction-giver'; technically, the person who directs an archer's aim.

49 *hard beset.* Hotly besieged.

91 *pawn for fealty.* Pledge for faithfulness.

Silvia, Valentine and Proteus. Illustration by Walter Crane, 1894

Val.   My lord, I will be thankful
To any happy messenger from thence.
   Duke. Know ye Don Antonio, your country-
    man?
   Val. Ay, my good lord, I know the gentleman
To be of worth and worthy estimation
And not without desert so well reputed.
   Duke. Hath he not a son?
   Val. Ay, my good lord; a son that well de-
    serves
The honour and regard of such a father.   60
   Duke. You know him well?
   Val. I know him as myself; for from our
    infancy
We have conversed and spent our hours together:
And though myself have been an idle truant,
Omitting the sweet benefit of time
To clothe mine age with angel-like perfection,
Yet hath Sir Proteus, for that's his name,
Made use and fair advantage of his days;
His years but young, but his experience old;
His head unmellow'd, but his judgement ripe; 70
And, in a word, for far behind his worth
Comes all the praises that I now bestow,
He is complete in feature and in mind
With all good grace to grace a gentleman.
   Duke. Beshrew me, sir, but if he make this
    good,
He is as worthy for an empress' love
As meet to be an emperor's counsellor.
Well, sir, this gentleman is come to me,
With commendation from great potentates;
And here he means to spend his time awhile: 80
I think 'tis no unwelcome news to you.
   Val. Should I have wish'd a thing, it had
    been he.
   Duke. Welcome him then according to his
    worth.
Silvia, I speak to you; and you, sir Thurio;
For Valentine, I need not cite him to it:
I will send him hither to you presently. [*Exit.*
   Val. This is the gentleman I told your lady-
    ship
Had come along with me, but that his mistress
Did hold his eyes lock'd in her crystal looks.
   Sil. Belike that now she hath enfranchised
    them   90
●Upon some other pawn for fealty.
   Val. Nay, sure, I think she holds them pri-
    soners still.
   Sil. Nay, then he should be blind; and, being
    blind,
How could he see his way to seek out you?
   Val. Why, lady, Love hath twenty pair of eyes.
   Thu. They say that Love hath not an eye
    at all.
   Val. To see such lovers, Thurio, as yourself:
Upon a homely object Love can wink.
   Sil. Have done, have done; here comes the
    gentleman.

         Enter PROTEUS. [*Exit* THURIO.

   Val. Welcome, dear Proteus! Mistress, I
    beseech you,   100
Confirm his welcome with some special favour.
   Sil. His worth is warrant for his welcome
    hither,
If this be he you oft have wish'd to hear from.
   Val. Mistress, it is: sweet lady, entertain him

To be my fellow-servant to your ladyship.
   Sil.   Too low a mistress for so high a servant.
   Pro.   Not so, sweet lady: but too mean a
      servant
To have a look of such a worthy mistress.
   Val.   Leave off discourse of disability:
Sweet lady, entertain him for your servant.   110
   Pro.   My duty will I boast of; nothing else.
• *Sil.*   And duty never yet did want his meed:
Servant, you are welcome to a worthless mistress.
   Pro.   I'll die on him that says so but yourself.
   Sil.   That you are welcome?
   Pro.   That you are worthless.

Re-enter THURIO.

   Thu.   Madam, my lord your father would
      speak with you.
   Sil.   I wait upon his pleasure.   Come, Sir
      Thurio,
Go with me.   Once more, new servant, welcome:
I'll leave you to confer of home affairs;
When you have done, we look to hear from you.
   Pro.   We'll both attend upon your ladyship.
              [*Exeunt Silvia and Thurio.*
   Val.   Now, tell me, how do all from whence
      you came?
• *Pro.*   Your friends are well and have them
      much commended.
   Val.   And how do yours?
   Pro.   I left them all in health.
   Val.   How does your lady? and how thrives
      your love?
   Pro.   My tales of love were wont to weary you;
I know you joy not in a love-discourse.
   Val.   Ay, Proteus, but that life is alter'd now:
I have done penance for contemning Love,
Whose high imperious thoughts have punish'd me
With bitter fasts, with penitential groans,
With nightly tears and daily heart-sore sighs;
For in revenge of my contempt of love,
Love hath chased sleep from my enthralled eyes
And made them watchers of mine own heart's
      sorrow.
O gentle Proteus, Love's a mighty lord
And hath so humbled me as I confess
There is no woe to his correction
Nor to his service no such joy on earth.
Now no discourse, except it be of love;   140
Now can I break my fast, dine, sup and sleep,
Upon the very naked name of love.
   Pro.   Enough; I read your fortune in your eye.
Was this the idol that you worship so?
   Val.   Even she; and is she not a heavenly
      saint?
   Pro.   No; but she is an earthly paragon.
   Val.   Call her divine.
   Pro.   I will not flatter her.
   Val.   O, flatter me; for love delights in praises.
   Pro.   When I was sick, you gave me bitter pills,
And I must minister the like to you.   150
   Val.   Then speak the truth by her; if not
      divine,
• Yet let her be a principality,
Sovereign to all the creatures on the earth.
• *Pro.*   Except my mistress.
   Val.   Sweet, except not any;
• Except thou wilt except against my love.
   Pro.   Have I not reason to prefer mine own?
• *Val.*   And I will help thee to prefer her too:

112 *meed.* Reward.

123 *have them much commended.* Have sent their warm
remembrances.

Valentine (Denholm Elliot) and Proteus (Derek
Godfrey), Stratford-upon-Avon, 1960

152 *principality.* First and principal of women, referring to the hierarchy of angels.

154 *Sweet.* Endearment applied to both men and
women.

155 *Except.* Unless.

157 *prefer.* Promote, advance.

167 *alone*. Unique.

172 *do not dream on thee*. Think about your feelings.

196 *Is it mine, or Valentine's praise*. Most modern editors have emended this to 'Is it mine eye, or Valentine's praise'.

207 *advice*. Knowledge.

209 *picture I have yet beheld*. Proteus may be merely referring to her appearance. Dr. Johnson thought that 'picture' meant 'portrait' and noted Shakespeare's mistake.

212 *no reason but*. No doubt that.

214 *compass*. Win.

Set design for a street in Milan by J. Gower Parks, Stratford-upon-Avon, 1938

She shall be dignified with this high honour—
To bear my lady's train, lest the base earth
Should from her vesture chance to steal a kiss 160
And, of so great a favour growing proud,
Disdain to root the summer-swelling flower
And make rough winter everlastingly.
   Pro. Why, Valentine, what braggardism is
     this?
   Val. Pardon me, Proteus: all I can is nothing
To her whose worth makes other worthies nothing;
● She is alone.
   Pro.   Then let her alone.
   Val. Not for the world: why, man, she is
     mine own,
And I as rich in having such a jewel
As twenty seas, if all their sand were pearl,   170
The water nectar and the rocks pure gold.
● Forgive me that I do not dream on thee,
Because thou see'st me dote upon my love.
My foolish rival, that her father likes
Only for his possessions are so huge,
Is gone with her along, and I must after,
For love, thou know'st, is full of jealousy.
   Pro. But she loves you?
   Val. Ay, and we are betroth'd: nay, more,
     our marriage-hour,
With all the cunning manner of our flight,   180
Determined of; how I must climb her window,
The ladder made of cords, and all the means
Plotted and 'greed on for my happiness.
Good Proteus, go with me to my chamber,
In these affairs to aid me with thy counsel.
   Pro. Go on before; I shall inquire you forth:
I must unto the road, to disembark
Some necessaries that I needs must use,
And then I'll presently attend you.
   Val. Will you make haste?   190
   Pro. I will.   [*Exit Valentine.*
Even as one heat another heat expels,
Or as one nail by strength drives out another,
So the remembrance of my former love
Is by a newer object quite forgotten.
● †Is it mine, or Valentine's praise,
Her true perfection, or my false transgression,
That makes me reasonless to reason thus?
She is fair; and so is Julia that I love—
That I did love, for now my love is thaw'd;   200
Which, like a waxen image 'gainst a fire,
Bears no impression of the thing it was.
Methinks my zeal to Valentine is cold,
And that I love him not as I was wont.
O, but I love his lady too too much,
And that's the reason I love him so little.
● How shall I dote on her with more advice,
That thus without advice begin to love her!
● 'Tis but her picture I have yet beheld,
And that hath dazzled my reason's light;   210
But when I look on her perfections,
● There is no reason but I shall be blind.
If I can check my erring love, I will;
● If not, to compass her I'll use my skill.   [*Exit.*

   SCENE V. *The same. A street.*

   Enter SPEED *and* LAUNCE *severally.*

   Speed. Launce! by mine honesty, welcome to
Milan!
   Launce. Forswear not thyself, sweet youth,
for I am not welcome. I reckon this always,

that a man is never undone till he be hanged,
nor never welcome to a place till some certain
● shot be paid and the hostess say 'Welcome!'

Speed. Come on, you madcap, I'll to the
alehouse with you presently; where, for one
shot of five pence, thou shalt have five thousand
welcomes. But, sirrah, how did thy master part
with Madam Julia?

Launce. Marry, after they closed in earnest,
they parted very fairly in jest.

Speed. But shall she marry him?

Launce. No.

Speed. How then? shall he marry her?

Launce. No, neither.

Speed. What, are they broken?

Launce. No, they are both as whole as a fish.

Speed. Why, then, how stands the matter
with them?

Launce. Marry, thus; when it stands well
with him, it stands well with her.

Speed. What an ass art thou! I understand
thee not.

Launce. What a block art thou, that thou
● canst not! My staff understands me.

Speed. What thou sayest?

Launce. Ay, and what I do too: look thee,
I'll but lean, and my staff understands me.

Speed. It stands under thee, indeed.

Launce. Why, stand-under and under-stand
is all one.

Speed. But tell me true, will't be a match?

Launce. Ask my dog: if he say ay, it will; if
he say, no, it will; if he shake his tail and say
nothing, it will.

Speed. The conclusion is then that it will.

Launce. Thou shalt never get such a secret
● from me but by a parable.

Speed. 'Tis well that I get it so. But, Launce,
how sayest thou, that my master is become a
notable lover?

Launce. I never knew him otherwise.

Speed. Than how?

● *Launce.* A notable lubber, as thou reportest
him to be.

Speed. Why, thou whoreson ass, thou mis-
takest me.   50

Launce. Why, fool, I meant not thee; I meant
thy master.

Speed. I tell thee, my master is become a hot
lover.

Launce. Why, I tell thee, I care not though
he burn himself in love. If thou wilt, go with me
to the alehouse; if not, thou art an Hebrew, a
Jew, and not worth the name of a Christian.

Speed. Why?

Launce. Because thou hast not so much cha-
● rity in thee as to go to the ale with a Christian.
Wilt thou go?

Speed. At thy service.   [*Exeunt.*

SCENE VI.   *The same.   The* DUKE'S *palace.*

Enter PROTEUS.

Pro. To leave my Julia, shall I be forsworn;
To love fair Silvia, shall I be forsworn;
To wrong my friend, I shall be much forsworn;
And even that power which gave me first my oath
Provokes me to this threefold perjury;
Love bade me swear and Love bids me forswear.

7 *shot.* Payment, reckoning at a tavern.

28 *understands me.* i.e. props me up.

Speed (Jack McGowran) and Launce (Patrick Wymark)
with dog, Stratford-upon-Avon, 1960

41 *by a parable.* Indirectly.

47 *lubber.* Lout.

61 *ale.* i.e. the 'Church-ale', a parish festival at which
ale was sold to raise funds.

13 *learn*. Teach.

17 *leave*. Cease, stop.

26 *Ethiope*. The common Elizabethan term for a black
African.

35 *Myself in counsel, his competitor*. i.e. with myself in
the secret (and), his associate.

37 *pretended*. Intended.

43 *drift*. Scheme.

Costume design for Julia by J. Gower Parks, Stratford-
upon-Avon, 1938

2 *conjure*. Beseech.

3 *table*. Writing tablet.

5 *lesson*. Instruct, teach. *Mean*. Means.

18 *inly*. Inward.

O sweet-suggesting Love, if thou hast sinn'd,
Teach me, thy tempted subject, to excuse it!
At first I did adore a twinkling star,
But now I worship a celestial sun.   10
Unheedful vows may heedfully be broken,
And he wants wit that wants resolved will
● To learn his wit to exchange the bad for better.
Fie, fie, unreverend tongue! to call her bad,
Whose sovereignty so oft thou hast preferr'd
With twenty thousand soul-confirming oaths.
● I cannot leave to love, and yet I do;
But there I leave to love where I should love.
Julia I lose and Valentine I lose:
If I keep them, I needs must lose myself;   20
If I lose them, thus find I by their loss
For Valentine myself, for Julia Silvia.
I to myself am dearer than a friend,
For love is still most precious in itself;
And Silvia—witness Heaven, that made her fair!—
● Shows Julia but a swarthy Ethiope.
I will forget that Julia is alive,
Remembering that my love to her is dead;
And Valentine I'll hold an enemy,
Aiming at Silvia as a sweeter friend.   30
I cannot now prove constant to myself,
Without some treachery used to Valentine.
This night he meaneth with a corded ladder
To climb celestial Silvia's chamber-window,
● Myself in counsel, his competitor.
Now presently I'll give her father notice
● Of their disguising and pretended flight;
Who, all enraged, will banish Valentine;
For Thurio, he intends, shall wed his daughter;
But, Valentine being gone, I'll quickly cross   40
By some sly trick blunt Thurio's dull proceeding.
Love, lend me wings to make my purpose swift,
● As thou hast lent me wit to plot this drift! [*Exit.*

SCENE VII.   *Verona.*   JULIA'S *house.*

Enter JULIA *and* LUCETTA.

Jul.   Counsel, Lucetta; gentle girl, assist me;
● And even in kind love I do conjure thee,
● Who art the table wherein all my thoughts
Are visibly charaċter'd and engraved,
● To lesson me and tell me some good mean
How, with my honour, I may undertake
A journey to my loving Proteus.
Luc.   Alas, the way is wearisome and long!
Jul.   A true-devoted pilgrim is not weary
To measure kingdoms with his feeble steps;   10
Much less shall she that hath Love's wings to fly,
And when the flight is made to one so dear,
Of such divine perfection, as Sir Proteus.
Luc.   Better forbear till Proteus make return.
Jul.   O, know'st thou not his looks are my
soul's food?
Pity the dearth that I have pined in,
By longing for that food so long a time.
● Didst thou but know the inly touch of love,
Thou wouldst as soon go kindle fire with snow
As seek to quench the fire of love with words. 20
Luc.   I do not seek to quench your love's hot
fire,
But qualify the fire's extreme rage,
Lest it should burn above the bounds of reason.
Jul.   The more thou damm'st it up, the more
it burns.
The current that with gentle murmur glides,

Thou know'st, being stopp'd, impatiently doth
    rage;
But when his fair course is not hindered,
He makes sweet music with the enamell'd stones,
●Giving a gentle kiss to every sedge
He overtaketh in his pilgrimage,   30
And so by many winding nooks he strays
With willing sport to the wild ocean.
Then let me go and hinder not my course:
I'll be as patient as a gentle stream
And make a pastime of each weary step,
Till the last step have brought me to my love;
And there I'll rest, as after much turmoil
●A blessed soul doth in Elysium.
    Luc.   But in what habit will you go along?
    Jul.   Not like a woman; for I would prevent
The loose encounters of lascivious men:
Gentle Lucetta, fit me with such weeds
As may beseem some well-reputed page.
    Luc.   Why, then, your ladyship must cut your
        hair.
    Jul.   No, girl; I'll knit it up in silken strings
●With twenty odd-conceited true-love knots.
●To be fantastic may become a youth
●Of greater time than I shall show to be.
    Luc.   What fashion, madam, shall I make your
        breeches?
    Jul.   That fits as well as 'Tell me, good my lord,
●What compass will you wear your farthingale?'
Why even what fashion thou best likest, Lucetta.
    Luc.   You must needs have them with a cod-
        piece, madam.
    Jul.   Out, out, Lucetta! that will be ill-
        favour'd.
●   _Luc._   A round hose, madam, now's not worth
        a pin,
●Unless you have a codpiece to stick pins on.
    Jul.   Lucetta, as thou lovest me, let me have
What thou thinkest meet and is most mannerly.
But tell me, wench, how will the world repute me
For undertaking so unstaid a journey?   60
I fear me, it will make me scandalized.
    Luc.   If you think so, then stay at home and
        go not.
    Jul.   Nay, that I will not.
    Luc.   Then never dream on infamy, but go.
If Proteus like your journey when you come,
No matter who's displeased when you are gone:
I fear me, he will scarce be pleased withal.
    Jul.   That is the least, Lucetta, of my fear:
A thousand oaths, an ocean of his tears
And instances of infinite of love   70
Warrant me welcome to my Proteus.
    Luc.   All these are servants to deceitful men.
    Jul.   Base men, that use them to so base effect!
But truer stars did govern Proteus' birth;
His words are bonds, his oaths are oracles,
His love sincere, his thoughts immaculate,
His tears pure messengers sent from his heart,
His heart as far from fraud as heaven from earth.
    Luc.   Pray heaven he prove so, when you come
        to him!
    Jul.   Now, as thou lovest me, do him not that
        wrong   80
To bear a hard opinion of his truth:
Only deserve my love by loving him;
And presently go with me to my chamber,
To take a note of what I stand in need of,
To furnish me upon my longing journey.

29 _sedge_. Grass-like plant growing in marshes.

38 _Elysium_. In classical mythology, the place where the blessed went after death.

46 _odd-conceited_. Elaborately odd.

47 _fantastic_. Fanciful.

48 _greater time_. Older years.

51 _compass_. Fashion. _Farthingale_. Hooped skirt.

55 _round hose_. Bulging breeches.

Costumes at the time of James I. The Countess of Somerset wears a farthingale. Illustration from J. R. Planché (1796–1880)

56 _to stick pins on_. Apparently one of the uses of the cod-piece.

90 *tarriance.* Delay.

Proteus and Valentine. Illustration by Walter Crane, 1894

34 *suggested.* Tempted.

47 *pretence.* Intention.

All that is mine I leave at thy dispose,
My goods, my lands, my reputation;
Only, in lieu thereof, dispatch me hence.
Come, answer not, but to it presently!
● I am impatient of my tarriance.   [*Exeunt.* 90

ACT III.

Scene I. *Milan.   The* Duke's *palace.*

Enter Duke, Thurio, *and* Proteus.

Duke. Sir Thurio, give us leave, I pray, awhile;
We have some secrets to confer about.
                                        [*Exit Thu.*
Now, tell me, Proteus, what's your will with me?
  Pro. My gracious lord, that which I would
         discover
The law of friendship bids me to conceal;
But when I call to mind your gracious favours
Done to me, undeserving as I am,
My duty pricks me on to utter that
Which else no worldly good should draw from me.
Know, worthy prince, Sir Valentine, my friend,
This night intends to steal away your daughter:
Myself am one made privy to the plot.
I know you have determined to bestow her
On Thurio, whom your gentle daughter hates;
And should she thus be stol'n away from you,
It would be much vexation to your age.
Thus, for my duty's sake, I rather chose
To cross my friend in his intended drift
Than, by concealing it, heap on your head
A pack of sorrows which would press you down,
Being unprevented, to your timeless grave.   21
  Duke. Proteus, I thank thee for thine honest
         care;
Which to requite, command me while I live.
This love of theirs myself have often seen,
Haply when they have judged me fast asleep,
And oftentimes have purposed to forbid
Sir Valentine her company and my court:
But fearing lest my jealous aim might err
And so unworthily disgrace the man,
A rashness that I ever yet have shunn'd,   30
I gave him gentle looks, thereby to find
That which thyself hast now disclosed to me.
And, that thou mayst perceive my fear of this,
● Knowing that tender youth is soon suggested,
I nightly lodge her in an upper tower,
The key whereof myself have ever kept;
And thence she cannot be convey'd away.
  Pro. Know, noble lord, they have devised a
         mean
How he her chamber-window will ascend
And with a corded ladder fetch her down;   40
For which the youthful lover now is gone
And this way comes he with it presently;
Where, if it please you, you may intercept him.
But, good my Lord, do it so cunningly
That my discovery be not aimed at;
For love of you, not hate unto my friend,
● Hath made me publisher of this pretence.
  Duke. Upon mine honour, he shall never know
That I had any light from thee of this.
  Pro. Adieu, my Lord; Sir Valentine is coming.
                                        [*Exit.* 50

Enter Valentine.

  Duke. Sir Valentine, whither away so fast?

Val. Please it your grace, there is a messenger
That stays to bear my letters to my friends,
And I am going to deliver them.
　Duke. Be they of much import?
　Val. The tenour of them doth but signify
My health and happy being at your court.
　Duke. Nay then, no matter; stay with me
　　awhile;
● I am to break with thee of some affairs
That touch me near, wherein thou must be secret.
'Tis not unknown to thee that I have sought　61
To match my friend Sir Thurio to my daughter.
　Val. I know it well, my Lord; and, sure, the
　　match
Were rich and honourable; besides, the gentle-
　　man
Is full of virtue, bounty, worth and qualities
Beseeming such a wife as your fair daughter:
Cannot your Grace win her to fancy him?
● *Duke.* No, trust me; she is peevish, sullen,
　　froward,
Proud, disobedient, stubborn, lacking duty,
Neither regarding that she is my child　70
Nor fearing me as if I were her father;
And, may I say to thee, this pride of hers,
Upon advice, hath drawn my love from her;
And, where I thought the remnant of mine age
Should have been cherish'd by her child-like
　　duty,
I now am full resolved to take a wife
And turn her out to who will take her in:
Then let her beauty be her wedding-dower;
For me and my possessions she esteems not.
　Val. What would your Grace have me to do
　　in this?　80
● *Duke.* †There is a lady in Verona here
Whom I affect; but she is nice and coy
And nought esteems my aged eloquence:
Now therefore would I have thee to my tutor—
For long agone I have forgot to court;
Besides, the fashion of the time is changed—
How and which way I may bestow myself
To be regarded in her sun-bright eye.
　Val. Win her with gifts, if she respect not
　　words:
Dumb jewels often in their silent kind　90
More than quick words do move a woman's mind.
　Duke. But she did scorn a present that I sent
　　her.
　Val. A woman sometimes scorns what best
　　contents her.
Send her another; never give her o'er;
For scorn at first makes after-love the more.
If she do frown, 'tis not in hate of you,
But rather to beget more love in you:
If she do chide, 'tis not to have you gone;
For why, the fools are mad, if left alone.
Take no repulse, whatever she doth say;　100
For 'get you gone,' she doth not mean 'away!'
Flatter and praise, commend, extol their graces;
● Though ne'er so black, say they have angels' faces.
That man that hath a tongue, I say, is no man,
If with his tongue he cannot win a woman.
　Duke. But she I mean is promised by her
　　friends
Unto a youthful gentleman of worth,
And kept severely from resort of men,
That no man hath access by day to her.
　Val. Why, then, I would resort to her by night.

59 *break with thee.* Disclose to you.

68 *froward.* Perverse.

Valentine (Denholm Elliot) and Duke (Eric Porter),
Stratford-upon-Avon, 1960

81 *in Verona.* i.e. of Verona, since the action takes place
in Milan.

103 *black.* Swarthy (i.e. ugly).

115 *shelving.* Overhanging.

117 *quaintly.* Skilfully.

121 *blood.* Good parentage.

135 *fashion me.* Adapt myself.

138 *engine.* Device. *proceeding.* Scheme.

144 *herald thoughts.* i.e. they go in advance of him.

145 *importune.* Command.

153 *Phaethon . . . Merops' son.* Phaethon was the son of Phoebus, the sun god, and Clymene (the wife of Merops). He persuaded his father to let him drive the sun-chariot but was unable to control the horses and was destroyed by a thunderbolt from Zeus.

Phaethon struck by a thunderbolt from Zeus. Engraving from Tonson's edition of Ovid's *Metamorphoses*, 1727

Duke. Ay, but the doors be lock'd and keys kept safe,   111
That no man hath recourse to her by night.
　Val. What lets but one may enter at her window?
　Duke. Her chamber is aloft, far from the ground,
And built so shelving that one cannot climb it
Without apparent hazard of his life.
　Val. Why then, a ladder quaintly made of cords,
To cast up, with a pair of anchoring hooks,
Would serve to scale another Hero's tower,
So bold Leander would adventure it.   120
　Duke. Now, as thou art a gentleman of blood,
Advise me where I may have such a ladder.
　Val. When would you use it? pray, sir, tell me that.
　Duke. This very night; for Love is like a child,
That longs for every thing that he can come by.
　Val. By seven o'clock I'll get you such a ladder.
　Duke. But, hark thee; I will go to her alone:
How shall I best convey the ladder thither?
　Val. It will be light, my lord, that you may bear it
Under a cloak that is of any length.   130
　Duke. A cloak as long as thine will serve the turn?
　Val. Ay, my good lord.
　Duke.　　　　　　Then let me see thy cloak:
I'll get me one of such another length.
　Val. Why, any cloak will serve the turn, my lord.
　Duke. How shall I fashion me to wear a cloak?
I pray thee, let me feel thy cloak upon me.
What letter is this same? What's here? 'To Silvia'!
And here an engine fit for my proceeding.
I'll be so bold to break the seal for once. [*Reads.*
'My thoughts do harbour with my Silvia nightly,
　And slaves they are to me that send them flying:
O, could their master come and go as lightly,
　Himself would lodge where senseless they are lying!
My herald thoughts in thy pure bosom rest them;
　While I, their king, that hither them importune,
Do curse the grace that with such grace hath bless'd them,
　Because myself do want my servants' fortune:
I curse myself, for they are sent by me,
That they should harbour where their lord would be.'
What's here?   150
　'Silvia, this night I will enfranchise thee.'
'Tis so; and here's the ladder for the purpose.
Why, Phaethon,—for thou art Merops' son,—
Wilt thou aspire to guide the heavenly car
And with thy daring folly burn the world?
Wilt thou reach stars, because they shine on thee?
Go, base intruder! overweening slave!
Bestow thy fawning smiles on equal mates,
And think my patience, more than thy desert,
Is privilege for thy departure hence: 160
Thank me for this more than for all the favours
Which all too much I have bestow'd on thee.
But if thou linger in my territories

Longer than swiftest expedition
Will give thee time to leave our royal court,
By heaven! my wrath shall far exceed the love
I ever bore my daughter or thyself.
Be gone! I will not hear thy vain excuse;
But, as thou lovest thy life, make speed from
  hence.   [*Exit.*
  Val.   And why not death rather than living
    torment?   170
To die is to be banish'd from myself;
And Silvia is myself: banish'd from her
Is self from self: a deadly banishment!
What light is light, if Silvia be not seen?
What joy is joy, if Silvia be not by?
Unless it be to think that she is by
And feed upon the shadow of perfection.
Except I be by Silvia in the night,
There is no music in the nightingale;
Unless I look on Silvia in the day,   180
There is no day for me to look upon;
• She is my essence, and I leave to be,
• If I be not by her fair influence
Foster'd, illumined, cherish'd, kept alive.
I fly not death, to fly his deadly doom:
Tarry I here, I but attend on death:
But, fly I hence, I fly away from life.

Enter PROTEUS *and* LAUNCE.

  Pro.   Run, boy, run, run, and seek him out.
• *Launce.*   Soho, soho!
  Pro.   What seest thou?   190
  Launce.   Him we go to find: there's not a
hair on's head but 'tis a Valentine.
  Pro.   Valentine?
  Val.   No.
  Pro.   Who then? his spirit?
  Val.   Neither.
  Pro.   What then?
  Val.   Nothing.
  Launce.   Can nothing speak? Master, shall I
    strike?
  Pro.   Who wouldst thou strike?   200
  Launce.   Nothing.
  Pro.   Villain, forbear.
  Launce.   Why, sir, I'll strike nothing: I pray
    you,—
  Pro.   Sirrah, I say, forbear. Friend Valentine,
    a word.
  Val.   My ears are stopt and cannot hear good
    news,
So much of bad already hath possess'd them.
  Pro.   Then in dumb silence will I bury mine,
For they are harsh, untuneable and bad.
  Val.   Is Silvia dead?
  Pro.   No, Valentine.   210
  Val.   No Valentine, indeed, for sacred Silvia.
Hath she forsworn me?
  Pro.   No, Valentine.
  Val.   No Valentine, if Silvia have forsworn me.
What is your news?
• *Launce.*   Sir, there is a proclamation that you
    are vanished.
  Pro.   That thou art banished—O, that's the
    news!—
From hence, from Silvia and from me thy friend.
  Val.   O, I have fed upon this woe already,
And now excess of it will make me surfeit.   220
Doth Silvia know that I am banished?

182 *essence.* Very being. *leave.* Cease.

183 *influence.* A reference to the influence of a star upon human beings.

189 *Soho.* A cry in hare-hunting and hawking.

Costume design for Launce by J. Gower Parks, Stratford-upon-Avon, 1938

216 *vanished.* Banished.

222 *doom.* Sentence.

250 *milk-white bosom.* Sixteenth century gowns had a small pocket in the inside of the bodice, often the receptacle for love-letters, tokens, etc.

256 *Regard.* Take notice of.

263 *one knave.* This implies single knavery as opposed to double or excessive knavery.

269 *gossips.* Sponsors at a child's baptism. Launce is saying that his love is not a virgin (maid) because she has had an illegitimate child.

271 *water-spaniel.* The spaniel was well-known for its fawning. Other qualities included finding hidden ducks by smell and retrieving.

272 *bare.* There are two meanings here: 'mere' and 'naked'.

274-277 *Imprimis . . . can milk.* The usual form of an Elizabethan inventory of goods. *jade.* There is a quibble here on 'a poor horse' and 'a woman of low morals'.

A milkmaid at the time of Shakespeare. Woodcut from *Roxburghe Ballads*, 17th century

Pro. Ay, ay; and she hath offer'd to the doom—
Which, unreversed, stands in effectual force—
A sea of melting pearl, which some call tears:
Those at her father's churlish feet she tender'd;
With them, upon her knees, her humble self;
Wringing her hands, whose whiteness so became them
As if but now they waxed pale for woe:
But neither bended knees, pure hands held up,
Sad sighs, deep groans, nor silver-shedding tears,
Could penetrate her uncompassionate sire;   231
But Valentine, if he be ta'en, must die.
Besides, her intercession chafed him so,
When she for thy repeal was suppliant,
That to close prison he commanded her,
With many bitter threats of biding there.
   Val. No more; unless the next word that thou speak'st
Have some malignant power upon my life:
If so, I pray thee, breathe it in mine ear,
As ending anthem of my endless dolour.   240
   Pro. Cease to lament for that thou canst not help,
And study help for that which thou lament'st.
Time is the nurse and breeder of all good.
Here if thou stay, thou canst not see thy love;
Besides, thy staying will abridge thy life.
Hope is a lover's staff; walk hence with that
And manage it against despairing thoughts.
Thy letters may be here, though thou art hence;
Which, being writ to me, shall be deliver'd
Even in the milk-white bosom of thy love.   250
The time now serves not to expostulate:
Come, I'll convey thee through the city-gate;
And, ere I part with thee, confer at large
Of all that may concern thy love-affairs.
As thou lovest Silvia, though not for thyself,
Regard thy danger, and along with me!
   Val. I pray thee, Launce, an if thou seest my boy,
Bid him make haste and meet me at the North-gate.
   Pro. Go, sirrah, find him out. Come, Valen-tine.
   Val. O my dear Silvia! Hapless Valentine!   260
[*Exeunt Val. and Pro.*
   Launce. I am but a fool, look you; and yet I have the wit to think my master is a kind of a knave: but that's all one, if he be but one knave. He lives not now that knows me to be in love; yet I am in love; but a team of horse shall not pluck that from me; nor who 'tis I love; and yet 'tis a woman; but what woman, I will not tell myself; and yet 'tis a milkmaid; yet 'tis not a maid, for she hath had gossips; yet 'tis a maid, for she is her master's maid, and serves for wages. She hath more qualities than a water-spaniel; which is much in a bare Christian. [*Pulling out a paper.*] Here is the cate-log of her condition. 'Imprimis: She can fetch and carry.' Why, a horse can do no more: nay, a horse cannot fetch, but only carry; therefore is she better than a jade. 'Item: She can milk;' look you, a sweet virtue in a maid with clean hands.

Enter SPEED.

   Speed. How now, Signior Launce! what news with your mastership?   280

Launce. With my master's ship? why, it is at sea.

Speed. Well, your old vice still; mistake the word. What news, then, in your paper?

Launce. The blackest news that ever thou heardest.

Speed. Why, man, how black?

Launce. Why, as black as ink.

Speed. Let me read them.

Launce. Fie on thee, jolt-head! thou canst not read.   291

Speed. Thou liest; I can.

Launce. I will try thee. Tell me this: who begot thee?

Speed. Marry, the son of my grandfather.

Launce. O illiterate loiterer! it was the son of thy grandmother: this proves that thou canst not read.

Speed. Come, fool, come; try me in thy paper.

● *Launce.* There; and Saint Nicholas be thy speed!   301

Speed. [*Reads*] 'Imprimis: She can milk.'

Launce. Ay, that she can.

Speed. 'Item: She brews good ale.'

Launce. And thereof comes the proverb: 'Blessing of your heart, you brew good ale.'

Speed. 'Item: She can sew.'

Launce. That's as much as to say, Can she so?

Speed. 'Item: She can knit.'   310

● *Launce.* What need a man care for a stock
● with a wench, when she can knit him a stock?

Speed. 'Item: She can wash and scour.'

Launce. A special virtue; for then she need not be washed and scoured.

Speed. 'Item: She can spin.'

● *Launce.* Then may I set the world on wheels, when she can spin for her living.

Speed. 'Item: She hath many nameless virtues.'   320

Launce. That's as much as to say, bastard virtues; that, indeed, know not their fathers and therefore have no names.

Speed. 'Here follow her vices.'

Launce. Close at the heels of her virtues.

Speed. 'Item: She is not to be kissed fasting, in respect of her breath.'

Launce. Well, that fault may be mended with a breakfast. Read on.

● *Speed.* 'Item: She hath a sweet mouth.' 330

Launce. That makes amends for her sour breath.

Speed. 'Item: She doth talk in her sleep.'

Launce. It's no matter for that, so she sleep not in her talk.

Speed. 'Item: She is slow in words.'

Launce. O villain, that set this down among her vices! To be slow in words is a woman's only virtue: I pray thee, out with't, and place it for her chief virtue.   340

Speed. 'Item: she is proud.'

Launce. Out with that too; it was Eve's legacy, and cannot be ta'en from her.

Speed. 'Item: She hath no teeth.'

Launce. I care not for that neither, because I love crusts.

● *Speed.* 'Item: She is curst.'

Launce. Well, the best is, she hath no teeth to bite.

300 *Saint Nicholas.* St. Nicholas was the patron saint of scholars.

311 *stock.* Dowry.

312 *stock.* The word means 'stocking' here.

317 *set the world on wheels.* Take life easily.

330 *sweet mouth.* A lecherous nature.

347 *curst.* Shrewish.

350 *praise.* Appraise, test.

355 *liberal.* Loose, wanton.

378 *gracious.* Acceptable.

388 *going.* Walking.

Launce: 'Thou must run for him . . .' Engraving by Kenny Meadows from Barry Cornwall's *Works of Shakspere*, 1846

Speed. 'Item: She will often praise her liquor.' 351
Launce. If her liquor be good, she shall: if she will not, I will; for good things should be praised.
Speed. 'Item: She is too liberal.'
Launce. Of her tongue she cannot, for that's writ down she is slow of; of her purse she shall not, for that I'll keep shut: now, of another thing she may, and that cannot I help. Well, proceed. 360
Speed. 'Item: She hath more hair than wit, and more faults than hairs, and more wealth than faults.'
Launce. Stop there; I'll have her: she was mine, and not mine, twice or thrice in that last article. Rehearse that once more.
Speed. 'Item: She hath more hair than wit,'—
Launce. More hair than wit? It may be; I'll prove it. The cover of the salt hides the salt, and therefore it is more than the salt; the hair that covers the wit is more than the wit, for the greater hides the less. What's next?
Speed. 'And more faults than hairs,'—
Launce. That's monstrous: O, that that were out!
Speed. 'And more wealth than faults.'
Launce. Why, that word makes the faults gracious. Well, I'll have her: and if it be a match, as nothing is impossible,—
Speed. What then? 380
Launce. Why, then will I tell thee—that thy master stays for thee at the North-gate.
Speed. For me?
Launce. For thee! ay, who art thou? he hath stayed for a better man than thee.
Speed. And must I go to him?
Launce. Thou must run to him, for thou hast stayed so long that going will scarce serve the turn.
Speed. Why didst not tell me sooner? pox of your love-letters! [*Exit.* 391
Launce. Now will he be swinged for reading my letter; an unmannerly slave, that will thrust himself into secrets! I'll after, to rejoice in the boy's correction. [*Exit.*

SCENE II. *The same. The* DUKE's *palace.*

Enter DUKE *and* THURIO.

Duke. Sir Thurio, fear not but that she will love you,
Now Valentine is banish'd from her sight.
Thu. Since his exile she hath despised me most,
Forsworn my company and rail'd at me,
That I am desperate of obtaining her.
Duke. This weak impress of love is as a figure
Trenched in ice, which with an hour's heat
Dissolves to water and doth lose his form.
A little time will melt her frozen thoughts
And worthless Valentine shall be forgot. 10

Enter PROTEUS.

How now, Sir Proteus! Is your countryman
According to our proclamation gone?
Pro. Gone, my good lord.
Duke. My daughter takes his going grievously.
Pro. A little time, my lord, will kill that grief.

Duke. So I believe; but Thurio thinks not so.
● Proteus, the good conceit I hold of thee—
For thou hast shown some sign of good desert—
Makes me the better to confer with thee.
  Pro. Longer than I prove loyal to your grace
Let me not live to look upon your grace.   21
  Duke. Thou know'st how willingly I would effect
The match between Sir Thurio and my daughter.
  Pro. I do, my lord.
  Duke. And also, I think, thou art not ignorant
How she opposes her against my will.
  Pro. She did, my lord, when Valentine was here.
  Duke. Ay, and perversely she persevers so.
What might we do to make the girl forget
The love of Valentine and love Sir Thurio?   30
  Pro. The best way is to slander Valentine
With falsehood, cowardice and poor descent,
Three things that women highly hold in hate.
  Duke. Ay, but she'll think that it is spoke in hate.
  Pro. Ay, if his enemy deliver it:
● Therefore it must with circumstance be spoken
By one whom she esteemeth as his friend.
  Duke. Then you must undertake to slander him.
  Pro. And that, my lord, I shall be loath to do:
'Tis an ill office for a gentleman,   40
Especially against his very friend.
  Duke. Where your good word cannot advantage him,
Your slander never can endamage him;
● Therefore the office is indifferent,
Being entreated to it by your friend.
  Pro. You have prevail'd, my lord: if I can do it
By aught that I can speak in his dispraise,
She shall not long continue love to him.
But say this weed her love from Valentine,
It follows not that she will love Sir Thurio.   50
  Thu. Therefore, as you unwind her love from him,
● Lest it should ravel and be good to none,
● You must provide to bottom it on me;
Which must be done by praising me as much
As you in worth dispraise Sir Valentine.
● *Duke.* And, Proteus, we dare trust you in this kind,
Because we know, on Valentine's report,
You are already Love's firm votary
And cannot soon revolt and change your mind.
Upon this warrant shall you have access   60
Where you with Silvia may confer at large;
● For she is lumpish, heavy, melancholy,
And, for your friend's sake, will be glad of you;
Where you may temper her by your persuasion
To hate young Valentine and love my friend.
  Pro. As much as I can do, I will effect:
But you, Sir Thurio, are not sharp enough;
● You must lay lime to tangle her desires
By wailful sonnets, whose composed rhymes
● Should be full-fraught with serviceable vows.   70
  Duke. Ay,
Much is the force of heaven-bred poesy.
  Pro. Say that upon the altar of her beauty
You sacrifice your tears, your sighs, your heart:
Write till your ink be dry, and with your tears
Moist it again, and frame some feeling line

17 *conceit.* Opinion.

36 *circumstance.* Circumlocution.

44 *indifferent.* Neither good nor bad.

52 *ravel.* Become entangled.

53 *to bottom it.* A skein or ball of wool was wound upon a core or 'bottom'.

56 *kind.* Kind of affair.

62 *lumpish.* Down in the dumps.

68 *lime.* Bird-lime (i.e. to trap her).

70 *serviceable vows.* Vows of service, devotion.

77 *discover such integrity*. Disclose such genuine devotion.

82 *elegies*. Love-poems.

85 *dump*. Mournful melody.

92 *sort*. Sort out.

Set design for the forest on the frontiers of Mantua by
J. Gower Parks, Stratford-upon-Avon, 1938

1 *passenger*. Traveller.

4 *rifle*. Rob.

10 *proper*. Handsome.

26 *rehearse*. Relate.

● That may discover such integrity:
For Orpheus' lute was strung with poets' sinews,
Whose golden touch could soften steel and stones,
Make tigers tame and huge leviathans   80
Forsake unsounded deeps to dance on sands.
● After your dire-lamenting elegies,
Visit by night your lady's chamber-window
With some sweet concert; to their instruments
● Tune a deploring dump: the night's dead silence
Will well become such sweet-complaining griev-
  ance.
This, or else nothing, will inherit her.
   Duke. This discipline shows thou hast been
   in love.
   Thu. And thy advice this night I'll put in
   practice.
Therefore, sweet Proteus, my direction-giver, 90
Let us into the city presently
● To sort some gentlemen well skill'd in music.
I have a sonnet that will serve the turn
To give the onset to thy good advice.
   Duke. About it, gentlemen!
   Pro. We'll wait upon your grace till after
   supper,
And afterward determine our proceedings.
   Duke. Even now about it! I will pardon you.
                                        [*Exeunt.*

ACT IV.

SCENE I. *The frontiers of Mantua. A forest.*

Enter certain Outlaws.

● *First Out.* Fellows, stand fast; I see a passenger.
   Sec. Out. If there be ten, shrink not, but
   down with 'em.

Enter VALENTINE *and* SPEED.

   Third Out. Stand, sir, and throw us that
   you have about ye:
● If not, we'll make you sit and rifle you.
   Speed. Sir; we are undone; these are the
   villains
That all the travellers do fear so much.
   Val. My friends,—
   First Out. That's not so, sir: we are your
   enemies.
   Sec. Out. Peace! we'll hear him.
● *Third Out.* Ay, by my beard, will we, for
   he's a proper man.   10
   Val. Then know that I have little wealth to
   lose:
A man I am cross'd with adversity;
My riches are these poor habiliments,
Of which if you should here disfurnish me,
You take the sum and substance that I have.
   Sec. Out. Whither travel you?
   Val. To Verona.
   First Out. Whence came you?
   Val. From Milan.
   Third Out. Have you long sojourned there?
   Val. Some sixteen months, and longer might
   have stay'd,
If crooked fortune had not thwarted me.
   First Out. What, were you banish'd thence?
   Val. I was.
   Sec. Out. For what offence?
● *Val.* For that which now torments me to re-
   hearse:

I kill'd a man, whose death I much repent;
But yet I slew him manfully in fight,
Without false vantage or base treachery.
 First Out. Why, ne'er repent it, if it were
  done so.   30
But were you banish'd for so small a fault?
 Val. I was, and held me glad of such a doom.
 Sec. Out. Have you the tongues?
 Val. My youthful travel therein made me
  happy,
Or else I often had been miserable.
 Third Out. By the bare scalp of Robin Hood's
  fat friar.
This fellow were a king for our wild faction!
 First Out. We'll have him. Sirs, a word.
 Speed. Master, be one of them; it's an
honourable kind of thievery.   40
 Val. Peace, villain!
 Sec. Out. Tell us this: have you any thing to
  take to?
 Val. Nothing but my fortune.
 Third Out. Know, then, that some of us are
  gentlemen,
Such as the fury of ungovern'd youth
Thrust from the company of awful men:
Myself was from Verona banished
For practising to steal away a lady,
An heir, and near allied unto the duke.
 Sec. Out. And I from Mantua, for a gentle-
  man,   50
Who, in my mood, I stabb'd unto the heart.
 First Out. And I for such like petty crimes
  as these.
But to the purpose—for we cite our faults,
That they may hold excused our lawless lives;
And partly, seeing you are beautified
With goodly shape and by your own report
A linguist and a man of such perfection
As we do in our quality much want—
 Sec. Out. Indeed, because you are a banish'd
  man,
Therefore, above the rest, we parley to you: 60
Are you content to be our general?
To make a virtue of necessity
And live, as we do, in this wilderness?
 Third Out. What say'st thou? wilt thou be of
  our consort?
Say ay, and be the captain of us all:
We'll do thee homage and be ruled by thee,
Love thee as our commander and our king.
 First Out. But if thou scorn our courtesy,
  thou diest.
 Sec. Out. Thou shalt not live to brag what we
  have offer'd.
 Val. I take your offer and will live with you,
Provided that you do no outrages   71
On silly women or poor passengers.
 Third Out. No, we detest such vile base prac-
  tices.
Come, go with us, we'll bring thee to our crews,
And show thee all the treasure we have got;
Which, with ourselves, all rest at thy dispose.
            [*Exeunt.*

SCENE II. *Milan. Outside the* DUKE'S *palace,*
  under SILVIA'S *chamber.*

Enter PROTEUS.

Pro. Already have I been false to Valentine

33 *tongues.* i.e. foreign languages.

34 *happy.* Proficient.

36 *fat friar.* Friar Tuck of the Robin Hood legend.

First Outlaw: '. . . Sirs, a word.' Engraving by Kenny
Meadows from Barry Cornwall's *Works of Shakspere,*
1846

42 *any thing to take to.* i.e. any means of subsistence.

46 *awful.* Lawful.

48 *practising.* Scheming.

51 *my mood.* A fit of anger.

58 *quality.* Profession.

60 *above the rest.* More than any other reason.

64 *consort.* Company.

72 *silly.* Harmless. *Poor passengers.* i.e. travellers who
have no money.

4 *prefer*. Advance.

Thurio and Proteus. Illustration by Walter Crane, 1894

27 *allycholly*. A corruption of 'melancholy'.

56 *likes*. Pleases.

And now I must be as unjust to Thurio
Under the colour of commending him,
● I have access my own love to prefer:
But Silvia is too fair, too true, too holy,
To be corrupted with my worthless gifts.
When I protest true loyalty to her,
She twits me with my falsehood to my friend:
When to her beauty I commend my vows,
She bids me think how I have been forsworn   10
In breaking faith with Julia whom I loved:
And notwithstanding all her sudden quips,
The least whereof would quell a lover's hope,
Yet, spaniel-like, the more she spurns my love,
The more it grows and fawneth on her still.
But here comes Thurio: now must we to her
     window,
And give some evening music to her ear.

Enter THURIO *and* Musicians.

Thu.   How now, Sir Proteus, are you crept
     before us?
Pro.   Ay, gentle Thurio: for you know that
     love
Will creep in service where it cannot go.   20
Thu. Ay, but I hope, sir, that you love not here.
Pro.   Sir, but I do; or else I would be hence.
Thu.   Who? Silvia?
Pro.   Ay, Silvia; for your sake.
Thu.   I thank you for your own.   Now, gen-
     tlemen,
Let's tune, and to it lustily awhile.

Enter, at a distance, Host, *and* JULIA *in
     boy's clothes.*

Host.   Now, my young guest, methinks you're
●allycholly: I pray you, why is it?
Jul.   Marry, mine host, because I cannot be
merry.
Host.   Come, we'll have you merry: I'll bring
you where you shall hear music and see the gen-
tleman that you asked for.
Jul.   But shall I hear him speak?
Host.   Ay, that you shall.
Jul.   That will be music.   [*Music plays.*
Host.   Hark, hark!
Jul.   Is he among these?
Host.   Ay: but, peace! let's hear 'em.

SONG.
Who is Silvia? what is she,
     That all our swains commend her?   40
Holy, fair and wise is she;
     The heaven such grace did lend her,
That she might admired be.

Is she kind as she is fair?
     For beauty lives with kindness.
Love doth to her eyes repair,
     To help him of his blindness,
And, being help'd, inhabits there.

Then to Silvia let us sing,
     That Silvia is excelling;   50
She excels each mortal thing
     Upon the dull earth dwelling:
To her let us garlands bring.

Host.   How now! are you sadder than you
were before?   How do you, man? the music
●likes you not.
Jul.   You mistake; the musician likes me not.

Host. Why, my pretty youth?
Jul. He plays false, father.
Host. How? out of tune on the strings?   60
Jul. Not so; but yet so false that he grieves
my very heart-strings.
Host. You have a quick ear.
Jul. Ay, I would I were deaf; it makes me
have a slow heart.
Host. I perceive you delight not in music.
Jul. Not a whit, when it jars so.
● *Host.* Hark, what fine change is in the music!
● *Jul.* Ay, that change is the spite.
Host. You would have them always play but
one thing?   71
Jul. I would always have one play but one
      thing.
But, host, doth this Sir Proteus that we talk on
Often resort unto this gentlewoman?
Host. I tell you what Launce, his man, told
● me: he loved her out of all nick.
Jul. Where is Launce?
Host. Gone to seek his dog; which to-mor-
row, by his master's command, he must carry for
a present to his lady.   80
Jul. Peace! stand aside: the company parts.
Pro: Sir Thurio, fear not you: I will so plead
That you shall say my cunning drift excels.
Thu. Where meet we?
Pro.   At Saint Gregory's well.
Thu.   Farewell.
          [*Exeunt Thu. and Musicians.*

          Enter SILVIA *above.*

Pro. Madam, good even to your ladyship.
Sil. I thank you for your music, gentlemen.
Who is that that spake?
Pro. One, lady, if you knew his pure heart's
      truth,
You would quickly learn to know him by his
      voice.
Sil. Sir Proteus, as I take it.   90
Pro. Sir Proteus, gentle lady, and your servant.
● *Sil.* What's your will?
Pro.   That I may compass yours.
Sil. You have your wish; my will is even this:
That presently you hie you home to bed.
Thou subtle, perjured, false, disloyal man!
● Think'st thou I am so shallow, so conceitless,
To be seduced by thy flattery,
That hast deceived so many with thy vows?
Return, return, and make thy love amends.
● For me, by this pale queen of night I swear,   100
I am so far from granting thy request
That I despise thee for thy wrongful suit,
And by and by intend to chide myself
Even for this time I spend in talking to thee.
Pro. I grant, sweet love, that I did love a lady;
But she is dead.
Jul. [*Aside*] 'Twere false, if I should speak it;
For I am sure she is not buried.
Sil. Say that she be; yet Valentine thy friend
Survives; to whom, thyself art witness,   110
I am betroth'd: and art thou not ashamed
To wrong him with thy importunacy?
Pro. I likewise hear that Valentine is dead.
Sil. And so suppose am I; for in his grave
Assure thyself my love is buried.
Pro. Sweet lady, let me rake it from the earth.
Sil. Go to thy lady's grave and call hers thence,

Elizabethan musicians. Detail from a frieze in Gilling
Castle, *c.* 1585

68 *change.* Variation.

69 *spite.* Injury.

76 *nick.* Reckoning. Accounts were kept in inns by
making 'nicks' (notches) on a stick.

92 *compass yours.* Gain your good will.

96 *conceitless.* Witless.

100 *pale queen of night.* The moon.

136 *by halidom*. A mild oath.

Set design for Duke's palace, under Silvia's chamber, by J. Gower Parks, Stratford-upon-Avon, 1938

8 *impose*. Command.

13 *remorseful*. Compassionate.

26 *repose*. Rely.

Or, at the least, in hers sepulchre thine.
 Jul. [*Aside*] He heard not that.
 Pro. Madam, if your heart be so obdurate,
Vouchsafe me yet your picture for my love, 121
The picture that is hanging in your chamber;
To that I'll speak, to that I'll sigh and weep:
For since the substance of your perfect self
Is else devoted, I am but a shadow;
And to your shadow will I make true love.
 Jul. [*Aside*] If 'twere a substance, you would, sure, deceive it,
And make it but a shadow, as I am.
 Sil. I am very loath to be your idol, sir;
But since your falsehood shall become you well
To worship shadows and adore false shapes, 131
Send to me in the morning and I'll send it:
And so, good rest.
 Pro.   As wretches have o'ernight
That wait for execution in the morn.
    [*Exeunt Pro. and Sil. severally.*
 Jul. Host, will you go?
 Host. By my halidom, I was fast asleep.
 Jul. Pray you, where lies Sir Proteus?
 Host. Marry, at my house. Trust me, I think 'tis almost day.
 Jul. Not so; but it hath been the longest night
That e'er I watch'd and the most heaviest. 141
    [*Exeunt.*

SCENE III. *The same.*

Enter EGLAMOUR.

 Egl. This is the hour that Madam Silvia
Entreated me to call and know her mind:
There's some great matter she'ld employ me in.
Madam, madam!

Enter SILVIA *above*.

 Sil.   Who calls?
 Egl.   Your servant and your friend;
One that attends your ladyship's command.
 Sil. Sir Eglamour, a thousand times good morrow.
 Egl. As many, worthy lady, to yourself:
According to your ladyship's impose,
I am thus early come to know what service
It is your pleasure to command me in. 10
 Sil. O Eglamour, thou art a gentleman—
Think not I flatter, for I swear I do not—
Valiant, wise, remorseful, well accomplish'd:
Thou art not ignorant what dear good will
I bear unto the banish'd Valentine,
Nor how my father would enforce me marry
Vain Thurio, whom my very soul abhors.
Thyself hast loved; and I have heard thee say
No grief did ever come so near thy heart
As when thy lady and thy true love died, 20
Upon whose grave thou vow'dst pure chastity.
Sir Eglamour, I would to Valentine,
To Mantua, where I hear he makes abode;
And, for the ways are dangerous to pass,
I do desire thy worthy company,
Upon whose faith and honour I repose.
Urge not my father's anger, Eglamour,
But think upon my grief, a lady's grief,
And on the justice of my flying hence,
To keep me from a most unholy match, 30
Which heaven and fortune still rewards with plagues.

I do desire thee, even from a heart
As full of sorrows as the sea of sands,
To bear me company and go with me.:
If not, to hide what I have said to thee,
That I may venture to depart alone.
• *Egl.* Madam, I pity much your grievances;
Which since I know they virtuously are placed,
I give consent to go along with you,
•Recking as little what betideth me   4C
As much I wish all good befortune you.
When will you go?
    Sil.   This evening coming.
    Egl. Where shall I meet you?
    Sil.   At Friar Patrick's cell,
Where I intend holy confession.
    Egl. I will not fail your ladyship.   Good
morrow, gentle lady.
    Sil. Good morrow, kind Sir Eglamour.
                        [*Exeunt severally.*

SCENE IV. *The same.*

Enter LAUNCE, *with his Dog.*

Launce.   When a man's servant shall play the
cur with him, look you, it goes hard: one that I
brought up of a puppy; one that I saved from
drowning, when three or four of his blind brothers
and sisters went to it.   I have taught him, even
as one would say precisely, 'thus I would teach a
dog.'   I was sent to deliver him as a present to
Mistress Silvia from my master; and I came no
sooner into the dining-chamber but he steps me
•to her trencher and steals her capon's leg: O,
•'tis a foul thing when a cur cannot keep himself
in all companies!   I would have, as one should
say, one that takes upon him to be a dog indeed,
to be, as it were, a dog at all things.   If I had
not had more wit than he, to take a fault upon
me that he did, I think verily he had been hanged
for't; sure as I live, he had suffered for't: you
shall judge.   He thrusts me himself into the company of three or four gentlemanlike dogs, under
the duke's table: he had not been there—bless
the mark!—a pissing while, but all the chamber
smelt him.   'Out with the dog!' says one: 'What
cur is that?' says another: 'Whip him out' says
the third: 'Hang him up' says the duke.   I,
having been acquainted with the smell before,
knew it was Crab, and goes me to the fellow that
whips the dogs: 'Friend,' quoth I, 'you mean to
whip the dog?'   'Ay, marry, do I,' quoth he.
'You do him the more wrong,' quoth I; ''twas I
•did the thing you wot of.'   He makes me no
more ado, but whips me out of the chamber.
How many masters would do this for his servant?
Nay, I'll be sworn, I have sat in the stocks for
puddings he hath stolen, otherwise he had been
executed; I have stood on the pillory for geese
he hath killed, otherwise he had suffered for't.
Thou thinkest not of this now.   Nay, I remember
the trick you served me when I took my leave of
Madam Silvia: did not I bid thee still mark me
and do as I do? when didst thou see me heave up
my leg and make water against a gentlewoman's
farthingale? didst thou ever see me do such a
trick?

Enter PROTEUS *and* JULIA.
    Pro. Sebastian is thy name?   I like thee well
•And will employ thee in some service presently.

37 *grievances.* Distresses.

40 *Recking.* Caring.

10 *trencher.* Wooden plate.

11 *keep himself.* Restrain himself.

30 *wot.* Know.

Launce: '. . . I have sat in the stocks for puddings he hath stolen'. Contemporary woodcut of stocks

45 *presently.* Immediately.

John Quick, 18th century English actor, as Launce.
Engraving from a design by Rhamberg, 1785

---

59 *squirrel*. This is a reference to the dog's small size.

60 *hangman boys*. Boys fit for the hangman, rough-necks.

68 *entertained*. Taken into service.

78 *deliver'd*. i.e. who gave.

Jul. In what you please: I'll do what I can.
Pro. I hope thou wilt. [*To Launce*] How now, you whoreson peasant!
Where have you been these two days loitering?
   Launce. Marry, sir, I carried Mistress Silvia the dog you bade me.   50
   Pro. And what says she to my little jewel?
   Launce. Marry, she says your dog was a cur, and tells you currish thanks is good enough for such a present.
   Pro. But she received my dog?
   Launce. No, indeed, did she not: here have I brought him back again.
   Pro. What, didst thou offer her this from me?
• *Launce.* Ay, sir; the other squirrel was stolen
• from me by the hangman boys in the market-place: and then I offered her mine own, who is a dog as big as ten of yours, and therefore the gift the greater.
   Pro. Go get thee hence, and find my dog again,
Or ne'er return again into my sight.
Away, I say! stay'st thou to vex me here?
                                              [*Exit Launce.*
A slave, that still an end turns me to shame!
• Sebastian, I have entertained thee,
Partly that I have need of such a youth
That can with some discretion do my business, 70
For 'tis no trusting to yond foolish lout,
But chiefly for thy face and thy behaviour,
Which, if my augury deceive me not,
Witness good bringing up, fortune and truth:
Therefore know thou, for this I entertain thee.
Go presently and take this ring with thee,
Deliver it to Madam Silvia:
• She loved me well deliver'd it to me.
   Jul. It seems you loved not her, to leave her token.
She is dead, belike?
   Pro.   Not so; I think she lives. 80
   Jul. Alas!
   Pro. Why dost thou cry 'alas'?
   Jul.   I cannot choose
But pity her.
   Pro.   Wherefore shouldst thou pity her?
   Jul. Because methinks that she loved you as well
As you do love your lady Silvia:
She dreams on him that has forgot her love;
You dote on her that cares not for your love.
'Tis pity love should be so contrary;
And thinking on it makes me cry 'alas!'
   Pro. Well, give her that ring and therewithal
This letter. That's her chamber. Tell my lady
I claim the promise for her heavenly picture.
Your message done, hie home unto my chamber,
Where thou shalt find me, sad and solitary. [*Exit.*
   Jul. How many women would do such a message?
Alas, poor Proteus! thou hast entertain'd
A fox to be the shepherd of thy lambs.
Alas, poor fool! why do I pity him
That with his very heart despiseth me?
Because he loves her, he despiseth me;   100
Because I love him, I must pity him.
This ring I gave him when he parted from me,
To bind him to remember my good will;
And now am I, unhappy messenger,
To plead for that which I would not obtain,

To carry that which I would have refused,
To praise his faith which I would have dispraised.
I am my master's true-confirmed love;
But cannot be true servant to my master,
Unless I prove false traitor to myself.   110
Yet will I woo for him, but yet so coldly
● As, heaven it knows, I would not have him speed.

Enter SILVIA, *attended.*

Gentlewoman, good day! I pray you, be my mean
To bring me where to speak with Madam Silvia.
    Sil.   What would you with her, if that I be she?
    Jul.   If you be she, I do entreat your patience
To hear me speak the message I am sent on.
    Sil.   From whom?
    Jul.   From my master, Sir Proteus, madam.
    Sil.   O, he sends you for a picture.   120
    Jul.   Ay, madam.
    Sil.   Ursula, bring my picture there.
Go give your master this: tell him from me,
One Julia, that his changing thoughts forget,
Would better fit his chamber than this shadow.
    Jul.   Madam, please you peruse this letter.—
● Pardon me, madam; I have unadvised
Deliver'd you a paper that I should not:
This is the letter to your ladyship.
    Sil.   I pray thee, let me look on that again.
    Jul.   It may not be; good madam, pardon me.
    Sil.   There, hold!
I will not look upon your master's lines:
I know they are stuff'd with protestations
● And full of new-found oaths; which he will break
As easily as I do tear his paper.
    Jul.   Madam, he sends your ladyship this ring.
    Sil.   The more shame for him that he sends
        it me;
For I have heard him say a thousand times
His Julia gave it him at his departure.   140
Though his false finger have profaned the ring,
Mine shall not do his Julia so much wrong.
    Jul.   She thanks you.
    Sil.   What say'st thou?
● *Jul.*   I thank you, madam, that you tender her.
Poor gentlewoman! my master wrongs her much.
    Sil.   Dost thou know her?
    Jul.   Almost as well as I do know myself:
To think upon her woes I do protest
That I have wept a hundred several times.   150
    Sil.   Belike she thinks that Proteus hath for-
        sook her.
    Jul.   I think she doth; and that's her cause of
        sorrow.
    Sil.   Is she not passing fair?
    Jul.   She hath been fairer, madam, than she is:
When she did think my master loved her well,
She, in my judgement, was as fair as you;
But since she did neglect her looking-glass
● And threw her sun-expelling mask away,
The air hath starved the roses in her cheeks
And pinch'd the lily-tincture of her face,   160
That now she is become as black as I.
    Sil.   How tall was she?
● *Jul.*   About my stature; for at Pentecost,
When all our pageants of delight were play'd,
Our youth got me to play the woman's part,
And I was trimm'd in Madam Julia's gown,
Which served me as fit, by all men's judgements,
As if the garment had been made for me:

112 *speed.* Succeed.

Silvia giving her portrait to Julia. Illustration by Walter Crane, 1894

127 *unadvised.* Inadvertently.

135 *new-found.* Newly invented.

145 *tender.* Think tenderly of.

158 *sun-expelling.* Fashionable Elizabethan women protected their complexions by wearing masks.

163 *Pentecost.* Whitsun (Pentecost) was the time when parishes and towns put on their traditional plays.

172 *Ariadne.* Ariadne, the daughter of Minos, king of Crete, helped Theseus in his encounter with the Minotaur. She ran away with him, but was then abandoned by him.

Ariadne. From a 19th century engraving

190 *tire.* Head-dress.

197 *grey.* Elizabethans meant 'blue' when they said 'grey eye'.

200 *respective.* Worthy of respect.

203 *senseless.* Lifeless, insensible.

9 *postern.* Small back or side door.

Silvia and Eglamour. Engraving from *Plays* published by F. C. and J. Rivington, 1823

Therefore I know she is about my height.
And at that time I made her weep agood,   170
For I did play a lamentable part:
● Madam, 'twas Ariadne passioning
For Theseus' perjury and unjust flight;
Which I so lively acted with my tears
That my poor mistress, moved therewithal,
Wept bitterly; and would I might be dead
If I in thought felt not her very sorrow!
  Sil.   She is beholding to thee, gentle youth.
Alas, poor lady, desolate and left!
I weep myself to think upon thy words.   180
Here, youth, there is my purse; I give thee this
For thy sweet mistress' sake, because thou lovest
    her.
Farewell.   [*Exit Silvia, with attendants.*
  Jul.   And she shall thank you for't, if e'er
    you know her.
A virtuous gentlewoman, mild and beautiful!
I hope my master's suit will be but cold,
Since she respects my mistress' love so much.
Alas, how love can trifle with itself!
Here is her picture: let me see; I think,
● If I had such a tire, this face of mine   190
Were full as lovely as is this of hers:
And yet the painter flatter'd her a little,
Unless I flatter with myself too much.
Her hair is auburn, mine is perfect yellow:
If that be all the difference in his love,
I'll get me such a colour'd periwig.
● Her eyes are grey as glass, and so are mine:
Ay, but her forehead's low, and mine's as high.
What should it be that he respects in her
● But I can make respective in myself,   200
If this fond Love were not a blinded god?
Come, shadow, come, and take this shadow up,
● For 'tis thy rival.   O thou senseless form,
Thou shalt be worshipp'd, kiss'd, loved and adored!
And, were there sense in his idolatry,
My substance should be statue in thy stead.
I'll use thee kindly for thy mistress' sake,
That used me so; or else, by Jove I vow,
I should have scratch'd out your unseeing eyes,
To make my master out of love with thee! [*Exit.*

ACT V.

Scene I. *Milan. An abbey.*

Enter Eglamour.

Egl.   The sun begins to gild the western sky;
And now it is about the very hour
That Silvia, at Friar Patrick's cell, should
    meet me.
She will not fail, for lovers break not hours,
Unless it be to come before their time;
So much they spur their expedition.
See where she comes.

Enter Silvia.

              Lady, a happy evening!
  Sil.   Amen, amen! Go on, good Eglamour,
● Out at the postern by the abbey-wall:
I fear I am attended by some spies.   10
  Egl.   Fear not: the forest is not three
    leagues off;
If we recover that, we are sure enough. [*Exeunt.*

SCENE II. *The same. The* DUKE'S *palace.*

Enter THURIO, PROTEUS, *and* JULIA.

Thu. Sir Proteus, what says Silvia to my
    suit?
Pro. O, sir, I find her milder than she was;
And yet she takes exceptions at your person.
Thu. What, that my leg is too long?
Pro. No; that it is too little.
Thu. I'll wear a boot, to make it somewhat
    rounder.
Jul. [*Aside*] But love will not be spurr'd to
    what it loathes.
Thu. What says she to my face?
Pro. She says it is a fair one.
Thu. Nay then, the wanton lies; my face is
    black.   10
Pro. But pearls are fair; and the old say-
    ing is,
Black men are pearls in beauteous ladies' eyes.
Jul. [*Aside*] 'Tis true; such pearls as put out
    ladies' eyes;
For I had rather wink than look on them.
Thu. How likes she my discourse?
Pro. Ill, when you talk of war.
Thu. But well, when I discourse of love and
    peace?
Jul. [*Aside*] But better, indeed, when you
    hold your peace.
Thu. What says she to my valour?
Pro. O, sir, she makes no doubt of that.   20
Jul. [*Aside*] She needs not, when she knows
    it cowardice.
Thu. What says she to my birth?
Pro. That you are well derived.
Jul. [*Aside*] True; from a gentleman to a
    fool.
Thu. Considers she my possessions?
Pro. O, ay; and pities them.
Thu. Wherefore?
Jul. [*Aside*] That such an ass should owe
    them.
Pro. That they are out by lease.
Jul. Here comes the duke.   30

Enter DUKE.

Duke. How now, Sir Proteus! how now,
    Thurio!
Which of you saw Sir Eglamour of late?
Thu.   Not I.
Pro.   Nor I.
Duke.   Saw you my daughter?
Pro.   Neither.
Duke. Why then,
She's fled unto that peasant Valentine;
And Eglamour is in her company.
'Tis true; for Friar Laurence met them both,
As he in penance wander'd through the forest;
Him he knew well, and guess'd that it was she,
But, being mask'd, he was not sure of it;   40
Besides, she did intend confession
At Patrick's cell this even; and there she
    was not;
These likelihoods confirm her flight from hence.
Therefore, I pray you, stand not to discourse,
But mount you presently and meet with me
Upon the rising of the mountain-foot
That leads toward Mantua, whither they are fled:
Dispatch, sweet gentlemen, and follow me. [*Exit.*

6 *boot.* i.e. riding boot.

10 *black.* Swarthy.

13 *pearls.* Julia quibbles on 'pearls' by taking it to mean
'cataracts'.

14 *wink.* Shut my eyes.

28 *owe.* Own.

29 *out by lease.* Let to others. Proteus may also be
referring to Thurio's mental endowments, which are no
longer under his control.

Duke: '. . . she . . . being masked'. Type of mask worn by
ladies at the time of James I. Illustration from J. R.
Planché (1796–1880)

49 *peevish.* Perverse.

Forest with outlaws. Engraving from Charles Knight's *Pictorial Edition of the Works of William Shakspere,* 1839–43

8 *Moyses.* Common Elizabethan form of the name 'Moses'.

2 *desert.* Deserted place.

6 *record.* Sing.

Thu. Why, this it is to be a peevish girl,
That flies her fortune when it follows her. 50
I'll after, more to be revenged on Eglamour
Than for the love of reckless Silvia. [*Exit.*
Pro. And I will follow, more for Silvia's love
Than hate of Eglamour that goes with her. [*Exit.*
Jul. And I will follow, more to cross that love
Than hate for Silvia that is gone for love. [*Exit.*

SCENE III. *The frontiers of Mantua.*
The forest.

Enter Outlaws *with* SILVIA.

First Out. Come, come,
Be patient; we must bring you to our captain.
Sil. A thousand more mischances than this one
Have learn'd me how to brook this patiently.
Sec. Out. Come, bring her away.
First Out. Where is the gentleman that was with her?
Third Out. Being nimble-footed, he hath outrun us,
But Moyses and Valerius follow him.
Go thou with her to the west end of the wood;
There is our captain: we'll follow him that's fled; 10
The thicket is beset; he cannot 'scape.
First Out. Come, I must bring you to our captain's cave:
Fear not; he bears an honourable mind,
And will not use a woman lawlessly.
Sil. O Valentine, this I endure for thee!
[*Exeunt.*

SCENE IV. *Another part of the forest.*

Enter VALENTINE.

Val. How use doth breed a habit in a man!
This shadowy desert, unfrequented woods,
I better brook than flourishing peopled towns:
Here can I sit alone, unseen of any,
And to the nightingale's complaining notes
Tune my distresses and record my woes.
O thou that dost inhabit in my breast,
Leave not the mansion so long tenantless,
Lest, growing ruinous, the building fall
And leave no memory of what it was! 10
Repair me with thy presence, Silvia;
Thou gentle nymph, cherish thy forlorn swain!
What halloing and what stir is this to-day?
These are my mates, that make their wills their law,
Have some unhappy passenger in chase.
They love me well; yet I have much to do
To keep them from uncivil outrages.
Withdraw thee, Valentine: who's this comes here?

Enter PROTEUS, SILVIA, *and* JULIA.

Pro. Madam, this service I have done for you,
Though you respect not aught your servant doth,
To hazard life and rescue you from him 21
That would have forced your honour and your love;
Vouchsafe me, for my meed, but one fair look;
A smaller boon than this I cannot beg
And less than this, I am sure, you cannot give.

Val. [*Aside*] How like a dream is this I see
and hear!
Love, lend me patience to forbear awhile.
Sil. O miserable, unhappy that I am!
Pro. Unhappy were you, madam, ere I came;
But by my coming I have made you happy. 30
Sil. By thy approach thou makest me most
unhappy.
Jul. [*Aside*] And me, when he approacheth
to your presence.
Sil. Had I been seized by a hungry lion,
I would have been a breakfast to the beast,
Rather than have false Proteus rescue me.
O, Heaven be judge how I love Valentine,
Whose life's as tender to me as my soul!
And full as much, for more there cannot be,
I do detest false perjured Proteus.
Therefore be gone; solicit me no more. 40
Pro. What dangerous action, stood it next to
death,
Would I not undergo for one calm look!
O, 'tis the curse in love, and still approved,
When women cannot love where they're beloved!
Sil. When Proteus cannot love where he's beloved.
Read over Julia's heart, thy first best love,
For whose dear sake thou didst then rend thy
faith
Into a thousand oaths; and all those oaths
Descended into perjury, to love me.
Thou hast no faith left now, unless thou'dst two;
And that's far worse than none; better have none
Than plural faith which is too much by one:
Thou counterfeit to thy true friend!
Pro.   In love
Who respects friend?
Sil.   All men but Proteus.
Pro. Nay, if the gentle spirit of moving words
Can no way change you to a milder form,
I'll woo you like a soldier, at arms' end,
And love you 'gainst the nature of love,—force ye.
Sil. O heaven!
Pro.   I'll force thee yield to my desire.
Val. Ruffian, let go that rude uncivil touch,
Thou friend of an ill fashion!
Pro.   Valentine! 61
Val. Thou common friend, that's without
faith or love,
For such is a friend now; treacherous man!
Thou hast beguiled my hopes; nought but mine
eye
Could have persuaded me: now I dare not say
I have one friend alive; thou wouldst disprove me.
Who should be trusted, when one's own right hand
Is perjured to the bosom? Proteus,
I am sorry I must never trust thee more,
But count the world a stranger for thy sake. 70
The private wound is deepest: O time most accurst,
'Mongst all foes that a friend should be the worst!
Pro. My shame and guilt confounds me.
Forgive me, Valentine: if hearty sorrow
Be a sufficient ransom for offence,
I tender 't here; I do as truly suffer
As e'er I did commit.
Val.   Then I am paid;
And once again I do receive thee honest.
Who by repentance is not satisfied
Is nor of heaven nor earth, for these are pleased.

31 *approach.* Amorous advances.

50 *unless thou'dst two.* i.e. unless you can be a faithful
love to both Julia and me at the same time.

57 *at arms' end.* At sword's point.

Valentine: 'Ruffian, let go that rude uncivil touch'.
Engraving from a design by F. Hayman, Hanmer's
edition of Shakespeare's works, 1744

62 *common.* Base.

86 *wag.* Boy.

Julia reveals herself to Proteus. Engraving from a painting by T. Stothard (1755–1834)

---

103 *cleft the root.* i.e. of her heart. The phrase alludes to 'cleaving the pin' in archery.

104 *this habit.* i.e. her boy's clothes.

117 *close.* Union.

126 *give back.* Back off.

127 *measure.* Reach (of a sword).

129 *Verona.* Thurio comes from Milan. Shakespeare has forgotten.

137 *means.* Efforts.

By penitence the Eternal's wrath's appeased: 81
And, that my love may appear plain and free,
All that was mine in Silvia I give thee.
 Jul. O me unhappy!   [*Swoons.*
 Pro. Look to the boy.
 • *Val.* Why, boy! why, wag! how now! what's
the matter? Look up; speak.
 Jul. O good sir, my master charged me to
deliver a ring to Madam Silvia, which, out of my
neglect, was never done.   90
 Pro. Where is that ring, boy?
 Jul.   Here 'tis; this is it.
 Pro. How! let me see:
Why, this is the ring I gave to Julia.
 Jul. O, cry you mercy, sir, I have mistook:
This is the ring you sent to Silvia.
 Pro. But how camest thou by this ring? At
my depart
I gave this unto Julia.
 Jul. And Julia herself did give it me;
And Julia herself hath brought it hither.
 Pro. How! Julia!   100
 Jul. Behold her that gave aim to all thy oaths,
And entertain'd 'em deeply in her heart.
• How oft hast thou with perjury cleft the root!
• O Proteus, let this habit make thee blush!
Be thou ashamed that I have took upon me
Such an immodest raiment, if shame live
In a disguise of love:
It is the lesser blot, modesty finds,
Women to change their shapes than men their
 minds.
 Pro. Than men their minds! 'tis true. O
 heaven! were man 110
But constant, he were perfect. That one error
Fills him with faults; makes him run through all
 the sins:
Inconstancy falls off ere it begins.
What is in Silvia's face, but I may spy
More fresh in Julia's with a constant eye?
 Val. Come, come, a hand from either:
• Let me be blest to make this happy close;
'Twere pity two such friends should be long foes.
 Pro. Bear witness, Heaven, I have my wish
 for ever.
 Jul. And I mine.   120

 Enter Outlaws, *with* DUKE *and* THURIO.

 Outlaws. A prize, a prize, a prize!
 Val. Forbear, forbear, I say! it is my lord
 the duke.
Your grace is welcome to a man disgraced,
Banished Valentine.
 Duke.   Sir Valentine!
 Thu. Yonder is Silvia; and Silvia's mine.
• *Val.* Thurio, give back, or else embrace thy
 death;
• Come not within the measure of my wrath;
Do not name Silvia thine; if once again,
• † Verona shall not hold thee. Here she stands:
Take but possession of her with a touch; 130
I dare thee but to breathe upon my love.
 Thu. Sir Valentine, I care not for her, I:
I hold him but a fool that will endanger
His body for a girl that loves him not:
I claim her not, and therefore she is thine.
 Duke. The more degenerate and base art
 thou,
• To make such means for her as thou hast done

And leave her on such slight conditions.
Now, by the honour of my ancestry,
I do applaud thy spirit, Valentine,   140
And think thee worthy of an empress' love:
Know then, I here forget all former griefs,
● Cancel all grudge, repeal thee home again,
● Plead a new state in thy unrival'd merit,
To which I thus subscribe: Sir Valentine,
Thou art a gentleman and well derived;
Take thou thy Silvia, for thou hast deserved her.
    Val. I thank your grace; the gift hath made
        me happy.
I now beseech you, for your daughter's sake,
To grant one boon that I shall ask of you.   150
    Duke. I grant it, for thine own, whate'er it be.
    Val. These banish'd men that I have kept
        withal
Are men endued with worthy qualities:
Forgive them what they have committed here
And let them be recall'd from their exile:
They are reformed, civil, full of good
And fit for great employment, worthy lord.
    Duke. Thou hast prevail'd; I pardon them
        and thee:
Dispose of them as thou know'st their deserts.
● Come, let us go: we will include all jars   160
● With triumphs, mirth and rare solemnity.
    Val. And, as we walk along, I dare be bold
With our discourse to make your grace to smile.
What think you of this page, my lord?
    Duke. I think the boy hath grace in him; he
        blushes.
    Val. I warrant you, my lord, more grace than
        boy.
    Duke. What mean you by that saying?
    Val. Please you, I'll tell you as we pass along,
That you will wonder what hath fortuned.
Come, Proteus; 'tis your penance but to hear   170
The story of your loves discovered:
That done, our day of marriage shall be yours;
One feast, one house, one mutual happiness.
                          [*Exeunt.*

143 *repeal.* Recall.

144 *Plead a new state.* Take up a new position (with regard to Valentine's merits).

160 *jars.* Disagreements.

161 *solemnity.* Festivity.

The Taming
of the Shrew

1592

The Play. In Elizabethan times the word 'shrew' was pronounced 'shrow', as we still do in Shrewsbury, and as the rhymes make clear in the play—there is a good deal of rhyme in it. It follows upon the heels of *The Comedy of Errors* and *The Two Gentlemen of Verona*; once Shakespeare got going he was a very rapid worker, as everything shows and Ben Jonson tells us.

In some contrast to those two plays the *Shrew* goes straight forward to its target, with one forward impulse, high spirits, and complete assurance of technique. It is a gleeful play, on a subject highly popular with the Elizabethans, and, dealing with 'the war between the sexes', has an archetypal situation to make play with. Hence its undying appeal. That it appealed much to Shakespeare and released his genius we can tell from its memorable characters: Kate the reformed shrew ('Kiss me, Kate'), her wooer Petruchio, and Christopher Sly, the Warwickshireman from Shakespeare's home-ground, who provides the framework for the play and watches the fun from up above in the gallery. These are the first of his unforgettable comic creations, along with Launce.

At the same time there is plenty that brings this original play into close association with the other two. The suitors gain access to the younger daughter, Bianca, under the guise of schooling her in books and music. We have several Latin tags from Ovid and Terence, the latter through the medium of Lyly's grammar, used in all schools. The names Tranio and Grumio come from Plautus. Classical references come easily and naturally in all the early plays, since Shakespeare was close to his schooling. Lucrece was in his mind—many references to her occur all through his work, as *Venus and Adonis* is close:

> Adonis painted by a running brook
> And Cytherea all in sedges hid.

Even more Italian phrases occur, which would come from his association with Florio, who was half-Italian, as was also the Dark Lady, Emilia Lanier. Her father was Baptista Bassano, and a leading character is a Baptista, father of Kate and Bianca.

A
Pleaſant Conceited

Hiſtorie, called The taming
of a Shrew.

As it was ſundry times acted by the
Right honorable the Earle of
Pembrook his ſeruants.

Printed at London by Peter Short and
are to be ſold by Cutbert Burbie, at his
ſhop at the Royall Exchange.
1594.

Far left: *The
quarto of a comedy
similar in title,
general conception
and plot to
Shakespeare's*
The Taming of
the Shrew *and
probably the basis
for his play*

Left: *A 19th
century engraving
of Barton-on-the-
Heath, the
Warwickshire
village*

A reference to Rheims reminds us of Marlowe, who had been sent there to report on the activities of the Catholic exiles. Lucentio 'hath been long studying at Rheims'—there is no reason why he should have studied there if Marlowe had not been close by. The *Shrew* was originally a Pembroke's play, a troupe for which Marlowe was also writing. It is not likely that the two writers should not have known each other well. The play was so popular that it was almost immediately pirated; it has remained popular ever since, to conquer new audiences through film and television.

The subject was ready to hand, but use was made of Gascoigne's *Supposes*, itself an adaptation from Ariosto. To this there is a direct reference in the last scene: Bianca marries the right lover, after the confusion made

> While counterfeit supposes bleared thine eyne.

Once more the young men are travelling abroad

> To seek their fortunes farther than at home,
> Where small experience grows.

Once more a trade-embargo is made use of, as in *The Comedy of Errors*:

> Your ships are stayed at Venice, and the Duke
> For private quarrel 'twixt your Duke and him
> Hath published and proclaimed it openly.

Again the utmost use is made of disguising to forward the intrigue of the plot. Shakespeare repeats himself, like any other writer—only more frequently, from the exigencies of the theatre, each time improving as he goes.

Background. The most original thing about the *Shrew* is the Induction, for which Shakespeare drew upon his Stratford background and his own early experience with a travelling troupe of players. Christopher Sly the tinker, for whose benefit the play is performed in the hall below, is old Sly's son of Barton-on-the-Heath—where Shakespeare's uncle and aunt, the Lamberts, lived. 'Ask Marian Hacket, the fat ale-wife of Wincot', possibly Wilmcote, where Shakespeare's mother came from. There were Hackets around Stratford, as we know from the parish registers; and there is 'old John Naps of Greet', not far away (it was misprinted as Greece, and editors have mostly been too timorous to correct it). Sly was a Stratford name, as E. K. Chambers pointed out.

A travelling troupe of players, heralded by their trumpet, are themselves introduced—as later in *Hamlet*. A boy-actor is dressed up to play the part of a lady, and appear as Sly's wife grieving for his long delusion (he has fallen asleep drunk); if the boy can't readily produce tears,

> An onion will do well for such a shift,
> Which in a napkin being close conveyed
> Shall in despite enforce a watery eye.

The players are to stay the night, and meanwhile are taken into the buttery for a meal—exactly as used to happen and Shakespeare had often experienced.

The drunken sleeper is to be carried up into the great chamber of the lordly country-house, hung around with wanton pictures, his head bathed in warm distilled water, and attendants are to 'burn sweet wood to make the lodging sweet'. When he awakes,

Strolling players arriving at an inn; in the background their later performance in the village square. Print from Scarron's Comical Romance of a Company of Stage Players, 1676

> Let one attend him with a silver basin
> Full of rose-water and bestrewed with flowers,
> Another bear the ewer, the third a diaper . . .

just as in an aristocratic mansion. When Sly awakes, to look down on the play below, it is just as the 'quality' would have looked from the usual gallery upon the goings-on in the great hall below. And in fact the Elizabethan proscenium in the theatre recapitulated the end of a hall, with its doors to buttery and kitchen, as we see in a college hall or historic house still.

Personal. We hear more than ever about hunting in this play; in the first scene a lord returns from hunting, with huntsman and train, and there follows a great deal of knowledgeable talk about the qualities of individual hounds. In Act IV an expert passage about hawking describes how Kate is gradually to be subdued, broken in and trained like a falcon, kept hungry and without sleep,

> To make her come and know her keeper's call;

all to be done gently and with the best intentions:

> This is a way to kill a wife with kindness.

The out-of-doors countryman knew about hawking, as about deer-hunting and coursing the hare—perhaps about keeping a wife in order too: Anne Shakespeare never raised her voice, though we know that the clever daughter Susanna ran the household later: she took after her father. He favoured bowls also, another gentlemanly sport (in those days):

> Well, forward, forward! Thus the bowl should run,
> And not unluckily against the bias.

Naturally the writer was not less well acquainted with the usages of printing and publishing. Lucentio is bidden to make sure of Bianca, 'cum privilegio ad imprimendum solum', as with the privilege of the sole right in printing: the copyright formula at the time. And we may catch a reference to contemporary writing in the references to 'cony-catching'—the arts of confidence-tricksters on which Robert Greene was writing his popular tracts. Something happened between Shakespeare and Greene which has been, alas, lost.[1]

Theme. The theme of the play was much to the fore in that age and the moral driven home was in keeping with it. Shakespeare's moral outlook, as a normal family man, was always conservative and conformist, unlike Marlowe's. It is important—in our day of revolution in the status of women, Women's Lib., and the rest of it—to get this right and not be anachronistic about it.

Shakespeare's view is the normal Elizabethan one. It is not in the least that he was unsympathetic to the rights and claims, or the duties, of women. So far from that, as a woman critic points out: 'Shakespeare's sympathy with and almost uncanny understanding of women characters is one of the distinguishing features of his comedy, as opposed to that of most of his contemporaries.' (Marlowe had no interest in women: he preferred boys.) The Elizabethan position was the traditional one of the Christian

[1] v. my *Shakespeare the Man,* 59–61.

Right: *Robert
Greene's pamphlet*
Conycatching *and
many of his other
pamphlets were
written to earn
quick money*

Far right: *Bess of
Hardwick,
Countess of
Shrewsbury, one
of the most
remarkable women
of the Elizabethan
age*

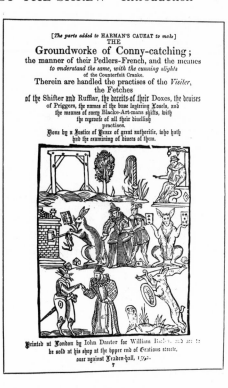

church, as laid down by St. Paul: 'Let women be subject to their husbands, as to the
Lord; for the husband is the head of the woman, as Christ is the head of the Church.'

What is more original in Shakespeare's play is that the man subdues the unbroken-in,
coltish jade that Kate is by comic means, outwardly roughly, but inwardly by love.
He really loves Kate, and the psychological subtlety—which only Shakespeare would
have been capable of—is that Kate has fallen for her man too, though she is too proud
and obstinate to confess it. She is reduced by firmness plus unmitigated love; and she
likes that: her man is a completely masculine type, as William Shakespeare was.

Petruchio never once lays hands on her, even though she slaps him. So that it is
utterly crude and psychologically wrong to bring Petruchio on the stage beating, or
ever even smacking, Kate: she is to be treated comically, and her uncouthness brought
home to her humorously with love. It is no less anachronistic and out of keeping to treat
what Shakespeare wrote as if it were ironical and he did not mean it when he said:

> Thy husband is thy lord, thy life, thy keeper,
> Thy head, thy sovereign; one that cares for thee
> And for thy maintenance; commits his body
> To painful labour both by sea and land,
> To watch the night in storms, the day in cold,
> Whilst thou liest warm at home, secure and safe.

Though a bit poetically emphatic, it is simply what William Shakespeare meant and all
Elizabethans thought. And fair enough: menfolk were exposed to all the hazards of
life by sea and land; women were secure at home, their chief hazard came from child-
birth.

Everybody in his proper place, according to order—the natural and social order.
There is no evidence that matrimonial relations were any more unhappy in his day than
in ours; actually they were far more stable and harmonious. Though women's place

was a secondary one in the struggles of the outer world—their kingdom was house and home—one cannot but allow that women were much to the fore in the Renaissance world. Such eminent rulers as Elizabeth I, Catherine de Medici and the successive women Regents of the Netherlands who made a better job of it than the menfolk did, are in the forefront; women could make remarkable careers for themselves, if along the royal road of matrimony—witness the famous Bess of Hardwick, ancestress of three dukedoms. Women had a foremost part in culture and as patrons of literature and the arts.

The whole play is an expression of, and in keeping with, the age. It was thought hardly proper for a younger sister, like Bianca, to be married off before the elder, such as Kate. We recall that the scrupulous Sir Thomas More passed over a younger sister, whom he would have preferred, to marry a shrewish eldest sister whom he did not wish to humiliate. Baptista will not bestow his younger daughter,

> Before I have a husband for the elder.

This sets the action in train. When disappointed in his suit, Hortensio declares:

> I will be married to a wealthy widow
> Ere three days pass, which hath as long loved me
> As I have loved this proud disdainful haggard.

This beckoning road was as open in Elizabethan society as in America today. Widows had by right one-third of their husband's income: this gave them a great advantage in the marriage market: witness the matrimonial careers of Lettice Knollys, Frances Walsingham, Frances Howard—each of them married four times, the first two to become countesses, the third a royal duchess, Duchess of Richmond and Lennox.[1] So great was the financial attraction of marrying a widow that a Bill in Parliament was preferred to discourage it on demographic grounds.

Further to its contemporary relevance, the continuing success of the play should bring home that it has a deeper, more universal appeal and probes to levels in human nature beyond the contemporary, the topical and controversial. William Shakespeare speaks home to the truth about human nature and society.

In this play we catch him here, there, and everywhere: in the virtuosity of his knowledge of horse-flesh; in the refinement of the senses in his increasing acquaintance with aristocratic life; in the endless punning and verbal play. Oddly enough, we are given less bawdy in this play, though there is a naughty suggestiveness in Sly's approach to the boy, acting the part of a wife, to go to bed with him—this never fails to raise a laugh; while the 'standing' joke is repeated from *The Two Gentlemen*:

> Page: I hope this reason stands for my excuse.
> Sly: Ay, it stands so that I may hardly tarry so long.

Text. The text of the play as it has come down to us from the First Folio is a fairly good one, probably from Shakespeare's working draft for performance. Written for Pembroke's early company, which ended in 1593, he would have carried it along with him to the Lord Chamberlain's when it came together next year. It quotes a number of catches and has snatches of song. The use of the Induction to put the play in its charming Stratford setting was not unprecedented—in production the opportunity should be taken to evoke Shakespeare's Warwickshire.

[1] v. my *Simon Forman: Sex and Society in Shakespeare's Age*, c.x.

THE TAMING OF THE SHREW.

DRAMATIS PERSONÆ.

A Lord.
CHRISTOPHER SLY, a tinker. } Persons in the
Hostess, Page, Players, Hunts- } Induction.
men, and Servants.

BAPTISTA, a rich gentleman of Padua.
VINCENTIO, an old gentleman of Pisa.
LUCENTIO, son to Vincentio, in love with Bianca.
PETRUCHIO, a gentleman of Verona, a suitor
to Katharina.
GREMIO, } suitors to Bianca.
HORTENSIO, }

TRANIO, } servants to Lucentio.
BIONDELLO, }
GRUMIO, } servants to Petruchio.
CURTIS, }
A Pedant.

KATHARINA, the shrew, } daughters to Baptista.
BIANCA, }
Widow.

Tailor, Haberdasher, and Servants attending on
Baptista and Petruchio.

SCENE: *Padua, and Petruchio's country house.*

Sly outside the alehouse. From C. Knight's *Pictorial
Edition of the Works of William Shakspere*, 1839–43

---

1 *pheeze.* A slang term meaning 'fix you'.

4 *Richard.* Sly means William.

5 *paucas pallabris.* A corruption of the Spanish *pocas
palabras* 'few words'.

6 *sessa.* Perhaps for 'assez' i.e. 'enough'; or 'cease'.

9 *denier.* A French coin worth a twelfth of a sou. *Go by,
Jeronimy.* 'Hieronimo beware; go by go by' from Kyd's
The Spanish Tragedy, had become a stock expression
implying haste.

12 *third-borough.* A petty constable.

Opposite: Petruchio throws the meat about the stage.
Engraving by H. Gravelot for Theobald's edition, 1773

● *A bullet beside a text line indicates an annotation in the
opposite column*

INDUCTION.

SCENE I. *Before an alehouse on a heath.*

Enter HOSTESS *and* SLY.

● *Sly.* I'll pheeze you, in faith.
  Host. A pair of stocks, you rogue!
  Sly. Ye are a baggage: the Slys are no rogues;
●look in the chronicles; we came in with Richard
●Conqueror. Therefore paucas pallabris; let the
●world slide: sessa!
  Host. You will not pay for the glasses you
have burst?
● *Sly.* No, not a denier. Go by, Jeronimy: go
to thy cold bed, and warm thee.   10
  Host. I know my remedy; I must go fetch
●the third-borough.   [*Exit.*
  Sly. Third, or fourth, or fifth borough, I'll
answer him by law: I'll not budge an inch, boy:
let him come, and kindly.   [*Falls asleep.*

17 *Brach.* Bitch-hound. *embossed.* Foaming at the mouth.

20 *in the coldest fault.* Where the scent was lost (cold).

23 *merest.* Absolutely.

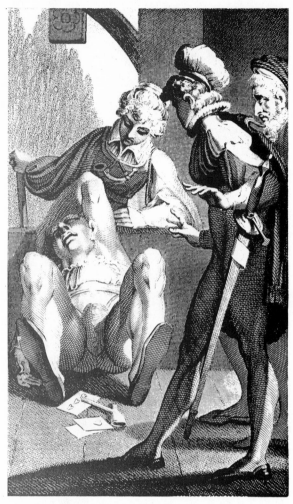

Lord: 'O monstrous beast!' Illustration by H. Fuseli from Steevens' *The Plays of William Shakspeare,* 1805

36 *practise.* Play a trick.

40 *brave.* Finely dressed.

46 *Carry him.* See introduction.

57 *diaper.* Towel.

64 *And when he says he is.* i.e. still mad.

68 *husbanded with modesty.* Carried through with moderation.

Horns winded.   Enter a Lord *from hunting, with his train.*

　　Lord.　Huntsman, I charge thee, tender well
　　　my hounds:
●†Brach Merriman, the poor cur is emboss'd;
And couple Clowder with the deep-mouth'd brach.
Saw'st thou not, boy, how Silver made it good
●At the hedge-corner, in the coldest fault?　　20
I would not lose the dog for twenty pound.
　　First Hun.　Why, Belman is as good as he,
　　　my lord;
●He cried upon it at the merest loss
And twice to-day pick'd out the dullest scent:
Trust me, I take him for the better dog.
　　Lord.　Thou art a fool: if Echo were as fleet,
I would esteem him worth a dozen such.
But sup them well and look unto them all:
To-morrow I intend to hunt again.
　　First Hun.　I will, my lord.　　30
　　Lord.　What's here? one dead, or drunk? See,
　　　doth he breathe?
　　Sec. Hun.　He breathes, my lord. Were he
　　　not warm'd with ale,
This were a bed but cold to sleep so soundly.

　　Lord.　O monstrous beast! how like a swine
　　　he lies!
Grim death, how foul and loathsome is thine image!
●Sirs, I will practise on this drunken man.
What think you, if he were convey'd to bed,
Wrapp'd in sweet clothes, rings put upon his
　　　fingers,
A most delicious banquet by his bed,
●And brave attendants near him when he wakes,
Would not the beggar then forget himself?　　41
　　First Hun.　Believe me, lord, I think he can-
　　　not choose.
　　Sec. Hun.　It would seem strange unto him
　　　when he waked.
　　Lord.　Even as a flattering dream or worthless
　　　fancy.
Then take him up and manage well the jest:
●Carry him gently to my fairest chamber
And hang it round with all my wanton pictures:
Balm his foul head in warm distilled waters
And burn sweet wood to make the lodging sweet:
Procure me music ready when he wakes,　　50
To make a dulcet and a heavenly sound;
And if he chance to speak, be ready straight
And with a low submissive reverence
Say 'What is it your honour will command?'
Let one attend him with a silver basin
Full of rose-water and bestrew'd with flowers;
●Another bear the ewer, the third a diaper,
And say 'Will't please your lordship cool your
　　　hands?'
Some one be ready with a costly suit
And ask him what apparel he will wear;　　60
Another tell him of his hounds and horse,
And that his lady mourns at his disease:
Persuade him that he hath been lunatic;
●†And when he says he is, say that he dreams,
For he is nothing but a mighty lord.
This do and do it kindly, gentle sirs:
It will be pastime passing excellent,
●If it be husbanded with modesty.
　　First Hun.　My lord, I warrant you we will
　　　play our part,
As he shall think by our true diligence　　70
He is no less than what we say he is.

Lord. Take him up gently and to bed with him;
And each one to his office when he wakes.
   [*Some bear out Sly.   A trumpet sounds.*
Sirrah, go see what trumpet 'tis that sounds:
      [*Exit Servingman.*
Belike, some noble gentleman that means,
Travelling some journey, to repose him here.

    Re-enter Servingman.

How now! who is it?
 Serv.   An't please your honour, players
That offer service to your lordship.
 Lord. Bid them come near.

    Enter Players.

     Now, fellows, you are welcome.
Players. We thank your honour.   80
Lord. Do you intend to stay with me to-night?
A Player. So please your lordship to accept
 our duty.
Lord. With all my heart.   This fellow I re-
 member,
Since once he play'd a farmer's eldest son:
'Twas where you woo'd the gentlewoman so well:
I have forgot your name; but, sure, that part
Was aptly fitted and naturally perform'd.
A Player. I think 'twas Soto that your honour
 means.
Lord. 'Tis very true: thou didst it excellent.
Well, you are come to me in happy time; 90
The rather for I have some sport in hand
• Wherein your cunning can assist me much.
There is a lord will hear you play to-night:
• But I am doubtful of your modesties;
Lest over-eyeing of his odd behaviour,—
For yet his honour never heard a play—
You break into some merry passion
And so offend him; for I tell you, sirs,
If you should smile he grows impatient.
 A Player. Fear not, my lord: we can contain
 ourselves,   100
• Were he the veriest antic in the world.
• *Lord.* Go, sirrah, take them to the buttery,
And give them friendly welcome every one:
Let them want nothing that my house affords.
    [*Exit one with the Players.*
Sirrah, go you to Barthol'mew my page,
• And see him dress'd in all suits like a lady:
That done, conduct him to the drunkard's cham-
 ber;
And call him 'madam,' do him obeisance.
Tell him from me, as he will win my love,
He bear himself with honourable action, 110
Such as he hath observed in noble ladies
Unto their lords, by them accomplished:
Such duty to the drunkard let him do
With soft low tongue and lowly courtesy,
And say 'What is't your honour will command,
Wherein your lady and your humble wife
May show her duty and make known her love?'
And then with kind embracements, tempting
 kisses,
And with declining head into his bosom,
Bid him shed tears, as being overjoy'd 120
To see her noble lord restored to health,
Who for this seven years hath esteemed him
No better than a poor and loathsome beggar:
And if the boy have not a woman's gift
To rain a shower of commanded tears,

Strolling players in an alehouse. Engraving from a painting by William Hogarth (1697–1764)

92 *cunning.* Skill.

94 *modesties.* Self-control.

101 *antic.* Buffoon.

102 *buttery.* A room where liquor was kept in butts.

106 *suits.* Points.

127 *close.* Secretly.

137 *spleen.* Mood.

2 *sack.* Sherry, a more gentlemanly drink.

First Servant: 'Will't please your lordship drink a cup of sack?' Engraving from a painting by C. W. Sharpe from Charles Knight's *The Works of Shakspere*, 1873–1876

8 *conserves of beef.* Salt beef.

9 *doublet.* A jacket.

19-21 *Burton-heath.* See introduction. *card-maker.* A card is an iron comb for preparing the wool for spinning. *bear-herd.* Leader of a tame bear.

24-25 *on the score.* Indebted: accounts were originally kept by scoring (notching) on sticks.

26-27 *bestraught.* Distraught.

An onion will do well for such a shift,
●Which in a napkin being close convey'd
Shall in despite enforce a watery eye.
See this dispatch'd with all the haste thou canst:
Anon I'll give thee more instructions.   130
                    [*Exit a Servingman.*
I know the boy will well usurp the grace,
Voice, gait and action of a gentlewoman:
I long to hear him call the drunkard husband,
And how my men will stay themselves from laughter
When they do homage to this simple peasant.
I'll in to counsel them; haply my presence
●May well abate the over-merry spleen
Which otherwise would grow into extremes.
                    [*Exeunt.*

SCENE II. *A bedchamber in the* Lord's *house.*

Enter aloft SLY, *with* Attendants; *some with apparel, others with basin and ewer and other appurtenances; and* Lord.

Sly. For God's sake, a pot of small ale.
●*First Serv.* Will't please your lordship drink a cup of sack?
Sec. Serv. Will't please your honour taste of these conserves?
Third Serv. What raiment will your honour wear to day?
Sly. I am Christophero Sly; call not me 'honour' nor 'lordship:' I ne'er drank sack in my life; and if you give me any conserves, give
●me conserves of beef: ne'er ask me what raiment
●I'll wear; for I have no more doublets than backs, no more stockings than legs, nor no more shoes than feet; nay, sometime more feet than shoes, or such shoes as my toes look through the over-leather.
Lord. Heaven cease this idle humour in your honour!
O, that a mighty man of such descent,
Of such possessions and so high esteem,
Should be infused with so foul a spirit!
Sly. What, would you make me mad? Am
●not I Christopher Sly, old Sly's son of Burton-heath, by birth a pedlar, by education a card-maker, by transmutation a bear-herd, and now by present profession a tinker? Ask Marian Hacket, the fat ale-wife of Wincot, if she know me not: if she say I am not fourteen pence on
●the score for sheer ale, score me up for the lyingest knave in Christendom. What! I am not be-
●straught: here's—
Third Serv. O, this it is that makes your lady mourn!
Sec. Serv. O, this is it that makes your servants droop!
Lord. Hence comes it that your kindred shuns your house,   30
As beaten hence by your strange lunacy.
O noble lord, bethink thee of thy birth,
Call home thy ancient thoughts from banishment
And banish hence these abject lowly dreams.
Look how thy servants do attend on thee,
Each in his office ready at thy beck.
Wilt thou have music? hark! Apollo plays
                    [*Music.*
And twenty caged nightingales do sing:
Or wilt thou sleep? we'll have thee to a couch

Softer and sweeter than the lustful bed   40
● On purpose trimm'd up for Semiramis.
Say thou wilt walk; we will bestrew the ground:
● Or wilt thou ride? thy horses shall be trapp'd,
Their harness studded all with gold and pearl.
Dost thou love hawking? thou hast hawks will soar
Above the morning lark: or wilt thou hunt?
● Thy hounds shall make the welkin answer them
And fetch shrill echoes from the hollow earth.
●   *First Serv.*   Say thou wilt course; thy grey-
                hounds are as swift
● As breathed stags, ay, fleeter than the roe.   50
●   *Sec. Serv.*   Dost thou love pictures? we will
                fetch thee straight
Adonis painted by a running brook,
And Cytherea all in sedges hid,
Which seem to move and wanton with her breath,
Even as the waving sedges play with wind.
●   *Lord.*   We'll show thee Io as she was a maid,
And how she was beguiled and surprised,
As lively painted as the deed was done.
●   *Third Serv.*   Or Daphne roaming through a
                thorny wood,
Scratching her legs that one shall swear she
                bleeds,   60
And at that sight shall sad Apollo weep,
So workmanly the blood and tears are drawn.
   Lord.   Thou art a lord and nothing but a
                lord:
Thou hast a lady far more beautiful
● Than any woman in this waning age.
   First Serv.   And till the tears that she hath
                shed for thee
Like envious floods o'er-run her lovely face,
She was the fairest creature in the world;
And yet she is inferior to none.
   Sly.   Am I a lord? and have I such a lady? 70
Or do I dream? or have I dream'd till now?
I do not sleep: I see, I hear, I speak;
I smell sweet savours and I feel soft things:
Upon my life, I am a lord indeed
And not a tinker nor Christophero Sly.
Well, bring our lady hither to our sight;
● And once again, a pot o' the smallest ale.
   Sec. Serv.   Will't please your mightiness to
                wash your hands?
O, how we joy to see your wit restored!   79
O, that once more you knew but what you are!
These fifteen years you have been in a dream;
Or when you waked, so waked as if you slept.
   Sly.   These fifteen years! by my fay, a goodly
                nap.
But did I never speak of all that time?
   First Serv.   O, yes, my lord, but very idle
                words:
For though you lay here in this goodly chamber,
Yet would you say ye were beaten out of door;
And rail upon the hostess of the house;
And say you would present her at the leet,
● Because she brought stone jugs and no seal'd
                quarts: 90
● Sometimes you would call out for Cicely Hacket.
   Sly.   Ay, the woman's maid of the house.
   Third Serv.   Why, sir, you know no house
                nor no such maid,
Nor no such men as you have reckon'd up,
As Stephen Sly and old John Naps of Greece
And Peter Turph and Henry Pimpernell

41 *Semiramis.* Legendary Assyrian Queen, notorious for her promiscuity.

43 *trapp'd.* Adorned.

47 *welkin.* Sky.

49 *course.* Hare-hunting.

50 *breathed.* Strong winded.

51-53 *Adonis . . . Cytherea all in sedges hid.* Venus, sometimes known as Cytherea, fell in love with the young hunter Adonis who was killed by a boar; cf. Shakespeare's *Venus and Adonis.*

56 *Io.* Io was beloved of Zeus who changed her into a heifer to outwit the jealousy of his wife Hera.

59 *Daphne.* The god Apollo fell in love with the nymph Daphne who was changed into a laurel tree when she prayed for help to avoid him.

Apollo pursuing Daphne. Detail from a painting by Domenichino (1581–1641) and assistants

65 *waning.* Decadent.

77 *smallest.* Weakest.

89 *present her at the leet.* Accuse her at the manor court.

90 *seal'd quarts.* Quart measures stamped with an official seal of approval.

91-92 *Sometimes . . . saw.* See introduction.

103 *Marry*. An oath 'by the Virgin Mary' originally, but by Shakespeare's day equivalent to 'indeed!'

107 *goodman*. Husband.

140 *comonty*. Sly means comedy. *gambold*. Gambol, a dance or caper.

143 *household stuff*. Household furnishings.

144 *history*. Story.

And twenty more such names and men as these
Which never were nor no man ever saw.
  Sly.   Now Lord be thanked for my good
      amends!
  All.   Amen.   100
  Sly.   I thank thee: thou shalt not lose by it.

Enter the Page *as a lady, with attendants.*

  Page.   How fares my noble lord?
  Sly.   Marry, I fare well; for here is cheer
      enough.
Where is my wife?
  Page.   Here, noble lord: what is thy will
      with her?
  Sly.   Are you my wife and will not call me
      husband?
My men should call me 'lord:' I am your good-
      man.
  Page.   My husband and my lord, my lord and
      husband;
I am your wife in all obedience.
  Sly.   I know it well.   What must I call her?
  Lord.   Madam.   111
  Sly.   Al'ce madam, or Joan madam?
  Lord.   'Madam,' and nothing else: so lords
      call ladies.
  Sly.   Madam wife, they say that I have dream'd
And slept above some fifteen year or more.
  Page.   Ay, and the time seems thirty unto me,
Being all this time abandon'd from your bed.
  Sly.   'Tis much.   Servants, leave me and her
      alone.
Madam, undress you and come now to bed.
  Page.   Thrice-noble lord, let me entreat of you
To pardon me yet for a night or two,   121
Or, if not so, until the sun be set:
For your physicians have expressly charged,
In peril to incur your former malady,
That I should yet absent me from your bed:
I hope this reason stands for my excuse.
  Sly.   Ay, it stands so that I may hardly tarry
so long.   But I would be loath to fall into my
dreams again: I will therefore tarry in despite of
the flesh and the blood.   130

Enter a Messenger.

  Mess.   Your honour's players, hearing your
      amendment,
Are come to play a pleasant comedy;
For so your doctors hold it very meet,
Seeing too much sadness hath congeal'd your
      blood,
And melancholy is the nurse of frenzy:
Therefore they thought it good you hear a play
And frame your mind to mirth and merriment,
Which bars a thousand harms and lengthens life.
  Sly.   Marry, I will, let them play it.   Is not
a comonty a Christmas gambold or a tumbling-
trick?   141
  Page.   No, my good lord; it is more pleasing
      stuff.
  Sly.   What, household stuff?
  Page.   It is a kind of history.
  Sly.   Well, we'll see't.   Come, madam wife,
sit by my side and let the world slip: we shall
ne'er be younger.
            Flourish.

ACT I.

Scene I. *Padua. A public place.*

Enter Lucentio *and his man* Tranio.

Luc. Tranio, since for the great desire I had
●To see fair Padua, nursery of arts,
I am arrived for fruitful Lombardy,
The pleasant garden of great Italy;
And by my father's love and leave am arm'd
With his good will and thy good company,
My trusty servant, well approved in all,
Here let us breathe and haply institute
●A course of learning and ingenious studies.
Pisa renown'd for grave citizens   10
Gave me my being and my father first,
A merchant of great traffic through the world,
Vincentio, come of the Bentivolii.
Vincentio's son brought up in Florence
●It shall become to serve all hopes conceived,
To deck his fortune with his virtuous deeds:
And therefore, Tranio, for the time I study,
Virtue and that part of philosophy
Will I apply that treats of happiness
By virtue specially to be achieved.   20
Tell me thy mind; for I have Pisa left
And am to Padua come, as he that leaves
●A shallow plash to plunge him in the deep
And with satiety seeks to quench his thirst.
● *Tra.* Mi perdonato, gentle master mine,
I am in all affected as yourself;
Glad that you thus continue your resolve
To suck the sweets of sweet philosophy.
Only, good master, while we do admire
This virtue and this moral discipline,   30
●Let's be no stoics nor no stocks, I pray;
Or so devote to Aristotle's checks
As Ovid be an outcast quite abjured:
●Balk logic with acquaintance that you have
And practise rhetoric in your common talk;
Music and poesy use to quicken you;
The mathematics and the metaphysics,
●Fall to them as you find your stomach serves you;
No profit grows where is no pleasure ta'en:
In brief, sir, study what you most affect.   40
● *Luc.* Gramercies, Tranio, well dost thou advise.
If, Biondello, thou wert come ashore,
We could at once put us in readiness,
And take a lodging fit to entertain
Such friends as time in Padua shall beget.
But stay a while: what company is this?
     Tra. Master, some show to welcome us to town.

Enter Baptista, Katharina, Bianca, Gremio, *and* Hortensio. Lucentio *and* Tranio *stand by.*

Bap. Gentlemen, importune me no farther,
For how I firmly am resolved you know;
That is, not to bestow my youngest daughter   50
Before I have a husband for the elder:
If either of you both love Katharina,
Because I know you well and love you well,
Leave shall you have to court her at your pleasure.
● *Gre.* [*Aside*] To cart her rather: she's too
          rough for me.
There, there, Hortensio, will you any wife?
     Kath. I pray you, sir, is it your will
●To make a stale of me amongst these mates?

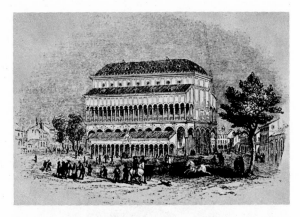

Padua, a public place. Engraving from Charles Knight's *Pictorial Edition of the Works of Shakspere*, 1839–43

---

2 *Padua.* Famous for its university.

9 *ingenious.* Intellectual.

15 *serve.* Fulfil.

23 *plash.* Pool.

25 *Mi perdonato.* Pardon me.

31 *stocks.* Posts with a pun on 'stoics'.

34 *Balk logic.* Bandy arguments.

38 *stomach.* Appetite.

41 *Gramercies.* Many thanks.

55 *cart.* Being taken through the streets in a cart was a common punishment for female offenders.

58 *stale.* Both a laughing-stock and a whore. *mates.* Low fellows.

62 *I wis.* Indeed. *it.* Marriage.

65 *paint your face.* Draw blood.

Ada Rehan, English Edwardian actress, as Kate.
Painting by Eliot Gregory (1854–1915)

69 *froward.* Wilful.

78 *peat.* Pet.

79 *Put finger in the eye.* Cry.

84 *Minerva.* Goddess of Wisdom.

85 *strange.* Unfriendly.

87 *mew.* Shut her up.

109 *blow our nails.* Wait patiently. *fast it fairly out.* Pass
the time.

110 *our cake's dough on both sides.* Our expectations
are disappointed.

117 *brooked parle.* Permitted discussion.

Hor. Mates, maid! how mean you that? no
    mates for you,
Unless you were of gentler, milder mould.   60
    Kath. I' faith, sir, you shall never need to fear:
● I wis it is not half way to her heart;
But if it were, doubt not her care should be
To comb your noddle with a three-legg'd stool
● And paint your face and use you like a fool.
    Hor. From all such devils, good Lord deliver us!
    Gre. And me too, good Lord!
    Tra. Hush, master! here's some good pastime
    toward:
● That wench is stark mad or wonderful froward.
    Luc. But in the other's silence do I see   70
Maid's mild behaviour and sobriety.
Peace, Tranio!
    Tra. Well said, master; mum! and gaze your
    fill.
    Bap. Gentlemen, that I may soon make good
What I have said, Bianca, get you in:
And let it not displease thee, good Bianca,
For I will love thee ne'er the less, my girl.
●   *Kath.* A pretty peat! it is best
● Put finger in the eye, an she knew why.
    Bian. Sister, content you in my discontent. 80
Sir, to your pleasure humbly I subscribe:
My books and instruments shall be my company,
On them to look and practise by myself.
●   *Luc.* Hark, Tranio! thou may'st hear Minerva
    speak.
●   *Hor.* Signior Baptista, will you be so strange?
Sorry am I that our good will effects
Bianca's grief.
●   *Gre.*   Why will you mew her up,
Signior Baptista, for this fiend of hell,
And make her bear the penance of her tongue?
    Bap. Gentlemen, content ye; I am resolved: 90
Go in, Bianca: [*Exit Bianca.*
And for I know she taketh most delight
In music, instruments and poetry,
Schoolmasters will I keep within my house,
Fit to instruct her youth. If you, Hortensio,
Or Signior Gremio, you, know any such,
Prefer them hither; for to cunning men
I will be very kind, and liberal
To mine own children in good bringing up:
And so farewell. Katharina, you may stay; 100
For I have more to commune with Bianca. [*Exit.*

    Kath. Why, and I trust I may go too, may
I not? What, shall I be appointed hours; as
though, belike, I knew not what to take, and
what to leave, ha?   [*Exit.*
    Gre. You may go to the devil's dam: your
gifts are so good, here's none will hold you.
Their love is not so great, Hortensio, but we may
● blow our nails together, and fast it fairly out:
● our cake's dough on both sides. Farewell: yet,
for the love I bear my sweet Bianca, if I can by
any means light on a fit man to teach her that
wherein she delights, I will wish him to her
father.
    Hor. So will I, Signior Gremio: but a word,
I pray. Though the nature of our quarrel yet
● never brooked parle, know now, upon advice, it
toucheth us both, that we may yet again have
access to our fair mistress and be happy rivals in
Bianca's love, to labour and effect one thing
specially.   121
    Gre. What's that, I pray?

Hor. Marry, sir, to get a husband for her sister.

Gre. A husband! a devil.

Hor. I say, a husband.

Gre. I say, a devil. Thinkest thou, Hortensio, though her father be very rich, any man is so very a fool to be married to hell?   129

Hor. Tush, Gremio, though it pass your patience and mine to endure her loud alarums, why, man, there be good fellows in the world, an a man could light on them, would take her with all faults, and money enough.

● *Gre.* I cannot tell; but I had as lief take her dowry with this condition, to be whipped at the
● high cross every morning.

Hor. Faith, as you say, there's small choice in rotten apples. But come; since this bar in
● law makes us friends, it shall be so far forth friendly maintained till by helping Baptista's eldest daughter to a husband we set his youngest free for a husband, and then have to't afresh.
● Sweet Bianca! Happy man be his dole! He that runs fastest gets the ring. How say you, Signior Gremio?

Gre. I am agreed; and would I had given him the best horse in Padua to begin his wooing that would thoroughly woo her, wed her and bed her and rid the house of her! Come on.   150

[*Exeunt Gremio and Hortensio.*

Tra. I pray, sir, tell me, is it possible
That love should of a sudden take such hold?

Luc. O Tranio, till I found it to be true,
I never thought it possible or likely;
But see, while idly I stood looking on,
● I found the effect of love in idleness:
And now in plainness do confess to thee,
That art to me as secret and as dear
● As Anna to the queen of Carthage was,
Tranio, I burn, I pine, I perish, Tranio,   160
If I achieve not this young modest girl.
Counsel me, Tranio, for I know thou canst;
Assist me, Tranio, for I know thou wilt.

Tra. Master, it is no time to chide you now;
● Affection is not rated from the heart:
If love have touch'd you, nought remains but so,
● 'Redime te captum quam queas minimo.'

Luc. Gramercies, lad, go forward; this contents:
The rest will comfort, for thy counsel's sound.

Tra. Master, you look'd so longly on the maid,
Perhaps you mark'd not what's the pith of all.

Luc. O yes, I saw sweet beauty in her face,
● Such as the daughter of Agenor had,
That made great Jove to humble him to her hand,
When with his knees he kiss'd the Cretan strand.

Tra. Saw you no more? mark'd you not how her sister
Began to scold and raise up such a storm
That mortal ears might hardly endure the din?

Luc. Tranio, I saw her coral lips to move
And with her breath she did perfume the air: 180
Sacred and sweet was all I saw in her.

Tra. Nay, then, 'tis time to stir him from his trance.
I pray, awake, sir: if you love the maid,
Bend thoughts and wits to achieve her. Thus it stands:
● Her elder sister is so curst and shrewd
That till the father rid his hands of her,

135 *as lief.* As soon.

137 *high cross.* The cross usually in the market place of a town.

140-143 *it shall be . . . to't afresh.* They may continue to be friends until they have found a husband for Kate, after which they can renew their rivalry.

144 *Happy man be his dole.* Proverbial: 'May his lot be happy'.

156 *love in idleness.* The pansy, supposed to be conducive to love.

159 *As Anna . . . Carthage.* Sister and confidante of Dido, queen of Carthage.

165 *rated from.* Scolded out of.

167 *'Redime . . . minimo'.* Ransom yourself from captivity as cheaply as you can. Quoted in Lily's *Latin Grammar* from Terence's play *Eunuchus*.

173 *daughter of Agenor.* Europa whom Jupiter wooed in the shape of a bull.

185 *curst.* Bad-tempered.

195 *jump.* Agree.

Costume designs for Tranio, Lucentio and Biondello
by Rosemary Vercoe, Stratford-upon-Avon, 1948

203 *Basta.* Enough. *I have it full.* See it clearly.

208 *port.* State.

210 *meaner.* Of lower status.

237 *descried.* Recognized.

Master, your love must live a maid at home;
And therefore has he closely mew'd her up,
Because she will not be annoy'd with suitors.
  Luc. Ah, Tranio, what a cruel father's he!
But art thou not advised, he took some care   191
To get her cunning schoolmasters to instruct her?
    Tra. Ay, marry, am I, sir; and now 'tis
      plotted.
    Luc. I have it, Tranio.
    Tra.   Master, for my hand,
●Both our inventions meet and jump in one.
    Luc. Tell me thine first.
    Tra.   You will be schoolmaster
And undertake the teaching of the maid:
That's your device.
    Luc.   It is: may it be done?
    Tra. Not possible; for who shall bear your
      part,
And be in Padua here Vincentio's son,   200
Keep house and ply his book, welcome his friends,
Visit his countrymen and banquet them?
● *Luc.* Basta; content thee, for I have it full.
We have not yet been seen in any house,
Nor can we be distinguish'd by our faces
For man or master; then it follows thus;
Thou shalt be master, Tranio, in my stead,
●Keep house and port and servants, as I should:
I will some other be, some Florentine,
●Some Neapolitan, or meaner man of Pisa.   210
'Tis hatch'd and shall be so: Tranio, at once
Uncase thee; take my colour'd hat and cloak:
When Biondello comes, he waits on thee;
But I will charm him first to keep his tongue.
    Tra. So had you need.
In brief, sir, sith it your pleasure is,
And I am tied to be obedient;
For so your father charged me at our parting,
'Be serviceable to my son,' quoth he,
Although I think 'twas in another sense;   220
I am content to be Lucentio,
Because so well I love Lucentio.
    Luc. Tranio, be so, because Lucentio loves:
And let me be a slave, to achieve that maid
Whose sudden sight hath thrall'd my wounded
      eye.
Here comes the rogue.

Enter BIONDELLO.

          Sirrah, where have you been?
    Bion. Where have I been! Nay, how now!
where are you? Master, has my fellow Tranio
stolen your clothes? Or you stolen his? or both?
pray, what's the news?   230
    Luc. Sirrah, come hither: 'tis no time to jest,
And therefore frame your manners to the time.
Your fellow Tranio here, to save my life,
Puts my apparel and my countenance on,
And I for my escape have put on his;
For in a quarrel since I came ashore
●I kill'd a man and fear I was descried:
Wait you on him, I charge you, as becomes,
While I make way from hence to save my life:
You understand me?
    Bion.   I, sir! ne'er a whit.   240
    Luc. And not a jot of Tranio in your mouth:
Tranio is changed into Lucentio.
    Bion. The better for him: would I were
      so too!

Tra.   So could I, faith, boy, to have the next
    wish after,
That Lucentio indeed had Baptista's youngest
    daughter.
But, sirrah, not for my sake, but your master's,
    I advise
You use your manners discreetly in all kind of
    companies:
When I am alone, why, then I am Tranio;
But in all places else your master Lucentio.   249
    Luc.   Tranio, let's go: one thing more rests,
that thyself execute, to make one among these
wooers: if thou ask me why, sufficeth, my rea-
sons are both good and weighty.   [*Exeunt.*

The presenters above speak.

First Serv.   My lord, you nod; you do not
    mind the play.
Sly.   Yes, by Saint Anne, do I. A good mat-
ter, surely: comes there any more of it?
Page.   My lord, 'tis but begun.
Sly.   'Tis a very excellent piece of work,
madam lady: would 'twere done!   259
                        [*They sit and mark.*

SCENE II. *Padua. Before* HORTENSIO'S *house.*

Enter PETRUCHIO *and his man* GRUMIO.

Pet.   Verona, for a while I take my leave,
To see my friends in Padua, but of all
My best beloved and approved friend,
Hortensio; and I trow this is his house.
Here, sirrah Grumio; knock, I say.
    Gru.   Knock, sir! whom should I knock? is
there any man has rebused your worship?
    Pet.   Villain, I say, knock me here soundly.
    Gru.   Knock you here, sir! why, sir, what am
I, sir, that I should knock you here, sir?   10
    Pet.   Villain, I say, knock me at this gate
And rap me well, or I'll knock your knave's pate.
    Gru.   My master is grown quarrelsome. I
    should knock you first,
And then I know after who comes by the worst.
    Pet.   Will it not be?
Faith, sirrah, an you'll not knock, I'll ring it;
I'll try how you can sol, fa, and sing it.
                   [*He wrings him by the ears.*
    Gru.   Help, masters, help! my master is mad.
    Pet.   Now, knock when I bid you, sirrah
    villain!

Enter HORTENSIO.

Hor.   How now! what's the matter? My old
friend Grumio! and my good friend Petruchio!
How do you all at Verona?
    Pet.   Signior Hortensio, come you to part
    the fray?
'Con tutto il cuore, ben trovato,' may I say.
    Hor.   'Alla nostra casa ben venuto, molto
honorato signor mio Petruchio.'
Rise, Grumio, rise: we will compound this
    quarrel.
    Gru.   Nay, 'tis no matter, sir, what he 'leges
in Latin. If this be not a lawful cause for me to
leave his service, look you, sir, he bid me knock
him and rap him soundly, sir: well, was it fit for
a servant to use his master so, being perhaps, for
aught I see, two and thirty, a pip out?
Whom would to God I had well knock'd at first,

4 *trow.* Believe.

7 *rebused.* Grumio's mistake; he means 'abused'.

8 *me.* i.e. for me.

Petruchio wrings Grumio by the ears. Engraving by
Kenny Meadows from Barry Cornwall's *The Works of
Shakspere*, 1846

24 *'Con tutto . . . trovato'.* With all my heart, well met.

25-26 *'Alla nostra . . . Petruchio'.* Welcome to our
house, my much honoured Signor Petruchio.

27 *compound.* Settle.

33 *two and thirty, a pip out.* In the card game 'thirty-
one', a pip was the marking on the card. The phrase
meant 'drunk'.

46 *heavy chance.* Sad happening.

52 *in a few.* i.e. words.

59 *come roundly.* Speak frankly.

Michael Williams as Petruchio, Royal Shakespeare Co,
1967

68 *burden.* Bass or obligato.

69 *Florentius.* Florent, the knight in Gower's *Confessio Amantis,* marries a hag who can tell him the answer to a riddle which will save his life.

70 *Sibyl.* A prophetess to whom Apollo gave as many years of life as she could hold grains of sand in her hand.

71 *Xanthippe.* Socrates' wife, a notorious shrew.

79 *aglet-baby.* A small figure that formed the tag on the end of a lace.

80 *trot.* Hag.

95 *board.* A pun on 'to board a vessel' and 'to win'.

Then had not Grumio come by the worst.
   Pet. A senseless villain! Good Hortensio,
I bade the rascal knock upon your gate
And could not get him for my heart to do it.
   Gru. Knock at the gate! O heavens! Spake
you not these words plain, 'Sirrah, knock me
here, rap me here, knock me well, and knock me
soundly'? And come you now with, 'knocking
at the gate'?
   Pet. Sirrah, be gone, or talk not, I advise you.
   Hor. Petruchio, patience; I am Grumio's
      pledge:
Why, this's a heavy chance 'twixt him and you,
Your ancient, trusty, pleasant servant Grumio.
And tell me now, sweet friend, what happy gale
Blows you to Padua here from old Verona?
   Pet. Such wind as scatters young men through
      the world   50
To seek their fortunes farther than at home
Where small experience grows.   But in a few,
Signior Hortensio, thus it stands with me:
Antonio, my father, is deceased;
And I have thrust myself into this maze,
Haply to wive and thrive as best I may:
Crowns in my purse I have and goods at home,
And so am come abroad to see the world.
   Hor. Petruchio, shall I then come roundly
      to thee
And wish thee to a shrewd ill-favour'd wife?   60
Thou'ldst thank me but a little for my counsel:
And yet I'll promise thee she shall be rich
And very rich: but thou'rt too much my friend,
And I'll not wish thee to her.
   Pet. Signior Hortensio, 'twixt such friends
      as we
Few words suffice; and therefore, if thou know
One rich enough to be Petruchio's wife,
As wealth is burden of my wooing dance,
Be she as foul as was Florentius' love,
As old as Sibyl and as curst and shrewd   70
As Socrates' Xanthippe, or a worse,
She moves me not, or not removes, at least,
Affection's edge in me, were she as rough
As are the swelling Adriatic seas:
I come to wive it wealthily in Padua;
If wealthily, then happily in Padua.
   Gru. Nay, look you, sir, he tells you flatly
what his mind is: why, give him gold enough and
marry him to a puppet or an aglet-baby; or an
old trot with ne'er a tooth in her head, though
she have as many diseases as two and fifty horses:
why, nothing comes amiss, so money comes withal.
   Hor. Petruchio, since we are stepp'd thus
      far in,
I will continue that I broach'd in jest.
I can, Petruchio, help thee to a wife
With wealth enough and young and beauteous,
Brought up as best becomes a gentlewoman:
Her only fault, and that is faults enough,
Is that she is intolerable curst
And shrewd and froward, so beyond all measure
That, were my state far worser than it is,   91
I would not wed her for a mine of gold.
   Pet. Hortensio, peace! thou know'st not gold's
      effect:
Tell me her father's name and 'tis enough;
For I will board her, though she chide as loud
As thunder when the clouds in autumn crack.
   Hor. Her father is Baptista Minola,

An affable and courteous gentleman:
Her name is Katharina Minola,
Renown'd in Padua for her scolding tongue.   100
   Pet. I know her father, though I know not her;
And he knew my deceased father well.
I will not sleep, Hortensio, till I see her;
And therefore let me be thus bold with you
• To give you over at this first encounter,
Unless you will accompany me thither.
   Gru. I pray you, sir, let him go while the
humour lasts.   O' my word, an she knew him as
well as I do, she would think scolding would do
little good upon him: she may perhaps call him
half a score knaves or so: why, that's nothing;
• an he begin once, he'll rail in his rope-tricks. I'll
• tell you what, sir, an she stand him but a little,
• he will throw a figure in her face and so disfigure
her with it that she shall have no more eyes to
see withal than a cat.   You know him not, sir.
   Hor. Tarry, Petruchio, I must go with thee,
For in Baptista's keep my treasure is:
He hath the jewel of my life in hold,
His youngest daughter, beautiful Bianca,   120
And her withholds from me and other more,
Suitors to her and rivals in my love,
Supposing it a thing impossible,
For those defects I have before rehearsed,
That ever Katharina will be woo'd;
Therefore this order hath Baptista ta'en,
That none shall have access unto Bianca
Till Katharine the curst have got a husband.
   Gru. Katharine the curst!
A title for a maid of all titles the worst.   130
   Hor. Now shall my friend Petruchio do me
     grace,
And offer me disguised in sober robes
To old Baptista as a schoolmaster
• Well seen in music, to instruct Bianca;
That so I may, by this device, at least
Have leave and leisure to make love to her
And unsuspected court her by herself.
   Gru. Here's no knavery! See, to beguile the
old folks, how the young folks lay their heads
together!   140

    Enter GREMIO, *and* LUCENTIO *disguised.*

Master, master, look about you: who goes there,
    ha?
   Hor. Peace, Grumio! it is the rival of my love.
Petruchio, stand by a while.
   Gru. A proper stripling and an amorous!
•   *Gre.* O, very well; I have perused the note.
Hark you, sir; I'll have them very fairly bound:
All books of love, see that at any hand;
And see you read no other lectures to her:
You understand me: over and beside
Signior Baptista's liberality,   150
• I'll mend it with a largess. Take your paper too,
And let me have them very well perfumed:
For she is sweeter than perfume itself
To whom they go to. What will you read to her?
   Luc. Whate'er I read to her, I'll plead for you
As for my patron, stand you so assured,
As firmly as yourself were still in place:
Yea, and perhaps with more successful words
Than you, unless you were a scholar, sir.
   Gre. O this learning, what a thing it is!   160
•   *Gru.* O this woodcock, what an ass it is!
   Pet. Peace, sirrah!

105 *give you over.* Leave you.

112 *rope-tricks.* Probably Grumio is trying to say rhetoric.

113 *stand.* Withstand.

114 *figure.* Figure of speech.

134 *seen.* Qualified.

145 *note.* A reading list for Bianca.

151 *mend it with largess.* Give additional gifts of money.

161 *woodcock.* Fool; the woodcock is a bird easily trapped.

Woodcock snares. Illustration from Henry Parrot's
Laquei Ridiculosi, or Springs for Woodcocks, 1613

170 *turn.* Requirement.

178 *bags.* i.e. money bags.

183 *Upon agreement . . . liking.* If we agree to his conditions.

Costume designs for Hortensio and Grumio by Rosemary Vercoe, Stratford-upon-Avon, 1948

211 *fear.* Frighten. *bugs.* Bugbears or bogeys.

Hor.   Grumio, mum! God save you, Signior
     Gremio.
Gre. And you are well met, Signior Hortensio.
Trow you whither I am going? To Baptista Minola.
I promised to inquire carefully
About a schoolmaster for the fair Bianca:
And by good fortune I have lighted well
On this young man, for learning and behaviour
● Fit for her turn, well read in poetry   170
And other books, good ones, I warrant ye.
Hor.   'Tis well; and I have met a gentleman
Hath promised me to help me to another,
A fine musician to instruct our mistress;
So shall I no whit be behind in duty
To fair Bianca, so beloved of me.
Gre.   Beloved of me; and that my deeds shall
     prove.
● *Gru.*   And that his bags shall prove.
Hor.   Gremio, 'tis now no time to vent our love:
Listen to me, and if you speak me fair,   180
I'll tell you news indifferent good for either.
Here is a gentleman whom by chance I met,
● Upon agreement from us to his liking,
Will undertake to woo curst Katharine,
Yea, and to marry her, if her dowry please.
Gre.   So said, so done, is well.
Hortensio, have you told him all her faults?
Pet.   I know she is an irksome brawling scold:
If that be all, masters, I hear no harm.
Gre.   No, say'st me so, friend? What coun-
     tryman?   190
Pet.   Born in Verona, old Antonio's son:
My father dead, my fortune lives for me;
And I do hope good days and long to see.
Gre.   O sir, such a life, with such a wife, were
     strange!
But if you have a stomach, to't i' God's name:
You shall have me assisting you in all.
But will you woo this wild-cat?
Pet.   Will I live?
Gru.   Will he woo her? ay, or I'll hang her.
Pet.   Why came I hither but to that intent?
Think you a little din can daunt mine ears?   200
Have I not in my time heard lions roar?
Have I not heard the sea puff'd up with winds
Rage like an angry boar chafed with sweat?
Have I not heard great ordnance in the field,
And heaven's artillery thunder in the skies?
Have I not in a pitched battle heard
Loud 'larums, neighing steeds, and trumpets'
     clang?
And do you tell me of a woman's tongue,
That gives not half so great a blow to hear
As will a chestnut in a farmer's fire?   210
● Tush, tush! fear boys with bugs.
Gru.   For he fears none.
Gre.   Hortensio, hark:
This gentleman is happily arrived,
My mind presumes, for his own good and ours.
Hor.   I promised we would be contributors
And bear his charge of wooing, whatsoe'er.
Gre. And so we will, provided that he win her.
Gru.   I would I were as sure of a good dinner.

Enter TRANIO *brave, and* BIONDELLO.

Tra.   Gentlemen, God save you. If I may
     be bold,
Tell me, I beseech you, which is the readiest way
To the house of Signior Baptista Minola?   221

Bion. He that has the two fair daughters:
is't he you mean?
  Tra. Even he, Biondello.
  Gre. Hark you, sir; you mean not her to—
  Tra. Perhaps, him and her, sir: what have
    you to do?
  Pet. Not her that chides, sir, at any hand, I
    pray.
  Tra. I love no chiders, sir.   Biondello, let's
    away.
  Luc. Well begun, Tranio.
  Hor.   Sir, a word ere you go;
Are you a suitor to the maid you talk of, yea or no?
  Tra. And if I be, sir, is it any offence?   231
  Gre. No; if without more words you will get
    you hence.
  Tra. Why, sir, I pray, are not the streets as
    free
For me as for you?
  Gre.   But so is not she.
  Tra. For what reason, I beseech you?
  Gre.   For this reason, if you'll know,
That she's the choice love of Signior Gremio.
  Hor. That she's the chosen of Signior Hor-
    tensio.
  Tra. Softly, my masters! if you be gentlemen,
Do me this right; hear me with patience.
Baptista is a noble gentleman,   240
To whom my father is not all unknown;
And were his daughter fairer than she is,
She may more suitors have and me for one.
● Fair Leda's daughter had a thousand wooers;
Then well one more may fair Bianca have:
And so she shall; Lucentio shall make one,
● Though Paris came in hope to speed alone.
  Gre. What! this gentleman will out-talk us all.
● *Luc.* Sir, give him head: I know he'll prove
    a jade.   249
  Pet. Hortensio, to what end are all these words?
  Hor. Sir, let me be so bold as ask you,
Did you yet ever see Baptista's daughter?
  Tra. No, sir; but hear I do that he hath two,
The one as famous for a scolding tongue
As is the other for beauteous modesty.
  Pet. Sir, sir, the first's for me; let her go by.
  Gre. Yea, leave that labour to great Hercules;
● And let it be more than Alcides' twelve.
  Pet. Sir, understand you this of me in sooth:
The youngest daughter whom you hearken for
Her father keeps from all access of suitors,   261
And will not promise her to any man
Until the elder sister first be wed:
The younger then is free and not before.
  Tra. If it be so, sir, that you are the man
● Must stead us all and me amongst the rest,
And if you break the ice and do this feat,
Achieve the elder, set the younger free
● For our access, whose hap shall be to have her
Will not so graceless be to be ingrate.   270
  Hor. Sir, you say well and well you do con-
    ceive;
And since you do profess to be a suitor,
You must, as we do, gratify this gentleman,
To whom we all rest generally beholding.
  Tra. Sir, I shall not be slack: in sign whereof,
● Please ye we may contrive this afternoon,
And quaff carouses to our mistress' health,
And do as adversaries do in law,
Strive mightily, but eat and drink as friends.

244 *Leda's daughter.* Helen of Troy.

247 *Paris.* The Trojan King's son who stole Helen from her husband.

Paris about to embark for Greece. Engraving from a relief in the Villa Ludosi, Rome

249 *jade.* A poor horse, and so he will soon give up.

258 *Alcides.* Another name for Hercules.

Derek Godfrey as Petruchio, Stratford-upon-Avon, 1962

266 *stead.* Help.

269 *hap.* Fortune.

276 *contrive.* While away.

282 *ben venuto.* Welcome.

3 *gawds.* Ornaments.

13 *Minion.* Minx.

17 *fair.* In finery.

26 *hilding.* Good-for-nothing.

Katherine: 'Her silence flouts me . . .' Katherine (Janet Suzman), Bianca (June Watts) and Baptista (Roy Kinnear), Royal Shakespeare Co, 1967

33 *dance bare-foot.* The custom for older unmarried sisters at their younger sister's wedding.

34 *lead apes in hell.* The fate of old maids, since they could not lead children into heaven.

Gru. Bion. O excellent motion!   Fellows, let's be gone.   280
Hor.   The motion's good indeed and be it so,
● Petruchio, I shall be your ben venuto. [*Exeunt.*

ACT II.

SCENE I.   *Padua.   A room in* BAPTISTA'S *house.*

Enter KATHARINA *and* BIANCA.

Bian.   Good sister, wrong me not, nor wrong yourself,
To make a bondmaid and a slave of me :
● That I disdain : but for these other gawds,
Unbind my hands, I'll pull them off myself,
Yea, all my raiment, to my petticoat ;
Or what you will command me will I do,
So well I know my duty to my elders.
Kath.   Of all thy suitors, here I charge thee, tell
Whom thou lovest best : see thou dissemble not.
Bian.   Believe me, sister, of all the men alive
I never yet beheld that special face   11
Which I could fancy more than any other.
● *Kath.* Minion, thou liest.   Is't not Hortensio?
Bian.   If you affect him, sister, here I swear
I'll plead for you myself, but you shall have him.
Kath.   O then, belike, you fancy riches more :
● You will have Gremio to keep you fair.
Bian.   Is it for him you do envy me so?
Nay then you jest, and now I well perceive
You have but jested with me all this while :   20
I prithee, sister Kate, untie my hands.
Kath.   If that be jest, then all the rest was so.
[*Strikes her.*

Enter BAPTISTA.

Bap.   Why, how now, dame! whence grows this insolence?
Bianca, stand aside.   Poor girl! she weeps.
Go ply thy needle ; meddle not with her.
● For shame, thou hilding of a devilish spirit,
Why dost thou wrong her that did ne'er wrong thee?
When did she cross thee with a bitter word?
Kath.   Her silence flouts me, and I'll be revenged.   [*Flies after Bianca.*
Bap.   What, in my sight?   Bianca, get thee in.
[*Exit Bianca.* 30
Kath.   What, will you not suffer me?   Nay, now I see
She is your treasure, she must have a husband ;
● I must dance bare-foot on her wedding day
● And for your love to her lead apes in hell.
Talk not to me : I will go sit and weep
Till I can find occasion of revenge.   [*Exit.*
Bap.   Was ever gentleman thus grieved as I?
But who comes here?

Enter GREMIO, LUCENTIO *in the habit of a mean man ;* PETRUCHIO, *with* HORTENSIO *as a musician ; and* TRANIO, *with* BIONDELLO *bearing a lute and books.*

Gre.   Good morrow, neighbour Baptista.
Bap.   Good morrow, neighbour Gremio.   God save you, gentlemen !   41
Pet.   And you, good sir !   Pray, have you not a daughter

Call'd Katharina, fair and virtuous?
    Bap. I have a daughter, sir, called Katharina.
    Gre. You are too blunt: go to it orderly.
    Pet. You wrong me, Signior Gremio: give
    me leave.
I am a gentleman of Verona, sir,
That, hearing of her beauty and her wit,
Her affability and bashful modesty,
Her wondrous qualities and mild behaviour,   50
Am bold to show myself a forward guest
Within your house, to make mine eye the witness
Of that report which I so oft have heard.
●And, for an entrance to my entertainment,
I do present you with a man of mine,
                    [*Presenting Hortensio.*

Cunning in music and the mathematics,
To instruct her fully in those sciences,
Whereof I know she is not ignorant:
Accept of him, or else you do me wrong:
His name is Licio, born in Mantua.   60
    Bap. You're welcome, sir; and he, for your
    good sake.
But for my daughter Katharine, this I know,
She is not for your turn, the more my grief.
    Pet. I see you do not mean to part with her,
Or else you like not of my company.
    Bap. Mistake me not; I speak but as I find.
Whence are you, sir? what may I call your name?
    Pet. Petruchio is my name; Antonio's son,
A man well known throughout all Italy.
    Bap. I know him well: you are welcome for
    his sake.   70
    Gre. Saving your tale, Petruchio, I pray,
Let us, that are poor petitioners, speak too:
●Baccare! you are marvellous forward.
    Pet. O, pardon me, Signior Gremio; I would
    fain be doing.
    Gre. I doubt it not, sir; but you will curse
    your wooing.
Neighbour, this is a gift very grateful, I am sure
of it. To express the like kindness, myself, that
have been more kindly beholding to you than any,
freely give unto you this young scholar [*presenting Lucentio*], that hath been long studying
at Rheims; as cunning in Greek, Latin, and
other languages, as the other in music and mathematics: his name is Cambio; pray, accept his
service.
    Bap. A thousand thanks, Signior Gremio.
Welcome, good Cambio. [*To Tranio*] But, gen-
tle sir, methinks you walk like a stranger: may
I be so bold to know the cause of your coming?
    Tra. Pardon me, sir, the boldness is mine own,
That, being a stranger in this city here,   90
Do make myself a suitor to your daughter,
Unto Bianca, fair and virtuous.
Nor is your firm resolve unknown to me,
In the preferment of the eldest sister.
This liberty is all that I request,
That, upon knowledge of my parentage,
I may have welcome 'mongst the rest that woo
And free access and favour as the rest:
And, toward the education of your daughters,
I here bestow a simple instrument,   100
And this small packet of Greek and Latin books:
If you accept them, then their worth is great.
    Bap. Lucentio is your name; of whence, I
    pray?
    Tra. Of Pisa, sir; son to Vincentio.

54 *entrance to my entertainment.* Admission for my reception.

Petruchio: 'I do present you with a man of mine, cunning in music . . .' From a contemporary engraving

73 *Baccare.* Stand back.

Pisa. Engraving from Charles Knight's *Pictorial Edition of the Works of William Shakspere*, 1839–43

113 *passing.* Very.

123 *in possession.* Upon marriage.

125 *widowhood.* Her estate as a widow.

127 *specialities.* Special contracts.

139 *speed.* Fortune.

141 *to the proof.* In tested armour.

148 *break her.* Tame her.

Hortensio: 'She hath broke the lute to me . . .' Hortensio (David Lyon), Baptista (Paul Brooke), Royal Shakespeare Co, 1978

150 *frets.* Pieces of gut tied across the fingerboard of the lute, later replaced by inlaid ridges of wood or metal.

Bap. A mighty man of Pisa; by report
I know him well: you are very welcome, sir.
Take you the lute, and you the set of books;
You shall go see your pupils presently.
Holla, within!

   Enter a Servant.
    Sirrah, lead these gentlemen
To my daughters; and tell them both,   110
These are their tutors: bid them use them well.
[*Exit Servant, with Lucentio and Hortensio,*
       Biondello following.
We will go walk a little in the orchard,
● And then to dinner. You are passing welcome,
And so I pray you all to think yourselves.
 Pet. Signior Baptista, my business asketh
  haste,
And every day I cannot come to woo.
You knew my father well, and in him me,
Left solely heir to all his lands and goods,
Which I have better'd rather than decreased:
Then tell me, if I get your daughter's love, 120
What dowry shall I have with her to wife?
 Bap. After my death the one half of my lands,
● And in possession twenty thousand crowns.
 Pet. And, for that dowry, I'll assure her of
● Her widowhood, be it that she survive me,
In all my lands and leases whatsoever:
● Let specialties be therefore drawn between us,
That covenants may be kept on either hand.
 Bap. Ay, when the special thing is well ob-
  tain'd,
That is, her love; for that is all in all.   130
 Pet. Why, that is nothing; for I tell you, father,
I am as peremptory as she proud-minded;
And where two raging fires meet together
They do consume the thing that feeds their fury:
Though little fire grows great with little wind,
Yet extreme gusts will blow out fire and all:
So I to her and so she yields to me;
For I am rough and woo not like a babe.
● *Bap.* Well mayst thou woo, and happy be
  thy speed!
But be thou arm'd for some unhappy words. 140
● *Pet.* Ay, to the proof; as mountains are for
  winds,
That shake not, though they blow perpetually.

   Re-enter HORTENSIO, *with his head broke.*
 Bap. How now, my friend! why dost thou
  look so pale?
 Hor. For fear, I promise you, if I look pale.
 Bap. What, will my daughter prove a good
  musician?
 Hor. I think she'll sooner prove a soldier:
Iron may hold with her, but never lutes.
● *Bap.* Why, then thou canst not break her to
  the lute?
 Hor. Why, no; for she hath broke the lute
  to me.
● I did but tell her she mistook her frets,   150
And bow'd her hand to teach her fingering;
When, with a most impatient devilish spirit,
'Frets, call you these?' quoth she; 'I'll fume
  with them:'
And, with that word, she struck me on the head,
And through the instrument my pate made way;
And there I stood amazed for a while,
As on a pillory, looking through the lute:

While she did call me rascal fiddler
● And twangling Jack; with twenty such vile terms,
As had she studied to misuse me so.   160
  Pet. Now, by the world, it is a lusty wench;
I love her ten times more than e'er I did:
O, how I long to have some chat with her!
  Bap. Well, go with me and be not so discom-
fited:
Proceed in practice with my younger daughter;
She's apt to learn and thankful for good turns.
Signior Petruchio, will you go with us,
Or shall I send my daughter Kate to you?
  Pet. I pray you do. [*Exeunt all but Petru-
chio.*] I will attend her here,
And woo her with some spirit when she comes.
Say that she rail; why then I'll tell her plain 171
She sings as sweetly as a nightingale:
Say that she frown; I'll say she looks as clear
As morning roses newly wash'd with dew:
Say she be mute and will not speak a word:
Then I'll commend her volubility,
And say she uttereth piercing eloquence:
If she do bid me pack, I'll give her thanks,
As though she bid me stay by her a week:
If she deny to wed, I'll crave the day   180
● When I shall ask the banns and when be married.
But here she comes; and now, Petruchio, speak.

Enter KATHARINA.

Good morrow, Kate; for that's your name, I hear.
  Kath. Well have you heard, but something
      hard of hearing:
They call me Katharine that do talk of me.
  Pet. You lie, in faith; for you are call'd plain
      Kate,
And bonny Kate and sometimes Kate the curst;
But Kate, the prettiest Kate in Christendom,
Kate of Kate Hall, my super-dainty Kate,   189
● For dainties are all Kates, and therefore, Kate,
Take this of me, Kate of my consolation;
Hearing thy mildness praised in every town,
Thy virtues spoke of, and thy beauty sounded,
Yet not so deeply as to thee belongs,
Myself am moved to woo thee for my wife.
● *Kath.* Moved! in good time: let him that
      moved you hither
Remove you hence: I knew you at the first
● You were a moveable.
  Pet.   Why, what's a moveable?
● *Kath.* A join'd-stool.
  Pet.   Thou hast hit it: come, sit on me.
  Kath. Asses are made to bear, and so are you.
  Pet. Women are made to bear, and so are you.
  Kath. No such jade as you, if me you mean.
  Pet. Alas! good Kate, I will not burden thee;
● For, knowing thee to be but young and light—
  Kath. Too light for such a swain as you to
      catch;
And yet as heavy as my weight should be.
● *Pet.* Should be! should—buzz!
  Kath.   Well ta'en, and like a buzzard.
● *Pet.* O slow-wing'd turtle! shall a buzzard
      take thee?
● *Kath.* Ay, for a turtle, as he takes a buzzard.
  Pet. Come, come, you wasp; i' faith, you are
      too angry.   210
  Kath. If I be waspish, best beware my sting.
  Pet. My remedy is then, to pluck it out.
  Kath. Ay, if the fool could find it where it lies.

159 *Jack.* Knave.

181 *banns.* The public announcement in church of the intention to marry.

Mrs F. R. Benson, the Edwardian actress, as Kate

190 *For dainties are all Kates.* A pun on 'cates' meaning delicacies.

196 *in good time.* Indeed.

198 *moveable.* A quibble on a piece of furniture (in French, *meuble*) and a changeable person.

199 *join'd stool.* A stool made by a joiner, particularly a night-stool, or commode, and a standard taunt.

204 *light.* Wanton.

207 *he.* Suggests 'bee' which in turn suggests 'buzz'. *buzzard.* A hawk that is untrainable; therefore a fool.

208 *turtle.* Turtle-dove.

209 *buzzard.* A buzzing insect.

Kate strikes Petruchio. Katherine (Peggy Ashcroft),
Petruchio (Peter O'Toole), Stratford-upon-Avon, 1960

222 *arms*. With a pun on coat of arms.

225 *A herald . . . books*. In the herald's books were
the names of those who bore coats-of-arms.

226 *crest*. The device upon a coat-of-arms. *coxcomb*. A
fool's cap.

228 *craven*. A cock that will not fight.

230 *crab*. Crab apple.

258 *halt*. Limp.

259 *and whom . . . command*. i.e. your servants.

260 *Dian*. Diana, goddess of the moon and chastity,
and hunting.

268 *keep you warm*. Take care of yourself.

Pet.   Who knows not where a wasp does wear
his sting? In his tail.
Kath.   In his tongue.
Pet.   Whose tongue?
Kath.   Yours, if you talk of tails: and so fare-
well.
Pet.   What, with my tongue in your tail? nay,
come again,
Good Kate; I am a gentleman.
Kath.   That I'll try. [*She strikes him.* 220
Pet.   I swear I'll cuff you, if you strike again.
• *Kath.*   So may you lose your arms:
If you strike me, you are no gentleman;
And if no gentleman, why then no arms.
• *Pet.*   A herald, Kate? O, put me in thy
books!
• *Kath.*   What is your crest? a coxcomb?
Pet.   A combless cock, so Kate will be my
hen.
• *Kath.*   No cock of mine; you crow too like a
craven.
Pet.   Nay, come, Kate, come; you must not
look so sour.
• *Kath.*   It is my fashion, when I see a crab. 230
Pet.   Why, here's no crab; and therefore
look not sour.
Kath.   There is, there is.
Pet.   Then show it me.
Kath.   Had I a glass, I would.
Pet.   What, you mean my face?
Kath.   Well aim'd of such a young one.
Pet.   Now, by Saint George, I am too young
for you.
Kath.   Yet you are wither'd.
Pet.   'Tis with cares.   240
Kath.   I care not.
Pet.   Nay, hear you, Kate: in sooth you scape
not so.
Kath.   I chafe you, if I tarry: let me go.
Pet.   No, not a whit: I find you passing gentle.
'Twas told me you were rough and coy and
sullen,
And now I find report a very liar;
For thou art pleasant, gamesome, passing cour-
teous,
But slow in speech, yet sweet as spring-time
flowers:
Thou canst not frown, thou canst not look askance,
Nor bite the lip, as angry wenches will,   250
Nor hast thou pleasure to be cross in talk,
But thou with mildness entertain'st thy wooers,
With gentle conference, soft and affable.
Why does the world report that Kate doth limp?
O slanderous world! Kate like the hazel-twig
Is straight and slender and as brown in hue
As hazel nuts and sweeter than the kernels.
• O, let me see thee walk: thou dost not halt.
• *Kath.*   Go, fool, and whom thou keep'st com-
mand.
Pet.   Did ever Dian so become a grove   260
As Kate this chamber with her princely gait?
O, be thou Dian, and let her be Kate;
And then let Kate be chaste and Dian sportful!
Kath.   Where did you study all this goodly
speech?
Pet.   It is extempore, from my mother-wit.
Kath.   A witty mother! witless else her son.
Pet.   Am I not wise?
• *Kath.*   Yes; keep you warm.

Pet. Marry, so I mean, sweet Katharine, in
  thy bed:
And therefore, setting all this chat aside,   270
Thus in plain terms: your father hath consented
That you shall be my wife; your dowry 'greed
  on;
And, will you, nill you, I will marry you.
• Now, Kate, I am a husband for your turn;
For, by this light, whereby I see thy beauty,
Thy beauty, that doth make me like thee well,
Thou must be married to no man but me;
For I am he am born to tame you Kate,
• And bring you from a wild Kate to a Kate
Conformable as other household Kates.   280
Here comes your father: never make denial;
I must and will have Katharine to my wife.

  Re-enter BAPTISTA, GREMIO, *and* TRANIO.

Bap. Now, Signior Petruchio, how speed you
  with my daughter?
Pet. How but well, sir? how but well?
It were impossible I should speed amiss.
  Bap. Why, how now, daughter Katharine!
  in your dumps?
  Kath. Call you me daughter? now, I promise
  you
You have show'd a tender fatherly regard,
To wish me wed to one half lunatic;
A mad-cap ruffian and a swearing Jack,   290
That thinks with oaths to face the matter out.
  Pet. Father, 'tis thus: yourself and all the
  world,
That talk'd of her, have talk'd amiss of her:
• If she be curst, it is for policy,
For she's not froward, but modest as the dove;
She is not hot, but temperate as the morn;
• For patience she will prove a second Grissel,
• And Roman Lucrece for her chastity:
And to conclude, we have 'greed so well together,
That upon Sunday is the wedding-day.   300
  Kath. I'll see thee hang'd on Sunday first.
  Gre. Hark, Petruchio; she says she'll see
  thee hang'd first.
• *Tra.* Is this your speeding? nay, then, good
  night our part!
  Pet. Be patient, gentlemen; I choose her for
  myself:
If she and I be pleased, what's that to you?
'Tis bargain'd 'twixt us twain, being alone,
That she shall still be curst in company.
I tell you, 'tis incredible to believe
How much she loves me: O, the kindest Kate!
She hung about my neck; and kiss on kiss   310
She vied so fast, protesting oath on oath,
That in a twink she won me to her love.
O, you are novices! 'tis a world to see,
How tame, when men and women are alone,
• A meacock wretch can make the curstest shrew.
Give me thy hand, Kate: I will unto Venice,
To buy apparel 'gainst the wedding-day.
Provide the feast, father, and bid the guests;
• I will be sure my Katharine shall be fine.
  Bap. I know not what to say: but give me
  your hands;   320
God send you joy, Petruchio! 'tis a match.
  Gre. Tra. Amen, say we: we will be wit-
  nesses.
  Pet. Father, and wife, and gentlemen, adieu;

274 *for your turn.* To suit you.

279 *wild Kate.* A play on wild cat.

294 *policy.* Tactics.

297 *Grissel.* Patient Griselda was the heroine of
Chaucer's *Clerk's Tale.*

Griselda gives up her daughter. Woodcut by Edward
Burne-Jones from *The Works of Geoffrey Chaucer,*
Kelmscott Press, 1896

298 *Lucrece.* A Roman matron who was the symbol of
chastity; rather than live dishonoured, she killed herself.
c.f. Shakespeare's *The Rape of Lucrece.*

303 *speeding.* Success.

315 *meacock.* Timid.

319 *fine.* Dressed.

329 *mart.* Bargain.

330 *fretting.* A pun on 'decaying' and 'chafing'.

341 *Skipper.* Flighty youth.

344 *he of both.* Whichever of the two.

353 *arras counterpoints.* Counterpanes worked in tapestry.

372 *jointure.* Settlement in the event of widowhood.

376 *argosy.* Rich merchant vessel.

Gremio: '. . . an argosy That now is lying in Marseilles' road'. Engraving from Charles Knight's *Pictorial Edition of the Works of William Shakspere,* 1939–43

377 *road.* Harbour.

380 *galliases.* Large sailing galleys.

I will to Venice; Sunday comes apace:
We will have rings and things and fine array;
And kiss me, Kate, we will be married o' Sunday.
[*Exeunt Petruchio and Katharina severally.*
 Gre. Was ever match clapp'd up so suddenly?
 Bap. Faith, gentlemen, now I play a merchant's part,
And venture madly on a desperate mart.
 Tra. 'Twas a commodity lay fretting by you:
'Twill bring you gain, or perish on the seas. 331
 Bap. The gain I seek is, quiet in the match.
 Gre. No doubt but he hath got a quiet catch.
But now, Baptista, to your younger daughter:
Now is the day we long have looked for:
I am your neighbour, and was suitor first.
 Tra. And I am one that love Bianca more
Than words can witness, or your thoughts can
  guess.
 Gre. Youngling, thou canst not love so dear
  as I.
 Tra. Greybeard, thy love doth freeze.
 Gre.   But thine doth fry. 340
Skipper, stand back: 'tis age that nourisheth.
 Tra. But youth in ladies' eyes that flourisheth.
 Bap. Content you, gentlemen: I will compound this strife:
'Tis deeds must win the prize; and he of both
That can assure my daughter greatest dower
Shall have my Bianca's love.
Say, Signior Gremio, what can you assure her?
 Gre. First, as you know, my house within the
  city
Is richly furnished with plate and gold;
Basins and ewers to lave her dainty hands; 350
My hangings all of Tyrian tapestry;
In ivory coffers I have stuff'd my crowns;
In cypress chests my arras counterpoints,
Costly apparel, tents, and canopies,
Fine linen, Turkey cushions boss'd with pearl,
Valance of Venice gold in needlework,
Pewter and brass and all things that belong
To house or housekeeping: then, at my farm
I have a hundred milch-kine to the pail,
Sixscore fat oxen standing in my stalls, 360
And all things answerable to this portion.
Myself am struck in years, I must confess;
And if I die to-morrow, this is hers,
If whilst I live she will be only mine.
 Tra. That 'only' came well in. Sir, list to me:
I am my father's heir and only son:
If I may have your daughter to my wife,
I'll leave her houses three or four as good,
Within rich Pisa walls, as any one
Old Signior Gremio has in Padua; 370
Besides two thousand ducats by the year
Of fruitful land, all which shall be her jointure.
What, have I pinch'd you, Signior Gremio?
 Gre. Two thousand ducats by the year of land!
My land amounts not to so much in all:
That she shall have; besides an argosy
That now is lying in Marseilles' road.
What, have I choked you with an argosy?
 Tra. Gremio, 'tis known my father hath no less
Than three great argosies; besides two galliases,
And twelve tight galleys: these I will assure her,
And twice as much, whate'er thou offer'st next.
 Gre. Nay, I have offer'd all, I have no more;
And she can have no more than all I have:
If you like me, she shall have me and mine.

Tra. Why, then the maid is mine from all the
world,
By your firm promise : Gremio is out-vied.
   Bap. I must confess your offer is the best ;
● And, let your father make her the assurance,
She is your own ; else, you must pardon me, 390
If you should die before him, where's her dower?
   Tra. That's but a cavil : he is old, I young.
   Gre. And may not young men die, as well as
old ?
   Bap. Well, gentlemen,
I am thus resolved : on Sunday next you know
My daughter Katharine is to be married :
Now, on the Sunday following, shall Bianca
Be bride to you, if you make this assurance ;
If not, to Signior Gremio :
And so, I take my leave, and thank you both.
   Gre. Adieu, good neighbour. [*Exit Baptista.*
            Now I fear thee not : 401
Sirrah young gamester, your father were a fool
To give thee all, and in his waning age
● Set foot under thy table : tut, a toy !
An old Italian fox is not so kind, my boy. [*Exit.*
   Tra. A vengeance on your crafty wither'd hide !
● Yet I have faced it with a card of ten.
'Tis in my head to do my master good :
I see no reason but supposed Lucentio
● Must get a father, call'd ' supposed Vincentio ;'
And that's a wonder : fathers commonly   411
Do get their children ; but in this case of wooing,
A child shall get a sire, if I fail not of my cun-
    ning.   [*Exit.*

ACT III.

SCENE I. *Padua.* BAPTISTA'S *house.*

Enter LUCENTIO, HORTENSIO, *and* BIANCA.

   Luc. Fiddler, forbear ; you grow too forward,
    sir :
Have you so soon forgot the entertainment
Her sister Katharine welcomed you withal ?
   Hor. But, wrangling pedant, this is
The patroness of heavenly harmony :
Then give me leave to have prerogative ;
And when in music we have spent an hour,
Your lecture shall have leisure for as much.
●   *Luc.* Preposterous ass, that never read so far
To know the cause why music was ordain'd ! 10
Was it not to refresh the mind of man
After his studies or his usual pain?
Then give me leave to read philosophy,
And while I pause, serve in your harmony.
   Hor. Sirrah, I will not bear these braves of
    thine.
   Bian. Why, gentlemen, you do me double
    wrong,
To strive for that which resteth in my choice :
● I am no breeching scholar in the schools ;
I'll not be tied to hours nor 'pointed times,
But learn my lessons as I please myself.   20
And, to cut off all strife, here sit we down :
Take you your instrument, play you the whiles ;
His lecture will be done ere you have tuned.
   Hor. You'll leave his lecture when I am in
    tune ?
   Luc. That will be never : tune your instrument.
   Bian. Where left we last ?

389 *assurance.* Guarantee.

404 *Set foot under thy table.* Become your dependent.
toy. A joke.

407 *faced it with a card of ten.* Successful bluffing.

410 *get.* Beget.

9 *Preposterous.* Literally, putting those things first
which should come later.

18 *breeching scholar.* Schoolboy liable for whipping.

Costume design for Bianca by Rosemary Vercoe, Stratford-upon-Avon, 1948

28-29 '*Hic ibat . . . senis*'. 'Here flowed the Simois; here is the Sigeian land; here had stood the towering palace of Priam'.

36 *bearing my port.* Behaving as I would.

37 *pantaloon.* A stock character in Italian comedy: an old man in baggy pants.

PANTALON
De la Comédie Italienne, qui joue dans
Arlequin Enfant, Perroquet, Statue.

Pantalon. Engraving from Claude Gillot (1673–1722)

50 *Pedascule.* Shakespeare has coined this diminutive of 'pedant'.

52-53 *Æacides Was Ajax.* Ajax, the Greek warrior, was also known as Aecus, after his grandfather.

67 *gamut.* The scale.

73 *accord.* Agreement.

80 *nice.* Precise.

Luc.   Here, madam:
  ' Hic ibat Simois; hic est Sigeia tellus;
     Hic steterat Priami regia celsa senis.'
Bian.   Construe them.   30
Luc. 'Hic ibat,' as I told you before, 'Simois,'
I am Lucentio, 'hic est,' son unto Vincentio of Pisa, 'Sigeia tellus,' disguised thus to get your love; 'Hic steterat,' and that Lucentio that comes a-wooing, 'Priami,' is my man Tranio, 'regia,' bearing my port, 'celsa senis,' that we might beguile the old pantaloon.
Hor.   Madam, my instrument's in tune.
Bian.   Let's hear.   O fie ! the treble jars.
Luc. Spit in the hole, man, and tune again.   40
Bian.   Now let me see if I can construe it:
'Hic ibat Simois,' I know you not, 'hic est Sigeia tellus,' I trust you not; 'Hic steterat Priami,' take heed he hear us not, 'regia,' presume not, 'celsa senis,' despair not.
Hor.   Madam, 'tis now in tune.
Luc.   All but the base.
Hor.   The base is right; 'tis the base knave that jars.
[*Aside*] How fiery and forward our pedant is !
Now, for my life, the knave doth court my love:
Pedascule, I 'll watch you better yet.   50
Bian.   In time I may believe, yet I mistrust.
Luc. Mistrust it not; for, sure, Æacides
Was Ajax, call'd so from his grandfather.
Bian.   I must believe my master; else, I promise you,
I should be arguing still upon that doubt:
But let it rest.   Now, Licio, to you:
Good masters, take it not unkindly, pray,
That I have been thus pleasant with you both.
Hor.   You may go walk, and give me leave a while:
My lessons make no music in three parts.   60
Luc. Are you so formal, sir ? well, I must wait,
[*Aside*] And watch withal; for, but I be deceived,
Our fine musician groweth amorous.
Hor.   Madam, before you touch the instrument,
To learn the order of my fingering,
I must begin with rudiments of art;
To teach you gamut in a briefer sort,
More pleasant, pithy and effectual,
Than hath been taught by any of my trade:
And there it is in writing, fairly drawn.   70
Bian.   Why, I am past my gamut long ago.
Hor.   Yet read the gamut of Hortensio.
Bian. [*Reads*] "'Gamut' I am, the ground of all accord,
     'A re,' to plead Hortensio's passion;
     'B mi,' Bianca, take him for thy lord,
        'C fa ut,' that loves with all affection:
     'D sol re,' one clef, two notes have I :
     'E la mi,' show pity, or I die."
Call you this gamut? tut, I like it not:
Old fashions please me best; I am not so nice,   80
To change true rules for old inventions.

Enter a Servant.

Serv.   Mistress, your father prays you leave your books
And help to dress your sister's chamber up:
You know to-morrow is the wedding-day.
Bian.   Farewell, sweet masters both; I must be gone.   [*Exeunt Bianca and Servant.*

Luc. Faith, mistress, then I have no cause to
   stay.   [*Exit.*
Hor. But I have cause to pry into this pedant:
Methinks he looks as though he were in love:
Yet if thy thoughts, Bianca, be so humble
●To cast thy wandering eyes on every stale,   90
●Seize thee that list: if once I find thee ranging,
Hortensio will be quit with thee by changing.
                                         [*Exit.*

SCENE II. *Padua.* *Before* BAPTISTA'S *house.*

Enter BAPTISTA, GREMIO, TRANIO, KATHARINA,
  BIANCA, LUCENTIO, *and* others, attendants.

Bap. [*To Tranio*] Signior Lucentio, this is the
   'pointed day.
That Katharine and Petruchio should be married,
And yet we hear not of our son-in-law.
What will be said? what mockery will it be,
To want the bridegroom when the priest attends
To speak the ceremonial rites of marriage!
What says Lucentio to this shame of ours?
Kath. No shame but mine: I must, forsooth,
   be forced
To give my hand opposed against my heart
●Unto a mad-brain rudesby full of spleen;   10
Who woo'd in haste and means to wed at leisure.
I told you, I, he was a frantic fool,
Hiding his bitter jests in blunt behaviour:
And, to be noted for a merry man,
He'll woo a thousand, 'point the day of marriage,
Make feasts, invite friends, and proclaim the banns;
Yet never means to wed where he hath woo'd.
Now must the world point at poor Katharine,
And say, 'Lo, there is mad Petruchio's wife,
If it would please him come and marry her!'   20
Tra. Patience, good Katharine, and Baptista
   too.
Upon my life, Petruchio means but well,
Whatever fortune stays him from his word:
Though he be blunt, I know him passing wise;
Though he be merry, yet withal he's honest.
Kath. Would Katharine had never seen him
   though!
[*Exit weeping, followed by Bianca and others.*
Bap. Go, girl; I cannot blame thee now to weep;
For such an injury would vex a very saint,
Much more a shrew of thy impatient humour.

Enter BIONDELLO.

Bion. Master, master! news, old news, and
such news as you never heard of!   31
Bap. Is it new and old too? how may that be?
Bion. Why, is it not news, to hear of Petru-
chio's coming?
Bap. Is he come?
Bion. Why, no, sir.
Bap. What then?
Bion. He is coming.
Bap. When will he be here?
Bion. When he stands where I am and sees
you there.   41
Tra. But say, what to thine old news?
Bion. Why, Petruchio is coming in a new hat
●and an old jerkin, a pair of old breeches thrice
●turned, a pair of boots that have been candle-
cases, one buckled, another laced, an old rusty
sword ta'en out of the town-armoury, with a
●broken hilt, and chapeless; with **two broken**

90 *stale.* Bait.

91 *Seize thee that list.* Let anyone who wants you take
you. *ranging.* Straying.

10 *rudesby full of spleen.* A rude fellow full of whims.

44 *jerkin.* A short jacket.

45-46 *candle-cases.* Old boots used to keep candle ends
in.

48 *chapeless.* Lacking the metal plates on the scabbard.

F. R. Benson, the Edwardian actor, as Petruchio

49 *points*. Laces used to fasten the hose to the doublet.

51-57 *glanders . . . near-legged before*. Biondello lists various diseases and defects of the horse.

57-64 *half-checked bit . . . packthread*. A detailed description of the horse's harness, cobbled together haphazardly.

68 *kersey*. Coarse wool.

69 *list*. Strip of border cloth.

70 *pricked*. Pinned.

Baptista: 'Why, sir, you know this is your wedding day.' Baptista (Derek Smith) and Petruchio (Alan Bates), Royal Shakespeare Co, 1973

● points: his horse hipped with an old mothy saddle and stirrups of no kindred; besides, possessed
● with the glanders and like to mose in the chine; troubled with the lampass, infected with the fashions, full of windgalls, sped with spavins, rayed with the yellows, past cure of the fives, stark spoiled with the staggers, begnawn with the bots, swayed in the back and shoulder-shotten;
● near-legged before and with a half-checked bit and a head-stall of sheep's leather which, being restrained to keep him from stumbling, hath been often burst and now repaired with knots; one girth six times pieced and a woman's crupper of velure, which hath two letters for her name fairly set down in studs, and here and there pieced with packthread.

Bap. Who comes with him?

Bion. O, sir, his lackey, for all the world caparisoned like the horse; with a linen stock on
● one leg and a kersey boot-hose on the other,
● gartered with a red and blue list; an old hat
● and 'the humour of forty fancies' pricked in't for a feather: a monster, a very monster in apparel, and not like a Christian footboy or a gentleman's lackey.

Tra. 'Tis some odd humour pricks him to this fashion;
Yet oftentimes he goes but mean-apparell'd.

Bap. I am glad he's come, howsoe'er he comes.

Bion. Why, sir, he comes not.

Bap. Didst thou not say he comes?

Bion. Who? that Petruchio came?

Bap. Ay, that Petruchio came.   80

Bion. No, sir; I say his horse comes, with him on his back.

Bap. Why, that's all one.

Bion. Nay, by Saint Jamy,
    I hold you a penny,
    A horse and a man
    Is more than one,
    And yet not many.

Enter PETRUCHIO *and* GRUMIO.

Pet. Come, where be these gallants? who's at home?

Bap. You are welcome, sir.

Pet.   And yet I come not well.   90

Bap. And yet you halt not.

Tra.   Not so well apparell'd
As I wish you were.

Pet. Were it better, I should rush in thus.
But where is Kate? where is my lovely bride?
How does my father? Gentles, methinks you frown:
And wherefore gaze this goodly company,
As if they saw some wondrous monument,
Some comet or unusual prodigy?

Bap. Why, sir, you know this is your wedding-day:
First were we sad, fearing you would not come;
Now sadder, that you come so unprovided.   101
Fie, doff this habit, shame to your estate,
An eye-sore to our solemn festival!

Tra. And tell us, what occasion of import
Hath all so long detain'd you from your wife,
And sent you hither so unlike yourself?

Pet. Tedious it were to tell, and harsh to hear:

Sufficeth, I am come to keep my word,
Though in some part enforced to digress;
Which, at more leisure, I will so excuse   110
As you shall well be satisfied withal.
But where is Kate? I stay too long from her:
The morning wears, 'tis time we were at church.
   Tra.   See not your bride in these unreverent
    robes :
Go to my chamber; put on clothes of mine.
   Pet.   Not I, believe me: thus I'll visit her.
   Bap.   But thus, I trust, you will not marry her.
   Pet.   Good sooth, even thus; therefore ha'
    done with words:
To me she's married, not unto my clothes:
Could I repair what she will wear in me,   120
As I can change these poor accoutrements,
'Twere well for Kate and better for myself.
But what a fool am I to chat with you,
When I should bid good morrow to my bride,
And seal the title with a lovely kiss !
              [*Exeunt Petruchio and Grumio.*
   Tra.   He hath some meaning in his mad
    attire :
We will persuade him, be it possible,
To put on better ere he go to church.
   Bap.   I'll after him, and see the event of this.
    [*Exeunt Baptista, Gremio, and attendants.*
   Tra.   But to her love concerneth us to add
Her father's liking: which to bring to pass,   131
As I before imparted to your worship,
I am to get a man,—whate'er he be,
It skills not much, we'll fit him to our turn,—
And he shall be Vincentio of Pisa;
And make assurance here in Padua
Of greater sums than I have promised.
So shall you quietly enjoy your hope,
And marry sweet Bianca with consent.
   Luc.   Were it not that my fellow-schoolmaster
Doth watch Bianca's steps so narrowly,   141
'Twere good, methinks, to steal our marriage;
Which once perform'd, let all the world say no,
I'll keep mine own, despite of all the world.
   Tra.   That by degrees we mean to look into,
And watch our vantage in this business:
We'll over-reach the greybeard, Gremio,
The narrow-prying father, Minola,
The quaint musician, amorous Licio;
All for my master's sake, Lucentio.   150

       Re-enter GREMIO.

Signior Gremio, came you from the church?
   Gre.   As willingly as e'er I came from school.
   Tra.   And is the bride and bridegroom coming
    home?
   Gre.   A bridegroom say you? 'tis a groom
    indeed,
A grumbling groom, and that the girl shall find.
   Tra.   Curster than she? why, 'tis impossible.
   Gre.   Why, he's a devil, a devil, a very fiend.
   Tra.   Why, she's a devil, a devil, the devil's
    dam.
   Gre.   Tut, she's a lamb, a dove, a fool to him !
I'll tell you, Sir Lucentio: when the priest   160
Should ask, if Katharine should be his wife,
'Ay, by gogs-wouns,' quoth he; and swore so loud,
That, all-amazed, the priest let fall the book;
And, as he stoop'd again to take it up
This mad-brain'd bridegroom took him such a cuff
That down fell priest and book and book and priest:

118   *Good sooth.* In truth, yes.

120   *wear.* Wear out.

134   *skills.* Matters.

149   *quaint.* Cunning.

174 *muscadel.* A sweet wine.

207-208 *The oats have . . . horses.* Grumio gets it backwards.

213 *be jogging . . . green.* Get an early start.

215 *jolly.* Domineering.

216 *Take it on you.* Assert yourself.

Katherine: 'Gentlemen, forward to the bridal dinner.' Engraving from a painting by Francis Wheatley (1747–1801)

' Now take them up,' quoth he, ' if any list.'
  Tra. What said the wench when he rose again?
  Gre. Trembled and shook ; for why, he stamp'd and swore,
As if the vicar meant to cozen him.   **170**
But after many ceremonies done,
He calls for wine : ' A health !' quoth he, as if
He had been aboard, carousing to his mates
After a storm ; quaff'd off the muscadel
And threw the sops all in the sexton's face ;
Having no other reason
But that his beard grew thin and hungerly
And seem'd to ask him sops as he was drinking.
This done, he took the bride about the neck
And kiss'd her lips with such a clamorous smack
That at the parting all the church did echo : **181**
And I seeing this came thence for very shame ;
And after me, I know, the rout is coming.
Such a mad marriage never was before :
Hark, hark ! I hear the minstrels play. [*Music.*

Re-enter PETRUCHIO, KATHARINA, BIANCA, BAPTISTA, HORTENSIO, GRUMIO, *and Train.*

  Pet. Gentlemen and friends, I thank you for your pains :
I know you think to dine with me to-day,
And have prepared great store of wedding cheer ;
But so it is, my haste doth call me hence,
And therefore here I mean to take my leave. **190**
  Bap. Is't possible you will away to-night?
  Pet. I must away to-day, before night come :
Make it no wonder ; if you knew my business,
You would entreat me rather go than stay.
And, honest company, I thank you all,
That have beheld me give away myself
To this most patient, sweet and virtuous wife :
Dine with my father, drink a health to me ;
For I must hence ; and farewell to you all.
  Tra. Let us entreat you stay till after dinner.
  Pet. It may not be.
  Gre.   Let me entreat you.
  Pet. It cannot be.
  Kath.   Let me entreat you. **201**
  Pet. I am content.
  Kath.   Are you content to stay?
  Pet. I am content you shall entreat me stay ;
But yet not stay, entreat me how you can.
  Kath. Now, if you love me, stay.
  Pet.   Grumio, my horse.
  Gru. Ay, sir, they be ready : the oats have eaten the horses.
  Kath. Nay, then,
Do what thou canst, I will not go to-day ; **210**
No, nor to-morrow, not till I please myself.
The door is open, sir ; there lies your way ;
You may be jogging whiles your boots are green ;
For me, I'll not be gone till I please myself :
'Tis like you'll prove a jolly surly groom,
That take it on you at the first so roundly.
  Pet. O Kate, content thee ; prithee, be not angry.
  Kath. I will be angry : what hast thou to do?
Father, be quiet : he shall stay my leisure. **219**
  Gre. Ay, marry, sir, now it begins to work.
  Kath. Gentlemen, forward to the bridal dinner :
I see a woman may be made a fool,
If she had not a spirit to resist.
  Pet. They shall go forward, Kate, at thy command.

Obey the bride, you that attend on her;
● Go to the feast, revel and domineer,
Carouse full measure to her maidenhead,
Be mad and merry, or go hang yourselves:
But for my bonny Kate, she must with me.
● Nay, look not big, nor stamp, nor stare, nor fret;
I will be master of what is mine own: 231
● She is my goods, my chattels; she is my house,
My household stuff, my field, my barn,
My horse, my ox, my ass, my any thing;
And here she stands, touch her whoever dare;
I'll bring mine action on the proudest he
That stops my way in Padua.   Grumio,
Draw forth thy weapon, we are beset with thieves;
Rescue thy mistress, if thou be a man.
Fear not, sweet wench, they shall not touch thee,
    Kate: 240
I'll buckler thee against a million.

    [*Exeunt Petruchio, Katharina, and Grumio.*

Bap. Nay, let them go, a couple of quiet ones.
Gre. Went they not quickly, I should die
    with laughing.
Tra. Of all mad matches never was the like.
Luc. Mistress, what's your opinion of your
    sister?
Bian. That, being mad herself, she's madly
    mated.
● *Gre.* I warrant him, Petruchio is Kated.
Bap. Neighbours and friends, though bride
    and bridegroom wants
For to supply the places at the table,   249
You know there wants no junkets at the feast.
Lucentio, you shall supply the bridegroom's place;
And let Bianca take her sister's room.
Tra. Shall sweet Bianca practise how to bride
    it?
Bap. She shall, Lucentio. Come, gentlemen,
    let's go.   [*Exeunt.*

ACT IV.

Scene I. Petruchio's *country house.*

Enter Grumio.

Gru. Fie, fie on all tired jades, on all mad
masters, and all foul ways! Was ever man so
● beaten? was ever man so rayed? was ever man
so weary? I am sent before to make a fire, and
they are coming after to warm them. Now, were
● not I a little pot and soon hot, my very lips
might freeze to my teeth, my tongue to the roof
of my mouth, my heart in my belly, ere I should
come by a fire to thaw me: but I, with blowing
the fire, shall warm myself; for, considering the
weather, a taller man than I will take cold.
Holla, ho! Curtis.

Enter Curtis.

Curt. Who is that calls so coldly?
Gru. A piece of ice: if thou doubt it, thou
mayst slide from my shoulder to my heel with no
greater a run but my head and my neck. A fire,
good Curtis.
Curt. Is my master and his wife coming,
Grumio?
Gru. O, ay, Curtis, ay: and therefore fire,
● fire; cast on no water.   21
Curt. Is she so hot a shrew as she's reported?

226 *domineer.* Carouse.

230 *big.* Threatening.

232-234 *She is . . . any thing.* Petruchio echoes the tenth commandment.

Petruchio: 'Fear not, sweet wench . . .' Drawing by C. R. Ryley (1752–1798)

247 *Kated.* Caught the Kate disease.

3 *rayed.* Dirtied.

6 *a little pot and soon hot.* Small men have quick tempers.

21 *cast on no water.* Grumio reverses the last line of a famous round 'Scotland Burning'.

27 *three-inch fool.* Very short. *I am no beast.* Grumio has identified himself as a 'beast' and by association his fellow servant Curtis, who is objecting.

29 *horn.* i.e. of a cuckold.

39 *thy duty.* Thy due.

43 *'Jack, boy! ho!'.* The beginning of a well-known catch.

45 *cony-catching.* Cheating.

49-50 *fustian.* Coarse cloth.

51 *jacks.* i.e. 'men servants' and leather drinking vessels'.

52 *jills.* i.e. 'maids' and 'metal drinking cups'; the cups held a gill, or quarter-pint. *carpets.* Table covers.

Grumio quarrelling with Curtis. Engraving by Kenny Meadows from Barry Cornwall's *The Works of Shakspere*, 1846

66 *sensible.* i.e. 'rational' and 'capable of being felt'.

68 *Imprimis.* First.

77-78 *bemoiled.* Muddied.

Gru. She was, good Curtis, before this frost: but, thou knowest, winter tames man, woman and beast; for it hath tamed my old master and my new mistress and myself, fellow Curtis.

Curt. Away, you three-inch fool! I am no beast.

Gru. Am I but three inches? why, thy horn is a foot; and so long am I at the least. But wilt thou make a fire, or shall I complain on thee to our mistress, whose hand, she being now at hand, thou shalt soon feel, to thy cold comfort, for being slow in thy hot office?

Curt. I prithee, good Grumio, tell me, how goes the world?

Gru. A cold world, Curtis, in every office but thine; and therefore fire: do thy duty, and have thy duty; for my master and mistress are almost frozen to death.   40

Curt. There's fire ready; and therefore, good Grumio, the news.

Gru. Why, 'Jack, boy! ho! boy!' and as much news as will thaw.

Curt. Come, you are so full of cony-catching!

Gru. Why, therefore fire; for I have caught extreme cold. Where's the cook? is supper ready, the house trimmed, rushes strewed, cobwebs swept; the serving-men in their new fustian, their white stockings, and every officer his wedding-garment on? Be the jacks fair within, the jills fair without, the carpets laid, and every thing in order?

Curt. All ready; and therefore, I pray thee, news.

Gru. First, know, my horse is tired; my master and mistress fallen out.

Curt. How?

Gru. Out of their saddles into the dirt; and thereby hangs a tale.   60

Curt. Let's ha't, good Grumio.

Gru. Lend thine ear.

Curt. Here.

Gru. There.   [*Strikes him.*

Curt. This is to feel a tale, not to hear a tale.

Gru. And therefore 'tis called a sensible tale: and this cuff was but to knock at your ear, and beseech listening. Now I begin: Imprimis, we came down a foul hill, my master riding behind my mistress,—   70

Curt. Both of one horse?

Gru. What's that to thee?

Curt. Why, a horse.

Gru. Tell thou the tale: but hadst thou not crossed me, thou shouldst have heard how her horse fell and she under her horse; thou shouldst have heard in how miry a place, how she was bemoiled, how he left her with the horse upon her, how he beat me because her horse stumbled, how she waded through the dirt to pluck him off me, how he swore, how she prayed, that never prayed before, how I cried, how the horses ran away, how her bridle was burst, how I lost my crupper, with many things of worthy memory, which now shall die in oblivion and thou return unexperienced to thy grave.

Curt. By this reckoning he is more shrew than she.

Gru. Ay; and that thou and the proudest of you all shall find when he comes home. But what talk I of this? Call forth Nathaniel, Joseph,

Nicholas, Philip, Walter, Sugarsop and the rest:
• let their heads be sleekly combed, their blue
coats brushed and their garters of an indifferent
knit: let them curtsy with their left legs and not
presume to touch a hair of my master's horse-
tail till they kiss their hands. Are they all ready?
   Curt. They are.
   Gru. Call them forth.
   Curt. Do you hear, ho? you must meet my
• master to countenance my mistress.   101
   Gru. Why, she hath a face of her own.
   Curt. Who knows not that?
   Gru. Thou, it seems, that calls for company
to countenance her.
   Curt. I call them forth to credit her.
   Gru. Why, she comes to borrow nothing of
them.

     Enter four or five Serving-men.

   Nath. Welcome home, Grumio!
   Phil. How now, Grumio!   110
   Jos. What, Grumio!
   Nich. Fellow Grumio!
   Nath. How now, old lad?
   Gru. Welcome, you;—how now, you;—what,
you;—fellow, you;—and thus much for greeting.
Now, my spruce companions, is all ready, and
all things neat?
   Nath. All things is ready. How near is our
master?   119
   Gru. E'en at hand, alighted by this; and
• therefore be not— Cock's passion, silence! I hear
my master.

     Enter PETRUCHIO *and* KATHARINA.

   Pet. Where be these knaves? What, no man
     at door
To hold my stirrup nor to take my horse!
Where is Nathaniel, Gregory, Philip?
   All Serv. Here, here, sir; here, sir.
   Pet. Here, sir! here, sir! here, sir! here, sir!
You logger-headed and unpolish'd grooms!
What, no attendance? no regard? no duty?
Where is the foolish knave I sent before?   130
   Gru. Here, sir; as foolish as I was before.
•   *Pet.* You peasant swain! you whoreson malt-
     horse drudge!
Did I not bid thee meet me in the park,
And bring along these rascal knaves with thee?
   Gru. Nathaniel's coat, sir, was not fully made,
• And Gabriel's pumps were all unpink'd i' the
     heel;
• There was no link to colour Peter's hat,
And Walter's dagger was not come from sheath-
     ing:
There were none fine but Adam, Ralph, and
     Gregory;
The rest were ragged, old, and beggarly;   140
Yet, as they are, here are they come to meet you.
   Pet. Go, rascals, go, and fetch my supper in.
           [*Exeunt Servants.*
[*Singing*] Where is the life that late I led—
Where are those—Sit down, Kate, and welcome.—
• Soud, soud, soud, soud!

     Re-enter Servants *with supper.*

Why, when, I say? Nay, good sweet Kate, be
     merry.

93 *blue.* The usual colour of servants' dress.

101 *countenance.* Honour.

121 *Cock's passion.* God's Passion.

Petruchio: 'Where be these knaves?' Engraving by
F. Hayman from Hanmer's *Works of Shakespeare,* 1744

132 *malt-horse drudge.* A brewer's horse on a treadmill
used to grind malt.

136 *unpink'd.* Undecorated by patterns punched in the
leather.

137 *link.* A burnt torch which provided blacking.

145 *Soud.* Most editors emend to 'Food'.

160 *beetle-headed.* Blockhead; a beetle was a mallet.

161 *have a stomach.* Are hungry, but also have a temper.

168 *trenchers.* Wooden platters.

Petruchio: 'There, take it to you, trenchers, cups and all.' Frontispiece to Rowe's edition of 1709

170 *I'll be with you straight.* I'll be even with you immediately.

175 *it engenders choler.* Roast meat was said to cause anger.

180 *for company.* Together.

Off with my boots, you rogues! you villains, when?
[*Sings*] It was the friar of orders grey,
        As he forth walked on his way:—
Out, you rogue! you pluck my foot awry: 150
Take that, and mend the plucking off the other.
                                    [*Strikes him.*
Be merry, Kate.   Some water, here; what, ho!
Where's my spaniel Troilus?   Sirrah, get you hence,
And bid my cousin Ferdinand come hither:
One, Kate, that you must kiss, and be acquainted with.
Where are my slippers?   Shall I have some water?

                    Enter one with water.

Come, Kate, and wash, and welcome heartily.
You whoreson villain! will you let it fall?
                                    [*Strikes him.*
   Kath.   Patience, I pray you; 'twas a fault unwilling.
   Pet.   A whoreson beetle-headed, flap-ear'd knave!   160
Come, Kate, sit down; I know you have a stomach.
Will you give thanks, sweet Kate; or else shall I?
What's this? mutton?
   First Serv.   Ay.
   Pet.   Who brought it?
   Peter.   I.
   Pet.   'Tis burnt; and so is all the meat.
What dogs are these!   Where is the rascal cook?
How durst you, villains, bring it from the dresser,
And serve it thus to me that love it not?
There, take it to you, trenchers, cups, and all:
        [*Throws the meat, &c. about the stage.*
You heedless joltheads and unmanner'd slaves!
What, do you grumble?   I'll be with you straight.
   Kath.   I pray you, husband, be not so disquiet: 171
The meat was well, if you were so contented.
   Pet.   I tell thee, Kate, 'twas burnt and dried away;
And I expressly am forbid to touch it,
For it engenders choler, planteth anger;
And better 'twere that both of us did fast,
Since, of ourselves, ourselves are choleric,
Than feed it with such over-roasted flesh.
Be patient; to-morrow 't shall be mended,
And, for this night, we'll fast for company: 180
Come, I will bring thee to thy bridal chamber.
                                    [*Exeunt.*

            Re-enter Servants *severally.*

   Nath.   Peter, didst ever see the like?
   Peter.   He kills her in her own humour.

                Re-enter CURTIS.

   Gru.   Where is he?
   Curt.   In her chamber, making a sermon of continency to her;
And rails, and swears, and rates, that she, poor soul,
Knows not which way to stand, to look, to speak,
And sits as one new-risen from a dream.   189
Away, away! for he is coming hither. [*Exeunt.*

Re-enter PETRUCHIO.

Pet. Thus have I politicly begun my reign,
And 'tis my hope to end successfully.
• My falcon now is sharp and passing empty;
• And till she stoop she must not be full-gorged,
• For then she never looks upon her lure.
• Another way I have to man my haggard,
To make her come and know her keeper's call,
• That is, to watch her, as we watch these kites
• That bate and beat and will not be obedient.
She eat no meat to-day, nor none shall eat;   200
Last night she slept not, nor to-night she shall
   not;
As with the meat, some undeserved fault
I'll find about the making of the bed;
And here I'll fling the pillow, there the bolster,
This way the coverlet, another way the sheets:
Ay, and amid this hurly I intend
That all is done in reverend care of her;
And in conclusion she shall watch all night:
And if she chance to nod I'll rail and brawl
And with the clamour keep her still awake.   210
This is a way to kill a wife with kindness;
And thus I'll curb her mad and headstrong
   humour.
He that knows better how to tame a shrew,
Now let him speak: 'tis charity to show. [*Exit.*

SCENE II. *Padua.* *Before* BAPTISTA'S *house.*

Enter TRANIO *and* HORTENSIO.

Tra. Is't possible, friend Licio, that Mistress
   Bianca
Doth fancy any other but Lucentio?
I tell you, sir, she bears me fair in hand.
Hor. Sir, to satisfy you in what I have said,
Stand by and mark the manner of his teaching.

Enter BIANCA *and* LUCENTIO.

Luc. Now, mistress, profit you in what you
   read?
Bian. What, master, read you? first resolve
   me that.
• *Luc.* I read that I profess, the Art to Love.
Bian. And may you prove, sir, master of your
   art!
Luc. While you, sweet dear, prove mistress
   of my heart!   10
Hor. Quick proceeders, marry! Now, tell
   me, I pray,
You that durst swear that your mistress Bianca
Loved none in the world so well as Lucentio.
Tra. O despiteful love! unconstant woman-
   kind!
I tell thee, Licio, this is wonderful.
Hor. Mistake no more: I am not Licio,
Nor a musician, as I seem to be;
But one that scorn to live in this disguise,
For such a one as leaves a gentleman,
• And makes a god of such a cullion: 20
Know, sir, that I am call'd Hortensio.
Tra. Signior Hortensio, I have often heard
Of your entire affection to Bianca;
And since mine eyes are witness of her lightness,
I will with you, if you be so contented,
Forswear Bianca and her love for ever.
Hor. See, how they kiss and court! Signior
   Lucentio.

King James I hawking. Engraving from Charles Knight's
Pictorial Edition of the Works of William Shakspere,
1839–43

193 *sharp.* Hungry.

194 *stoop.* Fly to the quarry.

195 *lure.* A device usually of feathers and meat on a
string to recall a hawk.

196 *man my haggard.* Tame my wild hawk.

198 *watch her.* Keep her awake.

199 *bate and beat.* Flap and flutter in an effort to escape.

8 *Art to love.* Ovid's *Ars Amatoria.*

Lucentio: 'I read that I profess, the Art to Love.'
Lucentio (Anthony Higgins) and Bianca (Zoe Wana-
maker), Royal Shakespeare Co, 1978

20 *cullion.* Low fellow.

34 *beastly*. Lasciviously.

35 *Would all . . . forsworn*. Would that she had only the one suitor.

57 *tricks . . . long*. Many tricks, with a reference to the card game 'thirty one'.

61 *An ancient angel*. A man of the good old stamp.

63 *mercatante*. Merchant.

Here is my hand, and here I firmly vow
Never to woo her more, but do forswear her,
As one unworthy all the former favours   30
That I have fondly flatter'd her withal.
   Tra.   And here I take the like unfeigned oath,
Never to marry with her though she would en-
   treat:
● Fie on her! see, how beastly she doth court him!
● *Hor.*   Would all the world but he had quite
   forsworn!
For me, that I may surely keep mine oath,
I will be married to a wealthy widow,
Ere three days pass, which hath as long loved me
As I have loved this proud disdainful haggard.
And so farewell, Signior Lucentio.   40
Kindness in women, not their beauteous looks,
Shall win my love: and so I take my leave,
In resolution as I swore before.   [*Exit.*
   Tra.   Mistress Bianca, bless you with such
   grace
As 'longeth to a lover's blessed case!
Nay, I have ta'en you napping, gentle love,
And have forsworn you with Hortensio.
   Bian.   Tranio, you jest: but have you both
   forsworn me?
   Tra.   Mistress, we have.
   Luc.   Then we are rid of Licio.
   Tra.   I' faith, he'll have a lusty widow now,
That shall be woo'd and wedded in a day.   51
   Bian.   God give him joy!
   Tra.   Ay, and he'll tame her.
   Bian.   He says so, Tranio.
   Tra.   Faith, he is gone unto the taming-school.
   Bian.   The taming-school! what, is there such
   a place?
   Tra.   Ay, mistress, and Petruchio is the master;
● That teacheth tricks eleven and twenty long,
To tame a shrew and charm her chattering
   tongue.

Enter BIONDELLO.

   Bion.   O master, master, I have watch'd so
   long
That I am dog-weary: but at last I spied   60
●†An ancient angel coming down the hill,
Will serve the turn.
   Tra.   What is he, Biondello?
● *Bion.*   Master, a mercatante, or a pedant,
I know not what; but formal in apparel,
In gait and countenance surely like a father.
   Luc.   And what of him, Tranio?
   Tra.   If he be credulous and trust my tale,
I'll make him glad to seem Vincentio,
And give assurance to Baptista Minola,
As if he were the right Vincentio.   70
Take in your love, and then let me alone.
       [*Exeunt Lucentio and Bianca.*

Enter a Pedant.

   Ped.   God save you, sir!
   Tra.   And you, sir! you are welcome.
Travel you far on, or are you at the farthest?
   Ped.   Sir, at the farthest for a week or two:
But then up farther, and as far as Rome;
And so to Tripoli, if God lend me life.
   Tra.   What countryman, I pray?
   Ped.   Of Mantua.
   Tra.   Of Mantua, sir? marry, God forbid!
And come to Padua, careless of your life?

Ped.   My life, sir! how, I pray? for that goes
    hard.   80
    Tra.   'Tis death for any one in Mantua
To come to Padua.   Know you not the cause?
Your ships are stay'd at Venice, and the duke,
For private quarrel 'twixt your duke and him,
Hath publish'd and proclaim'd it openly:
'Tis marvel, but that you are but newly come,
You might have heard it else proclaim'd about.
    Ped.   Alas! sir, it is worse for me than so;
For I have bills for money by exchange
From Florence and must here deliver them.   90
    Tra.   Well, sir, to do you courtesy,
This will I do, and this I will advise you:
First, tell me, have you ever been at Pisa?
    Ped.   Ay, sir, in Pisa have I often been,
Pisa renowned for grave citizens.
    Tra.   Among them know you one Vincentio?
    Ped.   I know him not, but I have heard of him;
A merchant of incomparable wealth.
    Tra.   He is my father, sir; and, sooth to say,
In countenance somewhat doth resemble you.   100
    Bion.   [*Aside*] As much as an apple doth an
    oyster, and all one.
    Tra.   To save your life in this extremity,
This favour will I do you for his sake;
And think it not the worst of all your fortunes
That you are like to Sir Vincentio.
His name and credit shall you undertake,
And in my house you shall be friendly lodged:
Look that you take upon you as you should;
You understand me, sir: so shall you stay
Till you have done your business in the city: 110
If this be courtesy, sir, accept of it.
    Ped.   O sir, I do; and will repute you ever
The patron of my life and liberty.
    Tra.   Then go with me to make the matter
    good.
This, by the way, I let you understand;
My father is here look'd for every day,
To pass assurance of a dower in marriage
'Twixt me and one Baptista's daughter here:
In all these circumstances I'll instruct you:
Go with me to clothe you as becomes you.   120
                       [*Exeunt.*

SCENE III.   *A room in* PETRUCHIO'S *house.*

Enter KATHARINA *and* GRUMIO.

    Gru.   No, no, forsooth; I dare not for my life.
    Kath.   The more my wrong, the more his
    spite appears:
What, did he marry me to famish me?
Beggars, that come unto my father's door,
Upon entreaty have a present alms;
If not, elsewhere they meet with charity:
But I, who never knew how to entreat,
Nor never needed that I should entreat,
Am starved for meat, giddy for lack of sleep,
With oaths kept waking and with brawling fed: 10
And that which spites me more than all these wants,
He does it under name of perfect love;
As who should say, if I should sleep or eat,
'Twere deadly sickness or else present death.
I prithee go and get me some repast;
I care not what, so it be wholesome food.
    Gru.   What say you to a neat's foot?
    Kath.   'Tis passing good: I prithee let me
    have it.

80 *goes hard.* This is serious.

101 *and all one.* Absolutely the same.

108 *take upon you.* Play your part.

Set design of Petruchio's house by Vivienne Kernot,
Stratford-upon-Avon, 1954

2 *The more my wrong.* The greater the wrong done to
me.

13 *As who should say.* As if to say.

17 *neat's.* Ox's.

19 *choleric*. Engendering anger.

32 *very name*. The mere name.

36 *amort*. Dejected.

43 *sorted to no proof*. Futile.

56 *fardingales*. Hooped skirts or petticoats.

Petruchio: 'With ruffs and cuffs and fardingales and things;' Woodcut of the clothes conscious Queen Elizabeth from Phillip Stubbs' *Anatomy of Abuses*, 1583

64 *porringer*. Small dish.

65 *lewd and filthy*. Vile and nasty.

66 *cockle*. i.e. cockle shell.

69 *fit the time*. Is fashionable.

Gru. I fear it is too choleric a meat.
How say you to a fat tripe finely broil'd?   20
 Kath. I like it well: good Grumio, fetch it me.
 Gru. I cannot tell; I fear 'tis choleric.
What say you to a piece of beef and mustard?
 Kath. A dish that I do love to feed upon.
 Gru. Ay, but the mustard is too hot a little.
 Kath. Why then, the beef, and let the mustard
   rest.
 Gru. Nay then, I will not: you shall have the
   mustard,
Or else you get no beef of Grumio.
 Kath. Then both, or one, or any thing thou wilt.
 Gru. Why then, the mustard without the beef.
 Kath. Go, get thee gone, thou false deluding
   slave,   [*Beats him.*
That feed'st me with the very name of meat:
Sorrow on thee and all the pack of you,
That triumph thus upon my misery!
Go, get thee gone, I say.

Enter PETRUCHIO *and* HORTENSIO *with meat.*

Pet. How fares my Kate? What, sweeting,
   all amort?
 Hor. Mistress, what cheer?
 Kath.   Faith, as cold as can be.
 Pet. Pluck up thy spirits; look cheerfully upon
   me.
Here, love; thou see'st how diligent I am
To dress thy meat myself and bring it thee: 40
I am sure, sweet Kate, this kindness merits thanks.
What, not a word? Nay, then thou lovest it not;
And all my pains is sorted to no proof.
Here, take away this dish.
 Kath.   I pray you, let it stand.
 Pet. The poorest service is repaid with thanks;
And so shall mine, before you touch the meat.
 Kath. I thank you, sir.
 Hor. Signior Petruchio, fie! you are to blame.
Come, Mistress Kate, I'll bear you company.
 Pet. [*Aside*] Eat it up all, Hortensio, if thou
   lovest me.   50
Much good do it unto thy gentle heart!
Kate, eat apace: and now, my honey love,
Will we return unto thy father's house
And revel it as bravely as the best,
With silken coats and caps and golden rings,
With ruffs and cuffs and fardingales and things;
With scarfs and fans and double change of bravery,
With amber bracelets, beads and all this knavery.
What, hast thou dined? The tailor stays thy
   leisure,
To deck thy body with his ruffling treasure.   60

Enter Tailor.

Come, tailor, let us see these ornaments;
Lay forth the gown.

Enter Haberdasher.

                      What news with you, sir?
 Hab. Here is the cap your worship did bespeak.
 Pet. Why, this was moulded on a porringer;
A velvet dish: fie, fie! 'tis lewd and filthy:
Why, 'tis a cockle or a walnut-shell,
A knack, a toy, a trick, a baby's cap:
Away with it! come, let me have a bigger.
 Kath. I'll have no bigger: this doth fit the time,
And gentlewomen wear such caps as these.   70
 Pet. When you are gentle, you shall have one too,

And not till then.

Hor. [*Aside*] That will not be in haste.

Kath. Why, sir, I trust I may have leave to speak;

And speak I will; I am no child, no babe:
Your betters have endured me say my mind,
And if you cannot, best you stop your ears.
My tongue will tell the anger of my heart,
Or else my heart concealing it will break,
And rather than it shall, I will be free
Even to the uttermost, as I please, in words.   80

Pet. Why, thou say'st true; it is a paltry cap,
● A custard-coffin, a bauble, a silken pie:
I love thee well, in that thou likest it not.

Kath. Love me or love me not, I like the cap;
And it I will have, or I will have none.

[*Exit Haberdasher.*

Pet. Thy gown? why, ay: come, tailor, let us see't.
● O mercy, God! what masquing stuff is here?
● What's this? a sleeve? 'tis like a demi-cannon:
What, up and down, carved like an apple-tart?
Here's snip and nip and cut and slish and slash,
● Like to a censer in a barber's shop: 91
Why, what, i' devil's name, tailor, call'st thou this?

Hor. [*Aside*] I see she's like to have neither cap nor gown.

Tai. You bid me make it orderly and well,
According to the fashion and the time.

Pet. Marry, and did; but if you be remember'd,
I did not bid you mar it to the time.
● Go, hop me over every kennel home,
For you shall hop without my custom, sir:
I'll none of it: hence! make your best of it.   100

Kath. I never saw a better-fashion'd gown,
● More quaint, more pleasing, nor more commendable:
Belike you mean to make a puppet of me.

Pet. Why, true; he means to make a puppet of thee.

Tai. She says your worship means to make a puppet of her.

Pet. O monstrous arrogance! Thou liest, thou thread, thou thimble,
● Thou yard, three-quarters, half-yard, quarter, nail!
● Thou flea, thou nit, thou winter-cricket thou!
Braved in mine own house with a skein of thread?
Away, thou rag, thou quantity, thou remnant;
● Or I shall so be-mete thee with thy yard
As thou shalt think on prating whilst thou livest!
I tell thee, I, that thou hast marr'd her gown.

Tai. Your worship is deceived; the gown is made
Just as my master had direction:
Grumio gave order how it should be done.

Gru. I gave him no order; I gave him the stuff.

Tai. But how did you desire it should be made?

Gru. Marry, sir, with needle and thread.   121

Tai. But did you not request to have it cut?
● *Gru.* Thou hast faced many things.

Tai. I have.
● *Gru.* Face not me: thou hast braved many men; brave not me; I will neither be faced nor braved. I say unto thee, I bid thy master cut out the gown; but I did not bid him cut it to pieces: ergo, thou liest.

Tai. Why, here is the note of the fashion to testify.   131

82 *Custard-coffin.* Custard crust.

87 *masquing.* Fit only for masques.

88 *demi-cannon.* A large cannon.

91 *censer.* Brazier for perfumes.

Tailors at work. Illustration from Comenius', *Orbis Sensualium Pictus*, 1689

98 *kennel.* Cutter.

102 *quaint.* Elegant.

109 *nail.* A measurement of cloth; two and a half inches.

110 *nit.* Louse's egg.

113 *be-mete.* Measure, with a pun on 'beat'.

123 *faced.* Meaning both 'defied' and 'trimmed'.

125 *braved.* Made fine clothes for, but also a pun on 'defied'.

138 *bottom*. Ball.

140 *compassed*. With a rounded edge.

142 *trunk sleeve*. Large puffed sleeve.

148 *prove upon thee*. Maintain by fighting.

150-151 *an I had . . . where*. If I had you in the right place.

153 *bill*. i.e. 'the note' and 'a weapon like a pike'. *mete-yard*. Yardstick.

Petruchio: 'Well, sir, in brief, the gown is not for me.'
Painting by C. R. Leslie (1794–1859)

182 *furniture*. Dress.

190 *dinner-time*. Mid-day.

194 *what*. Whatever.

Pet. Read it.
Gru. The note lies in's throat, if he say I said so.
Tai. [*Reads*] 'Imprimis, a loose-bodied gown:'
Gru. Master, if ever I said loose-bodied gown, sew me in the skirts of it, and beat me to death with a bottom of brown thread: I said a gown.
Pet. Proceed.
Tai. [*Reads*] 'With a small compassed cape:'
Gru. I confess the cape.   141
Tai. [*Reads*] 'With a trunk sleeve:'
Gru. I confess two sleeves.
Tai. [*Reads*] 'The sleeves curiously cut.'
Pet. Ay, there's the villany.
Gru. Error i' the bill, sir; error i the bill. I commanded the sleeves should be cut out and sewed up again; and that I'll prove upon thee, though thy little finger be armed in a thimble.
Tai. This is true that I say: an I had thee in place where, thou shouldst know it.   151
Gru. I am for thee straight: take thou the bill, give me thy mete-yard, and spare not me.
Hor. God-a-mercy, Grumio! then he shall have no odds.
Pet. Well, sir, in brief, the gown is not for me.
Gru. You are i' the right, sir: 'tis for my mistress.
Pet. Go, take it up unto thy master's use.
Gru. Villain, not for thy life: take up my mistress' gown for thy master's use!   161
Pet. Why, sir, what's your conceit in that?
Gru. O, sir, the conceit is deeper than you think for:
Take up my mistress' gown to his master's use!
O, fie, fie, fie!
Pet. [*Aside*] Hortensio, say thou wilt see the tailor paid.
Go take it hence; be gone, and say no more.
Hor. Tailor, I'll pay thee for thy gown to-morrow:
Take no unkindness of his hasty words:
Away! I say; commend me to thy master.   170
                                   [*Exit Tailor.*

Pet. Well, come, my Kate; we will unto your father's
Even in these honest mean habiliments:
Our purses shall be proud, our garments poor;
For 'tis the mind that makes the body rich;
And as the sun breaks through the darkest clouds,
So honour peereth in the meanest habit.
What is the jay more precious than the lark,
Because his feathers are more beautiful?
Or is the adder better than the eel,
Because his painted skin contents the eye?   180
O, no, good Kate; neither art thou the worse
For this poor furniture and mean array.
If thou account'st it shame, lay it on me;
And therefore frolic: we will hence forthwith,
To feast and sport us at thy father's house.
Go, call my men, and let us straight to him;
And bring our horses unto Long-lane end;
There will we mount, and thither walk on foot.
Let's see; I think 'tis now some seven o'clock,
And well we may come there by dinner-time. 190
Kath. I dare assure you, sir, 'tis almost two;
And 'twill be supper-time ere you come there.
Pet. It shall be seven ere I go to horse:
Look, what I speak, or do, or think to do,
You are still crossing it. Sirs, let't alone:

I will not go to-day; and ere I do,
It shall be what o'clock I say it is.
 Hor. [*Aside*] Why, so this gallant will command the sun.   [*Exeunt.*

SCENE IV. *Padua. Before* BAPTISTA'S *house.*

Enter TRANIO, *and the* Pedant *dressed like* VINCENTIO.

 Tra. Sir, this is the house: please it you that I call?
 Ped. Ay, what else? and but I be deceived
Signior Baptista may remember me,
Near twenty years ago, in Genoa,
● Where we were lodgers at the Pegasus.
 Tra. 'Tis well; and hold your own, in any case,
With such austerity as 'longeth to a father.
 Ped. I warrant you.

Enter BIONDELLO.

     But, sir, here comes your boy;
● 'Twere good he were school'd.
 Tra. Fear you not him.   Sirrah Biondello,
Now do your duty throughly, I advise you: 11
Imagine 'twere the right Vincentio.
 Bion. Tut, fear not me.
 Tra. But hast thou done thy errand to Baptista?
 Bion. I told him that your father was at Venice,
And that you look'd for him this day in Padua.
● *Tra.* Thou'rt a tall fellow: hold thee that to drink.
Here comes Baptista: set your countenance, sir.

Enter BAPTISTA *and* LUCENTIO.

Signior Baptista, you are happily met.
[*To the Pedant*] Sir, this is the gentleman I told you of: 20
I pray you, stand good father to me now,
Give me Bianca for my patrimony.
 Ped. Soft, son!
Sir, by your leave: having come to Padua
To gather in some debts, my son Lucentio
Made me acquainted with a weighty cause
Of love between your daughter and himself:
And, for the good report I hear of you
And for the love he beareth to your daughter
And she to him, to stay him not too long, 30
I am content, in a good father's care,
To have him match'd; and if you please to like
No worse than I, upon some agreement
Me shall you find ready and willing
With one consent to have her so bestow'd;
● For curious I cannot be with you,
Signior Baptista, of whom I hear so well.
 Bap. Sir, pardon me in what I have to say:
Your plainness and your shortness please me well.
Right true it is, your son Lucentio here 40
Doth love my daughter and she loveth him,
Or both dissemble deeply their affections:
And therefore, if you say no more than this,
That like a father you will deal with him
● And pass my daughter a sufficient dower,
The match is made, and all is done:
Your son shall have my daughter with consent.
 Tra. I thank you, sir.   Where then do you know best

5 *Pegasus.* The name of an inn.

9 *school'd.* Instructed about the role.

17 *tall.* Manly.

36 *curious.* Over particular.

45 *pass.* Settle upon.

49 *affied.* Betrothed.

50 *part's.* Party's.

53 *is hearkening.* Is eavesdropping.

59 *scrivener.* Notary.

61 *pittance.* Fare or meals.

70 *one mess . . . cheer.* One dish is all that you are likely to get.

81 *moralize.* Explain.

92 *assurance.* Legal guarantee. *assurance.* Agreement.

104-105 *appendix.* Companion.

● We be affied and such assurance ta'en
● As shall with either part's agreement stand ?   50
     Bap.   Not in my house, Lucentio; for, you
       know,
Pitchers have ears, and I have many servants:
● Besides, old Gremio is hearkening still;
And happily we might be interrupted.
     Tra.   Then at my lodging, an it like you:
There doth my father lie; and there, this night,
We'll pass the business privately and well.
Send for your daughter by your servant here;
● My boy shall fetch the scrivener presently.
The worst is this, that, at so slender warning,   60
● You are like to have a thin and slender pittance.
     Bap.   It likes me well. Biondello, hie you home,
And bid Bianca make her ready straight;
And, if you will, tell what hath happened,
Lucentio's father is arrived in Padua,
And how she's like to be Lucentio's wife.
     Bion.   I pray the gods she may with all my
       heart !
     Tra.   Dally not with the gods, but get thee
       gone.   [*Exit Bion.*
Signior Baptista, shall I lead the way?
● Welcome ! one mess is like to be your cheer: **70**
Come, sir; we will better it in Pisa.
     Bap.   I follow you.
       [*Exeunt Tranio, Pedant, and Baptista.*

       Re-enter BIONDELLO.

     Bion.   Cambio !
     Luc.   What sayest thou, Biondello?
     Bion.   You saw my master wink and laugh
upon you?
     Luc.   Biondello, what of that?
     Bion.   Faith, nothing; but has left me here
behind, to expound the meaning or moral of his
signs and tokens.   80
●   *Luc.*   I pray thee, moralize them.
     Bion.   Then thus. Baptista is safe, talking
with the deceiving father of a deceitful son.
     Luc.   And what of him?
     Bion.   His daughter is to be brought by you
to the supper.
     Luc.   And then?
     Bion.   The old priest of Saint Luke's church
is at your command at all hours.
     Luc.   And what of all this?   90
     Bion.   I cannot tell; expect they are busied
● about a counterfeit assurance: take you assurance
of her, 'cum privilegio ad imprimendum solum:'
to the church; take the priest, clerk, and some
sufficient honest witnesses:
If this be not that you look for, I have no more
       to say,
But bid Bianca farewell for ever and a day.
     Luc.   Hearest thou, Biondello?
     Bion.   I cannot tarry: I knew a wench mar-
ried in an afternoon as she went to the garden
for parsley to stuff a rabbit; and so may you, sir:
and so, adieu, sir.   My master hath appointed
me to go to Saint Luke's, to bid the priest be
● ready to come against you come with your appendix.   [*Exit.*
     Luc.   I may, and will, if she be so contented:
She will be pleased; then wherefore should I doubt?
Hap what hap may, I'll roundly go about her:
It shall go hard if Cambio go without her. [*Exit.*

SCENE V. *A public road.*

Enter PETRUCHIO, KATHARINA, HORTENSIO,
and Servants.

Pet. Come on, i' God's name; once more to-
    ward our father's.
Good Lord, how bright and goodly shines the
    moon!
Kath. The moon! the sun: it is not moonlight
    now.
Pet. I say it is the moon that shines so bright.
Kath. I know it is the sun that shines so bright.
Pet. Now, by my mother's son, and that's
    myself,
It shall be moon, or star, or what I list,
Or ere I journey to your father's house.
Go on, and fetch our horses back again.
Evermore cross'd and cross'd; nothing but cross'd!
    Hor.   Say as he says, or we shall never go. 11
    Kath.   Forward, I pray, since we have come
    so far,
And be it moon, or sun, or what you please:
• An if you please to call it a rush-candle,
Henceforth I vow it shall be so for me.
    Pet.   I say it is the moon.
    Kath.   I know it is the moon.
    Pet.   Nay, then you lie: it is the blessed sun.
    Kath.   Then, God be bless'd, it is the blessed
    sun:
But sun it is not, when you say it is not;
And the moon changes even as your mind.   20
What you will have it named, even that it is;
And so it shall be so for Katharine.
    Hor.   Petruchio, go thy ways; the field is won.
    Pet.   Well, forward, forward! thus the bowl
    should run,
• And not unluckily against the bias.
But, soft! company is coming here.

Enter VINCENTIO.

[*To Vincentio*] Good morrow, gentle mistress:
    where away?
Tell me, sweet Kate, and tell me truly too,
Hast thou beheld a fresher gentlewoman?
Such war of white and red within her cheeks! 30
What stars do spangle heaven with such beauty,
As those two eyes become that heavenly face?
Fair lovely maid, once more good day to thee.
Sweet Kate, embrace her for her beauty's sake.
    Hor.   A' will make the man mad, to make a
    woman of him.
    Kath.   Young budding virgin, fair and fresh
    and sweet,
Whither away, or where is thy abode?
Happy the parents of so fair a child;
Happier the man, whom favourable stars   40
Allot thee for his lovely bed-fellow!
    Pet.   Why, how now, Kate! I hope thou art
    not mad:
This is a man, old, wrinkled, faded, wither'd,
And not a maiden, as thou say'st he is.
    Kath.   Pardon, old father, my mistaking eyes,
That have been so bedazzled with the sun
That everything I look on seemeth green:
Now I perceive thou art a reverend father;
Pardon, I pray thee, for my mad mistaking.
    Pet.   Do, good old grandsire; and withal make
    known   50

14 *rush-candle.* A rush dipped in grease to serve as a
candle.

25 *bias.* The weight in the side of a bowl that determines its direction.

Bowling in the 14th century. Engraving from Joseph
Strutt's *Sports and Pastimes of the People of England*, 1810

76 *jealous.* Suspicious.

Costume design for Lucentio by Vivienne Kernot, Stratford-upon-Avon, 1954

5-6 *church o' your back.* See you married.

14 *toward.* Forward.

Which way thou travellest: if along with us,
We shall be joyful of thy company.
   Vin. Fair sir, and you my merry mistress,
That with your strange encounter much amazed
     me,
My name is call'd Vincentio; my dwelling Pisa;
And bound I am to Padua; there to visit
A son of mine, which long I have not seen.
   Pet. What is his name?
   Vin.   Lucentio, gentle sir.
   Pet. Happily met; the happier for thy son.
And now by law, as well as reverend age,   60
I may entitle thee my loving father:
The sister to my wife, this gentlewoman,
Thy son by this hath married.   Wonder not,
Nor be not grieved: she is of good esteem,
Her dowry wealthy, and of worthy birth;
Beside, so qualified as may beseem
The spouse of any noble gentleman.
Let me embrace with old Vincentio,
And wander we to see thy honest son,
Who will of thy arrival be full joyous.   70
   Vin. But is this true? or is it else your pleasure,
Like pleasant travellers, to break a jest
Upon the company you overtake?
   Hor. I do assure thee, father, so it is.
   Pet. Come, go along, and see the truth hereof;
● For our first merriment hath made thee jealous.
                      [Exeunt all but Hortensio.
   Hor. Well, Petruchio, this has put me in heart.
Have to my widow! and if she be froward,
Then hast thou taught Hortensio to be untoward.
                            [Exit.

ACT V.

SCENE I. *Padua.* *Before* LUCENTIO'S *house.*

GREMIO *discovered.* *Enter behind* BIONDELLO,
LUCENTIO, *and* BIANCA.

   Bion. Softly and swiftly, sir; for the priest is
ready.
   Luc. I fly, Biondello: but they may chance
to need thee at home; therefore leave us.
●   *Bion.* Nay, faith, I'll see the church o' your
back; and then come back to my master's as
soon as I can.
      [Exeunt Lucentio, Bianca, and Biondello.
   Gre. I marvel Cambio comes not all this while.

Enter PETRUCHIO, KATHARINA, VINCENTIO,
GRUMIO, *with* Attendants.

   Pet. Sir. here's the door, this is Lucentio's
     house:
My father's bears more toward the market-place;
Thither must I, and here I leave you, sir.   11
   Vin. You shall not choose but drink before
     you go:
I think I shall command your welcome here,
● And, by all likelihood, some cheer is toward.
                             [Knocks.
   Gre. They're busy within; you were best
knock louder.

Pedant *looks out of the window.*

   Ped. What's he that knocks as he would beat
down the gate?

Vin.   Is Signior Lucentio within, sir?

Ped.   He's within, sir, but not to be spoken withal.   21

Vin.   What if a man bring him a hundred pound or two, to make merry withal?

Ped.   Keep your hundred pounds to yourself: he shall need none, so long as I live.

Pet.   Nay, I told you your son was well beloved in Padua.   Do you hear, sir?   To leave frivolous circumstances, I pray you, tell Signior Lucentio that his father is come from Pisa and is here at the door to speak with him.   30

Ped.   Thou liest: his father is come from Padua and here looking out at the window.

Vin.   Art thou his father?

Ped.   Ay, sir; so his mother says, if I may believe her.

Pet.   [*To Vincentio*]   Why, how now, gentleman! why, this is flat knavery, to take upon you another man's name.

Ped.   Lay hands on the villain: I believe a' means to cozen somebody in this city under my countenance.   41

Re-enter BIONDELLO.

Bion.   I have seen them in the church together: God send 'em good shipping! But who is here? mine old master Vincentio! now we are undone and brought to nothing.

Vin.   [*Seeing Biondello*]   Come hither, crack-hemp.

Bion.   I hope I may choose, sir.

Vin.   Come hither, you rogue.   What, have you forgot me?   50

Bion.   Forgot you! no, sir: I could not forget you, for I never saw you before in all my life.

Vin.   What, you notorious villain, didst thou never see thy master's father, Vincentio?

Bion.   What, my old worshipful old master? yes, marry, sir: see where he looks out of the window.

Vin.   Is't so, indeed?   [*Beats Biondello.*

Bion.   Help, help, help! here's a madman will murder me.   [*Exit.*   61

Ped.   Help, son! help, Signior Baptista!   [*Exit from above.*

Pet.   Prithee, Kate, let's stand aside and see the end of this controversy.   [*They retire.*

Re-enter Pedant *below;* TRANIO, BAPTISTA, *and* Servants.

Tra.   Sir, what are you that offer to beat my servant?

Vin.   What am I, sir! nay, what are you, sir? O immortal gods! O fine villain! A silken doublet! a velvet hose! a scarlet cloak! and a copatain hat! O, I am undone! I am undone! while I play the good husband at home, my son and my servant spend all at the university.

Tra.   How now! what's the matter?

Bap.   What, is the man lunatic?

Tra.   Sir, you seem a sober ancient gentleman by your habit, but your words show you a madman.   Why, sir, what 'cerns it you if I wear pearl and gold?   I thank my good father, I am able to maintain it.   79

---

43   *good shipping.* Good luck.

46-47   *crack-hemp.* Gallows-bird.

69-70   *copatain hat.* High-crowned.

96 *forthcoming*. Available to stand trial.

111 *haled*. Molested, hauled away.

120 *supposes*. Illusions. See introduction. *eyne*. Eye.

121 *packing*. Plotting.

Diana Rigg as Bianca, Stratford-upon-Avon, 1962

Vin. Thy father! O villain! he is a sail-maker in Bergamo.

Bap. You mistake, sir, you mistake, sir. Pray, what do you think is his name?

Vin. His name! as if I knew not his name: I have brought him up ever since he was three years old, and his name is Tranio.

Ped. Away, away, mad ass! his name is Lucentio; and he is mine only son, and heir to the lands of me, Signior Vincentio.   89

Vin. Lucentio! O, he hath murdered his master! Lay hold on him, I charge you, in the duke's name. O, my son, my son! Tell me, thou villain, where is my son Lucentio?

Tra. Call forth an officer.

Enter one with an Officer.

Carry this mad knave to the gaol.   Father Baptista, I charge you see that he be forthcoming.

Vin. Carry me to the gaol!

Gre. Stay, officer: he shall not go to prison.

Bap. Talk not, Signior Gremio: I say he shall go to prison.   100

Gre. Take heed, Signior Baptista, lest you be cony-catched in this business: I dare swear this is the right Vincentio.

Ped. Swear, if thou darest.

Gre. Nay, I dare not swear it.

Tra. Then thou wert best say that I am not Lucentio.

Gre. Yes, I know thee to be Signior Lucentio.

Bap. Away with the dotard! to the gaol with him!   110

Vin. Thus strangers may be haled and abused: O monstrous villain!

Re-enter BIONDELLO, *with* LUCENTIO *and* BIANCA.

Bion. O! we are spoiled and—yonder he is: deny him, forswear him, or else we are all undone.

Luc. [*Kneeling*] Pardon, sweet father.

Vin. Lives my sweet son?

[*Exeunt Biondello, Tranio, and Pedant, as fast as may be.*

Bian. Pardon, dear father.

Bap. How hast thou offended? Where is Lucentio?

Luc. Here's Lucentio, Right son to the right Vincentio; That have by marriage made thy daughter mine, While counterfeit supposes blear'd thine eyne.

Gre. Here's packing, with a witness, to deceive us all!

Vin. Where is that damned villain Tranio, That faced and braved me in this matter so?

Bap. Why, tell me, is not this my Cambio?

Bian. Cambio is changed into Lucentio.

Luc. Love wrought these miracles. Bianca's love Made me exchange my state with Tranio, While he did bear my countenance in the town; And happily I have arrived at the last   130 Unto the wished haven of my bliss. What Tranio did, myself enforced him to; Then pardon him, sweet father, for my sake.

Vin. I'll slit the villain's nose, that would have sent me to the gaol.

Bap.   But do you hear, sir? have you married my daughter 'without asking my good will?

Vin.   Fear not, Baptista; we will content you, go to: but I will in, to be revenged for this villany.   [*Exit.* 140

Bap.   And I, to sound the depth of this knavery.   [*Exit.*

Luc.   Look not pale, Bianca; thy father will not frown.   [*Exeunt Lucentio and Bianca.*

Gre.   My cake is dough; but I'll in among the rest,
Out of hope of all, but my share of the feast.
                                                            [*Exit.*

Kath.   Husband, let's follow, to see the end of this ado.

Pet.   First kiss me, Kate, and we will.

Kath.   What, in the midst of the street?

Pet.   What, art thou ashamed of me?   150

Kath.   No, sir, God forbid; but ashamed to kiss.

Pet.   Why, then let's home again.   Come, sirrah, let's away.

Kath.   Nay, I will give thee a kiss: now pray thee, love, stay.

Pet.   Is not this well?   Come, my sweet Kate:
Better once than never, for never too late.
                                                          [*Exeunt.*

Scene II.   *Padua.* Lucentio's *house.*

Enter Baptista, Vincentio, Gremio, *the* Pedant, Lucentio, Bianca, Petruchio, Katharina, Hortensio, *and* Widow, Tranio, Biondello, *and* Grumio: *the Serving-men with Tranio bringing in a banquet.*

Luc.   At last, though long, our jarring notes agree:
And time it is, when raging war is done,
To smile at scapes and perils overblown.
My fair Bianca, bid my father welcome,
While I with self-same kindness welcome thine.
Brother Petruchio, sister Katharina,
And thou, Hortensio, with thy loving widow,
Feast with the best, and welcome to my house:
My banquet is to close our stomachs up,
After our great good cheer.   Pray you, sit down;
For now we sit to chat as well as eat.   11

Pet.   Nothing but sit and sit, and eat and eat!

Bap.   Padua affords this kindness, son Petruchio.

Pet.   Padua affords nothing but what is kind.

Hor.   For both our sakes, I would that word were true.

Pet.   Now, for my life, Hortensio fears his widow.

Wid.   Then never trust me, if I be afeard.

Pet.   You are very sensible, and yet you miss my sense:
I mean, Hortensio is afeard of you.

Wid.   He that is giddy thinks the world turns round.   20

Pet.   Roundly replied.

Kath.   Mistress, how mean you that?

Wid.   Thus I conceive by him.

Pet.   Conceives by me!   How likes Hortensio that?

Hor.   My widow says, thus she conceives her tale.

22 *conceive by.* Understand, but in the next line Petruchio puns on the meaning 'is pregnant by'.

The three couples. Centre, Petruchio (Keith Michell) and Kate (Barbara Jefford), George Devine's production, Stratford-upon-Avon, 1954

---

32 *mean*. Contemptible.

40 *Head, and butt*. Head and tails.

45 *bitter*. Sharp.

52 *slipp'd me*. Unleashed me.

58 *gird*. Gibe.

63 *sadness*. Seriousness.

Pet. Very well mended. Kiss him for that, good widow.
    Kath. 'He that is giddy thinks the world turns round:'
I pray you, tell me what you meant by that.
    Wid. Your husband, being troubled with a shrew,
Measures my husband's sorrow by his woe:
And now you know my meaning.   30
    Kath. A very mean meaning.
    Wid.   Right, I mean you.
• *Kath.* And I am mean indeed, respecting you.
    Pet. To her, Kate!
    Hor. To her, widow!
    Pet. A hundred marks, my Kate does put her down.
    Hor. That's my office.
    Pet. Spoke like an officer: ha' to thee, lad!
                            [*Drinks to Hortensio.*

    Bap. How likes Gremio these quick-witted folks?
    Gre. Believe me, sir, they butt together well.
• *Bian.* Head, and butt! an hasty-witted body
Would say your head and butt were head and horn.
    Vin. Ay, mistress bride, hath that awaken'd you?
    Bian. Ay, but not frighted me; therefore I'll sleep again.
    Pet. Nay, that you shall not: since you have begun,
• Have at you for a bitter jest or two!
    Bian. Am I your bird? I mean to shift my bush;
And then pursue me as you draw your bow.
You are welcome all.
                [*Exeunt Bianca, Katharina, and Widow.*

    Pet. She hath prevented me. Here, Signior Tranio,
This bird you aim'd at, though you hit her not;
Therefore a health to all that shot and miss'd. 51
• *Tra.* O, sir, Lucentio slipp'd me like his greyhound,
Which runs himself and catches for his master.
    Pet. A good swift simile, but something currish.
    Tra. 'Tis well, sir, that you hunted for yourself:
'Tis thought your deer does hold you at a bay.
    Bap. O ho, Petruchio! Tranio hits you now.
• *Luc.* I thank thee for that gird, good Tranio.
    Hor. Confess, confess, hath he not hit you here?
    Pet. A' has a little gall'd me, I confess;   60
And, as the jest did glance away from me,
'Tis ten to one it maim'd you two outright.
• *Bap.* Now, in good sadness, son Petruchio,
I think thou hast the veriest shrew of all.
    Pet. Well, I say no: and therefore for assurance
Let's each one send unto his wife;
And he whose wife is most obedient
To come at first when he doth send for her,
Shall win the wager which we will propose.
    Hor. Content. What is the wager?
    Luc.   Twenty crowns. 70
    Pet. Twenty crowns!

I'll venture so much of my hawk or hound,
But twenty times so much upon my wife.
Luc.   A hundred then.
Hor.   Content.
Pet.   A match! 'tis done.
Hor.   Who shall begin?
Luc.   That will I.
Go, Biondello, bid your mistress come to me.
  Bion.   I go.   [*Exit.*
● *Bap.*   Son, I'll be your half, Bianca comes.
  Luc.   I'll have no halves; I'll bear it all
    myself.

Re-enter BIONDELLO.

How now! what news?
  Bion.   Sir, my mistress sends you word   80
That she is busy and she cannot come.
  Pet.   How! she is busy and she cannot come!
Is that an answer?
  Gre.   Ay, and a kind one too:
Pray God, sir, your wife send you not a worse.
  Pet.   I hope, better.
  Hor.   Sirrah Biondello, go and entreat my wife
To come to me forthwith.   [*Exit Bion.*
  Pet.   O, ho! entreat her!
Nay, then she must needs come.
  Hor.   I am afraid, sir,
Do what you can, yours will not be entreated.

Re-enter BIONDELLO.

Now, where's my wife?   90
  Bion.   She says you have some goodly jest in
    hand:
She will not come; she bids you come to her.
  Pet.   Worse and worse; she will not come!
O vile,
Intolerable, not to be endured!
Sirrah Grumio, go to your mistress;
Say, I command her come to me. [*Exit Grumio.*
  Hor.   I know her answer.
  Pet.   What?
  Hor.   She will not.
  Pet.   The fouler fortune mine, and there an end.
● *Bap.*   Now, by my holidame, here comes
    Katharina!

Re-enter KATHARINA.

  Kath.   What is your will, sir, that you send
    for me?   100
  Pet.   Where is your sister, and Hortensio's
    wife?
  Kath.   They sit conferring by the parlour fire.
  Pet.   Go, fetch them hither: if they deny to
    come,
● Swinge me them soundly forth unto their hus-
    bands:
Away, I say, and bring them hither straight.
                 [*Exit Katharina.*
  Luc.   Here is a wonder, if you talk of a wonder.
  Hor.   And so it is: I wonder what it bodes.
  Pet.   Marry, peace it bodes, and love and
    quiet life,
● And awful rule and right supremacy;
And, to be short, what not, that's sweet and
    happy?   110
  Bap.   Now, fair befal thee, good Petruchio!

78 *I'll be your half.* I'll take on half the bet.

99 *holidame.* Holy Dame. i.e. the Virgin Mary; equivalent to 'bless my soul'.

104 *Swinge.* Beat.

Costume design for Kate by Vivienne Kernot, Stratford-upon-Avon, 1954

109 *awful.* Inspiring respect.

Vanessa Redgrave as Kate, Stratford-upon-Avon, 1962

129 *laying.* Betting.

161 *simple.* Silly.

The wager thou hast won; and I will add
Unto their losses twenty thousand crowns;
Another dowry to another daughter,
For she is changed, as she had never been.
   Pet. Nay, I will win my wager better yet
And show more sign of her obedience,
Her new-built virtue and obedience.
See where she comes and brings your froward wives
As prisoners to her womanly persuasion.   120

Re-enter KATHARINA, *with* BIANCA *and* Widow.

Katharine, that cap of yours becomes you not:
Off with that bauble, throw it under-foot.
   Wid. Lord, let me never have a cause to sigh,
Till I be brought to such a silly pass!
   Bian. Fie! what a foolish duty call you this?
   Luc. I would your duty were as foolish too:
The wisdom of your duty, fair Bianca,
Hath cost me an hundred crowns since sup-
      per-time.
• *Bian.* The more fool you, for laying on
      my duty.
   Pet. Katharine, I charge thee, tell these
      headstrong women   130
What duty they do owe their lords and husbands.
   Wid. Come, come, you're mocking: we will
      have no telling.
   Pet. Come on, I say; and first begin with her.
   Wid. She shall not.
   Pet. I say she shall: and first begin with her.
   Kath. Fie, fie! unknit that threatening unkind
      brow,
And dart not scornful glances from those eyes,
To wound thy lord, thy king, thy governor:
It blots thy beauty as frosts do bite the meads,
Confounds thy fame as whirlwinds shake fair
      buds,   140
And in no sense is meet or amiable.
A woman moved is like a fountain troubled,
Muddy, ill-seeming, thick, bereft of beauty;
And while it is so, none so dry or thirsty
Will deign to sip or touch one drop of it.
Thy husband is thy lord, thy life, thy keeper,
Thy head, thy sovereign; one that cares for thee,
And for thy maintenance commits his body
To painful labour both by sea and land,
To watch the night in storms, the day in cold, 150
Whilst thou liest warm at home, secure and
      safe;
And craves no other tribute at thy hands
But love, fair looks and true obedience;
Too little payment for so great a debt.
Such duty as the subject owes the prince
Even such a woman oweth to her husband;
And when she is froward, peevish, sullen, sour,
And not obedient to his honest will,
What is she but a foul contending rebel
And graceless traitor to her loving lord?   160
•I am ashamed that women are so simple
To offer war where they should kneel for peace,
Or seek for rule, supremacy and sway,
When they are bound to serve, love and obey.
Why are our bodies soft and weak and smooth,
Unapt to toil and trouble in the world,
But that our soft conditions and our hearts
Should well agree with our external parts?
Come, come, you froward and unable worms!
My mind hath been as big as one of yours,   170

My heart as great, my reason haply more,
To bandy word for word and frown for frown;
But now I see our lances are but straws,
Our strength as weak, our weakness past compare,
That seeming to be most which we indeed least
    are.
● Then vail your stomachs, for it is no boot,
And place your hands below your husband's foot:
In token of which duty, if he please,
My hand is ready; may it do him ease.
    Pet. Why, there's a wench! Come on, and
        kiss me, Kate.   180
    Luc. Well, go thy ways, old lad; for thou
        shalt ha't.
●   *Vin.* 'Tis a good hearing when children are
        toward.
    Luc. But a harsh hearing when women are
        froward.
    Pet. Come, Kate, we'll to bed.
● We three are married, but you two are sped.
● [*To Luc.*] 'Twas I won the wager, though you
        hit the white;
And, being a winner, God give you good night!
        [*Exeunt Petruchio and Katharina.*
    Hor. Now, go thy ways; thou hast tamed a
        curst shrew.
    Luc. 'Tis a wonder, by your leave, she will
        be tamed so.   [*Exeunt.*

176 *vail your stomachs.* Lower your pride.

Katherine: 'And place your hand below your husband's foot.' Petruchio (Alan Bates), Katherine (Susan Fleetwood), Royal Shakespeare Co, 1973

182 *'Tis . . . toward'.* It is pleasant to hear of children who are promising.

185 *sped.* Done for.

186 *hit the white.* Hit the bull's eye, but also a play on Bianca.

Love's Labour's Lost

1593

The Background. It has long been realised that this play was originally written for private performance. It is full of topicalities, references to contemporary events and characters; the themes out of which the play was constructed are contemporary and topical. This makes it easier to interpret, with a full and proper knowledge of what was going on at the time, and who was who. It is full of private jokes and allusions, some of which are lost, but that is no great loss, and the obscurer ones can be omitted in performance. The play is an acutely personal one, Shakespeare himself stamped in every line, his high spirits and sheer verbal cleverness, which sometimes carried him away, and makes some difficulties for us four hundred years later.

The very names of the play show how topical it was. The Protestant Henry of Navarre had been fighting for his right, his succession to the French throne since 1589. He was at the height of his popularity in England in August 1591, when an expedition under Essex went to his aid in Normandy—reawakening the memories and echoes of the war there, more than a century before, under Henry VI. Young Southampton went abroad to serve there, and shortly became the patron of the actor-dramatist. It was feared that Navarre would convert to Catholicism for the sake of the French throne— he was under instruction, and when he did so it gave grave concern to Elizabeth I; the issue of oath-breaking is glanced at in the play. Navarre, Berowne (Biron), Longaville (Longueville), Dumain (de Mayenne), were leading figures in France, and appear in the pamphlets published by Richard Field, Shakespeare's Stratford contemporary, who was contemporaneously printing *Venus and Adonis,* 1593 and *The Rape of Lucrece,* 1594.

The play, which has several references to the plague, belongs to the plague years 1592 and 1593, when the theatres were mostly closed and Shakespeare was free to write his two long poems and the Sonnets for his patron, and both *Love's Labour's Lost* and *A Midsummer Night's Dream* for the Southampton circle.

The very theme of the play is that of the first section of the Sonnets and of *Venus and Adonis*—of the young man who will not respond to the love of women. In the play the young king makes a vow with his friends to forego the society of women for a period. The play is a skit on this, a kind of lyrical farce. It has always been realised that Berowne,

Far left: *Henry of Navarre became king of France in 1589. This wood engraving shows his entry into Rouen 1596*

Left: *London under the Plague. Woodcut from the title page of John Taylor's* The Feareful Summer *1636*

in thinking this to be nonsense and laughing at it, speaks for Shakespeare:

> But love, first learnèd in a lady's eyes,
> Lives not alone immurèd in the brain,
> But with the motion of all elements,
> Courses as swift as thought in every power,
> And gives to every power a double power . . .

It is also obvious that Berowne's lady, Rosaline, is a portrait of Shakespeare's own mistress, the Dark Lady of the Sonnets, for they are described in closely similar language.

It has now at last been recognised that when Rosaline described Berowne, it is Shakespeare laughing at himself:

> but a merrier man,
> Within the limit of becoming mirth,

(a joke too, for Shakespeare was a bawdy writer)

> I never spent an hour's talk withal.
> His eye begets occasion for his wit;
> For every object that the one doth catch
> The other turns to a mirth-moving jest,
> Which his fair tongue—conceit's expositor—
> Delivers in such apt and gracious words
> That agèd ears play truant at his tales,
> And younger hearings are quite ravishèd,
> So sweet and voluble is his discourse.

And he goes on to laugh at his obviously known characteristics—his liking for women and food and plenty of sleep. It is all in keeping with external evidences about him, and with the picture of the euphoric, self-confident personality we derive from envious Robert Greene's attack on him in 1592.

Don Adriano de Armado, 'a fantastical Spaniard', is no less easily identifiable (and was in fact identified years ago by the historian, Martin Hume) with his immense conceit, his airs and graces, his inflated and flattering rhetoric. Philip II's ex-Secretary of State, Antonio Perez, was in England from April 1593 to July 1595, until he outwore his welcome and fatigued his sponsors, Essex and his secretary Anthony Bacon. Essex—Southampton's admired leader and friend—gave Perez an apartment at Essex House. So we have:

> Our Court, you know, is haunted
> With a refinèd traveller of Spain;
> A man in all the world's new fashion planted,
> That hath a mint of phrases in his brain;
> One who the music of his own vain tongue
> Doth ravish like enchanting harmony;
> A man of compliments . . .
> From tawny Spain . . .

Perez was a professional rhetorician, and his inflated language is made fun of throughout. He was a homosexual, and a great snob, so that to make him fall in love with Jacquenetta, 'a base wench, a country girl,' was an obvious hit.

So too with Holofernes, 'a schoolmaster', with his fantastic use of rare and odd words, which is ridiculed. John Florio was during these years Italian tutor to Southampton, living in his household. He later dedicated his Dictionary, *A World of Words,* to Southampton; but already, a couple of years before our play, in his *Second Fruits* of 1591, he had expressed a low view of English plays as 'neither right comedies nor right tragedies', but 'mere representations of histories, without any decorum'. This was fair enough comment on the three parts of *Henry VI*, which had won Shakespeare such popularity, and probably gained him Southampton's attention. Here was Shakespeare's

Right: *John Florio, Italian tutor to Southampton and translator of Montaigne. Engraving from the 1611 edition of Florio's dictionary* Queen Anna's New World of Words

Far right: *Title page of Florio's* A Worlde of Wordes, *1598*

return. That Florio was partly in mind we see from the proverb Shakespeare quotes from Florio's *First Fruits*:

> Venetia, Venetia,
> Chi non ti vede, non ti pretia.

'Venice, he who doth not see thee, doth not value thee.'

There are a number of parallel passages between Shakespeare and Florio; Italian phrases he could always have got from the tutor in Southampton's household, where the play probably had its first performance. That the play had its special relation to the Earl and his circle is corroborated by the fact that he had it produced again specially for James I at Southampton House in 1605.

Essex, and Southampton, knew Henry of Navarre, who had, in historical fact, received just such missions from the French royal ladies as that which is featured in the play; and, moreover, he became a patron of just such an Academy.

On the literary side, the contemporary pamphlet-war between the Cambridge intellectuals—Gabriel Harvey on one side, Robert Greene and Thomas Nashe on the other—is made use of to extract fun. The incorrigible young Nashe's pen was wickedly inspired whenever he thought of poor Harvey, ineffable, conceited don as he was. In the play Nashe features as 'tender Juvenal', by which he was referred to by Greene and others. He tried to bounce himself into Southampton's patronage with an unsolicited dedication, but this post was already pre-empted, and subsequently he gained the notice of Sir George Carey, Lord Chamberlain Hunsdon's son, who succeeded him as patron of Shakespeare's company. He lived in Blackfriars, where the Lord Chamberlain also had a house, as Richard Field his press. We see how definite and closely associated this circle was in just these years.

Character of the Play. We must always remember, in reading, that a play is a play is a play, and the actor-dramatist' thought and composed in scenes. The King and courtiers, the Princess and her ladies, speak in verse: their part, with its teasing love-interest, is romantic comedy. And at this period, when the Sonnets were being written, several sonnets appear in the play. The Armado and Holofernes scenes, and the yokels all in prose, are pure farce and should be played as such. The country clowns' presentation of the Nine Worthies ridicules the regular doggerel familiar on such Elizabethan occasions—though Shakespeare interposes a kind-hearted realistic touch when one of them breaks down:

> 'There, an't please you: a foolish mild man; an honest man, look you, and soon
> dashed! He is a marvellous good neighbour, faith, and a very good bowler; but,
> for Alisander—alas! you see how 'tis—a little o'er-parted'
> (i.e. the part is too much for him).

The masque of Muscovites which the courtiers present masked reflects the marked interest of the Elizabethans in Russia, since they were the first to open up direct Russian contact with the West through the voyages to Archangel. These were written up in Hakluyt's *Navigations*, the first edition of which had appeared a few years before, in 1589—and we know that Shakespeare, a keen and rapid reader, looked into Hakluyt. Embassies were exchanged, and Russian ambassadors were presented to the Queen. A pageant of Russians at the Gray's Inn Revels at Christmas time 1594 does not upset our dating of the play, for it was obviously revised, with additions, for public performance in 1597. As a professional to his finger-tips Shakespeare would naturally touch up a play written for a private occasion and a special audience when it came before the public.

Everything bespeaks the specialised appeal to the aristocratic audience for which it was written—notably the sophisticated wit of an intellectual kind; Elizabethans enjoyed this kind of sparring, which much attracted Shakespeare—the element that perhaps appeals least to us today. Caroline Spurgeon, in her perceptive book on his imagery, noticed how his senses became more refined with his entry into this aristocratic circle; and, sure enough, the 'base vulgar' have their strong smell.

There are, indeed, many personal touches. The schoolmasterly clichés—*pauca verba* (few words), *haud credo* (I don't think)—remind us of his schooldays and the information from a very early source that, for a time, he was a young usher in a country school. The passage at arms, with Dull misunderstanding the schoolmaster's *haud credo*, is based on a pun I elucidated years ago. Dull protests that it was not a *haud credo* (auld grey doe) but a pricket, i.e. a young buck. This again reminds us of Shakespeare's perfect fixation on hunting the deer in his early days. The Latin tag the schoolmaster quotes from Mantuan, the Renaissance poet popular in schools, goes back to them: 'Old Mantuan! who understands thee not loves thee not.' There is more about Elizabethan schooling and schoolmasters in Shakespeare than in any other dramatist of the time.

We are reminded of the university in the line,

Proceeded well, to stop all good proceeding!

For it was the regular term at Oxford for proceeding to one's M.A. He was acquainted with Oxford from passing through it on his way to and from London; actually, it is likely that the poet was present with his young patron, when Southampton, a Cambridge man, proceeded M.A. at Oxford the year before, in 1592.

From first to last, in spite of the disillusionment he suffered from his dark mistress (the Rosaline of the play, the equivocal distracting woman of the Sonnets), Shakespeare had a romantic conception of the love of men and women—unlike Marlowe or Francis Bacon or Ben Jonson. This has always been a strong element in his world-wide appeal. *Love's Labour's Lost*—the very title may have come from Florio's *First Fruits*, 'it were labour lost to speak of Love'—is a manifesto in favour of love and life, nature and natural feeling, against intellectualism, pedantry and affectation. Here we have Shakespeare—an edge is added to it by the fact that we have a naturally clever man, himself an intellectual, tilting against various absurd forms of intellectualism.

The play ends in parting, not the usual consummation of romantic love, and this is in keeping with the actual situation behind the play, which sparked it off and which it reflects: Southampton would not and did not marry for some years yet. Berowne (Shakespeare) has the last word and points to the exception that it is:

Our wooing doth not end like an old play:
Jack hath not Jill: these ladies' courtesy
Might well have made our sport a comedy.

We may be sure that Shakespeare played the part of Berowne in the original performance; it would be a proper idea to present Berowne as Shakespeare in producing the play today.

The characters are dismissed from the stage with a couple of magical songs. For all their pure poetry, they evoke for us the contemporary scene at Stratford more strongly than pages of prose description. It is winter time,

> When icicles hang by the wall,
>   And Dick the shepherd blows his nail,
> And Tom bears logs into the hall,
>   And milk comes frozen home in pail . . .
>
> When all aloud the wind doth blow,
>   And coughing drowns the parson's saw,
> And birds sit brooding in the snow,
>   And Marian's nose looks red and raw,
> When roasted crabs hiss in the bowl,
> Then nightly sings the staring owl:
>   Tu-whit,
> Tu-who, a merry note,
> While greasy Joan doth keel the pot.

Text. Cuthbert Burby printed the play in 1598, 'as it was presented before her Highness this last Christmas. Newly corrected and augmented.' Evidently the play had been revised for public performance. The editors of the First Folio in 1623 reprinted the play from the 1598 copy, with some checking from their prompt-book.

The revision, and the transmission, account for a certain number of misprints, textual confusions, and changes. These need not, however, detain us. Shakespeare had more urgent things to do, busy as he was, than to tie up loose ends to present a smooth surface, nor was he much concerned in the printing of his plays. He naturally changed his mind, from one draft to another, as any writer does; and Dr. Johnson, greatest of his critics—a mind on a par with his subject, as few are—observed that the dramatist sometimes scamped the ending of a play in a hurry, for the next was called for.

The play in production is the thing, and an admirable producer, Granville Barker, concludes that 'style' must be the keynote of any satisfactory production answering to Shakespeare's ideas. And that is in keeping with our conception of the stylishness of the young Southampton's circle, of which the actor-dramatist was the poet. Then, for all the fun and frolics, the posturing and caricaturing, at the end the shadow of reality falls upon the scene, with the messenger announcing the death of the Princess's father— she must withdraw and away: dramatically effective, it raises the end to a higher level, with a touch of emotion and reality to conclude the light-hearted matter.

LOVE'S LABOUR'S LOST.

DRAMATIS PERSONÆ.

FERDINAND, king of Navarre.
BIRON,
LONGAVILLE, } lords attending on the King.
DUMAIN,
BOYET, } lords attending on the Princess
MERCADE, } of France.
DON ADRIANO DE ARMADO, a fantastical
Spaniard.
SIR NATHANIEL, a curate.
HOLOFERNES, a schoolmaster.
DULL, a constable.

COSTARD, a clown.
MOTH, page to Armado.
A Forester.
The PRINCESS of France.
ROSALINE,
MARIA, } ladies attending on the
KATHARINE, } Princess.
JAQUENETTA, a country wench.
Lords, Attendants, &c.
SCENE: *Navarre.*

● *A bullet beside a text line indicates an annotation in the
opposite column*

ACT I.

SCENE I. *The king of Navarre's park.*

Enter FERDINAND, *king of* NAVARRE, BIRON,
LONGAVILLE, *and* DUMAIN.

   King. Let fame, that all hunt after in their
     lives,
Live register'd upon our brazen tombs
And then grace us in the disgrace of death;
● When, spite of cormorant devouring Time,
The endeavour of this present breath may buy
That honour which shall bate his scythe's keen
     edge
And make us heirs of all eternity.
Therefore, brave conquerors,—for so you are,
That war against your own affections
And the huge army of the world's desires,— 10
Our late edict shall strongly stand in force:
Navarre shall be the wonder of the world;
● Our court shall be a little Academe,
Still and contemplative in living art.
You three, Biron, Dumain, and Longaville,
Have sworn for three years' term to live with me
My fellow-scholars and to keep those statutes

4 *cormorant.* Greedy.

13 *Academe.* The name of Plato's school at Athens.
Italian nobles, particularly the Medici, set up similar
'schools' within their Court during the Renaissance.

Opposite : The arrival of the Princess of France. From a
painting by Thomas Stothard (1755–1834)

32 *all these.* His friends, the other three.

Costume design for Biron by J. Gower Parks for Regent's
Park Open Air Theatre, London, 1935

That are recorded in this schedule here:
Your oaths are pass'd; and now subscribe your
  names,
That his own hand may strike his honour down
That violates the smallest branch herein: 21
If you are arm'd to do as sworn to do,
Subscribe to your deep oaths, and keep it too.
   Long. I am resolved; 'tis but a three years'
   fast:
The mind shall banquet, though the body pine:
Fat paunches have lean pates, and dainty bits
Make rich the ribs, but bankrupt quite the wits.
   Dum. My loving lord, Dumain is mortified:
The grosser manner of these world's delights
He throws upon the gross world's baser slaves:
To love, to wealth, to pomp, I pine and die; 31
● With all these living in philosophy.
   Biron. I can but say their protestation over;
So much, dear liege, I have already sworn,
That is, to live and study here three years.
But there are other strict observances;
As, not to see a woman in that term,
Which I hope well is not enrolled there;
And one day in a week to touch no food
And but one meal on every day beside, 40
The which I hope is not enrolled there;
And then, to sleep but three hours in the night,
And not be seen to wink of all the day—
When I was wont to think no harm all night
And make a dark night too of half the day—
Which I hope well is not enrolled there:
O, these are barren tasks, too hard to keep,
Not to see ladies, study, fast, not sleep!
   King. Your oath is pass'd to pass away from
   these.
   Biron. Let me say no, my liege, an if you
   please: 50
I only swore to study with your grace
And stay here in your court for three years' space.
   Long. You swore to that, Biron, and to
   the rest.
   Biron. By yea and nay, sir, then I swore
   in jest.
What is the end of study? let me know.
   King. Why, that to know, which else we
   should not know.
   Biron. Things hid and barr'd, you mean,
   from common sense?
   King. Ay, that is study's god-like recompense.
   Biron. Come on, then; I will swear to study so,
To know the thing I am forbid to know: 60
As thus,—to study where I well may dine,
  When I to feast expressly am forbid;
Or study where to meet some mistress fine,
  When mistresses from common sense are hid;
Or, having sworn too hard a keeping oath,
Study to break it and not break my troth.
If study's gain be thus and this be so,
Study knows that which yet it doth not know:
Swear me to this, and I will ne'er say no.
   King. These be the stops that hinder study
   quite 70
And train our intellects to vain delight.
   Biron. Why, all delights are vain; but that
   most vain,
Which with pain purchased doth inherit pain:
As, painfully to pore upon a book
  To seek the light of truth; while truth the
  while

Doth falsely blind the eyesight of his look:
　Light seeking light doth light of light beguile:
So, ere you find where light in darkness lies,
Your light grows dark by losing of your eyes.
Study me how to please the eye indeed　　80
　By fixing it upon a fairer eye,
Who dazzling so, that eye shall be his heed
　And give him light that it was blinded by.
Study is like the heaven's glorious sun
　That will not be deep-search'd with saucy looks:
Small have continual plodders ever won
　Save base authority from others' books.
These earthly godfathers of heaven's lights
　That give a name to every fixed star
Have no more profit of their shining nights　90
　Than those that walk and wot not what
　　they are.
Too much to know is to know nought but fame;
And every godfather can give a name.
　King. How well he's read, to reason against
　　reading!
● *Dum.* Proceeded well, to stop all good pro-
　　ceeding!
　Long. He weeds the corn and still lets grow
　　the weeding.
● *Biron.* The spring is near when green geese
　　are a-breeding.
　Dum. How follows that?
　Biron. 　　　　　　Fit in his place and time.
　Dum. In reason nothing.
　Biron. 　　　　　Something then in rhyme.
● *King.* Biron is like an envious sneaping frost
　　　　That bites the first-born infants of
　　　　the spring. 　　　　　101
　Biron. Well, say I am; why should proud
　　summer boast
　　　　Before the birds have any cause to
　　　　sing?
Why should I joy in any abortive birth?
At Christmas I no more desire a rose
Than wish a snow in May's new-fangled mirth;
But like of each thing that in season grows.
So you, to study now it is too late,
Climb o'er the house to unlock the little gate.
　King. Well, sit you out: go home, Biron:
　　adieu. 　　　　　　　110
　Biron. No, my good lord; I have sworn to
　　stay with you:
● And though I have for barbarism spoke more
　　Than for that angel knowledge you can say,
Yet confident I'll keep what I have swore
　And bide the penance of each three years' day.
Give me the paper; let me read the same;
And to the strict'st decrees I'll write my name.
　King. How well this yielding rescues thee
　　from shame!
　Biron [*reads*]. 'Item, That no woman shall
come within a mile of my court:' Hath this been
proclaimed? 　　　　　　　121
　Long. Four days ago.
　Biron. Let's see the penalty. [*Reads*] 'On
pain of losing her tongue.' Who devised this
penalty?
　Long. Marry, that did I.
　Biron. Sweet lord, and why?
　Long. To fright them hence with that dread
　　penalty.
● *Biron.* A dangerous law against gentility!
　[*Reads*] 'Item, If any man be seen to talk

95 *Proceeded.* The word in university usage means to take an academic degree.

97 *green geese.* These were hatched in the autumn and sold in the spring. Green Goose Fair, held on Whit Monday, was a festive occasion for Elizabethan and Jacobean folk.

A typical English fair. Engraving from *Old England*, 1854

100 *sneaping.* Nipping.

112 *barbarism.* Lack of learning or culture.

129 *gentility.* Good manners.

Ferdinand, Dumain, Biron and Longaville. Illustration
by Norman Wilkinson from *Players' Shakespeare*, 1924

158 *in attainder*. Condemned to.

163 *haunted*. Visited by.

169 *complements*. Accomplishments.

171 *hight*. Is named.

172 *For interim*. For respite or relaxation.

174 *world's debate*. Warfare.

177 *minstrelsy*. i.e. entertainment.

184 *reprehend*. Represent.

185 *tharborough*. Thirdborough; lowest in the hierarchy of police officers.

with a woman within the term of three years, he
shall endure such public shame as the rest of the
court can possibly devise.'
This article, my liege, yourself must break;
　For well you know here comes in embassy
The French king's daughter with yourself to
　　　speak—
　A maid of grace and complete majesty—
About surrender up of Aquitaine
　To her decrepit, sick and bedrid father:
Therefore this article is made in vain,　　　140
　Or vainly comes the admired princess hither.
　King. What say you, lords? why, this was
　　　quite forgot.
　Biron. So study evermore is overshot:
While it doth study to have what it would
It doth forget to do the thing it should,
And when it hath the thing it hunteth most,
'Tis won as towns with fire, so won, so lost.
　King. We must of force dispense with this
　　　decree;
She must lie here on mere necessity.
　Biron. Necessity will make us all forsworn
　Three thousand times within this three years'
　　　space;　　　151
For every man with his affects is born,
　Not by might master'd but by special grace:
If I break faith, this word shall speak for me;
I am forsworn on 'mere necessity.'
So to the laws at large I write my name:
　　　　　　　　　　　　[*Subscribes.*
And he that breaks them in the least degree
● Stands in attainder of eternal shame:
　Suggestions are to other as to me;
But I believe, although I seem so loath,　　160
I am the last that will last keep his oath.
But is there no quick recreation granted?
● *King.* Ay, that there is.　Our court, you know,
　　　is haunted
With a refined traveller of Spain;
A man in all the world's new fashion planted,
　That hath a mint of phrases in his brain;
One whom the music of his own vain tongue
　Doth ravish like enchanting harmony;
● A man of complements, whom right and wrong
　Have chose as umpire of their mutiny:　　170
● This child of fancy that Armado hight
● 　For interim to our studies shall relate
In high-born words the worth of many a knight
● 　From tawny Spain lost in the world's debate.
How you delight, my lords, I know not, I;
But, I protest, I love to hear him lie
● And I will use him for my minstrelsy.
　Biron. Armado is a most illustrious wight,
A man of fire-new words, fashion's own knight.
　Long. Costard the swain and he shall be our
　　　sport;　　　180
And so to study, three years is but short.

　　　Enter DULL *with a letter, and* COSTARD.

　Dull. Which is the duke's own person?
　Biron. This, fellow: what wouldst?
● *Dull.* I myself reprehend his own person, for
● I am his grace's tharborough: but I would see his
own person in flesh and blood.
　Biron. This is he.
　Dull. Signior Arme—Arme—commends you.
There's villany abroad: this letter will tell you
more.　　　190

Cost. Sir, the contempts thereof are as touching me.

King. A letter from the magnificent Armado.

Biron. How low soever the matter, I hope in God for high words.

Long. A high hope for a low heaven : God grant us patience !

Biron. To hear? or forbear laughing?

Long. To hear meekly, sir, and to laugh moderately : or to forbear both.   200

Biron. Well, sir, be it as the style shall give us cause to climb in the merriness.

● *Cost.* The matter is to me, sir, as concerning Jaquenetta. The manner of it is, I was taken with the manner.

Biron. In what manner?

● *Cost.* In manner and form following, sir ; all those three : I was seen with her in the manor-house, sitting with her upon the form, and taken following her into the park ; which, put together, is in manner and form following. Now, sir, for the manner,—it is the manner of a man to speak to a woman : for the form,—in some form.

Biron. For the following, sir?

● *Cost.* As it shall follow in my correction : and God defend the right !

King. Will you hear this letter with attention?

Biron. As we would hear an oracle.

Cost. Such is the simplicity of man to hearken after the flesh.   220

● *King* [*reads*]. 'Great deputy, the welkin's
● vicegerent and sole dominator of Navarre, my soul's earth's god, and body's fostering patron.'

Cost. Not a word of Costard yet.

King [*reads*]. 'So it is,'—

Cost. It may be so : but if he say it is so, he
● is, in telling true, but so.

King. Peace !

Cost. Be to me and every man that dares not fight !   230

King. No words !

Cost. Of other men's secrets, I beseech you.

King [*reads*]. 'So it is, besieged with sable-coloured melancholy, I did commend the black-oppressing humour to the most wholesome physic of thy health-giving air ; and, as I am a gentle-
● man, betook myself to walk. The time when. About the sixth hour ; when beasts most graze, birds best peck, and men sit down to that nourishment which is called supper : so much for the time when. Now for the ground which ; which, I mean, I walked upon : it is ycleped thy park. Then for the place where ; where, I mean, I did encounter that obscene and most preposterous event, that draweth from my snow-white pen the ebon-coloured ink, which here thou viewest, beholdest, surveyest, or seest : but to the place where ; it standeth north-north-east and by east
● from the west corner of thy curious-knotted garden : there did I see that low-spirited swain, that base minnow of thy mirth,'—   251

Cost. Me?

King [*reads*]. 'that unlettered small-knowing soul,'—

Cost. Me?

King [*reads*]. 'that shallow vassal,'—

Cost. Still me?

King [*reads*]. 'which, as I remember, hight Costard,—

204-205 *taken with the manner*. i.e. 'caught in the act'.

207 *In manner and form following*. Another common expression of the period.

215 *correction*. Punishment.

221 *welkin*. Sky.

222 *sole dominator*. Ruler.

227 *but so*. Equivalent to the modern term 'so so'.

237-243 *The time when . . . the place where*. Standard legal terminology in Shakespeare's day. Such phrases are probably skits on legal phraseology.

249-250 *curious-knotted garden*. Intricately laid-out. Flower beds designed in different patterns or 'knots' were popular with Elizabethan gardeners.

A knotted garden. Engraving from *Old England*, 1854

Jaquenetta and Costard. Illustration by Norman Wilkinson from *Players' Shakespeare*, 1924

262-263 *continent canon.* The law enforcing restraint.

276 *weaker vessel.* The biblical term for woman.

283 *the best for the worst.* The very worst.

304-305 *mutton and porridge.* Mutton broth. 'Porridge' had the same meaning as 'pottage'. 'Mutton' was also a term for a loose woman.

Cost. O, me !   260

King [*reads*]. ' sorted and consorted, contrary
● to thy established proclaimed edict and continent
canon, which with,—O, with—but with this I
passion to say wherewith,—

Cost. With a wench.

King [*reads*]. 'with a child of our grandmother
Eve, a female ; or, for thy more sweet understanding, a woman. Him I, as my ever-esteemed
duty pricks me on, have sent to thee, to receive
the meed of punishment, by thy sweet grace's
officer, Anthony Dull ; a man of good repute,
carriage, bearing, and estimation.'

Dull. Me, an't shall please you ; I am Anthony
Dull.

King [*reads*]. 'For Jaquenetta,—so is the
● weaker vessel called which I apprehended with
the aforesaid swain,—I keep her as a vessel of
thy law's fury ; and shall, at the least of thy sweet
notice, bring her to trial. Thine, in all compli-
ments of devoted and heart-burning heat of duty.
          DON ADRIANO DE ARMADO.'

Biron. This is not so well as I looked for, but
the best that ever I heard.

● *King.* Ay, the best for the worst. But, sirrah,
what say you to this ?

Cost. Sir, I confess the wench.

King. Did you hear the proclamation ?

Cost. I do confess much of the hearing it, but
little of the marking of it.

King. It was proclaimed a year's imprisonment, to be taken with a wench.   290

Cost. I was taken with none, sir : I was taken
with a damsel.

King. Well, it was proclaimed 'damsel.'

Cost. This was no damsel neither, sir ; she
was a virgin.

King. It is so varied too ; for it was proclaimed
'virgin.'

Cost. If it were, I deny her virginity : I was
taken with a maid.

King. This maid will not serve your turn, sir.

Cost. This maid will serve my turn, sir.   301

King. Sir, I will pronounce your sentence :
you shall fast a week with bran and water.

● *Cost.* I had rather pray a month with mutton
and porridge.

King. And Don Armado shall be your keeper.
My Lord Biron, see him deliver'd o'er :
And go we, lords, to put in practice that
    Which each to other hath so strongly sworn.
        [*Exeunt King, Longaville, and Dumain.*
Biron. I'll lay my head to any good man's hat,
    These oaths and laws will prove an idle scorn.
Sirrah, come on.

Cost. I suffer for the truth, sir ; for true it is,
I was taken with Jaquenetta, and Jaquenetta is a
true girl ; and therefore welcome the sour cup of
prosperity ! Affliction may one day smile again ;
and till then, sit thee down, sorrow !   [*Exeunt.*

SCENE II.   *The same.*

Enter ARMADO *and* MOTH.

Arm. Boy, what sign is it when a man of
great spirit grows melancholy ?

Moth. A great sign, sir, that he will look sad.

Arm. Why, sadness is one and the self-same
thing, dear imp.

Moth. No, no; O Lord, sir, no.

Arm. How canst thou part sadness and melan-
•choly, my tender juvenal?

Moth. By a familiar demonstration of the
working, my tough senior.   10

Arm. Why tough senior? why tough senior?

Moth. Why tender juvenal? why tender juvenal?

• *Arm.* I spoke it, tender juvenal, as a congruent epitheton appertaining to thy young days,
which we may nominate tender.

• *Moth.* And I, tough senior, as an appertinent
title to your old time, which we may name tough.

Arm. Pretty and apt.

Moth. How mean you, sir? I pretty, and
my saying apt? or I apt, and my saying pretty?

Arm. Thou pretty, because little.

Moth. Little pretty, because little. Wherefore
apt?

Arm. And therefore apt, because quick.

Moth. Speak you this in my praise, master?

• *Arm.* In thy condign praise.

• *Moth.* I will praise an eel with the same praise.

Arm. What, that an eel is ingenious?

Moth. That an eel is quick.   30

Arm. I do say thou art quick in answers:
thou heatest my blood.

Moth. I am answered, sir.

Arm. I love not to be crossed.

Moth. [*Aside*] He speaks the mere contrary;
•crosses love not him.

Arm. I have promised to study three years
with the duke.

Moth. You may do it in an hour, sir.

Arm. Impossible.   40

Moth. How many is one thrice told?

Arm. I am ill at reckoning; it fitteth the
spirit of a tapster.

Moth. You are a gentleman and a gamester,
sir.

Arm. I confess both: they are both the varnish of a complete man.

Moth. Then, I am sure, you know how much
the gross sum of deuce-ace amounts to.

Arm. It doth amount to one more than two.

Moth. Which the base vulgar do call three.

Arm. True.

Moth. Why, sir, is this such a piece of study?
Now here is three studied, ere ye'll thrice wink:
and how easy it is to put 'years' to the word
'three,' and study three years in two words, the
•dancing horse will tell you.

Arm. A most fine figure!

Moth. To prove you a cipher.   59

Arm. I will hereupon confess I am in love:
and as it is base for a soldier to love, so am I in
love with a base wench. If drawing my sword
against the humour of affection would deliver me
from the reprobate thought of it, I would take Desire prisoner, and ransom him to any French courtier for a new-devised courtesy. I think scorn to
sigh: methinks I should outswear Cupid. Comfort me, boy: what great men have been in love?

Moth. Hercules, master.

Arm. Most sweet Hercules! More authority,
dear boy, name more; and, sweet my child, let
them be men of good repute and carriage.

Moth. Samson, master: he was a man of
good carriage, great carriage, for he carried the

8 *juvenal.* Juvenile. This term with its pun on the name of the Latin satirist was used by Greene and others as a nick-name for the poet, Thomas Nashe. 'Gallant young juvenal' was how he was described by Francis Meres in his catalogue of writers, *Palladis Tamia*, 1598. Moth, then, is Nashe.

Thomas Nashe (1567–1601). Woodcut from an Eliza-bethan cartoon

14-15 *congruent epitheton.* Fitting epithet.

17-18 *appertinent title to.* A title belonging to.

27 *condign.* Well-merited.

28 *an eel.* There is some joke here at Armado's expense, probably erotic.

36 *crosses.* Coins—with crosses on them. A common pun of the period.

57 *dancing horse.* This refers to Morocco, a trick-per-forming horse owned by Banks, frequently mentioned in Elizabethan and Jacobean literature.

Morocco, the 'dancing horse'. Nineteenth century engraving from a contemporary pamphlet, 1595

78 *rapier.* Duelling with the rapier was becoming increasingly fashionable at this time. Shakespeare's references to this new practice are uniformly disapproving.

82 *complexion.* This usually meant the colour of the skin; but it could also mean 'temperament' i.e. one of the four humours (bloody, phlegmatic, choleric and melancholic).

114-115 *the King and the Beggar.* The ballad of King Cophetua and the Beggar Maid, which Shakespeare refers to by name in Act IV, Scene I of this play, seems to be a favourite with him, since he mentions it several times.

King Cophetua and the Beggar Maid. Painting by Sir Edward Burne Jones (1833–98)

123 *rational hind.* Intelligent peasant.

136-137 *allowed for the day-woman.* Allowed in as a dairy-maid.

141 *That's hereby,* i.e. that's as maybe.

town-gates on his back like a porter: and he was in love.

   Arm.   O well-knit Samson! strong-jointed
Samson! I do excel thee in my rapier as much as thou didst me in carrying gates.   I am in love too.   Who was Samson's love, my dear Moth?

   Moth.   A woman, master.   81

   Arm.   Of what complexion?

   Moth.   Of all the four, or the three, or the two, or one of the four.

   Arm.   Tell me precisely of what complexion.

   Moth.   Of the sea-water green, sir.

   Arm.   Is that one of the four complexions?

   Moth.   As I have read, sir; and the best of them too.

   Arm.   Green indeed is the colour of lovers; but to have a love of that colour, methinks Samson had small reason for it.   He surely affected her for her wit.

   Moth.   It was so, sir; for she had a green wit.

   Arm.   My love is most immaculate white and red.

   Moth.   Most maculate thoughts, master, are masked under such colours.

   Arm.   Define, define, well-educated infant.

   Moth.   My father's wit and my mother's tongue, assist me!   101

   Arm.   Sweet invocation of a child; most pretty and pathetical!

Moth.   If she be made of white and red,
   Her faults will ne'er be known,
For blushing cheeks by faults are bred
   And fears by pale white shown:
Then if she fear, or be to blame,
   By this you shall not know,
For still her cheeks possess the same
   Which native she doth owe.   111
A dangerous rhyme, master, against the reason of white and red.

   Arm.   Is there not a ballad, boy, of the King and the Beggar?

   Moth.   The world was very guilty of such a ballad some three ages since: but I think now 'tis not to be found; or, if it were, it would neither serve for the writing nor the tune.

   Arm.   I will have that subject newly writ o'er, that I may example my digression by some mighty precedent.   Boy, I do love that country girl that I took in the park with the rational hind Costard: she deserves well.

   Moth.   [*Aside*] To be whipped; and yet a better love than my master.

   Arm.   Sing, boy; my spirit grows heavy in love.

   Moth.   And that's great marvel, loving a light wench.

   Arm.   I say, sing.   130

   Moth.   Forbear till this company be past.

Enter DULL, COSTARD, *and* JAQUENETTA.

   Dull.   Sir, the duke's pleasure is, that you keep Costard safe: and you must suffer him to take no delight nor no penance; but a' must fast three days a week.   For this damsel, I must keep her at the park: she is allowed for the day-woman.   Fare you well.

   Arm.   I do betray myself with blushing.   Maid!

   Jaq.   Man?

   Arm.   I will visit thee at the lodge.   140

   Jaq.   That's hereby.

Arm. I know where it is situate.
Jaq. Lord, how wise you are!
Arm. I will tell thee wonders.
• *Jaq.* With that face?
Arm. I love thee.
• *Jaq.* So I heard you say.
Arm. And so, farewell.
Jaq. Fair weather after you!
Dull. Come, Jaquenetta, away!   150
          [Exeunt Dull and Jaquenetta.
Arm. Villain, thou shalt fast for thy offences
ere thou be pardoned.
Cost. Well, sir, I hope, when I do it, I shall
• do it on a full stomach.
Arm. Thou shalt be heavily punished.
• *Cost.* I am more bound to you than your fellows, for they are but lightly rewarded.
Arm. Take away this villain; shut him up.
Moth. Come, you transgressing slave; away!
Cost. Let me not be pent up, sir: I will fast,
being loose.   161
• *Moth.* No, sir; that were fast and loose: thou
shalt to prison.
Cost. Well, if ever I do see the merry days of
desolation that I have seen, some shall see.
Moth. What shall some see?
Cost. Nay, nothing, Master Moth, but what
they look upon. It is not for prisoners to be too
silent in their words; and therefore I will say
nothing: I thank God I have as little patience as
another man; and therefore I can be quiet.   171
          [Exeunt Moth and Costard.
Arm. I do affect the very ground, which is
base, where her shoe, which is baser, guided by
her foot, which is basest, doth tread. I shall be
forsworn, which is a great argument of falsehood,
if I love. And how can that be true love which
is falsely attempted? Love is a familiar; Love is
a devil: there is no evil angel but Love. Yet
was Samson so tempted, and he had an excellent
strength; yet was Solomon so seduced, and he
had a very good wit. Cupid's butt-shaft is too
hard for Hercules' club; and therefore too much
• odds for a Spaniard's rapier. The first and second cause will not serve my turn; the passado
• he respects not, the duello he regards not: his
disgrace is to be called boy; but his glory is to
subdue men. Adieu, valour! rust, rapier! be
still, drum! for your manager is in love; yea, he
loveth. Assist me, some extemporal god of
• rhyme, for I am sure I shall turn sonnet. Devise, wit; write, pen; for I am for whole volumes
in folio.   *[Exit.*

ACT II.

Scene I. *The same.*

Enter the Princess of France, Rosaline, Maria,
Katharine, Boyet, Lords, *and other* Attendants.

Boyet. Now, madam, summon up your dearest spirits:
Consider who the king your father sends,
To whom he sends, and what's his embassy:
Yourself, held precious in the world's esteem,
To parley with the sole inheritor
Of all perfections that a man may owe,
Matchless Navarre; the plea of no less weight

145 *With that face.* i.e. 'you don't mean it'.

147 *So I heard you say.* Another piece of slang meaning 'you don't say'.

154 *full stomach.* With a good heart.

156-157 *fellows.* Servants.

162 *fast and loose.* An old cheating game usually associated with gypsies.

183-184 *first and second cause.* A reference to the etiquette of challenging to a duel. *passado.* A forward thrust of the sword.

Duelling with rapiers. Woodcut from J. Meyer's *Grandliche Beschreibung der Fryen . . .* 1570

185 *duello.* The rules and correct practice of duelling.

190 *turn sonnet.* Fashion or shape a sonnet.

Costume design for the Princess of France by James
Bailey, Stratford-upon-Avon, 1956

Than Aquitaine, a dowry for a queen.
Be now as prodigal of all dear grace
As Nature was in making graces dear   10
When she did starve the general world beside
And prodigally gave them all to you.
 Prin.   Good Lord Boyet, my beauty, though
   but mean,
Needs not the painted flourish of your praise:
Beauty is bought by judgement of the eye,
Not utter'd by base sale of chapmen's tongues:
I am less proud to hear you tell my worth
Than you much willing to be counted wise
In spending your wit in the praise of mine.
But now to task the tasker: good Boyet,   20
You are not ignorant, all-telling fame
Doth noise abroad, Navarre hath made a vow,
Till painful study shall outwear three years,
No woman may approach his silent court:
Therefore to's seemeth it a needful course,
Before we enter his forbidden gates,
To know his pleasure; and in that behalf,
Bold of your worthiness, we single you
As our best-moving fair solicitor.
Tell him, the daughter of the King of France, 30
On serious business, craving quick dispatch,
Importunes personal conference with his grace:
Haste, signify so much; while we attend,
Like humble-visaged suitors, his high will.
 Boyet.   Proud of employment, willingly I go.
 Prin.   All pride is willing pride, and yours
   is so.   [*Exit Boyet.*
Who are the votaries, my loving lords,
That are vow-fellows with this virtuous duke?
 First Lord.   Lord Longaville is one.
 Prin.   Know you the man?
 Mar.   I know him, madam: at a marriage-
   feast,   40
Between Lord Perigort and the beauteous heir
Of Jaques Falconbridge, solemnized
In Normandy, saw I this Longaville:
A man of sovereign parts he is esteem'd;
Well fitted in arts, glorious in arms:
Nothing becomes him ill that he would well.
The only soil of his fair virtue's gloss,
If virtue's gloss will stain with any soil,
Is a sharp wit match'd with too blunt a will;
Whose edge hath power to cut, whose will still
   wills   50
It should none spare that come within his power.
 Prin.   Some merry mocking lord, belike;
   is't so?
 Mar.   They say so most that most his hu-
   mours know.
 Prin.   Such short-lived wits do wither as
   they grow.
Who are the rest?
 Kath.   The young Dumain, a well-accom-
   plished youth,
Of all that virtue love for virtue loved:
Most power to do most harm, least knowing ill;
For he hath wit to make an ill shape good,
And shape to win grace though he had no wit. 60
I saw him at the Duke Alençon's once;
And much too little of that good I saw
Is my report to his great worthiness.
 Ros.   Another of these students at that time
Was there with him, if I have heard a truth.
Biron they call him; but a merrier man,
Within the limit of becoming mirth,

I never spent an hour's talk withal:
His eye begets occasion for his wit;
For every object that the one doth catch   70
The other turns to a mirth-moving jest,
Which his fair tongue, conceit's expositor,
Delivers in such apt and gracious words
That aged ears play truant at his tales
And younger hearings are quite ravished;
So sweet and voluble is his discourse.
   Prin. God bless my ladies! are they all in
     love,
That every one her own hath garnished
With such bedecking ornaments of praise?
   First Lord. Here comes Boyet.

        Re-enter BOYET.

● *Prin.*   Now, what admittance, lord? 80
   Boyet. Navarre had notice of your fair ap-
     proach;
And he and his competitors in oath
Were all address'd to meet you, gentle lady,
Before I came. Marry, thus much I have learnt:
He rather means to lodge you in the field,
Like one that comes here to besiege his court,
Than seek a dispensation for his oath,
● To let you enter his unpeopled house.
Here comes Navarre.

   Enter KING, LONGAVILLE, DUMAIN, BIRON,
      and Attendants.

   King. Fair princess, welcome to the court of
     Navarre.   90
   Prin. 'Fair' I give you back again; and
'welcome' I have not yet: the roof of this court
is too high to be yours; and welcome to the wide
fields too base to be mine.
   King. You shall be welcome, madam, to my
     court.
   Prin. I will be welcome, then: conduct me
     thither.
   King. Hear me, dear lady; I have sworn an
     oath.
   Prin. Our Lady help my lord! he'll be for-
     sworn.
● *King.* Not for the world, fair madam, by my
     will.
   Prin. Why, will shall break it; will and no-
     thing else.   100
   King. Your ladyship is ignorant what it is.
   Prin. Were my lord so, his ignorance were
     wise,
Where now his knowledge must prove ignorance.
● I hear your grace hath sworn out house-keeping:
'Tis deadly sin to keep that oath, my lord,
And sin to break it.
But pardon me, I am too sudden-bold:
To teach a teacher ill beseemeth me.
Vouchsafe to read the purpose of my coming,
● And suddenly resolve me in my suit.   110
   King. Madam, I will, if suddenly I may.
   Prin. You will the sooner, that I were away;
For you'll prove perjured if you make me stay.
   Biron. Did not I dance with you in Brabant
     once?
   Ros. Did not I dance with you in Brabant
     once?
   Biron. I know you did.
   Ros. How needless was it then to ask the
     question!

80 *admittance.* Permission to enter.

88 *unpeopled.* Without servants.

King: 'Fair princess, welcome . . .' Engraving from a design by L. du Guernier from Pope's *Works of Shakespeare*, 1728

99 *by my will.* Willingly.

104 *housekeeping.* Hospitality.

110 *suddenly.* Immediately.

Aquitaine, known as Guienne after the 13th century
(an English possession from 1152–1453). From Ortelius'
Epitome to the Theatre of the World, 1598

---

160 *We arrest your word.* Take your word as security.

Biron.   You must not be so quick.
Ros.   'Tis 'long of you that spur me with such
   questions.
Biron.   Your wit's too hot, it speeds too fast,
   'twill tire.   120
Ros.   Not till it leave the rider in the mire.
Biron.   What time o' day?
Ros.   The hour that fools should ask.
Biron.   Now fair befall your mask!
Ros.   Fair fall the face it covers!
Biron.   And send you many lovers!
Ros.   Amen, so you be none.
Biron.   Nay, then will I be gone.
King.   Madam, your father here doth intimate
The payment of a hundred thousand crowns; 130
Being but the one half of an entire sum
Disbursed by my father in his wars.
But say that he or we, as neither have,
Received that sum, yet there remains unpaid
A hundred thousand more; in surety of the
   which,
One part of Aquitaine is bound to us,
Although not valued to the money's worth.
If then the king your father will restore
But that one half which is unsatisfied,
We will give up our right in Aquitaine,   140
And hold fair friendship with his majesty.
But that, it seems, he little purposeth,
For here he doth demand to have repaid
A hundred thousand crowns; and not demands,
On payment of a hundred thousand crowns,
To have his title live in Aquitaine;
Which we much rather had depart withal
And have the money by our father lent
Than Aquitaine so gelded as it is.
Dear princess, were not his requests so far   150
From reason's yielding, your fair self should make
A yielding 'gainst some reason in my breast
And go well satisfied to France again.
   Prin.   You do the king my father too much
      wrong
And wrong the reputation of your name,
In so unseeming to confess receipt
Of that which hath so faithfully been paid.
   King.   I do protest I never heard of it:
And if you prove it, I'll repay it back
Or yield up Aquitaine.
• *Prin.*   We arrest your word.   160
Boyet, you can produce acquittances
For such a sum from special officers
Of Charles his father.
   King.   Satisfy me so.
   Boyet.   So please your grace, the packet is not
      come
Where that and other specialties are bound:
To-morrow you shall have a sight of them.
   King.   It shall suffice me: at which interview
All liberal reason I will yield unto.
Meantime receive such welcome at my hand
As honour without breach of honour may   170
Make tender of to thy true worthiness:
You may not come, fair princess, in my gates;
But here without you shall be so received
As you shall deem yourself lodged in my heart,
Though so denied fair harbour in my house.
Your own good thoughts excuse me, and farewell:
To-morrow shall we visit you again.
   Prin.   Sweet health and fair desires consort
      your grace!

King. Thy own wish wish ·I thee in every
  place !   [*Exit.*
Biron. Lady, I will commend you to mine
  own heart.   180
Ros. Pray you, do my commendations; I
would be glad to see it.
Biron. I would you heard it groan.
Ros. Is the fool sick?
Biron. Sick at the heart.
Ros. Alack, let it blood.
Biron. Would that do it good?
Ros. My physic says 'ay,'
Biron. Will you prick't with your eye?
Ros. No point, with my knife.   190
Biron. Now, God save thy life!
Ros. And yours from long living!
Biron. I cannot stay thanksgiving. [*Retiring.*
Dum. Sir, I pray you, a word: what lady is
  that same?

Boyet. The heir of Alencon, Katharine her
  name.
Dum. A gallant lady. Monsieur, fare you
  well.   [*Exit.*
Long. I beseech you a word: what is she in
  the white?
Boyet. A woman sometimes, an you saw her
  in the light.
Long. Perchance light in the light. I desire
  her name.
Boyet. She hath but one for herself; to desire
  that were a shame.   200
Long. Pray you, sir, whose daughter?
Boyet. Her mother's, I have heard.
Long. God's blessing on your beard!
Boyet. Good sir, be not offended.
She is an heir of Falconbridge.
Long. Nay, my choler is ended.
She is a most sweet lady.
Boyet. Not unlike, sir, that may be.
                                  [*Exit Long.*
Biron. What's her name in the cap?
Boyet. Rosaline, by good hap.   210
Biron. Is she wedded or no?
Boyet. To her will, sir, or so.
Biron. You are welcome, sir: adieu.
Boyet. Farewell to me, sir, and welcome to
  you.   [*Exit Biron.*
Mar. That last is Biron, the merry mad-cap
  lord:
Not a word with him but a jest.
Boyet.   And every jest but a word.
Prin. It was well done of you to take him at
  his word.
Boyet. I was as willing to grapple as he was
  to board.
Mar. Two hot sheeps, marry.
Boyet.   And wherefore not ships?
No sheep, sweet lamb, unless we feed on your
  lips.   220
Mar. You sheep, and I pasture: shall that
  finish the jest?
Boyet. So you grant pasture for me.
                             [*Offering to kiss her.*
Mar.   Not so, gentle beast:
My lips are no common, though several they be.
Boyet. Belonging to whom?
Mar.   To my fortunes and me.
Prin. Good wits will be jangling; but, gen-
  tles, agree:

Costume design for Rosaline by J. Gower Parks for
Holywell Park production, London, 1931

217 *take him at his word.* Talk to him in his own strain.

223 *several.* To quote Dr. Johnson '*several* is an enclosed field of a private proprietor; so Katherine says
her lips are private property'. cf Sonnet 137: 'Why
should my heart think that a several plot,/Which my
heart knows the wide world's common place?'

234 *behaviours*. Powers of expression.

235 *thorough*. Through.

246 *margent*. Literally, margins of a page; Boyet means the eyes.

249 *disposed*. Inclined to be merry.

258 *You are too hard for me*. More than I can manage.

Moth and Armado. Illustration by Norman Wilkinson from *Players' Shakespeare*, 1924

3 *Concolinel*. This could be the title of Moth's song, or merely a refrain.

5 *enlargement*. Freedom.

6 *festinately*. Quickly.

9 *French brawl*. A braule, French dance that was popular in England at this time.

12 *canary*. A lively Spanish dance.

This civil war of wits were much better used
On Navarre and his book-men; for here 'tis abused.
  Boyet. If my observation, which very seldom lies,
By the heart's still rhetoric disclosed with eyes,
Deceive me not now, Navarre is infected. 230
  Prin. With what?
  Boyet. With that which we lovers entitle affected.
  Prin. Your reason?
  Boyet. Why, all his behaviours did make their retire
To the court of his eye, peeping thorough desire:
His heart, like an agate, with your print impress'd,
Proud with his form, in his eye pride express'd:
His tongue, all impatient to speak and not see,
Did stumble with haste in his eyesight to be;
All senses to that sense did make their repair, 240
To feel only looking on fairest of fair:
Methought all his senses were lock'd in his eye,
As jewels in crystal for some prince to buy;
Who, tendering their own worth from where they were glass'd,
Did point you to buy them, along as you pass'd:
His face's own margent did quote such amazes
That all eyes saw his eyes enchanted with gazes.
I'll give you Aquitaine and all that is his,
An you give him for my sake but one loving kiss.
  Prin. Come to our pavilion: Boyet is disposed.
  Boyet. But to speak that in words which his eye hath disclosed. 250
I only have made a mouth of his eye,
By adding a tongue which I know will not lie.
  Ros. Thou art an old love-monger and speakest skilfully.
  Mar. He is Cupid's grandfather and learns news of him.
  Ros. Then was Venus like her mother, for her father is but grim.
  Boyet. Do you hear, my mad wenches?
  Mar.   No.
  Boyet.   What then, do you see?
  Ros. Ay, our way to be gone.
  Boyet.   You are too hard for me.
                            [*Exeunt*.

ACT III.

SCENE I. *The same*.

Enter ARMADO *and* MOTH.

  Arm. Warble, child; make passionate my sense of hearing.
  Moth. Concolinel.   [*Singing*.
  Arm. Sweet air! Go, tenderness of years;
take this key, give enlargement to the swain, bring
him festinately hither: I must employ him in a
letter to my love.
  Moth. Master, will you win your love with a
French brawl?
  Arm. How meanest thou? brawling in French?
  Moth. No, my complete master: but to jig off
a tune at the tongue's end, canary to it with your
feet, humour it with turning up your eyelids, sigh
a note and sing a note, sometime through the
throat, as if you swallowed love with singing love,
sometime through the nose, as if you snuffed up

love by smelling love; with your hat penthouse-like o'er the shop of your eyes; with your arms crossed on your thin-belly doublet like a rabbit on a spit; or your hands in your pocket like a man after the old painting; and keep not too long in one tune, but a snip and away. These are complements, these are humours; these betray nice wenches, that would be betrayed without these; and make them men of note—do you note me?—that most are affected to these.

Arm. How hast thou purchased this experience?

Moth. By my penny of observation.

Arm. But O,—but O,—

Moth. 'The hobby-horse is forgot.' 30

Arm. Callest thou my love 'hobby-horse'?

Moth. No, master; the hobby-horse is but a colt, and your love perhaps a hackney. But have you forgot your love?

Arm. Almost I had.

Moth. Negligent student! learn her by heart.

Arm. By heart and in heart, boy.

Moth. And out of heart, master: all those three I will prove.

Arm. What wilt thou prove? 40

Moth. A man, if I live; and this, by, in, and without, upon the instant: by heart you love her, because your heart cannot come by her; in heart you love her, because your heart is in love with her; and out of heart you love her, being out of heart that you cannot enjoy her.

Arm. I am all these three.

Moth. And three times as much more, and yet nothing at all.

Arm. Fetch hither the swain: he must carry me a letter. 51

Moth. A message well sympathized; a horse to be ambassador for an ass.

Arm. Ha, ha! what sayest thou?

Moth. Marry, sir, you must send the ass upon the horse, for he is very slow-gaited. But I go.

Arm. The way is but short: away!

Moth. As swift as lead, sir.

Arm. The meaning, pretty ingenious?
Is not lead a metal heavy, dull, and slow? 60

Moth. Minimè, honest master; or rather, master, no.

Arm. I say lead is slow.

Moth. You are too swift, sir, to say so:
Is that lead slow which is fired from a gun?

Arm. Sweet smoke of rhetoric!
He reputes me a cannon; and the bullet, that's he:
I shoot thee at the swain.

Moth. Thump then and I flee. [*Exit.*

Arm. A most acute juvenal; volable and free of grace!
By thy favour, sweet welkin, I must sigh in thy face:
Most rude melancholy, valour gives thee place.
My herald is return'd. 70

Re-enter MOTH *with* COSTARD.

Moth. A wonder, master! here's a costard broken in a shin.

Arm. Some enigma, some riddle: come, thy l'envoy; begin.

Cost. No egma, no riddle, no l'envoy; no salve †in the mail, sir: O, sir, plantain, a plain plantain! no l'envoy, no l'envoy; no salve, sir, but a plantain!

Arm. By virtue, thou enforcest laughter; thy

17 *penthouse.* Like an overhanging roof.

30 *The hobby-horse is forgot.* The hobby horse (an actor inside the frame of a horse) was a figure that accompanied morris dancing. This refrain from a popular ballad occurs in other plays of the time.

Hobby horse. Early 19th century drawing

33 *hackney.* A whore.

61 *Minimè.* By no means.

67 *volable.* Probably voluble.

71 *costard broken in a shin.* Costard: literally an apple, or slang for head, with probably some bawdy suggestion implied.

72 *l'envoy.* The send-off or address at the conclusion of a poem or a prose piece.

74 *plantain.* Plantain leaves were used to heal bruises.

85 *The fox, the ape and the bumble-bee.* This nonsensical rhyme probably contains a reference to the Gabriel Harvey v. Nashe polemic, the particular point of which is now lost.

102 *sold him a bargain, a goose.* Made a fool of him.

122 *Frances.* A whore. Nashe gives this name to the prostitute in his *Choise of Valentines :* another indication that Nashe was in mind.

131 *significant.* Sign (the letter).

Armado gives Moth a letter for Jaquenetta. Drawing by Edward Dayes (1763–1804)

silly thought my spleen ; the heaving of my lungs provokes me to ridiculous smiling. O, pardon me, my stars ! Doth the inconsiderate take salve for l'envoy, and the word l'envoy for a salve ? 80
   Moth. Do the wise think them other? is not
     l'envoy a salve ?
   Arm. No, page : it is an epilogue or discourse,
     to make plain
Some obscure precedence that hath tofore been
   sain.
I will example it :
       The fox, the ape and the humble-bee,
       Were still at odds, being but three.
There's the moral.   Now the l'envoy.
   Moth. I will add the l'envoy.   Say the moral
again.
   Arm. The fox, the ape, the humble-bee,   90
     Were still at odds, being but three.
   Moth. Until the goose came out of door,
     And stay'd the odds by adding four.
Now will I begin your moral, and do you follow
with my l'envoy.
       The fox, the ape and the humble-bee,
       Were still at odds, being but three.
   Arm. Until the goose came out of door,
     Staying the odds by adding four.
   Moth. A good l'envoy, ending in the goose :
would you desire more?   101
   Cost. The boy hath sold him a bargain, a goose,
    that's flat.
Sir, your pennyworth is good, an your goose be fat.
To sell a bargain well is as cunning as fast and
   loose :
Let me see ; a fat l'envoy ; ay, that's a fat goose.
   Arm. Come hither, come hither.   How did
    this argument begin?
   Moth. By saying that a costard was broken
    in a shin.
Then call'd you for the l'envoy.
   Cost. True, and I for a plantain : thus came
    your argument in ;
Then the boy's fat l'envoy, the goose that you
    bought ;   110
And he ended the market.
   Arm. But tell me ; how was there a costard
broken in a shin?
   Moth. I will tell you sensibly.
   Cost. Thou hast no feeling of it, Moth : I will
    speak that l'envoy :
I Costard, running out, that was safely within,
Fell over the threshold, and broke my shin.
   Arm. We will talk no more of this matter.
   Cost. Till there be more matter in the shin.
   Arm. Sirrah Costard, I will enfranchise thee.
   Cost. O, marry me to one Frances : I smell
some l'envoy, some goose, in this.
   Arm. By my sweet soul, I mean setting thee
at liberty, enfreedoming thy person : thou wert
immured, restrained, captivated, bound.
   Cost. True, true ; and now you will be my
purgation and let me loose.
   Arm. I give thee thy liberty, set thee from
durance ; and, in lieu thereof, impose on thee
nothing but this : bear this significant [*giving a
letter*] to the country maid Jaquenetta : there is
remuneration ; for the best ward of mine honour
is rewarding my dependents. Moth, follow. [*Exit.*
   Moth. Like the sequel, I. Signior Costard,
    adieu.

Cost. My sweet ounce of man's flesh! my incony Jew! [*Exit Moth.*
Now will I look to his remuneration. Remuneration! O, that's the Latin word for three farthings: three farthings—remuneration.—'What's the price of this inkle?'—'One penny.'—'No, I'll give you a remuneration:' why, it carries it. Remuneration! why, it is a fairer name than French crown. I will never buy and sell out of this word.

Enter BIRON.

Biron. O, my good knave Costard! exceedingly well met.
Cost. Pray you, sir, how much carnation ribbon may a man buy for a remuneration?
Biron. What is a remuneration?
Cost. Marry, sir, halfpenny farthing.   149
Biron. Why, then, three-farthing worth of silk.
Cost. I thank your worship: God be wi' you!
Biron. Stay, slave, I must employ thee:
As thou wilt win my favour, good my knave,
Do one thing for me that I shall entreat.
Cost. When would you have it done, sir?
Biron. This afternoon.
Cost. Well, I will do it, sir: fare you well.
Biron. Thou knowest not what it is.
Cost. I shall know, sir, when I have done it.
Biron. Why, villain, thou must know first.   160
Cost. I will come to your worship to-morrow morning.
Biron. It must be done this afternoon. Hark, slave, it is but this:
The princess comes to hunt here in the park,
And in her train there is a gentle lady;
When tongues speak sweetly, then they name her name,
And Rosaline they call her: ask for her;
And to her white hand see thou do commend 169
This seal'd-up counsel. There's thy guerdon; go.
  [*Giving him a shilling.*
Cost. Gardon, O sweet gardon! better than remuneration, a 'leven-pence farthing better: most sweet gardon! I will do it, sir, in print. Gardon! Remuneration! [*Exit.*
Biron. And I, forsooth, in love! I, that have been love's whip:
A very beadle to a humorous sigh;
A critic, nay, a night-watch constable;
A domineering pedant o'er the boy;
Than whom no mortal so magnificent!   180
This wimpled, whining, purblind, wayward boy;
This senior-junior, giant-dwarf, Dan Cupid;
Regent of love-rhymes, lord of folded arms,
The anointed sovereign of sighs and groans,
Liege of all loiterers and malcontents,
Dread prince of plackets, king of codpieces,
Sole imperator and great general
Of trotting 'paritors:—O my little heart!—
And I to be a corporal of his field,
And wear his colours like a tumbler's hoop!   190
What, I! I love! I sue! I seek a wife!
A woman, that is like a German clock,
Still a-repairing, ever out of frame,
And never going aright, being a watch,
But being watch'd that it may still go right!
Nay, to be perjured, which is worst of all;
And, among three, to love the worst of all;
A wightly wanton with a velvet brow,
With two pitch-balls stuck in her face for eyes;

136 *incony Jew.* 'Incony' is a term of endearment. 'Jew' appears in *A Midsummer Night's Dream* in the company of 'Juvenal', perhaps as an affectionate diminutive.

140 *inkle.* A kind of linen tape.

143 *out of this word.* Without using this word.

Biron: 'Hark, slave, it is but this:' Illustration by Gordon Browne from Henry Irving's *Shakespeare*, 1888

170-171 *guerdon . . . gardon.* A reward.

173 *in print.* Precisely, most carefully.

181 *wimpled.* Blindfold.

182 *Dan.* Variant of Don.

186 *plackets . . . codpieces.* 'Placket' was used of a petticoat or of the opening in it to a pocket. Codpiece was a bag-like appendage at the front of men's breeches or hose. In Elizabethan slang terms, 'placket' stood for 'woman'; 'codpiece' for 'man'.

188 *'paritors.* Dr. Johnson said that 'a paritor is the officer of the bishop's court who carried out citations; as citations are most frequently issued for fornication, the paritor is under Cupid's government'.

190 *tumbler's hoop.* A hoop twisted with coloured silks with which the tumbler did his tricks.

201 *Argus.* In classical mythology Argus, with his hundred eyes, was sent by Juno to watch over Io, so that Jupiter should not make love to her.

207 *Joan.* Joan is used for a lower class girl as opposed to a lady, as in the closing song to this play 'While greasy Joan doth keel the pot'.

8 *stand and play the murderer in.* Stands were commonly erected from which the driven deer were shot.

Ladies hunting, 14th century. Engraving from Joseph Strutt's *The Sports and Pastimes of the People of England,* 1810

22 *O heresy in fair, fit for these days.* This refers to Henry of Navarre's abjuring Protestantism for the sake of reconciling Catholics, especially Catholic Paris—'Paris is worth a Mass'—to his succession to the French throne. His conversion greatly disturbed his English allies, especially the Queen, and the breach of his word is glanced at in this play.

Ay, and, by heaven, one that will do the deed 200
● Though Argus were her eunuch and her guard:
And I to sigh for her! to watch for her!
To pray for her! Go to; it is a plague
That Cupid will impose for my neglect
Of his almighty dreadful little might.
Well, I will love, write, sigh, pray, sue and groan:
● Some men must love my lady and some Joan.
                                        [*Exit.*

ACT IV.

SCENE I. *The same.*

Enter the Princess, *and her train, a* Forester, BOYET, ROSALINE, MARIA, *and* KATHARINE.

  Prin. Was that the king, that spurr'd his horse so hard
Against the steep uprising of the hill?
  Boyet. I know not; but I think it was not he.
  Prin. Whoe'er a' was, a' show'd a mounting mind.
Well, lords, to-day we shall have our dispatch:
On Saturday we will return to France.
Then, forester, my friend, where is the bush
● That we must stand and play the murderer in?
  For. Hereby, upon the edge of yonder coppice;
A stand where you may make the fairest shoot. 10
  Prin. I thank my beauty, I am fair that shoot,
And thereupon thou speak'st the fairest shoot.
  For. Pardon me, madam, for I meant not so.
  Prin. What, what? first praise me and again say no?
O short-lived pride! Not fair? alack for woe!
  For. Yes, madam, fair.
  Prin.   Nay, never paint me now:
Where fair is not, praise cannot mend the brow.
Here, good my glass, take this for telling true:
Fair payment for foul words is more than due.
  For. Nothing but fair is that which you inherit. 20
  Prin. See, see, my beauty will be saved by merit!
● O heresy in fair, fit for these days!
A giving hand, though foul, shall have fair praise.
But come, the bow: now mercy goes to kill,
And shooting well is then accounted ill.
Thus will I save my credit in the shoot:
Not wounding, pity would not let me do't;
If wounding, then it was to show my skill,
That more for praise than purpose meant to kill.
And out of question so it is sometimes, 30
Glory grows guilty of detested crimes,
When, for fame's sake, for praise, an outward part,
We bend to that the working of the heart;
As I for praise alone now seek to spill
The poor deer's blood, that my heart means no ill.
  Boyet. Do not curst wives hold that self-sovereignty
Only for praise sake, when they strive to be
Lords o'er their lords?
  Prin.   Only for praise: and praise we may afford
To any lady that subdues a lord. 40
  Boyet. Here comes a member of the commonwealth.

Enter COSTARD.

Cost. God dig-you-den all! Pray you, which
is the head lady?
Prin. Thou shalt know her, fellow, by the
rest that have no heads.
Cost. Which is the greatest lady, the highest?
Prin. The thickest and the tallest.
Cost. The thickest and the tallest! it is so;
truth is truth.
An your waist, mistress, were as slender as my
wit,
One o' these maids' girdles for your waist should
be fit.   50
Are not you the chief woman? you are the
thickest here.
Prin. What's your will, sir? what's your
will?
Cost. I have a letter from Monsieur Biron to
one Lady Rosaline.
Prin. O, thy letter, thy letter! he's a good
friend of mine:
Stand aside, good bearer. Boyet, you can carve;
Break up this capon.
Boyet.   I am bound to serve.
This letter is mistook, it importeth none here;
It is writ to Jaquenetta.
Prin.   We will read it, I swear.
Break the neck of the wax, and every one give
ear.   59

Boyet [*reads*]. 'By heaven, that thou art fair,
is most infallible; true, that thou art beauteous;
truth itself, that thou art lovely. More fairer
than fair, beautiful than beauteous, truer than
truth itself, have commiseration on thy heroical
vassal! The magnanimous and most illustrate
king Cophetua set eye upon the pernicious and
indubitate beggar Zenelophon; and he it was
that might rightly say, *Veni, vidi, vici*; which to
annothanize in the vulgar,—O base and obscure
vulgar!—*videlicet*, He came, saw, and overcame:
he came, one; saw, two; overcame, three. Who
came? the king: why did he come? to see: why
did he see? to overcome: to whom came he? to
the beggar: what saw he? the beggar: who overcame he? the beggar. The conclusion is victory:
on whose side? the king's. The captive is enriched: on whose side? the beggar's. The catastrophe is a nuptial: on whose side? the king's:
no, on both in one, or one in both. I am the
king; for so stands the comparison: thou the
beggar; for so witnesseth thy lowliness. Shall I
command thy love? I may: shall I enforce thy
love? I could: shall I entreat thy love? I will.
What shalt thou exchange for rags? robes; for
tittles? titles; for thyself? me. Thus, expecting
thy reply, I profane my lips on thy foot, my eyes
on thy picture, and my heart on thy every part.
Thine, in the dearest design of industry,
                DON ADRIANO DE ARMADO.'
Thus dost thou hear the Nemean lion roar   90
  'Gainst thee, thou lamb, that standest as his
    prey.
Submissive fall his princely feet before,
  And he from forage will incline to play:
But if thou strive, poor soul, what art thou then?
Food for his rage, repasture for his den.
Prin. What plume of feathers is he that in-
dited this letter?

56 *capon.* There is a double meaning here. 'Capon'
means a 'chicken' and also 'love-letter'.

Boyet (Sebastian Shaw) reads the letter to Rosaline
(Estelle Kohler) and the Princess of France (Susan
Fleetwood), Royal Shakespeare Co, 1973

66 *Cophetua.* We have already had a reference to King
Cophetua and the Beggar Maid. Shakespeare mentions
the story again in *Romeo and Juliet, Richard II* and
2 Henry IV.

69 *annothanize.* Shakespeare's coinage for 'anatomize'
vulgar. The vernacular.

90 *Nemean lion.* A reference to the first labour of Hercules, recalled from Golding's *Ovid.*

101 *A phantasime, a Monarcho.* 'Phantasime' means a fantastic being. Monarcho was Queen Elizabeth's dwarf, a dwarf being a favourite appendage to a royal monarch, as at the Spanish Court.

110 *suitor.* This was pronounced 'shooter', and thus explains the quibble.

127 *hit it.* This was a popular catch, to be danced to.

134 *mark . . . prick . . . mete.* These are archery terms. 'Mark' means 'target'; 'prick' the bull's eye or spot in centre of the target; 'mete'—to aim at; all used with bawdy suggestiveness.

135 *Wide o' the bow hand.* Wide of the mark.

136 *clout.* The target mark.

Archers at the target. Illustration from *Le centre de l'amour, c.* 1600

What vane? what weathercock? did you **ever** hear better?
Boyet. I am much deceived but I remember **the** style.
Prin. Else your memory is bad, going o'er it erewhile.
Boyet. This Armado is a Spaniard, that keeps here in court;   100
A phantasime, a Monarcho, and one that makes sport
To the prince and his bookmates.
Prin.   Thou fellow, a word:
Who gave thee this letter?
Cost.   I told you; my lord.
Prin. To whom shouldst thou give it?
Cost.   From my lord to my lady.
Prin. From which lord to which lady?
Cost. From my lord Biron, a good master of mine,
To a lady of France that he call'd Rosaline.
Prin. Thou hast mistaken his letter. Come, lords, away.
[*To Ros.*] Here, sweet, put up this: 'twill be thine another day.
                    [*Exeunt Princess and train.*
Boyet. Who is the suitor? who is the suitor?
Ros.   Shall I teach you to know? 110
Boyet. Ay, my continent of beauty.
Ros.   Why, she that bears the bow.
Finely put off!
Boyet. My lady goes to kill horns; but, if thou marry,
Hang me by the neck, if horns that year miscarry.
Finely put on!
Ros. Well, then, I am the shooter.
Boyet.   And who is your deer?
Ros. If we choose by the horns, yourself come not near.
Finely put on, indeed!
Mar. You still wrangle with her, Boyet, and she strikes at the brow.
Boyet. But she herself is hit lower: have I hit her now?   120
Ros. Shall I come upon thee with an old saying, that was a man when King Pepin of France was a little boy, as touching the hit it?
Boyet. So I may answer thee with one as old, that was a woman when Queen Guinover of Britain was a little wench, as touching the hit it.
Ros. Thou canst not hit it, hit it, hit it,
Thou canst not hit it, my good man.
Boyet. An I cannot, cannot, cannot,
An I cannot, another can.   130
                    [*Exeunt Ros. and Kath.*
Cost. By my troth, most pleasant: how both did fit it!
Mar. A mark marvellous well shot, for they both did hit it.
Boyet. A mark! O, mark but that mark! A mark, says my lady!
Let the mark have a prick in't, to mete at, if it may be.
Mar. Wide o' the bow hand! i' faith, your hand is out.
Cost. Indeed, a' must shoot nearer, or he'll ne'er hit the clout.
Boyet. An if my hand be out, then belike your hand is in.

Cost. Then will she get the upshoot by cleaving the pin.

● *Mar.* Come, come, you talk greasily; your lips grow foul.

Cost. She's too hard for you at pricks, sir: challenge her to bowl.   140

● *Boyet.* I fear too much rubbing. Good night, my good owl. [*Exeunt Boyet and Maria.*

Cost. By my soul, a swain! a most simple clown!

Lord, Lord, how the ladies and I have put him down!

O' my troth, most sweet jests! most incony vulgar wit!

When it comes so smoothly off, so obscenely, as it were, so fit.

Armado o' th' one side,—O, a most dainty man!

To see him walk before a lady and to bear her fan!

To see him kiss his hand! and how most sweetly a' will swear!

And his page o' t' other side, that handful of wit!

Ah, heavens, it is a most pathetical nit!   150

● Sola, sola!   [*Shout within.*
                    [*Exit Costard, running.*

Scene II. *The same.*

Enter HOLOFERNES, SIR NATHANIEL, *and* DULL.

Nath. Very reverend sport, truly; and done
● in the testimony of a good conscience.

Hol. The deer was, as you know, sanguis, in
● blood; ripe as the pomewater, who now hangeth like a jewel in the ear of caelo, the sky, the welkin, the heaven; and anon falleth like a crab on the face of terra, the soil, the land, the earth.

Nath. Truly, Master Holofernes, the epithets are sweetly varied, like a scholar at the least:
● but, sir, I assure ye, it was a buck of the first head.

● *Hol.* Sir Nathaniel, haud credo.   11
● *Dull.* 'Twas not a haud credo; 'twas a pricket.

Hol. Most barbarous intimation! yet a kind of insinuation, as it were, in via, in way, of explication; facere, as it were, replication, or rather, ostentare, to show, as it were, his inclination, after his undressed, unpolished, uneducated, unpruned, untrained, or rather, unlettered, or ratherest, unconfirmed fashion, to insert again my haud credo for a deer.   20

Dull. I said the deer was not a haud credo; 'twas a pricket.

Hol. Twice-sod simplicity, bis coctus!
O thou monster Ignorance, how deformed dost thou look!

Nath. Sir, he hath never fed of the dainties that are bred in a book;

he hath not eat paper, as it were; he hath not drunk ink: his intellect is not replenished; he is only an animal, only sensible in the duller parts:

And such barren plants are set before us, that we thankful should be,

Which we of taste and feeling are, for those parts that do fructify in us more than he.   30

For as it would ill become me to be vain, indiscreet, or a fool,

● So were there a patch set on learning, to see him in a school:

But omne bene, say I; being of an old father's mind,

Many can brook the weather that love not the wind.

---

139 *greasily*. Indecently.

141 *rubbing*. A technical term used in the game of bowls.

151 *Sola*. A hunting halloo.

2 *the testimony of a good conscience*. The curate gives his blessing to this sport.

4 *pomewater*. A large, juicy apple popular in the 16th century.

10 *buck of the first head*. A mature, fully grown buck.

11 *haud credo*. Latin for 'I do not believe it'. Dull took this for 'awd (old) grey doe' and goes on to insist that it was not a doe but a buck.

12 *pricket*. A two-year old buck.

Stag-hunting at Nonesuch Palace. Detail from a painting, Flemish School

---

32 *patch*. Fool.

Miles Malleson as Sir Nathanial, Old Vic Theatre, London, 1949

---

37 *Dyctynna*. An unusual name for the moon. Shakespeare noticed this in the 2nd book of Golding's translation of Ovid's *Metamorphoses*.

41 *raught*. Reached.

54 *Perge*. Latin for 'proceed'.

56 *affect the letter*. Resort to alliteration.

71 *pia mater*. The brain.

80 *Mehercle!* By Hercules!

82-83 *vir sapit qui pauca loquitur*. A proverb meaning 'That man is wise that speaketh few things or words'— a tag from Lily's *Latin Grammar*

Dull. You two are book-men : can you tell me by your wit
What was a month old at Cain's birth, that's not five weeks old as yet?
• *Hol.* Dictynna, goodman Dull; Dictynna, goodman Dull.
Dull. What is Dictynna?
Nath. A title to Phœbe, to Luna, to the moon.
Hol. The moon was a month old when Adam was no more,   40
•And raught not to five weeks when he came to five-score.
The allusion holds in the exchange.
Dull. 'Tis true indeed; the collusion holds in the exchange.
Hol. God comfort thy capacity! I say, the allusion holds in the exchange.
Dull. And I say, the pollusion holds in the exchange; for the moon is never but a month old: and I say beside that, 'twas a pricket that the princess killed.
Hol. Sir Nathaniel, will you hear an extemporal epitaph on the death of the deer? And, to humour the ignorant, call I the deer the princess killed a pricket.
• *Nath.* Perge, good Master Holofernes, perge; so it shall please you to abrogate scurrility.
• *Hol.* I will something affect the letter, for it argues facility.
The preyful princess pierced and prick'd a pretty pleasing pricket;
Some say a sore; but not a sore, till now made sore with shooting.
The dogs did yell: put L to sore, then sorel jumps from thicket;   60
Or pricket sore, or else sorel; the people fall a-hooting.
If sore be sore, then L to sore makes fifty sores one sorel.
Of one sore I an hundred make by adding but one more L.
Nath. A rare talent!
Dull. [*Aside*] If a talent be a claw, look how he claws him with a talent.
Hol. This is a gift that I have, simple, simple; a foolish extravagant spirit, full of forms, figures, shapes, objects, ideas, apprehensions, motions, revolutions: these are begot in the ventricle of
•memory, nourished in the womb of pia mater, and delivered upon the mellowing of occasion. But the gift is good in those in whom it is acute, and I am thankful for it.
Nath. Sir, I praise the Lord for you: and so may my parishioners; for their sons are well tutored by you, and their daughters profit very greatly under you: you are a good member of the commonwealth.
• *Hol.* Mehercle, if their sons be ingenuous, they shall want no instruction; if their daughters
•be capable, I will put it to them: but vir sapit qui pauca loquitur; a soul feminine saluteth us.

Enter JAQUENETTA *and* COSTARD.

Jaq. God give you good morrow, master Parson.
Hol. Master Parson, quasi pers-on. An if one should be pierced, which is the one?
Cost. Marry, master schoolmaster, he that is likest to a hogshead.

Hol. Piercing a hogshead! a good lustre of conceit in a turf of earth; fire enough for a flint, pearl enough for a swine: 'tis pretty; it is well.

Jaq. Good master Parson, be so good as read me this letter: it was given me by Costard, and sent me from Don Armado: I beseech you, read it.

Hol. Fauste, precor gelida quando pecus omne sub umbra Ruminat,—and so forth. Ah, good old Mantuan! I may speak of thee as the traveller doth of Venice;

    Venetia, Venetia,
    Chi non ti vede non ti pretia.   100

Old Mantuan, old Mantuan! who understandeth thee not, loves thee not. Ut, re, sol, la, mi, fa. Under pardon, sir, what are the contents? or rather, as Horace says in his—What, my soul, verses?

Nath. Ay, sir, and very learned.

Hol. Let me hear a staff, a stanze, a verse; lege, domine.

Nath. [*reads*]

If love make me forsworn, how shall I swear to love?
  Ah, never faith could hold, if not to beauty vow'd! 110
Though to myself forsworn, to thee I'll faithful prove;
  Those thoughts to me were oaks, to thee like osiers bow'd.
Study his bias leaves and makes his book thine eyes,
  Where all those pleasures live that art would comprehend:
If knowledge be the mark, to know thee shall suffice;
  Well learned is that tongue that well can thee commend,
All ignorant that soul that sees thee without wonder;
  Which is to me some praise that I thy parts admire:
Thy eye Jove's lightning bears, thy voice his dreadful thunder,
  Which, not to anger bent, is music and sweet fire. 120
Celestial as thou art, O, pardon love this wrong,
That sings heaven's praise with such an earthly tongue.

Hol. You find not the apostraphas, and so miss the accent: let me supervise the canzonet. Here are only numbers ratified; but, for the elegancy, facility, and golden cadence of poesy, caret. Ovidius Naso was the man: and why, indeed, Naso, but for smelling out the odoriferous flowers of fancy, the jerks of invention? Imitari is nothing: so doth the hound his master, the ape his keeper, the tired horse his rider. But, damosella virgin, was this directed to you?

Jaq. Ay, sir, from one Monsieur Biron, one of the strange queen's lords.

Hol. I will overglance the superscript: 'To the snow-white hand of the most beauteous Lady Rosaline.' I will look again on the intellect of the letter, for the nomination of the party writing to the person written unto: 'Your ladyship's in all desired employment, BIRON.' Sir Nathaniel, this Biron is one of the votaries with the king; and here he hath framed a letter to a sequent of the stranger queen's, which accidentally, or by

89 *Piercing a hogshead.* 'Hogshead' was often used to describe a dull-witted person. 'Piercing a hogshead' was slang for getting drunk.

95-96 *Fauste . . . Ruminat.* 'I pray thee, Faustus, while our cattle ruminate in the cool shade.' These are the opening words to the first eclogue of Mantuan, a Renaissance poet whose Latin poems were used in schools as a textbook. This line was thrown about by both Harvey and Nashe in their pamphlet warfare.

99-100 *Venetia . . . pretia.* This proverb appears in Florio's *First Fruites* (1578) with the following translation: 'Venise who seeth thee not, praiseth thee not, but who seeth thee, it casteth hym well'.

102 *Ut, re, sol, la, mi, fa.* Holofernes is airing his knowledge of music but gets it wrong. The hexachord should run 'Ut, re, mi, fa, sol, la'!

109 *If love make me forsworn.* This sonnet was reprinted in *The Passionate Pilgrim* (1599).

124 *supervise the canzonet.* 'Look over' the short song or ditty.

137 *intellect.* Understanding, meaning.

156 *colourable colours.* i.e. plausible pretexts.

163-164 *undertake your ben venuto.* i.e. act as your sponsor and ensure your welcome.

171 *pauca verba.* Few words.

Costume design for Biron by J. Gower Parks, for Holywell Park production, London, 1931

2 *pitched a toil.* Laid a snare.

3 *toiling in a pitch.* Biron is no doubt referring to Rosaline's eyes ('two pitch-balls').

12-13 *lie in my throat.* Lie deeply.

the way of progression, hath miscarried.   Trip and go, my sweet; deliver this paper into the royal hand of the king: it may concern much. Stay not thy compliment; I forgive thy duty: adieu.

Jaq.   Good Costard, go with me. Sir, God save your life !   150

Cost.   Have with thee, my girl.

                                    [*Exeunt Cost. and Jaq.*

Nath.   Sir, you have done this in the fear of God, very religiously; and, as a certain father saith,—

Hol.   Sir, tell not me of the father; I do fear colourable colours.   But to return to the verses: did they please you, Sir Nathaniel?

Nath.   Marvellous well for the pen.

Hol.   I do dine to-day at the father's of a certain pupil of mine; where, if, before repast, it shall please you to gratify the table with a grace, I will, on my privilege I have with the parents of the foresaid child or pupil, undertake your ben venuto; where I will prove those verses to be very unlearned, neither savouring of poetry, wit, nor invention: I beseech your society.

Nath.   And thank you too; for society, saith the text, is the happiness of life.

Hol.   And, certes, the text most infallibly concludes it.   [*To Dull*] Sir, I do invite you too; you shall not say me nay: pauca verba. Away ! the gentles are at their game, and we will to our recreation.   [*Exeunt.*

SCENE III.   *The same.*

Enter BIRON, *with a paper.*

Biron.   The king he is hunting the deer; I am coursing myself: they have pitched a toil; I am toiling in a pitch,—pitch that defiles: defile ! a foul word.   Well, set thee down, sorrow ! for so they say the fool said, and so say I, and I the fool: well proved, wit !   By the Lord, this love is as mad as Ajax: it kills sheep; it kills me, I a sheep: well proved again o' my side !   I will not love: if I do, hang me; i' faith, I will not.   O, but her eye,—by this light, but for her eye, I would not love her; yes, for her two eyes.   Well, I do nothing in the world but lie, and lie in my throat.   By heaven, I do love: and it hath taught me to rhyme and to be melancholy; and here is part of my rhyme, and here my melancholy. Well, she hath one o' my sonnets already: the clown bore it, the fool sent it, and the lady hath it: sweet clown, sweeter fool, sweetest lady ! By the world, I would not care a pin, if the other three were in.   Here comes one with a paper: God give him grace to groan ! [*Stands aside.* 21

Enter the King, *with a paper.*

King.   Ay me !

Biron.   [*Aside*] Shot, by heaven !   Proceed, sweet Cupid: thou hast thumped him with thy bird-bolt under the left pap.   In faith, secrets !

King [*reads*].

So sweet a kiss the golden sun gives not
   To those fresh morning drops upon the rose,
As thy eye-beams, when their fresh rays have smote
   The night of dew that on my cheeks down flows:
Nor shines the silver moon one half so bright 30

Through the transparent bosom of the deep,
As doth thy face through **tears** of mine give light;
Thou shinest in every tear that I do weep:
No drop but as a coach doth carry thee;
So ridest thou triumphing in my woe.
Do but behold the tears that swell in me,
And they thy glory through my grief will show:
But do not love thyself; then thou wilt keep
My tears for glasses, and still make me weep.
O queen of queens! how far dost thou excel,   40
No thought can think, nor tongue of mortal **tell**.
How shall she know my griefs? I'll drop the
    paper:
Sweet leaves, shade folly.   Who is he comes here?
                            [*Steps aside.*
What, Longaville! and reading! listen, ear.
    Biron. Now, in thy likeness, one more fool
        appear!

Enter LONGAVILLE, *with a paper.*

    Long. Ay me, I am forsworn!
    Biron. Why, he comes in like a perjure,
wearing papers.
    King. In love, I hope: sweet fellowship in
        shame!
    Biron. One drunkard loves another of the
        name.   50
    Long. Am I the first that have been per-
        jured so?
    Biron. I could put thee in comfort.   Not by
two that I know:
Thou makest the triumviry, the corner-cap of
    society,
● The shape of Love's Tyburn that hangs up sim-
    plicity.
    Long. I fear these stubborn lines lack power
        to move.
O sweet Maria, empress of my love!
These numbers will I tear, and write in prose.
    Biron. O, rhymes are guards on wanton
        Cupid's hose:
Disfigure not his slop.
    Long.   This same shall go. [*Reads.*
● Did not the heavenly rhetoric of thine eye,   60
    'Gainst whom the world cannot hold argument,
    Persuade my heart to this false perjury?
    Vows for thee broke deserve not punishment.
    A woman I forswore; but I will prove,
    Thou being a goddess, I forswore not thee:
    My vow was earthly, thou a heavenly love;
    Thy grace being gain'd cures all disgrace in me.
    Vows are but breath, and breath a vapour is:
    Then thou, fair sun, which on my earth dost
        shine,
    Exhalest this vapour-vow; in thee it is: 70
    If broken then, it is no fault of mine:
    If by me broke, what fool is not so wise
    To lose an oath to win a paradise?
● *Biron.* This is the liver-vein, which makes
    flesh a deity,
A green goose a goddess: pure, pure idolatry.
God amend us, God amend! we are much out o'
    the way.
    Long. By whom shall I send this?—Com-
        pany! stay.   [*Steps aside.*
    Biron. All hid, all hid; an old infant play.
Like a demigod here sit I in the sky,
And wretched fools' secrets heedfully o'er-eye. 80

King: 'What, Longaville! and reading . . .' Engraving
by H. Fuseli from Steevens' *The Plays of Shakspeare,*
1805

---

54 *shape of Love's Tyburn.* The gallows were triangular
shaped and Longaville makes a third in the triumvirate
to be caught out.

60 *Did not the heavenly rhetoric of thine eye . . .* This
sonnet is reprinted in *The Passionate Pilgrim.*

74 *liver-vein.* The liver was considered the seat of passion; hence liver-vein means vein or style of love.

81 *More sacks to the mill.* A lot more to come.

82 *woodcocks.* Simpletons: four of the men have now been caught out.

94 *is not that a good word?* Is that not a kindness on my part?

98 *saucers.* Since Dumain's lady is a fever in his blood she might be let out, like blood in saucers, as in blood-letting. This is the meaning.

101-120 *On a day . . . thy love.* This poem appears in *The Passionate Pilgrim.*

Longaville: 'Dumain, thy love is far from charity . . .'
Engraving from a design by H. Gravelot for Theobald's edition of Shakespeare's works, 1744

●More sacks to the mill! O heavens, I have my wish!

    Enter DUMAIN, *with a paper.*

●Dumain transform'd! four woodcocks in a dish!
  Dum. O most divine Kate!
  Biron. O most profane coxcomb!
  Dum. By heaven, the wonder in a mortal eye!
  Biron. By earth, she is not, corporal, there you lie.
  Dum. Her amber hair for foul hath amber quoted.
  Biron. An amber-colour'd raven was well noted.
  Dum. As upright as the cedar.
  Biron.   Stoop, I say;
Her shoulder is with child.
  Dum.   As fair as day. 90
  Biron. Ay, as some days; but then no sun must shine.
  Dum. O that I had my wish!
  Long.   And I had mine!
  King. And I mine too, good Lord!
● *Biron.* Amen, so I had mine: is not that a good word?
  Dum. I would forget her; but a fever she
Reigns in my blood and will remember'd be.
  Biron. A fever in your blood! why, then incision
●Would let her out in saucers: sweet misprision!
  Dum. Once more I'll read the ode that I have writ.
  Biron. Once more I'll mark how love can vary wit. 100
  Dum. [*reads*]

●   On a day—alack the day!—
    Love, whose month is ever May,
    Spied a blossom passing fair
    Playing in the wanton air:
    Through the velvet leaves the wind,
    All unseen, can passage find;
    That the lover, sick to death,
    Wish himself the heaven's breath.
    Air, quoth he, thy cheeks may blow;
    Air, would I might triumph so! 110
    But, alack, my hand is sworn
    Ne'er to pluck thee from thy thorn;
    Vow, alack, for youth unmeet,
    Youth so apt to pluck a sweet!
    Do not call it sin in me,
    That I am forsworn for thee;
    Thou for whom Jove would swear
    Juno but an Ethiope were;
    And deny himself for Jove,
    Turning mortal for thy love. 120
This will I send and something else more plain,
That shall express my true love's fasting pain.
O, would the king, Biron, and Longaville,
Were lovers too! Ill, to example ill,
Would from my forehead wipe a perjured note;
For none offend where all alike do dote.
  Long. [*advancing*]. Dumain, thy love is far from charity,
That in love's grief desirest society:
You may look pale, but I should blush, I know,
To be o'erheard and taken napping so. 130
  King [*advancing*]. Come, sir, you blush; as his your case is such;
You chide at him, offending twice as much;

You do not love Maria; Longaville
Did never sonnet for her sake compile,
Nor never lay his wreathed arms athwart
His loving bosom to keep down his heart.
I have been closely shrouded in this bush
And mark'd you both and for you both did blush:
I heard your guilty rhymes, observed your fashion,
Saw sighs reek from you, noted well your passion:
Ay me! says one; O Jove! the other cries;   141
One, her hairs were gold, crystal the other's eyes:
[*To Long.*] You would for paradise break faith
      and troth;
[*To Dum.*] And Jove, for your love, would in-
      fringe an oath.
What will Biron say when that he shall hear
Faith so infringed, which such zeal did swear?
How will he scorn! how will he spend his wit!
How will he triumph, leap and laugh at it!
For all the wealth that ever I did see,
I would not have him know so much by me.   150
    Biron.   Now step I forth to whip hypocrisy.
                                    [*Advancing.*
Ah, good my liege, I pray thee, pardon me!
Good heart, what grace hast thou, thus to reprove
These worms for loving, that art most in love?
Your eyes do make no coaches; in your tears
There is no certain princess that appears;
You'll not be perjured, 'tis a hateful thing;
Tush, none but minstrels like of sonneting!
But are you not ashamed? nay, are you not,
All three of you, to be thus much o'ershot?   160
You found his mote; the king your mote did see;
But I a beam do find in each of three.
O, what a scene of foolery have I seen,
Of sighs, of groans, of sorrow and of teen!
O me, with what strict patience have I sat,
To see a king transformed to a gnat!
• To see great Hercules whipping a gig,
And profound Solomon to tune a jig,
• And Nestor play at push-pin with the boys,
And critic Timon laugh at idle toys!   170
Where lies thy grief, O, tell me, good Dumain?
And, gentle Longaville, where lies thy pain?
And where my liege's? all about the breast:
• A caudle, ho!
    King.   Too bitter is thy jest.
Are we betray'd thus to thy over-view?
    Biron.   Not you to me, but I betray'd by you:
I, that am honest; I, that hold it sin
To break the vow I am engaged in;
I am betray'd, by keeping company
† With men like men of inconstancy.   180
When shall you see me write a thing in rhyme?
Or groan for love? or spend a minute's time
In pruning me? When shall you hear that I
Will praise a hand, a foot, a face, an eye,
A gait, a state, a brow, a breast, a waist,
A leg, a limb?
    King.   Soft! whither away so fast?
A true man or a thief that gallops so?
    Biron.   I post from love: good lover, let me go.

    Enter JAQUENETTA *and* COSTARD.

Jaq.   God bless the king!
King.   What present hast thou there?
Cost.   Some certain treason.
King.   What makes treason here?   190
Cost.   Nay, it makes nothing, sir.
King.   If it mar nothing neither,

Costume design for Ferdinand by J. Gower Parks for
Holywell Park production, London, 1931

___

167 *whipping a gig.* Whirling a top; 'Whirligig' pre-
serves this word.

169 *push-pin.* A child's game in which pins were pushed
with the object of crossing those of another player.

174 *caudle.* A warm sweetened drink of thin gruel and
wine given to children and invalids. So Biron is
laughing at the King and his lords who have been
caught in the toils of love after all.

207 *make up the mess.* i.e. make up the party of four at table.

222 *Ind.* India.

239 *painted rhetoric.* Feigned speech.

The treason and you go in peace away together.
   Jaq. I beseech your grace, let this letter
    be read:
Our parson misdoubts it; 'twas treason, he said.
   King. Biron, read it over.
                  [Giving him the paper.
Where hadst thou it?
   Jaq. Of Costard.
   King. Where hadst thou it?
   Cost. Of Dun Adramadio, Dun Adramadio.
                [Biron tears the letter.
   King. How now! what is in you? why dost
    thou tear it?   200
   Biron. A toy, my liege, a toy: your grace
    needs not fear it.
   Long. It did move him to passion, and there-
    fore let's hear it.
   Dum. It is Biron's writing, and here is his
    name.   *[Gathering up the pieces.*
   Biron. [*To Costard*] Ah, you whoreson log-
    gerhead! you were born to do me shame.
Guilty, my lord, guilty! I confess, I confess.
   King. What?
● *Biron.* That you three fools lack'd me fool to
    make up the mess:
He, he, and you, and you, my liege, and I,
Are pick-purses in love, and we deserve to die.
O, dismiss this audience, and I shall tell you more.
   Dum. Now the number is even.
   Biron.   True, true; we are four.
Will these turtles be gone?
   King.   Hence, sirs; away!
   Cost. Walk aside the true folk, and let the
    traitors stay.
         [Exeunt Costard and Jaquenetta.
   Biron. Sweet lords, sweet lovers, O, let us
    embrace!
As true we are as flesh and blood can be:
The sea will ebb and flow, heaven show his face;
Young blood doth not obey an old decree:
We cannot cross the cause why we were born;
Therefore of all hands must we be forsworn.
   King. What, did these rent lines show some
    love of thine?   220
   Biron. Did they, quoth you? Who sees the
    heavenly Rosaline,
●That, like a rude and savage man of Ind,
At the first opening of the gorgeous east,
Bows not his vassal head and strucken blind
    Kisses the base ground with obedient breast?
What peremptory eagle-sighted eye
    Dares look upon the heaven of her brow,
That is not blinded by her majesty?
   King. What zeal, what fury hath inspired thee
    now?
My love, her mistress, is a gracious moon;   230
    She an attending star, scarce seen a light.
   Biron. My eyes are then no eyes, nor I Biron:
O, but for my love, day would turn to night!
Of all complexions the cull'd sovereignty
    Do meet, as at a fair, in her fair cheek,
Where several worthies make one dignity,
    Where nothing wants that want itself doth seek.
Lend me the flourish of all gentle tongues,—
● Fie, painted rhetoric! O, she needs it not:
To things of sale a seller's praise belongs,   240
    She passes praise; then praise too short doth
    blot.
A wither'd hermit, five-score winters worn,

Might shake off fifty, looking in her eye:
Beauty doth varnish age, as if new-born,
● And gives the crutch the cradle's infancy:
O, 'tis the sun that maketh all things shine.
  King. By heaven, thy love is black as ebony.
Biron. Is ebony like her? O wood divine!
A wife of such wood were felicity.
O, who can give an oath? where is a book? 250
That I may swear beauty doth beauty lack,
If that she learn not of her eye to look:
No face is fair that is not full so black.
King. O paradox! Black is the badge of hell,
The hue of dungeons and the suit of night;
And beauty's crest becomes the heavens well.
  Biron. Devils soonest tempt, resembling spirits
    of light.
O, if in black my lady's brows be deck'd,
It mourns that painting and usurping hair
Should ravish doters with a false aspect; 260
And therefore is she born to make black fair.
Her favour turns the fashion of the days,
For native blood is counted painting now;
And therefore red, that would avoid dispraise,
Paints itself black, to imitate her brow.
Dum. To look like her are chimney-sweepers
    black.
  Long. And since her time are colliers counted
    bright.
King. And Ethiopes of their sweet complexion
    crack.
  Dum. Dark needs no candles now, for dark is
    light.
Biron. Your mistresses dare never come in rain,
For fear their colours should be wash'd away.
King. 'Twere good, yours did; for, sir, to tell
    you plain,
I'll find a fairer face not wash'd to-day.
Biron. I'll prove her fair, or talk till doomsday
    here.
  King. No devil will fright thee then so much
    as she.
Dum. I never knew man hold vile stuff so dear.
  Long. Look, here's thy love: my foot and her
    face see.
Biron. O, if the streets were paved with thine
    eyes,
Her feet were much too dainty for such tread!
Dum. O vile! then, as she goes, what upward
    lies 280
The street should see as she walk'd overhead.
King. But what of this? are we not all in love?
  Biron. Nothing so sure; and thereby all for-
    sworn.
King. Then leave this chat; and, good Biron,
    now prove
Our loving lawful, and our faith not torn.
Dum. Ay, marry, there; some flattery for this
    evil.
  Long. O, some authority how to proceed;
● Some tricks, some quillets, how to cheat the devil.
  Dum. Some salve for perjury.
    Biron.   'Tis more than need.
Have at you, then, affection's men at arms. 290
Consider what you first did swear unto,
To fast, to study, and to see no woman;
Flat treason 'gainst the kingly state of youth.
Say, can you fast? your stomachs are too young;
And abstinence engenders maladies.
And where that you have vow'd to study, lords,

245 *crutch.* Metaphor for old age.

Biron: 'And therefore is she born to make black fair.'
Rosaline (Ruth Lodge), Stratford-upon-Avon, 1946

288 *quillets.* Subtleties, arguments.

322 *fiery numbers.* Refers to the odes and sonnets just read.

338 *cockled.* Shelled.

341 *Hesperides.* Hercules' last labour was to pick the golden apples of Hesperus which grew in a garden watched over by a dragon.

Apollo with lute. From a 19th century engraving

In that each of you have forsworn his book,
Can you still dream and pore and thereon look?
For when would you, my lord, or you, or you,
Have found the ground of study's excellence   300
Without the beauty of a woman's face?
[From women's eyes this doctrine I derive;
They are the ground, the books, the academes
From whence doth spring the true Promethean
        fire.]
Why, universal plodding poisons up
The nimble spirits in the arteries,
As motion and long-during action tires
The sinewy vigour of the traveller.
Now, for not looking on a woman's face,
You have in that forsworn the use of eyes   310
And study too, the causer of your vow;
For where is any author in the world
Teaches such beauty as a woman's eye?
Learning is but an adjunct to ourself
And where we are our learning likewise is:
Then when ourselves we see in ladies' eyes,
Do we not likewise see our learning there?
O, we have made a vow to study, lords,
And in that vow we have forsworn our books.
For when would you, my liege, or you, or you,
In leaden contemplation have found out   321
• Such fiery numbers as the prompting eyes
Of beauty's tutors have enrich'd you with?
Other slow arts entirely keep the brain;
And therefore, finding barren practisers,
Scarce show a harvest of their heavy toil:
But love, first learned in a lady's eyes,
Lives not alone immured in the brain;
But, with the motion of all elements,
Courses as swift as thought in every power,   330
And gives to every power a double power,
Above their functions and their offices.
It adds a precious seeing to the eye;
A lover's eyes will gaze an eagle blind;
A lover's ear will hear the lowest sound,
When the suspicious head of theft is stopp'd:
Love's feeling is more soft and sensible
• Than are the tender horns of cockled snails;
Love's tongue proves dainty Bacchus gross in
        taste:
For valour, is not Love a Hercules,   340
• Still climbing trees in the Hesperides?
Subtle as Sphinx; as sweet and musical
As bright Apollo's lute, strung with his hair;
And when Love speaks, the voice of all the
        gods
Make heaven drowsy with the harmony.
Never durst poet touch a pen to write
Until his ink were temper'd with Love's sighs;
O, then his lines would ravish savage ears
And plant in tyrants mild humility.
From women's eyes this doctrine I derive: 350
They sparkle still the right Promethean fire;
They are the books, the arts, the academes,
That show, contain and nourish all the world:
Else none at all in aught proves excellent.
Then fools you were these women to forswear,
Or keeping what is sworn, you will prove fools.
For wisdom's sake, a word that all men love,
Or for love's sake, a word that loves all men,
Or for men's sake, the authors of these women,
Or women's sake, by whom we men are men,   360
Let us once lose our oaths to find ourselves,
Or else we lose ourselves to keep our oaths.

It is religion to be thus forsworn,
For charity itself fulfils the law,
And who can sever love from charity?
    King. Saint Cupid, then! and, soldiers, to the
        field!
●   *Biron.* Advance your standards, and upon
        them, lords;
Pell-mell, down with them! but be first advised,
In conflict that you get the sun of them.
●   *Long.* Now to plain-dealing; lay these glozes by:
Shall we resolve to woo these girls of France?
    King. And win them too! therefore let us
        devise
Some entertainment for them in their tents.
    Biron. First, from the park let us conduct
        them thither;
Then homeward every man attach the hand
Of his fair mistress: in the afternoon
We will with some strange pastime solace them,
Such as the shortness of the time can shape;
For revels, dances, masks and merry hours
Forerun fair Love, strewing her way with flowers.
    King. Away, away! no time shall be omitted
That will betime, and may by us be fitted.
●*Biron.* Allons! allons! Sow'd cockle reap'd no
        corn;
And justice always whirls in equal measure:
Light wenches may prove plagues to men for-
        sworn;
If so, our copper buys no better treasure.
                            [*Exeunt.*

ACT V.

Scene I. *The same.*

Enter Holofernes, Sir Nathaniel, *and*
Dull.

● *Hol.* Satis quod suffict.
● *Nath.* I praise God for you, sir: your reasons
at dinner have been sharp and sententious;
●pleasant without scurrility, witty without affection,
audacious without impudency, learned without
opinion, and strange without heresy. I did converse this quondam day with a companion of the
king's, who is intituled, nominated, or called,
Don Adriano de Armado.
● *Hol.* Novi hominem tanquam te: his humour
is lofty, his discourse peremptory, his tongue
filed, his eye ambitious, his gait majestical, and
his general behaviour vain, ridiculous, and
●thrasonical. He is too picked, too spruce, too
●affected, too odd, as it were, too peregrinate, as
I may call it.
  Nath. A most singular and choice epithet.
                 [*Draws out his table-book.*
  Hol. He draweth out the thread of his ver-
bosity finer than the staple of his argument. I
abhor such fanatical phantasimes, such insociable
●and point-devise companions; such rackers of
orthography, as to speak dout, fine, when he
should say doubt; det, when he should pronounce debt,—d, e, b, t, not d, e, t: he clepeth a
calf, cauf; half, hauf; neighbour vocatur nebour;
neigh abbreviated ne. This is abhominable,—
●which he would call abbominable: it insinuateth
●† me of insanie: anne intelligis, domine? to make
frantic, lunatic.
● *Nath.* Laus Deo, bene intelligo.   30

367-369 *Advance . . . of them.* While couched in military terms, this speech is full of sexual puns.

370 *glozes.* Pretences.

383 *Sow'd . . . corn.* Sowed weeds yield no corn.

1 *Satis . . . sufficit.* Enough is as good as a feast.

2 *reasons.* Speeches.

4 *affection.* Affectation.

10 *Novi . . . te.* Another tag from Lily's *Latin Grammar*
meaning 'I know the man as well as I know you'.

14 *thrasonical.* Boastful. Thraso was a braggart in
Terence's play *Eunuchus.* *picked.* Exquisite.

15 *peregrinate.* Like a foreigner.

SD *table-book.* A book in which an Elizabethan would
note down matters of interest.

21 *point-devise.* Over precise. *rackers of orthography.*
Holofernes disapproves of those who fail to pronounce
according to the spelling, omitting the 'b' in 'doubt' and
'debt', which was pronounced in Elizabethan times.

27-28 *insinuateth . . . insanie.* i.e. it drives me frantic.

28 *anne . . . domine?* i.e. you understand, Sir?

30 *Laus . . . intelligo.* i.e. God be praised, I understand
well.

31-32 *Priscian . . . scratched.* Priscian was a 6th century grammarian; therefore 'Your Latin is a little faulty'.

33 *Videsne quis venit?* Do you see who comes?

34 *Video, et gaudeo.* I see and rejoice. These scraps of Latin illustrate the exchanges between master and pupil at the time.

41-42 *alms-basket.* The basket in which the remains from a feast was collected for the poor.

44 *honorificabilitudinitatibus.* Medieval Latin coinage meaning 'the state of being loaded with honours'.

45 *flap-dragon.* A flaming raisin, floating in liquor, to be snapped at in a Christmas game.

46 *peal.* As of bells.

49-50 *horn-book.* A leaf of paper, protected by transparent horn, from which children learned their ABC, etc.

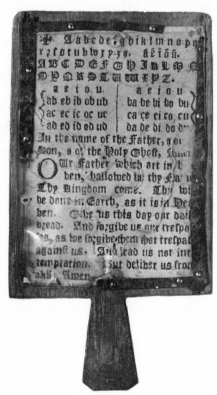

Hornbook. Seventeenth century

52 *pueritia.* Childishness.

55 *consonant.* Nonentity.

66 *wit-old.* A synonym for cuckold.

70 *gig.* Whipping top.

87-88 *charge-house . . . mountain.* Perhaps a by-word for a bad school.

Hol. Bon, bon, fort bon! Priscian **a** little scratched, 'twill serve.
Nath. Videsne quis venit?
Hol. Video, et gaudeo.

Enter ARMADO, MOTH, *and* COSTARD.

Arm. Chirrah!   [*To Moth.*
Hol. Quare chirrah, not sirrah?
Arm. Men of peace, well encountered.
Hol. Most military sir, salutation.
Moth. [*Aside to Costard*] They have been at a great feast of languages, and stolen the scraps.
Cost. O, they have lived long on the alms-basket of words. I marvel thy master hath not eaten thee for a word; for thou art not so long by the head as honorificabilitudinitatibus: thou art easier swallowed than a flap-dragon.
Moth. Peace! the peal begins.
Arm. [*To Hol.*] Monsieur, are you not lettered?
Moth. Yes, yes; he teaches boys the horn-book. What is a, b, spelt backward, with the horn on his head?   51
Hol. Ba, pueritia, with a horn added.
Moth. Ba, most silly sheep with a horn. You hear his learning.
Hol. Quis, quis, thou consonant?
Moth. The third of the five vowels, if you repeat them; or the fifth, if I.
Hol. I will repeat them,—a, e, i,—
Moth. The sheep: the other two concludes it,—o, u.   60
Arm. Now, by the salt wave of the Mediterraneum, a sweet touch, a quick venue of wit! snip, snap, quick and home! it rejoiceth my intellect: true wit!
Moth. Offered by a child to an old man; which is wit-old.
Hol. What is the figure? what is the figure?
Moth. Horns.
Hol. Thou disputest like an infant: go, whip thy gig.   70.
Moth. Lend me your horn to make one, and I will whip about your infamy circum circa,—a gig of a cuckold's horn.
Cost. An I had but one penny in the world, thou shouldst have it to buy gingerbread: hold, there is the very remuneration I had of thy master, thou halfpenny purse of wit, thou pigeon-egg of discretion. O, an the heavens were so pleased that thou wert but my bastard, what a joyful father wouldst thou make me! Go to; thou hast it ad dunghill, at the fingers' ends, as they say.
Hol. O, I smell false Latin; dunghill for unguem.
Arm. Arts-man, preambulate, we will be singuled from the barbarous. Do you not educate youth at the charge-house on the top of the mountain?
Hol. Or mons, the hill.
Arm. At your sweet pleasure, for the mountain.
Hol. I do, sans question.   91
Arm. Sir, it is the king's most sweet pleasure and affection to congratulate the princess at her pavilion in the posteriors of this day, which the rude multitude call the afternoon.
Hol. The posterior of the day, most generous

sir, is liable, congruent and measurable for the afternoon : the word is well culled, chose, sweet and apt, I do assure you, sir, I do assure.

Arm. Sir, the king is a noble gentleman, and
● my familiar, I do assure ye, very good friend : for what is inward between us, let it pass.   I do
● beseech thee, remember thy courtesy ; I beseech thee, apparel thy head : and among other important and most serious designs, and of great import indeed, too, but let that pass : for I must tell thee, it will please his grace, by the world, sometime to lean upon my poor shoulder, and
● with his royal finger, thus, dally with my excrement, with my mustachio ; but, sweet heart, let that pass.   By the world, I recount no fable : some certain special honours it pleaseth his greatness to impart to Armado, a soldier, a man of travel, that hath seen the world ; but let that pass.   The very all of all is,—but, sweet heart, I do implore secrecy,—that the king would have
● me present the princess, sweet chuck, with some delightful ostentation, or show, or pageant, or antique, or firework.   Now, understanding that the curate and your sweet self are good at such eruptions and sudden breaking out of mirth, as it were, I have acquainted you withal, to the end to crave your assistance.

● *Hol.* Sir, you shall present before her the Nine Worthies.   Sir, as concerning some entertainment of time, some show in the posterior of this day, to be rendered by our assistants, at the king's command, and this most gallant, illustrate, and learned gentleman, before the princess ; I say none so fit as to present the Nine Worthies. 130

Nath. Where will you find men worthy enough to present them ?

Hol. †Joshua, yourself ; myself and this gallant gentleman, Judas Maccabæus ; this swain, because of his great limb or joint, shall pass Pompey the Great ; the page, Hercules,—

Arm. Pardon, sir ; error : he is not quantity enough for that Worthy's thumb : he is not so big as the end of his club.

Hol. Shall I have audience ? he shall present
● Hercules in minority : his enter and exit shall be strangling a snake ; and I will have an apology for that purpose.

Moth. An excellent device ! so, if any of the audience hiss, you may cry 'Well done, Hercules ! now thou crushest the snake !' that is the way to make an offence gracious, though few have the grace to do it.

Arm. For the rest of the Worthies ?—

Hol. I will play three myself. 150

Moth. Thrice-worthy gentleman !

Arm. Shall I tell you a thing ?

Hol. We attend.

● *Arm.* We will have, if this fadge not, an antique.   I beseech you, follow.

● *Hol.* Via, goodman Dull ! thou hast spoken no word all this while.

Dull. Nor understood none neither, sir.

Hol. Allons ! we will employ thee.

Dull. I'll make one in a dance, or so ; or I will play 160
● On the tabor to the Worthies, and let them dance the hay.

Hol. Most dull, honest Dull ! To our sport, away !   [*Exeunt.*

101 *familiar.* Friend.

103 *remember thy courtesy.* Put on your hat.

109-110 *excrement.* Here refers to the moustache.

117 *chuck.* Chick or chicken.

124-125 *Nine Worthies.* Although the list varied with different authors, traditionally it comprised Hector of Troy, Alexander, Julius Caesar, Joshua, David, Judas Maccabaeus, Arthur, Charlemagne, and Sir Guy of Warwick : a popular number in pageants, Lord Mayor's shows, etc. Holofernes's Nine Worthies in the following scene include Pompey the Great and Hercules.

141-142 *Hercules . . . snake.* The child Hercules was said to have strangled two snakes while in his cradle.

154 *fadge.* Succeed.

156 *Via.* Forward.

161 *tabor.* A small drum. *dance the hay.* Country dance or reel.

Dancing to the drum. Woodcut from S. Bateman's *Doom,* 1581

2 *fairings*. Gifts and presents.

12 *shrewd unhappy gallows*. Unlucky gallows bird.

19 *mouse*. Term of endearment.

22 *in snuff*. A pun on the meanings 'in anger' and 'snuffing out a candle'; means therefore 'take it ill'.

Princess: 'Well bandied both . . .' Illustration by Gordon Browne from Henry Irving's *Shakespeare*, 1888

30 *favour*. A token of love; a gift.

33 *favour*. Face.

40 *Much in the letters*. The hand-writing is good.

42 *text B*. The lines twit Rosaline on being dark as ink.

43 *pencils*. Brushes used in a lady's make-up. If the joking is going to get personal, Rosaline is equal to the occasion.

44 *dominical*. The red letter S which marked Sundays in the old almanacs, and here a reference to Katherine's red or golden hair.

45 *O's*. Spotty or pimpled.

46 *shrows*. Shrews.

SCENE II.   *The same.*

Enter the Princess, KATHARINE, ROSALINE, *and* MARIA.

Prin.   Sweet hearts, we shall be rich ere we depart,
If fairings come thus plentifully in :
A lady wall'd about with diamonds !
Look you what I have from the loving king.
    Ros.   Madame, came nothing else along with that ?
    Prin.   Nothing but this ! yes, as much love in rhyme
As would be cramm'd up in a sheet of paper,
Writ o' both sides the leaf, margent and all,
That he was fain to seal on Cupid's name.
    Ros.   That was the way to make his godhead wax,   10
For he hath been five thousand years a boy.
    Kath.   Ay, and a shrewd unhappy gallows too.
    Ros.   You'll ne'er be friends with him ; a' kill'd your sister.
    Kath.   He made her melancholy, sad, and heavy ;
And so she died : had she been light, like you,
Of such a merry, nimble, stirring spirit,
She might ha' been a grandam ere she died :
And so may you ; for a light heart lives long.
    Ros.   What's your dark meaning, mouse, of this light word ?
    Kath.   A light condition in a beauty dark.   20
    Ros.   We need more light to find your meaning out.
    Kath.   You'll mar the light by taking it in snuff ;
Therefore I'll darkly end the argument.
    Ros.   Look, what you do, you do it still i' the dark.
    Kath.   So do not you, for you are a light wench.
    Ros.   Indeed I weigh not you, and therefore light.
    Kath.   You weigh me not ? O, that's you care not for me.
    Ros.   Great reason ; for 'past cure is still past care.'
    Prin.   Well bandied both ; a set of wit well play'd.
But, Rosaline, you have a favour too :   30
Who sent it ? and what is it ?
    Ros.   I would you knew :
An if my face were but as fair as yours,
My favour were as great ; be witness this.
Nay, I have verses too, I thank Biron :
The numbers true ; and, were the numbering too,
I were the fairest goddess on the ground :
I am compared to twenty thousand fairs.
O, he hath drawn my picture in his letter !
    Prin.   Any thing like ?
    Ros.   Much in the letters ; nothing in the praise.
    Prin.   Beauteous as ink ; a good conclusion.   41
    Kath.   Fair as a text B in a copy-book.
    Ros.   'Ware pencils, ho ! let me not die your debtor,
My red dominical, my golden letter :
O that your face were not so full of O's !
    Kath.   A pox of that jest ! and I beshrew all shrows.
    Prin.   But, Katharine, what was sent to you from fair Dumain ?
    Kath.   Madam, this glove.

Prin.   Did he not send you twain?
Kath. Yes, madam, and moreover
Some thousand verses of a faithful lover,   50
A huge translation of hypocrisy,
Vilely compiled, profound simplicity.
  Mar. This and these pearls to me sent Longaville:
The letter is too long by half a mile.
  Prin. I think no less.   Dost thou not wish in
   heart
The chain were longer and the letter short?
  Mar. Ay, or I would these hands might never
   part.
  Prin. We are wise girls to mock our lovers so.
  Ros. They are worse fools to purchase mocking so.
That same Biron I'll torture ere I go: 60
● O that I knew he were but in by the week!
How I would make him fawn and beg and seek
And wait the season and observe the times
And spend his prodigal wits in bootless rhymes
And shape his service wholly to my hests
● And make him proud to make me proud that jests!
● †So perttaunt-like would I o'ersway his state
That he should be my fool and I his fate.
  Prin. None are so surely caught, when they
   are catch'd,
As wit turn'd fool: folly, in wisdom hatch'd,   70
Hath wisdom's warrant and the help of school
And wit's own grace to grace a learned fool.
  Ros. The blood of youth burns not with such
   excess
As gravity's revolt to wantonness.
● *Mar.* Folly in fools bears not so strong a note
As foolery in the wise, when wit doth dote;
Since all the power thereof it doth apply
To prove, by wit, worth in simplicity.
  Prin. Here comes Boyet, and mirth is in his
   face.

Enter BOYET.

  Boyet. O, I am stabb'd with laughter! Where's
   her grace?   80
  Prin. Thy news, Boyet?
  Boyet.   Prepare, madam, prepare!
● Arm, wenches, arm! encounters mounted are
Against your peace: Love doth approach disguised,
Armed in arguments; you'll be surprised:
Muster your wits; stand in your own defence;
Or hide your heads like cowards, and fly hence.
● *Prin.* Saint Denis to Saint Cupid! What are
   they
That charge their breath against us? say, scout,
   say.
  Boyet. Under the cool shade of a sycamore
I thought to close mine eyes some half an hour;
When, lo! to interrupt my purposed rest,   91
Toward that shade I might behold address
The king and his companions: warily
I stole into a neighbour thicket by,
And overheard what you shall overhear;
That, by and by, disguised they will be here.
Their herald is a pretty knavish page,
● That well by heart hath conn'd his embassage:
Action and accent did they teach him there;
'Thus must thou speak,' and 'thus thy body bear:'
And ever and anon they made a doubt   101
● Presence majestical would put him out;

---

61 *in . . . week.* Well and truly caught.

66 *make . . . jests.* And gets himself up to impress me when I am merely jesting.

67 *perttaunt-like.* The winning card in a game of Post and Pair.

75 *note.* Black mark.

Boyet: 'Prepare, madam, prepare . . .' Illustration by Norman Wilkinson for *Players' Shakespeare*, 1924

---

82 *encounters.* Assailants.

87 *Saint Denis.* The patron saint of France.

98 *conn'd.* Learned by heart.

102 *Presence majestical.* Being before royalty.

109 *rubb'd his elbow.* An expression of satisfaction like rubbing one's hands. *fleer'd.* Grinned.

117 *spleen.* Outburst.

121 *Muscovites or Russians.* The Elizabethans were very conscious of Russia and Moscow since they were first to open up direct oceanic contact with Russia via Archangel. Many embassies were exchanged, and there were grand receptions of envoys by the Queen at Court. Shakespeare was familiar with accounts of the voyages from his reading of Hakluyt.

Boyet: ' . . . apparell'd thus, Like Muscovites or Russians . . .' Engraving from Charles Knight's *Pictorial Edition of the Works of William Shakspere,* 1839–43

135 *removes.* Exchanges.

141 *several.* Respective.

149 *kill . . . heart.* Discourage.

SD *Blackamoors.* African negroes or Moors. This reflects the increasing contemporary contacts with the African coasts and the Mediterranean.

' For,' quoth the king, ' an angel shalt thou see;
Yet fear not thou, but speak audaciously.'
The boy replied, ' An angel is not evil;
I should have fear'd her had she been a devil.'
With that, all laugh'd and clapp'd him on the
    shoulder,
Making the bold wag by their praises bolder:
●One rubb'd his elbow thus, and fleer'd and swore
A better speech was never spoke before;   110
Another, with his finger and his thumb,
Cried, ' Via! we will do't, come what will come;'
The third he caper'd, and cried, ' All goes well;'
The fourth turn'd on the toe, and down he fell.
With that, they all did tumble on the ground,
With such a zealous laughter, so profound,
●That in this spleen ridiculous appears,
To check their folly, passion's solemn tears.
    Prin. But what, but what, come they to visit
    us?
    Boyet. They do, they do; and are apparell'd
    thus,   120
●Like Muscovites or Russians, as I guess.
Their purpose is to parle, to court and dance;
And every one his love-feat will advance
Unto his several mistress, which they'll know
By favours several which they did bestow.
    Prin. And will they so? the gallants shall be
    task'd;
For, ladies, we will every one be mask'd;
And not a man of them shall have the grace,
Despite of suit, to see a lady's face.
Hold, Rosaline, this favour thou shalt wear,   130
And then the king will court thee for his dear;
Hold, take thou this, my sweet, and give me thine,
So shall Biron take me for Rosaline.
And change you favours too; so shall your loves
●Woo contrary, deceived by these removes.
    Ros. Come on, then; wear the favours most
    in sight.
    Kath. But in this changing what is your intent?
    Prin. The effect of my intent is to cross theirs:
They do it but in mocking merriment;
And mock for mock is only my intent.   140
●Their several counsels they unbosom shall
To loves mistook, and so be mock'd withal
Upon the next occasion that we meet,
With visages display'd, to talk and greet.
    Ros. But shall we dance, if they desire us to't?
    Prin. No, to the death, we will not move a foot;
Nor to their penn'd speech render we no grace,
But while 'tis spoke each turn away her face.
●   *Boyet.* Why, that contempt will kill the speak-
    er's heart,
And quite divorce his memory from his part.   150
    Prin. Therefore I do it; and I make no doubt
The rest will ne'er come in, if he be out.
There's no such sport as sport by sport o'erthrown,
To make theirs ours and ours none but our own:
So shall we stay, mocking intended game,
And they, well mock'd, depart away with shame.
                    [*Trumpets sound within.*

    Boyet. The trumpet sounds: be mask'd; the
    maskers come.   [*The Ladies mask.*

Enter Blackamoors with music; MOTH; *the*
    King, BIRON, LONGAVILLE, *and* DUMAIN, *in*
    Russian habits, and masked.

    Moth. All hail, the richest beauties on the
    earth!—

Boyet.   Beauties no richer than rich taffeta.
Moth.   A holy parcel of the fairest dames   160
    [*The Ladies turn their backs to him.*
That ever turn'd their—backs—to mortal views!
Biron.   [*Aside to Moth*] Their eyes, villain,
    their eyes.
Moth.   That ever turn'd their eyes to mortal
    views!—
Out—
Boyet.   True; out indeed.
Moth.   Out of your favours, heavenly spirits,
    vouchsafe
Not to behold—
Biron.   [*Aside to Moth*] Once to behold, rogue.
Moth.   Once to behold with your sun-beamed
    eyes,
——with your sun-beamed eyes—
Boyet.   They will not answer to that epithet;
You were best call it 'daughter-beamed eyes.'   171
Moth.   They do not mark me, and that brings
    me out.
Biron.   Is this your perfectness? be gone, you
    rogue!   [*Exit Moth.*
Ros.   What would these strangers? know their
    minds, Boyet:
If they do speak our language, 'tis our will
That some plain man recount their purposes:
Know what they would.
Boyet.   What would you with the princess?
Biron.   Nothing but peace and gentle visitation.
Ros.   What would they, say they?   180
Boyet.   Nothing but peace and gentle visitation.
Ros.   Why, that they have; and bid them so
    be gone.
Boyet.   She says, you have it, and you may be
    gone.
King.   Say to her, we have measured many
    miles
To tread a measure with her on this grass.
Boyet.   They say, that they have measured
    many a mile
To tread a measure with you on this grass.
Ros.   It is not so. Ask them how many inches
Is in one mile: if they have measured many,
The measure then of one is easily told.   190
Boyet.   If to come hither you have measured
    miles,
And many miles, the princess bids you tell
How many inches doth fill up one mile.
Biron.   Tell her, we measure them by weary
    steps.
Boyet.   She hears herself.
Ros.   How many weary steps,
Of many weary miles you have o'ergone,
Are number'd in the travel of one mile?
Biron.   We number nothing that we spend for
    you:
Our duty is so rich, so infinite,
That we may do it still without accompt.   200
Vouchsafe to show the sunshine of your face,
That we, like savages, may worship it.
Ros.   My face is but a moon, and clouded too.
King.   Blessed are clouds, to do as such clouds
    do!
Vouchsafe, bright moon, and these thy stars, to
    shine,
Those clouds removed, upon our watery eyne.
Ros.   O vain petitioner! beg a greater matter;
Thou now request'st but moonshine in the water.

The ladies with masks. Engraving by Kenny Meadows from Barry Cornwall's *The Works of Shakspere*, 1846

159 *taffeta.* Taffeta was used to make masks.

172 *mark.* Listen. *brings me out.* Puts me off.

179 *visitation.* Visit.

200 *accompt.* Account.

203 *clouded.* Masked.

208 *moonshine in the water.* An expression meaning 'foolish' or 'silly'.

209 *change*. A pun on the meanings 'a round in a dance' and 'changes of the moon'.

219 *nice*. Particular.

227 *Twice . . . you*. Some joke is lost here; see lines 245–6 below.

232 *treys*. Three in dice games. *nice*. Exact.

233 *Metheglin*. A Welsh drink made of honey like mead. *wort and malmsey*. Unfermented beer and a sweet wine.

235 *cog*. Cheat.

237 *gall*. A sore spot.

● *King.* Then, in our measure do but vouchsafe one change.
Thou bid'st me beg : this begging is not strange.
　Ros. Play, music, then ! Nay, you must do it soon.　　　　　　　[*Music plays.* 211
Not yet ! no dance ! Thus change I like the moon.
　King. Will you not dance ? How come you thus estranged ?
　Ros. You took the moon at full, but now she's changed.
　King. Yet still she is the moon, and I the man.
The music plays ; vouchsafe some motion to it.
　Ros. Our ears vouchsafe it.
　King.　　　　　　But your legs should do it.
　Ros. Since you are strangers and come here by chance,
●We'll not be nice : take hands. We will not dance.
　King. Why take we hands, then ?
　Ros.　　　　　　Only to part friends : 220
Curtsy, sweet hearts ; and so the measure ends.
　King. More measure of this measure ; be not nice.
　Ros. We can afford no more at such a price.
　King. Prize you yourselves : what buys your company ?
　Ros. Your absence only.
　King.　　　　　　That can never be.
　Ros. Then cannot we be bought : and so, adieu ;
●Twice to your visor, and half once to you.
　King. If you deny to dance, let's hold more chat.
　Ros. In private, then.
　King.　　　　　I am best pleased with that.
　　　　　　　　　　[*They converse apart.*

Biron. White-handed mistress, one sweet word with thee.　　　　　　　230
　Prin. Honey, and milk, and sugar ; there is three.
● *Biron.* Nay then, two treys, and if you grow so nice,
●Metheglin, wort, and malmsey : well run, dice !
There's half-a-dozen sweets.
　Prin.　　　　Seventh sweet, adieu :
●Since you can cog, I'll play no more with you.
　Biron. One word in secret.
　Prin.　　　　Let it not be sweet.
● *Biron.* Thou grievest my gall.
　Prin.　　　　Gall ! bitter.
　Biron.　　　　　　Therefore meet.
　　　　　　　　　[*They converse apart.*
　Dum. Will you vouchsafe with me to change a word ?
　Mar. Name it.
　Dum.　　　Fair lady,—
　Mar.　　　　Say you so ? Fair lord,—
Take that for your fair lady.
　Dum.　　　　Please it you, 240
As much in private, and I'll bid adieu.
　　　　　　　　　[*They converse apart.*
　Kath. What, was your vizard made without a tongue ?
　Long. I know the reason, lady, why you ask.
　Kath. O for your reason ! quickly, sir ; I long.
　Long. You have a double tongue within your mask,
And would afford my speechless vizard half.

Kath. Veal, quoth the Dutchman.   Is not 'veal' a calf?
Long. A calf, fair lady!
Kath.   No, a fair lord calf.
Long. Let's part the word.
Kath.   No, I'll not be your half:
Take all, and wean it; it may prove an ox.   250
Long. Look, how you butt yourself in these
   sharp mocks!
Will you give horns, chaste lady? do not so.
Kath. Then die a calf, before your horns do
   grow.
Long. One word in private with you, ere I die.
Kath. Bleat softly then; the butcher hears
   you cry.   [*They converse apart.*
Boyet. The tongues of mocking wenches are
   as keen
As is the razor's edge invisible,
Cutting a smaller hair than may be seen,
   Above the sense of sense; so sensible
Seemeth their conference; their conceits have
   wings   260
Fleeter than arrows, bullets, wind, thought, swift-
   er things.
Ros. Not one word more, my maids; break
   off, break off.
Biron. By heaven, all dry-beaten with pure
   scoff!
King. Farewell, mad wenches; you have
   simple wits.
Prin. Twenty adieus, my frozen Muscovits.
   [*Exeunt King, Lords, and Blackamoors.*
Are these the breed of wits so wonder'd at?
Boyet. Tapers they are, with your sweet
   breaths puff'd out.
Ros. Well-liking wits they have; gross, gross;
   fat, fat.
Prin. O poverty in wit, kingly-poor flout!
Will they not, think you, hang themselves to-
   night?   270
Or ever, but in vizards, show their faces?
This pert Biron was out of countenance quite.
Ros. O, they were all in lamentable cases!
The king was weeping-ripe for a good word.
Prin. Biron did swear himself out of all suit.
Mar. Dumain was at my service, and his sword:
   No point, quoth I; my servant straight was
   mute.
Kath. Lord Longaville said, I came o'er his
   heart;
And trow you what he call'd me?
Prin.   Qualm, perhaps.
Kath. Yes, in good faith.
Prin.   Go, sickness as thou art!   280
Ros. Well, better wits have worn plain sta-
   tute-caps.
But will you hear? the king is my love sworn.
Prin. And quick Biron hath plighted faith
   to me.
Kath. And Longaville was for my service born.
Mar. Dumain is mine, as sure as bark on tree.
Boyet. Madam, and pretty mistresses, give
   ear:
Immediately they will again be here
In their own shapes; for it can never be
They will digest this harsh indignity.
Prin. Will they return?
Boyet. They will, they will, God knows,   290
And leap for joy, though they are lame with blows:

Costume design for Katherine by J. Gower Parks for Holywell Park production, London, 1931

247-248 *Veal . . . lord calf.* Katherine is quibbling on 'veil' (mask), and also upon Longaville's name. Her last word was 'long'; and she now adds 'veal'.

249 *your half.* Your wife. We still say 'better half'.

250 *ox.* Fool.

263 *dry-beaten.* Bruised but not bloody.

281 *plain statute-caps.* The law required apprentices to wear plain woollen caps.

294 *blow.* Blossom.

297 *vailing.* Letting fall.

321 *pins . . . sleeve.* 'To make absolutely dependent'.
Biron is implying that the ladies are dependent on Boyet.

323 *carve.* Gesture.

325 *form.* Propriety.

326 *plays at tables.* Plays backgammon.

Playing backgammon. Seventeenth century engraving

328 *mean.* Tenor.

Therefore change favours; and, when they repair,
Blow like sweet roses in this summer air.
  ● *Prin.* How blow? how blow? speak to be
    understood.
    Boyet. Fair ladies mask'd are roses in their
    bud;
Dismask'd, their damask sweet commixture
  shown,
● Are angels vailing clouds, or roses blown.
    Prin. Avaunt, perplexity! What shall we do,
If they return in their own shapes to woo?
    Ros. Good madam, if by me you'll be advised,
Let's mock them still, as well known as disguised:
Let us complain to them what fools were here,
Disguised like Muscovites, in shapeless gear;
And wonder what they were and to what end
Their shallow shows and prologue vilely penn'd
And their rough carriage so ridiculous,
Should be presented at our tent to us.
    Boyet. Ladies, withdraw: the gallants are at
    hand.
    Prin. Whip to our tents, as roes run o'er land.
  [*Exeunt Princess, Rosaline, Katharine, and
                    Maria.*

Re-enter the King, Biron, Longaville, *and*
    Dumain, *in their proper habits.*

    King. Fair sir, God save you! Where's the
    princess?   310
    Boyet. Gone to her tent. Please it your
    majesty
Command me any service to her thither?
    King. That she vouchsafe me audience for
    one word.
    Boyet. I will; and so will she, I know, my
    lord.   [*Exit.*
    Biron. This fellow pecks up wit as pigeons
    pease,
And utters it again when God doth please:
He is wit's pedler, and retails his wares
At wakes and wassails, meetings, markets, fairs;
And we that sell by gross, the Lord doth know,
Have not the grace to grace it with such show.
● This gallant pins the wenches on his sleeve; 321
  Had he been Adam, he had tempted Eve;
● A' can carve too, and lisp: why, this is he
  That kiss'd his hand away in courtesy;
● This is the ape of form, monsieur the nice,
● That, when he plays at tables, chides the dice
  In honourable terms: nay, he can sing
● A mean most meanly; and in ushering
  Mend him who can: the ladies call him sweet;
The stairs, as he treads on them, kiss his feet:
This is the flower that smiles on every one, 331
To show his teeth as white as whale's bone;
And consciences, that will not die in debt,
Pay him the due of honey-tongued Boyet.
    King. A blister on his sweet tongue, with my
    heart,
That put Armado's page out of his part!
    Biron. See where it comes! Behaviour, what
    wert thou
Till this madman show'd thee? and what art thou
  now?

Re-enter the Princess, *ushered by* Boyet; Rosa-
    line, Maria, *and* Katharine.

    King. All hail, sweet madam, and fair time of
    day!

- *Prin.*   'Fair' in 'all hail' is foul, as I conceive.
  King.   Construe my speeches better, if you may.
    Prin.   Then wish me better; I will give you
        leave.
  King.   We came to visit you, and purpose now
  To lead you to our court; vouchsafe it then.
  Prin.   This field shall hold me; and so hold your
        vow:
  Nor God, nor I, delights in perjured men.
  King.   Rebuke me not for that which you pro-
        voke:
- The virtue of your eye must break my oath.
- *Prin.*   You nickname virtue; vice you should
        have spoke;
  For virtue's office never breaks men's troth.
  Now by my maiden honour, yet as pure   351
  As the unsullied lily, I protest,
  A world of torments though I should endure,
  I would not yield to be your house's guest;
  So much I hate a breaking cause to be
  Of heavenly oaths, vow'd with integrity.
  King.   O, you have lived in desolation here,
  Unseen, unvisited, much to our shame.
  Prin.   Not so, my lord; it is not so, I swear;
  We have had pastimes here and pleasant game:
  A mess of Russians left us but of late.   361
    King.   How, madam!   Russians!
    Prin.   Ay, in truth, my lord;
  Trim gallants, full of courtship and of state.
  Ros.   Madam, speak true.   It is not so, my
        lord:
- My lady, to the manner of the days,
  In courtesy gives undeserving praise.
  We four indeed confronted were with four
  In Russian habit: here they stay'd an hour,
  And talk'd apace; and in that hour, my lord,
  They did not bless us with one happy word.   370
  I dare not call them fools; but this I think,
  When they are thirsty, fools would fain have
        drink.
- *Biron.*   This jest is dry to me.   Fair gentle
        sweet,
  Your wit makes wise things foolish: when we
        greet,
  With eyes best seeing, heaven's fiery eye,
  By light we lose light: your capacity
  Is of that nature that to your huge store
  Wise things seem foolish and rich things but poor.

  Ros.   This proves you wise and rich, for in my
        eye,—
  Biron.   I am a fool, and full of poverty.   380
  Ros.   But that you take what doth to you
        belong,
  It were a fault to snatch words from my tongue.
  Biron.   O, I am yours, and all that I possess!
  Ros.   All the fool mine?
  Biron.   I cannot give you less.
  Ros.   Which of the vizards was it that you
        wore?
  Biron.   Where? when? what vizard? why de-
        mand you this?
  Ros.   There, then, that vizard; that super-
        fluous case
  That hid the worse and show'd the better face.
  King.   We are descried; they'll mock us now
        downright.
  Dum.   Let us confess and turn it to a jest.
  Prin.   Amazed, my lord? why looks your high-
        ness sad?   391

340 *'all hail'*. The Princess plays on the meanings of 'welcome' and 'ice shower'.

348 *virtue*. Force.

349 *nickname virtue*. Miscall goodness.

365 *to . . . days*. In the manner of the times.

373 *dry*. Poor.

407 *Three-piled*. Thick pile as in the finest velvet.

413 *russet*. Homespun cloth. *kersey*. Coarse woollen cloth.

417 *rage*. Madness.

419 '*Lord . . . us*'. This sign was put up on the doors of plague-infected houses. London experienced two severe outbreaks of the plague in 1592 and 1593.

422 *visited*. Infected with the plague.

423 *Lord's tokens*. The love-tokens given to the ladies by the lords, and a pun on the spots that indicated the plague.

Biron (Ian Richardson) proposes to Rosaline (Estelle Kohlet), Royal Shakespeare Co, 1973

426-427 *how . . . sue*. How can the plaintiff also incur the penalty? There is a pun on *sue* which has the meanings 'entreat' and 'to bring suit against'.

434 *well advised*. i.e. was it sensible?

Ros. Help, hold his brows! he'll swoon!
  Why look you pale?
Sea-sick, I think, coming from Muscovy.
  Biron. Thus pour the stars down plagues for
    perjury.
Can any face of brass hold longer out?
Here stand I: lady, dart thy skill at me;
  Bruise me with scorn, confound me with a
    flout;
Thrust thy sharp wit quite through my igno-
    rance;
Cut me to pieces with thy keen conceit;
And I will wish thee never more to dance,   400
  Nor never more in Russian habit wait.
O, never will I trust to speeches penn'd,
  Nor to the motion of a schoolboy's tongue,
Nor never come in vizard to my friend,
  Nor woo in rhyme, like a blind harper's song!
Taffeta phrases, silken terms precise,
  Three-piled hyperboles, spruce affectation,
Figures pedantical; these summer-flies
  Have blown me full of maggot ostentation:
I do forswear them; and I here protest,   410
  By this white glove,—how white the hand,
    God knows!—
Henceforth my wooing mind shall be express'd
  In russet yeas and honest kersey noes:
And, to begin, wench,—so God help me, la!—
My love to thee is sound, sans crack or flaw.
  Ros. Sans sans, I pray you.
  Biron.   Yet I have a trick
Of the old rage: bear with me, I am sick;
  I'll leave it by degrees. Soft, let us see:
Write, 'Lord have mercy on us' on those three;
  They are infected; in their hearts it lies;   420
They have the plague, and caught it of your
    eyes;
These lords are visited; you are not free,
For the Lord's tokens on you do I see.

  Prin. No, they are free that gave these tokens
    to us.
  Biron. Our states are forfeit: seek not to
    undo us.
  Ros. It is not so; for how can this be true,
That you stand forfeit, being those that sue?
  Biron. Peace! for I will not have to do with
    you.
  Ros. Nor shall not, if I do as I intend.
  Biron. Speak for yourselves; my wit is at an
    end.   430
  King. Teach us, sweet madam, for our rude
    transgression
Some fair excuse.
  Prin.   The fairest is confession.
Were not you here but even now disguised?
  King. Madam, I was.
  Prin.   And were you well advised?
  King. I was, fair madam.
  Prin.   When you then were here,
What did you whisper in your lady's ear?
  King. That more than all the world I did
    respect her.
  Prin. When she shall challenge this, you will
    reject her.
  King. Upon mine honour, no.
  Prin.   Peace, peace! forbear:
Your oath once broke, you force not to forswear.
  King. Despise me, when I break this oath of
    mine.   **441**

Prin. I will: and therefore keep it. Rosaline,
What did the Russian whisper in your ear?
 Ros. Madam, he swore that he did hold me
   dear
As precious eyesight, and did value me
Above this world; adding thereto moreover
That he would wed me, or else die my lover.
 Prin. God give thee joy of him! the noble
   lord
Most honourably doth uphold his word.
 King. What mean you, madam? by my life,
   my troth,   450
I never swore this lady such an oath.
 Ros. By heaven, you did; and to confirm it
   plain,
You gave me this: but take it, sir, again.
 King. My faith and this the princess I did
   give:
I knew her by this jewel on her sleeve.
 Prin. Pardon me, sir, this jewel did she wear;
And Lord Biron, I thank him, is my dear.
What, will you have me, or your pearl again?
 Biron. Neither of either; I remit both twain.
I see the trick on't: here was a consent,   460
Knowing aforehand of our merriment,
To dash it like a Christmas comedy:
Some carry-tale, some please-man, some slight
   zany,
Some mumble-news, some trencher-knight, some
   Dick,
That smiles his cheek in years and knows the trick
To make my lady laugh when she's disposed,
Told our intents before; which once disclosed,
The ladies did change favours: and then we,
Following the signs, woo'd but the sign of she.
Now, to our perjury to add more terror,   470
We are again forsworn, in will and error.
Much upon this it is: and might not you
   [*To Boyet.*
Forestall our sport, to make us thus untrue?
Do not you know my lady's foot by the squier,
  And laugh upon the apple of her eye?
And stand between her back, sir, and the fire,
   Holding a trencher, jesting merrily?
You put our page out: go, you are allow'd;
Die when you will, a smock shall be your shroud.
You leer upon me, do you? there's an eye   480
Wounds like a leaden sword.
 Boyet.   Full merrily
Hath this brave manage, this career, been run.
  Biron. Lo, he is tilting straight! Peace! I
   have done.

            Enter COSTARD.

Welcome, pure wit! thou partest a fair fray.
 Cost. O Lord, sir, they would know
Whether the three Worthies shall come in or no.
 Biron. What, are there but three?
 Cost.   No, sir; but it is vara fine,
For every one pursents three.
 Biron.   And three times thrice is nine.
 Cost. Not so, sir; under correction, sir; I hope
   it is not so.
You cannot beg us, sir, I can assure you, sir; we
   know what we know: 490
I hope, sir, three times thrice, sir,—
 Biron. Is not nine.
 Cost. Under correction, sir, we know where-
until it doth amount.

The Zanni, a foolish clown, was the servant of the pantaloon character in the *commedia dell' arte.* Etching by Jacques Callot (1592–1635)

460 *consent.* A compact.

462 *dash.* Make fun of.

463 *please-man . . . zany.* Flatterer . . . clown.

464 *mumble-news . . . trencher-knight . . . Dick.* Gossip . . . parasite . . . fellow.

465 *in years.* i.e. into wrinkles.

472 *Much . . . is.* i.e. that's how it is.

474 *know . . . squier.* Know how to please my lady. *squier.* Square.

475 *laugh . . . eye.* Joke intimately with her.

478 *allow'd.* A licensed fool.

481 *leaden sword.* Stage weapons were commonly made of lead.

482 *manage.* A short gallop at speed.

483 *straight.* Straightway.

490 *You . . . us.* You cannot prove us fools.

498 *reckoning*. Keeping accounts.

503 *parfect*. Costard means 'perform'. *Pompion*. Pumpkin: a joke on Pompeius Magnus, 'Pompey the Great'.

522 *our sport*. i.e. the Muscovite masque.

Costume design for Armado by J. Gower Parks for Holywell Park production, London, 1931

533-534 *fortuna de la guerra*. Fortune of war.

545-546 *hedge-priest*. Illiterate priest.

547 *Abate*. Except. *novum*. A dice game in which nine and five were the principal throws. Correctly therefore *Novem quinque*.

Biron. By Jove, I always took three threes for nine.
Cost. O Lord, sir, it were pity you should get
• your living by reckoning, sir.
Biron. How much is it?
Cost. O Lord, sir, the parties themselves, the actors, sir, will show whereuntil it doth amount: for mine own part, I am, as they say, but to
• parfect one man in one poor man, Pompion the Great, sir.
Biron. Art thou one of the Worthies?
Cost. It pleased them to think me worthy of Pompion the Great: for mine own part, I know not the degree of the Worthy, but I am to stand for him.
Biron. Go, bid them prepare.   510
Cost. We will turn it finely off, sir; we will take some care.   [*Exit.*
King. Biron, they will shame us: let them not approach.
Biron. We are shame-proof, my lord: and 'tis some policy
To have one show worse than the king's and his company.
King. I say they shall not come.
Prin. Nay, my good lord, let me o'errule you now:
That sport best pleases that doth least know how:
† Where zeal strives to content, and the contents
Dies in the zeal of that which it presents:
Their form confounded makes most form in mirth,
When great things labouring perish in their birth.
• *Biron.* A right description of our sport, my lord.

Enter ARMADO.

Arm. Anointed, I implore so much expense of thy royal sweet breath as will utter a brace of words.
                    [*Converses apart with the King, and delivers him a paper.*
Prin. Doth this man serve God?
Biron. Why ask you?
Prin. He speaks not like a man of God's making.
Arm. That is all one, my fair, sweet, honey monarch; for, I protest, the schoolmaster is exceeding fantastical; too too vain, too too vain:
• but we will put it, as they say, to fortuna de la guerra. I wish you the peace of mind, most royal couplement!   [*Exit.*
King. Here is like to be a good presence of Worthies. He presents Hector of Troy; the swain, Pompey the Great; the parish curate, Alexander; Armado's page, Hercules; the pedant, Judas Maccabæus: 540
And if these four Worthies in their first show thrive,
These four will change habits, and present the other five.
Biron. There is five in the first show.
King. You are deceived; 'tis not so.
• *Biron.* The pedant, the braggart, the hedge-priest, the fool and the boy:—
• † Abate throw at novum, and the whole world again
Cannot pick out five such, take each one in his vein.

King. The ship is under sail, and here she comes amain.

Enter COSTARD, *for Pompey.*

Cost. I Pompey am,—
Boyet.   You lie, you are not he. 550
Cost. I Pompey am,—
Boyet.   With libbard's head on knee.
Biron. Well said, old mocker: I must needs be friends with thee.
Cost. I Pompey am, Pompey surnamed the Big,—
Dum. The Great.
Cost. It is, 'Great,' sir:—
                       Pompey surnamed the Great;
That oft in field, with targe and shield, did make my foe to sweat:
And travelling along this coast, I here am come by chance,
And lay my arms before the legs of this sweet lass of France.
If your ladyship would say, 'Thanks, Pompey,' I had done.
Prin. Great thanks, great Pompey.   560
Cost. 'Tis not so much worth; but I hope I was perfect: I made a little fault in 'Great.'
Biron. My hat to a halfpenny, Pompey proves the best Worthy.

Enter SIR NATHANIEL, *for Alexander.*

Nath. When in the world I lived, I was the world's commander;
By east, west, north, and south, I spread my conquering might:
My scutcheon plain declares that I am Alisander,—
Boyet. Your nose says, no, you are not; for it stands too right.
Biron. Your nose smells 'no' in this, most tender-smelling knight.
Prin. The conqueror is dismay'd. Proceed, good Alexander.   570
Nath. When in the world I lived, I was the world's commander,—
Boyet. Most true, 'tis right; you were so, Alisander.
Biron. Pompey the Great,—
Cost. Your servant, and Costard.
Biron. Take away the conqueror, take away Alisander.
Cost. [*To Sir Nath.*] O, sir, you have overthrown Alisander the conqueror! You will be scraped out of the painted cloth for this: your lion, that holds his poll-axe sitting on a close-stool, will be given to Ajax: he will be the ninth Worthy. A conqueror, and afeard to speak! run away for shame, Alisander. [*Nath. retires.*] There, an't shall please you; a foolish mild man; an honest man, look you, and soon dashed. He is a marvellous good neighbour, faith, and a very good bowler: but, for Alisander,—alas, you see how 'tis,—a little o'erparted. But there are Worthies a-coming will speak their mind in some other sort.   590
Prin. Stand aside, good Pompey.

Enter HOLOFERNES, *for Judas; and* MOTH, *for Hercules.*

Hol. Great Hercules is presented by this imp,

551 *libbard's head.* Leopard's head.

556 *targe.* Small shield.

568 *Your nose . . . right.* Alexander's neck was somewhat awry.

579 *painted cloth.* Painted cloths decorated the interiors of Elizabethan houses, and the Nine Worthies were a common subject.

580 *lion.* Alexander's arms were a lion holding a battle-axe. *close-stool.* Stool with chamber pot.

Crest of Alexander. Woodcut by Jackson from Francis Douce's *Shakespeare and Ancient Manners*, 1837

581 *Ajax.* A pun on the word 'jakes' or privy.

585 *dashed.* Discouraged.

588 *o'erparted.* Given too big a part.

Holofernes (Derek Smith) and Moth (Tony Valls), Royal Shakespeare Co, 1973

593 *canis.* Dog.

595 *manus.* Hand.

596 *Quoniam.* Since.

597 *Ergo.* Therefore.

614 *cittern.* A guitar-like instrument.

Cittern player. Engraving from a 14th century manuscript

616 *Death's . . . ring.* A ring with a skull for decoration.

618 *falchion.* Sword.

620 *half-cheek.* Profile.

640 *Troyan.* A good fellow.

642-643 *clean-timbered.* Well built.

646 *small.* The leg below the calf.

●   Whose club kill'd Cerberus, that three-headed
    canis ;
   And when he was a babe, a child, a shrimp,
●   Thus did he strangle serpents in his manus.
● Quoniam he seemeth in minority,
●   Ergo I come with this apology.
   Keep some state in thy exit, and vanish.
                 [*Moth retires.*

    Judas I am,—
Dum.   A Judas !   600
Hol.   Not Iscariot, sir.
    Judas I am, ycliped Maccabæus.
Dum.   Judas Maccabæus clipt is plain Judas.
Biron.   A kissing traitor. How art thou proved
    Judas ?
Hol.   Judas I am,—
Dum.   The more shame for you, Judas.
Hol.   What mean you, sir ?
Boyet.   To make Judas hang himself.
Hol.   Begin, sir ; you are my elder.
Biron.   Well followed : Judas was hanged on
    an elder.   610
Hol.   I will not be put out of countenance.
Biron.   Because thou hast no face.
Hol.   What is this ?
● *Boyet.*   A cittern-head.
Dum.   The head of a bodkin.
● *Biron.*   A Death's face in a ring.
Long.   The face of an old Roman coin, scarce
    seen.
● *Boyet.*   The pommel of Cæsar's falchion.
Dum.   The carved-bone face on a flask.
● *Biron.*   Saint George's half-cheek in a brooch.
Dum.   Ay, and in a brooch of lead.   621
Biron.   Ay, and worn in the cap of a tooth-
    drawer.
   And now forward ; for we have put thee in coun-
    tenance.
Hol.   You have put me out of countenance.
Biron.   False ; we have given thee faces.
Hol.   But you have out-faced them all.
Biron.   An thou wert a lion, we would do so.
Boyet.   Therefore, as he is an ass, let him go.
   And so adieu, sweet Jude ! nay, why dost thou
    stay ?
Dum.   For the latter end of his name.   630
Biron.   For the ass to the Jude ; give it him :—
   Jud-as, away !
Hol.   This is not generous, not gentle, not
    humble.
Boyet.   A light for Monsieur Judas ! it grows
    dark, he may stumble.   [*Hol. retires.*
Prin.   Alas, poor Maccabæus, how hath he
    been baited !

        Enter ARMADO, *for Hector.*

Biron.   Hide thy head, Achilles : here comes
   Hector in arms.
Dum.   Though my mocks come home by me,
   I will now be merry.
● *King.*   Hector was but a Troyan in respect of
   this.   640
Boyet.   But is this Hector ?
● *King.*   I think Hector was not so clean-tim-
   bered.
Long.   His leg is too big for Hector's.
Dum.   More calf, certain.
● *Boyet.*   No ; he is best indued in the small.
Biron.   This cannot be Hector.

Dum.   He's a god or a painter; for he makes faces.

●   *Arm.*   The armipotent Mars, of lances the almighty,   650
Gave Hector a gift,—
Dum.   A gilt nutmeg.
Biron.   A lemon.
Long.   Stuck with cloves.
Dum.   No, cloven.
Arm.   Peace!—
The armipotent Mars, of lances the almighty,
    Gave Hector a gift, the heir of Ilion;
A man so breathed, that certain he would fight; yea
    From morn till night, out of his pavilion.   660
I am that flower,—
Dum.   That mint.
Long.   That columbine.
Arm.   Sweet Lord Longaville, rein thy tongue.
Long.   I must rather give it the rein, for it runs against Hector.
Dum.   Ay, and Hector's a greyhound.
Arm.   The sweet war-man is dead and rotten; sweet chucks, beat not the bones of the buried: when he breathed, he was a man.   But I will forward with my device. [*To the Princess*] Sweet royalty, bestow on me the sense of hearing.   670
Prin.   Speak, brave Hector: we are much delighted.
Arm.   I do adore thy sweet grace's slipper.
Boyet. [*Aside to Dum.*] Loves her by the foot.
Dum. [*Aside to Boyet*] He may not by the yard.
Arm.   This Hector far surmounted Hannibal,—
Cost.   The party is gone, fellow Hector, she is gone; she is two months on her way.
Arm.   What meanest thou?   680
Cost.   Faith, unless you play the honest Troyan, the poor wench is cast away: she's quick; the child brags in her belly already: 'tis yours.
Arm.   Dost thou infamonize me among potentates? thou shalt die.
Cost.   Then shall Hector be whipped for Jaquenetta that is quick by him and hanged for Pompey that is dead by him.
Dum.   Most rare Pompey!
Boyet.   Renowned Pompey!   690
Biron.   Greater than great, great, great, great Pompey!   Pompey the Huge!
Dum.   Hector trembles.
●   *Biron.*   Pompey is moved.   More Ates, more Ates! stir them on! stir them on!
Dum.   Hector will challenge him.
Biron.   Ay, if a' have no more man's blood in's belly than will sup a flea.
Arm.   By the north pole, I do challenge thee.
Cost.   I will not fight with a pole, like a northern man: I'll slash; I'll do it by the sword. I bepray you, let me borrow my arms again.
Dum.   Room for the incensed Worthies!
Cost.   I'll do it in my shirt.
Dum.   Most resolute Pompey!
●   *Moth.*   Master, let me take you a button-hole lower.   Do you not see Pompey is uncasing for the combat?   What mean you?   You will lose your reputation.
Arm.   Gentlemen and soldiers, pardon me; I will not combat in my shirt.   711

Costume design for Dumain by J. Gower Parks for Holywell Park productions, London, 1931

650 *armipotent.* Mighty in arms.

694 *Ates.* Spirits of discord and strife.

706-707 *take . . . lower.* A pun on the meanings 'help you off with your garment' and 'take you down a peg'.

Costume design for the Princess of France by J. Gower
Parks for Regent's Park Open Air Theatre, London, 1935

743 *liberal.* Free, or unrestrained.

745 *converse of breath.* Conversation.

752 *at his very loose.* At the last minute, from a term
in archery.

Dum. You may not deny it: Pompey hath
made the challenge.
Arm. Sweet bloods, I both may and will.
Biron. What reason have you for't?
Arm. The naked truth of it is, I have no
shirt; I go woolward for penance.
Boyet. True, and it was enjoined him in
Rome for want of linen: since when, I'll be
sworn, he wore none but a dishclout of Jaquenetta's, and that a' wears next his heart for a
favour.

Enter MERCADE.

Mer. God save you, madam!
Prin. Welcome, Mercade;
But that thou interrupt'st our merriment.
Mer. I am sorry, madam; for the news I bring
Is heavy in my tongue. The king your father—
Prin. Dead, for my life!
Mer. Even so; my tale is told.
Biron. Worthies, away! the scene begins to
cloud.   731
Arm. For mine own part, I breathe free
breath. I have seen the day of wrong through
the little hole of discretion, and I will right my-
self like a soldier.   [*Exeunt Worthies.*
King. How fares your majesty?
Prin. Boyet, prepare; I will away to-night.
King. Madam, not so; I do beseech you, stay.
Prin. Prepare, I say. I thank you, gracious
lords,
For all your fair endeavours; and entreat,   740
Out of a new-sad soul, that you vouchsafe
In your rich wisdom to excuse or hide
• The liberal opposition of our spirits,
If over-boldly we have borne ourselves
• In the converse of breath: your gentleness
Was guilty of it. Farewell, worthy lord!
A heavy heart bears not a nimble tongue:
Excuse me so, coming too short of thanks
For my great suit so easily obtain'd.
King. The extreme parts of time extremely
forms   750
All causes to the purpose of his speed,
• And often at his very loose decides
That which long process could not arbitrate:
And though the mourning brow of progeny
Forbid the smiling courtesy of love
The holy suit which fain it would convince,
Yet, since love's argument was first on foot,
Let not the cloud of sorrow justle it
From what it purposed; since, to wail friends lost
Is not by much so wholesome-profitable   760
As to rejoice at friends but newly found.
Prin. I understand you not: my griefs are
double.
Biron. Honest plain words best pierce the
ear of grief;
And by these badges understand the king.
For your fair sakes have we neglected time,
Play'd foul play with our oaths: your beauty,
ladies,
Hath much deform'd us, fashioning our humours
Even to the opposed end of our intents:
And what in us hath seem'd ridiculous,—
As love is full of unbefitting strains,   770
All wanton as a child, skipping and vain,
Form'd by the eye and therefore, like the eye,
Full of strange shapes, of habits and of forms,

Varying in subjects as the eye doth roll
To every varied object in his glance:
• Which parti-coated presence of loose love
Put on by us, if, in your heavenly eyes,
Have misbecomed our oaths and gravities,
Those heavenly eyes, that look into these faults,
• Suggested us to make.   Therefore, ladies,   780
Our love being yours, the error that love makes
Is likewise yours: we to ourselves prove false,
By being once false for ever to be true
To those that make us both,—fair ladies, you:
And even that falsehood, in itself a sin,
Thus purifies itself and turns to grace.

  Prin.   We have received your letters full of
   love;
Your favours, the ambassadors of love;
And, in our maiden council, rated them
At courtship, pleasant jest and courtesy,   790
• As bombast and as lining to the time:
• But more devout than this in our respects
Have we not been; and therefore met your loves
In their own fashion, like a merriment.
  Dum.   Our letters, madam, show'd much
   more than jest.
•   *Long.*   So did our looks.
  Ros.   We did not quote them so.
  King.   Now, at the latest minute of the hour,
Grant us your loves.
  Prin.   A time, methinks, too short
To make a world-without-end bargain in.
No, no, my lord, your grace is perjured much,
• Full of dear guiltiness; and therefore this: 801
If for my love, as there is no such cause,
You will do aught, this shall you do for me:
Your oath I will not trust; but go with speed
To some forlorn and naked hermitage,
Remote from all the pleasures of the world;
• There stay until the twelve celestial signs
Have brought about the annual reckoning.
If this austere insociable life
Change not your offer made in heat of blood;
If frosts and fasts, hard lodging and thin weeds
Nip not the gaudy blossoms of your love,
But that it bear this trial and last love;
Then, at the expiration of the year,
Come challenge me, challenge me by these de-
  serts,
And, by this virgin palm now kissing thine,
I will be thine; and till that instant shut
My woeful self up in a mourning house,
Raining the tears of lamentation
For the remembrance of my father's death.   820
If this thou do deny, let our hands part,
Neither intitled in the other's heart.
  King.   If this, or more than this, I would deny,
•   To flatter up these powers of mine with rest,
The sudden hand of death close up mine eye!
  Hence ever then my heart is in thy breast.
  [*Biron.*   And what to me, my love? and what
   to me?
  Ros.   You must be purged too, your sins are
   rack'd,
You are attaint with faults and perjury:
Therefore if you my favour mean to get,   830
A twelvemonth shall you spend, and never rest,
But seek the weary beds of people sick.]
  Dum.   But what to me, my love? but what to
   me?
A wife?

776 *parti-coated.* Wearing motley, the costume of the fool.

780 *Suggested.* Tempted.

791 *bombast.* Woollen stuffing.

792 *devout.* Serious.

796 *quote.* Regard.

801 *dear.* Grievous.

807 *signs.* The twelve signs of the Zodiac.

Areas of the human body affected by the signs of the Zodiac. Illustration from William Lilly's *Almanack Melhini Anglici Ephemeris,* 1681

824 *flatter up.* Gratify.

The princess and her ladies, the king and his lords with
Armado in the background, Old Vic, London, 1949

---

854 *flouts.* Mockeries or insults.

855 *estates.* Ranks.

Kath.   A beard, fair health, and honesty;
With three-fold love I wish you all these three.
  Dum. O, shall I say, I thank you, gentle wife?
  Kath. Not so, my lord; a twelvemonth and
     a day
I'll mark no words that smooth-faced wooers
     say:
Come when the king doth to my lady come;
Then, if I have much love, I'll give you some. 840
  Dum. I'll serve thee true and faithfully till
     then.
  Kath. Yet swear not, lest ye be forsworn again.
  Long. What says Maria?
  Mar.   At the twelvemonth's end
I'll change my black gown for a faithful friend.
  Long. I'll stay with patience; but the time is
     long.
  Mar. The liker you; few taller are so young.
  Biron. Studies my lady? mistress, look on me;
Behold the window of my heart, mine eye,
What humble suit attends thy answer there:
Impose some service on me for thy love.   850
  Ros. Oft have I heard of you, my Lord Biron,
Before I saw you; and the world's large tongue
Proclaims you for a man replete with mocks,
• Full of comparisons and wounding flouts,
• Which you on all estates will execute
That lie within the mercy of your wit.
To weed this wormwood from your fruitful brain,
And therewithal to win me, if you please,
Without the which I am not to be won,
You shall this twelvemonth term from day to day
Visit the speechless sick and still converse   861
With groaning wretches; and your task shall be,
With all the fierce endeavour of your wit
To enforce the pained impotent to smile.
  Biron. To move wild laughter in the throat of
     death?
It cannot be; it is impossible:
Mirth cannot move a soul in agony.
  Ros. Why, that's the way to choke a gibing
     spirit,
Whose influence is begot of that loose grace
Which shallow laughing hearers give to fools:
A jest's prosperity lies in the ear   871
Of him that hears it, never in the tongue
Of him that makes it: then, if sickly ears,
Deaf'd with the clamours of their own dear
     groans,
Will hear your idle scorns, continue then,
And I will have you and that fault withal;
But if they will not, throw away that spirit,
And I shall find you empty of that fault,
Right joyful of your reformation.
  Biron. A twelvemonth! well; befall what will
     befall,   880
I'll jest a twelvemonth in an hospital.
  Prin. [*To the King*] Ay, sweet my lord; and
     so I take my leave.
  King. No, madam; we will bring you on
     your way.
  Biron. Our wooing doth not end like an old
     play;
Jack hath not Jill: these ladies' courtesy
Might well have made our sport a comedy.
  King. Come, sir, it wants a twelvemonth and
     a day,
And then 'twill end.
  Biron.   That's too long for a play.

Re-enter ARMADO.

Arm.   Sweet majesty, vouchsafe me,—
Prin.   Was not that Hector?
Dum.   The worthy knight of Troy.   890
Arm.   I will kiss thy royal finger, and take leave. I am a votary; I have vowed to Jaquenetta to hold the plough for her sweet love three years. But, most esteemed greatness, will you
• hear the dialogue that the two learned men have compiled in praise of the owl and the cuckoo? it should have followed in the end of our show.
King.   Call them forth quickly; we will do so.
Arm.   Holla! approach.   900

Re-enter HOLOFERNES, NATHANIEL, MOTH,
      COSTARD, *and others.*

This side is Hiems, Winter, this Ver, the Spring; the one maintained by the owl, the other by the cuckoo. Ver, begin.

THE SONG.

SPRING.

When daisies pied and violets blue
   And lady-smocks all silver-white
And cuckoo-buds of yellow hue
   Do paint the meadows with delight,
The cuckoo then, on every tree,
Mocks married men; for thus sings he,
            Cuckoo;   910
Cuckoo, cuckoo: O word of fear,
Unpleasing to a married ear!
When shepherds pipe on oaten straws
   And merry larks are ploughmen's clocks,
• When turtles tread, and rooks, and daws,
   And maidens bleach their summer smocks,
The cuckoo then, on every tree,
Mocks married men; for thus sings he,
            Cuckoo;
Cuckoo, cuckoo: O word of fear,   920
Unpleasing to a married ear!

WINTER.

When icicles hang by the wall
   And Dick the shepherd blows his nail
And Tom bears logs into the hall
   And milk comes frozen home in pail
When blood is nipp'd and ways be foul,
Then nightly sings the staring owl,
            Tu-whit;
Tu-who, a merry note,
• While greasy Joan doth keel the pot.   930
When all aloud the wind doth blow
• And coughing drowns the parson's saw
And birds sit brooding in the snow
   And Marian's nose looks red and raw,
• When roasted crabs hiss in the bowl,
   Then nightly sings the staring owl,
            Tu-whit;
Tu-who, a merry note,
While greasy Joan doth keel the pot.

Arm.   The words of Mercury are harsh after the songs of Apollo. You that way: we this way.   [*Exeunt.*

895 *dialogue.* This was a popular form of debate in the Middle Ages.

Spring and Winter. Illustration by Norman Wilkinson from *Players' Shakespeare*, 1924

915 *turtles.* Turtle doves.

930 *keel.* i.e. to cool a hot or boiling liquid, by stirring, skimming, or pouring in something cold, to prevent it from boiling over.

932 *saw.* Maxim or proverb.

935 *crabs.* Crab apples.

'While greasy Joan doth keel the pot.' Engraving from Charles Knight's *Pictorial Edition of the Works of Shakspere*, 1834–43

A Midsummer Night's Dream

1594

The Occasion. The play was written, or adapted, for a wedding celebration. We know from Sonnet 106 that, in 1593, Shakespeare was reading Chaucer, from whose 'antique pen' had come the 'Knight's Tale', which provides the framework for the play; and we may infer from Sonnet 98 that he was thinking of a 'summer's story'. When we come to the close of the play, however, we find that it is Maytime, and the young lovers return from observing Mayday to grace the marriage of the elderly, stately couple, Duke Theseus and his betrothed Hippolyta.

This is obviously appropriate to the wedding of the elderly Privy Councillor and Vice-Chamberlain to the Queen, Sir Thomas Heneage and Southampton's mother, the Countess, on 2 May 1594. Moreover, this wedding was a private occasion, certainly not graced by the presence of the Queen, who did not favour it—we know independently that Heneage was out of favour with her that spring. For one thing, he was old—why should he want to marry?—and, for another, the Countess was a Catholic. From her point of view, it was a good protective move, for the Vice-Chamberlain was a staunch Protestant; her family needed protection, for her son had offended Lord Treasurer Burghley by breaking his promise to marry his grand-daughter and the Queen never favoured Southampton, for all his attractive ambivalence.

Nor is it at all probable that the actor-dramatist—who was all gentlemanly courtesy and tact—would confront the Virgin Queen on a first performance with—

> To live a barren sister all your life,
> Chanting faint hymns to the cold fruitless moon.

(Elizabeth was all too frequently hailed as Cynthia, the cold goddess of the moon, 'the mortal moon', etc.)

> But earthlier happy is the rose distilled
> Than that which, withering on the virgin thorn,
> Grows, lives and dies in single blessedness.

*Reconciliation of
Oberon and
Titania. Painting
by Sir Noel
Paton (1821–
1901)*

This is an image with which Shakespeare addressed his young patron in the Sonnets, urging him to marry; in it we recognise the Southampton theme.

So the marriage of the elderly couple was a private one, which the Queen did not attend—that is why little is known about it; we do not know where it took place, except in a private house, probably Southampton House in Holborn, its gardens running down Chancery Lane (we can still trace the shape of the site).

Character of the Play. The plot of the play—the double-plot of the elderly match and the complications of the young lovers at cross-purposes—is hardly important, though it provides the framework. What the world remembers are the twin elements of the fairy-tale and the performance of the 'rude mechanicals': the characters of Titania and Oberon, above all Puck; of Bottom the weaver and his crew of joiner, carpenter, bellows-mender, tinker and tailor, above all Bottom.

Though the fairy-tale is a primitive, archetypal form of literature, and there are other examples in the Elizabethan age, we may regard *A Midsummer Night's Dream* as a perennial inspiration and a fountain-source of fairy-tale literature ever after, up to our own day with Kipling's *Puck of Pook's Hill*. The play was a favourite with those elect spirits, Milton and Keats, as well as with the world in general. Even in Shakespeare's own day, his fellow Warwickshireman Drayton's charming 'Nymphydia' was greatly influenced by it, perhaps inspired by it.

How perceptive Quiller-Couch was in writing about Puck and Robin Goodfellow: rather than from books, 'it is even more likely that he brought all this fairy-stuff up to London in his own head, packed with nursery legends of his native Warwickshire. When will criticism learn to allow for the enormous drafts made by creative artists such as Shakespeare and Dickens upon their childhood?' Q. was himself a creative writer, and he knew.

The historian too can appreciate that Shakespeare never lost touch with his native Stratford. The mechanics are straight out of the streets and occupations of the country market-town we know so much about—after all, his father was a glover (as Drayton's was a butcher, Richard Field's a tanner), further down in Henley Street was blacksmith Hornby. It is like this very clever man, always ready for a joke, that the names of the artisans (Elizabethans called them 'mechanics') pun upon their occupations—a 'bottom' is the skein upon which the weaver winds his yarn, and so on. As for their performance, Shakespeare is caricaturing what he, the professional, had often seen in country plays and provincial performances. Once more, after they have been laughed off the stage, there is a kind-hearted comment that bespeaks the author: 'the best in this kind are but shadows, and the worst are no worse, if imagination amend them.'

There he is, speaking directly to our hearts.

Such are the elements that go to the making of this play: marriage and married love, love crossed and brought together again, the competing claims of love and friendship—so much to the fore in these years, in *The Two Gentlemen of Verona* and more powerfully in *The Merchant of Venice*. This theme is the very crux of the Sonnets, and what gives them their dramatic tension, almost like another play.

Scholars have traced the mingled elements out of which the play was blended. There is Chaucer, along with Shakespeare's favourite poet, Ovid. We know that he read the *Metamorphoses* in the original—and Beeston of the Globe Company told John Aubrey that 'he understood Latin pretty well, for he had been in his younger years a schoolmaster in the country'. Nevertheless, for a busy player and playwright, it was handier and more convenient to reach down Golding's translation, which he used more often. The chief contemporaries who influenced Shakespeare, apart from Marlowe, were Sidney and Spenser—from the latter comes Oberon. Bottom's woeful Pyramus and Thisbe play was suggested from Ovid.

Various touches serve to give us the contemporary background and make the play more real to us.

> The thrice three Muses mourning for the death
> Of learning, late deceased in beggary—

refers to the death of Robert Greene in penury and want some eighteen months earlier. Greene, a Cambridge man, always asserted his M.A. from both universities; and Shakespeare, who respected learning, several times payed tribute to his rival, Marlowe, in the Sonnets for his greater learning, as a university man: 'his well-refined pen', that 'worthier pen' and 'able spirit', whose favour from the young patron adds 'feathers to the learned's wing'. The reference continues:

> That is some satire, keen and critical,
> Not sorting with a nuptial ceremony—

which is appropriate enough to Greene's sharp and realistic cony-catching pamphlets and descriptions of low life, which were more successful than his plays; or even to the bitter attack on Shakespeare from his death-bed in 1592.

In the summer of that year the Queen had paid a visit to Oxford, when Southampton was made an M.A. That Shakespeare was in attendance we may well infer from the authentic note of the Duke's speech:

> Where I have come, great clerks have purposèd
> To greet me with premeditated welcomes;
> Where I have seen them shiver and look pale,
> Make periods in the midst of sentences,

> Throttle their practised accent in their fears,
> And in conclusion dumbly have broke off.

Upon occasion this was precisely what had happened to scared academics confronting Queen Elizabeth I.

The description of the disastrously wet summer of 1594 does not disturb our dating, for this play, too, being a private one in origin, would have been revised and expanded for public performance. It is a countryman who writes (and Shakespeare was a country-man, unlike Marlowe and Ben Jonson, who were townees):

>   the green corn
> Hath rotted ere his youth attained a beard.
> The fold stands empty in the drownèd field,
> And crows are fatted with the murrain flock,
> The nine men's morris is filled up with mud,
> And the quaint mazes in the wanton green
> For lack of tread are undistinguishable.

We are reminded that it was in the Cotswolds, on the threshold of Stratford, that morris dancing never died out, and from there was revived in this century.

The play is full of country lore, country activities and observations. There is Shakespeare's early passion for hunting:

> My love shall hear the music of my hounds.
> Uncouple in the western valley, let them go . . .

>   their heads are hung
> With ears that sweep away the morning dew,
> Crook-kneed, and dewlapped like Thessalian bulls;
> Slow in pursuit; but matched in mouth like bells,
> Each under each. A cry more tuneable
> Was never holla'ed to, nor cheered with horn.

This is a hunting man's enthusiasm—nothing like it in other Elizabethan dramatists. We note the sportsman's eye for birds:

> As wild geese that the creeping fowler eye,
> Or russet-pated choughs, many in sort,
> Rising and cawing at the gun's report,
> Sever themselves, and madly sweep the sky.

Or sounds:

> More tuneable than lark to shepherd's ear,
> When wheat is green, when hawthorn buds appear.

Country beliefs and superstitions, traditional lore, are woven into the texture of the play, which is largely fabricated out of them. Life is electrified by ghosts, who visit us by night; with dawn,

> At whose approach, ghosts, wandering here and there,
> Troop home to churchyards: damnèd spirits all,
> That in crossways and floods have burial.

At cross-roads suicides were buried.

> Now it is the time of night
>   That the graves, all gaping wide,
> Every one lets forth his sprite,
>   In the churchway paths to glide.

In the ghost-haunted churchway path at Stratford there was a charnel-house in his time.

Even the unimaginative E. K. Chambers saw that Puck, or Robin Goodfellow, was the most characteristic creation of *A Midsummer Night's Dream,* the symbol of what he calls a 'dramatic fantasy'. Puck comes straight out of folklore:

> are not you he
> That frights the maidens of the villagery,
> Skim milk, and sometimes labour in the quern,
> And bootless make the breathless housewife churn,
> And sometime make the drink to bear no barm,
> Mislead night-wanderers, laughing at their harm?

All this added a dimension to the simple lives of country folk, and lapped it round with poetry. Puck boasts of his feats:

> And sometime lurk I in a gossip's bowl,
> In very likeness of a roasted crab,
> And when she drinks against her lips I bob,
> And on her withered dewlap pour the ale.
> The wisest aunt, telling the saddest tale,
> Sometime for three-foot stool mistaketh me:
> Then slip I from her bum, down topples she,
> And 'tailor' cries, and falls into a cough.
> And then the whole choir hold their hips and laugh,
> And waxen in their mirth, and neeze, and swear
> A merrier hour was never wasted there.

Much of this play is in rhyme, and rhyme comes easily and naturally to a born poet—not to those who are not. The most moving poetry occurs in these evocative passages from country life and lore, for this is what was at heart with Shakespeare. He was an historically-minded, backward-looking man, inspired by the past and the life of the past, like Scott and Hardy—not a forward-looking, more superficial kind of writer, like Shaw or H. G. Wells. As an inspired painter, Samuel Palmer, wrote: 'The Past for poets', and he added, 'the Present for pigs.'

One gesture to the contemporary world is vouchsafed by the poet, a salute to the Queen—there are not many in Shakespeare (as against Spenser, for example), for he was aligned, through Southampton, with Essex who moved into dangerous opposition. (The movement can be traced in the Plays.) It is thought that the following may refer back to the Entertainments Leicester laid on for her at Kenilworth in 1575—which Shakespeare could have seen as a boy of eleven; for this was Leicester's last attempt to capture the Queen in marriage. Cupid aims

> At a fair Vestal, thronèd by the west . . .
> But I might see young Cupid's fiery shaft
> Quenched in the chaste beams of the wat'ry moon.
> And the imperial Votaress passed on
> In maiden meditation, fancy-free.

But we see Shakespeare's early genius at its most authentic in the comic transcripts from real life; as Dr. Johnson saw, his initial gift was for comedy—in keeping with his nature (compare Berowne).

Text. The text of this play has come down to us in very good state, probably from Shakespeare's own revised draft, and presents few problems. We must remember that it was not to the interest of the Company, or the author, to publish their plays: the theatre was their first and last concern, and they wanted to keep their property for theatrical performances. So great was Shakespeare's appeal that his plays were often pirated, got by memory—perhaps with the connivance of lesser actors—and printed in reported versions (the Bad Quartos).

This play was printed in a good quarto in 1600, 'as it hath been sundry times publicly acted by the Right Honourable the Lord Chamberlain's servants'. It was reprinted by Jaggard in 1619, and from this again in the First Folio of 1623, the great collection of all Shakespeare's work for the theatre, brought together by his fellows, Heming and Condell, in his honour. It was compared with the Company's own copy, as we know from a charming touch that has crept into the final Interlude, which is annotated:

> Tawyer, with a trumpet before them.

Tawyer was Heming's servant, who was buried in St. Saviour's, Southwark (the present cathedral) a couple of years later, in 1625. It brings the performers of this magical play vividly before us.

A MIDSUMMER-NIGHT'S DREAM.

DRAMATIS PERSONÆ.

THESEUS, Duke of Athens.
EGEUS, father to Hermia.
LYSANDER, } in love with Hermia.
DEMETRIUS,
PHILOSTRATE, master of the revels to Theseus.
QUINCE, a carpenter.
SNUG, a joiner.
BOTTOM, a weaver.
FLUTE, a bellows-mender.
SNOUT, a tinker.
STARVELING, a tailor.

HIPPOLYTA, queen of the Amazons, betrothed to Theseus.

HERMIA, daughter to Egeus, in love with Lysander.
HELENA, in love with Demetrius.

OBERON, king of the fairies.
TITANIA, queen of the fairies.
PUCK, or Robin Goodfellow.
PEASEBLOSSOM,
COBWEB,
MOTH, } fairies.
MUSTARDSEED,

Other fairies attending their King and Queen.
Attendants on Theseus and Hippolyta.

SCENE : *Athens, and a wood near it.*

● *A bullet beside a text line indicates an annotation in the opposite column*

ACT I.

SCENE I. *Athens. The palace of* THESEUS.

Enter THESEUS, HIPPOLYTA, PHILOSTRATE, *and* Attendants.

   The. Now, fair Hippolyta, our nuptial hour
Draws on apace; four happy days bring in
Another moon: but, O, methinks, how slow
● This old moon wanes! she lingers my desires,
● Like to a step-dame or a dowager
Long withering out a young man's revenue.
   Hip. Four days will quickly steep themselves
    in night;
Four nights will quickly dream away the time;

The palace of Theseus. Illustration by Paul Nash from *Players' Shakespeare,* 1924

4 *lingers.* Delays.

5-6 *dowager . . . revenue.* Like a widow whose income from the estate diminishes the heir's portion.

Opposite : Titania awakes. Painting by Henry Fuseli, 1793–4

15 *pāle companion.* i.e. melancholy.

16-17 *I woo'd . . . injuries.* Hippolyta, queen of the Amazons, had been conquered by Theseus in battle.

19 *With pomp, with triumph.* With parades and public festivities.

31 *feigning voice.* Soft voice. *feigning love.* Pretending love.

32 *stolen . . . fantasy.* Captured her imagination.

33 *gawds, conceits.* Trinkets, tokens.

45 *Immediately.* Expressly.

Costume design for Theseus by Norman Wilkinson, Savoy Theatre, London, 1914

54 *in this kind.* In this matter.

60 *concern my modesty.* Affect my reputation.

And then the moon, like to a silver bow
New-bent in heaven, shall behold the night   10
Of our solemnities.
    The.   Go, Philostrate,
Stir up the Athenian youth to merriments;
Awake the pert and nimble spirit of mirth:
Turn melancholy forth to funerals;
● The pale companion is not for our pomp.
                      [*Exit Philostrate.*
● Hippolyta, I woo'd thee with my sword,
And won thy love, doing thee injuries;
But I will wed thee in another key,
● With pomp, with triumph and with revelling.

    Enter EGEUS, HERMIA, LYSANDER, *and*
               DEMETRIUS.

    Ege. Happy be Theseus, our renowned duke!
    The. Thanks, good Egeus: what's the news
      with thee?   21
    Ege. Full of vexation come I, with complaint
Against my child, my daughter Hermia.
Stand forth, Demetrius. My noble lord,
This man hath my consent to marry her.
Stand forth, Lysander: and, my gracious duke,
This man hath bewitch'd the bosom of my child:
Thou, thou, Lysander, thou hast given her
    rhymes
And interchanged love-tokens with my child:
Thou hast by moonlight at her window sung   30
● With feigning voice verses of feigning love,
● And stolen the impression of her fantasy
● With bracelets of thy hair, rings, gawds, conceits,
Knacks, trifles, nosegays, sweetmeats, messen-
    gers
Of strong prevailment in unharden'd youth:
With cunning hast thou filch'd my daughter's
    heart,
Turn'd her obedience, which is due to me,
To stubborn harshness: and, my gracious duke,
Be it so she will not here before your grace
Consent to marry with Demetrius,   40
I beg the ancient privilege of Athens,
As she is mine, I may dispose of her:
Which shall be either to this gentleman
Or to her death, according to our law
● Immediately provided in that case.
    The. What say you, Hermia? be advised,
    fair maid:
To you your father should be as a god;
One that composed your beauties, yea, and one
To whom you are but as a form in wax
By him imprinted and within his power   50
To leave the figure or disfigure it.
Demetrius is a worthy gentleman.
    Her. So is Lysander.
    The.   In himself he is;
● But in this kind, wanting your father's voice,
The other must be held the worthier.
    Her. I would my father look'd but with my
    eyes.
    The. Rather your eyes must with his judge-
    ment look.
    Her. I do entreat your grace to pardon me.
I know not by what power I am made bold,
● Nor how it may concern my modesty,   60
In such a presence here to plead my thoughts;
But I beseech your grace that I may know
The worst that may befall me in this case,
If I refuse to wed Demetrius.

The. Either to die the death or to abjure
For ever the society of men.
Therefore, fair Hermia, question your desires;
•Know of your youth, examine well your blood,
Whether, if you yield not to your father's choice,
You can endure the livery of a nun,   70
•For aye to be in shady cloister mew'd,
To live a barren sister all your life,
Chanting faint hymns to the cold fruitless moon.
Thrice-blessed they that master so their blood,
•To undergo such maiden pilgrimage;
But earthlier happy is the rose distill'd,
Than that which withering on the virgin thorn
Grows, lives and dies in single blessedness.
    Her.   So will I grow, so live, so die, my lord,
Ere I will yield my virgin patent up   80
Unto his lordship, whose unwished yoke
My soul consents not to give sovereignty.
    The.   Take time to pause; and, by the next
        new moon—
The sealing-day betwixt my love and me,
For everlasting bond of fellowship—
Upon that day either prepare to die
For disobedience to your father's will,
Or else to wed Demetrius, as he would;
Or on Diana's altar to protest
For aye austerity and single life.   90
    Dem.   Relent, sweet Hermia: and, Lysander,
        yield
•Thy crazed title to my certain right.
    Lys.   You have her father's love, Demetrius;
Let me have Hermia's: do you marry him.
    Ege.   Scornful Lysander! true, he hath my
        love,
And what is mine my love shall render him.
And she is mine, and all my right of her
•I do estate unto Demetrius.
    Lys.   I am, my lord, as well derived as he,
As well possess'd; my love is more than his; 100
My fortunes every way as fairly rank'd,
•If not with vantage, as Demetrius';
And, which is more than all these boasts can be,
I am beloved of beauteous Hermia:
•Why should not I then prosecute my right?
•Demetrius, I'll avouch it to his head,
Made love to Nedar's daughter, Helena,
And won her soul; and she, sweet lady, dotes,
Devoutly dotes, dotes in idolatry,
•Upon this spotted and inconstant man.   110
    The.   I must confess that I have heard so
        much,
And with Demetrius thought to have spoke
        thereof;
But, being over-full of self-affairs,
My mind did lose it.   But, Demetrius, come;
And come, Egeus; you shall go with me,
I have some private schooling for you both.
For you, fair Hermia, look you arm yourself
To fit your fancies to your father's will;
Or else the law of Athens yields you up—
Which by no means we may extenuate—   120
To death, or to a vow of single life.
Come, my Hippolyta: what cheer, my love?
Demetrius and Egeus, go along:
I must employ you in some business
Against our nuptial and confer with you
Of something nearly that concerns yourselves.
    Ege.   With duty and desire we follow you.
        [*Exeunt all but Lysander and Hermia.*

F. R. Benson, English Edwardian actor, as Lysander

68 *blood.* Nature.

71 *mew'd.* A term used in falconry meaning 'caged'.

75 *maiden pilgrimage.* A life of chastity.

92 *crazed title.* Flawed claim.

98 *estate.* Bequeath.

102 *If not with vantage, as.* If not better than.

105 *prosecute.* Pursue.

106 *avouch it to his head.* Say it to his face.

110 *spotted.* Dishonourable.

131 *Beteem.* Supply.

135 *blood.* Rank.

143 *momentany.* Momentary.

145 *collied.* Black.

146 *spleen.* Flash, like a moment of anger.

156 *persuasion.* Principle.

167 *morn of May.* On the first day of May, the custom was to go to the woods, gather flowers and dance and sing.

Bringing in the Maypole. Engraving from *Old England*, 1854

170 *golden head.* Cupid's arrows of love were tipped with gold; those of dislike, with lead.

173 *Carthage queen.* Dido, queen of Carthage, threw herself on a pyre when her lover, the Trojan Aeneas, deserted her.

Lys. How now, my love! why is your cheek so pale?
How chance the roses there do fade so fast?
 Her. Belike for want of rain, which I could well   130
 • Beteem them from the tempest of my eyes.
 Lys. Ay me! for aught that I could ever read,
Could ever hear by tale or history,
The course of true love never did run smooth;
 • But, either it was different in blood,—
 Her. O cross! too high to be enthrall'd to low.
 Lys. Or else misgraffed in respect of years,—
 Her. O spite! too old to be engaged to young.
 Lys. Or else it stood upon the choice of friends,—
 Her. O hell! to choose love by another's eyes.
 Lys. Or, if there were a sympathy in choice,
War, death, or sickness did lay siege to it,
 • Making it momentany as a sound,
Swift as a shadow, short as any dream;
 • Brief as the lightning in the collied night,
 • That, in a spleen, unfolds both heaven and earth,
And ere a man hath power to say 'Behold!'
The jaws of darkness do devour it up:
So quick bright things come to confusion.
 Her. If then true lovers have been ever cross'd,
It stands as an edict in destiny: 151
Then let us teach our trial patience,
Because it is a customary cross,
As due to love as thoughts and dreams and sighs,
Wishes and tears, poor fancy's followers.
 • *Lys.* A good persuasion: therefore, hear me, Hermia.
I have a widow aunt, a dowager
Of great revenue, and she hath no child:
From Athens is her house remote seven leagues;
And she respects me as her only son.   160
There, gentle Hermia, may I marry thee;
And to that place the sharp Athenian law
Cannot pursue us. If thou lovest me then,
Steal forth thy father's house to-morrow night;
And in the wood, a league without the town,
Where I did meet thee once with Helena,
 • To do observance to a morn of May,
There will I stay for thee.
 Her.   My good Lysander!
I swear to thee, by Cupid's strongest bow,
 • By his best arrow with the golden head,   170
By the simplicity of Venus' doves,
By that which knitteth souls and prospers loves,
 • And by that fire which burn'd the Carthage queen,
When the false Troyan under sail was seen,
By all the vows that ever men have broke,
In number more than ever women spoke,
In that same place thou hast appointed me,
To-morrow truly will I meet with thee.
 Lys. Keep promise, love. Look, here comes Helena.

Enter HELENA.

 Her. God speed fair Helena! whither away?
 Hel. Call you me fair? that fair again unsay.
Demetrius loves your fair: O happy fair!
Your eyes are lode-stars; and your tongue's sweet air
More tuneable than lark to shepherd's ear,
When wheat is green, when hawthorn buds appear.
Sickness is catching: O, were favour so,
Yours would I catch, fair Hermia, ere I go;
My ear should catch your voice, my eye your eye,

My tongue should catch your tongue's sweet me-
      lody.
● Were the world mine, Demetrius being bated,
● The rest I'ld give to be to you translated.   191
O, teach me how you look, and with what art
You sway the motion of Demetrius' heart.
      Her. I frown upon him, yet he loves me still.
      Hel. O that your frowns would teach my
      smiles such skill!
      Her. I give him curses, yet he gives me love.
      Hel. O that my prayers could such affection
      move!
      Her. The more I hate, the more he follows me.
      Hel. The more I love, the more he hateth me.
      Her. His folly, Helena, is no fault of mine.
      Hel. None, but your beauty: would that fault
      were mine!   201
      Her. Take comfort: he no more shall see my
      face;
Lysander and myself will fly this place.
Before the time I did Lysander see,
Seem'd Athens as a paradise to me:
O, then, what graces in my love do dwell,
That he hath turn'd a heaven unto a hell!
      Lys. Helen, to you our minds we will unfold:
● To-morrow night, when Phœbe doth behold
Her silver visage in the watery glass,   210
Decking with liquid pearl the bladed grass,
A time that lovers' flights doth still conceal,
Through Athens' gates have we devised to steal.
      Her. And in the wood, where often you and I
Upon faint primrose-beds were wont to lie,
Emptying our bosoms of their counsel sweet,
There my Lysander and myself shall meet;
And thence from Athens turn away our eyes,
To seek new friends and stranger companies.
Farewell, sweet playfellow: pray thou for us;
And good luck grant thee thy Demetrius!   221
Keep word, Lysander: we must starve our sight
From lovers' food till morrow deep midnight.
      Lys. I will, my Hermia.   [*Exit Herm.*

      Helena, adieu:
As you on him, Demetrius dote on you! [*Exit.*
      Hel. How happy some o'er other some can be!
Through Athens I am thought as fair as she.
But what of that? Demetrius thinks not so;
He will not know what all but he do know:
And as he errs, doting on Hermia's eyes,   230
So I, admiring of his qualities:
● Things base and vile, holding no quantity,
Love can transpose to form and dignity:
Love looks not with the eyes, but with the mind;
And therefore is wing'd Cupid painted blind:
Nor hath Love's mind of any judgement taste;
Wings and no eyes figure unheedy haste:
And therefore is Love said to be a child,
Because in choice he is so oft beguiled.
As waggish boys in game themselves forswear,   240
So the boy Love is perjured every where:
● For ere Demetrius look'd on Hermia's eyne,
He hail'd down oaths that he was only mine;
And when this hail some heat from Hermia felt,
So he dissolved, and showers of oaths did melt.
I will go tell him of fair Hermia's flight:
Then to the wood will he to-morrow night
Pursue her; and for this intelligence
If I have thanks, it is a dear expense:
But herein mean I to enrich my pain,   250
To have his sight thither and back again. [*Exit.*

190 *bated.* Excepted.

191 *translated.* Transformed.

209 *Phœbe.* Diana, goddess of the Moon.

Helena. Illustration by Arthur Rackham, 1908

232 *quantity.* Substance.

242 *eyne.* Archaic plural form of 'eye'.

SD *Enter Quince* . . . The names of the clowns are suggestive of their trades. *Bottom* refers to a skein on which the weaver's thread is wound. *Quince* or *quine* was a wooden block used by carpenters. *Snug* means well-fitted and is appropriate for a joiner. *Flute* is another word for pipe and the bellows mender was also responsible for the pipes of the organ. *Snout* suggests the spout of a kettle which tinkers regularly might have to mend, while *Starveling* alludes to the proverbial skinniness of tailors.

Carpenters at work. A 15th century German woodcut

---

2 *generally*. Bottom means 'individually'.

10 *grow to a point*. Come to the point.

29 *condole*. Wail and lament.

31 *Ercles*. Hercules, a part in which an actor could rant.

32 *tear a cat*. A reference to Hercules killing a lion.

37 *Phibbus' car*. Phoebus' chariot.

52 *small*. Soft.

A 'jovial tinker'. From a contemporary woodcut

SCENE II. *Athens.* QUINCE'S *house.*

Enter QUINCE, SNUG, BOTTOM, FLUTE, SNOUT, *and* STARVELING.

Quin. Is all our company here?

Bot. You were best to call them generally, man by man, according to the scrip.

Quin. Here is the scroll of every man's name, which is thought fit, through all Athens, to play in our interlude before the duke and the duchess, on his wedding-day at night.

Bot. First, good Peter Quince, say what the play treats on, then read the names of the actors, and so grow to a point.   10

Quin. Marry, our play is, The most lamentable comedy, and most cruel death of Pyramus and Thisby.

Bot. A very good piece of work, I assure you, and a merry. Now, good Peter Quince, call forth your actors by the scroll. Masters, spread yourselves.

Quin. Answer as I call you. Nick Bottom, the weaver.

Bot. Ready. Name what part I am for, and proceed.   21

Quin. You, Nick Bottom, are set down for Pyramus.

Bot. What is Pyramus? a lover, or a tyrant?

Quin. A lover, that kills himself most gallant for love.

Bot. That will ask some tears in the true performing of it: if I do it, let the audience look to their eyes; I will move storms, I will condole in some measure. To the rest: yet my chief humour is for a tyrant: I could play Ercles rarely, or a part to tear a cat in, to make all split.

> The raging rocks
> And shivering shocks
> Shall break the locks
>   Of prison gates;
>   And Phibbus' car
> Shall shine from far
> And make and mar
>   The foolish Fates.   40

This was lofty! Now name the rest of the players. This is Ercles' vein, a tyrant's vein; a lover is more condoling.

Quin. Francis Flute, the bellows-mender.

Flu. Here, Peter Quince.

Quin. Flute, you must take Thisby on you.

Flu. What is Thisby? a wandering knight?

Quin. It is the lady that Pyramus must love.

Flu. Nay, faith, let not me play a woman; I have a beard coming.   50

Quin. That's all one: you shall play it in a mask, and you may speak as small as you will.

Bot. An I may hide my face, let me play Thisby too, I'll speak in a monstrous little voice, 'Thisne, Thisne;' 'Ah Pyramus, my lover dear! thy Thisby dear, and lady dear!'

Quin. No, no; you must play Pyramus: and, Flute, you Thisby.

Bot. Well, proceed.

Quin. Robin Starveling, the tailor.   60

Star. Here, Peter Quince.

Quin. Robin Starveling, you must play Thisby's mother. Tom Snout, the tinker.

Snout. Here, Peter Quince.

Quin. You, Pyramus' father: myself, Thisby's

father. Snug, the joiner; you, the lion's part:
and, I hope, here is a play fitted.

Snug. Have you the lion's part written? pray
you, if it be, give it me, for I am slow of study.

Quin. You may do it extempore, for it is
nothing but roaring.   71

Bot. Let me play the lion too: I will roar,
that I will do any man's heart good to hear me;
I will roar, that I will make the duke say 'Let
him roar again, let him roar again.'

Quin. An you should do it too terribly, you
would fright the duchess and the ladies, that
they would shriek; and that were enough to
hang us all.

All. That would hang us, every mother's son.

Bot. I grant you, friends, if that you should
fright the ladies out of their wits, they would
have no more discretion but to hang us: but I
will aggravate my voice so that I will roar you
as gently as any sucking dove; I will roar you
an 'twere any nightingale.

Quin. You can play no part but Pyramus;
for Pyramus is a sweet-faced man; a proper man,
as one shall see in a summer's day; a most lovely
gentleman-like man: therefore you must needs
play Pyramus.   91

Bot. Well, I will undertake it. What beard
were I best to play it in?

Quin. Why, what you will.

Bot. I will discharge it in either your straw-
colour beard, your orange-tawny beard, your
purple-in-grain beard, or your French-crown-
colour beard, your perfect yellow.

Quin. Some of your French crowns have no
hair at all, and then you will play barefaced.
But, masters, here are your parts: and I am to
entreat you, request you and desire you, to con
them by to-morrow night; and meet me in the
palace wood, a mile without the town, by moonlight; there will we rehearse, for if we meet in
the city, we shall be dogged with company, and
our devices known. In the meantime I will draw
a bill of properties, such as our play wants. I
pray you, fail me not.

Bot. We will meet; and there we may rehearse most obscenely and courageously. Take
pains; be perfect: adieu.

Quin. At the duke's oak we meet.

Bot. Enough; hold or cut bow-strings.

[*Exeunt.*

ACT II.

SCENE I. *A wood near Athens.*

Enter, from opposite sides, a Fairy, *and* PUCK.

Puck. How now, spirit! whither wander you?

Fai. Over hill, over dale,
    Thorough bush, thorough brier,
Over park, over pale,
    Thorough flood, thorough fire,
I do wander every where,
Swifter than the moon's sphere;
And I serve the fairy queen,
To dew her orbs upon the green.
The cowslips tall her pensioners be: 10
In their gold coats spots you see;
Those be rubies, fairy favours,
In those freckles live their savours:

84 *aggravate.* Bottom means 'moderate'.

97-98 *purple-in-grain.* A fast red dye. *French-crown-colour.* Gold, the colour of a French coin.

99 *crowns.* A reference to the baldness associated with the 'French disease'.

100 *barefaced.* A pun playing of the meanings 'bald' and 'brazen'.

111 *obscenely.* Bottom means 'seemly'.

114 *hold or cut bow-strings.* Hold firm or give up.

'Exeunt Bottom etc.' Illustration by W. Heath Robinson, 1914

4 *pale.* Enclosed land.

7 *moon's sphere.* The moon was thought to be enclosed in a hollow sphere which revolved around the earth.

9 *orbs.* Circles of darker green grass.

10 *pensioners.* Queen Elizabeth's bodyguard of young men were known as 'pensioners'.

20 *passing fell and wrath*. Very fierce and angry.

The changeling. From Max Reinhardt's and William Dieterle's film, USA, 1935

25 *trace*. Wander.

30 *square*. Argue.

34 *Robin Goodfellow*. In English folklore, a name of a particular goblin with capricious tricks.

36 *quern*. A manual mill for grinding grain.

38 *barm*. Yeast.

Puck. Detail from an engraving from a painting by Richard Dadd, 1841

48 *crab*. Crab apple.

56 *neeze*. Sneeze.

66-68 *Corin . . . Phillida*. Traditional names for lovers in pastoral poetry.

71 *buskin'd*. Booted.

Opposite : Oberon: 'Ill met by moonlight . . .' Engraving from Rowe's edition of Shakespeare's works, 1709

I must go seek some dewdrops here
And hang a pearl in every cowslip's ear.
Farewell, thou lob of spirits ; I'll be gone :
Our queen and all her elves come here anon.
    Puck.   The king doth keep his revels here to-
      night :
Take heed the queen come not within his sight ;
For Oberon is passing fell and wrath,   20
Because that she as her attendant hath
A lovely boy, stolen from an Indian king ;
She never had so sweet a changeling ;
And jealous Oberon would have the child
Knight of his train, to trace the forests wild ;
But she perforce withholds the loved boy,
Crowns him with flowers and makes him all her
    joy :
And now they never meet in grove or green,
By fountain clear, or spangled starlight sheen,
But they do square, that all their elves for fear 30
Creep into acorn-cups and hide them there.
    Fai.   Either I mistake your shape and making
      quite,
Or else you are that shrewd and knavish sprite
Call'd Robin Goodfellow : are not you he
That frights the maidens of the villagery ;
Skim milk, and sometimes labour in the quern
And bootless make the breathless housewife churn ;
And sometime make the drink to bear no barm ;
Mislead night-wanderers, laughing at their harm ?
Those that Hobgoblin call you and sweet Puck,
You do their work, and they shall have good luck :
Are not you he ?
    Puck.   Thou speak'st aright ;
I am that merry wanderer of the night.
I jest to Oberon and make him smile
When I a fat and bean-fed horse beguile,
Neighing in likeness of a filly foal :
And sometime lurk I in a gossip's bowl,
In very likeness of a roasted crab,
And when she drinks, against her lips I bob
And on her wither'd dewlap pour the ale.   50
The wisest aunt, telling the saddest tale,
Sometime for three-foot stool mistaketh me ;
Then slip I from her bum, down topples she,
And 'tailor' cries, and falls into a cough ;
And then the whole quire hold their hips and laugh,
And waxen in their mirth and neeze and swear
A merrier hour was never wasted there.
But, room, fairy ! here comes Oberon.
    Fai.   And here my mistress.   Would that he
      were gone !

Enter, from one side, OBERON, *with his train ; from the other,* TITANIA, *with hers.*

    Obe.   Ill met by moonlight, proud Titania. 60
    Tita.   What, jealous Oberon ! Fairies, skip
      hence :
I have forsworn his bed and company.
    Obe.   Tarry, rash wanton : am not I thy lord ?
    Tita.   Then I must be thy lady : but I know
When thou hast stolen away from fairy land,
And in the shape of Corin sat all day,
Playing on pipes of corn and versing love
To amorous Phillida.   Why art thou here,
Come from the farthest steppe of India ?
But that, forsooth, the bouncing Amazon,   70
Your buskin'd mistress and your warrior love,
To Theseus must be wedded, and you come
To give their bed joy and prosperity.

78-80 *Perigenia . . . Ægle . . . Ariadne . . . Antiopa.* All women Theseus had loved and left.

The Quarrel. Painting by Sir J. N. Paton (1821–1902)

85 *beached margent.* The beach.

86 *ringlets.* Hair in ringlets (or circular dances).

97 *murrion flock.* Flock dead of the murrain disease.

98 *nine men's morris.* A game similar to Hopscotch, but played on turf.

99 *quaint mazes.* Labyrinths marked out on village greens over which youths raced.

109 *Hiems'.* Winter's.

112 *childing.* Fruitful.

Titania: '. . . Neptune's yellow sands.' Illustration by W. Heath Robinson, 1914

Obe.   How canst thou thus for shame, Titania,
Glance at my credit with Hippolyta,
Knowing I know thy love to Theseus?
Didst thou not lead him through the glimmering
    night
●From Perigenia, whom he ravished?
And make him with fair Ægle break his faith,
With Ariadne and Antiopa?   80

  Tita.   These are the forgeries of jealousy:
And never, since the middle summer's spring,
Met we on hill, in dale, forest or mead,
By paved fountain or by rushy brook,
●Or in the beached margent of the sea,
●To dance our ringlets to the whistling wind,
But with thy brawls thou hast disturb'd our sport.
Therefore the winds, piping to us in vain,
As in revenge, have suck'd up from the sea
Contagious fogs; which falling in the land   90
Have every pelting river made so proud
That they have overborne their continents:
The ox hath therefore stretch'd his yoke in vain,
The ploughman lost his sweat, and the green corn
Hath rotted ere his youth attain'd a beard;
The fold stands empty in the drowned field,
●And crows are fatted with the murrion flock;
●The nine men's morris is fill'd up with mud,
●And the quaint mazes in the wanton green
For lack of tread are undistinguishable: 100
The human mortals want their winter here;
No night is now with hymn or carol blest:
Therefore the moon, the governess of floods,
Pale in her anger, washes all the air,
That rheumatic diseases do abound:
And thorough this distemperature we see
The seasons alter: hoary-headed frosts
Fall in the fresh lap of the crimson rose,
●And on old Hiems' thin and icy crown
An odorous chaplet of sweet summer buds   110
Is, as in mockery, set: the spring, the summer,
●The childing autumn, angry winter, change
Their wonted liveries, and the mazed world,
By their increase, now knows not which is which:
And this same progeny of evils comes
From our debate, from our dissension;
We are their parents and original.

  Obe.   Do you amend it then; it lies in you:
Why should Titania cross her Oberon?
I do but beg a little changeling boy,   120
To be my henchman.

  Tita.   Set your heart at rest:
The fairy land buys not the child of me.
His mother was a votaress of my order:
And, in the spiced Indian air, by night,
Full often hath she gossip'd by my side,
And sat with me on Neptune's yellow sands,
Marking the embarked traders on the flood,
When we have laugh'd to see the sails conceive
And grow big-bellied with the wanton wind;
Which she, with pretty and with swimming gait
Following,—her womb then rich with my young
    squire,—   131
Would imitate, and sail upon the land,
To fetch me trifles, and return again,
As from a voyage, rich with merchandise.
But she, being mortal, of that boy did die;
And for her sake do I rear up her boy,
And for her sake I will not part with him.

  Obe.   How long within this wood intend you
    stay?

Tita. Perchance till after Theseus' wedding-
    day.
If you will patiently dance in our round   140
And see our moonlight revels, go with us;
● If not, shun me, and I will spare your haunts.
    Obe. Give me that boy, and I will go with thee.
    Tita. Not for thy fairy kingdom.   Fairies,
    away!
We shall chide downright, if I longer stay.
               [Exit Titania with her train.
    Obe. Well, go thy way: thou shalt not from
    this grove
Till I torment thee for this injury.
My gentle Puck, come hither.   Thou rememberest
Since once I sat upon a promontory,
And heard a mermaid on a dolphin's back   150
Uttering such dulcet and harmonious breath
That the rude sea grew civil at her song
And certain stars shot madly from their spheres,
To hear the sea-maid's music.
    Puck.   I remember.
    Obe. That very time I saw, but thou couldst
    not,
Flying between the cold moon and the earth,
Cupid all arm'd: a certain aim he took
At a fair vestal throned by the west,
And loosed his love-shaft smartly from his bow,
As it should pierce a hundred thousand hearts; 160
But I might see young Cupid's fiery shaft
Quench'd in the chaste beams of the watery moon,
And the imperial votaress passed on,
In maiden meditation, fancy-free.
Yet mark'd I where the bolt of Cupid fell:
It fell upon a little western flower,
Before milk-white, now purple with love's wound,
● And maidens call it love-in-idleness.
Fetch me that flower; the herb I shew'd thee once:
The juice of it on sleeping eye-lids laid   170
Will make or man or woman madly dote
Upon the next live creature that it sees.
Fetch me this herb; and be thou here again
● Ere the leviathan can swim a league.
    Puck. I'll put a girdle round about the earth
In forty minutes.   *[Exit.*
    Obe.   Having once this juice,
I'll watch Titania when she is asleep,
And drop the liquor of it in her eyes.
The next thing then she waking looks upon,
Be it on lion, bear, or wolf, or bull,   180
On meddling monkey, or on busy ape,
She shall pursue it with the soul of love:
And ere I take this charm from off her sight,
As I can take it with another herb,
I'll make her render up her page to me.
But who comes here?   I am invisible;
And I will overhear their conference.

Enter DEMETRIUS, HELENA *following him.*

    Dem. I love thee not, therefore pursue me not.
Where is Lysander and fair Hermia?
The one I'll slay, the other slayeth me.   190
Thou told'st me they were stolen unto this wood;
● And here am I, and wode within this wood,
Because I cannot meet my Hermia.
Hence, get thee gone, and follow me no more.
●   *Hel.* You draw me, you hard-hearted adamant;
But yet you draw not iron, for my heart
● Is true as steel: leave you your power to draw,
And I shall have no power to follow you.

142 *spare.* Avoid.

Oberon: 'And heard a mermaid . . .' Illustration by
Arthur Rackham, 1908

168 *love-in-idleness.* Pansy.

174 *leviathan.* Whale.

Puck: 'I'll put a girdle . . .' Engraving from a painting by
H. Fuseli (1741–1825)

192 *wode.* Mad.

195 *adamant.* Magnet.

197 *leave you.* Give up.

231 *Apollo . . . chase.* In classical mythology Daphne is pursued by Apollo before being turned into a bay tree.

232 *griffin.* A fabulous creature with a lion's body and an eagle's head.

Griffin. Woodcut from S. Bateman's *Doom,* 1581

233 *bootless.* Useless.

251 *woodbine.* Honeysuckle.

252 *eglantine.* Sweet-briar.

256 *Weed.* Garment.

Dem.   Do I entice you? do I speak you fair?
Or, rather, do I not in plainest truth   200
Tell you, I do not, nor I cannot love you?
    Hel. And even for that do I love you the more.
I am your spaniel; and, Demetrius,
The more you beat me, I will fawn on you:
Use me but as your spaniel, spurn me, strike me,
Neglect me, lose me; only give me leave,
Unworthy as I am, to follow you.
What worser place can I beg in your love,—
And yet a place of high respect with me,—
Than to be used as you use your dog?   210
    Dem.   Tempt not too much the hatred of my
        spirit,
For I am sick when I do look on thee.
    Hel. And I am sick when I look not on you.
    Dem. You do impeach your modesty too much,
To leave the city and commit yourself
Into the hands of one that loves you not;
To trust the opportunity of night
And the ill counsel of a desert place
With the rich worth of your virginity.
    Hel. Your virtue is my privilege: for that   220
It is not night when I do see your face,
Therefore I think I am not in the night;
Nor doth this wood lack worlds of company,
For you in my respect are all the world:
Then how can it be said I am alone,
When all the world is here to look on me?
    Dem.   I'll run from thee and hide me in the
        brakes,
And leave thee to the mercy of wild beasts.
    Hel. The wildest hath not such a heart as you.
Run when you will, the story shall be changed;
● Apollo flies, and Daphne holds the chase;   231
● The dove pursues the griffin; the mild hind
● Makes speed to catch the tiger; bootless speed,
When cowardice pursues and valour flies.
    Dem. I will not stay thy questions; let me go:
Or, if thou follow me, do not believe
But I shall do thee mischief in the wood.
    Hel.   Ay, in the temple, in the town, the field,
You do me mischief. Fie, Demetrius!
Your wrongs do set a scandal on my sex: 240
We cannot fight for love, as men may do;
We should be woo'd and were not made to woo.
                                     [*Exit Dem.*
I'll follow thee and make a heaven of hell,
To die upon the hand I love so well.   [*Exit.*
    Obe.   Fare thee well, nymph: ere he do leave
        this grove,
Thou shalt fly him and he shall seek thy love.

                Re-enter PUCK.

Hast thou the flower there? Welcome, wanderer.
    Puck. Ay, there it is.
    Obe.   I pray thee, give it me.
I know a bank where the wild thyme blows,
Where oxlips and the nodding violet grows,   250
● †Quite over-canopied with luscious woodbine,
● With sweet musk-roses and with eglantine:
There sleeps Titania sometime of the night,
Lull'd in these flowers with dances and delight;
And there the snake throws her enamell'd skin,
● Weed wide enough to wrap a fairy in:
And with the juice of this I'll streak her eyes,
And make her full of hateful fantasies.
Take thou some of it, and seek through this
        grove:

A sweet Athenian lady is in love   260
With a disdainful youth: anoint his eyes;
But do it when the next thing he espies
May be the lady: thou shalt know the man
By the Athenian garments he hath on.
Effect it with some care that he may prove
More fond on her than she upon her love:
And look thou meet me ere the first cock crow.
 Puck. Fear not, my lord, your servant shall
  do so.   *[Exeunt.*

SCENE II. *Another part of the wood.*

Enter TITANIA, *with her train.*

 Tita. Come, now a roundel and a fairy song;
Then, for the third part of a minute, hence;
• Some to kill cankers in the musk-rose buds,
• Some war with rere-mice for their leathern wings,
 To make my small elves coats, and some keep
  back
The clamorous owl that nightly hoots and won-
  ders
• At our quaint spirits. Sing me now asleep;
Then to your offices and let me rest.

The Fairies sing.

You spotted snakes with double tongue,
 Thorny hedgehogs, be not seen; 10
Newts and blind-worms, do no wrong,
 Come not near our fairy queen.
• Philomel, with melody
 Sing in our sweet lullaby;
Lulla, lulla, lullaby, lulla, lulla, lullaby:
  Never harm,
  Nor spell nor charm,
 Come our lovely lady nigh;
So, good night, with lullaby.
Weaving spiders, come not here; 20

 Hence, you long-legg'd spinners, hence!
Beetles black, approach not near;
 Worm nor snail, do no offence.
  Philomel, with melody, &c.

A Fairy. Hence, away! now all is well:
 One aloof stand sentinel.
  [Exeunt Fairies. Titania sleeps.

Enter OBERON, *and squeezes the flower on
Titania's eyelids.*

 Obe. What thou seest when thou dost wake,
 Do it for thy true-love take,
 Love and languish for his sake:
• Be it ounce, or cat, or bear, 30
• Pard, or boar with bristled hair,
 In thy eye that shall appear
 When thou wakest, it is thy dear:
 Wake when some vile thing is near.
         [Exit.

Enter LYSANDER *and* HERMIA.

 Lys. Fair love, you faint with wandering in the
  wood;
• And to speak troth, I have forgot our way:
We'll rest us, Hermia, if you think it good,
 And tarry for the comfort of the day.

3 *cankers.* Grubs or caterpillars.

4 *rere-mice.* Bats.

7 *quaint.* Neat or dainty.

13 *Philomel.* The nightingale.

Oberon squeezing the flower on Titania's eyelids.
Oberon (Alan Howard), Titania (Sara Kestleman),
Puck (John Kane), Royal Shakespeare Co, 1970

30 *ounce.* Lynx.

31 *Pard.* Leopard.

36 *troth.* Truth.

45 *take the sense.* Understand my meaning.

46 *Love . . . conference.* Love makes lovers understand each other.

54 *beshrew.* Curse.

68 *approve.* Try.

78 *Churl.* A boor.

85 *charge.* Order.

88 *fond.* A pun playing on the meanings 'foolish' and 'doting'.

Helena: 'O, I am out of breath in this fond chase . . .'
Miss Cooper as Helena. From J. O. Halliwell's *Complete Works of Shakespeare*, 1853

Her.   Be it so, Lysander: find you out a bed;
For I upon this bank will rest my head.   40
   Lys.   One turf shall serve as pillow for us both;
One heart, one bed, two bosoms and one troth.
   Her.   Nay, good Lysander; for my sake, my dear,
Lie further off yet, do not lie so near.
   Lys.   O, take the sense, sweet, of my innocence!
Love takes the meaning in love's conference.
I mean, that my heart unto yours is knit
So that but one heart we can make of it;
Two bosoms interchained with an oath;
So then two bosoms and a single troth.   50
Then by your side no bed-room me deny;
For lying so, Hermia, I do not lie.
   Her.   Lysander riddles very prettily:
Now much beshrew my manners and my pride,
If Hermia meant to say Lysander lied.
But, gentle friend, for love and courtesy
Lie further off; in human modesty,
Such separation as may well be said
Becomes a virtuous bachelor and a maid,
So far be distant; and, good night, sweet friend:
Thy love ne'er alter till thy sweet life end!   61
   Lys.   Amen, amen, to that fair prayer, say I;
And then end life when I end loyalty!
Here is my bed: sleep give thee all his rest!
   Her.   With half that wish the wisher's eyes be press'd!   [*They sleep.*

Enter PUCK.

   Puck.   Through the forest have I gone,
     But Athenian found I none,
     On whose eyes I might approve
     This flower's force in stirring love.
     Night and silence.—Who is here?   70
     Weeds of Athens he doth wear:
     This is he, my master said,
     Despised the Athenian maid;
     And here the maiden, sleeping sound,
     On the dank and dirty ground.
     Pretty soul! she durst not lie
     Near this lack-love, this kill-courtesy.
     Churl, upon thy eyes I throw
     All the power this charm doth owe.
     When thou wakest, let love forbid   80
     Sleep his seat on thy eyelid:
     So awake when I am gone;
     For I must now to Oberon.   [*Exit.*

Enter DEMETRIUS *and* HELENA, *running.*

   Hel.   Stay, though thou kill me, sweet Demetrius.
   Dem.   I charge thee, hence, and do not haunt me thus.
   Hel.   O, wilt thou darkling leave me? do not so.
   Dem.   Stay, on thy peril: I alone will go.
                     [*Exit.*
   Hel.   O, I am out of breath in this fond chase!
The more my prayer, the lesser is my grace.
Happy is Hermia, wheresoe'er she lies;   90
For she hath blessed and attractive eyes.
How came her eyes so bright? Not with salt tears:
If so, my eyes are oftener wash'd than hers.

No, no, I am as ugly as a bear;
For beasts that meet me run away for fear:
Therefore no marvel though Demetrius
Do, as a monster, fly my presence thus.
What wicked and dissembling glass of mine
● Made me compare with Hermia's sphery eyne?
But who is here? Lysander! on the ground! 100
Dead? or asleep? I see no blood, no wound.
Lysander, if you live, good sir, awake.
   Lys. [*Awaking*] And run through fire I will
      for thy sweet sake.
● Transparent Helena! Nature shows art,
That through thy bosom makes me see thy heart.
Where is Demetrius? O, how fit a word
Is that vile name to perish on my sword!
   Hel. Do not say so, Lysander; say not so.
What though he love your Hermia? Lord, what
      though?
Yet Hermia still loves you: then be content. 110
   Lys. Content with Hermia! No; I do repent
The tedious minutes I with her have spent.
Not Hermia but Helena I love:
Who will not change a raven for a dove?
The will of man is by his reason sway'd;
And reason says you are the worthier maid.
Things growing are not ripe until their season:
So I, being young, till now ripe not to reason;
● And touching now the point of human skill,
Reason becomes the marshal to my will   120
And leads me to your eyes, where I o'erlook
Love's stories written in love's richest book.
   Hel. Wherefore was I to this keen mockery
      born?
When at your hands did I deserve this scorn?
Is 't not enough, is 't not enough, young man,
That I did never, no, nor never can,
Deserve a sweet look from Demetrius' eye,
But you must flout my insufficiency?
Good troth, you do me wrong, good sooth, you do,
In such disdainful manner me to woo.   130
But fare you well: perforce I must confess
I thought you lord of more true gentleness.
O, that a lady, of one man refused,
Should of another therefore be abused!   [*Exit.*
   Lys. She sees not Hermia. Hermia, sleep
      thou there:
And never mayst thou come Lysander near!
For as a surfeit of the sweetest things
The deepest loathing to the stomach brings,
Or as the heresies that men do leave
Are hated most of those they did deceive,   140
So thou, my surfeit and my heresy,
Of all be hated, but the most of me!
And, all my powers, address your love and might
To honour Helen and to be her knight!   [*Exit.*

   Her. [*Awaking*] Help me, Lysander, help
      me! do thy best
To pluck this crawling serpent from my breast!
Ay me, for pity! what a dream was here!
Lysander, look how I do quake with fear:
Methought a serpent eat my heart away,
And you sat smiling at his cruel prey.   150
Lysander! what, removed? Lysander! lord!
What, out of hearing? gone? no sound, no
      word?
Alack, where are you? speak, an if you hear;
Speak, of all loves! I swoon almost with fear.
No? then I well perceive you are not nigh:
Either death or you I'll find immediately. [*Exit.*

Costume designs for The Lovers. Illustration by Paul Nash from *Players' Shakespeare*, 1924

99 *sphery eyne.* Eyes like stars.

104 *Transparent.* Bright.

119-120 *And touching . . . will.* Reason, having at last matured, is now master of will.

4-5 *tiring-house.* Dressing room.

8 *bully.* Brother.

The mechanicals rehearse their play, Royal Shakespeare Co, 1970

14 *By'r lakin.* 'By our little lady'. *parlous.* Risky or dangerous.

25 *eight and six.* Alternative lines, in a ballad, of eight and six syllables.

40 *defect.* Bottom means 'effect'.

62 *disfigure.* Bottom means 'figure' i.e. represent.

ACT III.

SCENE I. *The wood. Titania lying asleep.*

Enter QUINCE, SNUG, BOTTOM, FLUTE, SNOUT,
and STARVELING.

Bot. Are we all met?

Quin. Pat, pat; and here's a marvellous convenient place for our rehearsal. This green plot shall be our stage, this hawthorn-brake our tiring-house; and we will do it in action as we will do it before the duke.

Bot. Peter Quince,—

Quin. What sayest thou, bully Bottom?

Bot. There are things in this comedy of Pyramus and Thisby that will never please. First, Pyramus must draw a sword to kill himself; which the ladies cannot abide. How answer you that?

Snout. By'r lakin, a parlous fear.

Star. I believe we must leave the killing out, when all is done.

Bot. Not a whit: I have a device to make all well. Write me a prologue; and let the prologue seem to say, we will do no harm with our swords and that Pyramus is not killed indeed; and, for the more better assurance, tell them that I Pyramus am not Pyramus, but Bottom the weaver: this will put them out of fear.

Quin. Well, we will have such a prologue; and it shall be written in eight and six.

Bot. No, make it two more; let it be written in eight and eight.

Snout. Will not the ladies be afeard of the lion?

Star. I fear it, I promise you.

Bot. Masters, you ought to consider with yourselves: to bring in—God shield us!—a lion among ladies, is a most dreadful thing; for there is not a more fearful wild-fowl than your lion living; and we ought to look to 't.

Snout. Therefore another prologue must tell he is not a lion.

Bot. Nay, you must name his name, and half his face must be seen through the lion's neck: and he himself must speak through, saying thus, or to the same defect,—'Ladies,'—or 'Fair ladies,—I would wish you,'—or 'I would request you,'—or 'I would entreat you,—not to fear, not to tremble: my life for yours. If you think I come hither as a lion, it were pity of my life: no, I am no such thing; I am a man as other men are;' and there indeed let him name his name, and tell them plainly he is Snug the joiner.

Quin. Well, it shall be so. But there is two hard things; that is, to bring the moonlight into a chamber; for, you know, Pyramus and Thisby meet by moonlight.   51

Snout. Doth the moon shine that night we play our play?

Bot. A calendar, a calendar! look in the almanac; find out moonshine, find out moonshine.

Quin. Yes, it doth shine that night.

Bot. Why, then may you leave a casement of the great chamber window, where we play, open, and the moon may shine in at the casement.

Quin. Ay; or else one must come in with a bush of thorns and a lanthorn, and say he comes to disfigure, or to present, the person of Moonshine. Then, there is another thing: we must have a

wall in the great chamber; for Pyramus and
Thisby, says the story, did talk through the
chink of a wall.

Snout.   You can never bring in a wall.   What
say you, Bottom?

Bot.   Some man or other must present Wall:
and let him have some plaster, or some loam, or
some rough-cast about him, to signify wall; and
let him hold his fingers thus, and through that
cranny shall Pyramus and Thisby whisper.

Quin.   If that may be, then all is well.   Come,
sit down, every mother's son, and rehearse your
parts.   Pyramus, you begin: when you have
spoken your speech, enter into that brake: and
so every one according to his cue.

Enter Puck *behind.*

● *Puck.*   What hempen home-spuns have we
        swaggering here,
So near the cradle of the fairy queen?   80
● What, a play toward!   I 'll be an auditor;
An actor too perhaps, if I see cause.

Quin.   Speak, Pyramus.   Thisby, stand forth.

Bot.   Thisby, the flowers of odious savours
        sweet,—

Quin.   Odours, odours.

Bot.   —— odours savours sweet:
So hath thy breath, my dearest Thisby dear.
But hark, a voice!   stay thou but here awhile,
        And by and by I will to thee appear.   [*Exit.*

Puck.   A stranger Pyramus than e'er played
        here.   [*Exit.*   90

Flu.   Must I speak now?

Quin.   Ay, marry, must you; for you must
understand he goes but to see a noise that he
heard, and is to come again.

Flu.   Most radiant Pyramus, most lily-white of
        hue,
Of colour like the red rose on triumphant brier,
● Most brisky juvenal and eke most lovely Jew,
As true as truest horse that yet would never
        tire,
● I 'll meet thee, Pyramus, at Ninny's tomb.

Quin.   'Ninus' tomb,' man: why, you must
not speak that yet; that you answer to Pyramus:
you speak all your part at once, cues and all.
Pyramus enter: your cue is past; it is, 'never
tire.'

Flu.   O,—As true as truest horse, that yet
would never tire.

Re-enter Puck, *and* Bottom *with an ass's head.*

Bot.   If I were fair, Thisby, I were only thine.

Quin.   O monstrous!   O strange!   we are
haunted.   Pray, masters!   fly, masters!   Help!
        [*Exeunt Quince, Snug, Flute, Snout, and
                Starveling.*

● *Puck.*   I 'll follow you, I 'll lead you about a
        round,
Through bog, through bush, through brake,
        through brier: 110
Sometime a horse I 'll be, sometime a hound,
A hog, a headless bear, sometime a fire;
And neigh, and bark, and grunt, and roar, and
        burn,
Like horse, hound, hog, bear, fire, at every turn.
        [*Exit.*

● *Bot.*   Why do they run away?   this is a knavery
of them to make me afeard.

Bottom (James Cagney) and Flute (Joe E. Brown).
From Max Reinhardt's and William Dieterle's film,
USA, 1935

97 *juvenal.* Youth.   *eke.* Also.

99 *Ninny.* Ninus founded Nineveh.

Quince: 'O monstrous! O strange!...' Engraving from
Hanmer's edition of Shakespeare's works, 1744

109 *round.* Round about.

115 *knavery.* Trick or joke.

128 *ousel cock*. Male blackbird.

130 *throstle*. Thrush.

131 *quill*. Pipe.

138 *give a bird the lie*. Contradict.

Titania (Muriel Pavlov) and Bottom (Anthony Quayle). George Devine's production, Stratford-upon-Avon, 1954

150 *gleek*. Jest or joke.

153-154 *enough . . . turn*. Enough for my own needs.

157 *rate*. Rank.

171 *humble-bees*. Bumble-bees.

Re-enter SNOUT.

Snout. O Bottom, thou art changed! what do I see on thee?

Bot. What do you see? you see an ass-head of your own, do you?   [*Exit Snout.* 120

Re-enter QUINCE.

Quin. Bless thee, Bottom! bless thee! thou art translated.   [*Exit.*

Bot. I see their knavery: this is to make an ass of me; to fright me, if they could. But I will not stir from this place, do what they can: I will walk up and down here, and I will sing, that they shall hear I am not afraid.   [*Sings.*

● 　The ousel cock so black of hue,
　　　With orange-tawny bill,
● 　The throstle with his note so true,   130
● 　The wren with little quill,—

Tita. [*Awaking*] What angel wakes me from my flowery bed?

Bot. [*Sings*]
The finch, the sparrow and the lark,
　The plain-song cuckoo gray,
Whose note full many a man doth mark,
　And dares not answer nay;—
for, indeed, who would set his wit to so foolish a
● bird? who would give a bird the lie, though he cry 'cuckoo' never so?

Tita. I pray thee, gentle mortal, sing again:
Mine ear is much enamour'd of thy note;   141
So is mine eye enthralled to thy shape;
And thy fair virtue's force perforce doth move me
On the first view to say, to swear, I love thee.

Bot. Methinks, mistress, you should have little reason for that: and yet, to say the truth, reason and love keep little company together now-a-days; the more the pity that some honest neighbours will not make them friends. Nay, I
● can gleek upon occasion.   150

Tita. Thou art as wise as thou art beautiful.

Bot. Not so, neither: but if I had wit enough
● to get out of this wood, I have enough to serve mine own turn.

Tita. Out of this wood do not desire to go:
Thou shalt remain here, whether thou wilt or no.
● I am a spirit of no common rate:
The summer still doth tend upon my state;
And I do love thee: therefore, go with me;
I'll give thee fairies to attend on thee,   160
And they shall fetch thee jewels from the deep,
And sing while thou on pressed flowers dost sleep:
And I will purge thy mortal grossness so
That thou shalt like an airy spirit go.
Peaseblossom! Cobweb! Moth! and Mustard-seed!

Enter PEASEBLOSSOM, COBWEB, MOTH, *and* MUSTARDSEED.

Peas. Ready.
Cob. 　　　And I.
Moth. 　　　　　And I.
Mus. 　　　　　　　And I.
All. 　　　　　　　　　Where shall we go?

Tita. Be kind and courteous to this gentleman;
Hop in his walks and gambol in his eyes;
Feed him with apricocks and dewberries,
With purple grapes, green figs, and mulberries;
● The honey-bags steal from the humble-bees,   171

And for night-tapers crop their waxen thighs
And light them at the fiery glow-worm's eyes,
To have my love to bed and to arise;
And pluck the wings from painted butterflies
To fan the moonbeams from his sleeping eyes:
Nod to him, elves, and do him courtesies.
   Peas.   Hail, mortal!
   Cob.   Hail!
   Moth.   Hail!   180
   Mus.   Hail!
   Bot.   I cry your worships mercy, heartily: I
beseech your worship's name.
   Cob.   Cobweb.
   Bot.   I shall desire you of more acquaintance,
good Master Cobweb: if I cut my finger, I shall
make bold with you.   Your name, honest gentle-
man?
   Peas.   Peaseblossom.
   Bot.   I pray you, commend me to Mistress
Squash, your mother, and to Master Peascod,
your father.   Good Master Peaseblossom, I shall
desire you of more acquaintance too.   Your name,
I beseech you, sir?
   Mus.   Mustardseed.
   Bot.   Good Master Mustardseed, I know your
patience well: that same cowardly, giant-like ox-
beef hath devoured many a gentleman of your
house: I promise you your kindred hath made
my eyes water ere now.   I desire your more ac-
quaintance, good Master Mustardseed.   201
   Tita.   Come, wait upon him; lead him to my
    bower.
The moon methinks looks with a watery eye;
And when she weeps, weeps every little flower,
   Lamenting some enforced chastity.
Tie up my love's tongue, bring him silently.
                    [*Exeunt.*

SCENE II.   *Another part of the wood.*

Enter OBERON.

   Obe.   I wonder if Titania be awaked;
Then, what it was that next came in her eye,
Which she must dote on in extremity.

Enter PUCK.

Here comes my messenger.
                 How now, mad spirit!
What night-rule now about this haunted grove?
   Puck.   My mistress with a monster is in love.
Near to her close and consecrated bower,
While she was in her dull and sleeping hour,
A crew of patches, rude mechanicals,
That work for bread upon Athenian stalls,   10
Were met together to rehearse a play
Intended for great Theseus' nuptial-day.
The shallowest thick-skin of that barren sort,
Who Pyramus presented, in their sport
Forsook his scene and enter'd in a brake:
When I did him at this advantage take,
An ass's nole I fixed on his head:
Anon his Thisbe must be answered,
And forth my mimic comes.   When they him spy,
As wild geese that the creeping fowler eye,   20
Or russet-pated choughs, many in sort,
Rising and cawing at the gun's report,
Sever themselves and madly sweep the sky,
So, at his sight, away his fellows fly;
And, at our stamp, here o'er and o'er one falls:

Peaseblossom, Cobweb, Moth and Mustardseed.
Illustration by Arthur Rackham, 1908

---

182 *mercy.* Thanks.

186 *Cobweb.* Cobwebs were used on cuts to stop the bleeding.

191 *Squash.* Unripe pea pod.

2 *next.* First.

5 *night-rule.* Night revelry.

9 *patches, rude mechanicals.* Fools, rough craftsmen.

13 *barren sort.* Foolish group.

17 *nole.* Noodle or head.

21 *russet-pated choughs.* Reddish-headed choughs; the chough is a bird of the crow family. *in sort.* Together.

36 *latch'd.* Moistened.

Olivia de Havilland as Hermia. From Max Reinhardt's and William Dieterle's film, USA, 1935

44 *Lay breath so bitter.* Speak so unkindly.

53 *whole earth.* Solid earth.

70 *O brave touch.* A fine exploit!

74 *misprised.* Mistaken.

He murder cries and help from Athens calls.
Their sense thus weak, lost with their fears thus
 strong,
Made senseless things begin to do them wrong;
For briers and thorns at their apparel snatch;
Some sleeves, some hats, from yielders all things
 catch. 30
I led them on in this distracted fear,
And left sweet Pyramus translated there:
When in that moment, so it came to pass,
Titania waked and straightway loved an ass.
 Obe.   This falls out better than I could devise.
But hast thou yet latch'd the Athenian's eyes
With the love-juice, as I did bid thee do?
 Puck.   I took him sleeping,—that is finish'd
 too,—
And the Athenian woman by his side;
That, when he waked, of force she must be
 eyed. 40

   Enter HERMIA *and* DEMETRIUS.

 Obe.   Stand close: this is the same Athenian.
 Puck.   This is the woman, but not this the man.
 Dem.   O, why rebuke you him that loves you so?
Lay breath so bitter on your bitter foe.
 Her.   Now I but chide; but I should use thee
 worse,
For thou, I fear, hast given me cause to curse.
If thou hast slain Lysander in his sleep,
Being o'er shoes in blood, plunge in the deep,
And kill me too.
The sun was not so true unto the day 50
As he to me: would he have stolen away
From sleeping Hermia?   I 'll believe as soon
This whole earth may be bored and that the moon
May through the centre creep and so displease
Her brother's noontide with the Antipodes.
It cannot be but thou hast murder'd him;
So should a murderer look, so dead, so grim.
 Dem.   So should the murder'd look, and so
 should I,
Pierced through the heart with your stern cruelty:
Yet you, the murderer, look as bright, as clear, 60
As yonder Venus in her glimmering sphere.
 Her.   What's this to my Lysander? where is
 he?
Ah, good Demetrius, wilt thou give him me?
 Dem.   I had rather give his carcass to my
 hounds.
 Her.   Out, dog! out, cur! thou drivest me
 past the bounds
Of maiden's patience.   Hast thou slain him, then?
Henceforth be never number'd among men!
O, once tell true, tell true, even for my sake!
Durst thou have look'd upon him being awake,
And hast thou kill'd him sleeping?   O brave
 touch! 70
Could not a worm, an adder, do so much?
An adder did it; for with doubler tongue
Than thine, thou serpent, never adder stung.
 Dem.   You spend your passion on a misprised
 mood:
I am not guilty of Lysander's blood;
Nor is he dead, for aught that I can tell.
 Her.   I pray thee, tell me then that he is well.
 Dem.   An if I could, what should I get there-
 fore?
 Her.   A privilege never to see me more.
And from thy hated presence part I so: 80

See me no more, whether he be dead or no.
         [*Exit.*
 Dem.   There is no following her in this fierce
  vein:
Here therefore for a while I will remain.
So sorrow's heaviness doth heavier grow
● For debt that bankrupt sleep doth sorrow owe;
Which now in some slight measure it will pay,
● If for his tender here I make some stay.
       [*Lies down and sleeps.*
 Obe.   What hast thou done? thou hast mis-
  taken quite
And laid the love-juice on some true-love's sight:
Of thy misprision must perforce ensue 90
Some true love turn'd and not a false turn'd true.
● *Puck.*   Then fate o'er-rules, that, one man
  holding troth,
A million fail, confounding oath on oath.
 Obe.   About the wood go swifter than the
  wind,
And Helena of Athens look thou find:
● All fancy-sick she is and pale of cheer,
With sighs of love, that costs the fresh blood dear:
By some illusion see thou bring her here:
● I'll charm his eyes against she do appear.
 Puck.   I go, I go; look how I go, 100
Swifter than arrow from the Tartar's bow. [*Exit.*
 Obe.   Flower of this purple dye,
   Hit with Cupid's archery,
   Sink in apple of his eye.
   When his love he doth espy,
   Let her shine as gloriously
   As the Venus of the sky.
   When thou wakest, if she be by,
   Beg of her for remedy.

     Re-enter PUCK.

 Puck.   Captain of our fairy band, 110
  Helena is here at hand;
  And the youth, mistook by me,
  Pleading for a lover's fee.
●   Shall we their fond pageant see?
  Lord, what fools these mortals be!
 Obe.   Stand aside: the noise they make
  Will cause Demetrius to awake.
 Puck.   Then will two at once woo one;
  That must needs be sport alone;
  And those things do best please me 120
  That befal preposterously.

   Enter LYSANDER *and* HELENA.

 Lys.   Why should you think that I should woo
  in scorn?
Scorn and derision never come in tears:
● Look, when I vow, I weep; and vows so born,
In their nativity all truth appears.
How can these things in me seem scorn to you,
Bearing the badge of faith, to prove them true?
 Hel.   You do advance your cunning more and
  more.
When truth kills truth, O devilish-holy fray!
These vows are Hermia's: will you give her o'er?
Weigh oath with oath, and you will nothing
  weigh: 131
Your vows to her and me, put in two scales,
Will even weigh, and both as light as tales.
 Lys.   I had no judgement when to her I swore.
 Hel.   Nor none, in my mind, now you give
  her o'er.

---

85 *For debt . . . owe.* Sorrow has caused lack of sleep.

87 *tender.* Offer.

Robert Helpmann as Oberon, Old Vic, London, 1954

92-93 *Then fate . . . oath.* Then fate rules supreme; one man in a million keeps faith, the rest break promise after promise.

96 *cheer.* Face.

99 *against.* By the time.

114 *fond pageant.* Foolish show.

124-125 *vows so . . . appears.* Tears prove the truth of these vows.

141 *Taurus.* A mountain range in Turkey.

'That pure congealed white, high Taurus snow . . .'
Engraving from Charles Knight's *Pictorial Edition of
the Works of William Shakspere,* 1839–43

150 *in souls.* Together.

152 *gentle.* Well-born.

157 *trim.* Fine (ironical).

175 *aby.* Buy.

177-180 *Dark . . . recompense.* In the darkness when the
eye cannot see, hearing becomes more acute.

188 *oes.* Orbs.

Lys. Demetrius loves her, and he loves not
   you.
Dem. [*Awaking*] O Helen, goddess, nymph,
   perfect, divine !
To what, my love, shall I compare thine eyne ?
Crystal is muddy.   O, how ripe in show
Thy lips, those kissing cherries, tempting grow !
• That pure congealed white, high Taurus' snow,
Fann'd with the eastern wind, turns to a crow
When thou hold'st up thy hand : O, let me kiss
This princess of pure white, this seal of bliss !
   Hel. O spite ! O hell ! I see you all are bent
To set against me for your merriment :
If you were civil and knew courtesy,
You would not do me thus much injury.
Can you not hate me, as I know you do,
• But you must join in souls to mock me too ?   150
If you were men, as men you are in show,
• You would not use a gentle lady so :
To vow, and swear, and superpraise my parts,
When I am sure you hate me with your hearts.
You both are rivals, and love Hermia ;
And now both rivals, to mock Helena :
• A trim exploit, a manly enterprise,
To conjure tears up in a poor maid's eyes
With your derision ! none of noble sort
Would so offend a virgin and extort   160
A poor soul's patience, all to make you sport.
   Lys. You are unkind, Demetrius ; be not so ;
For you love Hermia ; this you know I know :
And here, with all good will, with all my heart,
In Hermia's love I yield you up my part ;
And yours of Helena to me bequeath,
Whom I do love and will do till my death.
   Hel. Never did mockers waste more idle breath.
   Dem. Lysander, keep thy Hermia ; I will none :
If e'er I loved her, all that love is gone.   170
My heart to her but as guest-wise sojourn'd,
And now to Helen is it home return'd,
There to remain.
   Lys.   Helen, it is not so.
   Dem. Disparage not the faith thou dost not
   know,
• Lest, to thy peril, thou aby it dear.
Look, where thy love comes ; yonder is thy dear.

Re-enter HERMIA.

• *Her.* Dark night, that from the eye his func-
   tion takes,
The ear more quick of apprehension makes ;
Wherein it doth impair the seeing sense,
It pays the hearing double recompense.   180
Thou art not by mine eye, Lysander, found ;
Mine ear, I thank it, brought me to thy sound.
But why unkindly didst thou leave me so ?
   Lys. Why should he stay, whom love doth
   press to go ?
   Her. What love could press Lysander from
   my side ?
   Lys. Lysander's love, that would not let him
   bide,
Fair Helena, who more engilds the night
• Than all yon fiery oes and eyes of light.
Why seek'st thou me ? could not this make thee
   know,
The hate I bear thee made me leave thee so ?   190
   Her. You speak not as you think : it cannot be.
   Hel. Lo, she is one of this confederacy !
Now I perceive they have conjoin'd all three

To fashion this false sport, in spite of me.
- Injurious Hermia! most ungrateful maid!
Have you conspired, have you with these con-
  trived
To bait me with this foul derision?
Is all the counsel that we two have shared,
The sisters' vows, the hours that we have spent,
When we have chid the hasty-footed time   200
For parting us,—O, is it all forgot?
All school-days' friendship, childhood innocence?
- We, Hermia, like two artificial gods,
Have with our needles created both one flower,
Both on one sampler, sitting on one cushion,
Both warbling of one song, both in one key,
As if our hands, our sides, voices and minds,
- Had been incorporate.   So we grew together,
Like to a double cherry, seeming parted,
But yet an union in partition;   210
Two lovely berries moulded on one stem;
So, with two seeming bodies, but one heart;
- Two of the first, like coats in heraldry,
Due but to one and crowned with one crest.
And will you rent our ancient love asunder,
To join with men in scorning your poor friend?
It is not friendly, 'tis not maidenly:
Our sex, as well as I, may chide you for it,
Though I alone do feel the injury.

Her.   I am amazed at your passionate words.
I scorn you not: it seems that you scorn me.   221
Hel.   Have you not set Lysander, as in scorn,
To follow me and praise my eyes and face?
And made your other love, Demetrius,
Who even but now did spurn me with his foot,
To call me goddess, nymph, divine and rare,
Precious, celestial?   Wherefore speaks he this
To her he hates? and wherefore doth Lysander
Deny your love, so rich within his soul,
And tender me, forsooth, affection,   230
But by your setting on, by your consent?
What though I be not so in grace as you,
So hung upon with love, so fortunate,
But miserable most, to love unloved?
This you should pity rather than despise.
Her.   I understand not what you mean by this.
Hel.   Ay, do, persever, counterfeit sad looks,
- Make mouths upon me when I turn my back;
Wink each at other; hold the sweet jest up:
This sport, well carried, shall be chronicled.   240
If you have any pity, grace, or manners,
- You would not make me such an argument.
But fare ye well: 'tis partly my own fault;
Which death or absence soon shall remedy.
Lys.   Stay, gentle Helena; hear my excuse:
My love, my life, my soul, fair Helena!
Hel.   O excellent!
Her.   Sweet, do not scorn her so.
- *Dem.*   If she cannot entreat, I can compel.
Lys.   Thou canst compel no more than she
  entreat:
Thy threats have no more strength than her
  weak prayers.   250
Helen, I love thee; by my life, I do:
I swear by that which I will lose for thee,
To prove him false that says I love thee not.
Dem.   I say I love thee more than he can do.
Lys.   If thou say so, withdraw, and prove
  it too.
Dem.   Quick, come!
Her.   Lysander, whereto tends all this?

195 *Injurious.* Insulting.

Helena: 'O, is it all forgot? All school-days . . .'
Illustration by Gordon Browne from Henry Irving's
Shakespeare, 1888

203 *artificial.* Skilled in art.

208 *incorporate.* Joined in body.

213 *Two of the first.* An heraldic term. This means the
repetition of identical quarterings, i.e. Helena and
Hermia had but a single heart.

238 *Make . . . back.* Make faces behind my back.

242 *argument.* Object of mockery.

248 *entreat.* Prevail by pleading.

257 *Ethiope*. Blackamoor, referring to Hermia's dark complexion.

258-259 *Seem . . . go!* Demetrius is accusing Lysander of merely pretending to want to fight a duel.

267-268 *bond . . . bond*. A pun on the meanings 'chain' and 'a document binding parties on oath'.

272 *what news*. What news is this?

288 *puppet*. Doll. Hermia picks this up as an insulting reference to her height.

289 *that way . . . game*. So that's your line of attack.

Hermia (Zena Walker) and Lysander (Tony Britton), George Devine's production, Stratford-upon-Avon, 1954

300 *curst*. Shrewish.

  ● *Lys.* Away, you Ethiope!
  Dem.   †No, no; he'll . . .
●Seem to break loose; take on as you would
      follow,
  But yet come not: you are a tame man, go!
      Lys. Hang off, thou cat, thou burr! vile
          thing, let loose,   260
  Or I will shake thee from me like a serpent!
      Her. Why are you grown so rude? what
          change is this?
  Sweet love,—
      Lys.   Thy love! out, tawny Tartar, out!
  Out, loathed medicine! hated potion, hence!
      Her. Do you not jest?
      Hel.   Yes, sooth; and so do you.
      Lys. Demetrius, I will keep my word with thee.
  ● *Dem.* I would I had your bond, for I perceive
  A weak bond holds you: I'll not trust your word.
      Lys. What, should I hurt her, strike her,
          kill her dead?
  Although I hate her, I'll not harm her so.   270
      Her. What, can you do me greater harm
          than hate?
●Hate me! wherefore? O me! what news, my love!
  Am not I Hermia? are not you Lysander?
  I am as fair now as I was erewhile.
  Since night you loved me; yet since night you
      left me:
  Why, then you left me—O, the gods forbid!—
  In earnest, shall I say?
      Lys.   Ay, by my life;
  And never did desire to see thee more.
  Therefore be out of hope, of question, of doubt;
  Be certain, nothing truer; 'tis no jest   280
  That I do hate thee and love Helena.
      Her. O me! you juggler! you canker-blossom!
  You thief of love! what, have you come by night
  And stolen my love's heart from him?
      Hel.   Fine, i'faith!
  Have you no modesty, no maiden shame,
  No touch of bashfulness? What, will you tear
  Impatient answers from my gentle tongue?
●Fie, fie! you counterfeit, you puppet, you!
  ● *Her.* Puppet? why so? ay, that way goes
          the game.
  Now I perceive that she hath made compare 290
  Between our statures; she hath urged her height;
  And with her personage, her tall personage,
  Her height, forsooth, she hath prevail'd with him.
  And are you grown so high in his esteem,
  Because I am so dwarfish and so low?
  How low am I, thou painted maypole? speak;
  How low am I? I am not yet so low
  But that my nails can reach unto thine eyes.
      Hel. I pray you, though you mock me,
          gentlemen,
●Let her not hurt me: I was never curst;   300
  I have no gift at all in shrewishness;
  I am a right maid for my cowardice:
  Let her not strike me. You perhaps may think,
  Because she is something lower than myself,
  That I can match her.
      Her.   Lower! hark, again.
      Hel. Good Hermia, do not be so bitter with me.
  I evermore did love you, Hermia,
  Did ever keep your counsels, never wrong'd you;
  Save that, in love unto Demetrius,
  I told him of your stealth unto this wood.   310
  He follow'd you; for love I follow'd him;

But he hath chid me hence and threaten'd me
To strike me, spurn me, nay, to kill me too:
And now, so you will let me quiet go,
To Athens will I bear my folly back
And follow you no further: let me go:
You see how simple and how fond I am.
    Her. Why, get you gone: who is't that hinders
      you?
    Hel. A foolish heart, that I leave here behind.
    Her. What, with Lysander?
    Hel.   With Demetrius. 320
    Lys. Be not afraid; she shall not harm thee,
      Helena.
    Dem. No, sir, she shall not, though you take
      her part.
  ●   *Hel.* O, when she's angry, she is keen and
      shrewd!
She was a vixen when she went to school;
And though she be but little, she is fierce.
    Her. 'Little' again! nothing but 'low' and
      'little'!
Why will you suffer her to flout me thus?
Let me come to her.
    Lys.   Get you gone, you dwarf;
●You minimus, of hindering knot-grass made;
You bead, you acorn.
    Dem.   You are too officious 330
In her behalf that scorns your services.
Let her alone: speak not of Helena;
●Take not her part; for, if thou dost intend
Never so little show of love to her,
Thou shalt aby it.
    Lys.   Now she holds me not;
Now follow, if thou darest, to try whose right,
Of thine or mine, is most in Helena.
    Dem. Follow! nay, I'll go with thee, cheek
●   by jole. [*Exeunt Lysander and Demetrius.*
●   *Her.* You, mistress, all this coil is 'long of you:
Nay, go not back.
    Hel.   I will not trust you, I, 340
Nor longer stay in your curst company.
Your hands than mine are quicker for a fray,
My legs are longer though, to run away. [*Exit.*
    Her. I am amazed, and know not what to say.
                       [*Exit.*

    Obe. This is thy negligence: still thou mistakest,
Or else committ'st thy knaveries wilfully.
    Puck. Believe me, king of shadows, I mistook.
Did not you tell me I should know the man
By the Athenian garments he had on?
And so far blameless proves my enterprise, 350
That I have 'nointed an Athenian's eyes;
And so far am I glad it so did sort
As this their jangling I esteem a sport.
    Obe. Thou see'st these lovers seek a place to
      fight:
Hie therefore, Robin, overcast the night;
●The starry welkin cover thou anon
●With drooping fog as black as Acheron,
And lead these testy rivals so astray
As one come not within another's way.
Like to Lysander sometime frame thy tongue,
●Then stir Demetrius up with bitter wrong; 361
And sometime rail thou like Demetrius;
And from each other look thou lead them thus,
Till o'er their brows death-counterfeiting sleep
With leaden legs and batty wings doth creep:
Then crush this herb into Lysander's eye;
Whose liquor hath this virtuous property,

323 *keen and shrewd.* Bitter and sharp-tongued.

329 *knot-grass.* A weed supposed to stunt growth.

333 *intend.* Pretend.

338 *jole.* Jowl.

339 *all this . . . you.* All this turmoil is due to you.

Costume designs for Titania and Oberon. Illustration
by Paul Nash from *Players' Shakespeare*, 1924

356 *welkin.* Sky.

357 *Acheron.* A river in the Underworld.

361 *wrong.* Insult.

The Lovers' Quarrel (Ross Alexander, Dick Powell, Jean Muir, and Olivia de Havilland). From Max Reinhardt's and William Dieterle's film, USA, 1935

369 *wonted.* Usual.

370 *derision.* Ludicrous diversion.

373 *With league.* In a union. *date.* Duration.

379 *dragons.* Dragons drew the chariot of Night.

380 *Aurora's harbinger.* The morning star.

381-387 *ghosts . . . night.* Ghosts of people who lacked a proper funeral, like those dead from drowning and suicide, were buried at cross-roads. At night these spirits wandered, but returned to their graves by sunrise.

387 *aye.* Ever.

389 *morning's love.* Either Aurora herself or her lover Cephalus.

402 *drawn.* Sword in hand.

409 *recreant.* Coward.

To take from thence all error with his might,
And make his eyeballs roll with wonted sight.
When they next wake, all this derision   370
Shall seem a dream and fruitless vision,
And back to Athens shall the lovers wend,
With league whose date till death shall never end.
Whiles I in this affair do thee employ,
I'll to my queen and beg her Indian boy;
And then I will her charmed eye release
From monster's view, and all things shall be peace.
          Puck.   My fairy lord, this must be done with haste,
For night's swift dragons cut the clouds full fast,
And yonder shines Aurora's harbinger;   380
At whose approach, ghosts, wandering here and there,
Troop home to churchyards: damned spirits all,
That in crossways and floods have burial,
Already to their wormy beds are gone;
For fear lest day should look their shames upon,
They wilfully themselves exile from light
And must for aye consort with black-brow'd night.
          Obe.   But we are spirits of another sort:
I with the morning's love have oft made sport,
And, like a forester, the groves may tread,   390
Even till the eastern gate, all fiery-red,
Opening on Neptune with fair blessed beams,
Turns into yellow gold his salt green streams,
But, notwithstanding, haste; make no delay:
We may effect this business yet ere day. [*Exit.*
          Puck.   Up and down, up and down,
          I will lead them up and down:
          I am fear'd in field and town:
          Goblin, lead them up and down.
Here comes one.   400

          Re-enter LYSANDER.

     Lys.   Where art thou, proud Demetrius? speak thou now.
     Puck.   Here, villain; drawn and ready. Where art thou?
     Lys.   I will be with thee straight.
     Puck.   Follow me, then,
To plainer ground.
          [*Exit Lysander, as following the voice.*

          Re-enter DEMETRIUS.

     Dem.   Lysander! speak again:
Thou runaway, thou coward, art thou fled?
Speak! In some bush? Where dost thou hide thy head?
     Puck.   Thou coward, art thou bragging to the stars,
Telling the bushes that thou look'st for wars,
And wilt not come? Come, recreant; come, thou child;
I'll whip thee with a rod: he is defiled   410
That draws a sword on thee.
     Dem.   Yea, art thou there?
     Puck.   Follow my voice: we'll try no manhood here.   [*Exeunt.*

          Re-enter LYSANDER.

     Lys.   He goes before me and still dares me on:
When I come where he calls, then he is gone.
The villain is much lighter-heel'd than I:
I follow'd fast, but faster he did fly;
That fallen am I in dark uneven way,
And here will rest me. [*Lies down.*] Come, thou gentle day!

For if but once thou show me thy grey light,
I'll find Demetrius and revenge this spite. [*Sleeps.*

Re-enter PUCK *and* DEMETRIUS.

Puck. Ho, ho, ho! Coward, why comest
    thou not?   421
• *Dem.* Abide me, if thou darest; for well I wot
Thou runn'st before me, shifting every place,
And darest not stand, nor look me in the face.
Where art thou now?
Puck.   Come hither: I am here.
Dem. Nay, then, thou mock'st me. Thou
    shalt buy this dear,
If ever I thy face by daylight see:
Now, go thy way. Faintness constraineth me
To measure out my length on this cold bed.
By day's approach look to be visited.   430
                 [*Lies down and sleeps.*

Re-enter HELENA.

Hel. O weary night, O long and tedious night,
• Abate thy hours! Shine comforts from the east,
That I may back to Athens by daylight,
    From these that my poor company detest:
And sleep, that sometimes shuts up sorrow's eye,
Steal me awhile from mine own company.
                 [*Lies down and sleeps.*
Puck. Yet but three? Come one more;
    Two of both kinds makes up four.
    Here she comes, curst and sad:
    Cupid is a knavish lad,   440
    Thus to make poor females mad.

Re-enter HERMIA.

Her. Never so weary, never so in woe,
Bedabbled with the dew and torn with briers,
I can no further crawl, no further go;
    My legs can keep no pace with my desires.
Here will I rest me till the break of day.
Heavens shield Lysander, if they mean a fray!
                 [*Lies down and sleeps.*
Puck.   On the ground
      Sleep sound:
      I'll apply   450
      To your eye,
    Gentle lover, remedy.
    [*Squeezing the juice on Lysander's eyes.*
      When thou wakest,
      Thou takest
      True delight
      In the sight
    Of thy former lady's eye:
    And the country proverb known,
    That every man should take his own,
    In your waking shall be shown: 460
      Jack shall have Jill;
      Nought shall go ill;
The man shall have his mare again, and all shall
    be well.   [*Exit.*

ACT IV.

SCENE I. *The same.* LYSANDER, DEMETRIUS,
  HELENA, *and* HERMIA *lying asleep*

Enter TITANIA *and* BOTTOM; PEASEBLOSSOM,
  COBWEB, MOTH, MUSTARDSEED, *and other*
  Fairies attending; OBERON *behind unseen.*

Tita. Come, sit thee down upon this flowery bed,
•   While I thy amiable cheeks do coy,

Puck (Mickey Rooney) and Hermia (Olivia de Havilland). From Max Reinhardt's and William Dieterle's film, USA, 1935

422 *well I wot.* I know well.

432 *Abate.* Shorten.

Puck placing the flower juice on Lysander's eyes. Engraving from a design by H. Gravelot from Theobald's edition of Shakespeare's works, 1744

2 *coy.* Caress.

Illustration by Katherine Cameron, 1916

20 *neaf*. Hand or fist.

21 *leave your courtesy*. Stop bowing.

25 *Cavalery*. Cavalier.

31 *tongs and the bones*. Instruments used in country music.

35 *bottle*. Bundle.

41 *exposition*. Bottom means 'disposition'.

Opposite above : Bottom : 'Scratch my head . . .' Engraving from a painting by H. Fuseli (1741–1825)

Opposite below : Titania awakes. Engraving from a painting by H. Fuseli (1741–1825)

And stick musk-roses in thy sleek smooth head,
    And kiss thy fair large ears, my gentle joy.
Bot. Where's Peaseblossom?
Peas. Ready.
Bot. Scratch my head, Peaseblossom. Where's Mounsieur Cobweb?
Cob. Ready.
Bot. Mounsieur Cobweb, good mounsieur, get you your weapons in your hand, and kill me a red-hipped humble-bee on the top of a thistle ; and, good mounsieur, bring me the honey-bag. Do not fret yourself too much in the action, mounsieur ; and, good mounsieur, have a care the honey-bag break not ; I would be loath to have you overflown with a honey-bag, signior. Where's Mounsieur Mustardseed?
Mus. Ready.
Bot. Give me your neaf, Mounsieur Mustard-seed. Pray you, leave your courtesy, good mounsieur.
Mus. What's your will?
Bot. Nothing, good mounsieur, but to help Cavalery Cobweb to scratch. I must to the bar-ber's, mounsieur ; for methinks I am marvellous hairy about the face ; and I am such a tender ass, if my hair do but tickle me, I must scratch.
Tita. What, wilt thou hear some music, my sweet love? 29
Bot. I have a reasonable good ear in music. Let's have the tongs and the bones.
Tita. Or say, sweet love, what thou desirest to eat.
Bot. Truly, a peck of provender : I could munch your good dry oats. Methinks I have a great desire to a bottle of hay : good hay, sweet hay, hath no fellow.
Tita. I have a venturous fairy that shall seek The squirrel's hoard, and fetch thee new nuts.
Bot. I had rather have a handful or two of dried peas. But, I pray you, let none of your people stir me : I have an exposition of sleep come upon me. 42
Tita. Sleep thou, and I will wind thee in my arms.
Fairies, be gone, and be all ways away.
                    [*Exeunt fairies.*
So doth the woodbine the sweet honeysuckle
Gently entwist ; the female ivy so
Enrings the barky fingers of the elm.
O, how I love thee ! how I dote on thee !
                    [*They sleep.*

Enter PUCK.

Obe. [*Advancing*] Welcome, good Robin.
    See'st thou this sweet sight?
Her dotage now I do begin to pity : 50
For, meeting her of late behind the wood,
Seeking sweet favours for this hateful fool,
I did upbraid her and fall out with her ;
For she his hairy temples then had rounded
With coronet of fresh and fragrant flowers ;
And that same dew, which sometime on the buds
Was wont to swell like round and orient pearls,
Stood now within the pretty flowerets' eyes
Like tears that did their own disgrace bewail.
When I had at my pleasure taunted her 60
And she in mild terms begg'd my patience,
I then did ask of her her changeling child ;
Which straight she gave me, and her fairy sent

66 *imperfection*. Defect caused by the juice.

76 *Dian's bud*. This is probably the *agnus castus* or Chaste Tree which was thought to preserve chastity. *Cupid's flower*. The pansy.

108 *observation*. Observing the traditional rites associated with the first day of May.

109 *vaward*. Vanguard or early morning.

111 *Uncouple*. Unleash.

Theseus: 'We will, fair queen, up to the mountain's top . . .' Illustration by Arthur Rackham, 1908

117 *bay'd*. Brought to bay.

118 *hounds of Sparta*. In classical times these dogs were famed for their speed and ability to follow a scent.

119 *chiding*. Baying.

To bear him to my bower in fairy land.
And now I have the boy, I will undo
●This hateful imperfection of her eyes:
And, gentle Puck, take this transformed scalp
From off the head of this Athenian swain;
That, he awaking when the other do,
May all to Athens back again repair   70
And think no more of this night's accidents
But as the fierce vexation of a dream.
But first I will release the fairy queen.
     Be as thou wast wont to be;
     See as thou wast wont to see:
●   Dian's bud o'er Cupid's flower
     Hath such force and blessed power.
Now, my Titania; wake you, my sweet queen.
  Tita.   My Oberon! what visions have I seen!
Methought I was enamour'd of an ass.   80
  Obe.   There lies your love.
  Tita.   How came these things to pass?
O, how mine eyes do loathe his visage now!
  Obe.   Silence awhile. Robin, take off this head.
Titania, music call; and strike more dead
Than common sleep of all these five the sense.
  Tita.   Music, ho! music, such as charmeth
     sleep!   [*Music, still.*
  Puck.   Now, when thou wakest, with thine
     own fool's eyes peep.
  Obe.   Sound, music! **Come,** my queen, take
     hands with me,   89
And rock the ground whereon these sleepers be.
Now thou and I are new in amity
And will to-morrow midnight solemnly
Dance in Duke Theseus' house triumphantly
And bless it to all fair prosperity:
There shall the pairs of faithful lovers be
Wedded, with Theseus, all in jollity.
  Puck.   Fairy king, attend, and mark:
     I do hear the morning lark.
  Obe.   Then, my queen, in silence sad,
     Trip we after night's shade: 100
     We the globe can compass soon,
     Swifter than the wandering moon.
  Tita.   Come, my lord, and in our flight
     Tell me how it came this night
     That I sleeping here was found
     With these mortals on the ground.
                 [*Exeunt.*
                 [*Horns winded within.*

Enter THESEUS, HIPPOLYTA, EGEUS, *and train.*
  The.   Go, one of you, find out the forester;
●For now our observation is perform'd;
●And since we have the vaward of the day,
My love shall hear the music of my hounds.   110
●Uncouple in the western valley; let them go:
Dispatch, I say, and find the forester.
            [*Exit an Attendant.*
We will, fair queen, up to the mountain's top
And mark the musical confusion
Of hounds and echo in conjunction.
  Hip.   I was with Hercules and Cadmus once,
●When in a wood of Crete they bay'd the bear
●With hounds of Sparta: never did I hear
●Such gallant chiding; for, besides the groves,
The skies, the fountains, every region near   120
Seem'd all one mutual cry: I never heard
So musical a discord, such sweet thunder.
  The.   My hounds are bred out of the Spartan
     kind,

So flew'd, so sanded, and their heads are hung
With ears that sweep away the morning dew;
Crook-knee'd, and dew-lapp'd like Thessalian
        bulls;
Slow in pursuit, but match'd in mouth like bells,
Each under each.   A cry more tuneable
Was never holla'd to, nor cheer'd with horn,
In Crete, in Sparta, nor in Thessaly: 130
Judge when you hear.   But, soft! what nymphs
        are these?
        Ege.   My lord, this is my daughter here
                asleep;
And this, Lysander; this Demetrius is;
This Helena, old Nedar's Helena:
I wonder of their being here together.
        The.   No doubt they rose up early to observe
The rite of May, and, hearing our intent,
Came here in grace of our solemnity.
But speak, Egeus; is not this the day
That Hermia should give answer of her choice?
        Ege.   It is, my lord.   141
        The.   Go, bid the huntsmen wake them with
                their horns. [*Horns and shout within. Lys.,
                Dem., Hel., and Her., wake and start up.*
Good morrow, friends.   Saint Valentine is past:
Begin these wood-birds but to couple now?
        Lys.   Pardon, my lord.
        The.   I pray you all, stand up.
I know you two are rival enemies:
How comes this gentle concord in the world,
That hatred is so far from jealousy,
To sleep by hate, and fear no enmity?
        Lys.   My lord, I shall reply amazedly,   150
Half sleep, half waking: but as yet, I swear,
I cannot truly say how I came here;
But, as I think,—for truly would I speak,
And now I do bethink me, so it is,—
I came with Hermia hither: our intent
Was to be gone from Athens, where we might,
Without the peril of the Athenian law.
        Ege.   Enough, enough, my lord; you have
                enough:
I beg the law, the law, upon his head.
They would have stolen away; they would,
        Demetrius,   160
Thereby to have defeated you and me,
You of your wife and me of my consent,
Of my consent that she should be your wife.
        Dem.   My lord, fair Helen told me of their
                stealth,
Of this their purpose hither to this wood;
And I in fury hither follow'd them,
Fair Helena in fancy following me.
But, my good lord, I wot not by what power,—
But by some power it is,—my love to Hermia,
Melted as the snow, seems to me now   170
As the remembrance of an idle gawd
Which in my childhood I did dote upon;
And all the faith, the virtue of my heart,
The object and the pleasure of mine eye,
Is only Helena.   To her, my lord,
Was I betroth'd ere I saw Hermia:
But, like in sickness, did I loathe this food;
But, as in health, come to my natural taste,
Now I do wish it, love it, long for it,
And will for evermore be true to it.   180
        The.   Fair lovers, you are fortunately met:
Of this discourse we more will hear anon.
Egeus, I will overbear your will;

124 *flew'd.* Lipped. *sanded.* Of a sandy colour.

127-128 *but match'd . . . each.* The quality of the barking of the hounds is important to the huntsman. They should be of different but blending tones like a peal of bells.

Theseus and Hippolyta discover the sleeping lovers. Engraving from Charles Knight's *Pictorial Edition of the Works of William Shakspere,* 1839–43

138 *in grace of our solemnity.* In honour of the marriage rite.

143 *Saint Valentine.* Birds were believed to choose their mates on St. Valentine's Day.

Lysander (Albert Finney) and Hermia (Priscilla Morgan), Stratford-upon-Avon, 1959

186 *something worn*. Late.

193 *parted*. Out of focus.

211 *go about*. Try to.

214 *patched*. Referring to the parti-coloured dress, or motley that fools wore.

224 *at her death*. At Thisbe's death.

4 *transported*. Carried away by the spirits.

14 *of naught*. Naughty.

For in the temple, by and by, with us
These couples shall eternally be knit:
●And, for the morning now is something worn,
Our purposed hunting shall be set aside.
Away with us to Athens; three and three,
We'll hold a feast in great solemnity.
Come, Hippolyta.   190
      [Exeunt The., Hip., Ege., and train.
  Dem.   These things seem small and undistinguishable,
Like far-off mountains turned into clouds.
● *Her.*   Methinks I see these things with parted
     eye,
When every thing seems double.
  Hel.   So methinks:
And I have found Demetrius like a jewel,
Mine own, and not mine own.
  Dem.   Are you sure
That we are awake?   It seems to me
That yet we sleep, we dream.   Do not you think
The duke was here, and bid us follow him?   199
  Her.   Yea; and my father.
  Hel.   And Hippolyta.
  Lys.   And he did bid us follow to the temple.
  Dem.   Why, then, we are awake: let's follow
     him;
And by the way let us recount our dreams.
                      [Exeunt.
  Bot. [*Awaking*] When my cue comes, call me, and I will answer: my next is, 'Most fair Pyramus.'   Heigh-ho!   Peter Quince!   Flute, the bellows-mender!   Snout, the tinker!   Starveling! God's my life, stolen hence, and left me asleep! I have had a most rare vision.   I have had a dream, past the wit of man to say what dream it
●was: man is but an ass, if he go about to expound this dream.   Methought I was—there is no man can tell what.   Methought I was,—and methought
●I had,—but man is but a patched fool, if he will offer to say what methought I had.   The eye of man hath not heard, the ear of man hath not seen, man's hand is not able to taste, his tongue to conceive, nor his heart to report, what my dream was.   I will get Peter Quince to write a ballad of this dream: it shall be called Bottom's Dream, because it hath no bottom; and I will sing it in the latter end of a play, before the duke: peradventure, to make it the more gra-
●cious,† I shall sing it at her death.   [*Exit.*

SCENE II.   *Athens.*   QUINCE'S *house.*

Enter QUINCE, FLUTE, SNOUT, *and*
STARVELING.

  Quin.   Have you sent to Bottom's house? is he come home yet?
  Star.   He cannot be heard of.   Out of doubt
●he is transported.
  Flu.   If he come not, then the play is marred: it goes not forward, doth it?
  Quin.   It is not possible: you have not a man in all Athens able to discharge Pyramus but he.
  Flu.   No, he hath simply the best wit of any handicraft man in Athens.   10
  Quin.   Yea, and the best person too; and he is a very paramour for a sweet voice.
  Flu.   You must say 'paragon:' a paramour is,
●God bless us, a thing of naught.

Enter Snug.

Snug. Masters, the duke is coming from the temple, and there is two or three lords and ladies more married: if our sport had gone forward, we had all been made men.

Flu. O sweet bully Bottom! Thus hath he lost sixpence a day during his life; he could not have 'scaped sixpence a day: an the duke had not given him sixpence a day for playing Pyramus, I'll be hanged; he would have deserved it: sixpence a day in Pyramus, or nothing.

Enter Bottom.

Bot. Where are these lads? where are these hearts?

Quin. Bottom! O most courageous day! O most happy hour!

Bot. Masters, I am to discourse wonders: but ask me not what; for if I tell you, I am no true Athenian. I will tell you every thing, right as it fell out.

Quin. Let us hear, sweet Bottom.

Bot. Not a word of me. All that I will tell you is, that the duke hath dined. Get your apparel together, good strings to your beards, new ribbons to your pumps; meet presently at the palace; every man look o'er his part; for the short and the long is, our play is preferred. In any case, let Thisby have clean linen; and let not him that plays the lion pare his nails, for they shall hang out for the lion's claws. And, most dear actors, eat no onions nor garlic, for we are to utter sweet breath; and I do not doubt but to hear them say, it is a sweet comedy. No more words: away! go, away!   [*Exeunt.*

ACT V.

Scene I. *Athens. The palace of* Theseus.

Enter Theseus, Hippolyta, Philostrate, Lords, *and* Attendants.

Hip. 'Tis strange, my Theseus, that these lovers speak of.

The. More strange than true: I never may believe
These antique fables, nor these fairy toys.
Lovers and madmen have such seething brains,
Such shaping fantasies, that apprehend
More than cool reason ever comprehends.
The lunatic, the lover and the poet
Are of imagination all compact:
One sees more devils than vast hell can hold,
That is, the madman: the lover, all as frantic, 10
Sees Helen's beauty in a brow of Egypt:
The poet's eye, in a fine frenzy rolling,
Doth glance from heaven to earth, from earth to heaven;
And as imagination bodies forth
The forms of things unknown, the poet's pen
Turns them to shapes and gives to airy nothing
A local habitation and a name.
Such tricks hath strong imagination,
That, if it would but apprehend some joy,
It comprehends some bringer of that joy;   20
Or in the night, imagining some fear,
How easy is a bush supposed a bear!
Hip. But all the story of the night told over,
And all their minds transfigured so together,

18 *made.* Men who have had their fortunes made.

20 *sixpence a day.* A pension of sixpence a day for life.

26 *hearts.* Good fellows.

37 *pumps.* Shoes.

39 *preferred.* Chosen.

3 *antique.* Fantastic.

5 *shaping fantasies.* Fantasies of the creative imagination.

The poet. Drawing by J. H. Mortimer, 1775

11 *brow of Egypt.* Face of a gypsy.

14 *bodies forth.* Gives concrete form to.

39 *abridgement*. Entertainment.

Theseus and the Centaur. Engraving of a Greek sculpture from Charles Knight's *Pictorial Edition of the Works of William Shakspere*, 1839–43

48-49 '*The riot . . . rage*'. The 'Thracian singer', Orpheus, was torn to death by the drunken female followers of the god Bacchus.

50 *device*. Spectacle.

52 *thrice three Muses*. In classical mythology each of the nine sister Muses presided over one branch of knowledge or art.

55 *Not sorting with*. Not suitable for.

74 *unbreathed*. Unexercised.

More witnesseth than fancy's images
And grows to something of great constancy;
But, howsoever, strange and admirable.
    The. Here come the lovers, full of joy and
    mirth.

Enter LYSANDER, DEMETRIUS, HERMIA, *and*
    HELENA.

Joy, gentle friends! joy and fresh days of love
Accompany your hearts!
    Lys.   More than to us   30
Wait in your royal walks, your board, your bed!
    The. Come now; what masques, what dances
    shall we have,
To wear away this long age of three hours
Between our after-supper and bed-time?
Where is our usual manager of mirth?
What revels are in hand? Is there no play,
To ease the anguish of a torturing hour?
Call Philostrate.
    Phil.   Here, mighty Theseus.
    The. Say, what abridgement have you for this
    evening?
What masque? what music? How shall we be-
    guile   40
The lazy time, if not with some delight?
    Phil. There is a brief how many sports are
    ripe:
Make choice of which your highness will see first.
                  [Giving a paper.
    The. [*Reads*] 'The battle with the Centaurs, to
    be sung
By an Athenian eunuch to the harp.'
We'll none of that: that have I told my love,
In glory of my kinsman Hercules.
[*Reads*] 'The riot of the tipsy Bacchanals,
Tearing the Thracian singer in their rage.'
That is an old device; and it was play'd   50
When I from Thebes came last a conqueror
[*Reads*] 'The thrice three Muses mourning for
    the death
Of Learning, late deceased in beggary.'
That is some satire, keen and critical,
Not sorting with a nuptial ceremony.
[*Reads*] 'A tedious brief scene of young Pyramus
And his love Thisbe; very tragical mirth.'
Merry and tragical! tedious and brief!
    That is, hot ice and wondrous strange snow.
How shall we find the concord of this discord? 60
    Phil. A play there is, my lord, some ten words
    long,
Which is as brief as I have known a play;
But by ten words, my lord, it is too long,
Which makes it tedious; for in all the play
There is not one word apt, one player fitted:
And tragical, my noble lord, it is;
For Pyramus therein doth kill himself.
Which, when I saw rehearsed, I must confess,
Made mine eyes water; but more merry tears
The passion of loud laughter never shed.   70
    The. What are they that do play it?
    Phil. Hard-handed men that work in Athens
    here,
Which never labour'd in their minds till now,
And now have toil'd their unbreathed memories
With this same play, against your nuptial.
    The. And we will hear it.
    Phil.   No, my noble lord;
It is not for you: I have heard it over,

And it is nothing, nothing in the world;
Unless you can find sport in their intents,
● Extremely stretch'd and conn'd with cruel pain, 80
To do you service.
       The.   I will hear that play;
For never anything can be amiss,
When simpleness and duty tender it.
Go, bring them in: and take your places, ladies.
                                 [*Exit Philostrate.*
● *Hip.* I love not to see wretchedness o'ercharged
And duty in his service perishing.
       The. Why, gentle sweet, you shall see no
           such thing.
       Hip. He says they can do nothing in this
           kind.
       The. The kinder we, to give them thanks for
           nothing.
Our sport shall be to take what they mistake: 90
● And what poor duty cannot do, noble respect
† Takes it in might, not merit.
● Where I have come, great clerks have purposed
To greet me with premeditated welcomes;
Where I have seen them shiver and look pale,
● Make periods in the midst of sentences,
Throttle their practised accent in their fears
And in conclusion dumbly have broke off,
Not paying me a welcome.   Trust me, sweet,
Out of this silence yet I pick'd a welcome;   100
And in the modesty of fearful duty
I read as much as from the rattling tongue
Of saucy and audacious eloquence.
Love, therefore, and tongue-tied simplicity
● In least speak most, to my capacity.

          Re-enter PHILOSTRATE.

● *Phil.* So please your grace, the Prologue is
           address'd.
       The. Let him approach. [*Flourish of trumpets.*

          Enter QUINCE *for the* Prologue.

Pro. If we offend, it is with our good will.
   That you should think, we come not to offend,
But with good will. To show our simple skill, 110
   That is the true beginning of our end.
Consider then we come but in despite.
   We do not come as minding to content you,
Our true intent is.   All for your delight
   We are not here.   That you should here repent
       you,
● The actors are at hand and by their show
You shall know all that you are like to know.
● *The.* This fellow doth not stand upon points.
       Lys. He hath rid his prologue like a rough
● colt; he knows not the stop.   A good moral, my
lord: it is not enough to speak, but to speak true.
       Hip. Indeed he hath played on his prologue
like a child on a recorder; a sound, but not in
government.
       The. His speech was like a tangled chain;
nothing impaired, but all disordered.   Who is
next?

          Enter PYRAMUS *and* THISBE, WALL,
              MOONSHINE, *and* LION.

Pro. Gentles, perchance you wonder at this
       show;
   But wonder on, till truth make all things plain.
This man is Pyramus, if you would know;   130

80 *stretch'd and conn'd.* Strained and learned.

85-86 *I love . . . perishing.* I do not enjoy seeing poor people struggling with something they are incapable of performing.

F. R. Benson, English Edwardian actor, as Theseus, Court Theatre, London, 1915

91-92 *And what . . . merit.* The noble mind recognizes the effort made and does not simply judge the result.

93 *clerks.* Scholars.

96 *periods.* Full stops.

105 *to my capacity.* In my view.

106 *address'd.* Ready.

116 *show.* The mimed dumb show that usually accompanied the prologue.

118 *points.* Punctuation or niceties.

120 *stop.* An equestrian term for pulling up a horse, or a mark in punctuation—a punning, double meaning.

The Mechanicals performing their play, George Devine's production Stratford-upon-Avon, 1954

140 *hight.* Called.

143 *did fall.* Let fall.

152 *At large.* At length.

164 *right and sinister.* Right and left, perhaps meaning horizontal.

166 *lime and hair.* Plaster.

183 *sensible.* Conscious.

This beauteous lady Thisby is certain.
This man, with lime and rough-cast, doth present
  Wall, that vile Wall which did these lovers
    sunder ;
And through Wall's chink, poor souls, they are
    content
  To whisper. At the which let no man wonder.
This man, with lanthorn, dog, and bush of thorn,
  Presenteth Moonshine ; for, if you will know,
By moonshine did these lovers think no scorn
  To meet at Ninus' tomb, there, there to woo.
● This grisly beast, which Lion hight by name, 140
The trusty Thisby, coming first by night,
  Did scare away, or rather did affright ;
● And, as she fled, her mantle she did fall,
  Which Lion vile with bloody mouth did stain.
Anon comes Pyramus, sweet youth and tall,
  And finds his trusty Thisby's mantle slain :
Whereat, with blade, with bloody blameful blade,
  He bravely broach'd his boiling bloody breast ;
And Thisby, tarrying in mulberry shade,
  His dagger drew, and died. For all the rest,
Let Lion, Moonshine, Wall, and lovers twain 151
● At large discourse, while here they do remain.
[*Exeunt Prologue, Pyramus, Thisbe, Lion, and*
                Moonshine.
   The. I wonder if the lion be to speak.
   Dem. No wonder, my lord : one lion may,
when many asses do.
   Wall. In this same interlude it doth befall
That I, one Snout by name, present a wall ;
And such a wall, as I would have you think,
That had in it a crannied hole or chink,
Through which the lovers, Pyramus and Thisby,
Did whisper often very secretly. 161
This loam, this rough-cast and this stone doth
  show
That I am that same wall ; the truth is so :
● And this the cranny is, right and sinister,
Through which the fearful lovers are to whisper.
●   *The.* Would you desire lime and hair to speak
better ?
   Dem. It is the wittiest partition that ever I
heard discourse, my lord.

       Re-enter PYRAMUS.

   The. Pyramus draws near the wall : silence !
   Pyr. O grim-look'd night ! O night with hue
  so black ! 171
O night, which ever art when day is not !
O night , O night ! alack, alack, alack,
  I fear my Thisby's promise is forgot !
And thou, O wall, O sweet, O lovely wall,
  That stand'st between her father's ground and
    mine !
Thou wall, O wall, O sweet and lovely wall,
  Show me thy chink, to blink through with mine
    eyne !   [*Wall holds up his fingers.*
Thanks, courteous wall : Jove shield thee well for
  this !
But what see I ? No Thisby do I see. 180
O wicked wall, through whom I see no bliss !
  Cursed be thy stones for thus deceiving me !
●   *The.* The wall, methinks, being sensible, should
curse again.
   Pyr. No, in truth, sir, he should not. 'De-
ceiving me' is Thisby's cue : she is to enter now,
and I am to spy her through the wall. You shall

see, it will fall pat as I told you.   Yonder she comes.

Re-enter THISBE.

This.   O wall, full often hast thou heard my moans,   190
For parting my fair Pyramus and me!
My cherry lips have often kiss'd thy stones,
Thy stones with lime and hair knit up in thee.
Pyr.   I see a voice: now will I to the chink,
To spy an I can hear my Thisby's face.
Thisby!
This.   My love thou art, my love I think.
Pyr.   Think what thou wilt, I am thy lover's grace;
And, like Limander, am I trusty still.
This.   And I like Helen, till the Fates me kill.
Pyr.   Not Shafalus to Procrus was so true.
This.   As Shafalus to Procrus, I to you.
Pyr.   O, kiss me through the hole of this vile wall!
This.   I kiss the wall's hole, not your lips at all.
Pyr.   Wilt thou at Ninny's tomb meet me straightway?
This.   'Tide life, 'tide death, I come without delay.   [*Exeunt Pyramus and Thisbe.*
Wall.   Thus have I, Wall, my part discharged so;
And, being done, thus Wall away doth go. [*Exit.*
The.   Now is the mural down between the two neighbours.
Dem.   No remedy, my lord, when walls are so wilful to hear without warning.   211
Hip.   This is the silliest stuff that ever I heard.
The.   The best in this kind are but shadows; and the worst are no worse, if imagination amend them.
Hip.   It must be your imagination then, and not theirs.
The.   If we imagine no worse of them than they of themselves, they may pass for excellent men.   Here come two noble beasts in, a man and a lion.   221

Re-enter LION *and* MOONSHINE.

Lion.   You, ladies, you, whose gentle hearts do fear
The smallest monstrous mouse that creeps on floor,
May now perchance both quake and tremble here,
When lion rough in wildest rage doth roar.
Then know that I, one Snug the joiner, am
A lion-fell, nor else no lion's dam;
For, if I should as lion come in strife
Into this place, 'twere pity on my life.
The.   A very gentle beast, and of a good conscience.   231
Dem.   The very best at a beast, my lord, that e'er I saw.
Lys.   This lion is a very fox for his valour.
The.   True; and a goose for his discretion.
Dem.   Not so, my lord; for his valour cannot carry his discretion; and the fox carries the goose.
The.   His discretion, I am sure, cannot carry his valour; for the goose carries not the fox. It is well: leave it to his discretion, and let us listen to the moon.

199 *Limander.* Probably Leander who every night swam the Hellespont to visit Hero.

200 *Helen.* Probably Hero since Helen of Troy is hardly an example of fidelity.

201 *Shafalus to Procrus.* Probably Cephalus and Procris, another pair of legendary lovers.

213 *in this kind.* Of this sort, i.e. plays.

227 *fell.* Fierce.

229 *'twere . . . life.* More than my life is worth.

237 *carry.* Overcome.

273

Costume designs for The Clowns. Illustration by Paul Nash from *Players' Shakespeare*, 1924

243 *Lanthorn.* Lanterns were often made of horn.

244-245 *horns on his head.* A cuckold was said to have horns, and this is the subject of frequent jokes.

246 *no crescent.* Not waxing.

254 *in snuff.* A pun on the meanings 'offended' and 'in need of putting out'.

274 *moused.* Shaken.

283 *dole.* Grief.

290 *Fates.* The three fates spun the thread that determined the length of a human's life.

291 *thrum.* The loose end of the warp thread.

296 *frame.* Create.

● *Moon.* This lanthorn doth the horned moon
present ;—
● *Dem.* He should have worn the horns on his
head.
● *The.* He is no crescent, and his horns are invisible within the circumference.
Moon. This lanthorn doth the horned moon
present ;
Myself the man i' the moon do seem to be.
The. This is the greatest error of all the rest:
the man should be put into the lanthorn. How is
it else the man i' the moon?
Dem. He dares not come there for the candle ;
● for, you see, it is already in snuff.
Hip. I am aweary of this moon : would he
would change !
The. It appears, by his small light of discretion, that he is in the wane ; but yet, in courtesy,
in all reason, we must stay the time.
Lys. Proceed, Moon.   260
Moon. All that I have to say, is, to tell you
that the lanthorn is the moon ; I, the man in the
moon ; this thorn-bush, my thorn-bush ; and this
dog, my dog.
Dem. Why, all these should be in the lanthorn ;
for all these are in the moon. But, silence ! here
comes Thisbe.

Re-enter THISBE.

This. This is old Ninny's tomb. Where is
my love ?
Lion. [*Roaring*] Oh——   [*Thisbe runs off.*
Dem. Well roared, Lion.   270
The. Well run, Thisbe.
Hip. Well shone, Moon. Truly, the moon
shines with a good grace.
[*The Lion shakes Thisbe's mantle, and exit.*
● *The.* Well moused, Lion.
Lys. And so the lion vanished.
Dem. And then came Pyramus.

Re-enter PYRAMUS.

Pyr. Sweet Moon, I thank thee for thy sunny
beams ;
I thank thee, Moon, for shining now so bright ;
For, by thy gracious, golden, glittering gleams,
I trust to take of truest Thisby sight.   280
But stay, O spite !
But mark, poor knight,
● What dreadful dole is here !
Eyes, do you see ?
How can it be ?
O dainty duck ! O dear !
Thy mantle good,
What, stain'd with blood !
Approach, ye Furies fell !
● O Fates, come, come,   290
● Cut thread and thrum ;
Quail, crush, conclude, and quell !
The. This passion, and the death of a dear
friend, would go near to make a man look sad.
Hip. Beshrew my heart, but I pity the man.
● *Pyr.* O wherefore, Nature, didst thou lions
frame ?
Since lion vile hath here deflower'd my dear :
Which is—no, no—which was the fairest dame
That lived, that loved, that liked, that look'd
with cheer.

Come, tears, confound ;   300
   Out, sword, and wound
The pap of Pyramus ;
   Ay, that left pap,
   Where heart doth hop : [*Stabs himself.*
Thus die I, thus, thus, thus.
   Now am I dead,
   Now am I fled ;
My soul is in the sky :
   Tongue, lose thy light ;
   Moon, take thy flight : [*Exit Moonshine.*
Now die, die, die, die, die.   [*Dies.*
   Dem.   No die but an ace, for him ; for he is
but one.
   Lys.   Less than an ace, man ; for he is dead ;
he is nothing.
   The.   With the help of a surgeon he might yet
recover, and prove an ass.
   Hip.   How chance Moonshine is gone before
Thisbe comes back and finds her lover ?
   The.   She will find him by starlight.   Here
she comes ; and her passion ends the play.   321

Re-enter THISBE.

   Hip.   Methinks she should not use a long one
for such a Pyramus : I hope she will be brief.
   Dem.   A mote will turn the balance, which
Pyramus, which Thisbe, is the better ; he for a
man, God warrant us ; she for a woman, God
bless us.
   Lys.   She hath spied him already with those
sweet eyes.
   Dem.   And thus she means, videlicet :—   330
   This.   Asleep, my love ?
   What, dead, my dove ?
O Pyramus, arise !
   Speak, speak.   Quite dumb ?
   Dead, dead ?   A tomb
Must cover thy sweet eyes.
   These lily lips,
   This cherry nose,
These yellow cowslip cheeks,
   Are gone, are gone :   340
   Lovers, make moan :
His eyes were green as leeks.
   O Sisters Three,
   Come, come to me,
With hands as pale as milk ;
   Lay them in gore,
   Since you have shore
With shears his thread of silk.
   Tongue, not a word :
   Come, trusty sword ;   350
Come, blade, my breast imbrue :
                    [*Stabs herself.*
   And, farewell, friends ;
   Thus Thisby ends :
Adieu, adieu, adieu.   [*Dies.*
   The.   Moonshine and Lion are left to bury
the dead.
   Dem.   Ay, and Wall too.
   Bot. [*Starting up*] No, I assure you ; the wall
is down that parted their fathers.   Will it please
you to see the epilogue, or to hear a Bergomask
dance between two of our company ?   361
   The.   No epilogue, I pray you ; for your play
needs no excuse.   Never excuse ; for when the
players are all dead, there need none to be blamed.

324   *mote.* A small particle.

326   *warrant.* Defend.

330   *videlicet.* From the Latin 'one may see'; or 'as follows'.

Flute as Thisbe ; costume design by Norman Wilkinson, Savoy Theatre, London, 1914

343   *Sisters Three.* The three Fates.

347   *shore.* Shorn.

351   *imbrue.* Stain with blood.

360   *Bergomask.* A country dance named after Bergamo in Italy.

370 *iron tongue.* Bell.

371 *fairy time.* Midnight when the fairies and ghosts came out.

374 *palpable-gross.* Obviously silly or stupid.

381 *fordone.* Tired out.

382 *brands.* Logs.

391 *triple Hecate's.* Hecate ruled in three realms, i.e. she was Diana on Earth, Cynthia in Heaven, and Proserpine in Hades. *team.* Her chariot was drawn by black horses or dragons.

Hecate. Print by William Blake, 1795

397 *behind the door.* From behind the door.

423 *take his gait.* Make his way.

Marry, if he that writ it had played Pyramus and hanged himself in Thisbe's garter, it would have been a fine tragedy: and so it is, truly; and very notably discharged.   But, come, your Bergomask: let your epilogue alone.   [*A dance.*
• The iron tongue of midnight hath told twelve:
• Lovers, to bed; 'tis almost fairy time.   371
  I fear we shall out-sleep the coming morn
  As much as we this night have overwatch'd.
• This palpable-gross play hath well beguiled
  The heavy gait of night.   Sweet friends, to bed.
  A fortnight hold we this solemnity,
  In nightly revels and new jollity.   [*Exeunt.*

Enter PUCK.

Puck.   Now the hungry lion roars,
      And the wolf behowls the moon;
    Whilst the heavy ploughman snores,   380
•   All with weary task fordone.
•   Now the wasted brands do glow,
      Whilst the screech-owl, screeching loud,
    Puts the wretch that lies in woe
      In remembrance of a shroud.
    Now it is the time of night
      That the graves all gaping wide,
    Every one lets forth his sprite,
      In the church-way paths to glide:
    And we fairies, that do run   390
•   By the triple Hecate's team,
    From the presence of the sun,
      Following darkness like a dream,
    Now are frolic: not a mouse
    Shall disturb this hallow'd house:
    I am sent with broom before,
•   To sweep the dust behind the door.

Enter OBERON *and* TITANIA *with their train.*

Obe.   Through the house give glimmering light,
      By the dead and drowsy fire:
    Every elf and fairy sprite   400
      Hop as light as bird from brier;
    And this ditty, after me,
    Sing, and dance it trippingly.
Tita.   First, rehearse your song by rote,
      To each word a warbling note:
    Hand in hand, with fairy grace,
    Will we sing, and bless this place.
                [*Song and dance.*
Obe.   Now, until the break of day,
    Through this house each fairy stray.
    To the best bride-bed will we,   410
    Which by us shall blessed be;
    And the issue there create
    Ever shall be fortunate.
    So shall all the couples three
    Ever true in loving be;
    And the blots of Nature's hand
    Shall not in their issue stand:
    Never mole, hare lip, nor scar,
    Nor mark prodigious, such as are
    Despised in nativity,   420
    Shall upon their children be.
    With this field-dew consecrate,
•   Every fairy take his gait;
    And each several chamber bless,
    Through this palace, with sweet peace;
    And the owner of it blest

Ever shall in safety rest.
Trip away ; make no stay ;
Meet me all by break of day.
    [*Exeunt Oberon, Titania, and train.*
Puck.   If we shadows have offended,   430
Think but this, and all is mended,
That you have but slumber'd here
While these visions did appear.
● And this weak and idle theme,
● No more yielding but a dream,
Gentles, do not reprehend :
If you pardon, we will mend :
And, as I am an honest Puck,
If we have unearned luck
● Now to 'scape the serpent's tongue,   440
We will make amends ere long ;
Else the Puck a liar call :
So, good night unto you all.
● Give me your hands, if we be friends,
And Robin shall restore amends.   [*Exit.*

Oberon : 'Trip away . . .' Painting by T. von Holst (1810–1844)

434 *idle*. Foolish.

435 *No more yielding*. Means 'no more than a dream'.

440 *serpent's tongue*. The hisses from an audience.

444 *Give me your hands*. Applaud.

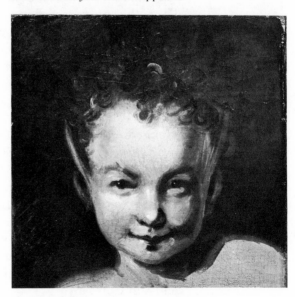

Puck or Robin Goodfellow. Painting after Sir Joshua Reynolds (1723–1792)

The Merchant
of Venice

1596

THE ALERT DRAMATIST with his ear to the ground for what would appeal—what we would call box-office returns—ever since he began successfully with the *Henry VI* plays, found a topical subject to hand for *The Merchant of Venice*. For, at the time and for long afterwards, the play was often referred to as 'The Jew of Venice'; Shylock was the dominant character, the one who remains above all the rest in the mind, and the play relates to the theme that has had so terrible a resonance in our time: the Jew in Europe and the evil phenomenon of anti-Semitism. It is necessary to confront it directly and simply, without flinching.

Europe has had a shocking record in regard to the Jews—to my mind unforgivable— reaching its evil climax in our demotic days with Belsen and Dachau, and all the rest. The 16th century record was nothing like so bad, and Jewish characteristics, the addiction to money and usury, etc, were regarded as matter for comedy—as were other national characteristics, Scotch, Irish, Dutch, German, French, or Spanish, as in *The Two Gentlemen of Verona* and again in this play, good for a laugh from the groundlings. It must be realised that, to the Elizabethans, Shylock was a comic character, though we may think of him as more tragic.

Background. He derives directly from Barabas, the leading figure in Marlowe's savage, farcical play, *The Jew of Malta*. With the popular excitement over the Lopez affair running high in 1594, Marlowe's play was revived by the Admiral's Company and given some fifteen performances later that year. The Chamberlain's men saw their chance to go one better, as their actor-dramatist certainly did with the play he wrote for them. Marlowe's play was the chief influence upon his mind, though Shakespeare placed the action once more in the setting of a familiar Italian story, from the collection called *Il Pecorone*, contemporary with Boccaccio. He fused these two main elements into a play which has been always successful—particularly, we note, perhaps significantly, in Germany.

Dr. Lopez, the Queen's physician, we repeat, had been shockingly handled in England. He had been too successful for some people's taste—and that had somewhat

Venice : Piazetta and Doge's Palace from the Bacino. 18th century painting from the studio of Canaletto

gone to his head; he dabbled dangerously in political intelligence and he had made aspersions against Essex's sexual health. It was Essex who ran him down, made it a point of 'honour' to bring him down. The humane Queen never believed that Lopez intended to poison her, but could not hold up for ever the popular clamour against him. We must remember (a), Shakespeare's indirect affiliation to Essex through Southampton; (b), his usual conformity with popular opinion. Considering that, it is rather wonderful what he made out of the play, though we today may feel sensitive about it—far more than the Victorians, with whom it was very popular.

On the other hand it provides an illuminating contrast with Marlowe's play: the contrasting genius of the two men stands out sharply. Marlowe's Barabas is a comic villain, savagely belaboured and brought to book for the delight of the pit. Shakespeare begins with the popular representation of Skylock as a Jew to be despised, but his humanity cannot help breaking in. Shylock *has* been wronged, and 'hath not a Jew eyes? hath not a Jew hands, organs, dimensions, senses, affections, passions? fed with the same food, hurt with the same weapons, subject to the same diseases, healed by the same means, warmed and cooled by the same winter and summer, as a Christian is?' Here is the real

Shakespeare: a very different soul from Marlowe, for all that he owed to him.

There are virtual quotations from Marlowe, besides phrases and other flecks—Shakespeare's infallible ear picked up and registered everything usable. An Elizabethan audience found it funny when the Jew's daughter ran away to marry a Christian—though we may not. Shylock's outburst is as follows:

> My daughter! O my ducats! O my daughter!
> Fled with a Christian! O my Christian ducats!

The words are practically the same as Marlowe's, the situation repeated from his play. The Elizabethans laughed at the absconding Jessica playing fast and loose with his money: 'Your daughter spent in Genoa, as I heard, one night, fourscore ducats.' I do not find that funny. One critic says reasonably that, in this disturbing play, Shakespeare 'tries to have it both ways'.

In fact, though he does try to even up the scales, they are tipped against Shylock: one cannot say that he receives justice. So no wonder he lingers in everybody's mind, no comic figure but an ambivalent one, hovering between comedy and tragedy. From the beginning one sympathises with him at the ill-treatment he has received from Antonio:

> Fair sir, you spat on me on Wednesday last,
> You spurned me such a day, another time
> You called me dog: and for these courtesies
> I'll lend you thus much moneys?

When he demands his pound of flesh, however, the audience would recognise the reference to Lopez, *lupus*, the wolf:

> thy currish spirit
> Governed a wolf, who hanged for human slaughter . . .
> . . . thy desires
> Are wolvish, bloody, starved and ravenous.

The idea of exacting a pound of flesh is to us melodramatic and unconvincing, yet it comes with the story and the very phrase has entered into common usage. The medievals, infantile as they were, believed even worse of the Jews. One cannot think that Shylock receives any kind of justice when Antonio generously remits one half of his goods, to claim the other half—provided he becomes a Christian and leaves everything to his absconding daughter and her husband. The Elizabethans evidently thought that that was good enough for him.

The Elizabethan Age. Everything bespeaks the time, and there is no difficulty about dating.

> . . . my wealthy *Andrew* docked in sand,
> Vailing her high top lower than her ribs
> To kiss her burial—

refers to the Spanish galleon, the *St. Andrew,* which ran aground and was taken at the capture of Cadiz in the summer of 1596. She nearly ran aground again when being brought up-Channel. In the play Antonio's ship is reported wrecked in the Narrow Seas, on the Goodwin Sands. The play belongs to that autumn.

> Plucking the grass to know where sits the wind,
> Prying in maps for ports, and piers and roads,

in the first scene, watching out for their argosies upon the high seas—this is precisely what one finds the merchants who were clients of Simon Forman doing at the time. [1]

The Queen herself was an accomplished orator, and there is every likelihood that the perambulating actor would have heard her perform:

> And there is such confusion in my powers
> As, after some oration fairly spoke
> By a belovèd prince, there doth appear
> Among the buzzing pleasèd multitude,
> Where every something being blent together,
> Turns to a wild of nothing, save of joy
> Expressed and not expressed.

Jokes against neighbour nations and their characteristics were common fare, then as now. Here again is the Scot: 'he hath a neighbourly charity in him, for he borrowed a box of the ear of the Englishman, and swore he would pay him again when he was able.' The Elizabethans thought drunkenness the endemic vice of Germans. Portia, when asked how she liked her German suitor, replies: 'Very vilely in the morning when he is sober, and most vilely in the afternoon when he is drunk: when he is best, he is a little worse than a man, and when he is worst he is little better than a beast.' When Portia says to Antonio's friend, Bassanio:

> I fear you speak upon the rack
> Where men enforcèd do speak any thing,

we reflect that there the brutality of the age stands revealed, the rack in the background. But was it any worse than ours abroad, four hundred years on?

Personal. We turn with relief from these barbs to make fools laugh to the personal touches that bring Shakespeare before us. Here is the love of sports and outdoor activities so obvious in the plays he wrote when younger:

> In my schooldays, when I had lost one shaft,
> I shot his fellow of the self-same flight
> The self-same way, with more advisèd watch
> To find the other forth, and by adventuring both
> I oft found both.

The archery-butts at Stratford were on the low-lying ground by the bridge—one often thinks of them, and the schoolboy, when passing over it. Had he a particular experience in mind when he wrote?—

> All things that are
> Are with more spirit chasèd than enjoyed.

[1] v. my *Simon Forman*, c. VIII.

We hear the echo from the Sonnet:

> The expense of spirit in a waste of shame
> Is lust in action . . .
> Enjoyed no sooner but despisèd straight.

Much has been made of the friendship theme, the intimate feeling by which Bassanio would sacrifice everything to save Antonio:

> But life itself, my wife, and all the world
> Are not with me esteemed above your life.
> I would lose all, ay, sacrifice them all
> Here to this devil, to deliver you.

On which the spirited Portia, something of a feminist, comments:

> Your wife would give you little thanks for that
> If she were by to hear you make the offer.

However, the friendship theme is subordinate to the far more powerful emotions aroused around Shylock. And the love theme around Portia is cool and subdued, the choosing among suitors, with its dramatic appeal for a rather simple audience, is hardly moving to a modern one: it is a commonplace of the traditional story Shakespeare is adapting.

It may be worth observing the report of Portia:

> she doth stray about
> By holy crosses where she kneels and prays
> For happy wedlock hours.

Wayside crosses were a feature of Elizabethan England, and there were still old-fashioned people to pray at them. Of course the action of the play is in Italy; Shakespeare was a conforming member of the Church of England, but an old-fashioned one to whom the terms and habits of the old faith came naturally: priests are priests, people cross themselves, we hear of holy unction and holy bread; oaths are the old ones, 'Marry' and 'by our Lady', 'by the mass' and 'by God's wounds', the conservative Queen's customary oath.

The play is, as usual, fairly sprinkled with the classical allusions, figures and images, that welled up from his schooling. The last Act is different in character from the dramatic tensions of the previous Acts: it is intensely lyrical and magical, drenched in moonlight and music. (In our time it has inspired Vaughan Williams' 'Serenade to Music'.) But when the disparate images of Troilus and Cressida, along with Thisbe, occur we can see Shakespeare with his Chaucer open before him at the pages where they occur together. Those famous broken paragraphs of verse, each beginning, 'In such a night,' marvellously evoke moonlit Belmont.

> In such a night
> Stood Dido with a willow in her hand
> Upon the wild sea banks, and waft her love
> To come again to Carthage.

Perhaps he was thinking of Marlowe and his *Dido*—as certainly he was when he wrote that Portia's

> sunny locks
> Hang on her temples like a golden fleece,
> Which makes her seat of Belmont Colchos' strand.

So in the poem written in rivalry with *Venus and Adonis* had Marlowe described Southampton's:

> His dangling tresses that were never shorn,
> Had they been cut and unto Colchos borne,
> Would have allured the venturous youth of Greece
> To hazard more than for the golden fleece.

There is more music than ever in this play. We are given the charming song:

> Tell me where is Fancy bred,
> Or in the heart, or in the head?

Much of the last Act is performed to the sound of music, and we have Shakespeare's tribute to its power, which was evidently spoken from his heart:

> The man that hath no music in himself,
> Nor is not moved with concord of sweet sounds,
> Is fit for treasons, stratagems, and spoils,
> The motions of his spirit are dull as night,
> And his affections dark as Erebus.

The action is spun out by the intrigue about Portia's ring, which Bassanio gave away to procure the learned doctor (Portia in disguise) to plead Antonio's case and save his life. Thus, when all is resolved, the comedy is dismissed with Shakespeare's characteristic (and popular) bawdy: Gratiano says,

> But were the day come, I should wish it dark
> Till I were couching with the doctor's clerk.
> Well, while I live, I'll fear no other thing
> So sore, as keeping safe Nerissa's ring.

Text. The text is a good one, a quarto published in 1600; E. K. Chambers 'saw no reason why the copy used for [it] should not have been in Shakespeare's hand'. It was reprinted in the First Folio, with a few additions of stage directions from the Company's prompt-book.

Merchant of Venice

Act 3, Scene 3

Shylock Follow not,
Ill have no speaking, I will have my bond

THE MERCHANT OF VENICE.

DRAMATIS PERSONÆ.

The DUKE OF VENICE.
The PRINCE OF MOROCCO, } suitors to Portia.
The PRINCE OF ARRAGON, }
ANTONIO, a merchant of Venice.
BASSANIO, his friend, suitor likewise to Portia.
SALANIO,
SALARINO, } friends to Antonio and Bassanio.
GRATIANO,
SALERIO,
LORENZO, in love with Jessica.
SHYLOCK, a rich Jew.
TUBAL, a Jew, his friend.
LAUNCELOT GOBBO, the clown, servant to Shylock.

OLD GOBBO, father to Launcelot.
LEONARDO, servant to Bassanio.
BALTHASAR, } servants to Portia.
STEPHANO, }
PORTIA, a rich heiress.
NERISSA, her waiting-maid.
JESSICA, daughter to Shylock.

Magnificoes of Venice, Officers of the Court of Justice, Gaoler, Servants to Portia, and other Attendants.

SCENE: *Partly at Venice, and partly at Belmont, the seat of Portia, on the Continent.*

● *A bullet beside a text line indicates an annotation in the opposite column*

ACT I.

SCENE I. *Venice. A street.*

Enter ANTONIO, SALARINO, *and* SALANIO.

Ant. In sooth, I know not why I am so sad:
It wearies me; you say it wearies you;
But how I caught it, found it, or came by it,
What stuff 'tis made of, whereof it is born,
I am to learn;
And such a want-wit sadness makes of me,
That I have much ado to know myself.
   Salar. Your mind is tossing on the ocean;
●There, where your argosies with portly sail,
Like signiors and rich burghers on the flood,   10
Or, as it were, the pageants of the sea,
Do overpeer the petty traffickers,
That curtsy to them, do them reverence,
As they fly by them with their woven wings.
   Salan. Believe me, sir, had I such venture forth,
The better part of my affections would
Be with my hopes abroad. I should be still

Venice in the 15th century. From Schedel's *Liber Chronicorum*, 1493

9 *argosies.* Large merchant ships.

Opposite: Frontispiece from an 1800 *Shakspere.* Engraving from a design by W. M. Craig

285

27 *Andrew.* The name of the Spanish galleon which was captured by Essex at Cadiz in 1596.

28 *Vailing.* Lowering.

50 *Janus.* The two-faced god of Roman mythology; as god of gates he faced both ways.

Salarino: 'Now, by two-headed Janus . . .' Engraving from Charles Knight's *Pictorial Edition of the Works of William Shakspere,* 1839–43

56 *Nestor.* The old veteran amongst the Greek commanders at Troy.

SD *Enter . . . Gratiano.* Graziano was the name of the comic doctor in the Italian *commedia dell'arte.* Gratiano plays the 'fool's part' in the scene.

74 *respect upon.* Regard for.

Plucking the grass, to know where sits the wind,
Peering in maps for ports and piers and roads;
And every object that might make me fear   20
Misfortune to my ventures, out of doubt
Would make me sad.
   Salar.   My wind cooling my broth
Would blow me to an ague, when I thought
What harm a wind too great at sea might do.
I should not see the sandy hour-glass run,
But I should think of shallows and of flats,
●And see my wealthy Andrew dock'd in sand,
●Vailing her high-top lower than her ribs
To kiss her burial.   Should I go to church
And see the holy edifice of stone,   30
And not bethink me straight of dangerous rocks,
Which touching but my gentle vessel's side,
Would scatter all her spices on the stream,
Enrobe the roaring waters with my silks,
And, in a word, but even now worth this,
And now worth nothing? Shall I have the thought
To think on this, and shall I lack the thought
That such a thing bechanced would make me sad?
But tell not me; I know, Antonio
Is sad to think upon his merchandise.   40
   Ant. Believe me, no: I thank my fortune for it,
My ventures are not in one bottom trusted,
Nor to one place; nor is my whole estate
Upon the fortune of this present year:
Therefore my merchandise makes me not sad.
   Salar. Why, then you are in love.
   Ant.   Fie, fie!
   Salar. Not in love neither?   Then let us say you are sad,
Because you are not merry: and 'twere as easy
For you to laugh and leap and say you are merry,
●Because you are not sad.   Now, by two-headed Janus,   50
Nature hath framed strange fellows in her time:
Some that will evermore peep through their eyes
And laugh like parrots at a bag-piper,
And other of such vinegar aspect
That they'll not show their teeth in way of smile,
●Though Nestor swear the jest be laughable.

Enter BASSANIO, LORENZO, *and* GRATIANO.

   Salan. Here comes Bassanio, your most noble kinsman,
Gratiano and Lorenzo.   Fare ye well:
We leave you now with better company.
   Salar. I would have stay'd till I had made you merry,   60
If worthier friends had not prevented me.
   Ant. Your worth is very dear in my regard.
I take it, your own business calls on you
And you embrace the occasion to depart.
   Salar. Good morrow, my good lords.
   Bass. Good signiors both, when shall we laugh? say, when?
You grow exceeding strange: must it be so?
   Salar. We'll make our leisures to attend on yours.
                 [Exeunt Salarino and Salanio.

   Lor. My Lord Bassanio, since you have found Antonio,
We two will leave you: but at dinner-time,   70
I pray you, have in mind where we must meet.
   Bass. I will not fail you.
   Gra. You look not well, Signior Antonio;
●You have too much respect upon the world:

They lose it that do buy it with much care :
Believe me, you are marvellously changed.
    Ant.   I hold the world but as the world,
        Gratiano ;
A stage where every man must play a part,
And mine a sad one.
    Gra.   Let me play the fool :
With mirth and laughter let old wrinkles come,
And let my liver rather heat with wine   81
Than my heart cool with mortifying groans.
Why should a man, whose blood is warm within,
Sit like his grandsire cut in alabaster ?
Sleep when he wakes and creep into the jaundice
By being peevish ?   I tell thee what, Antonio—
I love thee, and it is my love that speaks—
There are a sort of men whose visages
Do cream and mantle like a standing pond,
And do a wilful stillness entertain,   90
With purpose to be dress'd in an opinion
Of wisdom, gravity, profound conceit,
As who should say 'I am Sir Oracle,
And when I ope my lips let no dog bark !'
O my Antonio, I do know of these
That therefore only are reputed wise
For saying nothing, when, I am very sure,
If they should speak, would almost damn those ears
Which, hearing them, would call their brothers
        fools.
I'll tell thee more of this another time :   100
But fish not, with this melancholy bait,
● For this fool gudgeon, this opinion.
Come, good Lorenzo.   Fare ye well awhile :
I'll end my exhortation after dinner.
    Lor.   Well, we will leave you then till dinner-
        time :
I must be one of these same dumb wise men,
For Gratiano never lets me speak.
    Gra.   Well, keep me company but two years moe,
Thou shalt not know the sound of thine own tongue.
    Ant.   Farewell : I'll grow a talker for this gear.
    Gra.   Thanks, i' faith, for silence is only com-
    mendable
● In a neat's tongue dried and a maid not vendible.
           [*Exeunt Gratiano and Lorenzo.*

    Ant.   Is that any thing now?
    Bass.   Gratiano speaks an infinite deal of no-
thing, more than any man in all Venice.   His
reasons are as two grains of wheat hid in two
bushels of chaff : you shall seek all day ere you
find them, and when you have them, they are
not worth the search.
    Ant.   Well, tell me now what lady is the same
To whom you swore a secret pilgrimage,   120
That you to-day promised to tell me of?
    Bass.   'Tis not unknown to you, Antonio,
How much I have disabled mine estate,
● By something showing a more swelling port
Than my faint means would grant continuance :
Nor do I now make moan to be abridged
From such a noble rate ; but my chief care
Is to come fairly off from the great debts
Wherein my time something too prodigal
● Hath left me gaged.   To you, Antonio,   130
I owe the most, in money and in love,
And from your love I have a warranty
To unburden all my plots and purposes
How to get clear of all the debts I owe.
    Ant.   I pray you, good Bassanio, let me know it ;
And if it stand, as you yourself still do,

The Fool. From an early 19th century engraving

---

102 *gudgeon.* A small fresh-water fish used as bait.

112 *neat's tongue.* Ox-tongue (dried or cured). *maid not vendible.* Old maid.

124 *port.* Life-style.

130 *gaged.* Bound.

154 *To wind about my love with circumstance.* To beat about the bush.

160 *prest.* Willing.

170 *golden fleece.* Jason and the Argonauts found the Golden Fleece in Colchos and won it with the help of Medea, the King's daughter who, like Portia's father, subjected the Argonauts to three tests.

175 *thrift.* Success, profit.

181 *rack'd.* Stretched.

Dorothy Tutin as Portia, Stratford-upon-Avon, 1960

Within the eye of honour, be assured,
My purse, my person, my extremest means,
Lie all unlock'd to your occasions.
   Bass. In my school-days, when I had lost one shaft,   140
I shot his fellow of the self-same flight
The self-same way with more advised watch,
To find the other forth, and by adventuring both
I oft found both: I urge this childhood proof,
Because what follows is pure innocence.
I owe you much, and, like a wilful youth,
That which I owe is lost; but if you please
To shoot another arrow that self way
Which you did shoot the first, I do not doubt,
As I will watch the aim, or to find both   150
Or bring your latter hazard back again
And thankfully rest debtor for the first.
   Ant. You know me well, and herein spend but time
● To wind about my love with circumstance;
And out of doubt you do me now more wrong
In making question of my uttermost
Than if you had made waste of all I have:
Then do but say to me what I should do
That in your knowledge may by me be done,
● And I am prest unto it: therefore, speak.   160
   Bass. In Belmont is a lady richly left;
And she is fair and, fairer than that word,
Of wondrous virtues: sometimes from her eyes
I did receive fair speechless messages:
Her name is Portia, nothing undervalued
To Cato's daughter, Brutus' Portia:
Nor is the wide world ignorant of her worth,
For the four winds blow in from every coast
Renowned suitors, and her sunny locks
● Hang on her temples like a golden fleece;   170
Which makes her seat of Belmont Colchos' strand,
And many Jasons come in quest of her.
O my Antonio, had I but the means
To hold a rival place with one of them,
● I have a mind presages me such thrift,
That I should questionless be fortunate!
   Ant. Thou know'st that all my fortunes are at sea;
Neither have I money nor commodity
To raise a present sum: therefore go forth;
Try what my credit can in Venice do: 180
● That shall be rack'd, even to the uttermost,
To furnish thee to Belmont, to fair Portia.
Go, presently inquire, and so will I,
Where money is, and I no question make
To have it of my trust or for my sake. [*Exeunt.*

SCENE II. *Belmont. A room in* PORTIA'S *house.*

Enter PORTIA *and* NERISSA.

   Por. By my troth, Nerissa, my little body is aweary of this great world.
   Ner. You would be, sweet madam, if your miseries were in the same abundance as your good fortunes are: and yet, for aught I see, they are as sick that surfeit with too much as they that starve with nothing. It is no mean happiness therefore, to be seated in the mean: superfluity comes sooner by white hairs, but competency lives longer.   10
   Por. Good sentences and well pronounced.
   Ner. They would be better, if well followed.
   Por. If to do were as easy as to know what

were good to do, chapels had been churches and poor men's cottages princes' palaces.   It is a good divine that follows his own instructions: I can easier teach twenty what were good to be done, than be one of the twenty to follow mine own teaching.   The brain may devise laws for the blood, but a hot temper leaps o'er a cold decree: such a hare is madness the youth, to skip o'er the meshes of good counsel the cripple.   But this reasoning is not in the fashion to choose me a husband.   O me, the word 'choose!'   I may neither choose whom I would nor refuse whom I dislike; so is the will of a living daughter curbed by the will of a dead father.   Is it not hard, Nerissa, that I cannot choose one nor refuse none?   29

Ner.   Your father was ever virtuous; and holy men at their death have good inspirations: therefore the lottery, that he hath devised in these three chests of gold, silver and lead, whereof who chooses his meaning chooses you, will, no doubt, never be chosen by any rightly but one who shall rightly love.   But what warmth is there in your affection towards any of these princely suitors that are already come?

Por.   I pray thee, over-name them; and as thou namest them, I will describe them; and, according to my description, level at my affection.

Ner.   First, there is the Neapolitan prince.

Por.   Ay, that's a colt indeed, for he doth nothing but talk of his horse; and he makes it a great appropriation to his own good parts, that he can shoe him himself.   I am much afeard my lady his mother played false with a smith.

Ner.   Then there is the County Palatine.

Por.   He doth nothing but frown, as who should say 'If you will not have me, choose:' he hears merry tales and smiles not: I fear he will prove the weeping philosopher when he grows old, being so full of unmannerly sadness in his youth.   I had rather be married to a death's-head with a bone in his mouth than to either of these.   God defend me from these two!

Ner.   How say you by the French lord, Monsieur Le Bon?

Por.   God made him, and therefore let him pass for a man.   In truth, I know it is a sin to be a mocker: but, he! why, he hath a horse better than the Neapolitan's, a better bad habit of frowning than the Count Palatine; he is every man in no man; if a throstle sing, he falls straight a capering: he will fence with his own shadow: if I should marry him, I should marry twenty husbands.   If he would despise me, I would forgive him, for if he love me to madness, I shall never requite him.   70

Ner.   What say you, then, to Falconbridge, the young baron of England?

Por.   You know I say nothing to him, for he understands not me, nor I him: he hath neither Latin, French, nor Italian, and you will come into the court and swear that I have a poor pennyworth in the English.   He is a proper man's picture, but, alas, who can converse with a dumb-show?   How oddly he is suited!   I think he bought his doublet in Italy, his round hose in France, his bonnet in Germany and his behaviour every where.

26-27 *will . . . will.* There is a pun here on Portia's choice and her father's testament.

43 *Neapolitan prince.* The Neapolitans were recognised for their horsemanship.

49 *County Palatine.* Count Palatine, that is, a count of the Palatinate, a German region which extended on both sides of the middle Rhine.

53 *weeping philosopher.* Heraclitus, a gloomy Greek philosopher.

55-56 *death's-head with a bone in his mouth.* Skull and cross-bones.

65 *throstle.* Thrush.

79 *suited.* Dressed.

Portia: 'I think he bought . . . his round hose in France, his bonnet in Germany'. French and German contemporary costumes, from Chambers's *Pictorial History of England*, 1851

88-89 *Frenchman became his surety.* A reference to the traditional alliance between France and Scotland.

104 *rhenish wine.* Wine from the Rhineland.

116 *Sibylla.* The ancient prophetess, the sibyl of Cumae.

Ner. What think you of the Scottish lord, his neighbour?

Por. That he hath a neighbourly charity in him, for he borrowed a box of the ear of the Englishman and swore he would pay him again when he was able: I think the Frenchman became his surety and sealed under for another.

Ner. How like you the young German, the Duke of Saxony's nephew? 91

Por. Very vilely in the morning, when he is sober, and most vilely in the afternoon, when he is drunk: when he is best, he is a little worse than a man, and when he is worst, he is little better than a beast: an the worst fall that ever fell, I hope I shall make shift to go without him.

Ner. If he should offer to choose, and choose the right casket, you should refuse to perform your father's will, if you should refuse to accept him.

Por. Therefore, for fear of the worst, I pray thee, set a deep glass of rhenish wine on the contrary casket, for if the devil be within and that temptation without, I know he will choose it. I will do any thing, Nerissa, ere I'll be married to a sponge.

Ner. You need not fear, lady, the having any of these lords: they have acquainted me with their determinations; which is, indeed, to return to their home and to trouble you with no more suit, unless you may be won by some other sort than your father's imposition depending on the caskets.

Por. If I live to be as old as Sibylla, I will die as chaste as Diana, unless I be obtained by the manner of my father's will. I am glad this parcel of wooers are so reasonable, for there is not one among them but I dote on his very absence, and I pray God grant them a fair departure.

Ner. Do you not remember, lady, in your father's time, a Venetian, a scholar and a soldier, that came hither in company of the Marquis of Montferrat?

Por. Yes, yes, it was Bassanio; as I think, he was so called.

Ner. True, madam: he, of all the men that ever my foolish eyes looked upon, was the best deserving a fair lady. 131

Por. I remember him well, and I remember him worthy of thy praise.

Enter a Serving-man.

How now! what news?

Serv. The four strangers seek for you, madam, to take their leave: and there is a forerunner come from a fifth, the Prince of Morocco, who brings word the prince his master will be here to-night. 139

Por. If I could bid the fifth welcome with so good a heart as I can bid the other four farewell, I should be glad of his approach: if he have the condition of a saint and the complexion of a devil, I had rather he should shrive me than wive me.
Come, Nerissa. Sirrah, go before.
Whiles we shut the gates upon one wooer, another
knocks at the door. [*Exeunt.*

SCENE III. *Venice. A public place.*

Enter BASSANIO *and* SHYLOCK.

Shy. Three thousand ducats; well.

Bass. Ay, sir, for three months.

Shy. For three months; well.

Bass. For the which, as I told you, Antonio shall be bound.

Shy. Antonio shall become bound; well.

Bass. May you stead me? will you pleasure me? shall I know your answer?

Shy. Three thousand ducats for three months and Antonio bound. 10

Bass. Your answer to that.

Shy. Antonio is a good man.

Bass. Have you heard any imputation to the contrary?

Shy. Oh, no, no, no, no: my meaning in saying he is a good man is to have you understand me that he is sufficient. Yet his means are in supposition: he hath an argosy bound to Tripolis, another to the Indies; I understand, moreover, upon the Rialto, he hath a third at Mexico, a fourth for England, and other ventures he hath, squandered abroad. But ships are but boards, sailors but men: there be land-rats and water-rats, water-thieves and land-thieves, I mean pirates, and then there is the peril of waters, winds and rocks. The man is, notwithstanding, sufficient. Three thousand ducats; I think I may take his bond.

Bass. Be assured you may.

Shy. I will be assured I may; and, that I may be assured, I will bethink me. May I speak with Antonio?

Bass. If it please you to dine with us.

Shy. Yes, to smell pork; to eat of the habitation which your prophet the Nazarite conjured the devil into. I will buy with you, sell with you, talk with you, walk with you, and so following, but I will not eat with you, drink with you, nor pray with you. What news on the Rialto? Who is he comes here? 40

Enter ANTONIO.

Bass. This is Signior Antonio.

Shy. [*Aside*] How like a fawning publican he looks!
I hate him for he is a Christian,
But more for that in low simplicity
He lends out money gratis and brings down
The rate of usance here with us in Venice.
If I can catch him once upon the hip,
I will feed fat the ancient grudge I bear him.
He hates our sacred nation, and he rails,
Even there where merchants most do congregate,
On me, my bargains and my well-won thrift, 51
Which he calls interest. Cursed be my tribe,
If I forgive him!

Bass.   Shylock, do you hear?

Shy. I am debating of my present store,
And, by the near guess of my memory,
I cannot instantly raise up the gross
Of full three thousand ducats. What of that?
Tubal, a wealthy Hebrew of my tribe,
Will furnish me. But soft! how many months
Do you desire? [*To Ant.*] Rest you fair, good
         signior; 60
Your worship was the last man in our mouths.

Set design for a Venetian street by F. Lloyd, 1856

---

1 *ducats.* The ducat was a Venetian gold coin.

7 *stead.* Help or assist.

17 *sufficient.* Acceptable as surety.

20 *Rialto.* The Exchange of Venice, where the Venetian merchants met twice a day.

Shylock and Bassanio. Engraving by Kenny Meadows from Barry Cornwall's *The Works of Shakespere*, 1846

35-36 *conjured the devil into.* A reference to the destruction of the Gaderene swine, St. Mark's Gospel, 5.

42 *fawning publican.* Tax-gatherer, a term of abuse.

47 *upon the hip.* At a disadvantage.

72-91 *When Jacob grazed . . . steal it not.* This passage paraphrases *Genesis* 27 and 30. Shylock argues that Jacob thrived by breeding sheep and received God's blessing. So too can money be made to breed and is likewise blessed.

80 *eanlings.* Young lambs.

112 *You call me misbeliever, cut-throat dog.* In Venice Jews were obliged to wear a circle of yellow cloth sewn into the breast of the outer garment, a long, loose coat of gaberdine.

William Charles Macready, the Victorian actor, as Shylock, Theatre Royal, Drury Lane, London, 1841

Ant. Shylock, although I neither lend nor
  borrow
By taking nor by giving of excess,
Yet, to supply the ripe wants of my friend,
I'll break a custom.   Is he yet possess'd
How much ye would?
  Shy.   Ay, ay, three thousand ducats.
  Ant. And for three months.
  Shy. I had forgot; three months; you told
  me so.
Well then, your bond; and let me see; but
  hear you;
Methought you said you neither lend nor borrow
Upon advantage.
  Ant.   I do never use it.   71
● *Shy.* When Jacob grazed his uncle Laban's
  sheep—
This Jacob from our holy Abram was,
As his wise mother wrought in his behalf,
The third possessor; ay, he was the third—
  Ant. And what of him? did he take interest?
  Shy. No, not take interest, not, as you would
  say,
Directly interest: mark what Jacob did.
When Laban and himself were compromised
● That all the eanlings which were streak'd and pied
Should fall as Jacob's hire, the ewes, being rank,
In the end of autumn turned to the rams,
And, when the work of generation was
Between these woolly breeders in the act,
The skilful shepherd peel'd me certain wands
And, in the doing of the deed of kind,
He stuck them up before the fulsome ewes,
Who then conceiving did in eaning time
Fall parti-colour'd lambs, and those were Jacob's.
This was a way to thrive, and he was blest: 90
And thrift is blessing, if men steal it not.
  Ant. This was a venture, sir, that Jacob
    served for;
A thing not in his power to bring to pass,
But sway'd and fashion'd by the hand of heaven.
Was this inserted to make interest good?
Or is your gold and silver ewes and rams?
  Shy. I cannot tell; I make it breed as fast:
But note me, signior.
  Ant.   Mark you this, Bassanio,
The devil can cite Scripture for his purpose.
An evil soul producing holy witness   100
Is like a villain with a smiling cheek,
A goodly apple rotten at the heart:
O, what a goodly outside falsehood hath!
  Shy. Three thousand ducats; 'tis a good
    round sum.
Three months from twelve; then, let me see;
    the rate—
  Ant. Well, Shylock, shall we be beholding
    to you?
  Shy. Signior Antonio, many a time and oft

In the Rialto you have rated me
About my moneys and my usances:
Still have I borne it with a patient shrug,   110
For sufferance is the badge of all our tribe.
● You call me misbeliever, cut-throat dog,
And spit upon my Jewish gaberdine,
And all for use of that which is mine own.
Well then, it now appears you need my help:
Go to, then; you come to me, and you say
'Shylock, we would have moneys:' you say so;
You, that did void your rheum upon my beard

And foot me as you spurn a stranger cur
Over your threshold: moneys is your suit.   120
What should I say to you?   Should I not say
'Hath a dog money? is it possible
A cur can lend three thousand ducats?'   Or
Shall I bend low and in a bondman's key,
With bated breath and whispering humbleness,
Say this;
'Fair sir, you spit on me on Wednesday last;
You spurn'd me such a day; another time
You call'd me dog; and for these courtesies
I'll lend you thus much moneys'?   130
   Ant.   I am as like to call thee so again,
To spit on thee again, to spurn thee too.
If thou wilt lend this money, lend it not
As to thy friends; for when did friendship take
A breed for barren metal of his friend?
But lend it rather to thine enemy,
Who, if he break, thou mayst with better face
Exact the penalty.
   Shy.   Why, look you, how you storm!
I would be friends with you and have your love,
Forget the shames that you have stain'd me with,
● Supply your present wants and take no doit   141
Of usance for my moneys, and you'll not hear me:
This is kind I offer.
   Bass.   This were kindness.
   Shy.   This kindness will I show.
Go with me to a notary, seal me there
● Your single bond; and, in a merry sport,
If you repay me not on such a day,
In such a place, such sum or sums as are
Express'd in the condition, let the forfeit
Be nominated for an equal pound   150
Of your fair flesh, to be cut off and taken
In what part of your body pleaseth me.
   Ant.   Content, i' faith: I'll seal to such a bond
And say there is much kindness in the Jew.
   Bass.   You shall not seal to such a bond for me:
I'll rather dwell in my necessity.
   Ant.   Why, fear not, man; I will not forfeit it:
Within these two months, that's a month before
This bond expires, I do expect return
Of thrice three times the value of this bond.   160
   Shy.   O father Abram, what these Chris-
     tians are,
Whose own hard dealings teaches them suspect
The thoughts of others!   Pray you, tell me this;
If he should break his day, what should I gain
By the exaction of the forfeiture?
A pound of man's flesh taken from a man
Is not so estimable, profitable neither,
As flesh of muttons, beefs, or goats.   I say,
To buy his favour, I extend this friendship:
If he will take it, so; if not, adieu;   170
And, for my love, I pray you wrong me not.
   Ant.   Yes, Shylock, I will seal unto this bond.
   Shy.   Then meet me forthwith at the notary's;
Give him direction for this merry bond,
And I will go and purse the ducats straight,
See to my house, left in the fearful guard
Of an unthrifty knave, and presently
I will be with you.
   Ant.   Hie thee, gentle Jew.   [*Exit Shylock.*
The Hebrew will turn Christian: he grows kind.
   Bass.   I like not fair terms and a villain's mind.
   Ant.   Come on: in this there can be no dismay;
My ships come home a month before the day.
                   [*Exeunt.*

Antonio (Anthony Nicholls), Bassanio (Basil Hoskins)
and Shylock (Emlyn Williams), Stratford-upon-Avon,
1956

---

141 *doit.* A very small sum worth half a farthing.

146 *single bond.* Made with one person alone, without
security.

17 *scanted*. Restricted.

Morocco: 'I pray you, lead me to the caskets'. Engraving from a design by F. Hayman for Hanmer's edition of Shakespeare's works, 1744

25 *Sophy*. King of Persia.

26 *Sultan Solyman*. The Sultan of Turkey who in 1535 fought an unsuccessful campaign against the Persians.

32 *Lichas*. The servant who unwittingly brought Hercules (Alcides) the poisoned garment that caused his death.

4 *Launcelot Gobbo*. From the Italian *'gobbo'*, hunchbacked.

Gobbo, the hunchback from *commedia dell'arte*. Etching by Jacques Callot (1592–1635)

ACT II.

SCENE I. *Belmont. A room in* PORTIA'S *house.*

Flourish of cornets. Enter the PRINCE OF MOROCCO *and his train;* PORTIA, NERISSA, *and others attending.*

Mor.   Mislike me not for my complexion,
The shadow'd livery of the burnish'd sun,
To whom I am a neighbour and near bred.
Bring me the fairest creature northward born,
Where Phœbus' fire scarce thaws the icicles,
And let us make incision for your love,
To prove whose blood is reddest, his or mine.
I tell thee, lady, this aspect of mine
Hath fear'd the valiant: by my love, I swear
The best-regarded virgins of our clime   10
Have loved it too: I would not change this hue,
Except to steal your thoughts, my gentle queen.
Por.   In terms of choice I am not solely led
By nice direction of a maiden's eyes;
Besides, the lottery of my destiny
Bars me the right of voluntary choosing:
But if my father had not scanted me
And hedged me by his wit, to yield myself
His wife who wins me by that means I told you,
Yourself, renowned prince, then stood as fair   20
As any comer I have look'd on yet
For my affection.
Mor.   Even for that I thank you:
Therefore, I pray you, lead me to the caskets
To try my fortune.   By this scimitar
That slew the Sophy and a Persian prince
That won three fields of Sultan Solyman,
I would outstare the sternest eyes that look,
Outbrave the heart most daring on the earth,
Pluck the young sucking cubs from the she-bear,
Yea, mock the lion when he roars for prey,   30
To win thee, lady.   But, alas the while!
If Hercules and Lichas play at dice
Which is the better man, the greater throw
May turn by fortune from the weaker hand:
So is Alcides beaten by his page;
And so may I, blind fortune leading me,
Miss that which one unworthier may attain,
And die with grieving.
Por.   You must take your chance,
And either not attempt to choose at all
Or swear before you choose, if you choose wrong
Never to speak to lady afterward   41
In way of marriage: therefore be advised.
Mor.   Nor will not.   Come, bring me unto
my chance.
Por.   First, forward to the temple: after dinner
Your hazard shall be made.
Mor.   Good fortune then!
To make me blest or cursed'st among men.
                              [*Cornets, and exeunt.*

SCENE II. *Venice.   A street.*

Enter LAUNCELOT.

Laun.   Certainly my conscience will serve me to run from this Jew my master.   The fiend is at mine elbow and tempts me saying to me 'Gobbo, Launcelot Gobbo, good Launcelot,' or 'good Gobbo,' or 'good Launcelot Gobbo, use your legs, take the start, run away.'   My conscience says 'No; take heed, honest Launcelot;

take heed, honest Gobbo,' or, as aforesaid, 'honest Launcelot Gobbo; do not run; scorn running with thy heels.' Well, the most courageous fiend bids me pack: 'Via!' says the fiend; 'away!' says the fiend; 'for the heavens, rouse up a brave mind,' says the fiend, 'and run.' Well, my conscience, hanging about the neck of my heart, says very wisely to me 'My honest friend Launcelot, being an honest man's son,' or rather an honest woman's son; for, indeed, my father did something smack, something grow to, he had a kind of taste; well, my conscience says 'Launcelot, budge not.' 'Budge,' says the fiend. 'Budge not,' says my conscience. 'Conscience,' say I, 'you counsel well;' 'Fiend,' say I, 'you counsel well:' to be ruled by my conscience, I should stay with the Jew my master, who, God bless the mark, is a kind of devil; and, to run away from the Jew, I should be ruled by the fiend, who, saving your reverence, is the devil himself. Certainly the Jew is the very devil incarnal; and, in my conscience, my conscience is but a kind of hard conscience, to offer to counsel me to stay with the Jew. The fiend gives the more friendly counsel: I will run, fiend; my heels are at your command; I will run.

Enter Old GOBBO, *with a basket.*

Gob. Master young man, you, I pray you, which is the way to master Jew's?

Laun. [*Aside*] O heavens, this is my true-
• begotten father! who, being more than sand-blind, high-gravel blind, knows me not: I will try confusions with him.

Gob. Master young gentleman, I pray you, which is the way to master Jew's?   41

Laun. Turn up on your right hand at the next turning, but, at the next turning of all, on your left; marry, at the very next turning, turn of no hand, but turn down indirectly to the Jew's house.

• *Gob.* By God's sonties, 'twill be a hard way to hit. Can you tell me whether one Launcelot, that dwells with him, dwell with him or no?

• *Laun.* Talk you of young Master Launcelot? [*Aside*] Mark me now; now will I raise the waters. Talk you of young Master Launcelot?

Gob. No master, sir, but a poor man's son: his father, though I say it, is an honest exceeding poor man and, God be thanked, well to live.

Laun. Well, let his father be what a' will, we talk of young Master Launcelot.

Gob. Your worship's friend and Launcelot, sir.

Laun. But I pray you, ergo, old man, ergo, I beseech you, talk you of young Master Launcelot?

Gob. Of Launcelot, an't please your mastership.

Laun. Ergo, Master Launcelot. Talk not of Master Launcelot, father; for the young gentleman, according to Fates and Destinies and such odd sayings, the Sisters Three and such branches of learning, is indeed deceased, or, as you would say in plain terms, gone to heaven.

Gob. Marry, God forbid! the boy was the very staff of my age, my very prop.   70

Laun. Do I look like a cudgel or a hovel-post, a staff or a prop? Do you know me, father?

Gob. Alack the day, I know you not, young

Drinkwater Meadows as Old Gobbo, Princess's Theatre, London, 1858

37-38 *sand-blind.* Almost blind (semi-blind). *high-gravel.* A pun on 'sand'.

47 *sonties.* Saints.

50 *Master Launcelot.* A term applied to an employer. Launcelot pretends to his father that he has improved his station and is no longer a servant.

Old Gobbo and Launcelot. Engraving by Kenny Meadows from Barry Cornwall's *The Works of Shakspere*, 1846

---

100 *fill-horse*. Draught-horse.

110 *set up my rest*. Determined.

128 *Gramercy*. Many thanks.

133 *infection*. Affection.

139 *cater-cousins*. Close friends.

gentleman : but, I pray you, tell me, is my boy, God rest his soul, alive or dead ?

Laun.   Do you not know me, father ?

Gob.   Alack, sir, I am sand-blind ; I know you not.

Laun.   Nay, indeed, if you had your eyes, you might fail of the knowing me : it is a wise father that knows his own child. Well, old man, I will tell you news of your son : give me your blessing : truth will come to light ; murder cannot be hid long ; a man's son may, but at the length truth will out.

Gob.   Pray you, sir, stand up : I am sure you are not Launcelot, my boy.

Laun.   Pray you, let's have no more fooling about it, but give me your blessing : I am Launcelot, your boy that was, your son that is, your child that shall be.   91

Gob.   I cannot think you are my son.

Laun.   I know not what I shall think of that : but I am Launcelot, the Jew's man, and I am sure Margery your wife is my mother.

Gob.   Her name is Margery, indeed : I'll be sworn, if thou be Launcelot, thou art mine own flesh and blood. Lord worshipped might he be ! what a beard hast thou got ! thou hast got more hair on thy chin than Dobbin my fill-horse has on his tail.   101

Laun.   It should seem, then, that Dobbin's tail grows backward : I am sure he had more hair of his tail than I have of my face when I last saw him.

Gob.   Lord, how art thou changed ! How dost thou and thy master agree ? I have brought him a present. How 'gree you now ?

Laun.   Well, well : but, for mine own part, as I have set up my rest to run away, so I will not rest till I have run some ground. My master's a very Jew : give him a present ! give him a halter : I am famished in his service ; you may tell every finger I have with my ribs. Father, I am glad you are come : give me your present to one Master Bassanio, who, indeed, gives rare new liveries : if I serve not him, I will run as far as God has any ground. O rare fortune ! here comes the man : to him, father ; for I am a Jew, if I serve the Jew any longer.   120

Enter BASSANIO, *with* LEONARDO *and other followers.*

Bass.   You may do so ; but let it be so hasted that supper be ready at the farthest by five of the clock. See these letters delivered ; put the liveries to making, and desire Gratiano to come anon to my lodging.   [*Exit a Servant.*

Laun.   To him, father.

Gob.   God bless your worship !

Bass.   Gramercy ! wouldst thou aught with me ?

Gob.   Here's my son, sir, a poor boy,—

Laun.   Not a poor boy, sir, but the rich Jew's man ; that would, sir, as my father shall specify—

Gob.   He hath a great infection, sir, as one would say, to serve,—

Laun.   Indeed, the short and the long is, I serve the Jew, and have a desire, as my father shall specify—

Gob.   His master and he, saving your worship's reverence, are scarce cater-cousins—

Laun. To be brief, the very truth is that the Jew, having done me wrong, doth cause me, as
• my father, being, I hope, an old man, shall frutify unto you—

Gob. I have here a dish of doves that I would bestow upon your worship, and my suit is—

• *Laun.* In very brief, the suit is impertinent to myself, as your worship shall know by this honest old man ; and, though I say it, though old man, yet poor man, my father.

Bass. One speak for both. What would you?

Laun. Serve you, sir.   151

• *Gob.* That is the very defect of the matter, sir.

Bass. I know thee well ; thou hast obtain'd thy suit :
Shylock thy master spoke with me this day,
• And hath preferr'd thee, if it be preferment
To leave a rich Jew's service, to become
The follower of so poor a gentleman.

Laun. The old proverb is very well parted between my master Shylock and you, sir : you have the grace of God, sir, and he hath enough.

Bass. Thou speak'st it well. Go, father, with thy son.
Take leave of thy old master and inquire
My lodging out. Give him a livery
• More guarded than his fellows' : see it done.

Laun. Father, in. I cannot get a service, no ;
I have ne'er a tongue in my head. Well, if any
• man in Italy have a fairer table which doth offer to swear upon a book, I shall have good fortune.
Go to, here's a simple line of life : here's a small trifle of wives : alas, fifteen wives is nothing !
eleven widows and nine maids is a simple coming-in for one man : and then to 'scape drowning thrice, and to be in peril of my life with the edge of a feather-bed ; here are simple scapes. Well, if Fortune be a woman, she's a good wench for
• this gear. Father, come ; I'll take my leave of the Jew in the twinkling of an eye.

               [*Exeunt Launcelot and Old Gobbo.*

Bass. I pray thee, good Leonardo, think on this :
These things being bought and orderly bestow'd,
Return in haste, for I do feast to-night   180
My best-esteem'd acquaintance : hie thee, go.

Leon. My best endeavours shall be done herein.

            Enter GRATIANO.

Gra. Where is your master?

Leon.   Yonder, sir, he walks. [*Exit.*

Gra. Signior Bassanio !

Bass. Gratiano !

Gra. I have a suit to you.

Bass.   You have obtain'd it.

Gra. You must not deny me : I must go with you to Belmont.

Bass. Why, then you must. But hear thee, Gratiano ;
Thou art too wild, too rude and bold of voice ;
Parts that become thee happily enough   191
And in such eyes as ours appear not faults ;
But where thou art not known, why, there they show
Something too liberal. Pray thee, take pain
To allay with some cold drops of modesty
Thy skipping spirit, lest through thy wild behaviour

142-143 *frutify.* Certify.

146 *impertinent.* Launcelot means 'pertinent'.

152 *defect.* Effect.

155 *preferr'd.* Recommended for advancement.

164 *guarded.* Braided.

J. B. Buckstone, the Victorian actor, as Launcelot Gobbo. From J. O. Halliwell's *The Complete Works of William Shakspere*, 1853

167 *table.* Palm of the hand.

176 *gear.* Business.

205 *ostent*. Appearance.

1 *slink away in supper-time*. Shakespeare makes use of the masque as part of the evening's entertainment. It occurs in many of his plays. Inigo Jones produced some of his most famous designs for the masques of Ben Jonson.

Zenobia from Ben Jonson's *Masque of Queens*, 1609.
Design by Inigo Jones

I be misconstrued in the place I go to
And lose my hopes.
    Gra.   Signior Bassanio, hear me:
If I do not put on a sober habit,   199
Talk with respect and swear but now and then,
Wear prayer-books in my pocket, look demurely,
Nay more, while grace is saying, hood mine eyes
Thus with my hat, and sigh and say 'amen,'
Use all the observance of civility,
Like one well studied in a sad ostent
To please his grandam, never trust me more.
    Bass.   Well, we shall see your bearing.
    Gra.   Nay, but I bar to-night: you shall not gauge me
By what we do to-night.
    Bass.   No, that were pity:
I would entreat you rather to put on   210
Your boldest suit of mirth, for we have friends
That purpose merriment.   But fare you well:
I have some business.
    Gra.   And I must to Lorenzo and the rest:
But we will visit you at supper-time.   [*Exeunt.*

SCENE III.   *The same.   A room in* SHYLOCK'S *house.*

Enter JESSICA *and* LAUNCELOT.

    Jes.   I am sorry thou wilt leave my father so:
Our house is hell, and thou, a merry devil,
Didst rob it of some taste of tediousness.
But fare thee well, there is a ducat for thee:
And, Launcelot, soon at supper shalt thou see
Lorenzo, who is thy new master's guest:
Give him this letter; do it secretly;
And so farewell: I would not have my father
See me in talk with thee.   9
    Laun.   Adieu! tears exhibit my tongue.   Most beautiful pagan, most sweet Jew! if a Christian did not play the knave and get thee, I am much deceived.   But, adieu: these foolish drops do something drown my manly spirit: adieu.
    Jes.   Farewell, good Launcelot.
                      [*Exit Launcelot.*
Alack, what heinous sin is it in me
To be ashamed to be my father's child!
But though I am a daughter to his blood,
I am not to his manners.   O Lorenzo,
If thou keep promise, I shall end this strife,   20
Become a Christian and thy loving wife. [*Exit.*

SCENE IV.   *The same.   A street.*

Enter GRATIANO, LORENZO, SALARINO, *and* SALANIO.

    Lor.   Nay, we will slink away in supper-time,
Disguise us at my lodging and return,
All in an hour.
    Gra.   We have not made good preparation.
    Salar.   We have not spoke us yet of torch-bearers.
    Salan.   'Tis vile, unless it may be quaintly order'd,
And better in my mind not undertook.
    Lor.   'Tis now but four o'clock: we have two hours
To furnish us.

Enter LAUNCELOT, *with a letter.*

Friend Launcelot, what's the news?
Laun.   An it shall please you to break up this,
it shall seem to signify.   11
Lor.   I know the hand : in faith, 'tis a fair hand ;
And whiter than the paper it writ on
Is the fair hand that writ.
Gra.   Love-news, in faith.
Laun.   By your leave, sir.
Lor.   Whither goest thou?
Laun.   Marry, sir, to bid my old master the
Jew to sup to-night with my new master the
Christian.
Lor.   Hold here, take this : tell gentle Jessica
I will not fail her ; speak it privately.   21
Go, gentlemen,   [*Exit Launcelot.*
Will you prepare you for this masque to-night?
I am provided of a torch-bearer.
Salar.   Ay, marry, I 'll be gone about it straight.
Salan.   And so will I.
Lor.   Meet me and Gratiano
At Gratiano's lodging some hour hence.
Salar.   'Tis good we do so.
                              [*Exeunt Salar. and Salan.*
Gra.   Was not that letter from fair Jessica ?
Lor.   I must needs tell thee all.   She hath
          directed   30
How I shall take her from her father's house,
What gold and jewels she is furnish'd with,
What page's suit she hath in readiness.
If e'er the Jew her father come to heaven,
It will be for his gentle daughter's sake :
And never dare misfortune cross her foot,
Unless she do it under this excuse,
That she is issue to a faithless Jew.
Come, go with me ; peruse this as thou goest :
Fair Jessica shall be my torch-bearer.   [*Exeunt.*

SCENE V. *The same. Before* SHYLOCK'S *house.*

Enter SHYLOCK *and* LAUNCELOT.

Shy.   Well, thou shalt see, thy eyes shall be
          thy judge,
The difference of old Shylock and Bassanio :—
What, Jessica !—thou shalt not gormandise,
As thou hast done with me :—What, Jessica !—
And sleep and snore, and rend apparel out ;—
Why, Jessica, I say !
Laun.   Why, Jessica !
Shy.   Who bids thee call?   I do not bid thee
          call.
Laun.   Your worship was wont to tell me that
I could do nothing without bidding.

Enter JESSICA.

Jes.   Call you? what is your will?   10
Shy.   I am bid forth to supper, Jessica :
There are my keys.   But wherefore should I go?
I am not bid for love ; they flatter me :
But yet I 'll go in hate, to feed upon
The prodigal Christian.   Jessica, my girl,
Look to my house.   I am right loath to go :
There is some ill a-brewing towards my rest,
For I did dream of money-bags to-night.
Laun.   I beseech you, sir, go : my young
master doth expect your reproach.   20
Shy.   So do I his.

20 *gentle.* A pun on 'gentile'.

Shylock and Jessica. Illustration by Thomas Lowinsky
from *Players' Shakespeare*, 1923

20 *reproach.* Launcelot means 'approach'.

33 *varnish'd faces*. Refers to the visors of the masquers.

43 *Jewess' eye*. A Jew's eye denoted wealth.

44 *Hagar's offspring*. Hagar was a gentile and bond-woman to Abraham's wife, Sarah. Her son, Ishmael, was an out-cast or 'wild man'.

Shylock: 'What says that fool of Hagar's offspring'.
Painting by Robert Smirke (1752–1845)

46 *patch*. Fool.

5-7 *O, ten times faster . . . faith unforfeited*. The doves of Venus attend a betrothal more readily than they would a marriage.

14 *younker*. Young fellow.

15 *scarfed bark*. Ship decorated with flags.

Laun. And they have conspired together, I will not say you shall see a masque; but if you do, then it was not for nothing that my nose fell a-bleeding on Black-Monday last at six o'clock i' the morning, falling out that year on Ash-Wednesday was four year, in the afternoon.

Shy. What, are there masques? Hear you me, Jessica:
Lock up my doors; and when you hear the drum
And the vile squealing of the wry-neck'd fife,   30
Clamber not you up to the casements then,
Nor thrust your head into the public street
● To gaze on Christian fools with varnish'd faces,
But stop my house's ears, I mean my casements:
Let not the sound of shallow foppery enter
My sober house.   By Jacob's staff, I swear,
I have no mind of feasting forth to-night:
But I will go.   Go you before me, sirrah;
Say I will come.
Laun. I will go before, sir.   Mistress, look out at window, for all this;   41
  There will come a Christian by,
●   Will be worth a Jewess' eye.   [*Exit.*
● *Shy.* What says that fool of Hagar's offspring, ha?
Jes. His words were 'Farewell mistress;' nothing else.
● *Shy.* The patch is kind enough, but a huge feeder;
Snail-slow in profit, and he sleeps by day
More than the wild-cat: drones hive not with me;
Therefore I part with him, and part with him
To one that I would have him help to waste   50
His borrow'd purse.   Well, Jessica, go in:
Perhaps I will return immediately:
Do as I bid you; shut doors after you:
Fast bind, fast find.
A proverb never stale in thrifty mind.   [*Exit.*
Jes. Farewell; and if my fortune be not crost,
I have a father, you a daughter, lost.   [*Exit.*

SCENE VI.   *The same.*

Enter GRATIANO *and* SALARINO, *masqued.*

Gra. This is the pent-house under which Lorenzo
Desired us to make stand.
Salar.   His hour is almost past.
Gra. And it is marvel he out-dwells his hour,
For lovers ever run before the clock.
● *Salar.* O, ten times faster Venus' pigeons fly
To seal love's bonds new-made, than they are wont
To keep obliged faith unforfeited!
Gra. That ever holds: who riseth from a feast
With that keen appetite that he sits down?
Where is the horse that doth untread again   10
His tedious measures with the unbated fire
That he did pace them first? All things that are,
Are with more spirit chased than enjoy'd.
● How like a younker or a prodigal
● The scarfed bark puts from her native bay,
Hugg'd and embraced by the strumpet wind!
How like the prodigal doth she return,
With over-weather'd ribs and ragged sails,
Lean, rent and beggar'd by the strumpet wind!
Salar. Here comes Lorenzo: more of this hereafter.   20

Enter LORENZO.

Lor. Sweet friends, your patience for my
    long abode;
Not I, but my affairs, have made you wait:
When you shall please to play the thieves for
    wives,
I'll watch as long for you then.   Approach;
Here dwells my father Jew.   Ho! who's within?

Enter JESSICA, *above, in boy's clothes.*

Jes. Who are you?   Tell me, for more cer-
    tainty,
Albeit I'll swear that I do know your tongue.
    Lor. Lorenzo, and thy love.
    Jes. Lorenzo, certain, and my love indeed,
For who love I so much?   And now who knows
But you, Lorenzo, whether I am yours?   31
    Lor. Heaven and thy thoughts are witness
        that thou art.
    Jes. Here, catch this casket; it is worth
        the pains.
I am glad 'tis night, you do not look on me,
• For I am much ashamed of my exchange:
But love is blind and lovers cannot see
The pretty follies that themselves commit;
For if they could, Cupid himself would blush
To see me thus transformed to a boy.
    Lor. Descend, for you must be my torch-
        bearer.   40
    Jes. What, must I hold a candle to my
        shames?
• They in themselves, good sooth, are too too light.
• Why, 'tis an office of discovery, love;
And I should be obscured.
    Lor.   So are you, sweet,
Even in the lovely garnish of a boy.
But come at once;
For the close night doth play the runaway,
And we are stay'd for at Bassanio's feast.
    Jes. I will make fast the doors, and gild my-
        self
With some more ducats, and be with you straight.
                            [*Exit above.* 50
    Gra. Now, by my hood, a Gentile and no
        Jew.
    Lor. Beshrew me but I love her heartily;
For she is wise, if I can judge of her,
And fair she is, if that mine eyes be true,
And true she is, as she hath proved herself,
And therefore, like herself, wise, fair and true,
Shall she be placed in my constant soul.

Enter JESSICA, *below.*

What, art thou come?   On, gentlemen; away!
Our masquing mates by this time for us stay.
                [*Exit with Jessica and Salarino.*

Enter ANTONIO.

Ant. Who's there?   60
Gra. Signior Antonio!
Ant. Fie, fie, Gratiano!   where are all the
    rest?
'Tis nine o'clock: our friends all stay for you.
No masque to-night: the wind is come about;
Bassanio presently will go aboard:
I have sent twenty out to seek for you.
    Gra. I am glad on't: I desire no more delight
Than to be under sail and gone to-night. [*Exeunt.*

35 *exchange.* Disguise as a boy.

42 *light.* Wanton or flippant.

43 *discovery.* Jessica is saying that her escape could be revealed.

30 *disabling*. Disparagement.

41 *Hyrcanian deserts*. South of the Caspian sea.

50 *base*. Lead is a base metal.

51 *cerecloth*. The waxed sheet used for embalming.

SCENE. VII. *Belmont. A room in*
PORTIA'S *house*.

Flourish of cornets.   Enter PORTIA, *with the*
PRINCE OF MOROCCO, *and their trains*.

Por. Go draw aside the curtains and discover
The several caskets to this noble prince.
Now make your choice.
   Mor. The first, of gold, who this inscription
      bears,
'Who chooseth me shall gain what many men
      desire ;'
The second, silver, which this promise carries,
'Who chooseth me shall get as much as he de-
      serves ;'
This third, dull lead, with warning all as blunt,
'Who chooseth me must give and hazard all he
      hath.'
How shall I know if I do choose the right?   10
   Por. The one of them contains my picture,
      prince :
If you choose that, then I am yours withal.
   Mor. Some god direct my judgement! Let me
      see ;
I will survey the inscriptions back again.
What says this leaden casket?
'Who chooseth me must give and hazard all he
      hath.'
Must give : for what? for lead? hazard for lead?
This casket threatens.   Men that hazard all
Do it in hope of fair advantages :
A golden mind stoops not to shows of dross ;   20
I'll then nor give nor hazard aught for lead.
What says the silver with her virgin hue?
'Who chooseth me shall get as much as he de-
      serves.'
As much as he deserves ! Pause there, Morocco,
And weigh thy value with an even hand :
If thou be'st rated by thy estimation,
Thou dost deserve enough ; and yet enough
May not extend so far as to the lady :
And yet to be afeard of my deserving
●Were but a weak disabling of myself.   30
As much as I deserve !   Why, that's the lady :
I do in birth deserve her, and in fortunes,
In graces and in qualities of breeding ;
But more than these, in love I do deserve.
What if I stray'd no further, but chose here?
Let's see once more this saying graved in gold ;
'Who chooseth me shall gain what many men
      desire.'
Why, that's the lady ; all the world desires her ;
From the four corners of the earth they come,
To kiss this shrine, this mortal-breathing saint : 40
●The Hyrcanian deserts and the vasty wilds
Of wide Arabia are as throughfares now
For princes to come view fair Portia :
The watery kingdom, whose ambitious head
Spits in the face of heaven, is no bar
To stop the foreign spirits, but they come,
As o'er a brook, to see fair Portia.
One of these three contains her heavenly picture.
Is 't like that lead contains her? 'Twere damnation
●To think so base a thought : it were too gross   50
●To rib her cerecloth in the obscure grave.
Or shall I think in silver she's immured,
Being ten times undervalued to tried gold?
O sinful thought !   Never so rich a gem

Was set in worse than gold.   They have in Eng-
    land
A coin that bears the figure of an angel
Stamped in gold, but that's insculp'd upon;
But here an angel in a golden bed
Lies all within.   Deliver me the key:
Here do I choose, and thrive I as I may!   60
    Por.   There, take it, prince; and if my form
        lie there,
Then I am yours. [*He unlocks the golden casket.*
    Mor.   O hell! what have we here?
A carrion Death, within whose empty eye
There is a written scroll!   I'll read the writing.
[*Reads*] All that glisters is not gold;
            Often have you heard that told:
            Many a man his life hath sold
            But my outside to behold:
            Gilded tombs do worms infold.
            Had you been as wise as bold,   70
            Young in limbs, in judgement old,
            Your answer had not been inscroll'd:
            Fare you well; your suit is cold.

        Cold, indeed; and labour lost:
        Then, farewell, heat, and welcome, frost!
Portia, adieu.   I have too grieved a heart
To take a tedious leave: thus losers part.
        [*Exit with his train.   Flourish of cornets.*
    Por.   A gentle riddance.   Draw the curtains, go.
Let all of his complexion choose me so. [*Exeunt.*

SCENE VIII.   *Venice.   A street.*

Enter SALARINO *and* SALANIO.

Salar.   Why, man, I saw Bassanio under sail:
With him is Gratiano gone along;
And in their ship I am sure Lorenzo is not.
    Salan.   The villain Jew with outcries raised
        the duke,
Who went with him to search Bassanio's ship.
    Salar.   He came too late, the ship was under
        sail:
But there the duke was given to understand
That in a gondola were seen together
Lorenzo and his amorous Jessica:
Besides, Antonio certified the duke   10
They were not with Bassanio in his ship.
    Salan.   I never heard a passion so confused,
So strange, outrageous, and so variable,
As the dog Jew did utter in the streets:
'My daughter! O my ducats! O my daughter!
Fled with a Christian! O my Christian ducats!
Justice! the law! my ducats, and my daughter!
A sealed bag, two sealed bags of ducats,
Of double ducats, stolen from me by my daughter!
And jewels, two stones, two rich and precious
    stones,   20
Stolen by my daughter! Justice! find the girl;
She hath the stones upon her, and the ducats.'
    Salar.   Why, all the boys in Venice follow
        him,
Crying, his stones, his daughter, and his ducats.
    Salan.   Let good Antonio look he keep his day,
Or he shall pay for this.
    Salar.   Marry, well remember'd.
I reason'd with a Frenchman yesterday,
Who told me, in the narrow seas that part
The French and English, there miscarried
A vessel of our country richly fraught: 30

75 *farewell, heat, and welcome, frost.* An inversion of
the old proverb.

Morocco: 'Here do I choose . . .' Engraving from a
design by H. Gravelot from Theobald's edition of
Shakespeare's works, 1740

25 *keep his day.* Fulfil the bond.

27 *reason'd.* Talked.

39 *Slubber.* Perform carelessly or hastily. *servitor.* Servant.

Costume design for the Prince of Arragon by Alan Tagg, Stratford-upon-Avon, 1956

I thought upon Antonio when he told me;
And wish'd in silence that it were not his.
   Salan. You were best to tell Antonio what
     you hear;
Yet do not suddenly, for it may grieve him.
   Salar. A kinder gentleman treads not the
     earth.
I saw Bassanio and Antonio part:
Bassanio told him he would make some speed
Of his return: he answer'd, 'Do not so;
• Slubber not business for my sake, Bassanio,
But stay the very riping of the time;   40
And for the Jew's bond which he hath of me,
Let it not enter in your mind of love:
Be merry, and employ your chiefest thoughts
To courtship and such fair ostents of love
As shall conveniently become you there:'
And even there, his eye being big with tears,
Turning his face, he put his hand behind him,
And with affection wondrous sensible
He wrung Bassanio's hand; and so they parted.
   Salan. I think he only loves the world for
     him.   50
I pray thee, let us go and find him out
And quicken his embraced heaviness
With some delight or other.
   Salar.   Do we so. [*Exeunt.*

SCENE IX.   *Belmont. A room in* PORTIA'S
house.

Enter NERISSA *with a* Servitor.

   Ner. Quick, quick, I pray thee; draw the
     curtain straight:
The Prince of Arragon hath ta'en his oath,
And comes to his election presently.

Flourish of cornets. Enter the PRINCE OF
ARRAGON, PORTIA, *and their trains.*

   Por. Behold, there stand the caskets, noble
     prince:
If you choose that wherein I am contain'd,
Straight shall our nuptial rites be solemnized:
But if you fail, without more speech, my lord,
You must be gone from hence immediately.
   Ar. I am enjoin'd by oath to observe three
     things:
First, never to unfold to any one   10
Which casket 'twas I chose; next, if I fail
Of the right casket, never in my life
To woo a maid in way of marriage:
Lastly,
If I do fail in fortune of my choice,
Immediately to leave you and be gone.
   Por. To these injunctions every one doth
     swear
That comes to hazard for my worthless self.
   Ar. And so have I address'd me. Fortune
     now
To my heart's hope! Gold; silver; and base lead.
'Who chooseth me must give and hazard all he
     hath.'   21
You shall look fairer, ere I give or hazard.
What says the golden chest? ha! let me see:
'Who chooseth me shall gain what many men
     desire.'
What many men desire! that 'many' may be
     meant
By the fool multitude, that choose by show,

Not learning more than the fond eye doth teach;
• Which pries not to the interior, but, like the martlet,
Builds in the weather on the outward wall,
Even in the force and road of casualty.   30
I will not choose what many men desire,
• Because I will not jump with common spirits
And rank me with the barbarous multitudes.
Why, then to thee, thou silver treasure-house;
Tell me once more what title thou dost bear:
'Who chooseth me shall get as much as he deserves:'
And well said too; for who shall go about
• To cozen fortune and be honourable
Without the stamp of merit?   Let none presume
To wear an undeserved dignity.   40
• O, that estates, degrees and offices
Were not derived corruptly, and that clear honour
Were purchased by the merit of the wearer!
• How many then should cover that stand bare!
How many be commanded that command!
How much low peasantry would then be glean'd
From the true seed of honour! and how much honour
Pick'd from the chaff and ruin of the times
To be new-varnish'd!   Well, but to my choice:
'Who chooseth me shall get as much as he deserves.'   50
• I will assume desert.   Give me a key for this,
And instantly unlock my fortunes here.
                    [*He opens the silver casket.*
    Por.   Too long a pause for that which you find there.
    Ar.   What's here? the portrait of a blinking idiot,
Presenting me a schedule!   I will read it.
How much unlike art thou to Portia!
How much unlike my hopes and my deservings!
'Who chooseth me shall have as much as he deserves.'
Did I deserve no more than a fool's head?
Is that my prize? are my deserts no better?   60
    Por.   To offend, and judge, are distinct offices
And of opposed natures.
    Ar.   What is here?

[*Reads*] The fire seven times tried this:
          Seven times tried that judgement is,
          That did never choose amiss.
          Some there be that shadows kiss;
          Such have but a shadow's bliss:
•   There be fools alive, I wis,
•   Silver'd o'er; and so was this.
          Take what wife you will to bed,   70
          I will ever be your head:
          So be gone: you are sped.

          Still more fool I shall appear
          By the time I linger here:
          With one fool's head I came to woo,
          But I go away with two.
          Sweet, adieu.   I'll keep my oath,
•   Patiently to bear my wroth.
                    [*Exeunt Arragon and train.*

    Por.   Thus hath the candle singed the moth.
O, these deliberate fools! when they do choose,
They have the wisdom by their wit to lose.   81
    Ner.   The ancient saying is no heresy,
Hanging and wiving goes by destiny.
    Por.   Come, draw the curtain, Nerissa.

28 *martlet.* A swift or house martin.

32 *jump.* Agree.

38 *cozen.* Deceive.

41 *estates, degrees and offices.* Possessions, social rank and public appointments.

44 *cover.* Wear hats. The head was uncovered in the presence of a superior.

51 *assume desert.* i.e. claim what I deserve.

68 *I wis.* Certainly.

69 *Silver'd o'er.* Silver-haired and therefore looking wise. *and so was this.* It is probable that Arragon is looking at his own reflection in a silver mirror.

78 *wroth.* 'Truth', meaning misfortune, was intended, rather than 'wrath'.

89 *sensible regreets*. Substantial greetings, not words alone, but gifts.

90 *commends . . . breath*. Commendations and courteous speech.

101 *Bassanio, lord Love*. Since Cupid is mentioned in the preceding line Portia is saying, 'Cupid, may this newcomer be Bassanio'.

10 *knapped ginger*. Nibbled ginger. Old women were supposed to need and like ginger to restore their sexual appetite.

12-13 *slips of prolixity*. Prolix.

17 *full stop*. i.e. stop this runaway talk and come to the point.

32 *fledged*. Ready to fly. *complexion*. Nature.

Shylock: 'You knew . . . none so well as you, of my daughter's flight'. From a painting by Sir John Gilbert, 1864

Enter a Servant.

Serv.   Where is my lady?
Por.   Here: what would my lord?
Serv.   Madam, there is alighted at your gate
A young Venetian, one that comes before
To signify the approaching of his lord;
● From whom he bringeth sensible regreets,
● To wit, besides commends and courteous breath,
Gifts of rich value.   Yet I have not seen   91
So likely an ambassador of love:
A day in April never came so sweet,
To show how costly summer was at hand,
As this fore-spurrer comes before his lord.
Por.   No more, I pray thee: I am half afeard
Thou wilt say anon he is some kin to thee,
Thou spend'st such high-day wit in praising him.
Come, come, Nerissa; for I long to see
Quick Cupid's post that comes so mannerly.   100
● *Ner.*   Bassanio, lord Love, if thy will it be!
[*Exeunt.*

ACT III.

Scene I.   *Venice.   A street.*

Enter Salanio *and* Salarino.

Salan.   Now, what news on the Rialto?
Salar.   Why, yet it lives there unchecked that Antonio hath a ship of rich lading wrecked on the narrow seas; the Goodwins, I think they call the place; a very dangerous flat and fatal, where the carcases of many a tall ship lie buried, as they say, if my gossip Report be an honest woman of her word.
Salan.   I would she were as lying a gossip in
● that as ever knapped ginger or made her neighbours believe she wept for the death of a third
● husband.   But it is true, without any slips of prolixity or crossing the plain highway of talk, that the good Antonio, the honest Antonio,——
O that I had a title good enough to keep his name company!—
Salar.   Come, the full stop.
Salan.   Ha! what sayest thou?   Why, the end is, he hath lost a ship.
Salar.   I would it might prove the end of his losses.   21
Salan.   Let me say 'amen' betimes, lest the devil cross my prayer, for here he comes in the likeness of a Jew.

Enter Shylock.

How now, Shylock! what news among the merchants?
Shy.   You knew, none so well, none so well as you, of my daughter's flight.
Salar.   That's certain: I, for my part, knew the tailor that made the wings she flew withal.   30
Salan.   And Shylock, for his own part, knew
● the bird was fledged; and then it is the complexion of them all to leave the dam.
Shy.   She is damned for it.
Salar.   That's certain, if the devil may be her judge.
Shy.   My own flesh and blood to rebel!
Salan.   Out upon it, old carrion! rebels it at these years?   39
Shy.   I say, my daughter is my flesh and blood.
Salar.   There is more difference between thy

flesh and hers than between jet and ivory; more
• between your bloods than there is between red
wine and rhenish. But tell us, do you hear
whether Antonio have had any loss at sea or no?

Shy. There I have another bad match: a
bankrupt, a prodigal, who dare scarce show his
head on the Rialto; a beggar, that was used to
come so smug upon the mart; let him look to his
bond: he was wont to call me usurer; let him
look to his bond: he was wont to lend money for
a Christian courtesy; let him look to his bond.

Salar. Why, I am sure, if he forfeit, thou
wilt not take his flesh: what's that good for?

Shy. To bait fish withal: if it will feed nothing
else, it will feed my revenge. He hath disgraced
me, and hindered me half a million; laughed at
my losses, mocked at my gains, scorned my
nation, thwarted my bargains, cooled my friends,
heated mine enemies; and what's his reason? I
• am a Jew. Hath not a Jew eyes? hath not a
Jew hands, organs, dimensions, senses, affections,
passions? fed with the same food, hurt with the
same weapons, subject to the same diseases,
healed by the same means, warmed and cooled
by the same winter and summer, as a Christian
is? If you prick us, do we not bleed? if you
tickle us, do we not laugh? if you poison us, do we
not die? and if you wrong us, shall we not revenge?
If we are like you in the rest, we will resemble
you in that. If a Jew wrong a Christian, what
is his humility? Revenge. If a Christian wrong
a Jew, what should his sufferance be by Christian
example? Why, revenge. The villany you teach
me, I will execute, and it shall go hard but I will
better the instruction.

Enter a Servant.

Serv. Gentlemen, my master Antonio is at
his house and desires to speak with you both.

Salar. We have been up and down to seek him.

Enter Tubal.

Salan. Here comes another of the tribe: a
third cannot be matched, unless the devil himself
turn Jew. [*Exeunt Salan., Salar., and Servant*.

Shy. How now, Tubal! what news from
Genoa? hast thou found my daughter?

Tub. I often came where I did hear of her,
but cannot find her.

Shy. Why, there, there, there, there! a diamond gone, cost me two thousand ducats in
Frankfort! The curse never fell upon our nation
till now; I never felt it till now: two thousand
ducats in that; and other precious, precious jewels.
I would my daughter were dead at my foot, and
the jewels in her ear! would she were hearsed at
my foot, and the ducats in her coffin! No news
of them? Why, so: and I know not what's
spent in the search: why, thou loss upon loss! the
thief gone with so much, and so much to find the
• thief; and no satisfaction, no revenge: nor no ill
luck stirring but what lights on my shoulders; no
sighs but of my breathing; no tears but of my
shedding.   101

Tub. Yes, other men have ill luck too: Antonio,
as I heard in Genoa,—

Shy. What, what, what? ill luck, ill luck?

Tub. Hath an argosy cast away, coming from
Tripolis.

43-44 *red wine and rhenish*. Shakespeare is contrasting
the rich red blood of Jessica with the thin blood
(Rhenish wine) of her father.

61-76 *Hath not a Jew eyes? . . . the instruction*. Hazlitt
said of Edmund Kean speaking these words that he was
'worth a wilderness of monkeys that have aped humanity'.

Shylock with Tubal. Engraving by Kenny Meadows
from Barry Cornwall's *The Works of Shakspere*, 1846

98-101 *nor no ill luck . . . my shedding*. At the Stratford-
upon-Avon production in 1962 Peter O'Toole empha-
sized these rhythms by beating his breast at every
repetition of 'my'. At their formal mourning, Jews
accompany the ritualized wailing by beating the breast
until tears are shed.

131 *fee me an officer.* Engage a Sheriff's officer (whose duty it was to make arrests).

135 *synagogue.* This is to prepare an oath.

18 *naughty.* Wicked.

22 *peize.* To weigh down and so retard.

Shy. I thank God, I thank God. Is't true, is't true?

Tub. I spoke with some of the sailors that escaped the wreck.   110

Shy. I thank thee, good Tubal: good news, good news! ha, ha! where? in Genoa?

Tub. Your daughter spent in Genoa, as I heard, in one night fourscore ducats.

Shy. Thou stickest a dagger in me: I shall never see my gold again: fourscore ducats at a sitting! fourscore ducats!

Tub. There came divers of Antonio's creditors in my company to Venice, that swear he cannot choose but break.   120

Shy. I am very glad of it: I'll plague him; I'll torture him: I am glad of it.

Tub. One of them showed me a ring that he had of your daughter for a monkey.

Shy. Out upon her! Thou torturest me, Tubal: it was my turquoise; I had it of Leah when I was a bachelor: I would not have given it for a wilderness of monkeys.

Tub. But Antonio is certainly undone.

Shy. Nay, that's true, that's very true. Go, Tubal, fee me an officer; bespeak him a fortnight before. I will have the heart of him, if he forfeit; for, were he out of Venice, I can make what merchandise I will. Go, go, Tubal, and meet me at our synagogue; go, good Tubal; at our synagogue, Tubal.   [*Exeunt.*

SCENE II. *Belmont. A room in* PORTIA'S *house.*

Enter BASSANIO, PORTIA, GRATIANO, NERISSA, *and* Attendants.

Por. I pray you, tarry: pause a day or two
Before you hazard; for, in choosing wrong,
I lose your company: therefore forbear awhile.
There's something tells me, but it is not love,
I would not lose you; and you know yourself,
Hate counsels not in such a quality.
But lest you should not understand me well,—
And yet a maiden hath no tongue but thought,—
I would detain you here some month or two
Before you venture for me.   I could teach you
How to choose right, but I am then forsworn; 11
So will I never be: so may you miss me;
But if you do, you'll make me wish a sin,
That I had been forsworn.   Beshrew your eyes,
They have o'erlook'd me and divided me;
One half of me is yours, the other half yours,
Mine own, I would say; but if mine, then yours,
And so all yours.   O, these naughty times
Put bars between the owners and their rights!
And so, though yours, not yours.   Prove it so,
Let fortune go to hell for it, not I.   21
I speak too long; but 'tis to peize the time,
To eke it and to draw it out in length,
To stay you from election.

Bass.   Let me choose;
For as I am, I live upon the rack.

Por. Upon the rack, Bassanio! then confess
What treason there is mingled with your love.

Bass. None but that ugly treason of mistrust,
Which makes me fear the enjoying of my love:
There may as well be amity and life   30
'Tween snow and fire, as treason and my love.

Por. Ay, but I fear you speak upon the rack,
Where men enforced do speak anything.

Bass. Promise me life, and I'll confess the
    truth.
Por. Well then, confess and live.
Bass.   'Confess' and 'love'
Had been the very sum of my confession:
O happy torment, when my torturer
Doth teach me answers for deliverance!
But let me to my fortune and the caskets.
    Por. Away, then! I am lock'd in one of
        them :   40
If you do love me, you will find me out.
Nerissa and the rest, stand all aloof.
Let music sound while he doth make his choice;
Then, if he lose, he makes a swan-like end,
Fading in music: that the comparison
May stand more proper, my eye shall be the
        stream
And watery death-bed for him.   He may win;
And what is music then?   Then music is
Even as the flourish when true subjects bow
To a new-crowned monarch: such it is   50
As are those dulcet sounds in break of day
That creep into the dreaming bridegroom's ear
And summon him to marriage.   Now he goes,
● With no less presence, but with much more love,
Than young Alcides, when he did redeem
The virgin tribute paid by howling Troy
To the sea-monster: I stand for sacrifice ;
● The rest aloof are the Dardanian wives,
With bleared visages, come forth to view
The issue of the exploit.   Go, Hercules!   60
Live thou, I live: with much much more dismay
I view the fight than thou that makest the fray.

Music, whilst BASSANIO *comments on the caskets
                to himself.*

SONG.
Tell me where is fancy bred,
    Or in the heart or in the head?
    How begot, how nourished?
            Reply, reply.
    It is engender'd in the eyes,
    With gazing fed; and fancy dies
    In the cradle where it lies.
            Let us all ring fancy's knell: 70
            I'll begin it,—Ding, dong, bell.
All. Ding, dong, bell.
Bass. So may the outward shows be least
        themselves:
The world is still deceived with ornament.
In law, what plea so tainted and corrupt
But, being season'd with a gracious voice,
Obscures the show of evil?   In religion,
What damned error, but some sober brow
Will bless it and approve it with a text,
Hiding the grossness with fair ornament?   80
There is no vice so simple but assumes
Some mark of virtue on his outward parts :
How many cowards, whose hearts are all as false
As stairs of sand, wear yet upon their chins
The beards of Hercules and frowning Mars,
Who, inward search'd, have livers white as milk;
● And these assume but valour's excrement
To render them redoubted!   Look on beauty,
And you shall see 'tis purchased by the weight;
Which therein works a miracle in nature,   90
Making them lightest that wear most of it :
● So are those crisped snaky golden locks
Which make such wanton gambols with the wind,

54-55 *with much more love . . . redeem.* Hercules
(Alcides) rescued Hesione not for love but for the
horses which her father, the King of Troy, had
promised him.

58 *Dardanian.* Trojan.

87 *excrement.* Outward growth.

92 *crisped snaky golden locks.* Courtesans were painted
by the Venetian painters of the Renaissance with
crimped gold hair.

Two courtesans. Painting by Vittore Carpaccio (*c.* 1465–
c. 1522)

94 *supposed fairness.* Fictitious beauty.

97 *guiled.* Treacherous.

141 *by note.* By a bill of dues.

Bassanio: 'I come . . . to give and to receive'. Engraving
from a painting by Richard Westall (1765–1836)

• Upon supposed fairness, often known
  To be the dowry of a second head,
  The skull that bred them in the sepulchre.
• Thus ornament is but the guiled shore
  To a most dangerous sea; the beauteous scarf
  †Veiling an Indian beauty; in a word,   99
  The seeming truth which cunning times put on
  To entrap the wisest. Therefore, thou gaudy gold,
  Hard food for Midas, I will none of thee;
  Nor none of thee, thou pale and common drudge
  'Tween man and man: but thou, thou meagre
      lead,
  Which rather threatenest than dost promise aught,
  Thy paleness moves me more than eloquence;
  And here choose I: joy be the consequence!
      Por. [*Aside*] How all the other passions fleet
          to air,
  As doubtful thoughts, and rash-embraced despair,
  And shuddering fear, and green-eyed jealousy!
  O love,   111
  Be moderate; allay thy ecstasy;
  In measure rein thy joy; scant this excess.
  I feel too much thy blessing: make it less,
  For fear I surfeit.
      Bass.   What find I here?
          [*Opening the leaden casket.*

  Fair Portia's counterfeit! What demi-god
  Hath come so near creation? Move these eyes?
  Or whether, riding on the balls of mine,
  Seem they in motion? Here are sever'd lips,
  Parted with sugar breath: so sweet a bar   120
  Should sunder such sweet friends. Here in her
      hairs
  The painter plays the spider and hath woven
  A golden mesh to entrap the hearts of men
  Faster than gnats in cobwebs: but her eyes,—
  How could he see to do them? having made one,
  Methinks it should have power to steal both his
  And leave itself unfurnish'd. Yet look, how far
  The substance of my praise doth wrong this
      shadow
  In underprizing it, so far this shadow
  Doth limp behind the substance. Here's the
      scroll,   130
  The continent and summary of my fortune.
      [*Reads*] You that choose not by the view,
          Chance as fair and choose as true!
          Since this fortune falls to you,
          Be content and seek no new.
          If you be well pleased with this
          And hold your fortune for your bliss,
          Turn you where your lady is
          And claim her with a loving kiss.
  A gentle scroll. Fair lady, by your leave;   140
• I come by note, to give and to receive.
  Like one of two contending in a prize,
  That thinks he hath done well in people's eyes,
  Hearing applause and universal shout,
  Giddy in spirit, still gazing in a doubt
  Whether those peals of praise be his or no;
  So, thrice-fair lady, stand I, even so;
  As doubtful whether what I see be true,
  Until confirm'd, sign'd, ratified by you.
      Por. You see me, Lord Bassanio, where I stand,
  Such as I am: though for myself alone   151
  I would not be ambitious in my wish,
  To wish myself much better; yet, for you
  I would be trebled twenty times myself;
  A thousand times more fair, ten thousand times

More rich;
That only to stand high in your account,
I might in virtues, beauties, livings, friends,
Exceed account; but the full sum of me
● † Is sum of something, which, to term in gross,
Is an unlesson'd girl, unschool'd, unpractised; 161
Happy in this, she is not yet so old
† But she may learn; happier than this,
She is not bred so dull but she can learn;
Happiest of all is that her gentle spirit
Commits itself to yours to be directed,
As from her lord, her governor, her king.
Myself and what is mine to you and yours
Is now converted: but now I was the lord
Of this fair mansion, master of my servants, 170
Queen o'er myself; and even now, but now,
This house, these servants and this same myself
Are yours, my lord: I give them with this ring;
Which when you part from, lose, or give away,
Let it presage the ruin of your love
● And be my vantage to exclaim on you.
    Bass. Madam, you have bereft me of all words,
Only my blood speaks to you in my veins;
And there is such confusion in my powers,
As, after some oration fairly spoke   180
By a beloved prince, there doth appear
Among the buzzing pleased multitude;
Where every something, being blent together,
Turns to a wild of nothing, save of joy,
Express'd and not express'd. But when this ring
Parts from this finger, then parts life from hence:
O, then be bold to say Bassanio's dead!
    Ner. My lord and lady, it is now our time,
That have stood by and seen our wishes prosper,
To cry, good joy: good joy, my lord and lady!
    Gra. My lord Bassanio and my gentle lady,
I wish you all the joy that you can wish;
For I am sure you can wish none from me:
And when your honours mean to solemnize
The bargain of your faith, I do beseech you,
Even at that time I may be married too.
    Bass. With all my heart, so thou canst get a
        wife.
    Gra. I thank your lordship, you have got me
        one.
My eyes, my lord, can look as swift as yours:
● You saw the mistress, I beheld the maid;   200
● You loved, I loved for intermission.
No more pertains to me, my lord, than you.
Your fortune stood upon the casket there,
And so did mine too, as the matter falls;
For wooing here until I sweat again,
● And swearing till my very roof was dry
With oaths of love, at last, if promise last,
I got a promise of this fair one here
To have her love, provided that your fortune
Achieved her mistress.

    Por.   Is this true, Nerissa? 210
    Ner. Madam, it is, so you stand pleased withal.
    Bass. And do you, Gratiano, mean good faith?
    Gra. Yes, faith, my lord.
    Bass. Our feast shall be much honour'd in
your marriage.
    Gra. We'll play with them the first boy for a
thousand ducats.
● *Ner.* What, and stake down?
    Gra. No; we shall ne'er win at that sport,
and stake down.   220
But who comes here? Lorenzo and his infidel?

160 *sum of something.* Portia modestly sets aside her wealth.

176 *vantage to exclaim on you.* Opportunity to protest.

200 *maid.* Nerissa was a 'waiting-gentlewoman', therefore worthy to marry a gentleman.

201 *intermission.* To pass the time.

206 *roof.* i.e. of his mouth.

218 *stake down.* A wager, with a lewd quibble.

Robert Shaw and Marigold Charlesworth as Gratiano and Nerissa, Stratford-upon-Avon, 1953

Denholm Elliot as Bassanio, Stratford-upon-Avon, 1960

What, and my old Venetian friend Salerio?

Enter LORENZO, JESSICA, *and* SALERIO,
a Messenger from Venice.

Bass. Lorenzo and Salerio, welcome hither;
If that the youth of my new interest here
Have power to bid you welcome. By your leave,
I bid my very friends and countrymen,
Sweet Portia, welcome.
Por.   So do I, my lord:
They are entirely welcome.
Lor. I thank your honour. For my part, my
lord,
My purpose was not to have seen you here; 230
But meeting with Salerio by the way,
He did intreat me, past all saying nay,
To come with him along.
Saler.   I did, my lord;
And I have reason for it. Signor Antonio
Commends him to you. [*Gives Bassanio a letter.*
Bass.   Ere I ope his letter,
I pray you, tell me how my good friend doth.
Saler. Not sick, my lord, unless it be in mind;
Nor well, unless in mind: his letter there
Will show you his estate.
Gra. Nerissa, cheer yon stranger; bid her
welcome.   240
Your hand, Salerio: what's the news from Venice?
How doth that royal merchant, good Antonio?
I know he will be glad of our success;
We are the Jasons, we have won the fleece.
Saler. I would you had won the fleece that
he hath lost.
Por. There are some shrewd contents in yon
same paper,
That steals the colour from Bassanio's cheek:
Some dear friend dead; else nothing in the world
Could turn so much the constitution
Of any constant man. What, worse and worse!
With leave, Bassanio; I am half yourself, 251
And I must freely have the half of anything
That this same paper brings you.
Bass.   O sweet Portia,
Here are a few of the unpleasant'st words
That ever blotted paper! Gentle lady,
When I did first impart my love to you,
I freely told you, all the wealth I had
Ran in my veins, I was a gentleman;
And then I told you true: and yet, dear lady,
Rating myself at nothing, you shall see
How much I was a braggart. When I told you
My state was nothing, I should then have told you
That I was worse than nothing; for, indeed,
I have engaged myself to a dear friend,
Engaged my friend to his mere enemy,
To feed my means. Here is a letter, lady;
The paper as the body of my friend,
And every word in it a gaping wound,
Issuing life-blood. But is it true, Salerio?
Have all his ventures fail'd? What, not one hit?
From Tripolis, from Mexico and England, 271
From Lisbon, Barbary and India?
And not one vessel 'scape the dreadful touch
Of merchant-marring rocks?
Saler.   Not one, my lord.
Besides, it should appear, that if he had
The present money to discharge the Jew,
He would not take it. Never did I know
A creature, that did bear the shape of man,

So keen and greedy to confound a man:
He plies the duke at morning and at night,   280
• And doth impeach the freedom of the state,
If they deny him justice: twenty merchants,
• The duke himself, and the magnificoes
• Of greatest port, have all persuaded with him;
• But none can drive him from the envious plea
Of forfeiture, of justice and his bond.
    Jes.   When I was with him I have heard him
        swear
To Tubal and to Chus, his countrymen,
That he would rather have Antonio's flesh
Than twenty times the value of the sum   290
That he did owe him: and I know, my lord,
If law, authority and power deny not,
It will go hard with poor Antonio.
    Por.   Is it your dear friend that is thus in
        trouble?
    Bass.   The dearest friend to me, the kindest
        man,
The best-condition'd and unwearied spirit
In doing courtesies, and one in whom
The ancient Roman honour more appears
Than any that draws breath in Italy.
    Por.   What sum owes he the Jew?   300
    Bass.   For me three thousand ducats.
    Por.   What, no more?
Pay him six thousand, and deface the bond;
Double six thousand, and then treble that,
Before a friend of this description
Shall lose a hair through Bassanio's fault.
First go with me to church and call me wife,
And then away to Venice to your friend;
For never shall you lie by Portia's side
With an unquiet soul.   You shall have gold
To pay the petty debt twenty times over: 310
When it is paid, bring your true friend along.
My maid Nerissa and myself meantime
Will live as maids and widows.   Come, away!
For you shall hence upon your wedding-day:
Bid your friends welcome, show a merry cheer:
Since you are dear bought, I will love you dear.
But let me hear the letter of your friend.
    Bass. [*Reads*] Sweet Bassanio, my ships have
all miscarried, my creditors grow cruel, my es-
tate is very low, my bond to the Jew is forfeit;
and since in paying it, it is impossible I should
live, all debts are cleared between you and I, if I
might but see you at my death. Notwithstanding, use your pleasure: if your love do not
persuade you to come, let not my letter.
    Por.   O love, dispatch all business, and be
        gone!
    Bass.   Since I have your good leave to go
        away,
I will make haste: but, till I come again,
No bed shall e'er be guilty of my stay,
    No rest be interposer 'twixt us twain.   330
                                    [*Exeunt.*

SCENE III.   *Venice. A street.*

Enter SHYLOCK, SALARINO, ANTONIO, *and*
                Gaoler.

    Shy.   Gaoler, look to him: tell not me of
        mercy;
This is the fool that lent out money gratis:
Gaoler, look to him.
    Ant.   Hear me yet, good Shylock.

281 *impeach.* Challenge.

283 *magnificoes.* The chief men of Venice.

Leonardo Loredan, Doge of Venice from 1501 to 1521.
Painting by Giovanni Bellini (d. 1516)

284 *port.* Dignity.

285 *envious.* Malicious.

9 *fond.* Foolish.

Shylock, Salarino, Antonio and the gaoler. Engraving from a painting by Richard Westall (1765–1836)

27 *commodity.* Trading facilities.

32 *bated.* Reduced.

2 *conceit.* Conception.

Shy. I'll have my bond; speak not against
    my bond:
I have sworn an oath that I will have my bond.
Thou call'dst me dog before thou hadst a cause;
But, since I am a dog, beware my fangs:
The duke shall grant me justice.   I do wonder,
● Thou naughty gaoler, that thou art so fond
To come abroad with him at his request.   10
    Ant. I pray thee, hear me speak.
    Shy. I'll have my bond; I will not hear thee
        speak:
I'll have my bond; and therefore speak no more.
I'll not be made a soft and dull-eyed fool,
To shake the head, relent, and sigh, and yield
To Christian intercessors.   Follow not;
I'll have no speaking: I will have my bond.
                                                    [*Exit.*
    Salar. It is the most impenetrable cur
That ever kept with men.
    Ant.   Let him alone:
I'll follow him no more with bootless prayers. 20
He seeks my life; his reason well I know:
I oft deliver'd from his forfeitures
Many that have at times made moan to me;
Therefore he hates me.
    Salar.   I am sure the duke
Will never grant this forfeiture to hold.
    Ant. The duke cannot deny the course of law:
● For the commodity that strangers have
With us in Venice, if it be denied,
Will much impeach the justice of his state;
Since that the trade and profit of the city   30
Consisteth of all nations.   Therefore, go:
● These griefs and losses have so bated me,
That I shall hardly spare a pound of flesh
To-morrow to my bloody creditor.
Well, gaoler, on.   Pray God, Bassanio come
To see me pay his debt, and then I care not!
                                                  [*Exeunt.*

SCENE IV. *Belmont.   A room in* PORTIA'S
                house.

Enter PORTIA, NERISSA, LORENZO, JESSICA,
            and BALTHASAR.

    Lor. Madam, although I speak it in your
        presence,
● You have a noble and a true conceit
Of god-like amity; which appears most strongly
In bearing thus the absence of your lord.
But if you knew to whom you show this honour,
How true a gentleman you send relief,
How dear a lover of my lord your husband,
I know you would be prouder of the work
Than customary bounty can enforce you.
    Por. I never did repent for doing good,   10
Nor shall not now: for in companions
That do converse and waste the time together,
Whose souls do bear an equal yoke of love,
There must be needs a like proportion
Of lineaments, of manners and of spirit;
Which makes me think that this Antonio,
Being the bosom lover of my lord,
Must needs be like my lord.   If it be so,
How little is the cost I have bestow'd
In purchasing the semblance of my soul   20
From out the state of hellish misery!
This comes too near the praising of myself;

Therefore no more of it: hear other things.
Lorenzo, I commit into your hands
● The husbandry and manage of my house
Until my lord's return: for mine own part,
I have toward heaven breathed a secret vow
To live in prayer and contemplation,
Only attended by Nerissa here,
Until her husband and my lord's return: 30
There is a monastery two miles off;
And there will we abide.   I do desire you
● Not to deny this imposition;
The which my love and some necessity
Now lays upon you.
    Lor.   Madam, with all my heart;
I shall obey you in all fair commands.
    Por.   My people do already know my mind,
And will acknowledge you and Jessica
In place of Lord Bassanio and myself.
And so farewell, till we shall meet again.   40
    Lor.   Fair thoughts and happy hours attend
        on you!
    Jes.   I wish your ladyship all heart's content.
    Por.   I thank you for your wish, and am well
        pleased
To wish it back on you: fare you well, Jessica.
        [*Exeunt Jessica and Lorenzo.*

Now, Balthasar,
As I have ever found thee honest-true,
So let me find thee still.   Take this same letter,
And use thou all the endeavour of a man
● In speed to Padua: see thou render this
Into my cousin's hand, Doctor Bellario;   50
And, look, what notes and garments he doth
        give thee,
Bring them, I pray thee, with imagined speed
● Unto the tranect, to the common ferry
Which trades to Venice.   Waste no time in words,
But get thee gone: I shall be there before thee.
    Balth.   Madam, I go with all convenient
        speed.   [*Exit.*
    Por.   Come on, Nerissa; I have work in hand
That you yet know not of: we'll see our husbands
Before they think of us.
    Ner.   Shall they see us?
    Por.   They shall, Nerissa; but in such a
        habit,   60
● That they shall think we are accomplished
With that we lack.   I'll hold thee any wager,
When we are both accoutred like young men,
I'll prove the prettier fellow of the two,
And wear my dagger with the braver grace,
And speak between the change of man and boy
With a reed voice, and turn two mincing steps
Into a manly stride, and speak of frays
Like a fine bragging youth, and tell quaint lies,
How honourable ladies sought my love,   70
Which I denying, they fell sick and died;
I could not do withal; then I'll repent,
And wish, for all that, that I had not kill'd them;
And twenty of these puny lies I'll tell,
That men shall swear I have discontinued school
Above a twelvemonth.   I have within my mind
● A thousand raw tricks of these bragging Jacks,
Which I will practise.
    Ner.   Why, shall we turn to men?
    Por.   Fie, what a question's that,
If thou wert near a lewd interpreter!   80
But come, I'll tell thee all my whole device
When I am in my coach, which stays for us

25 *husbandry and manage.* Ordering and management.

33 *imposition.* Command.

49 *Padua.* The university renowned for the study of Civil Law.

Padua University, famous for its School of Law. From a contemporary Italian engraving

53 *tranect.* Crossing.

61 *accomplished.* Equipped.

77 *Jacks.* Knaves.

19 *Scylla . . . Charybdis.* Scylla, a nymph who was transformed into a monster, preyed on mariners who attempted to pass between her cave and the whirlpool of Charybdis, in the Straits of Messina.

24 *enow.* Enough.

57 *'cover'.* Lay the cloth. Launcelot puns on 'cover' meaning the head covered as a sign of rank.

At the park gate; and therefore haste away,
For we must measure twenty miles to-day.
[*Exeunt.*

SCENE V.   *The same.   A garden.*

Enter LAUNCELOT *and* JESSICA.

Laun. Yes, truly; for, look you, the sins of the father are to be laid upon the children: therefore, I promise ye, I fear you. I was always plain with you, and so now I speak my agitation of the matter: therefore be of good cheer, for truly I think you are damned. There is but one hope in it that can do you any good; and that is but a kind of bastard hope neither.

Jes. And what hope is that, I pray thee?   10

Laun. Marry, you may partly hope that your father got you not, that you are not the Jew's daughter.

Jes. That were a kind of bastard hope, indeed: so the sins of my mother should be visited upon me.

Laun. Truly then I fear you are damned both by father and mother: thus when I shun Scylla, your father, I fall into Charybdis, your mother: well, you are gone both ways.   20

Jes. I shall be saved by my husband; he hath made me a Christian.

Laun. Truly, the more to blame he: we were Christians enow before; e'en as many as could well live, one by another. This making of Christians will raise the price of hogs: if we grow all to be pork-eaters, we shall not shortly have a rasher on the coals for money.

Enter LORENZO.

Jes. I'll tell my husband, Launcelot, what you say: here he comes.   30

Lor. I shall grow jealous of you shortly, Launcelot, if you thus get my wife into corners.

Jes. Nay, you need not fear us, Lorenzo: Launcelot and I are out. He tells me flatly, there is no mercy for me in heaven, because I am a Jew's daughter: and he says, you are no good member of the commonwealth, for in converting Jews to Christians, you raise the price of pork.   39

Lor. I shall answer that better to the commonwealth than you can the getting up of the negro's belly: the Moor is with child by you, Launcelot.

Laun. It is much that the Moor should be more than reason: but if she be less than an honest woman, she is indeed more than I took her for.

Lor. How every fool can play upon the word! I think the best grace of wit will shortly turn into silence, and discourse grow commendable in none only but parrots. Go in, sirrah; bid them prepare for dinner.

Laun. That is done, sir; they have all stomachs.

Lor. Goodly Lord, what a wit-snapper are you! then bid them prepare dinner.

Laun. That is done too, sir; only 'cover' is the word.

Lor. Will you cover then, sir?

Laun. Not so, sir, neither; I know my duty.

● *Lor.* Yet more quarrelling with occasion ! Wilt
thou show the whole wealth of thy wit in an instant ? I pray thee, understand a plain man in
his plain meaning : go to thy fellows ; bid them
cover the table, serve in the meat, and we will
come in to dinner.

    Laun. For the table, sir, it shall be served in ;
for the meat, sir, it shall be covered ; for your
● coming in to dinner, sir, why, let it be as humours
and conceits shall govern.   [*Exit.*

● *Lor.* O dear discretion, how his words are
    suited !   70
The fool hath planted in his memory
An army of good words ; and I do know
A many fools, that stand in better place,
Garnish'd like him, that for a tricksy word
● Defy the matter. How cheer'st thou, Jessica ?
And now, good sweet, say thy opinion,
How dost thou like the Lord Bassanio's wife ?

    Jes. Past all expressing. It is very meet
The Lord Bassanio live an upright life ;
For, having such a blessing in his lady,   80
He finds the joys of heaven here on earth ;
†And if on earth he do not mean it, then
In reason he should never come to heaven.
Why, if two gods should play some heavenly match
And on the wager lay two earthly women,
And Portia one, there must be something else
● Pawn'd with the other, for the poor rude world
Hath not her fellow.

    Lor.   Even such a husband
Hast thou of me as she is for a wife.

    Jes. Nay, but ask my opinion too of that. 90

    Lor. I will anon : first, let us go to dinner.

    Jes. Nay, let me praise you while I have a
    stomach.

    Lor. No, pray thee, let it serve for table-talk ;
Then, howsoe'er thou speak'st, 'mong other things
I shall digest it.

    Jes.   Well, I'll set you forth. [*Exeunt.*

ACT IV.

Scene I. *Venice. A court of justice.*

Enter the Duke, *the* Magnificoes, Antonio,
Bassanio, Gratiano, Salerio, *and others.*

    Duke. What, is Antonio here ?

    Ant. Ready, so please your grace.

    Duke. I am sorry for thee : thou art come to
    answer
A stony adversary, an inhuman wretch
Uncapable of pity, void and empty
From any dram of mercy.

    Ant.   I have heard
Your grace hath ta'en great pains to qualify
His rigorous course ; but since he stands obdurate
And that no lawful means can carry me
Out of his envy's reach, I do oppose   10
My patience to his fury, and am arm'd
To suffer, with a quietness of spirit,
The very tyranny and rage of his.

    Duke. Go one, and call the Jew into the court.

    Saler. He is ready at the door : he comes, my
    lord.

Enter Shylock.

    Duke. Make room, and let him stand before
our face.

60 *quarrelling with occasion.* Disputing at every opportunity.

68-69 *humours and conceits.* Whims and fancies.

70 *discretion.* Discrimination.

75 *Defy the matter.* Refuse to make sense.

87 *Pawn'd.* Staked.

92 *stomach.* Appetite.

Henry Mellon, the Victorian actor, as the Duke,
Princess's Theatre, London, 1858

21 *apparent.* Seeming.

26 *moiety.* Portion.

43 *my humour.* i.e. my whim.

50 *affection.* Inclination, desire.

62 *losing suit.* Shylock is prepared to lose three thousand ducats in order to get his 'weight of carrion flesh'.

Charles Macklin, the 18th century actor, as Shylock, 1775

Shylock, the world thinks, and I think so too,
That thou but lead'st this fashion of thy malice
To the last hour of act; and then 'tis thought
Thou'lt show thy mercy and remorse more strange
● Than is thy strange apparent cruelty;   21
And where thou now exact'st the penalty,
Which is a pound of this poor merchant's flesh,
Thou wilt not only loose the forfeiture,
But, touch'd with human gentleness and love,
● Forgive a moiety of the principal;
Glancing an eye of pity on his losses,
That have of late so huddled on his back,
Enow to press a royal merchant down
And pluck commiseration of his state   30
From brassy bosoms and rough hearts of flint,
From stubborn Turks and Tartars, never train'd
To offices of tender courtesy.
We all expect a gentle answer, Jew.

　Shy.   I have possess'd your grace of what I
　　purpose;
And by our holy Sabbath have I sworn
To have the due and forfeit of my bond:
If you deny it, let the danger light
Upon your charter and your city's freedom.
You'll ask me, why I rather choose to have   40
A weight of carrion flesh than to receive
Three thousand ducats: I'll not answer that:
● But, say, it is my humour: is it answer'd?
What if my house be troubled with a rat
And I be pleased to give ten thousand ducats
To have it baned?   What, are you answer'd yet?
Some men there are love not a gaping pig;
Some, that are mad if they behold a cat;
And others, when the bagpipe sings i' the nose,
● Cannot contain their urine: for affection,   50
Mistress of passion, sways it to the mood
Of what it likes or loathes.   Now, for **your**
　　answer:
As there is no firm reason to be render'd,
Why he cannot abide a gaping pig;
Why he, a harmless necessary cat;
†Why he, a woollen bag-pipe; but of force
Must yield to such inevitable shame
As to offend, himself being offended;
So can I give no reason, nor I will not,
More than a lodged hate and a certain loathing
I bear Antonio, that I follow thus   61
● A losing suit against him.   Are you answer'd?
　Bass.   This is no answer, thou unfeeling man,
To excuse the current of thy cruelty.
　Shy.   I am not bound to please thee with my
　　answers.
　Bass.   Do all men kill the things they do not
　　love?
　Shy.   Hates any man the thing he would not
　　kill?
　Bass.   Every offence is not a hate at first.
　Shy.   What, wouldst thou have a serpent sting
　　thee twice?
　Ant.   I pray you, think you question with the
　　Jew: 70
You may as well go stand upon the beach
And bid the main flood bate his usual height;
You may as well use question with the wolf
Why he hath made the ewe bleat for the lamb;
You may as well forbid the mountain pines
To wag their high tops and to make no noise,
When they are fretten with the gusts of heaven;
You may as well do any thing most hard,

As seek to soften that—than which what's hard-
    er?—
His Jewish heart: therefore, I do beseech you, 80
Make no more offers, use no farther means,
But with all brief and plain conveniency
Let me have judgement and the Jew his will.
    Bass.   For thy three thousand ducats here is six.
    Shy.   If every ducat in six thousand ducats
Were in six parts and every part a ducat,
I would not draw them; I would have my bond.
    Duke.   How shalt thou hope for mercy, render-
    ing none?
    Shy.   What judgement shall I dread, doing no
    wrong?
You have among you many a purchased slave, 90
Which, like your asses and your dogs and mules,
You use in abject and in slavish parts,
Because you bought them: shall I say to you,
Let them be free, marry them to your heirs?
Why sweat they under burthens? let their beds
Be made as soft as yours and let their palates
Be season'd with such viands?   You will answer
'The slaves are ours:' so do I answer you:
The pound of flesh, which I demand of him,
Is dearly bought; 'tis mine and I will have it. 100
If you deny me, fie upon your law!
There is no force in the decrees of Venice.
I stand for judgement: answer; shall I have it?
    Duke.   Upon my power I may dismiss this
    court,
Unless Bellario, a learned doctor,
Whom I have sent for to determine this,
Come here to-day.
    Saler.   My lord, here stays without
A messenger with letters from the doctor,
New come from Padua.
    Duke.   Bring us the letters; call the messenger.
    Bass.   Good cheer, Antonio!   What, man,
    courage yet!   111
The Jew shall have my flesh, blood, bones and all,
Ere thou shalt lose for me one drop of blood.
    Ant.   I am a tainted wether of the flock,
Meetest for death: the weakest kind of fruit
Drops earliest to the ground; and so let me:
You cannot better be employ'd, Bassanio,
Than to live still and write mine epitaph.

    Enter NERISSA, *dressed like a lawyer's clerk.*

    Duke.   Came you from Padua, from Bellario?
    Ner.   From both, my lord.   Bellario greets
    your grace.   [*Presenting a letter.* 120

    Bass.   Why dost thou whet thy knife so
    earnestly?
    Shy.   To cut the forfeiture from that bankrupt
    there.
    Gra.   Not on thy sole, but on thy soul, harsh
    Jew,
Thou makest thy knife keen; but no metal can,
No, not the hangman's axe, bear half the keenness
Of thy sharp envy.   Can no prayers pierce thee?
    Shy.   No, none that thou hast wit enough to
    make.
• *Gra.*   O, be thou damn'd, inexecrable dog!
And for thy life let justice be accused.
Thou almost makest me waver in my faith 130
To hold opinion with Pythagoras,
That souls of animals infuse themselves
Into the trunks of men: thy currish spirit
•Govern'd a wolf, who, hang'd for human slaughter,

Bassanio: 'Why dost thou whet thy knife so earnestly?'
Engraving by H. Fuseli from Steevens's edition, 1805

128 *inexecrable.* i.e. that cannot be denounced too much.

134 *Govern'd a wolf.* This is probably a reference to the execution of Dr. Lopez (*lupus:* Latin for 'wolf'). See introduction.

Roderigo Lopez, Elizabeth I's Jewish physician, who was executed for treason (probably unjustly) in 1594. From a contemporary engraving.

182 *must the Jew be merciful.* Here, 'must' carries the sense of inevitabilility, not of compulsion. Portia assumes that Shylock will be merciful.

Peggy Ashcroft as Portia, Queens Theatre, London, 1936

Even from the gallows did his fell soul fleet,
And, whilst thou lay'st in thy unhallow'd dam,
Infused itself in thee; for thy desires
Are wolvish, bloody, starved and ravenous..
   Shy. Till thou canst rail the seal from off my
        bond,
Thou but offend'st thy lungs to speak so loud:
Repair thy wit, good youth, or it will fall   **141**
To cureless ruin. I stand here for law.
   Duke. This letter from Bellario doth commend
A young and learned doctor to our court.
Where is he?
   Ner.   He attendeth here hard by,
To know your answer, whether you'll admit him.
   Duke. With all my heart. Some three or four
      of you
Go give him courteous conduct to this place.
Meantime the court shall hear Bellario's letter.
   Clerk. [*Reads*] Your grace shall understand
that at the receipt of your letter I am very sick:
but in the instant that your messenger came, in
loving visitation was with me a young doctor of
Rome; his name is Balthasar. I acquainted him
with the cause in controversy between the Jew
and Antonio the merchant: we turned o'er many
books together: he is furnished with my opinion;
which, bettered with his own learning, the greatness whereof I cannot enough commend, comes
with him, at my importunity, to fill up your
grace's request in my stead. I beseech you, let
his lack of years be no impediment to let him lack
a reverend estimation; for I never knew so young
a body with so old a head. I leave him to your
gracious acceptance, whose trial shall better publish his commendation.
   Duke. You hear the learn'd Bellario, what he
      writes:
And here, I take it, is the doctor come.

   Enter PORTIA, *dressed like a doctor of laws.*
Give me your hand. Come you from old Bellario?
   Por. I did, my lord.
   Duke.   You are welcome: take your place.
Are you acquainted with the difference   **171**
That holds this present question in the court?
   Por. I am informed throughly of the cause.
Which is the merchant here, and which the Jew?
   Duke. Antonio and old Shylock, both stand
      forth.
   Por. Is your name Shylock?
   Shy.   Shylock is my name.
   Por. Of a strange nature is the suit you follow;
Yet in such rule that the Venetian law
Cannot impugn you as you do proceed.
You stand within his danger, do you not?   **180**
   Ant. Ay, so he says.
   Por.   Do you confess the bond?
   Ant. I do.
   Por.   Then must the Jew be merciful.
   Shy. On what compulsion must I? tell me that.
   Por. The quality of mercy is not strain'd,
It droppeth as the gentle rain from heaven
Upon the place beneath: it is twice blest;
It blesseth him that gives and him that takes:
'Tis mightiest in the mightiest: it becomes
The throned monarch better than his crown;
His sceptre shows the force of temporal power,
The attribute to awe and majesty,   **191**
Wherein doth sit the dread and fear of kings;

But mercy is above this sceptred sway;
It is enthroned in the hearts of kings,
It is an attribute to God himself;
And earthly power doth then show likest God's
When mercy seasons justice.   Therefore, Jew,
Though justice be thy plea, consider this,
That, in the course of justice, none of us
Should see salvation: we do pray for mercy;   200
And that same prayer doth teach us all to render
The deeds of mercy.   I have spoke thus much
To mitigate the justice of thy plea;
Which if thou follow, this strict court of Venice
Must needs give sentence 'gainst the merchant
    there.
  Shy.   My deeds upon my head!   I crave the
    law,
The penalty and forfeit of my bond.
  Por.   Is he not able to discharge the money?
  Bass.   Yes, here I tender it for him in the
    court;
Yea, twice the sum: if that will not suffice,   210
I will be bound to pay it ten times o'er,
On forfeit of my hands, my head, my heart:
If this will not suffice, it must appear
That malice bears down truth.   And I beseech you,
Wrest once the law to your authority:
To do a great right, do a little wrong,
And curb this cruel devil of his will.
  Por.   It must not be; there is no power in
    Venice
Can alter a decree established:
'Twill be recorded for a precedent,   220
And many an error by the same example
Will rush into the state: it cannot be.
  • *Shy.*   A Daniel come to judgement! yea, a
    Daniel!
O wise young judge, how I do honour thee!
  Por.   I pray you, let me look upon the bond.
  Shy.   Here 'tis, most reverend doctor, here
    it is.
  Por.   Shylock, there's thrice thy money offer'd
    thee.
  Shy.   An oath, an oath, I have an oath in
    heaven:
Shall I lay perjury upon my soul?
No, not for Venice.
  Por.   Why, this bond is forfeit;   230
And lawfully by this the Jew may claim
A pound of flesh, to be by him cut off
Nearest the merchant's heart.   Be merciful:
Take thrice thy money; bid me tear the bond.
  Shy.   When it is paid according to the tenour.
It doth appear you are a worthy judge;
You know the law, your exposition
Hath been most sound: I charge you by the law,
Whereof you are a well-deserving pillar,
Proceed to judgement: by my soul I swear   240
There is no power in the tongue of man
To alter me: I stay here on my bond.
  Ant.   Most heartily I do beseech the court
To give the judgement.
  Por.   Why then, thus it is:
You must prepare your bosom for his knife.
  Shy.   O noble judge! O excellent young man!
  Por.   For the intent and purpose of the law
Hath full relation to the penalty,
Which here appeareth due upon the bond.
  Shy.   'Tis very true: O wise and upright
    judge!
                             250

"It must not be. There is no power in Venice
Can alter a decree established."
"Portia".   Ellen Terry

Ellen Terry as Portia. Late 19th century illustration by
W. Morton

223 *Daniel.* This refers to the story of Susannah and
the Elders, and is apt since Daniel was a 'young youth'.
Daniel convicted the Elders 'by their own mouth' in
much the same way as Portia convicts Shylock.

How much more elder art thou than thy looks!
  Por.   Therefore lay bare your bosom.
  Shy.   Ay, his breast:
So says the bond: doth it not, noble judge?
'Nearest his heart:' those are the very words.
  Por.   It is so. Are there balance here to
      weigh
The flesh?
  Shy.   I have them ready.
  Por.   Have by some surgeon, Shylock, on your
      charge,
To stop his wounds, lest he do bleed to death.
  Shy.   Is it so nominated in the bond?
  Por.   It is not so express'd: but what of that?
'Twere good you do so much for charity.   261
  Shy.   I cannot find it; 'tis not in the bond.
  Por.   You, merchant, have you any thing to
      say?
  Ant.   But little: I am arm'd and well pre-
      pared.
Give me your hand, Bassanio: fare you well!
Grieve not that I am fallen to this for you;
For herein Fortune shows herself more kind
Than is her custom: it is still her use
To let the wretched man outlive his wealth,
To view with hollow eye and wrinkled brow   270
An age of poverty; from which lingering penance
Of such misery doth she cut me off.
Commend me to your honourable wife:
Tell her the process of Antonio's end;
Say how I loved you, speak me fair in death;
And, when the tale is told, bid her be judge
Whether Bassanio had not once a love.
Repent but you that you shall lose your friend,
And he repents not that he pays your debt;
For if the Jew do cut but deep enough,   280
I'll pay it presently with all my heart.
  Bass.   Antonio, I am married to a wife
Which is as dear to me as life itself;
But life itself, my wife, and all the world,
Are not with me esteem'd above thy life:
I would lose all, ay, sacrifice them all
Here to this devil, to deliver you.
  Por.   Your wife would give you little thanks
      for that,
If she were by, to hear you make the offer.
  Gra.   I have a wife, whom, I protest, I love:
I would she were in heaven, so she could   291
Entreat some power to change this currish Jew.
  Ner.   'Tis well you offer it behind her back;
The wish would make else an unquiet house.
  Shy.   These be the Christian husbands. I
      have a daughter;
Would any of the stock of Barrabas
Had been her husband rather than a Christian!
                                    [*Aside.*
We trifle time: I pray thee, pursue sentence.
  Por.   A pound of that same merchant's flesh
      is thine:
The court awards it, and the law doth give it.
  Shy.   Most rightful judge!   301
  Por.   And you must cut this flesh from off
      his breast:
The law allows it, and the court awards it.
  Shy.   Most learned judge! A sentence! Come,
      prepare!
  Por.   Tarry a little; there is something else.
This bond doth give thee here no jot of blood;
The words expressly are 'a pound of flesh:'

Portia: 'Have by some surgeon, Shylock . . .' Maria Ann Pope and Charles Macklin in an 18th century production

Opposite: Antonio: 'Give me your hand, Bassanio: fare you well!' Detail from a painting by Robert Smirke (1752–1845)

Portia's judgement. Drawing by P. J. de Loutherberg (1740–1812)

Shylock: 'pay the bond thrice . . .' Engraving from Rowe's edition of the works of Shakespeare, 1709

Take then thy bond, take thou thy pound of
  flesh;
But, in the cutting it, if thou dost shed
One drop of Christian blood, thy lands and goods
Are, by the laws of Venice, confiscate   311
Unto the state of Venice.
  Gra. O upright judge! Mark, Jew: O learned
    judge!
  Shy. Is that the law?
  Por.   Thyself shalt see the act:
For, as thou urgest justice, be assured
Thou shalt have justice, more than thou desirest.
  Gra. O learned judge! Mark, Jew: a learned
    judge!
  Shy. I take this offer, then; pay the bond
    thrice
And let the Christian go.
  Bass.   Here is the money.
  Por. Soft!   320
The Jew shall have all justice; soft! no haste:
He shall have nothing but the penalty.
  Gra. O Jew! an upright judge, a learned
    judge!
  Por. Therefore prepare thee to cut off the flesh.
Shed thou no blood, nor cut thou less nor more
But just a pound of flesh: if thou cut'st more
Or less than a just pound, be it but so much
As makes it light or heavy in the substance,
Or the division of the twentieth part
Of one poor scruple, nay, if the scale do turn 330
But in the estimation of a hair,
Thou diest and all thy goods are confiscate.
  Gra. A second Daniel, a Daniel, Jew!
Now, infidel, I have you on the hip.
  Por. Why doth the Jew pause? take thy for-
    feiture.
  Shy. Give me my principal, and let me go.
  Bass. I have it ready for thee; here it is.
  Por. He hath refused it in the open court:
He shall have merely justice and his bond.   339
  Gra. A Daniel, still say I, a second Daniel!
I thank thee, Jew, for teaching me that word.
  Shy. Shall I not have barely my principal?
  Por. Thou shalt have nothing but the forfeiture,
To be so taken at thy peril, Jew.
  Shy. Why, then the devil give him good of it!
I'll stay no longer question.
  Por.   Tarry, Jew:
The law hath yet another hold on you.
It is enacted in the laws of Venice,
If it be proved against an alien
That by direct or indirect attempts   350
He seek the life of any citizen,
The party 'gainst the which he doth contrive
Shall seize one half his goods; the other half
Comes to the privy coffer of the state;
And the offender's life lies in the mercy
Of the duke only, 'gainst all other voice.
In which predicament, I say, thou stand'st;
For it appears, by manifest proceeding,
That indirectly and directly too
Thou hast contrived against the very life   360
Of the defendant; and thou hast incurr'd
The danger formerly by me rehearsed.
Down therefore and beg mercy of the duke.
  Gra. Beg that thou mayst have leave to hang
    thyself:
And yet, thy wealth being forfeit to the state,
Thou hast not left the value of a cord;

Therefore thou must be hang'd at the state's charge.
   Duke. That thou shalt see the difference of
     our spirits,
I pardon thee thy life before thou ask it:
For half thy wealth, it is Antonio's;   370
The other half comes to the general state,
Which humbleness may drive unto a fine.
   Por. Ay, for the state, not for Antonio.
   Shy. Nay, take my life and all; pardon not that:
You take my house when you do take the prop
That doth sustain my house; you take my life
When you do take the means whereby I live.
   Por. What mercy can you render him, Antonio?
   Gra. A halter gratis; nothing else, for God's
     sake.
   Ant. So please my lord the duke and all the
     court   380
• To quit the fine for one half of his goods,
I am content; so he will let me have
• The other half in use, to render it,
Upon his death, unto the gentleman
That lately stole his daughter:
Two things provided more, that, for this favour,
He presently become a Christian;
The other, that he do record a gift,
Here in the court, of all he dies possess'd,
Unto his son Lorenzo and his daughter.   390
   Duke. He shall do this, or else I do recant
The pardon that I late pronounced here.
   Por. Art thou contented, Jew? what dost thou
     say?
   Shy. I am content.
   Por.   Clerk, draw a deed of gift.
   Shy. I pray you, give me leave to go from
     hence;
I am not well: send the deed after me,
And I will sign it.
   Duke.   Get thee gone, but do it.
   Gra. In christening shalt thou have two god-
     fathers:
Had I been judge, thou shouldst have had ten more,
To bring thee to the gallows, not the font.   400
                 [Exit Shylock.
   Duke. Sir, I entreat you home with me to dinner.
   Por. I humbly do desire your grace of pardon:
I must away this night toward Padua,
And it is meet I presently set forth.
   Duke. I am sorry that your leisure serves you
     not.
Antonio, gratify this gentleman,
For, in my mind, you are much bound to him.
             [Exeunt Duke and his train.

   Bass. Most worthy gentleman, I and my friend
Have by your wisdom been this day acquitted
Of grievous penalties; in lieu whereof,   410
Three thousand ducats, due unto the Jew,
We freely cope your courteous pains withal.
   Ant. And stand indebted, over and above,
In love and service to you evermore.
   Por. He is well paid that is well satisfied;
And I, delivering you, am satisfied
And therein do account myself well paid:
My mind was never yet more mercenary.
I pray you, know me when we meet again:
I wish you well, and so I take my leave.   420
   Bass. Dear sir, of force I must attempt you
     further:
Take some remembrance of us, as a tribute,
Not as a fee: grant me two things, I pray you,

381 *To quit.* To remit.

383 *in use.* In trust.

Portia, Gratiano, the Duke and Shylock. Illustration by
Thomas Lowinsky from *Players' Shakespeare,* 1923

Shylock: 'give me leave to go . . .' Engraving from a
painting by Sir John Gilbert (1817–97)

16 *old swearing.* Plenty of swearing.

Not to deny me, and to pardon me.
   Por. You press me far, and therefore I will
    yield.
[*To Ant.*] Give me your gloves, I'll wear them
    for your sake;
[*To Bass.*] And, for your love, I'll take this
    ring from you:
Do not draw back your hand; I'll take no more;
And you in love shall not deny me this.
   Bass. This ring, good sir, alas, it is a trifle!
I will not shame myself to give you this.   431
   Por. I will have nothing else but only this;
And now methinks I have a mind to it.
   Bass. There's more depends on this than on
    the value.
The dearest ring in Venice will I give you,
And find it out by proclamation:
Only for this, I pray you, pardon me.
   Por. I see, sir, you are liberal in offers:
You taught me first to beg; and now methinks
You teach me how a beggar should be answer'd.
   Bass. Good sir, this ring was given me by my
    wife;   441
And when she put it on, she made me vow
That I should neither sell nor give nor lose it.
   Por. That 'scuse serves many men to save
    their gifts.
An if your wife be not a mad-woman,
And know how well I have deserved the ring,
She would not hold out enemy for ever,
For giving it to me.   Well, peace be with you!
           [Exeunt Portia and Nerissa.
   Ant. My Lord Bassanio, let him have the
    ring:
Let his deservings and my love withal   450
Be valued 'gainst your wife's commandment.
   Bass. Go, Gratiano, run and overtake him;
Give him the ring, and bring him, if thou canst,
Unto Antonio's house: away! make haste.
              [Exit Gratiano.
Come, you and I will thither presently;
And in the morning early will we both
Fly toward Belmont: come, Antonio. [*Exeunt.*

      SCENE II. *The same. A street.*

      Enter PORTIA *and* NERISSA.

   Por. Inquire the Jew's house out, give him
    this deed
And let him sign it: we'll away to-night
And be a day before our husbands home:
This deed will be well welcome to Lorenzo.

      Enter GRATIANO.

   Gra. Fair sir, you are well o'erta'en:
My Lord Bassanio upon more advice
Hath sent you here this ring, and doth entreat
Your company at dinner.
   Por.   That cannot be:
His ring I do accept most thankfully:
And so, I pray you, tell him: furthermore,   10
I pray you, show my youth old Shylock's house.
   Gra. That will I do.
   Ner.   Sir, I would speak with you.
[*Aside to Por.*] I'll see if I can get my hus-
    band's ring,
Which I did make him swear to keep for ever.
   Por. [*Aside to Ner.*] Thou mayst, I warrant.
  •   We shall have old swearing

That they did give the rings away to men;
But we'll outface them, and outswear them too.
[*Aloud*] Away! make haste: thou know'st where
   I will tarry.
  Ner.   Come, good sir, will you show me to
   this house?   [*Exeunt.*

ACT V.

SCENE I.   *Belmont. Avenue to* PORTIA'S *house.*

Enter LORENZO *and* JESSICA.

  Lor.   The moon shines bright: in such a night
   as this,
When the sweet wind did gently kiss the trees
And they did make no noise, in such a night
Troilus methinks mounted the Troyan walls
And sigh'd his soul toward the Grecian tents,
Where Cressid lay that night.
  Jes.   In such a night
Did Thisbe fearfully o'ertrip the dew
And saw the lion's shadow ere himself
And ran dismay'd away.
  Lor.   In such a night
Stood Dido with a willow in her hand   10
Upon the wild sea banks and waft her love
To come again to Carthage.
  Jes.   In such a night
Medea gather'd the enchanted herbs
That did renew old Æson.
  Lor.   In such a night
Did Jessica steal from the wealthy Jew
And with an unthrift love did run from Venice
As far as Belmont.
  Jes.   In such a night
Did young Lorenzo swear he loved her well,
Stealing her soul with many vows of faith
And ne'er a true one.
  Lor.   In such a night   20
Did pretty Jessica, like a little shrew,
Slander her love, and he forgave it her.
  Jes.   I would out-night you, did no body come;
But, hark, I hear the footing of a man.

Enter STEPHANO.

  Lor.   Who comes so fast in silence of the night?
  Steph.   A friend.
  Lor.   A friend! what friend? your name, I
   pray you, friend?
  Steph.   Stephano is my name; and I bring
   word
My mistress will before the break of day
Be here at Belmont: she doth stray about   30
By holy crosses, where she kneels and prays
For happy wedlock hours.
  Lor.   Who comes with her?
  Steph.   None but a holy hermit and her maid.
I pray you, is my master yet return'd?
  Lor.   He is not, nor we have not heard from
   him.
But go we in, I pray thee, Jessica,
And ceremoniously let us prepare
Some welcome for the mistress of the house.

Enter LAUNCELOT.

  Laun.   Sola, sola! wo ha, ho! sola, sola!
  Lor.   Who calls?   40
  Laun.   Sola! did you see Master Lorenzo?
Master Lorenzo, sola, sola!

Lorenzo and Jessica in the avenue to Portia's house.
Engraving from Charles Knight's *Pictorial Edition of
the Works of William Shakspere*, 1839–43

31 *crosses.* Roadside crosses were common in both
England and Italy.

39 *Sola, sola!* A hunting cry.

59 *patines*. The shallow gold or silver dish from which Holy Communion was served.

60 *smallest orb*. A reference to 'the music of the spheres', an accepted idea in Shakespeare's day.

63 *immortal souls*. i.e. immortal souls can hear the music of the spheres.

79 *the poet*. Presumably Ovid.

81 *stockish*. Unfeeling, blockish.

87 *Erebus*. A dark place on the way to Hades.

99 *without respect*. This means that nothing is absolutely good, but only relatively.

Lor.   Leave hollaing, man: here.

Laun.   Sola! where? where?

Lor.   Here.

Laun.   Tell him there's a post come from my master, with his horn full of good news: my master will be here ere morning.   [*Exit.*

Lor.   Sweet soul, let's in, and there expect their coming.

And yet no matter: why should we go in?   50

My friend Stephano, signify, I pray you,

Within the house, your mistress is at hand;

And bring your music forth into the air.

[*Exit Stephano.*

How sweet the moonlight sleeps upon this bank!

Here will we sit and let the sounds of music

Creep in our ears: soft stillness and the night

Become the touches of sweet harmony.

Sit, Jessica.   Look how the floor of heaven

● Is thick inlaid with patines of bright gold:

● There's not the smallest orb which thou behold'st

But in his motion like an angel sings,   61

Still quiring to the young-eyed cherubins;

● Such harmony is in immortal souls;

But whilst this muddy vesture of decay

Doth grossly close it in, we cannot hear it.

Enter Musicians.

Come, ho! and wake Diana with a hymn:

With sweetest touches pierce your mistress' ear

And draw her home with music.   [*Music.*

Jes.   I am never merry when I hear sweet music.

Lor.   The reason is, your spirits are attentive: 70

For do but note a wild and wanton herd,

Or race of youthful and unhandled colts,

Fetching mad bounds, bellowing and neighing loud,

Which is the hot condition of their blood;

If they but hear perchance a trumpet sound,

Or any air of music touch their ears,

You shall perceive them make a mutual stand,

Their savage eyes turn'd to a modest gaze

● By the sweet power of music: therefore the poet

Did feign that Orpheus drew trees, stones and floods;   80

● Since nought so stockish, hard and full of rage,

But music for the time doth change his nature.

The man that hath no music in himself,

Nor is not moved with concord of sweet sounds,

Is fit for treasons, stratagems and spoils;

The motions of his spirit are dull as night

● And his affections dark as Erebus:

Let no such man be trusted.   Mark the music.

Enter PORTIA *and* NERISSA.

Por.   That light we see is burning in my hall.

How far that little candle throws his beams!   90

So shines a good deed in a naughty world.

Ner.   When the moon shone, we did not see the candle.

Por.   So doth the greater glory dim the less:

A substitute shines brightly as a king

Until a king be by, and then his state

Empties itself, as doth an inland brook

Into the main of waters.   Music! hark!

Ner.   It is your music, madam, of the house.

● *Por.*   Nothing is good, I see, without respect:

Methinks it sounds much sweeter than by day.

Opposite : Lorenzo: 'How sweet the moonlight sleeps...'
Engraving from a painting by W. Hodges (1744–97)

109-110 *Endymion . . . awaked.* Lorenzo is likened to Endymion, and Jessica to Diana who caused him to sleep on Latmos.

SD *tucket.* A flourish on a trumpet.

127 *We should hold day with the Antipodes.* 'If you would always walk in the night, it would be day with us, as it is now on the other side of the globe'.

Bassanio presents Antonio to Portia. Engraving by Kenny Meadows from Barry Cornwall's *The Works of Shakspere,* 1846

141 *breathing courtesy.* Welcome of mere words.

144 *gelt.* A eunuch.

148 *posy.* An inscription engraved on the inside of a ring.

Ner.   Silence bestows that virtue on it, madam.
Por.   The crow doth sing as sweetly as the lark
When neither is attended, and I think
The nightingale, if she should sing by day,
When every goose is cackling, would be thought
No better a musician than the wren.
How many things by season season'd are
To their right praise and true perfection!
● Peace, ho! the moon sleeps with Endymion
And would not be awaked.   [*Music ceases.*

   Lor.   That is the voice,   110
Or I am much deceived, of Portia.
   Por.   He knows me as the blind man knows the cuckoo,
By the bad voice.
   Lor.   Dear lady, welcome home.
   Por.   We have been praying for our husbands' healths,
Which speed, we hope, the better for our words.
Are they return'd?
   Lor.   Madam, they are not yet;
But there is come a messenger before,
To signify their coming.
   Por.   Go in, Nerissa;
Give order to my servants that they take
No note at all of our being absent hence;   120
Nor you, Lorenzo; Jessica, nor you.
                 [*A tucket sounds.*
   Lor.   Your husband is at hand; I hear his trumpet:
We are no tell-tales, madam; fear you not.
   Por.   This night methinks is but the daylight sick;
It looks a little paler: 'tis a day,
Such as the day is when the sun is hid.

   Enter BASSANIO, ANTONIO, GRATIANO, *and*
             their followers.

● *Bass.*   We should hold day with the Antipodes,
If you would walk in absence of the sun.
   Por.   Let me give light, but let me not be light;
For a light wife doth make a heavy husband,   130
And never be Bassanio so for me:
But God sort all!   You are welcome home, my lord.
   Bass.   I thank you, madam.   Give welcome to my friend.
This is the man, this is Antonio,
To whom I am so infinitely bound.
   Por.   You should in all sense be much bound to him,
For, as I hear, he was much bound for you.
   Ant.   No more than I am well acquitted of.
   Por.   Sir, you are very welcome to our house:
It must appear in other ways than words,   140
● Therefore I scant this breathing courtesy.
   Gra.   [*To Ner.*] By yonder moon I swear you do me wrong;
In faith, I gave it to the judge's clerk:
● Would he were gelt that had it, for my part,
Since you do take it, love, so much at heart.
   Por.   A quarrel, ho, already! what's the matter?
   Gra.   About a hoop of gold, a paltry ring
● That she did give me, whose posy was
For all the world like cutler's poetry
Upon a knife, 'Love me, and leave me not.'   150
   Ner.   What talk you of the posy or the value?
You swore to me, when I did give it you,

That you would wear it till your hour of death
And that it should lie with you in your grave:
Though not for me, yet for your vehement oaths,
You should have been respective and have
    kept it.
Gave it a judge's clerk! no, God's my judge,
The clerk will ne'er wear hair on's face that
    had it.
  Gra. He will, an if he live to be a man.
  Ner. Ay, if a woman live to be a man. 160
  Gra. Now, by this hand, I gave it to a youth,
• A kind of boy, a little scrubbed boy,
No higher than thyself, the judge's clerk,
A prating boy, that begg'd it as a fee:
I could not for my heart deny it him.
  Por. You were to blame, I must be plain
    with you,
To part so slightly with your wife's first gift;
A thing stuck on with oaths upon your finger
And so riveted with faith unto your flesh.
I gave my love a ring and made him swear 170
Never to part with it; and here he stands;
I dare be sworn for him he would not leave it
Nor pluck it from his finger, for the wealth
That the world masters. Now, in faith, Gratiano,
You give your wife too unkind a cause of grief:
An 'twere to me, I should be mad at it.
  Bass. [*Aside*] Why, I were best to cut my
    left hand off
And swear I lost the ring defending it.
  Gra. My Lord Bassanio gave his ring away
Unto the judge that begg'd it and indeed 180
Deserved it too; and then the boy, his clerk,
That took some pains in writing, he begg'd mine;
And neither man nor master would take aught
But the two rings.
  Por.   What ring gave you, my lord?
Not that, I hope, which you received of me.
  Bass. If I could add a lie unto a fault,
I would deny it; but you see my finger
Hath not the ring upon it; it is gone.
  Por. Even so void is your false heart of truth.
By heaven, I will ne'er come in your bed 190
Until I see the ring.
  Ner.   Nor I in yours
Till I again see mine.
  Bass.   Sweet Portia,
If you did know to whom I gave the ring,
If you did know for whom I gave the ring
And would conceive for what I gave the ring
And how unwillingly I left the ring,
When nought would be accepted but the ring,
You would abate the strength of your displeasure.
  Por. If you had known the virtue of the ring,
Or half her worthiness that gave the ring, 200
Or your own honour to contain the ring,
You would not then have parted with the ring.
What man is there so much unreasonable,
If you had pleased to have defended it
• With any terms of zeal, wanted the modesty
To urge the thing held as a ceremony?
Nerissa teaches me what to believe:
I'll die for't but some woman had the ring.
  Bass. No, by my honour, madam, by my soul,
• No woman had it, but a civil doctor, 210
Which did refuse three thousand ducats of me
And begg'd the ring; the which I did deny him
And suffer'd him to go displeased away;
Even he that did uphold the very life

Antonio, Jessica, Portia, Lorenzo and Nerissa. Illustration by Thomas Lowinsky from *Players' Shakespeare*, 1923

---

162 *scrubbed.* Stunted.

205-206 *wanted . . . To urge.* i.e. so wanted moderation that he would have urged. *ceremony.* Sacred symbol.

210 *civil doctor.* A quibble on 'doctor of Civil Law' and 'polite doctor'.

226 *liberal.* A pun implying 'free in giving' and 'licentious'.

230 *Argus.* He was supposed to have a hundred eyes.

237 *pen.* A bawdy pun.

Of my dear friend.   What should I say, sweet
    lady?
I was enforced to send it after him;
I was beset with shame and courtesy;
My honour would not let ingratitude
So much besmear it.   Pardon me, good lady;
For, by these blessed candles of the night,   220
Had you been there, I think you would have
    begg'd
The ring of me to give the worthy doctor.

    Por.   Let not that doctor e'er come near my
    house:
Since he hath got the jewel that I loved,
And that which you did swear to keep for me,
I will become as liberal as you;
I'll not deny him any thing I have,
No, not my body nor my husband's bed:
Know him I shall, I am well sure of it:
Lie not a night from home; watch me like
    Argus: 230
If you do not, if I be left alone,
Now, by mine honour, which is yet mine own,
I'll have that doctor for my bedfellow.
    Ner.   And I his clerk; therefore be well
    advised
How you do leave me to mine own protection.
    Gra.   Well, do you so: let not me take him,
    then;
For if I do, I'll mar the young clerk's pen.
    Ant.   I am the unhappy subject of these
    quarrels.
    Por.   Sir, grieve not you; you are welcome
    notwithstanding.
    Bass.   Portia, forgive me this enforced wrong;
And, in the hearing of these many friends,   241
I swear to thee, even by thine own fair eyes,
Wherein I see myself—
    Por.   Mark you but that!
In both my eyes he doubly sees himself;
In each eye, one: swear by your double self,
And there's an oath of credit.
    Bass.   Nay, but hear me:
Pardon this fault, and by my soul I swear
I never more will break an oath with thee.
    Ant.   I once did lend my body for his wealth;
Which, but for him that had your husband's ring,
Had quite miscarried: I dare be bound again,
My soul upon the forfeit, that your lord
Will never more break faith advisedly.
    Por.   Then you shall be his surety.   Give him
    this
And bid him keep it better than the other.
    Ant.   Here, Lord Bassanio; swear to keep
    this ring.
    Bass.   By heaven, it is the same I gave the
    doctor!
    Por.   I had it of him: pardon me, Bassanio;
For, by this ring, the doctor lay with me.   259
    Ner.   And pardon me, my gentle Gratiano;
For that same scrubbed boy, the doctor's clerk,
In lieu of this last night did lie with me.
    Gra.   Why, this is like the mending of high-
    ways
In summer, where the ways are fair enough:
What, are we cuckolds ere we have deserved it?
    Por.   Speak not so grossly.   You are all
    amazed:
Here is a letter; read it at your leisure;
It comes from Padua, from Bellario:

There you shall find that Portia was the doctor,
Nerissa there her clerk: Lorenzo here   270
Shall witness I set forth as soon as you
And even but now return'd; I have not yet
Enter'd my house.   Antonio, you are welcome;
And I have better news in store for you
Than you expect: unseal this letter soon;
There you shall find three of your argosies
Are richly come to harbour suddenly:
You shall not know by what strange accident
I chanced on this letter.
   Ant.   I am dumb.
   Bass.   Were you the doctor and I knew you
     not?   280
   Gra.   Were you the clerk that is to make me
     cuckold?
   Ner.   Ay, but the clerk that never means to
     do it,
Unless he live until he be a man.
   Bass.   Sweet doctor, you shall be my bed-
     fellow:
When I am absent, then lie with my wife.
   Ant.   Sweet lady, you have given me life and
     living:
For here I read for certain that my ships
Are safely come to road.
   Por.   How now, Lorenzo!
My clerk hath some good comforts too for you.
   Ner.   Ay, and I'll give them him without a
     fee.   290
There do I give to you and Jessica,
From the rich Jew, a special deed of gift,
After his death, of all he dies possess'd of.
   Lor.   Fair ladies, you drop manna in the way
Of starved people.
   Por.   It is almost morning,
And yet I am sure you are not satisfied
Of these events at full.   Let us go in;
● And charge us there upon inter'gatories,
And we will answer all things faithfully.
   Gra.   Let it be so: the first inter'gatory   300
That my Nerissa shall be sworn on is,
Whether till the next night she had rather stay,
Or go to bed now, being two hours to day:
But were the day come, I should wish it dark,
That I were couching with the doctor's clerk.
Well, while I live I'll fear no other thing
● So sore as keeping safe Nerissa's ring. [*Exeunt*

298 *inter'gatories*. These were a list of questions put,
on oath, to a witness.

307 *Nerissa's ring*. A bawdy pun.

Gratiano (Jeffery Dench), Nerissa (Patsy Byrne),
Bassanio (Peter McEnery) and Portia (Janet Suzman),
Royal Shakespeare Co, 1965

As You Like It

1598

THIS PLAY IS PURE COMEDY, with a pastoral background, and a few touches of more serious intent. Shakespeare took the story from his contemporary Thomas Lodge's *Rosalynde, Euphues' Golden Legacie.* The characters that impress themselves on our memory are Rosalind herself and to some extent her lover Orlando, though more from his situation as a younger brother done out of his proper inheritance; and the 'melancholy' Jacques, an old disillusioned libertine, whose comments on life provide a tart contrast, useful stiffening, to the love-banter. The subject enables the dramatist to have some fun at the expense of love-talk of various kinds. One sort is the silly passion the shepherdess Phebe conceives for Rosalind disguised as a youth, who sends her packing back to her proper swain, Silvius, who entertains a similarly disdained passion for Phebe.

The whole atmosphere is that of so many Elizabethan songs of 'nymphs and shepherds', and forest life where 'they fleet the time carelessly, as they did in the golden world'. This care-free life is contrasted with that of the Court, since the Duke of the play has had his place usurped by his brother and has taken to the woods. The theme is carried forward in some charming songs, in counterpoint: 'Under the greenwood tree', and 'Blow, blow thou winter wind.' The music for 'It was a lover and his lass' was composed by Thomas Morley, the madrigalist, who lived in the parish of St. Helen's, Bishopsgate, about the time Shakespeare lodged there.

Background. There are more references than usual to place this play in its time. In 1598 the poem Marlowe was writing when he died in 1593, *Hero and Leander*, was at length published; that Marlowe was much in Shakespeare's mind is evident from several specific references and associative phrases. Jove and his page Ganymede are a commonplace of the classics; Rosalind, in taking the guise of a youth, takes the name of Ganymede. But Marlowe had begun his play, *Dido*, with their dallying; one can hardly doubt that it came back to Shakespeare, since we have his touching reference, the only one in which he virtually cited a fellow-writer by name, since it is Marlowe's famous line that he quotes:

Rosalind.
Drawing by C.
Wilhelm for
Princes Theatre
production,
Manchester, 1896

> Dead shepherd, now I find thy saw of might:
> 'Who ever loved that loved not at first sight?'

Shakespeare would have known well how his fellow and rival came by his end: stupidity 'strikes a man more dead than a great reckoning in a little room'. The fatal quarrel in the tavern at Deptford had arisen, according to the inquest, over 'le reckoning'. As for love, 'Leander, he would have lived many a fair year, if it had not been for a hot midsummer night; for, good youth, he went but forth to wash him in the Hellespont and, being taken with the cramp, was drowned—and the foolish chroniclers of that age found it was "Hero of Sestos".'

Francis Meres did not mention the play in his list of Shakespeare's work early in 1598: it fairly clearly belongs to later that year.

The voyages of this time were hardly less in mind: Shakespeare picked up everything that was going at the time. Perhaps particularly those to the South Sea, i.e. the Pacific, for those were the most sensational, involving the passage through the Straits of Magellan into the Spanish preserve. Thomas Cavendish had achieved this and followed Drake in circumnavigating the globe in 1587–8; he was again in the Straits of Magellan in 1592; Richard Hawkins penetrated into the Pacific, where he and his ship were captured in 1594. Rosalind considers 'an inch of delay' in hearing about her lover 'a South Sea of discovery'. Her affection 'hath an unknown bottom, like the Bay of Portugal'—so familiar to the Elizabethan seamen. The morose Jacques considered Touchstone's brain 'as dry as the remainder biscuit after a voyage'.

The Age. The time is brought home to us in many an authentic touch. 'Be it known unto all men by these presents' is the regular formula with which writs and bills began, preambles to serving notice on people. Good old Adam, the faithful family retainer, who bore the exhausted Orlando on his shoulders—the tradition is that Shakespeare played the part of Adam—exemplified

> The constant service of the antique world,
> When service sweat for duty, not for meed [reward].
> Thou art not for the fashion of these times,
> When none will sweat but for promotion.

The usurping Duke pushes Orlando's brother out of doors, and orders his officers to

> Make an extent upon his house and lands—

the regular form when taking possession of property.

A 'why' is as 'plain as the way to parish church'—how that simple phrase brings the age before us! Rosalind describes Orlando and his love verses in these terms: 'O most gentle pulpiter! What tedious homily of love have you wearied your parishioners withal, and never cried "Have patience, good people!" ' Evidently parsons in their pulpits sometimes did—though in the Book of Homilies read in church there is none on Love. Cynical Jacques' comment on Orlando's pretty love-speeches is this: 'have you not been acquainted with goldsmiths' wives and conned them out of their rings?' We hear of 'painted cloths' that hung in people's houses, of tilts and tilting that were a feature of Court life, and the executioner asking pardon on the scaffold before letting fall his axe—no less a feature of the age. 'The howling of Irish wolves against the moon' is a phrase that might have occurred at any time; but Irish amenities were much to the fore in this year 1598, that of the worst disaster to English arms at the rout of the Yellow Ford, which distinguished the opening of O'Neill's[1] rebellion in Ulster.

Themes. A main theme of the play is the contrast between Court and Country. The good Duke has been banished and has taken to the forest with his faithful followers; other characters take refuge there from their troubles and trials—his daughter Rosalind is sent away from Court, and is accompanied by the bad Duke's daughter, Celia. Orlando takes refuge from the persecution of his brother. Before long everybody ends up in the forest, even the usurping Duke and the unkind brother are converted from their wicked ways.

All this provides a theme which recommends itself to Shakespeare's sceptical view of the world. Touchstone says, 'if thou never wast at Court thou never sawest good manners'. To which the countryman, Corin, replies: 'those that are good manners at the Court are as ridiculous in the country as the behaviour of the country is most mockable at the Court'. At Court people kiss hands, and courtiers' hands sweat as well as shepherds': the grease from handling sheep is as wholesome as the perfume courtiers use from civet, 'the very uncleanly flux of a cat'. Touchstone, the clown, claims to be a courtier: 'I have trod a measure [i.e. a dance]; I have flattered a lady; I have been politic [i.e. insincere] with my friend, smooth with mine enemy; I have undone three tailors; I have had four quarrels, and like to have fought one.'

An underlying theme is that of faithfulness and simplicity against sophisticated selfishness and cruelty. The action is set going by an elder brother doing a younger out of his inheritance: 'he lets me feed with his hinds, bars me the place of a brother and mines my gentility with my education'. Orlando reproaches his brother: 'my father charged you in his will to give me good education: you have trained me like a peasant, obscuring and hiding from me all gentleman-like qualities.' We may be sure that this theme had real significance for Shakespeare, who was very much set on being ranked as a gentleman and, unlike many denizens of the theatre, behaved like one.

We can catch something of him in personal reflections dropped in passing: it is Adam who says,

> Know you not, master, to some kind of men
> Their graces serve them but as enemies?

And again,

> . . . in my youth I never did apply
> Hot and rebellious liquors in my blood,

[1] Hugh O'Neill, native prince, known to the English as the Earl of Tyrone

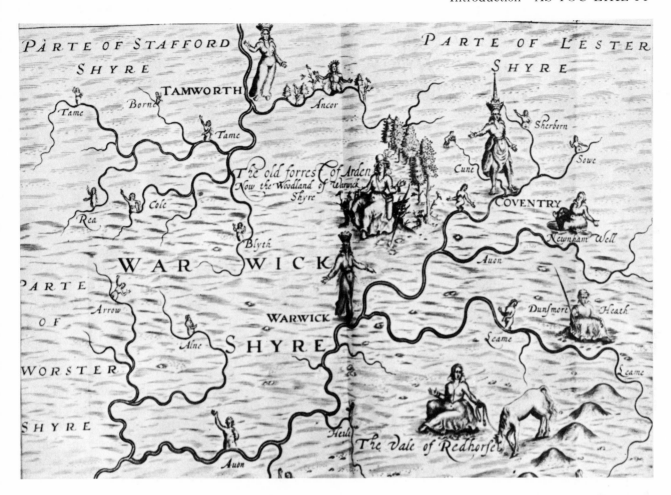

Nor did not with unbashful forehead woo
The means of weakness and debility.

Shakespeare always speaks against drunkenness, as against ingratitude: the winter wind in the forest is not so unkind as man's ingratitude. Where the same sentiment is enforced again and again we may be sure that it meant something special to the author. Here too we see the normal social man (so unlike Marlowe), accepting his place in society with its duties, obligations and pleasures:

If ever you have looked on better days,
If ever been where bells have knolled to church,
If ever sat at any good man's feast,
If ever from your eyelids wiped a tear
And know what 'tis to pity and be pitied . . .

There, we may be sure, we have the man, and we note phrases from church-service and the Bible, the Prodigal Son eating husks with hogs, etc.

Warwickshire. It is vaguely suggested that the forest is the Ardennes, but everything shows that it is Arden, from which Shakespeare's parents came, the background of his own youth, that he has in mind, along with the shepherd and shepherdesses of the Cotswolds. A familiar enough sight at Stratford must have been

. . . the whining schoolboy, with his satchel
And shining morning face, creeping like snail
Unwillingly to school.

We have the sheepcotes and bounds of feed (i.e. fences), the little cots, up in the Cotswold uplands. Twice we have the phrase an 'inland man' as indicating good manners, against the rough ways of the uplands, portrayed in the country folk, William and Audrey. A country vicar is made fun of in Sir Oliver Martext ('Sir' was the usual appellation of a curate, one who was not a Master of Arts). The description of the cottage:

down in the neighbour bottom,
The rank of osiers by the murmuring stream—

makes one think of the situation of Anne Hathaway's cottage. Even 'the acres of the rye', where in springtime 'these pretty folks would lie', applied well enough in his time to the way across the fields of rye to Shottery.

William Shakespeare was a home-keeping man, so far as his profession allowed: he never lost touch with family and home, and was able to live there more in his last years, in the best house in the town from the proceeds of his life of hard work. Jacques, who has travelled abroad, to turn cynic, is thus addressed by Rosalind: 'look you lisp and wear strange suits, disable all the benefits of your own country . . . or I will scarce think you have swam in a gondola.' And in portraying Jacques Shakespeare was able to aim a hit at the contemporary cult of melancholy—exemplified, for example, by the dramatist, John Ford. Jacques asserts that he has 'neither the scholar's melancholy, which is emulation [i.e. competitiveness, envy—true enough]; nor the musician's, which is fantastical [compare Dowland's famous 'Lacrymae']; nor the courtier's, which is proud; nor the soldier's, which is ambitious; nor the lawyer's, which is politic.' All

Above: *The 'whining schoolboy' from the Second Age of Man. From the painting by Robert Smirke R.A. (1752–1845)*

Right: *Nineteenth century engraving of Anne Hathaway's cottage at Shottery, near Stratford-upon-Avon*

these shafts reach home, and we could give notorious illustrations of them from personages of the time.

The asides are more interesting than the love-talk, the baiting and banter, which strikes us today as contrived—a good deal of it in keeping with rules of Elizabethan rhetoric; though here, as always, the dramatist reveals what a clever man he was to be able to keep it going: 'conceit's expositor', as he had described himself. Much of this is perhaps to be played in high style, with a smile upon it, as if half-parody, in inverted commas.

Theatre. The consciousness of his profession, the theatre itself, is ever-present as through all his work, in the Sonnets too. It finds expression in a famous oration of Jacques:

> All the world's a stage,
> And all the men and women merely players:
> They have their exits and their entrances,
> And one man in his time plays many parts.

Though this was a Renaissance commonplace, developed in terms of rhetoric, it is too real and vivid not to reflect personal observation: the whining schoolboy, the swearing, duelling soldier, the fat J.P. full of capon and wise saws, the lean and slippered pantaloon—old age, seen in terms of the stage.

We can envisage the boy-actors who took the parts of Rosalind and Celia for we are told: the former tall and fair, the other 'low and browner'. The play has, as often later, a masque-like ending with Hymen entering to marry up the couples. Once more, the sudden improbable changes that take place in the characters of the bad Duke and the wicked brother, would not have bothered Elizabethans. And there is a characteristically personal Epilogue, original for being spoken by a lady—Rosalind. 'I charge you, O women, for the love you bear to men, to like as much of this play as please you. And I charge you, O men, for the love you bear to women—as I perceive by your simpering, none of you hates them—that between you and the women the play may please.' How like Shakespeare!—polite and courteous, positively propitiating, the way to be popular; and how unlike Ben Jonson, whose attitude to the public was always, 'take it or leave it, as you please.' In this year the friendly, gentlemanly Shakespeare gave the rumbustious Ben his chance, by welcoming his play, *Every Man in his Humour*, to the Company and himself performing in it.

In this same year, the Admiral's men produced their Robin Hood plays; here was the Chamberlain's *riposte* at the end of the year.

Text. The text is a good one, from the First Folio. Shakespeare's plays were so popular that the Company tried again and again to protect its rights by having the publication of a play 'stayed', i.e. asserting its right to publish, then withholding publication. For it was stage-performances that mattered to the Company and to Shakespeare as a leading member of it, financially dependent on it. This was his living, not publishing his works. In 1600 four of the Company's plays were thus stayed: *As You Like It, Much Ado About Nothing, Henry V* and Jonson's success with *Every Man in his Humour*. Thus there is no Quarto of *As You Like It*, and the play would have been lost to us if Shakespeare's good fellows, Heming and Condell, had not specially gathered his plays together to do him exceptional honour.

AS YOU LIKE IT.

DRAMATIS PERSONÆ.

DUKE, living in banishment.
FREDERICK, his brother, and usurper of his dominions.
AMIENS,⎫ lords attending on the banished
JAQUES,⎭ duke.
LE BEAU, a courtier attending upon Frederick.
CHARLES, wrestler to Frederick.
OLIVER,
JAQUES,⎬ sons of Sir Rowland de Boys.
ORLANDO,
ADAM,⎫ servants to Oliver.
DENNIS,⎭
TOUCHSTONE, a clown.

SIR OLIVER MARTEXT, a vicar.
CORIN,⎫ shepherds.
SILVIUS,⎭
WILLIAM, a country fellow, in love with Audrey.
A person representing Hymen.
ROSALIND, daughter to the banished duke.
CELIA, daughter to Frederick.
PHEBE, a shepherdess.
AUDREY, a country wench.

Lords, pages, and attendants, &c.

SCENE: *Oliver's house; Duke Frederick's court; and the Forest of Arden.*

● *A bullet beside a text line indicates an annotation in the opposite column*

ACT I.

SCENE I. *Orchard of* OLIVER'S *house.*

Enter ORLANDO *and* ADAM.

Orl. As I remember, Adam, it was upon this fashion; bequeathed me by will but poor a thousand crowns, and, as thou sayest, charged my brother, on his blessing, to breed.me well: and
● there begins my sadness. My brother Jaques he keeps at school, and report speaks goldenly of his profit: for my part, he keeps me rustically at home, or, to speak more properly, stays me here at home unkept; for call you that keeping for a gentleman of my birth, that differs not from the

Set design for Orchard of Oliver's house by Motley, Stratford-upon-Avon, 1952

5 *Jaques.* Pronounced 'Jak-es'.

Opposite: Third age of man—the lover. Drawing by J. A. Atkinson (1775–*c.* 1833)

341

12 *fair with their feeding*. Well fed.

13 *manage*. Technical term for the training of horses.

19 *countenance*. Attitude.

20 *hinds*. Farm labourers.

21-22 *mines my gentility with my education*. i.e. undermines my gentility with my lack of education.

31 *what make you here?* What are you doing here?

38-39 *be naught awhile*. Go away.

49 *courtesy of nations*. Custom.

54 *reverence*. The respect due to their father.

55 *boy*. Used contemptuously.

56-57 *too young in this*. i.e. inferior when it comes to wrestling.

76 *allottery*. Share.

stalling of an ox? His horses are bred better;
●for, besides that they are fair with their feeding,
●they are taught their manage, and to that end
riders dearly hired: but I, his brother, gain
nothing under him but growth; for the which his
animals on his dunghills are as much bound to
him as I. Besides this nothing that he so plentifully gives me, the something that nature gave
●me his countenance seems to take from me: he
●lets me feed with his hinds, bars me the place of
●a brother, and, as much as in him lies, mines my
gentility with my education. This is it, Adam,
that grieves me; and the spirit of my father,
which I think is within me, begins to mutiny
against this servitude: I will no longer endure
it, though yet I know no wise remedy how to
avoid it.

Adam. Yonder comes my master, your brother.

Orl. Go apart, Adam, and thou shalt hear
how he will shake me up.   30

Enter OLIVER.

● *Oli.* Now, sir! what make you here?

Orl. Nothing: I am not taught to make any
thing.

Oli. What mar you then, sir?

Orl. Marry, sir, I am helping you to mar that
which God made, a poor unworthy brother of
yours, with idleness.

● *Oli.* Marry, sir, be better employed, and be
naught awhile.   39

Orl. Shall I keep your hogs and eat husks
with them? What prodigal portion have I spent,
that I should come to such penury?

Oli. Know you where you are, sir?

Orl. O, sir, very well: here in your orchard.

Oli. Know you before whom, sir?

Orl. Ay, better than him I am before knows
me. I know you are my eldest brother; and, in
the gentle condition of blood, you should so know
●me. The courtesy of nations allows you my
better, in that you are the first-born; but the
same tradition takes not away my blood, were
there twenty brothers betwixt us: I have as much
of my father in me as you; albeit, I confess, your
●coming before me is nearer to his reverence.

● *Oli.* What, boy!

● *Orl.* Come, come, elder brother, you are too
young in this.

Oli. Wilt thou lay hands on me, villain?

Orl. I am no villain; I am the youngest son
of Sir Rowland de Boys; he was my father, and
he is thrice a villain that says such a father begot
villains. Wert thou not my brother, I would not
take this hand from thy throat till this other had
pulled out thy tongue for saying so: thou hast
railed on thyself.

Adam. Sweet masters, be patient: for your
father's remembrance, be at accord.

Oli. Let me go, I say.

Orl. I will not, till I please: you shall hear
me. My father charged you in his will to give
me good education: you have trained me like a
peasant, obscuring and hiding from me all gentleman-like qualities. The spirit of my father
grows strong in me, and I will no longer endure
it: therefore allow me such exercises as may be-
●come a gentleman, or give me the poor allottery

my father left me by testament; with that I will go buy my fortunes.

Oli. And what wilt thou do? beg, when that is spent? Well, sir, get you in: I will not long be troubled with you; you shall have some part of your will: I pray you, leave me.

Orl. I will no further offend you than becomes me for my good.

Oli. Get you with him, you old dog.

Adam. Is 'old dog' my reward? Most true, I have lost my teeth in your service. God be with my old master! he would not have spoke such a word.   [*Exeunt Orlando and Adam.*

Oli. Is it even so? begin you to grow upon me? I will physic your rankness, and yet give no thousand crowns neither.   Holla, Dennis!

Enter DENNIS.

Den. Calls your worship?

Oli. Was not Charles, the duke's wrestler, here to speak with me?

Den. So please you, he is here at the door and importunes access to you.

Oli. Call him in. [*Exit Dennis.*] 'Twill be a good way; and to-morrow the wrestling is.

Enter CHARLES.

Cha. Good morrow to your worship.   100

Oli. Good Monsieur Charles, what's the new news at the new court?

Cha. There's no news at the court, sir, but the old news: that is, the old duke is banished by his younger brother the new duke; and three or four loving lords have put themselves into voluntary exile with him, whose lands and revenues enrich the new duke; therefore he gives them good leave to wander.

Oli. Can you tell if Rosalind, the duke's daughter, be banished with her father?   111

Cha. O, no; for the duke's daughter, her cousin, so loves her, being ever from their cradles bred together, that she would have followed her exile, or have died to stay behind her. She is at the court, and no less beloved of her uncle than his own daughter; and never two ladies loved as they do.

Oli. Where will the old duke live?

Cha. They say he is already in the forest of Arden, and a many merry men with him; and there they live like the old Robin Hood of England: they say many young gentlemen flock to him every day, and fleet the time carelessly, as they did in the golden world.

Oli. What, you wrestle to-morrow before the new duke?

Cha. Marry, do I, sir; and I came to acquaint you with a matter. I am given, sir, secretly to understand that your younger brother Orlando hath a disposition to come in disguised against me to try a fall. To-morrow, sir, I wrestle for my credit; and he that escapes me without some broken limb shall acquit him well. Your brother is but young and tender; and, for your love, I would be loath to foil him, as I must, for my own honour, if he come in: therefore, out of my love to you, I came hither to acquaint you withal, that either you might stay him from his intendment or brook such disgrace well as he

---

90-91 *grow upon me.* Take liberties. *physic your rankness.* Cure your insolence.

Charles: '. . . the old duke is banished . . . and three or four loving lords.' Costume design for First Forest Lord by C. Lovat Fraser, 1919

---

121 *Arden.* The Ardennes on the borders of Belgium and Luxembourg; Shakespeare's audience would, however, have thought of the forest of Arden in Warwickshire.

124 *fleet.* Pass.

125 *golden world.* The Golden Age of classical times.

140 *intendment.* Intention.

162-63 *anatomize*. Dissect, describe.

167 *go alone again*. i.e. walk without help.

177 *misprised*. Despised.

Rosalind and Celia. Costume designs by Cyril Mahoney

6 *learn*. Teach.

14 *righteously tempered*. Well directed.

shall run into, in that it is a thing of his own search and altogether against my will.

Oli. Charles, I thank thee for thy love to me, which thou shalt find I will most kindly requite. I had myself notice of my brother's purpose herein and have by underhand means laboured to dissuade him from it, but he is resolute. I'll tell thee, Charles: it is the stubbornest young fellow of France, full of ambition, an envious emulator of every man's good parts, a secret and villanous contriver against me his natural brother: therefore use thy discretion; I had as lief thou didst break his neck as his finger. And thou wert best look to't; for if thou dost him any slight disgrace or if he do not mightily grace himself on thee, he will practise against thee by poison, entrap thee by some treacherous device and never leave thee till he hath ta'en thy life by some indirect means or other; for, I assure thee, and almost with tears I speak it, there is not one so young and so villanous this day living. I speak but brotherly of him; but should I anatomize him to thee as he is, I must blush and weep and thou must look pale and wonder.

Cha. I am heartily glad I came hither to you. If he come to-morrow, I'll give him his payment: if ever he go alone again, I'll never wrestle for prize more: and so God keep your worship!

Oli. Farewell, good Charles. [*Exit Charles.*] Now will I stir this gamester: I hope I shall see an end of him; for my soul, yet I know not why, hates nothing more than he. Yet he's gentle, never schooled and yet learned, full of noble device, of all sorts enchantingly beloved, and indeed so much in the heart of the world, and especially of my own people, who best know him, that I am altogether misprised: but it shall not be so long; this wrestler shall clear all: nothing remains but that I kindle the boy thither; which now I'll go about.   [*Exit.* 180

SCENE II. *Lawn before the* DUKE'S *palace.*

Enter CELIA *and* ROSALIND.

Cel. I pray thee, Rosalind, sweet my coz, be merry.

Ros. Dear Celia, I show more mirth than I am mistress of; and would you yet I were merrier? Unless you could teach me to forget a banished father, you must not learn me how to remember any extraordinary pleasure.

Cel. Herein I see thou lovest me not with the full weight that I love thee. If my uncle, thy banished father, had banished thy uncle, the duke my father, so thou hadst been still with me, I could have taught my love to take thy father for mine: so wouldst thou, if the truth of thy love to me were so righteously tempered as mine is to thee.

Ros. Well, I will forget the condition of my estate, to rejoice in yours.

Cel. You know my father hath no child but I, nor none is like to have: and, truly, when he dies, thou shalt be his heir, for what he hath taken away from thy father perforce, I will render thee again in affection; by mine honour, I will; and when I break that oath, let me turn monster: therefore, my sweet Rose, my dear Rose, be merry.

Ros. From henceforth I will, coz, and devise sports. Let me see; what think you of falling in love?

Cel. Marry, I prithee, do, to make sport withal: but love no man in good earnest; nor no • further in sport neither than with safety of a pure blush thou mayst in honour come off again.

Ros. What shall be our sport, then?

Cel. Let us sit and mock the good housewife Fortune from her wheel, that her gifts may henceforth be bestowed equally.

Ros. I would we could do so, for her benefits are mightily misplaced, and the bountiful blind woman doth most mistake in her gifts to women.

Cel. 'Tis true; for those that she makes fair she scarce makes honest, and those that she makes honest she makes very ill-favouredly.

Ros. Nay, now thou goest from Fortune's office to Nature's: Fortune reigns in gifts of the world, not in the lineaments of Nature.

Enter TOUCHSTONE.

Cel. No? when Nature hath made a fair creature, may she not by Fortune fall into the fire? Though Nature hath given us wit to flout at Fortune, hath not Fortune sent in this fool to cut off the argument? 50

Ros. Indeed, there is Fortune too hard for • Nature, when Fortune makes Nature's natural the cutter-off of Nature's wit.

Cel. Peradventure this is not Fortune's work neither, but Nature's; who perceiveth our natural wits too dull to reason of such goddesses and hath sent this natural for our whetstone; for always the dulness of the fool is the whetstone of the wits. How now, wit! whither wander you?

Touch. Mistress, you must come away to your father. 61

Cel. Were you made the messenger?

Touch. No, by mine honour, but I was bid to come for you.

Ros. Where learned you that oath, fool?

Touch. Of a certain knight that swore by his honour they were good pancakes and swore by his honour the mustard was naught: now I'll stand to it, the pancakes were naught and the mustard was good, and yet was not the knight forsworn. 71

Cel. How prove you that, in the great heap of your knowledge?

Ros. Ay, marry, now unmuzzle your wisdom.

Touch. Stand you both forth now: stroke your chins, and swear by your beards that I am a knave.

Cel. By our beards, if we had them, thou art.

Touch. By my knavery, if I had it, then I were; but if you swear by that that is not, you are not forsworn: no more was this knight, swearing by his honour, for he never had any; or if he had, he had sworn it away before ever he saw those pancakes or that mustard.

Cel. Prithee, who is't that thou meanest?

Touch. One that old Frederick, your father, loves.

Cel. My father's love is enough to honour him: enough! speak no more of him; you'll be • whipped for taxation one of these days. 91

31-32 *than with safety . . . come off again.* i.e. than you may come out of the affair with honour and nothing lost save a pure blush.

52 *natural.* Born fool.

Tom King, 18th century English actor, as Touchstone. Engraving from Bell's edition of *Shakespeare*, 1775

91 *taxation.* Criticism.

107 *colour*. Kind.

Costume design for Le Beau by J. Gower Parks, Open Air Theatre, Regent's Park, London, 1935

113 *keep not my rank*. i.e. rating as a wit, with quibble on 'rank' as ill-smelling.

131 *bills*. Proclamations. Rosalind mocks their regular formal opening.

Touch. The more pity, that fools may not speak wisely what wise men do foolishly.

Cel. By my troth, thou sayest true; for since the little wit that fools have was silenced, the little foolery that wise men have makes a great show. Here comes Monsieur Le Beau.

Ros. With his mouth full of news.

Cel. Which he will put on us, as pigeons feed their young. 100

Ros. Then shall we be news-crammed.

Cel. All the better; we shall be the more marketable.

Enter LE BEAU.

Bon jour, Monsieur Le Beau: what's the news?

Le Beau. Fair princess, you have lost much good sport.

• *Cel.* Sport! of what colour?

Le Beau. What colour, madam! how shall I answer you?

Ros. As wit and fortune will. 110

Touch. Or as the Destinies decree.

Cel. Well said: that was laid on with a trowel.

• *Touch.* Nay, if I keep not my rank,—

Ros. Thou losest thy old smell.

Le Beau. You amaze me, ladies: I would have told you of good wrestling, which you have lost the sight of.

Ros. Yet tell us the manner of the wrestling.

Le Beau. I will tell you the beginning; and, if it please your ladyships, you may see the end; for the best is yet to do; and here, where you are, they are coming to perform it.

Cel. Well, the beginning, that is dead and buried.

Le Beau. There comes an old man and his three sons,—

Cel. I could match this beginning with an old tale.

Le Beau. Three proper young men, of excellent growth and presence. 130

• *Ros.* With bills on their necks, 'Be it known unto all men by these presents.'

Le Beau. The eldest of the three wrestled with Charles, the duke's wrestler; which Charles in a moment threw him and broke three of his ribs, that there is little hope of life in him: so he served the second, and so the third. Yonder they lie; the poor old man, their father, making such pitiful dole over them that all the beholders take his part with weeping. 140

Ros. Alas!

Touch. But what is the sport, monsieur, that the ladies have lost?

Le Beau. Why, this that I speak of.

Touch. Thus men may grow wiser every day: it is the first time that ever I heard breaking of ribs was sport for ladies.

Cel. Or I, I promise thee.

Ros. But is there any else longs to see this broken music in his sides? is there yet another dotes upon rib-breaking? Shall we see this wrestling, cousin?

Le Beau. You must, if you stay here; for here is the place appointed for the wrestling, and they are ready to perform it.

Cel. Yonder, sure, they are coming: let us now stay and see it.

Flourish. Enter DUKE FREDERICK, Lords,
ORLANDO, CHARLES, *and* Attendants.

Duke F. Come on: since the youth will not
be entreated, his own peril on his forwardness.

Ros. Is yonder the man?   160

Le Beau. Even he, madam.

Cel. Alas, he is too young! yet he looks successfully.

Duke F. How now, daughter and cousin!
are you crept hither to see the wrestling?

Ros. Ay, my liege, so please you give us
leave.

Duke F. You will take little delight in it, I
• can tell you; there is such odds in the man.   In
pity of the challenger's youth I would fain dissuade him, but he will not be entreated.   Speak
to him, ladies; see if you can move him.

Cel. Call him hither, good Monsieur Le Beau.

Duke F. Do so: I 'll not be by.

Le Beau. Monsieur the challenger, the prin-
cesses call for you.

Orl. I attend them with all respect and duty.

Ros. Young man, have you challenged Charles
the wrestler?   179

Orl. No, fair princess; he is the general challenger: I come but in, as others do, to try with
him the strength of my youth.

Cel. Young gentleman, your spirits are too
bold for your years.   You have seen cruel proof
of this man's strength: if you saw yourself with
your eyes or knew yourself with your judgement,
the fear of your adventure would counsel you to
a more equal enterprise.   We pray you, for your
own sake, to embrace your own safety and give
over this attempt.   190

Ros. Do, young sir; your reputation shall not
therefore be misprised: we will make it our suit
to the duke that the wrestling might not go forward.

Orl. I beseech you, punish me not with your
hard thoughts; wherein I confess me much guilty,
to deny so fair and excellent ladies any thing.
But let your fair eyes and gentle wishes go with
me to my trial: wherein if I be foiled, there is
• but one shamed that was never gracious; if killed,
but one dead that is willing to be so: I shall do
my friends no wrong, for I have none to lament
me, the world no injury, for in it I have nothing;
only in the world I fill up a place, which may be
better supplied when I have made it empty.

Ros. The little strength that I have, I would
it were with you.

Cel. And mine, to eke out hers.

Ros. Fare you well: pray heaven I be deceived in you!   210

Cel. Your heart's desires be with you!

Cha. Come, where is this young gallant that
is so desirous to lie with his mother earth?

Orl. Ready, sir; but his will hath in it a more
• modest working.

Duke F. You shall try but one fall.

Cha. No, I warrant your grace, you shall not
entreat him to a second, that have so mightily
persuaded him from a first.   219

Orl. An you mean to mock me after, you should
not have mocked me before: but come your ways.

Ros. Now Hercules be thy speed, young man!

Cel. I would I were invisible, to catch the
strong fellow by the leg.   [*They wrestle.*

169 *odds in the man.* i.e. the odds are in favour of
Charles.

Before the wrestling bout. Engraving from a painting
by Daniel Maclise (1806–1870)

200 *gracious.* Graced (by favours).

215 *working.* Endeavour.

Wrestling scene. Charles thrown by Orlando. Painting by Francis Hayman, 1744

230 *well breathed.* Warmed up.

254 *Sticks me at heart.* Grieves me.

Rosalind gives a chain to Orlando. Engraving from a painting by J. Downman (*c.* 1750–1824)

263 *quintain.* A post used for tilting.

268 *Have with you.* Come on.

Ros. O excellent young man!
Cel. If I had a thunderbolt in mine eye, I can tell who should down. [*Shout. Charles is thrown.*
Duke F. No more, no more.
Orl. Yes, I beseech your grace: I am not yet
●well breathed.   230
Duke F. How dost thou, Charles?
Le Beau. He cannot speak, my lord.
Duke F. Bear him away. What is thy name, young man?
Orl. Orlando, my liege; the youngest son of Sir Rowland de Boys.
Duke F. I would thou hadst been son to some man else:
The world esteem'd thy father honourable,
But I did find him still mine enemy:
Thou shouldst have better pleased me with this deed,   240
Hadst thou descended from another house.
But fare thee well; thou art a gallant youth:
I would thou hadst told me of another father.
      [*Exeunt Duke Fred., train, and Le Beau.*
Cel. Were I my father, coz, would I do this?
Orl. I am more proud to be Sir Rowland's son,
His youngest son; and would not change that calling,
To be adopted heir to Frederick.
Ros. My father loved Sir Rowland as his soul,
And all the world was of my father's mind:
Had I before known this young man his son,
I should have given him tears unto entreaties, 250
Ere he should thus have ventured.
Cel.   Gentle cousin,
Let us go thank him and encourage him:
My father's rough and envious disposition
●Sticks me at heart. Sir, you have well deserved:
If you do keep your promises in love
But justly, as you have exceeded all promise,
Your mistress shall be happy.
Ros.   Gentleman,
      [*Giving him a chain from her neck.*
Wear this for me, one out of suits with fortune,
That could give more, but that her hand lacks means.
Shall we go, coz?
Cel.   Ay. Fare you well, fair gentleman.
Orl. Can I not say, I thank you? My better parts   261
Are all thrown down, and that which here stands up
●Is but a quintain, a mere lifeless block.
Ros. He calls us back: my pride fell with my fortunes;
I'll ask him what he would. Did you call, sir?
Sir, you have wrestled well and overthrown
More than your enemies.
Cel.   Will you go, coz?
● *Ros.* Have with you. Fare you well.
      [*Exeunt Rosalind and Celia.*
Orl. What passion hangs these weights upon my tongue?
I cannot speak to her, yet she urged conference.
O poor Orlando, thou art overthrown!   271
Or Charles or something weaker masters thee.

Re-enter LE BEAU.

Le Beau. Good sir, I do in friendship counsel you
To leave this place. Albeit you have deserved

High commendation, true applause and love,
Yet such is now the duke's condition
That he misconstrues all that you have done.
● The duke is humorous : what he is indeed,
More suits you to conceive than I to speak of.
  Orl. I thank you, sir : and, pray you, tell me
  this ;   280
Which of the two was daughter of the duke
That here was at the wrestling ?
  Le Beau. Neither his daughter, if we judge
  by manners ;
● But yet indeed the lesser is his daughter :
The other is daughter to the banish'd duke,
And here detain'd by her usurping uncle,
To keep his daughter company ; whose loves
Are dearer than the natural bond of sisters.
But I can tell you that of late this duke
Hath ta'en displeasure 'gainst his gentle niece,
Grounded upon no other argument   291
But that the people praise her for her virtues
And pity her for her good father's sake ;
And, on my life, his malice 'gainst the lady
Will suddenly break forth. Sir, fare you well :
Hereafter, in a better world than this,
I shall desire more love and knowledge of you.
  Orl. I rest much bounden to you : fare you
  well.   [*Exit Le Beau.*
● Thus must I from the smoke into the smother ;
From tyrant duke unto a tyrant brother : 300
But heavenly Rosalind !   [*Exit.*

SCENE III. *A room in the palace.*

Enter CELIA *and* ROSALIND.

Cel. Why, cousin ! why, Rosalind ! Cupid
have mercy ! not a word ?
 Ros. Not one to throw at a dog.
 Cel. No, thy words are too precious to be
cast away upon curs ; throw some of them at me ;
come, lame me with reasons.
 Ros. Then there were two cousins laid up ;
when the one should be lamed with reasons and
the other mad without any.
 Cel. But is all this for your father ? 10
● *Ros.* No, some of it is for my child's father.
O, how full of briers is this working-day world !
 Cel. They are but burs, cousin, thrown upon
thee in holiday foolery : if we walk not in the
trodden paths, our very petticoats will catch them.
 Ros. I could shake them off my coat : these
burs are in my heart.
● *Cel.* Hem them away.
 Ros. I would try, if I could cry 'hem' and
have him.   20
 Cel. Come, come, wrestle with thy affections.
 Ros. O, they take the part of a better wrestler
than myself !
● *Cel.* O, a good wish upon you ! you will try
in time, in despite of a fall. But, turning these
jests out of service, let us talk in good earnest : is
it possible, on such a sudden, you should fall into
so strong a liking with old Sir Rowland's youngest
son ?
 Ros. The duke my father loved his father
dearly.   31
 Cel. Doth it therefore ensue that you should
love his son dearly ? By this kind of chase, I
should hate him, for my father hated his father
dearly ; yet I hate not Orlando.

278 *humorous.* Moody.

284 *lesser.* Smaller (in height).

299 *smoke into the smother.* i.e. bad to worse.

11 *my child's father.* i.e. the man I shall marry.

18 *Hem them away.* Cough them away.

24-25 *try in time.* This suggests that she will try a fall
with Orlando, with a sexual implication.

Duke Frederick: 'Mistress, dispatch you . . . from our court!' Design by Ronald Searle, Mermaid Theatre production, Royal Exchange, London, 1953

55 *purgation.* Clearing from guilt.

77 *Juno's swans.* Swans traditionally drew the chariot of Venus. The birds sacred to Juno were in fact geese, but geese and swans were frequently confused in ancient mythology. In Greek art, swans were depicted harnessed together.

Ros. No, faith, hate him not, for my sake.
Cel. Why should I not? doth he not deserve well?
Ros. Let me love him for that, and do you love him because I do. Look, here comes the duke.   41
Cel. With his eyes full of anger.

Enter Duke Frederick, *with* Lords.

Duke F. Mistress, dispatch you with your safest haste
And get you from our court.
Ros.   Me, uncle?
Duke F.   You, cousin:
Within these ten days if that thou be'st found
So near our public court as twenty miles,
Thou diest for it.
Ros.   I do beseech your grace,
Let me the knowledge of my fault bear with me:
If with myself I hold intelligence
Or have acquaintance with mine own desires, 50
If that I do not dream or be not frantic,—
As I do trust I am not—then, dear uncle,
Never so much as in a thought unborn
Did I offend your highness.
Duke F.   Thus do all traitors:
• If their purgation did consist in words,
They are as innocent as grace itself:
Let it suffice thee that I trust thee not.
Ros. Yet your mistrust cannot make me a traitor:
Tell me whereon the likelihood depends.
Duke F. Thou art thy father's daughter; there's enough.   60
Ros. So was I when your highness took his dukedom;
So was I when your highness banish'd him:
Treason is not inherited, my lord;
Or, if we did derive it from our friends,
What's that to me? my father was no traitor:
Then, good my liege, mistake me not so much
To think my poverty is treacherous.
Cel. Dear sovereign, hear me speak.
Duke F. Ay, Celia; we stay'd her for your sake,
Else had she with her father ranged along. 70
Cel. I did not then entreat to have her stay;
It was your pleasure and your own remorse:
I was too young that time to value her;
But now I know her: if she be a traitor,
Why so am I; we still have slept together,
Rose at an instant, learn'd, play'd, eat together,
• And wheresoe'er we went, like Juno's swans,
Still we went coupled and inseparable.
Duke F. She is too subtle for thee; and her smoothness,
Her very silence and her patience   80
Speak to the people, and they pity her.
Thou art a fool: she robs thee of thy name;
And thou wilt show more bright and seem more virtuous
When she is gone.   Then open not thy lips:
Firm and irrevocable is my doom
Which I have pass'd upon her; she is banish'd.
Cel. Pronounce that sentence then on me, my liege:
I cannot live out of her company.
Duke F. You are a fool. You, niece, provide yourself:
If you outstay the time, upon mine honour, 90

And in the greatness of my word, you die.
[*Exeunt Duke Frederick and Lords.*
Cel. O my poor Rosalind, whither wilt
  thou go?
Wilt thou change fathers? I will give thee mine.
I charge thee, be not thou more grieved than I am.
  Ros. I have more cause.
  Cel.   Thou hast not, cousin;
Prithee, be cheerful: know'st thou not, the duke
Hath banish'd me, his daughter?
  Ros.   That he hath not.
  Cel. No, hath not? Rosalind lacks then the
  love
Which teacheth thee that thou and I am one:
Shall we be sunder'd? shall we part, sweet girl?
No: let my father seek another heir.   101
Therefore devise with me how we may fly,
Whither to go and what to bear with us;
And do not seek to take your change upon you,
To bear your griefs yourself and leave me out;
For, by this heaven, now at our sorrows pale,
Say what thou canst, I'll go along with thee.
  Ros. Why, whither shall we go?
  Cel. To seek my uncle in the forest of Arden.
  Ros. Alas, what danger will it be to us,   110
Maids as we are, to travel forth so far!
Beauty provoketh thieves sooner than gold.
  Cel. I'll put myself in poor and mean attire
●And with a kind of umber smirch my face;
The like do you: so shall we pass along
And never stir assailants.
  Ros.   Were it not better,
Because that I am more than common tall,
●That I did suit me all points like a man?
●A gallant curtle-axe upon my thigh,   119
A boar-spear in my hand; and—in my heart
Lie there what hidden woman's fear there will—
●We'll have a swashing and a martial outside,
As many other mannish cowards have
That do outface it with their semblances.
  Cel. What shall I call thee when thou art
  a man?
  Ros. I'll have no worse a name than Jove's
  own page;
And therefore look you call me Ganymede.
But what will you be call'd?
  Cel. Something that hath a reference to my
  state;
No longer Celia, but Aliena.   130
● *Ros.* But, cousin, what if we assay'd to steal
The clownish fool out of your father's court?
Would he not be a comfort to our travel?
  Cel. He'll go along o'er the wide world
  with me;
Leave me alone to woo him. Let's away,
And get our jewels and our wealth together,
Devise the fittest time and safest way
To hide us from pursuit that will be made
After my flight. Now go we in content
To liberty and not to banishment. [*Exeunt.* 140

ACT II.

SCENE I. *The Forest of Arden.*

Enter DUKE *senior,* AMIENS, *and two or
three* Lords, *like foresters.*

  Duke S. Now, my co-mates and brothers in
  exile,
Hath not old custom made this life more sweet

114 *umber.* Brown earth.

118 *suit me all points.* Dress myself in all ways.

119 *curtle-axe.* Cutlass or short sword.

122 *swashing.* Swaggering.

Ganymede, Jove's page in classical mythology. From a
19th century engraving

131 *assay'd.* Attempted.

5 *penalty of Adam.* Expulsion from Paradise.

13 *toad.* Elizabethans believed that the toad had a precious stone in its head which was an antidote to poison.

Mythical toad with jewel. Illustration from *Ortus Sanitatus*, 1495

24 *forked heads.* Barbed arrows.

33 *sequester'd.* Separated.

44 *moralize.* Draw morals from.

Jaques and the wounded stag. Detail from a landscape by Sir G. Beaumont (1753–1827)

Than that of painted pomp? Are not these woods
More free from peril than the envious court?
● Here feel we but the penalty of Adam,
The seasons' difference, as the icy fang
And churlish chiding of the winter's wind,
Which, when it bites and blows upon my body,
Even till I shrink with cold, I smile and say
'This is no flattery: these are counsellors   10
That feelingly persuade me what I am.'
Sweet are the uses of adversity,
● Which, like the toad, ugly and venomous,
Wears yet a precious jewel in his head;
And this our life exempt from public haunt
Finds tongues in trees, books in the running
    brooks,
Sermons in stones and good in every thing.
I would not change it.
    Ami.   Happy is your grace,
That can translate the stubbornness of fortune
Into so quiet and so sweet a style.   20
    Duke S.   Come, shall we go and kill us
    venison?
And yet it irks me the poor dappled fools,
Being native burghers of this desert city,
● Should in their own confines with forked heads
Have their round haunches gored.
    First Lord.   Indeed, my lord,
The melancholy Jaques grieves at that,
And, in that kind, swears you do more usurp
Than doth your brother that hath banish'd you.
To-day my Lord of Amiens and myself
Did steal behind him as he lay along   30
Under an oak whose antique root peeps out
Upon the brook that brawls along this wood:
● To the which place a poor sequester'd stag,
That from the hunter's aim had ta'en a hurt,
Did come to languish, and indeed, my lord,
The wretched animal heaved forth such groans
That their discharge did stretch his leathern coat
Almost to bursting, and the big round tears
Coursed one another down his innocent nose
In piteous chase; and thus the hairy fool,   40
Much marked of the melancholy Jaques,
Stood on the extremest verge of the swift brook,
Augmenting it with tears.
    Duke S.   But what said Jaques?
● Did he not moralize this spectacle?
    First Lord.   O, yes, into a thousand similes.
First, for his weeping into the needless stream;
'Poor deer,' quoth he 'thou makest a testament
As worldlings do, giving thy sum of more
To that which had too much:' then, being there
    alone,
Left and abandon'd of his velvet friends,   50
' 'Tis right,' quoth he; 'thus misery doth part
The flux of company:' anon a careless herd,
Full of the pasture, jumps along by him
And never stays to greet him; 'Ay,' quoth Jaques,
'Sweep on, you fat and greasy citizens;
'Tis just the fashion: wherefore do you look
Upon that poor and broken bankrupt there?'
Thus most invectively he pierceth through
The body of the country, city, court,
Yea, and of this our life, swearing that we   60
Are mere usurpers, tyrants and what's worse,
To fright the animals and to kill them up
In their assign'd and native dwelling-place.
    Duke S.   And did you leave him in this con-
    templation?

Sec. Lord. We did, my lord, weeping and commenting
Upon the sobbing deer.
Duke S.   Show me the place:
• I love to cope him in these sullen fits,
For then he's full of matter.
First Lord. I'll bring you to him straight.
[*Exeunt.*

SCENE II. *A room in the palace.*

Enter DUKE FREDERICK, *with* Lords.

Duke F. Can it be possible that no man saw them?
It cannot be: some villains of my court
Are of consent and sufferance in this.
First Lord. I cannot hear of any that did see her.
The ladies, her attendants of her chamber,
Saw her a-bed, and in the morning early
They found the bed untreasured of their mistress.
• *Sec. Lord.* My lord, the roynish clown, at whom so oft
Your grace was wont to laugh, is also missing.
Hisperia, the princess' gentlewoman,   10
Confesses that she secretly o'erheard
Your daughter and her cousin much commend
The parts and graces of the wrestler
That did but lately foil the sinewy Charles;
And she believes, wherever they are gone,
That youth is surely in their company.
Duke F. Send to his brother; fetch that gallant hither;
If he be absent, bring his brother to me;
I'll make him find him: do this suddenly,
And let not search and inquisition quail   20
To bring again these foolish runaways. [*Exeunt.*

SCENE III. *Before* OLIVER'S *house.*

Enter ORLANDO *and* ADAM, *meeting.*

Orl. Who's there?
Adam. What, my young master? O my gentle master!
O my sweet master! O you memory
Of old Sir Rowland! why, what make you here?
Why are you virtuous? why do people love you?
And wherefore are you gentle, strong and valiant?
• Why would you be so fond to overcome
• The bonny priser of the humorous duke?
Your praise is come too swiftly home before you.
Know you not, master, to some kind of men   10
Their graces serve them but as enemies?
No more do yours: your virtues, gentle master,
Are sanctified and holy traitors to you.
O, what a world is this, when what is comely
Envenoms him that bears it!
Orl. Why, what's the matter?
Adam.   O unhappy youth!
Come not within these doors; within this roof
The enemy of all your graces lives:
Your brother—no, no brother; yet the son—
Yet not the son, I will not call him son   20
Of him I was about to call his father—
Hath heard your praises, and this night he means
To burn the lodging where you use to lie
And you within it: if he fail of that,
He will have other means to cut you off.
• I overheard him and his practices.

Costume design for Duke Frederick by J. Gower Parks,
Open Air Theatre, Regent's Park, London, 1935

67 *cope*. Encounter.

8 *roynish*. Scurvy, coarse.

7 *fond*. Foolish.

8 *bonny priser*. Strong prize-fighter.

26 *practices*. Plots.

37 *diverted blood*. Hostile blood relation.

58 *meed*. Reward.

68 *low*. Humble.

Rosalind (Janet Suzman), Celia (Rowena Cooper) and Touchstone (Patrick Stewart), Royal Shakespeare Co, 1968

This is no place; this house is but a butchery:
Abhor it, fear it, do not enter it.
   Orl. Why, whither, Adam, wouldst thou have
     me go?
   Adam. No matter whither, so you come not
     here.   30
   Orl. What, wouldst thou have me go and beg
     my food?
Or with a base and boisterous sword enforce
A thievish living on the common road?
This I must do, or know not what to do:
Yet this I will not do, do how I can;
I rather will subject me to the malice
● Of a diverted blood and bloody brother.
   Adam. But do not so. I have five hundred
     crowns,
The thrifty hire I saved under your father,
Which I did store to be my foster-nurse   40
When service should in my old limbs lie lame
And unregarded age in corners thrown:
Take that, and He that doth the ravens feed,
Yea, providently caters for the sparrow,
Be comfort to my age! Here is the gold;
All this I give you. Let me be your servant:
Though I look old, yet I am strong and lusty;
For in my youth I never did apply
Hot and rebellious liquors in my blood,
Nor did not with unbashful forehead woo   50
The means of weakness and debility;
Therefore my age is as a lusty winter,
Frosty, but kindly: let me go with you;
I 'll do the service of a younger man
In all your business and necessities.
   Orl. O good old man, how well in thee ap-
     pears
The constant service of the antique world,
● When service sweat for duty, not for meed!
Thou art not for the fashion of these times,
Where none will sweat but for promotion,   60
And having that, do choke their service up
Even with the having: it is not so with thee.
But, poor old man, thou prunest a rotten tree,
That cannot so much as a blossom yield
In lieu of all thy pains and husbandry.
But come thy ways; we 'll go along together,
And ere we have thy youthful wages spent,
● We 'll light upon some settled low content.
   Adam. Master, go on, and I will follow thee,
To the last gasp, with truth and loyalty.   70
From seventeen years till now almost fourscore
Here lived I, but now live here no more.
At seventeen years many their fortunes seek;
But at fourscore it is too late a week:
Yet fortune cannot recompense me better
Than to die well and not my master's debtor.
                          [Exeunt.

     SCENE IV. *The Forest of Arden.*

Enter ROSALIND *for* GANYMEDE, CELIA *for*
    ALIENA, *and* TOUCHSTONE.

   Ros. O Jupiter, how weary are my spirits!
   Touch. I care not for my spirits, if my legs
were not weary.
   Ros. I could find in my heart to disgrace my
man's apparel and to cry like a woman; but I
must comfort the weaker vessel, as doublet and
hose ought to show itself courageous to petticoat:
therefore courage, good Aliena!

Cel. I pray you, bear with me; I cannot go
no further.   10
Touch. For my part, I had rather bear with
you than bear you; yet I should bear no cross if
I did bear you, for I think you have no money
in your purse.
Ros. Well, this is the forest of Arden.
Touch. Ay, now am I in Arden; the more
fool I; when I was at home, I was in a better
place: but travellers must be content.
Ros. Ay, be so, good Touchstone.

Enter CORIN *and* SILVIUS.

Look you, who comes here; a young man and an
old in solemn talk.   21
    Cor. That is the way to make her scorn you
      still.
    Sil. O Corin, that thou knew'st how I do
      love her!
    Cor. I partly guess; for I have loved ere now.
    Sil. No, Corin, being old, thou canst not
      guess,
Though in thy youth thou wast as true a lover
As ever sigh'd upon a midnight pillow:
But if thy love were ever like to mine—
As sure I think did never man love so—
How many actions most ridiculous   30
Hast thou been drawn to by thy fantasy?
    Cor. Into a thousand that I have forgotten.
    Sil. O, thou didst then ne'er love so heartily!
If thou remember'st not the slightest folly
That ever love did make thee run into,
Thou hast not loved:
Or if thou hast not sat as I do now,
Wearying thy hearer in thy mistress' praise,
Thou hast not loved:
Or if thou hast not broke from company   40
Abruptly, as my passion now makes me,
Thou hast not loved.
O Phebe, Phebe, Phebe!   [*Exit.*
    Ros. Alas, poor shepherd! searching of thy
      wound,
I have by hard adventure found mine own.
    Touch. And I mine. I remember, when I
was in love I broke my sword upon a stone and
bid him take that for coming a-night to Jane
Smile; and I remember the kissing of her batlet
and the cow's dugs that her pretty chopt hands
had milked; and I remember the wooing of a
peascod instead of her, from whom I took two
cods and, giving her them again, said with weeping tears 'Wear these for my sake.' We that
are true lovers run into strange capers; but as all
is mortal in nature, so is all nature in love mortal
in folly.
    Ros. Thou speakest wiser than thou art ware
      of.
    Touch. Nay, I shall ne'er be ware of mine own
wit till I break my shins against it.   60
    Ros. Jove, Jove! this shepherd's passion
      Is much upon my fashion.
    Touch. And mine; but it grows something
      stale with me.
    Cel. I pray you, one of you question yond man
If he for gold will give us any food:
I faint almost to death.
    Touch.   Holla, you clown!
    Ros. Peace, fool: he's not thy kinsman.

12 *cross.* Elizabethan coins were stamped with crosses.

Shepherds with their flock. Woodcut from Edmund
Spenser's *The Shepherd's Calendar,* 1611

31 *fantasy.* Fancy.

44 *searching of.* Probing.

49 *batlet.* A bat used in washing clothes.

50 *chopt.* Chapped.

52 *peascod.* Pea-pods or peascods were used as love
tokens. Touchstone quibbles on cods, i.e. testicles.

55-57 *as all is mortal in nature . . . mortal in folly.* As
nature is subject to death so love is subject to folly.

81 *recks.* Reckons.

83 *cote.* Cottage.

94 *mend.* Improve.

Cor.   Who calls?
Touch.   Your betters, sir.
Cor.   Else are they very wretched.
Ros.   Peace, I say.   Good even to you, friend.
Cor.   And to you, gentle sir, and to you all.
Ros.   I prithee, shepherd, if that love or gold
Can in this desert place buy entertainment,
Bring us where we may rest ourselves and feed:
Here's a young maid with travel much oppress'd
And faints for succour.
Cor.   Fair sir, I pity her
And wish, for her sake more than for mine own,
My fortunes were more able to relieve her;
But I am shepherd to another man
And do not shear the fleeces that I graze:
My master is of churlish disposition   80
● And little recks to find the way to heaven
By doing deeds of hospitality:
● Besides, his cote, his flocks and bounds of feed
Are now on sale, and at our sheepcote now,
By reason of his absence, there is nothing
That you will feed on; but what is, come see,
And in my voice most welcome shall you be.
Ros.   What is he that shall buy his flock and
       pasture?
Cor.   That young swain that you saw here but
       erewhile,
That little cares for buying any thing.   90
Ros.   I pray thee, if it stand with honesty,
Buy thou the cottage, pasture and the flock,
And thou shalt have to pay for it of us.
● *Cel.*   And we will mend thy wages.   I like
       this place,
And willingly could waste my time in it.
Cor.   Assuredly the thing is to be sold:
Go with me: if you like upon report
The soil, the profit and this kind of life,
I will your very faithful feeder be
And buy it with your gold right suddenly.   100
                              [*Exeunt.*

SCENE V.   *The forest.*

Enter AMIENS, JAQUES, *and others.*

SONG.

Ami.   Under the greenwood tree
           Who loves to lie with me,
           And turn his merry note
           Unto the sweet bird's throat,
       Come hither, come hither, come hither:
           Here shall he see
           No enemy
       But winter and rough weather.

Jaq.   More, more, I prithee, more.
Ami.   It will make you melancholy, Monsieur Jaques.   11
Jaq.   I thank it.   More, I prithee, more.   I
can suck melancholy out of a song, as a weasel
sucks eggs.   More, I prithee, more.
Ami.   My voice is ragged: I know I cannot
please you.
Jaq.   I do not desire you to please me; I do
desire you to sing.   Come, more; another stanzo:
call you 'em stanzos?
Ami.   What you will, Monsieur Jaques.   20
Jaq.   Nay, I care not for their names; they
owe me nothing.   Will you sing?

Ami. More at your request than to please myself.

Jaq. Well then, if ever I thank any man, I'll thank you; but that they call compliment is like • the encounter of two dog-apes, and when a man thanks me heartily, methinks I have given him a • penny and he renders me the beggarly thanks. Come, sing; and you that will not, hold your tongues.

• *Ami.* Well, I'll end the song. Sirs, cover the while; the duke will drink under this tree. He hath been all this day to look you.

Jaq. And I have been all this day to avoid him. He is too disputable for my company: I think of as many matters as he, but I give heaven thanks and make no boast of them. Come, warble, come.

SONG.

> Who doth ambition shun   [*All together here.*
> And loves to live i' the sun,   41
> Seeking the food he eats
> And pleased with what he gets,
> Come hither, come hither, come hither:
>   Here shall he see
>   No enemy
> But winter and rough weather.

Jaq. I'll give you a verse to this note that I made yesterday in despite of my invention.

Ami. And I'll sing it.   50

Jaq. Thus it goes:—

> If it do come to pass
> That any man turn ass,
> Leaving his wealth and ease,
> A stubborn will to please,
> Ducdame, ducdame, ducdame:
>   Here shall he see
>   Gross fools as he,
> An if he will come to me.

Ami. What's that 'ducdame'?   60

Jaq. 'Tis a Greek invocation, to call fools into a circle. I'll go sleep, if I can; if I cannot, I'll rail against all the first-born of Egypt.

• *Ami.* And I'll go seek the duke: his banquet is prepared.   [*Exeunt severally.*

SCENE VI. *The forest.*

Enter ORLANDO *and* ADAM.

Adam. Dear master, I can go no further: O, I die for food! Here lie I down, and measure out my grave. Farewell, kind master.

Orl. Why, how now, Adam! no greater heart in thee? Live a little; comfort a little; cheer thyself a little. If this uncouth forest yield any thing savage, I will either be food for it or bring • it for food to thee. Thy conceit is nearer death than thy powers. For my sake be comfortable; hold death awhile at the arm's end: I will here be with thee presently; and if I bring thee not something to eat, I will give thee leave to die: but if thou diest before I come, thou art a mocker of my labour. Well said! thou lookest cheerly, and I'll be with thee quickly. Yet thou liest in the bleak air: come, I will bear thee to some shelter; and thou shalt not die for lack of a dinner, if there live any thing in this desert. Cheerly, good Adam!   [*Exeunt.*

27 *dog-apes.* Baboons.

29 *beggarly thanks.* Effusive, like a beggar's.

32-33 *cover the while.* Lay the table.

56 *Ducdame.* Deliberate nonsense.

64 *banquet.* A light meal of wine and fruit.

8 *conceit.* Imagination.

Orlando: '... I will bear thee to some shelter'. Set design for forest by Motley, Stratford-upon-Avon, 1952

5 *compact of jars.* Always in disagreement.

6 *discord in the spheres.* The harmony of the spheres was an ancient idea: the planets were supposed to give out musical notes.

13 *motley.* The parti-coloured garment of the domestic fool.

Costume design for the Fool (Touchstone) by C. Wilhelm, Princes Theatre, Manchester 1896

20 *poke.* Pocket.

21 *lack-lustre.* Sad.

53-55 *He that a fool . . . senseless of the bob.* He against whom a fool scores a hit is very foolish—even if he smarts under the gibe—if he does not pretend to be insensible to it.

57 *squandering glances.* Random jests.

SCENE VII. *The forest.*

A table set out. Enter DUKE *senior,* AMIENS, *and* Lords *like outlaws.*

Duke S. I think he be transform'd into a beast;
For I can no where find him like a man.
  First Lord. My lord, he is but even now gone hence:
Here was he merry, hearing of a song.
  Duke S. If he, compact of jars, grow musical,
We shall have shortly discord in the spheres.
Go, seek him: tell him I would speak with him.

Enter JAQUES.

  First Lord. He saves my labour by his own approach.
  Duke S. Why, how now, monsieur! what a life is this,
That your poor friends must woo your company?
What, you look merrily! 11
  Jaq. A fool, a fool! I met a fool i' the forest,
A motley fool; a miserable world!
As I do live by food, I met a fool;
Who laid him down and bask'd him in the sun,
And rail'd on Lady Fortune in good terms,
In good set terms and yet a motley fool.
'Good morrow, fool,' quoth I. 'No, sir,' quoth he,
'Call me not fool till heaven hath sent me fortune:'
And then he drew a dial from his poke, 20
And, looking on it with lack-lustre eye,
Says very wisely, 'It is ten o'clock:
Thus we may see,' quoth he, 'how the world wags:
'Tis but an hour ago since it was nine,
And after one hour more 'twill be eleven;
And so, from hour to hour, we ripe and ripe,
And then, from hour to hour, we rot and rot;
And thereby hangs a tale.' When I did hear
The motley fool thus moral on the time,
My lungs began to crow like chanticleer, 30
That fools should be so deep-contemplative,
And I did laugh sans intermission
An hour by his dial. O noble fool!
A worthy fool! Motley's the only wear.
  Duke S. What fool is this?
  Jaq. O worthy fool! One that hath been a courtier,
And says, if ladies be but young and fair,
They have the gift to know it: and in his brain,
Which is as dry as the remainder biscuit
After a voyage, he hath strange places cramm'd
With observation, the which he vents 41
In mangled forms. O that I were a fool!
I am ambitious for a motley coat.
  Duke S. Thou shalt have one.
  Jaq.   It is my only suit;
Provided that you weed your better judgements
Of all opinion that grows rank in them
That I am wise. I must have liberty
Withal, as large a charter as the wind,
To blow on whom I please; for so fools have;
And they that are most galled with my folly, 50
They most must laugh. And why, sir, must they so?
The 'why' is plain as way to parish church:
He that a fool doth very wisely hit
Doth very foolishly, although he smart,
Not to seem senseless of the bob: if not,
The wise man's folly is anatomized
Even by the squandering glances of the fool.
Invest me in my motley; give me leave

To speak my mind, and I will through and
    through
Cleanse the foul body of the infected world,   60
If they will patiently receive my medicine.
    Duke S.   Fie on thee! I can tell what thou
    wouldst do.
● *Jaq.*   What, for a counter, would I do but
    good?
    Duke S.   Most mischievous foul sin, in chid-
    ing sin:
For thou thyself hast been a libertine,
● As sensual as the brutish sting itself;
● And all the embossed sores and headed evils,
That thou with license of free foot hast caught,
Wouldst thou disgorge into the general world.
    Jaq.   Why, who cries out on pride,   70
That can therein tax any private party?
Doth it not flow as hugely as the sea,
● †Till that the weary very means do ebb?
What woman in the city do I name,
When that I say the city-woman bears
The cost of princes on unworthy shoulders?
Who can come in and say that I mean her,
When such a one as she such is her neighbour?
● Or what is he of basest function
● That says his bravery is not on my cost,   80
Thinking that I mean him, but therein suits
His folly to the mettle of my speech?
There then; how then? what then?   Let me see
    wherein
My tongue hath wrong'd him: if it do him right,
Then he hath wrong'd himself; if he be free,
Why then my taxing like a wild-goose flies,
Unclaim'd of any man.   But who comes here?

Enter ORLANDO, *with his sword drawn.*

    Orl.   Forbear, and eat no more.
    Jaq.   Why, I have eat none yet.
    Orl.   Nor shalt not, till necessity be served.
    Jaq.   Of what kind should this cock come of?
    Duke S.   Art thou thus bolden'd, man, by
    thy distress,   91
Or else a rude despiser of good manners,
That in civility thou seem'st so empty?
    Orl.   You touch'd my vein at first: the thorny
    point
Of bare distress hath ta'en from me the show
● Of smooth civility: yet am I inland bred
And know some nurture.   But forbear, I say:
He dies that touches any of this fruit
Till I and my affairs are answered.
    Jaq.   An you will not be answered with rea-
son, I must die.   101
    Duke S.   What would you have?   Your gen-
    tleness shall force
More than your force move us to gentleness.
    Orl.   I almost die for food; and let me have it.
    Duke S.   Sit down and feed, and welcome to
    our table.
    Orl.   Speak you so gently?   Pardon me, I
    pray you:
I thought that all things had been savage here;
And therefore put I on the countenance
Of stern commandment.   But whate'er you are
That in this desert inaccessible,   110
Under the shade of melancholy boughs,
Lose and neglect the creeping hours of time;
If ever you have look'd on better days,
If ever been where bells have knoll'd to church,

63 *counter.* Worthless coin.

66 *brutish sting.* Carnal passion.

67 *embossed.* Swollen.

73 *Till that the weary very means do ebb.* i.e. until the
very means of wealth are exhausted.

79 *function.* Occupation.

80 *bravery.* Fine clothes.

96 *inland.* i.e. not rustic or awkward.

An Elizabethan meal out of doors: From *Le centre de
l'amour c.* 1600

Jaques: '. . . At first the infant, Mewling and puking in the nurse's arms.' Engraving from a painting by Robert Smirke (1752–1845)

Jaques: '. . . And then the lover'. Engraving from a painting by Robert Smirke (1752–1845)

150 *pard.* Leopard.

156 *modern instances.* Commonplace or trite examples.

158 *pantaloon.* The stock Old Man of Italian *commedia dell'arte.*

Opposite : Second, fourth, fifth, sixth and seventh ages of man. Drawings by J. A. Atkinson (1752–*c.* 1833)

If ever sat at any good man's feast,
If ever from your eyelids wiped a tear
And know what 'tis to pity and be pitied,
Let gentleness my strong enforcement be :
In the which hope I blush, and hide my sword.
   Duke S.   True is it that we have seen better
     days,   120
And have with holy bell been knoll'd to church
And sat at good men's feasts and wiped our eyes
Of drops that sacred pity hath engender'd :
And therefore sit you down in gentleness
And take upon command what help we have
That to your wanting may be minister'd.
   Orl.   Then but forbear your food a little while,
Whiles, like a doe, I go to find my fawn
And give it food.   There is an old poor man,
Who after me hath many a weary step   130
Limp'd in pure love : till he be first sufficed,
Oppress'd with two weak evils, age and hunger,
I will not touch a bit.
   Duke S.   Go find him out,
And we will nothing waste till you return.
   Orl.   I thank ye ; and be blest for your good
     comfort !   [*Exit.*
   Duke S.   Thou seest we are not all alone un-
     happy :
This wide and universal theatre
Presents more woeful pageants than the scene
Wherein we play in.
   Jaq.   All the world's a stage,
And all the men and women merely players :   140
They have their exits and their entrances ;
And one man in his time plays many parts,
His acts being seven ages.   At first the infant,
Mewling and puking in the nurse's arms.
And then the whining school-boy, with his satchel
And shining morning face, creeping like snail
Unwillingly to school.   And then the lover,
Sighing like furnace, with a woeful ballad
Made to his mistress' eyebrow.   Then a soldier,
• Full of strange oaths and bearded like the pard,
Jealous in honour, sudden and quick in quarrel,
Seeking the bubble reputation
Even in the cannon's mouth. And then the justice,
In fair round belly with good capon lined,
With eyes severe and beard of formal cut,
• Full of wise saws and modern instances ;
And so he plays his part.   The sixth age shifts
• Into the lean and slipper'd pantaloon,
With spectacles on nose and pouch on side,   159
His youthful hose, well saved, a world too wide
For his shrunk shank ; and his big manly voice,
Turning again toward childish treble, pipes
And whistles in his sound.   Last scene of all,
That ends this strange eventful history,
Is second childishness and mere oblivion,
Sans teeth, sans eyes, sans taste, sans every thing.

     Re-enter ORLANDO, *with* ADAM.

   Duke S. Welcome.   Set down your venerable
     burden
And let him feed.
   Orl.   I thank you most for him.
   Adam.   So had you need :
I scarce can speak to thank you for myself.   170
   Duke S.   Welcome ; fall to : I will not trouble
     you
As yet, to question you about your fortunes.
Give us some music ; and, good cousin, sing.

Medieval musicians. From a 14th century manuscript

194 *limn'd*. Portrayed.

16 *of such a nature*. i.e. whose duty it is.

2 *thrice-crowned queen of night*. The goddess of the moon was Luna in the sky, Diana on earth and Hecate in the underworld.

4 *Thy huntress'*. Rosalind, a maiden, came under the protection of Diana.

6 *character*. Inscribe.

Song.

Ami.   Blow, blow, thou winter wind,
Thou art not so unkind
As man's ingratitude;
Thy tooth is not so keen,
Because thou art not seen,
Although thy breath be rude.   179
Heigh-ho! sing, heigh-ho! unto the green holly:
Most friendship is feigning, most loving mere folly:
Then, heigh-ho, the holly!
This life is most jolly.

Freeze, freeze, thou bitter sky,
That dost not bite so nigh
As benefits forgot:
Though thou the waters warp,
Thy sting is not so sharp
As friend remember'd not.
Heigh-ho! sing, &c.   190

Duke S.   If that you were the good Sir Rowland's son,
As you have whisper'd faithfully you were,
And as mine eye doth his effigies witness
Most truly limn'd and living in your face,
Be truly welcome hither: I am the duke
That loved your father: the residue of your fortune,
Go to my cave and tell me.   Good old man,
Thou art right welcome as thy master is.
Support him by the arm.   Give me your hand,
And let me all your fortunes understand. [*Exeunt.*

ACT III.

Scene I.   *A room in the palace.*

Enter Duke Frederick, Lords, *and* Oliver.

Duke F.   Not see him since?   Sir, sir, that cannot be:
But were I not the better part made mercy,
I should not seek an absent argument
Of my revenge, thou present.   But look to it:
Find out thy brother, wheresoe'er he is;
Seek him with candle; bring him dead or living
Within this twelvemonth, or turn thou no more
To seek a living in our territory.
Thy lands and all things that thou dost call thine
Worth seizure do we seize into our hands,   10
Till thou canst quit thee by thy brother's mouth
Of what we think against thee.
Oli.   O that your highness knew my heart in this!
I never loved my brother in my life.
Duke F.   More villain thou.   Well, push him out of doors;
And let my officers of such a nature
Make an extent upon his house and lands:
Do this expediently and turn him going. [*Exeunt.*

Scene II.   *The forest.*

Enter Orlando, *with a paper.*

Orl.   Hang there, my verse, in witness of my love:
And thou, thrice-crowned queen of night, survey
With thy chaste eye, from thy pale sphere above,
Thy huntress' name that my full life doth sway.
O Rosalind! these trees shall be my books
And in their barks my thoughts I 'll character;
That every eye which in this forest looks
Shall see thy virtue witness'd every where.

Run, run, Orlando; carve on every tree
The fair, the chaste and unexpressive she. [*Exit.*

Enter CORIN *and* TOUCHSTONE.

Cor. And how like you this shepherd's life,
Master Touchstone?

Touch. Truly, shepherd, in respect of itself,
it is a good life; but in respect that it is a shepherd's life, it is naught. In respect that it is
solitary, I like it very well; but in respect that it
is private, it is a very vile life. Now, in respect
it is in the fields, it pleaseth me well; but in
respect it is not in the court, it is tedious. As it
is a spare life, look you, it fits my humour well;
but as there is no more plenty in it, it goes much
against my stomach. Hast any philosophy in
thee, shepherd?

Cor. No more but that I know the more one
sickens the worse at ease he is; and that he that
wants money, means and content is without three
good friends; that the property of rain is to wet
and fire to burn; that good pasture makes fat
sheep, and that a great cause of the night is lack
of the sun; that he that hath learned no wit by
● nature nor art may complain of good breeding or
comes of a very dull kindred.

Touch. Such a one is a natural philosopher.
Wast ever in court, shepherd?

Cor. No, truly.

Touch. Then thou art damned.

Cor. Nay, I hope.

Touch. Truly, thou art damned, like an ill-
roasted egg all on one side.   39

Cor. For not being at court? Your reason.

Touch. Why, if thou never wast at court,
thou never sawest good manners; if thou never
sawest good manners, then thy manners must
be wicked; and wickedness is sin, and sin is
● damnation. Thou art in a parlous state, shepherd.

Cor. Not a whit, Touchstone: those that are
good manners at the court are as ridiculous in
the country as the behaviour of the country is
most mockable at the court. You told me you
salute not at the court, but you kiss your hands:
that courtesy would be uncleanly, if courtiers
were shepherds.

Touch. Instance, briefly; come, instance.

Cor. Why, we are still handling our ewes,
● and their fells, you know, are greasy.

Touch. Why, do not your courtier's hands
sweat? and is not the grease of a mutton as
wholesome as the sweat of a man? Shallow,
shallow. A better instance, I say; come.

Cor. Besides, our hands are hard.   60

Touch. Your lips will feel them the sooner.
Shallow again. A more sounder instance, come.

Cor. And they are often tarred over with
the surgery of our sheep; and would you have
us kiss tar? The courtier's hands are perfumed
● with civet.

● *Touch.* Most shallow man! thou worms-meat,
in respect of a good piece of flesh indeed! Learn
● of the wise, and perpend: civet is of a baser birth
than tar, the very uncleanly flux of a cat. Mend
the instance, shepherd.   71

Cor. You have too courtly a wit for me:
I'll rest.

Touch. Wilt thou rest damned? God help

31 *complain of.* i.e. complain of the lack of good breeding.

45 *parlous.* Perilous.

Arcadian shepherds. From M. A. de Dominis' *De
Republica Ecclesiastica*, 1617

A nobleman and his lady. From a 17th century woodcut

55 *fells.* Fleeces.

66 *civet.* The glandular secretions of the civet cat were
used in perfumes.

67 *worms-meat.* Food for worms.

69 *perpend.* Consider.

75 *make incision in.* Operate on.

79-80 *content with my harm.* Put up with my misfortunes.

85 *bell-wether.* The leader of the flock.

Rosalind reading. Illustration by Arthur Hopkins, 1916

103-104 *butter-women's rank to market.* i.e. the rhymes jog like farm women jogging to market.

114 *to cart.* Prostitutes were often publicly carted through the streets.

119 *false gallop.* A canter.

124 *graff.* Graft.

thee, shallow man! God make incision in thee! thou art raw.

Cor. Sir, I am a true labourer: I earn that I eat, get that I wear, owe no man hate, envy no man's happiness, glad of other men's good, content with my harm, and the greatest of my pride is to see my ewes graze and my lambs suck.

Touch. That is another simple sin in you, to bring the ewes and the rams together and to offer to get your living by the copulation of cattle; to be bawd to a bell-wether, and to betray a she-lamb of a twelvemonth to a crooked-pated, old, cuckoldly ram, out of all reasonable match. If thou beest not damned for this, the devil himself will have no shepherds; I cannot see else how thou shouldst 'scape.   90

Cor. Here comes young Master Ganymede, my new mistress's brother.

Enter ROSALIND, *with a paper, reading.*

Ros. From the east to western Ind,
      No jewel is like Rosalind.
      Her worth, being mounted on the wind,
      Through all the world bears Rosalind.
      All the pictures fairest lined
      Are but black to Rosalind.
      Let no fair be kept in mind
      But the fair of Rosalind.   100

Touch. I'll rhyme you so eight years together, dinners and suppers and sleeping-hours excepted: it is the right butter-women's rank to market.

Ros. Out, fool!

Touch. For a taste:
      If a hart do lack a hind,
      Let him seek out Rosalind.
      If the cat will after kind,
      So be sure will Rosalind.   110
      Winter garments must be lined,
      So must slender Rosalind.
      They that reap must sheaf and bind;
      Then to cart with Rosalind.
      Sweetest nut hath sourest rind,
      Such a nut is Rosalind.
      He that sweetest rose will find
      Must find love's prick and Rosalind.

This is the very false gallop of verses: why do you infect yourself with them?   120

Ros. Peace, you dull fool! I found them on a tree.

Touch. Truly, the tree yields bad fruit.

Ros. I'll graff it with you, and then I shall graff it with a medlar: then it will be the earliest fruit i' the country; for you'll be rotten ere you be half ripe, and that's the right virtue of the medlar.

Touch. You have said; but whether wisely or no, let the forest judge.   130

Enter CELIA, *with a writing.*

Ros. Peace!
Here comes my sister, reading: stand aside.

Cel. [*Reads*]
      Why should this a desert be?
        For it is unpeopled? No:
      Tongues I'll hang on every tree,
        That shall civil sayings show:
      Some, how brief the life of man
        Runs his erring pilgrimage,

That the stretching of a span
        Buckles in his sum of age;   140
Some, of violated vows
        'Twixt the souls of friend and friend:
But upon the fairest boughs,
        Or at every sentence end,
Will I Rosalinda write,
        Teaching all that read to know
The quintessence of every sprite
        Heaven would in little show.
Therefore Heaven Nature charged
        That one body should be fill'd   150
With all graces wide-enlarged:
        Nature presently distill'd
Helen's cheek, but not her heart,
        Cleopatra's majesty,
Atalanta's better part,
        Sad Lucretia's modesty.
Thus Rosalind of many parts
        By heavenly synod was devised,
Of many faces, eyes and hearts,
        To have the touches dearest prized.   160
Heaven would that she these gifts should
        have,
And I to live and die her slave.

Ros. O most gentle pulpiter! what tedious homily of love have you wearied your parishioners withal, and never cried 'Have patience, good people'!
Cel. How now! back, friends! Shepherd, go off a little.   Go with him, sirrah.
Touch. Come, shepherd, let us make an honourable retreat; though not with bag and baggage, yet with scrip and scrippage.   171
        [*Exeunt Corin and Touchstone.*
Cel. Didst thou hear these verses?
Ros. O, yes, I heard them all, and more too; for some of them had in them more feet than the verses would bear.
Cel. That's no matter: the feet might bear the verses.
Ros. Ay, but the feet were lame and could not bear themselves without the verse and therefore stood lamely in the verse.   180
Cel. But didst thou hear without wondering how thy name should be hanged and carved upon these trees?
Ros. I was seven of the nine days out of the wonder before you came; for look here what I found on a palm-tree.   I was never so berhymed since Pythagoras' time, that I was an Irish rat, which I can hardly remember.
Cel. Trow you who hath done this?
Ros. Is it a man?   190
Cel. And a chain, that you once wore, about his neck.   Change you colour?
Ros. I prithee, who?
Cel. O Lord, Lord! it is a hard matter for friends to meet; but mountains may be removed with earthquakes and so encounter.
Ros. Nay, but who is it?
Cel. Is it possible?
Ros. Nay, I prithee now with most petitionary vehemence, tell me who it is.   200
Cel. O wonderful, wonderful, and most wonderful wonderful! and yet again wonderful, and after that, out of all hooping!
Ros. Good my complexion! dost thou think, though I am caparisoned like a man, I have a

171 *scrip and scrippage.* Shepherd's pouch.

187 *Pythagoras.* He believed in the transmigration of souls.

188 *Irish rat.* An Irish superstition was that rats could be killed by incantations.

203 *out of all hooping.* Beyond all measure.

Celia: 'O wonderful, wonderful . . .' Rosalind (Peggy Ashcroft) and Celia (Valerie Tudor), Old Vic Theatre, London, 1955

Virginia McKenna as Rosalind, Old Vic Theatre, London, 1955

207 *South-sea of discovery*. i.e. as long and tedious as a voyage to the South Sea, the Pacific.

227 *sad brow and true maid*. Seriously and honestly.

238 *Gargantua*. Rabelais' giant.

245 *atomies*. Atoms, motes.

257 *'holla'*. 'Halt'.

258 *curvets*. Prances.

doublet and hose in my disposition? One inch of ●delay more is a South-sea of discovery; I prithee, tell me who is it quickly, and speak apace. I would thou couldst stammer, that thou mightst pour this concealed man out of thy mouth, as wine comes out of a narrow-mouthed bottle, either too much at once, or none at all. I prithee, take the cork out of thy mouth that I may drink thy tidings.

Cel. So you may put a man in your belly.

Ros. Is he of God's making? What manner of man? Is his head worth a hat, or his chin worth a beard?

Cel. Nay, he hath but a little beard.

Ros. Why, God will send more, if the man will be thankful: let me stay the growth of his beard, if thou delay me not the knowledge of his chin.

Cel. It is young Orlando, that tripped up the wrestler's heels and your heart both in an instant.

Ros. Nay, but the devil take mocking: speak, ●sad brow and true maid.

Cel. I' faith, coz, 'tis he.

Ros. Orlando?

Cel. Orlando.   230

Ros. Alas the day! what shall I do with my doublet and hose? What did he when thou sawest him? What said he? How looked he? Wherein went he? What makes he here? Did he ask for me? Where remains he? How parted he with thee? and when shalt thou see him again? Answer me in one word.

● *Cel.* You must borrow me Gargantua's mouth first: 'tis a word too great for any mouth of this age's size. To say ay and no to these particulars is more than to answer in a catechism.   241

Ros. But doth he know that I am in this forest and in man's apparel? Looks he as freshly as he did the day he wrestled?

● *Cel.* It is as easy to count atomies as to resolve the propositions of a lover; but take a taste of my finding him, and relish it with good observance. I found him under a tree, like a dropped acorn.

Ros. It may well be called Jove's tree, when it drops forth such fruit.   250

Cel. Give me audience, good madam.

Ros. Proceed.

Cel. There lay he, stretched along, like a wounded knight.

Ros. Though it be pity to see such a sight, it well becomes the ground.

● *Cel.* Cry 'holla' to thy tongue, I prithee; it ●curvets unseasonably. He was furnished like a hunter.   259

Ros. O, ominous! he comes to kill my heart.

Cel. I would sing my song without a burden: thou bringest me out of tune.

Ros. Do you not know I am a woman? when I think, I must speak. Sweet, say on.

Cel. You bring me out. Soft! comes he not here?

Enter ORLANDO *and* JAQUES.

Ros. 'Tis he: slink by, and note him.

Jaq. I thank you for your company; but, good faith, I had as lief have been myself alone.   270

Orl. And so had I; but yet, for fashion sake, I thank you too for your society.

Jaq. God be wi' you: let's meet as little as we can.

Orl. I do desire we may be better strangers.

Jaq. I pray you, mar no more trees with writing love-songs in their barks.

● *Orl.* I pray you, mar no moe of my verses with reading them ill-favouredly.

Jaq. Rosalind is your love's name? 280

Orl. Yes, just.

Jaq. I do not like her name.

Orl. There was no thought of pleasing you when she was christened.

Jaq. What stature is she of?

Orl. Just as high as my heart.

Jaq. You are full of pretty answers. Have you not been acquainted with goldsmiths' wives,
● and conned them out of rings? 289

● *Orl.* Not so; but I answer you right painted cloth, from whence you have studied your questions.

Jaq. You have a nimble wit: I think 'twas made of Atalanta's heels. Will you sit down with me? and we two will rail against our mistress the world and all our misery.

Orl. I will chide no breather in the world but myself, against whom I know most faults.

Jaq. The worst fault you have is to be in love. 300

Orl. 'Tis a fault I will not change for your best virtue. I am weary of you.

Jaq. By my troth, I was seeking for a fool when I found you.

Orl. He is drowned in the brook: look but in, and you shall see him.

Jaq. There I shall see mine own figure.

Orl. Which I take to be either a fool or a cipher.

Jaq. I'll tarry no longer with you: farewell, good Signior Love. 310

Orl. I am glad of your departure: adieu, good Monsieur Melancholy.   [*Exit Jaques.*

Ros. [*Aside to Celia*] I will speak to him like a saucy lackey and under that habit play the knave with him. Do you hear, forester?

Orl. Very well: what would you?

Ros. I pray you, what is't o' clock?

Orl. You should ask me what time o' day: there's no clock in the forest. 319

Ros. Then there is no true lover in the forest; else sighing every minute and groaning every hour would detect the lazy foot of Time as well as a clock.

Orl. And why not the swift foot of Time? had not that been as proper?

Ros. By no means, sir: Time travels in divers paces with divers persons. I'll tell you who Time ambles withal, who Time trots withal, who Time gallops withal and who he stands still withal.

Orl. I prithee, who doth he trot withal?

Ros. Marry, he trots hard with a young maid between the contract of her marriage and the day it is solemnized: if the interim be but a se'nnight, Time's pace is so hard that it seems the length of seven year.

Orl. Who ambles Time withal?

Ros. With a priest that lacks Latin and a rich man that hath not the gout, for the one sleeps easily because he cannot study and the other lives merrily because he feels no pain, the one lacking the burden of lean and wasteful learning,

278 *moe.* More.

289 *conned them out of rings.* Learned them by heart from the rings within which 'love-poesies' were engraved.

290-291 *right painted cloth.* Hangings painted with pictures and mottoes.

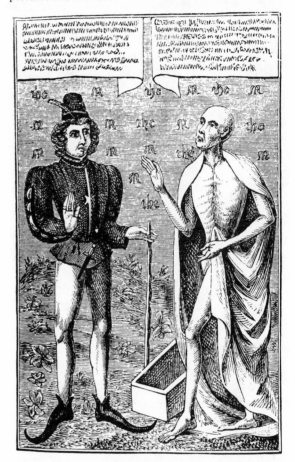

This copy of a medieval painted cloth shows Man conversing with Death. Engraving from Charles Knight's *Pictorial Edition of the Works of Shakspere*, 1839-1843

Edith Evans as Rosalind with Michael Redgrave as Orlando, Old Vic Theatre, London, 1936

357 *cony.* Rabbit.

358 *kindled.* Born.

383 *quotidian.* Daily fever.

393 *blue eye.* i.e. with dark circles.

393-394 *unquestionable.* Not to be spoken to.

401-402 *point-device.* Neat and trim.

the other knowing no burden of heavy tedious penury; these Time ambles withal.

Orl. Who doth he gallop withal?

Ros. With a thief to the gallows, for though he go as softly as foot can fall, he thinks himself too soon there.

Orl. Who stays it still withal?

Ros. With lawyers in the vacation; for they sleep between term and term and then they perceive not how Time moves. 351

Orl. Where dwell you, pretty youth?

Ros. With this shepherdess, my sister; here in the skirts of the forest, like fringe upon a petticoat.

Orl. Are you native of this place?

Ros. As the cony that you see dwell where she is kindled.

Orl. Your accent is something finer than you could purchase in so removed a dwelling. 360

Ros. I have been told so of many: but indeed an old religious uncle of mine taught me to speak, who was in his youth an inland man; one that knew courtship too well, for there he fell in love. I have heard him read many lectures against it, and I thank God I am not a woman, to be touched with so many giddy offences as he hath generally taxed their whole sex withal.

Orl. Can you remember any of the principal evils that he laid to the charge of women? 370

Ros. There were none principal; they were all like one another as half-pence are, every one fault seeming monstrous till his fellow-fault came to match it.

Orl. I prithee, recount some of them.

Ros. No, I will not cast away my physic but on those that are sick. There is a man haunts the forest, that abuses our young plants with carving 'Rosalind' on their barks; hangs odes upon hawthorns and elegies on brambles, all, forsooth, deifying the name of Rosalind: if I could meet that fancy-monger, I would give him some good counsel, for he seems to have the quotidian of love upon him.

Orl. I am he that is so love-shaked: I pray you, tell me your remedy.

Ros. There is none of my uncle's marks upon you: he taught me how to know a man in love; in which cage of rushes I am sure you are not prisoner. 390

Orl. What were his marks?

Ros. A lean cheek, which you have not, a blue eye and sunken, which you have not, an unquestionable spirit, which you have not, a beard neglected, which you have not; but I pardon you for that, for simply your having in beard is a younger brother's revenue: then your hose should be ungartered, your bonnet unbanded, your sleeve unbuttoned, your shoe untied and every thing about you demonstrating a careless desolation; but you are no such man; you are rather point-device in your accoutrements as loving yourself than seeming the lover of any other.

Orl. Fair youth, I would I could make thee believe I love.

Ros. Me believe it! you may as soon make her that you love believe it; which, I warrant, she is apter to do than to confess she does: that is one of the points in the which women still give the lie to their consciences. But, in good sooth, are you he that hangs the verses on the trees, wherein Rosalind is so admired?

Orl. I swear to thee, youth, by the white hand of Rosalind, I am that he, that unfortunate he.

Ros. But are you so much in love as your rhymes speak?

Orl. Neither rhyme nor reason can express how much. 419

Ros. Love is merely a madness, and, I tell you, deserves as well a dark house and a whip as madmen do: and the reason why they are not so punished and cured is, that the lunacy is so ordinary that the whippers are in love too. Yet I profess curing it by counsel.

Orl. Did you ever cure any so?

Ros. Yes, one, and in this manner. He was to imagine me his love, his mistress; and I set him every day to woo me: at which time would I, being but a moonish youth, grieve, be effeminate, changeable, longing and liking, proud, fantastical, apish, shallow, inconstant, full of tears, full of smiles, for every passion something and for no passion truly any thing, as boys and women are for the most part cattle of this colour; would now like him, now loathe him; then entertain him, then forswear him; now weep for him, then spit at him; that I drave my suitor from his mad humour of love to a living humour of madness; which was, to forswear the full stream of the world and to live in a nook merely monastic. And thus I cured him; and this way will I take upon me to wash your liver as clean as a sound sheep's heart, that there shall not be one spot of love in't.

Orl. I would not be cured, youth.

Ros. I would cure you, if you would but call me Rosalind and come every day to my cote and woo me.

Orl. Now, by the faith of my love, I will: tell me where it is. 450

Ros. Go with me to it and I'll show it you: and by the way you shall tell me where in the forest you live. Will you go?

Orl. With all my heart, good youth.

Ros. Nay, you must call me Rosalind. Come, sister, will you go? [*Exeunt.*

SCENE III. *The forest.*

Enter TOUCHSTONE *and* AUDREY; JAQUES *behind.*

Touch. Come apace, good Audrey: I will fetch up your goats, Audrey. And how, Audrey? am I the man yet? doth my simple feature content you?

Aud. Your features! Lord warrant us! what features?

Touch. I am here with thee and thy goats, as the most capricious poet, honest Ovid, was among the Goths.

Jaq. [*Aside*] O knowledge ill-inhabited, worse than Jove in a thatched house! 11

Touch. When a man's verses cannot be understood, nor a man's good wit seconded with the forward child Understanding, it strikes a man more dead than a great reckoning in a little room. Truly, I would the gods had made thee poetical.

443 *liver.* Supposed to be the seat of passion.

Touchstone: 'And how, Audrey? Am I the man yet?'
Illustration by H. M. Brock, 1916

3 *feature.* Appearance.

8 *honest Ovid.* Ironical; for unchastity Ovid was banished from Rome and forced to live among the Goths, pronounced 'goats'; 'capricious', from its derivation, is another quibble on goats.

11 *Jove in a thatched house.* Jove, in disguise, once visited earth and was entertained by an old couple, Baucis and Philemon, in their humble cottage.

15 *great reckoning.* A large bill; a pun on 'reckoning', i.e. Marlowe's death in the tavern at Deptford. See introduction.

Audrey and Touchstone. Illustration by Steven Spurrier, 1916

32 *material*. Practical, to the point.

36 *foul*. Not handsome.

51 *horn-beasts*. A reference to the horns of the cuckold.

Touchstone (Paul Rogers), Sir Oliver Martex (John Wood) and Audrey (Rachel Roberts), Old Vic Theatre, London, 1950

76 *'ild*. Reward.

77 *toy*. Trifle.

Aud. I do not know what 'poetical' is : is it honest in deed and word ? is it a true thing ?

Touch. No, truly ; for the truest poetry is the most feigning ; and lovers are given to poetry, and what they swear in poetry may be said as lovers they do feign.

Aud. Do you wish then that the gods had made me poetical ?

Touch. I do, truly ; for thou swearest to me thou art honest : now, if thou wert a poet, I might have some hope thou didst feign.

Aud. Would you not have me honest ?

Touch. No, truly, unless thou wert hard-favoured ; for honesty coupled to beauty is to have honey a sauce to sugar.   31

Jaq. [*Aside*] A material fool !

Aud. Well, I am not fair ; and therefore I pray the gods make me honest.

Touch. Truly, and to cast away honesty upon a foul slut were to put good meat into an unclean dish.

Aud. I am not a slut, though I thank the gods I am foul.   39

Touch. Well, praised be the gods for thy foulness ! sluttishness may come hereafter. But be it as it may be, I will marry thee, and to that end I have been with Sir Oliver Martext, the vicar of the next village, who hath promised to meet me in this place of the forest and to couple us.

Jaq. [*Aside*] I would fain see this meeting.

Aud. Well, the gods give us joy !

Touch. Amen. A man may, if he were of a fearful heart, stagger in this attempt ; for here we have no temple but the wood, no assembly but horn-beasts. But what though ? Courage ! As horns are odious, they are necessary. It is said, 'many a man knows no end of his goods :' right ; many a man has good horns, and knows no end of them. Well, that is the dowry of his wife ; 'tis none of his own getting. Horns ? Even so. Poor men alone ? No, no ; the noblest deer hath them as huge as the rascal. Is the single man therefore blessed ? No : as a walled town is more worthier than a village, so is the forehead of a married man more honourable than the bare brow of a bachelor ; and by how much defence is better than no skill, by so much is a horn more precious than to want. Here comes Sir Oliver.

Enter SIR OLIVER MARTEXT.

Sir Oliver Martext, you are well met : will you dispatch us here under this tree, or shall we go with you to your chapel ?

Sir Oli. Is there none here to give the woman ?

Touch. I will not take her on gift of any man.

Sir Oli. Truly, she must be given, or the marriage is not lawful.   71

Jaq. [*Advancing*] Proceed, proceed : I'll give her.

Touch. Good even, good Master What-ye-call't : how do you, sir ? You are very well met : God 'ild you for your last company : I am very glad to see you : even a toy in hand here, sir : nay, pray be covered.

Jaq. Will you be married, motley ?   79

Touch. As the ox hath his bow, sir, the horse his curb and the falcon her bells, so man hath his desires ; and as pigeons bill, so wedlock would be nibbling.

Jaq. And will you, being a man of your breeding, be married under a bush like a beggar? Get you to church, and have a good priest that can tell you what marriage is: this fellow will but join you together as they join wainscot; then one of you will prove a shrunk panel and, like green timber, warp, warp. 90

Touch. [*Aside*] I am not in the mind but I were better to be married of him than of another: for he is not like to marry me well; and not being well married, it will be a good excuse for me hereafter to leave my wife.

Jaq. Go thou with me, and let me counsel thee.

Touch. Come, sweet Audrey:
We must be married, or we must live in bawdry.
Farewell, good Master Oliver: not,— 100
  O sweet Oliver,
  O brave Oliver,
Leave me not behind thee:
but,—
  Wind away,
  Begone, I say,
I will not to wedding with thee.
[*Exeunt Jaques, Touchstone and Audrey.*
Sir Oli. 'Tis no matter: ne'er a fantastical knave of them all shall flout me out of my calling.
[*Exit.* 109

SCENE IV. *The forest.*

Enter ROSALIND *and* CELIA.

Ros. Never talk to me; I will weep.

Cel. Do, I prithee; but yet have the grace to consider that tears do not become a man.

Ros. But have I not cause to weep?

Cel. As good cause as one would desire; therefore weep.

Ros. His very hair is of the dissembling colour.

Cel. Something browner than Judas's: marry, his kisses are Judas's own children. 10

Ros. I' faith, his hair is of a good colour.

Cel. An excellent colour: your chestnut was ever the only colour.

Ros. And his kissing is as full of sanctity as the touch of holy bread.

Cel. He hath bought a pair of cast lips of Diana: a nun of winter's sisterhood kisses not more religiously; the very ice of chastity is in them.

Ros. But why did he swear he would come this morning, and comes not? 21

Cel. Nay, certainly, there is no truth in him.

Ros. Do you think so?

Cel. Yes; I think he is not a pick-purse nor a horse-stealer, but for his verity in love, I do think him as concave as a covered goblet or a worm-eaten nut.

Ros. Not true in love?

Cel. Yes, when he is in; but I think he is not in. 30

Ros. You have heard him swear downright he was.

Cel. 'Was' is not 'is:' besides, the oath of a lover is no stronger than the word of a tapster; they are both the confirmer of false reckonings. He attends here in the forest on the duke your father.

Katherine Hepburn as Rosalind, Old Vic Theatre, London, 1950

7-8 *dissembling colour.* Reddish, like Judas.

26 *concave.* Hollow.

45 *traverse, athwart.* Across.

46 *puisny.* Inferior, puny.

23 *cicatrice and capable impressure.* Scar and visible mark.

Ros. I met the duke yesterday and had much question with him: he asked me of what parentage I was; I told him, of as good as he; so he laughed and let me go. But what talk we of fathers, when there is such a man as Orlando?

Cel. O, that's a brave man! he writes brave verses, speaks brave words, swears brave oaths
● and breaks them bravely, quite traverse, athwart
● the heart of his lover; as a puisny tilter, that spurs his horse but on one side, breaks his staff like a noble goose: but all's brave that youth mounts and folly guides. Who comes here?

Enter CORIN.

Cor. Mistress and master, you have oft inquired   50
After the shepherd that complain'd of love,
Who you saw sitting by me on the turf,
Praising the proud disdainful shepherdess
That was his mistress.
Cel.   Well, and what of him?
Cor. If you will see a pageant truly play'd,
Between the pale complexion of true love
And the red glow of scorn and proud disdain,
Go hence a little and I shall conduct you,
If you will mark it.
Ros.   O, come, let us remove:
The sight of lovers feedeth those in love.   60
Bring us to this sight, and you shall say
I'll prove a busy actor in their play.   [*Exeunt.*

SCENE V. *Another part of the forest.*

Enter SILVIUS *and* PHEBE.

Sil. Sweet Phebe, do not scorn me; do not, Phebe;
Say that you love me not, but say not so
In bitterness. The common executioner,
Whose heart the accustom'd sight of death makes hard,
Falls not the axe upon the humbled neck
But first begs pardon: will you sterner be
†Than he that dies and lives by bloody drops?

Enter ROSALIND, CELIA, *and* CORIN, *behind.*

Phe. I would not be thy executioner:
I fly thee, for I would not injure thee.
Thou tell'st me there is murder in mine eye: 10
'Tis pretty, sure, and very probable,
That eyes, that are the frail'st and softest things,
Who shut their coward gates on atomies,
Should be call'd tyrants, butchers, murderers!
Now I do frown on thee with all my heart;
And if mine eyes can wound, now let them kill thee:
Now counterfeit to swoon; why now fall down;
Or if thou canst not, O, for shame, for shame,
Lie not, to say mine eyes are murderers!
Now show the wound mine eye hath made in thee: 20
Scratch thee but with a pin, and there remains
Some scar of it; lean but upon a rush,
● The cicatrice and capable impressure
Thy palm some moment keeps; but now mine eyes,
Which I have darted at thee, hurt thee not,
Nor, I am sure, there is no force in eyes
That can do hurt.
Sil.   O dear Phebe,

If ever,—as that ever may be near,—
● You meet in some fresh cheek the power of **fancy,**
Then shall you know the wounds invisible   30
That love's keen arrows make.
    Phe.   But till that time
Come not thou near me: and when that time
    comes,
Afflict me with thy mocks, pity me not ;
As till that time I shall not pity thee.
    Ros.   And why, I pray you? Who might be
    your mother,
That you insult, exult, and all at once,
Over the wretched? What though you have no
    beauty,—
As, by my faith, I see no more in you
Than without candle may go dark to bed—
Must you be therefore proud and pitiless?   40
Why, what means this? Why do you look on me?
I see no more in you than in the ordinary
● Of nature's sale-work. 'Od's my little life,
I think she means to tangle my eyes too !
No, faith, proud mistress, hope not after it :
'Tis not your inky brows, your black silk hair,
● Your bugle eyeballs, nor your cheek of cream,
That can entame my spirits to your worship.
You foolish shepherd, wherefore do you follow her,
Like foggy south puffing with wind and rain ?   50
You are a thousand times a properer man
Than she a woman : 'tis such fools as you
That makes the world full of ill-favour'd children :
'Tis not her glass, but you, that flatters her ;
And out of you she sees herself more proper
Than any of her lineaments can show her.
But, mistress, know yourself : down on your knees,
And thank heaven, fasting, for a good man's love :
For I must tell you friendly in your ear,
Sell when you can : you are not for all markets :
Cry the man mercy ; love him ; take his offer : 61
Foul is most foul, being foul to be a scoffer.
So take her to thee, shepherd : fare you well.
    Phe. Sweet youth, I pray you, chide **a** year
    together :
I had rather hear you chide than this man woo.
    Ros.   He's fallen in love with your foulness
and she'll fall in love with my anger. If it be so,
as fast as she answers thee with frowning looks,
I'll sauce her with bitter words. Why look you
so upon me ?   70
    Phe. For no ill will I bear you.
    Ros. I pray you, do not fall in love with me,
For I am falser than vows made in wine :
Besides, I like you not. If you will know my house,
'Tis at the tuft of olives here hard by.
Will you go, sister ? Shepherd, ply her hard.
Come, sister. Shepherdess, look on him better,
And be not proud : though all the world could see,
None could be so abused in sight as he.   80
Come, to our flock.
                [*Exeunt Rosalind, Celia and Corin.*
● *Phe.* Dead shepherd, now I find thy saw of might,
'Who ever loved that loved not at first sight?'
    Sil. Sweet Phebe,—
    Phe.   Ha, what say'st thou, Silvius?
    Sil. Sweet Phebe, pity me.
    Phe. Why, I am sorry for thee, gentle Silvius.
    Sil. Wherever sorrow is, relief would be :
If you do sorrow at my grief in love,
By giving love your sorrow and my grief
● Were both extermined.

29 *fancy.* Love.

43 *sale-work.* Ready-made goods.

47 *bugle.* A glass bead, with black centre.

82 *saw.* Wise saying.

An Elizabethan shepherdess. From a contemporary woodcut

89 *extermined.* Expunged.

108 *carlot.* Peasant.

Silvius (Emrys Jones) and Phebe (Dorothy Tutin), Old
Vic production, Bristol, 1950

Phe.   Thou hast my love: is not that neigh-
    bourly?   90
Sil.   I would have you.
Phe.   Why, that were covetousness.
Silvius, the time was that I hated thee,
And yet it is not that I bear thee love;
But since that thou canst talk of love so well,
Thy company, which erst was irksome to me,
I will endure, and I'll employ thee too:
But do not look for further recompense
Than thine own gladness that thou art employ'd.
   Sil.   So holy and so perfect is my love,
And I in such a poverty of grace,   100
That I shall think it a most plenteous crop
To glean the broken ears after the man
That the main harvest reaps: loose now and then
A scatter'd smile, and that I'll live upon.
   Phe.   Know'st thou the youth that spoke to me
    erewhile?
   Sil.   Not very well, but I have met him oft;
And he hath bought the cottage and the bounds
That the old carlot once was master of.
   Phe.   Think not I love him, though I ask for
    him;
'Tis but a peevish boy; yet he talks well;   110
But what care I for words? yet words do well
When he that speaks them pleases those that hear.
It is a pretty youth: not very pretty:
But, sure, he's proud, and yet his pride becomes
    him:
He'll make a proper man: the best thing in him
Is his complexion; and faster than his tongue
Did make offence his eye did heal it up.
He is not very tall; yet for his years he's tall:
His leg is but so so; and yet 'tis well:
There was a pretty redness in his lip,   120
A little riper and more lusty red
Than that mix'd in his cheek; 'twas just the dif-
    ference
Betwixt the constant red and mingled damask.
There be some women, Silvius, had they mark'd
    him
In parcels as I did, would have gone near
To fall in love with him; but, for my part,
I love him not nor hate him not; and yet
I have more cause to hate him than to love him:
For what had he to do to chide at me?
He said mine eyes were black and my hair black:
And, now I am remember'd, scorn'd at me: 131
I marvel why I answer'd not again:
But that's all one; omittance is no quittance.
I'll write to him a very taunting letter,
And thou shalt bear it: wilt thou, Silvius?
   Sil.   Phebe, with all my heart.
   Phe.   I'll write it straight;
The matter's in my head and in my heart:
I will be bitter with him and passing short.
Go with me, Silvius.   [*Exeunt.*

ACT IV.

SCENE I. *The forest.*

Enter ROSALIND, CELIA, *and* JAQUES.

   Jaq.   I prithee, pretty youth, let me be better
acquainted with thee.
   Ros.   They say you are a melancholy fellow.
   Jaq.   I am so; I do love it better than laughing.
   Ros.   Those that are in extremity of either are

abominable fellows and betray themselves to every
● modern censure worse than drunkards.

Jaq. Why, 'tis good to be sad and say nothing.

Ros. Why then, 'tis good to be a post.   9

Jaq. I have neither the scholar's melancholy,
which is emulation, nor the musician's, which is
fantastical, nor the courtier's, which is proud, nor
the soldier's, which is ambitious, nor the lawyer's,
● which is politic, nor the lady's, which is nice, nor
the lover's, which is all these: but it is a melancholy of mine own, compounded of many simples,
extracted from many objects, and indeed the sundry contemplation of my travels, in which my
often rumination wraps me in a most humorous
sadness.   20

Ros. A traveller! By my faith, you have great
reason to be sad: I fear you have sold your own
lands to see other men's; then, to have seen
much and to have nothing, is to have rich eyes
and poor hands.

Jaq. Yes, I have gained my experience.

Ros. And your experience makes you sad: I
had rather have a fool to make me merry than
experience to make me sad; and to travel for it too!

Enter ORLANDO.

Orl. Good day and happiness, dear Rosalind!

Jaq. Nay, then, God be wi' you, an you talk
in blank verse.   [*Exit.*

Ros. Farewell, Monsieur Traveller: look you
● lisp and wear strange suits, disable all the benefits
of your own country, be out of love with your
nativity and almost chide God for making you
that countenance you are, or I will scarce think
you have swam in a gondola. Why, how now,
Orlando! where have you been all this while?
You a lover! An you serve me such another trick,
never come in my sight more.   41

Orl. My fair Rosalind, I come within an hour
of my promise.

Ros. Break an hour's promise in love! He
that will divide a minute into a thousand parts
and break but a part of the thousandth part of a
minute in the affairs of love, it may be said of
him that Cupid hath clapped him o' the shoulder,
but I'll warrant him heart-whole.

Orl. Pardon me, dear Rosalind.   50

Ros. Nay, an you be so tardy, come no more
in my sight: I had as lief be wooed of a snail.

Orl. Of a snail?

Ros. Ay, of a snail; for though he comes
slowly, he carries his house on his head; a better
jointure, I think, than you make a woman: besides, he brings his destiny with him.

Orl. What's that?

Ros. Why, horns, which such as you are fain
to be beholding to your wives for: but he comes
armed in his fortune and prevents the slander of
his wife.

Orl. Virtue is no horn-maker; and my Rosalind is virtuous.

Ros. And I am your Rosalind.

Cel. It pleases him to call you so; but he hath
● a Rosalind of a better leer than you.

Ros. Come, woo me, woo me, for now I am in
a holiday humour and like enough to consent.
What would you say to me now, an I were your
very very Rosalind?   71

Orl. I would kiss before I spoke.

7 *modern.* Common.

14 *nice.* Particular.

34 *lisp.* Affect a foreign accent.

Dorothea Baird, English Edwardian actress, as Rosalind

67 *leer.* Look.

74 *gravelled*. At a loss.

85 *ranker*. Coarser, less pure.

97 *videlicet*. Namely (a legal term).

Rosalind: '. . . he went but forth to wash him in the Hellespont.' Engraving from Charles Knight's *Pictorial Edition of the Works of Shakspere, 1839–1843*

138 *commission*. Authority.

140 *goes before*. Anticipates.

Ros. Nay, you were better speak first, and when you were gravelled for lack of matter, you might take occasion to kiss. Very good orators, when they are out, they will spit; and for lovers lacking—God warn us!—matter, the cleanliest shift is to kiss.

Orl. How if the kiss be denied?

Ros. Then she puts you to entreaty, and there begins new matter.   81

Orl. Who could be out, being before his beloved mistress?

Ros. Marry, that should you, if I were your mistress, or I should think my honesty ranker than my wit.

Orl. What, of my suit?

Ros. Not out of your apparel, and yet out of your suit. Am not I your Rosalind?

Orl. I take some joy to say you are, because I would be talking of her.   91

Ros. Well in her person I say I will not have you.

Orl. Then in mine own person I die.

Ros. No, faith, die by attorney. The poor world is almost six thousand years old, and in all this time there was not any man died in his own person, videlicet, in a love-cause. Troilus had his brains dashed out with a Grecian club; yet he did what he could to die before, and he is one of the patterns of love. Leander, he would have lived many a fair year, though Hero had turned nun, if it had not been for a hot midsummer night; for, good youth, he went but forth to wash him in the Hellespont and being taken with the cramp was drowned: and the foolish chroniclers of that age found it was 'Hero of Sestos.' But these are all lies: men have died from time to time and worms have eaten them, but not for love.

Orl. I would not have my right Rosalind of this mind, for, I protest, her frown might kill me.

Ros. By this hand, it will not kill a fly. But come, now I will be your Rosalind in a more coming-on disposition, and ask me what you will, I will grant it.

Orl. Then love me, Rosalind.

Ros. Yes, faith, will I, Fridays and Saturdays and all.

Orl. And wilt thou have me?

Ros. Ay, and twenty such.

Orl. What sayest thou?   120

Ros. Are you not good?

Orl. I hope so.

Ros. Why then, can one desire too much of a good thing? Come, sister, you shall be the priest and marry us. Give me your hand, Orlando. What do you say, sister?

Orl. Pray thee, marry us.

Cel. I cannot say the words.

Ros. You must begin, 'Will you, Orlando—'

Cel. Go to. Will you, Orlando, have to wife this Rosalind?   131

Orl. I will.

Ros. Ay, but when?

Orl. Why now; as fast as she can marry us.

Ros. Then you must say 'I take thee, Rosalind, for wife.'

Orl. I take thee, Rosalind, for wife.

Ros. I might ask you for your commission; but I do take thee, Orlando, for my husband: there's a girl goes before the priest; and certainly a woman's thought runs before her actions.   141

Orl.   So do all thoughts; they are winged.

Ros.   Now tell me how long you would have her after you have possessed her.

Orl.   For ever and a day.

Ros.   Say 'a day,' without the 'ever.'   No, no, Orlando; men are April when they woo, December when they wed: maids are May when they are maids, but the sky changes when they are wives.   I will be more jealous of thee than a Barbary cock-pigeon over his hen, more clamorous than a parrot against rain, more new-fangled than an ape, more giddy in my desires than a monkey: I will weep for nothing, like Diana in the fountain, and I will do that when you are disposed to be merry; I will laugh like a hyen, and that when thou art inclined to sleep.

Orl.   But will my Rosalind do so?

Ros.   By my life, she will do as I do.

Orl.   O, but she is wise.   160

Ros.   Or else she could not have the wit to do this: the wiser, the waywarder: make the doors upon a woman's wit and it will out at the casement; shut that and 'twill out at the key-hole; stop that, 'twill fly with the smoke out at the chimney.

Orl.   A man that had a wife with such a wit, ● he might say 'Wit, whither wilt?'

Ros.   Nay, you might keep that check for it till you met your wife's wit going to your neighbour's bed.   171

Orl.   And what wit could wit have to excuse that?

Ros.   Marry, to say she came to seek you there.   You shall never take her without her answer, unless you take her without her tongue.   O, that woman that cannot make her fault her husband's occasion, let her never nurse her child herself, for she will breed it like a fool!

Orl.   For these two hours, Rosalind, I will leave thee.   181

Ros.   Alas! dear love, I cannot lack thee two hours.

Orl.   I must attend the duke at dinner: by two o'clock I will be with thee again.

Ros.   Ay, go your ways, go your ways; I knew what you would prove: my friends told me as much, and I thought no less: that flattering tongue of yours won me: 'tis but one cast away, and so, come, death!   Two o'clock is your hour?

Orl.   Ay, sweet Rosalind.   191

Ros.   By my troth, and in good earnest, and so God mend me, and by all pretty oaths that are not dangerous, if you break one jot of your promise or come one minute behind your hour, I will think you the most pathetical break-promise and the most hollow lover and the most unworthy of her you call Rosalind that may be chosen out of the gross band of the unfaithful: therefore beware my censure and keep your promise.   200

Orl.   With no less religion than if thou wert indeed my Rosalind: so adieu.

Ros.   Well, Time is the old justice that examines all such offenders, and let Time try: adieu.
                                          [*Exit Orlando.*

Cel.   You have simply misused our sex in your love-prate: we must have your doublet and hose plucked over your head, and show the world what the bird hath done to her own nest.

Ros.   O coz, coz, coz, my pretty little coz,

Margaret Leighton as Rosalind and Laurence Harvey as Orlando, Stratford-upon-Avon, 1952

---

168 *'Wit, whither wilt?'* A common phrase to curb someone's tongue.

216 *bastard of Venus.* Cupid.

222 *shadow.* Shady place.

The English manner of cutting up the deer. From George Turbeville's *The Noble Art of Venerie*, 1575

that thou didst know how many fathom deep I am in love! But it cannot be sounded: my affection hath an unknown bottom, like the bay of Portugal.

Cel. Or rather, bottomless, that as fast as you pour affection in, it runs out.

● *Ros.* No, that same wicked bastard of Venus that was begot of thought, conceived of spleen and born of madness, that blind rascally boy that abuses every one's eyes because his own are out, let him be judge how deep I am in love. I'll tell thee, Aliena, I cannot be out of the sight of
● Orlando: I'll go find a shadow and sigh till he come.

Cel. And I'll sleep.   [*Exeunt.*

SCENE II. *The forest.*

Enter JAQUES, Lords, *and* Foresters.

Jaq. Which is he that killed the deer?
A Lord. Sir, it was I.
Jaq. Let's present him to the duke, like a Roman conqueror; and it would do well to set the deer's horns upon his head, for a branch of victory. Have you no song, forester, for this purpose?
For. Yes, sir.
Jaq. Sing it: 'tis no matter how it be in tune, so it make noise enough.   10

SONG.

For. What shall he have that kill'd the deer?
His leather skin and horns to wear.
            Then sing him home;
         [*The rest shall bear this burden.*
Take thou no scorn to wear the horn;
It was a crest ere thou wast born:
            Thy father's father wore it,
            And thy father bore it:
The horn, the horn, the lusty horn
Is not a thing to laugh to scorn. [*Exeunt.*

SCENE III. *The forest.*

Enter ROSALIND *and* CELIA.

Ros. How say you now? Is it not past two o'clock? and here much Orlando!
Cel. I warrant you, with pure love and troubled brain, he hath ta'en his bow and arrows and is gone forth to sleep. Look, who comes here.

Enter SILVIUS.

Sil. My errand is to you, fair youth;
My gentle Phebe bid me give you this:
I know not the contents; but, as I guess
By the stern brow and waspish action
Which she did use as she was writing of it,   10
It bears an angry tenour: pardon me;
I am but as a guiltless messenger.
    Ros. Patience herself would startle at this letter
And play the swaggerer; bear this, bear all:
She says I am not fair, that I lack manners;
She calls me proud, and that she could not love me,
Were man as rare as phœnix. 'Od's my will!
Her love is not the hare that I do hunt:
Why writes she so to me? Well, shepherd, well,
This is a letter of your own device.   20
    Sil. No, I protest, I know not the contents:

Phebe did write it.

Ros.   Come, come, you are a fool
And turn'd into the extremity of love.
I saw her hand: she has a leathern hand,
● A freestone-colour'd hand; I verily did think
That her old gloves were on, but 'twas her hands:
She has a huswife's hand; but that's no matter:
I say she never did invent this letter;
This is a man's invention and his hand.

Sil.   Sure, it is hers.   30
Ros.   Why, 'tis a boisterous and a cruel style,
A style for challengers; why, she defies me,
Like Turk to Christian: women's gentle brain
Could not drop forth such giant-rude invention,
Such Ethiope words, blacker in their effect
Than in their countenance.   Will you hear the
     letter?

Sil.   So please you, for I never heard it yet;
Yet heard too much of Phebe's cruelty.

Ros.   She Phebes me: mark how the tyrant
     writes.   [*Reads.*
          Art thou god to shepherd turn'd,   40
          That a maiden's heart hath burn'd?
Can a woman rail thus?

Sil.   Call you this railing?

Ros. [*Reads*]
          Why, thy godhead laid apart,
          Warr'st thou with a woman's heart?
Did you ever hear such railing?
          Whiles the eye of man did woo me,
          That could do no vengeance to me.
Meaning me a beast.

●   If the scorn of your bright eyne   50
          Have power to raise such love in mine,
          Alack, in me what strange effect
          Would they work in mild aspect!
          Whiles you chid me, I did love;
          How then might your prayers move!
          He that brings this love to thee
          Little knows this love in me:
          And by him seal up thy mind;
          Whether that thy youth and kind
          Will the faithful offer take   60
          Of me and all that I can make;
          Or else by him my love deny,
          And then I'll study how to die.

Sil.   Call you this chiding?
Cel.   Alas, poor shepherd!
Ros.   Do you pity him? no, he deserves no
pity.   Wilt thou love such a woman?   What, to
make thee an instrument and play false strains
upon thee! not to be endured!   Well, go your
way to her, for I see love hath made thee a tame
snake, and say this to her: that if she love me,
I charge her to love thee; if she will not, I will
never have her unless thou entreat for her.   If
you be a true lover, hence, and not a word; for
here comes more company.   [*Exit Silvius.*

Enter OLIVER.

Oli.   Good morrow, fair ones: pray you, if you
     know,
Where in the purlieus of this forest stands
A sheep-cote fenced about with olive trees?

Cel.   West of this place, down in the neighbour
     bottom:
● The rank of osiers by the murmuring stream   80
Left on your right hand brings you to the place.
But at this hour the house doth keep itself;

25 *freestone.* Sandstone, between yellow and brown in colour.

50 *eyne.* Eyes.

80 *rank of osiers.* Row of willows.

Silvius gives Rosalind a letter. Engraving from Rowe's edition of the works of Shakespeare, 1709

Orlando rescues Oliver from the lion. Engraving from a
painting by Raphael West (1769–1850)

There's none within.
 Oli. If that an eye may profit by a tongue,
Then should I know you by description;
Such garments and such years: 'The boy is fair,
Of female favour, and bestows himself
Like a ripe sister: the woman low
And browner than her brother.' Are not you
The owner of the house I did enquire for? 90
 Cel. It is no boast, being ask'd, to say we are.
 Oli. Orlando doth commend him to you both,
And to that youth he calls his Rosalind
He sends this bloody napkin. Are you he?
 Ros. I am: what must we understand by this?
 Oli. Some of my shame; if you will know of me
What man I am, and how, and why, and where
This handkercher was stain'd.
 Cel.   I pray you, tell it.
 Oli. When last the young Orlando parted
  from you
He left a promise to return again 100
Within an hour, and pacing through the forest,
Chewing the food of sweet and bitter fancy,
Lo, what befel! he threw his eye aside,
And mark what object did present itself:
Under an oak, whose boughs were moss'd with age
And high top bald with dry antiquity,
A wretched ragged man, o'ergrown with hair,
Lay sleeping on his back: about his neck
A green and gilded snake had wreathed itself,
Who with her head nimble in threats approach'd
The opening of his mouth; but suddenly, 111
Seeing Orlando, it unlink'd itself,
And with indented glides did slip away
Into a bush: under which bush's shade
A lioness, with udders all drawn dry,
Lay couching, head on ground, with catlike watch,
When that the sleeping man should stir; for 'tis
The royal disposition of that beast
To prey on nothing that doth seem as dead:
This seen, Orlando did approach the man 120
And found it was his brother, his elder brother.
 Cel. O, I have heard him speak of that same
  brother;
And he did render him the most unnatural
That lived amongst men.
 Oli.   And well he might so do,
For well I know he was unnatural.
 Ros. But, to Orlando: did he leave him there,
Food to the suck'd and hungry lioness?
 Oli. Twice did he turn his back and purposed
  so;
But kindness, nobler ever than revenge,
And nature, stronger than his just occasion, 130
Made him give battle to the lioness,
Who quickly fell before him: in which hurtling
From miserable slumber I awaked.
 Cel. Are you his brother?
 Ros.   Was't you he rescued?
 Cel. Was't you that did so oft contrive to kill
  him?
 Oli. 'Twas I; but 'tis not I: I do not shame
To tell you what I was, since my conversion
So sweetly tastes, being the thing I am.
 Ros. But, for the bloody napkin?
 Oli.   By and by.
When from the first to last betwixt us two 140
Tears our recountments had most kindly bathed,
As how I came into that desert place:—
In brief, he led me to the gentle duke,

Who gave me fresh array and entertainment,
Committing me unto my brother's love;
Who led me instantly unto his cave,
There stripp'd himself, and here upon his arm
The lioness had torn some flesh away,
Which all this while had bled; and now he fainted
And cried, in fainting, upon Rosalind.   150
Brief, I recover'd him, bound up his wound;
And, after some small space, being strong at heart,
He sent me hither, stranger as I am,
To tell this story, that you might excuse
His broken promise, and to give this napkin
Dyed in his blood unto the shepherd youth
That he in sport doth call his Rosalind.
                         [*Rosalind swoons.*

Cel. Why, how now, Ganymede! sweet Ganymede!

Oli. Many will swoon when they do look on
blood.

Cel. There is more in it.   Cousin Ganymede!

Oli. Look, he recovers.   161

Ros. I would I were at home.

Cel.   We'll lead you thither.
I pray you, will you take him by the arm?

Oli. Be of good cheer, youth: you a man!
you lack a man's heart.

Ros. I do so, I confess it.   Ah, sirrah, a body
would think this was well counterfeited!   I pray
you, tell your brother how well I counterfeited.
Heigh-ho!   169

Oli. This was not counterfeit: there is too
great testimony in your complexion that it was a
passion of earnest.

Ros. Counterfeit, I assure you.

Oli. Well then, take a good heart and counterfeit to be a man.

Ros. So I do: but, i'faith, I should have been
a woman by right.

Cel. Come, you look paler and paler: pray
you, draw homewards.   Good sir, go with us.

Oli. That will I, for I must bear answer back
How you excuse my brother, Rosalind.   181

Ros. I shall devise something: but, I pray
you, commend my counterfeiting to him.   Will
you go?   [*Exeunt.*

ACT V.

Scene I.   *The forest.*

Enter Touchstone *and* Audrey.

Touch. We shall find a time, Audrey; patience, gentle Audrey.

Aud. Faith, the priest was good enough, for
all the old gentleman's saying.

Touch. A most wicked Sir Oliver, Audrey, a
most vile Martext.   But, Audrey, there is a
youth here in the forest lays claim to you.

Aud. Ay, I know who 'tis; he hath no interest in me in the world: here comes the man
you mean.   10

Touch. It is meat and drink to me to see a
clown: by my troth, we that have good wits
have much to answer for; we shall be flouting;
we cannot hold.

Enter William.

Will. Good even, Audrey.

Aud. God ye good even, William.

Rosalind swoons. Engraving from a painting by Robert Smirke (1752-1845)

---

172 *passion of earnest.* Genuine emotion.

4 *old gentleman's.* i.e. Jaques.

13 *flouting.* Mocking.

48 *ipse*. He himself.

60 *bastinado*. Fighting with cudgels.

61 *bandy with thee in faction*. Compete with you in arguments and insults.

62 *policy*. Stratagems.

Will. And good even to you, sir.

Touch. Good even, gentle friend. Cover thy head, cover thy head; nay, prithee, be covered. How old are you, friend?   20

Will. Five and twenty, sir.

Touch. A ripe age. Is thy name William?

Will. William, sir.

Touch. A fair name. Wast born i' the forest here?

Will. Ay, sir, I thank God.

Touch. 'Thank God;' a good answer. Art rich?

Will. Faith, sir, so so.

Touch. 'So so' is good, very good, very excellent good; and yet it is not; it is but so so. Art thou wise?   31

Will. Ay, sir, I have a pretty wit.

Touch. Why, thou sayest well. I do now remember a saying, 'The fool doth think he is wise, but the wise man knows himself to be a fool.' The heathen philosopher, when he had a desire to eat a grape, would open his lips when he put it into his mouth; meaning thereby that grapes were made to eat and lips to open. You do love this maid?   40

Will. I do, sir.

Touch. Give me your hand. Art thou learned?

Will. No, sir.

Touch. Then learn this of me: to have, is to have; for it is a figure in rhetoric that drink, being poured out of a cup into a glass, by filling the one doth empty the other; for all your writers
• do consent that ipse is he: now, you are not ipse, for I am he.

Will. Which he, sir?   50

Touch. He, sir, that must marry this woman. Therefore, you clown, abandon,—which is in the vulgar leave,—the society,—which in the boorish is company,—of this female,—which in the common is woman; which together is, abandon the society of this female, or, clown, thou perishest; or, to thy better understanding, diest; or, to wit, I kill thee, make thee away, translate thy life into death, thy liberty into bondage: I will deal
• in poison with thee, or in bastinado, or in steel;
• I will bandy with thee in faction; I will o'er-run
• thee with policy; I will kill thee a hundred and fifty ways: therefore tremble, and depart.

Aud. Do, good William.

Will. God rest you merry, sir.   [*Exit.*

Enter CORIN.

Cor. Our master and mistress seeks you; come, away, away!

Touch. Trip, Audrey! trip, Audrey! I attend, I attend.   [*Exeunt.*

SCENE II.   *The forest.*

Enter ORLANDO *and* OLIVER.

Orl. Is't possible that on so little acquaintance you should like her? that but seeing you should love her? and loving woo? and, wooing, she should grant? and will you persever to enjoy her?

Oli. Neither call the giddiness of it in question, the poverty of her, the small acquaintance, my sudden wooing, nor her sudden consenting; but say with me, I love Aliena; say with her that she loves me; consent with both that we may enjoy each other: it shall be to your good; for my father's house and all the revenue that was old Sir Rowland's will I estate upon you, and here live and die a shepherd.

Orl. You have my consent. Let your wedding be to-morrow: thither will I invite the duke and all's contented followers. Go you and prepare Aliena; for look you, here comes my Rosalind.

Enter ROSALIND.

Ros. God save you, brother.   20
Oli. And you, fair sister.   [*Exit.*
Ros. O, my dear Orlando, how it grieves me to see thee wear thy heart in a scarf!
Orl. It is my arm.
Ros. I thought thy heart had been wounded with the claws of a lion.
Orl. Wounded it is, but with the eyes of a lady.
Ros. Did your brother tell you how I counterfeited to swoon when he showed me your handkercher?   30
Orl. Ay, and greater wonders than that.
Ros. O, I know where you are: nay, 'tis true: there was never any thing so sudden but the fight
• of two rams and Cæsar's thrasonical brag of 'I came, saw, and overcame:' for your brother and my sister no sooner met but they looked, no sooner looked but they loved, no sooner loved but they sighed, no sooner sighed but they asked one another the reason, no sooner knew the reason but they sought the remedy; and in these degrees have they made a pair of stairs to mar-
• riage which they will climb incontinent, or else be incontinent before marriage: they are in the very wrath of love and they will together; clubs cannot part them.
Orl. They shall be married to-morrow, and I will bid the duke to the nuptial. But, O, how bitter a thing it is to look into happiness through another man's eyes! By so much the more shall I to-morrow be at the height of heart-heaviness, by how much I shall think my brother happy in having what he wishes for.
Ros. Why then, to-morrow I cannot serve your turn for Rosalind?
Orl. I can live no longer by thinking.
Ros. I will weary you then no longer with idle talking. Know of me then, for now I speak to some purpose, that I know you are a gentle-
• man of good conceit: I speak not this that you should bear a good opinion of my knowledge, insomuch I say I know you are; neither do I labour for a greater esteem than may in some little measure draw a belief from you, to do yourself good and not to grace me. Believe then, if you please, that I can do strange things: I have, since I was three year old, conversed with a magician, most profound in his art and yet not damnable. If you do love Rosalind so near the heart as your gesture cries it out, when your brother marries Aliena, shall you marry her: I know into what straits of fortune she is driven; and it is not impossible to me, if it appear not
• inconvenient to you, to set her before your eyes to-morrow human as she is and without any danger.
Orl. Speakest thou in sober meanings?
Ros. By my life, I do; which I tender dearly,

Ronald Pickup as Rosalind and Jeremy Brett as Orlando, National Theatre, London, 1968–1969

34 *thrasonical.* Boast like Thraso, the braggart soldier in Terence's *Eunuchus.*

42 *incontinent.* Immediately (with a double meaning).

59 *good conceit.* Intelligence.

73 *inconvenient.* Inappropriate.

119 *Irish wolves.* There were still wolves in Ireland, extinct in England.

Touchstone and Audrey. Engraving from a painting by John Pettie (1839–1893)

though I say I am a magician. Therefore, put you in your best array; bid your friends; for if you will be married to-morrow, you shall, and to Rosalind, if you will. 81

Enter SILVIUS *and* PHEBE.

Look, here comes a lover of mine and a lover of hers.

   Phe. Youth, you have done me much ungentleness,
To show the letter that I writ to you.

   Ros. I care not if I have: it is my study
To seem despiteful and ungentle to you:
You are there followed by a faithful shepherd;
Look upon him, love him; he worships you.

   Phe. Good shepherd, tell this youth what 'tis to love.

   Sil. It is to be all made of sighs and tears;
And so am I for Phebe. 91

   Phe. And I for Ganymede.

   Orl. And I for Rosalind.

   Ros. And I for no woman.

   Sil. It is to be all made of faith and service;
And so am I for Phebe.

   Phe. And I for Ganymede.

   Orl. And I for Rosalind.

   Ros. And I for no woman.

   Sil. It is to be all made of fantasy, 100
All made of passion and all made of wishes,
All adoration, duty, and observance,
All humbleness, all patience and impatience,
† All purity, all trial, all observance;
And so am I for Phebe.

   Phe. And so am I for Ganymede.

   Orl. And so am I for Rosalind.

   Ros. And so am I for no woman.

   Phe. If this be so, why blame you me to love you? 110

   Sil. If this be so, why blame you me to love you?

   Orl. If this be so, why blame you me to love you?

   Ros. Who do you speak to, 'Why blame you me to love you?'

   Orl. To her that is not here, nor doth not hear.

   Ros. Pray you, no more of this; 'tis like the
● howling of Irish wolves against the moon. [*To Sil.*] I will help you, if I can: [*To Phe.*] I would love you, if I could. To-morrow meet me all together. [*To Phe.*] I will marry you, if ever I marry woman, and I'll be married to-morrow: [*To Orl.*] I will satisfy you, if ever I satisfied man, and you shall be married to-morrow: [*To Sil.*] I will content you, if what pleases you contents you, and you shall be married to-morrow. [*To Orl.*] As you love Rosalind, meet: [*To Sil.*] as you love Phebe, meet: and as I love no woman, I'll meet. So fare you well: I have left you commands. 131

   Sil. I'll not fail, if I live.

   Phe. Nor I.

   Orl. Nor I. [*Exeunt.*

SCENE III. *The forest.*

Enter TOUCHSTONE *and* AUDREY.

   Touch. To-morrow is the joyful day, Audrey; to-morrow will we be married.

   Aud. I do desire it with all my heart; and I

hope it is no dishonest desire to desire to be a woman of the world. **Here come two of the banished duke's pages.**

Enter two Pages.

First Page. Well met, honest gentleman.
Touch. By my troth, well met. Come, sit, sit, and a song.   9
Sec. Page. We are for you: sit i' the middle.
First Page. Shall we clap into't roundly, without hawking or spitting or saying we are hoarse, which are the only prologues to a bad voice?
Sec. Page. I'faith, i'faith; and both in a tune, like two gipsies on a horse.

SONG.

It was a lover and his lass,
    With a hey, and a ho, and a hey nonino,
That o'er the green corn-field did pass
    In the spring time, the only pretty ring time,
When birds do sing, hey ding a ding, ding: 21
Sweet lovers love the spring.

Between the acres of the rye,
    With a hey, and a ho, and a hey nonino,
These pretty country folks would lie,
    In spring time, &c.

This carol they began that hour,
    With a hey, and a ho, and a hey nonino,
How that a life was but a flower
    In spring time, &c.   30

And therefore take the present time,
    With a hey, and a ho, and a hey nonino;
For love is crowned with the prime
    In spring time, &c.

Touch. Truly, young gentlemen, though there was no great matter in the ditty, yet the note was very untuneable.
First Page. You are deceived, sir: we kept time, we lost not our time.
Touch. By my troth, yes; I count it but time lost to hear such a foolish song. God be wi' you; and God mend your voices! Come, Audrey.   [*Exeunt.*

SCENE IV. *The forest.*

Enter DUKE senior, AMIENS, JAQUES, ORLANDO, OLIVER, *and* CELIA.

Duke S. Dost thou believe, Orlando, that the boy
Can do all this that he hath promised?
Orl. I sometimes do believe, and sometimes do not;
†As those that fear they hope, and know they fear.

Enter ROSALIND, SILVIUS, *and* PHEBE.

Ros. Patience once more, whiles our compact is urged:
You say, if I bring in your Rosalind,
You will bestow her on Orlando here?
Duke S. That would I, had I kingdoms to give with her.
Ros. And you say, you will have her, when I bring her?
Orl. That would I, were I of all kingdoms king.   10
Ros. You say, you'll marry me, if I be willing?

4 *dishonest.* Unchaste.

Music to 'It was a lover and his lass'. From a manuscript

37 *untuneable.* Unmusical, disagreeable to the ear.

Costume design for Duke Senior, J. Gower Parks, Open Air Theatre, Regent's Park, London, 1935

4 *fear they hope.* Fear they only hope.

45 *measure*. Stately dance.

Victorian actors, Mrs H. Marston and Mr Younge as Audrey and Touchstone, Sadler's Wells Theatre, London, 1848

65-66 *swift and sententious*. Quick-witted and pointed.

68 *dulcet diseases*. 'Pleasant weaknesses'.

Phe.   That will I, should I die the hour after.
Ros.   But if you do refuse to marry me,
You'll give yourself to this most faithful shepherd?
Phe.   So is the bargain.
Ros.   You say, that you'll have Phebe, if she
    will?
Sil.   Though to have her and death were both
    one thing.
Ros.   I have promised to make all this matter
    even.
Keep you your word, O duke, to give your daughter;
You yours, Orlando, to receive his daughter: 20
Keep your word, Phebe, that you'll marry me,
Or else refusing me, to wed this shepherd:
Keep your word, Silvius, that you'll marry her,
If she refuse me: and from hence I go,
To make these doubts all even.
                    [*Exeunt Rosalind and Celia.*
Duke S.   I do remember in this shepherd boy
Some lively touches of my daughter's favour.
Orl.   My lord, the first time that I ever saw
    him
Methought he was a brother to your daughter:
But, my good lord, this boy is forest-born,   30
And hath been tutor'd in the rudiments
Of many desperate studies by his uncle,
Whom he reports to be a great magician,
Obscured in the circle of this forest.

Enter TOUCHSTONE *and* AUDREY.

Jaq.   There is, sure, another flood toward, and these couples are coming to the ark. Here comes a pair of very strange beasts, which in all tongues are called fools.
Touch.   Salutation and greeting to you all!
Jaq.   Good my lord, bid him welcome: this is the motley-minded gentleman that I have so often met in the forest: he hath been a courtier, he swears.
Touch.   If any man doubt that, let him put me to my purgation. I have trod a measure; I have flattered a lady; I have been politic with my friend, smooth with mine enemy; I have undone three tailors; I have had four quarrels, and like to have fought one.
Jaq.   And how was that ta'en up?   50
Touch.   Faith, we met, and found the quarrel was upon the seventh cause.
Jaq.   How seventh cause? Good my lord, like this fellow.
Duke S.   I like him very well.
Touch.   God 'ild you, sir; I desire you of the like. I press in here, sir, amongst the rest of the country copulatives, to swear and to forswear; according as marriage binds and blood breaks: a poor virgin, sir, an ill-favoured thing, sir, but mine own; a poor humour of mine, sir, to take that that no man else will: rich honesty dwells like a miser, sir, in a poor house; as your pearl in your foul oyster.
Duke S.   By my faith, he is very swift and sententious.
Touch.   According to the fool's bolt, sir, and such dulcet diseases.
Jaq.   But, for the seventh cause; how did you find the quarrel on the seventh cause?   70
Touch.   Upon a lie seven times removed:— bear your body more seeming, Audrey:—as thus, sir. I did dislike the cut of a certain courtier's

beard : he sent me word, if I said his beard was not cut well, he was in the mind it was : this is called the Retort Courteous. If I sent him word again 'it was not well cut,' he would send me word, he cut it to please himself : this is called the Quip Modest. If again 'it was not well cut,' he disabled my judgement : this is called the Reply Churlish. If again 'it was not well cut,' he would answer, I spake not true : this is called the Reproof Valiant. If again 'it was not well cut,' he would say, I lied : this is called the Countercheck Quarrelsome : and so to the Lie Circumstantial and the Lie Direct.

Jaq. And how oft did you say his beard was not well cut?

Touch. I durst go no further than the Lie Circumstantial, nor he durst not give me the Lie Direct ; and so we measured swords and parted.

Jaq. Can you nominate in order now the degrees of the lie?

Touch. O sir, we quarrel in print, by the book ; as you have books for good manners : I will name you the degrees. The first, the Retort Courteous ; the second, the Quip Modest ; the third, the Reply Churlish ; the fourth, the Reproof Valiant ; the fifth, the Countercheck Quarrelsome ; the sixth, the Lie with Circumstance ; the seventh, the Lie Direct. All these you may avoid but the Lie Direct ; and you may avoid that too, with an If. I knew when seven justices could not take up a quarrel, but when the parties were met themselves, one of them thought but of an If, as, ' If you said so, then I said so ;' and they shook hands and swore brothers. Your If is the only peace-maker ; much virtue in If.

Jaq. Is not this a rare fellow, my lord? he's as good at any thing and yet a fool.   110

Duke S. He uses his folly like a stalking-horse and under the presentation of that he shoots his wit.

　　　Enter Hymen, Rosalind, *and* Celia.

　　　　　Still Music.

Hym. Then is there mirth in heaven,
　　When earthly things made even
　　　　Atone together.
　　Good duke, receive thy daughter :
　　Hymen from heaven brought her,
　　　　Yea, brought her hither,
　　That thou mightst join her hand with his
　　Whose heart within his bosom is.   121

Ros. [*To duke*] To you I give myself, for I am yours.
[*To Orl.*] To you I give myself, for I am yours.

Duke S. If there be truth in sight, you are my daughter.

Orl. If there be truth in sight, you are my Rosalind.

Phe. If sight and shape be true,
Why then, my love adieu !

Ros. I'll have no father, if you be not he :
I'll have no husband, if you be not he :
Nor ne'er wed woman, if you be not she.   130

Hym. Peace, ho ! I bar confusion :
　　'Tis I must make conclusion
　　　　Of these most strange events :
　　Here's eight that must take hands
　　To join in Hymen's bands,
　　　　If truth holds true contents.

112 *presentation.* Pretence. *Hymen.* The god of marriage.

116 *Atone.* Be joined, are at one.

Rosalind : 'To you I give myself, for I am yours.' Engraving from a painting by William Hamilton (1751–1801)

Ada Rehan as Rosalind, Lyceum Theatre, London,
1890

_____

179 *shrewd.* Sharp.

You and you no cross shall part :
You and you are heart in heart :
You to his love must accord,
Or have a woman to your lord :   140
You and you are sure together,
As the winter to foul weather.
Whiles a wedlock-hymn we sing,
Feed yourselves with questioning ;
That reason wonder may diminish,
How thus we met, and these things finish.

SONG.
Wedding is great Juno's crown :
    O blessed bond of board and bed !
'Tis Hymen peoples every town ;
    High wedlock then be honoured :   150
Honour, high honour and renown,
To Hymen, god of every town !

Duke S. O my dear niece, welcome thou art
    to me !
Even daughter, welcome, in no less degree.
    Phe. I will not eat my word, now thou art mine ;
Thy faith my fancy to thee doth combine.

Enter JAQUES DE BOYS.

Jaq. de B. Let me have audience for a word
    or two :
I am the second son of old Sir Rowland,
That bring these tidings to this fair assembly.
Duke Frederick, hearing how that every day 160
Men of great worth resorted to this forest,
Address'd a mighty power ; which were on foot,
In his own conduct, purposely to take
His brother here and put him to the sword :
And to the skirts of this wild wood he came ;
Where meeting with an old religious man,
After some question with him, was converted
Both from his enterprise and from the world,
His crown bequeathing to his banish'd brother,
And all their lands restored to them again   170
That were with him exiled.   This to be true,
I do engage my life.
    Duke S.   Welcome, young man ;
Thou offer'st fairly to thy brothers' wedding :
To one his lands withheld, and to the other
A land itself at large, a potent dukedom.
First, in this forest let us do those ends
That here were well begun and well begot :
And after, every of this happy number
• That have endured shrewd days and nights with us
Shall share the good of our returned fortune, 180
According to the measure of their states.
Meantime, forget this new-fall'n dignity
And fall into our rustic revelry.
Play, music ! And you, brides and bridegrooms all,
With measure heap'd in joy, to the measures fall.
    Jaq. Sir, by your patience.   If I heard you
        rightly,
The duke hath put on a religious life
And thrown into neglect the pompous court?
    Jaq de B. He hath.
    Jaq. To him will I : out of these convertites
There is much matter to be heard and learn'd. 191
[*To duke*] You to your former honour I be-
        queath ;
Your patience and your virtue well deserves it :
[*To Orl.*] You to a love that your true faith doth
        merit :
[*To Oli.*] You to your land and love and great

allies :

[*To Sil.*] You to a long and well-deserved bed :

[*To Touch.*] And you to wrangling ; for thy
loving voyage

Is but for two months victuall'd.   So, to your
pleasures :

I am for other than for dancing measures.

    Duke S. Stay, Jaques, stay.   **200**

    Jaq. To see no pastime I : what you would have
I 'll stay to know at your abandon'd cave. [*Exit.*

    Duke S. Proceed, proceed : we will begin these
      rites,

As we do trust they 'll end, in true delights,

                        [*A dance.*

EPILOGUE.

    Ros. It is not the fashion to see the lady the
epilogue ; but it is no more unhandsome than to
see the lord the prologue.   If it be true that good
wine needs no bush, 'tis true that a good play
needs no epilogue ; yet to good wine they do use
good bushes, and good plays prove the better by the
help of good epilogues.   What a case am I in
then, that am neither a good epilogue nor cannot
insinuate with you in the behalf of a good play !
I am not furnished like a beggar, therefore to
beg will not become me : my way is to conjure
you ; and I 'll begin with the women.   I charge
you, O women, for the love you bear to men, to
like as much of this play as please you : and I
charge you, O men, for the love you bear to
women—as I perceive by your simpering, none
of you hates them—that between you and the
women the play may please.   If I were a woman
I would kiss as many of you as had beards that
pleased me, complexions that liked me and breaths
that I defied not : and, I am sure, as many as
have good beards or good faces or sweet breaths
will, for my kind offer, when I make curtsy, bid
me farewell.   [*Exeunt.*

207-208 *good wine needs no bush.* From Roman times
taverns hung a 'bush' outside to advertise their liquor ;
so this proverb means that good things need no
advertisement.

Vintner's with bush under sign. From a medieval
manuscript

Much Ado About Nothing

1599

THE COMEDY IN MUCH ADO is set against a more serious, if rather melodramatic, story than its predecessor, and the love-combat of Beatrice and Benedick is an improvement on Rosalind and Orlando. It harks back in a way to Petruchio and Kate, but in altogether wittier and more sophisticated fashion. Shakespeare found a promising story in Bandello's collection, which he knew both in Italian and in French. He tightened up the action and concentrated it for dramatic effect, at one point preferring Ariosto's version of the tale in Sir John Harington's recent translation of *Orlando Furioso* (1591), while some hints came from Spenser's *Faerie Queene* (1590), a prodigious influence for Elizabethan writers.

So there is little point in the pedantic hunt for remote and improbable 'sources' in studying Shakespeare: he took from what was ready to hand, often what was recent, that which seemed to him to offer the makings of a play, and then made it. He crossed it with a sub-plot, adding characters and inventions of his own, as a composer would take a musical theme and combine it with another to create further permutations. What we remember from *Much Ado* are the characters of Beatrice and Benedick, as Charles I noted in his copy of the Second Folio, and as Berlioz named his opera based on the play. Hardly less memorable are Dogberry and Verges, the constable and head-borough, officers of the watch, who are convincing, if comic, transcripts from local life. They are absurd but completely real.

It is arresting that Shakespeare should have chosen the name Hero for his heroine, upon whom a wicked trick is played to place her chastity under suspicion and her marriage in jeopardy: plenty of other names were available, but *Hero and Leander* (whose name also occurs) was ready to hand. It is perhaps not without significance that the bastard brother of the Prince of Arragon was called Don John. Philip II's bastard brother, Don John, was a familiar figure to the Elizabethans. In the play he is a despicable character, who wants to ruin Hero's marriage to Claudio out of pure malice —a forerunner of Iago in *Othello*. A good deal in the play verges on the tragic, reminding us of *Romeo and Juliet*, or is to appear again in *The Winter's Tale* (as was the pastoral element of *As You Like It*). For Shakespeare constantly repeated situations and themes, re-using his basic elements, improving and refining upon his characters.

Date. The play is usually dated to 1599, and this is corroborated by various circumstances. There is a tell-tale reference—

> like favourites,
> Made proud by princes, that advance their pride
> Against that power that bred it.

This exactly expresses what Essex was doing at that moment: advanced and favoured by the Queen, indeed spoiled by her, he was now challenging not only her popularity but her rule. Through his relationship to Southampton, this was Shakespeare's alignment, and he still had hopes of the gallant chivalrous figure that Essex was—Philip Sidney's heir—and expressed them. Here was the choice, the agonising crux, out of which *Troilus and Cressida* was to come. A reference to Troilus also comes in this play: Shakespeare's mind was full of echoes and reverberations, conscious and subconscious. Hence too the revealing images that spring up at any moment, almost involuntarily. No writer was ever more fortunate.

Owing to the publication of the play in 1600 from a theatre-copy we know that Dogberry was played by the Company's brilliant comedian, Will Kemp, who left the Chamberlain's men later this year. Verges was played by Richard Cowley, who had come on from Strange's, and lived in Shoreditch, as Shakespeare did at first, according to Aubrey. Balthasar was played by the minstrel, Jack Wilson, who sang the lovely song:

> Sigh no more, ladies, sigh no more,
> Men were deceivers ever . . .

to counterpoint the theme.

The Age. Many touches bring the background to the fore. Beatrice begins by regarding Benedick as the plague: 'God help the noble Claudio, if he have caught the Benedick'. But we remember that *carduus benedictus* was a remedy for heart-disease. 'I charge thee on thy allegiance' was the regular form of an arrest, or warning before it. There are several references to writing in itself, with a ballad-maker's pen—even the news was sung in the form of ballads then—and to sonneteering. Some names 'run smoothly in the even road of a blank verse', but Benedick cannot express love in rhyme: 'I have tried: I can find out no rhyme to "lady" but "baby", an innocent rhyme; for "scorn", "horn", a hard rhyme; for "school", "fool", a babbling rhyme. Very ominous endings: no, I was not born under a rhyming planet.' Here we are permitted a glimpse of Shakespeare at his own work: himself *was* born under a rhyming planet, and rhymes came easily to him, though much of this play is in prose.

We note the usual hoary old jokes about horns, and cuckolding, of which heterosexual Elizabethans could never have enough—a whole song is devoted to it in *As You Like It* : to us boring, the appeal of the joke hardly intelligible. The literary background of one such joke—

> In time the savage bull doth bear the yoke—

is more interesting, for it is a line from Kyd's immensely successful *Spanish Tragedy* which the magpie memory of the actor has retained. Kyd's line comes from one of Watson's Sonnets, and both Kyd and Watson were close friends of Marlowe. *The*

*Christina of
Denmark, Duchess
of Milan, in
mourning clothes.
Painting c. 1538
by Hans Holbein*

Spanish Tragedy was acted by Strange's men, with whom Shakespeare had some early association. Can he have acted in it?

A passing reference to the Duchess of Milan's gown suggests interesting possibilities. Hero's waiting woman says, 'I saw the Duchess of Milan's gown that they praise so.' To which Hero says, 'O, that exceeds, they say.' Margaret: 'By my troth, 'tis but a nightgown in respect of yours.' Holbein's famous portrait of Christina, Duchess of Milan, does indeed look like a night-gown, the long black gown of a young widow. Can Shakespeare have seen the picture? Zuccaro claimed to have seen it in the house of Henry, second Earl of Pembroke,[1] patron of the Company with which Shakespeare (and Marlowe) had brief associations. We must needs point out that this was *not* the son, William, third Earl—for the benefit of those who wish to confuse themselves.

To come down to earth, we hear of a Scotch jig—we did not know that there was such a special kind, 'hot and hasty, and full as fantastical'. Jokes about national idiosyncrasies never fail, in this like Shaw's rallying the English, which brought him such success in our time. We have a hit at foreigners' clothing: 'like a German from the waist downward, all slops; and a Spaniard from the hip upwards, no doublet.' We may well see William Shakespeare in the reflection, 'what a pretty thing man is when he goes in his doublet and hose and leaves off his wit!' Or in, 'if a man do not erect in this age his own tomb ere he dies, he shall live no longer in monument than the bell rings and the widow weeps.'

Dogberry and Verges. When all is said, we probably remember best today Shakespeare's transcripts from real life: out of the artificial comedy of *The Two Gentlemen of Verona,* Launce and his dog; from *A Midsummer Night's Dream,* Bottom the weaver and his rude mechanicals. This comic realism reaches an absurd height with the constable, Dogberry, and his lieutenant, Verges. These local officers of the watch provided regular farcical fare for the stage, but there is an extra-ordinary verisimilitude in Shakespeare's portrayal, for all that it is a caricature.

John Aubrey tells us that 'Ben Jonson and he did gather humours of men daily wherever they came'—no doubt: the proper way of writers at all times, observing human fooleries. The humour of the Constable, evidently Dogberry, 'he happened to take at Grendon in Bucks'—presumably Grendon Underwood, along the road from London to Bicester, thence on to Oxford or Stratford.

[1] v. Roy Strong, *The English Icon,* 347.

Beatrice and Benedick at the dance in Leonato's house. Engraving of Princess's Theatre production, London, 1858

The beast that bears me, tired with my woe,
Plods daily on, to bear that weight in me,
As if by some instinct the wretch did know
His rider loved not speed, being made from thee.

But those years were over now, in 1599.

Dogberry and Verges are delicious fools, better than all the professional jesters. Their language is perfectly convincing, for all that it is larded with what would later be called malapropisms.

Dogberry: This is your charge: you shall comprehend [sc. apprehend] all vagrom men; you are to bid any man stand, in the Prince's name.

Second Watch: How if 'a will not stand?

Dogberry: Why then, take no note of him but let him go; and presently call the rest of the watch together and thank God you are rid of a knave.

Verges. If he will not stand when he is bidden, he is none of the Prince's subjects. [The usual bawdy joke, with gestures, about standing.]

Dogberry: True, and they are to meddle with none but the Prince's subjects. You shall also make no noise in the streets, for, for the watch to babble and to talk is most tolerable and not to be endured.'

The authenticity of this may be seen from a fascinating letter from the great Lord Burghley to Walsingham, the Queen's principal ministers, when the hue and cry was up for the Babington conspirators.[1]

[1] The conspiracy's aim was to kill Elizabeth, to place Mary Stuart on the throne.

'Sir, As I came from London homeward in my coach, I saw at every town's end the number of ten or twelve standing with long staves, and until I came to Enfield I thought no other of them but that they had stayed for avoiding of the rain, or to drink at some alehouse, for so they did stand under pentices at alehouses. But at Enfield finding a dozen in a plump, when there was no rain, I bethought myself that they were appointed as watchmen, for the apprehending of such as are missing. And thereupon I called some of them to me apart, and asked them wherefore they stood there. And one of them answered, "To take three young men." And demanding how they should know the persons, one answered with these words, "Marry, my lord, by intelligence of their favour." "What mean you by that?" quoth I. "Marry," said they, "one of the parties hath a hooked nose." "And have you," quoth I, "no other mark?" "No," saith they. And then I asked who appointed them. And they answered one Banks, a

A constable of the watch. Illustration from the manuscript, Album of G. Holtzschuher of Nuremburg

head constable, whom I willed to be sent to me. Surely, sir, whosoever had the charge from you hath used the matter negligently. For these watchmen stand so openly in plumps as no suspected person will come near them; and if they be no better instructed but to find three persons by one of them having a hooked nose, they may miss thereof.'[1]

It is perfect Shakespearean dialogue, and just like the scene in *Much Ado*. It is pleasant to record that, all the same, the Babington conspirators were rounded up nearby at Harrow. Similarly, in the play, Dogberry and his fellows managed to get the truth out of Don John's villainous agent, Borachio, who bids 'Stand thee close then, under this pent-house, for it drizzles rain, and I will, like a true drunkard, utter all to thee.' He confesses to the trick by which Hero was accused wrongfully.

Dogberry: Flat burglary as ever was committed.

First Watch: And that Count Claudio did mean, upon his words, to disgrace Hero before the whole assembly, and not marry her.
Dogberry: O villain! thou wilt be condemned into everlasting redemption [sc. perdition] for this.

We may well conclude that the intrigue, which provided occasion for this—the plot Shakespeare made use of from his 'sources'—is less important than these marvellous scenes from real life.

Benedick and Beatrice. In the story Hero is at first framed by the odious Borachio enacting a love-scene at her chamber-window with her waiting-woman dressed up to resemble her. Claudio is taken in by this and disclaims her at the very wedding ceremony in church. Hero swoons at the disgrace, and is taken up for dead. Beatrice has more spirit. 'Is he not approved in the height a villain, that hath slandered, scorned, dishonoured my kinswoman? O that I were a man! What, bear her in hand until they come to take hands; and then, with public accusation, uncovered slander, unmitigated rancour—O God, that I were a man! I would eat his heart in the market-place.'

We see that Beatrice is a real woman, and her love-contests with Benedick are naturally more powerful and realistic than the romantic-pastoral of Rosalind and Orlando. However, we must let the play speak for itself. *Much Ado* was always popular; Leonard Digges, whose family were acquainted with Shakespeare, testified:

> let but Beatrice
> And Benedick be seen, lo, in a trice
> The cockpit, galleries, boxes all are full.

A tribute of another kind is the fact that, a few years later, Heywood's *Fair Maid of the Exchange* (1607) has many borrowings from *Much Ado*.

Text. The text is a good one, from the first Quarto of 1600, in spite of the Company staying publication—and evidently from a theatre prompt-book, for in places it has the names of the actors, or descriptions of characters (e.g. 'Bastard' for Don John) instead of the names of the *dramatis personae*. Clearly not revised by Shakespeare for any publication, it was used for the text in the First Folio, with a few corrections and misprints.

[1] q. from the State Papers in my *The England of Elizabeth,* 357.

MUCH ADO ABOUT NOTHING.

DRAMATIS PERSONÆ.

DON PEDRO, prince of Arragon.
DON JOHN, his bastard brother.
CLAUDIO, a young lord of Florence.
BENEDICK, a young lord of Padua.
LEONATO, governor of Messina.
ANTONIO, his brother.
BALTHASAR, attendant on Don Pedro.
CONRADE, } followers of Don John.
BORACHIO, }
FRIAR FRANCIS.
DOGBERRY, a constable.

VERGES, a headborough.
A Sexton.
A Boy.

HERO, daughter to Leonato.
BEATRICE, niece to Leonato.
MARGARET, } gentlewomen attending on
URSULA, } Hero.

Messengers, Watch, Attendants, &c.

SCENE: *Messina.*

● *A bullet beside a text line indicates an annotation in the opposite column*

ACT I.

SCENE I. *Before* LEONATO'S *house.*

Enter LEONATO, HERO, *and* BEATRICE, *with a* Messenger.

Leon. I learn in this letter that Don Peter of Arragon comes this night to Messina.

Mess. He is very near by this: he was not three leagues off when I left him.

Leon. How many gentlemen have you lost in this action?

Mess. But few of any sort, and none of name.

Leon. A victory is twice itself when the achiever brings home full numbers. I find here that Don Peter hath bestowed much honour on a young Florentine called Claudio. 11

Mess. Much deserved on his part and equally remembered by Don Pedro: he hath borne himself beyond the promise of his age, doing, in the figure of a lamb, the feats of a lion: he hath indeed better bettered expectation than you must expect of me to tell you how.

View of Messina. Engraving from Charles Knight's *Pictorial Edition of the Works of William Shakspere,* 1839–43

Opposite : Hero swoons. Engraving from a painting by William Hamilton (1751–1801)

397

39 *set up his bills.* Posted notices.

40 *at the flight.* To a shooting contest.

41 *subscribed for.* Accepted on behalf of.

42 *at the bird-bolt.* Small blunt-headed arrow for the cross bow.

47 *meet.* Even.

51 *holp.* Helped.

Googie Withers as Beatrice, Stratford-upon-Avon, 1958

69 *difference.* A distinguishing mark (in heraldry).

77 *block.* The form on which a hat is made, i.e. fashion.

Beatrice: 'He wears his faith but as the fashion of his hat'. Engraving from Charles Knight's *Pictorial Edition of the Works of William Shakspere*, 1839–43

Leon.   He hath an uncle here in Messina will be very much glad of it.

Mess.   I have already delivered him letters, and there appears much joy in him; even so much that joy could not show itself modest enough without a badge of bitterness.

Leon.   Did he break out into tears?

Mess.   In great measure.

Leon.   A kind overflow of kindness: there are no faces truer than those that are so washed. How much better is it to weep at joy than to joy at weeping!

Beat.   I pray you, is Signior Mountanto returned from the wars or no?   31

Mess.   I know none of that name, lady: there was none such in the army of any sort.

Leon.   What is he that you ask for, niece?

Hero.   My cousin means Signior Benedick of Padua.

Mess.   O, he's returned; and as pleasant as ever he was.

● *Beat.*   He set up his bills here in Messina and
● challenged Cupid at the flight; and my uncle's
● fool, reading the challenge, subscribed for Cupid,
● and challenged him at the bird-bolt. I pray you, how many hath he killed and eaten in these wars? But how many hath he killed? for indeed I promised to eat all of his killing.

Leon.   Faith, niece, you tax Signior Benedick
● too much; but he'll be meet with you, I doubt it not.

Mess.   He hath done good service, lady, in these wars.

Beat.   You had musty victual, and he hath
● holp to eat it: he is a very valiant trencher-man; he hath an excellent stomach.

Mess.   And a good soldier too, lady.

Beat.   And a good soldier to a lady: but what is he to a lord?

Mess.   A lord to a lord, a man to a man; stuffed with all honourable virtues.

Beat.   It is so, indeed; he is no less than a stuffed man: but for the stuffing,—well, we are all mortal.   60

Leon.   You must not, sir, mistake my niece There is a kind of merry war betwixt Signior Benedick and her: they never meet but there's a skirmish of wit between them.

Beat.   Alas! he gets nothing by that. In our last conflict four of his five wits went halting off, and now is the whole man governed with one: so that if he have wit enough to keep himself
● warm, let him bear it for a difference between himself and his horse; for it is all the wealth that he hath left, to be known a reasonable creature. Who is his companion now? He hath every month a new sworn brother.

Mess.   Is't possible?

Beat.   Very easily possible: he wears his faith but as the fashion of his hat; it ever changes with
● the next block.

Mess.   I see, lady, the gentleman is not in your books.

Beat.   No; an he were, I would burn my study. But, I pray you, who is his companion? Is there no young squarer now that will make a voyage with him to the devil?

Mess.   He is most in the company of the right noble Claudio.

Beat.   O Lord, he will hang upon him like a

disease: he is sooner caught than the pestilence, and the taker runs presently mad. God help the noble Claudio! if he have caught the Benedick, it will cost him a thousand pound ere a' be cured.

Mess. I will hold friends with you, lady. 91

Beat. Do, good friend.

● *Leon.* You will never run mad, niece.

Beat. No, not till a hot January.

Mess. Don Pedro is approached.

Enter DON PEDRO, DON JOHN, CLAUDIO, BENEDICK, *and* BALTHASAR.

D. Pedro. Good Signior Leonato, you are
● come to meet your trouble: the fashion of the world is to avoid cost, and you encounter it.

Leon. Never came trouble to my house in the likeness of your grace: for trouble being gone, comfort should remain; but when you depart from me, sorrow abides and happiness takes his leave.

D. Pedro. You embrace your charge too willingly. I think this is your daughter.

Leon. Her mother hath many times told me so.

Bene. Were you in doubt, sir, that you asked her?

Leon. Signior Benedick, no; for then were you a child.

D. Pedro. You have it full, Benedick: we may guess by this what you are, being a man. Truly, the lady fathers herself. Be happy, lady; for you are like an honourable father.

Bene. If Signior Leonato be her father, she
● would not have his head on her shoulders for all Messina, as like him as she is.

Beat. I wonder that you will still be talking, Signior Benedick: nobody marks you.

Bene. What, my dear Lady Disdain! are you yet living? 120

Beat. Is it possible disdain should die while she hath such meet food to feed it as Signior Benedick? Courtesy itself must convert to disdain, if you come in her presence.

Bene. Then is courtesy a turncoat. But it is certain I am loved of all ladies, only you excepted: and I would I could find in my heart that I had not a hard heart; for, truly, I love none.

Beat. A dear happiness to women: they would else have been troubled with a pernicious suitor. I thank God and my cold blood, I am of your humour for that: I had rather hear my dog bark at a crow than a man swear he loves me.

Bene. God keep your ladyship still in that mind! so some gentleman or other shall 'scape a predestinate scratched face.

Beat. Scratching could not make it worse, an 'twere such a face as yours were.

● *Bene.* Well, you are a rare parrot-teacher.

Beat. A bird of my tongue is better than a beast of yours. 141

Bene. I would my horse had the speed of your tongue, and so good a continuer. But keep your way, i' God's name; I have done.

● *Beat.* You always end with a jade's trick: I know you of old.

D. Pedro. That is the sum of all, Leonato. Signior Claudio and Signior Benedick, my dear friend Leonato hath invited you all. I tell him we shall stay here at the least a month; and he heartily prays some occasion may detain us longer.

93 *run mad.* i.e. fall madly in love.

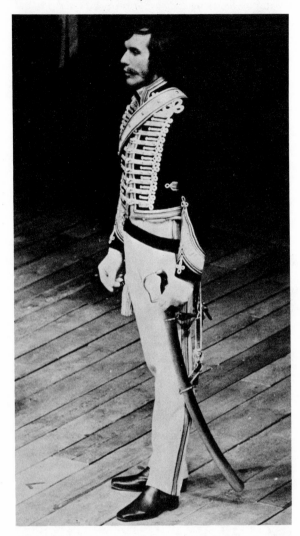

Robin Ellis as Don Pedro, Royal Shakespeare Co, 1976

97 *trouble.* i.e. trouble of entertaining the Prince and his entourage.

115 *head.* i.e. with its beard and grey hair.

139 *parrot-teacher.* i.e. chatterbox.

145 *jade.* Old horse.

186-187 *flouting Jack.* Mocking fellow. *Cupid is a good hare-finder and Vulcan a rare carpenter.* i.e. talk nonsense (Cupid was blind and Vulcan a blacksmith).

204 *sigh away Sundays.* i.e. on Sundays he will feel his bondage more keenly.

George Alexander, the Edwardian actor, as Benedick, St James's Theatre, London, 1898

I dare swear he is no hypocrite, but prays from his heart.

Leon. If you swear, my lord, you shall not be forsworn. [*To Don John*] Let me bid you welcome, my lord : being reconciled to the prince your brother, I owe you all duty.

D. John. I thank you : I am not of many words, but I thank you.

Leon. Please it your grace lead on ?   160

D. Pedro. Your hand, Leonato ; we will go together.

[*Exeunt all except Benedick and Claudio.*

Claud. Benedick, didst thou note the daughter of Signior Leonato ?

Bene. I noted her not ; but I looked on her.

Claud. Is she not a modest young lady ?

Bene. Do you question me, as an honest man should do, for my simple true judgement ; or would you have me speak after my custom, as being a professed tyrant to their sex ?   170

Claud. No ; I pray thee speak in sober judgement.

Bene. Why, i' faith, methinks she's too low for a high praise, too brown for a fair praise and too little for a great praise : only this commendation I can afford her, that were she other than she is, she were unhandsome ; and being no other but as she is, I do not like her.

Claud. Thou thinkest I am in sport : I pray thee tell me truly how thou likest her.   180

Bene. Would you buy her, that you inquire after her ?

Claud. Can the world buy such a jewel ?

Bene. Yea, and a case to put it into. But speak you this with a sad brow ? or do you play
• the flouting Jack, to tell us Cupid is a good hare-finder and Vulcan a rare carpenter ? Come, in what key shall a man take you, to go in the song ?

Claud. In mine eye she is the sweetest lady that ever I looked on.   190

Bene. I can see yet without spectacles and I see no such matter : there's her cousin, an she were not possessed with a fury, exceeds her as much in beauty as the first of May doth the last of December. But I hope you have no intent to turn husband, have you ?

Claud. I would scarce trust myself, though I had sworn the contrary, if Hero would be my wife.

Bene. Is't come to this ? In faith, hath not the world one man but he will wear his cap with suspicion ? Shall I never see a bachelor of three-score again ? Go to, i' faith ; an thou wilt needs thrust thy neck into a yoke, wear the print of it
• and sigh away Sundays. Look ; Don Pedro is returned to seek you.

Re-enter DON PEDRO.

D. Pedro. What secret hath held you here, that you followed not to Leonato's ?

Bene. I would your grace would constrain me to tell.

D. Pedro. I charge thee on thy allegiance.

Bene. You hear, Count Claudio : I can be secret as a dumb man ; I would have you think so ; but, on my allegiance, mark you this, on my allegiance. He is in love. With who ? now that is your grace's part. Mark how short his answer is ;—With Hero, Leonato's short daughter.

Claud. If this were so, so were it uttered.

Bene. Like the old tale, my lord : 'it is not so, nor 'twas not so, but, indeed, God forbid it should be so.' 220

Claud. If my passion change not shortly, God forbid it should be otherwise.

D. Pedro. Amen, if you love her ; for the lady is very well worthy.

Claud. You speak this to fetch me in, my lord.

D. Pedro. By my troth, I speak my thought.

Claud. And, in faith, my lord, I spoke mine.

Bene. And, by my two faiths and troths, my lord, I spoke mine.

Claud. That I love her, I feel. 230

D. Pedro. That she is worthy, I know.

Bene. That I neither feel how she should be loved nor know how she should be worthy, is the opinion that fire cannot melt out of me : I will die in it at the stake.

D. Pedro. Thou wast ever an obstinate heretic in the despite of beauty.

Claud. And never could maintain his part but in the force of his will.

Bene. That a woman conceived me, I thank her ; that she brought me up, I likewise give her most humble thanks : but that I will have a recheat winded in my forehead, or hang my bugle in an invisible baldrick, all women shall pardon me. Because I will not do them the wrong to mistrust any, I will do myself the right to trust none ; and the fine is, for the which I may go the finer, I will live a bachelor.

D. Pedro. I shall see thee, ere I die, look pale with love. 250

Bene. With anger, with sickness, or with hunger, my lord, not with love : prove that ever I lose more blood with love than I will get again with drinking, pick out mine eyes with a ballad-maker's pen and hang me up at the door of a brothel-house for the sign of blind Cupid.

D. Pedro. Well, if ever thou dost fall from this faith, thou wilt prove a notable argument.

Bene. If I do, hang me in a bottle like a cat and shoot at me ; and he that hits me, let him be clapped on the shoulder, and called Adam. 261

D. Pedro. Well, as time shall try :
'In time the savage bull doth bear the yoke.'

Bene. The savage bull may ; but if ever the sensible Benedick bear it, pluck off the bull's horns and set them in my forehead : and let me be vilely painted, and in such great letters as they write 'Here is good horse to hire,' let them signify under my sign 'Here you may see Benedick the married man.' 270

Claud. If this should ever happen, thou wouldst be horn-mad.

D. Pedro. Nay, if Cupid have not spent all his quiver in Venice, thou wilt quake for this shortly.

Bene. I look for an earthquake too, then.

D. Pedro. Well, you will temporize with the hours. In the meantime, good Signior Benedick, repair to Leonato's : commend me to him and tell him I will not fail him at supper ; for indeed he hath made great preparation. 280

Bene. I have almost matter enough in me for such an embassage ; and so I commit you—

Claud. To the tuition of God : From my house, if I had it,—

D. Pedro. The sixth of July : Your loving friend, Benedick.

225 *fetch me in.* Get me to confess.

242-43 *recheat winded.* The huntsman's call sounded.

244 *baldrick.* Belt.

261 *Adam.* Adam Bell, a famous archer.

Don Pedro : "'In time the savage bull doth bear the yoke'". Emblem of matrimony from Cesare Ripa's *Iconologia*, 1603

272 *horn-mad.* Furious, with a quip on a cuckold's horns.

274 *Venice.* Notorious in Shakespeare's day for its sexual licence.

276-277 *temporize with the hours.* Soften as time goes by.

285 *sixth of July.* Old midsummer's day.

289 *basted.* With tacking stitches.

319 *The fairest grant is the necessity.* i.e. the best gift is made when it is most needed.

10 *thick-pleached.* Lined with interwoven boughs.

Costume design for Claudio by Voytek, Royal Shakespeare Co, 1971

Bene. Nay, mock not, mock not. The body of your discourse is sometime guarded with frag-
● ments, and the guards are but slightly basted on neither : ere you flout old ends any further, examine your conscience : and so I leave you.
[*Exit.* 291
Claud. My liege, your highness now may do me good.
D. Pedro. My love is thine to teach : teach it but how,
And thou shalt see how apt it is to learn
Any hard lesson that may do thee good.
Claud. Hath Leonato any son, my lord?
D. Pedro. No child but Hero ; she's his only heir.
Dost thou affect her, Claudio?
Claud.   O, my lord,
When you went onward on this ended action,
I look'd upon her with a soldier's eye,   300
That liked, but had a rougher task in hand
Than to drive liking to the name of love :
But now I am return'd and that war-thoughts
Have left their places vacant, in their rooms
Come thronging soft and delicate desires,
All prompting me how fair young Hero is,
Saying, I liked her ere I went to wars.
D. Pedro. Thou wilt be like a lover pre-sently
And tire the hearer with a book of words.
If thou dost love fair Hero, cherish it,   310
And I will break with her and with her father
And thou shalt have her.   Was't not to this end
That thou began'st to twist so fine a story?
Claud. How sweetly you do minister to love,
That know love's grief by his complexion !
But lest my liking might too sudden seem,
I would have salved it with a longer treatise.
D. Pedro. What need the bridge much broader than the flood?
● The fairest grant is the necessity.
Look, what will serve is fit : 'tis once, thou lovest,   320
And I will fit thee with the remedy.
I know we shall have revelling to-night :
I will assume thy part in some disguise
And tell fair Hero I am Claudio,
And in her bosom I 'll unclasp my heart
And take her hearing prisoner with the force
And strong encounter of my amorous tale ;
Then after to her father will I break ;
And the conclusion is, she shall be thine.
In practice let us put it presently. [*Exeunt.* 330

SCENE II. *A room in* LEONATO'S *house.*

Enter LEONATO *and* ANTONIO, *meeting.*

Leon. How now, brother ! Where is my cousin, your son? hath he provided this music?
Ant. He is very busy about it. But, brother, I can tell you strange news that you yet dreamt not of.
Leon. Are they good?
Ant. As the event stamps them : but they have a good cover ; they show well outward. The prince and Count Claudio, walking in a
● thick-pleached alley in mine orchard, were thus much overheard by a man of mine : the prince discovered to Claudio that he loved my niece your daughter and meant to acknowledge it

this night in a dance; and if he found her accordant, he meant to take the present time by the top and instantly break with you of it.

Leon. Hath the fellow any wit that told you this?

Ant. A good sharp fellow: I will send for him; and question him yourself.   20

Leon. No, no; we will hold it as a dream till it appear itself: but I will acquaint my daughter withal, that she may be the better prepared for an answer, if peradventure this be true. Go you and tell her of it. [*Enter attendants.*] Cousins, you know what you have to do. O, I cry you mercy, friend; go you with me, and I will use your skill. Good cousin, have a care this busy time.   [*Exeunt.*

Scene III.   *The same.*

Enter Don John *and* Conrade.

Con. What the good-year, my lord! why are you thus out of measure sad?

D. John. There is no measure in the occasion that breeds; therefore the sadness is without limit.

Con. You should hear reason.

D. John. And when I have heard it, what blessing brings it?

Con. If not a present remedy, at least a patient sufferance.   10

D. John. I wonder that thou, being, as thou
● sayest thou art, born under Saturn, goest about to apply a moral medicine to a mortifying mischief. I cannot hide what I am: I must be sad when I have cause and smile at no man's jests, eat when I have stomach and wait for no man's leisure, sleep when I am drowsy and tend on no man's business, laugh when I am merry and claw no man in his humour.

Con. Yea, but you must not make the full show of this till you may do it without controlment. You have of late stood out against your brother, and he hath ta'en you newly into his grace; where it is impossible you should take true root but by the fair weather that you make yourself: it is needful that you frame the season for your own harvest.

D. John. I had rather be a canker in a hedge than a rose in his grace, and it better fits my blood to be disdained of all than to fashion a carriage to rob love from any: in this, though I cannot be said to be a flattering honest man, it must not be denied but I am a plain-dealing
● villain. I am trusted with a muzzle and enfranchised with a clog; therefore I have decreed not to sing in my cage. If I had my mouth, I would bite; if I had my liberty, I would do my liking: in the meantime let me be that I am and seek not to alter me.

Con. Can you make no use of your discontent?   40

D. John. I make all use of it, for I use it only.

Who comes here?

Enter Borachio.

What news, Borachio?

Bora. I came yonder from a great supper: the prince your brother is royally entertained by

12 *Saturn.* Planet of gloomy influence, hence saturnine.

Don John: 'I had rather be a canker in a hedge . . .' Engraving of a cankered rose from Charles Knight's *Pictorial Edition of the Works of William Shakspere,* 1839–43

34-35 *I am trusted with a muzzle and enfranchised with a clog.* i.e. muzzled and hobbled.

58 *March-chick.* Precocious youngster.

60 *entertained for a perfumer.* Employed as a fumigator.

22 *curst.* Ill-tempered.

Julia Neilson, the Edwardian actress, as Beatrice, St James's Theatre, London, 1898

Leonato; and I can give you intelligence of an intended marriage.

D. John. Will it serve for any model to build mischief on? What is he for a fool that betroths himself to unquietness?   50

Bora. Marry, it is your brother's right hand.

D. John. Who? the most exquisite Claudio?

Bora. Even he.

D. John. A proper squire! And who, and who? which way looks he?

Bora. Marry, on Hero, the daughter and heir of Leonato.

● *D. John.* A very forward March-chick! How came you to this?

● *Bora.* Being entertained for a perfumer, as I was smoking a musty room, comes me the prince and Claudio, hand in hand, in sad conference: I whipt me behind the arras; and there heard it agreed upon that the prince should woo Hero for himself, and having obtained her, give her to Count Claudio.

D. John. Come, come, let us thither: this may prove food to my displeasure. That young start-up hath all the glory of my overthrow: if I can cross him any way, I bless myself every way. You are both sure, and will assist me?   71

Con. To the death, my lord.

D. John. Let us to the great supper: their cheer is the greater that I am subdued. Would the cook were of my mind! Shall we go prove what's to be done?

Bora. We'll wait upon your lordship.

[*Exeunt.*

ACT II.

SCENE I. *A hall in* LEONATO's *house.*

Enter LEONATO, ANTONIO, HERO, BEATRICE, *and others.*

Leon. Was not Count John here at supper?

Ant. I saw him not.

Beat. How tartly that gentleman looks! I never can see him but I am heart-burned an hour after.

Hero. He is of a very melancholy disposition.

Beat. He were an excellent man that were made just in the midway between him and Benedick: the one is too like an image and says nothing, and the other too like my lady's eldest son, evermore tattling.   11

Leon. Then half Signior Benedick's tongue in Count John's mouth, and half Count John's melancholy in Signior Benedick's face,—

Beat. With a good leg and a good foot, uncle, and money enough in his purse, such a man would win any woman in the world, if a' could get her good-will.

Leon. By my troth, niece, thou wilt never get thee a husband, if thou be so shrewd of thy tongue.   21

● *Ant.* In faith, she's too curst.

Beat. Too curst is more than curst: I shall lessen God's sending that way; for it is said, 'God sends a curst cow short horns;' but to a cow too curst he sends none.

Leon. So, by being too curst, God will send you no horns.

Beat. Just, if he send me no husband; for

the which blessing I am at him upon my knees every morning and evening.   Lord, I could not endure a husband with a beard on his face: I
● had rather lie in the woollen.

Leon. You may light on a husband that hath no beard.

Beat. What should I do with him? dress him in my apparel and make him my waiting-gentle-woman? He that hath a beard is more than a youth, and he that hath no beard is less than a man: and he that is more than a youth is not for me, and he that is less than a man, I am not for
● him: therefore I will even take sixpence in earnest of the bear-ward, and lead his apes into hell.

Leon. Well, then, go you into hell?

Beat. No, but to the gate; and there will the devil meet me, like an old cuckold, with horns on his head, and say 'Get you to heaven, Beatrice, get you to heaven; here's no place for you maids:' so deliver I up my apes, and away to Saint Peter for the heavens; he shows me where the bachelors sit, and there live we as merry as the day is long.

Ant. [*To Hero*] Well, niece, I trust you will be ruled by your father.

Beat. Yes, faith; it is my cousin's duty to make curtsy and say 'Father, as it please you.' But yet for all that, cousin, let him be a handsome fellow, or else make another curtsy and say 'Father, as it please me.'

Leon. Well, niece, I hope to see you one day fitted with a husband.   61

Beat. Not till God make men of some other metal than earth. Would it not grieve a woman to be overmastered with a piece of valiant dust? to make an account of her life to a clod of way-ward marl? No, uncle, I'll none: Adam's sons are my brethren; and, truly, I hold it a sin to match in my kindred.

Leon. Daughter, remember what I told you: if the prince do solicit you in that kind, you know your answer.   71

Beat. The fault will be in the music, cousin, if you be not wooed in good time: if the prince be too important, tell him there is measure in every thing and so dance out the answer. For, hear me, Hero: wooing, wedding, and repenting,
● is as a Scotch jig, a measure, and a cinque pace: the first suit is hot and hasty, like a Scotch jig, and full as fantastical; the wedding, mannerly-modest, as a measure, full of state and ancientry; and then comes repentance and, with his bad legs, falls into the cinque pace faster and faster, till he sink into his grave.

Leon. Cousin, you apprehend passing shrewdly.

Beat. I have a good eye, uncle; I can see a church by daylight.

Leon. The revellers are entering, brother: make good room.   [*All put on their masks.*

Enter DON PEDRO, CLAUDIO, BENEDICK, BAL-THASAR, DON JOHN, BORACHIO, MAR-GARET, URSULA, *and others, masked.*

● *D. Pedro.* Lady, will you walk about with your friend?   90

Hero. So you walk softly and look sweetly and say nothing, I am yours for the walk; and especially when I walk away.

D. Pedro. With me in your company?

33 *in the woollen.* Between blankets, without sheets.

42-43 *in earnest of.* As an advance payment. *bear-ward.* Bearkeeper. *lead his apes into hell.* Said of women who died single.

77 *cinque pace.* A lively dance.

90 *walk about.* i.e. pair off for the dance.

Masked dancers. From a contemporary engraving

98 *the lute should be like the case.* i.e. your face like your mask.

99 *Philemon.* The peasant who gave hospitality to Jove.

114 *clerk.* i.e. who answered responses in church.

135 *'Hundred Merry Tales'.* A common jest-book of the time.

Diana Wynyard as Beatrice and Anthony Quayle as Benedick, Stratford-upon-Avon, 1949

148 *fleet.* Company.

149 *boarded.* Closed in on.

155 *partridge wing.* On which there is very little meat.

Hero. I may say so, when I please.
D. Pedro. And when please you to say so?
Hero. When I like your favour; for God
●defend the lute should be like the case!
● *D. Pedro.* My visor is Philemon's roof; within the house is Jove.   100
Hero. Why, then, your visor should be thatched.
D. Pedro. Speak low, if you speak love.
                                [Drawing her aside.

Balth. Well, I would you did like me.
Marg. So would not I, for your own sake; for I have many ill qualities.
Balth. Which is one?
Marg. I say my prayers aloud.
Balth. I love you the better: the hearers may cry, Amen.   110
Marg. God match me with a good dancer!
Balth. Amen.
Marg. And God keep him out of my sight
●when the dance is done! Answer, clerk.
Balth. No more words: the clerk is answered.
Urs. I know you well enough; you are Signior Antonio.
Ant. At a word, I am not.
Urs. I know you by the waggling of your head.   120
Ant. To tell you true, I counterfeit him.
Urs. You could never do him so ill-well, unless you were the very man. Here's his dry hand up and down: you are he, you are he.
Ant. At a word, I am not.
Urs. Come, come, do you think I do not know you by your excellent wit? can virtue hide itself? Go to, mum, you are he: graces will appear, and there's an end.
Beat. Will you not tell me who told you so?
Bene. No, you shall pardon me.   131
Beat. Nor will you not tell me who you are?
Bene. Not now.
Beat. That I was disdainful, and that I had
●my good wit out of the 'Hundred Merry Tales:'
—well, this was Signior Benedick that said so.
Bene. What's he?
Beat. I am sure you know him well enough.
Bene. Not I, believe me.
Beat. Did he never make you laugh?   140
Bene. I pray you, what is he?
Beat. Why, he is the prince's jester: a very dull fool; only his gift is in devising impossible slanders: none but libertines delight in him; and the commendation is not in his wit, but in his villany; for he both pleases men and angers them, and then they laugh at him and beat him.
●I am sure he is in the fleet: I would he had
●boarded me.
Bene. When I know the gentleman, I'll tell him what you say.   151
Beat. Do, do: he'll but break a comparison or two on me; which, peradventure not marked or not laughed at, strikes him into melancholy;
●and then there's a partridge wing saved, for the fool will eat no supper that night. [*Music.*] We must follow the leaders.
Bene. In every good thing.
Beat. Nay, if they lead to any ill, I will leave them at the next turning.   160
                        [*Dance. Then exeunt all except Don John, Borachio, and Claudio.*

D. John. Sure my brother is amorous on Hero and hath withdrawn her father to break with him about it. The ladies follow her and but one visor remains.

Bora. And that is Claudio: I know him by his bearing.

D. John. Are not you Signior Benedick?

Claud. You know me well; I am he.

D. John. Signior, you are very near my brother in his love: he is enamoured on Hero; I pray you, dissuade him from her: she is no equal for his birth: you may do the part of an honest man in it.

Claud. How know you he loves her?

D. John. I heard him swear his affection.

Bora. So did I too; and he swore he would marry her to-night.

D. John. Come, let us to the banquet.

[*Exeunt Don John and Borachio.*

Claud. Thus answer I in name of Benedick,
But hear these ill news with the ears of Claudio.
'Tis certain so; the prince wooes for himself. 181
Friendship is constant in all other things
Save in the office and affairs of love:
Therefore all hearts in love use their own tongues;
Let every eye negotiate for itself
And trust no agent; for beauty is a witch
Against whose charms faith melteth into blood.
This is an accident of hourly proof,
Which I mistrusted not. Farewell, therefore,
    Hero!

Re-enter BENEDICK.

Bene. Count Claudio?   190

Claud. Yea, the same.

Bene. Come, will you go with me?

Claud. Whither?

Bene. Even to the next willow, about your own business, county. What fashion will you wear the garland of? about your neck, like an usurer's chain? or under your arm, like a lieutenant's scarf? You must wear it one way, for the prince hath got your Hero.

Claud. I wish him joy of her.   200

Bene. Why, that's spoken like an honest drovier: so they sell bullocks. But did you think the prince would have served you thus?

Claud. I pray you, leave me.

Bene. Ho! now you strike like the blind man: 'twas the boy that stole your meat, and you'll beat the post.

Claud. If it will not be, I'll leave you. [*Exit.*

Bene. Alas, poor hurt fowl! now will he creep into sedges. But that my Lady Beatrice should know me, and not know me! The prince's fool! Ha? It may be I go under that title because I am merry. Yea, but so I am apt to do myself wrong; I am not so reputed: it is the base, though bitter, disposition of Beatrice that puts the world into her person, and so gives me out. Well, I'll be revenged as I may.

Re-enter DON PEDRO.

D. Pedro. Now, signior, where's the count? did you see him?

Bene. Troth, my lord, I have played the part of Lady Fame. I found him here as melancholy as a lodge in a warren: I told him, and I think I told him true, that your grace had got the good

222 *lodge in a warren.* Gamekeeper's lodge in a park.

H. Beerbohm Tree as Benedick, His Majesty's Theatre, London, 1905

241 *If their singing answer.* i.e. if it turns out as you say.

251-53 *great thaw.* i.e. when roads are impassable and people have to stay at home. *impossible conveyance.* Incredible skill.

Hercules. From a 19th century engraving

263 *Ate in good apparel.* The goddess of discord in a fair shape.

276 *Prester John.* Mythical priest-king thought to rule over Ethiopia.

277 *Cham.* Khan of the Mongols.

will of this young lady; and I offered him my company to a willow-tree, either to make him a garland, as being forsaken, or to bind him up a rod, as being worthy to be whipped.

D. Pedro. To be whipped! What's his fault?

Bene. The flat transgression of a school-boy, who, being overjoyed with finding a birds' nest, shows it his companion, and he steals it.   231

D. Pedro. Wilt thou make a trust a transgression? The transgression is in the stealer.

Bene. Yet it had not been amiss the rod had been made, and the garland too; for the garland he might have worn himself, and the rod he might have bestowed on you, who, as I take it, have stolen his birds' nest.

D. Pedro. I will but teach them to sing, and restore them to the owner.   240

Bene. If their singing answer your saying, by my faith, you say honestly.

D. Pedro. The Lady Beatrice hath a quarrel to you: the gentleman that danced with her told her she is much wronged by you.

Bene. O, she misused me past the endurance of a block! an oak but with one green leaf on it would have answered her; my very visor began to assume life and scold with her. She told me, not thinking I had been myself, that I was the prince's jester, that I was duller than a great thaw; huddling jest upon jest with such impossible conveyance upon me that I stood like a man at a mark, with a whole army shooting at me. She speaks poniards, and every word stabs: if her breath were as terrible as her terminations, there were no living near her; she would infect to the north star. I would not marry her, though she were endowed with all that Adam had left him before he transgressed: she would have made Hercules have turned spit, yea, and have cleft his club to make the fire too. Come, talk not of her: you shall find her the infernal Ate in good apparel. I would to God some scholar would conjure her; for certainly, while she is here, a man may live as quiet in hell as in a sanctuary; and people sin upon purpose, because they would go thither; so, indeed, all disquiet, horror and perturbation follows her.

D. Pedro. Look, here she comes.   270

Re-enter CLAUDIO, BEATRICE, HERO, *and* LEONATO.

Bene. Will your grace command me any service to the world's end? I will go on the slightest errand now to the Antipodes that you can devise to send me on; I will fetch you a toothpicker now from the furthest inch of Asia, bring you the length of Prester John's foot, fetch you a hair off the great Cham's beard, do you any embassage to the Pigmies, rather than hold three words' conference with this harpy. You have no employment for me?   280

D. Pedro. None, but to desire your good company.

Bene. O God, sir, here's a dish I love not: I cannot endure my Lady Tongue.   [*Exit.*

D. Pedro. Come, lady, come; you have lost the heart of Signior Benedick.

Beat. Indeed, my lord, he lent it me awhile; and I gave him use for it, a double heart for his single one: marry, once before he won it of me with false dice, therefore your grace may well say I have lost it.   291

D. Pedro. You have put him down, lady, you have put him down.

Beat. So I would not he should do me, my lord, lest I should prove the mother of fools. I have brought Count Claudio, whom you sent me to seek.

D. Pedro. Why, how now, count! wherefore are you sad?

Claud. Not sad, my lord.   300

D. Pedro. How then? sick?

Claud. Neither, my lord.

Beat. The count is neither sad, nor sick, nor merry, nor well; but civil count, civil as an orange, and something of that jealous complexion.

• *D. Pedro.* I' faith, lady, I think your blazon to be true; though, I'll be sworn, if he be so, his conceit is false. Here, Claudio, I have wooed in thy name, and fair Hero is won: I have broke with her father, and his good will obtained: name the day of marriage, and God give thee joy!

Leon. Count, take of me my daughter, and with her my fortunes: his grace hath made the match, and all grace say Amen to it.

Beat. Speak, count, 'tis your cue.

Clau. Silence is the perfectest herald of joy: I were but little happy, if I could say how much. Lady, as you are mine, I am yours: I give away myself for you and dote upon the exchange. 320

Beat. Speak, cousin; or, if you cannot, stop his mouth with a kiss, and let not him speak neither.

D. Pedro. In faith, lady, you have a merry heart.

Beat. Yea, my lord; I thank it, poor fool, it keeps on the windy side of care. My cousin tells him in his ear that he is in her heart.

Claud. And so she doth, cousin.

• *Beat.* Good Lord, for alliance! Thus goes every one to the world but I, and I am sunburnt; I may sit in a corner and cry heigh-ho for a husband!

D. Pedro. Lady Beatrice, I will get you one.

Beat. I would rather have one of your father's getting. Hath your grace ne'er a brother like you? Your father got excellent husbands, if a maid could come by them.

D. Pedro. Will you have me, lady?

Beat. No, my lord, unless I might have another for working-days: your grace is too costly to wear every day. But, I beseech your grace, pardon me: I was born to speak all mirth and no matter.

D. Pedro. Your silence most offends me, and to be merry best becomes you; for, out of question, you were born in a merry hour.

Beat. No, sure, my lord, my mother cried; but then there was a star danced, and under that was I born. Cousins, God give you joy! 350

Leon. Niece, will you look to those things I told you of?

Beat. I cry you mercy, uncle. By your grace's pardon.   [*Exit.*

D. Pedro. By my troth, a pleasant-spirited lady.

Leon. There's little of the melancholy element in her, my lord: she is never sad but when

307 *blazon.* Description.

330-332 *goes every one to the world.* i.e. everyone gets married. *sunburnt.* i.e. dried up and browned.

Ellen Terry as Beatrice, Lyceum Theatre, London, 1882

she sleeps, and not ever sad then; for I have heard my daughter say, she hath often dreamed of unhappiness and waked herself with laughing.

D. Pedro. She cannot endure to hear tell of a husband.

Leon. O, by no means: she mocks all her wooers out of suit.

D. Pedro. She were an excellent wife for Benedick.

Leon. O Lord, my lord, if they were but a week married, they would talk themselves mad.

D. Pedro. County Claudio, when mean you to go to church?   371

Claud. To-morrow, my lord: time goes on crutches till love have all his rites.

Leon. Not till Monday, my dear son, which is hence a just seven-night; and a time too brief, too, to have all things answer my mind.

D. Pedro. Come, you shake the head at so long a breathing: but, I warrant thee, Claudio, the time shall not go dully by us. I will in the interim undertake one of Hercules' labours; which is, to bring Signior Benedick and the Lady Beatrice into a mountain of affection the one with the other. I would fain have it a match, and I doubt not but to fashion it, if you three will but minister such assistance as I shall give you direction.

Leon. My lord, I am for you, though it cost me ten nights' watchings.

Claud. And I, my lord.

D. Pedro. And you too, gentle Hero?

Hero. I will do any modest office, my lord, to help my cousin to a good husband.   391

D. Pedro. And Benedick is not the unhopefullest husband that I know. Thus far can I praise him; he is of a noble strain, of approved valour and confirmed honesty. I will teach you how to humour your cousin, that she shall fall in love with Benedick; and I, with your two helps, will so practise on Benedick that, in despite of his quick wit and his queasy stomach, he shall fall in love with Beatrice. If we can do this, Cupid is no longer an archer: his glory shall be ours, for we are the only love-gods. Go in with me, and I will tell you my drift.   *[Exeunt.*

SCENE II. *The same.*

Enter Don John *and* Borachio.

D. John. It is so; the Count Claudio shall marry the daughter of Leonato.

Bora. Yea, my lord; but I can cross it.

D. John. Any bar, any cross, any impediment will be medicinable to me: I am sick in displeasure to him, and whatsoever comes athwart his affection ranges evenly with mine. How canst thou cross this marriage?

Bora. Not honestly, my lord; but so covertly that no dishonesty shall appear in me.   10

D. John. Show me briefly how.

Bora. I think I told your lordship a year since, how much I am in the favour of Margaret, the waiting gentlewoman to Hero.

D. John. I remember.

Bora. I can, at any unseasonable instant of the night, appoint her to look out at her lady's chamber window.

D. John.   What life is in that, to be the death of this marriage?   20

Bora.   The poison of that lies in you to temper. Go you to the prince your brother; spare not to tell him that he hath wronged his honour in marrying the renowned Claudio—whose estimation do you mightily hold up—to a contaminated stale, such a one as Hero.

D. John.   What proof shall I make of that?

Bora.   Proof enough to misuse the prince, to vex Claudio, to undo Hero and kill Leonato. Look you for any other issue?   30

D. John.   Only to despite them, I will endeavour any thing.

Bora.   Go, then; find me a meet hour to draw Don Pedro and the Count Claudio alone: tell them that you know that Hero loves me; intend a kind of zeal both to the prince and Claudio, as,—in love of your brother's honour, who hath made this match, and his friend's reputation, who is thus like to be cozened with the semblance of a maid,—that you have discovered thus.   They will scarcely believe this without trial: offer them instances; which shall bear no less likelihood than to see me at her chamber-window, hear me †call Margaret Hero, hear Margaret term me Claudio; and bring them to see this the very night before the intended wedding,—for in the meantime I will so fashion the matter that Hero shall be absent,—and there shall appear such seeming truth of Hero's disloyalty that jealousy shall be called assurance and all the preparation overthrown.   51

D. John.   Grow this to what adverse issue it can, I will put it in practice.   Be cunning in the working this, and thy fee is a thousand ducats.

Bora.   Be you constant in the accusation, and my cunning shall not shame me.

D. John.   I will presently go learn their day of marriage.   [*Exeunt.*

SCENE III.   LEONATO'S *orchard.*

Enter BENEDICK.

Bene.   Boy!

Enter Boy.

Boy.   Signior?

Bene.   In my chamber-window lies a book: bring it hither to me in the orchard.

Boy.   I am here already, sir.

Bene.   I know that; but I would have thee hence, and here again. [*Exit Boy.*] I do much wonder that one man, seeing how much another man is a fool when he dedicates his behaviours to love, will, after he hath laughed at such shallow follies in others, become the argument of his own scorn by falling in love: and such a man is Claudio. I have known when there was no music with him but the drum and the fife; and now had he rather hear the tabor and the pipe: I have known when he would have walked ten mile a-foot to see a good armour; and now will he lie ten nights awake, carving the fashion of a new doublet. He was wont to speak plain and to the purpose, like an honest man and a soldier; and now is he turned orthography; his words are a very fantastical banquet, just so many strange dishes. May I be so converted and see with

39 *cozened.* Cheated.

49-50 *jealousy shall be called assurance.* Suspicion shall be called certainty.

15 *tabor.* Small drum.

Benedick: '. . . now will he lie ten nights awake, carving the fashion of a new doublet'. Woodcut of the Englishman who loves new fashions from Andrew Boorde's *The Fyrst Boke of the Introduction of Knowledge,* 1562

21 *orthography.* Pedantic in his speech.

35 *noble . . . angel.* Benedick puns on the names of two Elizabethan coins.

45 *We'll fit the kid-fox with a pennyworth.* i.e. we'll give the crafty young fellow what he bargained for.

Balthasar: 'Because you talk of wooing, I will sing.'
Drawing by Mariano Andrew, 1949

these eyes? I cannot tell; I think not: I will not be sworn but love may transform me to an oyster; but I'll take my oath on it, till he have made an oyster of me, he shall never make me such a fool. One woman is fair, yet I am well; another is wise, yet I am well; another virtuous, yet I am well; but till all graces be in one woman, one woman shall not come in my grace. Rich she shall be, that's certain; wise, or I'll none; virtuous, or I'll never cheapen her; fair, or I'll never look on her; mild, or come not near
• me; noble, or not I for an angel; of good discourse, an excellent musician, and her hair shall be of what colour it please God. Ha! the prince and Monsieur Love! I will hide me in the arbour.
[*Withdraws.*

Enter DON PEDRO, CLAUDIO, *and* LEONATO.

D. Pedro. Come, shall we hear this music?
Claud. Yea, my good lord. How still the evening is, 40
As hush'd on purpose to grace harmony!
D. Pedro. See you where Benedick hath hid himself?
Claud. O, very well, my lord: the music ended,
• We'll fit the kid-fox with a pennyworth.

Enter BALTHASAR *with Music.*

D. Pedro. Come, Balthasar, we'll hear that song again.
Balth. O, good my lord, tax not so bad a voice
To slander music any more than once.
D. Pedro. It is the witness still of excellency
To put a strange face on his own perfection.
I pray thee, sing, and let me woo no more. 50
Balth. Because you talk of wooing, I will sing;
Since many a wooer doth commence his suit
To her he thinks not worthy, yet he wooes,
Yet will he swear he loves.
D. Pedro.   Now, pray thee, come;
Or, if thou wilt hold longer argument,
Do it in notes.
Balth.   Note this before my notes;
There's not a note of mine that's worth the noting.
D. Pedro. Why, these are very crotchets that he speaks;
Note, notes, forsooth, and nothing.   [*Air.*
Bene. Now, divine air! now is his soul ravished! Is it not strange that sheeps' guts should hale souls out of men's bodies? Well, a horn for my money, when all's done.

The Song.

Balth. Sigh no more, ladies, sigh no more,
      Men were deceivers ever,
   One foot in sea and one on shore,
      To one thing constant never:
   Then sigh not so, but let them go,
      And be you blithe and bonny,
   Converting all your sounds of woe 70
      Into Hey nonny, nonny.

   Sing no more ditties, sing no moe,
      Of dumps so dull and heavy;
   The fraud of men was ever so,
      Since summer first was leavy:
      Then sigh not so, &c.

D. Pedro. By my troth, a good song.

Balth.   And an ill singer, my lord.

D. Pedro.   Ha, no, no, faith ; thou singest well
● enough for a shift.   80

Bene.   An he had been a dog that should have
howled thus, they would have hanged him : and
I pray God his bad voice bode no mischief.   I had
as lief have heard the night-raven, come what
plague could have come after it.

D. Pedro.   Yea, marry, dost thou hear, Balthasar?   I pray thee, get us some excellent music ;
for to-morrow night we would have it at the Lady
Hero's chamber-window.

Balth.   The best I can, my lord.   90

D. Pedro.   Do so : farewell. [*Exit Balthasar.*]
Come hither, Leonato.   What was it you told me
of to-day, that your niece Beatrice was in love
with Signior Benedick?

Claud.   O, ay : stalk on, stalk on ; the fowl
sits.   I did never think that lady would have
loved any man.

Leon.   No, nor I neither ; but most wonderful
that she should so dote on Signior Benedick, whom
she hath in all outward behaviours seemed ever
to abhor.   101

Bene.   Is't possible?   Sits the wind in that
corner?

Leon.   By my troth, my lord, I cannot tell what
to think of it but that she loves him with an enraged affection ; it is past the infinite of thought.

D. Pedro.   May be she doth but counterfeit.

Claud.   Faith, like enough.

Leon.   O God, counterfeit !   There was never
counterfeit of passion came so near the life of passion as she discovers it.   111

D. Pedro.   Why, what effects of passion shows
she?

Claud.   Bait the hook well ; this fish will bite.

Leon.   What effects, my lord?   She will sit
you, you heard my daughter tell you how.

Claud.   She did, indeed.

D. Pedro.   How, how, I pray you?   You amaze
me : I would have thought her spirit had been
invincible against all assaults of affection.   120

Leon.   I would have sworn it had, my lord ;
especially against Benedick.

Bene.   I should think this a gull, but that the
white-bearded fellow speaks it : knavery cannot,
sure, hide himself in such reverence.

Claud.   He hath ta'en the infection : hold it up.

D. Pedro.   Hath she made her affection known
to Benedick?

Leon.   No ; and swears she never will : that's
her torment.   130

Claud.   'Tis true, indeed ; so your daughter
says : 'Shall I,' says she, 'that have so oft encountered him with scorn, write to him that I
love him?'

Leon.   This says she now when she is beginning to write to him ; for she'll be up twenty times
a night, and there will she sit in her smock till
she have writ a sheet of paper : my daughter tells
us all.

Claud.   Now you talk of a sheet of paper, I
remember a pretty jest your daughter told us of.

Leon.   O, when she had writ it and was reading it over, she found Benedick and Beatrice between the sheet?

Claud.   That.

Leon.   O, she tore the letter into a thousand

80 *shift*. Makeshift performance.

Alan Howard as Benedick, Royal Shakespeare Co, 1968

413

Costume design for Benedick by Voytek, Royal Shakespeare Co, 1971

161 *discover.* Reveal.

164 *alms.* Good deed.

170 *blood.* Passion.

176 *daffed.* Set aside, doffed.

halfpence; railed at herself, that she should be so immodest to write to one that she knew would flout her; 'I measure him,' says she, 'by my own spirit; for I should flout him, if he writ to me; yea, though I love him, I should.' 151

Claud. Then down upon her knees she falls, weeps, sobs, beats her heart, tears her hair, prays, curses; 'O sweet Benedick! God give me patience!'

Leon. She doth indeed; my daughter says so: and the ecstasy hath so much overborne her that my daughter is sometime afeard she will do a desperate outrage to herself: it is very true.

D. Pedro. It were good that Benedick knew of it by some other, if she will not discover it. 161

Claud. To what end? He would make but a sport of it and torment the poor lady worse.

D. Pedro. An he should, it were an alms to hang him. She's an excellent sweet lady; and, out of all suspicion, she is virtuous.

Claud. And she is exceeding wise.

D. Pedro. In every thing but in loving Benedick.

Leon. O, my lord, wisdom and blood combating in so tender a body, we have ten proofs to one that blood hath the victory. I am sorry for her, as I have just cause, being her uncle and her guardian.

D. Pedro. I would she had bestowed this dotage on me: I would have daffed all other respects and made her half myself. I pray you, tell Benedick of it, and hear what a' will say.

Leon. Were it good, think you?

Claud. Hero thinks surely she will die; for she says she will die, if he love her not, and she will die, ere she make her love known, and she will die, if he woo her, rather than she will bate one breath of her accustomed crossness.

D. Pedro. She doth well: if she should make tender of her love, 'tis very possible he'll scorn it; for the man, as you know all, hath a contemptible spirit.

Claud. He is a very proper man.

D. Pedro. He hath indeed a good outward happiness. 191

Claud. Before God! and, in my mind, very wise.

D. Pedro. He doth indeed show some sparks that are like wit.

Claud. And I take him to be valiant.

D. Pedro. As Hector, I assure you: and in the managing of quarrels you may say he is wise; for either he avoids them with great discretion, or undertakes them with a most Christian-like fear. 200

Leon. If he do fear God, a' must necessarily keep peace: if he break the peace, he ought to enter into a quarrel with fear and trembling.

D. Pedro. And so will he do; for the man doth fear God, howsoever it seems not in him by some large jests he will make. Well, I am sorry for your niece. Shall we go seek Benedick, and tell him of her love?

Claud. Never tell him, my lord: let her wear it out with good counsel.

Leon. Nay, that's impossible: she may wear her heart out first. 210

D. Pedro. Well, we will hear further of it by your daughter: let it cool the while. I love Benedick well; and I could wish he would modestly examine himself, to see how much he is unworthy so good a lady.

Leon. My lord, will you walk? dinner is ready.

Claud. If he do not dote on her upon this, I will never trust my expectation.   220

D. Pedro. Let there be the same net spread for her; and that must your daughter and her gentlewomen carry. The sport will be, when they hold one an opinion of another's dotage, • and no such matter: that's the scene that I would see, which will be merely a dumb-show. Let us send her to call him in to dinner.

[*Exeunt Don Pedro, Claudio, and Leonato.*

Bene. [*Coming forward*] This can be no trick: the conference was sadly borne. They have the truth of this from Hero. They seem to pity the lady: it seems her affections have their full bent. Love me! why, it' must be requited. I hear how I am censured: they say I will bear myself proudly, if I perceive the love come from her; they say too that she will rather die than give any sign of affection. I did never think to marry: I must not seem proud: happy are they that hear their detractions and can put them to mending. They say the lady is fair; 'tis a truth, I can bear them witness; and virtuous; 'tis so, I cannot reprove it; and wise, but for loving me; by my troth, it is no addition to her wit, nor no great argument of her folly, for I will be horribly in love with her. I may chance have some odd quirks and remnants of wit broken on me, because I have railed so long against marriage: but doth not the appetite alter? a man loves the meat in his youth that he cannot endure in his age. Shall quips and sentences and these paper bullets of the brain awe a man from the career of his humour? No, the world must be peopled. When I said I would die a bachelor, I did not think I should live till I were married. Here comes Beatrice. By this day! she's a fair lady: I do spy some marks of love in her.

Enter BEATRICE.

Beat. Against my will I am sent to bid you come in to dinner.

Bene. Fair Beatrice, I thank you for your pains.

Beat. I took no more pains for those thanks than you take pains to thank me: if it had been painful, I would not have come.   261

Bene. You take pleasure then in the message?

Beat. Yea, just so much as you may take • upon a knife's point and choke a daw withal. You have no stomach, signior: fare you well.

[*Exit.*

Bene. Ha! 'Against my will I am sent to bid you come in to dinner;' there's a double meaning in that. 'I took no more pains for those thanks than you took pains to thank me;' that's as much as to say, Any pains that I take for you is as easy as thanks. If I do not take pity of her, I am a villain; if I do not love her, I am a Jew. I will go get her picture.   [*Exit.*

ACT III.

SCENE I. LEONATO'S *garden.*

Enter HERO, MARGARET, *and* URSULA.

Hero. Good Margaret, run thee to the parlour; There shalt thou find my cousin Beatrice

225 *no such matter.* There is nothing of the kind.

264 *daw.* Jackdaw, fool.

Costume design for Beatrice by Voytek, Royal Shakespeare Co, 1971

14 *presently.* Immediately.

24 *lapwing.* Peewit, plover.

36 *haggerds.* Wild hawks.

Hero and Ursula with Beatrice concealed. Engraving from a painting by Rev. M. W. Peters (d. 1814)

Proposing with the prince and Claudio :
Whisper her ear and tell her, I and Ursula
Walk in the orchard and our whole discourse
Is all of her ; say that thou overheard'st us ;
And bid her steal into the pleached bower,
Where honeysuckles, ripen'd by the sun,
Forbid the sun to enter, like favourites,
Made proud by princes, that advance their pride
Against that power that bred it : there will she
    hide her,   11
To listen our purpose.   This is thy office ;
Bear thee well in it and leave us alone.
  Marg. I'll make her come, I warrant you,
    presently.   [*Exit.*
  Hero. Now, Ursula, when Beatrice doth come,
As we do trace this alley up and down,
Our talk must only be of Benedick.
When I do name him, let it be thy part
To praise him more than ever man did merit :
My talk to thee must be how Benedick   20
Is sick in love with Beatrice. Of this matter
Is little Cupid's crafty arrow made,
That only wounds by hearsay.

         Enter BEATRICE, *behind.*
                  Now begin ;
For look where Beatrice, like a lapwing, runs
Close by the ground, to hear our conference.
  Urs. The pleasant'st angling is to see the fish
Cut with her golden oars the silver stream,
And greedily devour the treacherous bait :
So angle we for Beatrice ; who even now
Is couched in the woodbine coverture.   30
Fear you not my part of the dialogue.
  Hero. Then go we near her, that her ear lose
    nothing
Of the false sweet bait that we lay for it.
              [*Approaching the bower.*
No, truly, Ursula, she is too disdainful ;
I know her spirits are as coy and wild
As haggerds of the rock.
  Urs.   But are you sure
That Benedick loves Beatrice so entirely ?
  Hero. So says the prince and my new-trothed
    lord.
  Urs. And did they bid you tell her of it,
    madam ?
  Hero. They did entreat me to acquaint her of it ;
But I persuaded them, if they loved Benedick, 41
To wish him wrestle with affection,
And never to let Beatrice know of it.
  Urs. Why did you so ? Doth not the gentleman
Deserve as full as fortunate a bed
As ever Beatrice shall couch upon ?
  Hero. O god of love ! I know he doth deserve
As much as may be yielded to a man :
But Nature never framed a woman's heart
Of prouder stuff than that of Beatrice ;   50
Disdain and scorn ride sparkling in her eyes,
Misprising what they look on, and her wit
Values itself so highly that to her
All matter else seems weak : she cannot love,
Nor take no shape nor project of affection,
She is so self-endeared.
  Urs.   Sure, I think so ;
And therefore certainly it were not good
She knew his love, lest she make sport at it.
  Hero. Why, you speak truth. I never yet
    saw man,

How wise, how noble, young, how rarely fea-
      tured,   60
But she would spell him backward: if fair-faced,
She would swear the gentleman should be her
      sister;
•If black, why, Nature, drawing of an antique,
Made a foul blot; if tall, a lance ill-headed;
If low, an agate very vilely cut;
If speaking, why, a vane blown with all winds;
If silent, why, a block moved with none.
So turns she every man the wrong side out
And never gives to truth and virtue that
Which simpleness and merit purchaseth.   70
   Urs. Sure, sure, such carping is not com-
      mendable.
   Hero. No, not to be so odd and from all
      fashions
As Beatrice is, cannot be commendable:
But who dare tell her so? If I should speak,
She would mock me into air; O, she would laugh
      me
Out of myself, press me to death with wit.
Therefore let Benedick, like cover'd fire,
Consume away in sighs, waste inwardly:
It were a better death than die with mocks,
Which is as bad as die with tickling.   80
   Urs. Yet tell her of it: hear what she will say.
   Hero. No; rather I will go to Benedick
And counsel him to fight against his passion.
And, truly, I'll devise some honest slanders
To stain my cousin with: one doth not know
How much an ill word may empoison liking.
   Urs. O, do not do your cousin such a wrong.
She cannot be so much without true judgement—
Having so swift and excellent a wit
As she is prized to have—as to refuse   90
So rare a gentleman as Signior Benedick.
   Hero. He is the only man of Italy,
Always excepted my dear Claudio.
   Urs. I pray you, be not angry with me,
      madam,
Speaking my fancy: Signior Benedick,
For shape, for bearing, argument and valour,
Goes foremost in report through Italy.
   Hero. Indeed, he hath an excellent good
      name.
   Urs. His excellence did earn it, ere he had it.
When are you married, madam?   100
   Hero. Why, every day, to-morrow. Come,
      go in:
I'll show thee some attires, and have thy counsel
Which is the best to furnish me to-morrow.
• *Urs.* She's limed, I warrant you: we have
      caught her, madam.
   Hero. If it prove so, then loving goes by haps:
Some Cupid kills with arrows, some with traps.
                     [*Exeunt Hero and Ursula.*

   Beat. [*Coming forward*] What fire is in mine
      ears? Can this be true?
      Stand I condemn'd for pride and scorn so
      much?
Contempt, farewell! and maiden pride, adieu!
   No glory lives behind the back of such.   110
And, Benedick, love on; I will requite thee,
   Taming my wild heart to thy loving hand:
If thou dost love, my kindness shall incite thee
   To bind our loves up in a holy band;
For others say thou dost deserve, and I
Believe it better than reportingly.   [*Exit.*

63 *antique*. Grotesque figure.

104 *limed*. Snared.

Ursula: 'She's limed, I warrant you'. Drawing by
Thomas Stothard (1755–1834)

18 *Hang him, truant!* i.e. hang him for a rogue.

21 *toothache.* Supposed common with lovers.

24 *hang . . . draw.* A joke upon the capital punishment of hanging (by the neck until half-dead), drawing (the bowels from the body and displaying them to the victim) and quartering (the still living body).

27 *humour or a worm.* Reputedly, the causes of tooth decay.

36 *slops.* Loose breeches.

Claudio: '. . . the barber's man hath been seen with him'. Barber with customer, early 17th century. Illustration from J. O. Halliwell's edition of Shakespeare's works, 1853–65

50 *civet.* Fashionable perfume from the secretions of the civet cat.

SCENE II. *A room in* LEONATO'S *house*.

Enter DON PEDRO, CLAUDIO, BENEDICK, *and* LEONATO.

D. Pedro. I do but stay till your marriage be consummate, and then go I toward Arragon.

Claud. I'll bring you thither, my lord, if you'll vouchsafe me.

D. Pedro. Nay, that would be as great a soil in the new gloss of your marriage as to show a child his new coat and forbid him to wear it. I will only be bold with Benedick for his company; for, from the crown of his head to the sole of his foot, he is all mirth: he hath twice or thrice cut Cupid's bow-string and the little hangman dare not shoot at him; he hath a heart as sound as a bell and his tongue is the clapper, for what his heart thinks his tongue speaks.

Bene. Gallants, I am not as I have been.

Leon. So say I: methinks you are sadder.

Claud. I hope he be in love.

• *D. Pedro.* Hang him, truant! there's no true drop of blood in him, to be truly touched with love: if he be sad, he wants money.   20

• *Bene.* I have the toothache.

D. Pedro. Draw it.

Bene. Hang it!

• *Claud.* You must hang it first, and draw it afterwards.

D. Pedro. What! sigh for the toothache?

• *Leon.* Where is but a humour or a worm.

Bene. Well, every one can master a grief but he that has it.

Claud. Yet say I, he is in love.   30

D. Pedro. There is no appearance of fancy in him, unless it be a fancy that he hath to strange disguises; as, to be a Dutchman to-day, a Frenchman to-morrow, or in the shape of two countries at once, as, a German from the waist downward,

• all slops, and a Spaniard from the hip upward, no doublet. Unless he have a fancy to this foolery, as it appears he hath, he is no fool for fancy, as you would have it appear he is.

Claud. If he be not in love with some woman, there is no believing old signs: a' brushes his hat o' mornings; what should that bode?   42

D. Pedro. Hath any man seen him at the barber's?

Claud. No, but the barber's man hath been seen with him, and the old ornament of his cheek hath already stuffed tennis-balls.

Leon. Indeed, he looks younger than he did, by the loss of a beard.

• *D. Pedro.* Nay, a' rubs himself with civet: can you smell him out by that?   51

Claud. That's as much as to say, the sweet youth's in love.

D. Pedro. The greatest note of it is his melancholy.

Claud. And when was he wont to wash his face?

D. Pedro. Yea, or to paint himself? for the which, I hear what they say of him.

Claud. Nay, but his jesting spirit; which is now crept into a lute-string and now governed by stops.

D. Pedro. Indeed, that tells a heavy tale for him: conclude, conclude he is in love.

Claud. Nay, but I know who loves him.

D. Pedro.   That would I know too : I warrant, one that knows him not.

● *Claud.*   Yes, and his ill conditions ; and, in de-
●spite of all, dies for him.

D. Pedro.   She shall be buried with her face upwards.   71

Bene.   Yet is this no charm for the toothache. Old signior, walk aside with me : I have studied eight or nine wise words to speak to you, which
●these hobby-horses must not hear.

[*Exeunt Benedick and Leonato.*

D. Pedro.   For my life, to break with him about Beatrice.

Claud.   'Tis even so.   Hero and Margaret have by this played their parts with Beatrice ; and then the two bears will not bite one another when they meet.   81

Enter DON JOHN.

D. John.   My lord and brother, God save you !

D. Pedro.   Good den, brother.

D. John.   If your leisure served, I would speak with you.

D. Pedro.   In private ?

D. John.   If it please you : yet Count Claudio may hear ; for what I would speak of concerns him.

D. Pedro.   What's the matter ?   90

D. John.   [*To Claudio*] Means your lordship to be married to-morrow ?

D. Pedro.   You know he does.

D. John.   I know not that, when he knows what I know.

Claud.   If there be any impediment, I pray you discover it.

D. John.   You may think I love you not : let that appear hereafter, and aim better at me by that I now will manifest.   For my brother, I think he holds you well, and in dearness of heart hath holp to effect your ensuing marriage ;— surely suit ill spent and labour ill bestowed.

D. Pedro.   Why, what's the matter ?

D. John.   I came hither to tell you ; and, cir- cumstances shortened, for she has been too long a talking of, the lady is disloyal.

Claud.   Who, Hero ?

D. John.   Even she ; Leonato's Hero, your Hero, every man's Hero.   110

Claud.   Disloyal ?

D. John.   The word is too good to paint out her wickedness ; I could say she were worse : think you of a worse title, and I will fit her to it. Wonder not till further warrant : go but with me to-night, you shall see her chamber-window en- tered, even the night before her wedding-day : if you love her then, to-morrow wed her ; but it would better fit your honour to change your mind.

Claud.   May this be so ?   120

D. Pedro.   I will not think it.

D. John.   If you dare not trust that you see, confess not that you know : if you will follow me, I will show you enough ; and when you have seen more and heard more, proceed accordingly.

Claud.   If I see any thing to-night why I should not marry her to-morrow, in the congre- gation, where I should wed, there will I shame her.

D. Pedro.   And, as I wooed for thee to obtain her, I will join with thee to disgrace her.   130

D. John.   I will disparage her no farther till

68 *ill conditions.* Bad qualities.

69 *dies for him.* Falls for him, with a sexual innuendo.

75 *hobby-horses.* Buffoons.

Dogberry: 'Are you good men and true?' Engraving from Charles Knight's *Pictorial Edition of the Works of William Shakspere,* 1839–43

---

9 *desartless.* Malapropism for 'deserving'.

26 *vagrom.* Vagrant.

44 *bills.* Halberds.

you are my witnesses: bear it coldly but till midnight, and let the issue show itself.

D. Pedro.   O day untowardly turned!

Claud.   O mischief strangely thwarting!

D. John.   O plague right well prevented! so will you say when you have seen the sequel.

[*Exeunt.*

SCENE III.   *A street.*

Enter DOGBERRY *and* VERGES *with the Watch.*

Dog.   Are you good men and true?

Verg.   Yea, or else it were pity but they should suffer salvation, body and soul.

Dog.   Nay, that were a punishment too good for them, if they should have any allegiance in them, being chosen for the prince's watch.

Verg.   Well, give them their charge, neighbour Dogberry.

Dog.   First, who think you the most desartless man to be constable?   10

First Watch.   Hugh Otecake, sir, or George Seacole; for they can write and read.

Dog.   Come hither, neighbour Seacole. God hath blessed you with a good name: to be a well-favoured man is the gift of fortune; but to write and read comes by nature.

Sec. Watch.   Both which, master constable,—

Dog.   You have: I knew it would be your answer. Well, for your favour, sir, why, give God thanks, and make no boast of it; and for your writing and reading, let that appear when there is no need of such vanity. You are thought here to be the most senseless and fit man for the constable of the watch; therefore bear you the lantern. This is your charge: you shall comprehend all vagrom men; you are to bid any man stand, in the prince's name.

Sec. Watch.   How if a' will not stand?

Dog.   Why, then, take no note of him, but let him go; and presently call the rest of the watch together and thank God you are rid of a knave.

Verg.   If he will not stand when he is bidden, he is none of the prince's subjects.

Dog.   True, and they are to meddle with none but the prince's subjects. You shall also make no noise in the streets; for for the watch to babble and to talk is most tolerable and not to be endured.

Watch.   We will rather sleep than talk: we know what belongs to a watch.   40

Dog.   Why, you speak like an ancient and most quiet watchman; for I cannot see how sleeping should offend: only, have a care that your bills be not stolen. Well, you are to call at all the ale-houses, and bid those that are drunk get them to bed.

Watch.   How if they will not?

Dog.   Why, then, let them alone till they are sober: if they make you not then the better answer, you may say they are not the men you took them for.   51

Watch.   Well, sir.

Dog.   If you meet a thief, you may suspect him, by virtue of your office, to be no true man; and, for such kind of men, the less you meddle or make with them, why, the more is for your honesty.

Watch.   If we know him to be a thief, shall we not lay hands on him?

Dog. Truly, by your office, you may; but I think they that touch pitch will be defiled: the most peaceable way for you, if you do take a thief, is to let him show himself what he is and steal out of your company.

Verg. You have been always called a merciful man, partner.

Dog. Truly, I would not hang a dog by my will, much more a man who hath any honesty in him.

Verg. If you hear a child cry in the night, you must call to the nurse and bid her still it. 70

Watch. How if the nurse be asleep and will not hear us?

Dog. Why, then, depart in peace, and let the child wake her with crying; for the ewe that will not hear her lamb when it baes will never answer a calf when he bleats.

Verg. 'Tis very true.

Dog. This is the end of the charge:—you, constable, are to present the prince's own person: if you meet the prince in the night, you may stay him.   81

Verg. Nay, by'r lady, that I think a' cannot.

Dog. Five shillings to one on't, with any man
• that knows the statues, he may stay him: marry, not without the prince be willing; for, indeed, the watch ought to offend no man; and it is an offence to stay a man against his will.

Verg. By'r lady, I think it be so.

Dog. Ha, ah, ha! Well, masters, good night: an there be any matter of weight chances, call up me: keep your fellows' counsels and your own; and good night. Come, neighbour.

Watch. Well, masters, we hear our charge: let us go sit here upon the church-bench till two, and then all to bed.

Dog. One word more, honest neighbours. I pray you, watch about Signior Leonato's door; for the wedding being there to-morrow, there is a
• great coil to-night. Adieu: be vigitant, I beseech you.   [*Exeunt Dogberry and Verges.* 101

Enter BORACHIO *and* CONRADE.

Bora. What, Conrade!

Watch. [*Aside*] Peace! stir not.

Bora. Conrade, I say!

Con. Here, man; I am at thy elbow.

Bora. Mass, and my elbow itched; I thought
• there would a scab follow.

Con. I will owe thee an answer for that: and now forward with thy tale.

Bora. Stand thee close, then, under this penthouse, for it drizzles rain; and I will, like a true drunkard, utter all to thee.

Watch. [*Aside*] Some treason, masters: yet stand close.

Bora. Therefore know I have earned of Don John a thousand ducats.

Con. Is it possible that any villany should be so dear?

Bora. Thou shouldst rather ask if it were possible any villany should be so rich; for when rich villains have need of poor ones, poor ones may make what price they will.

Con. I wonder at it.

Bora. That shows thou art unconfirmed. Thou

85 *statues*. i.e. for statutes, laws.

100 *coil*. Bustle.

Dogberry (John Woodvine) and the Watch, Royal Shakespeare Co, 1976

107 *scab follow*. A pun on 'scurvy fellow'.

143 *reechy*. Grimy.

144 *Bel's priests*. Baal's priests.

183 *lock*. Love-lock, or curl.

190-191 *commodity*. Merchandise.

Ancient watchmen. Engraving from Charles Knight's *Pictorial Edition of the Works of William Shakspere*, 1839–43

knowest that the fashion of a doublet, or a hat, or a cloak, is nothing to a man.

Con.   Yes, it is apparel.

Bora.   I mean, the fashion.

Con.   Yes, the fashion is the fashion.

Bora.   Tush! I may as well say the fool's the fool.   But seest thou not what a deformed thief this fashion is?

Watch.   [*Aside*] I know that Deformed; a' has been a vile thief this seven year; a' goes up and down like a gentleman: I remember his name.

Bora.   Didst thou not hear somebody?

Con.   No; 'twas the vane on the house.

Bora.   Seest thou not, I say, what a deformed thief this fashion is? how giddily a' turns about all the hot bloods between fourteen and five-and-thirty? sometimes fashioning them like Pharaoh's soldiers in the reechy painting, sometime like god Bel's priests in the old church-window, sometime like the shaven Hercules in the smirched worm-eaten tapestry, where his codpiece seems as massy as his club?

Con.   All this I see; and I see that the fashion wears out more apparel than the man.   But art not thou thyself giddy with the fashion too, that thou hast shifted out of thy tale into telling me of the fashion?

Bora.   Not so, neither: but know that I have to-night wooed Margaret, the Lady Hero's gentlewoman, by the name of Hero: she leans me out at her mistress' chamber-window, bids me a thousand times good night,—I tell this tale vilely: —I should first tell thee how the prince, Claudio and my master, planted and placed and possessed by my master Don John, saw afar off in the orchard this amiable encounter.   161

Con.   And thought they Margaret was Hero?

Bora.   Two of them did, the prince and Claudio; but the devil my master knew she was Margaret; and partly by his oaths, which first possessed them, partly by the dark night, which did deceive them, but chiefly by my villany, which did confirm any slander that Don John had made, away went Claudio enraged; swore he would meet her, as he was appointed, next morning at the temple, and there, before the whole congregation, shame her with what he saw o'er night and send her home again without a husband.

First Watch.   We charge you, in the prince's name, stand!

Sec. Watch.   Call up the right master constable.   We have here recovered the most dangerous piece of lechery that ever was known in the commonwealth.   181

First Watch.   And one Deformed is one of them: I know him; a' wears a lock.

Con.   Masters, masters,—

Sec. Watch.   You'll be made bring Deformed forth, I warrant you.

Con.   Masters,—

First Watch.   Never speak: we charge you let us obey you to go with us.

Bora.   We are like to prove a goodly commodity, being taken up of these men's bills.   191

Con.   A commodity in question, I warrant you.   Come, we'll obey you.   [*Exeunt.*

SCENE IV.   HERO'S *apartment.*

Enter HERO, MARGARET, *and* URSULA.

Hero. Good Ursula, wake my cousin Beatrice, and desire her to rise.

Urs. I will, lady.

Hero. And bid her come hither.

Urs. Well.   [*Exit.*

● *Marg.* Troth, I think your other rabato were better.

Hero. No, pray thee, good Meg, I'll wear this.

Marg. By my troth, 's not so good; and I warrant your cousin will say so.   10

Hero. My cousin's a fool, and thou art another: I'll wear none but this.

● *Marg.* I like the new tire within excellently, if the hair were a thought browner; and your gown's a most rare fashion, i' faith. I saw the Duchess of Milan's gown that they praise so.

Hero. O, that exceeds, they say.

● *Marg.* By my troth, 's but a night-gown in ●respect of yours: cloth o' gold, and cuts, and ●laced with silver, set with pearls, down sleeves, side sleeves, and skirts, round underborne with a ●bluish tinsel: but for a fine, quaint, graceful and excellent fashion, yours is worth ten on 't.

Hero. God give me joy to wear it! for my heart is exceeding heavy.

Marg. 'Twill be heavier soon by the weight of a man.

Hero. Fie upon thee! art not ashamed?

Marg. Of what, lady? of speaking honourably? Is not marriage honourable in a beggar? Is not your lord honourable without marriage? I think you would have me say, 'saving your reverence, a husband:' an bad thinking do not wrest true speaking, I'll offend nobody: is there any harm in 'the heavier for a husband'? None, I think, an it be the right husband and the right ●wife; otherwise 'tis light, and not heavy: ask my Lady Beatrice else; here she comes.

Enter BEATRICE.

Hero. Good morrow, coz.

Beat. Good morrow, sweet Hero.   40

Hero. Why, how now? do you speak in the sick tune?

Beat. I am out of all other tune, methinks.

Marg. Clap's into 'Light o' love;' that goes ●without a burden: do you sing it, and I'll dance it.

● *Beat.* Ye light o' love, with your heels! then, if your husband have stables enough, you'll see ●he shall lack no barns.

Marg. O illegitimate construction! I scorn that with my heels.   51

Beat. 'Tis almost five o'clock, cousin; 'tis time you were ready. By my troth, I am exceeding ill: heigh-ho!

Marg. For a hawk, a horse, or a husband?

Beat. For the letter that begins them all, H.

● *Marg.* Well, an you be not turned Turk, ●there's no more sailing by the star.

● *Beat.* What means the fool, trow?

Marg. Nothing I; but God send every one their heart's desire!   61

Hero. These gloves the count sent me; they are an excellent perfume.

Beat. I am stuffed, cousin; I cannot smell.

6 *rabato.* Ruff.

13 *tire.* Decorative head-dress.

18 *night-gown.* Dressing gown.

19 *cuts.* Slits to show colour underneath.

20-21 *down sleeves, side sleeves.* The first were long sleeves; the second hung loose. *underborne.* stiffened out underneath.

22 *quaint.* Elegant.

Elaborate ruffs and headdresses from the time of Elizabeth I. Illustration from Phillip Stubbes's *Anatomy of the Abuses in England*, 1583

37 *light.* Pun on 'wanton'.

45 *burden.* Second or bass part, with further sexual implication.

47 *with your heels.* Light-heeled meant 'unchaste'.

49 *barns.* Bairns.

57 *turned Turk.* Changed faith.

58 *star.* Polar star.

59 *trow.* I wonder.

68 *professed apprehension.* Set up claim as a wit.

73-74 *Carduus Benedictus.* Holy-thistle, a herb much used medicinally.

78 *moral.* Hidden meaning.

83 *list.* Please.

18 *palabras.* Be brief.

23 *tedious.* Dogberry understands 'tedious' to mean 'rich'.

Louis Calvert as Dogberry, His Majesty's Theatre, London, 1905

Marg. A maid, and stuffed! there's goodly catching of cold.

Beat. O, God help me! God help me! how long have you professed apprehension?

Marg. Ever since you left it. Doth not my wit become me rarely? 70

Beat. It is not seen enough, you should wear it in your cap. By my troth, I am sick.

Marg. Get you some of this distilled Carduus Benedictus, and lay it to your heart: it is the only thing for a qualm.

Hero. There thou prickest her with a thistle.

Beat. Benedictus! why Benedictus? you have some moral in this Benedictus.

Marg. Moral! no, by my troth, I have no moral meaning; I meant, plain holy-thistle. You may think perchance that I think you are in love: nay, by'r lady, I am not such a fool to think what I list, nor I list not to think what I can, nor indeed I cannot think, if I would think my heart out of thinking, that you are in love or that you will be in love or that you can be in love. Yet Benedick was such another, and now is he become a man: he swore he would never marry, and yet now, in despite of his heart, he eats his meat without grudging: and how you may be converted I know not, but methinks you look with your eyes as other women do.

Beat. What pace is this that thy tongue keeps?

Marg. Not a false galiop.

Re-enter URSULA.

Urs. Madam, withdraw: the prince, the count, Signior Benedick, Don John, and all the gallants of the town, are come to fetch you to church.

Hero. Help to dress me, good coz, good Meg, good Ursula. [*Exeunt.*

SCENE V. *Another room in* LEONATO'S *house.*

Enter LEONATO, *with* DOGBERRY *and* VERGES.

Leon. What would you with me, honest neighbour?

Dog. Marry, sir, I would have some confidence with you that decerns you nearly.

Leon. Brief, I pray you; for you see it is a busy time with me.

Dog. Marry, this it is, sir.

Verg. Yes, in truth it is, sir.

Leon. What is it, my good friends?

Dog. Goodman Verges, sir, speaks a little off the matter: an old man, sir, and his wits are not so blunt as, God help, I would desire they were; but, in faith, honest as the skin between his brows.

Verg. Yes, I thank God I am as honest as any man living that is an old man and no honester than I.

Dog. Comparisons are odorous: palabras, neighbour Verges.

Leon. Neighbours, you are tedious. 20

Dog. It pleases your worship to say so, but we are the poor duke's officers; but truly, for mine own part, if I were as tedious as a king, I could find it in my heart to bestow it all of your worship.

Leon. All thy tediousness on me, ah?

Dog. Yea, an 'twere a thousand pound more than 'tis; for I hear as good exclamation on your worship as of any man in the city; and though I be but a poor man, I am glad to hear it. 30

Verg. And so am I.

Leon. I would fain know what you have to say.

Verg. Marry, sir, our watch to-night, excepting your worship's presence, ha' ta'en a couple of as arrant knaves as any in Messina.

Dog. A good old man, sir; he will be talking: as they say, When the age is in, the wit is out: God help us! it is a world to see. Well said, i' faith, neighbour Verges: well, God's a good man; an two men ride of a horse, one must ride behind. An honest soul, i' faith, sir; by my troth he is, as ever broke bread; but God is to be worshipped; all men are not alike; alas, good neighbour!

Leon. Indeed, neighbour, he comes too short of you.

Dog. Gifts that God gives.

Leon. I must leave you.

Dog. One word, sir: our watch, sir, have indeed comprehended two aspicious persons, and we would have them this morning examined before your worship.

Leon. Take their examination yourself and bring it me: I am now in great haste, as it may appear unto you.

Dog. It shall be suffigance.

Leon. Drink some wine ere you go: fare you well.

Enter a Messenger.

Mess. My lord, they stay for you to give your daughter to her husband. 60

Leon. I'll wait upon them: I am ready.

[*Exeunt Leonato and Messenger.*

Dog. Go, good partner, go, get you to Francis Seacole; bid him bring his pen and inkhorn to the gaol: we are now to examination these men.

Verg. And we must do it wisely.

Dog. We will spare for no wit, I warrant you: here's that shall drive some of them to a non-come: only get the learned writer to set down our excommunication and meet me at the gaol.

[*Exeunt.*

ACT IV.

Scene I. *A church.*

Enter Don Pedro, Don John, Leonato, Friar Francis, Claudio, Benedick, Hero, Beatrice, *and attendants.*

Leon. Come, Friar Francis, be brief; only to the plain form of marriage, and you shall recount their particular duties afterwards.

Friar. You come hither, my lord, to marry this lady.

Claud. No.

Leon. To be married to her: friar, you come to marry her.

Friar. Lady, you come hither to be married to this count. 10

Hero. I do.

Friar. If either of you know any inward impediment why you should not be conjoined, I charge you, on your souls, to utter it.

Claud. Know you any, Hero?

Hero. None, my lord.

67-68 *here's that.* i.e. his brain. *non-come.* i.e. nonplus.

The cathedral of Messina. Engraving from Charles Knight's *Pictorial Edition of the Works of William Shakspere, 1839–43*

42 *luxurious.* Lustful.

53 *large.* Broad, immodest.

The marriage scene. Illustration of Gordon Craig's production, Lyceum Theatre, London, 1882

66 *stale.* Prostitute.

Friar.   Know you any, count?
Leon.   I dare make his answer, none.
Claud.   O, what men dare do! what men may do! what men daily do, not knowing what they do!   21
Bene.   How now! interjections? Why, then, some be of laughing, as, ah, ha, he!
Claud.   Stand thee by, friar.   Father, by your leave:
Will you with free and unconstrained soul
Give me this maid, your daughter?
Leon.   As freely, son, as God did give her me.
Claud.   And what have I to give you back, whose worth
May counterpoise this rich and precious gift?
D. Pedro.   Nothing, unless you render her again.   30
Claud.   Sweet prince, you learn me noble thankfulness.
There, Leonato, take her back again:
Give not this rotten orange to your friend;
She's but the sign and semblance of her honour.
Behold how like a maid she blushes here!
O, what authority and show of truth
Can cunning sin cover itself withal!
Comes not that blood as modest evidence
To witness simple virtue? Would you not swear,
All you that see her, that she were a maid,   40
By these exterior shows? But she is none:
●She knows the heat of a luxurious bed;
Her blush is guiltiness, not modesty.
Leon.   What do you mean, my lord?
Claud.   Not to be married,
Not to knit my soul to an approved wanton.
Leon.   Dear my lord, if you, in your own proof,
Have vanquish'd the resistance of her youth,
And made defeat of her virginity,—
Claud.   I know what you would say: if I have known her,
You will say she did embrace me as a husband,
And so extenuate the 'forehand sin: 51
No, Leonato,
●I never tempted her with word too large;
But, as a brother to his sister, show'd
Bashful sincerity and comely love.
Hero.   And seem'd I ever otherwise to you?
Claud.   Out on thee! Seeming! I will write against it:
You seem to me as Dian in her orb,
As chaste as is the bud ere it be blown;
But you are more intemperate in your blood   60
Than Venus, or those pamper'd animals
That rage in savage sensuality.
Hero.   Is my lord well, that he doth speak so wide?
Leon.   Sweet prince, why speak not you?
D. Pedro.   What should I speak?
I stand dishonour'd, that have gone about
●To link my dear friend to a common stale.
Leon.   Are these things spoken, or do I but dream?
D. John.   Sir, they are spoken, and these things are true.
Bene.   This looks not like a nuptial.
Hero.   True! O God!
Claud.   Leonato, stand I here?   70
Is this the prince? is this the prince's brother?
Is this face Hero's? are our eyes our own?

Leon. All this is so: but what of this, my lord?
Claud. Let me but move one question to your
  daughter;
● And, by that fatherly and kindly power
That you have in her, bid her answer truly.
 Leon. I charge thee do so, as thou art
  my child.
 Hero. O, God defend me! how am I beset!
What kind of catechising call you this?

 Claud. To make you answer truly to your
  name.   80
 Hero. Is it not Hero? Who can blot that name
With any just reproach?
 Claud.   Marry, that can Hero;
Hero itself can blot out Hero's virtue.
What man was he talk'd with you yesternight
Out at your window betwixt twelve and one?
Now, if you are a maid, answer to this.
 Hero. I talk'd with no man at that hour,
  my lord.
 D. Pedro. Why, then are you no maiden.
  Leonato,
I am sorry you must hear: upon mine honour,
Myself, my brother and this grieved count 90
Did see her, hear her, at that hour last night
Talk with a ruffian at her chamber-window;
Who hath indeed, most like a liberal villain,
Confess'd the vile encounters they have had
A thousand times in secret.
 D. John. Fie, fie! they are not to be named,
  my lord,
Not to be spoke of:
There is not chastity enough in language
Without offence to utter them. Thus, pretty lady,
I am sorry for thy much misgovernment. 100
 Claud. O Hero, what a Hero hadst thou been,
If half thy outward graces had been placed
About thy thoughts and counsels of thy heart!
But fare thee well, most foul, most fair! farewell,
Thou pure impiety and impious purity!
For thee I'll lock up all the gates of love,
● And on my eyelids shall conjecture hang,
To turn all beauty into thoughts of harm,
And never shall it more be gracious.
 Leon. Hath no man's dagger here a point for
  me?   [*Hero swoons.* 110
 Beat. Why, how now, cousin! wherefore sink
  you down?
 D. John. Come, let us go. These things,
  come thus to light,
Smother her spirits up.
 [*Exeunt Don Pedro, Don John, and Claudio.*
 Bene. How doth the lady?
 Beat.   Dead, I think. Help, uncle!
Hero! why, Hero! Uncle! Signior Benedick!
  Friar!
 Leon. O Fate! take not away thy heavy hand.
Death is the fairest cover for her shame
That may be wish'd for.
 Beat.   How now, cousin Hero!
 Friar. Have comfort, lady.
 Leon. Dost thou look up?   120
 Friar. Yea, wherefore should she not?
 Leon. Wherefore! Why, doth not every earthly
  thing
Cry shame upon her? Could she here deny
● The story that is printed in her blood?
Do not live, Hero; do not ope thine eyes:
For, did I think thou wouldst not quickly die,

75 *kindly.* Natural.

107 *conjecture.* Suspicion.

Beatrice: 'Why, how now, cousin! wherefore sink you
down?' Engraving from a design by F. Hayman from
Hanmer's edition of Shakespeare's works, 1744

124 *in her blood.* Blushes.

128 *rearward.* In the aftermath.

130 *frame.* Plan.

168 *experimental seal.* Stamp of experience.

Costume design for Hero by Voytek, Royal Shakespeare
Co, 1971

Thought I thy spirits were stronger than thy
    shames,
●Myself would, on the rearward of reproaches,
Strike at thy life.   Grieved I, I had but one?
●Chid I for that at frugal nature's frame?   130
O, one too much by thee!   Why had I one?
Why ever wast thou lovely in my eyes?
Why had I not with charitable hand
Took up a beggar's issue at my gates,
Who smirched thus and mired with infamy,
I might have said 'No part of it is mine;
This shame derives itself from unknown loins'?
But mine and mine I loved and mine I praised
And mine that I was proud on, mine so much
That I myself was to myself not mine,   140
Valuing of her,—why, she, O, she is fallen
Into a pit of ink, that the wide sea
Hath drops too few to wash her clean again
And salt too little which may season give
To her foul-tainted flesh!

    Bene.   Sir, sir, be patient.
For my part, I am so attired in wonder,
I know not what to say.

    Beat.   O, on my soul, my cousin is belied!

    Bene.   Lady, were you her bedfellow last
    night?

    Beat.   No, truly not; although, until last
    night,   150
I have this twelvemonth been her bedfellow.

    Leon.   Confirm'd, confirm'd! O, that is stronger
    made
Which was before barr'd up with ribs of iron!
Would the two princes lie, and Claudio lie,
Who loved her so, that, speaking of her foulness,
Wash'd it with tears?   Hence from her! let her
    die.

    Friar.   Hear me a little; for I have only been
Silent so long and given way unto
†This course of fortune. . . .
By noting of the lady I have mark'd   160
A thousand blushing apparitions
To start into her face, a thousand innocent shames
In angel whiteness beat away those blushes;
And in her eye there hath appear'd a fire,
To burn the errors that these princes hold
Against her maiden truth.   Call me a fool;
Trust not my reading nor my observations,
●Which with experimental seal doth warrant
The tenour of my book; trust not my age,
My reverence, calling, nor divinity,   170
If this sweet lady lie not guiltless here
Under some biting error.

    Leon.   Friar, it cannot be.
Thou seest that all the grace that she hath left
Is that she will not add to her damnation
A sin of perjury; she not denies it:
Why seek'st thou then to cover with excuse
That which appears in proper nakedness?

    Friar.   Lady, what man is he you are accused
    of?

    Hero.   They know that do accuse me; I know
    none:
If I know more of any man alive   180
Than that which maiden modesty doth warrant,
Let all my sins lack mercy!   O my father,
Prove you that any man with me conversed
At hours unmeet, or that I yesternight
Maintain'd the change of words with any creature,
Refuse me, hate me, torture me to death!

Friar. There is some strange misprision in
the princes.
Bene. Two of them have the very bent of
honour;
And if their wisdoms be misled in this,
The practice of it lives in John the bastard,   190
Whose spirits toil in frame of villanies.

Leon. I know not. If they speak but truth
of her,
These hands shall tear her; if they wrong her
honour,
The proudest of them shall well hear of it.
Time hath not yet so dried this blood of mine,
Nor age so eat up my invention,
Nor fortune made such havoc of my means,
Nor my bad life reft me so much of friends,
But they shall find, awaked in such a kind,
Both strength of limb and policy of mind,   200
Ability in means and choice of friends,
To quit me of them throughly.
Friar.   Pause awhile,
And let my counsel sway you in this case.
Your daughter here the princes left for dead:
Let her awhile be secretly kept in,
And publish it that she is dead indeed;
Maintain a mourning ostentation
And on your family's old monument
Hang mournful epitaphs and do all rites
That appertain unto a burial.   210
Leon. What shall become of this? what will
this do?
Friar. Marry, this well carried shall on her
behalf
Change slander to remorse; that is some good:
But not for that dream I on this strange course,
But on this travail look for greater birth.
She dying, as it must be so maintain'd,
Upon the instant that she was accused,
Shall be lamented, pitied and excused
Of every hearer: for it so falls out
That what we have we prize not to the worth   220
Whiles we enjoy it, but being lack'd and lost,
Why, then we rack the value, then we find
The virtue that possession would not show us
Whiles it was ours. So will it fare with Claudio:
When he shall hear she died upon his words,
The idea of her life shall sweetly creep
Into his study of imagination,
And every lovely organ of her life
Shall come apparell'd in more precious habit,
More moving-delicate and full of life,   230
Into the eye and prospect of his soul,
Than when she lived indeed; then shall he mourn,
If ever love had interest in his liver,
And wish he had not so accused her,
No, though he thought his accusation true.
Let this be so, and doubt not but success
Will fashion the event in better shape
Than I can lay it down in likelihood.
But if all aim but this be levell'd false,
The supposition of the lady's death   240
Will quench the wonder of her infamy:
And if it sort not well, you may conceal her,
As best befits her wounded reputation,
In some reclusive and religious life,
Out of all eyes, tongues, minds and injuries.
Bene. Signior Leonato, let the friar advise you:
And though you know my inwardness and love
Is very much unto the prince and Claudio,

187 *misprision.* Mistake.

196 *invention.* Inventiveness, cunning.

200 *policy of mind.* Power of mind.

222 *rack.* Stretch.

227 *study of imagination.* Brooding contemplation.

233 *liver.* Seat of passion.

247 *inwardness.* Intimacy.

254 *strange sores strangely they strain the cure.* i.e. a desperate disease requires a desperate cure.

266 *even.* Direct, easy.

277 *eat it.* i.e. then deny the oath.

Beatrice: 'Kill Claudio'. Drawing by Samuel Shelley (1750?–1808)

305-306 *bear her in hand.* Lead her on, delude her.

Yet, by mine honour, I will deal in this
As secretly and justly as your soul   250
Should with your body.
 Leon.   Being that I flow in grief,
The smallest twine may lead me.
 Friar. 'Tis well consented : presently away ;
 For to strange sores strangely they strain the
  cure.
Come, lady, die to live : this wedding-day
 Perhaps is but prolong'd : have patience and
  endure.
    [*Exeunt all but Benedick and Beatrice.*
 Bene. Lady Beatrice, have you wept all this
  while ?
 Beat. Yea, and I will weep a while longer.
 Bene. I will not desire that.
 Beat. You have no reason ; I do it freely. 260
 Bene. Surely I do believe your fair cousin is
wronged.
 Beat. Ah, how much might the man deserve
of me that would right her !
 Bene. Is there any way to show such friendship ?
 Beat. A very even way, but no such friend.
 Bene. May a man do it ?
 Beat. It is a man's office, but not yours.
 Bene. I do love nothing in the world so well
as you : is not that strange ?   270
 Beat. As strange as the thing I know not. It
were as possible for me to say I loved nothing so
well as you : but believe me not ; and yet I lie
not ; I confess nothing, nor I deny nothing. I
am sorry for my cousin.
 Bene. By my sword, Beatrice, thou lovest me.
 Beat. Do not swear, and eat it.
 Bene. I will swear by it that you love me ; and
I will make him eat it that says I love not you.
 Beat. Will you not eat your word ?   280
 Bene. With no sauce that can be devised to it.
I protest I love thee.
 Beat. Why, then, God forgive me !
 Bene. What offence, sweet Beatrice ?
 Beat. You have stayed me in a happy hour : I
was about to protest I loved you.
 Bene. And do it with all thy heart.
 Beat. I love you with so much of my heart
that none is left to protest.
 Bene. Come, bid me do any thing for thee. 290
 Beat. Kill Claudio.
 Bene. Ha ! not for the wide world.
 Beat. You kill me to deny it. Farewell.
 Bene. Tarry, sweet Beatrice.
 Beat. I am gone, though I am here : there is
no love in you : nay, I pray you, let me go.
 Bene. Beatrice,—
 Beat. In faith, I will go.
 Bene. We'll be friends first.
 Beat. You dare easier be friends with me than
fight with mine enemy.   301
 Bene. Is Claudio thine enemy ?

 Beat. Is he not approved in the height a villain,
that hath slandered, scorned, dishonoured my
kinswoman ? O that I were a man ! What, bear
her in hand until they come to take hands ; and
then, with public accusation, uncovered slander,
unmitigated rancour,—O God, that I were a man !
I would eat his heart in the market-place.
 Bene. Hear me, Beatrice,—   310
 Beat. Talk with a man out at a window ! A
proper saying !

Bene. Nay, but, Beatrice,—

Beat. Sweet Hero! She is wronged, she is slandered, she is undone.

Bene. Beat—

Beat. Princes and counties! Surely, a princely testimony, a goodly count, Count Comfect; a sweet gallant, surely! O that I were a man for his sake! or that I had any friend would be a man for my sake! But manhood is melted into courtesies, valour into compliment, and men are only turned into tongue, and trim ones too: he is now as valiant as Hercules that only tells a lie and swears it. I cannot be a man with wishing, therefore I will die a woman with grieving.

Bene. Tarry, good Beatrice. By this hand, I love thee.

Beat. Use it for my love some other way than swearing by it.   330

Bene. Think you in your soul the Count Claudio hath wronged Hero?

Beat. Yea, as sure as I have a thought or a soul.

Bene. Enough, I am engaged; I will challenge him. I will kiss your hand, and so I leave you. By this hand, Claudio shall render me a dear account. As you hear of me, so think of me. Go, comfort your cousin: I must say she is dead: and so, farewell.   [*Exeunt.* 340

SCENE II. *A prison.*

Enter DOGBERRY, VERGES, *and* Sexton, *in gowns; and the* Watch, *with* CONRADE *and* BORACHIO.

Dog. Is our whole dissembly appeared?

Verg. O, a stool and a cushion for the sexton.

Sex. Which be the malefactors?

Dog. Marry, that am I and my partner.

Verg. Nay, that's certain; we have the exhibition to examine.

Sex. But which are the offenders that are to be examined? let them come before master constable.

Dog. Yea, marry, let them come before me. What is your name, friend?   11

Bora. Borachio.

Dog. Pray, write down, Borachio. Yours, sirrah?

Con. I am a gentleman, sir, and my name is Conrade.

Dog. Write down, master gentleman Conrade. Masters, do you serve God?

Con. } Yea, sir, we hope.
Bora. }

Dog. Write down, that they hope they serve God: and write God first; for God defend but God should go before such villains! Masters, it is proved already that you are little better than false knaves; and it will go near to be thought so shortly. How answer you for yourselves?

Con. Marry, sir, we say we are none.

Dog. A marvellous witty fellow, I assure you; but I will go about with him. Come you hither, sirrah; a word in your ear: sir, I say to you, it is thought you are false knaves.   30

Bora. Sir, I say to you we are none.

Dog. Well, stand aside. 'Fore God, they are both in a tale. Have you writ down, that they are none?

317 *counties.* Counts.

318 *Count Comfect.* A confectionary count.

Set design for the gaol scene by Mariano Andreu, Stratford-upon-Avon, 1950

5-6 *exhibition.* i.e. for commission.

33 *in a tale.* In collusion.

The Examination of Conrade and Borachio. Painting by Robert Smirke (1752–1845)

38 *eftest*. Easiest.

69 *opinioned*. i.e. for pinioned.

70 *Let them be in the hands*. i.e. be bound.

2 *second*. Assist.

Sex. Master constable, you go not the way to examine : you must call forth the watch that are their accusers.

Dog. Yea, marry, that's the eftest way. Let the watch come forth. Masters, I charge you, in the prince's name, accuse these men.   40

First Watch. This man said, sir, that Don John, the prince's brother, was a villain.

Dog. Write down Prince John a villain. Why, this is flat perjury, to call a prince's brother villain.

Bora. Master constable,—

Dog. Pray thee, fellow, peace : I do not like thy look, I promise thee.

Sex. What heard you him say else ?

Sec. Watch. Marry, that he had received a thousand ducats of Don John for accusing the Lady Hero wrongfully.   51

Dog. Flat burglary as ever was committed.

Verg. Yea, by mass, that it is.

Sex. What else, fellow ?

First Watch. And that Count Claudio did mean, upon his words, to disgrace Hero before the whole assembly, and not marry her.

Dog. O villain ! thou wilt be condemned into everlasting redemption for this.

Sex. What else ?   60

Watch. This is all.

Sex. And this is more, masters, than you can deny. Prince John is this morning secretly stolen away ; Hero was in this manner accused, in this very manner refused, and upon the grief of this suddenly died. Master constable, let these men be bound, and brought to Leonato's : I will go before and show him their examination.   [*Exit*.

Dog. Come, let them be opinioned.

Verg. † Let them be in the hands—   70

Con. Off, coxcomb !

Dog. God's my life, where 's the sexton ? let him write down the prince's officer coxcomb. Come, bind them. Thou naughty varlet !

Con. Away ! you are an ass, you are an ass.

Dog. Dost thou not suspect my place ? dost thou not suspect my years ? O that he were here to write me down an ass ! But, masters, remember that I am an ass ; though it be not written down, yet forget not that I am an ass. No, thou villain, thou art full of piety, as shall be proved upon thee by good witness. I am a wise fellow, and, which is more, an officer, and, which is more, a householder, and, which is more, as pretty a piece of flesh as any is in Messina, and one that knows the law, go to ; and a rich fellow enough, go to ; and a fellow that hath had losses, and one that hath two gowns and every thing handsome about him. Bring him away. O that I had been writ down an ass !   [*Exeunt*.   90

ACT V.

SCENE I. *Before* LEONATO'S *house*.

Enter LEONATO *and* ANTONIO.

Ant. If you go on thus, you will kill yourself ; And 'tis not wisdom thus to second grief Against yourself.

Leon.   I pray thee, cease thy counsel, Which falls into mine ears as profitless As water in a sieve : give not me counsel ;

Nor let no comforter delight mine ear
But such a one whose wrongs do suit with mine.
Bring me a father that so loved his child,
Whose joy of her is overwhelm'd like mine,
And bid him speak of patience;   10
Measure his woe the length and breadth of mine
And let it answer every strain for strain,
As thus for thus and such a grief for such,
In every lineament, branch, shape, and form:
If such a one will smile and stroke his beard,
●† Bid sorrow wag, cry 'hem!' when he should
        groan,
● Patch grief with proverbs, make misfortune drunk
With candle-wasters; bring him yet to me,
And I of him will gather patience.
But there is no such man: for, brother, men   20
Can counsel and speak comfort to that grief
Which they themselves not feel; but, tasting it,
Their counsel turns to passion, which before
● Would give preceptial medicine to rage,
Fetter strong madness in a silken thread,
Charm ache with air and agony with words:
No, no; 'tis all men's office to speak patience
To those that wring under the load of sorrow,
But no man's virtue nor sufficiency
To be so moral when he shall endure   30
The like himself. Therefore give me no counsel:
My griefs cry louder than advertisement.
    Ant. Therein do men from children nothing
        differ.
    Leon. I pray thee, peace. I will be flesh
        and blood;
For there was never yet philosopher
That could endure the toothache patiently,
However they have writ the style of gods
● And made a push at chance and sufferance.
    Ant. Yet bend not all the harm upon yourself;
Make those that do offend you suffer too.   40
    Leon. There thou speak'st reason: nay, I
        will do so.
My soul doth tell me Hero is belied;
And that shall Claudio know; so shall the prince
And all of them that thus dishonour her.
    Ant. Here comes the prince and Claudio
        hastily.

            Enter Don Pedro *and* Claudio.

D. Pedro. Good den, good den.
Claud.   Good day to both of you.
Leon. Hear you, my lords,—
D. Pedro.   We have some haste, Leonato.
Leon. Some haste, my lord! well, fare you
        well, my lord:
Are you so hasty now? well, all is one.
D. Pedro. Nay, do not quarrel with us, good
        old man.   50
Ant. If he could right himself with quarrel-
        ing,
Some of us would lie low.
Claud.   Who wrongs him?
Leon. Marry, thou dost wrong me; thou dis-
        sembler, thou:—
Nay, never lay thy hand upon thy sword;
I fear thee not.
Claud.   Marry, beshrew my hand,
If it should give your age such cause of fear:
In faith, my hand meant nothing to my sword.
● *Leon.* Tush, tush, man; never fleer and jest
        at me:

16 *wag.* Depart.

17-18 *make misfortune drunk With candle-wasters.*
Drown misfortune in philosophy.

24 *preceptial medicine.* Remedial advice.

38 *made a push at.* Scoffed at.

58 *fleer.* Sneer.

75 *nice fence*. Skill at fencing.

78 *daff*. Put aside.

82 *Win me and wear me*. Proverbial form of challenge: 'win first before boasting'.

84 *foining*. Thrusting.

Antonio: 'Sir boy, I'll whip you from your foining fence'. Duelling in the 17th century, from a contemporary woodcut

___

94 *Scambling*. Scuffling.

95 *cog*. Cheat.

96 *anticly*. Grotesquely.

102 *wake*. Disturb.

I speak not like a dotard nor a fool,
As under privilege of age to brag   60
What I have done being young, or what would do
Were I not old.   Know, Claudio, to thy head,
Thou hast so wrong'd mine innocent child and me
That I am forced to lay my reverence by
And, with grey hairs and bruise of many days,
Do challenge thee to trial of a man.
I say thou hast belied mine innocent child;
Thy slander hath gone through and through her
          heart,
And she lies buried with her ancestors;
O, in a tomb where never scandal slept,   70
Save this of hers, framed by thy villany!
    Claud.   My villany?
    Leon.   Thine, Claudio; thine, I say.
    D. Pedro.   You say not right, old man.
    Leon.   My lord, my lord,
I'll prove it on his body, if he dare,
Despite his nice fence and his active practice,
His May of youth and bloom of lustihood.
    Claud.   Away! I will not have to do with you.
    Leon.   Canst thou so daff me?   Thou hast
          kill'd my child:
If thou kill'st me, boy, thou shalt kill a man.
    Ant.   He shall kill two of us, and men indeed:
But that's no matter; let him kill one first;   81
Win me and wear me; let him answer me.
Come, follow me, boy; come, sir boy, come, fol-
          low me:
Sir boy, I'll whip you from your foining fence;
Nay, as I am a gentleman, I will.
    Leon.   Brother,—
    Ant.   Content yourself.   God knows I loved
          my niece;
And she is dead, slander'd to death by villains,
That dare as well answer a man indeed
As I dare take a serpent by the tongue: 90
Boys, apes, braggarts, Jacks, milksops!
    Leon.   Brother Antony,—
    Ant.   Hold you content.   What, man! I know
          them, yea,
And what they weigh, even to the utmost
          scruple,—
Scambling, out-facing, fashion-monging boys,
That lie and cog and flout, deprave and slander,
Go anticly, show outward hideousness,
And speak off half a dozen dangerous words,
How they might hurt their enemies, if they durst;
And this is all.
    Leon.   But, brother Antony,—
    Ant.   Come, 'tis no matter: 100
Do not you meddle; let me deal in this.
    D. Pedro.   Gentlemen both, we will not wake
          your patience.
My heart is sorry for your daughter's death:
But, on my honour, she was charged with nothing
But what was true and very full of proof.
    Leon.   My lord, my lord,—
    D. Pedro.   I will not hear you.
    Leon.   No?   Come, brother; away! I will be
          heard.
    Ant.   And shall, or some of us will smart for it.
             [*Exeunt Leonato and Antonio.*
    D. Pedro.   See, see; here comes the man we
          went to seek.   110

      Enter BENEDICK.

    Claud.   Now, signior, what news?

Bene. Good day, my lord.

D. Pedro. Welcome, signior: you are almost come to part almost a fray.

Claud. We had like to have had our two noses snapped off with two old men without teeth.

D. Pedro. Leonato and his brother. What thinkest thou? Had we fought, I doubt we should have been too young for them.

Bene. In a false quarrel there is no true valour. I came to seek you both.   121

Claud. We have been up and down to seek thee; for we are high-proof melancholy and would fain have it beaten away. Wilt thou use thy wit?

Bene. It is in my scabbard: shall I draw it?

D. Pedro. Dost thou wear thy wit by thy side?

Claud. Never any did so, though very many have been beside their wit. I will bid thee draw, as we do the minstrels; draw, to pleasure us.

D. Pedro. As I am an honest man, he looks pale. Art thou sick, or angry?   131

Claud. What, courage, man! What though care killed a cat, thou hast mettle enough in thee to kill care.

Bene. Sir, I shall meet your wit in the career, an you charge it against me. I pray you choose another subject.

Claud. Nay, then, give him another staff: this last was broke cross.

D. Pedro. By this light, he changes more and more: I think he be angry indeed.   141

Claud. If he be, he knows how to turn his girdle.

Bene. Shall I speak a word in your ear?

Claud. God bless me from a challenge!

Bene. [*Aside to Claudio*] You are a villain; I jest not: I will make it good how you dare, with what you dare, and when you dare. Do me right, or I will protest your cowardice. You have killed a sweet lady, and her death shall fall heavy on you. Let me hear from you.   151

Claud. Well, I will meet you, so I may have good cheer.

D. Pedro. What, a feast, a feast?

Claud. I' faith, I thank him; he hath bid me to a calf's head and a capon; the which if I do not carve most curiously, say my knife's naught. Shall I not find a woodcock too?

Bene. Sir, your wit ambles well; it goes easily.

D. Pedro. I'll tell thee how Beatrice praised thy wit the other day. I said, thou hadst a fine wit: 'True,' said she, 'a fine little one.' 'No,' said I, 'a great wit:' 'Right,' says she, 'a great gross one.' 'Nay,' said I, 'a good wit:' 'Just,' said she, 'it hurts nobody.' 'Nay,' said I, 'the gentleman is wise:' 'Certain,' said she, 'a wise gentleman.' 'Nay,' said I, 'he hath the tongues:' 'That I believe,' said she, 'for he swore a thing to me on Monday night, which he forswore on Tuesday morning; there's a double tongue; there's two tongues.' Thus did she, an hour together, trans-shape thy particular virtues: yet at last she concluded with a sigh, thou wast the properest man in Italy.

Claud. For the which she wept heartily and said she cared not.

D. Pedro. Yea, that she did; but yet, for all that, an if she did not hate him deadly, she would love him dearly: the old man's daughter told us all.   180

129 *as we do the minstrels.* i.e. draw out their instruments.

135 *in the career.* At full charge.

139 *broke cross.* Snapped in the middle.

156-158 *calf's head . . . capon . . . woodcock.* i.e. a fool, a weakling and a simpleton.

William Charles Macready, the Victorian actor, as Benedick, Theatre Royal, Drury Lane, London, 1842

205-206 *a giant to an ape . . . to such a man.* Much bigger than an ape, but then the ape is wiser than he.

208 *sad.* Serious.

230-231 *division.* Arrangement. *one meaning well suited,* i.e. one point neatly set out.

Claud. All, all; and, moreover, God saw him when he was hid in the garden.

D. Pedro. But when shall we set the savage bull's horns on the sensible Benedick's head?

Claud. Yea, and text underneath, 'Here dwells Benedick the married man'?

Bene. Fare you well, boy: you know my mind. I will leave you now to your gossip-like humour: you break jests as braggarts do their blades, which, God be thanked, hurt not. My lord, for your many courtesies I thank you: I must discontinue your company: your brother the bastard is fled from Messina: you have among you killed a sweet and innocent lady. For my Lord Lackbeard there, he and I shall meet: and, till then, peace be with him. [*Exit.*

D. Pedro. He is in earnest.

Claud. In most profound earnest; and, I'll warrant you, for the love of Beatrice.

D. Pedro. And hath challenged thee.   200

Claud. Most sincerely.

D. Pedro. What a pretty thing man is when he goes in his doublet and hose and leaves off his wit!

Claud. He is then a giant to an ape; but then is an ape a doctor to such a man.

D. Pedro. But, soft you, let me be: pluck up, my heart, and be sad. Did he not say, my brother was fled?

Enter DOGBERRY, VERGES, *and the* Watch, *with* CONRADE *and* BORACHIO.

Dog. Come you, sir: if justice cannot tame you, she shall ne'er weigh more reasons in her balance: nay, an you be a cursing hypocrite once, you must be looked to.

D. Pedro. How now? two of my brother's men bound! Borachio one!

Claud. Hearken after their offence, my lord.

D. Pedro. Officers, what offence have these men done?

Dog. Marry, sir, they have committed false report; moreover, they have spoken untruths; secondarily, they are slanders; sixth and lastly, they have belied a lady; thirdly, they have verified unjust things; and, to conclude, they are lying knaves.

D. Pedro. First, I ask thee what they have done; thirdly, I ask thee what's their offence; sixth and lastly, why they are committed; and, to conclude, what you lay to their charge.

Claud. Rightly reasoned, and in his own division; and, by my troth, there's one meaning well suited.   231

D. Pedro. Who have you offended, masters, that you are thus bound to your answer? this learned constable is too cunning to be understood: what's your offence?

Bora. Sweet prince, let me go no farther to mine answer: do you hear me, and let this count kill me. I have deceived even your very eyes: what your wisdoms could not discover, these shallow fools have brought to light; who in the night overheard me confessing to this man how Don John your brother incensed me to slander the Lady Hero, how you were brought into the orchard and saw me court Margaret in Hero's garments, how you disgraced her, when you should marry her: my villany they have

upon record; which I had rather seal with my
death than repeat over to my shame. The lady
is dead upon mine and my master's false accusation; and, briefly, I desire nothing but the reward of a villain.

    D. Pedro. Runs not this speech like iron
      through your blood?

    Claud. I have drunk poison whiles he ut-
      ter'd it.

    D. Pedro. But did my brother set thee on
      to this?

    Bora. Yea, and paid me richly for the practice
of it.

    D. Pedro. He is composed and framed of
      treachery:

And fled he is upon this villany.

    Claud. Sweet Hero! now thy image doth
      appear

In the rare semblance that I loved it first.   260

    Dog. Come, bring away the plaintiffs: by
this time our sexton hath reformed Signior Leonato of the matter: and, masters, do not forget to
specify, when time and place shall serve, that
I am an ass.

    Verg. Here, here comes master Signior Leo-
nato, and the sexton too.

Re-enter LEONATO *and* ANTONIO, *with the*
Sexton.

    Leon. Which is the villain? let me see his eyes,
That, when I note another man like him,   270
I may avoid him: which of these is he?

    Bora. If you would know your wronger,
      look on me.

    Leon. Art thou the slave that with thy breath
      hast kill'd
Mine innocent child?

    Bora.   Yea, even I alone.

    Leon. No, not so, villain; thou beliest thyself:
Here stand a pair of honourable men;
A third is fled, that had a hand in it.
I thank you, princes, for my daughter's death:
Record it with your high and worthy deeds:
'Twas bravely done, if you bethink you of it.

    Claud. I know not how to pray your patience;
Yet I must speak. Choose your revenge yourself;
Impose me to what penance your invention
Can lay upon my sin: yet sinn'd I not
But in mistaking.

    D. Pedro.   By my soul, nor I:
And yet, to satisfy this good old man,
I would bend under any heavy weight
That he'll enjoin me to.

    Leon. I cannot bid you bid my daughter live;
That were impossible: but, I pray you both,
Possess the people in Messina here   291
How innocent she died; and if your love
● Can labour aught in sad invention,
Hang her an epitaph upon her tomb
And sing it to her bones, sing it to-night:
To-morrow morning come you to my house,
And since you could not be my son-in-law,
Be yet my nephew: my brother hath a daughter,
Almost the copy of my child that's dead,
And she alone is heir to both of us: 300
Give her the right you should have given her
      cousin,
And so dies my revenge.

    Claud.   O noble sir,

293 *invention.* Poetic devising.

Costume design for Don John by Voytek, Royal
Shakespeare Co, 1971

328 *God save the foundation.* Dogberry answers as if he had received alms from a religious house.

Benedick (Donald Sinden) writing a sonnet, Royal Shakespeare Co, 1976

9 *come over me.* A sexual quibble.

10 *below stairs.* i.e. and never become mistress of the house.

Your over-kindness doth wring tears from me!
I do embrace your offer; and dispose
For henceforth of poor Claudio.
 Leon. To-morrow then I will expect your
  coming;
To-night I take my leave. This naughty man
Shall face to face be brought to Margaret,
Who I believe was pack'd in all this wrong,
Hired to it by your brother.
 Bora.   No, by my soul, she was not,
Nor knew not what she did when she spoke to me,
But always hath been just and virtuous 312
In any thing that I do know by her.
 Dog. Moreover, sir, which indeed is not under
white and black, this plaintiff here, the offender,
did call me ass: I beseech you, let it be remembered in his punishment. And also, the watch
heard them talk of one Deformed: they say he
wears a key in his ear and a lock hanging by it,
and borrows money in God's name, the which he
hath used so long and never paid that now men
grow hard-hearted and will lend nothing for God's
sake: pray you, examine him upon that point.
 Leon. I thank thee for thy care and honest
  pains.
 Dog. Your worship speaks like a most thankful
and reverend youth; and I praise God for you.
 Leon. There's for thy pains.
 ● *Dog.* God save the foundation!
 Leon. Go, I discharge thee of thy prisoner,
and I thank thee. 330
 Dog. I leave an arrant knave with your worship; which I beseech your worship to correct
yourself, for the example of others. God keep your
worship! I wish your worship well; God restore
you to health! I humbly give you leave to depart;
and if a merry meeting may be wished, God pro-
hibit it! Come, neighbour.
   [*Exeunt Dogberry and Verges.*
 Leon. Until to-morrow morning, lords, farewell.
 Ant. Farewell, my lords: we look for you
  to-morrow.
 D. Pedro. We will not fail.
 Claud.   To-night I'll mourn with Hero.
 Leon. [*To the Watch*] Bring you these fellows on. We'll talk with Margaret, 341
How her acquaintance grew with this lewd fellow.
   [*Exeunt, severally.*

   SCENE II. LEONATO'S *garden.*

Enter BENEDICK *and* MARGARET, *meeting.*

 Bene. Pray thee, sweet Mistress Margaret,
deserve well at my hands by helping me to the
speech of Beatrice.
 Marg. Will you then write me a sonnet in
praise of my beauty?
 Bene. In so high a style, Margaret, that no
man living shall come over it; for, in most comely
truth, thou deservest it.
 ● *Marg.* To have no man come over me! why,
● shall I always keep below stairs? 10
 Bene. Thy wit is as quick as the greyhound's
mouth; it catches.
 Marg. And yours as blunt as the fencer's foils,
which hit, but hurt not.
 Bene. A most manly wit, Margaret; it will

not hurt a woman : and so, I pray thee, call Bea-
• trice : I give thee the bucklers.
   Marg.   Give us the swords; we have bucklers
of our own.
   Bene.   If you use them, Margaret, you must
• put in the pikes with a vice ; and they are danger-
ous weapons for maids.
   Marg.   Well, I will call Beatrice to you, who
I think hath legs.
   Bene.   And therefore will come.
                      [*Exit Margaret.*

   [*Sings*]   The god of love,
            That sits above,
    And knows me, and knows me,
       How pitiful I deserve,—

• I mean in singing ; but in loving, Leander the good
swimmer, Troilus the first employer of pandars, and
• a whole bookful of these quondam carpet-mongers,
whose names yet run smoothly in the even road
of a blank verse, why, they were never so truly
turned over and over as my poor self in love.
Marry, I cannot show it in rhyme ; I have tried :
I can find out no rhyme to 'lady' but 'baby,' an
innocent rhyme ; for 'scorn,' 'horn,' a hard rhyme ;
for 'school,' 'fool,' a babbling rhyme ; very ominous endings : no, I was not born under a rhyming
planet, nor I cannot woo in festival terms.   41

   Enter BEATRICE.
Sweet Beatrice, wouldst thou come when I called
thee ?
   Beat.   Yea, signior, and depart when you bid me.
   Bene.   O, stay but till then !
   Beat.   'Then' is spoken ; fare you well now :
and yet, ere I go, let me go with that I came ;
which is, with knowing what hath passed between
you and Claudio.
   Bene.   Only foul words ; and thereupon I will
kiss thee.   51
   Beat.   Foul words is but foul wind, and foul
wind is but foul breath, and foul breath is noisome ;
therefore I will depart unkissed.
   Bene.   Thou hast frighted the word out of his
right sense, so forcible is thy wit.   But I must tell
thee plainly, Claudio undergoes my challenge ;
and either I must shortly hear from him, or I will
subscribe him a coward.   And, I pray thee now,
tell me for which of my bad parts didst thou first
fall in love with me ?   61
   Beat.   For them all together ; which maintained
so politic a state of evil that they will not admit
any good part to intermingle with them.   But for
which of my good parts did you first suffer love
for me ?
   Bene.   Suffer love ! a good epithet ! I do suffer
love indeed, for I love thee against my will.
   Beat.   In spite of your heart, I think ; alas, poor
heart !   If you spite it for my sake, I will spite it
for yours ; for I will never love that which my
friend hates.
   Bene.   Thou and I are too wise to woo peace-
ably.
   Beat.   It appears not in this confession : there's
not one wise man among twenty that will praise
himself.
   Bene.   An old, an old instance, Beatrice, that
lived in the time of good neighbours.   If a man do
not erect in this age his own tomb ere he dies, he

17 *bucklers.* Small shields. 'To give the bucklers'
acknowledged defeat.

21 *pikes.* Spikes mounted on the bucklers. *Vice.* Screw.

30-31 *Leander the good swimmer, Troilus the first employer of pandars.* Leander swam the Hellespont every
night to visit his love, Hero ; Troilus used Pandarus as a
go-between in wooing Cressida.

32 *quondam carpet-mongers.* Former ladies men.

85 *rheum.* Tears.

98 *old coil.* Great confusion.

The Epitaph Scene. Engraving from a design by H. Gravelot for Theobald's edition of Shakespeare's works, 1773

---

5 *guerdon.* Recompense.

shall live no longer in monument than the bell rings and the widow weeps.

Beat. And how long is that, think you?

Bene. Question: why, an hour in clamour and a quarter in **rheum**: therefore is it most expedient for the wise, if Don Worm, his conscience, find no impediment to the contrary, to be the trumpet of his own virtues, as I am to myself. So much for praising myself, who, I myself will bear witness, is praiseworthy: and now tell me, how doth your cousin? 91

Beat. Very ill.

Bene. And how do you?

Beat. Very ill too.

Bene. Serve God, love me and mend. There will I leave you too, for here comes one in haste.

Enter URSULA.

Urs. Madam, you must come to your uncle. Yonder's old coil at home: it is proved my Lady Hero hath been falsely accused, the prince and Claudio mightily abused; and Don John is the author of all, who is fled and gone. Will you come presently?

Beat. Will you go hear this news, signior?

Bene. I will live in thy heart, die in thy lap and be buried in thy eyes; and moreover I will go with thee to thy uncle's. [*Exeunt.*

SCENE III. *A church.*

Enter DON PEDRO, CLAUDIO, *and three or four with tapers.*

Claud. Is this the monument of Leonato?

A Lord. It is, my lord.

Claud. [*Reading out of a scroll*]

> Done to death by slanderous tongues
>   Was the Hero that here lies:
> Death, in guerdon of her wrongs,
>   Gives her fame which never dies.
> So the life that died with shame
> Lives in death with glorious fame.

> Hang thou there upon the tomb,
> Praising her when I am dumb.   10

Now, music, sound, and sing your solemn hymn.

SONG.

> Pardon, goddess of the night,
> Those that slew thy virgin knight;
> For the which, with songs of woe,
> Round about her tomb they go.
>   Midnight, assist our moan;
>   Help us to sigh and groan,
>   Heavily, heavily:
>   Graves, yawn and yield your dead,
>   Till death be uttered,   20
>   Heavily, heavily.

Claud. Now, unto thy bones good night!
     Yearly will I do this rite.

D. Pedro. Good morrow, masters; put your torches out:

The wolves have prey'd; and look, the gentle day,

Before the wheels of Phœbus, round about

Dapples the drowsy east with spots of grey.

Thanks to you all, and leave us: fare you well.

Claud. Good morrow, masters: each his several way.

D. Pedro.   Come, let us hence, and put on
    other weeds;   30
And then to Leonato's we will go.
  • *Claud.*   And Hymen now with luckier issue
    speed's
Than this for whom we render'd up this woe.
                    [*Exeunt.*

SCENE IV.   *A room in* LEONATO'S *house.*

Enter LEONATO, ANTONIO, BENEDICK, BEA-
TRICE, MARGARET, URSULA, FRIAR FRANCIS,
and HERO.

  Friar.   Did I not tell you she was innocent?
  Leon.   So are the prince and Claudio, who
    accused her
Upon the error that you heard debated:
But Margaret was in some fault for this,
Although against her will, as it appears
In the true course of all the question.
  Ant.   Well, I am glad that all things sort so
    well.
  Bene.   And so am I, being else by faith en-
    forced
To call young Claudio to a reckoning for it.
  Leon.   Well, daughter, and you gentlewomen
    all,   10
Withdraw into a chamber by yourselves,
And when I send for you, come hither mask'd.
                  [*Exeunt Ladies.*
The prince and Claudio promised by this hour
To visit me.   You know your office, brother:
You must be father to your brother's daughter,
And give her to young Claudio.
  Ant.   Which I will do with confirm'd coun-
    tenance.
  Bene.   Friar, I must entreat your pains, I
    think.
  Friar.   To do what, signior?
  Bene.   To bind me, or undo me; one of them.
Signior Leonato, truth it is, good signior,   21
Your niece regards me with an eye of favour.
  Leon.   That eye my daughter lent her: 'tis
    most true.
  Bene.   And I do with an eye of love requite
    her.
  Leon.   The sight whereof I think you had
    from me,
From Claudio and the prince: but what's your
    will?
  Bene.   Your answer, sir, is enigmatical:
But, for my will, my will is your good will
May stand with ours, this day to be conjoin'd
In the state of honourable marriage: 30
In which, good friar, I shall desire your help.
  Leon.   My heart is with your liking.
  Friar.   And my help.
Here comes the prince and Claudio.

Enter DON PEDRO *and* CLAUDIO, *and two or
three others.*

  D. Pedro.   Good morrow to this fair assembly.
  Leon.   Good morrow, prince; good morrow,
    Claudio:
We here attend you.   Are you yet determined
To-day to marry with my brother's daughter?
  • *Claud.*   I'll hold my mind, were she an Ethiope.
  Leon.   Call her forth, brother; here's the friar
    ready.   [*Exit Antonio.*

32 *Hymen.* God of marriage.

38 *Ethiope.* Black African.

46-47 *Europa . . . noble beast in love.* Europe, with
allusion to Europa, carried off by Jove in the form of a
bull.

Claudio: 'Another Hero!' Engraving from a painting by
Francis Wheatley (1747–1801)

D. Pedro. Good morrow, Benedick. Why,
 what's the matter,   40
That you have such a February face,
So full of frost, of storm and cloudiness?
 Claud. I think he thinks upon the savage
 bull.
Tush, fear not, man; we'll tip thy horns with
 gold
And all Europa shall rejoice at thee,
•As once Europa did at lusty Jove,
When he would play the noble beast in love.
 Bene. Bull Jove, sir, had an amiable low;
And some such strange bull leap'd your father's
 cow,
And got a calf in that same noble feat   50
Much like to you, for you have just his bleat.
 Claud. For this I owe you: here comes other
 reckonings.

Re-enter ANTONIO, *with the* Ladies *masked.*

Which is the lady I must seize upon?
 Ant. This same is she, and I do give you her.
 Claud. Why, then she's mine. Sweet, let
 me see your face.
 Leon. No, that you shall not, till you take
 her hand
Before this friar and swear to marry her.
 Claud. Give me your hand: before this holy
 friar,
I am your husband, if you like of me.
 Hero. And when I lived, I was your other
 wife: [*Unmasking.* 60
And when you loved, you were my other husband.
 Claud. Another Hero!
 Hero.   Nothing certainer:
One Hero died defiled, but I do live,
And surely as I live, I am a maid.
 D. Pedro. The former Hero! Hero that is
 dead!
 Leon. She died, my lord, but whiles her slan-
 der lived.
 Friar. All this amazement can I qualify;
When after that the holy rites are ended,
I'll tell you largely of fair Hero's death:
Meantime let wonder seem familiar,   70
And to the chapel let us presently.
 Bene. Soft and fair, friar. Which is Beatrice?
 Beat. [*Unmasking*] I answer to that name.
 What is your will?
 Bene. Do not you love me?
 Beat.   Why, no; no more than reason.
 Bene. Why, then your uncle and the prince
 and Claudio
Have been deceived; they swore you did.
 Beat. Do not you love me?
 Bene.   Troth, no; no more than reason.
 Beat. Why, then my cousin Margaret and
 Ursula
Are much deceived; for they did swear you did.
 Bene. They swore that you were almost sick
 for me.   80
 Beat. They swore that you were well-nigh
 dead for me.
 Bene. 'Tis no such matter. Then you do not
 love me?
 Beat. No, truly, but in friendly recompense.
 Leon. Come, cousin, I am sure you love the
 gentleman.

Claud. And I'll be sworn upon't that he loves
    her;
For here's a paper written in his hand,
A halting sonnet of his own pure brain,
Fashion'd to Beatrice.
    Hero.   And here's another
Writ in my cousin's hand, stolen from her pocket,
Containing her affection unto Benedick.   90
    Bene. A miracle! here's our own hands against
our hearts. Come, I will have thee; but, by
this light, I take thee for pity.
    Beat. I would not deny you; but, by this
good day, I yield upon great persuasion; and
partly to save your life, for I was told you were
in a consumption.
    Bene. Peace! I will stop your mouth.
                    [*Kissing her.*
    D. Pedro. How dost thou, Benedick, the
married man?   100
    Bene. I'll tell thee what, prince; a college of
wit-crackers cannot flout me out of my humour.
Dost thou think I care for a satire or an epigram?
● No: if a man will be beaten with brains, a' shall
wear nothing handsome about him. In brief,
since I do purpose to marry, I will think nothing
to any purpose that the world can say against it;
and therefore never flout at me for what I have
said against it; for man is a giddy thing, and this
is my conclusion. For thy part, Claudio, I did
think to have beaten thee; but in that thou art
like to be my kinsman, live unbruised and love
my cousin.
    Claud. I had well hoped thou wouldst have
denied Beatrice, that I might have cudgelled
● thee out of thy single life, to make thee a double-
dealer; which, out of question, thou wilt be, if
my cousin do not look exceeding narrowly to thee.
    Bene. Come, come, we are friends: let's have
a dance ere we are married, that we may lighten
our own hearts and our wives' heels.   121
    Leon. We'll have dancing afterward.
    Bene. First, of my word; therefore play, music.
Prince, thou art sad; get thee a wife, get thee a
wife: there is no staff more reverend than one
tipped with horn.

                Enter a Messenger.

    Mess. My lord, your brother John is ta'en in
    flight,
And brought with armed men back to Messina.
    Bene. Think not on him till to-morrow: I'll
devise thee brave punishments for him. Strike
up, pipers.   [*Dance.* 131
                    [*Exeunt.*

Benedick: 'Peace! I will stop your mouth'. Benedick
(John Gielgud) and Beatrice (Peggy Ashcroft), Palace
Theatre, London, 1955

104-105 *if a man will be beaten with brains, a' shall
wear nothing handsome about him.* i.e. if a man is afraid of
witticisms he will hardly dare to put on his best suit.

116-117 *double-dealer.* Married man but unfaithful.

The Merry Wives of Windsor

1599-1600

THIS PERENNIALLY SUCCESSFUL PLAY is the most purely amusing, from beginning to end, that Shakespeare ever wrote. It is of course a farce, though it has some continuity with the comic scenes in *Henry IV*, particularly in the characters of Falstaff and Mistress Quickly, who is given a larger part in the intrigue here; Justice Shallow appears again, with a different ninny for companion, his cousin Slender; Falstaff's followers, Bardolph and Nym, make a brief appearance, Pistol with his grandiloquent talk is retained. For the rest, there are as admirable comic creations as anywhere in Shakespeare: Mistress Ford and her jealous husband, whom Falstaff would cuckold, and the marvellous caricatures of Sir Hugh Evans, the Welsh curate and schoolmaster, and Dr. Caius, the French physician, each of whom 'makes fritters of English' in his own way.

Shakespeare never wrote anything funnier—and the play has proved an inspiration to other artists in other fields, particularly music, with Nicolai's opera, Verdi's *Falstaff* and Vaughan Williams' *Sir John in Love*.

This last title gives the theme, for it is a new Falstaff, or aspect of him: the would-be seducer of a respectable citizen's wife of Windsor—his idea of making love (continuous with his behaviour with Doll Tearsheet at the Boar's Head in East Cheap). It is the same old reprobate, with the same virtuosity of language in recounting his misadventures as that with which he had regaled Prince Hal.

The Occasion. It is evident that Shakespeare enjoyed writing this piece, such spirits and such merriment—the theme inspired him to these new comic creations, and to a superb piece of craftsmanship. (The poet Auden was fool enough to call it 'Shakespeare's worst play'—not much sense of humour there!) This is the more remarkable, and yet it demonstrates the complete mastery he had achieved, in that the work was obviously the answer to a royal command, and written at speed. An old tradition has it that the Queen expressed a wish to see Sir John in love—that was true to her, by the way: the language that surrounded her was that of love, demanded by the ageing virgin. And why should not she have been as disappointed as other people were at the absence of Falstaff from *Henry V*, when they had been promised more of him?

The play was put together rapidly, leaving various unimportant loose ends, and almost wholly in prose. It has, however, a more ceremonial ending in verse, evidently suited, or adapted, for a Garter Feast, probably at Windsor, with which Shakespeare was well acquainted from performances there. It is not known precisely which Garter Feast—the practical dramatist was always ready to tailor his piece for the occasion—nor does it greatly matter. The play's the thing.

Nor again do 'sources', beloved of pedants, matter. The Italian *novelle* familiar to Shakespeare are full of seducers of other men's wives—and Shakespeare himself was sufficiently experienced in the subject without book; the theme of the jealous husband, which admirably counterpoints Falstaff's attempts to board the wife—

Boarding call you it? I'll be sure to keep him above deck'—

owes something to Ben Jonson's jealous husband in *Every Man in his Humour,* in which Shakespeare acted in 1598. He did not act in Jonson's *Every Man out of his Humour* next year; but the considerable play that is made of, and at the expense of, 'humours' reflects Shakespeare's recent experience. *The Merry Wives* is evidently posterior to these, and common sense indicates that it comes after *Henry IV* and *Henry V*.

There had been some trouble over names in these plays, which is not without contemporary significance and calls attention to the real historical background, as opposed

Right: *Ben Jonson whose* Everyman in His Humour *had some influence on* The Merry Wives of Windsor

Far right: *The Execution of Sir John Oldcastle, the famous Lollard of Henry V's reign. Falstaff was originally called Sir John Oldcastle. Woodcut from Holinshed's* Chronicles, *1587*

to literary conjecturing without solid foundation. Falstaff was originally called Sir John Oldcastle, from the famous Lollard of Henry V's reign. But Oldcastle was a collateral ancestor of Lord Cobham. William Brooke, 7th Lord Cobham, was the father-in-law of Sir Robert Cecil, opposed to Essex and his party, which was Shakespeare's affiliation. The Brookes objected to Oldcastle being portrayed as the profligate Sir John on the stage, and 'Falstaff' had to be substituted. When the 1st Lord Chamberlain Hunsdon died, in July 1596, he was succeeded as Chamberlain by Lord Cobham. This Cobham died in April 1597, when the second Lord Hunsdon succeeded him as Lord Chamberlain, and of course as patron of Shakespeare's Company. Again it was understandable that Lord Cobham should object to the family name of Brooke being made ridiculous as that under which the jealous husband solicits Falstaff's attentions to test his wife's fidelity. Shakespeare had to change the name Brooke to Broome. Now these people, both Hunsdon and Cobham, lived in Blackfriars, with which Shakespeare had long associations. So these shafts went home more closely than people have realised, though there is further evidence that Falstaff jokes had private references now lost to us, but laughed at in the Southampton circle.[1] Actually, Cobham was made a Knight of the Garter in 1599 and entertained the Queen in Blackfriars in 1600; if *The Merry Wives* was performed on either of those occasions there would be all the more reason to change the name of Brooke.

[1] cf. my *Shakespeare the Man,* 162.

Background. Windsor provides the stage-set, as it were: the Castle in the background, the Castle ditch where Page, Shallow and Slender 'couch till we see the light of our fairies', who are to torment Falstaff at Herne's Oak, of medieval folklore, in the Great Park. We hear of the Pettyward and the Park-ward, and the way to Frogmore; Slender expected to marry Ann Page at Eton, Dr. Caius likewise at the deanery by St. George's Chapel; while Falstaff is tumbled from the dirty-linen basket into the Thames at Datchet Mead.

But Shakespeare has drawn upon his experience of small-town life at Stratford for his *bourgeois* farce. Blank verse, the language of romance, and music are for Court and courtiers; none of this in *The Merry Wives* until we come to the fairies and the compliment to the Queen and her Order of the Garter at the end. Otherwise the characters are mainly drawn from middle-class citizenry, and speak prose. The Fords and Pages are respectable townsfolk. So is the Welsh cleric-schoolmaster, Evans; Shakespeare's school had had a Jenkins for schoolmaster in his time. Dr. Caius speaks French and broken English. The scenes between Henry V and his French princess Catherine, in *Henry V,* are mostly in French; and we know that Shakespeare was lodging in the French household of the Montjoies in Silver Street shortly after 1600, and probably before. Falstaff claims that Page's wife had examined his parts 'with most judicious *oeillades*'. Now where did Shakespeare get that surprising French word from?

The whole scene in which young William is put through his Latin accidence by Sir Hugh Evans is straight out of Shakespeare's schooling—while Mistress Quickly's ear is alert to the bawdy suggestions she suspects in declining such words as 'horum, harum, horum'. Though she is now Dr. Caius' respectable housekeeper her inclinations are to be as much of a bawd as ever—she has not changed her spots from the Boar's Head. Justice Shallow is still the old wag of his Gloucestershire garden, interested in the form of the greyhounds racing on the Cotswolds. We hear of Banbury cheese and an even more familiar memory in the glover's great round paring-knife, which Shakespeare must have handled himself in his youth. The joke about luces in Shallow's coat-of-arms may go back to the Lucys of Charlecote, whom Shakespeare had reason to know; Sir Thomas Lucy died about this time, in 1600.

Contemporary London is evoked in Falstaff's dismissive image of 'the lisping hawthorn buds that come like women in men's apparel and smell like Bucklersbury in simple-time'—sissies evidently, who smelt better than ordinary Elizabethans. Sackerson is mentioned, the bear that performed at Paris Garden, near the Globe on the South Bank, so famous as to be a character in his own right. Sir John denies to Mistress Ford that he has also been making up to her friend, Mistress Page: 'thou mightest as well say I love to walk by the Counter-gate, which is as hateful to me as the reek of a lime-kiln'— the Counter being the prison for debtors.

Oddly enough—though not oddly for the reading man Shakespeare was—literary references are as much present in this play as sport and frolics. Sir John—his being a knight is his one claim to any respect—pays his attentions to the *bourgeoise* Mistress Ford in the inflated Court-language of love caricatured, with a line from Sidney's *Astrophil and Stella* :

Have I caught thee, my heavenly jewel?

Marlowe's famous poem, 'Come live with me and by my love', is garbled by Evans:

To shallow rivers to whose falls ......
Melodious birds sings madrigals;
There will we make our beds of roses
And a thousand fragrant posies.

Anne Page and
Slender. *Drawing
by J. M. Wright
(1776–1866)*

The Company would seem to have had a Welsh actor, man or boy, in its cast at the time—and this beautifully constructed play had a good part for almost everybody. Marlowe's Dr. Faustus and Mephistopheles are not forgotten.

A couple of references show that Shakespeare had been reading Ralegh's *Discovery . . . of Guiana*, which came out in 1596. Falstaff assures Pistol and Nym that Mistress Page 'did so course o'er my exteriors with such a greedy intention that the appetite of her eye did seem to scorch me up like a burning-glass. She bears the purse too; she is a region in Guiana, all gold and bounty. I will be 'cheator [punning on escheator and cheater] to them both, and they shall be exchequers to me. They shall be my East and West Indies, and I will trade to them both.' It was in Ralegh that Shakespeare had been reading about the man-eaters, the Anthropophagi, and formed his own word out of it by analogy with Carthaginian. When Simple inquires for Falstaff at the Garter Inn the Host says, 'there's his chamber, his house, his castle [did Shakespeare still think of him as Oldcastle?], his standing-bed and truckle-bed. Go, knock and call. He'll speak like an Anthropophaginian unto thee.' The room was new-painted with the story of the Prodigal, by the way—as the White Swan at Stratford still has a room painted with that of Tobit and the Angel.

A phrase from the Prayer Book appears, quoted by Evans. 'What phrase is this, "He hears with ear"?' Why, it is affectations'. It evidently struck Shakespeare's ear at church as odd, as it used to mine. Mistress Ford considered that Falstaff's disposition and his words 'do no more adhere and keep place together than the Hundredth Psalm to the tune of "Greensleeves".' William Shakespeare evidently attended church, like a good townsman, at Stratford. But what did he do in London? Southampton House was a nest of Catholics, a refuge for priests—and 'priest' and 'by the mass' are the words that come readily to Shakespeare. On Falstaff's second attempt on Mistress Ford's virtue he has to be smuggled out of the house as the fat Witch of Brentford, and beaten as such.

> Mrs. Ford: Nay, by the mass . . . he [her husband] beat him most
> unpitifully, methought.
> Mrs. Page: I'll have the cudgel hallowed and hung o'er the altar—it hath
> done meritorious service.

William Shakespeare was familiar not only with the traditional terms of the old faith but was on terms with Catholic usages.

448

The ninny Slender, whom his friends put up to marry Ann Page, sighs, 'I had rather than forty shillings I had my Book of Songs and Sonnets here': that is Tottel's Miscellany, the best known anthology of Shakespeare's youth, which would have provided Slender with some love-talk, in which he was wanting.

The Order of the Garter. The play is firmly related to the Order of the Garter and must have been produced at one or other of its feasts—possibly even Cobham's in 1600, the name Brooke having been removed. The Quarto version of the play (1602), which has the original Brooke instead of Broome, also has a tell-tale 'cozen-Gar-mombles', altered later to 'Cozen-Germans'. In 1592 Count Mompelgart had visited England and, though anxious to be made a Knight of the Garter, went away without paying his debts. Evans reports that 'there is three cozen-garmombles [Germans] that has cozened all the hosts of Readins, of Maidenhead, of Colebrook, of horses and money.' The Count continued to pester the Queen for the Order; as Duke of Württemberg he got it in 1597, though she did not bother to send him the insignia.

To end all the jolly rough and tumble various characters disguise themselves as fairies to scare the timorous Falstaff at Herne's Oak.

> Elves, list your names; silence, you airy toys!
> Cricket, to Windsor chimneys shalt thou leap:
> Where fires thou find'st unraked and hearths unswept,
> There pinch the maids as blue as bilberry:
> Our radiant Queen hates sluts and sluttery.

The credulous Falstaff is terrified: he knows that to speak to the fairies is death.

> Search Windsor Castle, elves, within and out,
> Strew good luck, ouphs, on every sacred room,
> That it may stand till the perpetual doom,
> In state as wholesome as in state 'tis fit,
> Worthy the owner and the owner it.

As for the Order:

> The several chairs of Order look you scour
> With juice of balm and every precious flower—
> Each fair instalment, coat, and several crest
> With loyal blazon, evermore be blest . . .

And *Honi soit qui mal y pense* write—it is nice to note that the poet respected the mute e in the manner of French verse—

> In emerald tufts, flowers purple, blue, and white . . .
> Buckled below fair knighthood's bending knee.

Text. The authoritative text is that of the First Folio, from the Company's prompt-book as copied from Shakespeare's manuscript by the regular scribe, Ralph Crane. In the process some gaps occurred, which an earlier Quarto of the play, of 1602, has helped to fill—as, for instance, in the admirable text of our leading textual scholar, Fredson Bowers, in the (American) Pelican Shakespeare.

THE
MERRY WIVES OF WINDSOR.

DRAMATIS PERSONÆ.

SIR JOHN FALSTAFF.
FENTON, a gentleman.
SHALLOW, a country justice.
SLENDER, cousin to Shallow.
FORD,
PAGE, } two gentlemen dwelling at Windsor.
WILLIAM PAGE, a boy, son to Page.
SIR HUGH EVANS, a Welsh parson.
DOCTOR CAIUS, a French physician.
Host of the Garter Inn.
BARDOLPH,
PISTOL, } sharpers attending on Falstaff.
NYM,

ROBIN, page to Falstaff.
SIMPLE, servant to Slender.
RUGBY, servant to Doctor Caius.

MISTRESS FORD.
MISTRESS PAGE.
ANNE PAGE, her daughter.
MISTRESS QUICKLY, servant to Doctor Caius.

Servants to Page, Ford, &c.

SCENE: *Windsor, and the neighbourhood.*

• *A bullet beside a text line indicates an annotation in the opposite column*

ACT I.

SCENE I. *Windsor. Before* PAGE'S *house.*

Enter JUSTICE SHALLOW, SLENDER, *and* SIR HUGH EVANS.

Shal. Sir Hugh, persuade me not; I will
•make a Star-chamber matter of it: if he were
twenty Sir John Falstaffs, he shall not abuse
Robert Shallow, esquire.
Slen. In the county of Gloucester, justice of
•peace and 'Coram.'
• *Shal.* Ay, cousin Slender, and 'Custalorum.'
Slen. Ay, and 'Rato-lorum' too; and a gentleman born, master parson; who writes himself
•'Armigero,' in any bill, warrant, quittance, or
obligation, 'Armigero.'   11

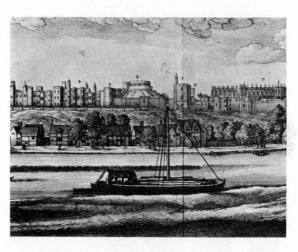

View of Windsor Castle. Engraving by Wenceslas Hollar from Elias Ashmole's *The Institution, Laws and Ceremonies of the Most Noble Order of the Garter,* 1672

2 *Star-chamber.* The Court of the Star Chamber (so-called because the ceiling was decorated with stars) dealt with serious disturbances of the peace, etc.

6 *'Coram'.* i.e. of the quorum, those justices whose presence was necessary to form a bench of magistrates.

7 *'Custalorum'.* i.e. *Custos Rotulorum,* the keeper of the county records.

10 *'Armigero'.* i.e. for armiger, Esquire, one entitled to have a coat of arms.

Opposite: Slender with Anne Page. Painting by A. W. Callcott, 1835

16 *luces*. Pikes. This may also be an allusion to the coat of arms of the Lucy family of Charlecote.

20 *passant*. Walking.

24 *quarter*. Add another coat of arms to my own (by marrying).

36 *meet*. Fitting.

Costume design for Shallow by Theodore Komisar-jevsky, Stratford-upon-Avon, 1935

39 *vizaments*. i.e. advisements.

56 *pribbles and prabbles*. Petty quarrels.

Shal. Ay, that I do; and have done any time these three hundred years.

Slen. All his successors gone before him hath done't; and all his ancestors that come after him may: they may give the dozen white luces in their coat.

Shal. It is an old coat.

Evans. The dozen white louses do become an old coat well; it agrees well, passant; it is a familiar beast to man, and signifies love.   21

Shal. The luce is the fresh fish; the salt fish is an old coat.

Slen. I may quarter, coz.

Shal. You may, by marrying.

Evans. It is marring indeed, if he quarter it.

Shal. Not a whit.

Evans. Yes, py'r lady; if he has a quarter of your coat, there is but three skirts for yourself, in my simple conjectures: but that is all one. If Sir John Falstaff have committed disparagements unto you, I am of the church, and will be glad to do my benevolence to make atonements and compremises between you.

Shal. The council shall hear it; it is a riot.

Evans. It is not meet the council hear a riot; there is no fear of Got in a riot: the council, look you, shall desire to hear the fear of Got, and not to hear a riot; take your vizaments in that.

Shal. Ha! o' my life, if I were young again, the sword should end it.   41

Evans. It is petter that friends is the sword, and end it: and there is also another device in my prain, which peradventure prings goot discretions with it: there is Anne Page, which is daughter to Master Thomas Page, which is pretty virginity.

Slen. Mistress Anne Page? She has brown hair, and speaks small like a woman.

Evans. It is that fery person for all the orld, as just as you will desire; and seven hundred pounds of moneys, and gold and silver, is her grandsire upon his death's-bed—Got deliver to a joyful resurrections!—give, when she is able to overtake seventeen years old: it were a goot motion if we leave our pribbles and prabbles, and desire a marriage between Master Abraham and Mistress Anne Page.

Slen. Did her grandsire leave her seven hundred pound?   60

Evans. Ay, and her father is make her a petter penny.

Slen. I know the young gentlewoman; she has good gifts.

Evans. Seven hundred pounds and possibilities is goot gifts.

Shal. Well, let us see honest Master Page. Is Falstaff there?

Evans. Shall I tell you a lie? I do despise a liar as I do despise one that is false, or as I despise one that is not true. The knight, Sir John, is there; and, I beseech you, be ruled by your well-willers. I will peat the door for Master Page. [*Knocks*] What, hoa! Got pless your house here!

Page. [*Within*] Who's there?

Enter PAGE.

Evans. Here is Got's plessing, and your friend, and Justice Shallow; and here young

Master Slender, that peradventures shall tell you another tale, if matters grow to your likings.

Page. I am glad to see your worships well. I thank you for my venison, Master Shallow. 81

Shal. Master Page, I am glad to see you: much good do it your good heart! I wished your venison better; it was ill killed. How doth good Mistress Page?—and I thank you always with my heart, la! with my heart.

Page. Sir, I thank you.

Shal. Sir, I thank you; by yea and no, I do.

Page. I am glad to see you, good Master Slender. 90

● *Slen.* How does your fallow greyhound, sir?
● I heard say he was outrun on Cotsall.

Page. It could not be judged, sir.

Slen. You'll not confess, you'll not confess.

● *Shal.* That he will not. 'Tis your fault, 'tis your fault; 'tis a good dog.

Page. A cur, sir.

Shal. Sir, he's a good dog, and a fair dog: can there be more said? he is good and fair. Is Sir John Falstaff here? 100

Page. Sir, he is within; and I would I could do a good office between you.

Evans. It is spoke as a Christians ought to speak.

Shal. He hath wronged me, Master Page.

Page. Sir, he doth in some sort confess it.

Shal. If it be confessed, it is not redressed: is not that so, Master Page? He hath wronged me; indeed he hath; at a word, he hath, believe me: Robert Shallow, esquire, saith, he is wronged.

Page. Here comes Sir John. 111

Enter SIR JOHN FALSTAFF, BARDOLPH, NYM, *and* PISTOL.

Fal. Now, Master Shallow, you'll complain of me to the king?

Shal. Knight, you have beaten my men, killed my deer, and broke open my lodge.

Fal. But not kissed your keeper's daughter?

Shal. Tut, a pin! this shall be answered.

Fal. I will answer it straight; I have done all this. That is now answered.

Shal. The council shall know this. 120

Fal. 'Twere better for you if it were known in counsel: you'll be laughed at.

● *Evans.* Pauca verba, Sir John; goot worts.

Fal. Good worts! good cabbage. Slender, I broke your head: what matter have you against me?

Slen. Marry, sir, I have matter in my head against you; and against your cony-catching rascals, Bardolph, Nym, and Pistol.

● *Bard.* You Banbury cheese! 130

Slen. Ay, it is no matter.

Pist. How now, Mephostophilus!

Slen. Ay, it is no matter.

● *Nym.* Slice, I say! pauca, pauca: slice! that's my humour.

Slen. Where's Simple, my man? Can you tell, cousin?

Evans. Peace, I pray you. Now let us understand. There is three umpires in this matter, ● as I understand; that is, Master Page, fidelicet Master Page; and there is myself, fidelicet my-

91 *fallow.* Fawn-coloured.

92 *Cotsall.* The Cotswold Hills in Gloucestershire, a great coursing centre.

95 *fault.* Misfortune.

James Quin (1693–1766) as Falstaff

123 *Pauca verba.* Few words. *worts.* Evans means 'words'; Falstaff understands 'plants'.

130 *Banbury cheese.* Banbury cheese was very thin.

134 *Slice.* i.e. as one would a cheese.

140 *fidelicet.* i.e. for videlicet, namely.

158 *seven groats in mill-sixpences.* The groat was worth fourpence; the mill-sixpence had milled edges.

159 *Edward shovel-boards.* Shillings dating from the reign of Edward VI and used in the game of shovel-board.

Playing shovelboard. From *Le centre de l'amour c.* 1600

164 *mountain-foreigner.* Abusive term for Welshman.

165 *latten bilbo.* Sword made of mixed metal.

166 *labras.* Lips.

170 *'marry trap'.* A term of abuse.

171 *run the nuthook's humour on me.* Threaten me with a constable.

177 *Scarlet and John.* Will Scarlet and Little John, companions of Robin Hood. The allusion is to Bardolph's red complexion.

183 *fap.* Drunk.

184 *conclusions passed the careires.* i.e. matters got out of hand.

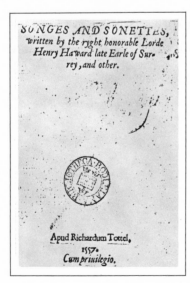

Title page of Richard Tottel's *Book of Songs and Sonnets,* 1577

self; and the three party is, lastly and finally, mine host of the Garter.

Page. We three, to hear it and end it between them.

Evans. Fery goot: I will make a prief of it in my note-book; and we will afterwards ork upon the cause with as great discreetly as we can.

Fal. Pistol!

Pist. He hears with ears.   150

Evans. The tevil and his tam! what phrase is this, 'He hears with ear'? why, it is affectations.

Fal. Pistol, did you pick Master Slender's purse?

Slen. Ay, by these gloves, did he, or I would I might never come in mine own great chamber again else, of seven groats in mill-sixpences, and two Edward shovel-boards, that cost me two shilling and two pence a-piece of Yead Miller, by these gloves.   161

Fal. Is this true, Pistol?

Evans. No; it is false, if it is a pick-purse.

Pist. Ha, thou mountain-foreigner! Sir John and master mine,

I combat challenge of this latten bilbo.

Word of denial in thy labras here!

Word of denial: froth and scum, thou liest!

Slen. By these gloves, then, 'twas he.

Nym. Be avised, sir, and pass good humours: I will say 'marry trap' with you, if you run the nuthook's humour on me; that is the very note of it.

Slen. By this hat, then, he in the red face had it; for though I cannot remember what I did when you made me drunk, yet I am not altogether an ass.

Fal. What say you, Scarlet and John?

Bard. Why, sir, for my part, I say the gentleman had drunk himself out of his five sentences.   180

Evans. It is his five senses: fie, what the ignorance is!

Bard. And being fap, sir, was, as they say, cashiered; and so conclusions passed the careires.

Slen. Ay, you spake in Latin then too; but 'tis no matter: I'll ne'er be drunk whilst I live again, but in honest, civil, godly company, for this trick: if I be drunk, I'll be drunk with those that have the fear of God, and not with drunken knaves.   190

Evans. So Got udge me, that is a virtuous mind.

Fal. You hear all these matters denied, gentlemen; you hear it.

Enter ANNE PAGE, *with wine;* MISTRESS FORD *and* MISTRESS PAGE, *following.*

Page. Nay, daughter, carry the wine in; we'll drink within.   [*Exit Anne Page.*

Slen. O heaven! this is Mistress Anne Page.

Page. How now, Mistress Ford!

Fal. Mistress Ford, by my troth, you are very well met: by your leave, good mistress.   200
                              [*Kisses her.*

Page. Wife, bid these gentlemen welcome. Come, we have a hot venison pasty to dinner: come, gentlemen, I hope we shall drink down all unkindness.

                    [*Exeunt all except Shal., Slen., and Evans.*

Slen. I had rather than forty shillings I had
● my Book of Songs and Sonnets here.

Enter SIMPLE.

How now, Simple! where have you been? I
must wait on myself, must I? You have not the
Book of Riddles about you, have you?

Sim. Book of Riddles! why, did you not lend
it to Alice Shortcake upon All-hallowmas last, a
fortnight afore Michaelmas?

Shal. Come, coz; come, coz; we stay for you.
A word with you, coz; marry, this, coz: there
● is, as 'twere, a tender, a kind of tender, made
afar off by Sir Hugh here. Do you understand me?

Slen. Ay, sir, you shall find me reasonable; if
it be so, I shall do that that is reason.

Shal. Nay, but understand me.

Slen. So I do, sir.   220

Evans. Give ear to his motions, Master Slender: I will description the matter to you, if you
be capacity of it.

Slen. Nay, I will do as my cousin Shallow
says: I pray you, pardon me; he's a justice of
peace in his country, simple though I stand here.

Evans. But that is not the question: the question is concerning your marriage.

Shal. Ay, there's the point, sir.

Evans. Marry, is it; the very point of it; to
Mistress Anne Page.   231

Slen. Why, if it be so, I will marry her upon
any reasonable demands.

Evans. But can you affection the 'oman? Let
us command to know that of your mouth or of
your lips; for divers philosophers hold that the
lips is parcel of the mouth. Therefore, precisely,
can you carry your good will to the maid?

Shal. Cousin Abraham Slender, can you love
her?   240

Slen. I hope, sir, I will do as it shall become
one that would do reason.

Evans. Nay, Got's lords and his ladies! you
must speak possitable, if you can carry her your
desires towards her.

Shal. That you must. Will you, upon good
dowry, marry her?

Slen. I will do a greater thing than that, upon
your request, cousin, in any reason.

Shal. Nay, conceive me, conceive me, sweet
coz: what I do is to pleasure you, coz. Can you
love the maid?

Slen. I will marry her, sir, at your request:
but if there be no great love in the beginning, yet
heaven may decrease it upon better acquaintance,
when we are married and have more occasion to
know one another; I hope, upon familiarity will
grow more contempt: but if you say, 'Marry
her,' I will marry her; that I am freely dissolved,
and dissolutely.   260

Evans. It is a fery discretion answer; save the
fall is in the ort 'dissolutely:' the ort is, according to our meaning, 'resolutely:' his meaning is
good.

Shal. Ay, I think my cousin meant well.

Slen. Ay, or else I would I might be hanged, la!

Shal. Here comes fair Mistress Anne.

Re-enter ANNE PAGE.

Would I were young for your sake, Mistress
Anne!

206 *Book of Songs and Sonnets.* The most popular
anthology of poetry first published by Richard Tottel
in 1557.

215 *tender.* Proposal.

Slender. Detail from a drawing by J. Coghlan (early
19th century)

296 *veneys.* Bouts.

307 *Sackerson.* Famous bear that performed at Paris Garden, near the Globe on the South Bank.

Slender: 'I have seen Sackerson loose twenty times'. Engraving from Charles Knight's *Pictorial Edition of the Works of Shakspere,* 1839–43

316 *By cock and pie.* A mild oath.

Slender: 'Mistress Anne, yourself shall go first.' Engraving from a painting by Robert Smirke (1752–1845)

Anne. The dinner is on the table; my father desires your worships' company.   271

Shal. I will wait on him, fair Mistress Anne.

Evans. Od's plessed will! I will not be absence at the grace. [*Exeunt Shallow and Evans.*

Anne. Will't please your worship to come in, sir?

Slen. No, I thank you, forsooth, heartily; I am very well.

Anne. The dinner attends you, sir.

Slen. I am not a-hungry, I thank you, forsooth. Go, sirrah, for all you are my man, go wait upon my cousin Shallow. [*Exit Simple.*] A justice of peace sometime may be beholding to his friend for a man. I keep but three men and a boy yet, till my mother be dead: but what though? yet I live like a poor gentleman born.

Anne. I may not go in without your worship: they will not sit till you come.

Slen. I' faith, I'll eat nothing; I thank you as much as though I did.   291

Anne. I pray you, sir, walk in.

Slen. I had rather walk here, I thank you. I bruised my shin th' other day with playing at sword and dagger with a master of fence; three veneys for a dish of stewed prunes; and, by my troth, I cannot abide the smell of hot meat since. Why do your dogs bark so? be there bears i' the town?

Anne. I think there are, sir; I heard them talked of.   301

Slen. I love the sport well; but I shall as soon quarrel at it as any man in England. You are afraid, if you see the bear loose, are you not?

Anne. Ay, indeed, sir.

Slen. That's meat and drink to me, now. I have seen Sackerson loose twenty times, and have taken him by the chain; but, I warrant you, the women have so cried and shrieked at it, that it passed: but women, indeed, cannot abide 'em; they are very ill-favoured rough things.

Re-enter PAGE.

Page. Come, gentle Master Slender, come; we stay for you.

Slen. I'll eat nothing, I thank you, sir.

Page. By cock and pie, you shall not choose, sir! come, come.

Slen. Nay, pray you, lead the way.

Page. Come on, sir.

Slen. Mistress Anne, yourself shall go first.

Anne. Not I, sir; pray you, keep on.   321

Slen. Truly, I will not go first; truly, la! I will not do you that wrong.

Anne. I pray you, sir.

Slen. I'll rather be unmannerly than troublesome. You do yourself wrong, indeed, la!
[*Exeunt.*

SCENE II.   *The same.*

Enter SIR HUGH EVANS *and* SIMPLE.

Evans. Go your ways, and ask of Doctor Caius' house which is the way: and there dwells one Mistress Quickly, which is in the manner of his nurse, or his dry nurse, or his cook, or his laundry, his washer, and his wringer.

Sim. Well, sir.

Evans. Nay, it is petter yet. Give her this letter; for it is a 'oman that altogether's acquaintance with Mistress Anne Page: and the letter is, to desire and require her to solicit your master's desires to Mistress Anne Page. I pray you, be gone: I will make an end of my dinner; there's pippins and cheese to come.   [*Exeunt.*

SCENE III.   *A room in the Garter Inn.*

Enter FALSTAFF, HOST, BARDOLPH, NYM, PISTOL, *and* ROBIN.

Fal. Mine host of the Garter!

Host. What says my bully-rook? speak scholarly and wisely.

Fal. Truly, mine host, I must turn away some of my followers.

Host. Discard, bully Hercules; cashier: let them wag; trot, trot.

Fal. I sit at ten pounds a week.

Host. Thou'rt an emperor, Cæsar, Keisar, and Pheezar. I will entertain Bardolph; he shall draw, he shall tap: said I well, bully Hector?

Fal. Do so, good mine host.

Host. I have spoke; let him follow. [*To Bard.*] Let me see thee froth and lime: I am at a word; follow.   [*Exit.*

Fal. Bardolph, follow him. A tapster is a good trade: an old cloak makes a new jerkin; a withered serving-man a fresh tapster. Go; adieu.   20

Bard. It is a life that I have desired: I will thrive.

Pist. O base Hungarian wight! wilt thou the spigot wield?   [*Exit Bardolph.*

Nym. He was gotten in drink: is not the humour conceited?

Fal. I am glad I am so acquit of this tinderbox: his thefts were too open; his filching was like an unskilful singer; he kept not time.

Nym. The good humour is to steal at a minute's rest.   31

Pist. 'Convey,' the wise it call. 'Steal!' foh! a fico for the phrase!

Fal. Well, sirs, I am almost out at heels.

Pist. Why, then, let kibes ensue.

Fal. There is no remedy; I must cony-catch; I must shift.

Pist. Young ravens must have food.

Fal. Which of you know Ford of this town?

Pist. I ken the wight: he is of substance good.   41

Fal. My honest lads, I will tell you what I am about.

Pist. Two yards, and more.

Fal. No quips now, Pistol! Indeed, I am in the waist two yards about; but I am now about no waste; I am about thrift. Briefly, I do mean to make love to Ford's wife: I spy entertainment in her; she discourses, she carves, she gives the leer of invitation: I can construe the action of her familiar style; and the hardest voice of her behaviour, to be Englished rightly, is, 'I am Sir John Falstaff's.'

Pist. He hath studied her will, and translated her will, out of honesty into English.

Set design for the Garter Inn, Stratford-upon-Avon, 1945

---

2 *bully-rook.* Brave chap.

10 *Pheezar.* Probably 'vizier'.

15 *froth and lime.* i.e. serve ale with a large head of foam and wine adulterated with lime to make it sparkle.

23 *Hungarian wight.* Beggarly fellow.

33 *fico.* Fig.

35 *kibes.* Chilblains.

51 *hardest voice.* Most severe interpretation.

60 *angels*. Elizabethan coins bearing the figure of the angel Michael and worth ten shillings each.

68 *œillades*. Amorous glances.

76 *Guiana*. A reference to Sir Walter Ralegh's expedition of 1595.

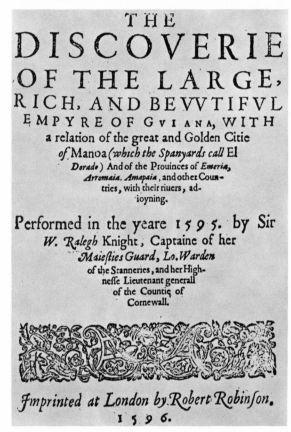

THE
DISCOVERIE
OF THE LARGE,
RICH, AND BEVVTIFVL
EMPYRE OF GVIANA, WITH
a relation of the great and Golden Citie
of Manoa *(which the Spanyards call* El
Dorado*)* And of the Prouinces of *Emeria,*
Arromaia. Amapaia, and other Coun-
tries, with their riuers, ad-
ioyning.

Performed in the yeare 1595. by Sir
W. *Ralegh* Knight, Captaine of her
Maiefties Guard, Lo. Warden
of the Stanneries, and her High-
neffe Lieutenant generall
of the Countie of
Cornewall.

Imprinted at London by Robert Robinfon.
1596.

Title page of Sir Walter Ralegh's narrative, *The Dis-coverie . . . of Guiana*, 1596

77 *cheater*. Escheators, offices of the Exchequer who dealt with lands due to the Crown.

83 *Pandarus*. Cressida's uncle, who acted as a go-between in the wooing of Cressida by Troilus.

89 *pinnace*. Small, fast-sailing ship.

94 *gourd and fullam*. Types of false dice.

96 *Tester*. Elizabethan sixpence.

101 *welkin*. Sky.

Nym. The anchor is deep: will that humour pass?

Fal. Now, the report goes she has all the rule of her husband's purse: he hath a legion of angels.   60

Pist. As many devils entertain; and 'To her, boy,' say I.

Nym. The humour rises; it is good: humour me the angels.

Fal. I have writ me here a letter to her: and here another to Page's wife, who even now gave me good eyes too, examined my parts with most judicious œillades; sometimes the beam of her view gilded my foot, sometimes my portly belly.

Pist. Then did the sun on dunghill shine. 70

Nym. I thank thee for that humour.

Fal. O, she did so course o'er my exteriors with such a greedy intention, that the appetite of her eye did seem to scorch me up like a burning-glass! Here's another letter to her: she bears the purse too; she is a region in Guiana, all gold and bounty. I will be cheater to them both, and they shall be exchequers to me; they shall be my East and West Indies, and I will trade to them both. Go bear thou this letter to Mistress Page; and thou this to Mistress Ford: we will thrive, lads, we will thrive.

Pist. Shall I Sir Pandarus of Troy become,
And by my side wear steel? then, Lucifer take all!

Nym. I will run no base humour: here, take the humour-letter: I will keep the haviour of reputation.

Fal. [*To Robin*] Hold, sirrah, bear you these letters tightly;
Sail like my pinnace to these golden shores.
Rogues, hence, avaunt! vanish like hailstones, go;
Trudge, plod away o' the hoof; seek shelter, pack!
Falstaff will learn the humour of the age,
French thrift, you rogues; myself and skirted page.
                         [*Exeunt Falstaff and Robin.*

Pist. Let vultures gripe thy guts! for gourd
         and fullam holds,
And high and low beguiles the rich and poor:
Tester I'll have in pouch when thou shalt lack,
Base Phrygian Turk!

Nym. I have operations which be humours of revenge.

Pist. Wilt thou revenge?   100

Nym. By welkin and her star!

Pist. With wit or steel?

Nym. With both the humours, I:
I will discuss the humour of this love to Page.

Pist. And I to Ford shall eke unfold
         How Falstaff, varlet vile,
      His dove will prove, his gold will hold,
         And his soft couch defile.

Nym. My humour shall not cool: I will incense Page to deal with poison; I will possess him with yellowness, for the † revolt of mine is dangerous: that is my true humour.

Pist. Thou art the Mars of malecontents: I second thee; troop on.   [*Exeunt.*

SCENE IV. *A room in* DOCTOR CAIUS'S *house.*

Enter MISTRESS QUICKLY, SIMPLE, *and* RUGBY.

Quick. What, John Rugby! I pray thee, go to the casement, and see if you can see my master, Master Doctor Caius, coming. If he do, i' faith, and find any body in the house, here will be an old abusing of God's patience and the king's English.

Rug. I'll go watch.

Quick. Go; and we'll have a posset for't soon
● at night, in faith, at the latter end of a sea-coal fire. [*Exit Rugby.*]   An honest, willing, kind fellow, as ever servant shall come in house with-
● al, and, I warrant you, no tell-tale nor no breed-bate: his worst fault is, that he is given to prayer; he is something peevish that way: but nobody but has his fault; but let that pass. Peter Simple, you say your name is?

Sim. Ay, for fault of a better.

Quick. And Master Slender's your master?

Sim. Ay, forsooth.

Quick. Does he not wear a great round beard, like a glover's paring-knife?   21

Sim. No, forsooth: he hath but a little wee
● face, with a little yellow beard, a Cain-coloured beard.

Quick. A softly-sprighted man, is he not?

Sim. Ay, forsooth: but he is as tall a man of his hands as any is between this and his head;
● he hath fought with a warrener.

Quick. How say you? O, I should remember him: does he not hold up his head, as it were, and strut in his gait?   31

Sim. Yes, indeed, does he.

Quick. Well, heaven send Anne Page no worse fortune! Tell Master Parson Evans I will do what I can for your master: Anne is a good girl, and I wish—

Re-enter RUGBY.

Rug. Out, alas! here comes my master.
● *Quick.* We shall all be shent. Run in here, good young man; go into this closet: he will not stay long. [*Shuts Simple in the closet.*] What, John Rugby! John! what, John, I say! Go, John, go inquire for my master; I doubt he be not well, that he comes not home.   43

[*Singing*] And down, down, adown-a, &c.

Enter DOCTOR CAIUS.

Caius. Vat is you sing? I do not like des toys. Pray you, go and vetch me in my closet un boitier vert, a box, a green-a box: do intend vat I speak? a green-a box.

Quick. Ay, forsooth; I'll fetch it you. [*Aside*] I am glad he went not in himself: if he had
● found the young man, he would have been horn-mad.   52
● *Caius.* Fe, fe, fe, fe! ma foi, il fait fort chaud. Je m'en vais a la cour—la grande affaire.

Quick. Is it this, sir?
● *Caius.* Oui; mette le au mon pocket: depeche, quickly. Vere is dat knave Rugby?

Quick. What, John Rugby! John!

Rug. Here, sir!

Caius. You are John Rugby, and you are Jack Rugby. Come, take-a your rapier, and come after my heel to the court.   62

Rug. 'Tis ready, sir, here in the porch.

Caius. By my trot, I tarry too long. Od's
● me! Qu'ai-j'oublie! dere is some simples in my closet, dat I vill not for the varld I shall leave behind.

9 *sea-coal.* Coal brought by sea from Newcastle.

12-13 *breed-bate.* Trouble maker.

Eliza Winstanley, the Victorian actress, as Mistress Quickly. From J. O. Halliwell's *The Complete Works of Shakspere*, 1853

23 *Cain-coloured.* Reddish-yellow, traditionally the colour of Cain's hair.

28 *warrener.* Gamekeeper.

38 *shent.* Scolded.

51-52 *horn-mad.* Enraged like a horned animal about to charge.

53-54 *ma foi . . . la grande affaire.* On my word, it is very hot. I am going to the court—important business.

56 *mette la au mon pocket.* Put it in my pocket.

65 *Qu'ai-j'oublie!* What have I forgotten. *simples.* Medicinal herbs.

71 *larron.* Thief.

Dr Caius, Mistress Quickly and Simple. Engraving from Bell's edition of *Shakespeare,* 1774

92 *baille.* Fetch.

123 *Jack.* Rascal.

129 *what, the good-jer.* i.e. what the devil.

Quick. Ay me, he'll find the young man there, and be mad!

Caius. O diable, diable! vat is in my closet? Villain! larron! [*Pulling Simple out.*] Rugby, my rapier!   72

Quick. Good master, be content.

Caius. Wherefore shall I be content-a?

Quick. The young man is an honest man.

Caius. What shall de honest man do in my closet? dere is no honest man dat shall come in my closet.

Quick. I beseech you, be not so phlegmatic. Hear the truth of it: he came of an errand to me from Parson Hugh.   81

Caius. Vell.

Sim. Ay, forsooth; to desire her to—

Quick. Peace, I pray you.

Caius. Peace-a your tongue. Speak-a your tale.

Sim. To desire this honest gentlewoman, your maid, to speak a good word to Mistress Anne Page for my master in the way of marriage.

Quick. This is all, indeed, la! but I'll ne'er put my finger in the fire, and need not.   91

Caius. Sir Hugh send-a you? Rugby, baille me some paper. Tarry you a little-a while.

[*Writes.*

Quick. [*Aside to Simple*] I am glad he is so quiet: if he had been throughly moved, you should have heard him so loud and so melancholy. But notwithstanding, man, I'll do you your master what good I can: and the very yea and the no is, the French doctor, my master,—I may call him my master, look you, for I keep his house; and I wash, wring, brew, bake, scour, dress meat and drink, make the beds, and do all myself,—

Sim. [*Aside to Quickly*] 'Tis a great charge to come under one body's hand.

Quick. [*Aside to Simple*] Are you avised o' that? you shall find it a great charge: and to be up early and down late; but notwithstanding,—to tell you in your ear; I would have no words of it,—my master himself is in love with Mistress Anne Page: but notwithstanding that, I know Anne's mind,—that's neither here nor there.

Caius. You jack'nape, give-a this letter to Sir Hugh; by gar, it is a shallenge: I will cut his troat in de park; and I will teach a scurvy jack-a-nape priest to meddle or make. You may be gone; it is not good you tarry here. By gar, I will cut all his two stones; by gar, he shall not have a stone to throw at his dog. [*Exit Simple.*

Quick. Alas, he speaks but for his friend. 120

Caius. It is no matter-a ver dat: do not you tell-a me dat I shall have Anne Page for myself? By gar, I vill kill de Jack priest; and I have appointed mine host of de Jarteer to measure our weapon. By gar, I will myself have Anne Page.

Quick. Sir, the maid loves you, and all shall be well. We must give folks leave to prate: what, the good-jer!

Caius. Rugby, come to the court with me. By gar, if I have not Anne Page, I shall turn your head out of my door. Follow my heels, Rugby.   [*Exeunt Caius and Rugby.*

Quick. You shall have An fool's-head of your own. No, I know Anne's mind for that: never a woman in Windsor knows more of Anne's mind than I do; nor can do more than I do with her, I thank heaven.

Fent. [*Within*] Who's within there? ho!

● *Quick.* Who's there, I trow! Come near the house, I pray you.   141

Enter FENTON.

Fent. How now, good woman! how dost thou?

Quick. The better that it pleases your good worship to ask.

Fent. What news? how does pretty Mistress Anne?

Quick. In truth, sir, and she is pretty, and honest, and gentle; and one that is your friend, I can tell you that by the way; I praise heaven for it.   151

Fent. Shall I do any good, thinkest thou? shall I not lose my suit?

Quick. Troth, sir, all is in his hands above: but notwithstanding, Master Fenton, I'll be sworn on a book, she loves you. Have not your worship a wart above your eye?

Fent. Yes, marry, have I; what of that?

● *Quick.* Well, thereby hangs a tale: good faith, it is such another Nan; but, I detest, an honest maid as ever broke bread: we had an hour's talk of that wart. I shall never laugh but in that maid's company! But indeed she is
● given too much to allicholy and musing: but for you—well, go to.

Fent. Well, I shall see her to-day. Hold, there's money for thee; let me have thy voice in my behalf: if thou seest her before me, commend me.

Quick. Will I? i' faith, that we will; and I will tell your worship more of the wart the next time we have confidence; and of other wooers.

Fent. Well, farewell; I am in great haste now.

Quick. Farewell to your worship. [*Exit Fenton.*] Truly, an honest gentleman: but Anne loves him not; for I know Anne's mind as well as another does. Out upon't! what have I forgot?   [*Exit.* 180

ACT II.

SCENE I. *Before* PAGE'S *house*.

Enter MISTRESS PAGE, *with a letter*.

Mrs Page. What, have I scaped love-letters in the holiday-time of my beauty, and am I now a subject for them? Let me see.   [*Reads.*

'Ask me no reason why I love you; for though Love use Reason for his physician, he admits him not for his counsellor. You are not young, no more am I; go to then, there's sympathy: you are merry, so am I; ha, ha! then there's
● more sympathy: you love sack, and so do I; would you desire better sympathy? Let it suffice thee, Mistress Page,—at the least, if the love of soldier can suffice,—that I love thee. I will not say, pity me; 'tis not a soldier-like phrase: but I say, love me. By me,

> Thine own true knight,
> By day or night,

140 *trow.* Wonder.

160 *it is such another Nan.* i.e. it is such a remarkable Nan. *detest.* i.e. protest.

164 *allicholy.* i.e. for melancholy.

9 *sack.* Wine from Spain or the Canaries.

Fanny Elizabeth Fitzwilliam, the Victorian actress, as Mistress Page. From J. O. Halliwell's *The Complete Works of Shakspere*, 1853

20 *Herod of Jewry*. In the miracle plays Herod was played as an outright villain.

23-24 *Flemish drunkard*. Regarded as the most drunken in Europe.

52 *hack*. Behave promiscuously.

53 *article of thy gentry*. Character of your rank.

Mistress Page: 'Letter for letter . . .' Engraving from a painting by Rev. M. W. Peters (*d*.1814)

81-82 *Mount Pelion*. In classical mythology the Titans, when they rebelled against the gods, placed Mount Pelion on Mount Ossa in their effort to reach Mount Olympus.

83 *turtles*. Turtledoves.

Or any kind of light,
With all his might
For thee to fight,   JOHN FALSTAFF.'
● What a Herod of Jewry is this! O wicked, wicked world! One that is well-nigh worn to pieces with age to show himself a young gallant!
● What an unweighed behaviour hath this Flemish drunkard picked—with the devil's name!—out of my conversation, that he dares in this manner assay me? Why, he hath not been thrice in my company! What should I say to him? I was then frugal of my mirth: Heaven forgive me! Why, I'll exhibit a bill in the parliament for the putting down of men. How shall I be revenged on him? for revenged I will be, as sure as his guts are made of puddings.

Enter MISTRESS FORD.

Mrs Ford. Mistress Page! trust me, I was going to your house.
Mrs Page. And, trust me, I was coming to you. You look very ill.
Mrs Ford. Nay, I'll ne'er believe that; I have to show to the contrary.
Mrs Page. Faith, but you do, in my mind.
Mrs Ford. Well, I do then; yet I say I could show you to the contrary. O Mistress Page, give me some counsel!
Mrs Page. What's the matter, woman?
Mrs Ford. O woman, if it were not for one trifling respect, I could come to such honour!
Mrs Page. Hang the trifle, woman! take the honour. What is it? dispense with trifles; what is it?
Mrs Ford. If I would but go to hell for an eternal moment or so, I could be knighted.   50
Mrs Page. What? thou liest! Sir Alice Ford!
● These knights will hack; and so thou shouldst
● not alter the article of thy gentry.
Mrs Ford. We burn daylight: here, read, read; perceive how I might be knighted. I shall think the worse of fat men, as long as I have an eye to make difference of men's liking: and yet he would not swear; praised women's modesty; and gave such orderly and well-behaved reproof to all uncomeliness, that I would have sworn his disposition would have gone to the truth of his words; but they do no more adhere and keep place together than the Hundredth Psalm to the tune of 'Green Sleeves.' What tempest, I trow, threw this whale, with so many tuns of oil in his belly, ashore at Windsor? How shall I be revenged on him? I think the best way were to entertain him with hope, till the wicked fire of lust have melted him in his own grease. Did you ever hear the like?   70
Mrs Page. Letter for letter, but that the name of Page and Ford differs! To thy great comfort in this mystery of ill opinions, here's the twin-brother of thy letter: but let thine inherit first; for, I protest, mine never shall. I warrant he hath a thousand of these letters, writ with blank space for different names,—sure, more, —and these are of the second edition: he will print them, out of doubt; for he cares not what he puts into the press, when he would put us two.
● I had rather be a giantess, and lie under Mount Pelion. Well, I will find you twenty lascivious
● turtles ere one chaste man.

Mrs Ford. Why, this is the very same; the very hand, the very words. What doth he think of us?

Mrs Page. Nay, I know not: it makes me almost ready to wrangle with mine own honesty. I'll entertain myself like one that I am not acquainted withal; for, sure, unless he know some strain in me, that I know not myself, he would never have boarded me in this fury.

Mrs Ford. 'Boarding,' call you it? I'll be sure to keep him above deck.

Mrs Page. So will I: if he come under my hatches, I'll never to sea again. Let's be revenged on him: let's appoint him a meeting; give him a show of comfort in his suit and lead him on with a fine-baited delay, till he hath pawned his horses to mine host of the Garter. 100

Mrs Ford. Nay, I will consent to act any villany against him, that may not sully the chariness of our honesty. O, that my husband saw this letter! it would give eternal food to his jealousy.

Mrs Page. Why, look where he comes; and my good man too: he's as far from jealousy as I am from giving him cause; and that I hope is an unmeasurable distance.

Mrs Ford. You are the happier woman. 110

Mrs Page. Let's consult together against this greasy knight. Come hither. [*They retire.*

Enter FORD *with* PISTOL, *and* PAGE *with* NYM.

Ford. Well, I hope it be not so.

Pist. Hope is a curtal dog in some affairs:
Sir John affects thy wife.

Ford. Why, sir, my wife is not young.

Pist. He wooes both high and low, both rich and poor,
Both young and old, one with another, Ford;
He loves the gallimaufry: Ford, perpend.

Ford. Love my wife! 120

Pist. With liver burning hot. Prevent, or go thou,
Like Sir Actæon he, with Ringwood at thy heels:
O, odious is the name!

Ford. What name, sir?

Pist. The horn, I say. Farewell.
Take heed, have open eye, for thieves do foot by night:
Take heed, ere summer comes or cuckoo-birds do sing.
Away, Sir Corporal Nym!
Believe it, Page; he speaks sense. [*Exit.*

Ford. [*Aside*] I will be patient; I will find out this. 131

Nym. [*To Page*] And this is true; I like not the humour of lying. He hath wronged me in some humours: I should have borne the humoured letter to her; but I have a sword and it shall bite upon my necessity. He loves your wife; there's the short and the long. My name is Corporal Nym; I speak and I avouch; 'tis true: my name is Nym and Falstaff loves your wife. Adieu. I love not the humour of bread and cheese, and there's the humour of it. Adieu. [*Exit.* 141

Page. 'The humour of it,' quoth a'! here's a fellow frights English out of his wits.

Ford. I will seek out Falstaff.

Page. I never heard such a drawling, affecting rogue.

92 *boarded me in this fury.* i.e. made advances to me in this impetuous fashion.

114 *curtal.* Dock-tailed; therefore unreliable.

119 *gallimaufry.* Variety, mixture. *perpend.* Think on it.

122 *Actæon.* In classical mythology, the hunter who was turned into a stag after seeing Diana bathing and was torn to pieces by his own hounds. *Ringwood.* Traditional name for a hound.

Death of Actaeon. Detail from a painting by Titian (d.1576)

148 *Cataian.* Sharper (like a native of Cathay).

An inhabitant of China (Cathay). From John Speed's
A Prospect of the Most Famous Parts of the World, 1631

201 *Cavaleiro-justice.* Gallant justice.

Ford.   If I do find it: well.

Page.   I will not believe such a Cataian, though
the priest o' the town commended him for a true
man.   150

Ford.   'Twas a good sensible fellow: well.

Page.   How now, Meg!
        [*Mrs Page and Mrs Ford come forward.*

Mrs Page.   Whither go you, George? Hark
you.

Mrs Ford.   How now, sweet Frank! why art
thou melancholy?

Ford.   I melancholy! I am not melancholy.
Get you home, go.

Mrs Ford.   Faith, thou hast some crotchets in
thy head.   Now, will you go, Mistress Page?

Mrs Page.   Have with you.   You'll come to
dinner, George. [*Aside to Mrs Ford*] Look who
comes yonder: she shall be our messenger to this
paltry knight.

Mrs Ford. [*Aside to Mrs Page*] Trust me, I
thought on her: she'll fit it.

Enter MISTRESS QUICKLY.

Mrs Page.   You are come to see my daughter
Anne?

Quick.   Ay, forsooth; and, I pray, how does
good Mistress Anne?   170

Mrs Page.   Go in with us and see: we have an
hour's talk with you.
        [*Exeunt Mrs Page, Mrs Ford, and
                                Mrs Quickly.*

Page.   How now, Master Ford!

Ford.   You heard what this knave told me,
did you not?

Page.   Yes: and you heard what the other
told me?

Ford.   Do you think there is truth in them?

Page.   Hang 'em, slaves! I do not think the
knight would offer it: but these that accuse him
in his intent towards our wives are a yoke of
his discarded men; very rogues, now they be out
of service.

Ford.   Were they his men?

Page.   Marry, were they.

Ford.   I like it never the better for that. Does
he lie at the Garter?

Page.   Ay, marry, does he. If he should intend this voyage towards my wife, I would turn
her loose to him; and what he gets more of her
than sharp words, let it lie on my head.   191

Ford.   I do not misdoubt my wife; but I would
be loath to turn them together. A man may be
too confident: I would have nothing lie on my
head: I cannot be thus satisfied.

Page.   Look where my ranting host of the
Garter comes: there is either liquor in his pate or
money in his purse when he looks so merrily.

Enter HOST.

How now, mine host!

Host.   How now, bully-rook! thou'rt a gentleman.   Cavaleiro-justice, I say!   201

Enter SHALLOW.

Shal.   I follow, mine host, I follow. Good
even and twenty, good Master Page! Master
Page, will you go with us? we have sport in
hand.

Host. Tell him, cavaleiro-justice; tell him, bully-rook.

Shal. Sir, there is a fray to be fought between Sir Hugh the Welsh priest and Caius the French doctor.   210

Ford. Good mine host o' the Garter, a word with you.   [*Drawing him aside.*

Host. What sayest thou, my bully-rook?

Shal. [*To Page*] Will you go with us to behold it? My merry host hath had the measuring of their weapons; and, I think, hath appointed them contrary places; for, believe me, I hear the parson is no jester. Hark, I will tell you what our sport shall be.   [*They converse apart.*

Host. Hast thou no suit against my knight, my guest-cavaleire?   221

Ford. None, I protest: but I'll give you a pottle of burnt sack to give me recourse to him and tell him my name is Brook; only for a jest.

Host. My hand, bully; thou shalt have egress and regress;—said I well?—and thy name shall be Brook. It is a merry knight. Will you go, †An-heires?

Shal. Have with you, mine host.

Page. I have heard the Frenchman hath good skill in his rapier.   231

Shal. Tut, sir, I could have told you more. In these times you stand on distance, your passes, stoccadoes, and I know not what: 'tis the heart, Master Page; 'tis here, 'tis here. I have seen the time, with my long sword I would have made you four tall fellows skip like rats.

Host. Here, boys, here, here! shall we wag?

Page. Have with you. I had rather hear them scold than fight.   240

[*Exeunt Host, Shal., and Page.*

Ford. Though Page be a secure fool, and stands so firmly on his wife's frailty, yet I cannot put off my opinion so easily: she was in his company at Page's house; and what they made there, I know not. Well, I will look further into't: and I have a disguise to sound Falstaff. If I find her honest, I lose not my labour; if she be otherwise, 'tis labour well bestowed.   [*Exit.*

SCENE II. *A room in the Garter Inn.*

Enter FALSTAFF *and* PISTOL.

Fal. I will not lend thee a penny.

Pist. Why, then the world's mine oyster, Which I with sword will open.

Fal. Not a penny. I have been content, sir, you should lay my countenance to pawn: I have grated upon my good friends for three reprieves for you and your coach-fellow Nym; or else you had looked through the grate, like a geminy of baboons. I am damned in hell for swearing to gentlemen my friends, you were good soldiers and tall fellows; and when Mistress Bridget lost the handle of her fan, I took't upon mine honour thou hadst it not.

Pist. Didst not thou share? hadst thou not fifteen pence?

Fal. Reason, you rogue, reason: thinkest thou I'll endanger my soul gratis? At a word, hang no more about me, I am no gibbet for you. Go. A short knife and a throng! To your manor of Pickt-hatch! Go. You'll not bear a letter for me, you rogue! you stand upon your

223 *pottle of burnt sack.* Two quart tankard of mulled wine.

224 *Brook.* See introduction.

228 *An-heires.* Probably Dutch *mynheers* (masters).

234 *stoccadoes.* Thrusts.

236 *long sword.* A heavy weapon no longer fashionable in 1600.

The long sword at the time of Henry VIII. Illustration from Egerton Castle's *Schools and Masters of Fence,* 1885

8 *geminy.* Pair.

18 *short knife and a throng.* i.e. be a cut purse, operating with a short knife in a crowd.

19 *manor of Pickt-hatch.* A disreputable area of London.

27 *cat-a-mountain*. Wild cat.

28 *red-lattice*. Ale-house; many alehouses had red-latticed windows.

'Enter MISTRESS QUICKLY.' Illustration by Joseph Fletcher, 1916

61 *canaries*. i.e. for quandary.

79 *pensioners*. Gentlemen of the royal bodyguard.

honour   Why, thou unconfinable baseness, it is as much as I can do to keep the terms of my honour precise: I, I, I myself sometimes, leaving the fear of God on the left hand and hiding mine honour in my necessity, am fain to shuffle, to hedge and to lurch; and yet you, rogue, will
● ensconce your rags, your cat-a-mountain looks,
● your red-lattice phrases, and your bold-beating oaths, under the shelter of your honour! You will not do it, you!   30
   Pist.   I do relent: what would thou more of man?

        Enter ROBIN.
   Rob.   Sir, here's a woman would speak with you.
   Fal.   Let her approach.

    Enter MISTRESS QUICKLY.
   Quick.   Give your worship good morrow.
   Fal.   Good morrow, good wife.
   Quick.   Not so, an't please your worship.
   Fal.   Good maid, then.
   Quick.   I'll be sworn,
As my mother was, the first hour I was born.
   Fal.   I do believe the swearer.   What with me?
   Quick.   Shall I vouchsafe your worship a word or two?
   Fal.   Two thousand, fair woman: and I'll vouchsafe thee the hearing.
   Quick.   There is one Mistress Ford, sir:—I pray, come a little nearer this ways:—I myself dwell with Master Doctor Caius,—
   Fal.   Well, on: Mistress Ford, you say,—
   Quick.   Your worship says very true: I pray your worship, come a little nearer this ways.   50
   Fal.   I warrant thee, nobody hears; mine own people, mine own people.
   Quick.   Are they so?   God bless them and make them his servants!
   Fal.   Well, Mistress Ford; what of her?
   Quick.   Why, sir, she's a good creature.   Lord, Lord! your worship's a wanton!   Well, heaven forgive you and all of us, I pray!
   Fal.   Mistress Ford; come, Mistress Ford,—
   Quick.   Marry, this is the short and the long
● of it; you have brought her into such a canaries as 'tis wonderful.   The best courtier of them all, when the court lay at Windsor, could never have brought her to such a canary.   Yet there has been knights, and lords, and gentlemen, with their coaches, I warrant you, coach after coach, letter after letter, gift after gift; smelling so sweetly, all musk, and so rushling, I warrant you, in silk and gold; and in such alligant terms; and in such wine and sugar of the best and the fairest, that would have won any woman's heart; and, I warrant you, they could never get an eye-wink of her: I had myself twenty angels given me this morning; but I defy all angels, in any such sort, as they say, but in the way of honesty: and, I warrant you, they could never get her so much as sip on a cup with the proudest of them all: and yet there has been earls, nay, which is more,
● pensioners; but, I warrant you, all is one with her.   80
   Fal.   But what says she to me? be brief, my good she-Mercury.
   Quick.   Marry, she hath received your letter, for the which she thanks you a thousand times;

and she gives you to notify that her husband will be absence from his house between ten and eleven.

Fal. Ten and eleven?

Quick. Ay, forsooth; and then you may come and see the picture, she says, that you wot of: Master Ford, her husband, will be from home. Alas! the sweet woman leads an ill life with him: he's a very jealousy man: she leads a very
• frampold life with him, good heart.

Fal. Ten and eleven. Woman, commend me to her; I will not fail her.

Quick. Why, you say well. But I have another messenger to your worship. Mistress Page hath her hearty commendations to you too: and let me tell you in your ear, she's as fartuous a civil modest wife, and one, I tell you, that will not miss you morning nor evening prayer, as any is in Windsor, whoe'er be the other: and she bade me tell your worship that her husband is seldom from home; but she hopes there will come a time. I never knew a woman so dote upon a man: surely I think you have charms, la; yes, in truth.

Fal. Not I, I assure thee: setting the attraction of my good parts aside I have no other charms.   111

Quick. Blessing on your heart for't!

Fal. But, I pray thee, tell me this: has Ford's wife and Page's wife acquainted each other how they love me?

Quick. That were a jest indeed! they have not so little grace, I hope: that were a trick indeed! But Mistress Page would desire you to send her your little page, of all loves: her husband has a marvellous infection to the little page; and truly Master Page is an honest man. Never a wife in Windsor leads a better life than she does: do what she will, say what she will, take all, pay
• all, go to bed when she list, rise when she list, all is as she will: and truly she deserves it; for if there be a kind woman in Windsor, she is one. You must send her your page; no remedy.

Fal. Why, I will.

Quick. Nay, but do so, then: and, look you, he may come and go between you both; and in
• any case have a nay-word, that you may know one another's mind, and the boy never need to understand any thing; for 'tis not good that children should know any wickedness: old folks, you know, have discretion, as they say, and know the world.

Fal. Fare thee well: commend me to them both: there's my purse; I am yet thy debtor. Boy, go along with this woman. [*Exeunt Mistress Quickly and Robin.*] This news distracts me!
• *Pist.* This punk is one of Cupid's carriers: Clap on more sails; pursue; up with your fights: Give fire: she is my prize, or ocean whelm them all!   [*Exit.*

Fal. Sayest thou so, old Jack? go thy ways; I'll make more of thy old body than I have done. Will they yet look after thee? Wilt thou, after the expense of so much money, be now a gainer? Good body, I thank thee. Let them say 'tis grossly done; so it be fairly done, no matter.

Enter BARDOLPH.

Bard. Sir John, there's one Master Brook

94 *frampold.* Disagreeable.

124 *list.* Please.

131 *nay-word.* Watchword.

141 *punk.* Strumpet.

H. Beerbohm Tree who played Falstaff in both *The Merry Wives of Windsor* (1889–1902) and *Henry IV Part I* (1896)

Falstaff in the Garter Inn. Detail from a painting by
C. R. Leslie (1794–1859)

211 *meed*. Reward.

below would fain speak with you, and be acquainted with you; and hath sent your worship
a morning's draught of sack.

Fal. Brook is his name?

Bard. Ay, sir.

Fal. Call him in. [*Exit Bardolph.*] Such
Brooks are welcome to me, that o'erflow such
liquor. Ah, ha! Mistress Ford and Mistress
Page, have I encompassed you? go to; via!

Re-enter BARDOLPH, *with* FORD *disguised.*

Ford. Bless you, sir!   160

Fal. And you, sir! Would you speak with me?

Ford. I make bold to press with so little preparation upon you.

Fal. You're welcome. What's your will?
Give us leave, drawer.   [*Exit Bardolph.*

Ford. Sir, I am a gentleman that have spent
much; my name is Brook.

Fal. Good Master Brook, I desire more acquaintance of you.

Ford. Good Sir John, I sue for yours: not to
charge you; for I must let you understand I
think myself in better plight for a lender than
you are: the which hath something emboldened
me to this unseasoned intrusion; for they say, if
money go before, all ways do lie open.

Fal. Money is a good soldier, sir, and will on.

Ford. Troth, and I have a bag of money here
troubles me: if you will help to bear it, Sir John,
take all, or half, for easing me of the carriage.

Fal. Sir, I know not how I may deserve to be
your porter.   181

Ford. I will tell you, sir, if you will give me
the hearing.

Fal. Speak, good Master Brook: I shall be
glad to be your servant.

Ford. Sir, I hear you are a scholar.—I will
be brief with you,—and you have been a man
long known to me, though I had never so good
means, as desire, to make myself acquainted with
you. I shall discover a thing to you, wherein I
must very much lay open mine own imperfection:
but, good Sir John, as you have one eye upon my
follies, as you hear them unfolded, turn another
into the register of your own; that I may pass
with a reproof the easier, sith you yourself know
how easy it is to be such an offender.

Fal. Very well, sir; proceed.

Ford. There is a gentlewoman in this town;
her husband's name is Ford.

Fal. Well, sir.   200

Ford. I have long loved her, and, I protest
to you, bestowed much on her; followed her
with a doting observance; engrossed opportunities to meet her; fee'd every slight occasion that
could but niggardly give me sight of her; not
only bought many presents to give her, but have
given largely to many to know what she would
have given; briefly, I have pursued her as love
hath pursued me; which hath been on the wing
of all occasions. But whatsoever I have merited,
either in my mind or in my means, meed, I am
sure, I have received none; unless experience be
a jewel that I have purchased at an infinite rate,
and that hath taught me to say this:

'Love like a shadow flies when substance love
          pursues;
Pursuing that that flies, and flying what pursues.'

Fal. Have you received no promise of satisfaction at her hands?

Ford. Never.

Fal. Have you importuned her to such a purpose?   221

Ford. Never.

Fal. Of what quality was your love, then?

Ford. Like a fair house built on another man's ground; so that I have lost my edifice by mistaking the place where I erected it.

Fal. To what purpose have you unfolded this to me?

Ford. When I have told you that, I have told you all. Some say, that though she appear honest to me, yet in other places she enlargeth her mirth so far that there is shrewd construction made of her. Now, Sir John, here is the heart of my purpose: you are a gentleman of excellent breeding, admirable discourse, of great admittance, authentic in your place and person, generally allowed for your many war-like, court-like, and learned preparations.

Fal. O, sir!

Ford. Believe it, for you know it. There is money; spend it, spend it; spend more; spend all I have; only give me so much of your time in exchange of it, as to lay an amiable siege to the honesty of this Ford's wife: use your art of wooing; win her to consent to you: if any man may, you may as soon as any.

Fal. Would it apply well to the vehemency of your affection, that I should win what you would enjoy? Methinks you prescribe to yourself very preposterously.   250

Ford. O, understand my drift. She dwells so securely on the excellency of her honour, that the folly of my soul dares not present itself: she is too bright to be looked against. Now, could I come to her with any detection in my hand, my desires had instance and argument to commend themselves: I could drive her then from the ward of her purity, her reputation, her marriage-vow, and a thousand other her defences, which now are too too strongly embattled against me. What say you to't, Sir John?   261

Fal. Master Brook, I will first make bold with your money; next, give me your hand; and last, as I am a gentleman, you shall, if you will, enjoy Ford's wife.

Ford. O good sir!

Fal. I say you shall.

Ford. Want no money, Sir John; you shall want none.

Fal. Want no Mistress Ford, Master Brook; you shall want none. I shall be with her, I may tell you, by her own appointment; even as you came in to me, her assistant or go-between parted from me: I say I shall be with her between ten and eleven; for at that time the jealous rascally knave her husband will be forth. Come you to me at night; you shall know how I speed.

Ford. I am blest in your acquaintance. Do you know Ford, sir?   280

Fal. Hang him, poor cuckoldly knave! I know him not: yet I wrong him to call him poor; they say the jealous wittolly knave hath masses of money; for the which his wife seems to me well-favoured. I will use her as the key

258 *ward.* Guard.

283 *wittolly.* Cuckoldy.

290 *mechanical salt-butter.* Base cheap-living.

300 *Epicurean.* Sensual.

311 *Amaimon . . . Lucifer . . . Barbason.* Names of devils.

The horned cuckold, his unfaithful wife and the seducer. Woodcut from the *Roxburghe Ballads*, 17th century

316-318 *Fleming . . . the Welshman . . . an Irishman.* The Flemings were said to be partial to butter; the Welsh to cheese; and the Irish to strong liquor.

of the cuckoldly rogue's coffer; and there's my harvest-home.

Ford. I would you knew Ford, sir, that you might avoid him if you saw him.

Fal. Hang him, mechanical salt-butter rogue! I will stare him out of his wits; I will awe him with my cudgel: it shall hang like a meteor o'er the cuckold's horns. Master Brook, thou shalt know I will predominate over the peasant, and thou shalt lie with his wife. Come to me soon at night. Ford's a knave, and I will aggravate his style; thou, Master Brook, shalt know him for knave and cuckold. Come to me soon at night. [*Exit.*

Ford. What a damned Epicurean rascal is this! My heart is ready to crack with impatience. Who says this is improvident jealousy? my wife hath sent to him; the hour is fixed; the match is made. Would any man have thought this? See the hell of having a false woman! My bed shall be abused, my coffers ransacked, my reputation gnawn at; and I shall not only receive this villanous wrong, but stand under the adoption of abominable terms, and by him that does me this wrong. Terms! names! Amaimon sounds well; Lucifer, well; Barbason, well; yet they are devils' additions, the names of fiends: but Cuckold! Wittol!—Cuckold! the devil himself hath not such a name. Page is an ass, a secure ass: he will trust his wife; he will not be jealous. I will rather trust a Fleming with my butter, Parson Hugh the Welshman with my cheese, an Irishman with my aqua-vitæ bottle, or a thief to walk my ambling gelding, than my wife with herself: then she plots, then she ruminates, then she devises; and what they think in their hearts they may effect, they will break their hearts but they will effect. God be praised for my jealousy! Eleven o'clock the hour. I will prevent this, detect my wife, be revenged on Falstaff, and laugh at Page. I will about it; better three hours too soon than a minute too late. Fie, fie, fie! cuckold! cuckold! cuckold! [*Exit.*

SCENE III. *A field near Windsor.*

Enter CAIUS *and* RUGBY.

Caius. Jack Rugby!
Rug. Sir?
Caius. Vat is de clock, Jack?
Rug. 'Tis past the hour, sir, that Sir Hugh promised to meet.
Caius. By gar, he has save his soul, dat he is no come; he has pray his Pible well, dat he is no come: by gar, Jack Rugby, he is dead already, if he be come.
Rug. He is wise, sir; he knew your worship would kill him, if he came.   11
Caius. By gar, de herring is no dead so as I vill kill him. Take your rapier, Jack; I vill tell you how I vill kill him.
Rug. Alas, sir, I cannot fence.
Caius. Villany, take your rapier.
Rug. Forbear; here's company.

Enter HOST, SHALLOW, SLENDER, *and* PAGE.

Host. Bless thee, bully doctor!
Shal. Save you, Master Doctor Caius!

Page. Now, good master doctor!   20
Slen. Give you good morrow, sir.
Caius. Vat be all you, one, two, tree, four, come for?
• *Host.* To see thee fight, to see thee foin, to
• see thee traverse; to see thee here, to see thee
• there; to see thee pass thy punto, thy stock, thy
• reverse, thy distance, thy montant.   Is he dead,
• my Ethiopian? is he dead, my Francisco? ha,
• bully! What says my Æsculapius? my Galen?
my heart of elder? ha! is he dead, bully stale? is
he dead?   31
Caius. By gar, he is de coward Jack priest of de vorld; he is not show his face.
• *Host.* Thou art a Castalion-King-Urinal. Hector of Greece, my boy!
Caius. I pray you, bear vitness that me have stay six or seven, two, tree hours for him, and he is no come.
Shal. He is the wiser man, master doctor: he is a curer of souls, and you a curer of bodies; if you should fight, you go against the hair of your professions.   Is it not true, Master Page?
Page. Master Shallow, you have yourself been a great fighter, though now a man of peace.
Shal. Bodykins, Master Page, though I now be old and of the peace, if I see a sword out, my finger itches to make one.   Though we are justices and doctors and churchmen, Master Page, we have some salt of our youth in us; we are the sons of women, Master Page.   51
Page. 'Tis true, Master Shallow.
Shal. It will be found so, Master Page. Master Doctor Caius, I am come to fetch you home.   I am sworn of the peace: you have showed yourself a wise physician, and Sir Hugh hath shown himself a wise and patient churchman.   You must go with me, master doctor.
Host. Pardon, guest-justice.   A word, Moun-
• seur Mockwater.   60
Caius. Mock-vater! vat is dat?
Host. Mock-water, in our English tongue, is valour, bully.
Caius. By gar, den, I have as mush mock-vater as de Englishman.   Scurvy jack-dog priest! by gar, me vill cut his ears.
• *Host.* He will clapper-claw thee tightly, bully.
Caius. Clapper-de-claw! vat is dat?
Host. That is, he will make thee amends.   70
Caius. By gar, me do look he shall clapper-de-claw me; for, by gar, me vill have it.
Host. And I will provoke him to't, or let him wag.
Caius. Me tank you for dat.
Host. And, moreover, bully,—but first, master guest, and Master Page, and eke Cavaleiro Slender, go you through the town to Frogmore.
                                        [*Aside to them.*
Page. Sir Hugh is there, is he?
Host. He is there: see what humour he is in; and I will bring the doctor about by the fields. Will it do well?
Shal. We will do it.
Page, Shal., and Slen. Adieu, good master doctor.   [*Exeunt Page, Shal., and Slen.*
Caius. By gar, me vill kill de priest; for he speak for a jack-an-ape to Anne Page.

24 *foin.* Thrust.

25 *traverse.* Move from side to side.

26 *punto.* Thrust with the point of a sword. *Stock.* Thrust with the point of a dagger.

27 *montant.* Upward thrust.

28 *Francisco.* Frenchman.

29 *Æsculapius.* God of medicine. *Galen.* Ancient Greek authority on medicine, still regarded as authoritative in Shakespeare's time.

Aesculapius, the Greek god of medicine and healing. From a 19th century engraving

34 *Castalion-King-Urinal.* An insult veiled as a compliment; the Castilian king was Philip II of Spain.

60 *Mockwater.* A continuation of the 'stale-urinal' image.

67 *clapper-claw.* Maul.

90 *Frogmore.* Then a small village near Windsor.

5-6 *pittie-ward.* Towards Windsor Little Park. *park-ward.* Towards Windsor Great Park.

14 *costard.* Head (also the name of a large apple).

17-26 *To shallow rivers . . . etc.* A garbled version of Marlowe's poem 'The Passionate Shepherd to His Love'.

25 *vagram.* Confusing 'fragrant' and 'vagrant'.

Host. Let him die: sheathe thy impatience, throw cold water on thy choler: go about the fields with me through Frogmore: I will bring thee where Mistress Anne Page is, at a farm-house a-feasting; and thou shalt woo her. Cried I aim? said I well?
Caius. By gar, me dank you vor dat: by gar, I love you; and I shall procure-a you de good guest, de earl, de knight, de lords, de gentlemen, my patients.
Host. For the which I will be thy adversary toward Anne Page. Said I well?
Caius. By gar, 'tis good; vell said. 100
Host. Let us wag, then.
Caius. Come at my heels, Jack Rugby.
[*Exeunt.*

ACT III.

SCENE I. *A field near Frogmore.*

Enter SIR HUGH EVANS *and* SIMPLE.

Evans. I pray you now, good Master Slender's serving-man, and friend Simple by your name, which way have you looked for Master Caius, that calls himself doctor of physic?
Sim. Marry, sir, the pittie-ward, the park-ward, every way; old Windsor way, and every way but the town way.
Evans. I most fehemently desire you you will also look that way.
Sim. I will, sir. [*Exit.* 10
Evans. 'Pless my soul, how full of chollors I am, and trempling of mind! I shall be glad if he have deceived me. How melancholies I am! I will knog his urinals about his knave's costard when I have good opportunities for the ork. 'Pless my soul! [*Sings.*
To shallow rivers, to whose falls
Melodious birds sings madrigals;
There will we make our peds of roses,
And a thousand fragrant posies. 20
To shallow—
Mercy on me! I have a great dispositions to cry.
[*Sings.*
Melodious birds sing madrigals—
When as I sat in Pabylon—
And a thousand vagram posies.
To shallow &c.

Re-enter SIMPLE.

Sim. Yonder he is coming, this way, Sir Hugh.
Evans. He's welcome. [*Sings.*
To shallow rivers, to whose falls—
Heaven prosper the right! What weapons is he?
Sim. No weapons, sir. There comes my master, Master Shallow, and another gentleman, from Frogmore, over the stile, this way.
Evans. Pray you, give me my gown; or else keep it in your arms.

Enter PAGE, SHALLOW, *and* SLENDER.

Shal. How now, master Parson! Good morrow, good Sir Hugh. Keep a gamester from the dice, and a good student from his book, and it is wonderful.
Slen. [*Aside*] Ah, sweet Anne Page! 40
Page. 'Save you, good Sir Hugh!

Evans. 'Pless you from his mercy sake, all of you!

Shal. What, the sword and the word! do you study them both, master parson?

Page. And youthful still! in your doublet and hose this raw rheumatic day!

Evans. There is reasons and causes for it.

Page. We are come to you to do a good office, master parson.   50

Evans. Fery well: what is it?

Page. Yonder is a most reverend gentleman, who, belike having received wrong by some person, is at most odds with his own gravity and patience that ever you saw.

Shal. I have lived fourscore years and upward; I never heard a man of his place, gravity and learning, so wide of his own respect.

Evans. What is he?

Page. I think you know him; Master Doctor Caius, the renowned French physician.   61

Evans. Got's will, and his passion of my heart! I had as lief you would tell me of a mess of porridge.

Page. Why?

Evans. He has no more knowledge in Hibocrates and Galen,—and he is a knave besides; a cowardly knave as you would desires to be acquainted withal.

Page. I warrant you, he's the man should fight with him.   71

Slen. [*Aside*] O sweet Anne Page!

Shal. It appears so by his weapons. Keep them asunder: here comes Doctor Caius.

Enter HOST, CAIUS, *and* RUGBY.

Page. Nay, good master parson, keep in your weapon.

Shal. So do you, good master doctor.

Host. Disarm them, and let them question: let them keep their limbs whole and hack our English.   80

Caius. I pray you, let-a me speak a word with your ear. Vherefore vill you not meet-a me?

Evans. [*Aside to Caius*] Pray you, use your patience: in good time.

Caius. By gar, you are de coward, de Jack dog, John ape.

Evans. [*Aside to Caius*] Pray you, let us not be laughing-stocks to other men's humours; I desire you in friendship, and I will one way or other make you amends. [*Aloud*] I will knog your urinals about your knave's cogscomb for missing your meetings and appointments.   92

Caius. Diable! Jack Rugby,—mine host de Jarteer,—have I not stay for him to kill him? have I not, at de place I did appoint?

Evans. As I am a Christians soul now, look you, this is the place appointed: I'll be judgement by mine host of the Garter.

Host. Peace, I say, Gallia and Gaul, French and Welsh, soul-curer and body-curer!   100

Caius. Ay, dat is very good; excellent.

Host. Peace, I say! hear mine host of the Garter. Am I politic? am I subtle? am I a Machiavel? Shall I lose my doctor? no; he gives me the potions and the motions. Shall I lose my parson, my priest, my Sir Hugh? no: he gives me the proverbs and the no-verbs. Give me thy hand, terrestrial; so. Give me thy hand,

Page: 'Nay, good Master Parson, keep in your weapon'. Engraving from Rowe's edition of Shakespeare's works, 1709

91 *cogscomb.* Coxcomb (head).

120-121 *vlouting-stog.* i.e. flouting-stock, laughing stock.

123 *scall.* Scabby. *cogging companion.* Cheating rogue.

Ellen Terry as Mistress Page, Her Majesty's Theatre, London, 1902

18 *weathercock.* Robin wears a feather in his cap.

34 *twelve score.* i.e. yards.

celestial; so. Boys of art, I have deceived you both; I have directed you to wrong places: your hearts are mighty, your skins are whole, and let burnt sack be the issue. Come, lay their swords to pawn. Follow me, lads of peace; follow, follow, follow.

Shal. Trust me, a mad host. Follow, gentlemen, follow.

Slen. [*Aside*] O sweet Anne Page!
       [*Exeunt Shal., Slen., Page, and Host.*

Caius. Ha, do I perceive dat? have you make-a de sot of us, ha, ha?

Evans. This is well; he has made us his vlouting-stog. I desire you that we may be friends; and let us knog our prains together to be revenge on this same scall, scurvy, cogging companion, the host of the Garter.

Caius. By gar, with all my heart. He promise to bring me where is Anne Page; by gar, he deceive me too.

Evans. Well, I will smite his noddles. Pray you, follow.   [*Exeunt.*

SCENE II. *A street.*

Enter MISTRESS PAGE *and* ROBIN.

Mrs Page. Nay, keep your way, little gallant; you were wont to be a follower, but now you are a leader. Whether had you rather lead mine eyes, or eye your master's heels?

Rob. I had rather, forsooth, go before you like a man than follow him like a dwarf.

Mrs Page. O, you are a flattering boy: now I see you'll be a courtier.

Enter FORD.

Ford. Well met, Mistress Page. Whither go you?   10

Mrs Page. Truly, sir, to see your wife. Is she at home?

Ford. Ay; and as idle as she may hang together, for want of company. I think, if your husbands were dead, you two would marry.

Mrs Page. Be sure of that,—two other husbands.

Ford. Where had you this pretty weathercock?

Mrs Page. I cannot tell what the dickens his name is my husband had him of. What do you call your knight's name, sirrah?   21

Rob. Sir John Falstaff.

Ford. Sir John Falstaff!

Mrs Page. He, he; I can never hit on's name. There is such a league between my good man and he! Is your wife at home indeed?

Ford. Indeed she is.

Mrs Page. By your leave, sir: I am sick till I see her.   [*Exeunt Mrs Page and Robin.*

Ford. Has Page any brains? hath he any eyes? hath he any thinking? Sure, they sleep; he hath no use of them. Why, this boy will carry a letter twenty mile, as easy as a cannon will shoot point-blank twelve score. He pieces out his wife's inclination; he gives her folly motion and advantage: and now she's going to my wife, and Falstaff's boy with her. A man may hear this shower sing in the wind. And Falstaff's boy with her! Good plots, they are laid; and our revolted wives share damnation together. Well; I will take him, then torture my wife, pluck the borrowed veil of modesty from the so seeming Mistress Page, divulge Page himself for a secure and wilful Actæon; and to these violent proceedings all my neighbours shall cry aim. [*Clock heard.*] The clock gives me my cue, and my assurance bids me search: there I shall find Falstaff: I shall be rather praised for this than mocked; for it is as positive as the earth is firm that Falstaff is there: I will go.   50

Enter PAGE, SHALLOW, SLENDER, HOST, SIR HUGH EVANS, CAIUS, *and* RUGBY.

Shal., Page, &c.   Well met, Master Ford.
Ford.   Trust me, a good knot: I have good cheer at home; and I pray you all go with me.
Shal.   I must excuse myself, Master Ford.
Slen.   And so must I, sir: we have appointed to dine with Mistress Anne, and I would not break with her for more money than I'll speak of.
Shal.   We have lingered about a match between Anne Page and my cousin Slender, and this day we shall have our answer.   60
Slen.   I hope I have your good will, father Page.
Page.   You have, Master Slender; I stand wholly for you: but my wife, master doctor, is for you altogether.
Caius.   Ay, be-gar; and de maid is love-a me: my nursh-a Quickly tell me so mush.
Host.   What say you to young Master Fenton? he capers, he dances, he has eyes of youth, he writes verses, he speaks holiday, he smells April and May: he will carry't, he will carry't; 'tis in his buttons; he will carry't.   71
Page.   Not by my consent, I promise you. The gentleman is of no having: he kept company with the wild prince and Poins; he is of too high a region; he knows too much. No, he shall not knit a knot in his fortunes with the finger of my substance: if he take her, let him take her simply; the wealth I have waits on my consent, and my consent goes not that way.
Ford.   I beseech you heartily, some of you go home with me to dinner: besides your cheer, you shall have sport; I will show you a monster. Master doctor, you shall go; so shall you, Master Page; and you, Sir Hugh.
Shal.   Well, fare you well: we shall have the freer wooing at Master Page's.
          [*Exeunt Shal. and Slen.*
Caius.   Go home, John Rugby; I come anon.
          [*Exit Rugby.*
Host.   Farewell, my hearts: I will to my honest knight Falstaff, and drink canary with him.
          [*Exit.*
Ford.   [*Aside*] I think I shall drink in pipe-wine first with him; I'll make him dance. Will you go, gentles?
All.   Have with you to see this monster.
          [*Exeunt.*

SCENE III.   *A room in* FORD'S *house.*

Enter MISTRESS FORD *and* MISTRESS PAGE.

Mrs Ford.   What, John! What, Robert!
Mrs Page.   Quickly, quickly! Is the buck-basket—
Mrs Ford.   I warrant. What, Robin, I say!

45 *cry aim.* Shout applause.

69 *speaks holiday.* Talks gaily.

70-71 *'tis in his buttons.* i.e. it is obvious that he will win.

74 *wild prince and Poins.* i.e. Prince Hal and his companion Poins in *1* and *2 Henry IV.*

78 *simply.* As she is, without a dowry.

90-91 *pipe-wine.* Wine from the 'pipe' or cask; with a pun on the whine of a pipe.

2-3 *buck-basket.* Dirty linen basket.

14 *whitsters*. Bleachers.

15 *Datchet-mead*. Meadow between Windsor Little Park and the Thames.

22 *eyas-musket*. Fledgling sparrow-hawk.

27 *Jack-a-Lent*. i.e. brightly dressed puppet.

43 *pumpion*. Pumpkin.

45 *Have I caught thee, my heavenly jewel?* Quoted, not quite accurately, from Sidney's *Astrophil and Stella*.

Falstaff and Mistress Ford. Painting by George Clint (1770–1854)

50 *cog*. Lie.

60-61 *ship-tire*. Headdress shaped like a ship. *tire-valiant*. Fanciful headdress. *of Venetian admittance*. Fashionable in Venice.

Enter Servants *with a basket*.

Mrs Page. Come, come, come.
Mrs Ford. Here, set it down.
Mrs Page. Give your men the charge ; we must be brief.
Mrs Ford. Marry, as I told you before, John and Robert, be ready here hard by in the brew-house : and when I suddenly call you, come forth, and without any pause or staggering take this basket on your shoulders : that done, trudge with it in all haste, and carry it among the whitsters in Datchet-mead, and there empty it in the muddy ditch close by the Thames side.
Mrs Page. You will do it ?
Mrs Ford. I ha' told them over and over ; they lack no direction. Be gone, and come when you are called.   [*Exeunt Servants*. 20
Mrs Page. Here comes little Robin.

Enter ROBIN.

Mrs Ford. How now, my eyas-musket ! what news with you ?
Rob. My master, Sir John, is come in at your back-door, Mistress Ford, and requests your company.
Mrs Page. You little Jack-a-Lent, have you been true to us ?
Rob. Ay, I'll be sworn. My master knows not of your being here and hath threatened to put me into everlasting liberty if I tell you of it ; for he swears he'll turn me away.
Mrs Page. Thou'rt a good boy : this secrecy of thine shall be a tailor to thee and shall make thee a new doublet and hose. I'll go hide me.
Mrs Ford. Do so. Go tell thy master I am alone. [*Exit Robin*.] Mistress Page, remember you your cue.
Mrs Page. I warrant thee ; if I do not act it, hiss me.   [*Exit*. 41
Mrs Ford. Go to, then : we'll use this un-wholesome humidity, this gross watery pumpion ; we'll teach him to know turtles from jays.

Enter FALSTAFF.

Fal. Have I caught thee, my heavenly jewel ? Why, now let me die, for I have lived long enough : this is the period of my ambition : O this blessed hour !
Mrs Ford. O sweet Sir John !
Fal. Mistress Ford, I cannot cog, I cannot prate, Mistress Ford. Now shall I sin in my wish : I would thy husband were dead : I'll speak it before the best lord ; I would make thee my lady.
Mrs Ford. I your lady, Sir John ! alas, I should be a pitiful lady !
Fal. Let the court of France show me such another. I see how thine eye would emulate the diamond : thou hast the right arched beauty of the brow that becomes the ship-tire, the tire-valiant, or any tire of Venetian admittance. 61
Mrs Ford. A plain kerchief, Sir John : my brows become nothing else ; nor that well neither.
Fal. By the Lord, thou art a traitor to say so : thou wouldst make an absolute courtier ; and the firm fixture of thy foot would give an ex-

cellent motion to thy gait in a semi-circled farthingale. I see what thou wert, if Fortune thy foe were not, Nature thy friend. Come, thou canst not hide it. 71

Mrs Ford. Believe me, there's no such thing in me.

Fal. What made me love thee? let that persuade thee there's something extraordinary in thee. Come, I cannot cog and say thou art this and that, like a many of these lisping hawthorn-buds, that come like women in men's apparel, ●and smell like Bucklersbury in simple time; I cannot: but I love thee; none but thee; and thou deservest it. 81

Mrs Ford. Do not betray me, sir. I fear you love Mistress Page.

Fal. Thou mightst as well say I love to ●walk by the Counter-gate, which is as hateful to me as the reek of a lime-kiln.

Mrs Ford. Well, heaven knows how I love you; and you shall one day find it.

Fal. Keep in that mind; I'll deserve it.

Mrs Ford. Nay, I must tell you, so you do; or else I could not be in that mind. 91

Rob. [*Within*] Mistress Ford, Mistress Ford! here's Mistress Page at the door, sweating and blowing and looking wildly, and would needs speak with you presently.

Fal. She shall not see me: I will ensconce me behind the arras.

Mrs Ford. Pray you, do so: she's a very tattling woman. [*Falstaff hides himself.*

Re-enter MISTRESS PAGE *and* ROBIN.

What's the matter? how now! 100

Mrs Page. O Mistress Ford, what have you done? You're shamed, you're overthrown, you're undone for ever!

Mrs Ford. What's the matter, good Mistress Page?

Mrs Page. O well-a-day, Mistress Ford! having an honest man to your husband, to give him such cause of suspicion!

Mrs Ford. What cause of suspicion?

Mrs Page. What cause of suspicion! Out upon you! how am I mistook in you! 111

Mrs Ford. Why, alas, what's the matter?

Mrs Page. Your husband's coming hither, woman, with all the officers in Windsor, to search for a gentleman that he says is here now in the house by your consent, to take an ill advantage of his absence: you are undone.

Mrs Ford. 'Tis not so, I hope.

Mrs Page. Pray heaven it be not so, that you have such a man here! but 'tis most certain your husband's coming, with half Windsor at his heels, to search for such a one. I come before to tell you. If you know yourself clear, why, I am glad of it; but if you have a friend here, convey, convey him out. Be not amazed; call all your senses to you; defend your reputation, or bid farewell to your good life for ever.

Mrs Ford. What shall I do? There is a gentleman my dear friend; and I fear not mine own shame so much as his peril: I had rather than a thousand pound he were out of the house.

Mrs Page. For shame! never stand 'you had rather' and 'you had rather:' your husband's

79 *Bucklersbury.* London street where herbs were sold. *simple time.* Summer, when herbs were collected and sold.

Bucklersbury, a street in the City of London. Engraving from Charles Knight's *Pictorial Edition of the Works of William Shakspere,* 1839–43

85 *Counter-gate.* Debtors' prison in the City of London. Prisons were notorious for their foul smells.

140 *bucking.* Washing. *whiting-time.* Bleaching time.

Falstaff in the linen basket. Engraving by H. Gravelot from a design by F. Hayman for Hanmer's edition of Shakespeare's works, 1744

156 *cowl-staff.* Pole used so that two could carry the basket. *drumble.* Dawdle.

167 *Buck.* The word plays on three meanings: 1) clothes for washing, 2) male deer (symbol of the cuckold) 3) to copulate.

Opposite : Falstaff: 'I love thee. Help me away. Let me creep in here . . .' Engraving from a painting by Rev. M. W. Peters (*d.*1814)

here at hand; bethink you of some conveyance: in the house you cannot hide him. O, how have you deceived me! Look, here is a basket: if he be of any reasonable stature, he may creep in here; and throw foul linen upon him, as if it were going to bucking: or—it is whiting-time—send him by your two men to Datchet-mead. 141

Mrs Ford. He's too big to go in there. What shall I do?

Fal. [*Coming forward*] Let me see't, let me see't, O, let me see't! I'll in, I'll in. Follow your friend's counsel. I'll in.

Mrs Page. What, Sir John Falstaff! Are these your letters, knight?

Fal. I love thee. Help me away. Let me creep in here. I'll never— 150
[*Gets into the basket; they cover him with foul linen.*

Mrs Page. Help to cover your master, boy. Call your men, Mistress Ford. You dissembling knight!

Mrs Ford. What, John! Robert! John!
[*Exit Robin.*

Re-enter Servants.

Go take up these clothes here quickly. Where's the cowl-staff? look, how you drumble! Carry them to the laundress in Datchet-mead; quickly, come.

Enter FORD, PAGE, CAIUS, *and* SIR HUGH EVANS.

Ford. Pray you, come near: if I suspect without cause, why then make sport at me; then let me be your jest; I deserve it. How now! whither bear you this?

Serv. To the laundress, forsooth.

Mrs Ford. Why, what have you to do whither they bear it? You were best meddle with buck-washing.

Ford. Buck! I would I could wash myself of the buck! Buck, buck, buck! Ay, buck; I warrant you, buck; and of the season too, it shall appear. [*Exeunt Servants with the basket.*] Gentlemen, I have dreamed to-night; I'll tell you my dream. Here, here, here be my keys: ascend my chambers; search, seek, find out: I'll warrant we'll unkennel the fox. Let me stop this way first. [*Locking the door.*] So, now uncape.

Page. Good Master Ford, be contented: you wrong yourself too much.

Ford. True, Master Page. Up, gentlemen; you shall see sport anon: follow me, gentlemen.
[*Exit.* 180

Evans. This is fery fantastical humours and jealousies.

Caius. By gar, 'tis no the fashion of France; it is not jealous in France.

Page. Nay, follow him, gentlemen; see the issue of his search.
[*Exeunt Page, Caius, and Evans.*

Mrs Page. Is there not a double excellency in this?

Mrs Ford. I know not which pleases me better, that my husband is deceived, or Sir John.

Mrs Page. What a taking was he in when your husband asked who was in the basket!

Mrs Ford. I am half afraid he will have need

247 *a-birding*. Hunting small birds.

Pheasant hawking. Engraving by F. Barlow, 1671

of washing; so throwing him into the water will do him a benefit.

Mrs Page. Hang him, dishonest rascal! I would all of the same strain were in the same distress.

Mrs Ford. I think my husband hath some special suspicion of Falstaff's being here; for I never saw him so gross in his jealousy till now.

Mrs Page. I will lay a plot to try that; and we will yet have more tricks with Falstaff: his dissolute disease will scarce obey this medicine.

Mrs Ford. Shall we send that foolish carrion, Mistress Quickly, to him, and excuse his throwing into the water; and give him another hope, to betray him to another punishment?

Mrs Page. We will do it: let him be sent for to-morrow, eight o'clock, to have amends.   210

Re-enter FORD, PAGE, CAIUS, *and* SIR HUGH EVANS.

Ford. I cannot find him: may be the knave bragged of that he could not compass.

Mrs Page. [*Aside to Mrs Ford*] Heard you that?

Mrs Ford. You use me well, Master Ford, do you?

Ford. Ay, I do so.

Mrs Ford. Heaven make you better than your thoughts!

Ford. Amen!   220

Mrs Page. You do yourself mighty wrong, Master Ford.

Ford. Ay, ay; I must bear it.

Evans. If there be any pody in the house, and in the chambers, and in the coffers, and in the presses, heaven forgive my sins at the day of judgement!

Caius. By gar, nor I too: there is no bodies.

Page. Fie, fie, Master Ford! are you not ashamed? What spirit, what devil suggests this imagination? I would not ha' your distemper in this kind for the wealth of Windsor Castle.

Ford. 'Tis my fault, Master Page: I suffer for it.

Evans. You suffer for a pad conscience: your wife is as honest a 'omans as I will desires among five thousand, and five hundred too.

Caius. By gar, I see 'tis an honest woman.

Ford. Well, I promised you a dinner. Come, come, walk in the Park: I pray you, pardon me; I will hereafter make known to you why I have done this. Come, wife; come, Mistress Page. I pray you, pardon me; pray heartily, pardon me.

Page. Let's go in, gentlemen; but, trust me, we'll mock him. I do invite you to-morrow morning to my house to breakfast: after, we'll a-birding together; I have a fine hawk for the bush. Shall it be so?

Ford. Any thing.

Evans. If there is one, I shall make two in the company.   251

Caius. If dere be one or two, I shall make-a the turd.

Ford. Pray you, go, Master Page.

Evans. I pray you now, remembrance to-morrow on the lousy knave, mine host.

Caius. Dat is good; by gar, with all my heart!

Evans. A lousy knave, to have his gibes and his mockeries!   [*Exeunt.* 260

SCENE IV.   *A room in* PAGE'S *house.*

Enter FENTON *and* ANNE PAGE.

Fent. I see I cannot get thy father's love;
Therefore no more turn me to him, sweet Nan.
    Anne. Alas, how then?
    Fent.   Why, thou must be thyself.
He doth object I am too great of birth;
• And that, my state being gall'd with my expense,
I seek to heal it only by his wealth:
Besides these, other bars he lays before me,
My riots past, my wild societies;
And tells me 'tis a thing impossible
I should love thee but as a property.   10
    Anne. May be he tells you true.
    Fent. No, heaven so speed me in my time to
        come!
Albeit I will confess thy father's wealth
Was the first motive that I woo'd thee, Anne:
Yet, wooing thee, I found thee of more value
Than stamps in gold or sums in sealed bags;
And 'tis the very riches of thyself
That now I aim at.
    Anne.   Gentle Master Fenton,
Yet seek my father's love; still seek it, sir:
If opportunity and humblest suit   20
Cannot attain it, why, then,—hark you hither!
                        [*They converse apart.*

Enter SHALLOW, SLENDER, *and* MISTRESS
                QUICKLY.

Shal. Break their talk, Mistress Quickly: my
kinsman shall speak for himself.
• *Slen.* I'll make a shaft or a bolt on 't: 'slid,
'tis but venturing.
    Shal. Be not dismayed.
    Slen. No, she shall not dismay me: I care not
for that, but that I am afeard.
    Quick. Hark ye; Master Slender would speak
a word with you.   30
    Anne. I come to him.   [*Aside*] This is my
        father's choice.
O, what a world of vile ill-favour'd faults
Looks handsome in three hundred pounds a-year!
    Quick. And how does good Master Fenton?
Pray you, a word with you.
    Shal. She's coming; to her, coz. O boy, thou
hadst a father!
    Slen. I had a father, Mistress Anne; my uncle
can tell you good jests of him. Pray you, uncle,
tell Mistress Anne the jest, how my father stole
two geese out of a pen, good uncle.   41
    Shal. Mistress Anne, my cousin loves you.
    Slen. Ay, that I do; as well as I love any
woman in Gloucestershire.
    Shal. He will maintain you like a gentle-
woman.
• *Slen.* Ay, that I will, come cut and long-tail,
under the degree of a squire.
    Shal. He will make you a hundred and fifty
pounds jointure.   50
    Anne. Good Master Shallow, let him woo for
himself.
    Shal. Marry, I thank you for it; I thank you
for that good comfort. She calls you, coz: I'll
leave you.

5 *gall'd.* Reduced.

Anne: 'Gentle Master Fenton, Yet seek my father's love.'
Dyson Lovell as Fenton and Judi Dench as Anne Page,
Old Vic Theatre, London, 1959

24 *shaft or a bolt on 't.* i.e. try it this way or another.
'slid. God's eyelid.

47 *come cut and long-tail.* i.e. no matter who or what is
concerned.

68 *happy man be his dole.* i.e. good luck to the man who wins you.

Anne Page. Detail from a painting by A. W. Callcott (1779–1844)

Anne. Now, Master Slender,—
Slen. Now, good Mistress Anne,—
Anne. What is your will?
Slen. My will! 'od's heartlings, that's a pretty jest indeed! I ne'er made my will yet, I thank heaven; I am not such a sickly creature, I give heaven praise.   62
Anne. I mean, Master Slender, what would you with me?
Slen. Truly, for mine own part, I would little or nothing with you. Your father and my uncle hath made motions: if it be my luck, so; if not, happy man be his dole! They can tell you how things go better than I can: you may ask your father; here he comes.   70

Enter PAGE *and* MISTRESS PAGE.

Page. Now, Master Slender: love him, daughter Anne.
Why, how now! what does Master Fenton here?
You wrong me, sir, thus still to haunt my house:
I told you, sir, my daughter is disposed of.
Fent. Nay, Master Page, be not impatient.
Mrs Page. Good Master Fenton, come not to my child.
Page. She is no match for you.
Fent. Sir, will you hear me?
Page.   No, good Master Fenton.
Come, Master Shallow; come, son Slender, in.
Knowing my mind, you wrong me, Master Fenton.
                    [*Exeunt Page, Shal., and Slen.*
Quick. Speak to Mistress Page.
Fent. Good Mistress Page, for that I love your daughter
In such a righteous fashion as I do,
Perforce, against all checks, rebukes and manners,
I must advance the colours of my love
And not retire: let me have your good will.
Anne. Good mother, do not marry me to yond fool.
Mrs Page. I mean it not; I seek you a better husband.
Quick. That's my master, master doctor.
Anne. Alas, I had rather be set quick i' the earth   90
And bowl'd to death with turnips!
Mrs Page. Come, trouble not yourself. Good Master Fenton,
I will not be your friend nor enemy:
My daughter will I question how she loves you,
And as I find her, so am I affected.
Till then farewell, sir: she must needs go in;
Her father will be angry.
Fent. Farewell, gentle mistress: farewell, Nan.
                    [*Exeunt Mrs Page and Anne.*
Quick. This is my doing, now: 'Nay,' said I, 'will you cast away your child on a fool, and a physician? Look on Master Fenton:' this is my doing.
Fent. I thank thee; and I pray thee, once to-night
Give my sweet Nan this ring: there's for thy pains.
Quick. Now heaven send thee good fortune!
[*Exit Fenton.*] A kind heart he hath: a woman would run through fire and water for such a kind heart. But yet I would my master had Mistress Anne; or I would Master Slender had her; or, in sooth, I would Master Fenton had her: I will

do what I can for them all three; for so I have promised, and I'll be as good as my word; but speciously for Master Fenton. Well, I must of another errand to Sir John Falstaff from my two mistresses: what a beast am I to slack it! [*Exit.*

SCENE V.   *A room in the Garter Inn.*

Enter FALSTAFF *and* BARDOLPH.

Fal. Bardolph, I say,—
Bard. Here, sir.
• *Fal.* Go fetch me a quart of sack; put a toast in't. [*Exit Bard.*] Have I lived to be carried in a basket, like a barrow of butcher's offal, and to be thrown in the Thames? Well, if I be served such another trick, I'll have my brains ta'en out and buttered, and give them to a dog for a new-year's gift. The rogues slighted me into the river with as little remorse as they would have drowned a blind bitch's puppies, fifteen i' the litter: and you may know by my size that I have a kind of alacrity in sinking; if the bottom were as deep as hell, I should down. I had been drown-ed, but that the shore was shelvy and shallow,— a death that I abhor; for the water swells a man; and what a thing should I have been when I had been swelled! I should have been a mountain of
• mummy.

Re-enter BARDOLPH *with sack.*

Bard. Here's Mistress Quickly, sir, to speak with you.   21
Fal. Come, let me pour in some sack to the Thames water; for my belly's as cold as if I had
• swallowed snowballs for pills to cool the reins. Call her in.
Bard. Come in, woman!

Enter MISTRESS QUICKLY.

Quick. By your leave; I cry you mercy: give your worship good morrow.
Fal. Take away these chalices. Go brew me a pottle of sack finely.   30
Bard. With eggs, sir?
Fal. Simple of itself; I'll no pullet-sperm in my brewage. [*Exit Bardolph.*] How now!
Quick. Marry, sir, I come to your worship from Mistress Ford.
Fal. Mistress Ford! I have had ford enough; I was thrown into the ford; I have my belly full of ford.
Quick. Alas the day! good heart, that was not her fault: she does so take on with her
• men; they mistook their erection.   41
Fal. So did I mine, to build upon a foolish woman's promise.
Quick. Well, she laments, sir, for it, that it would yearn your heart to see it. Her husband goes this morning a-birding; she desires you once more to come to her between eight and nine: I must carry her word quickly: she'll make you amends, I warrant you.
Fal. Well, I will visit her: tell her so; and bid her think what a man is: let her consider his frailty, and then judge of my merit.   52
Quick. I will tell her.
Fal. Do so. Between nine and ten, sayest thou?
Quick. Eight and nine, sir.
Fal. Well, be gone: I will not miss her.

3 *toast.* Hot toast was frequently put into wine or beer.

Falstaff: 'The rogues slighted me into the river.' Engraving from Charles Knight's *Pictorial Edition of the Works of William Shakspere*, 1839–43

19 *mummy.* Dead flesh.

24 *reins.* Loins.

41 *erection.* i.e. for 'direction'.

71-72 *Cornuto.* Horned beast, cuckold.

99 *hinds.* Servants.

111 *bell-wether.* The leading ram of the flock around whose neck a bell was hung.

113 *peck.* Vessel that would hold a peck (quarter of a bushel).

Quick. Peace be with you, sir.   [*Exit.*
Fal. I marvel I hear not of Master Brook; he sent me word to stay within: I like his money well. O, here he comes.   60

Enter FORD.

Ford. Bless you, sir!
Fal. Now, master Brook, you come to know what hath passed between me and Ford's wife?
Ford. That, indeed, Sir John, is my business.
Fal. Master Brook, I will not lie to you: I was at her house the hour she appointed me.
Ford. And sped you, sir?
Fal. Very ill-favouredly, Master Brook.
Ford. How so, sir? Did she change her determination?   70
Fal. No, master Brook; but the peaking Cornuto her husband, Master Brook, dwelling in a continual 'larum of jealousy, comes me in the instant of our encounter, after we had embraced, kissed, protested, and, as it were, spoke the prologue of our comedy; and at his heels a rabble of his companions, thither provoked and instigated by his distemper, and, forsooth, to search his house for his wife's love.
Ford. What, while you were there?   80
Fal. While I was there.
Ford. And did he search for you, and could not find you?
Fal. You shall hear. As good luck would have it, comes in one Mistress Page; gives intelligence of Ford's approach; and, in her invention and Ford's wife's distraction, they conveyed me into a buck-basket.
Ford. A buck-basket!
Fal. By the Lord, a buck-basket! rammed me in with foul shirts and smocks, socks, foul stockings, greasy napkins; that, Master Brook, there was the rankest compound of villanous smell that ever offended nostril.
Ford. And how long lay you there?
Fal. Nay, you shall hear, Master Brook, what I have suffered to bring this woman to evil for your good. Being thus crammed in the basket, a couple of Ford's knaves, his hinds, were called forth by their mistress to carry me in the name of foul clothes to Datchet-lane: they took me on their shoulders; met the jealous knave their master in the door, who asked them once or twice what they had in their basket: I quaked for fear, lest the lunatic knave would have searched it; but fate, ordaining he should be a cuckold, held his hand. Well: on went he for a search, and away went I for foul clothes. But mark the sequel, Master Brook: I suffered the pangs of three several deaths; first, an intolerable fright, to be detected with a jealous rotten bell-wether; next, to be compassed, like a good bilbo, in the circumference of a peck, hilt to point, heel to head; and then, to be stopped in, like a strong distillation, with stinking clothes that fretted in their own grease: think of that,—a man of my kidney,—think of that,—that am as subject to heat as butter; a man of continual dissolution and thaw: it was a miracle to 'scape suffocation. And in the height of this bath, when I was more than half stewed in grease, like a Dutch dish, to be thrown into the Thames, and cooled, glowing hot,

in that surge, like a horse-shoe; think of that,—hissing hot,—think of that, Master Brook.

Ford. In good sadness, sir, I am sorry that for my sake you have suffered all this. My suit then is desperate; you'll undertake her no more?

Fal. Master Brook, I will be thrown into Etna, as I have been into Thames, ere I will leave her thus. Her husband is this morning gone a-birding: I have received from her another embassy of meeting; 'twixt eight and nine is the hour, Master Brook.

Ford. 'Tis past eight already, sir.

Fal. Is it? I will then address me to my appointment. Come to me at your convenient leisure, and you shall know how I speed; and the conclusion shall be crowned with your enjoying her. Adieu. You shall have her, Master Brook; Master Brook, you shall cuckold Ford.   [*Exit.*

Ford. Hum! ha! is this a vision? is this a dream? do I sleep? Master Ford, awake! awake, Master Ford! there's a hole made in your best coat, Master Ford. This 'tis to be married! this 'tis to have linen and buck-baskets! Well, I will proclaim myself what I am: I will now take the lecher; he is at my house; he cannot 'scape me; 'tis impossible he should; he cannot creep into a halfpenny purse, nor into a pepper-box: but, lest the devil that guides him should aid him, I will search impossible places. Though what I am I cannot avoid, yet to be what I would not shall not make me tame: if I have horns to make one mad, let the proverb go with me: I'll be horn-mad.   [*Exit.*

ACT IV.

SCENE I. *A street.*

Enter MISTRESS PAGE, MISTRESS QUICKLY, *and* WILLIAM.

Mrs Page. Is he at Master Ford's already, think'st thou?

Quick. Sure he is by this, or will be presently: but, truly, he is very courageous mad about his throwing into the water. Mistress Ford desires you to come suddenly.

Mrs Page. I'll be with her by and by; I'll but bring my young man here to school. Look, where his master comes; 'tis a playing-day, I see.

Enter SIR HUGH EVANS.

How now, Sir Hugh! no school to-day?   10

Evans. No; Master Slender is let the boys leave to play.

Quick. Blessing of his heart!

Mrs Page. Sir Hugh, my husband says my son profits nothing in the world at his book. I pray you, ask him some questions in his accidence.

Evans. Come hither, William; hold up your head; come.

Mrs Page. Come on, sirrah; hold up your head; answer your master, be not afraid.   20

Evans. William, how many numbers is in nouns?

Will. Two.

Quick. Truly, I thought there had been one number more, because they say, "'Od's nouns.'

Evans. Peace your tattlings! What is 'fair,' William?

143-144 *a hole made in your best coat.* i.e. there is a fault in something you thought impeccable.

Evans: 'William, how many numbers is in nouns?' Painting by Robert Smirke (1752–1845)

25 *'Od's nouns'.* God's wounds.

Pegg Woffington, one of Garrick's leading ladies, as Mrs Ford, 1751

---

29 *Polecats.* Slang term for prostitutes.

55 *caret.* Missing; Mistress Quickly mistakes it for 'carrot'.

68 *to hick and to hack.* To hiccup (from drink) and to wench.

81 *preeches.* i.e. breeches (meaning 'whipped').

84 *sprag.* Lively.

Will. Pulcher.

Quick. Polecats ! there are fairer things than polecats, sure.   30

Evans. You are a very simplicity 'oman : I pray you, peace.   What is 'lapis,' William ?

Will. A stone.

Evans. And what is 'a stone,' William ?

Will. A pebble.

Evans. No, it is 'lapis :' I pray you, remember in your prain.

Will. Lapis.

Evans. That is a good William.   What is he, William, that does lend articles ?   40

Will. Articles are borrowed of the pronoun, and be thus declined, Singulariter, nominativo, hic, hæc, hoc.

Evans. Nominativo, hig, hag, hog ; pray you, mark : genitivo, hujus.   Well, what is your accusative case ?

Will. Accusativo, hinc.

Evans. I pray you, have your remembrance, child ; accusativo, hung, hang, hog.

Quick. 'Hang-hog' is Latin for bacon, I warrant you.   51

Evans. Leave your prabbles, 'oman.   What is the focative case, William ?

Will. O,—vocativo, O.

Evans. Remember, William ; focative is caret.

Quick. And that's a good root.

Evans. 'Oman, forbear.

Mrs Page. Peace !

Evans. What is your genitive case plural, William ?   60

Will. Genitive case !

Evans. Ay.

Will. Genitive,—horum, harum, horum.

Quick. Vengeance of Jenny's case ! fie on her ! never name her, child, if she be a whore.

Evans. For shame, 'oman.

Quick. You do ill to teach the child such words : he teaches him to hick and to hack, which they'll do fast enough of themselves, and to call 'horum :' fie upon you !   70

Evans. 'Oman, art thou lunatics ? hast thou no understandings for thy cases and the numbers of the genders ?   Thou art as foolish Christian creatures as I would desires.

Mrs Page. Prithee, hold thy peace.

Evans. Show me now, William, some declensions of your pronouns.

Will. Forsooth, I have forgot.

Evans. It is qui, quæ, quod : if you forget your 'quies,' your 'quæs,' and your 'quods,' you must be preeches.   Go your ways, and play ; go.

Mrs Page. He is a better scholar than I thought he was.

Evans. He is a good sprag memory.   Farewell, Mistress Page.

Mrs Page. Adieu, good Sir Hugh.

[*Exit Sir Hugh.*]

Get you home, boy.   Come, we stay too long.

[*Exeunt.*

SCENE II.   *A room in* FORD'S *house.*

Enter FALSTAFF *and* MISTRESS FORD.

Fal. Mistress Ford, your sorrow hath eaten up my sufferance.   I see you are obsequious in your love, and I profess requital to a hair's breadth; not only, Mistress Ford, in the simple office of love, but in all the accoutrement, complement and ceremony of it. But are you sure of your husband now?

Mrs Ford. He's a-birding, sweet Sir John.

Mrs Page. [*Within*] What, ho, gossip Ford! what, ho! 10

Mrs Ford. Step into the chamber, Sir John.
[*Exit Falstaff.*

Enter MISTRESS PAGE.

Mrs Page. How now, sweetheart! who's at home besides yourself?

Mrs Ford. Why, none but mine own people.

Mrs Page. Indeed!

Mrs Ford. No, certainly. [*Aside to her*] Speak louder.

Mrs Page. Truly, I am so glad you have nobody here.

Mrs Ford. Why? 20

Mrs Page. Why, woman, your husband is in his old lunes again: he so takes on yonder with my husband; so rails against all married mankind; so curses all Eve's daughters, of what complexion soever; and so buffets himself on the forehead, crying, 'Peer out, peer out!' that any madness I ever yet beheld seemed but tameness, civility and patience, to this his distemper he is in now: I am glad the fat knight is not here.

Mrs Ford. Why, does he talk of him? 30

Mrs Page. Of none but him; and swears he was carried out, the last time he searched for him, in a basket; protests to my husband he is now here, and hath drawn him and the rest of their company from their sport, to make another experiment of his suspicion: but I am glad the knight is not here; now he shall see his own foolery.

Mrs Ford. How near is he, Mistress Page?

Mrs Page. Hard by; at street end; he will be here anon. 41

Mrs Ford. I am undone! The knight is here.

Mrs Page. Why then you are utterly shamed, and he's but a dead man. What a woman are you!—Away with him, away with him! better shame than murder.

Mrs Ford. Which way should he go? how should I bestow him? Shall I put him into the basket again?

Re-enter FALSTAFF.

Fal. No, I'll come no more i' the basket. May I not go out ere he come? 51

Mrs Page. Alas, three of Master Ford's brothers watch the door with pistols, that none shall issue out; otherwise you might slip away ere he came. But what make you here?

Fal. What shall I do? I'll creep up into the chimney.

Mrs Ford. There they always use to discharge their birding-pieces. Creep into the kiln-hole.

Fal. Where is it? 60

Mrs Ford. He will seek there, on my word. Neither press, coffer, chest, trunk, well, vault, but he hath an abstract for the remembrance of such places, and goes to them by his note: there is no hiding you in the house.

Fal. I'll go out then.

Mrs Page. If you go out in your own sem-

22 *lunes.* Fits of lunacy.

Falstaff: 'I'll creep up into the chimney.' Illustration by Henry Bunbury (1750–1811)

80-81 *thrummed hat.* Hat made of short tufts of wool.

Different types of mufflers worn by Elizabethan women. Engraving from Francis Douce's *Illustrations of Shakespeare,* 1839

---

109 *Still swine eat all the draff.* A proverb meaning that the quiet are often the most wicked.

122 *Youth in a basket!* Triumphant lover.

123 *ging.* Gang.

blance, you die, Sir John.   Unless you go out disguised—

Mrs Ford.   How might we disguise him?   70

Mrs Page.   Alas the day, I know not !   There is no woman's gown big enough for him; otherwise he might put on a hat, a muffler and a kerchief, and so escape.

Fal.   Good hearts, devise something: any extremity rather than a mischief.

Mrs Ford.   My maid's aunt, the fat woman of Brentford, has a gown above.

Mrs Page.   On my word, it will serve him: •she's as big as he is: and there's her thrummed hat and her muffler too.   Run up, Sir John.

Mrs Ford.   Go, go, sweet Sir John: Mistress Page and I will look some linen for your head.

Mrs Page.   Quick, quick! we'll come dress you straight: put on the gown the while.   85
[*Exit Falstaff.*

Mrs Ford.   I would my husband would meet him in this shape: he cannot abide the old woman of Brentford; he swears she's a witch; forbade her my house and hath threatened to beat her.

Mrs Page.   Heaven guide him to thy husband's cudgel, and the devil guide his cudgel afterwards !

Mrs Ford.   But is my husband coming?

Mrs Page.   Ay, in good sadness, is he; and talks of the basket too, howsoever he hath had intelligence.

Mrs Ford.   We'll try that; for I'll appoint my men to carry the basket again, to meet him at the door with it, as they did last time.

Mrs Page.   Nay, but he'll be here presently: let's go dress him like the witch of Brentford.

Mrs Ford.   I'll first direct my men what they shall do with the basket.   Go up; I'll bring linen for him straight.   [*Exit.*

Mrs Page.   Hang him, dishonest varlet! we cannot misuse him enough.

We'll leave a proof, by that which we will do,
Wives may be merry, and yet honest too:
We do not act that often jest and laugh;
• 'Tis old, but true, Still swine eats all the draff.
[*Exit.*

Re-enter MISTRESS FORD *with two* Servants.

Mrs Ford.   Go, sirs, take the basket again on your shoulders: your master is hard at door; if he bid you set it down, obey him: quickly, dispatch.   [*Exit.*

First Serv.   Come, come, take it up.

Sec. Serv.   Pray heaven it be not full of knight again.

First Serv.   I hope not; I had as lief bear so much lead.

Enter FORD, PAGE, SHALLOW, CAIUS, *and* SIR HUGH EVANS.

Ford.   Ay, but if it prove true, Master **Page,** have you any way then to unfool me again?   Set down the basket, villain!   Somebody call my •wife.   Youth in a basket !   O you pandarly ras- •cals ! there's a knot, a ging, a pack, a conspiracy against me: now shall the devil be shamed. What, wife, I say !   Come, come forth !   Behold what honest clothes you send forth to bleaching !

Page.   Why, this passes, Master Ford; you are not to go loose any longer; you must be pinioned.

Evans. Why, this is lunatics! this is mad as a mad dog!   131
Shal. Indeed, Master Ford, this is not well, indeed.
Ford. So say I too, sir.

Re-enter MISTRESS FORD.

Come hither, Mistress Ford; Mistress Ford, the honest woman, the modest wife, the virtuous creature, that hath the jealous fool to her husband! I suspect without cause, mistress, do I?
Mrs Ford. Heaven be my witness you do, if you suspect me in any dishonesty.   140
Ford. Well said, brazen-face! hold it out. Come forth, sirrah!
[*Pulling clothes out of the basket.*
Page. This passes!
Mrs Ford. Are you not ashamed? let the clothes alone.
Ford. I shall find you anon.
Evans. 'Tis unreasonable! Will you take up your wife's clothes? Come away.
Ford. Empty the basket, I say!
Mrs Ford. Why, man, why?   150
Ford. Master Page, as I am a man, there was one conveyed out of my house yesterday in this basket: why may not he be there again? In my house I am sure he is: my intelligence is true; my jealousy is reasonable. Pluck me out all the linen.
Mrs Ford. If you find a man there, he shall die a flea's death.
Page. Here's no man.
Shal. By my fidelity, this is not well, Master Ford; this wrongs you.   161
Evans. Master Ford, you must pray, and not follow the imaginations of your own heart: this is jealousies.
Ford. Well, he's not here I seek for.
Page. No, nor nowhere else but in your brain.
Ford. Help to search my house this one time. If I find not what I seek, show no colour for my extremity; let me for ever be your table-sport; let them say of me, 'As jealous as Ford, that searched a hollow walnut for his wife's leman.' Satisfy me once more; once more search with me.
Mrs Ford. What, ho, Mistress Page! come you and the old woman down; my husband will come into the chamber.
Ford. Old woman! what old woman's that?
Mrs Ford. Why, it is my maid's aunt of Brentford.
Ford. A witch, a quean, an old cozening quean! Have I not forbid her my house? She comes of errands, does she? We are simple men; we do not know what's brought to pass under the profession of fortune-telling. She works by charms, by spells, by the figure, and such daubery as this is, beyond our element: we know nothing. Come down, you witch, you hag, you; come down, I say!
Mrs Ford. Nay, good, sweet husband! Good gentlemen, let him not strike the old woman. 190

Re-enter FALSTAFF *in woman's clothes, and* MISTRESS PAGE.

Mrs Page. Come, Mother Prat; come, give me your hand.

172 *leman.* Lover.

180 *quean.* Jade, disreputable woman.

Mistress Page and Falstaff disguised. Detail from a drawing by John Thurston (1744–1822)

Ford: 'Out of my door . . . you hag.' Drawing by S. H. Grimm (1733–1794)

195 *ronyon.* Mangy creature.

237 *period.* Stop.

2 *the duke.* An allusion to Count Mömpelgart, later Duke of Württemberg, who visited England in 1592. See introduction.

Frederick, Duke of Württemberg who, after visiting Windsor, wished to be elected to the Order of the Garter. Elizabeth I finally agreed in 1597

Ford. I'll prat her. [*Beating him*] Out of my door, you witch, you hag, you baggage, you polecat, you ronyon! out, out! I'll conjure you, I'll fortune-tell you.   [*Exit Falstaff.*
Mrs Page. Are you not ashamed? I think you have killed the poor woman.
Mrs Ford. Nay, he will do it. 'Tis a goodly credit for you.   200
Ford. Hang her, witch!
Evans. By yea and no, I think the 'oman is a witch indeed: I like not when a 'oman has a great peard; I spy a great peard under his muffler.
Ford. Will you follow, gentlemen? I beseech you, follow; see but the issue of my jealousy: if I cry out thus upon no trail, never trust me when I open again.
Page. Let's obey his humour a little further: come, gentlemen.   211
[*Exeunt Ford, Page, Shal., Caius, and Evans.*
Mrs Page. Trust me, he beat him most pitifully.
Mrs Ford. Nay, by the mass, that he did not; he beat him most unpitifully, methought.
Mrs Page. I'll have the cudgel hallowed and hung o'er the altar; it hath done meritorious service.
Mrs Ford. What think you? may we, with the warrant of womanhood and the witness of a good conscience, pursue him with any further revenge?   222
Mrs Page. The spirit of wantonness is, sure, scared out of him: if the devil have him not in fee-simple, with fine and recovery, he will never, I think, in the way of waste, attempt us again.
Mrs Ford. Shall we tell our husbands how we have served him?
Mrs Page. Yes, by all means; if it be but to scrape the figures out of your husband's brains. If they can find in their hearts the poor unvirtuous fat knight shall be any further afflicted, we two will still be the ministers.
Mrs Ford. I'll warrant they'll have him publicly shamed: and methinks there would be no period to the jest, should he not be publicly shamed.
Mrs Page. Come, to the forge with it then; shape it: I would not have things cool. [*Exeunt.*

SCENE III.   *A room in the Garter Inn.*

Enter HOST *and* BARDOLPH.

Bard. Sir, the Germans desire to have three of your horses: the duke himself will be tomorrow at court, and they are going to meet him.
Host. What duke should that be comes so secretly? I hear not of him in the court. Let me speak with the gentlemen: they speak English?
Bard. Ay, sir; I'll call them to you.
Host. They shall have my horses; but I'll make them pay; I'll sauce them: they have had my house a week at command; I have turned away my other guests: they must come off; I'll sauce them. Come.   [*Exeunt.*

SCENE IV.   *A room in* FORD'S *house.*

Enter PAGE, FORD, MISTRESS PAGE, MISTRESS
FORD, *and* SIR HUGH EVANS.

Evans. 'Tis one of the best discretions of a
'oman as ever I did look upon.
Page. And did he send you both these letters
at an instant?
Mrs Page. Within a quarter of an hour.
Ford. Pardon me, wife. Henceforth do what
thou wilt;
I rather will suspect the sun with cold
Than thee with wantonness: now doth thy honour
stand,
In him that was of late an heretic,
As firm as faith.
Page.   'Tis well, 'tis well; no more: 10
Be not as extreme in submission
As in offence.
But let our plot go forward: let our wives
Yet once again, to make us public sport,
Appoint a meeting with this old fat fellow,
Where we may take him and disgrace him for it.
Ford. There is no better way than that they
spoke of.
Page. How? to send him word they'll meet
him in the park at midnight? Fie, fie! he'll
never come.
Evans. You say he has been thrown in the
rivers and has been grievously peaten as an old
'oman: methinks there should be terrors in him
that he should not come; methinks his flesh is
punished, he shall have no desires.
Page. So think I too.
Mrs Ford. Devise but how you'll use him
when he comes,
And let us two devise to bring him thither.
Mrs Page. There is an old tale goes that
Herne the hunter,
Sometime a keeper here in Windsor forest,
Doth all the winter-time, at still midnight,   30
Walk round about an oak, with great ragg'd horns;
And there he blasts the tree and takes the cattle
● And makes milch-kine yield blood and shakes a
chain
In a most hideous and dreadful manner:
You have heard of such a spirit, and well you
know
● The superstitious idle-headed eld
Received and did deliver to our age
This tale of Herne the hunter for a truth.
Page. Why, yet there want not many that do
fear
In deep of night to walk by this Herne's oak: 40
But what of this?
Mrs Ford.   Marry, this is our device;
That Falstaff at that oak shall meet with us.
Page. Well, let it not be doubted but he'll
come:
And in this shape when you have brought him
thither,
What shall be done with him? what is your plot?
Mrs Page. That likewise have we thought
upon, and thus:
Nan Page my daughter and my little son
And three or four more of their growth we'll dress
● Like urchins, ouphes and fairies, green and white,
With rounds of waxen tapers on their heads,   50

Mistress Page: 'Sometime a keeper here in Windsor forest'. Engraving from Charles Knight's *Pictorial Edition of the Works of William Shakspere,* 1893–43

33 *milch-kine.* Dairy cattle.

36 *eld.* People of earlier times.

49 *ouphes.* Elves, goblins.

67 *jack-an-apes.* Monkey.

70 *vizards.* Visors, masks.

10 *Anthropophaginian.* Cannibal. See introduction.

Mexican Indians with the skulls of their victims. Engraving by Theodor de Bry in *Historia Americae* Part 9, 1601

And rattles in their hands: upon a sudden,
As Falstaff, she and I, are newly met,
Let them from forth a sawpit rush at once
With some diffused song: upon their sight,
We two in great amazedness will fly:
Then let them all encircle him about
And, fairy-like, to pinch the unclean knight,
And ask him why, that hour of fairy revel,
In their so sacred paths he dares to tread
In shape profane.
 Mrs Ford. And till he tell the truth, 60
Let the supposed fairies pinch him sound
And burn him with their tapers.
 Mrs Page. The truth being known,
We'll all present ourselves, dis-horn the spirit,
And mock him home to Windsor.
 Ford. The children must
Be practised well to this, or they'll ne'er do't.
 Evans. I will teach the children their be-
haviours; and I will be like a jack-an-apes also,
to burn the knight with my taber.
 Ford. That will be excellent. I'll go buy
them vizards. 70
 Mrs Page. My Nan shall be the queen of all
  the fairies,
Finely attired in a robe of white.
 Page. That silk will I go buy. [*Aside*] And
 in that time
Shall Master Slender steal my Nan away
And marry her at Eton. Go send to Falstaff
 straight.
 Ford. Nay, I'll to him again in name of Brook:
He'll tell me all his purpose: sure, he'll come.
 Mrs Page. Fear not you that. Go get us
 properties
And tricking for our fairies.
 Evans. Let us about it: it is admirable plea-
sures and fery honest knaveries. 81
   [*Exeunt Page, Ford, and Evans.*
 Mrs Page. Go, Mistress Ford,
Send quickly to Sir John, to know his mind.
     [*Exit Mrs Ford.*
I'll to the doctor: he hath my good will,
And none but he, to marry with Nan Page.
That Slender, though well landed, is an idiot;
And he my husband best of all affects.
The doctor is well money'd, and his friends
Potent at court: he, none but he, shall have her,
Though twenty thousand worthier come to crave
 her. [*Exit.* 90

SCENE V. *A room in the Garter Inn.*

Enter HOST *and* SIMPLE.

 Host. What wouldst thou have, boor? what,
thick-skin? speak, breathe, discuss; brief, short,
quick, snap.
 Sim. Marry, sir, I come to speak with Sir
John Falstaff from Master Slender.
 Host. There's his chamber, his house, his
castle, his standing-bed and truckle-bed; 'tis
painted about with the story of the Prodigal,
fresh and new. Go knock and call; he'll speak
like an Anthropophaginian unto thee: knock,
I say. 11
 Sim. There's an old woman, a fat woman,
gone up into his chamber: I'll be so bold as stay,
sir, till she come down; I come to speak with her,
indeed.

Host. Ha! a fat woman! the knight may be robbed: I'll call. Bully knight! bully Sir John! speak from thy lungs military: art thou there? it is thine host, thine Ephesian, calls.

Fal. [*Above*] How now, mine host! 20

Host. Here's a Bohemian-Tartar tarries the coming down of thy fat woman. Let her descend, bully, let her descend; my chambers are honourable: fie! privacy? fie!

Enter FALSTAFF.

Fal. There was, mine host, an old fat woman even now with me; but she's gone.

Sim. Pray you, sir, was't not the wise woman of Brentford?

Fal. Ay, marry, was it, mussel-shell: what would you with her? 30

Sim. My master, sir, Master Slender, sent to her, seeing her go thorough the streets, to know, sir, whether one Nym, sir, that beguiled him of a chain, had the chain or no.

Fal. I spake with the old woman about it.

Sim. And what says she, I pray, sir?

Fal. Marry, she says that the very same man that beguiled Master Slender of his chain cozened him of it.

Sim. I would I could have spoken with the woman herself; I had other things to have spoken with her too from him. 42

Fal. What are they? let us know.

Host. Ay, come; quick.

Sim. I may not conceal them, sir.

Host. Conceal them, or thou diest.

Sim. Why, sir, they were nothing but about Mistress Anne Page; to know if it were my master's fortune to have her or no.

Fal. 'Tis, 'tis his fortune. 50

Sim. What, sir?

Fal. To have her, or no. Go; say the woman told me so.

Sim. May I be bold to say so, sir?

Fal. Ay, sir; like who more bold.

Sim. I thank your worship: I shall make my master glad with these tidings. [*Exit.*

Host. Thou art clerkly, thou art clerkly, Sir John. Was there a wise woman with thee?

Fal. Ay, that there was, mine host; one that hath taught me more wit than ever I learned before in my life; and I paid nothing for it neither, but was paid for my learning.

Enter BARDOLPH.

Bard. Out, alas, sir! cozenage, mere cozenage!

Host. Where be my horses? speak well of them, varletto.

Bard. Run away with the cozeners; for so soon as I came beyond Eton, they threw me off from behind one of them, in a slough of mire; and set spurs and away, like three German devils, three Doctor Faustuses. 71

Host. They are gone but to meet the duke, villain: do not say they be fled; Germans are honest men.

Enter SIR HUGH EVANS.

Evans. Where is mine host?

Host. What is the matter, sir?

Evans. Have a care of your entertainments: there is a friend of mine come to town, tells me

19 *Ephesian.* Boon companion.

21 *Bohemian-Tartar.* Savage, wild-man.

An inhabitant of Tartary. From John Speed's *A Prospect of the Most Famous Parts of the World*, 1631

58 *clerkly.* Scholarly.

71 *Doctor Faustuses.* A reference to Marlowe's *Doctor Faustus.*

80-81 *Readins . . . Maidenhead . . . Colebrook.* Reading, Maidenhead and modern Colnbrook were all villages close to Windsor.

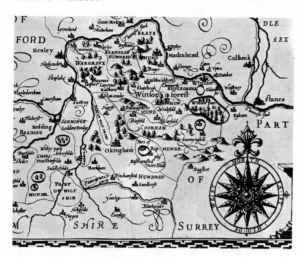

The Windsor area of Berkshire. From John Speed's *Theatre of the Empire of Great Britaine, 1611–12*

100 *liquor.* Grease.

104 *primero.* Card game.

there is three cozen germans that has cozened all
● the hosts of Readins, of Maidenhead, of Colebrook, of horses and money.   I tell you for good will, look you : you are wise and full of gibes and vlouting-stocks, and 'tis not convenient you should be cozened.   Fare you well.   [*Exit.*

Enter DOCTOR CAIUS.

Caius.   Vere is mine host de Jarteer?
Host.   Here, master doctor, in perplexity and doubtful dilemma.
Caius.   I cannot tell vat is dat : but it is tell-a me dat you make grand preparation for a duke de Jamany : by my trot, dere is no duke dat the court is know to come.   I tell you for good vill : adieu.   [*Exit.* 91
Host.   Hue and cry, villain, go !   Assist me, knight.   I am undone !   Fly, run, hue and cry, villain !   I am undone !   [*Exeunt Host and Bard.*
Fal.   I would all the world might be cozened ; for I have been cozened and beaten too.   If it should come to the ear of the court, how I have been transformed and how my transformation hath been washed and cudgelled, they would melt me
● out of my fat drop by drop and liquor fishermen's boots with me : I warrant they would whip me with their fine wits till I were as crest-fallen as a dried pear.   I never prospered since I forswore
● myself at primero.   Well, if my wind were but long enough to say my prayers, I would repent.

Enter MISTRESS QUICKLY.

Now, whence come you?
Quick.   From the two parties, forsooth.
Fal.   The devil take one party and his dam the other !   and so they shall be both bestowed.   I have suffered more for their sakes, more than the villanous inconstancy of man's disposition is able to bear.
Quick.   And have not they suffered?   Yes, I warrant ; speciously one of them ; Mistress Ford, good heart, is beaten black and blue, that you cannot see a white spot about her.
Fal.   What tellest thou me of black and blue? I was beaten myself into all the colours of the rainbow ; and I was like to be apprehended for the witch of Brentford : but that my admirable dexterity of wit, my counterfeiting the action of an old woman, delivered me, the knave constable had set me i' the stocks, i' the common stocks, for a witch.
Quick.   Sir, let me speak with you in your chamber : you shall hear how things go ; and, I warrant, to your content.   Here is a letter will say somewhat.   Good hearts, what ado here is to bring you together !   Sure, one of you does not serve heaven well, that you are so crossed.   130
Fal.   Come up into my chamber.   [*Exeunt.*

SCENE VI.   *Another room in the Garter Inn.*

Enter FENTON *and* HOST.

Host.   Master Fenton, talk not to me ; my mind is heavy : I will give over all.
Fent.   Yet hear me speak.   Assist me in my purpose,
And, as I am a gentleman, I'll give thee

A hundred pound in gold more than your loss.

Host. I will hear you, Master Fenton; and I
will at the least keep your counsel.

Fent. From time to time I have acquainted you
With the dear love I bear to fair Anne Page;
Who mutually hath answer'd my affection,   10
So far forth as herself might be her chooser,
Even to my wish: I have a letter from her
Of such contents as you will wonder at;
• The mirth whereof so larded with my matter,
That neither singly can be manifested,
Without the show of both; fat Falstaff
Hath a great scene: the image of the jest
I'll show you here at large. Hark, good mine host.
To-night at Herne's oak, just'twixt twelve and one,
Must my sweet Nan present the Fairy Queen; 20
The purpose why, is here: in which disguise,
While other jests are something rank on foot,
Her father hath commanded her to slip
Away with Slender and with him at Eton
Immediately to marry: she hath consented:
Now, sir,
Her mother, ever strong against that match
And firm for Doctor Caius, hath appointed
That he shall likewise shuffle her away,
While other sports are tasking of their minds, 30
• And at the deanery, where a priest attends,
Straight marry her: to this her mother's plot
She seemingly obedient likewise hath
Made promise to the doctor. Now, thus it rests:
Her father means she shall be all in white,
And in that habit, when Slender sees his time
To take her by the hand and bid her go,
She shall go with him: her mother hath intended,
The better to denote her to the doctor,
• For they must all be mask'd and vizarded,   40
• That quaint in green she shall be loose enrobed,
With ribands pendent, flaring 'bout her head;
And when the doctor spies his vantage ripe,
To pinch her by the hand, and, on that token,
The maid hath given consent to go with him.

Host. Which means she to deceive, father or
        mother?

Fent. Both, my good host, to go along with me:
And here it rests, that you'll procure the vicar
To stay for me at church 'twixt twelve and one,
And, in the lawful name of marrying,   50
To give our hearts united ceremony.

Host. Well, husband your device; I'll to the
        vicar:
Bring you the maid, you shall not lack a priest.

Fent. So shall I evermore be bound to thee;
Besides, I'll make a present recompense. [*Exeunt.*

ACT V.

Scene I. *A room in the Garter Inn.*

Enter Falstaff *and* Mistress Quickly.

Fal. Prithee, no more prattling; go. I'll hold.
This is the third time; I hope good luck lies in
odd numbers. Away! go. They say there is
divinity in odd numbers, either in nativity, chance,
or death. Away!

Quick. I'll provide you a chain; and I'll do
what I can to get you a pair of horns.

Fal. Away, I say; time wears: hold up your
• head, and mince.   [*Exit Mrs Quickly.*

14 *larded with my matter.* i.e. intermingled with what
concerns me.

31 *deanery.* This was attached to St. George's Chapel
in Windsor Castle.

View of the west end of St George's Chapel, Windsor.
Engraving by Wenceslas Hollar from Elias Ashmole's
*The Institutions, Laws and Ceremonies of the Most Noble
Order of the Garter,* 1672

40 *vizarded.* Disguised.

41 *quaint.* Elegant.

9 *mince.* Walk away (in an affected manner).

23-25 *Goliath . . . beam ;* A biblical reference. *Life is a shuttle.* Proverbial saying again alluding to the Bible.

Page: '. . . we'll couch i'the castle ditch'. Engraving from Charles Knight's *Pictorial Edition of the Works of William Shakspere,* 1839–43

6-7 '*mum . . . budget*'. 'Mumbudget' means 'silence'.

Enter FORD.

How now, Master Brook ! Master Brook, the matter will be known to-night, or never. Be you in the Park about midnight, at Herne's oak, and you shall see wonders.

Ford. Went you not to her yesterday, sir, as you told me you had appointed?

Fal. I went to her, Master Brook, as you see, like a poor old man : but I came from her, Master Brook, like a poor old woman. That same knave Ford, her husband, hath the finest mad devil of jealousy in him, Master Brook, that ever governed frenzy. I will tell you : he beat me grievously, in the shape of a woman ; for in the shape of man, Master Brook, I fear not Goliath with a weaver's beam ; because I know also life is a shuttle. I am in haste ; go along with me : I'll tell you all, Master Brook. Since I plucked geese, played truant and whipped top, I knew not what 'twas to be beaten till lately. Follow me : I'll tell you strange things of this knave Ford, on whom to-night I will be revenged, and I will deliver his wife into your hand. Follow. Strange things in hand, Master Brook ! Follow.
[*Exeunt.*

SCENE II. *Windsor Park.*

Enter PAGE, SHALLOW, *and* SLENDER.

Page. Come, come ; we'll couch i' the castle-ditch till we see the light of our fairies. Remember, son Slender, my daughter.

Slen. Ay, forsooth ; I have spoke with her and we have a nay-word how to know one another : I come to her in white, and cry 'mum ;' she cries 'budget ;' and by that we know one another.

Shal. That's good too : but what needs either your 'mum' or her 'budget?' the white will decipher her well enough. It hath struck ten o'clock.

Page. The night is dark ; light and spirits will become it well. Heaven prosper our sport ! No man means evil but the devil, and we shall know him by his horns. Let's away ; follow me.
[*Exeunt.*

SCENE III. *A street leading to the Park.*

Enter MISTRESS PAGE, MISTRESS FORD, *and* DOCTOR CAIUS.

Mrs Page. Master doctor, my daughter is in green : when you see your time, take her by the hand, away with her to the deanery, and dispatch it quickly. Go before into the Park : we two must go together.

Caius. I know vat I have to do. Adieu.

Mrs Page. Fare you well, sir. [*Exit Caius.*] My husband will not rejoice so much at the abuse of Falstaff as he will chafe at the doctor's marrying my daughter : but 'tis no matter ; better a little chiding than a great deal of heart-break. 11

Mrs Ford. Where is Nan now and her troop of fairies, and the Welsh devil Hugh?

Mrs Page. They are all couched in a pit hard by Herne's oak, with obscured lights ; which, at the very instant of Falstaff's and our meeting, they will at once display to the night.

Mrs Ford. That cannot choose but amaze him.

Mrs Page. If he be not amazed, he will be mocked; if he be amazed, he will every way be mocked.   .21

Mrs Ford. We'll betray him finely.

Mrs Page. Against such lewdsters and their lechery
Those that betray them do no treachery.

Mrs Ford. The hour draws on. To the oak, to the oak!   [*Exeunt.*

SCENE IV. *Windsor Park.*

Enter SIR HUGH EVANS *disguised, with others as Fairies.*

Evans. Trib, trib, fairies; come; and remember your parts: be pold, I pray you; follow me into the pit; and when I give the watch-'ords, do as I pid you: come, come; trib, trib. [*Exeunt*

SCENE V. *Another part of the Park.*

Enter FALSTAFF *disguised as Herne.*

Fal. The Windsor bell hath struck twelve; the minute draws on. Now, the hot-blooded gods assist me! Remember, Jove, thou wast a bull for thy Europa; love set on thy horns. O powerful love! that, in some respects, makes a beast a man, in some other, a man a beast. You were also, Jupiter, a swan for the love of Leda. O omnipotent Love! how near the god drew to the complexion of a goose! A fault done first in the form of a beast. O Jove, a beastly fault! And then another fault in the semblance of a fowl; think on't, Jove; a foul fault! When gods have hot backs, what shall poor men do? For me, I am here a Windsor stag; and the fattest, I think, i' the forest. Send me a cool rut-time, Jove, or who can blame me to piss my tallow? Who comes here? my doe?

Enter MISTRESS FORD *and* MISTRESS PAGE.

Mrs Ford. Sir John! art thou there, my deer? my male deer?

Fal. My doe with the black scut! Let the sky rain potatoes; let it thunder to the tune of Green Sleeves, hail kissing-comfits and snow eringoes; let there come a tempest of provocation, I will shelter me here.

Mrs Ford. Mistress Page is come with me, sweetheart.

Fal. Divide me like a bribe buck, each a haunch: I will keep my sides to myself, my shoulders for the fellow of this walk, and my horns I bequeath your husbands. Am I a woodman, ha? Speak I like Herne the hunter? Why, now is Cupid a child of conscience; he makes restitution. As I am a true spirit, welcome!
                                              [*Noise within.*

Mrs Page. Alas, what noise?

Mrs Ford. Heaven forgive our sins!

Fal. What should this be?

Mrs Ford.⎰
Mrs Page.⎱ Away, away!   [*They run off.*

Fal. I think the devil will not have me damned, lest the oil that's in me should set hell on fire; he would never else cross me thus.   40

3-4 *Jove, thou wast a bull for thy Europa.* Jove abducted Europa by appearing as a bull and when she climbed on his back swam across the sea with her.

13 *hot backs.* Strong sexual desires.

15-16 *cool . . . tallow.* Falstaff is asking for cool weather because lust is hot and likely to melt away his fat.

20 *scut.* Short tail of rabbit or deer.

21 *potatoes.* i.e. sweet potatoes, thought to be aphrodisiacs.

22-23 *kissing comfits and snow eringoes.* i.e. sugar-plums to sweeten the breath and candied roots of the sea-holly, another supposed aphrodisiac.

27 *bribe.* Stolen.

29 *fellow of this walk.* The keeper in charge of that part of the park.

Falstaff with Mistress Page and Mistress Ford. Engraving by H. Fuseli from George Steevens' *The Plays of William Shakspeare,* 1805.

52 *wink and couch.* i.e. close my eyes and lie hidden.

55 *Raise up the organs of her fantasy.* i.e. let her imagination have free rein.

65 *several chairs of order.* Individual stalls in the choir of St. George's Chapel, Windsor, belonging to the Knights of the Order of the Garter.

67 *instalment.* Particular stall. *coat.* i.e. of arms. *several.* Individual.

68 *blazon.* Heraldic shield or coat of arms.

73 '*Honi soit qui mal y pense*'. The motto of the Order of the Garter (Evil be to him who thinks evil).

Knights of the Order of the Garter. Engraving by Wenceslas Hollar from Elias Ashmole's *The Institutions, Laws and Ceremonies of the Most Noble Order of the Garter*, 1672

77 *charactery.* Writing.

Enter SIR HUGH EVANS, *disguised as before;* PISTOL, *as Hobgoblin;* MISTRESS QUICKLY, ANNE PAGE, *and others, as Fairies, with tapers.*

Quick.   Fairies, black, grey, green, and white,
You moonshine revellers, and shades of night.
You orphan heirs of fixed destiny,
Attend your office and your quality.
Crier Hobgoblin, make the fairy oyes.
    Pist.   Elves, list your names; silence, you airy toys.
Cricket, to Windsor chimneys shalt thou leap:
Where fires thou find'st unraked and hearths unswept,
There pinch the maids as blue as bilberry:
Our radiant queen hates sluts and sluttery.   50
    Fal.   They are fairies; he that speaks to them shall die:
• I'll wink and couch: no man their works must eye.
                    [*Lies down upon his face.*
    Evans.   Where's Bede? Go you, and where you find a maid
That, ere she sleep, has thrice her prayers said,
• Raise up the organs of her fantasy;
Sleep she as sound as careless infancy:
But those as sleep and think not on their sins,
Pinch them, arms, legs, backs, shoulders, sides and shins.
    Quick.   About, about;
Search Windsor Castle, elves, within and out: 60
Strew good luck, ouphes, on every sacred room:
That it may stand till the perpetual doom,
In state as wholesome as in state 'tis fit,
Worthy the owner, and the owner it.
• The several chairs of order look you scour
With juice of balm and every precious flower:
• Each fair instalment, coat, and several crest,
• With loyal blazon, evermore be blest!
And nightly, meadow-fairies, look you sing,
Like to the Garter's compass, in a ring: 70
The expressure that it bears, green let it be,
More fertile-fresh than all the field to see;
• And ' Honi soit qui mal y pense' write
In emerald tufts, flowers purple, blue, and white;
Like sapphire, pearl and rich embroidery,
Buckled below fair knighthood's bending knee:
• Fairies use flowers for their charactery.
Away; disperse: but till 'tis one o'clock,
Our dance of custom round about the oak
Of Herne the hunter, let us not forget.   80
    Evans.   Pray you, lock hand in hand; yourselves in order set;
And twenty glow-worms shall our lanterns be,
To guide our measure round about the tree.
But, stay; I smell a man of middle-earth.
    Fal.   Heavens defend me from that Welsh fairy, lest he transform me to a piece of cheese!
    Pist.   Vile worm, thou wast o'erlook'd even in thy birth.
    Quick.   With trial-fire touch me his finger-end:
If he be chaste, the flame will back descend
And turn him to no pain; but if he start,   90
It is the flesh of a corrupted heart.
    Pist.   A trial, come.
    Evans.   Come, will this wood take fire?
                    [*They burn him with their tapers.*
    Fal.   Oh, Oh, Oh!
    Quick.   Corrupt, corrupt, and tainted in desire!

About him, fairies; sing a scornful rhyme;
And, as you trip, still pinch him to your time.

SONG.

Fie on sinful fantasy!
Fie on lust and luxury!
Lust is but a bloody fire,
Kindled with unchaste desire,   100
Fed in heart, whose flames aspire
As thoughts do blow them, higher and higher.
Pinch him, fairies, mutually;
Pinch him for his villany;
Pinch him, and burn him, and turn him about,
Till candles and starlight and moonshine be out.

During this song they pinch FALSTAFF. DOC-
TOR CAIUS *comes one way, and steals away
a boy in green;* SLENDER *another way,
and takes off a boy in white; and* FENTON
comes, and steals away Mrs ANNE PAGE.
*A noise of hunting is heard within.   All
the Fairies run away.* FALSTAFF *pulls
off his buck's head, and rises.*

Enter PAGE, FORD, MISTRESS PAGE *and*
MISTRESS FORD.

Page. Nay, do not fly; I think we have
watch'd you now:
Will none but Herne the hunter serve your turn?
Mrs Page. I pray you, come, hold up the
jest no higher.
Now, good Sir John, how like you Windsor wives?
See you these, husband? do not these fair yokes
Become the forest better than the town?
Ford. Now, sir, who's a cuckold now? Master Brook, Falstaff's a knave, a cuckoldly knave;
here are his horns, Master Brook: and, Master
Brook, he hath enjoyed nothing of Ford's but
his buck-basket, his cudgel, and twenty pounds
of money, which must be paid to Master Brook;
his horses are arrested for it, Master Brook.
Mrs Ford. Sir John, we have had ill luck;
we could never meet.   I will never take you for
my love again; but I will always count you my
deer.
Fal. I do begin to perceive that I am made
an ass.
Ford. Ay, and an ox too: both the proofs are
extant.
Fal. And these are not fairies?   I was three
or four times in the thought they were not fairies:
and yet the guiltiness of my mind, the sudden
surprise of my powers, drove the grossness of the
foppery into a received belief, in despite of the
teeth of all rhyme and reason, that they were
fairies.   See now how wit may be made a Jack-
a-Lent, when 'tis upon ill employment!
Evans. Sir John Falstaff, serve Got, and
leave your desires, and fairies will not pinse you.
Ford. Well said, fairy Hugh.
Evans. And leave your jealousies too, I pray
you.   140
Ford. I will never mistrust my wife again,
till thou art able to woo her in good English.
Fal. Have I laid my brain in the sun and
dried it, that it wants matter to prevent so gross
o'erreaching as this?   Am I ridden with a Welsh
goat too? shall I have a coxcomb of frize?   'Tis
time I were choked with a piece of toasted cheese.

Fairies pinch Falstaff. Engraving from a painting by
Robert Smirke (1752–1845)

146 *coxcomb of frize.* Fool's cap of coarse woollen
cloth.

Falstaff (George Weir) with Ford and Page, Stratford-upon-Avon, 1902

153 *late-walking.* Staying out late at nights.

167 *metheglins.* Welsh mead.

172-173 *is a plummet o'er me.* i.e. has overwhelmed me.

197 *swinged.* Beaten.

Evans. Seese is not good to give putter; your belly is all putter.

Fal. 'Seese' and 'putter'! have I lived to stand at the taunt of one that makes fritters of English? This is enough to be the decay of lust and late-walking through the realm.

Mrs Page. Why, Sir John, do you think, though we would have thrust virtue out of our hearts by the head and shoulders and have given ourselves without scruple to hell, that ever the devil could have made you our delight?

Ford. What, a hodge-pudding? a bag of flax?

Mrs Page. A puffed man?   160

Page. Old, cold, withered and of intolerable entrails?

Ford. And one that is as slanderous as Satan?

Page. And as poor as Job?

Ford. And as wicked as his wife?

Evans. And given to fornications, and to taverns and sack and wine and metheglins, and to drinkings and swearings and starings, pribbles and prabbles?

Fal. Well, I am your theme: you have the start of me; I am dejected; I am not able to answer the Welsh flannel; ignorance itself is a plummet o'er me: use me as you will.

Ford. Marry, sir, we'll bring you to Windsor, to one Master Brook, that you have cozened of money, to whom you should have been a pandar: over and above that you have suffered, I think to repay that money will be a biting affliction.

Page. Yet be cheerful, knight: thou shalt eat a posset to-night at my house; where I will desire thee to laugh at my wife, that now laughs at thee: tell her Master Slender hath married her daughter.

Mrs Page. [*Aside*] Doctors doubt that: if Anne Page be my daughter, she is, by this, Doctor Caius' wife.

Enter SLENDER.

Slen. Whoa, ho! ho, father Page!

Page. Son, how now! how now, son! have you dispatched?

Slen. Dispatched! I'll make the best in Gloucestershire know on't; would I were hanged, la, else!

Page. Of what, son?

Slen. I came yonder at Eton to marry Mistress Anne Page, and she's a great lubberly boy. If it had not been i' the church, I would have swinged him, or he should have swinged me. If I did not think it had been Anne Page, would I might never stir!—and 'tis a postmaster's boy.

Page. Upon my life, then, you took the wrong.   201

Slen. What need you tell me that? I think so, when I took a boy for a girl. If I had been married to him, for all he was in woman's apparel, I would not have had him.

Page. Why, this is your own folly. Did not I tell you how you should know my daughter by her garments?

Slen. I went to her in white, and cried 'mum,' and she cried 'budget,' as Anne and I had appointed; and yet it was not Anne, but a postmaster's boy.

Mrs Page. Good George, be not angry: I knew of your purpose; turned my daughter into green; and, indeed, she is now with the doctor at the deanery, and there married.

Enter CAIUS.

Caius. Vere is Mistress Page? By gar, I am cozened: I ha' married un garçon, a boy; un paysan, by gar, a boy; it is not Anne Page: by gar, I am cozened.   220
Mrs Page. Why, did you take her in green?
Caius. Ay, by gar, and 'tis a boy: by gar, I'll raise all Windsor.   [*Exit.*
Ford. This is strange. Who hath got the right Anne?
Page. My heart misgives me: here comes Master Fenton.

Enter FENTON *and* ANNE PAGE.

How now, Master Fenton!
Anne. Pardon, good father! good my mother, pardon!
Page. Now, mistress, how chance you went not with Master Slender?   231
Mrs Page. Why went you not with master doctor, maid?
Fent. You do amaze her: hear the truth of it.
You would have married her most shamefully,
Where there was no proportion held in love.
The truth is, she and I, long since contracted,
Are now so sure that nothing can dissolve us.
The offence is holy that she hath committed;
And this deceit loses the name of craft,
Of disobedience, or unduteous title,   240
● Since therein she doth evitate and shun
A thousand irreligious cursed hours,
Which forced marriage would have brought upon her.
Ford. Stand not amazed; here is no remedy:
In love the heavens themselves do guide the state;
Money buys lands, and wives are sold by fate.
Fal. I am glad, though you have ta'en a special stand to strike at me, that your arrow hath glanced.
Page. Well, what remedy? Fenton, heaven give thee joy!   250
What cannot be eschew'd must be embraced.
Fal. When night-dogs run, all sorts of deer are chased.
Mrs Page. Well, I will muse no further.
Master Fenton,
Heaven give you many, many merry days!
Good husband, let us every one go home,
And laugh this sport o'er by a country fire;
Sir John and all.
Ford.   Let it be so. Sir John,
To Master Brook you yet shall hold your word;
For he to-night shall lie with Mistress Ford.
                           [*Exeunt.*

241 *evitate.* Avoid.

Anne Page (Vanessa Miles) and Fenton (Roger Rees)
Royal Shakespeare Co, 1968

Twelfth Night

1601

TWELFTH NIGHT, OR WHAT YOU WILL is the last of Shakespeare's romantic comedies. John Manningham, a young barrister of Middle Temple, saw it performed on Candlemas day in their splendid hall, which has survived the barbarity of our time. 2 February 1601–2: 'at our feast we had a play called *Twelfth Night, or What You Will*, much like the Comedy of Errors or *Menaechmi* in Plautus, but most like and near to that in Italian called *Inganni*. A good practice in it to make the Steward believe his Lady was in love with him, by counterfeiting a letter as from his Lady in general terms, telling him what she liked best in him, and prescribing his gesture in smiling, his apparel, etc; and then, when he came to practice, making him believe they took him to be mad.'

We see from this what Elizabethans most appreciated in a play: some piece of sharp practice, some notable act of cozening at which they all shouted out, as well as the love-scenes which similarly stimulated them to acts of love, produced assignations, sent them hurrying home to their wives or, as we are told, to the stews along the South Bank. (Perhaps the City Fathers were right, and the theatres were hardly schools of morals.)

Malvolio. It is somewhat curious that the unappealing character of Malvolio should so dominate people's impression of the play. That perceptive reader, Charles I, a cultivated connoisseur of the arts—unlike the detestable Puritans—registered as much by noting 'Malvolio' beside the play in his copy of the Second Folio. Something of this may be owing to the sheer originality of the character. Malvolio is in love with himself, a narcissist and that is something quite new and different. His mistress, the Countess Olivia, diagnoses what is wrong with him: 'you are sick of self-love, Malvolio, and taste with a distempered appetite.' There follows a sharp psychological observation 'to be generous, guiltless and of free disposition is to take those things for bird-bolts that you deem cannon-bullets.' That is, Malvolio took things too seriously (Ben Jonson was like that, the good-humoured Shakespeare the opposite).

Though we must not take Malvolio for a Puritan, he is somewhat puritanical: the minx Maria says only that 'sometimes he is a kind of puritan'. He takes his job as the Countess' steward seriously and much objects to the caterwauling her ruffianly uncle, Sir Toby Belch, keeps up with boon companions in the hall below—(Sir Toby is also

Above: *Middle Temple Hall, where* Twelfth Night *was performed, and commented on by a young barrister, John Manningham*

Left: *Malvolio with Olivia and Maria. Illustration by W. Heath Robinson, 1908*

engaged in heavily fleecing the simpleton, Sir Andrew Aguecheek.) So far we can only sympathise with Malvolio, trying in vain to keep order in the nursery.

His self-love and conceit, his perfectly honest pride in his job, are his undoing: they lay him open to the trick that is played upon him, of making him believe that the Countess is in love with him. He has no sense of humour, always a preservative. Maria then thinks up another trick, of having him confined in a dark hole of the house, while the Clown dresses up as a minister, Sir Topas, to exorcise the evil spirit from him. All this is very Elizabethan, though the nonsense of exorcising is still with us today, and people are such fools that it sometimes even works.

Perhaps it is not so surprising, after all, that this unattractive character has attracted most attention, and even most sympathy, out of the play. Shakespeare may have got the name, and one or two others, from a couple of Italian plays he looked at—Manningham noticed one of them; but the story was suggested by one of those in a recent book of Barnaby Rich. Shakespeare would seem to be conveying by the name the ill-will the Steward felt for the crew of roisterers and drunks below stairs. From the first his was the part that drew the crowd:

> The cockpit, galleries, boxes are all full
> To hear Malvolio that cross-gartered gull.

It is to be feared that hearty Elizabethans—no sensitive Victorians—much enjoyed his persecution and treatment. Still he remains to us the most interesting person in the play.

The Play. The characters of the main plot are less interesting. The love-sick Duke goes on mooning about the Countess Olivia, who cannot respond to him (and perhaps no wonder) and is hardly sympathetic. The Countess herself is much more so; she at any rate is a personality and has a will of her own, though she throws herself at the head of Viola disguised as an attractive youth. (How ambivalent Elizabethan comedy was—had need to be, with all those boy-actors!) The romantic love-talk is the usual commonplace; when it comes to Olivia's declaration of love in form it is in rhyme.

The more original and memorable characters are the lesser ones. Maria is a very well-depicted minx. Sir Toby Belch is authentic enough, the kind of old ruffian grandees had to put up with in their great houses, for he was a poor relation. Sir Andrew Aguecheek belongs to the tribe of Shakespeare's simple-minded country gentlemen, who exist to be taken in and laughed at, like Slender in *The Merry Wives* or even Justice Shallow.

Feste the Clown offers more of a problem. He has quite an important part to play, but we must face the fact that it is Elizabethan jesting, the role of the licensed jester—like the wit-combats of the earlier comedies—that has most of all dated and appeals to us least. Verbal wit is such diaphanous stuff—William Shakespeare, clever man that he was, had a great fondness for it.

With Feste an important new personality entered the cast of the Company. Will Kemp had departed, a boisterous, extrovert personality in the line of the famous clown, Tarleton, and his place was taken by Robert Armin. Armin was a subtler personality, introvert, temperamental, possibly somewhat *décousu*—which made him right for the wonderfully touching part of the Fool in *King Lear*, written for him; touched with poetry and melancholy, like so many clowns of genius, he was a writer himself, but again discontinuous. The lovely songs of this play are sung by him.

Music. This is the most musical of all the plays—not only in songs and catches but in the whole atmosphere, which is drenched in music, like the Belmont Act of *The Merchant of Venice*. It begins, as it ends, with music:

> If music be the food of love, play on;
> Give me excess of it, that, surfeiting,
> The appetite may sicken, and so die.
> —That strain again! It had a dying fall.

Of course music *is* the food of love, and it is the accompaniment to the romantic love-talk. Then there are the songs:

> O mistress mine, where are you roaming?
> O, stay and hear: your true love's coming . . .

One's heart turns over at the music to it, possibly Morley's:

> What is love? 'tis not hereafter
> Present mirth hath present laughter,
>   What's to come is still unsure.

It is the Duke again who asks for an old song:

> The spinsters and the knitters in the sun
> And the free maids that weave their thread with bones
> Do use to chant it.

The whole age was intensely musical, and people made their own music: they did not get it canned. So Feste sings a song that goes to the heart of this play, suffused as it is with the music of melancholy:

> Come away, come away, death,
> And in sad cypress let me be laid . . .

The play ends with a folksong, which places the whole thing in the perspective of time:

> When that I was and a little tiny boy,
> With hey, ho, the wind and the rain . . .

There are, too, Sir Toby's roaring catches and snatches. 'Hold thy peace, thou knave', 'Three merry men be we', 'There dwelt a man in Babylon, lady, lady!' 'O, the twelfth day of December'—i.e. the Twelfth night of the Christmas holidays and junketings.

Then there are the dances. 'Why dost not thou go to church in a galliard and come home in a coranto? My very walk should be a jig.' Sir Toby's 'passy measures pavin' would be a rather slow pavan. And at a time when people had to make their own entertainments there were numerous games—here we have tray-trip and cherry-pit. Bear-baiting was a familiar spectacle in the towns: Viola, disguised as a youth, is terrified at the thought of a duel with the timid Aguecheek (who is equally scared): Cesario (Viola) 'pants and looks pale, as if a bear were at his heels'. A typical piece of Shakespeare

bawdy follows: 'a little thing would make me tell them how much I lack of a man'.

Personal. Some reflections point as usual to the man writing.

> O spirit of love! how quick and fresh art thou,
> That, notwithstanding thy capacity
> Receiveth as the sea . . .

we remember the 'capacious' image applied to the Dark Lady in the Sonnets, and then—

> nought enters there . . .
> But falls into abatement and low price,
> Even in a minute.

It is 'the expense of spirit' again, no sooner had but despisèd straight. The Duke thinks that a woman should take an older than herself (though Shakespeare had taken a woman to wife who was much his elder):

> So wears she to him,
> So sways she level in her husband's heart;

for men's

> fancies are more giddy and unfirm,
> More longing, wavering, sooner lost and worn
> Than women's are.

No doubt that spoke for William Shakespeare. On the other hand, there were women who could not take the beating of too strong a passion:

>   no woman's heart
> So big, to hold so much: they lack retention.

That had certainly been true of Emilia Lanier:

>   Alas, their love may be called appetite . . .
>   That suffer surfeit, cloyment and revolt.

He had experienced both.

The Age. As usual many touches bespeak the time, give us a picture of it, and help us to place the play in its perspective. There are no Italian phrases now as in the days of Florio, but there are French phrases, as noticeably in *The Merry Wives*. These would be the years when Shakespeare was lodging with the Montjoies. The Countess Olivia betrothed herself to Sebastian (twin brother of Viola-Cesario) by 'mutual joinder' of hands, 'strengthened by interchangement of your rings'. Handfasting, betrothal with a ring before witnesses made a legal contract of marriage in those days. And this is precisely what 'Master Shakespeare' himself effected in 1602 at Madame Montjoie's motion for the daughter of the house and Stephen Bellot, the apprentice at tire- and wig-making. (There is a passage about different sorts and fashions of 'tires' contemporaneously in *The Merry Wives*.)

The songs help us to date the play. A version of 'O mistress mine' appeared in 1599, 'Farewell, dear heart, since I must needs be gone' in 1600. 'The new map with the augmentation to the Indies' refers to Mollineux's map of the world, on a new projection of 1599. Fabian ticks off Sir Toby with 'you are now sailed into the North of my lady's opinion, where you will hang like an icicle on a Dutchman's beard'. The Dutchman was William Barentz, of the Barentz Sea, and his recent Arctic voyage of 1596–7. A couple of references to the Sophy (or Shah) of Persia relate to the account of the Shirley brothers' journey and treatment there, recently published in 1600. Everything shows Shakespeare with attentive ear to the ground picking up everything going on at the time.

Orsino, Duke of Bracchiano, paid a visit to the Queen in January 1601; Shakespeare used his name for his Duke. That is all we can say. From his constant performances at Court he *may* have picked up a hint for Malvolio from Sir William Knollys, Comptroller of the Household, who was a bit of a sourpuss—the Knollyses were puritanically inclined—though he made a fool of himself over Mary Fitton. 'Policy I hate: I had as lief be a Brownist as a politician.' Both terms were derogatory at the time: by politics Elizabethans meant unscrupulous party intrigue, faction-fighting; politicians meant not the estimable, unself-interested figures of today, but more like Machiavellian intriguers or shop-stewards. And to be a Brownist was ludicrous sectarianism: William Browne gave the church-authorities a lot of trouble (besides beating his wife) by starting a separatist Puritan sect; he ultimately suffered a relapse into conformity and sense.

Shakespeare's 'bed of Ware', exceptionally large even for that time, when people largely shared beds, we can still happily see at the Victoria and Albert Museum.

Text. The text presents few difficulties; first printed, probably from the Company's prompt book, it is a good text, with the usual misprints. One misprint remains unexplained: 'the lady of the Strachy married the yeoman of the wardrobe'. Why should not 'Strachy' be a misprint for Sophy, to which there are two other references?

[1] c.f. 'The True Story of Mary Fitton', in my *Discoveries and Reviews*.

TWELFTH NIGHT;

OR, WHAT YOU WILL.

DRAMATIS PERSONÆ.

ORSINO, Duke of Illyria.
SEBASTIAN, brother to Viola.
ANTONIO, a sea captain, friend to Sebastian.
A Sea Captain, friend to Viola.
VALENTINE, } gentlemen attending on the
CURIO, } Duke.
SIR TOBY BELCH, uncle to Olivia.
SIR ANDREW AGUECHEEK.
MALVOLIO, steward to Olivia.

FABIAN,
FESTE, a Clown, } servants to Olivia.
OLIVIA.
VIOLA.
MARIA, Olivia's woman.
Lords, Priests, Sailors, Officers, Musicians, and other Attendants.
SCENE: *A city in Illyria, and the sea-coast near it.*

● *A bullet beside a text line indicates an annotation in the opposite column*

ACT I.

SCENE I. *The* DUKE'S *palace.*

Enter DUKE, CURIO, *and other* LORDS; *Musicians* attending.

Duke. If music be the food of love, play on;
Give me excess of it, that, surfeiting,
The appetite may sicken, and so die.
●That strain again! it had a dying fall:
O, it came o'er my ear like the sweet sound,
That breathes upon a bank of violets,
Stealing and giving odour! Enough; no more:
'Tis not so sweet now as it was before.
●O spirit of love! how quick and fresh art thou,
That, notwithstanding thy capacity   10
Receiveth as the sea, nought enters there,
●Of what validity and pitch soe'er,
But falls into abatement and low price,
●Even in a minute: so full of shapes is fancy
●That it alone is high fantastical.

4 *fall.* Cadence.

9 *quick.* Lively.

12 *validity and pitch.* Value and height.

14 *fancy.* Love.

15 *high fantastical.* Highly imaginative.

Opposite : Malvolio, cross-gartered, with Olivia and Maria. Engraving from Bell's edition of *Shakespeare,* 1774

509

21-23 *I turn'd . . . me.* This image refers to the myth in which the goddess Diana turns the hunter Actaeon into a deer as punishment for seeing her naked. He is then torn apart by his own dogs.

26 *seven years' heat.* Seven summers.

30 *season.* Salt is a preservative, and Olivia will preserve her love in tears.

35 *golden shaft.* Cupid's golden arrows induced love, those of lead, hatred.

37 *liver, brain and heart.* The Elizabethans believed that the liver was the seat of passion, the brain of reason, and the heart of emotion.

39 *self.* Sole.

2 *Illyria.* In Roman times, a province that bordered the East coast of the Adriatic.

4 *Elysium.* Heaven or, in mythology, the islands of the blessed after death.

11 *driving.* Drifting.

15 *Arion.* A Greek musician who threw himself into the sea to escape being killed by sailors. A dolphin, who had been charmed by his songs, carried him safely to shore.

27 *Orsino.* The name may have been suggested by the Duke of Bracciano, Virginio Orsino, who visited the English court in 1601.

Don Virginio Orsino, Duke of Bracciano

Cur.   Will you go hunt, my lord?
Duke.   What, Curio?
Cur.   The hart.
Duke.   Why, so I do, the noblest that I have:
O, when mine eyes did see Olivia first,
Methought she purged the air of pestilence!   20
• That instant was I turn'd into a hart;
And my desires, like fell and cruel hounds,
E'er since pursue me.

Enter VALENTINE.

                    How now! what news from her?
Val.   So please my lord, I might not be admitted;
But from her handmaid do return this answer:
• The element itself, till seven years' heat,
Shall not behold her face at ample view;
But, like a cloistress, she will veiled walk
And water once a day her chamber round
• With eye-offending brine: all this to season   30
A brother's dead love, which she would keep fresh
And lasting in her sad remembrance.
Duke.   O, she that hath a heart of that fine frame

To pay this debt of love but to a brother,
• How will she love, when the rich golden shaft
Hath kill'd the flock of all affections else
• That live in her; when liver, brain and heart,
These sovereign thrones, are all supplied, and fill'd
• Her sweet perfections with one self king!
Away before me to sweet beds of flowers: 40
Love-thoughts lie rich when canopied with bowers.
                                    [*Exeunt.*

SCENE II.   *The sea-coast.*

Enter VIOLA, *a* Captain, *and* Sailors.

Vio.   What country, friends, is this?
• *Cap.*   This is Illyria, lady.
Vio.   And what should I do in Illyria?
• My brother he is in Elysium.
Perchance he is not drown'd: what think you, sailors?
Cap.   It is perchance that you yourself were saved.
Vio.   O my poor brother! and so perchance may he be.
Cap.   True, madam: and, to comfort you with chance,
Assure yourself, after our ship did split,
When you and those poor number saved with you
• Hung on our driving boat, I saw your brother,   11
Most provident in peril, bind himself,
Courage and hope both teaching him the practice,
To a strong mast that lived upon the sea;
• Where, like Arion on the dolphin's back,
I saw him hold acquaintance with the waves
So long as I could see.
Vio.   For saying so, there's gold:
Mine own escape unfoldeth to my hope,
Whereto thy speech serves for authority,   20
The like of him.   Know'st thou this country?
Cap.   Ay, madam, well; for I was bred and born
Not three hours' travel from this very place.
Vio.   Who governs here?
Cap.   A noble duke, in nature as in name.
Vio.   What is his name?
• *Cap.*   Orsino.

Vio.   Orsino! I have heard my father name
him:
He was a bachelor then.
   Cap.   And so is now, or was so very late;   30
For but a month ago I went from hence,
And then 'twas fresh in murmur,—as, you know,
What great ones do the less will prattle of,—
That he did seek the love of fair Olivia.
   Vio.   What's she?
   Cap.   A virtuous maid, the daughter of a count
That died some twelvemonth since, then leaving
her
In the protection of his son, her brother,
Who shortly also died: for whose dear love,
They say, she hath abjured the company   40
And sight of men.
   Vio.   O that I served that lady
And might not be delivered to the world,
Till I had made mine own occasion mellow,
What my estate is!
   Cap.   That were hard to compass;
Because she will admit no kind of suit,
No, not the duke's.
   Vio.   There is a fair behaviour in thee, captain;
And though that nature with a beauteous wall
Doth oft close in pollution, yet of thee
I will believe thou hast a mind that suits   50
With this thy fair and outward character.
I prithee, and I'll pay thee bounteously,
Conceal me what I am, and be my aid
For such disguise as haply shall become
The form of my intent. I'll serve this duke:
Thou shalt present me as an eunuch to him:
It may be worth thy pains; for I can sing
And speak to him in many sorts of music
That will allow me very worth his service.
What else may hap to time I will commit;   60
Only shape thou thy silence to my wit.
   Cap.   Be you his eunuch, and your mute I'll be:
When my tongue blabs, then let mine eyes not see.
   Vio.   I thank thee: lead me on.   [*Exeunt.*

SCENE III. OLIVIA'S *house.*

Enter SIR TOBY BELCH *and* MARIA.

   Sir To.   What a plague means my niece, to
take the death of her brother thus? I am sure
care's an enemy to life.
   Mar.   By my troth, Sir Toby, you must come
in earlier o' nights: your cousin, my lady, takes
great exceptions to your ill hours.
   Sir To.   Why, let her except, before excepted.
   Mar.   Ay, but you must confine yourself within
the modest limits of order.   9
   Sir To.   Confine! I'll confine myself no finer
than I am: these clothes are good enough to
drink in; and so be these boots too: an they be
not, let them hang themselves in their own straps.
   Mar.   That quaffing and drinking will undo
you: I heard my lady talk of it yesterday; and
of a foolish knight that you brought in one night
here to be her wooer.
   Sir To.   Who, Sir Andrew Aguecheek?
   Mar.   Ay, he.
   Sir To.   He's as tall a man as any's in Illyria.
   Mar.   What's that to the purpose?   21
   Sir To.   Why, he has three thousand ducats a
year.

42-44 *And might . . . is.* I shall declare myself when I think the time is appropriate.

59 *allow.* Prove or show.

61 *wit.* Plan.

62 *mute.* Dumb servant.

Laurence Olivier as Sir Toby Belch, Old Vic Theatre, London, 1937

5 *cousin.* In Elizabethan times, a term widely used to denote kinship.

7 *except, before excepted.* A legal phrase meaning, 'with the exceptions previously excluded'.

10 *Confine.* Sir Toby quibbles on the meanings 'to limit' and 'to clothe'.

20 *tall.* Fine or prosperous.

22 *ducats.* Gold or silver coins of varying value in different European countries.

27 *viol-de-gamboys.* Viola da gamba, a stringed instrument that was the ancestor of the violoncello.

30 *natural.* A pun on the meanings 'through nature' and 'like an idiot or fool'.

37 *substractors.* Detractors.

43 *coystrill.* A rogue.

44 *parish-top.* A large top kept in every village, to be whipped in frosty weather, that the peasants might be kept warm by exercise.

Parish-top. Engraving from Charles Knight's *Pictorial Edition of the Works of William Shakspere*, 1839–43

45 *Castiliano vulgo.* A nonsensical expression, like saying 'to speak Spanish'.

73 *'thought is free'.* The proverbial reply to the question 'Do you think I am a fool'?

74 *buttery-bar.* The ledge on the top of the buttery-hatch to rest tankards on.

77 *dry.* A double meaning. Maria implies 'thirsty', but also 'sexual impotence'.

79 *I can . . . dry.* This refers to the saying 'Fools have wit enough to keep themselves dry'.

81 *dry jest.* Dull joke.

85 *canary.* A sweet wine from the Canary Islands.

Mar. Ay, but he'll have but a year in all these ducats: he's a very fool and a prodigal.

Sir To. Fie, that you'll say so! he plays o' the viol-de-gamboys, and speaks three or four languages word for word without book, and hath all the good gifts of nature.   29

Mar. He hath indeed, almost natural: for besides that he's a fool, he's a great quarreller; and but that he hath the gift of a coward to allay the gust he hath in quarrelling, 'tis thought among the prudent he would quickly have the gift of a grave.

Sir To. By this hand, they are scoundrels and substractors that say so of him.   Who are they?

Mar. They that add, moreover, he's drunk nightly in your company.   39

Sir To. With drinking healths to my niece: I'll drink to her as long as there is a passage in my throat and drink in Illyria: he's a coward and a coystrill that will not drink to my niece till his brains turn o' the toe like a parish-top.   What, wench! Castiliano vulgo! for here comes Sir Andrew Agueface.

Enter Sir Andrew Aguecheek.

Sir And. Sir Toby Belch! how now, Sir Toby Belch!

Sir To. Sweet Sir Andrew!

Sir And. Bless you, fair shrew.   50

Mar. And you too, sir.

Sir To. Accost, Sir Andrew, accost.

Sir And. What's that?

Sir To. My niece's chambermaid.

Sir And. Good Mistress Accost, I desire better acquaintance.

Mar. My name is Mary, sir.

Sir And. Good Mistress Mary Accost,—

Sir To. You mistake, knight: 'accost' is front her, board her, woo her, assail her.   60

Sir And. By my troth, I would not undertake her in this company.   Is that the meaning of 'accost'?

Mar. Fare you well, gentlemen.

Sir To. An thou let part so, Sir Andrew, would thou mightst never draw sword again.

Sir And. An you part so, mistress, I would I might never draw sword again.   Fair lady, do you think you have fools in hand?

Mar. Sir, I have not you by the hand.   70

Sir And. Marry, but you shall have; and here's my hand.

Mar. Now, sir, 'thought is free:' I pray you, bring your hand to the buttery-bar and let it drink.

Sir And. Wherefore, sweet-heart? what's your metaphor?

Mar. It's dry, sir.

Sir And. Why, I think so: I am not such an ass but I can keep my hand dry.   But what's your jest?   80

Mar. A dry jest, sir.

Sir And. Are you full of them?

Mar. Ay, sir, I have them at my fingers' ends: marry, now I let go your hand, I am barren.
                                                            [*Exit.*

Sir To. O knight, thou lackest a cup of canary: when did I see thee so put down?

Sir And. Never in your life, I think; unless you see canary put me down.   Methinks sometimes I have no more wit than a Christian or an ordinary man has: but I am a great eater of beef and I believe that does harm to my wit. 91

Sir To. No question.

Sir And. An I thought that, I'ld forswear it. I'll ride home to-morrow, Sir Toby.

Sir To. Pourquoi, my dear knight?

Sir And. What is 'pourquoi'? do or not do? I would I had bestowed that time in the tongues that I have in fencing, dancing and bear-baiting: O, had I but followed the arts!

Sir To. Then hadst thou had an excellent head of hair. 101

Sir And. Why, would that have mended my hair?

Sir To. Past question; for thou seest it will not curl by nature.

Sir And. But it becomes me well enough, does't not?

Sir To. Excellent; it hangs like flax on a distaff; and I hope to see a housewife take thee between her legs and spin it off. 110

Sir And. Faith, I'll home to-morrow, Sir Toby: your niece will not be seen; or if she be, it's four to one she'll none of me: the count himself here hard by woos her.

Sir To. She'll none o' the count: she'll not match above her degree, neither in estate, years, nor wit; I have heard her swear't. Tut, there's life in't, man.

Sir And. I'll stay a month longer. I am a fellow o' the strangest mind i' the world; I delight in masques and revels sometimes altogether. 121

Sir To. Art thou good at these kickshawses, knight?

Sir And. As any man in Illyria, whatsoever he be, under the degree of my betters; and yet I will not compare with an old man.

Sir To. What is thy excellence in a galliard, knight?

Sir And. Faith, I can cut a caper.

Sir To. And I can cut the mutton to't. 130

Sir And. And I think I have the back-trick simply as strong as any man in Illyria.

Sir To. Wherefore are these things hid? wherefore have these gifts a curtain before 'em? are they like to take dust, like Mistress Mall's picture? why dost thou not go to church in a galliard and come home in a coranto? My very walk should be a jig; I would not so much as make water but in a sink-a-pace. What dost thou mean? Is it a world to hide virtues in? I did think, by the excellent constitution of thy leg, it was formed under the star of a galliard.

Sir And. Ay, 'tis strong, and it does indifferent well in a flame-coloured stock. Shall we set about some revels?

Sir To. What shall we do else? were we not born under Taurus?

Sir And. Taurus! That's sides and heart.

Sir To. No, sir; it is legs and thighs. Let me see thee caper: ha! higher: ha, ha! excellent! [*Exeunt.* 151

SCENE IV. *The* DUKE'S *palace.*

Enter VALENTINE, *and* VIOLA *in man's attire.*

Val. If the duke continue these favours towards you, Cesario, you are like to be much ad-

90 *eater of beef*. Too much beef was believed to make men dull.

97 *tongues*. A pun on 'tongs' which Sir Toby takes up in his reply about 'head of hair'.

109 *distaff*. A staff used in spinning.

122 *kickshawses*. Trifles, from the French *quelque chose*.

127 *galliard*. A dance in triple time involving a 'caper' on the fifth step.

129 *caper*. A pun on the meanings 'leap' and on the sauce eaten with mutton.

131 *back-trick*. A series of reverse steps in a dance.

135 *Mistress Mall*. Pictures were protected from dust and sun by curtains.

137 *coranto*. A running dance.

139 *sink-a-pace*. A galliard of five steps. From the French *cinq pas*.

147 *Taurus*. Each sign of the zodiac was believed to influence a specific part of the body. Taurus was associated with the throat and neck; both Sir Toby and Sir Andrew are wrong.

Sir Toby: 'No, sir; it is legs and thighs. Let me see thee caper'. Engraving by Kenny Meadows from Barry Cornwall's *The Works of Shakspere*, 1846

5 *humour*. Changeable temperament.

15 *address thy gait*. Go.

Duke: 'Surprise her with discourse of my dear faith'.
Claire Bloom as Viola and John Neville as Orsino, Old
Vic Theatre, London, 1954

28 *nuncio*. Messenger.

32 *rubious*. Ruby-red. *pipe*. High boyish voice.

35 *constellation*. Character (because the Elizabethans
believed it was determined by the position of the stars
at birth).

41 *barful strife*. An effort full of obstacles.

6 *fear no colours*. Military standards, but also a pun on
'collars'.

7 *Make that good*. Explain it.

9 *lenten*. Sparse, because Lent was a time of fasting.

vanced: he hath known you but three days, and
already you are no stranger.
 ● *Vio.*   You either fear his humour or my negligence, that you call in question the continuance
of his love : is he inconstant, sir, in his favours?
   Val.   No, believe me.
   Vio.   I thank you.   Here comes the count.

Enter DUKE, CURIO, *and* Attendants.

   Duke.   Who saw Cesario, ho ?   10
   Vio.   On your attendance, my lord ; here.
   Duke.   Stand you a while aloof.   Cesario,
Thou know'st no less but all ; I have unclasp'd
To thee the book even of my secret soul :
 ● Therefore, good youth, address thy gait unto her ;
Be not denied access, stand at her doors,
And tell them, there thy fixed foot shall grow
Till thou have audience.
   Vio.   Sure, my noble lord,
If she be so abandon'd to her sorrow
As it is spoke, she never will admit me.   20
   Duke.   Be clamorous and leap all civil bounds
Rather than make unprofited return.
   Vio.   Say I do speak with her, my lord, what
         then?
   Duke.   O, then unfold the passion of my love,
Surprise her with discourse of my dear faith :
It shall become thee well to act my woes ;
She will attend it better in thy youth
 ● Than in a nuncio's of more grave aspect.
   Vio.   I think not so, my lord.
   Duke.   Dear lad, believe it ;
For they shall yet belie thy happy years,   30
That say thou art a man : Diana's lip
 ● Is not more smooth and rubious ; thy small pipe
Is as the maiden's organ, shrill and sound,
And all is semblative a woman's part.
 ● I know thy constellation is right apt
For this affair.   Some four or five attend him ;
All, if you will ; for I myself am best
When least in company.   Prosper well in this,
And thou shalt live as freely as thy lord,
To call his fortunes thine.
   Vio.   I'll do my best   40
 ● To woo your lady : [*Aside*] yet, a barful strife !
Whoe'er I woo, myself would be his wife.
                                        [*Exeunt.*

SCENE V.   OLIVIA'S *house.*

Enter MARIA *and* CLOWN.

   Mar.   Nay, either tell me where thou hast
been, or I will not open my lips so wide as a
bristle may enter in way of thy excuse : my lady
will hang thee for thy absence.
   Clo.   Let her hang me : he that is well hanged
 ● in this world needs to fear no colours.
 ● *Mar.*   Make that good.
   Clo.   He shall see none to fear.
 ● *Mar.*   A good lenten answer : I can tell thee
where that saying was born, of 'I fear no colours.'
   Clo.   Where, good Mistress Mary ?   11
   Mar.   In the wars ; and that may you be bold
to say in your foolery.
   Clo.   Well, God give them wisdom that have
it ; and those that are fools, let them use their
talents.
   Mar.   Yet you will be hanged for being so

long absent; or to be turned away, is not that as good as a hanging to you? 19

Clo. Many a good hanging prevents a bad marriage; and, for turning away, let summer bear it out.

Mar. You are resolute, then?

Clo. Not so, neither; but I am resolved on two points.

Mar. That if one break, the other will hold; or, if both break, your gaskins fall.

Clo. Apt, in good faith; very apt. Well, go thy way; if Sir Toby would leave drinking, thou wert as witty a piece of Eve's flesh as any in Illyria. 31

Mar. Peace, you rogue, no more o' that. Here comes my lady: make your excuse wisely, you were best. [*Exit.*

Clo. Wit, an't be thy will, put me into good fooling! Those wits, that think they have thee, do very oft prove fools; and I, that am sure I lack thee, may pass for a wise man: for what says Quinapalus? 'Better a witty fool than a foolish wit.' 40

Enter Lady OLIVIA *with* MALVOLIO.

God bless thee, lady!

Oli. Take the fool away.

Clo. Do you not hear, fellows? Take away the lady.

Oli. Go to, you're a dry fool; I'll no more of you: besides, you grow dishonest.

Clo. Two faults, madonna, that drink and good counsel will amend: for give the dry fool drink, then is the fool not dry: bid the dishonest man mend himself; if he mend, he is no longer dishonest; if he cannot let the botcher mend him. Any thing that's mended is but patched: virtue that transgresses is but patched with sin; and sin that amends is but patched with virtue. If that this simple syllogism will serve, so; if it will not, what remedy? As there is no true cuckold but calamity, so beauty's a flower. The lady bade take away the fool; therefore, I say again, take her away.

Oli. Sir, I bade them take away you. 60

Clo. Misprision in the highest degree! Lady, cucullus non facit monachum; that's as much to say as I wear not motley in my brain. Good madonna, give me leave to prove you a fool.

Oli. Can you do it?

Clo. Dexteriously, good madonna.

Oli. Make your proof.

Clo. I must catechize you for it, madonna: good my mouse of virtue, answer me.

Oli. Well, sir, for want of other idleness, I'll bide your proof. 71

Clo. Good madonna, why mournest thou?

Oli. Good fool, for my brother's death.

Clo. I think his soul is in hell, madonna.

Oli. I know his soul is in heaven, fool.

Clo. The more fool, madonna, to mourn for your brother's soul being in heaven. Take away the fool, gentlemen.

Oli. What think you of this fool, Malvolio? doth he not mend? 80

Mal. Yes, and shall do till the pangs of death shake him: infirmity, that decays the wise, doth ever make the better fool.

Clo. God send you, sir, a speedy infirmity, for

Maria: 'Yet you will be hanged for being so long absent'. Illustration by W. Heath Robinson, 1908

25 *points.* Subjects, but Maria puns on a second meaning i.e. the laces that held up breeches.

27 *gaskins.* Wide, loose trousers.

39 *Quinapalus.* Feste invents a philosopher.

51 *botcher.* A repairer of clothes; a worker less skilled than a craftsman.

55 *simple syllogism.* Like the fool's parti-coloured motley, no man is all bad or all good; he is a patchwork of sin and virtue.

61 *Misprision.* Misapprehension.

62 *cucullus non facit monachum.* 'A cowl does not make a monk'.

69 *mouse.* Term of endearment.

80 *mend.* Improve.

91 *ordinary fool.* A jester who was paid to perform in inns.

92-93 *out of his guard.* Defenceless; taken from fencing parlance.

95 *set.* Using memorized jokes and incapable of spontaneous ad libbing.

96 *fools' zanies.* A fool's assistants.

100 *bird-bolts.* Blunt missiles for a crossbow.

101 *allowed.* Licensed.

105 *Now Mercury . . . leasing.* May the God of deceit make you a good liar.

123 *pia mater.* Brain.

129 *pickle-herring.* Sir Toby is blaming pickled herrings for his drunken hiccoughing.

Sir Toby: 'give me faith, say I . . .' Illustration by W. Heath Robinson, 1908

140 *above heat.* Above normal body temperature.

142 *crowner.* Coroner.

the better increasing your folly! Sir Toby will be sworn that I am no fox; but he will not pass his word for two pence that you are no fool.

Oli. How say you to that, Malvolio?

Mal. I marvel your ladyship takes delight in such a barren rascal: I saw him put down the other day with an ordinary fool that has no more brain than a stone. Look you now, he's out of his guard already; unless you laugh and minister occasion to him, he is gagged. I protest, I take these wise men, that crow so at these set kind of fools, no better than the fools' zanies.

Oli. O, you are sick of self-love, Malvolio, and taste with a distempered appetite. To be generous, guiltless and of free disposition, is to take those things for bird-bolts that you deem cannon-bullets: there is no slander in an allowed fool, though he do nothing but rail; nor no railing in a known discreet man, though he do nothing but reprove.

Clo. Now Mercury endue thee with leasing, for thou speakest well of fools!

Re-enter MARIA.

Mar. Madam, there is at the gate a young gentleman much desires to speak with you.

Oli. From the Count Orsino, is it?

Mar. I know not, madam: 'tis a fair young man, and well attended.   111

Oli. Who of my people hold him in delay?

Mar. Sir Toby, madam, your kinsman.

Oli. Fetch him off, I pray you; he speaks nothing but madman: fie on him! [*Exit Maria.*] Go you, Malvolio: if it be a suit from the count, I am sick, or not at home; what you will, to dismiss it. [*Exit Malvolio.*] Now you see, sir, how your fooling grows old, and people dislike it.

Clo. Thou hast spoke for us, madonna, as if thy eldest son should be a fool; whose skull Jove cram with brains! for,—here he comes,—one of thy kin has a most weak pia mater.

Enter SIR TOBY.

Oli. By mine honour, half drunk. What is he at the gate, cousin?

Sir To. A gentleman.

Oli. A gentleman! what gentleman?

Sir To. 'Tis a gentleman here—a plague o' these pickle-herring! How now, sot!

Clo. Good Sir Toby!   130

Oli. Cousin, cousin, how have you come so early by this lethargy?

Sir To. Lechery! I defy lechery. There's one at the gate.

Oli. Ay, marry, what is he?

Sir To. Let him be the devil, an he will, I care not: give me faith, say I. Well, it's all one.   [*Exit.*

Oli. What's a drunken man like, fool?

Clo. Like a drowned man, a fool and a mad man: one draught above heat makes him a fool; the second mads him; and a third drowns him.

Oli. Go thou and seek the crowner, and let him sit o' my coz; for he's in the third degree of drink, he's drowned: go, look after him.

Clo. He is but mad yet, madonna; and the fool shall look to the madman.   [*Exit.*

Re-enter MALVOLIO.

Mal. Madam, yond young fellow swears he will speak with you. I told him you were sick; he takes on him to understand so much, and therefore comes to speak with you. I told him you were asleep; he seems to have a foreknowledge of that too, and therefore comes to speak with you. What is to be said to him, lady? he's fortified against any denial.

Oli. Tell him he shall not speak with me.

Mal. Has been told so; and he says, he'll ● stand at your door like a sheriff's post, and be the supporter to a bench, but he'll speak with you.

Oli. What kind o' man is he?

Mal. Why, of mankind.   160

Oli. What manner of man?

Mal. Of very ill manner; he'll speak with you, will you or no.

Oli. Of what personage and years is he?

Mal. Not yet old enough for a man, nor young ● enough for a boy; as a squash is before 'tis a ● peascod, or a codling when 'tis almost an apple: ● 'tis with him in standing water, between boy and man. He is very well-favoured and he speaks very shrewishly; one would think his mother's milk were scarce out of him.   171

Oli. Let him approach: call in my gentlewoman.

Mal. Gentlewoman, my lady calls.   [*Exit.*

Re-enter MARIA.

Oli. Give me my veil: come, throw it o'er my face.
We'll once more hear Orsino's embassy.

Enter VIOLA, *and* Attendants.

Vio. The honourable lady of the house, which is she?

Oli. Speak to me; I shall answer for her. Your will?   180

Vio. Most radiant, exquisite and unmatchable beauty,—I pray you, tell me if this be the lady of the house, for I never saw her: I would be loath to cast away my speech, for besides that it is excellently well penned, I have taken great pains to con it. Good beauties, let me sustain no ● scorn; I am very comptible, even to the least sinister usage.

Oli. Whence came you, sir?   189

Vio. I can say little more than I have studied, and that question's out of my part. Good gentle one, give me modest assurance if you be the lady of the house, that I may proceed in my speech.

Oli. Are you a comedian?

● *Vio.* No, my profound heart: and yet, by the very fangs of malice I swear, I am not that I play. Are you the lady of the house?

Oli. If I do not usurp myself, I am.

Vio. Most certain, if you are she, you do ● usurp yourself; for what is yours to bestow is ● not yours to reserve. But this is from my commission: I will on with my speech in your praise, and then show you the heart of my message.

Oli. Come to what is important in't: I forgive you the praise.

Vio. Alas, I took great pains to study it, and 'tis poetical.

Malvolio. Drawing by Percy Anderson, 1922

157 *Sheriff's post.* Posts were placed in front of mayors' and sheriffs' doors.

166 *squash.* An unripe pea-pod.

167 *codling.* An unripe apple.

168 *standing water.* The turn of the tide.

187-188 *I am . . . sinister usage.* I am sensitive to the smallest slight.

195 *No, my profound heart.* No, in all sincerity.

200 *usurp yourself.* Viola chides Olivia that by not marrying she is wrong herself.

201-202 *from my commission.* Outside my instructions.

213 *time of moon*. The moon was associated with lunacy.

217 *swabber*. The hand who washes the decks. *hull*. drift.

218 *giant*. An ironic reference to Maria's small size.

233 *divinity*. A theological dissertation.

251 *curtain*. This refers to the curtain that was hung over a picture to protect it against sun and dust.

252-253 *such a one I was this present*. This is a portrait of me, at present.

Olivia: '. . . 'is't not well done?' Painting by C. R. Leslie (1794–1859)

255 *in grain*. Colour fast. Olivia is refuting any suggestion that she might be wearing cosmetics.

273 *nonpareil*. Incomparable.

Opposite : Olivia unveiling. Engraving from a design by F. Hayman for Hanmer's edition of Shakespeare's works, 1744

Oli. It is the more like to be feigned : I pray you, keep it in. I heard you were saucy at my gates, and allowed your approach rather to wonder at you than to hear you. If you be not mad, be gone; if you have reason, be brief: 'tis not that time of moon with me to make one in so skipping a dialogue.

Mar. Will you hoist sail, sir? here lies your way.

Vio. No, good swabber; I am to hull here a little longer. Some mollification for your giant, sweet lady. Tell me your mind: I am a messenger.   220

Oli. Sure, you have some hideous matter to deliver, when the courtesy of it is so fearful. Speak your office.

Vio. It alone concerns your ear. I bring no overture of war, no taxation of homage: I hold the olive in my hand; my words are as full of peace as matter.

Oli. Yet you began rudely. What are you? what would you?   229

Vio. The rudeness that hath appeared in me have I learned from my entertainment. What I am, and what I would, are as secret as maidenhead; to your ears, divinity, to any other's, profanation.

Oli. Give us the place alone: we will hear this divinity. [*Exeunt Maria and Attendants.*] Now, sir, what is your text?

Vio. Most sweet lady,—

Oli. A comfortable doctrine, and much may be said of it. Where lies your text?   240

Vio. In Orsino's bosom.

Oli. In his bosom! In what chapter of his bosom?

Vio. To answer by the method, in the first of his heart.

Oli. O, I have read it: it is heresy. Have you no more to say?

Vio. Good madam, let me see your face.

Oli. Have you any commission from your lord to negotiate with my face? You are now out of your text: but we will draw the curtain and show you the picture. Look you, sir, such a one I was this present: is't not well done?   [*Unveiling.*

Vio. Excellently done, if God did all.

Oli. 'Tis in grain, sir; 'twill endure wind and weather.

Vio. 'Tis beauty truly blent, whose red and white
Nature's own sweet and cunning hand laid on:
Lady, you are the cruell'st she alive,
If you will lead these graces to the grave   260
And leave the world no copy.

Oli. O, sir, I will not be so hard-hearted; I will give out divers schedules of my beauty: it shall be inventoried, and every particle and utensil labelled to my will: as, item, two lips, indifferent red; item, two grey eyes, with lids to them; item, one neck, one chin, and so forth. Were you sent hither to praise me?

Vio. I see you what you are, you are too proud;
But, if you were the devil, you are fair.   270
My lord and master loves you: O, such love
Could be but recompensed, though you were crown'd
The nonpareil of beauty !

Viola (Dorothy Tutin) and Olivia (Geraldine McEwan),
Stratford-upon-Avon, 1958

___

279 *In voices well divulged*. Well spoken of.

280 *in dimension*. Physically.

287 *willow*. The tree associated with the unrequited
love.

288 *my soul*. i.e. Olivia.

291 *Halloo*. Cry loudly; there is also a pun here on
'hallow', meaning to honour.

297 *state*. Social class.

312 *blazon*. Coat of arms.

320 *county's man*. Count's man.

322 *flatter*. Arouse hope.

329 *owe*. Own.

Oli.   How does he love me?
Vio.   With adorations, fertile tears,
With groans that thunder love, with sighs of fire.
   Oli.   Your lord does know my mind; I cannot
      love him:
Yet I suppose him virtuous, know him noble,
Of great estate, of fresh and stainless youth;
● In voices well divulged, free, learn'd and valiant;
● And in dimension and the shape of nature   280
A gracious person: but yet I cannot love him;
He might have took his answer long ago.
   Vio.   If I did love you in my master's flame,
With such a suffering, such a deadly life,
In your denial I would find no sense;
I would not understand it.
   Oli.   Why, what would you?
●   *Vio.*   Make me a willow cabin at your gate,
● And call upon my soul within the house;
Write loyal cantons of contemned love
And sing them loud even in the dead of night;
● Halloo your name to the reverberate hills   291
And make the babbling gossip of the air
Cry out 'Olivia!'   O, you should not rest
Between the elements of air and earth,
But you should pity me!
   Oli.   You might do much.
What is your parentage?
●   *Vio.*   Above my fortunes, yet my state is well:
I am a gentleman.
   Oli.   Get you to your lord;
I cannot love him: let him send no more;
Unless, perchance, you come to me again,   300
To tell me how he takes it.   Fare you well:
I thank you for your pains: spend this for me.
   Vio.   I am no fee'd post, lady; keep your
      purse:
My master, not myself, lacks recompense.
Love make his heart of flint that you shall love;
And let your fervour, like my master's, be
Placed in contempt!   Farewell, fair cruelty.
                                                    [*Exit.*

   Oli.   'What is your parentage?'
'Above my fortunes, yet my state is well:
I am a gentleman.'   I'll be sworn thou art;   310
Thy tongue, thy face, thy limbs, actions and
      spirit,
● Do give thee five-fold blazon: not too fast: soft,
      soft!
Unless the master were the man.   How now!
Even so quickly may one catch the plague?
Methinks I feel this youth's perfections
With an invisible and subtle stealth
To creep in at mine eyes.   Well, let it be.
What ho, Malvolio!

                  Re-enter MALVOLIO.

   Mal.   Here, madam, at your service.
   Oli.   Run after that same peevish messenger,
● The county's man: he left this ring behind him,
Would I or not: tell him I'll none of it.   321
● Desire him not to flatter with his lord,
Nor hold him up with hopes; I am not for him:
If that the youth will come this way to-morrow,
I'll give him reasons for't: hie thee, Malvolio.
   Mal.   Madam, I will.   [*Exit.*
   Oli.   I do I know not what, and fear to find
Mine eye too great a flatterer for my mind.
● Fate, show thy force: ourselves we do not owe;
What is decreed must be, and be this so. [*Exit.*

ACT II.

SCENE I. *The sea-coast.*

Enter ANTONIO *and* SEBASTIAN.

Ant. Will you stay no longer? nor will you not that I go with you?

Seb. By your patience, no. My stars shine darkly over me: the malignancy of my fate might
● perhaps distemper yours; therefore I shall crave of you your leave that I may bear my evils alone: it were a bad recompense for your love, to lay any of them on you.

Ant. Let me yet know of you whither you are bound. 10
● *Seb.* No, sooth, sir: my determinate voyage
● is mere extravagancy. But I perceive in you so excellent a touch of modesty, that you will not extort from me what I am willing to keep in; therefore it charges me in manners the rather to express myself. You must know of me then, Antonio, my name is Sebastian, which I called Roderigo. My father was that Sebastian of Messaline, whom I know you have heard of. He left behind him myself and a sister, both born in an hour: if the heavens had been pleased, would we had so ended! but you, sir, altered that; for some hour
● before you took me from the breach of the sea was my sister drowned.

Ant. Alas the day!

Seb. A lady, sir, though it was said she much resembled me, was yet of many accounted beautiful: but, though I could not with such estimable wonder overfar believe that, yet thus far I will boldly publish her; she bore a mind that envy could not but call fair. She is drowned already, sir, with salt water, though I seem to drown her remembrance again with more.

Ant. Pardon me, sir, your bad entertainment.

Seb. O good Antonio, forgive me your trouble.

Ant. If you will not murder me for my love, let me be your servant.

Seb. If you will not undo what you have done, that is, kill him whom you have recovered, desire it not. Fare ye well at once: my bosom is full
● of kindness, and I am yet so near the manners of my mother, that upon the least occasion more
● mine eyes will tell tales of me. I am bound to the Count Orsino's court: farewell. [*Exit.*

Ant. The gentleness of all the gods go with thee!
I have many enemies in Orsino's court,
Else would I very shortly see thee there.
But, come what may, I do adore thee so,
That danger shall seem sport, and I will go. 49
[*Exit.*

SCENE II. *A street.*

Enter VIOLA, MALVOLIO *following.*

Mal. Were not you even now with the Countess Olivia?

Vio. Even now, sir; on a moderate pace I have since arrived but hither.

Mal. She returns this ring to you, sir: you might have saved me my pains, to have taken it away yourself. She adds, moreover, that you should put your lord into a desperate assurance she will none of him: and one thing more, that

Antonio and Sebastian. Nineteenth century costume designs

5 *distemper.* Affect for the worse.

11-12 *sooth.* Truth. *my determinate . . . extravagancy.* My intention to travel is mere whim.

12-16 *But I perceive . . . express myself.* I see you are too polite to ask questions, so I will tell you who I am.

23 *breach.* Surf.

41-42 *near the . . . mother.* Near tears.

43 *tell tales of me.* Betray me.

13 *She took the ring of me*. Viola lies to protect Olivia.

20 *She made good view of me*. She stared at me.

29 *pregnant enemy*. Wily devil.

30 *proper-false*. Handsome deceivers.

34 *fadge*. Turn out.

William Farren, 19th century actor, as Sir Andrew
Aguecheek

2-3 *'diluculo surgere'*. 'It is most healthy to rise at dawn';
a tag from Lily's *Latin Grammar*.

10 *four elements*. The Elizabethans believed that everything was composed of earth, air, fire and water.

17 *the picture of 'we three'*. A picture of two fools or
donkeys, with the viewer making the third.

18 *catch*. A song sung in a round.

23-25 *Pigrogromitus . . . Queubus*. Example of mock
learning that Feste delights in.

26 *leman*. Sweetheart.

27 *impeticos thy gratillity*. More nonsense, but meaning 'pocket thy gratuity'.

28 *whipstock*. Whiphandle.

you be never so hardy to come again in his affairs, unless it be to report your lord's taking of
this.   Receive it so.

● *Vio.*   She took the ring of me: I'll none of it.
   Mal.   Come, sir, you peevishly threw it to
her; and her will is, it should be so returned: if
it be worth stooping for, there it lies in your eye;
if not, be it his that finds it.   [*Exit.*
   Vio.   I left no ring with her: what means this
      lady?
Fortune forbid my outside have not charm'd her!
● She made good view of me; indeed, so much,   20
That sure methought her eyes had lost her tongue,
For she did speak in starts distractedly.
She loves me, sure; the cunning of her passion
Invites me in this churlish messenger.
None of my lord's ring! why, he sent her none.
I am the man: if it be so, as 'tis,
Poor lady, she were better love a dream.
Disguise, I see, thou art a wickedness,
● Wherein the pregnant enemy does much.
● How easy is it for the proper-false   30
In women's waxen hearts to set their forms!
Alas, our frailty is the cause, not we!
For such as we are made of, such we be.
● How will this fadge? my master loves her dearly;
And I, poor monster, fond as much on him;
And she, mistaken, seems to dote on me.
What will become of this?   As I am man,
My state is desperate for my master's love;
As I am woman,—now alas the day!—
What thriftless sighs shall poor Olivia breathe!
O time! thou must untangle this, not I;   41
It is too hard a knot for me to untie!   [*Exit.*

SCENE III.   OLIVIA'S *house*.

Enter SIR TOBY *and* SIR ANDREW.

   Sir To.   Approach, Sir Andrew: not to be a-bed
● after midnight is to be up betimes; and 'diluculo
surgere,' thou know'st,—
   Sir And.   Nay, by my troth, I know not: but
I know, to be up late is to be up late.
   Sir To.   A false conclusion: I hate it as an
unfilled can.   To be up after midnight and to go
to bed then, is early: so that to go to bed after
midnight is to go to bed betimes.   Does not our
● life consist of the four elements?   10
   Sir And.   Faith, so they say; but I think it
rather consists of eating and drinking.
   Sir To.   Thou'rt a scholar; let us therefore eat
and drink.   Marian, I say! a stoup of wine!

Enter CLOWN.

   Sir And.   Here comes the fool, i' faith.
   Clo.   How now, my hearts! did you never
● see the picture of 'we three'?   Now let's have a catch.
● *Sir To.*   Welcome, ass.   Now let's have a catch.
   Sir And.   By my troth, the fool has an excellent breast.   I had rather than forty shillings I
had such a leg, and so sweet a breath to sing, as
the fool has.   In sooth, thou wast in very gracious
● fooling last night, when thou spokest of Pigrogromitus, of the Vapians passing the equinoctial of
Queubus: 'twas very good, i' faith.   I sent thee
● sixpence for thy leman: hadst thou it?
● *Clo.*   I did impeticos thy gratillity; for Malvolio's
● nose is no whipstock: my lady has a white hand,
and the Myrmidons are no bottle-ale houses.

Sir And. Excellent! why, this is the best fooling, when all is done.   Now, a song.   31
Sir To. Come on; there is sixpence for you: let's have a song.
Sir And. There's a testril of me too: if one knight give a—
Clo. Would you have a love-song, or a song of good life?
Sir To. A love-song, a love-song.
Sir And. Ay, ay: I care not for good life.
Clo. [Sings]
O mistress mine, where are you roaming?   40
O, stay and hear; your true love's coming,
   That can sing both high and low:
Trip no further, pretty sweeting;
Journeys end in lovers meeting,
   Every wise man's son doth know.
Sir And. Excellent good, i' faith.
Sir To. Good, good.
Clo. [Sings]
What is love? 'tis not hereafter;
Present mirth hath present laughter;
   What's to come is still unsure: 50
In delay there lies no plenty;
Then come kiss me, sweet and twenty,
   Youth's a stuff will not endure.
Sir And. A mellifluous voice, as I am true knight.
Sir To. A contagious breath.
Sir And. Very sweet and contagious, i' faith.
Sir To. To hear by the nose, it is dulcet in contagion.   But shall we make the welkin dance indeed? shall we rouse the night-owl in a catch that will draw three souls out of one weaver? shall we do that?
Sir And. An you love me, let's do't: I am dog at a catch.
Clo. By'r lady, sir, and some dogs will catch well.
Sir And. Most certain.   Let our catch be, 'Thou knave.'
Clo. 'Hold thy peace, thou knave,' knight? I shall be constrained in't to call thee knave, knight.   70
Sir And. 'Tis not the first time I have constrained one to call me knave.   Begin, fool: it begins 'Hold thy peace.'
Clo. I shall never begin if I hold my peace.
Sir And. Good, i' faith.   Come, begin.
[*Catch sung.*

Enter MARIA.

Mar. What a caterwauling do you keep here! If my lady have not called up her steward Malvolio and bid him turn you out of doors, never trust me.   79
Sir To. My lady's a Cataian, we are politicians, Malvolio's a Peg-a-Ramsey, and 'Three merry men be we.'   Am not I consanguineous? am I not of her blood? Tillyvally.   Lady! [*Sings*] 'There dwelt a man in Babylon, lady, lady!'
Clo. Beshrew me, the knight's in admirable fooling.
Sir And. Ay, he does well enough if he be disposed, and so do I too: he does it with a better grace, but I do it more natural.
Sir To. [Sings] 'O, the twelfth day of December,'—   91
Mar. For the love o' God, peace!

34 *testril.* Sixpence.

56 *contagious breath.* Catchy song.

58-59 *To hear . . . contagion.* If we could hear with our nose, we might call it sweet smelling. *welkin.* Sky.

61 *three souls out of one weaver.* Move intensely; weavers were often Puritans addicted to singing psalms.

63-64 *I am dog at.* Good at.

Maria: 'What a caterwauling do you keep here!' From an early 19th century engraving

80 *Cataian.* A native of Cathay (China), a rogue.

81 *Peg-a-Ramsey.* A popular ballad about a spying wife.

Baliol Holloway as Malvolio, Stratford-upon-Avon, 1922

---

97 *coziers'*. Cobblers'.

101 *Sneck up*. Go hang.

124-125 *cakes and ale*. These were associated with church festivals and therefore disapproved of by the Puritans.

129 *chain*. Steward's chain of office.

134 *Go shake your ears*. Implies Malvolio is an ass.

145 *gull*. Deceive.

146 *nayword*. Byword.

160 *time-pleaser*. Sycophant.

Enter MALVOLIO.

Mal. My masters, are you mad? or what are you? Have you no wit, manners, nor honesty, but to gabble like tinkers at this time of night? Do ye make an alehouse of my lady's house, that ye squeak out your coziers' catches without any mitigation or remorse of voice? Is there no respect of place, persons, nor time in you?

Sir To. We did keep time, sir, in our catches. Sneck up!   101

Mal. Sir Toby, I must be round with you. My lady bade me tell you, that, though she harbours you as her kinsman, she's nothing allied to your disorders. If you can separate yourself and your misdemeanours, you are welcome to the house; if not, an it would please you to take leave of her, she is very willing to bid you farewell.

Sir To. 'Farewell, dear heart, since I must needs be gone.'   110

Mar. Nay, good Sir Toby.

Clo. 'His eyes do show his days are almost done.'

Mal. Is't even so?

Sir To. 'But I will never die.'

Clo. Sir Toby, there you lie.

Mal. This is much credit to you.

Sir To. 'Shall I bid him go?'

Clo. 'What an if you do?'

Sir To. 'Shall I bid him go, and spare not?'

Clo. 'O no, no, no, no, you dare not.'   121

Sir To. Out o' tune, sir: ye lie. Art any more than a steward? Dost thou think, because thou art virtuous, there shall be no more cakes and ale?

Clo. Yes, by Saint Anne, and ginger shall be hot i' the mouth too.

Sir To. Thou'rt i' the right. Go, sir, rub your chain with crums. A stoup of wine, Maria!

Mal. Mistress Mary, if you prized my lady's favour at any thing more than contempt, you would not give means for this uncivil rule: she shall know of it, by this hand.   [*Exit.*

Mar. Go shake your ears.

Sir And. 'Twere as good a deed as to drink when a man's a-hungry, to challenge him the field, and then to break promise with him and make a fool of him.

Sir To. Do't, knight: I'll write thee a challenge; or I'll deliver thy indignation to him by word of mouth.   141

Mar. Sweet Sir Toby, be patient for to-night: since the youth of the count's was to-day with my lady, she is much out of quiet. For Monsieur Malvolio, let me alone with him: if I do not gull him into a nayword, and make him a common recreation, do not think I have wit enough to lie straight in my bed: I know I can do it.

Sir To. Possess us, possess us; tell us something of him.   150

Mar. Marry, sir, sometimes he is a kind of puritan.

Sir And. O, if I thought that, I'ld beat him like a dog!

Sir To. What, for being a puritan? thy exquisite reason, dear knight?

Sir And. I have no exquisite reason for't, but I have reason good enough.

Mar. The devil a puritan that he is, or any thing constantly, but a time-pleaser; an affected

• ass, that cons state without book and utters it by great swarths: the best persuaded of himself, so crammed, as he thinks, with excellencies, that it is his grounds of faith that all that look on him love him; and on that vice in him will my revenge find notable cause to work.

Sir To. What wilt thou do?

Mar. I will drop in his way some obscure epistles of love; wherein, by the colour of his beard, the shape of his leg, the manner of his gait, the expressure of his eye, forehead, and complexion, he shall find himself most feelingly
• personated. I can write very like my lady your niece: on a forgotten matter we can hardly make distinction of our hands.

Sir To. Excellent! I smell a device.

Sir And. I have 't in my nose too.

Sir To. He shall think, by the letters that thou wilt drop, that they come from my niece, and that she's in love with him.   180

Mar. My purpose is, indeed, a horse of that colour.

Sir And. And your horse now would make him an ass.

Mar. Ass, I doubt not.

Sir And. O, 'twill be admirable!

Mar. Sport royal, I warrant you: I know my physic will work with him. I will plant you two, and let the fool make a third, where he shall find the letter: observe his construction of it. For this night, to bed, and dream on the event. Farewell.   [*Exit.*
• *Sir To.* Good night, Penthesilea.

Sir And. Before me, she's a good wench.
• *Sir To.* She's a beagle, true-bred, and one that adores me: what o' that?

Sir And. I was adored once too.

Sir To. Let's to bed, knight. Thou hadst need send for more money.
• *Sir And.* If I cannot recover your niece, I am a foul way out.   201

Sir To. Send for money, knight: if thou hast
• her not i' the end, call me cut.

Sir And. If I do not, never trust me, take it how you will.
• *Sir To.* Come, come, I'll go burn some sack; 'tis too late to go to bed now: come, knight; come, knight.   [*Exeunt.*

Scene IV. *The* Duke's *palace.*

Enter Duke, Viola, Curio, *and others.*

Duke. Give me some music. Now, good morrow, friends.
Now, good Cesario, but that piece of song,
• That old and antique song we heard last night:
Methought it did relieve my passion much,
• More than light airs and recollected terms
Of these most brisk and giddy-paced times:
Come, but one verse.

Cur. He is not here, so please your lordship, that should sing it.

Duke. Who was it?   10

Cur. Feste, the jester, my lord; a fool that the lady Olivia's father took much delight in. He is about the house.

Duke. Seek him out, and play the tune the while.   [*Exit Curio. Music plays.*
Come hither, boy: if ever thou shalt love,

161 *cons state without book.* Learns courtly speeches by heart.

173 *personated.* Described.

Maria: 'Sport royal, I warrant you'. Engraving from a painting by William Hamilton (1751–1801)

193 *Penthesilea.* Queen of the Amazons.

195 *beagle.* Small, intelligent hunting dog.

200 *recover.* Gain.

203 *cut.* Gelded.

206 *burn some sack.* Warm some sherry.

3 *antique.* Quaint.

5 *recollected terms.* Studied phrases.

18 *motions.* Emotions.

38 *hold the bent.* Endure the strain. A term from archery.

45 *spinsters.* Spinsters; also, unmarried women.

46 *bones.* Bone bobbins used in lace-making.

47 *silly.* Simple. *sooth.* In fact.

Study for *Twelfth Night* by W. H. Deverell (1827–54)

53 *cypress.* A coffin made of cypress.

In the sweet pangs of it remember me;
For such as I am all true lovers are,
●Unstaid and skittish in all motions else,
Save in the constant image of the creature
That is beloved.   How dost thou like this tune?
   Vio.   It gives a very echo to the seat   21
Where Love is throned.
   Duke.   Thou dost speak masterly:
My life upon't, young though thou art, thine eye
Hath stay'd upon some favour that it loves:
Hath it not, boy?
   Vio.   A little, by your favour.
   Duke.   What kind of woman is't?
   Vio.   Of your complexion.
   Duke.   She is not worth thee, then.   What
     years, i' faith?
   Vio.   About your years, my lord.
   Duke.   Too old, by heaven: let still the woman
     take   30
An elder than herself: so wears she to him,
So sways she level in her husband's heart:
For, boy, however we do praise ourselves,
Our fancies are more giddy and unfirm,
More longing, wavering, sooner lost and worn,
Than women's are.
   Vio.   I think it well, my lord.
   Duke.   Then let thy love be younger than
     thyself,
●Or thy affection cannot hold the bent;
For women are as roses, whose fair flower
Being once display'd, doth fall that very hour. 40
   Vio.   And so they are: alas, that they are so;
To die, even when they to perfection grow!

       Re-enter CURIO *and* CLOWN.

   Duke.   O, fellow, come, the song we had last
     night.
Mark it, Cesario, it is old and plain;
●The spinsters and the knitters in the sun
●And the free maids that weave their thread with
     bones
●Do use to chant it: it is silly sooth,
And dallies with the innocence of love,
Like the old age.
   Clo.   Are you ready, sir?   50
   Duke.   Ay; prithee, sing.   [*Music.*

        SONG.

   Clo.   Come away, come away, death,
     And in sad cypress let me be laid;
   Fly away, fly away, breath;
     I am slain by a fair cruel maid.
   My shroud of white, stuck all with yew,
     O, prepare it!
   My part of death, no one so true
     Did share it.

   Not a flower, not a flower sweet,   60
     On my black coffin let there be strown;
   Not a friend, not a friend greet
     My poor corpse, where my bones shall
      be thrown:
   A thousand thousand sighs to save,
     Lay me, O, where
   Sad true lover never find my grave,
     To weep there!

   Duke.   There's for thy pains.
   Clo.   No pains, sir; I take pleasure in singing,
sir.   70

Duke. I'll pay thy pleasure then.

Clo. Truly, sir, and pleasure will be paid, one time or another.

Duke. Give me now leave to leave thee.

● *Clo.* Now, the melancholy god protect thee; and the tailor make thy doublet of changeable
●taffeta, for thy mind is a very opal. I would have men of such constancy put to sea, that their business might be every thing and their intent every where; for that's it that always makes a good voyage of nothing. Farewell.   81

                                   [*Exit.*

Duke. Let all the rest give place.

                  [*Curio and Attendants retire.*

                         Once more, Cesario,
Get thee to yond same sovereign cruelty:
Tell her, my love, more noble than the world,
Prizes not quantity of dirty lands;
The parts that fortune hath bestow'd upon her,
Tell her, I hold as giddily as fortune;
● But 'tis that miracle and queen of gems
● That nature pranks her in attracts my soul.

    Vio. But if she cannot love you, sir?   90

    Duke. I cannot be so answer'd.

    Vio.   Sooth, but you must.
Say that some lady, as perhaps there is,
Hath for your love as great a pang of heart
As you have for Olivia: you cannot love her;
You tell her so; must she not then be answer'd?

    Duke. There is no woman's sides
Can bide the beating of so strong a passion
As love doth give my heart; no woman's heart
So big, to hold so much; they lack retention.
Alas, their love may be call'd appetite,   100
No motion of the liver, but the palate,
That suffer surfeit, cloyment and revolt;
But mine is all as hungry as the sea,
And can digest as much: make no compare
Between that love a woman can bear me
And that I owe Olivia.

    Vio.   Ay, but I know—

    Duke. What dost thou know?

    Vio. Too well what love women to men may owe:
In faith, they are as true of heart as we.
My father had a daughter loved a man,   110
As it might be, perhaps, were I a woman,
I should your lordship.

    Duke.   And what's her history?

    Vio. A blank, my lord. She never told her love,
But let concealment, like a worm i' the bud,
Feed on her damask cheek: she pined in thought,
And with a green and yellow melancholy
She sat like patience on a monument,
Smiling at grief. Was not this love indeed?
We men may say more, swear more: but indeed
● Our shows are more than will; for still we prove
Much in our vows, but little in our love.   121

    Duke. But died thy sister of her love, my boy?

    Vio. I am all the daughters of my father's house,
And all the brothers too: and yet I know not.
Sir, shall I to this lady?

    Duke.   Ay, that's the theme.
To her in haste; give her this jewel; say,
My love can give no place, bide no denay.

                                  [*Exeunt.*

75 *melancholy god.* Saturn.

77-80 *I would have . . . every where.* Feste comments that the Duke's changeable disposition makes him suitable to go to sea where his going hither and thither could prove profitable.

88 *that miracle . . .gems.* Her beauty.

89 *pranks.* Adorn.

Diana Rigg as Viola and Alan Howard as the Duke, Royal Shakespeare Co, 1966

120 *Our shows are more than will.* We display more emotion than we really feel.

2 *scruple*. A scrap.

6 *sheep-biter*. A dog that attacks sheep. Therefore a man that chases after 'mutton' i.e. women.

17 *metal of India*. Gold.

23 *Close*. Hide.

26 *tickling*. Trout can be caught by stroking them. Malvolio is to be caught by flattery.

28 *affect*. Admire.

29 *fancy*. Fall in love.

36 *jets*. Struts.

46 *Jezebel*. The harlot wife of King Ahab of Israel. Sir Andrew reveals his ignorance by this totally inappropriate reference.

48 *blows him*. Puffs him up.

Malvolio: 'Calling my officers about me, in my branched velvet gown'. Walter Hudd as Malvolio, His Majesty's Theatre, London, 1947

51 *stone-bow*. A cross-bow that shoots stones.

58 *the humour of state*. The manner of an important personage.

59 *after a demure travel of regard*. After looking around gravely.

SCENE V.   OLIVIA'S *garden*.

Enter SIR TOBY, SIR ANDREW, *and* FABIAN.

Sir To.   Come thy ways, Signior Fabian.

Fab.   Nay, I'll come: if I lose a scruple of this sport, let me be boiled to death with melancholy.

Sir To.   Wouldst thou not be glad to have the niggardly rascally sheep-biter come by some notable shame?

Fab.   I would exult, man: you know, he brought me out o' favour with my lady about a bear-baiting here.   10

Sir To.   To anger him we'll have the bear again; and we will fool him black and blue: shall we not, Sir Andrew?

Sir And.   An we do not, it is pity of our lives.

Sir To.   Here comes the little villain.

Enter MARIA.

How now, my metal of India!

Mar.   Get ye all three into the box-tree: Malvolio's coming down this walk: he has been yonder i' the sun practising behaviour to his own shadow this half hour: observe him, for the love of mockery; for I know this letter will make a contemplative idiot of him.   Close, in the name of jesting!   Lie thou there [*throws down a letter*]; for here comes the trout that must be caught with tickling.   [*Exit.*

Enter MALVOLIO.

Mal.   'Tis but fortune; all is fortune.   Maria once told me she did affect me: and I have heard herself come thus near, that, should she fancy, it should be one of my complexion.   Besides, she uses me with a more exalted respect than any one else that follows her.   What should I think on 't?

Sir To.   Here's an overweening rogue!

Fab.   O, peace!   Contemplation makes a rare turkey-cock of him: how he jets under his advanced plumes!

Sir And.   'Slight, I could so beat the rogue!

Sir To.   Peace, I say.

Mal.   To be Count Malvolio!   40

Sir To.   Ah, rogue!

Sir And.   Pistol him, pistol him.

Sir To.   Peace, peace!

Mal.   There is example for 't; the lady of the Strachy married the yeoman of the wardrobe.

Sir And.   Fie on him, Jezebel!

Fab.   O, peace! now he's deeply in: look how imagination blows him.

Mal.   Having been three months married to her, sitting in my state,—   50

Sir To.   O, for a stone-bow, to hit him in the eye!

Mal.   Calling my officers about me, in my branched velvet gown; having come from a day-bed, where I have left Olivia sleeping,—

Sir To.   Fire and brimstone!

Fab.   O, peace, peace!

Mal.   And then to have the humour of state; and after a demure travel of regard, telling them I know my place as I would they should do theirs, to ask for my kinsman Toby,—   61

Sir To. Bolts and shackles!

Fab. O peace, peace, peace! now, now.

Mal. Seven of my people, with an obedient
start, make out for him: I frown the while; and
perchance wind up my watch, or play with my—
some rich jewel. Toby approaches; courtesies
there to me,—

Sir To. Shall this fellow live?

Fab. Though our silence be drawn from us
with cars, yet peace.   71

Mal. I extend my hand to him thus, quench-
ing my familiar smile with an austere regard of
control,—

Sir To. And does not Toby take you a blow
o' the lips then?

Mal. Saying, 'Cousin Toby, my fortunes
having cast me on your niece give me this prerogative of speech,'—

Sir To. What, what?   80

Mal. 'You must amend your drunkenness.'

Sir To. Out, scab!

Fab. Nay, patience, or we break the sinews
of our plot.

Mal. 'Besides, you waste the treasure of your
time with a foolish knight,'—

Sir And. That's me, I warrant you.

Mal. 'One Sir Andrew,'—

Sir And. I knew 'twas I; for many do call
me fool.   90

Mal. What employment have we here?

[*Taking up the letter*

Fab. Now is the woodcock near the gin.

Sir To. O, peace! and the spirit of humours
intimate reading aloud to him!

Mal. By my life, this is my lady's hand:
these be her very C's, her U's and her T's; and
thus makes she her great P's. It is, in contempt
of question, her hand.

Sir And. Her C's, her U's and her T's: why
that?   100

Mal. [*Reads*] 'To the unknown beloved, this,
and my good wishes:'—her very phrases! By
your leave, wax. Soft! and the impressure her
Lucrece, with which she uses to seal: 'tis my
lady. To whom should this be?

Fab. This wins him, liver and all.

Mal. [*Reads*]

    Jove knows I love:
      But who?
    Lips, do not move;
    No man must know.   110

'No man must know.' What follows? the numbers altered! 'No man must know:' if this
should be thee, Malvolio?

Sir To. Marry, hang thee, brock!

Mal. [*Reads*]

    I may command where I adore;
      But silence, like a Lucrece knife,
    With bloodless stroke my heart doth gore:
    M, O, A, I, doth sway my life.

Fab. A fustian riddle!

Sir To. Excellent wench, say I.   120

Mal. 'M, O, A, I, doth sway my life.' Nay,
but first, let me see, let me see, let me see.

Fab. What dish o' poison has she dressed him!

Sir To. And with what wing the staniel
checks at it!

Mal. 'I may command where I adore.' Why,
she may command me: I serve her; she is my

Malvolio: 'To the unknown beloved . . .' Nicol William-
son as Malvolio, Royal Shakespeare Co, 1974

104 *Lucrece.* A signet ring depicting Lucrece, a Roman
matron who stabbed herself after being raped; therefore
a symbol of chastity.

114 *brock.* Badger.

119 *fustian.* Worthless.

124 *staniel.* A small hawk.

125 *checks at it.* Swerves to snatch at it.

128-129 *formal capacity*. Normal intelligence.

135 *Sowter*. A hound's name.

140 *faults*. Breaks in scent.

141 *consonancy*. Consistency.

142 *probation*. Scrutiny.

144 *O shall end*. Shall end in-crying.

152 *crush*. Squeeze a meaning.

155 *revolve*. Consider.

163 *tang*. Resound.

164-165 *trick of singularity*. The affectation of eccentricity.

173 *champain*. Open country.

176 *point-devise*. Precise.

178 *jade*. Deceive.

184 *strange*. Haughty.

Malvolio: 'Jove, I thank thee: I will smile . . .' Illustration by Charles E. Brock, 1916

lady. Why, this is evident to any formal capacity; there is no obstruction in this: and the end,—what should that alphabetical position portend? If I could make that resemble something in me,—Softly! M, O, A, I,—
Sir To. O, ay, make up that: he is now at a cold scent.
Fab. Sowter will cry upon't for all this, though it be as rank as a fox.
Mal. M,—Malvolio; M,—why, that begins my name.
Fab. Did not I say he would work it out? the cur is excellent at faults.   140
Mal. M,—but then there is no consonancy in the sequel; that suffers under probation: A should follow, but O does.
Fab. And O shall end, I hope.
Sir To. Ay, or I'll cudgel him, and make him cry O!
Mal. And then I comes behind.
Fab. Ay, an you had any eye behind you, you might see more detraction at your heels than fortunes before you.   150
Mal. M, O, A, I; this simulation is not as the former: and yet, to crush this a little, it would bow to me, for every one of these letters are in my name. Soft! here follows prose.
[*Reads*] 'If this fall into thy hand, revolve. In my stars I am above thee; but be not afraid of greatness: some are born great, some achieve greatness and some have greatness thrust upon 'em. Thy Fates open their hands; let thy blood and spirit embrace them; and, to inure thyself to what thou art like to be, cast thy humble slough and appear fresh. Be opposite with a kinsman, surly with servants; let thy tongue tang arguments of state; put thyself into the trick of singularity: she thus advises thee that sighs for thee. Remember who commended thy yellow stockings, and wished to see thee ever cross-gartered: I say, remember. Go to, thou art made, if thou desirest to be so; if not, let me see thee a steward still, the fellow of servants, and not worthy to touch Fortune's fingers. Farewell. She that would alter services with thee,

THE FORTUNATE-UNHAPPY.'

Daylight and champain discovers not more: this is open. I will be proud, I will read politic authors, I will baffle Sir Toby, I will wash off gross acquaintance, I will be point-devise the very man. I do not now fool myself, to let imagination jade me; for every reason excites to this, that my lady loves me. She did commend my yellow stockings of late, she did praise my leg being cross-gartered; and in this she manifests herself to my love, and with a kind of injunction drives me to these habits of her liking. I thank my stars I am happy. I will be strange, stout, in yellow stockings, and cross-gartered, even with the swiftness of putting on. Jove and my stars be praised! Here is yet a postscript.
[*Reads*] 'Thou canst not choose but know who I am. If thou entertainest my love, let it appear in thy smiling; thy smiles become thee well; therefore in my presence still smile, dear my sweet, I prithee.'
Jove, I thank thee: I will smile; I will do everything that thou wilt have me.   [*Exit.*
Fab. I will not give my part of this sport for

a pension of thousands to be paid from the
Sophy.
　Sir To. I could marry this wench for this
device.　　　　　　　　　　　　　　　　200
　Sir And. So could I too.
　Sir To. And ask no other dowry with her
but such another jest.
　Sir And. Nor I neither.
　Fab. Here comes my noble gull-catcher.

Re-enter MARIA.

　Sir To. Wilt thou set thy foot o' my neck?
　Sir And. Or o' mine either?
　Sir To. Shall I play my freedom at tray-trip,
and become thy bond-slave?
　Sir And. I' faith, or I either?　　　　210
　Sir To. Why, thou hast put him in such a
dream, that when the image of it leaves him he
must run mad.
　Mar. Nay, but say true; does it work upon
him?
　Sir To. Like aqua-vitæ with a midwife.
　Mar. If you will then see the fruits of the
sport, mark his first approach before my lady: he
will come to her in yellow stockings, and 'tis a
colour she abhors, and cross-gartered, a fashion
she detests; and he will smile upon her, which
will now be so unsuitable to her disposition,
being addicted to a melancholy as she is, that
it cannot but turn him into a notable contempt.
If you will see it, follow me.
　Sir To. To the gates of Tartar, thou most
excellent devil of wit!
　Sir And. I'll make one too.　　　*[Exeunt.*

ACT III.

Scene I. Olivia's *garden.*

Enter Viola, *and* Clown *with a tabor.*

　Vio. Save thee, friend, and thy music: dost
thou live by thy tabor?
　Clo. No, sir, I live by the church.
　Vio. Art thou a churchman?
　Clo. No such matter, sir: I do live by the
church; for I do live at my house, and my house
doth stand by the church.
　Vio. So thou mayst say, the king lies by a
beggar, if a beggar dwell near him; or, the
church stands by thy tabor, if thy tabor stand by
the church.　　　　　　　　　　　　11
　Clo. You have said, sir. To see this age! A
sentence is but a cheveril glove to a good wit:
how quickly the wrong side may be turned outward!
　Vio. Nay, that's certain; they that dally
nicely with words may quickly make them
wanton.
　Clo. I would, therefore, my sister had had
no name, sir.　　　　　　　　　　　20
　Vio. Why, man?
　Clo. Why, sir, her name's a word; and to
dally with that word might make my sister wanton. But indeed words are very rascals since
bonds disgraced them.
　Vio. Thy reason, man?
　Clo. Troth, sir, I can yield you none without
words; and words are grown so false, I am loath
to prove reason with them.

198 *Sophy.* The Shah of Persia. See introduction.

Costume design for Maria by J. Gower Parks, New
Theatre, London, 1932

205 *gull-catcher.* A trapper of fools.

208 *tray-trip.* A dice-game in which three (tray) was
important.

226 *Tartar.* Tartarus, the classical name of Hell.

2 *tabor.* A small drum.

13 *cheveril.* Kid.

16-17 *dally nicely.* Play subtly.

18 *wanton.* Equivocal, but also 'unchaste', which is the
meaning that the clown picks up in his reply.

Dorothy Tutin as Viola and Max Adrian as Feste, Royal Shakespeare Co, 1960

48 *pass upon.* Make fun of.

50 *commodity.* Consignment.

55 *these.* Coins that Viola had given him.

57 *use.* Interest.

58 *Pandarus.* The go-between in the love affair of Troilus and Cressida.

62 *Cressida . . . beggar.* In Henryson's *Testament of Cresseid*, the heroine ends her days as a leper and a beggar.

71 *haggard.* A wild hawk.

75 *folly-fall'n.* Acting foolishly. *taint their wit.* Betray their good sense.

78-79 *Dieu . . . serviteur.* God keep you, sir. And you too, your servant.

86 *list.* Goal.

Vio. I warrant thou art a merry fellow and carest for nothing.   31
   Clo. Not so, sir, I do care for something; but in my conscience, sir, I do not care for you: if that be to care for nothing, sir, I would it would make you invisible.
   Vio. Art not thou the Lady Olivia's fool?
   Clo. No, indeed, sir; the Lady Olivia has no folly: she will keep no fool, sir, till she be married; and fools are as like husbands as pilchards are to herrings; the husband's the bigger: I am indeed not her fool, but her corrupter of words.
   Vio. I saw thee late at the Count Orsino's.
   Clo. Foolery, sir, does walk about the orb like the sun, it shines every where. I would be sorry, sir, but the fool should be as oft with your master as with my mistress: I think I saw your wisdom there.
   Vio. Nay, an thou pass upon me, I'll no more with thee. Hold, there's expenses for thee.
   Clo. Now Jove, in his next commodity of hair, send thee a beard!   51
   Vio. By my troth, I'll tell thee, I am almost sick for one; [*Aside*] though I would not have it grow on my chin. Is thy lady within?
   Clo. Would not a pair of these have bred, sir?
   Vio. Yes, being kept together and put to use.
   Clo. I would play Lord Pandarus of Phrygia, sir, to bring a Cressida to this Troilus.
   Vio. I understand you, sir; 'tis well begged.
   Clo. The matter, I hope, is not great, sir, begging but a beggar: Cressida was a beggar. My lady is within, sir. I will construe to them whence you come; who you are and what you would are out of my welkin, I might say 'element,' but the word is over-worn.   [*Exit.*
   Vio. This fellow is wise enough to play the fool;
And to do that well craves a kind of wit:
He must observe their mood on whom he jests,
The quality of persons, and the time,   70
And, like the haggard, check at every feather
That comes before his eye. This is a practice
As full of labour as a wise man's art:
For folly that he wisely shows is fit;
But wise men, folly-fall'n, quite taint their wit.

Enter Sir Toby, *and* Sir Andrew.

   Sir To. Save you, gentleman.
   Vio. And you, sir.
   Sir And. Dieu vous garde, monsieur.
   Vio. Et vous aussi; votre serviteur.
   Sir And. I hope, sir, you are; and I am yours.   81
   Sir To. Will you encounter the house? my niece is desirous you should enter, if your trade be to her.
   Vio. I am bound to your niece, sir; I mean, she is the list of my voyage.
   Sir To. Taste your legs, sir; put them to motion.
   Vio. My legs do better understand me, sir, than I understand what you mean by bidding me taste my legs.   91
   Sir To. I mean, to go, sir, to enter.
   Vio. I will answer you with gait and entrance. But we are prevented.

Enter OLIVIA *and* MARIA.

Most excellent accomplished lady, the heavens
rain odours on you!

Sir And. That youth's a rare courtier: 'Rain
odours;' well.

Vio. My matter hath no voice, lady, but to
your own most pregnant and vouchsafed ear. 100

Sir And. 'Odours,' 'pregnant' and 'vouchsafed:' I'll get 'em all three all ready.

Oli. Let the garden door be shut, and leave
me to my hearing. [*Exeunt Sir Toby, Sir Andrew, and Maria.*] Give me your hand, sir.

Vio. My duty, madam, and most humble service.

Oli. What is your name?

Vio. Cesario is your servant's name, fair princess.

Oli. My servant, sir! 'Twas never merry world
Since lowly feigning was call'd compliment: 110
You're servant to the Count Orsino, youth.

Vio.   And he is yours, and his must needs be
yours:
Your servant's servant is your servant, madam.

Oli.   For him, I think not on him: for his
thoughts,
Would they were blanks, rather than fill'd with
me!

Vio.   Madam, I come to whet your gentle
thoughts
On his behalf.

Oli.   O, by your leave, I pray you,
I bade you never speak again of him:
But, would you undertake another suit,
I had rather hear you to solicit that   120
Than music from the spheres.

Vio.   Dear lady,—

Oli. Give me leave, beseech you. I did send,
After the last enchantment you did here,
A ring in chase of you: so did I abuse
Myself, my servant and, I fear me, you:
Under your hard construction must I sit,
To force that on you, in a shameful cunning,
Which you knew none of yours: what might you
think?
Have you not set mine honour at the stake
And baited it with all the unmuzzled thoughts 130
That tyrannous heart can think? To one of your
receiving
Enough is shown: a cypress, not a bosom,
Hideth my heart.   So, let me hear you speak.

Vio.   I pity you.

Oli.   That's a degree to love.

Vio. No, not a grize; for 'tis a vulgar proof,
That very oft we pity enemies.

Oli. Why, then, methinks 'tis time to smile
again.
O world, how apt the poor are to be proud!
If one should be a prey, how much the better
To fall before the lion than the wolf!   140
[*Clock strikes.*

The clock upbraids me with the waste of time.
Be not afraid, good youth, I will not have you:
And yet, when wit and youth is come to harvest,
Your wife is like to reap a proper man:
There lies your way, due west.

Vio. Then westward-ho! Grace and good dis-
position
Attend your ladyship!
You'll nothing, madam, to my lord by me?

---

100 *pregnant and vouchsafed.* Quick to understand and graciously granted.

Olivia: 'Give me your hand, sir'. Olivia (Lisa Harrow) and Viola (Judi Dench), Royal Shakespeare Co, 1971

109 *'Twas . . . world,* A proverbial phrase meaning the world has changed for the worse.

121 *music from the spheres.* The Elizabethans believed that the rotation of the stars and the planets produced celestial music.

126 *construction.* Interpretation.

129 *at the stake.* An image from bear-baiting, where the bear was tied to a stake and harassed by dogs.

131 *receiving.* Understanding.

132 *cypress.* The dark foliage was taken as a symbol of mourning.

135 *grize.* Step. *vulgar proof.* Common knowledge.

160 *love's . . . noon.* Love cannot be hidden.

163 *maugre.* In spite of.

12 *argument.* Evidence.

14 *'Slight.* By God's light.

26 *balked.* Missed.

29-30 *a Dutchman's beard.* An allusion to the explorer William Barentz. See introduction.

Oli. Stay:
I prithee, tell me what thou think'st of me.   150
   Vio. That you do think you are not what you
      are.
   Oli. If I think so, I think the same of you.
   Vio. Then think you right: I am not what I
      am.
   Oli. I would you were as I would have you be!
   Vio. Would it be better, madam, than I am?
I wish it might, for now I am your fool.
   Oli. O, what a deal of scorn looks beautiful
In the contempt and anger of his lip!
A murderous guilt shows not itself more soon
• Than love that would seem hid: love's night is
      noon.   160
Cesario, by the roses of the spring,
By maidhood, honour, truth and every thing,
• I love thee so, that, maugre all thy pride,
Nor wit nor reason can my passion hide.
Do not extort thy reasons from this clause,
For that I woo, thou therefore hast no cause;
But rather reason thus with reason fetter,
Love sought is good, but given unsought is better.
   Vio. By innocence I swear, and by my youth,
I have one heart, one bosom and one truth,   170
And that no woman has; nor never none
Shall mistress be of it, save I alone.
And so adieu, good madam: never more
Will I my master's tears to you deplore.
   Oli. Yet come again; for thou perhaps mayst
      move
That heart, which now abhors, to like his love.
                                    [*Exeunt.*

SCENE II.   OLIVIA'S *house.*

Enter SIR TOBY, SIR ANDREW, *and* FABIAN.

   Sir And. No, faith, I'll not stay a jot longer.
   Sir To. Thy reason, dear venom, give thy
reason.
   Fab. You must needs yield your reason, Sir
Andrew.
   Sir And. Marry, I saw your niece do more
favours to the count's serving-man than ever she
bestowed upon me; I saw 't i' the orchard.
   Sir To. Did she see thee the while, old boy?
tell me that.   10
   Sir And. As plain as I see you now.
• *Fab.* This was a great argument of love in her
toward you.
• *Sir And.* 'Slight, will you make an ass o' me?
   Fab. I will prove it legitimate, sir, upon the
oaths of judgement and reason.
   Sir To. And they have been grand-jurymen
since before Noah was a sailor.
   Fab. She did show favour to the youth in
your sight only to exasperate you, to awake your
dormouse valour, to put fire in your heart, and
brimstone in your liver. You should then have
accosted her; and with some excellent jests, fire-
new from the mint, you should have banged the
youth into dumbness. This was looked for at
• your hand, and this was balked: the double gilt
of this opportunity you let time wash off, and you
are now sailed into the north of my lady's opinion;
• where you will hang like an icicle on a Dutchman's beard, unless you do redeem it by some
laudable attempt either of valour or policy.   31
   Sir And. An't be any way, it must be with

valour; for policy I hate: I had as lief be a
Brownist as a politician.

Sir To. Why, then, build me thy fortunes upon
the basis of valour. Challenge me the count's
youth to fight with him; hurt him in eleven places:
my niece shall take note of it; and assure thyself, there is no love-broker in the world can
more prevail in man's commendation with woman
than report of valour.   41

Fab. There is no way but this, Sir Andrew.

Sir And. Will either of you bear me a challenge to him?

Sir To. Go, write it in a martial hand; be
curst and brief; it is no matter how witty, so it be
eloquent and full of invention: taunt him with the
license of ink: if thou thou'st him some thrice, it
shall not be amiss; and as many lies as will lie in
thy sheet of paper, although the sheet were big
enough for the bed of Ware in England, set 'em
down: go, about it. Let there be gall enough in
thy ink, though thou write with a goose-pen, no
matter: about it.

Sir And. Where shall I find you?

Sir To. We'll call thee at the cubiculo: go.
                        [*Exit Sir Andrew.*

Fab. This is a dear manakin to you, Sir Toby.

Sir To. I have been dear to him, lad, some
two thousand strong, or so.

Fab. We shall have a rare letter from him:
but you'll not deliver't?   61

Sir To. Never trust me, then; and by all
means stir on the youth to an answer. I think
oxen and wainropes cannot hale them together.
For Andrew, if he were opened, and you find so
much blood in his liver as will clog the foot of a
flea, I'll eat the rest of the anatomy.

Fab. And his opposite, the youth, bears in
his visage no great presage of cruelty.

Enter MARIA.

Sir To. Look, where the youngest wren of
nine comes.   71

Mar. If you desire the spleen, and will laugh
yourselves into stitches, follow me. Yond gull
Malvolio is turned heathen, a very renegado; for
there is no Christian, that means to be saved
by believing rightly, can ever believe such impossible passages of grossness. He's in yellow
stockings.

Sir To. And cross-gartered?   79

Mar. Most villanously; like a pedant that
keeps a school i' the church. I have dogged
him, like his murderer. He does obey every
point of the letter that I dropped to betray him:
he does smile his face into more lines than is
in the new map with the augmentation of the
Indies: you have not seen such a thing as 'tis.
I can hardly forbear hurling things at him. I
know my lady will strike him: if she do, he'll
smile and take't for a great favour.

Sir To. Come, bring us, bring us where he is.
                        [*Exeunt.* 90

SCENE III. *A street.*

Enter SEBASTIAN *and* ANTONIO.

Seb. I would not by my will have troubled you;
But, since you make your pleasure of your pains,
I will no further chide you.

34 *Brownist.* A follower of Robert Browne, a Puritan.

46 *curst.* Difficult.

48 *thou thou'st.* Address him as 'thou' (which was used for familiars and inferiors).

51 *bed of Ware.* A famous bed, almost eleven feet square, now in the Victoria and Albert Museum, London.

The bed of Ware

52 *gall.* Sir Toby puns on the two meanings; the first, 'bitterness', and the second, one of the ingredients of ink.

56 *cubiculo.* Chamber.

57 *manakin.* Puppet.

64 *wainropes.* Waggon-ropes.

66 *blood in his liver.* The liver was the seat of courage and therefore a lack of blood would indicate cowardice.

70 *the youngest wren.* The wren, one of the smallest birds, usually lays about nine eggs. The last hatched is the smallest; so Maria was acted by a small boy.

72 *the spleen.* A fit of laughter.

77 *passages.* Pieces.

85-86 *the new map . . . Indies.* Mollineux published a map of the world in 1599 which showed the East Indies and North America in greater detail than any before. Maria compares the net-work of rhumb-lines on the map to the wrinkles on Malvolio's face.

8 *jealousy.* Anxiety.

16 *uncurrent.* Worthless.

17 *worth.* Means.

26 *the count his galleys.* The Count's galleys.

28 *it . . . answer'd.* It would be difficult to make a defence.

31 *quality.* Nature.

34 *traffic's.* Trade's.

36 *lapsed.* Caught.

45 *store.* i.e. of money.

46 *idle markets.* Unnecessary purchases.

5 *sad.* Grave.

Ant. I could not stay behind you: my desire,
More sharp than filed steel, did spur me forth;
And not all love to see you, though so much
As might have drawn one to a longer voyage,
●But jealousy what might befall your travel,
Being skilless in these parts; which to a stranger,
Unguided and unfriended, often prove   10
Rough and unhospitable: my willing love,
The rather by these arguments of fear,
Set forth in your pursuit.
Seb.   My kind Antonio,
I can no other answer make but thanks,
†And thanks; and ever......oft good turns
●Are shuffled off with such uncurrent pay:
●But, were my worth as is my conscience firm,
You should find better dealing.   What's to do?
Shall we go see the reliques of this town?
Ant.   To-morrow, sir: best first go see your
                    lodging.   20
Seb.   I am not weary, and 'tis long to night:
I pray you, let us satisfy our eyes
With the memorials and the things of fame
That do renown this city.
Ant.   Would you'ld pardon me;
I do not without danger walk these streets:
●Once, in a sea-fight, 'gainst the count his galleys
I did some service; of such note indeed,
●That were I ta'en here it would scarce be
                    answer'd.
Seb.   Belike you slew great number of his
                    people.
Ant.   The offence is not of such a bloody
                    nature;   30
●Albeit the quality of the time and quarrel
Might well have given us bloody argument.
It might have since been answer'd in repaying
●What we took from them; which, for traffic's sake,
Most of our city did: only myself stood out;
●For which, if I be lapsed in this place,
I shall pay dear.
Seb.   Do not then walk too open.
Ant.   It doth not fit me.   Hold, sir, here's
                    my purse.
In the south suburbs, at the Elephant,
Is best to lodge: I will bespeak our diet,   40
Whiles you beguile the time and feed your
                    knowledge
With viewing of the town: there shall you
                    have me.
Seb.   Why I your purse?
Ant.   Haply your eye shall light upon some toy
●You have desire to purchase; and your store,
●I think, is not for idle markets, sir.
Seb.   I'll be your purse-bearer and leave you
For an hour.
Ant.   To the Elephant.
Seb.   I do remember. [*Exeunt.*

SCENE IV.   OLIVIA'S *garden.*

Enter OLIVIA *and* MARIA.

Oli.   I have sent after him: he says he'll come;
How shall I feast him? what bestow of him?
For youth is bought more oft than begg'd or
                    borrow'd.
I speak too loud.
●Where is Malvolio? he is sad and civil,
And suits well for a servant with my fortunes:
Where is Malvolio?

Mar. He's coming, madam; but in very
● strange manner. He is, sure, possessed, madam.
Oli. Why, what's the matter? does he rave?
Mar. No, madam, he does nothing but smile:
your ladyship were best to have some guard
about you, if he come; for, sure, the man is
tainted in's wits.
Oli. Go call him hither. [*Exit Maria.*] I
am as mad as he,
If sad and merry madness equal be.

Re-enter MARIA, *with* MALVOLIO.

How now, Malvolio!
Mal. Sweet lady, ho, ho.
Oli. Smilest thou?
I sent for thee upon a sad occasion.   20
Mal. Sad, lady! I could be sad: this does
make some obstruction in the blood, this cross-
gartering; but what of that? if it please the eye
● of one, it is with me as the very true sonnet is,
● 'Please one, and please all.'
Oli. Why, how dost thou, man? what is the
matter with thee?
Mal. Not black in my mind, though yellow
in my legs. It did come to his hands, and com-
mands shall be executed: I think we do know
● the sweet Roman hand.   31
Oli. Wilt thou go to bed, Malvolio?
Mal. To bed! ay, sweet-heart, and I'll come
to thee.
Oli. God comfort thee! Why dost thou smile
so and kiss thy hand so oft?
Mar. How do you, Malvolio?
Mal. At your request! yes; nightingales
answer daws.
Mar. Why appear you with this ridiculous
boldness before my lady?   41
Mal. 'Be not afraid of greatness:' 'twas well
writ.
Oli. What meanest thou by that, Malvolio?
Mal. 'Some are born great,'—
Oli. Ha!
Mal. 'Some achieve greatness,'—
Oli. What sayest thou?
Mal. 'And some have greatness thrust upon
them.'   50
Oli. Heaven restore thee!
Mal. 'Remember who commended thy yellow
stockings,'—
Oli. Thy yellow stockings!
Mal. 'And wished to see thee cross-gartered.'
Oli. Cross-gartered!
Mal. 'Go to, thou art made, if thou desirest
to be so;'—
Oli. Am I made?   59
Mal. 'If not, let me see thee a servant still.'
● *Oli.* Why, this is very midsummer madness.

Enter Servant.

Ser. Madam, the young gentleman of the
Count Orsino's is returned: I could hardly en-
treat him back: he attends your ladyship's
pleasure.
Oli. I'll come to him. [*Exit Servant.*]
Good Maria, let this fellow be looked to.
Where's my cousin Toby? Let some of my
people have a special care of him: I would not
● have him miscarry for the half of my dowry. 70
[*Exeunt Olivia and Maria.*

9 *possessed.* i.e. by devils.

Malvolio: 'Sweet lady, ho, ho'. Engraving from a
painting by John Henry Ramberg (1763–1840)

24 *sonnet.* Song.

25 *'Please one, and please all'.* The refrain of a popular
ballad.

31 *Roman hand.* Italic handwriting.

61 *midsummer madness.* Proverbially a time associated
with madness and oddity.

70 *miscarry.* Come to harm.

Mal. O, ho! do you come near me now? no worse man than Sir Toby to look to me! This concurs directly with the letter: she sends him on purpose, that I may appear stubborn to him; for she incites me to that in the letter. 'Cast thy humble slough,' says she; 'be opposite with a kinsman, surly with servants; let thy tongue tang with arguments of state; put thyself into the trick of singularity;' and consequently sets down the manner how; as, a sad face, a reverend carriage, a slow tongue, in the habit of some sir of note, and so forth. I have limed her; but it is Jove's doing, and Jove make me thankful! And when she went away now, 'Let this fellow be looked to:' fellow! not Malvolio, nor after my degree, but fellow. Why, every thing adheres together, that no dram of a scruple, no scruple of a scruple, no obstacle, no incredulous or unsafe circumstance—What can be said? Nothing that can be can come between me and the full prospect of my hopes. Well, Jove, not I, is the doer of this, and he is to be thanked.

Re-enter MARIA, *with* SIR TOBY *and* FABIAN.

Sir To. Which way is he, in the name of sanctity? If all the devils of hell be drawn in little, and Legion himself possessed him, yet I'll speak to him.

Fab. Here he is, here he is. How is't with you, sir? how is't with you, man?

Mal. Go off; I discard you: let me enjoy my private: go off. 100

Mar. Lo, how hollow the fiend speaks within him! did not I tell you? Sir Toby, my lady prays you to have a care of him.

Mal. Ah, ha! does she so?

Sir To. Go to, go to; peace, peace; we must deal gently with him: let me alone. How do you, Malvolio? how is't with you? What, man! defy the devil: consider, he's an enemy to mankind.

Mal. Do you know what you say? 110

Mar. La you, an you speak ill of the devil, how he takes it at heart! Pray God, he be not bewitched!

Fab. Carry his water to the wise woman.

Mar. Marry, and it shall be done to-morrow morning, if I live. My lady would not lose him for more than I'll say.

Mal. How now, mistress!

Mar. O Lord!

Sir To. Prithee, hold thy peace; this is not the way: do you not see you move him? let me alone with him. 122

Fab. No way but gentleness; gently, gently: the fiend is rough, and will not be roughly used.

Sir To. Why, how now, my bawcock! how dost thou, chuck?

Mal. Sir!

Sir To. Ay, Biddy, come with me. What, man! 'tis not for gravity to play at cherry-pit with Satan: hang him, foul collier! 130

Mar. Get him to say his prayers, good Sir Toby, get him to pray.

Mal. My prayers, minx!

Mar. No, I warrant you, he will not hear of godliness.

Mal. Go, hang yourselves all! you are idle

Malvolio in Olivia's garden. Detail from a painting by Daniel Maclise, 1829

71 *come near me.* Begin to understand.

74 *stubborn.* Hostile.

82 *limed.* Caught (as birds are snared with sticky bird lime).

84 *fellow.* Malvolio believes that Olivia implies 'companion' and not the other meaning 'menial'.

87 *dram.* A measure of one eighth of an ounce. *scruple.* Has a double meaning; 'doubt' and 'one third of a dram'.

95 *Legion.* The unclean spirits that possessed a madman: see Mark, 5, ix.

100 *private.* Privacy.

121 *move him.* Upset him.

125 *bawcock.* Fine fellow, from the French *beau coq.*

126 *chuck.* Chick.

128 *Biddy.* Chicken from 'chickabiddy'.

129 *cherry-pit.* Cherry stone; a child's game with cherry stones.

130 *foul collier.* i.e. the Devil.

Opposite : Malvolio cross-gartered. Engraving from a design by H. Gravelot for Theobald's edition, 1773

137 *element*. Sphere of life.

142 *genius*. Soul.

145 *take . . . taint*. Be exposed and spoilt.

Maria. Engraving from a painting by Augustus Egg (1818–63)

148-149 *in a dark . . . bound*. The usual treatment for mad or disturbed people.

156 *May morning*. Mayday game.

169 *blow of the law*. Infringing the law (by causing a breach of the peace).

181 *o' the windy side*. On the safe side.

194 *bum-baily*. A bailiff or sheriff's officer who arrested debtors.

198-199 *approbation*. Credit.

shallow things: I am not of your element: you shall know more hereafter.   [*Exit*.
Sir To. Is't possible?
Fab. If this were played upon a stage now, I could condemn it as an improbable fiction.   141
Sir To. His very genius hath taken the infection of the device, man.
Mar. Nay, pursue him now, lest the device take air and taint.
Fab. Why, we shall make him mad indeed.
Mar. The house will be the quieter.
Sir To. Come, we'll have him in a dark room and bound. My niece is already in the belief that he's mad: we may carry it thus, for our pleasure and his penance, till our very pastime, tired out of breath, prompt us to have mercy on him: at which time we will bring the device to the bar and crown thee for a finder of madmen. But see, but see.

Enter SIR ANDREW.

Fab. More matter for a May morning.
Sir And. Here's the challenge, read it: I warrant there's vinegar and pepper in't.
Fab. Is't so saucy?
Sir And. Ay, is't, I warrant him: do but read.   161
Sir To. Give me. [*Reads*] 'Youth, whatsoever thou art, thou art but a scurvy fellow.'
Fab. Good, and valiant.
Sir To. [*Reads*] 'Wonder not, nor admire not in thy mind, why I do call thee so, for I will show thee no reason for't.'
Fab. A good note; that keeps you from the blow of the law.   169
Sir To. [*Reads*] 'Thou comest to the lady Olivia, and in my sight she uses thee kindly: but thou liest in thy throat; that is not the matter I challenge thee for.'
Fab. Very brief, and to exceeding good sense —less.
Sir To. [*Reads*] 'I will waylay thee going home; where if it be thy chance to kill me,'—
Fab. Good.
Sir To. [*Reads*] 'Thou killest me like a rogue and a villain.'   180
Fab. Still you keep o' the windy side of the law: good.
Sir To. [*Reads*] 'Fare thee well; and God have mercy upon one of our souls! He may have mercy upon mine; but my hope is better, and so look to thyself. Thy friend, as thou usest him, and thy sworn enemy,   ANDREW AGUECHEEK.'
If this letter move him not, his legs cannot: I'll give't him.
Mar. You may have very fit occasion for't: he is now in some commerce with my lady, and will by and by depart.
Sir To. Go, Sir Andrew; scout me for him at the corner of the orchard like a bum-baily: so soon as ever thou seest him, draw; and, as thou drawest, swear horrible; for it comes to pass oft that a terrible oath, with a swaggering accent sharply twanged off, gives manhood more approbation than ever proof itself would have earned him. Away!   200
Sir And. Nay, let me alone for swearing.
                                                [*Exit*.
Sir To. Now will not I deliver his letter: for

the behaviour of the young gentleman gives him out to be of good capacity and breeding; his employment between his lord and my niece confirms no less: therefore this letter, being so excellently ignorant, will breed no terror in the youth: he
• will find it comes from a clodpole.   But, sir, I will deliver his challenge by word of mouth; set upon Aguecheek a notable report of valour; and drive the gentleman, as I know his youth will aptly receive it, into a most hideous opinion of his rage, skill, fury and impetuosity.   This will so fright them both that they will kill one another
• by the look, like cockatrices.

Re-enter OLIVIA, *with* VIOLA.

Fab.   Here he comes with your niece: give them way till he take leave, and presently after him.

Sir To.   I will meditate the while upon some horrid message for a challenge.   220
      [*Exeunt Sir Toby, Fabian, and Maria.*
Oli.   I have said too much unto a heart of stone
• And laid mine honour too unchary out:
There's something in me that reproves my fault;
But such a headstrong potent fault it is,
That it but mocks reproof.
Vio.   With the same 'haviour that your passion bears
Goes on my master's grief.
Oli.   Here, wear this jewel for me, 'tis my picture;
Refuse it not; it hath no tongue to vex you;
And I beseech you come again to-morrow.   230
What shall you ask of me that I'll deny,
That honour saved may upon asking give?
Vio.   Nothing but this; your true love for my master.
Oli.   How with mine honour may I give him that
Which I have given to you?
Vio.   I will acquit you.
Oli.   Well, come again to-morrow: fare thee well:
A fiend like thee might bear my soul to hell.
                                             [*Exit.*

Re-enter SIR TOBY *and* FABIAN.

Sir To.   Gentleman, God save thee.
Vio.   And you, sir.   239
Sir To.   That defence thou hast, betake thee to't: of what nature the wrongs are thou hast done him, I know not; but thy intercepter, full of despite, bloody as the hunter, attends thee at the
• orchard-end: dismount thy tuck, be yare in thy preparation, for thy assailant is quick, skilful and deadly.
Vio.   You mistake, sir; I am sure no man hath any quarrel to me: my remembrance is very free and clear from any image of offence done to any man.   250
Sir To.   You'll find it otherwise, I assure you: therefore, if you hold your life at any price, betake you to your guard; for your opposite hath in him what youth, strength, skill and wrath can furnish man withal.
Vio.   I pray you, sir, what is he?
• *Sir To.*   He is knight, dubbed with unhatched
• rapier and on carpet consideration; but he is a

208   *clodpole.* Blockhead.

215   *cockatrices.* Mythical serpents that could kill by looks.

222   *unchary.* Openly.

Costume design for Olivia by Norman Wilkinson, 1912

244   *dismount thy tuck.* Draw thy sword. *yare.* Quick.

257   *unhatched.* Unhacked or unused in battle.

258   *on carpet consideration.* One knighted not for military services.

262-263 *Hob, nob.* Have it, have it not.

265 *conduct.* Escort.

275 *meddle.* Fight.

286 *mortal arbitrement.* Mortal combat.

302 *firago.* Virago.

303-304 *stuck in.* Thrust, from the Italian *stoccado.*

305 *on the answer, he pays you.* On the return, he kills you.

320 *to take up.* To settle.

322 *He is . . . him.* He is as terrified of him.

devil in private brawl: souls and bodies hath he divorced three; and his incensement at this moment is so implacable, that satisfaction can be none but by pangs of death and sepulchre. Hob, nob, is his word; give't or take't.

Vio. I will return again into the house and desire some conduct of the lady. I am no fighter. I have heard of some kind of men that put quarrels purposely on others, to taste their valour: belike this is a man of that quirk.

Sir To. Sir, no; his indignation derives itself out of a very competent injury: therefore, get you on and give him his desire. Back you shall not to the house, unless you undertake that with me which with as much safety you might answer him: therefore, on, or strip your sword stark naked; for meddle you must, that's certain, or forswear to wear iron about you.

Vio. This is as uncivil as strange. I beseech you, do me this courteous office, as to know of the knight what my offence to him is: it is something of my negligence, nothing of my purpose.

Sir To. I will do so. Signior Fabian, stay you by this gentleman till my return.   [*Exit.*

Vio. Pray you, sir, do you know of this matter?

Fab. I know the knight is incensed against you, even to a mortal arbitrement; but nothing of the circumstance more.

Vio. I beseech you, what manner of man is he?   289

Fab. Nothing of that wonderful promise, to read him by his form, as you are like to find him in the proof of his valour. He is, indeed, sir, the most skilful, bloody and fatal opposite that you could possibly have found in any part of Illyria. Will you walk towards him? I will make your peace with him if I can.

Vio. I shall be much bound to you for't: I am one that had rather go with sir priest than sir knight: I care not who knows so much of my mettle.   [*Exeunt.* 300

Re-enter SIR TOBY, *with* SIR ANDREW.

Sir To. Why, man, he's a very devil; I have not seen such a firago. I had a pass with him, rapier, scabbard and all, and he gives me the stuck in with such a mortal motion, that it is inevitable; and on the answer, he pays you as surely as your feet hit the ground they step on. They say he has been fencer to the Sophy.

Sir And. Pox on't, I'll not meddle with him.

Sir To. Ay, but he will not now be pacified: Fabian can scarce hold him yonder.   310

Sir And. Plague on't, an I thought he had been valiant and so cunning in fence, I'ld have seen him damned ere I'ld have challenged him. Let him let the matter slip, and I'll give him my horse, grey Capilet.

Sir To. I'll make the motion: stand here, make a good show on't: this shall end without the perdition of souls. [*Aside*] Marry, I'll ride your horse as well as I ride you.   319

Re-enter FABIAN *and* VIOLA.

[*To Fab.*] I have his horse to take up the quarrel: I have persuaded him the youth's a devil.

Fab. He is as horribly conceited of him; and

pants and looks pale, as if a bear were at his heels.

Sir To. [*To Vio.*] There's no remedy, sir; he will fight with you for's oath sake: marry, he hath better bethought him of his quarrel, and he finds that now scarce to be worth talking of: therefore draw, for the supportance of his vow; he protests he will not hurt you.   330

Vio. [*Aside*] Pray God defend me! A little thing would make me tell them how much I lack of a man.

Fab. Give ground, if you see him furious.

Sir To. Come, Sir Andrew, there's no remedy; the gentleman will, for his honour's sake,
• have one bout with you; he cannot by the duello avoid it: but he has promised me, as he is a gentleman and a soldier, he will not hurt you. Come on; to't.   340

Sir And. Pray God, he keep his oath!

Vio. I do assure you, 'tis against my will.
                            [*They draw.*

Enter ANTONIO.

Ant. Put up your sword. If this young gentleman
Have done offence, I take the fault on me:
If you offend him, I for him defy you.

Sir To. You, sir! why, what are you?

Ant. One, sir, that for his love dares yet do more
Than you have heard him brag to you he will.

• *Sir To.* Nay, if you be an undertaker, I am for you.   [*They draw.* 350

Enter Officers.

Fab. O good Sir Toby, hold! here come the officers.

Sir To. I'll be with you anon.

Vio. Pray, sir, put your sword up, if you please.

• *Sir And.* Marry, will I, sir; and, for that I promised you, I'll be as good as my word: he will bear you easily and reins well.

First Off. This is the man; do thy office.

Sec. Off. Antonio, I arrest thee at the suit of Count Orsino.   361

Ant. You do mistake me, sir.

• *First Off.* No, sir, no jot; I know your favour well,
Though now you have no sea-cap on your head.
Take him away: he knows I know him well.

Ant. I must obey. [*To Vio.*] This comes with seeking you:
But there's no remedy; I shall answer it.
What will you do, now my necessity
Makes me to ask you for my purse? It grieves me
Much more for what I cannot do for you   370
Than what befalls myself. You stand amazed;
But be of comfort.

Sec. Off. Come, sir, away.

Ant. I must entreat of you some of that money.

Vio. What money, sir?
For the fair kindness you have show'd me here,
And, part, being prompted by your present trouble,
Out of my lean and low ability
I'll lend you something: my having is not much;
• I'll make division of my present with you: 380
Hold there's half my coffer.

Sir Andrew: 'Pray God, he keep his oath!' Illustration by W. Heath Robinson, 1908

337 *duello.* Duelling code.

349 *an undertaker.* One who takes up the challenge for another.

356-357 *for that . . . you.* His grey horse.

363 *favour.* Face.

380 *present.* Present means.

Ant.   Will you deny me now?
Is't possible that my deserts to you
Can lack persuasion? Do not tempt my misery,
Lest that it make me so unsound a man
As to upbraid you with those kindnesses
That I have done for you.
Vio.   I know of none;
Nor know I you by voice or any feature:
I hate ingratitude more in a man
Than lying, vainness, babbling, drunkenness,
Or any taint of vice whose strong corruption 390
Inhabits our frail blood.
Ant.   O heavens themselves!
Sec. Off. Come, sir, I pray you, go.
Ant. Let me speak a little. This youth that
        you see here
I snatch'd one half out of the jaws of death,
Relieved him with such sanctity of love,
And to his image, which methought did promise
Most venerable worth, did I devotion.
First Off. What's that to us? The time goes
        by: away!
Ant. But O how vile an idol proves this god!
Thou hast, Sebastian, done good feature shame.
In nature there's no blemish but the mind; 401
None can be call'd deform'd but the unkind:
Virtue is beauty, but the beauteous evil
Are empty trunks o'erflourish'd by the devil.
First Off. The man grows mad: away with
        him! Come, come, sir.
Ant. Lead me on.   [*Exit with Officers.*
Vio. Methinks his words do from such pas-
        sion fly,
That he believes himself: so do not I.
Prove true, imagination, O, prove true,
That I, dear brother, be now ta'en for you! 410
Sir To. Come hither, knight; come hither,
Fabian: we'll whisper o'er a couplet or two of
most sage saws.
Vio. He named Sebastian: I my brother know
Yet living in my glass; even such and so
In favour was my brother, and he went
Still in this fashion, colour, ornament,
For him I imitate: O, if it prove,
Tempests are kind and salt waves fresh in love.
                              [*Exit.*
Sir To. A very dishonest paltry boy, and
more a coward than a hare: his dishonesty ap-
pears in leaving his friend here in necessity and
denying him; and for his cowardship, ask Fabian.
Fab. A coward, a most devout coward, re-
ligious in it.
Sir And. 'Slid, I'll after him again and beat
him.
Sir To. Do; cuff him soundly, but never
draw thy sword.
Sir And. An I do not,—   [*Exit.* 430
Fab. Come, let's see the event.
Sir To. I dare lay any money 'twill be nothing yet.   [*Exeunt.*

ACT IV.

SCENE I. *Before* OLIVIA'S *house.*

Enter SEBASTIAN *and* CLOWN.

Clo. Will you make me believe that I am not
sent for you?

382 *deserts*. Claims.

402 *unkind*. Hard-hearted or unnatural.

404 *o'erflourish'd*. Ornamented, implying to conceal
what was within.

414-415 *I my . . . glass.* I am the living image of my
brother, or in my glass I see my brother.

Costume design for Viola and Sebastian by J. Gower
Parks, New Theatre, London, 1933

420 *dishonest*. Dishonourable.

426 *'Slid*. By God's eyelid.

Opposite: The duel scene. (above) Engraving from a
design by H. Hofmann from E. Dowden's *Shakespeare
Scenes and Characters*, 1876. (below) Eighteenth century
engraving showing David Garrick as Sir Toby

5 *held out.* Maintained.

14 *lubber.* A lout.

15 *cockney.* Fop, or spoilt child.

19 *Greek.* Buffoon.

24-25 *after . . . purchase.* At a high price, because twelve years' rent was equal to the purchase price of land.

43 *fleshed.* Initiated into blood-shed.

47 *malapert.* Impudent.

Olivia: 'Hold, Toby; on thy life . . .' Engraving from Charles Knight's *Pictorial Edition of the Works of William Shakspere,* 1839–43

55 *Rudesby.* Ruffian.

57 *extent.* 'In law, a writ of execution, whereby goods are seized for the king. It is therefore taken here for violence in general'. (Dr. Johnson).

60 *botch'd up.* Crudely patched up.

62 *Beshrew.* Curse.

Seb. Go to, go to, thou art a foolish fellow: Let me be clear of thee.

Clo. Well held out, i' faith! No, I do not know you; nor I am not sent to you by my lady, to bid you come speak with her; nor your name is not Master Cesario; nor this is not my nose neither. Nothing that is so is so.

Seb. I prithee, vent thy folly somewhere else: Thou know'st not me.   11

Clo. Vent my folly! he has heard that word of some great man and now applies it to a fool. Vent my folly! I am afraid this great lubber, the world, will prove a cockney. I prithee now, ungird thy strangeness and tell me what I shall vent to my lady: shall I vent to her that thou art coming?

Seb. I prithee, foolish Greek, depart from me: There's money for thee: if you tarry longer,   20 I shall give worse payment.

Clo. By my troth, thou hast an open hand. These wise men that give fools money get themselves a good report—after fourteen years' purchase.

Enter SIR ANDREW, SIR TOBY, *and* FABIAN.

Sir And. Now, sir, have I met you again? there's for you.

Seb. Why, there's for thee, and there, and there.
Are all the people mad?

Sir To. Hold, sir, or I'll throw your dagger o'er the house.   31

Clo. This will I tell my lady straight: I would not be in some of your coats for two pence. [*Exit.*

Sir To. Come on, sir; hold.

Sir And. Nay, let him alone: I'll go another way to work with him; I'll have an action of battery against him, if there be any law in Illyria: though I struck him first, yet it's no matter for that.

Seb. Let go thy hand.   40

Sir To. Come, sir, I will not let you go. Come, my young soldier, put up your iron: you are well fleshed; come on.

Seb. I will be free from thee. What wouldst thou now? If thou darest tempt me further, draw thy sword.

Sir To. What, what? Nay, then I must have an ounce or two of this malapert blood from you.

Enter OLIVIA.

Oli. Hold, Toby; on thy life I charge thee, hold!

Sir To. Madam!   50

Oli. Will it be ever thus? Ungracious wretch, Fit for the mountains and the barbarous caves, Where manners ne'er were preach'd! out of my sight!
Be not offended, dear Cesario.
Rudesby, be gone!
[*Exeunt Sir Toby, Sir Andrew, and Fabian.*
                                I prithee, gentle friend,
Let thy fair wisdom, not thy passion, sway
In this uncivil and unjust extent
Against thy peace. Go with me to my house,
And hear thou there how many fruitless pranks
This ruffian hath botch'd up, that thou thereby 60
Mayst smile at this: thou shalt not choose but go:
Do not deny. Beshrew his soul for me,

He started one poor heart of mine in thee.

Seb. What relish is in this? how runs the stream?
Or I am mad, or else this is a dream:

Let fancy still my sense in Lethe steep;
If it be thus to dream, still let me sleep!

Oli. Nay, come, I prithee; would thou 'ldst
be ruled by me!

Seb. Madam, I will.

Oli. O, say so, and so be! [*Exeunt.*

SCENE II. OLIVIA'S *house.*

Enter MARIA *and* CLOWN.

Mar. Nay, I prithee, put on this **gown** and
this beard; make him believe thou art Sir Topas
the curate: do it quickly; I'll call Sir Toby the
whilst. [*Exit.*

Clo. Well, I'll put it on, and I will dissemble
myself in 't; and I would I were the first that
ever dissembled in such a gown. I am not tall
enough to become the function well, nor lean
enough to be thought a good student; but to be
said an honest man and a good housekeeper goes
as fairly as to say a careful man and a great
scholar. The competitors enter.

Enter SIR TOBY *and* MARIA.

Sir To. Jove bless thee, master Parson.

Clo. Bonos dies, Sir Toby: for, as the old
hermit of Prague, that never saw pen and ink,
very wittily said to a niece of King Gorboduc,
'That that is is;' so I, being master Parson, am
master Parson; for, what is 'that' but 'that,'
and 'is' but 'is'?

Sir To. To him, Sir Topas. 20

Clo. What, ho, I say! peace in this prison!

Sir To. The knave counterfeits well; a good
knave.

Mal. [*Within*] Who calls there?

Clo. Sir Topas the curate, who comes to visit
Malvolio the lunatic.

Mal. Sir Topas, Sir Topas, good Sir Topas,
go to my lady.

Clo. Out, hyperbolical fiend! how vexest thou
this man! talkest thou nothing but of ladies? 30

Sir To. Well said, master Parson.

Mal. Sir Topas, never was man thus wronged:
good Sir Topas, do not think I am mad: they
have laid me here in hideous darkness.

Clo. Fie, thou dishonest Satan! I call thee
by the most modest terms; for I am one of those
gentle ones that will use the devil himself with
courtesy: sayest thou that house is dark?

Mal. As hell, Sir Topas. 39

Clo. Why, it hath bay windows transparent
as barricadoes, and the clearstores toward the
south north are as lustrous as ebony; and yet
complainest thou of obstruction?

Mal. I am not mad, Sir Topas: I say to you,
this house is dark.

Clo. Madman, thou errest: I say, there is no
darkness but ignorance; in which thou art more
puzzled than the Egyptians in their fog.

Mal. I say, this house is as dark as ignorance,
though ignorance were as dark as hell; and I
say, there was never man thus abused. I am no
more mad than you are: make the trial of it in
any constant question.

63 *started.* Roused.

64 *relish.* Meaning.

66 *Lethe.* The river of oblivion in Hades.

2 *Topas.* A semi-precious stone supposed to cure lunacy. Also the hero of Chaucer's satirical romance *Rime of Sir Topas*.

10 *housekeeper.* Solid citizen.

12 *competitors.* Confederates.

14 *Bonos dies.* 'Good day' in bad Latin.

15 *hermit of Prague.* Another example of Feste's mockery of the practice of citing authority.

16 *King Gorboduc.* Mythical British king.

29 *hyperbolical.* Extravagant.

41 *barricadoes.* Barricades. *clearstores.* Windows high up in a wall.

Malvolio: 'I am not mad, Sir Topas'. Engraving by Kenny Meadows from Barry Cornwall's *The Works of Shakspere*, 1846

48 *Egyptians in their fog.* One of the plagues that Moses called down on Egypt was a darkness lasting three days.

53 *constant.* Rational.

Malvolio: 'Sir Topas, Sir Topas!' Engraving by H. Fuseli from Steevens's edition, 1805

54 *Pythagoras*. A Greek philosopher who believed in the transmigration of souls.

68 *for all waters*. I can turn my hand to anything.

74 *delivered*. Released.

81 *perdy*. By God, from the French *par Dieu*.

92-93 *besides your five wits*. Mad. The wits were analogous with the five senses and consisted of memory, common wit, estimation, imagination and fantasy.

99 *propertied*. Treated me like a (theatrical) property.

102-103 *the minister is here*. For the next few lines the clown alternates between his own voice and that of Sir Topas.

112 *shent*. Reproved.

Clo. What is the opinion of Pythagoras concerning wild fowl?
Mal. That the soul of our grandam might haply inhabit a bird.
Clo. What thinkest thou of his opinion?
Mal. I think nobly of the soul, and no way approve his opinion.   60
Clo. Fare thee well. Remain thou still in darkness: thou shalt hold the opinion of Pythagoras ere I will allow of thy wits, and fear to kill a woodcock, lest thou dispossess the soul of thy grandam. Fare thee well.
Mal. Sir Topas, Sir Topas!
Sir To. My most exquisite Sir Topas!
Clo. Nay, I am for all waters.
Mar. Thou mightst have done this without thy beard and gown: he sees thee not.   70
Sir To. To him in thine own voice, and bring me word how thou findest him: I would we were well rid of this knavery. If he may be conveniently delivered, I would he were, for I am now so far in offence with my niece that I cannot pursue with any safety this sport to the upshot. Come by and by to my chamber.
[*Exeunt Sir Toby and Maria.*

Clo. [*Singing*] 'Hey, Robin, jolly Robin,
               Tell me how thy lady does.'
Mal. Fool!   80
Clo. 'My lady is unkind, perdy.'
Mal. Fool!
Clo. 'Alas, why is she so?'
Mal. Fool, I say!
Clo. 'She loves another'—Who calls, ha?
Mal. Good fool, as ever thou wilt deserve well at my hand, help me to a candle, and pen, ink and paper: as I am a gentleman, I will live to be thankful to thee for't.
Clo. Master Malvolio?   90
Mal. Ay, good fool.
Clo. Alas, sir, how fell you besides your five wits?
Mal. Fool, there was never man so notoriously abused: I am as well in my wits, fool, as thou art.
Clo. But as well? then you are mad indeed, if you be no better in your wits than a fool.
Mal. They have here propertied me; keep me in darkness, send ministers to me, asses, and do all they can to face me out of my wits.   101
Clo. Advise you what you say; the minister is here. Malvolio, Malvolio, thy wits the heavens restore! endeavour thyself to sleep, and leave thy vain bibble babble.
Mal. Sir Topas!
Clo. Maintain no words with him, good fellow. Who, I, sir? not I, sir. God be wi' you, good Sir Topas. Marry, amen. I will, sir, I will.
Mal. Fool, fool, fool, I say!   110
Clo. Alas, sir, be patient. What say you, sir? I am shent for speaking to you.
Mal. Good fool, help me to some light and some paper: I tell thee, I am as well in my wits as any man in Illyria.
Clo. Well-a-day that you were, sir!
Mal. By this hand, I am. Good fool, some ink, paper and light; and convey what I will set down to my lady: it shall advantage thee more than ever the bearing of letter did.   120
Clo. I will help you to't. But tell me true,

are you not mad indeed? or do you but counterfeit?

Mal. Believe me, I am not; I tell thee true.

Clo. Nay, I'll ne'er believe a madman till I
see his brains. I will fetch you light and paper
and ink.

Mal. Fool, I'll requite it in the highest degree: I prithee, be gone.

Clo. [*Singing*] I am gone, sir,   130
   And anon, sir,
  I'll be with you again,
   In a trice,
  Like to the old Vice,
  Your need to sustain;
  Who, with dagger of lath,
  In his rage and his wrath,
   Cries, ah, ha! to the devil:
  Like a mad lad,
  Pare thy nails, dad;   140
   † Adieu, good man devil. [*Exit.*

SCENE III. OLIVIA'S *garden.*

Enter SEBASTIAN.

Seb. This is the air; that is the glorious sun;
This pearl she gave me, I do feel't and see't;
And though 'tis wonder that enwraps me thus,
Yet 'tis not madness. Where's Antonio, then?
I could not find him at the Elephant:
Yet there he was; and there I found this credit,
That he did range the town to seek me out.
His counsel now might do me golden service;
For though my soul disputes well with my sense,
That this may be some error, but no madness,   10
Yet doth this accident and flood of fortune
So far exceed all instance, all discourse,
That I am ready to distrust mine eyes
And wrangle with my reason that persuades me
To any other trust but that I am mad
Or else the lady's mad; yet, if 'twere so,
She could not sway her house, command her fol-
  lowers,
Take and give back affairs and their dispatch
With such a smooth, discreet and stable bearing
As I perceive she does: there's something in't   20
That is deceiveable. But here the lady comes.

Enter OLIVIA *and* Priest.

Oli. Blame not this haste of mine. If you
  mean well,
Now go with me and with this holy man
Into the chantry by: there, before him,
And underneath that consecrated roof,
Plight me the full assurance of your faith;
That my most jealous and too doubtful soul
May live at peace. He shall conceal it
Whiles you are willing it shall come to note,
What time we will our celebration keep   30
According to my birth. What do you say?

Seb. I'll follow this good man, and go with
  you;
And, having sworn truth, ever will be true.

Oliv. Then lead the way, good father; and
  heavens so shine,
That they may fairly note this act of mine!
          [*Exeunt.*

134 *Vice.* A stock character in the Morality plays who carried a wooden dagger with which he would try to pare the Devil's nails.

12 *instance.* Precedent. *discourse.* Reason.

21 *deceiveable.* Deceptive.

Olivia: 'Blame not this haste of mine'. Drawing by William Hamilton (1751–1801)

24 *chantry by.* Nearby chapel.

26 *Plight me.* Olivia is asking for a betrothal ceremony in the presence of a witness, which was almost as binding as the marriage ceremony.

30 *celebration.* Marriage ceremony.

22 *abused.* Deceived.

23-24 *conclusions to be as kisses.* If conclusions be compared to kisses. *four negatives make your two affirmatives.* A common jest of the period that the 'no, no, no, no', of a coy lady actually mean 'yes, yes'.

35 *grace.* A play on the meanings 1) the title of the Duke; 2) generosity; and 3) virtue.

40 *the third pays for all.* The original form of the saying 'Third time lucky'.

41 *triplex.* Triple time in music.

42 *bells of Saint Bennet.* This may refer to the bells of St. Benet Hithe, a church across the river from the Globe.

56 *Vulcan.* The blacksmith of the gods in mythology.

Vulcan. From a 19th century engraving

57 *bawbling.* Trifling.

59 *scathful.* Destructive.

ACT V.

SCENE I.   *Before* OLIVIA'S *house.*

Enter CLOWN *and* FABIAN.

Fab.   Now, as thou lovest me, let me see his letter.

Clo.   Good Master Fabian, grant me another request.

Fab.   Any thing.

Clo.   Do not desire to see this letter.

Fab.   This is, to give a dog, and in recompense desire my dog again.

Enter DUKE, VIOLA, CURIO, *and* Lords.

Duke.   Belong you to the Lady Olivia, friends?

Clo.   Ay, sir; we are some of her trappings.   10

Duke.   I know thee well: how dost thou, my good fellow?

Clo.   Truly, sir, the better for my foes and the worse for my friends.

Duke.   Just the contrary; the better for thy friends.

Clo.   No, sir, the worse.

Duke.   How can that be?

Clo.   Marry, sir, they praise me and make an ass of me; now my foes tell me plainly I am an ass: so that by my foes, sir, I profit in the knowledge of myself, and by my friends I am abused: so that, conclusions to be as kisses, if your four negatives make your two affirmatives, why then, the worse for my friends and the better for my foes.

Duke.   Why, this is excellent.

Clo.   By my troth, sir, no; though it please you to be one of my friends.

Duke.   Thou shalt not be the worse for me: there's gold.   31

Clo.   But that it would be double-dealing, sir, I would you could make it another.

Duke.   O, you give me ill counsel.

Clo.   Put your grace in your pocket, sir, for this once, and let your flesh and blood obey it.

Duke.   Well, I will be so much a sinner, to be a double-dealer: there's another.

Clo.   Primo, secundo, tertio, is a good play; and the old saying is, the third pays for all: the triplex, sir, is a good tripping measure; or the bells of Saint Bennet, sir, may put you in mind; one, two, three.

Duke.   You can fool no more money out of me at this throw: if you will let your lady know I am here to speak with her, and bring her along with you, it may awake my bounty further.

Clo.   Marry, sir, lullaby to your bounty till I come again. I go, sir; but I would not have you to think that my desire of having is the sin of covetousness: but, as you say, sir, let your bounty take a nap, I will awake it anon.   [*Exit.*

Vio.   Here comes the man, sir, that did rescue me.

Enter ANTONIO *and* Officers.

Duke.   That face of his I do remember well;
Yet, when I saw it last, it was besmear'd
As black as Vulcan in the smoke of war:
A bawbling vessel was he captain of,
For shallow draught and bulk unprizable;
With which such scathful grapple did he make

With the most noble bottom of our fleet,　60
That very envy and the tongue of loss
Cried fame and honour on him. What's the
　matter?
First Off. Orsino, this is that Antonio
That took the Phœnix and her fraught from
　Candy;
And this is he that did the Tiger board,
When your young nephew Titus lost his leg:
Here in the streets, desperate of shame and state,
In private brabble did we apprehend him.
　Vio. He did me kindness, sir, drew on
　　my side;
But in conclusion put strange speech upon me: 70
I know not what 'twas but distraction.
　Duke. Notable pirate! thou salt-water thief!
What foolish boldness brought thee to their
　mercies,
Whom thou, in terms so bloody and so dear,
Hast made thine enemies?
　Ant.　　　　　　　Orsino, noble sir,
Be pleased that I shake off these names you
　give me:
Antonio never yet was thief or pirate,
Though I confess, on base and ground enough,
Orsino's enemy. A witchcraft drew me hither:
That most ingrateful boy there by your side,　80
From the rude sea's enraged and foamy mouth
Did I redeem; a wreck past hope he was:
His life I gave him and did thereto add
My love, without retention or restraint,
All his in dedication; for his sake
Did I expose myself, pure for his love,
Into the danger of this adverse town;
Drew to defend him when he was beset:
Where being apprehended, his false cunning,
Not meaning to partake with me in danger,　90
Taught him to face me out of his acquaintance,
And grew a twenty years removed thing
While one would wink; denied me mine own
　purse,
Which I had recommended to his use
Not half an hour before.
　Vio.　　　　　　How can this be?
　Duke. When came he to this town?
　Ant. To-day, my lord; and for three months
　before,
No interim, not a minute's vacancy,
Both day and night did we keep company.

　　　Enter OLIVIA *and* Attendants.

　Duke. Here comes the countess: now heaven
　　walks on earth.　　　　　　　100
But for thee, fellow; fellow, thy words are mad-
　ness:
Three months this youth hath tended upon me;
But more of that anon. Take him aside.
　Oli. What would my lord, but that he may
　　not have,
Wherein Olivia may seem serviceable?
Cesario, you do not keep promise with me.
　Vio. Madam!
　Duke. Gracious Olivia,—
　Oli. What do you say, Cesario? Good my
　　lord,—　　　　　　　109
　Vio. My lord would speak; my duty hushes me.
　Oli. If it be aught to the old tune, my lord,
It is as fat and fulsome to mine ear
As howling after music.

60 *bottom.* Ship.

64 *fraught.* Freight. *Candy.* Candia, Crete.

67 *desperate.* Recklessly ignoring.

68 *brabble.* Brawl.

71 *distraction.* Madness.

78 *on base and ground.* With sound grounds.

91 *to face me out of his acquaintance.* To deny any
acquaintance with me.

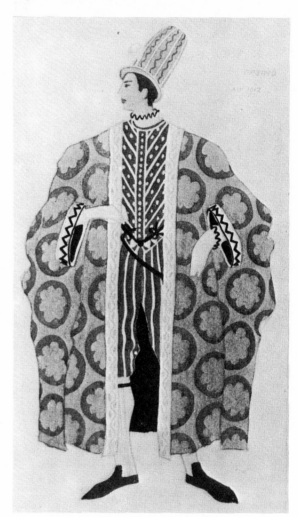

Costume design for Orsino by Norman Wilkinson, 1912

121 *Egyptian thief.* Heliodorus, in his *Ethiopica*, records the tale of the bandit Thyamis who tried to kill the woman he loved, rather than let her fall into the hands of his enemies.

126 *screws me.* Wrenches.

129 *tender dearly.* Love dearly.

139 *More, by all mores.* More than all comparisons.

Costume design for Viola by Norman Wilkinson, 1912

148 *sirrah.* Customary form of address to an inferior.

150 *strangle thy propriety.* Deny your identity i.e. as Olivia's husband.

164 *function.* Official capacity as a priest.

Duke.   Still so cruel?
Oli. Still so constant, lord.
Duke. What, to perverseness? you uncivil lady,
To whose ingrate and unauspicious altars
My soul the faithfull'st offerings hath breathed out
That e'er devotion tender'd! What shall I do?
Oli.   Even what it please my lord, that shall
become him.
Duke. Why should I not, had I the heart
to do it,   120
Like to the Egyptian thief at point of death,
Kill what I love?—a savage jealousy
That sometime savours nobly. But hear me this:
Since you to non-regardance cast my faith,
And that I partly know the instrument
That screws me from my true place in your
favour,
Live you the marble-breasted tyrant still;
But this your minion, whom I know you love,
And whom, by heaven I swear, I tender dearly,
Him will I tear out of that cruel eye,   130
Where he sits crowned in his master's spite.
Come, boy, with me; my thoughts are ripe in
mischief:
I'll sacrifice the lamb that I do love,
To spite a raven's heart within a dove.
Vio.   And I, most jocund, apt and willingly,
To do you rest, a thousand deaths would die.
Oli. Where goes Cesario?
Vio.   After him I love
More than I love these eyes, more than my life,
More, by all mores, than e'er I shall love wife.
If I do feign, you witnesses above   140
Punish my life for tainting of my love!
Oli.   Ay me, detested! how am I beguiled!
Vio.   Who does beguile you? who does do you
wrong?
Oli.   Hast thou forgot thyself? is it so long?
Call forth the holy father.
Duke.   Come, away!
Oli. Whither, my lord? Cesario, husband, stay.
Duke. Husband!
Oli.   Ay, husband: can he that deny?
Duke. Her husband, sirrah!
Vio.   No, my lord, not I.
Oli. Alas, it is the baseness of thy fear
That makes thee strangle thy propriety: 150
Fear not, Cesario; take thy fortunes up;
Be that thou know'st thou art, and then thou art
As great as that thou fear'st.

Enter Priest.

                         O, welcome, father!
Father, I charge thee, by thy reverence,
Here to unfold, though lately we intended
To keep in darkness what occasion now
Reveals before 'tis ripe, what thou dost know
Hath newly pass'd between this youth and me.
Priest.   A contract of eternal bond of love,
Confirm'd by mutual joinder of your hands,   160
Attested by the holy close of lips,
Strengthen'd by interchangement of your rings;
And all the ceremony of this compact
Seal'd in my function, by my testimony:
Since when, my watch hath told me, toward
my grave
I have travell'd but two hours.
Duke. O thou dissembling cub! what wilt
thou be

When time hath sow'd a grizzle on thy case?
Or will not else thy craft so quickly grow,
That thine own trip shall be thine overthrow? 170
Farewell, and take her; but direct thy feet
Where thou and I henceforth may never meet.
 Vio. My lord, I do protest—
 Oli.   O, do not swear!
Hold little faith, though thou hast too much fear.

Enter SIR ANDREW.

 Sir And. For the love of God, a surgeon!
Send one presently to Sir Toby.
 Oli. What's the matter?
 Sir And. He has broke my head across and
has given Sir Toby a bloody coxcomb too: for the
love of God, your help! I had rather than forty
pound I were at home.   181
 Oli. Who has done this, Sir Andrew?
 Sir And. The count's gentleman, one Cesario:
we took him for a coward, but he's the very devil
incardinate.
 Duke. My gentleman, Cesario?
 Sir And. 'Od's lifelings, here he is! You
broke my head for nothing; and that that I did,
I was set on to do't by Sir Toby.
 Vio. Why do you speak to me? I never hurt
     you: 190
You drew your sword upon me without cause;
But I bespake you fair, and hurt you not.
 Sir And. If a bloody coxcomb be a hurt, you
have hurt me: I think you set nothing by a
bloody coxcomb.

Enter SIR TOBY *and* CLOWN.

Here comes Sir Toby halting; you shall hear
more: but if he had not been in drink, he would
have tickled you othergates than he did.
 Duke. How now, gentleman! how is't with
     you?   200
 Sir To. That's all one: has hurt me, and
there's the end on't. Sot, didst see Dick surgeon, sot?
 Clo. O, he's drunk, Sir Toby, an hour agone;
his eyes were set at eight i' the morning.
 Sir To. Then he's a rogue, † and a passy measures panyn: I hate a drunken rogue.
 Oli. Away with him! Who hath made this
havoc with them?
 Sir And. I'll help you, Sir Toby, because
we'll be dressed together.   211
 Sir To. Will you help? an ass-head and a
coxcomb and a knave, a thin-faced knave, a gull!
 Oli. Get him to bed, and let his hurt be look'd
to.   [*Exeunt Clown, Fabian, Sir Toby, and
                                     Sir Andrew.*

Enter SEBASTIAN.

 Seb. I am sorry, madam, I have hurt your
     kinsman;
But, had it been the brother of my blood,
I must have done no less with wit and safety.
You throw a strange regard upon me, and by that
I do perceive it hath offended you: 220
Pardon me, sweet one, even for the vows
We made each other but so late ago.
 Duke. One face, one voice, one habit, and
     two persons,
A natural perspective, that is and is not!
 Seb. Antonio, O my dear Antonio!

168 *grizzle.* Grey hairs. *case.* Skin, as of a fox.

179 *coxcomb.* Head.

185 *incardinate.* Sir Andrew means 'incarnate'.

187 *'Od's lifelings.* By God's life.

196 *halting.* Limping.

198 *othergates.* Otherwise.

205 *set.* Closed.

206-207 *passy measures.* A slow stately dance. *panyn.*
Paynim; a heathen.

Couple dancing the Passy Pavan. Engraving by F. W.
Fairholt for J. O. Halliwell's edition of Shakespeare's
works, 1853–65.

218 *with wit and safety.* With due regard for my own
safety.

223 *habit.* Clothing.

224 *perspective.* Optical illusion.

234-235 *Nor can there . . . every where.* Nor can I be here and everywhere, unlike God.

241 *suited.* Dressed.

244 *dimension grossly clad.* Bodily form.

245 *Which from the . . . participate.* Which I have had from birth.

246 *as the rest goes even.* As everything else fits.

256 *lets.* Prevents.

259 *cohere and jump.* Come together and agree.

267 *bias.* Inclination.

272 *the glass seems true.* The optical illusion is proving to be real.

278 *orbed continent.* The sphere of the sun.

283 *durance.* Imprisoned.

Lily Brayton as Viola, Her Majesty's Theatre, London, 1901

How have the hours rack'd and tortured me,
Since I have lost thee !
   Ant. Sebastian are you?
   Seb.   Fear'st thou that, Antonio?
   Ant. How have you made division of your-
self?
An apple, cleft in two, is not more twin   230
Than these two creatures. Which is Sebastian?
   Oli. Most wonderful !
   Seb. Do I stand there? I never had a bro-
ther ;
• Nor can there be that deity in my nature,
Of here and every where. I had a sister,
Whom the blind waves and surges have devour'd.
Of charity, what kin are you to me?
What countryman? what name? what parentage?
   Vio. Of Messaline : Sebastian was my father ;
Such a Sebastian was my brother too,   240
• So went he suited to his watery tomb :
If spirits can assume both form and suit
You come to fright us.
   Seb.   A spirit I am indeed ;
• But am in that dimension grossly clad
• Which from the womb I did participate.
• Were you a woman, as the rest goes even,
I should my tears let fall upon your cheek,
And say 'Thrice-welcome, drowned Viola !'
   Vio. My father had a mole upon his brow.
   Seb. And so had mine.   250
   Vio. And died that day when Viola from her
birth
Had number'd thirteen years.
   Seb. O, that record is lively in my soul !
He finished indeed his mortal act
That day that made my sister thirteen years.
•   *Vio.* If nothing lets to make us happy both
But this my masculine usurp'd attire,
Do not embrace me till each circumstance
• Of place, time, fortune, do cohere and jump
That I am Viola : which to confirm,   260
I'll bring you to a captain in this town,
Where lie my maiden weeds ; by whose gentle
help
I was preserved to serve this noble count.
All the occurrence of my fortune since
Hath been between this lady and this lord.
   Seb. [*To Olivia*] So comes it, lady, you have
been mistook :
• But nature to her bias drew in that.
You would have been contracted to a maid ;
Nor are you therein, by my life, deceived,
You are betroth'd both to a maid and man. 270
   Duke. Be not amazed ; right noble is his
blood.
• If this be so, as yet the glass seems true,
I shall have share in this most happy wreck.
[*To Viola*] Boy, thou hast said to me a thousand
times
Thou never shouldst love woman like to me.
   Vio. And all those sayings will I over-swear ;
And all those swearings keep as true in soul
• As doth that orbed continent the fire
That severs day from night.
   Duke.   Give me thy hand ;
And let me see thee in thy woman's weeds. 280

   Vio. The captain that did bring me first on
shore
Hath my maid's garments : he upon some action
• Is now in durance, at Malvolio's suit,

A gentleman, and follower of my lady's.
● *Oli.* He shall enlarge him: fetch Malvolio
hither:
And yet, alas, now I remember me,
They say, poor gentleman, he's much distract.

Re-enter CLOWN *with a letter, and* FABIAN.

● A most extracting frenzy of mine own
From my remembrance clearly banish'd his.
How does he, sirrah?   290
● *Clo.* Truly, madam, he holds Belzebub at the
staves's end as well as a man in his case may do:
has here writ a letter to you; I should have given
't you to-day morning, but as a madman's epistles
● are no gospels, so it skills not much when they
are delivered.
Oli. Open 't, and read it.
Clo. Look then to be well edified when the
fool delivers the madman. [*Reads*] 'By the Lord,
madam,'—   300
Oli. How now! art thou mad?
Clo. No, madam, I do but read madness: an
your ladyship will have it as it ought to be, you
● must allow Vox.
Oli. Prithee, read i' thy right wits.
Clo. So I do, madonna; but to read his right
● wits is to read thus: therefore perpend, my princess, and give ear.
Oli. Read it you, sirrah.   [*To Fabian.*
Fab. [*Reads*] 'By the Lord, madam, you wrong
me, and the world shall know it: though you
have put me into darkness and given your drunken
cousin rule over me, yet have I the benefit of my
senses as well as your ladyship. I have your own
letter that induced me to the semblance I put on;
with the which I doubt not but to do myself much
right, or you much shame. Think of me as you
please. I leave my duty a little unthought of and
speak out of my injury.
                     THE MADLY-USED MALVOLIO.'
Oli. Did he write this?   320
Clo. Ay, madam.
Duke. This savours not much of distraction.
Oli. See him deliver'd, Fabian; bring him
      hither.   [*Exit Fabian.*
My lord, so please you, these things further
      thought on,
To think me as well a sister as a wife,
One day shall crown the alliance on 't, so please
      you,
● Here at my house and at my proper cost.
● *Duke.* Madam, I am most apt to embrace
      your offer.
[*To Viola*] Your master quits you; and for your
      service done him,
So much against the mettle of your sex,   330
So far beneath your soft and tender breeding,
And since you call'd me master for so long,
Here is my hand: you shall from this time be
Your master's mistress.
      Oli.   A sister! you are she.

Re-enter FABIAN, *with* MALVOLIO.

Duke. Is this the madman?
Oli.   Ay, my lord, this same.
How now, Malvolio!
      Mal.   Madam, you have done me wrong,
Notorious wrong.
      Oli.   Have I, Malvolio? no.

285 *enlarge.* Release.

288 *extracting.* Drawing every thought from the mind.

291-292 *he holds Belzebub . . . staves's end.* He holds the
devil at bay.

295 *skills.* Matters.

304 *Vox.* Appropriately loud voice for speaking in
public.

307 *perpend.* Notice.

327 *proper.* Own.

328 *apt.* Ready.

Richard Yates, 18th century English actor, as Malvolio,
1776

340 *from it*. Differently.

347 *lighter*. Lesser.

351 *geck and gull*. Fool and dupe.

355 *out of*. Beyond.

358 *presupposed*. Suggested.

360 *practice*. Trick.

Fabian: 'Good madam, hear me speak . . .' Illustration by W. Heath Robinson, 1908

369 *parts*. Traits of character.

371 *importance*. Importunity.

377 *baffled*. Ridiculed.

385 *whirligig*. Spinning top.

391 *convents*. Agrees.

Mal. Lady, you have.   Pray you, peruse that
        letter.
You must not now deny it is your hand:
● Write from it, if you can, in hand or phrase;   340
Or say 'tis not your seal, not your invention:
You can say none of this: well, grant it then
And tell me, in the modesty of honour,
Why you have given me such clear lights of
        favour,
Bade me come smiling and cross-garter'd to you,
To put on yellow stockings and to frown
● Upon Sir Toby and the lighter people;
And, acting this in an obedient hope,
Why have you suffer'd me to be imprison'd,
Kept in a dark house, visited by the priest,   350
● And made the most notorious geck and gull
That e'er invention play'd on? tell me why.
    Oli. Alas, Malvolio, this is not my writing,
Though, I confess, much like the character:
● But out of question 'tis Maria's hand.
And now I do bethink me, it was she
First told me thou wast mad; then camest in
        smiling,
● And in such forms which here were presupposed
Upon thee in the letter.   Prithee, be content:
● This practice hath most shrewdly pass'd upon
        thee;   360
But when we know the grounds and authors of it,
Thou shalt be both the plaintiff and the judge
Of thine own cause.
    Fab.   Good madam, hear me speak,
And let no quarrel nor no brawl to come
Taint the condition of this present hour,
Which I have wonder'd at.   In hope it shall not,
Most freely I confess, myself and Toby
Set this device against Malvolio here,
● Upon some stubborn and uncourteous parts
We had conceived against him: Maria writ   370
● The letter at Sir Toby's great importance;
In recompense whereof he hath married her.
How with a sportful malice it was follow'd,
May rather pluck on laughter than revenge;
If that the injuries be justly weigh'd
That have on both sides pass'd.
    ● *Oli.* Alas, poor fool, how have they baffled
        thee!

    Clo. Why, 'some are born great, some achieve
greatness, and some have greatness thrown upon
them.'   I was one, sir, in this interlude; one Sir
Topas, sir; but that's all one.   'By the Lord,
fool, I am not mad.'   But do you remember?
'Madam, why laugh you at such a barren rascal?
an you smile not, he's gagged:' and thus the
● whirligig of time brings in his revenges.
    Mal. I'll be revenged on the whole pack of
you.   [*Exit.*
    Oli. He hath been most notoriously abused.
    Duke. Pursue him, and entreat him to a peace:
He hath not told us of the captain yet: 390
● When that is known and golden time convents,
A solemn combination shall be made
Of our dear souls.   Meantime, sweet sister,
We will not part from hence.   Cesario, come;
For so you shall be, while you are a man;
But when in other habits you are seen,
Orsino's mistress and his fancy's queen.
                    [*Exeunt all, except Clown.*
    Clo. [*Sings*]
        When that I was and a little tiny boy,

With hey, ho, the wind and the rain,
A foolish thing was but a toy,   400
   For the rain it raineth every day.

But when I came to man's estate,
   With hey, ho, &c.
'Gainst knaves and thieves men shut their
     gate,
   For the rain, &c.

But when I came, alas! to wive,
   With hey, ho, &c.
By swaggering could I never thrive,
   For the rain, &c.

But when I came unto my beds,   410
   With hey, ho, &c.
• With toss-pots still had drunken heads,
   For the rain, &c.

A great while ago the world begun,
   With hey, ho, &c.
But that's all one, our play is done,
   And we'll strive to please you every day.
                     [*Exit.*

Clown: 'For the rain it raineth every day'. Illustration by W. Heath Robinson, 1908

412 *toss-pots.* Drunkards.

Clown: '. . . toss-pots still had drunken heads'. Illustration by W. Heath Robinson, 1908

Troilus and Cressida

1602

THE YEARS 1600–1602 were critical years, both in politics and in the theatre. To understand *Troilus and Cressida* we have to set it in the contemporary perspective: without a knowledge of that people have not known how to take it, and critics have been more than usually off the mark. In Shakespeare's own profession these years were marked by the notorious War of the Theatres. This was sparked off by Ben Jonson's explosive, quarrelsome temper, in a quarrel he made with Marston, for whom Dekker too entered the fray and took up the cudgels. The parties wrote against each other, produced their plays caricaturing each other, and this involved the Chamberlain's Company to some extent, since the men's companies were aligned against the revived boys' companies, whose shrill voices suited the satires, the invective and personal abuse that flew to and fro.

Shakespeare characteristically kept out of the quarrel, though he was affected by it, and traces remain in both *Hamlet* and *Troilus and Cressida*. The upshot of the War of the Theatres was very important: Comedy was never the same again. It ended the reign of romantic comedy which had prevailed through the 1590's, of which Shakespeare's last example was *Twelfth Night*. Henceforth the future of comedy was with Ben Jonson's satiric comedy, which was not congenial to Shakespeare's genius.

Nevertheless he provided his own example of it in *Troilus and Cressida*—a more scathing, brilliant and memorable example than anybody else's. It is almost as if Jonathan Swift had taken to writing a play. *Troilus and Cressida* is one of the most remarkable plays that Shakespeare ever wrote, but it has always been 'caviare to the general'. A play that goes so much to the heart of human folly, and exposes it in its most glaring manifestations—love, politics and war—can hardly be expected to be taken to the great heart of the people. But it was not intended for them; it was intended for a private, sophisticated audience, probably at one of the Inns of Court.

This has led to much unnecessary argumentation about what kind of a play it is. It is a satirical comedy, and to be played as such. The play's reference to Ben Jonson and the controversy in the theatres is clear. In his *Poetaster* in 1601 Jonson had brought on his Prologue Armed 'in well erected confidence' against his detractors. That was typical of him. It was no less characteristic of Shakespeare next year to mark himself off from

Ben, with a gentle reproof, by also bringing on a Prologue armed, not in confidence of author's pen or actor's voice, but suited to the argument of the play.

The political events of those years are no less important than the literary and dramatic, for politics and war are equal themes of the play with love and its disillusionment. Politics in the last years of the Queen's reign were dominated by the furious and febrile faction-fighting, dizzily led by Essex and his party, jostling for position to dominate the situation at Elizabeth's death and to control the accession of Scottish James. The situation was a critical one, people's tempers were on edge; the war with Spain was still going on and on, as it had done for nearly twenty years, pointlessly it seemed, as there appeared no end. The crisis burst openly with Essex's attempted *coup* to get possession of the Queen, in February 1601, his outbreak into the City, hoping for support, the fiasco for which he paid with his life on the scaffold, and his leading supporter, Southampton, with a suspended death-sentence. He spent the remaining two years of the Queen's life in the Tower.

It was all heart-breaking for her; and we cannot suppose that it did not go near the bone with William Shakespeare. For he had owed so much to Southampton, and this association shaped his alignment. The governmental side in the lacerating faction-fighting was led by the Cecils (backed by the Queen), and Shakespeare expressed something of what his friends felt about old Lord Burghley in old Polonius. While Shakespeare's affections and sympathies were with Essex and Southampton (as many literary folks were), his mind was always with government and authority. He saw that the Queen and her government were right, his friends irresponsible and wrong.

Nothing is more sickening than to see one's friends steering straight for disaster. Observing it all—as Shakespeare did from close at hand, his mind and heart divided, his sympathies torn in two—accounts in part for the searing disillusionment of the play, its acuity and excruciating psychological incisiveness. It is, after all, not very funny, it is much more satire than comedy. 'Fools on both sides' is the reflection of the disillusioned author, so profoundly disturbed that he never wrote more brilliantly. And the play contains some of his deepest reflections on politics.

The Play. The whole atmosphere is of that queasy time, when people's nerves were on edge—the people resented the death of Essex, always popular, though he had asked for it and made it inevitable. There is a phrase in the play that expresses it.

> There is no help,
> The bitter disposition of the time
> Will have it so.

There are recognisable touches of Essex and his situation:

> He is so plaguey-proud that the death-tokens of it
> Cry 'No recovery'.

That was exactly like him: he never would make submission, so that the situation was beyond repair. Upon his fall:

> What the declined is
> He shall as soon read in the eyes of others
> As feel in his own fall; for men, like butterflies,
> Show not their mealy wings but to the summer,

> And not a man, for being simply man,
> Hath any honour but honour for those honours
> That are without him—as place, riches, and favour . . .

And so it goes on, as Shakespeare had observed from nearby, frequently performing (and watching) at Court.

An Elizabethan audience knew what to expect from the story of Troilus—no romantic illusions about love, but the disillusionment of a fool, who has fallen for a tart, or no better than a tart, who is Cressida. They are brought together, in a sense sold to each other, by the archetypal Pandarus, one of the most vivid creations. Even more striking is the cynic Thersites, who plays the part of jester and chorus together, commenting on and railing against the various sorts of idiocy incarnate—the blockhead Ajax, the arrogant Achilles, his gilded boy-friend Patroclus, the empty-headed Helen, not much better than Cressida—and all in the most astonishing virtuosity of invective. (Swift never achieved better.) Against all these are arrayed a few decent characters in contrast: Agamemnon is noble, Nestor respect-worthy though platitudinous, lastly, Ulysses through whom Shakespeare expresses his profound political understanding.

The war goes on and on—and all because the beautiful Helen had been carried off from her Greek husband by Paris to Troy: Helen of Troy. Could it conceivably have been worth it? The issue is discussed between Hector and his brother Paris (both of whom were to die for her). Hector argues:

> Let Helen go.
> Since the first sword was drawn about this question,
> Every tithe-soul 'mongst many thousand dismes
> Hath been as dear as Helen—I mean, of ours.
> If we have lost so many tenths of ours
> To guard a thing not ours, nor worth to us—
> Had it our name—the value of one ten,

why not give her up? The only reply Paris can give is:

> But I would have the soil of her fair rape
> Wiped off in honourable keeping her—

a foolish argument. After arguing against it, Hector ends up by proposing to keep her:

> For 'tis a cause that hath no mean dependence
> Upon our joint and several dignities.

The anti-climax is laughable, in flagrant contradiction with his whole argument. On the Greek side Diomedes, who is to cuckold Troilus with Cressida, agrees as to Helen:

> She's bitter to her country. Hear me, Paris:
> For every false drop in her bawdy veins
> A Grecian's life hath sunk; for every scruple
> Of her contaminated carrion weight
> A Trojan hath been slain; since she could speak
> She hath not given so many good words breath
> As for her Greeks and Trojans suffered death.

An intelligent audience of young lawyers would enjoy the to-and-fro of the debate, and the railing contests, like wit-combats, that go on around Thersites. But this ragged and scurrilous cynic has the last word on the issue:

> After this, the vengeance on the whole camp! or, rather the Neapolitan
> bone-ache [i.e. syphilis]. For that, methinks, is the curse dependent on those
> that war for a placket [i.e. a whore].

(The long-continuing war had introduced a good deal of syphilis into England.) The Trojan war would continue to the destruction of Troy.

Troilus and Cressida. The image of the destruction of Troy was what had always impressed Shakespeare's imagination, not the chivalric fighting fools. We know what Falstaff thought about the Elizabethan code of 'honour', and the unnumbered asses of young men who got killed fighting duels (William Shakespeare never involved himself in this nonsense, as Marlowe and Ben Jonson did). Hector argued sensibly,

> these moral laws
> Of nature and of nations speak aloud
> To have her back returned—

and then goes on to allow 'honour' (emotional preference) to overrule his reason:

> Mine honour keeps the weather of my fate.
> Life every man holds dear; but the dear man
> Holds honour far more precious-dear than life.

So, of course, he is killed by the great Achilles. But Achilles would not come out of his tent, until moved by passion at Hector's killing his boy-friend, Patroclus. And Achilles kills Hector when he is unarmed—one sees how much honour Shakespeare thought there was in that!

Nor was there anything but contempt in his rendering of Troilus' passion for Cressida, and his portrayal of the two characters, the one foolish, the other false. In this he was in keeping with the traditional medieval view, which he derived from Caxton. But his portrayal of the characters was his own; one wonders how much his own experience went into the rendering. When Cressida breaks her plighted word to Troilus to go with a Greek, her excuse is:

> The error of our eye directs the mind . . .
> Minds swayed by eyes are full of turpitude.

Troilus can hardly believe the evidence of his own eyes, her assignation with another; his heart wishes him to believe contrary to the evidence: an obstinate hope

> That doth invert th'attest of eyes and ears,

as if they were the deceivers. This is precisely the experience expressed in Sonnet 137:

> Thou blind fool, love, what dost thou to mine eyes
> That they behold and see not what they see? . . .

561

Troilus is in the situation William Shakespeare had known from experience.

Political Wisdom. The disillusionment with love is less interesting intellectually than the reflections of wise Ulysses on the facts of politics and society. It is in this century that we have come to appreciate better Shakespeare's mature and responsible thought in this sphere. A normal man, a family man, grafted into society, his thinking here is so much more responsible than that of intellectuals like Marlowe and Jonson, odd men out. It is precisely because Shakespeare was a more sensitive man, who hated cruelty and suffering, that he realised how, if the order of society is shaken, it only leads to yet more suffering—as we have seen in the revolutions of our time. So his reflections on these matters are as relevant today as when they were written.

There must be order in human society, as in the universe:

> How could communities,
> Degrees in schools, and brotherhoods in cities,
> Peaceful commerce from dividable shores . . .
> Prerogative of age, crowns, sceptres, laurels,
> But by degree, stand in authentic place?

When order is broken down in society, Shakespeare well understood that it is reduced to a power struggle:

> Then everything includes itself in power,
> Power into will, will into appetite;
> And appetite, an universal wolf . . .
> Must make perforce an universal prey,
> And last eat up itself.

How exactly we have seen that borne out in the revolutions of our time, when impartial authority and just government have handed over to military dictatorships in African states, preying on neighbours or within themselves. Or in the spawn of revolution eating each other up—nine members of Lenin's Politburo liquidated by their fellow, Stalin. Or Hitler's murders of his former comrades. Shakespeare knew far better what to expect of humans than those who entertain liberal illusions about them.

Ulysses says a great deal more on this head: on faction-fighting, for example, the party and personal envies that impede common purpose.

The Age. At the end of Elizabeth's reign the opposing factions of Essex and Ralegh were both war-minded, all for action and going on fighting. Ulysses who speaks for political judgment, condemns them:

> They tax our policy and call it cowardice,
> Count wisdom as no member of the war,
> Forestall prescience, and esteem no act
> But that of hand.

They disparaged and discounted

> the still and mental parts
> That do contrive how many hands shall strike,

and calculate the nation's resources, what it could afford, and what was 'the enemy's weight'.

Shakespeare, as always, shared the view of authority and sympathised with the difficulties of government, rather than the simple (often personal) resentments of opposition. He had by now taken Essex's measure:

> Things small as nothing, for request's sake only,
> He makes important . . .

This is exactly as Essex behaved with the Queen, always pressing her for jobs for his own followers, like Bacon. It was intolerable. Then, when he could not get his way, he would retire from Court and sulk, with Southampton, just like Achilles with Patroclus.

It is given to the wise Ulysses (as it might be clever Robert Cecil) to flatter the foolish Ajax to the top of his bent, and to Thersites to express what is thought of the fighting fools—in terms of contemporary bull-baiting:

> The cuckold and the cuckold-maker are at it.
> Now, bull! now, dog! 'Loo, Paris, 'loo! now
> My doubled-horned Spartan! 'loo, Paris, loo!
> The bull has the game! Ware horns, ho!

The stage itself, as always with the actor-dramatist, provides images. To amuse Achilles his minion Patroclus mimics the other Greek leaders,

> . . . like a strutting player whose conceit
> Lies in his hamstring, and doth think it rich
> To hear the wooden dialogue and sound
> Twixt his stretched footing and the scaffoldage.

Text. The play was first mentioned in a blocking entry in the Stationers' Register in February 1603. In 1609 (the year in which the *Sonnets* were published by Thomas Thorp, who had got hold of the manuscript from their only possessor) a Quarto of this play was published, a good text apparently from a draft of Shakespeare's own manuscript. The Folio text followed this, with a few changes. But the Quarto has an interesting Preface, calling it 'a new play, never staled by the stage, never clapper-clawed with the palms of the vulgar'. This implies that it had been written for private production. It continues with praise of comedies, 'especially this author's comedies, that are so framed to the life that they serve for the most common commentaries of all the actions of our lives'. It proceeds to boost Shakespeare: 'And believe this, that, when he is gone and his comedies out of sale, you will scramble for them.' In fact they never have gone out of sale or ceased to hold the stage. Even this, the most rebarbative of the comedies, has received a marked revival in our time, to which it is highly relevant and for which it holds a message.

TROILUS AND CRESSIDA.

DRAMATIS PERSONÆ.

PRIAM, king of Troy.
HECTOR,
TROILUS,
PARIS, } his sons.
DEIPHOBUS,
HELENUS,
MARGARELON, a bastard son of Priam.
ÆNEAS,
ANTENOR, } Trojan commanders.
CALCHAS, a Trojan priest, taking part with
the Greeks.
PANDARUS, uncle to Cressida.
AGAMEMNON, the Grecian general.
MENELAUS, his brother.
ACHILLES,
AJAX,
ULYSSES,
NESTOR, } Grecian princes.
DIOMEDES,
PATROCLUS,

THERSITES, a deformed and scurrilous Gre-
cian.
ALEXANDER, servant to Cressida.
Servant to Troilus.
Servant to Paris.
Servant to Diomedes.

HELEN, wife to Menelaus.
ANDROMACHE, wife to Hector.
CASSANDRA, daughter to Priam, a pro-
phetess.
CRESSIDA, daughter to Calchas.

Trojan and Greek Soldiers, and Attendants.

SCENE: *Troy, and the Grecian camp
before it.*

William Brereton, the 18th century actor, as Troilus.
Engraving from Bell's *Shakespeare*, 1776

● *A bullet beside a text line indicates an annotation in the
opposite column*

2 *orgulous.* Proud.

Opposite : Troilus and Cressida watched by Pandarus.
Engraved from a painting by V. W. Bromley (1848–
1877)

PROLOGUE.

IN **Troy**, there lies the scene. From isles of
Greece
●The princes orgulous, their high blood chafed,
Have to the port of Athens sent their ships,

7 *Phrygia.* Western Asia Minor.

Map of Phrygia. From Homer's *Iliad*, translated by Alexander Pope, 1743 edition

11 *Tenedos.* Troy's port.

13 *Dardan.* Trojan.

16-17 *Dardan . . . Antenorides.* The names of the six gates of Troy.

19 *Sperr up.* Bolt in.

6 *gear.* Business.

10 *fonder.* More foolish.

18 *bolting.* Sifting.

28 *blench.* Flinch.

Fraught with the ministers and instruments
Of cruel war: sixty and nine, that wore
Their crownets regal, from the Athenian bay
● Put forth toward Phrygia; and their vow is made
To ransack Troy, within whose strong immures
The ravish'd Helen, Menelaus' queen,
With wanton Paris sleeps; and that's the quarrel.
● To Tenedos they come;
And the deep-drawing barks do there disgorge
● Their warlike fraughtage: now on Dardan plains
The fresh and yet unbruised Greeks do pitch
Their brave pavilions: Priam's six-gated city,
● Dardan, and Tymbria, Helias, Chetas, Troien,
And Antenorides, with massy staples
And corresponsive and fulfilling bolts,
● Sperr up the sons of Troy.
Now expectation, tickling skittish spirits,   20
On one and other side, Trojan and Greek,
Sets all on hazard: and hither am I come
A prologue arm'd, but not in confidence
Of author's pen or actor's voice, but suited
In like conditions as our argument,
To tell you, fair beholders, that our play
Leaps o'er the vaunt and firstlings of those broils,
Beginning in the middle, starting thence away
To what may be digested in a play.
Like or find fault; do as your pleasures are: 30
Now good or bad, 'tis but the chance of war.

ACT I.

SCENE I. *Troy. Before Priam's palace.*

Enter TROILUS *armed, and* PANDARUS.

   Tro. Call here my varlet; I'll unarm again:
Why should I war without the walls of Troy,
That find such cruel battle here within?
Each Trojan that is master of his heart,
Let him to field; Troilus, alas! hath none.
● *Pan.* Will this gear ne'er be mended?
   Tro. The Greeks are strong and skilful to their strength,
Fierce to their skill and to their fierceness valiant;
But I am weaker than a woman's tear,
● Tamer than sleep, fonder than ignorance,   10
Less valiant than the virgin in the night
And skilless as unpractised infancy.
   Pan. Well, I have told you enough of this: for my part, I'll not meddle nor make no further. He that will have a cake out of the wheat must needs tarry the grinding.
   Tro. Have I not tarried?
● *Pan.* Ay, the grinding; but you must tarry the bolting.
   Tro. Have I not tarried?
   Pan. Ay, the bolting, but you must tarry the leavening.   20
   Tro. Still have I tarried.
   Pan. Ay, to the leavening; but here's yet in the word 'hereafter' the kneading, the making of the cake, the heating of the oven and the baking; nay, you must stay the cooling too, or you may chance to burn your lips.
   Tro. Patience herself, what goddess e'er she be,
● Doth lesser blench at sufferance than I do.

At Priam's royal table do I sit;
And when fair Cressid comes into my thoughts,—
So, traitor! 'When she comes!' When is she
    thence ?   31
Pan.   Well, she looked yesternight fairer than
ever I saw her look, or any woman else.
Tro.   I was about to tell thee :—when my heart,
• As wedged with a sigh, would rive in twain,
Lest Hector or my father should perceive me,
I have, as when the sun doth light a storm,
Buried this sigh in wrinkle of a smile :
But sorrow, that is couch'd in seeming gladness,
Is like that mirth fate turns to sudden sadness. 40
Pan.   An her hair were not somewhat darker
than Helen's—well, go to—there were no more
comparison between the women : but, for my part,
she is my kinswoman; I would not, as they term
it, praise her : but I would somebody had heard
her talk yesterday, as I did.   I will not dispraise
your sister Cassandra's wit, but—
Tro.   O Pandarus! I tell thee, Pandarus,—
When I do tell thee, there my hopes lie drown'd,
Reply not in how many fathoms deep   50
They lie indrench'd.   I tell thee I am mad
In Cressid's love : thou answer'st 'she is fair;'
Pour'st in the open ulcer of my heart
Her eyes, her hair, her cheek, her gait, her voice,
Handlest in thy discourse, O, that her hand,
In whose comparison all whites are ink,
Writing their own reproach, to whose soft seizure
• The cygnet's down is harsh and spirit of sense
Hard as the palm of ploughman : this thou tell'st
    me,
As true thou tell'st me, when I say I love her; 60
But, saying thus, instead of oil and balm,
Thou lay'st in every gash that love hath given me
The knife that made it.
Pan.   I speak no more than truth.
Tro.   Thou dost not speak so much.
Pan.   Faith, I'll not meddle in't.   Let her be
as she is : if she be fair, 'tis the better for her; an
she be not, she has the mends in her own hands.
Tro.   Good Pandarus, how now, Pandarus!
Pan.   I have had my labour for my travail; ill-
thought on of her and ill-thought on of you; gone
between and between, but small thanks for my
labour.
Tro.   What, art thou angry, Pandarus? what,
with me?
Pan.   Because she's kin to me, therefore she's
not so fair as Helen : an she were not kin to me,
• she would be as fair on Friday as Helen is on
Sunday.   But what care I?   I care not an she
were a black-a-moor; 'tis all one to me.   80
Tro.   Say I she is not fair?
Pan.   I do not care whether you do or no.   She's
• a fool to stay behind her father; let her to the
Greeks; and so I'll tell her the next time I see
her : for my part, I'll meddle nor make no more
i' the matter.
Tro.   Pandarus,—
Pan.   Not I.
Tro.   Sweet Pandarus,—
Pan.   Pray you, speak no more to me : I will
leave all as I found it, and there an end.   91
            [*Exit Pandarus.   An alarum.*

Tro.   Peace, you ungracious clamours! peace,
    rude sounds!
Fools on both sides! Helen must needs be fair,

35 *wedged.* Cloven.

58 *spirit of sense.* i.e. the sense of touch.

78-79 *Helen . . . Sunday.* As Helen dressed in her Sunday finery.

83 *her father.* Calchas deserted to the Greeks when he
heard it foretold that the Trojans would lose the war.

101 *Daphne.* To escape Apollo's pursuit, this nymph was turned into a bay tree.

109 *sorts.* Is suitable.

Menelaus and Paris in combat. Engraving from Homer's *Iliad*, translated by Alexander Pope, 1743 edition

115 *horn.* The symbol of the cuckold.

12 *noise.* Rumour.

When with your blood you daily paint her thus.
I cannot fight upon this argument;
It is too starved a subject for my sword.
But Pandarus,—O gods, how do you plague me!
I cannot come to Cressid but by Pandar;
And he's as tetchy to be woo'd to woo,
As she is stubborn-chaste against all suit.   100
Tell me, Apollo, for thy Daphne's love,
What Cressid is, what Pandar, and what we?
Her bed is India; there she lies, a pearl:
Between our Ilium and where she resides,
Let it be call'd the wild and wandering flood,
Ourself the merchant, and this sailing Pandar
Our doubtful hope, our convoy and our bark.

Alarum.   Enter ÆNEAS.

Æne.   How now, Prince Troilus! wherefore
     not afield?
Tro.   Because not there: this woman's an-
     swer sorts,
For womanish it is to be from thence.   110
What news, Æneas, from the field to-day?
Æne.   That Paris is returned home and hurt.
Tro.   By whom, Æneas?
Æne.   Troilus, by Menelaus.
Tro.   Let Paris bleed: 'tis but a scar to scorn;
Paris is gored with Menelaus' horn.   [*Alarum.*
Æne.   Hark, what good sport is out of town
     to-day!
Tro.   Better at home, if ' would I might' were
     ' may.'
But to the sport abroad: are you bound thither?
Æne.   In all swift haste.
Tro.   Come, go we then together.
                              [*Exeunt.*

SCENE II.   *The same.   A street.*

Enter CRESSIDA *and* ALEXANDER.

Cres.   Who were those went by?
Alex.   Queen Hecuba and Helen.
Cres.   And whither go they?
Alex.   Up to the eastern tower,
Whose height commands as subject all the vale,
To see the battle.   Hector, whose patience
Is, as a virtue, fix'd, to-day was moved:
He chid Andromache and struck his armorer,
And, like as there were husbandry in war,
Before the sun rose he was harness'd light,
And to the field goes he; where every flower
Did, as a prophet, weep what it foresaw   10
In Hector's wrath.
Cres.   What was his cause of anger?
Alex.   The noise goes, this: there is among
     the Greeks
A lord of Trojan blood, nephew to Hector;
They call him Ajax.
Cres.   Good; and what of him?
Alex.   They say he is a very man per se,
And stands alone.
Cres.   So do all men, unless they are drunk,
sick, or have no legs.
Alex.   This man, lady, hath robbed many
beasts of their particular additions; he is as
valiant as the lion, churlish as the bear, slow as
the elephant: a man into whom nature hath so
crowded humours that his valour is crushed into
folly, his folly sauced with discretion: there is no
man hath a virtue that he hath not a glimpse of,

nor any man an attaint but he carries some stain of it: he is melancholy without cause, and merry against the hair: he hath the joints of every thing, but every thing so out of joint that he is
• a gouty Briareus, many hands and no use, or
• purblind Argus, all eyes and no sight.   31

Cres. But how should this man, that makes me smile, make Hector angry?

• *Alex.* They say he yesterday coped Hector in the battle and struck him down, the disdain and shame whereof hath ever since kept Hector fasting and waking.

Cres. Who comes here?

Alex. Madam, your uncle Pandarus.

Enter PANDARUS.

Cres. Hector's a gallant man.   40

Alex. As may be in the world, lady.

Pan. What's that? what's that?

Cres. Good morrow, uncle Pandarus.

• *Pan.* Good morrow, cousin Cressid: what do you talk of? Good morrow, Alexander. How
• do you, cousin? When were you at Ilium?

Cres. This morning, uncle.

Pan. What were you talking of when I came? Was Hector armed and gone ere ye came to Ilium? Helen was not up, was she?   50

Cres. Hector was gone, but Helen was not up.

Pan. E'en so: Hector was stirring early.

Cres. That were we talking of, and of his anger.

Pan. Was he angry?

Cres. So he says here.

Pan. True, he was so: I know the cause too: he'll lay about him to-day, I can tell them that: and there's Troilus will not come far behind him; let them take heed of Troilus, I can tell them that too.   61

Cres. What, is he angry too?

Pan. Who, Troilus? Troilus is the better man of the two.

Cres. O Jupiter! there's no comparison.

Pan. What, not between Troilus and Hector? Do you know a man if you see him?

Cres. Ay, if I ever saw him before and knew him.

Pan. Well, I say Troilus is Troilus.   70

Cres. Then you say as I say; for, I am sure, he is not Hector.

Pan. No, nor Hector is not Troilus in some degrees.

Cres. 'Tis just to each of them; he is himself.

Pan. .Himself! Alas, poor Troilus! I would he were.

Cres. So he is.

• *Pan.* Condition, I had gone barefoot to India.

Cres. He is not Hector.   81

Pan. Himself! no, he's not himself: would a' were himself! Well, the gods are above; time must friend or end: well, Troilus, well: I would my heart were in her body. No, Hector is not a better man than Troilus.

Cres. Excuse me.

Pan. He is elder.

Cres. Pardon me, pardon me.   89

Pan. Th' other's not come to't; you shall tell me another tale, when th' other's come to't. Hector shall not have his wit this year.

30 *Briareus.* A giant with a hundred hands.

31 *Argus.* A mythical character with a hundred eyes.

34 *coped.* Overcame.

44 *cousin.* A term denoting kinship.

46 *Ilium.* The palace of Priam.

80 *Condition.* On condition that. Pandarus means even if he had to go barefoot to India, he wishes Troilus were himself again.

Pandarus (David Waller) and Cressida (Francesca Annis), Royal Shakespeare Co, 1976

Pandarus and Cressida. Woodcut by Edward Burne-Jones, from William Morris's *Kelmscott Chaucer*, 1896

101 *favour.* Complexion.

129 *lifter.* Thief.

142 *stand to.* A sexual innuendo.

Cres. He shall not need it, if he have his own.
Pan. Nor his qualities.
Cres. No matter.
Pan. Nor his beauty.
Cres. 'Twould not become him; his own's better.
Pan. You have no judgement, niece: Helen herself swore th' other day, that Troilus, for a brown favour—for so 'tis, I must confess,—not brown neither,—
Cres. No, but brown.
Pan. 'Faith, to say truth, brown and not brown.
Cres. To say the truth, true and not true.
Pan. She praised his complexion above Paris.
Cres. Why, Paris hath colour enough.
Pan. So he has.   109
Cres. Then Troilus should have too much: if she praised him above, his complexion is higher than his; he having colour enough, and the other higher, is too flaming a praise for a good complexion. I had as lief Helen's golden tongue had commended Troilus for a copper nose.
Pan. I swear to you, I think Helen loves him better than Paris.
Cres. Then she's a merry Greek indeed.
Pan. Nay, I am sure she does. She came to him th' other day into the compassed window,—and, you know, he has not past three or four hairs on his chin,—
Cres. Indeed, a tapster's arithmetic may soon bring his particulars therein to a total.
Pan. Why, he is very young: and yet will he, within three pound, lift as much as his brother Hector.
Cres. Is he so young a man and so old a lifter?   129
Pan. But to prove to you that Helen loves him: she came and puts me her white hand to his cloven chin—
Cres. Juno have mercy! how came it cloven?
Pan. Why, you know, 'tis dimpled: I think his smiling becomes him better than any man in all Phrygia.
Cres. O, he smiles valiantly.
Pan. Does he not?
Cres. O yes, an 'twere a cloud in autumn. 139
Pan. Why, go to, then: but to prove to you that Helen loves Troilus,—
Cres. Troilus will stand to the proof, if you'll prove it so.
Pan. Troilus! why, he esteems her no more than I esteem an addle egg.
Cres. If you love an addle egg as well as you love an idle head, you would eat chickens i' the shell.
Pan. I cannot choose but laugh, to think how she tickled his chin: indeed, she has a marvellous white hand, I must needs confess,—   151

Cres. Without the rack.
Pan. And she takes upon her to spy a white hair on his chin.
Cres. Alas, poor chin! many a wart is richer.
Pan. But there was such laughing! Queen Hecuba laughed that her eyes ran o'er.
Cres. With mill-stones.
Pan. And Cassandra laughed.
Cres. But there was more temperate fire under the pot of her eyes: did her eyes run o'er too? 161

Pan. And Hector laughed.

Cres. At what was all this laughing?

Pan. Marry, at the white hair that Helen spied on Troilus' chin.

Cres. An't had been a green hair, I should have laughed too.

Pan. They laughed not so much at the hair as at his pretty answer.

Cres. What was his answer? 170

Pan. Quoth she, 'Here's but two and fifty hairs on your chin, and one of them is white.'

Cres. This is her question.

Pan. That's true; make no question of that. 'Two and fifty hairs,' quoth he, 'and one white: that white hair is my father, and all the rest are his sons.' 'Jupiter!' quoth she, 'which of these hairs is Paris my husband?' 'The forked one,' quoth he, 'pluck't out, and give it him.' But there was such laughing! and Helen so blushed, and Paris so chafed, and all the rest so laughed, that it passed.

Cres. So let it now; for it has been a great while going by.

Pan. Well, cousin, I told you a thing yesterday; think on't.

Cres. So I do.

Pan. I'll be sworn 'tis true; he will weep you, an 'twere a man born in April. 189

Cres. And I'll spring up in his tears, an 'twere a nettle against May. [*A retreat sounded.*

Pan. Hark! they are coming from the field: shall we stand up here, and see them as they pass toward Ilium? good niece, do, sweet niece Cressida.

Cres. At your pleasure.

Pan. Here, here, here's an excellent place; here we may see most bravely: I'll tell you them all by their names as they pass by; but mark Troilus above the rest. 200

Cres. Speak not so loud.

ÆNEAS *passes.*

Pan. That's Æneas: is not that a brave man? he's one of the flowers of Troy, I can tell you: but mark Troilus; you shall see anon.

ANTENOR *passes.*

Cres. Who's that?

Pan. That's Antenor: he has a shrewd wit, I can tell you; and he's a man good enough: he's one o' the soundest judgements in Troy, whosoever, and a proper man of person. When comes Troilus? I'll show you Troilus anon: if he see me, you shall see him nod at me.

Cres. Will he give you the nod?

Pan. You shall see.

Cres. If he do, the rich shall have more.

HECTOR *passes.*

Pan. That's Hector, that, that, look you, that; there's a fellow! Go thy way, Hector! There's a brave man, niece. O brave Hector! Look how he looks! there's a countenance! is't not a brave man?

Cres. O, a brave man! 220

Pan. Is a' not? it does a man's heart good. Look you what hacks are on his helmet! look you yonder, do you see? look you there: there's no

177 *sons*. Priam had fifty sons.

191 *against*. Expecting.

198 *bravely*. Excellently.

214 *the rich shall have more*. i.e. you will be even more foolish.

224 *take't off who will.* A common phrase meaning 'deny it, if you can'.

228 *lid.* Eyelid.

Cressida watches Troilus ride back from battle. Woodcut by Edward Burne-Jones from William Morris's *Kelmscott Chaucer*, 1896

280 *date.* Dates were used to sweeten pastry, but Cressida is also playing on the idea of being out of date.

283 *ward.* A defensive position in fencing.

●jesting; there's laying on, take't off who will, as they say: there be hacks!
  Cres. Be those with swords?
  Pan. Swords! any thing, he cares not; an the
●devil come to him, it's all one: by God's lid, it does one's heart good.   Yonder comes Paris, yonder comes Paris.   230

PARIS *passes.*

Look ye yonder, niece; is't not a gallant man too, is't not? Why, this is brave now. Who said he came hurt home to-day? he's not hurt: why, this will do Helen's heart good now, ha! Would I could see Troilus now! You shall see Troilus anon.

HELENUS *passes.*

  Cres. Who's that?
  Pan. That's Helenus. I marvel where Troilus is. That's Helenus. I think he went not forth to-day. That's Helenus.   240
  Cres. Can Helenus fight, uncle?
  Pan. Helenus? no. Yes, he'll fight indifferent well. I marvel where Troilus is. Hark! do you not hear the people cry 'Troilus'? Helenus is a priest.
  Cres. What sneaking fellow comes yonder?

TROILUS *passes.*

  Pan. Where? yonder? that's Deiphobus. 'Tis Troilus! there's a man, niece! Hem! Brave Troilus! the prince of chivalry!
  Cres. Peace, for shame, peace!   250
  Pan. Mark him; note him. O brave Troilus! Look well upon him, niece: look you how his sword is bloodied, and his helm more hacked than Hector's, and how he looks, and how he goes! O admirable youth! he ne'er saw three and twenty. Go thy way, Troilus, go thy way! Had I a sister were a grace, or a daughter a goddess, he should take his choice. O admirable man! Paris? Paris is dirt to him; and, I warrant, Helen, to change, would give an eye to boot.   260
  Cres. Here come more.

Forces *pass.*

  Pan. Asses, fools, dolts! chaff and bran, chaff and bran! porridge after meat! I could live and die i' the eyes of Troilus. Ne'er look, ne'er look: the eagles are gone: crows and daws, crows and daws! I had rather be such a man as Troilus than Agamemnon and all Greece.
  Cres. There is among the Greeks Achilles, a better man than Troilus.   269
  Pan. Achilles! a drayman, a porter, a very camel.
  Cres. Well, well.
  Pan. 'Well, well!' Why, have you any discretion? have you any eyes? do you know what a man is? Is not birth, beauty, good shape, discourse, manhood, learning, gentleness, virtue, youth, liberality, and such like, the spice and salt that season a man?
  Cres. Ay, a minced man: and then to be
●baked with no date in the pie, for then the man's date's out.   281
  Pan. You are such a woman! one knows not
●at what ward you lie.
  Cres. Upon my back, to defend my belly;

upon my wit, to defend my wiles; upon my
secrecy, to defend mine honesty; my mask, to
defend my beauty; and you, to defend all these:
and at all these wards I lie, at a thousand
watches.

Pan. Say one of your watches.   290

Cres. Nay, I'll watch you for that; and that's
one of the chiefest of them too: if I cannot ward
what I would not have hit, I can watch you for
telling how I took the blow; unless it swell past
hiding, and then it's past watching.

Pan. You are such another!

Enter TROILUS'S Boy.

Boy. Sir, my lord would instantly speak with
you.

Pan. Where?   299

Boy. At your own house; there he unarms him.

Pan. Good boy, tell him I come. [*Exit Boy.*]
I doubt he be hurt.   Fare ye well, good niece.

Cres. Adieu, uncle.

Pan. I'll be with you, niece, by and by.

Cres. To bring, uncle?

Pan. Ay, a token from Troilus.

Cres. By the same token, you are a bawd.

                                    [*Exit Pandarus.*

Words, vows, gifts, tears, and love's full sacrifice,
He offers in another's enterprise:
But more in Troilus thousand fold I see   310
Than in the glass of Pandar's praise may be;
Yet hold I off.   Women are angels, wooing:
Things won are done; joy's soul lies in the doing.
That she beloved knows nought that knows not
         this:
Men prize the thing ungain'd more than it is:
That she was never yet that ever knew
Love got so sweet as when desire did sue.
Therefore this maxim out of love I teach:
Achievement is command; ungain'd, beseech:
Then though my heart's content firm love doth
         bear,   320
Nothing of that shall from mine eyes appear.

                                    [*Exeunt.*

SCENE III.   *The Grecian camp.   Before
Agamemnon's tent.*

Sennet. Enter AGAMEMNON, NESTOR, ULYSSES,
MENELAUS, *and others.*

Agam.   Princes,
What grief hath set the jaundice on your cheeks?
The ample proposition that hope makes
In all designs begun on earth below
Fails in the promised largeness: checks and dis-
         asters
Grow in the veins of actions highest rear'd,
As knots, by the conflux of meeting sap,
Infect the sound pine and divert his grain
Tortive and errant from his course of growth.
Nor, princes, is it matter new to us   10
That we come short of our suppose so far
That after seven years' siege yet Troy walls stand;
Sith every action that hath gone before,
Whereof we have record, trial did draw
Bias and thwart, not answering the aim,
And that unbodied figure of the thought
That gave't surmised shape.   Why then, you
         princes,
Do you with cheeks abash'd behold our works,

Costume design for Cressida by Leslie Hurry, Stratford-
upon-Avon, 1960

286 *honesty.* Chastity.

289 *watches.* Guards and divisions of the night.

290 *watches.* Prayers.

291 *watch you.* Guard against.

302 *doubt.* Fear.

312 *wooing.* When being wooed.

9 *Tortive and errant.* Distorted and wandering.

15 *Bias.* Awry. *thwart.* Across.

38 *Boreas*. The North wind.

39 *Thetis*. A sea-nymph, the mother of Achilles, here used to personify the sea.

48 *breese*. Gadfly.

65 *hatch'd in silver*. Grey haired.

78 *specialty of rule*. The proper order in the chain of command.

And call them shames? which are indeed nought
    else
But the protractive trials of great Jove   20
To find persistive constancy in men:
The fineness of which metal is not found
In fortune's love; for then the bold and coward,
The wise and fool, the artist and unread,
The hard and soft, seem all affined and kin:
But, in the wind and tempest of her frown,
Distinction, with a broad and powerful fan,
Puffing at all, winnows the light away;
And what hath mass or matter, by itself
Lies rich in virtue and unmingled.   30
    Nest. With due observance of thy godlike seat,
Great Agamemnon, Nestor shall apply
Thy latest words.   In the reproof of chance
Lies the true proof of men: the sea being smooth,
How many shallow bauble boats dare sail
Upon her patient breast, making their way
With those of nobler bulk!
 •But let the ruffian Boreas once enrage
 •The gentle Thetis, and anon behold
The strong-ribb'd bark through liquid mountains
    cut,   40
Bounding between the two moist elements,
Like Perseus' horse: where's then the saucy boat
Whose weak untimber'd sides but even now
Co-rivall'd greatness?   Either to harbour fled,
Or made a toast for Neptune.   Even so
Doth valour's show and valour's worth divide
In storms of fortune; for in her ray and bright-
    ness
 •The herd hath more annoyance by the breese
Than by the tiger; but when the splitting wind
Makes flexible the knees of knotted oaks,   50
And flies fled under shade, why, then the thing
    of courage
As roused with rage with rage doth sympathize,
And with an accent tuned in selfsame key
Retorts to chiding fortune.
    Ulyss.   Agamemnon,
Thou great commander, nerve and bone of Greece,
Heart of our numbers, soul and only spirit,
In whom the tempers and the minds of all
Should be shut up, hear what Ulysses speaks.
Besides the applause and approbation
The which, [*To Agamemnon*] most mighty for
    thy place and sway,   60
[*To Nestor*] And thou most reverend for thy
    stretch'd-out life
I give to both your speeches, which were such
As Agamemnon and the hand of Greece
Should hold up high in brass, and such again
 •As venerable Nestor, hatch'd in silver,
Should with a bond of air, strong as the axletree
On which heaven rides, knit all the Greekish ears
To his experienced tongue, yet let it please both,
Thou great, and wise, to hear Ulysses speak.
    Agam. Speak, Prince of Ithaca; and be't of
    less expect   70
That matter needless, of importless burden,
Divide thy lips, than we are confident,
When rank Thersites opes his mastic jaws,
We shall hear music, wit and oracle.

    Ulyss. Troy, yet upon his basis, had been down,
And the great Hector's sword had lack'd a master,
But for these instances.
 •The specialty of rule hath been neglected:
And, look, how many Grecian tents do stand

Hollow upon this plain, so many hollow factions.
When that the general is not like the hive   81
To whom the foragers shall all repair,
●What honey is expected? Degree being viz-
    arded,
The unworthiest shows as fairly in the mask.
The heavens themselves, the planets and this
    centre
Observe degree, priority and place,
●Insisture, course, proportion, season, form,
Office and custom, in all line of order;
And therefore is the glorious planet Sol
In noble eminence enthroned and sphered   90
Amidst the other; whose medicinable eye
Corrects the ill aspects of planets evil,
●And posts, like the commandment of a king,
Sans check to good and bad: but when the
    planets
In evil mixture to disorder wander,
What plagues and what portents! what mutiny!
What raging of the sea! shaking of earth!
Commotion in the winds! frights, changes, hor-
    rors,
Divert and crack, rend and deracinate
The unity and married calm of states   100
Quite from their fixure! O, when degree is
    shaked,
Which is the ladder to all high designs,
The enterprise is sick! How could communities,
Degrees in schools and brotherhoods in cities,
Peaceful commerce from dividable shores,
The primogenitive and due of birth,
Prerogative of age, crowns, sceptres, laurels,
But by degree, stand in authentic place?
Take but degree away, untune that string,
And, hark, what discord follows! each thing
    meets   110
●In mere oppugnancy: the bounded waters
Should lift their bosoms higher than the shores
And make a sop of all this solid globe:
Strength should be lord of imbecility,
And the rude son should strike his father dead:
Force should be right; or rather, right and wrong,
Between whose endless jar justice resides,
Should lose their names, and so should justice too.
Then every thing includes itself in power,
Power into will, will into appetite;   120
And appetite, an universal wolf,
So doubly seconded with will and power,
Must make perforce an universal prey,
And last eat up himself. Great Agamemnon,
This chaos, when degree is suffocate,
Follows the choking.
And this neglection of degree it is
That by a pace goes backward, with a purpose
It hath to climb. The general's disdain'd
By him one step below, he by the next,   130
That next by him beneath; so every step,
Exampled by the first pace that is sick
Of his superior, grows to an envious fever
Of pale and bloodless emulation:
And 'tis this fever that keeps Troy on foot,
Not her own sinews. To end a tale of length,
Troy in our weakness stands, not in her strength.
    Nest. Most wisely hath Ulysses here dis-
        cover'd
The fever whereof all our power is sick.
    Agam. The nature of the sickness found,
        Ulysses,   140

83 *Degree.* Established rank.

87 *Insisture.* Regularity.

93 *posts.* Travels swiftly.

111 *mere oppugnancy.* Total opposition.

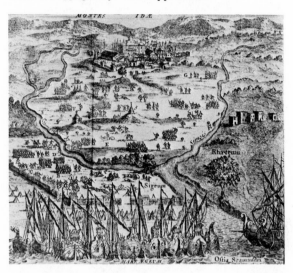

Map of Troy. From Homer's *Iliad*, translated by
Alexander Pope, 1743 edition

152 *topless deputation.* Highest authority.

153-156 *like a . . . scaffoldage.* See introduction.

159 *unsquared.* Rough.

160 *Typhon.* A monster with a very loud voice.

Ulysses: '. . . as like as Vulcan and his wife.' Painting of Vulcan and Venus by François Boucher (1703-1770)

174 *gorget.* A piece of armour for the neck.

178 *spleen.* Considered to be the seat of anger and bitter laughter in Elizabethan anatomy.

189 *In such a rein.* So arrogantly.

What is the remedy?
  Ulyss. The great Achilles, whom opinion crowns
The sinew and the forehand of our host,
Having his ear full of his airy fame,
Grows dainty of his worth and in his tent
Lies mocking our designs: with him Patroclus
Upon a lazy bed the livelong day
Breaks scurril jests,
And with ridiculous and awkward action,
Which, slanderer, he imitation calls,   150
He pageants us.   Sometime, great Agamemnon,
•Thy topless deputation he puts on,
•And, like a strutting player, whose conceit
Lies in his hamstring, and doth think it rich
To hear the wooden dialogue and sound
'Twixt his stretch'd footing and the scaffoldage,—
Such to-be-pitied and o'er-wrested seeming
He acts thy greatness in: and when he speaks,
•'Tis like a chime a-mending; with terms un-
    squared,
•Which, from the tongue of roaring Typhon
    dropp'd,   160
Would seem hyperboles. At this fusty stuff
The large Achilles, on his press'd bed lolling,
From his deep chest laughs out a loud applause;
Cries 'Excellent! 'tis Agamemnon just.
Now play me Nestor; hem, and stroke thy beard,
As he being drest to some oration.'
That's done, as near as the extremest ends
Of parallels, as like as Vulcan and his wife:
Yet god Achilles still cries 'Excellent!
'Tis Nestor right. Now play him me, Patroclus,
Arming to answer in a night alarm.'   171
And then, forsooth, the faint defects of age
Must be the scene of mirth; to cough and spit,
•And, with a palsy-fumbling on his gorget,
Shake in and out the rivet: and at this sport
Sir Valour dies; cries 'O, enough, Patroclus;
Or give me ribs of steel! I shall split all
•In pleasure of my spleen.' And in this fashion,
All our abilities, gifts, natures, shapes,
Severals and generals of grace exact,   180
Achievements, plots, orders, preventions,
Excitements to the field, or speech for truce,
Success or loss, what is or is not, serves
As stuff for these two to make paradoxes.

  Nest. And in the imitation of these twain—
Who, as Ulysses says, opinion crowns
With an imperial voice—many are infect.
Ajax is grown self-will'd, and bears his head
•In such a rein, in full as proud a place
As broad Achilles; keeps his tent like him;   190
Makes factious feasts; rails on our state of war,
Bold as an oracle, and sets Thersites,
A slave whose gall coins slanders like a mint,
To match us in comparisons with dirt,
To weaken and discredit our exposure,
How rank soever rounded in with danger.

  Ulyss. They tax our policy, and call it cow-
    ardice,
Count wisdom as no member of the war,
Forestall prescience and esteem no act
But that of hand: the still and mental parts,   200
That do contrive how many hands shall strike,
When fitness calls them on, and know by measure
Of their observant toil the enemies' weight,—
Why, this hath not a finger's dignity:
They call this bed-work, mappery, closet-war;

So that the ram that batters down the wall,
For the great swing and rudeness of his poise,
They place before his hand that made the engine,
Or those that with the fineness of their souls
By reason guide his execution.   210
● *Nest.* Let this be granted, and Achilles' horse
Makes many Thetis' sons.   [*A tucket.*
  Agam. What trumpet? look, Menelaus.
  Men. From Troy.

Enter Æneas.

  Agam. What would you 'fore our tent?
  Æne. Is this great Agamemnon's tent, I pray
    you?
  Agam. Even this.
  Æne. May one, that is a herald and a prince,
Do a fair message to his kingly ears?
  Agam. With surety stronger than Achilles'
    arm   220
'Fore all the Greekish heads, which with one voice
Call Agamemnon head and general.
  Æne. Fair leave and large security. How may
A stranger to those most imperial looks
Know them from eyes of other mortals?
  Agam.   How!
  Æne. Ay;
I ask, that I might waken reverence,
And bid the cheek be ready with a blush
Modest as morning when she coldly eyes
The youthful Phœbus: 230
Which is that god in office, guiding men?
Which is the high and mighty Agamemnon?
  Agam. This Trojan scorns us; or the men of
    Troy
Are ceremonious courtiers.
  Æne. Courtiers as free, as debonair, unarm'd,
As bending angels; that's their fame in peace:
But when they would seem soldiers, they have
    galls,
● Good arms, strong joints, true swords; and, Jove's
    accord,
Nothing so full of heart. But peace, Æneas,
Peace, Trojan; lay thy finger on thy lips!   240
The worthiness of praise distains his worth,
If that the praised himself bring the praise forth:
But what the repining enemy commends,
That breath fame blows; that praise, sole pure,
    transcends.
  Agam. Sir, you of Troy, call you yourself
    Æneas?
  Æne. Ay, Greek, that is my name.
  Agam. What's your affair, I pray you?
  Æne. Sir, pardon; 'tis for Agamemnon's ears.
  Agam. He hears nought privately that comes
    from Troy.
  Æne. Nor I from Troy come not to whisper
    him: 250
I bring a trumpet to awake his ear,
To set his sense on the attentive bent,
And then to speak.
  Agam.   Speak frankly as the wind;
It is not Agamemnon's sleeping hour:
That thou shalt know, Trojan, he is awake,
He tells thee so himself.
  Æne.   Trumpet, blow loud,
Send thy brass voice through all these lazy tents;
And every Greek of mettle, let him know,
What Troy means fairly shall be spoke aloud.
                              [*Trumpet sounds.*

211-212 *Let this . . . sons.* If that be admitted, Achilles' soldiers are worth more than Achilles himself.

238 *Jove's accord.* i.e. God willing.

Costume design for Aeneas by Leslie Hurry, Stratford-upon-Avon, 1960

296 *beaver*. The face guard of the helmet.

297 *vantbrace*. Armour for the forearm.

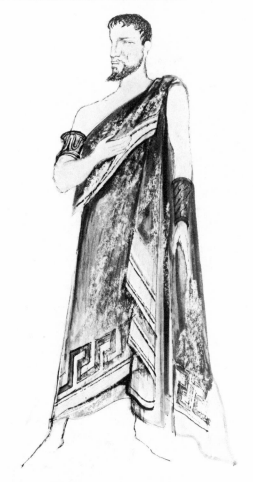

Costume design for Agamemnon by Leslie Hurry, Stratford-upon-Avon, 1960

We have, great Agamemnon, here in Troy   260
A prince call'd Hector,—Priam is his father,—
Who in this dull and long-continued truce
Is rusty grown: he bade me take a trumpet,
And to this purpose speak. Kings, princes, lords!
If there be one among the fair'st of Greece
That holds his honour higher than his ease,
That seeks his praise more than he fears his
      peril,
That knows his valour, and knows not his fear,
That loves his mistress more than in confession,
With truant vows to her own lips he loves,   270
And dare avow her beauty and her worth
In other arms than hers,—to him this challenge.
Hector, in view of Trojans and of Greeks,
Shall make it good, or do his best to do it,
He hath a lady, wiser, fairer, truer,
Than ever Greek did compass in his arms,
And will to-morrow with his trumpet call
Midway between your tents and walls of Troy,
To rouse a Grecian that is true in love:
If any come, Hector shall honour him;   280
If none, he'll say in Troy when he retires,
The Grecian dames are sunburnt and not worth
The splinter of a lance.   Even so much.
      Agam. This shall be told our lovers, Lord
      Æneas;
If none of them have soul in such a kind,
We left them all at home: but we are soldiers;
And may that soldier a mere recreant prove,
That means not, hath not, or is not in love!
If then one is, or hath, or means to be,   289
That one meets Hector; if none else, I am he.
      Nest. Tell him of Nestor, one that was a man
When Hector's grandsire suck'd: he is old now;
But if there be not in our Grecian host
One noble man that hath one spark of fire,
To answer for his love, tell him from me
• I'll hide my silver beard in a gold beaver
• And in my vantbrace put this wither'd brawn,
And meeting him will tell him that my lady
Was fairer than his grandam and as chaste
As may be in the world: his youth in flood,   300
I'll prove this truth with my three drops of blood.
      Æne. Now heavens forbid such scarcity of
      youth!
      Ulyss. Amen.
      Agam. Fair Lord Æneas, let me touch your
      hand;
To our pavilion shall I lead you, sir.
Achilles shall have word of this intent;
So shall each lord of Greece, from tent to tent:
Yourself shall feast with us before you go
And find the welcome of a noble foe.
      [*Exeunt all but Ulysses and Nestor.*

      Ulyss. Nestor!   310
      Nest. What says Ulysses?
      Ulyss. I have a young conception in my brain;
Be you my time to bring it to some shape.
      Nest. What is't?
      Ulyss. This 'tis:
Blunt wedges rive hard knots: the seeded pride
That hath to this maturity blown up
In rank Achilles must or now be cropp'd,
Or, shedding, breed a nursery of like evil,
To overbulk us all.
      Nest.   Well, and how?   320
      Ulyss. This challenge that the gallant Hector
      sends,

However it is spread in general name,
Relates in purpose only to Achilles.
   Nest. The purpose is perspicuous even as substance,
•Whose grossness little characters sum up:
And, in the publication, make no strain,
But that Achilles, were his brain as barren
As banks of Libya,—though, Apollo knows,
'Tis dry enough,—will, with great speed of judgement,
Ay, with celerity, find Hector's purpose   330
Pointing on him.
   Ulyss. And wake him to the answer, think you?
   Nest. Yes, 'tis most meet: whom may you else oppose,
That can from Hector bring his honour off,
If not Achilles? Though 't be a sportful combat,
Yet in the trial much opinion dwells;
For here the Trojans taste our dear'st repute
With their finest palate: and trust to me, Ulysses,
•Our imputation shall be oddly poised
In this wild action; for the success,   340
•Although particular, shall give a scantling
Of good or bad unto the general;
And in such indexes, although small pricks
To their subsequent volumes, there is seen
The baby figure of the giant mass
Of things to come at large. It is supposed
He that meets Hector issues from our choice;
And choice, being mutual act of all our souls,
Makes merit her election, and doth boil,
As 'twere from forth us all, a man distill'd   350
Out of our virtues; who miscarrying,
What heart receives from hence the conquering part,
To steel a strong opinion to themselves?
Which entertain'd, limbs are his instruments,
In no less working than are swords and bows
Directive by the limbs.
   Ulyss. Give pardon to my speech:
Therefore 'tis meet Achilles meet not Hector.
Let us, like merchants, show our foulest wares,
And think, perchance, they'll sell; if not,   360
The lustre of the better yet to show,
Shall show the better. Do not consent
That ever Hector and Achilles meet;
For both our honour and our shame in this
Are dogg'd with two strange followers.

   Nest. I see them not with my old eyes: what are they?
   Ulyss. What glory our Achilles shares from Hector,
Were he not proud, we all should share with him:
But he already is too insolent;
And we were better parch in Afric sun   370
Than in the pride and salt scorn of his eyes,
Should he 'scape Hector fair: if he were foil'd,
•Why then, we did our main opinion crush
In taint of our best man. No, make a lottery;
And, by device, let blockish Ajax draw
The sort to fight with Hector: among ourselves
Give him allowance for the better man;
•For that will physic the great Myrmidon
Who broils in loud applause, and make him fall
•His crest that prouder than blue Iris bends.   380
If the dull brainless Ajax come safe off,
We'll dress him up in voices: if he fail,

325 *Whose grossness . . . sum up.* Whose large size can be computed in small figures.

339 *Our . . . poised.* Our reputation shall be unequally balanced.

341 *scantling.* Small piece.

373-374 *we did . . . best man.* In the defeat of our best man we lose our reputation.

378 *Myrmidon.* Achilles, who was head of the Thessalian Myrmidons.

380 *Iris.* The rainbow.

392 *tarre*. Incite.

6-7 *botchy core*. Running sore.

15 *vinewedst*. Mildewed.

20 *red murrain*. Plague with red spots.

27 *porpentine*. Porcupine.

Porcupine. Woodcut from Edward Topsell's *The History of Four-footed Beasts*, 1607

37 *Cerberus*. The watchdog that guarded the entrance to Hades. *Proserpina*. Queen of the Underworld.

41 *Cobloaf*. A small round loaf of bread.

42 *pun*. Pound.

49 *assinego*. Little ass.

Yet go we under our opinion still
That we have better men.   But, hit or miss,
Our project's life this shape of sense assumes:
Ajax employ'd plucks down Achilles' plumes.
　Nest. Ulysses,
Now I begin to relish thy advice;
And I will give a taste of it forthwith
To Agamemnon: go we to him straight.　　390
Two curs shall tame each other: pride alone
●Must tarre the mastiffs on, as 'twere their bone.
　　　　　　　　　　　　　　　　　[Exeunt.

ACT II.

Scene I.　*A part of the Grecian camp.*

Enter Ajax *and* Thersites.

　Ajax. Thersites!
　Ther. Agamemnon, how if he had boils? full, all over, generally?
　Ajax. Thersites!
　Ther. And those boils did run? say so: did
●not the general run then? were not that a botchy core?
　Ajax. Dog!
　Ther. Then would come some matter from him; I see none now.　　　　　　　　　　10
　Ajax. Thou bitch-wolf's son, canst thou not hear? [*Beating him*] Feel, then.
　Ther. The plague of Greece upon thee, thou mongrel beef-witted lord!
●　*Ajax.* Speak then, thou vinewedst leaven, speak: I will beat thee into handsomeness.
　Ther. I shall sooner rail thee into wit and holiness: but, I think, thy horse will sooner con an oration than thou learn a prayer without book.
●Thou canst strike, canst thou? a red murrain o' thy jade's tricks!　　　　　　　　　　21
　Ajax. Toadstool, learn me the proclamation.
　Ther. Dost thou think I have no sense, thou strikest me thus?
　Ajax. The proclamation!
　Ther. Thou art proclaimed a fool, I think.
●　*Ajax.* Do not, porpentine, do not: my fingers itch.
　Ther. I would thou didst itch from head to foot and I had the scratching of thee; I would make thee the loathsomest scab in Greece. When thou art forth in the incursions, thou strikest as slow as another.
　Ajax. I say, the proclamation!
　Ther. Thou grumblest and railest every hour on Achilles, and thou art as full of envy at his
●greatness as Cerberus is at Proserpina's beauty, ay, that thou barkest at him.
　Ajax. Mistress Thersites!
　Ther. Thou shouldst strike him.　　　　40
●　*Ajax.* Cobloaf!
●　*Ther.* He would pun thee into shivers with his fist, as a sailor breaks a biscuit.
　Ajax. [*Beating him*] You whoreson cur!
　Ther. Do, do.
　Ajax. Thou stool for a witch!
　Ther. Ay, do, do; thou sodden-witted lord! thou hast no more brain than I have in mine
●elbows; an assinego may tutor thee: thou scurvy-valiant ass! thou art here but to thrash Trojans; and thou art bought and sold among those of any wit, like a barbarian slave.   If thou use to beat

me, I will begin at thy heel, and tell what thou art by inches, thou thing of no bowels, thou!

Ajax. You dog!

Ther. You scurvy lord!

Ajax. [*Beating him*] You cur!

Ther. Mars his idiot! do, rudeness; do, camel; do, do.   59

Enter ACHILLES *and* PATROCLUS.

Achil. Why, how now, Ajax! wherefore do you thus? How now, Thersites! what's the matter, man?

Ther. You see him there, do you?

Achil. Ay; what's the matter?

Ther. Nay, look upon him.

Achil. So I do: what's the matter?

Ther. Nay, but regard him well.

Achil. 'Well!' why, I do so.

Ther. But yet you look not well upon him; for, whosoever you take him to be, he is Ajax. 70

Achil. I know that, fool.

Ther. Ay, but that fool knows not himself.

Ajax. Therefore I beat thee.

Ther. Lo, lo, lo, lo, what modicums of wit he utters! his evasions have ears thus long. I have bobbed his brain more than he has beat my bones: I will buy nine sparrows for a penny, and his pia mater is not worth the ninth part of a sparrow. This lord, Achilles, Ajax, who wears his wit in his belly and his guts in his head, I'll tell you what I say of him.   81

Achil. What?

Ther. I say, this Ajax—

[*Ajax offers to beat him.*

Achil. Nay, good Ajax.

Ther. Has not so much wit—

Achil. Nay, I must hold you.

Ther. As will stop the eye of Helen's needle, for whom he comes to fight.

Achil. Peace, fool!

Ther. I would have peace and quietness, but the fool will not: he there: that he: look you there.

Ajax. O thou damned cur! I shall—

Achil. Will you set your wit to a fool's?

Ther. No, I warrant you; for a fool's will shame it.

Patr. Good words, Thersites.

Achil. What's the quarrel?

Ajax. I bade the vile owl go learn me the tenour of the proclamation, and he rails upon me.

Ther. I serve thee not.   101

Ajax. Well, go to, go to.

Ther. I serve here voluntary.

Achil. Your last service was sufferance, 'twas not voluntary: no man is beaten voluntary: Ajax was here the voluntary, and you as under an impress.

Ther. E'en so; a great deal of your wit, too, lies in your sinews, or else there be liars. Hector shall have a great catch, if he knock out either of your brains: a' were as good crack a fusty nut with no kernel.

Achil. What, with me too, Thersites?

Ther. There's Ulysses and old Nestor, whose wit was mouldy ere your grandsires had nails on their toes, yoke you like draught-oxen and make you plough up the wars.

Achil. What, what?

75 *ears thus long.* i.e. as long as an ass.

77-78 *pia mater.* Fine membrane enclosing the brain.

107 *impress.* Compulsion or impressment.

Costume design for Thersites by Malcolm Pride, Stratford-upon-Avon, 1954

126 *brach.* Bitch.

16 *tent.* A probe for wounds.

17-23 *Let Helen . . . one ten.* See introduction.

19 *dismes.* A tenth or tithe.

28 *counters.* Metal discs without value used for calculation.

29 *The past . . . infinite.* His infinite greatness which is past or beyond all measuring.

Ther. Yes, good sooth: to, Achilles! to, Ajax! to! 120
Ajax. I shall cut out your tongue.
Ther. 'Tis no matter; I shall speak as much as thou afterwards.
Patr. No more words, Thersites; peace!
Ther. I will hold my peace when Achilles' brach bids me, shall I?
Achil. There's for you, Patroclus.
Ther. I will see you hanged, like clotpoles, ere I come any more to your tents: I will keep where there is wit stirring and leave the faction of fools. 			[*Exit.*
Patr. A good riddance.
Achil. Marry, this, sir, is proclaim'd through all our host:
That Hector, by the fifth hour of the sun,
Will with a trumpet 'twixt our tents and Troy
To-morrow morning call some knight to arms
That hath a stomach; and such a one that dare
Maintain—I know not what: 'tis trash. Farewell.
Ajax. Farewell. Who shall answer him?
Achil. I know not: 'tis put to lottery; otherwise 140
He knew his man.
Ajax. O, meaning you. I will go learn more of it. 			[*Exeunt.*

SCENE II. *Troy.   A room in Priam's palace.*

Enter PRIAM, HECTOR, TROILUS, PARIS, *and* HELENUS.

Pri. After so many hours, lives, speeches spent,
Thus once again says Nestor from the Greeks:
'Deliver Helen, and all damage else—
As honour, loss of time, travail, expense,
Wounds, friends, and what else dear that is consumed
In hot digestion of this cormorant war—
Shall be struck off.' Hector, what say you to't?
Hect. Though no man lesser fears the Greeks than I
As far as toucheth my particular,
Yet, dread Priam, 10
There is no lady of more softer bowels,
More spongy to suck in the sense of fear,
More ready to cry out 'Who knows what follows?'
Than Hector is: the wound of peace is surety,
Surety secure; but modest doubt is call'd
The beacon of the wise, the tent that searches
To the bottom of the worst.   Let Helen go:
Since the first sword was drawn about this question,
Every tithe soul, 'mongst many thousand dismes,
Hath been as dear as Helen; I mean, of ours: 20
If we have lost so many tenths of ours,
To guard a thing not ours nor worth to us,
Had it our name, the value of one ten,
What merit's in that reason which denies
The yielding of her up?
Tro. 			Fie, fie, my brother!
Weigh you the worth and honour of a king
So great as our dread father in a scale
Of common ounces? will you with counters sum
The past proportion of his infinite?
And buckle in a waist most fathomless 30
With spans and inches so diminutive
As fears and reasons? fie, for godly shame!
Hel. No marvel, though you bite so sharp at reasons,

You are so empty of them. Should not our father
Bear the great sway of his affairs with reasons,
Because your speech hath none that tells him so?

   Tro. You are for dreams and slumbers, brother
         priest;
You fur your gloves with reason.   Here are your
         reasons:
You know an enemy intends you harm;
You know a sword employ'd is perilous,   40
And reason flies the object of all harm:
Who marvels then, when Helenus beholds
A Grecian and his sword, if he do set
The very wings of reason to his heels
And fly like chidden Mercury from Jove,
Or like a star disorb'd? Nay, if we talk of reason,
Let's shut our gates and sleep: manhood and
         honour
Should have hare-hearts, would they but fat their
         thoughts
With this cramm'd reason: reason and respect
Make livers pale and lustihood deject.   50
   Hect. Brother, she is not worth what she doth
         cost
The holding.
   Tro.   What is aught, but as 'tis valued?
   Hect.   But value dwells not in particular will;
It holds his estimate and dignity
As well wherein 'tis precious of itself
As in the prizer: 'tis mad idolatry
To make the service greater than the god;
And the will dotes that is attributive
To what infectiously itself affects,
Without some image of the affected merit.   60
   Tro. I take to-day a wife, and my election
Is led on in the conduct of my will;
My will enkindled by mine eyes and ears,
Two traded pilots 'twixt the dangerous shores
Of will and judgement: how may I avoid,
Although my will distaste what it elected,
The wife I chose? there can be no evasion
To blench from this and to stand firm by honour:
We turn not back the silks upon the merchant,
When we have soil'd them, nor the remainder
         viands   70
We do not throw in unrespective sieve,
Because we now are full.   It was thought meet
Paris should do some vengeance on the Greeks:
Your breath of full consent bellied his sails;
The seas and winds, old wranglers, took a truce
And did him service: he touch'd the ports desired,
And for an old aunt whom the Greeks held captive,
He brought a Grecian queen, whose youth and
         freshness
Wrinkles Apollo's, and makes stale the morning.
Why keep we her? the Grecians keep our aunt:
Is she worth keeping? why, she is a pearl,   81
Whose price hath launch'd above a thousand ships,
And turn'd crown'd kings to merchants.
If you'll avouch 'twas wisdom Paris went—
As you must needs, for you all cried 'Go, go,'—
If you'll confess he brought home noble prize—
As you must needs, for you all clapp'd your hands,
And cried 'Inestimable!'—why do you now
The issue of your proper wisdoms rate,
And do a deed that fortune never did,   90
Beggar the estimation which you prized
Richer than sea and land? O, theft most base,
That we have stol'n what we do fear to keep!
But, thieves, unworthy of a thing so stol'n,

46 *star disorb'd.* A shooting star.

48 *hare-hearts.* The Folio reads *hard.*

58 *attributive.* Subject.

59 *affects.* Desires.

64 *traded.* Practised.

77 *aunt.* Priam's sister was abducted by Telamon, King of Salamis and father of Ajax.

91 *estimation.* The esteemed object.

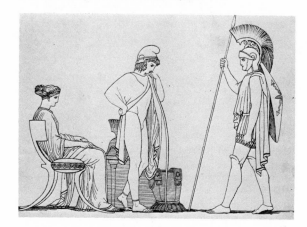

Hector and Paris. Engraving by John Flaxman from Homer's *Iliad*, translated by Alexander Pope, 1793

96 *warrant.* Defend.

Cassandra: 'Cry, Trojans, cry!' Engraving by Kenny Meadows from Barry Cornwall's *The Works of Shakspere*, 1846

110 *firebrand.* Before the birth of Paris, Hecuba dreamed she gave birth to a firebrand.

130 *convince.* Convict.

136 *propugnation.* Defence.

That in their country did them that disgrace,
● We fear to warrant in our native place!
   Cas. [*Within*] Cry, Trojans, cry!
   Pri.   What noise? what shriek is this?
   Tro. 'Tis our mad sister, I do know her voice.
   Cas. [*Within*] Cry, Trojans!
   Hect. It is Cassandra.   100

Enter CASSANDRA, *raving.*

   Cas. Cry, Trojans, cry! lend me ten thousand
     eyes,
And I will fill them with prophetic tears.
   Hect. Peace, sister, peace!
   Cas. Virgins and boys, mid-age and wrinkled
     eld,
Soft infancy, that nothing canst but cry,
Add to my clamours! let us pay betimes
A moiety of that mass of moan to come.
Cry, Trojans, cry! practise your eyes with tears!
Troy must not be, nor goodly Ilion stand;
● Our firebrand brother, Paris, burns us all.   110
Cry, Trojans, cry! a Helen and a woe:
Cry, cry! Troy burns, or else let Helen go. [*Exit.*
   Hect. Now, youthful Troilus, do not these
     high strains
Of divination in our sister work
Some touches of remorse? or is your blood
So madly hot that no discourse of reason,
Nor fear of bad success in a bad cause,
Can qualify the same?
   Tro.   Why, brother Hector,
We may not think the justness of each act
Such and no other than event doth form it,   120
Nor once deject the courage of our minds,
Because Cassandra's mad: her brain-sick raptures
Cannot distaste the goodness of a quarrel
Which hath our several honours all engaged
To make it gracious.   For my private part,
I am no more touch'd than all Priam's sons:
And Jove forbid there should be done amongst us
Such things as might offend the weakest spleen
To fight for and maintain!
●   *Par.* Else might the world convince of levity
As well my undertakings as your counsels: 131
But I attest the gods, your full consent
Gave wings to my propension and cut off
All fears attending on so dire a project.
For what, alas, can these my single arms?
● What propugnation is in one man's valour,
To stand the push and enmity of those
This quarrel would excite?   Yet, I protest,
Were I alone to pass the difficulties
And had as ample power as I have will,   140
Paris should ne'er retract what he hath done,
Nor faint in the pursuit.
   Pri.   Paris, you speak
Like one besotted on your sweet delights:
You have the honey still, but these the gall;
So to be valiant is no praise at all.
   Par. Sir, I propose not merely to myself
The pleasures such a beauty brings with it;
But I would have the soil of her fair rape
Wiped off, in honourable keeping her.
What treason were it to the ransack'd queen, 150
Disgrace to your great worths and shame to me,
Now to deliver her possession up
On terms of base compulsion!   Can it be
That so degenerate a strain as this
Should once set footing in your generous bosoms?

There's not the meanest spirit on our party
Without a heart to dare or sword to draw
When Helen is defended, nor none so noble
Whose life were ill bestow'd or death unfamed
Where Helen is the subject; then, I say,   160
Well may we fight for her whom, we know well,
The world's large spaces cannot parallel.
        Hect.   Paris and Troilus, you have both said well,
And on the cause and question now in hand
Have glozed, but superficially; not much
Unlike young men, whom Aristotle thought
●Unfit to hear moral philosophy:
The reasons you allege do more conduce
To the hot passion of distemper'd blood
Than to make up a free determination   170
'Twixt right and wrong, for pleasure and revenge
Have ears more deaf than adders to the voice
Of any true decision.   Nature craves
All dues be render'd to their owners: now,
What nearer debt in all humanity
Than wife is to the husband?   If this law
●Of nature be corrupted through affection,
And that great minds, of partial indulgence
To their benumbed wills, resist the same,
There is a law in each well-order'd nation   180
To curb those raging appetites that are
Most disobedient and refractory.
If Helen then be wife to Sparta's king,
As it is known she is, these moral laws
Of nature and of nations speak aloud
To have her back return'd: thus to persist
In doing wrong extenuates not wrong,
But makes it much more heavy. Hector's opinion
Is this in way of truth; yet ne'ertheless,
●My spritely brethren, I propend to you   190
In resolution to keep Helen still,
For 'tis a cause that hath no mean dependance
Upon our joint and several dignities.
        Tro.   Why, there you touch'd the life of our design:
Were it not glory that we more affected
●Than the performance of our heaving spleens,
I would not wish a drop of Trojan blood
Spent more in her defence.   But, worthy Hector,
She is a theme of honour and renown,
A spur to valiant and magnanimous deeds,   200
Whose present courage may beat down our foes,
And fame in time to come canonize us;
For, I presume, brave Hector would not lose
So rich advantage of a promised glory
As smiles upon the forehead of this action
For the wide world's revenue.
        Hect.   I am yours,
You valiant offspring of great Priamus.
I have a roisting challenge sent amongst
The dull and factious nobles of the Greeks
Will strike amazement to their drowsy spirits: 210
●I was advertised their great general slept,
●Whilst emulation in the army crept:
This, I presume, will wake him.   [*Exeunt.*

        Scene III.   *The Grecian camp. Before
                      Achilles' tent.*

        Enter Thersites, *solus.*

        Ther.   How now, Thersites! what, lost in the
labyrinth of thy fury! Shall the elephant Ajax
carry it thus? he beats me, and I rail at him:

167 *moral.* Political.

177 *affection.* Appetite.

190 *propend.* Incline.

196 *spleens.* Angry passions.

211 *advertised.* Advised or informed.

212 *emulation.* Jealous rivalry.

6 *'Sfoot*. God's foot.

8 *enginer*. A soldier concerned with devices to assault or undermine city walls.

14 *caduceus*. Mercury's staff.

Mercury with his caduceus. From a 19th century engraving

19-22 *After this . . . placket*. See introduction.

28 *slipped*. A pun on 'slip', a counterfeit brass coin covered in gold or silver.

33 *blood*. Passion.

36 *lazars*. Lepers.

55 *decline*. To go through, in a grammatical sense.

O, worthy satisfaction! would it were otherwise; that I could beat him, whilst he railed at me. 'Sfoot, I'll learn to conjure and raise devils, but I'll see some issue of my spiteful execrations. Then there's Achilles, a rare enginer! If Troy be not taken till these two undermine it, the walls will stand till they fall of themselves. O thou great thunder-darter of Olympus, forget that thou art Jove, the king of gods, and, Mercury, lose all the serpentine craft of thy caduceus, if ye take not that little little less than little wit from them that they have! which short-armed ignorance itself knows is so abundant scarce, it will not in circumvention deliver a fly from a spider, without drawing their massy irons and cutting the web. After this, the vengeance on the whole camp! or rather, the bone-ache! for that, methinks, is the curse dependant on those that war for a placket. I have said my prayers and devil Envy say Amen. What ho! my Lord Achilles!

Enter PATROCLUS.

Patr. Who's there? Thersites! Good Thersites, come in and rail.

Ther. If I could have remembered a gilt counterfeit, thou wouldst not have slipped out of my contemplation: but it is no matter; thyself upon thyself! The common curse of mankind, folly and ignorance, be thine in great revenue! heaven bless thee from a tutor, and discipline come not near thee! Let thy blood be thy direction till thy death! then if she that lays thee out says thou art a fair corse, I'll be sworn and sworn upon't she never shrouded any but lazars. Amen. Where's Achilles?

Patr. What, art thou devout? wast thou in prayer?

Ther. Ay: the heavens hear me!   40

Enter ACHILLES.

Achil. Who's there?

Patr. Thersites, my lord.

Achil. Where, where? Art thou come? why, my cheese, my digestion, why hast thou not served thyself in to my table so many meals? Come, what's Agamemnon?

Ther. Thy commander, Achilles. Then tell me, Patroclus, what's Achilles?

Patr. Thy lord, Thersites: then tell me, I pray thee, what's thyself?   50

Ther. Thy knower, Patroclus: then tell me, Patroclus, what art thou?

Patr. Thou mayst tell that knowest.

Achil. O, tell, tell.

Ther. I'll decline the whole question. Agamemnon commands Achilles; Achilles is my lord; I am Patroclus' knower, and Patroclus is a fool.

Patr. You rascal!

Ther. Peace, fool! I have not done.   60

Achil. He is a privileged man. Proceed, Thersites.

Ther. Agamemnon is a fool; Achilles is a fool; Thersites is a fool, and, as aforesaid, Patroclus is a fool.

Achil. Derive this; come.

Ther. Agamemnon is a fool to offer to command Achilles; Achilles is a fool to be com-

manded of Agamemnon; Thersites is a fool to
• serve such a fool, and Patroclus is a fool positive.
    Patr. Why am I a fool?   71
    Ther. Make that demand of the prover. It
suffices me thou art Look you, who comes
here?
    Achil. Patroclus, I'll speak with nobody.
Come in with me, Thersites.   [*Exit.*
•   *Ther.* Here is such patchery, such juggling
and such knavery! all the argument is a cuckold
and a whore; a good quarrel to draw emulous
factions and bleed to death upon. Now, the dry
• serpigo on the subject! and war and lechery
confound all!   [*Exit.*

    Enter AGAMEMNON, ULYSSES, NESTOR,
        DIOMEDES, *and* AJAX.

    Agam. Where is Achilles?
    Patr. Within his tent; but ill disposed, my
    lord.
    Agam. Let it be known to him that we are
    here.
• He shent our messengers; and we lay by
• Our appertainments, visiting of him:
Let him be told so; lest perchance he think
We dare not move the question of our place, 89
Or know not what we are.
    Patr.   I shall say so to him. [*Exit.*
    Ulyss. We saw him at the opening of his tent:
He is not sick.
    Ajax. Yes, lion-sick, sick of proud heart:
you may call it melancholy, if you will favour
the man; but, by my head, 'tis pride: but why,
why? let him show us the cause. A word, my
lord.   [*Takes Agamemnon aside.*
    Nest. What moves Ajax thus to bay at him?
    Ulyss. Achilles hath inveigled his fool from
him.   100
    Nest. Who, Thersites?
    Ulyss. He.
    Nest. Then will Ajax lack matter, if he have
lost his argument.
    Ulyss. No, you see, he is his argument that
has his argument, Achilles.
    Nest. All the better; their fraction is more
our wish than their faction: but it was a strong
composure a fool could disunite.
    Ulyss. The amity that wisdom knits not, folly
may easily untie. Here comes Patroclus. 111

    Re-enter PATROCLUS.

    Nest. No Achilles with him.
    Ulyss. The elephant hath joints, but none
for courtesy: his legs are legs for necessity, not
for flexure.
    Patr. Achilles bids me say, he is much sorry,
If any thing more than your sport and pleasure
Did move your greatness and this noble state
To call upon him; he hopes it is no other
But for your health and your digestion sake, 120
An after-dinner's breath.
    Agam.   Hear you, Patroclus:
We are too well acquainted with these answers:
But his evasion, wing'd thus swift with scorn,
Cannot outfly our apprehensions.
Much attribute he hath, and much the reason
Why we ascribe it to him; yet all his virtues,
Not virtuously on his own part beheld,
Do in our eyes begin to lose their gloss,

70 *positive.* Absolute.

77 *patchery.* Roguery.

81 *serpigo.* A spreading skin disease.

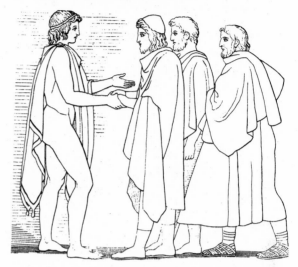

The embassy to Achilles. Engraving by John Flaxman
from Homer's *Iliad*, translated by Alexander Pope, 1793

86 *shent.* Scolded.

87 *appertainments.* Dignities.

138 *humorous*. Capricious and whimsical.

139 *pettish lunes*. Ill-humoured changes, like the moon.

176 *In will . . . self-admission*. Wilfully and with self-approval.

179-180 *Things small . . . important*. See introduction.

Costume design for Ajax by Leslie Hurry, Stratford-upon-Avon, 1960

Yea, like fair fruit in an unwholesome dish,
Are like to rot untasted.   Go and tell him,   130
We come to speak with him; and you shall
      not sin,
If you do say we think him over-proud
And under-honest, in self-assumption greater
Than in the note of judgement; and worthier than
      himself
Here tend the savage strangeness he puts on,
Disguise the holy strength of their command,
And underwrite in an observing kind
● His humorous predominance; yea, watch
● His pettish lunes, his ebbs, his flows, as if
The passage and whole carriage of this action   140
Rode on his tide.   Go tell him this, and add,
That if he overhold his price so much,
We'll none of him; but let him, like an engine
Not portable, lie under this report:
'Bring action hither, this cannot go to war:
A stirring dwarf we do allowance give
Before a sleeping giant.'   Tell him so.
      Patr. I shall; and bring his answer presently.
                                    [*Exit.*
      Agam. In second voice we'll not be satisfied;
We come to speak with him. Ulysses, enter you.
                                    [*Exit Ulysses.*
      Ajax. What is he more than another?   151
      Agam. No more than what he thinks he is.
      Ajax. Is he so much? Do you not think he
thinks himself a better man than I am?
      Agam. No question.
      Ajax. Will you subscribe his thought, and
say he is?
      Agam. No, noble Ajax; you are as strong,
as valiant, as wise, no less noble, much more
gentle, and altogether more tractable.   160
      Ajax. Why should a man be proud? How
doth pride grow? I know not what pride is.
      Agam. Your mind is the clearer, Ajax, and
your virtues the fairer. He that is proud eats
up himself: pride is his own glass, his own
trumpet, his own chronicle; and whatever praises
itself but in the deed, devours the deed in the
praise.
      Ajax. I do hate a proud man, as I hate the
engendering of toads.   170
      Nest. Yet he loves himself: is't not strange?
                                    [*Aside.*

            Re-enter ULYSSES.

      Ulyss. Achilles will not to the field to-
morrow.
      Agam. What's his excuse?
      Ulyss.   He doth rely on none,
But carries on the stream of his dispose
Without observance or respect of any,
● In will peculiar and in self-admission.
      Agam. Why will he not upon our fair request
Untent his person and share the air with us?
● *Ulyss.* Things small as nothing, for request's
      sake only,
He makes important: possess'd he is with great-
      ness,   180
And speaks not to himself but with a pride
That quarrels at self-breath: imagined worth
Holds in his blood such swoln and hot discourse
That 'twixt his mental and his active parts
Kingdom'd Achilles in commotion rages
And batters down himself: what should I say?

He is so plaguy proud that the death-tokens of it
Cry 'No recovery.'
 Agam.   Let Ajax go to him.
Dear lord, go you and greet him in his tent:
'Tis said he holds you well, and will be led 190
At your request a little from himself.
 Ulyss. O Agamemnon, let it not be so!
We'll consecrate the steps that Ajax makes
When they go from Achilles: shall the proud
   lord
That bastes his arrogance with his own seam
And never suffers matter of the world
Enter his thoughts, save such as do revolve
And ruminate himself, shall he be worshipp'd
Of that we hold an idol more than he?
No, this thrice worthy and right valiant lord 200
Must not so stale his palm, nobly acquired;
Nor, by my will, assubjugate his merit,
As amply titled as Achilles is,
By going to Achilles:
That were to enlard his fat already pride
And add more coals to Cancer when he burns
With entertaining great Hyperion.
This lord go to him! Jupiter forbid,
And say in thunder 'Achilles go to him.'

 Nest. [*Aside to Dio.*] O, this is well; he
  rubs the vein of him. 210
 Dio. [*Aside to Nest.*] And how his silence
  drinks up this applause!
 Ajax. If I go to him, with my armed fist
I'll pash him o'er the face.
 Agam. O, no, you shall not go.
 Ajax. An a' be proud with me, I'll pheeze
  his pride:
Let me go to him.
 Ulyss. Not for the worth that hangs upon
  our quarrel.
 Ajax. A paltry, insolent fellow!
 Nest. How he describes himself!
 Ajax. Can he not be sociable? 220
 Ulyss. The raven chides blackness.
 Ajax. I'll let his humours blood.
 Agam. He will be the physician that should
be the patient.
 Ajax. An all men were o' my mind,—
 Ulyss. Wit would be out of fashion.
 Ajax. A' should not bear it so, a' should eat
swords first: shall pride carry it?
 Nest. An 'twould, you'ld carry half.
 Ulyss. A' would have ten shares. 230
 Ajax. I will knead him; I'll make him supple.
 Nest. He's not yet through warm: force him
with praises: pour in, pour in; his ambition is
dry.
 Ulyss. [*To Agam.*] My lord, you feed too
much on this dislike.
 Nest. Our noble general, do not do so.
 Dio. You must prepare to fight without Achilles.
 Ulyss. Why, 'tis this naming of him does him
  harm.
Here is a man—but 'tis before his face; 240
I will be silent.
 Nest.   Wherefore should you so?
He is not emulous, as Achilles is.
 Ulyss. Know the whole world, he is as valiant.
 Ajax. A whoreson dog, that shall palter thus
  with us!
Would he were a Trojan!
 Nest. What a vice were it in Ajax now,

187 *death-tokens.* Plague spots that indicated death.

195 *seam.* Fat or grease.

201 *stale his palm.* Sully his honour.

206 *Cancer.* Summer begins under the sign of Cancer.

207 *Hyperion.* Sun.

215 *pheeze.* Beat.

222 *let his humours blood.* By blood-letting cure him
of his excessive pride.

244 *palter.* Play games.

Costume design for Agamemnon by Leslie Hurry,
Stratford-upon-Avon, 1960

250 *strange*. Haughty.

258 *Milo*. A famous athlete who carried a bull on his shoulders. *addition*. Title.

16 *Grace*. A quibble on the title of a Duke.

Costume design for Ulysses by Leslie Hurry, Stratford-upon-Avon, 1960

Ulyss.   If he were proud,—
Dio.   Or covetous of praise,—
Ulyss.   Ay, or surly borne,—
Dio.   Or strange, or self-affected!   250
Ulyss.   Thank the heavens, lord, thou art of
    sweet composure;
Praise him that got thee, she that gave thee
    suck:
Famed be thy tutor, and thy parts of nature
Thrice famed, beyond all erudition:
But he that disciplined thy arms to fight,
Let Mars divide eternity in twain,
And give him half: and, for thy vigour,
Bull-bearing Milo his addition yield
To sinewy Ajax.   I will not praise thy wisdom,
Which, like a bourn, a pale, a shore, confines 260
Thy spacious and dilated parts: here's Nestor;
Instructed by the antiquary times,
He must, he is, he cannot but be wise:
But pardon, father Nestor, were your days
As green as Ajax' and your brain so temper'd,
You should not have the eminence of him,
But be as Ajax.
Ajax.   Shall I call you father?
Nest.   Ay, my good son.
Dio.   Be ruled by him, Lord Ajax.
Ulyss.   There is no tarrying here; the hart
    Achilles
Keeps thicket.   Please it our great general 270
To call together all his state of war;
Fresh kings are come to Troy: to-morrow
We must with all our main of power stand fast:
And here's a lord,—come knights from east to
    west,
And cull their flower, Ajax shall cope the best.
Agam.   Go we to council.   Let Achilles sleep:
Light boats sail swift, though greater hulks draw
    deep.   [*Exeunt.*

ACT III.

Scene I.   *Troy.   Priam's palace.*

Enter a Servant *and* Pandarus.

Pan.   Friend, you! pray you, a word: do not you follow the young Lord Paris?
Serv.   Ay, sir, when he goes before me.
Pan.   You depend upon him, I mean?
Serv.   Sir, I do depend upon the lord.
Pan.   You depend upon a noble gentleman; I must needs praise him.
Serv.   The lord be praised!
Pan.   You know me, do you not?
Serv.   Faith, sir, superficially.   10
Pan.   Friend, know me better; I am the Lord Pandarus.
Serv.   I hope I shall know your honour better.
Pan.   I do desire it.
Serv.   You are in the state of grace.
Pan.   Grace! not so, friend; honour and lordship are my titles. [*Music within.*] What music is this?
Serv.   I do but partly know, sir: it is music in parts.   20
Pan.   Know you the musicians?
Serv.   Wholly, sir.
Pan.   Who play they to?
Serv.   To the hearers, sir.
Pan.   At whose pleasure, friend?

Serv. At mine, sir, and theirs that love music.
Pan. Command, I mean, friend.
Serv. Who shall I command, sir?
Pan. Friend, we understand not one another:
I am too courtly and thou art too cunning. At
whose request do these men play?   31
Serv. That's to't indeed, sir: marry, sir, at
the request of Paris my lord, who's there in person; with him, the mortal Venus, the heart-blood
of beauty, love's invisible soul,—
Pan. Who, my cousin Cressida?
Serv. No, sir, Helen: could you not find out
that by her attributes?
Pan. It should seem, fellow, that thou hast
not seen the Lady Cressida. I come to speak
with Paris from the Prince Troilus: I will make
a complimental assault upon him, for my business
seethes.
● *Serv.* Sodden business! there's a stewed
phrase indeed!

Enter PARIS *and* HELEN, *attended.*

Pan. Fair be to you, my lord, and to all this
fair company! fair desires, in all fair measure,
fairly guide them! especially to you, fair queen!
fair thoughts be your fair pillow!   49
Helen. Dear lord, you are full of fair words.
Pan. You speak your fair pleasure, sweet
● queen. Fair prince, here is good broken music.
Par. You have broke it, cousin: and, by my
life, you shall make it whole again; you shall
piece it out with a piece of your performance.
Nell, he is full of harmony.
Pan. Truly, lady, no.
Helen. O, sir,—
Pan. Rude, in sooth; in good sooth, very
rude.   60
Par. Well said, my lord! well, you say so
● in fits.
Pan. I have business to my lord, dear queen.
My lord, will you vouchsafe me a word?
Helen. Nay, this shall not hedge us out: we'll
hear you sing, certainly.
Pan. Well, sweet queen, you are pleasant
with me. But, marry, thus, my lord: my dear
lord and most esteemed friend, your brother
Troilus,—   70
Helen. My Lord Pandarus; honey-sweet
lord,—
Pan. Go to, sweet queen, go to:—commends
himself most affectionately to you,—
● *Helen.* You shall not bob us out of our melody: if you do, our melancholy upon your head!
Pan. Sweet queen, sweet queen! that's a
sweet queen, i' faith.
Helen. And to make a sweet lady sad is a
sour offence.   80
Pan. Nay, that shall not serve your turn;
that shall it not, in truth, la. Nay, I care not
for such words; no, no. And, my lord, he desires you, that if the king call for him at supper,
you will make his excuse.
Helen. My Lord Pandarus,—
Pan. What says my sweet queen, my very
very sweet queen?
Par. What exploit's in hand? where sups he
to-night?   90
Helen. Nay, but, my lord,—
Pan. What says my sweet queen? My cou-

44 *stewed.* With a pun on the meanings 'boil' and 'brothel'.

Paris (Glyn Grain) and Helen (Polly Adams), National
Theatre, London, 1976

52 *broken music.* Part music for different instruments.

62 *fits.* Divisions of a song.

75 *bob.* Cheat.

95 *disposer*. Mistress.

97 *wide*. i.e. of the mark.

111 *twain*. Estranged.

118 *you may*. i.e. have your joke.

130 *sore*. A pun on the meaning 'wound' with bawdy innuendo.

Pandarus (Anthony Quayle), Paris (Basil Hoskins) and Helen (Barbara Jefford), Stratford-upon-Avon, 1954

sin will fall out with you.   You must not know where he sups.

  • *Par.*   I'll lay my life, with my disposer Cressida.

  • *Pan.*   No, no, no such matter; you are wide: come, your disposer is sick.

Par.   Well, I'll make excuse.

Pan.   Ay, good my lord.   Why should you say Cressida? no, your poor disposer's sick.   101

Par.   I spy.

Pan.   You spy! what do you spy?   Come, give me an instrument.   Now, sweet queen.

Helen.   Why, this is kindly done.

Pan.   My niece is horribly in love with a thing you have, sweet queen.

Helen.   She shall have it, my lord, if it be not my lord Paris.

Pan.   He! no, she'll none of him; they two
 • are twain.   111

Helen.   Falling in, after falling out, may make them three.

Pan.   Come, come, I'll hear no more of this; I'll sing you a song now.

Helen.   Ay, ay, prithee now.   By my troth, sweet lord, thou hast a fine forehead.

  • *Pan.*   Ay, you may, you may.

Helen.   Let thy song be love: this love will undo us all.   O Cupid, Cupid, Cupid!   120

Pan.   Love! ay, that it shall, i' faith.

Par.   Ay, good now, love, love, nothing but love.

Pan.   In good troth, it begins so.   [*Sings.*
Love, love, nothing but love, still more!
    For, O, love's bow
    Shoots buck and doe:
    The shaft confounds,
    Not that it wounds,
  • But tickles still the sore.   130
These lovers cry Oh! oh! they die!
    Yet that which seems the wound to kill,
Doth turn oh! oh! to ha! ha! he!
    So dying love lives still:
Oh! oh! a while, but ha! ha! ha!
Oh! oh! groans out for ha! ha! ha!
Heigh-ho!

Helen.   In love, i' faith, to the very tip of the nose.   139

Par.   He eats nothing but doves, love, and that breeds hot blood, and hot blood begets hot thoughts, and hot thoughts beget hot deeds, and hot deeds is love.

Pan.   Is this the generation of love? hot blood, hot thoughts, and hot deeds? Why, they are vipers: is love a generation of vipers? Sweet lord, who's a-field to-day?

Par.   Hector, Deiphobus, Helenus, Antenor, and all the gallantry of Troy: I would fain have armed to-day, but my Nell would not have it so. How chance my brother Troilus went not?   151

Helen.   He hangs the lip at something: you know all, Lord Pandarus.

Pan.   Not I, honey-sweet queen.   I long to hear how they sped to-day.   You'll remember your brother's excuse?

Par.   To a hair.

Pan.   Farewell, sweet queen.

Helen.   Commend me to your niece.

Pan.   I will, sweet queen.   [*Exit.* 160
                [*A retreat sounded.*

Par.   They're come from field: let us to
  Priam's hall,
To greet the warriors. Sweet Helen, I must
  woo you
To help unarm our Hector: his stubborn buckles,
With these your white enchanting fingers touch'd,
Shall more obey than to the edge of steel
Or force of Greekish sinews; you shall do more
● Than all the island kings,—disarm great Hector.
  Helen.   'Twill make us proud to be his servant,
  Paris;
Yea, what he shall receive of us in duty
Gives us more palm in beauty than we have,   170
Yea, overshines ourself.
  Par.   Sweet, above thought I love thee.
                                    [*Exeunt.*

SCENE II.   *The same.   Pandarus' orchard.*

Enter PANDARUS *and* TROILUS' Boy, *meeting.*

  Pan.   How now! where's thy master? at my
cousin Cressida's?
  Boy.   No, sir; he stays for you to conduct him
thither.
  Pan.   O, here he comes.

Enter TROILUS.

How now, how now!
  Tro.   Sirrah, walk off.   [*Exit Boy.*
  Pan.   Have you seen my cousin?
  Tro.   No, Pandarus: I stalk about her door,
● Like a strange soul upon the Stygian banks   10
● Staying for waftage.   O, be thou my Charon,
And give me swift transportation to those fields
Where I may wallow in the lily-beds
Proposed for the deserver!   O gentle Pandarus,
From Cupid's shoulder pluck his painted wings,
And fly with me to Cressid!
  Pan.   Walk here i' the orchard, I'll bring her
straight.   [*Exit.*
  Tro.   I am giddy; expectation whirls me round.
The imaginary relish is so sweet   20
That it enchants my sense: what will it be,
When that the watery palate tastes indeed
Love's thrice repured nectar? death, I fear me,
Swooning destruction, or some joy too fine,
Too subtle-potent, tuned too sharp in sweetness,
For the capacity of my ruder powers:
I fear it much; and I do fear besides,
● That I shall lose distinction in my joys;
As doth a battle, when they charge on heaps
The enemy flying.   30

Re-enter PANDARUS.

  Pan.   She's making her ready, she'll come
straight: you must be witty now.   She does so
blush, and fetches her wind so short, as if she
● were frayed with a sprite: I'll fetch her.   It is
the prettiest villain: she fetches her breath as
short as a new-ta'en sparrow.   [*Exit.*
  Tro.   Even such a passion doth embrace my
  bosom:
My heart beats thicker than a feverous pulse;
● And all my powers do their bestowing lose,
Like vassalage at unawares encountering   40
The eye of majesty.

Re-enter PANDARUS *with* CRESSIDA.

  Pan.   Come, come, what need you blush?

167 *island kings.* Kings from the Greek islands.

10 *Stygian.* Of the river Styx, the river of Hades.

11 *waftage.* Passage. *Charon.* The ferryman of dead
souls who helped them across the river.

28 *distinction.* Power to distinguish.

34 *frayed with a sprite.* Frightened by a ghost.

39 *bestowing.* Use.

45 *watched*. Not allowed to sleep, which is how hawks were tamed.

48 *fills*. Shafts of a cart.

49 *this curtain*. Veil.

52 *rub on*. A cry from the game of bowls urging a bowl past an obstacle. *mistress*. The object-ball in a game of bowls.

53 *in fee-farm*. A grant in perpetuity.

61-62 '*In . . . interchangeably*'. A legal formula usually ending with 'have set their hands and seals'.

Troilus: 'O Cressida, how often have I wished me thus!'
Engraving by Kenny Meadows from Barry Cornwall's
The Works of Shakspere, 1846

100 *reversion*. Expectation.

shame's a baby. Here she is now: swear the oaths now to her that you have sworn to me.
● What, are you gone again? you must be watched ere you be made tame, must you? Come your ways, come your ways; an you draw backward,
● we'll put you i' the fills. Why do you not speak
● to her? Come, draw this curtain, and let's see your picture. Alas the day, how loath you are to offend daylight! an 'twere dark, you'ld close
● sooner. So, so; rub on, and kiss the mistress.
● How now! a kiss in fee-farm! build there, carpenter; the air is sweet. Nay, you shall fight your hearts out ere I part you. The falcon as the tercel, for all the ducks i' the river: go to, go to.

Tro. You have bereft me of all words, lady.

Pan. Words pay no debts, give her deeds: but she'll bereave you o' the deeds too, if she call your activity in question. What, billing
● again? Here's 'In witness whereof the parties interchangeably'—Come in, come in: I'll go get a fire.   [*Exit.*

Cres. Will you walk in, my lord?

Tro. O Cressida, how often have I wished me thus!

Cres. Wished, my lord! The gods grant,—O my lord!

Tro. What should they grant? what makes this pretty abruption? What too curious dreg espies my sweet lady in the fountain of our love?

Cres. More dregs than water, if my fears have eyes.

Tro. Fears make devils of cherubins; they never see truly.

Cres. Blind fear, that seeing reason leads, finds safer footing than blind reason stumbling without fear: to fear the worst oft cures the worse.   79

Tro. O, let my lady apprehend no fear: in all Cupid's pageant there is presented no monster.

Cres. Nor nothing monstrous neither?

Tro. Nothing, but our undertakings; when we vow to weep seas, live in fire, eat rocks, tame tigers; thinking it harder for our mistress to devise imposition enough than for us to undergo any difficulty imposed. This is the monstruosity in love, lady, that the will is infinite and the execution confined, that the desire is boundless and the act a slave to limit.   90

Cres. They say all lovers swear more performance than they are able and yet reserve an ability that they never perform, vowing more than the perfection of ten and discharging less than the tenth part of one. They that have the voice of lions and the act of hares, are they not monsters?

Tro. Are there such? such are not we: praise us as we are tasted, allow us as we prove; our head shall go bare till merit crown it: no perfec-
● tion in reversion shall have a praise in present: we will not name desert before his birth, and, being born, his addition shall be humble. Few words to fair faith: Troilus shall be such to Cressid as what envy can say worst shall be a mock for his truth, and what truth can speak truest not truer than Troilus.

Cres. Will you walk in, my lord?

Re-enter PANDARUS.

Pan. What, blushing still? have you not done talking yet?   109

Cres. Well, uncle, what folly I commit, I dedicate to you.

Pan. I thank you for that: if my lord get a boy of you, you'll give him me. Be true to my lord: if he flinch, chide me for it.

Tro. You know now your hostages; your uncle's word and my firm faith.

Pan. Nay, I'll give my word for her too: our kindred, though they be long ere they are wooed, they are constant being won: they are burs, I can tell you; they'll stick where they are thrown.

Cres. Boldness comes to me now, and brings me heart.   121
Prince Troilus, I have loved you night and day
For many weary months.

Tro. Why was my Cressid then so hard to win?

Cres. Hard to seem won: but I was won, my lord,
With the first glance that ever—pardon me—
If I confess much, you will play the tyrant.
I love you now; but not, till now, so much
But I might master it: in faith, I lie;   129
My thoughts were like unbridled children, grown
Too headstrong for their mother. See, we fools!
Why have I blabb'd? who shall be true to us,
When we are so unsecret to ourselves?
But, though I loved you well, I woo'd you not:
And yet, good faith, I wish'd myself a man,
Or that we women had men's privilege
Of speaking first. Sweet, bid me hold my tongue,
For in this rapture I shall surely speak
The thing I shall repent. See, see, your silence,
Cunning in dumbness, from my weakness draws
• My very soul of counsel! stop my mouth.   141

Tro. And shall, albeit sweet music issues thence.

Pan. Pretty, i' faith.

Cres. My lord, I do beseech you, pardon me;
'Twas not my purpose, thus to beg a kiss:
I am ashamed. O heavens! what have I done?
For this time will I take my leave, my lord.

Tro. Your leave, sweet Cressid!

Pan. Leave! an you take leave till to-morrow
morning,—   150

Cres. Pray you, content you.

Tro.   What offends you, lady?

Cres. Sir, mine own company.

Tro.   You cannot shun
Yourself.

Cres. Let me go and try:
I have a kind of self resides with you;
But an unkind self, that itself will leave,
To be another's fool. I would be gone:
Where is my wit? I know not what I speak.

Tro. Well know they what they speak that
speak so wisely.

Cres. Perchance, my lord, I show more craft
than love;   160
• And fell so roundly to a large confession,
To angle for your thoughts: but you are wise,
Or else you love not, for to be wise and love
Exceeds man's might; that dwells with gods
above.

Tro. O that I thought it could be in a woman—
As, if it can, I will presume in you—
To feed for aye her lamp and flames of love;
• To keep her constancy in plight and youth,
Outliving beauty's outward, with a mind
That doth renew swifter than blood decays! 170

141 *very soul of counsel.* Inmost secret thoughts.

161 *large.* Unhampered.

168 *youth.* Freshness.

Cressida: 'Sweet, bid me hold my tongue . . .' Troilus and Cressida embrace. Woodcut by Edward Burne-Jones, from William Morris's *Kelmscott Chaucer*, 1896

595

184 *plantage.* Plants whose growth was thought to be influenced by the moon.

185 *turtle.* Turtle dove.

186 *adamant.* Magnet or lodestone.

190 *numbers.* Metre in poetry.

201 *Pard.* Leopard.

Pandarus leads Cressida to Troilus. Wood engraving by Eric Gill from Chaucer's *Troilus and Criseyde,* 1927

Or that persuasion could but thus convince me,
That my integrity and truth to you
Might be affronted with the match and weight
Of such a winnow'd purity in love;
How were I then uplifted! but, alas!
I am as true as truth's simplicity
And simpler than the infancy of truth.
  Cres.   In that I'll war with you.
  Tro.   O virtuous fight,
When right with right wars who shall be most
    right!   179
True swains in love shall in the world to come
Approve their truths by Troilus: when their
    rhymes,
Full of protest, of oath and big compare,
Want similes, truth tired with iteration,
●As true as steel, as plantage to the moon,
●As sun to day, as turtle to her mate,
●As iron to adamant, as earth to the centre,
Yet, after all comparisons of truth,
As truth's authentic author to be cited,
'As true as Troilus' shall crown up the verse,
And sanctify the numbers.
  Cres.   Prophet may you be! 190
●If I be false, or swerve a hair from truth,
When time is old and hath forgot itself,
When waterdrops have worn the stones of Troy,
And blind oblivion swallow'd cities up,
And mighty states characterless are grated
To dusty nothing, yet let memory,
From false to false, among false maids in love,
Upbraid my falsehood! when they've said 'as
    false
As air, as water, wind, or sandy earth,
As fox to lamb, as wolf to heifer's calf,   200
●Pard to the hind, or stepdame to her son,'
'Yea,' let them say, to stick the heart of false-
    hood,
'As false as Cressid.'
  Pan.   Go to, a bargain made: seal it, seal it;
I'll be the witness.   Here I hold your hand, here
my cousin's.   If ever you prove false one to ano-
ther, since I have taken such pains to bring you
together, let all pitiful goers-between be called to
the world's end after my name; call them all
Pandars; let all constant men be Troiluses, all
false women Cressids, and all brokers-between
Pandars! say, amen.
  Tro.   Amen.
  Cres.   Amen.
  Pan.   Amen.   Whereupon I will show you a
chamber with a bed; which bed, because it shall
not speak of your pretty encounters, press it to
death: away!
And Cupid grant all tongue-tied maidens here
Bed, chamber, Pandar to provide this gear!   220
                          [*Exeunt.*

SCENE III.   *The Grecian camp.   Before Achilles'
tent.*

Enter AGAMEMNON, ULYSSES, DIOMEDES, NES-
    TOR, AJAX, MENELAUS, *and* CALCHAS.

  Cal. Now, princes, for the service I have done
    you,
The advantage of the time prompts me aloud
To call for recompense.   Appear it to your mind
†That, through the sight I bear in things to love,
I have abandon'd Troy, left my possession,

Incurr'd a traitor's name; exposed myself,
From certain and possess'd conveniences,
To doubtful fortunes; sequestering from me all
That time, acquaintance, custom and condition
Made tame and most familiar to my nature.   10
And here, to do you service, am become
As new into the world, strange, unacquainted:
● I do beseech you, as in way of taste,
To give me now a little benefit,
Out of those many register'd in promise,
Which, you say, live to come in my behalf.
    Agam.   What wouldst thou of us, Trojan?
      make demand.
    Cal.   You have a Trojan prisoner, call'd An-
      tenor,
Yesterday took: Troy holds him very dear.
Oft have you—often have you thanks therefore—
Desired my Cressid in right great exchange,   21
Whom Troy hath still denied: but this Antenor,
● I know, is such a wrest in their affairs
That their negotiations all must slack,
Wanting his manage; and they will almost
Give us a prince of blood, a son of Priam,
In change of him: let him be sent, great princes,
And he shall buy my daughter; and her presence
Shall quite strike off all service I have done,
In most accepted pain.
    Agam.   Let Diomedes bear him, 30
And bring us Cressid hither: Calchas shall have
What he requests of us.   Good Diomed,
Furnish you fairly for this interchange:
Withal bring word if Hector will to-morrow
Be answer'd in his challenge: Ajax is ready.
    Dio.   This shall I undertake; and 'tis a burden
Which I am proud to bear.
        [*Exeunt Diomedes and Calchas.*

Enter ACHILLES *and* PATROCLUS, *before their
       tent.*

    Ulyss.   Achilles stands i' the entrance of his
      tent:
Please it our general to pass strangely by him,
As if he were forgot; and, princes all,   40
Lay negligent and loose regard upon him:
I will come last.   'Tis like he'll question me
● Why such unplausive eyes are bent on him:
If so, I have derision medicinable,
To use between your strangeness and his pride,
Which his own will shall have desire to drink:
It may do good: pride hath no other glass
To show itself but pride, for supple knees
Feed arrogance and are the proud man's fees.
    Agam.   We'll execute your purpose, and put on
A form of strangeness as we pass along: 51
So do each lord, and either greet him not,
Or else disdainfully, which shall shake him more
Than if not look'd on.   I will lead the way.
    Achil.   What, comes the general to speak
      with me?
You know my mind, I'll fight no more 'gainst
      Troy.
    Agam.   What says Achilles? would he aught
      with us?
    Nest.   Would you, my lord, aught with the
      general?
    Achil.   No.
    Nest.   Nothing, my lord.   60
    Agam.   The better.
        [*Exeunt Agamemnon and Nestor.*

13   *taste.* Foretaste.

23   *wrest.* A tuning key for stringed instruments.

43   *unplausive.* Disapproving.

79 *mealy*. Powdery.

89 *At ample point*. To the full.

96 *how . . . parted*. However richly endowed.

99 *owes*. Owns.

109 *speculation*. Power of sight.

112 *position*. Proposition.

114 *circumstance*. Exposition.

Achil. Good day, good day.
Men. How do you? how do you?   [*Exit*.
Achil. What, does the cuckold scorn me?
Ajax. How now, Patroclus!
Achil. Good morrow, Ajax.
Ajax. Ha?
Achil. Good morrow.
Ajax. Ay, and good next day too.   [*Exit*.
Achil. What mean these fellows? Know they
   not Achilles?   70
   Patr. They pass by strangely: they were
      used to bend,
To send their smiles before them to Achilles;
To come as humbly as they used to creep
To holy altars.
   Achil.   What, am I poor of late?
'Tis certain, greatness, once fall'n out with for-
   tune,
Must fall out with men too: what the declined is
He shall as soon read in the eyes of others
As feel in his own fall; for men, like butterflies,
● Show not their mealy wings but to the summer,
And not a man, for being simply man,   80

Hath any honour, but honour for those honours
That are without him, as place, riches, favour,
Prizes of accident as oft as merit:
Which when they fall, as being slippery standers,
The love that lean'd on them as slippery too,
Do one pluck down another and together
Die in the fall. But 'tis not so with me:
Fortune and I are friends: I do enjoy
● At ample point all that I did possess,
Save these men's looks: who do, methinks, find
   out   90
Something not worth in me such rich beholding
As they have often given. Here is Ulysses:
I'll interrupt his reading.
How now, Ulysses!
   Ulyss.   Now, great Thetis' son!
   Achil. What are you reading?
   Ulyss.   A strange fellow here
● Writes me: 'That man, how dearly ever parted,
How much in having, or without or in,
Cannot make boast to have that which he hath,
● Nor feels not what he owes, but by reflection;
As when his virtues shining upon others   100
Heat them and they retort that heat again
To the first giver.'
   Achil.   This is not strange, Ulysses.
The beauty that is borne here in the face
The bearer knows not, but commends itself
To others' eyes; nor doth the eye itself,
That most pure spirit of sense, behold itself,
Not going from itself; but eye to eye opposed
Salutes each other with each other's form;
● For speculation turns not to itself,
Till it hath travell'd and is mirror'd there 110
Where it may see itself. This is not strange at
   all.
●   *Ulyss.* I do not strain at the position,—
It is familiar,—but at the author's drift;
● Who, in his circumstance, expressly proves
That no man is the lord of any thing,
Though in and of him there be much consisting,
Till he communicate his parts to others;
Nor doth he of himself know them for aught
Till he behold them form'd in the applause
Where they're extended; who, like an arch,
   reverberates   120

The voice again, or, like a gate of steel
Fronting the sun, receives and renders back
His figure and his heat.   I was much wrapt in
    this ;
And apprehended here immediately
The unknown Ajax.
Heavens, what a man is there ! a very horse,
That has he knows not what.   Nature, what
    things there are
● Most abject in regard and dear in use !
What things again most dear in the esteem
And poor in worth !   Now shall we see to-mor-
    row—   130
An act that very chance doth throw upon him—
Ajax renown'd.   O heavens, what some men do,
While some men leave to do !
How some men creep in skittish fortune's hall,
Whiles others play the idiots in her eyes !
How one man eats into another's pride,
● While pride is fasting in his wantonness !
To see these Grecian lords !—why, even already
They clap the lubber Ajax on the shoulder,
As if his foot were on brave Hector's breast   140
And great Troy shrieking.

    Achil.   I do believe it ; for they pass'd by me
As misers do by beggars, neither gave to me
Good word nor look : what, are my deeds forgot?
    Ulyss.   Time hath, my lord, a wallet at his
    back,
Wherein he puts alms for oblivion,
A great-sized monster of ingratitudes :
Those scraps are good deeds past ; which are
    devour'd
As fast as they are made, forgot as soon
As done : perseverance, dear my lord,   150
Keeps honour bright : to have done is to hang
● Quite out of fashion, like a rusty mail
In monumental mockery.   Take the instant way ;
For honour travels in a strait so narrow,
Where one but goes abreast : keep then the path ;
For emulation hath a thousand sons
That one by one pursue : if you give way,
● Or hedge aside from the direct forthright,
Like to an enter'd tide, they all rush by
And leave you hindmost ;   160
Or, like a gallant horse fall'n in first rank,
Lie there for pavement to the abject rear,
O'er-run and trampled on : then what they do in
    present,
Though less than yours in past, must o'ertop
    yours ;
For time is like a fashionable host
That slightly shakes his parting guest by the hand,
And with his arms outstretch'd, as he would fly,
Grasps in the comer : welcome ever smiles,
And farewell goes out sighing.   O, let not virtue
    seek
Remuneration for the thing it was ;·   170
For beauty, wit,
High birth, vigour of bone, desert in service,
Love, friendship, charity, are subjects all
To envious and calumniating time.
One touch of nature makes the whole world kin,
● That all with one consent praise new-born gawds,
Though they are made and moulded of things
    past,
And give to dust that is a little gilt
More laud than gilt o'er-dusted.
The present eye praises the present object :   180

128 *regard.* Estimation. *dear in use.* Invaluable in action.

137 *wantonness.* Arrogance.

152 *mail.* Armour.

158 *direct forthright.* Straight path.

176 *gawds.* Trifles.

Costume design for Ulysses by Malcolm Pride, Stratford-upon-Avon, 1954

194 *one of Priam's daughters*. Polyxena.

197 *Plutus*. Plutus, patron of wealth, was often confused with Pluto, god of the underworld.

201 *relation*. Report.

209 *Pyrrhus*. Son of Achilles.

228 *shrewdly*. Severely.

231 *Seals . . . danger*. Commits one to undertake unknown dangers.

Patrochus (Jeremy Brett), Ulysses (Richard Wordsworth) and Achilles (Charles Grey), Old Vic, 1956

Then marvel not, thou great and complete man,
That all the Greeks begin to worship Ajax;
Since things in motion sooner catch the eye
Than what not stirs.   The cry went once on thee,
And still it might, and yet it may again,
If thou wouldst not entomb thyself alive
And case thy reputation in thy tent;
Whose glorious deeds, but in these fields of late,
Made emulous missions 'mongst the gods themselves
And drave great Mars to faction.
   Achil.   Of this my privacy 190
I have strong reasons.
   Ulyss.   But 'gainst your privacy
The reasons are more potent and heroical:
'Tis known, Achilles, that you are in love
With one of Priam's daughters.
   Achil.   Ha! known!
   Ulyss.   Is that a wonder?
The providence that's in a watchful state
Knows almost every grain of Plutus' gold,
Finds bottom in the uncomprehensive deeps,
Keeps place with thought and almost, like the gods,
Does thoughts unveil in their dumb cradles. 200
There is a mystery—with whom relation
Durst never meddle—in the soul of state;
Which hath an operation more divine
Than breath or pen can give expressure to:
All the commerce that you have had with Troy
As perfectly is ours as yours, my lord;
And better would it fit Achilles much
To throw down Hector than Polyxena:
But it must grieve young Pyrrhus now at home,
When fame shall in our islands sound her trump,
And all the Greekish girls shall tripping sing, 211
'Great Hector's sister did Achilles win,
But our great Ajax bravely beat down him.'
Farewell, my lord: I as your lover speak:
The fool slides o'er the ice that you should break.
                         [*Exit.*
   Patr.   To this effect, Achilles, have I moved you:
A woman impudent and mannish grown
Is not more loathed than an effeminate man
In time of action.   I stand condemn'd for this;
They think my little stomach to the war 220
And your great love to me restrains you thus:
Sweet, rouse yourself; and the weak wanton Cupid
Shall from your neck unloose his amorous fold,
And, like a dew-drop from the lion's mane,
Be shook to air.
   Achil.   Shall Ajax fight with Hector?
   Patr.   Ay, and perhaps receive much honour by him.
   Achil.   I see my reputation is at stake;
My fame is shrewdly gored.
   Patr.   O, then, beware;
Those wounds heal ill that men do give themselves:
Omission to do what is necessary 230
Seals a commission to a blank of danger;
And danger, like an ague, subtly taints
Even then when we sit idly in the sun.
   Achil.   Go call Thersites hither, sweet Patroclus:
I'll send the fool to Ajax and desire him
To invite the Trojan lords after the combat

To see us here unarm'd: I have a woman's longing,
An appetite that I am sick withal,
● To see great. Hector in his weeds of peace,
To talk with him and to behold his visage, 240
Even to my full of view.

Enter THERSITES.

A labour saved!

Ther. A wonder!

Achil. What?

Ther. Ajax goes up and down the field, asking for himself.

Achil. How so?

Ther. He must fight singly to-morrow with Hector, and is so prophetically proud of an heroical cudgelling that he raves in saying nothing.

Achil. How can that be? 250

Ther. Why, he stalks up and down like a peacock,—a stride and a stand: ruminates like an hostess that hath no arithmetic but her brain to set down her reckoning: bites his lip with a politic regard, as who should say 'There were wit in this head, an 'twould out;' and so there is, but it lies as coldly in him as fire in a flint, which will not show without knocking. The man's undone for ever; for if Hector break not his neck i' the combat, he'll break 't himself in vain-glory. He knows not me: I said 'Good morrow, Ajax;' and he replies 'Thanks, Agamemnon.' What think you of this man that takes me for the general? He's grown a very land-fish, languageless, a monster. A plague of opinion! a man may wear it on both sides, like a leather jerkin.

Achil. Thou must be my ambassador to him, Thersites.

Ther. Who, I? why, he'll answer nobody; he professes not answering: speaking is for beggars; he wears his tongue in's arms. I will put on his presence: let Patroclus make demands to me, you shall see the pageant of Ajax.

Achil. To him, Patroclus: tell him I humbly desire the valiant Ajax to invite the most valorous Hector to come unarmed to my tent, and to procure safe-conduct for his person of the magnanimous and most illustrious six-or-seven-times-honoured captain-general of the Grecian army, Agamemnon, et cetera. Do this. 280

Patr. Jove bless great Ajax!

Ther. Hum!

Patr. I come from the worthy Achilles,—

Ther. Ha!

Patr. Who most humbly desires you to invite Hector to his tent,—

Ther. Hum!

Patr. And to procure safe-conduct from Agamemnon.

Ther. Agamemnon! 290

Patr. Ay, my lord.

Ther. Ha!

Patr. What say you to 't?

Ther. God b' wi' you, with all my heart.

Patr. Your answer, sir.

Ther. If to-morrow be a fair day, by eleven o'clock it will go one way or other: howsoever, he shall pay for me ere he has me.

Patr. Your answer, sir.

Ther. Fare you well, with all my heart. 300

Achil. Why, but he is not in this tune, is he?

Ther. No, but he's out o' tune thus. What

239 *weeds.* Clothes.

Thersites (John Nettles), Achilles (Robin Ellis) and Patroclus (Paul Moriarty), Royal Shakespeare Co, 1976

306 *catlings*. Strings of catgut for musical instruments.

11 *question of*. Communication allowed by.

21-22 *Anchises . . . Venus*. Father and mother of Aeneas.

music will be in him when Hector has knocked
out his brains, I know not; but, I am sure, none,
unless the fiddler Apollo get his sinews to make
catlings on.

Achil. Come, thou shalt bear a letter to him
straight.

Ther. Let me bear another to his horse; for
that's the more capable creature.   310

Achil. My mind is troubled, like a fountain
stirr'd;
And I myself see not the bottom of it.
                              [*Exeunt Achilles and Patroclus.*

Ther. Would the fountain of your mind were
clear again, that I might water an ass at it! I
had rather be a tick in a sheep than such a valiant
ignorance.   [*Exit.*

ACT IV.

Scene I.   *Troy.   A street.*

Enter, from one side, Æneas, *and* Servant *with
a torch; from the other,* Paris, Deiphobus,
Antenor, Diomedes, *and others, with
torches.*

Par. See, ho! who is that there?
Dei.   It is the Lord Æneas.
Æne. Is the prince there in person?
Had I so good occasion to lie long
As you, Prince Paris, nothing but heavenly busi-
ness
Should rob my bed-mate of my company.

Dio. That's my mind too. Good morrow, Lord
Æneas.

Par. A valiant Greek, Æneas,—take his
hand,—
Witness the process of your speech, wherein
You told how Diomed, a whole week by days,
Did haunt you in the field.

Æne.   Health to you, valiant sir, 10
During all question of the gentle truce;
But when I meet you arm'd, as black defiance
As heart can think or courage execute.

Dio. The one and other Diomed embraces.
Our bloods are now in calm; and, so long, health!
But when contention and occasion meet,
By Jove, I'll play the hunter for thy life
With all my force, pursuit and policy.

Æne. And thou shalt hunt a lion, that will fly
With his face backward.   In humane gentleness,
Welcome to Troy! now, by Anchises' life,   21
Welcome, indeed!   By Venus' hand I swear,
No man alive can love in such a sort
The thing he means to kill more excellently.

Dio. We sympathise: Jove, let Æneas live,
If to my sword his fate be not the glory,
A thousand complete courses of the sun!
But, in mine emulous honour, let him die,
With every joint a wound, and that to-morrow!

Æne. We know each other well.   30

Dio. We do; and long to know each other worse.

Par. This is the most despiteful gentle greet-
ing,
The noblest hateful love, that e'er I heard of.
What business, lord, so early?

Æne. I was sent for to the king; but why, I
know not.

Par. His purpose meets you: 'twas to bring
this Greek

To Calchas' house, and there to render him,
For the enfreed Antenor, the fair Cressid:
Let's have your company, or, if you please,
● Haste there before us: I constantly do think— 40
Or rather, call my thought a certain knowledge—
My brother Troilus lodges there to-night:
Rouse him and give him note of our approach,
● With the whole quality wherefore: I fear
We shall be much unwelcome.
　　Æne.　　　　　　That I assure you:
Troilus had rather Troy were borne to Greece
Than Cressid borne from Troy.
　　Par.　　　　　　There is no help;
The bitter disposition of the time
Will have it so.　On, lord; we'll follow you.
　　Æne. Good morrow, all. [*Exit with Servant.*
　　Par. And tell me, noble Diomed, faith, tell
　　　　me true,　　　　　　　　　　　　51
Even in the soul of sound good-fellowship,
Who, in your thoughts, merits fair Helen best,
Myself or Menelaus?
　　Dio.　　　　　Both alike:
He merits well to have her, that doth seek her,
Not making any scruple of her soilure,
With such a hell of pain and world of charge,
And you as well to keep her, that defend her,
Not palating the taste of her dishonour,
With such a costly loss of wealth and friends: 60
He, like a puling cuckold, would drink up
● The lees and dregs of a flat tamed piece;
You, like a lecher, out of whorish loins
Are pleased to breed out your inheritors:
Both merits poised, each weighs nor less nor more;
But he as he, the heavier for a whore.
　　Par. You are too bitter to your countrywoman.
● *Dio.* She's bitter to her country: hear me,
　　　　Paris:
For every false drop in her bawdy veins
A Grecian's life hath sunk; for every scruple　70
Of her contaminated carrion weight,
A Trojan hath been slain: since she could speak,
She hath not given so many good words breath
As for her Greeks and Trojans suffer'd death.
● *Par.* Fair Diomed, you do as chapmen do,
Dispraise the thing that you desire to buy:
But we in silence hold this virtue well,
We'll but commend what we intend to sell.
Here lies our way.　　　　　　[*Exeunt.*

Scene II.　*The same.　Court of Pandarus'
house.*

Enter Troilus *and* Cressida.

Tro. Dear, trouble not yourself: the morn is
　　cold.
　　Cres. Then, sweet my lord, I'll call mine
　　uncle down:
He shall unbolt the gates.
　　Tro.　　　　　Trouble him not;
To bed, to bed: sleep kill those pretty eyes,
And give as soft attachment to thy senses
As infants' empty of all thought!
　　Cres.　　　　　Good morrow, then.
　　Tro. I prithee now, to bed.
　　Cres.　　　　Are you a-weary of me?
　　Tro. O Cressida! but that the busy day,
Waked by the lark, hath roused the ribald crows,
And dreaming night will hide our joys no longer,
I would not from thee.

40 *constantly.* Firmly.

44 *quality.* Explanation.

62 *flat tamed piece.* A comparison with an opened flask of wine in which the contents have gone flat.

68-74 *She's bitter . . . death.* See introduction.

Diomed: 'She's bitter to her country . . .' Painting of Helen of Troy by Frederick Sandys (1829–1904)

75 *chapmen.* Traders.

Cressida: 'Night hath been too brief'. Wood engraving
by Eric Gill from Chaucer's *Troilus and Criseyde*, 1927

33 *capocchia.* Simpleton.

34 *bugbear.* Hobgoblin.

52 *import.* Concern.

Cres.   Night hath been too brief.
Tro. Beshrew the witch! with venomous wights
    she stays
As tediously as hell, but flies the grasps of love
With wings more momentary-swift than thought.
You will catch cold, and curse me.
Cres.   Prithee, tarry:
You men will never tarry.
O foolish Cressid! I might have still held off,
And then you would have tarried. Hark! there's
    one up.
Pan. [*Within*] What, 's all the doors open here?
Tro. It is your uncle.   20
Cres. A pestilence on him! now will he be
    mocking:
I shall have such a life!

Enter PANDARUS.

Pan. How now, how now! how go maiden-
heads? Here, you maid! where's my cousin
Cressid?
Cres. Go hang yourself, you naughty mocking
    uncle!
You bring me to do, and then you flout me too.
Pan. To do what? to do what? let her say
what: what have I brought you to do?
Cres. Come, come, beshrew your heart! you'll
    ne'er be good,   30
Nor suffer others.
Pan. Ha, ha! Alas, poor wretch! ah, poor
● capocchia! hast not slept to-night? would he not,
● a naughty man, let it sleep? a bugbear take him!
Cres. Did not I tell you? Would he were
    knock'd i' the head! [*Knocking within.*
Who's that at door? good uncle, go and see.
My lord, come you again into my chamber:
You smile and mock me, as if I meant naughtily.
Tro. Ha, ha!   39
Cres. Come, you are deceived, I think of no
    such thing. [*Knocking within.*
How earnestly they knock! Pray you, come in:
I would not for half Troy have you seen here.
                    [*Exeunt Troilus and Cressida.*
Pan. Who's there? what's the matter? will
you beat down the door? How now! what's the
matter?

Enter ÆNEAS.

Æne. Good morrow, lord, good morrow.
Pan. Who's there? my Lord Æneas! By my
    troth,
I knew you not: what news with you so early?
Æne. Is not Prince Troilus here?
Pan. Here! what should he do here?   50
Æne. Come, he is here, my lord; do not
    deny him:
● It doth import him much to speak with me.
Pan. Is he here, say you? 'tis more than I
know, I'll be sworn: for my own part, I came in
late. What should he do here?
Æne. Who!—nay, then: come, come, you'll
do him wrong ere you're ware: you'll be so
true to him, to be false to him: do not you know
of him, but yet go fetch him hither; go.

Re-enter TROILUS.

Tro. How now! what's the matter?   60

Æne. My lord, I scarce have leisure to
      salute you,
My matter is so rash : there is at hand
Paris your brother, and Deiphobus,
The Grecian Diomed, and our Antenor
Deliver'd to us ; and for him forthwith,
Ere the first sacrifice, within this hour,
We must give up to Diomedes' hand
The Lady Cressida.
      Tro.   Is it so concluded?
      Æne. By Priam and the general state of
      Troy :
They are at hand and ready to effect it.   70
      Tro. How my achievements mock me !
I will go meet them : and, my Lord Æneas,
We met by chance ; you did not find me here.
      Æne. Good, good, my lord ; the secrets of
      nature
Have not more gift in taciturnity.
                    [*Exeunt Troilus and Æneas.*
      Pan. Is 't possible? no sooner got but lost?
The devil take Antenor ! the young prince will
go mad : a plague upon Antenor ! I would they
had broke 's neck !

Re-enter CRESSIDA.

      Cres. How now ! what's the matter? who
was here?   81
      Pan. Ah, ah !
      Cres. Why sigh you so profoundly? where 's
my lord? gone ! Tell me, sweet uncle, what's
the matter?
      Pan. Would I were as deep under the earth
as I am above !
      Cres. O the gods ! what's the matter?
      Pan. Prithee, get thee in : would thou hadst
ne'er been born ! I knew thou wouldst be his
death. O, poor gentleman ! A plague upon
Antenor !
      Cres. Good uncle, I beseech you, on my
knees I beseech you, what's the matter?
      Pan. Thou must be gone, wench, thou must
be gone ; thou art changed for Antenor : thou
must to thy father, and be gone from Troilus :
'twill be his death ; 'twill be his bane ; he cannot
bear it.
      Cres. O you immortal gods ! I will not go.
      Pan. Thou must.   101
      Cres. I will not, uncle : I have forgot my
      father ;
I know no touch of consanguinity ;
No kin, no love, no blood, no soul so near me
As the sweet Troilus. O you gods divine !
Make Cressid's name the very crown of false-
      hood,
If ever she leave Troilus ! Time, force, and
      death,
Do to this body what extremes you can ;
But the strong base and building of my love
Is as the very centre of the earth,   110
Drawing all things to it. I 'll go in and weep,—
      Pan. Do, do.
      Cres. Tear my bright hair and scratch my
      praised cheeks,
Crack my clear voice with sobs and break my
      heart
With sounding Troilus. I will not go from Troy.
                              [*Exeunt.*

4 *violenteth*. Rages.

14 *spectacles*. With a pun on the meanings of 'sights' and 'glasses'.

35 *injury of chance*. Bad luck.

Edith Evans as Cressida, English Stage Society production, London, 1912–1913

SCENE III. *The same. Street before Pandarus' house.*

Enter PARIS, TROILUS, ÆNEAS, DEIPHOBUS, ANTENOR, *and* DIOMEDES.

Par. It is great morning, and the hour prefix'd
Of her delivery to this valiant Greek
Comes fast upon.   Good my brother Troilus,
Tell you the lady what she is to do,
And haste her to the purpose.
Tro.   Walk into her house;
I'll bring her to the Grecian presently:
And to his hand when I deliver her,
Think it an altar, and thy brother Troilus
A priest there offering to it his own heart.   [*Exit.*
Par. I know what 'tis to love;   10
And would, as I shall pity, I could help!
Please you walk in, my lords.   [*Exeunt.*

SCENE IV. *The same. Pandarus' house.*

Enter PANDARUS *and* CRESSIDA.

Pan. Be moderate, be moderate.
Cres. Why tell you me of moderation?
The grief is fine, full, perfect, that I taste,
And violenteth in a sense as strong
As that which causeth it: how can I moderate it?
If I could temporise with my affection,
Or brew it to a weak and colder palate,
The like allayment could I give my grief:
My love admits no qualifying dross;
No more my grief, in such a precious loss.   10
Pan. Here, here, here he comes.

Enter TROILUS.

Ah, sweet ducks!
Cres. O Troilus! Troilus! [*Embracing him.*
Pan. What a pair of spectacles is here! Let me embrace too.   'O heart,' as the goodly saying is,

   '—— O heart, heavy heart,
      Why sigh'st thou without breaking?'
where he answers again,
      'Because thou canst not ease thy smart 20
      By friendship nor by speaking.'
There was never a truer rhyme.   Let us cast away nothing, for we may live to have need of such a verse: we see it, we see it.   How now, lambs?
Tro. Cressid, I love thee in so strain'd a purity,
That the bless'd gods, as angry with my fancy,
More bright in zeal than the devotion which
Cold lips blow to their deities, take thee from me.
Cres. Have the gods envy?   30
Pan. Ay, ay, ay, ay; 'tis too plain a case.
Cres. And is it true that I must go from Troy?
Tro. A hateful truth.
Cres.   What, and from Troilus too?
Tro. From Troy and Troilus.
Cres.   Is it possible?
Tro. And suddenly; where injury of chance
Puts back leave-taking, justles roughly by
All time of pause, rudely beguiles our lips

Of all rejoindure, forcibly prevents
Our lock'd embrasures, strangles our dear vows
Even in the birth of our own labouring breath : 40
We two, that with so many thousand sighs
Did buy each other, must poorly sell ourselves
With the rude brevity and discharge of one.
Injurious time now with a robber's haste
Crams his rich thievery up, he knows not how :
As many farewells as be stars in heaven,
● With distinct breath and consign'd kisses to
    them,
He fumbles up into a loose adieu,
And scants us with a single famish'd kiss,
Distasted with the salt of broken tears.   50
    Æne. [*Within*] My lord, is the lady ready?
●   *Tro.* Hark! you are call'd : some say the
    Genius so
Cries 'come' to him that instantly must die.
Bid them have patience ; she shall come anon.
    Pan. Where are my tears? rain, to lay this
wind, or my heart will be blown up by the root.
                      [*Exit.*

    Cres. I must then to the Grecians?
    Tro.   No remedy.
    Cres. A woful Cressid 'mongst the merry
    Greeks!
When shall we see again?
    Tro. Hear me, my love : be thou but true
    of heart,—   60
    Cres. I true! how now! what wicked deem
    is this?
    Tro. Nay, we must use expostulation kindly,
For it is parting from us :
I speak not 'be thou true,' as fearing thee,
● For I will throw my glove to Death himself,
● That there's no maculation in thy heart :
But 'be thou true,' say I, to fashion in
My sequent protestation ; be thou true,
And I will see thee.
    Cres. O, you shall be exposed, my lord, to
    dangers   70
As infinite as imminent! but I'll be true.
    Tro. And I'll grow friend with danger. Wear
    this sleeve.
    Cres. And you this glove. When shall I
    see you?
    Tro. I will corrupt the Grecian sentinels,
To give thee nightly visitation.
But yet be true.
    Cres.   O heavens! 'be true' again!
    Tro. Hear why I speak it, love :
The Grecian youths are full of quality ;
They're loving, well composed with gifts of
    nature,
Flowing and swelling o'er with arts and ex-
    ercise :   80
● How novelty may move, and parts with person,
Alas, a kind of godly jealousy—
Which, I beseech you, call a virtuous sin—
Makes me afeard.
    Cres.   O heavens! you love me not.
    Tro. Die I a villain, then!
In this I do not call your faith in question
So mainly as my merit : I cannot sing,
● Nor heel the high lavolt, nor sweeten talk,
Nor play at subtle games ; fair virtues all,
● To which the Grecians are most prompt and
    pregnant :   90
But I can tell that in each grace of these

47 *With distinct . . . them.* Each separate 'farewell' with
an individual kiss.

52 *Genius.* A guardian spirit.

Troilus: 'Hear me, my love : be thou but true of heart'.
Engraving by Kenny Meadows from Barry Cornwall's
The Complete Works of Shakspere, 1857–1859

65 *throw my glove.* Challenge.

66 *maculation.* Stain.

81 *parts.* Talents.

88 *lavolt.* A lively dance for two people.

90 *pregnant.* Ready.

134 *I'll answer to my lust.* I'll do as I please.

139 *brave.* Boast.

Cressida leaves Troilus to go with Diomed. Woodcut by Edward Burne-Jones, from William Morris's *Kelmscott Chaucer*, 1896

There lurks a still and dumb-discoursive devil
That tempts most cunningly: but be not tempted.
  Cres. Do you think I will?
  Tro. No.
But something may be done that we will not:
And sometimes we are devils to ourselves,
When we will tempt the frailty of our powers,
Presuming on their changeful potency.
  Æne. [*Within*] Nay, good my lord,—
  Tro.   Come, kiss; and let us part. 100
  Par. [*Within*] Brother Troilus!
  Tro.   Good brother, come you hither;
And bring Æneas and the Grecian with you.
  Cres. My lord, will you be true?
  Tro. Who, I? alas, it is my vice, my fault:
Whiles others fish with craft for great opinion,
I with great truth catch mere simplicity;
Whilst some with cunning gild their copper
    crowns,
With truth and plainness I do wear mine bare.
Fear not my truth: the moral of my wit
Is 'plain and true;' there's all the reach of it. 110

Enter ÆNEAS, PARIS, ANTENOR, DEIPHOBUS,
    and DIOMEDES.

Welcome, Sir Diomed! here is the lady
Which for Antenor we deliver you:
At the port, lord, I'll give her to thy hand;
And by the way possess thee what she is.
Entreat her fair; and, by my soul, fair Greek,
If e'er thou stand at mercy of my sword,
Name Cressid, and thy life shall be as safe
As Priam is in Ilion.
  Dio.   Fair Lady Cressid,
So please you, save the thanks this prince
    expects:
The lustre in your eye, heaven in your cheek, 120
Pleads your fair usage; and to Diomed
You shall be mistress, and command him wholly.
  Tro. Grecian, thou dost not use me cour-
    teously,
To shame the zeal of my petition to thee
In praising her: I tell thee, lord of Greece,
She is as far high-soaring o'er thy praises
As thou unworthy to be call'd her servant.
I charge thee use her well, even for my charge;
For, by the dreadful Pluto, if thou dost not,
Though the great bulk Achilles be thy guard, 130
I'll cut thy throat.
  Dio.   O, be not moved, Prince Troilus:
Let me be privileged by my place and message,
To be a speaker free; when I am hence,
● I'll answer to my lust: and know you, lord,
I'll nothing do on charge: to her own worth
She shall be prized; but that you say 'be't so,'
I'll speak it in my spirit and honour, 'no.'
  Tro. Come, to the port. I'll tell thee, Diomed,
● This brave shall oft make thee to hide thy head.
Lady, give me your hand, and, as we walk, 140
To our own selves bend we our needful talk.
    [*Exeunt Troilus, Cressida, and Diomedes.*
                [*Trumpet within.*
  Par. Hark! Hector's trumpet.
  Æne.   How have we spent this morning!
The prince must think me tardy and remiss,
That swore to ride before him to the field.
  Par. 'Tis Troilus' fault: come, come, to field
    with him.

Dei. Let us make ready straight.
 Æne. Yea, with a bridegroom's fresh alacrity,
Let us address to tend on Hector's heels:
The glory of our Troy doth this day lie   149
On his fair worth and single chivalry. [*Exeunt.*

SCENE V. *The Grecian camp. Lists set out.*

Enter AJAX, *armed;* AGAMEMNON, ACHILLES,
PATROCLUS, MENELAUS, ULYSSES, NESTOR,
and others.

 • *Agam.* Here art thou in appointment fresh
      and fair,
 • Anticipating time with starting courage.
Give with thy trumpet a loud note to Troy,
Thou dreadful Ajax; that the appalled air
May pierce the head of the great combatant
And hale him hither.
 Ajax.   Thou, trumpet, there's my purse.
Now crack thy lungs, and split thy brazen pipe:
 • Blow, villain, till thy sphered bias cheek
 • Outswell the colic of puff'd Aquilon:
Come, stretch thy chest, and let thy eyes spout
      blood;   10
Thou blow'st for Hector.   [*Trumpet sounds.*
 Ulyss. No trumpet answers.
 Achil.   'Tis but early days.
 Agam. Is not yond Diomed, with Calchas'
      daughter?
 Ulyss. 'Tis he, I ken the manner of his gait;
He rises on the toe: that spirit of his
In aspiration lifts him from the earth.

Enter DIOMEDES, *with* CRESSIDA.

 Agam. Is this the Lady Cressid?
 Dio.   Even she.
 Agam. Most dearly welcome to the Greeks,
      sweet lady.
 Nest. Our general doth salute you with a kiss.
 Ulyss. Yet is the kindness but particular; 20
'Twere better she were kiss'd in general.
 Nest. And very courtly counsel: I'll begin.
So much for Nestor.
 Achil. I'll take that winter from your lips,
      fair lady: ·
Achilles bids you welcome.
 Men. I had good argument for kissing once.
 Patr. But that's no argument for kissing now;
 • For thus popp'd Paris in his hardiment,
And parted thus you and your argument.
 Ulyss. O deadly gall, and theme of all our
      scorns!   30
For which we lose our heads to gild his horns.
 Patr. The first was Menelaus' kiss; this,
      mine:
Patroclus kisses you.
 Men. O, this is trim!
 Patr. Paris and I kiss evermore for him.
 Men. I'll have my kiss, sir. Lady, by your
      leave.
 Cres. In kissing, do you render or receive?
 • *Patr.* Both take and give.
 Cres.   I'll make my match to live.
The kiss you take is better than you give;
Therefore no kiss.
 • *Men.* I'll give you boot, I'll give you three
      for one.   40

1 *appointment.* Equipment.

2 *starting.* Enthusiastic.

8 *bias.* Puffed out.

9 *Aquilon.* The north wind.

Cressida (Rosemary Harris) is introduced to the Greek
commanders, Old Vic Theatre, London, 1956

28 *hardiment.* Boldness.

37 *I'll make . . . live.* I will wager my life.

40 *boot.* Odds.

45 *filip.* Tap.

Ulysses: 'May I, sweet lady, beg a kiss of you?' Engraving by Kenny Meadows from Barry Cornwall's *The Works of Shakspere,* 1846

62 *sluttish spoils of opportunity.* Promiscuous women who succumb to every opportunity.

73 *securely.* Over-confidently.

87 *maiden.* Bloodless.

Cres. You're an odd man; give even, or give none.

Men. An odd man, lady! every man is odd.

Cres. No, Paris is not; for you know 'tis true,
That you are odd, and he is even with you.

● *Men.* You fillip me o' the head.

Cres.   No, I'll be sworn.

Ulyss. It were no match, your nail against his horn.
May I, sweet lady, beg a kiss of you?

Cres. You may.

Ulyss.   I do desire it.

Cres.   Why, beg, then.

Ulyss. Why then for Venus' sake, give me a kiss,
When Helen is a maid again, and his.   50

Cres. I am your debtor, claim it when 'tis due.

Ulyss. Never's my day, and then a kiss of you.

Dio. Lady, a word: I'll bring you to your father.   [*Exit with Cressida.*

Nest. A woman of quick sense.

Ulyss.   Fie, fie upon her!
There's language in her eye, her cheek, her lip,
Nay, her foot speaks; her wanton spirits look out
At every joint and motive of her body.
O, these encounterers, so glib of tongue,
That give accosting welcome ere it comes,
And wide unclasp the tables of their thoughts 60
To every ticklish reader! set them down
● For sluttish spoils of opportunity
And daughters of the game.   [*Trumpet within.*

All. The Trojans' trumpet.

Agam.   Yonder comes the troop.

Enter HECTOR, *armed;* ÆNEAS, TROILUS, *and other* Trojans, *with* Attendants.

Æne. Hail, all you state of Greece! what shall be done
To him that victory commands? or do you purpose
A victor shall be known? will you the knights
Shall to the edge of all extremity
Pursue each other, or shall be divided
By any voice or order of the field?   70
Hector bade ask.

Agam.   Which way would Hector have it?

Æne. He cares not; he'll obey conditions.

● *Achil.* 'Tis done like Hector; but securely done,
A little proudly, and great deal misprizing
The knight opposed.

Æne.   If not Achilles, sir,
What is your name?

Achil.   If not Achilles, nothing.

Æne. Therefore Achilles: but, whate'er, know this:
In the extremity of great and little,
Valour and pride excel themselves in Hector;
The one almost as infinite as all,   80
The other blank as nothing.   Weigh him well,
And that which looks like pride is courtesy.
This Ajax is half made of Hector's blood:
In love whereof, half Hector stays at home;
Half heart, half hand, half Hector comes to seek
This blended knight, half Trojan and half Greek.

● *Achil.* A maiden battle, then? O, I perceive you.

Re-enter DIOMEDES.

Agam.   Here is Sir Diomed.   Go, gentle
   knight,
Stand by our Ajax: as you and Lord Æneas
Consent upon the order of their fight,   90
So be it; either to the uttermost,
• Or else a breath: the combatants being kin
Half stints their strife before their strokes begin.
             [*Ajax and Hector enter the lists.*
Ulyss.   They are opposed already.
Agam.   What Trojan is that same that looks
   so heavy?
Ulyss.   The youngest son of Priam, a true
   knight,
Not yet mature, yet matchless, firm of word,
• Speaking in deeds and deedless in his tongue;
Not soon provoked nor being provoked soon
   calm'd;
His heart and hand both open and both free; 100
For what he has he gives, what thinks he shows;
Yet gives he not till judgement guide his bounty,
Nor dignifies an impair thought with breath;
Manly as Hector, but more dangerous;
• For Hector in his blaze of wrath subscribes
To tender objects, but he in heat of action
Is more vindicative than jealous love:
They call him Troilus, and on him erect
A second hope, as fairly built as Hector.
Thus says Æneas; one that knows the youth 110
• Even to his inches, and with private soul
Did in great Ilion thus translate him to me.
          [*Alarum.   Hector and Ajax fight.*

Agam.   They are in action.
Nest.   Now, Ajax, hold thine own!
Tro.   Hector, thou sleep'st;
Awake thee!
Agam.   His blows are well disposed: there,
   Ajax!
Dio.   You must no more.   [*Trumpets cease.*
Æne.   Princes, enough, so please you.
Ajax.   I am not warm yet; let us fight again.
Dio.   As Hector pleases.
Hect.   Why, then will I no more:
Thou art, great lord, my father's sister's son, 120
A cousin-german to great Priam's seed;
The obligation of our blood forbids
A gory emulation 'twixt us twain:
Were thy commixtion Greek and Trojan so
That thou couldst say 'This hand is Grecian all,
And this is Trojan; the sinews of this leg
All Greek, and this all Troy; my mother's blood
Runs on the dexter cheek, and this sinister
Bounds in my father's;' by Jove multipotent,
Thou shouldst not bear from me a Greekish
   member 130
Wherein my sword had not impressure made
Of our rank feud: but the just gods gainsay
That any drop thou borrow'dst from thy mother,
My sacred aunt, should by my mortal sword
Be drain'd!   Let me embrace thee, Ajax:
By him that thunders, thou hast lusty arms;
Hector would have them fall upon him thus:
Cousin, all honour to thee!
Ajax.   I thank thee, Hector:
Thou art too gentle and too free a man:
I came to kill thee, cousin, and bear hence 140
A great addition earned in thy death.
• *Hect.*   Not Neoptolemus so mirable,

92 *breath.* Exercise.

98 *deedless in his tongue.* Modest in word.

105-106 *subscribes . . . objects.* Has compassion for the
weak.

111 *with private soul.* Secretly.

Hector and Ajax fight. Engraving by John Flaxman from
Homer's *Iliad*, translated by Alexander Pope, 1793
edition

142 *Neoptolemus.* Although usually applied to Achilles'
son Pyrrhus, here it is probably Achilles himself.
mirable. Marvellous.

143 *Oyes.* The cry of heralds to secure attention.

156 *expecters.* The waiting Trojans.

162 *portly.* Imposing.

169 *hollow bias-drawing.* Insincere flattery.

179 *quondam.* Former.

Nestor: 'As hot as Perseus, spur thy Phrygian steed . . .'
Pegasus, the winged horse of Perseus. From a 19th
century engraving

●On whose bright crest Fame with her loud'st
  Oyes
Cries 'This is he,' could promise to himself
A thought of added honour torn from Hector.
 Æne. There is expectance here from both the
  sides,
What further you will do.
 Hect.   We'll answer it;
The issue is embracement: Ajax, farewell.
 Ajax. If I might in entreaties find success—
As seld I have the chance—I would desire 150
My famous cousin to our Grecian tents.
 Dio. 'Tis Agamemnon's wish, and great
  Achilles
Doth long to see unarm'd the valiant Hector.
 Hect. Æneas, call my brother Troilus to me,
And signify this loving interview
●To the expecters of our Trojan part;
Desire them home. Give me thy hand, my
  cousin;
I will go eat with thee and see your knights.
 Ajax. Great Agamemnon comes to meet us
  here.
 Hect. The worthiest of them tell me name by
  name;   160
But for Achilles, mine own searching eyes
●Shall find him by his large and portly size.
 Agam. Worthy of arms! as welcome as to one
That would be rid of such an enemy;
But that's no welcome: understand more clear,
What's past and what's to come is strew'd with
  husks
And formless ruin of oblivion;
But in this extant moment, faith and troth,
●Strain'd purely from all hollow bias-drawing,
Bids thee, with most divine integrity, 170
From heart of very heart, great Hector, welcome.
 Hect. I thank thee, most imperious Aga-
  memnon.
 Agam. [*To Troilus*] My well-famed lord of
  Troy, no less to you.
 Men. Let me confirm my princely brother's
  greeting:
You brace of warlike brothers, welcome hither.
 Hect. Who must we answer?
 Æne.   The noble Menelaus.
 Hect. O, you, my lord? by Mars his gauntlet,
  thanks!
Mock not, that I affect the untraded oath;
●Your quondam wife swears still by Venus' glove:
She's well, but bade me not commend her to you.
 Men. Name her not now, sir; she's a deadly
  theme.   181
 Hect. O, pardon; I offend.
 Nest. I have, thou gallant Trojan, seen thee oft
Labouring for destiny make cruel way
Through ranks of Greekish youth, and I have
  seen thee,
As hot as Perseus, spur thy Phrygian steed,
Despising many forfeits and subduements,
When thou hast hung thy advanced sword i' the
  air,
Not letting it decline on the declined,
That I have said to some my standers by 190
'Lo, Jupiter is yonder, dealing life!'
And I have seen thee pause and take thy breath,
When that a ring of Greeks have hemm'd thee in,
Like an Olympian wrestling: this have I seen;
But this thy countenance, still lock'd in steel,

•I never saw till now.   I knew thy grandsire,
And once fought with him : he was a soldier good ;
But, by great Mars, the captain of us all,
Never like thee.   Let an old man embrace thee ;
And, worthy warrior, welcome to our tents.   200
 Æne. 'Tis the old Nestor.
 Hect. Let me embrace thee, good old chro-
  nicle,
That hast so long walk'd hand in hand with time :
Most reverend Nestor, I am glad to clasp thee.
 Nest. I would my arms could match thee in
  contention,
As they contend with thee in courtesy.
 Hect. I would they could.
 Nest. Ha !
By this white beard, I'ld fight with thee to-
  morrow.   209
Well, welcome, welcome !—I have seen the time.
 Ulyss. I wonder now how yonder city stands
When we have here her base and pillar by us.
• *Hect.* I know your favour, Lord Ulysses, well.
Ah, sir, there's many a Greek and Trojan dead,
Since first I saw yourself and Diomed
In Ilion, on your Greekish embassy.
 Ulyss. Sir, I foretold you then what would
  ensue :
My prophecy is but half his journey yet ;
For yonder walls, that pertly front your town,
Yond towers, whose wanton tops do buss the
  clouds,   220
Must kiss their own feet.
 Hect.   I must not believe you :
There they stand yet, and modestly I think,
The fall of every Phrygian stone will cost
A drop of Grecian blood : the end crowns all,
And that old common arbitrator, Time,
Will one day end it.
 Ulyss.   So to him we leave it.
Most gentle and most valiant Hector, welcome :
After the general, I beseech you next
To feast with me and see me at my tent.
 Achil. I shall forestall thee, Lord Ulysses,
  thou !   230
Now, Hector, I have fed mine eyes on thee ;
I have with exact view perused thee, Hector,
•And quoted joint by joint.
 Hect.   Is this Achilles?
 Achil. I am Achilles.
 Hect. Stand fair, I pray thee : let me look on
  thee.
 Achil. Behold thy fill.
 Hect.   Nay, I have done already.
 Achil. Thou art too brief : I will the second
  time,
As I would buy thee, view thee limb by limb.
 Hect. O, like a book of sport thou'lt read
  me o'er ;   239
But there's more in me than thou understand'st.
Why dost thou so oppress me with thine eye?
 Achil. Tell me, you heavens, in which part
  of his body
Shall I destroy him? whether there, or there, or
  there?
That I may give the local wound a name
And make distinct the very breach whereout
Hector's great spirit flew : answer me, heavens !
 Hect. It would discredit the blest gods,
  proud man,
To answer such a question : stand again :

196 *grandsire*. Laomedon.

213 *favour*. Face.

233 *quoted*. Scrutinized.

Costume design for Achilles by Malcolm Pride, Stratford-upon-Avon, 1954

255 *stithied*. Forged.

267 *pelting*. Paltry.

269 *fell*. Fierce.

272 *convive*. Feast.

'Think'st thou to catch my life so pleasantly
As to prenominate in nice conjecture   250
Where thou wilt hit me dead?
   Achil.   I tell thee, yea.
   Hect.   Wert thou an oracle to tell me so,
I'ld not believe thee. Henceforth guard thee
    well;
For I'll not kill thee there, nor there, nor there;
● But, by the forge that stithied Mars his helm,
I'll kill thee every where, yea, o'er and o'er.
You wisest Grecians, pardon me this brag;
His insolence draws folly from my lips;
But I'll endeavour deeds to match these words,
Or may I never—
   Ajax.   Do not chafe thee, cousin: 260
And you, Achilles, let these threats alone,
Till accident or purpose bring you to't:
You may have every day enough of Hector,
If you have stomach; the general state, I fear,
Can scarce entreat you to be odd with him.
   Hect.   I pray you, let us see you in the field:
● We have had pelting wars, since you refused
The Grecians' cause.
   Achil.   Dost thou entreat me, Hector?
● To-morrow do I meet thee, fell as death;
To-night all friends.
   Hect.   Thy hand upon that match. 270
   Agam.   First, all you peers of Greece, go to
    my tent;
● There in the full convive we: afterwards,
As Hector's leisure and your bounties shall
Concur together, severally entreat him.
Beat loud the tabourines, let the trumpets blow,
That this great soldier may his welcome know.
       [*Exeunt all except Troilus and Ulysses.*
   Tro.   My Lord Ulysses, tell me, I beseech
    you,
In what place of the field doth Calchas keep?
   Ulyss.   At Menelaus' tent, most princely
    Troilus:
There Diomed doth feast with him to-night; 280
Who neither looks upon the heaven nor earth,
But gives all gaze and bent of amorous view
On the fair Cressid.
   Tro.   Shall I, sweet lord, be bound to you so
    much,
After we part from Agamemnon's tent,
To bring me thither?
   Ulyss.   You shall command me, sir.
As gentle tell me, of what honour was
This Cressida in Troy? Had she no lover there
That wails her absence?
   Tro.   O, sir, to such as boasting show their
    scars   290
A mock is due. Will you walk on, my lord?
She was beloved, she loved; she is, and doth:
But still sweet love is food for fortune's tooth.
                           [*Exeunt.*

ACT V.

Scene I. *The Grecian camp. Before Achilles'
tent.*

Enter Achilles *and* Patroclus.

   Achil.   I'll heat his blood with Greekish wine
    to-night,
Which with my scimitar I'll cool to-morrow.
Patroclus, let us feast him to the height.

Patr.   Here comes Thersites.

Enter THERSITES.

Achil.   How now, thou core of envy!
Thou crusty batch of nature, what's the news?

Ther.   Why, thou picture of what thou seemest,
and idol of idiot-worshippers, here's a letter for
thee.

Achil.   From whence, fragment?

Ther.   Why, thou full dish of fool, from Troy.

Patr.   Who keeps the tent now?   11

● *Ther.*   The surgeon's box, or the patient's
wound.

Patr.   Well said, adversity! and what need
these tricks?

Ther.   Prithee, be silent, boy; I profit not by
thy talk: thou art thought to be Achilles' male
varlet.

Patr.   Male varlet, you rogue! what's that?

Ther.   Why, his masculine whore.   Now, the
rotten diseases of the south, the guts-griping,
● ruptures, catarrhs, loads o' gravel i' the back,
lethargies, cold palsies, raw eyes, dirt-rotten
● livers, wheezing lungs, bladders full of imposthume, sciaticas, limekilns i' the palm, incurable
● bone-ache, and the rivelled fee-simple of the
tetter, take and take again such preposterous
discoveries!

Patr.   Why, thou damnable box of envy, thou,
what meanest thou to curse thus?   30

Ther.   Do I curse thee?

● *Patr.*   Why, no, you ruinous butt, you whoreson indistinguishable cur, no.

Ther.   No! why art thou then exasperate,
● thou idle immaterial skein of sleave-silk, thou
green sarcenet flap for a sore eye, thou tassel of
a prodigal's purse, thou?   Ah, how the poor
world is pestered with such waterflies, diminu-
tives of nature!

Patr.   Out, gall!   40

Ther.   Finch-egg!

Achil.   My sweet Patroclus, I am thwarted
          quite
From my great purpose in to-morrow's battle.
Here is a letter from Queen Hecuba,
A token from her daughter, my fair love,
Both taxing me and gaging me to keep
An oath that I have sworn.   I will not break it:
Fall Greeks; fail fame; honour or go or stay;
My major vow lies here, this I'll obey.
Come, come, Thersites, help to trim my tent: 50
This night in banqueting must all be spent.
Away, Patroclus!

[*Exeunt Achilles and Patroclus.*

Ther.   With too much blood and too little
brain, these two may run mad; but, if with too much
brain and too little blood they **do,** I'll be a curer
of madmen.   Here's Agamemnon, an honest
● fellow enough, and one that loves quails; but he
has not so much brain as ear-wax: and the
goodly transformation of Jupiter there, his brother, the bull,—the primitive statue, and oblique
memorial of cuckolds; a thrifty shoeing-horn in
a chain, hanging at his brother's leg,—to what
form but that he is, should wit larded with malice
and malice forced with wit turn him to?   To an
ass, were nothing; he is both ass and ox: to an
ox, were nothing; he is both ox and ass.   To be
● a dog, a mule, a cat, a fitchew, a toad, a lizard,

12 *The surgeon's . . . wound.* Thersites quibbles on
'tent' meaning a probe for a wound.

22 *gravel i' the back.* Stones in the kidney.

24-25 *imposthume.* Abscess. *limekilns.* Burnings.

26-27 *rivelled . . . tetter.* Wrinkled, chronic state of skin
eruption.

32 *ruinous butt.* Ruined cask.

35 *sleave-silk.* Floss silk.

36 *sarcenet.* Silk.

57 *quails.* Harlots.

67 *fitchew.* Fitch or polecat.

68 *puttock.* Kite.

82 *draught.* Cesspool.

102 *leave to see.* Not see.

Elspeth Keith as Thersites, Elizabethan Stage Society, London, 1912–1913

an owl, a puttock, or a herring without a roe, I would not care; but to be Menelaus! I would conspire against destiny.   Ask me not what I would be, if I were not Thersites; for I care not to be the louse of a lazar, so I were not Menelaus. Hoy-day! spirits and fires!

Enter HECTOR, TROILUS, AJAX, AGAMEMNON, ULYSSES, NESTOR, MENELAUS, *and* DIO-MEDES, *with lights.*

Agam.   We go wrong, we go wrong.
Ajax.   No, yonder 'tis; There, where we see the lights.
Hect.   I trouble you.
Ajax.   No, not a whit.
Ulyss.   Here comes himself to guide you.

Re-enter ACHILLES.

Achil.   Welcome, brave Hector; welcome, princes all.
Agam.   So now, fair Prince of Troy, I bid good night.
Ajax commands the guard to tend on you.
Hect.   Thanks and good night to the Greeks' general.   80
Men.   Good night, my lord.
Hect.   Good night, sweet Lord Menelaus.
Ther.   Sweet draught: 'sweet' quoth 'a! sweet sink, sweet sewer.
Achil.   Good night and welcome, both at once, to those
That go or tarry.
Agam.   Good night.
           [*Exeunt Agamemnon and Menelaus.*
Achil.   Old Nestor tarries; and you too, Diomed,
Keep Hector company an hour or two.
Dio.   I cannot, lord; I have important business,
The tide whereof is now.   Good night, great Hector.   90
Hect.   Give me your hand.
Ulyss.   [*Aside to Troilus*] Follow his torch; he goes to Calchas' tent:
I'll keep you company.
Tro.   Sweet sir, you honour me.
Hect.   And so, good night.
                 [*Exit Diomedes; Ulysses and
                               Troilus following.*
Achil.   Come, come, enter my tent.
[*Exeunt Achilles, Hector, Ajax, and Nestor.*
Ther.   That same Diomed's a false-hearted rogue, a most unjust knave; I will no more trust him when he leers than I will a serpent when he hisses: he will spend his mouth, and promise, like Brabbler the hound; but when he performs, astronomers foretell it; it is prodigious, there will come some change; the sun borrows of the moon, when Diomed keeps his word.   I will rather leave to see Hector, than not to dog him: they say he keeps a Trojan drab, and uses the traitor Calchas' tent: I'll after.   Nothing but lechery! all incontinent varlets!   [*Exit.*

SCENE II.   *The same.   Before Calchas' tent.*

Enter DIOMEDES.

Dio.   What, are you up here, ho? speak.
Cal.   [*Within*] Who calls?

Dio. Diomed. Calchas, I think. Where's
    your daughter?
Cal. [*Within*] She comes to you.

Enter TROILUS *and* ULYSSES, *at a distance;*
after them, THERSITES.

Ulyss. Stand where the torch may not dis-
    cover us.

Enter CRESSIDA.

Tro. Cressid comes forth to him.
Dio.   How now, my charge!
Cres. Now, my sweet guardian! Hark, a
    word with you.   [*Whispers.*
Tro. Yea, so familiar!
Ulyss. She will sing any man at first sight.
Ther. And any man may sing her, if he can
● take her cliff; she's noted.   11
Dio. Will you remember?
Cres. Remember! yes.
Dio. Nay, but do, then;
And let your mind be coupled with your words.
Tro. What should she remember?
Ulyss. List.
Cres. Sweet honey Greek, tempt me no more
    to folly.
Ther. Roguery!
Dio. Nay, then,—   20
Cres. I'll tell you what,—
Dio. Foh, foh! come, tell a pin: you are for-
    sworn.
Cres. In faith, I cannot: what would you
    have me do?
Ther. A juggling trick,—to be secretly open.
Dio. What did you swear you would bestow
    on me?
Cres. I prithee, do not hold me to mine oath;
Bid me do any thing but that, sweet Greek.
Dio. Good night.
Tro. Hold, patience!
Ulyss. How now, Trojan!   30
Cres. Diomed,—
Dio. No, no, good night: I'll be your fool
    no more.
Tro. Thy better must.
Cres. Hark, one word in your ear.
Tro. O plague and madness!
Ulyss. You are moved, prince; let us depart,
    I pray you,
Lest your displeasure should enlarge itself
To wrathful terms: this place is dangerous;
The time right deadly; I beseech you, go.
Tro. Behold, I pray you!
Ulyss.   Nay, good my lord, go off:
You flow to great distraction; come, my lord. 41
Tro. I pray thee, stay.
Ulyss.   You have not patience; come.
Tro. I pray you, stay; by hell and all hell's
    torments,
I will not speak a word!
Dio.   And so, good night.
Cres. Nay, but you part in anger.
Tro.   Doth that grieve thee?
O wither'd truth!
Ulyss.   Why, how now, lord!
Tro.   By Jove,
I will be patient.
Cres.   Guardian!—why, Greek!
Dio. Foh, foh! adieu; you palter.

11 *cliff.* Clef, a musical symbol with a play on 'cleft', the crotch of the body. *noted.* Notorious, and a pun on music which has been set down.

Cressida: 'Sweet honey Greek, tempt me no more to folly . . .' Engraving from a painting by Angelica Kauffman (1741–1807)

55 *Luxury.* Lechery.

56 *potato.* The sweet potato was believed to sexually excite.

Cressida: 'Here, Diomed, keep this sleeve...' Engraving from Bell's *Works* ... 1773–74

91 *Diana's waiting-women.* The stars.

Cres.   In faith, I do not: come hither once again.
Ulyss.   You shake, my lord, at something:
will you go?   50
You will break out.
Tro.   She strokes his cheek!
Ulyss.   Come, come.
Tro.   Nay, stay; by Jove, I will not speak a word:
There is between my will and all offences
A guard of patience: stay a little while.
• *Ther.*   How the devil Luxury, with his fat
• rump and potato-finger, tickles these together!
Fry, lechery, fry!
Dio.   But will you, then?
Cres.   In faith, I will, la; never trust me else.
Dio.   Give me some token for the surety of it. 60
Cres.   I'll fetch you one.   [*Exit.*
Ulyss.   You have sworn patience.
Tro.   Fear me not, sweet lord;
I will not be myself, nor have cognition
Of what I feel: I am all patience.

Re-enter CRESSIDA.

Ther.   Now the pledge; now, now, now!
Cres.   Here, Diomed, keep this sleeve.
Tro.   O beauty! where is thy faith?
Ulyss.   My lord,—
Tro.   I will be patient; outwardly I will.
Cres.   You look upon that sleeve; behold it well.
He loved me—O false wench!—Give't me again.
Dio.   Whose was't?   71
Cres.   It is no matter, now I have't again.
I will not meet with you to-morrow night:
I prithee, Diomed, visit me no more.
Ther.   Now she sharpens: well said, whet-stone!
Dio.   I shall have it.
Cres.   What, this?
Dio.   Ay, that.
Cres.   O, all you gods! O pretty, pretty pledge!
Thy master now lies thinking in his bed
Of thee and me, and sighs, and takes my glove,
And gives memorial dainty kisses to it,   80
As I kiss thee.   Nay, do not snatch it from me;
He that takes that doth take my heart withal.
Dio.   I had your heart before, this follows it.
Tro.   I did swear patience.
Cres.   You shall not have it, Diomed; faith, you shall not;
I'll give you something else.
Dio.   I will have this: whose was it?
Cres.   It is no matter.
Dio.   Come, tell me whose it was.
Cres.   'Twas one's that loved me better than you will.
But, now you have it, take it.
Dio.   Whose was it? 90
• *Cres.*   By all Diana's waiting-women yond,
And by herself, I will not tell you whose.
Dio.   To-morrow will I wear it on my helm,
And grieve his spirit that dares not challenge it.
Tro.   Wert thou the devil, and worest it on thy horn,
It should be challenged.
Cres.   Well, well, 'tis done, 'tis past: and yet it is not;

I will not keep my word.
Dio.   Why, then, farewell;
Thou never shalt mock Diomed again.
    Cres.   You shall not go: one cannot speak a
        word,   100
But it straight starts you.
    Dio.   I do not like this fooling.
    Ther.   Nor I, by Pluto: but that that likes
not you pleases me best.
    Dio.   What, shall I come? the hour?
    Cres.   Ay, come:—O Jove!—do come:—I
shall be plagued.
    Dio.   Farewell till then.
    Cres.   Good night: I prithee, come.
                              [*Exit Diomedes.*

Troilus, farewell! one eye yet looks on thee;
But with my heart the other eye doth see.
Ah, poor our sex! this fault in us I find,
● The error of our eye directs our mind: 110
What error leads must err; O, then conclude
Minds sway'd by eyes are full of turpitude. [*Exit.*
    Ther.   A proof of strength she could not pub-
        lish more,
Unless she said 'My mind is now turn'd whore.'
    Ulyss.   All's done, my lord.
    Tro.   It is.
    Ulyss.   Why stay we, then?
    Tro.   To make a recordation to my soul
Of every syllable that here was spoke.
But if I tell how these two did co-act,
Shall I not lie in publishing a truth?
Sith yet there is a credence in my heart,   120
An esperance so obstinately strong,
● That doth invert the attest of eyes and ears,
As if those organs had deceptious functions,
Created only to calumniate.
↬ Was Cressid here?
    Ulyss.   I cannot conjure, Trojan.
    Tro.   She was not, sure.
    Ulyss.   Most sure she was.
    Tro.   Why, my negation hath no taste of
        madness.
    Ulyss.   Nor mine, my lord: Cressid was here
        but now.
    Tro.   Let it not be believed for womanhood!
Think, we had mothers; do not give advantage
To stubborn critics, apt, without a theme,   131
● For depravation, to square the general sex
By Cressid's rule: rather think this not Cressid.
    Ulyss.   What hath she done, prince, that can
        soil our mothers?
    Tro.   Nothing at all, unless that this were she.
●   *Ther.*   Will he swagger himself out on 's own
        eyes?
    Tro.   This she? no, this is Diomed's Cressida:
If beauty have a soul, this is not she;
If souls guide vows, if vows be sanctimonies,
If sanctimony be the gods' delight,   140
● If there be rule in unity itself,
● This is not she.   O madness of discourse,
That cause sets up with and against itself!
● Bi-fold authority! where reason can revolt
Without perdition, and loss assume all reason
Without revolt: this is, and is not, Cressid.
Within my soul there doth conduce a fight
Of this strange nature that a thing inseparate
Divides more wider than the sky and earth,
And yet the spacious breadth of this division   150
Admits no orifex for a point as subtle

Diomed: 'What, shall I come? the hour?' Woodcut by
Edward Burne-Jones from William Morris's *Kelmscott
Chaucer*, 1896

110-112   *The error . . . turpitude.* See introduction.

122   *That doth . . . ears.* See introduction.

125   *conjure.* i.e. conjure up spirits.

132   *to square.* To measure.

136   *Will he . . . eyes?* Will he convince himself out of the
evidence of his own eyes?

141   *rule in unity.* The principle that an individual is
indivisible.

142   *discourse.* Reason.

144   *Bi-fold authority.* The double authority of reason.

144-146   *where reason . . . revolt.* Where reason can
rebel against the evidence without unreason (madness),
while lack of trust in the evidence of the senses assumes
itself to be reasonable (cf. Shakespeare on his Dark
Lady in the Sonnets).

152 *Ariachne's . . . woof.* The thread of a spider. Arachne was a weaver whom the jealous Athene turned into a spider.

153 *Instance.* Proof.

158 *orts.* Left-overs.

161 *half attach'd.* Half as much affected.

170 *casque.* Helmet.

173 *Constringed.* Compressed together.

185 *Have with you.* I am ready to go.

Andromache: 'My dreams will, sure, prove ominous . . .'
Engraving by Kenny Meadows from Barry Cornwall's
The Works of Shakspere, 1846

●As Ariachne's broken woof to enter.
●Instance, O instance! strong as Pluto's gates;
Cressid is mine, tied with the bonds of heaven:
Instance, O instance! strong as heaven itself;
The bonds of heaven are slipp'd, dissolved, and
   loosed;
And with another knot, five-finger-tied,
●The fractions of her faith, orts of her love,
The fragments, scraps, the bits and greasy relics
Of her o'er-eaten faith, are bound to Diomed. 160
● *Ulyss.* May worthy Troilus be half attach'd
With that which here his passion doth express?
    Tro. Ay, Greek; and that shall be divulged
    well
In characters as red as Mars his heart
Inflamed with Venus: never did young man fancy
With so eternal and so fix'd a soul.
Hark, Greek: as much as I do Cressid love,
So much by weight hate I her Diomed:
That sleeve is mine that he'll bear on his helm;
●Were it a casque composed by Vulcan's skill, 170
My sword should bite it: not the dreadful spout
Which shipmen do the hurricano call,
●Constringed in mass by the almighty sun,
Shall dizzy with more clamour Neptune's ear
In his descent than shall my prompted sword
Falling on Diomed.
    Ther. He'll tickle it for his concupy.
    Tro. O Cressid! O false Cressid! false, false,
    false!
Let all untruths stand by thy stained name,
And they'll seem glorious.
    Ulyss.   O, contain yourself; 180
Your passion draws ears hither.

Enter ÆNEAS.

    Æne. I have been seeking you this hour, my
    lord:
Hector, by this, is arming him in Troy;
Ajax, your guard, stays to conduct you home.
● *Tro.* Have with you, prince. My courteous
    lord, adieu.
Farewell, revolted fair! and, Diomed,
Stand fast, and wear a castle on thy head!
    Ulyss. I'll bring you to the gates.
    Tro. Accept distracted thanks.
        [*Exeunt Troilus, Æneas, and Ulysses.*
    Ther. Would I could meet that rogue Diomed!
I would croak like a raven; I would bode, I
would bode. Patroclus will give me any thing
for the intelligence of this whore: the parrot will
not do more for an almond than he for a commo-
dious drab. Lechery, lechery; still, wars and
lechery; nothing else holds fashion: a burning
devil take them!   [*Exit.*

SCENE III. *Troy. Before Priam's palace.*

Enter HECTOR and ANDROMACHE.

    And. When was my lord so much ungently
    temper'd,
To stop his ears against admonishment?
Unarm, unarm, and do not fight to-day.
    Hect. You train me to offend you; get you in:
By all the everlasting gods, I'll go!
    And. My dreams will, sure, prove ominous
    to the day.
    Hect. No more, I say.

Enter CASSANDRA.

Cas.   Where is my brother Hector?
And.   Here, sister; arm'd, and bloody in
    intent.
Consort with me in loud and dear petition,
Pursue we him on knees; for I have dream'd 10
Of bloody turbulence, and this whole night
Hath nothing been but shapes and forms of
    slaughter.
Cas. O, 'tis true.
Hect.   Ho! bid my trumpet sound.
Cas. No notes of sally, for the heavens, sweet
    brother.
Hect.   Be gone, I say: the gods have heard
    me swear.
Cas. The gods are deaf to hot and peevish
    vows:
They are polluted offerings, more abhorr'd
Than spotted livers in the sacrifice.
And. O, be persuaded! do not count it holy
To hurt by being just: it is as lawful,   20
For we would give much, to use violent thefts,
And rob in the behalf of charity.
  Cas. It is the purpose that makes strong the
    vow;
But vows to every purpose must not hold:
Unarm, sweet Hector.
Hect.   Hold you still, I say;
● Mine honour keeps the weather of my fate:
Life every man holds dear; but the brave man
Holds honour far more precious-dear than life.

Enter TROILUS.

How now, young man! mean'st thou to fight to-
    day?
  And. Cassandra, call my father to persuade. 30
                         [*Exit Cassandra.*
  Hect. No, faith, young Troilus; doff thy har-
    ness, youth;
I am to-day i' the vein of chivalry:
Let grow thy sinews till their knots be strong,
And tempt not yet the brushes of the war.
Unarm thee, go, and doubt thou not, brave boy,
I'll stand to-day for thee and me and Troy.
  Tro. Brother, you have a vice of mercy in
    you,
Which better fits a lion than a man.
  Hect. What vice is that, good Troilus? chide
    me for it.
  Tro. When many times the captive Grecian
    falls,   40
Even in the fan and wind of your fair sword,
You bid them rise, and live.
  Hect. O, 'tis fair play.
  Tro.   Fool's play, by heaven, Hector.
  Hect. How now! how now!
  Tro.   For the love of all the gods,
Let's leave the hermit pity with our mothers,
And when we have our armours buckled on,
The venom'd vengeance ride upon our swords,
● Spur them to ruthful work, rein them from ruth.
  Hect. Fie, savage, fie!
  Tro.   Hector, then 'tis wars.
  Hect. Troilus, I would not have you fight
    to-day.   50
  Tro. Who should withhold me?
Not fate, obedience, nor the hand of Mars
Beckoning with fiery truncheon my retire;

Hector and Andromache. Engraving by John Flaxman from the 1793 edition of Alexander Pope's translation of Homer's *Iliad*

26 *weather.* The windward, and therefore the safe side.

48 *ruth.* Pity.

86 *antics.* Clowns.

101 *tisick.* Cough.

Not Priamus and Hecuba on knees,
Their eyes o'ergalled with recourse of tears;
Nor you, my brother, with your true sword drawn,
Opposed to hinder me, should stop my way,
But by my ruin.

Re-enter CASSANDRA, *with* PRIAM.

Cas.   Lay hold upon him, Priam, hold him fast:
He is thy crutch; now if thou lose thy stay,   60
Thou on him leaning, and all Troy on thee,
Fall all together.
Pri.   Come, Hector, come, go back:
Thy wife hath dream'd; thy mother hath had
      visions;
Cassandra doth foresee; and I myself
Am like a prophet suddenly enrapt
To tell thee that this day is ominous:
Therefore, come back.
Hect.   Æneas is a-field;
And I do stand engaged to many Greeks,
Even in the faith of valour, to appear
This morning to them.
Pri.   Ay, but thou shalt not go.
Hect.   I must not break my faith.   71
You know me dutiful; therefore, dear sir,
Let me not shame respect; but give me leave
To take that course by your consent and voice,
Which you do here forbid me, royal Priam.
Cas.   O Priam, yield not to him!
And.   Do not, dear father.
Hect.   Andromache, I am offended with you:
Upon the love you bear me, get you in.
                           [*Exit Andromache.*
Tro.   This foolish, dreaming, superstitious girl
Makes all these bodements.
Cas.   O, farewell, dear Hector!
Look, how thou diest! look, how thy eye turns
      pale!   81
Look, how thy wounds do bleed at many vents!
Hark, how Troy roars! how Hecuba cries out!
How poor Andromache shrills her dolours forth!
Behold, distraction, frenzy and amazement,
Like witless antics, one another meet,
And all cry, Hector! Hector's dead! O Hector!
Tro.   Away! away!
Cas.   Farewell: yet, soft! Hector, I take my
      leave:
Thou dost thyself and all our Troy deceive. [*Exit.*
Hect.   You are amazed, my liege, at her ex-
      claim: 91
Go in and cheer the town: we'll forth and fight,
Do deeds worth praise and tell you them at night.
Pri.   Farewell: the gods with safety stand
      about thee!
[*Exeunt severally Priam and Hector. Alarums.*
Tro.   They are at it, hark! Proud Diomed,
      believe,
I come to lose my arm, or win my sleeve.

Enter PANDARUS.

Pan.   Do you hear, my lord? do you hear?
Tro.   What now?
Pan.   Here's a letter come from yond poor girl.
Tro.   Let me read.   100
Pan.   A whoreson tisick, a whoreson rascally
tisick so troubles me, and the foolish fortune of
this girl; and what one thing, what another, that
I shall leave you one o' these days: and I have a
rheum in mine eyes too, and such an ache in my

Opposite : Cassandra: 'Look, how thou diest! look, how
thy eye turns pale! Look, how thy wounds do bleed at
many vents!' Painting of Cassandra by George Romney
(1734–1802)

1 *clapper-clawing*. Mauling.

9 *sleeveless*. Useless.

18 *to proclaim barbarism*. To say that the spheres of authority which denote the civilized state are in chaos.

Warriors prepare for battle. Nineteenth century engraving from a 5th century B.C. painting on a drinking cup

bones that, unless a man were cursed, I cannot tell what to think on't.   What says she there?

   Tro. Words, words, mere words, no matter from the heart;
The effect doth operate another way.   109
                      [Tearing the letter.
Go, wind, to wind, there turn and change together.
My love with words and errors still she feeds;
But edifies another with her deeds.
                      [Exeunt severally.

SCENE IV.   *Plains between Troy and the Grecian camp.*

   Alarums: excursions.   Enter THERSITES.

   Ther. Now they are clapper-clawing one another; I'll go look on. That dissembling abominable varlet, Diomed, has got that same scurvy doting foolish young knave's sleeve of Troy there in his helm: I would fain see them meet; that that same young Trojan ass, that loves the whore there, might send that Greekish whoremasterly villain, with the sleeve, back to the dissembling luxurious drab, of a sleeveless errand. O' the t'other side, the policy of those crafty swearing rascals, that stale old mouse-eaten dry cheese, Nestor, and that same dog-fox, Ulysses, is not proved worth a blackberry: they set me up, in policy, that mongrel cur, Ajax, against that dog of as bad a kind, Achilles: and now is the cur Ajax prouder than the cur Achilles, and will not arm to-day; whereupon the Grecians begin to proclaim barbarism, and policy grows into an ill opinion.   Soft! here comes sleeve, and t'other.

   Enter DIOMEDES, TROILUS *following.*

   Tro. Fly not; for shouldst thou take the river Styx,   20
I would swim after.
   Dio.   Thou dost miscall retire:
I do not fly, but advantageous care
Withdrew me from the odds of multitude:
Have at thee!
   Ther. Hold thy whore, Grecian!—now for thy whore, Trojan!—now the sleeve, now the sleeve!
        [Exeunt Troilus and Diomedes, fighting.

   Enter HECTOR.

   Hect. What art thou, Greek? art thou for Hector's match?
Art thou of blood and honour?
   Ther. No, no, I am a rascal; a scurvy railing knave; a very filthy rogue.   31
   Hect. I do believe thee: live.   *[Exit.*
   Ther. God-a-mercy, that thou wilt believe me; but a plague break thy neck for frighting me! What's become of the wenching rogues? I think they have swallowed one another: I would laugh at that miracle: yet, in a sort, lechery eats itself.   I'll seek them.   *[Exit.*

SCENE V.   *Another part of the plains.*

   Enter DIOMEDES *and a* Servant.

   Dio. Go, go, my servant, take thou Troilus' horse;
Present the fair steed to my lady Cressid:
Fellow, commend my service to her beauty;

Tell her I have chastised the amorous Trojan,
And am her knight by proof.
 Serv.   I go, my lord. [*Exit.*
   Enter AGAMEMNON.

 Agam. Renew, renew! The fierce Polydamas
Hath beat down Menon: bastard Margarelon
Hath Doreus prisoner,
•And stands colossus-wise, waving his beam,
Upon the pashed corses of the kings   10
Epistrophus and Cedius: Polyxenes is slain,
Amphimachus and Thoas deadly hurt,
Patroclus ta'en or slain, and Palamedes
•Sore hurt and bruised: the dreadful Sagittary
Appals our numbers: haste we, Diomed,
To reinforcement, or we perish all.

   Enter NESTOR.

 Nest. Go, bear Patroclus' body to Achilles;
And bid the snail-paced Ajax arm for shame.
There is a thousand Hectors in the field:
Now here he fights on Galathe his horse, 20
And there lacks work; anon he's there afoot,
•And there they fly or die, like scaled sculls
Before the belching whale; then is he yonder,
And there the strawy Greeks, ripe for his edge,
Fall down before him, like the mower's swath:
Here, there, and every where, he leaves and takes,
Dexterity so obeying appetite
That what he will he does, and does so much
That proof is call'd impossibility.

   Enter ULYSSES.

 Ulyss. O, courage, courage, princes! great
  Achilles   30
Is arming, weeping, cursing, vowing vengeance:
Patroclus' wounds have roused his drowsy blood,
Together with his mangled Myrmidons,
That noseless, handless, hack'd and chipp'd, come
  to him,
Crying on Hector. Ajax hath lost a friend
And foams at mouth, and he is arm'd and at it,
Roaring for Troilus, who hath done to-day
Mad and fantastic execution,
Engaging and redeeming of himself
With such a careless force and forceless care 40
As if that luck, in very spite of cunning,
Bade him win all.

   Enter AJAX.

 Ajax. Troilus! thou coward Troilus! [*Exit.*
 Dio.   Ay, there, there.
 Nest. So, so, we draw together.

   Enter ACHILLES.

 Achil.   Where is this Hector?
Come, come, thou boy-queller, show thy face;
Know what it is to meet Achilles angry:
Hector! where's Hector? I will none but Hector.
         [*Exeunt.*

SCENE VI. *Another part of the plains.*

   Enter AJAX.

 Ajax. Troilus, thou coward Troilus, show thy
  head!

   Enter DIOMEDES.

 Dio. Troilus, I say! where's Troilus?
 Ajax.   What wouldst thou?

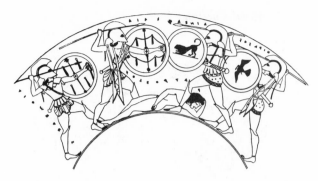

The battle over the body of Patroclus. Nineteenth century engraving from a classical Greek vase painting

9 *beam.* Lance.

14 *Sagittary.* A centaur who helped the Trojans with his superb archery.

22 *sculls.* Early form of the word 'school'. i.e. of fish.

Troilus (Denholm Elliot) and Ajax (Paul Hardwick) fight, Stratford-upon-Avon, 1960

11 *cogging.* Cheating.

29 *frush.* Smash.

Achilles takes to the field. Nineteenth century engraving from a classical Greek vase painting

---

5 *Empale him.* Surround him.

9-12 *The cuckold . . . ho!* Thersites uses the language of bear-baiting.

Dio. I would correct him.
Ajax. Were I the general, thou shouldst have my office
Ere that correction.   Troilus, I say! what, Troilus!

Enter TROILUS.

Tro. O traitor Diomed! turn thy false face, thou traitor,
And pay thy life thou owest me for my horse!
Dio. Ha, art thou there?
Ajax. I'll fight with him alone: stand, Diomed.
Dio. He is my prize; I will not look upon. 10
• *Tro.* Come, both you cogging Greeks; have at you both!   [*Exeunt, fighting.*

Enter HECTOR.

Hect. Yea, Troilus? O, well fought, my youngest brother!

Enter ACHILLES.

Achil. Now do I see thee, ha! have at thee, Hector!
Hect. Pause, if thou wilt.
Achil. I do disdain thy courtesy, proud Trojan:
Be happy that my arms are out of use:
My rest and negligence befriends thee now,
But thou anon shalt hear of me again;
Till when, go seek thy fortune.   [*Exit.*
Hect.   Fare thee well:
I would have been much more a fresher man, 20
Had I expected thee.   How now, my brother!

Re-enter TROILUS.

Tro. Ajax hath ta'en Æneas: shall it be?
No, by the flame of yonder glorious heaven,
He shall not carry him: I'll be ta'en too,
Or bring him off: fate, hear me what I say!
I reck not though I end my life to-day.   [*Exit.*

Enter one in sumptuous armour.

Hect. Stand, stand, thou Greek; thou art a goodly mark:
No? wilt thou not?   I like thy armour well;
• I'll frush it and unlock the rivets all,
But I'll be master of it: wilt thou not, beast, abide?
Why, then fly on, I'll hunt thee for thy hide. 31
[*Exeunt.*

SCENE VII.   *Another part of the plains.*

Enter ACHILLES, *with* Myrmidons.

Achil. Come here about me, you my Myrmidons;
Mark what I say.   Attend me where I wheel:
Strike not a stroke, but keep yourselves in breath:
And when I have the bloody Hector found,
• Empale him with your weapons round about;
In fellest manner execute your aims.
Follow me, sirs, and my proceedings eye:
It is decreed Hector the great must die. [*Exeunt.*

Enter MENELAUS *and* PARIS, *fighting: then*
THERSITES.

• *Ther.* The cuckold and the cuckold-maker are at it.   Now, bull! now, dog! 'Loo, Paris, 'loo! now my double-henned sparrow! 'loo, Paris, 'loo! The bull has the game: ware horns, ho!
[*Exeunt Paris and Menelaus.*

Enter MARGARELON.

Mar.   Turn, slave, and fight.
Ther.   What art thou?
Mar   A bastard son of Priam's.
Ther.   I am a bastard too; I love bastards: I
am a bastard begot, bastard instructed, bastard
in mind, bastard in valour, in every thing illegitimate.   One bear will not bite another, and
wherefore should one bastard?   Take heed,
the quarrel's most ominous to us: if the son of a
whore fight for a whore, he tempts judgement:
farewell, bastard.   [*Exit.*
Mar.   The devil take thee, coward!   [*Exit.*

SCENE VIII.   *Another part of the plains.*

Enter HECTOR.

Hect.   Most putrefied core, so fair without,
Thy goodly armour thus hath cost thy life.
Now is my day's work done; I'll take good
    breath:
Rest, sword; thou hast thy fill of blood and death.
          [*Puts off his helmet and hangs his shield
                                      behind him.*

Enter ACHILLES *and* Myrmidons.

Achil.   Look, Hector, how the sun begins to
    set;
How ugly night comes breathing at his heels:
• Even with the vail and darking of the sun,
To close the day up, Hector's life is done.
    Hect.   I am unarm'd; forego this vantage,
    Greek.
    Achil.   Strike, fellows, strike; this is the man
    I seek.   [*Hector falls.* 10
So, Ilion, fall thou next! now, Troy, sink down!
Here lies thy heart, thy sinews, and thy bone.
On, Myrmidons, and cry you all amain,
'Achilles hath the mighty Hector slain.'
                              [*A retreat sounded.*
Hark! a retire upon our Grecian part.
    Myr.   The Trojan trumpets sound the like,
    my lord.
    Achil.   The dragon wing of night o'erspreads
    the earth,
• And, stickler-like, the armies separates.
My half-supp'd sword, that frankly would have
    fed,
Pleased with this dainty bait, thus goes to bed. 20
                              [*Sheathes his sword.*
Come, tie his body to my horse's tail;
Along the field I will the Trojan trail. [*Exeunt.*

SCENE IX.   *Another part of the plains.*

Enter AGAMEMNON, AJAX, MENELAUS, NESTOR,
DIOMEDES, *and others, marching.   Shouts
within.*

    Agam.   Hark! hark! what shout is that?
    Nest.   Peace, drums!
[*Within*]   Achilles! Achilles! Hector's slain!
    Achilles!
• *Dio.*   The bruit is, Hector's slain, and by
    Achilles.
    Ajax.   If it be so, yet bragless let it be;
Great Hector was a man as good as he.
    Agam.   March patiently along: let one be sent
To pray Achilles see us at our tent.

7 *vail.* Setting.

Achilles slays Hector.   Nineteenth century engraving
from a Greek vase painting of the 6th century B.C.

18 *stickler-like.* Like an umpire of a duel.

4 *bruit.* Noise.

Achilles drags the body of Hector around the walls of Troy. Engraving by John Flaxman from Homer's *Iliad*, translated by Alexander Pope, 1793 edition

13-14 *But dare . . . dangers in.* Face any immediate danger that men or gods prepare.

19 *Niobes.* Niobe, weeping for her dead children, was turned to stone, but still continued to weep.

Niobe. From a 19th century engraving

25 *Titan.* Hyperion, the sun-god.

46-47 *painted cloths.* Rooms were hung with cloths painted with figures and symbols.

If in his death the gods have us befriended,   9
Great Troy is ours, and our sharp wars are ended.
[*Exeunt, marching.*

SCENE X.   *Another part of the plains.*

Enter ÆNEAS *and* Trojans.

Æne.   Stand, ho! yet are we masters of the field:
Never go home; here starve we out the night.

Enter TROILUS.

Tro.   Hector is slain.
All.   Hector! the gods forbid!
Tro.   He's dead; and at the murderer's horse's tail,
In beastly sort, dragg'd through the shameful field.
Frown on, you heavens, effect your rage with speed!
Sit, gods, upon your thrones, and smile at Troy!
I say, at once let your brief plagues be mercy,
And linger not our sure destructions on!   9
Æne.   My lord, you do discomfort all the host.
Tro.   You understand me not that tell me so:
I do not speak of flight, of fear, of death,
But dare all imminence that gods and men
Address their dangers in.   Hector is gone:
Who shall tell Priam so, or Hecuba?
Let him that will a screech-owl aye be call'd,
Go in to Troy, and say there, Hector's dead:
There is a word will Priam turn to stone;
Make wells and Niobes of the maids and wives,
Cold statues of the youth, and, in a word,   20
Scare Troy out of itself.   But, march away:
Hector is dead; there is no more to say.
Stay yet.   You vile abominable tents,
Thus proudly pight upon our Phrygian plains,
Let Titan rise as early as he dare.
I'll through and through you! and, thou great-sized coward,
No space of earth shall sunder our two hates:
I'll haunt thee like a wicked conscience still,
That mouldeth goblins swift as frenzy's thoughts.
Strike a free march to Troy! with comfort go: 30
Hope of revenge shall hide our inward woe.
[*Exeunt Æneas and Trojans.*

As TROILUS *is going out, enter, from the other side,* PANDARUS.

Pan.   But hear you, hear you!
Tro.   Hence, broker-lackey! ignomy and shame
Pursue thy life, and live aye with thy name! [*Exit.*
Pan.   A goodly medicine for my aching bones!
O world! world! world! thus is the poor agent despised!   O traitors and bawds, how earnestly are you set a-work, and how ill requited! why should our endeavour be so loved and the performance so loathed? what verse for it? what instance for it?   Let me see: 41

Full merrily the humble-bee doth sing,
Till he hath lost his honey and his sting;
And being once subdued in armed tail,
Sweet honey and sweet notes together fail.

Good traders in the flesh, set this in your painted cloths.
As many as be here of pandar's hall,

Your eyes, half out, weep out at Pandar's fall;
Or if you cannot weep, yet give some groans, 50
Though not for me, yet for your aching bones.
● Brethren and sisters of the hold-door trade,
Some two months hence my will shall here be
      made:
It should be now, but that my fear is this,
● Some galled goose of Winchester would hiss:
Till then I'll sweat and seek about for eases,
And at that time bequeathe you my diseases.
                                    [*Exit.*

52 *hold-door trade*. Pandering.

55 *galled goose of Winchester*. A prostitute affected with venereal disease. The brothels of Southwark were located on land belonging to the see of Winchester.

All's Well
That Ends Well

1603

It is usual to refer to *All's Well* and *Measure for Measure,* which go together, as problem plays; they are certainly not comedies in the usual sense of the term, except that at the end all's well and they have happy endings. They are both very serious plays: *Measure for Measure* has much that is tragic; *All's Well* has never been thought of as an attractive play, but its intellectual interest is immense. The subject did not fire Shakespeare's imagination, as *Measure for Measure* did, it gives the impression of being thought out, rather than felt along the heart and nerves. Perhaps it was experimental, and he was at a loss for something new, perhaps he was tired, as he well might be. He was getting older, a conflict between the older and younger generation is one theme. The verse is bare, uninspired, sometimes congested with thought. It looks as if he were filling in, as a writer does, by drawing on what he had known personally: it adds intensely to the interest of the work and its significance for the author.

The Story. He drew on a familiar story that goes back to Boccaccio, then changed details, as usual, to make a play out of it, and filled it out with his own inventions— particularly the character of Parolles, the braggadocio soldier, whom Charles I thought the most striking. Shaw considered the Countess's 'the most beautiful old woman's part ever written', and certainly the women win all round; the men show up very poorly, except for the ailing King of France, who is noble and pathetic. The Countess has a teen-age son, Count Bertram, fatherless, volatile, light-hearted. Helena, daughter of a famous doctor, who is dead, is in love with him; but he is beyond her reach, far out of her class, and will not marry. (Where have we met this young man before?)

The King is sick of an incurable disease. Helena cures him by the art learned from her father, and procures as her reward the King's command upon the young Count to marry her. Thus enforced, he refuses to consummate the marriage and goes off to the wars in Italy, attended by the braggart Parolles. In the fighting he acquits himself bravely; Parolles is an arrant coward, a man of words—a lesser Falstaff without the merriment. (There is little merriment in this play.)

The Count, who will not marry, wants to seduce a chaste Florentine girl, appropriately called Diana (a 'Capilet', observe). Helena follows him to Italy and entraps him by the 'bed-trick', beloved of Elizabethans, substituting herself, his proper wife, for the girl. Rings are exchanged, by which the consummation is proved and the Count is rounded up by the women. The good old Countess has stood by Helena all along, willing to receive her as her daughter, in preference to the son who has fallen down on his duty, and earned the King's disfavour. In the end the Count is caught and makes his submission—needs must—and all is well.

But where have we met all this before? As the best editor of the play remarks, one must consider 'the creative interplay between author and environment, the fact that the feelings of the author are a creative part of the climate of opinion in which he lives.'[1] Of course—as with any creative writer.

Contemporary. Many contemporary touches indicate the new age into which the country, and its dramatist, were moving. Early in 1603 the old Queen sickened and died. Again it was a year of severe plague; sickness and death were all about. The King's sickness dominates the first part of the play and motivates the action of the whole. We are instructed to see this in terms of folk-tale, and indeed it has its anthropological significance. But it is also contemporary. The King has been given up by the learned doctors of 'the congregated College', and he could not 'prostitute our past-cure malady to empirics'. The Royal College of Physicians contained the learned doctors and they led the persecution of the disdained empirics, who sometimes effected surprising cures.[2] The professional physicians adhered to the traditional authority of Galen, empirics were apt to follow the new teaching of Paracelsus. Helena effects the King's cure, the courtiers are amazed: 'to be relinquished of the artists—both of Galen and of Paracelsus—of all the learned Fellows . . . that gave him out incurable!'

There had been no curing the old Queen: Elizabeth I died in March 1603, and a new world opened up: the Jacobean age. Older people did not like it: Shakespeare's fellow-Warwickshireman, Drayton, detested it and the new generation that knew not David. The old King says of his young lords:

> but they may jest
> Till their own scorn return to them unnoted
> Ere they can hide their levity in honour.

The King agrees with the young Count's father:

> 'Let me not live', quoth he,
> 'After my flame lacks oil, to be the snuff
> Of younger spirits, whose apprehensive senses
> All but new things disdain; whose judgments are
> Mere fathers of their garments; whose constancies
> Expire before their fashions.'

Did this speak for William Shakespeare too, in the new age opening before them?

It was a crass and vulgar world, without the dignity which the historic figure of Elizabeth I had imposed, and Scotch James and his Danish Queen—both given to tippling—were incapable of emulating. Parolles is a figure of the new society, with its opportunism and its false values: 'Simply the thing I am shall make me live', he declares after his exposure. In a world of fools, such as Parolles can

> by foolery thrive:
> There's place and means for every man alive.

[1] G. K. Hunter, in the *Arden Shakespeare* edition, liii.

[2] cf. My *Simon Forman*, c. 111.

Class. In an unstable society the issue of Class becomes uncomfortably sharpened; in an older, traditional world people know their place and are more content. We have noticed Shakespeare occupying himself with the theme of gentility, about which he had reason to be conscious, in *As You Like It*. The issue of Class is acute in *All's Well*, for Helena's love for the Count is an 'ambitious love' as she recognises, and a doctor's daughter is disqualified from marrying a nobleman—except for the miraculous cure she has effected.

As to the miracle Shakespeare puts something very significant into the mouth of an old lord. 'They say miracles are past, and we have our philosophical persons to make modern and familiar things supernatural and causeless. Hence it is that we make trifles of terrors, ensconcing ourselves into seeming knowledge, when we should submit ourselves to an unknown fear.' Evidently Shakespeare was no superficial rationalist: he had an old-time view of the mystery of things, closer to the old faith.

The Countess is firm in these values; she respects the 'honesty' (i.e. honourableness, in Elizabethan meaning) of Helena's lower-class origin, but sets more store by the 'goodness' she achieves. 'I have those hopes of her good that her education promises her dispositions she inherits—which makes her fair gifts fairer.' The son scorns Helena for her origin:

> She had her breeding at my father's charge—
> A poor physician's daughter my wife! Disdain
> Rather corrupt me ever!

The King replies in a long speech which gives the message of the play.

> Strange is it that our bloods—
> Of colour, weight, and heat poured all together
> Would quite confound distinction—yet stands off
> In differences so mighty.

In disliking a physician's daughter the Count overlooks innate quality for the name. (We may reflect, cynically, that a king could afford to ignore such distinctions—as Henry VIII did, Elizabeth I not.) Shakespeare draws the moral in rhymed couplets some people have found uncongenial—but he uses them, as Elizabethans did, to enforce moral lessons, for didactic sentences, incantations.

> From lowest place when virtuous things proceed,
> The place is dignified by the doer's deed . . .

> Honours thrive
> When rather from our acts we them derive
> Than our foregoers. The mere word's a slave,
> Debauched on every tomb, on every grave,
> A lying trophy, and as oft is dumb,
> Where dust and damned oblivion is the tomb
> Of honoured bones indeed.

That is a pretty trenchant statement for an age which set such store by raising magnificent family monuments, with their trophies and epitaphs, in the churches where altars, shrines and images of the saints had stood. And it shows that, for all his proper respect for degree and gentility, Shakespeare had no illusions, no falsification of values underneath. Himself had certainly earned his place in society from his acts, his quality and achievement: *Non sans droit.*

The King is enraged with the Count, who has dishonoured him by his disrespect— 'My honour's at the stake'—and makes him obey, contracting him to Helena with 'Proud, scornful boy'. One must remember that 'Boy!' was a term of insult with Elizabethans; the Count is several times thus described: he is an adolescent. His values are false.

After his enforced marriage the Count compounds his misconduct by stealing away from Court to the war in Italy, to cheat Helena of her marital rights. This earns the 'everlasting displeasure of the King, who had even tuned his bounty to sing happiness to him.' His mother pleads for him that it was

English Edwardian actor, Lewis Ball, as the Countess of Rousillon's clown

> Natural rebellion done i' th'blade of youth.

(This was the burden of the Countess of Southampton's plea for her son after his rebellion with Essex—and everybody accepted the plea of his youth, though he was not so young: a delayed adolescent.) When the Count is rounded up by the women, roped and tied, and all is forgiven, the King is gracious:

> I am not a day of season,
> For thou may'st see a sunshine and a hail
> In me at once. But to the brightest beams
> Distracted clouds give way. So stand thou forth;
> The time is fair again.

This was precisely what was said of Elizabeth I, and how she kept order in the nursery by alternating storm and sunshine: after an overcast sky, what bliss when all was clear in the firmament again!

Helena also excuses the Count's stealing away, regarding herself as responsible for his being driven from 'the sportive Court, where thou wast shot at by fair eyes'. In the war abroad he served, bravely enough, as General of Horse. On the news of his wife's presumed death a companion comments, 'the great dignity that his valour hath here acquired for him shall at home be encountered with a shame as ample'—for he would be held responsible for her death. I think we may diagnose that his real fault was irresponsibility, the failure of a teen-age or delayed adolescent to face the responsibilities of adult life.

This is the theme of the Sonnets: the young lord who will not do his duty by his family, marry and carry it on—and yet allows himself to betray his friend with his friend's mistress. Ironically enough, the Count uses Shakespeare's argument with his young Lord against the Florentine girl's chastity:

> You are no maiden but a monument . . .
> And now you should be as your mother was
> When your sweet self was got.

Diana replies with an image which, for all its being a commonplace, is from the Sonnets:

> when you have our roses,
> You barely leave our thorns to prick ourselves.

633

Helena's comment is the forceful one:

> But, O strange men!
> That can such sweet use make of what they hate,
> When saucy trusting of the cozened thoughts
> Defiles the pitchy night; so lust doth play
> With what it loathes for that which is away.

Here is 'the expense of spirit in a waste of shame is lust in action' again—Shakespeare's love-hate complex about sex, which was to reach such depths shortly in *King Lear*.

For the moment, we may take it that his attitude is that of the sceptical relativism he usually enforces: 'How mightily sometimes we make us comforts of our losses! And how mightily some other times we drown our gain in tears!' And the conclusion?—

> 'The web of our life is of a mingled yarn, good and ill together; our virtues would be proud if our faults whipped them not, and our crimes would despair if they were not cherished by our virtues.'

This is Shakespeare's regular signature-tune. It is as well that he ends his comedy with,

> Mine eyes smell onions; I shall weep anon.
> Good Tom Drum, lend me a handkercher—

we should hardly know it for a comedy else.

Personal. Two references to the sack of Troy, and to Cressida, indicate that the recent *Troilus and Cressida* was still in mind. Though the satire is much less savage than in that play, there are satirical reflections on the code of honour, on Court affectations, and on the war, still not yet brought to an end: 'the muster-file, rotten and sound, upon my life, amounts not to fifteen thousand poll; half of the which dare not shake the snow from off their cassocks lest they shake themselves to pieces.' Parolles regards Captain Dumaine (note the name from *Love's Labour's Lost*) as good enough to instruct the doubling of files at Mile-End, where the musters were trained—and where Justice Shallow had watched 'a little quiver fellow' manage his piece.

Shakespeare's reading in the Voyages has a reflection:

> Thus, Indian-like,
> Religious in mine error, I adore
> The sun that looks upon his worshipper.

Contemporary religious controversy receives a hit from the Clown: 'If men could be contented to be what they are, there were no fear in marriage; for young Charbon the Puritan and old Poysam, the Papist, howsoever their hearts are severed in religion, their heads are both one; they may jowl horns together like any deer i'th'herd.' Here is the hoary old joke about horns and cuckolding again. We may note that the Clown's patter is suggestive rather than outright bawdy, though there is some of that. For the rest, the Clown's wit dates more than anything else. Probably the funniest episode is the uncasing of Parolles. The cult of melancholy is glanced at: 'I know a man that had this trick of melancholy sold a goodly manor for a song.'

634

The bed-trick—the trick that is played upon the young Count to get him to bed with his own wife—was popular with Elizabethans, if not with us. Any notable act of cozenage gave them pleasure in the theatre, and Count Bertram was fair game. Diana puts the point as it appeared, and appealed, to them:

> Only, in this disguise, I think't no sin
> To cozen him that would unjustly win.

It is to be observed once more how Shakespeare tips the balance in favour of his women.

Background. Professor Hunter comments that 'Shakespeare had some knowledge of French, and the atmosphere of the play is decidedly French; the names . . . seem to indicate a mind at work strongly imbued with a consciousness of French meanings'. But, of course, Shakespeare was lodging with the Montjoies in Silver Street in these years.

And what are we to make of the close parallels between the young Count and the young Earl Shakespeare had known so closely? Everything shows that Southampton's mother, the Countess, was a charming woman, who never lost the good will of the Queen for all her son's escapades and worse. He, too, was fatherless and irresponsible; he had dishonoured Lord Burghley by breaking his word to marry his granddaughter and, rather than do it, had stolen off from Court to France. Later on, from France again he meant to go further, into Italy, but was brought back by Essex to marry his cousin ('shot at with fair eyes'), one of the Queen's Court ladies, Elizabeth Vernon, at the last moment of her pregnancy. Over and over he earned the Queen's disfavour. Essex made him General of Horse abroad in Ireland (like the young Count Bertram in Italy), where he acquitted himself bravely. The Queen cashiered him. In the end, when he followed Essex into rebellion, the only plea for him was his youth and immaturity.

Southampton, too, had his Parolles—a braggadocio Captain Piers Edmonds, whom the Earl made his corporal-general when he was General of the Horse: 'he ate and drank at his table and lay in his tent. The Earl of Southampton would cull and hug him in his arms and play wantonly with him.'[1] Essex would take this professional soldier for coach-rides with him. Did Shakespeare know the fellow? It is not unlikely, and the type is familiar.

Text. The text, from the First Folio is a fair one and offers few difficulties. These, however, are fascinating, for they appear to indicate a copy from the author's own manuscript. For, as in *Much Ado, Romeo and Juliet,* and 2 *Henry IV,* the name occasionally given is that of the rôle and not that of the character. Professor Hunter concludes, 'it looks as if Shakespeare was finding out, in the course of composition, what to call these characters; if this inference is correct then the manuscript behind the Folio must represent a stage at which the play was still being composed.'

[1] *Salisbury Mss.,* (Hist. Mss. Com.), XI, 94, 108.

ALL'S WELL THAT ENDS WELL.

DRAMATIS PERSONÆ.

KING OF FRANCE.
DUKE OF FLORENCE.
BERTRAM, Count of Rousillon.
LAFEU, an old lord.
PAROLLES, a follower of Bertram.
Steward, } servants to the Countess of
Clown, } Rousillon.
A Page.

COUNTESS OF ROUSILLON, mother to Bertram.

HELENA, a gentlewoman protected by the Countess.
An old Widow of Florence.
DIANA, daughter to the Widow.
VIOLENTA, } neighbours and friends to the
MARIANA, } Widow.
Lords, Officers, Soldiers, &c., French and Florentine.

SCENE: *Rousillon; Paris; Florence; Marseilles.*

● *A bullet beside a text line indicates an annotation in the opposite column*

ACT I.

SCENE I. *Rousillon. The* COUNT'S *palace.*

Enter BERTRAM, *the* COUNTESS OF ROUSILLON, HELENA, *and* LAFEU, *all in black.*

Count. In delivering my son from me, I bury a second husband.

Ber. And I in going, madam, weep o'er my father's death anew: but I must attend his majesty's command, to whom I am now in ward, evermore in subjection.

Laf. You shall find of the king a husband,
●madam; you, sir, a father: he that so generally
●is at all times good must of necessity hold his virtue to you; whose worthiness would stir it up where it wanted rather than lack it where there is such abundance.

Count. What hope is there of his majesty's amendment?

Laf. He hath abandoned his physicians, madam; under whose practices he hath persecuted

Countess: 'In delivering my son from me, I bury a second husband'. Engraving by Kenny Meadows from Barry Cornwall's *Works of Shakspere*, 1846

Opposite: Parolles betrays Bertram and his army. Engraving from Rowe's edition of Shakespeare, 1709

8 *generally*. To the general public.

9 *hold*. Continue.

39 *fistula.* A long, pipe-like ulcer.

45-52 *I have those . . . goodness.* See introduction.

62-63 *I do . . . it too.* Helena is seen to grieve for her father, but she has another grief within her.

71-73 *thy blood . . . birthright.* The Countess is hoping that her son's inherited qualities will combine with his own good disposition.

time with hope, and finds no other advantage in the process but only the losing of hope by time.

Count. This young gentlewoman had a father,—O, that 'had'! how sad a passage 'tis!—whose skill was almost as great as his honesty; had it stretched so far, would have made nature immortal, and death should have play for lack of work. Would, for the king's sake, he were living! I think it would be the death of the king's disease.

Laf. How called you the man you speak of, madam?

Count. He was famous, sir, in his profession, and it was his great right to be so: Gerard de Narbon.   31

Laf. He was excellent indeed, madam: the king very lately spoke of him admiringly and mourningly: he was skilful enough to have lived still, if knowledge could be set up against mortality.

Ber. What is it, my good lord, the king languishes of?

● *Laf.* A fistula, my lord.

Ber. I heard not of it before.   40

Laf. I would it were not notorious. Was this gentlewoman the daughter of Gerard de Narbon?

Count. His sole child, my lord, and be-
● queathed to my overlooking. I have those hopes of her good that her education promises; her dispositions she inherits, which makes fair gifts fairer; for where an unclean mind carries virtuous qualities, there commendations go with pity; they are virtues and traitors too: in her they are the better for their simpleness; she derives her honesty and achieves her goodness.

Laf. Your commendations, madam, get from her tears.

Count. 'Tis the best brine a maiden can season her praise in. The remembrance of her father never approaches her heart but the tyranny of her sorrows takes all livelihood from her cheek. No more of this, Helena; go to, no more; lest it be rather thought you affect a sorrow than have it.   61

● *Hel.* I do affect a sorrow indeed, but I have it too.

Laf. Moderate lamentation is the right of the dead, excessive grief the enemy to the living.

Count. If the living be enemy to the grief, the excess makes it soon mortal.

Ber. Madam, I desire your holy wishes.

Laf. How understand we that?

Count. Be thou blest, Bertram, and succeed thy father   70
● In manners, as in shape! thy blood and virtue
Contend for empire in thee, and thy goodness
Share with thy birthright! Love all, trust a few,
Do wrong to none: be able for thine enemy
Rather in power than use, and keep thy friend
Under thy own life's key: be check'd for silence,
But never tax'd for speech. What heaven more
    will,
That thee may furnish and my prayers pluck
    down,
Fall on thy head! Farewell, my lord;
'Tis an unseason'd courtier; good my lord,   80
Advise him.

Laf.   He cannot want the best
That shall attend his love.

Count. Heaven bless him! Farewell, Bertram.
                                        [*Exit.*
Ber. [*To Helena*] The best wishes that can be
forged in your thoughts be servants to you! Be
comfortable to my mother, your mistress, and
make much of her.
Laf. Farewell, pretty lady: you must hold
the credit of your father.
                    [*Exeunt Bertram and Lafeu.*
Hel. O, were that all! I think not on my
    father;   90
And these great tears grace his remembrance
    more
Than those I shed for him. What was he like?
I have forgot him: my imagination
● Carries no favour in't but Bertram's.
I am undone: there is no living, none,
If Bertram be away. 'Twere all one
That I should love a bright particular star
And think to wed it, he is so above me:
● In his bright radiance and collateral light
Must I be comforted, not in his sphere.   100
The ambition in my love thus plagues itself:
The hind that would be mated by the lion
Must die for love. 'Twas pretty, though a plague,
To see him every hour; to sit and draw
His arched brows, his hawking eye, his curls,
● In our heart's table; heart too capable
● Of every line and trick of his sweet favour:
But now he's gone, and my idolatrous fancy
Must sanctify his reliques. Who comes here?

Enter PAROLLES.

[*Aside*] One that goes with him: I love him for
    his sake;   110
And yet I know him a notorious liar,
● Think him a great way fool, solely a coward;
Yet these fix'd evils sit so fit in him,
● That they take place, when virtue's steely bones
†Look bleak i' the cold wind: withal, full oft we see
Cold wisdom waiting on superfluous folly.
Par. Save you, fair queen!
Hel. And you, monarch!
Par. No.
Hel. And no.   120
Par. Are you meditating on virginity?
Hel. Ay. You have some stain of soldier in
you: let me ask you a question. Man is enemy
to virginity; how may we barricado it against him?
Par. Keep him out.
Hel. But he assails; and our virginity, though
valiant, in the defence yet is weak: unfold to us
some warlike resistance.
● *Par.* There is none: man, sitting down before
you, will undermine you and blow you up.   130
Hel. Bless our poor virginity from underminers
and blowers up! Is there no military policy, how
virgins might blow up men?
Par. Virginity being blown down, man will
quicklier be blown up: marry, in blowing him
down again, with the breach yourselves made,
you lose your city. It is not politic in the commonwealth of nature to preserve virginity. Loss
of virginity is rational increase and there was
never virgin got till virginity was first lost. That
you were made of is metal to make virgins.
Virginity by being once lost may be ten times
found; by being ever kept, it is ever lost: 'tis too
cold a companion; away with 't!

94 *favour.* Beloved face.

99 *collateral light.* Planets were thought to move in
concentric, parallel spheres. Helena in her lower
sphere will have to be content with seeing the light from
Bertram.

106 *table.* Records.

Helena: '. . . to sit and draw His arched brows . . . his
curls In our heart's table.' This illustration shows the
drawer inscribing the outlines of his friend on a table
held against the friend's heart. From Geoffrey Witney's
A Choice of Emblems, 1586

107 *trick.* Expression.

112 *a great way.* Mostly.

114 *take place.* Take precedence.

129 *sitting down.* Besieging.

152 *sanctified limit.* Consecrated ground. Parolles is saying that virginity is as sinful as suicide, because it murders itself by having no offspring. (cf. Shakespeare to Southampton in the Sonnets.)

157 *inhibited.* Forbidden.

172 *date.* A pun on the meanings 'fruit' and 'age'. The second meaning is taken up in the end of the sentence with 'in the cheek'.

181-187 *A mother . . . disaster.* These are the epithets of love poetry, and Helena is imagining Bertram using them on the ladies at court.

188 *adoptious christendoms.* Christian names.

189 *gossips.* Is godfather to.

198-199 *Might with . . . think.* It is unfortunate that our good wishes to our friends cannot be manifested in action.

LITTLE HELEN FAREWELL ACT·I·SC·I

Parolles and Helena. Illustration by Byam Shaw, *Chiswick Shakespeare c.* 1900

Hel. I will stand for 't a little, though therefore I die a virgin.

Par. There's little can be said in 't; 'tis against the rule of nature. To speak on the part of virginity, is to accuse your mothers; which is most infallible disobedience. He that hangs himself is a virgin: virginity murders itself; and should be buried in highways out of all sanctified limit, as a desperate offendress against nature. Virginity breeds mites, much like a cheese; consumes itself to the very paring, and so dies with feeding his own stomach. Besides, virginity is peevish, proud, idle, made of self-love, which is the most inhibited sin in the canon. Keep it not; you cannot choose but lose by 't: out with 't! within ten year it will make itself ten, which is a goodly increase; and the principal itself not much the worse: away with 't!

Hel. How might one do, sir, to lose it to her own liking?

Par. Let me see: marry, ill, to like him that ne'er it likes. 'Tis a commodity will lose the gloss with lying; the longer kept, the less worth: off with 't while 'tis vendible; answer the time of request. Virginity, like an old courtier, wears her cap out of fashion: richly suited, but unsuitable: just like the brooch and the tooth-pick, which wear not now. Your date is better in your pie and your porridge than in your cheek: and your virginity, your old virginity, is like one of our French withered pears, it looks ill, it eats drily; marry, 'tis a withered pear; it was formerly better; marry, yet 'tis a withered pear: will you any thing with it?

Hel. †Not my virginity yet......
There shall your master have a thousand loves,
A mother and a mistress and a friend,   181
A phœnix, captain and an enemy,
A guide, a goddess, and a sovereign,
A counsellor, a traitress, and a dear;
His humble ambition, proud humility,
His jarring concord, and his discord dulcet,
His faith, his sweet disaster; with a world
Of pretty, fond, adoptious christendoms,
That blinking Cupid gossips. Now shall he—
I know not what he shall. God send him well!
The court's a learning place, and he is one—   191
  Par. What one, i' faith?
  Hel. That I wish well. 'Tis pity—
  Par. What's pity?
  Hel. That wishing well had not a body in 't,
Which might be felt; that we, the poorer born,
Whose baser stars do shut us up in wishes,
Might with effects of them follow our friends,
And show what we alone must think, which never
Returns us thanks.   200

Enter Page.

Page. Monsieur Parolles, my lord calls for you.
                                              [*Exit.*
Par. Little Helen, farewell: if I can remember thee, I will think of thee at court.
Hel. Monsieur Parolles, you were born under a charitable star.
Par. Under Mars, I.
Hel. I especially think, under Mars.
Par. Why under Mars?
Hel. The wars have so kept you under that you must needs be born under Mars.   210

Par. When he was predominant.

Hel. When he was retrograde, I think, rather.

Par. Why think you so?

Hel. You go so much backward when you fight.

Par. That's for advantage.

Hel. So is running away, when fear proposes
the safety: but the composition that your valour
and fear makes in you is a virtue of a good wing,
and I like the wear well.   219

Par. I am so full of businesses, I cannot
answer thee acutely. I will return perfect
courtier; in the which, my instruction shall serve
to naturalize thee, so thou wilt be capable of a
courtier's counsel and understand what advice
shall thrust upon thee; else thou diest in thine
unthankfulness, and thine ignorance makes thee
away: farewell. When thou hast leisure, say thy
prayers; when thou hast none, remember thy
friends: get thee a good husband, and use him as
he uses thee: so, farewell.   [*Exit.* 230

Hel. Our remedies oft in ourselves do lie,
Which we ascribe to heaven: the fated sky
Gives us free scope, only doth backward pull
Our slow designs when we ourselves are dull.
What power is it which mounts my love so high,
That makes me see, and cannot feed mine eye?
The mightiest space in fortune nature brings
To join like likes and kiss like native things.
Impossible be strange attempts to those   239
That weigh their pains in sense and do suppose
What hath been cannot be: who ever strove
To show her merit, that did miss her love?
The king's disease—my project may deceive me,
But my intents are fix'd and will not leave me.
                                [*Exit.*

SCENE II. *Paris. The* KING'S *palace.*

Flourish of cornets. Enter the KING OF FRANCE,
with letters, and divers Attendants.

King. The Florentines and Senoys are by the
        ears;
Have fought with equal fortune and continue
A braving war.

First Lord.   So 'tis reported, sir.

King. Nay, 'tis most credible; we here re-
ceive it
A certainty, vouch'd from our cousin Austria,
With caution that the Florentine will move us
For speedy aid; wherein our dearest friend
Prejudicates the business and would seem
To have us make denial.

First Lord.   His love and wisdom,
Approved so to your majesty, may plead   10
For amplest credence.

King.   He hath arm'd our answer,
And Florence is denied before he comes:
Yet, for our gentlemen that mean to see
The Tuscan service, freely have they leave
To stand on either part.

Sec. Lord.   It well may serve
A nursery to our gentry, who are sick
For breathing and exploit.

King.   What's he comes here?

Enter BERTRAM, LAFEU, *and* PAROLLES.

First Lord. It is the Count Rousillon, my
        good lord,

218 *of a good wing.* Capable of swift flight; a term of approbation in falconry, but not for a soldier.

223 *naturalize.* Familiarize.

232 *fated.* Fateful, because the sky and its planets influence life and character.

237-238 *The mightiest . . . things.* Although fortune and status may separate people, nature or love can overcome these obstacles and draw them together.

View of Paris. Engraving from Knight's *Pictorial Edition of the Works of Shakspere,* 1839–1843

1 *Senoys.* Siennese.

17 *breathing.* Exercise.

20 *curious.* Careful.

33-35 *but they . . . honour.* See introduction.

41 *His tongue obey'd his hand.* As the chime of a clock is directed by the hands, his tongue was governed by his honour.

Michael Denison as Bertram, Stratford-upon-Avon, 1955

42 *another place.* A higher rank.

55-63 *'Let me not . . . fashions'.* See introduction.

Young Bertram.
   King.   Youth, thou bear'st thy father's face;
● Frank nature, rather curious than in haste,   20
Hath well composed thee. Thy father's moral parts
Mayst thou inherit too! Welcome to Paris.
   Ber. My thanks and duty are your majesty's.
   King. I would I had that corporal soundness now,
As when thy father and myself in friendship
First tried our soldiership! He did look far
Into the service of the time and was
Discipled of the bravest: he lasted long;
But on us both did haggish age steal on
And wore us out of act. It much repairs me 30
To talk of your good father. In his youth
He had the wit which I can well observe
● To-day in our young lords; but they may jest
Till their own scorn return to them unnoted
Ere they can hide their levity in honour:
† So like a courtier, contempt nor bitterness
Were in his pride or sharpness; if they were,
His equal had awaked them, and his honour,
Clock to itself, knew the true minute when
Exception bid him speak, and at this time 40
● His tongue obey'd his hand: who were below him
● He used as creatures of another place
And bow'd his eminent top to their low ranks,
Making them proud of his humility,
† In their poor praise he humbled. Such a man
Might be a copy to these younger times;
Which, follow'd well, would demonstrate them now
But goers backward.
   Ber.   His good remembrance, sir,
Lies richer in your thoughts than on his tomb;
So in approof lives not his epitaph 50
As in your royal speech.
   King. Would I were with him! He would always say—
Methinks I hear him now; his plausive words
He scatter'd not in ears, but grafted them,
● To grow there and to bear,—'Let me not live,'—
This his good melancholy oft began,
On the catastrophe and heel of pastime,
When it was out,—'Let me not live,' quoth he,
'After my flame lacks oil, to be the snuff
Of younger spirits, whose apprehensive senses 60
All but new things disdain; whose judgements are
Mere fathers of their garments; whose constancies
Expire before their fashions.' This he wish'd:
I after him do after him wish too,
Since I nor wax nor honey can bring home,
I quickly were dissolved from my hive,
To give some labourers room.
   Sec. Lord.   You are loved, sir;
They that least lend it you shall lack you first.
   King. I fill a place, I know't. How long is't, count,
Since the physician at your father's died? 70
He was much famed.
   Ber.   Some six months since, my lord.
   King. If he were living, I would try him yet.
Lend me an arm; the rest have worn me out
With several applications: nature and sickness
Debate it at their leisure. Welcome, count;
My son's no dearer.
   Ber.   Thank your majesty.
                      [Exeunt. Flourish.

SCENE III. *Rousillon. The* COUNT'S *palace.*

Enter COUNTESS, Steward, *and* Clown.

Count. I will now hear; what say you of this gentlewoman?

● *Stew.* Madam, the care I have had to even your content, I wish might be found in the calendar of my past endeavours; for then we wound our modesty and make foul the clearness of our deservings, when of ourselves we publish them.

Count. What does this knave here? Get you gone, sirrah: the complaints I have heard of you I do not all believe: 'tis my slowness that I do not; for I know you lack not folly to commit them, and have ability enough to make such knaveries yours.

Clo. 'Tis not unknown to you, madam, I am a poor fellow.

Count. Well, sir.

Clo. No, madam, 'tis not so well that I am poor, though many of the rich are damned: but,
● if I may have your ladyship's good will to go to the world, Isbel the woman and I will do as we may.   21

Count. Wilt thou needs be a beggar?

Clo. I do beg your good will in this case.

Count. In what case?

● *Clo.* In Isbel's case and mine own. Service is no heritage: and I think I shall never have the blessing of God till I have issue o' my body; for
● they say barnes are blessings.

Count. Tell me thy reason why thou wilt marry.

Clo. My poor body, madam, requires it: I am driven on by the flesh; and he must needs go that the devil drives.

Count. Is this all your worship's reason?

Clo. Faith, madam, I have other holy reasons, such as they are.

Count. May the world know them?

Clo. I have been, madam, a wicked creature, as you and all flesh and blood are; and, indeed, I do marry that I may repent.

Count. Thy marriage, sooner than thy wickedness.   41

Clo. I am out o' friends, madam; and I hope to have friends for my wife's sake.

Count. Such friends are thine enemies, knave.

Clo. You're shallow, madam, in great friends for the knaves come to do that for me which I
● am aweary of. He that ears my land spares my team and gives me leave to in the crop; if I be his cuckold, he's my drudge: he that comforts my wife is the cherisher of my flesh and blood; he that cherishes my flesh and blood loves my flesh and blood; he that loves my flesh and blood is my friend: ergo, he that kisses my wife is my friend.
● If men could be contented to be what they are, there were no fear in marriage; for young Charbon the puritan and old Poysam the papist, howsome'er their hearts are severed in religion, their heads are both one; they may joul horns together, like any deer i' the herd.

Count. Wilt thou ever be a foul-mouthed and calumnious knave?   61

Clo. A prophet I, madam; and I speak the truth the next way:

    For I the ballad will repeat,
      Which men full true shall find;

3-4 *even your content.* Give satisfaction.

19-20 *go to the world.* Get married.

25-26 *Service is no heritage.* Service brings little to be bequeathed.

28 *barnes.* Bairns, children.

47 *ears.* Cultivates.

54-59 *If men . . . i' the herd.* See introduction.

Court jester. Drawing from a medieval manuscript.

643

67 *kind*. Nature.

Helen of Troy. Engraving from a design by S. Shelley, 1789

89 *tithe-woman*. i.e. the one good woman in ten.

92 *mend the lottery*. Make the odds better.

97 *honesty*. Chastity.

98-100 *it will wear . . . heart*. Required by law to wear the surplice which they disapproved of, puritan clergy wore it over the black gown of the Calvinists as a sign of their independence.

114 *stranger sense*. Other ears.

124 *sithence*. Since.

> Your marriage comes by destiny,
>   Your cuckoo sings by kind.

Count.   Get you gone, sir; I'll talk with you more anon.

Stew.   May it please you, madam, that he bid Helen come to you: of her I am to speak.   71

Count.   Sirrah, tell my gentlewoman I would speak with her; Helen, I mean.

Clo.   Was this fair face the cause, quoth she,
>   Why the Grecians sacked Troy?
> Fond done, done fond,
>   Was this King Priam's joy?
> With that she sighed as she stood,
> With that she sighed as she stood,
>   And gave this sentence then;   80
> Among nine bad if one be good,
> Among nine bad if one be good,
>   There's yet one good in ten.

Count.   What, one good in ten? you corrupt the song, sirrah.

Clo.   One good woman in ten, madam; which is a purifying o' the song: would God would serve the world so all the year! we'd find no fault with the tithe-woman, if I were the parson. One in ten, quoth a'! An we might have a good woman born but one every blazing star, or at an earthquake, 'twould mend the lottery well: a man may draw his heart out, ere a' pluck one.

Count.   You'll be gone, sir knave, and do as I command you.

Clo.   That man should be at woman's command, and yet no hurt done! Though honesty be no puritan, yet it will do no hurt; it will wear the surplice of humility over the black gown of a big heart. I am going, forsooth: the business is for Helen to come hither.   [*Exit*. 101

Count.   Well, now.

Stew.   I know, madam, you love your gentlewoman entirely.

Count.   Faith, I do: her father bequeathed her to me; and she herself, without other advantage, may lawfully make title to as much love as she finds: there is more owing her than is paid; and more shall be paid her than she'll demand.

Stew.   Madam, I was very late more near her than I think she wished me: alone she was, and did communicate to herself her own words to her own ears; she thought, I dare vow for her, they touched not any stranger sense. Her matter was, she loved your son: Fortune, she said, was no goddess, that had put such difference betwixt their two estates; Love no god, that would not extend his might, only where qualities were level; Dian no queen of virgins, that would suffer her poor knight surprised, without rescue in the first assault or ransom afterward. This she delivered in the most bitter touch of sorrow that e'er I heard virgin exclaim in: which I held my duty speedily to acquaint you withal; sithence, in the loss that may happen, it concerns you something to know it.

Count.   You have discharged this honestly; keep it to yourself: many likelihoods informed me of this before, which hung so tottering in the balance that I could neither believe nor misdoubt. Pray you, leave me: stall this in your bosom; and I thank you for your honest care: I will speak with you further anon.   [*Exit Steward*.

Enter HELENA.

Even so it was with me when I was young:
● If ever we are nature's, these are ours; this thorn
Doth to our rose of youth rightly belong;
● Our blood to us, this to our blood is born;
It is the show and seal of nature's truth,
Where love's strong passion is impress'd in youth:
By our remembrances of days foregone,   140
†Such were our faults, or then we thought them
          none.
Her eye is sick on 't: I observe her now.

  Hel. What is your pleasure, madam?
  Count.   You know, Helen,
I am a mother to you.
  Hel. Mine honourable mistress.
  Count.   Nay, a mother:
Why not a mother? When I said 'a mother,'
Methought you saw a serpent: what's in 'mother,'
That you start at it? I say, I am your mother;
And put you in the catalogue of those
That were enwombed mine: 'tis often seen   150
Adoption strives with nature and choice breeds
A native slip to us from foreign seeds:
You ne'er oppress'd me with a mother's groan,
Yet I express to you a mother's care:
God's mercy, maiden! does it curd thy blood
To say I am thy mother? What's the matter,
That this distemper'd messenger of wet,
● The many-colour'd Iris, rounds thine eye?
Why? that you are my daughter?
  Hel.   That I am not.
  Count. I say, I am your mother.
  Hel.   Pardon, madam: 160
The Count Rousillon cannot be my brother:
I am from humble, he from honour'd name;
No note upon my parents, his all noble:
My master, my dear lord he is; and I
His servant live, and will his vassal die:
He must not be my brother.
  Count.   Nor I your mother?
  Hel. You are my mother, madam; would you
          were,—
So that my lord your son were not my brother,—
Indeed my mother! or were you both our mothers,
I care no more for than I do for heaven,   170
So I were not his sister. Can't no other,
But, I your daughter, he must be my brother?
  Count. Yes, Helen, you might be my daughter-
          in-law:
God shield you mean it not! daughter and mother
So strive upon your pulse. What, pale again?
My fear hath catch'd your fondness: now I see
The mystery of your loneliness, and find
● Your salt tears' head: now to all sense 'tis gross
You love my son; invention is ashamed,
Against the proclamation of thy passion,   180
To say thou dost not: therefore tell me true;
But tell me then, 'tis so; for, look, thy cheeks
Confess it, th' one to th' other; and thine eyes
See it so grossly shown in thy behaviours
That in their kind they speak it: only sin
And hellish obstinacy tie thy tongue,
That truth should be suspected. Speak, is 't so?
● If it be so, you have wound a goodly clew;
If it be not, forswear 't: howe'er, I charge thee,
As heaven shall work in me for thine avail,   190
To tell me truly.
  Hel.   Good madam, pardon me!
  Count. Do you love my son?

Greek goddess, Iris. From a 19th century engraving

178 *gross.* Evident.

188 *clew.* Ball of twine.

197 *appeach'd.* Accused you.

208 *captious and intenible.* Capable of receiving, but not of retaining.

216 *cites.* Reflects.

218-219 *that your . . . love.* i.e. that your chastity and passion were (paradoxically) at one.

Costume design for Helena by Tanya Moisewitch, Stratford-upon-Avon, 1958–1959

230 *general sovereignty.* i.e. as universal panaceas.

232-233 *As notes . . . in note.* As prescriptions whose powers were stronger than were recognized.

250 *receipt.* Cure.

Hel.   Your pardon, noble mistress!
Count. Love you my son?
Hel.   Do not you love him, madam?
Count. Go not about; my love hath in't a bond,
Whereof the world takes note: come, come, disclose
The state of your affection; for your passions
● Have to the full appeach'd.
    Hel.   Then, I confess,
Here on my knee, before high heaven and you,
That before you, and next unto high heaven,
I love your son.   200
My friends were poor, but honest; so's my love:
Be not offended; for it hurts not him
That he is loved of me: I follow him not
By any token of presumptuous suit;
Nor would I have him till I do deserve him;
Yet never know how that desert should be.
I know I love in vain, strive against hope;
● Yet in this captious and intenible sieve
I still pour in the waters of my love
And lack not to lose still: thus, Indian-like,   210
Religious in mine error, I adore
The sun, that looks upon his worshipper,
But knows of him no more.   My dearest madam,
Let not your hate encounter with my love
For loving where you do: but if yourself,
● Whose aged honour cites a virtuous youth,
Did ever in so true a flame of liking
● Wish chastely and love dearly, that your Dian
Was both herself and love; O, then, give pity
To her, whose state is such that cannot choose
But lend and give where she is sure to lose;   221
That seeks not to find that her search implies,
But riddle-like lives sweetly where she dies!
    Count. Had you not lately an intent,—speak truly,—
To go to Paris?
    Hel.   Madam, I had.
    Count.   Wherefore? tell true.
    Hel. I will tell truth; by grace itself I swear.
You know my father left me some prescriptions
Of rare and proved effects, such as his reading
And manifest experience had collected
● For general sovereignty; and that he will'd me
In heedfull'st reservation to bestow them,   231
● As notes whose faculties inclusive were
More than they were in note: amongst the rest
There is a remedy, approved, set down,
To cure the desperate languishings whereof
The king is render'd lost.
    Count.   This was your motive
For Paris, was it? speak.
    Hel. My lord your son made me to think of this;
Else Paris and the medicine and the king
Had from the conversation of my thoughts   240
Haply been absent then.
    Count.   But think you, Helen,
If you should tender your supposed aid,
He would receive it? he and his physicians
Are of a mind; he, that they cannot help him,
They, that they cannot help: how shall they credit
A poor unlearned virgin, when the schools,
Embowell'd of their doctrine, have left off
The danger to itself?
    Hel.   There's something in't,
More than my father's skill, which was the greatest
● Of his profession, that his good receipt   250
Shall for my legacy be sanctified

By the luckiest stars in heaven: and, would your
  honour
But give me leave to try success, I 'ld venture
The well-lost life of mine on his grace's cure
By such a day and hour.
    Count.   Dost thou believe 't?
    Hel. Ay, madam, knowingly.
    Count. Why, Helen, thou shalt have my leave
    and love,
Means and attendants and my loving greetings
To those of mine in court: I 'll stay at home
And pray God's blessing into thy attempt: 260
Be gone to-morrow; and be sure of this,
What I can help thee to thou shalt not miss.
                              [*Exeunt.*

ACT II.

Scene I. *Paris.* *The* King's *palace.*

Flourish of cornets. *Enter the* King, *attended
with divers young* Lords *taking leave for the
Florentine war;* Bertram, *and* Parolles.

    King. Farewell, young lords; these warlike
    principles
Do not throw from you: and you, my lords, fare-
  well:
Share the advice betwixt you; if both gain, all
The gift doth stretch itself as 'tis received,
And is enough for both.
    First Lord.   'Tis our hope, sir,
•After well enter'd soldiers, to return
And find your grace in health.
    King. No, no, it cannot be; and yet my heart
•Will not confess he owes the malady
That doth my life besiege. Farewell, young
  lords;   10
Whether I live or die, be you the sons
•Of worthy Frenchmen: let higher Italy,—
•†Those bated that inherit but the fall
•Of the last monarchy,—see that you come
Not to woo honour, but to wed it; when
The bravest questant shrinks, find what you seek,
That fame may cry you loud: I say, farewell.
    Sec. Lord. Health, at your bidding, serve your
    majesty!
    King. Those girls of Italy, take heed of
    them:
They say, our French lack language to deny, 20
If they demand: beware of being captives,
Before you serve.
    Both.   Our hearts receive your warnings.
    King. Farewell. Come hither to me.
                      [*Exit, attended.*
    First Lord. O my sweet lord, that you will
    stay behind us!
    Par. 'Tis not his fault, the spark.
    Sec. Lord.   O, 'tis brave wars!
    Par. Most admirable: I have seen those wars.
•   *Ber.* I am commanded here, and kept a coil
    with
'Too young' and 'the next year' and ''tis too
  early.'
    Par. An thy mind stand to 't, boy, steal away
    bravely.
•   *Ber.* I shall stay here the forehorse to a smock,
•Creaking my shoes on the plain masonry, 31
Till honour be bought up and no sword worn

6 *After well enter'd.* After becoming experienced.

9 *he owes.* It owns.

12 *higher.* Probably upper Italy.

13 *bated.* Weakened.

14 *the last monarchy.* Perhaps the Holy Roman Empire.

27 *kept a coil with.* Fussed over.

30 *forehorse to a smock.* The lead horse in a team driven by a woman.

31 *plain masonry.* Smooth floors.

36-37 *our parting . . . body*. Parting from you is like being torn apart.

53 *list*. Limit.

54-55 *wear . . . time*. Are fashionable.

57 *received star*. Popular fashion.

70 *across*. A term from tilting meaning a clumsy blow.

77 *canary*. A lively dance.

79 *King Pepin*. Father of Charlemain.

But one to dance with! By heaven, I'll steal away.
First Lord. There's honour in the theft.
Par.   Commit it, count.
Sec. Lord. I am your accessary; and so, farewell.
Ber. I grow to you, and our parting is a tortured body.
First Lord. Farewell, captain.
Sec. Lord. Sweet Monsieur Parolles!
Par. Noble heroes, my sword and yours are kin. Good sparks and lustrous, a word, good metals: you shall find in the regiment of the Spinii one Captain Spurio, with his cicatrice, an emblem of war, here on his sinister cheek; it was this very sword entrenched it: say to him, I live; and observe his reports for me.
First Lord. We shall, noble captain.
                              [*Exeunt Lords.*
Par. Mars dote on you for his novices! what will ye do?
Ber. Stay: the king.   50

Re-enter KING. BERTRAM *and* PAROLLES *retire*.

Par. [*To Ber.*] Use a more spacious ceremony to the noble lords; you have restrained yourself within the list of too cold an adieu: be more expressive to them: for they wear themselves in the cap of the time, there do muster true gait, eat, speak, and move under the influence of the most received star; and though the devil lead the measure, such are to be followed: after them, and take a more dilated farewell.
Ber. And I will do so.   60
Par. Worthy fellows; and like to prove most sinewy sword-men.
                        [*Exeunt Bertram and Parolles.*

Enter LAFEU.

Laf. [*Kneeling*] Pardon, my lord, for me and for my tidings.
King. I'll fee thee to stand up.
Laf. Then here's a man stands, that has brought his pardon.
I would you had kneel'd, my lord, to ask me mercy,
And that at my bidding you could so stand up.
King. I would I had; so I had broke thy pate,
And ask'd thee mercy for't.
Laf. Good faith, across: but, my good lord, 'tis thus;   70
Will you be cured of your infirmity?
King. No.
Laf. O, will you eat no grapes, my royal fox?
Yes, but you will my noble grapes, an if
My royal fox could reach them: I have seen a medicine
That's able to breathe life into a stone,
Quicken a rock, and make you dance canary
With spritely fire and motion; whose simple touch
Is powerful to araise King Pepin, nay,
To give great Charlemain a pen in's hand   80
And write to her a love-line.
King.   What 'her' is this?
Laf. Why, Doctor She: my lord, there's one arrived,

If you will see her: now, by my faith and honour,
If seriously I may convey my thoughts
In this my light deliverance, I have spoke
With one that, in her sex, her years, profession,
Wisdom and constancy, hath amazed me more
Than I dare blame my weakness: will you see
    her,
For that is her demand, and know her business?
That done, laugh well at me.
    King.   Now, good Lafeu, 90
Bring in the admiration; that we with thee
May spend our wonder too, or take off thine
• By wondering how thou took'st it.
    Laf.   Nay, I'll fit you,
And not be all day neither.   [*Exit.*
    King. Thus he his special nothing ever pro-
logues.

Re-enter LAFEU, *with* HELENA.

    Laf. Nay, come your ways.
    King.   This haste hath wings indeed.
    Laf. Nay, come your ways;
This is his majesty; say your mind to him:
A traitor you do look like; but such traitors
• His majesty seldom fears: I am Cressid's uncle,
That dare leave two together; fare you well. 101
                         [*Exit.*
•   *King.* Now, fair one, does your business fol-
low us?
    Hel. Ay, my good lord.
Gerard de Narbon was my father;
• In what he did profess, well found.
    King.   I knew him.
    Hel. The rather will I spare my praises
    towards him;
Knowing him is enough. On's bed of death
Many receipts he gave me; chiefly one,
Which, as the dearest issue of his practice,
And of his old experience the only darling,   110
He bade me store up, as a triple eye,
Safer than mine own two, more dear; I have so;
And, hearing your high majesty is touch'd
With that malignant cause wherein the honour
Of my dear father's gift stands chief in power,
I come to tender it and my appliance
With all bound humbleness.
    King.   We thank you, maiden;
But may not be so credulous of cure,
When our most learned doctors leave us and
• The congregated college have concluded   120
That labouring art can never ransom nature
From her inaidible estate; I say we must not
So stain our judgement, or corrupt our hope,
To prostitute our past-cure malady
To empirics, or to dissever so
Our great self and our credit, to esteem
A senseless help when help past sense we deem.
    Hel. My duty then shall pay me for my pains:
I will no more enforce mine office on you;
Humbly entreating from your royal thoughts 130
A modest one, to bear me back again.
    King. I cannot give thee less, to be call'd
    grateful:
Thou thought'st to help me; and such thanks
    I give
As one near death to those that wish him live:
But what at full I know, thou know'st no part,
I knowing all my peril, thou no art.
    Hel. What I can do can do no hurt to try,

93 *fit.* Satisfy.

100 *Cressid's uncle.* Pandarus was the go-between in
the love affair between Cressida and Troilus.

Helena, Lafeu and the King. Engraving from design by
F. Hayman, Hanmer's edition, 1743

102 *follow us.* Concern us.

105 *found.* Skilful.

120-125 *The congregated ... empirics.* See introduction.

King of France (Alec Guinness) and Helena (Irene Worth), Stratford, Ontario, 1953

---

138 *set up your rest.* 'Stake your all', from the card game Primero.

153 *square . . . shows.* Base suppositions on appearance.

167 *Hesperus.* The evening star.

168 *pilot's glass.* Hour glass.

181 *sense saves.* Makes sense.

190 *flinch in property.* Fail in what I have promised.

Since you set up your rest 'gainst remedy
He that of greatest works is finisher
Oft does them by the weakest minister: 140
So holy writ in babes hath judgement shown,
When judges have been babes; great floods have
    flown
From simple sources, and great seas have dried
When miracles have by the greatest been denied.
Oft expectation fails and most oft there
Where most it promises, and oft it hits
Where hope is coldest and despair most fits.
   King. I must not hear thee; fare thee well,
    kind maid;
Thy pains not used must by thyself be paid:
Proffers not took reap thanks for their reward.   150
   Hel. Inspired merit so by breath is barr'd:
It is not so with Him that all things knows
As 'tis with us that square our guess by shows;
But most it is presumption in us when
The help of heaven we count the act of men.
Dear sir, to my endeavours give consent;
Of heaven, not me, make an experiment.
I am not an impostor that proclaim
Myself against the level of mine aim;
But know I think and think I know most sure 160
My art is not past power nor you past cure.
    King. Art thou so confident? within what
    space
Hopest thou my cure?
   Hel.   The great'st grace lending grace,
Ere twice the horses of the sun shall bring
Their fiery torcher his diurnal ring,
Ere twice in murk and occidental damp
Moist Hesperus hath quench'd his sleepy lamp,
Or four and twenty times the pilot's glass
Hath told the thievish minutes how they pass,
What is infirm from your sound parts shall fly, 170
Health shall live free and sickness freely die.
   King. Upon thy certainty and confidence
What darest thou venture?
   Hel.   Tax of impudence,
A strumpet's boldness, a divulged shame
Traduced by odious ballads: my maiden's name
Sear'd otherwise; nay, worse—if worse—extended
With vilest torture let my life be ended.
   King. Methinks in thee some blessed spirit
    doth speak
His powerful sound within an organ weak:
And what impossibility would slay   180
In common sense, sense saves another way.
Thy life is dear; for all that life can rate
Worth name of life in thee hath estimate,
Youth, beauty, wisdom, courage, all
That happiness and prime can happy call:
Thou this to hazard needs must intimate
Skill infinite or monstrous desperate.
Sweet practiser, thy physic I will try,
That ministers thine own death if I die.
   Hel. If I break time, or flinch in property 190
Of what I spoke, unpitied let me die,
And well deserved: not helping, death's my fee;
But, if I help, what do you promise me?
    King. Make thy demand.
   Hel.   But will you make it even?
    King. Ay, by my sceptre and my hopes of
    heaven.
   Hel. Then shalt thou give me with thy kingly
    hand
What husband in thy power I will command:

Exempted be from me the arrogance
To choose from forth the royal blood of France,
My low and humble name to propagate   200
With any branch or image of thy state;
But such a one, thy vassal, whom I know
Is free for me to ask, thee to bestow.
   King. Here is my hand; the premises ob-
     served,
Thy will by my performance shall be served:
So make the choice of thy own time, for I,
Thy resolved patient, on thee still rely.
More should I question thee, and more I must,
Though more to know could not be more to trust,
From whence thou camest, how tended on:
     but rest   210
Unquestion'd welcome and undoubted blest.
Give me some help here, ho! If thou proceed
As high as word, my deed shall match thy meed.
     [*Flourish. Exeunt.*

SCENE II. *Rousillon. The* COUNT'S *palace.*

Enter COUNTESS *and* CLOWN.

   Count. Come on, sir; I shall now put you to
the height of your breeding.
   Clo. I will show myself highly fed and lowly
taught: I know my business is but to the court.
   Count. To the court! why, what place make
you special, when you put off that with such contempt? But to the court!
   Clo. Truly, madam, if God have lent a man
any manners, he may easily put it off at court:
he that cannot make a leg, put off's cap, kiss his
hand and say nothing, has neither leg, hands, lip,
nor cap; and indeed such a fellow, to say precisely, were not for the court; but for me, I have
an answer will serve all men.
   Count. Marry, that's a bountiful answer that
fits all questions.
   Clo. It is like a barber's chair that fits all buttocks, the pin-buttock, the quatch-buttock, the
brawn buttock, or any buttock.
   Count. Will your answer serve fit to all questions?   21
   Clo. As fit as ten groats is for the hand of an
attorney, as your French crown for your taffeta
punk, as Tib's rush for Tom's forefinger, as a
pancake for Shrove Tuesday, a morris for Mayday, as the nail to his hole, the cuckold to his
horn, as a scolding quean to a wrangling knave,
as the nun's lip to the friar's mouth, nay, as the
pudding to his skin.
   Count. Have you, I say, an answer of such
fitness for all questions?   31
   Clo. From below your duke to beneath your
constable, it will fit any question.
   Count. It must be an answer of most monstrous
size that must fit all demands.
   Clo. But a trifle neither, in good faith, if the
learned should speak truth of it: here it is, and
all that belongs to't. Ask me if I am a courtier:
it shall do you no harm to learn.   39
   Count. To be young again, if we could: I
will be a fool in question, hoping to be the wiser by
your answer. I pray you, sir, are you a courtier?
   Clo. O Lord, sir! There's a simple putting off.
More, more, a hundred of them.
   Count. Sir, I am a poor friend of yours, that
loves you.

3-4 *highly . . . taught.* Referring to the proverb, 'Better
fed than taught'.

10 *make a leg.* Curtsy.

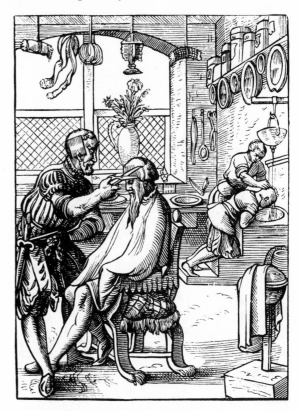

Clown: 'It is like a barber's chair . . .' Illustration from an
early 16th century engraving

22 *ten groats.* The usual attorney's fee.

23 *French crown.* A pun on a 'French coin' and a 'bald
head', symptom of the French disease. i.e. syphilis.

24 *punk.* Whore. *rush.* A ring made of rushes, used in
rustic marriages.

47 *Thick*. Quickly.

1-6 *They say . . . fear.* See introduction.

7 *argument*. Topic.

10 *artists*. Doctors.

12 *Galen and Paracelsus.* Galen was a Greek physician of the second century and Paracelsus a Swiss doctor of the sixteenth century.

Galen. From Andrew Boorde's *A Dyetary of Helth*, 1547

Clo. O Lord, sir! Thick, thick, spare not me.

Count. I think, sir, you can eat none of this homely meat.

Clo. O Lord, sir! Nay, put me to 't, I warrant you.   51

Count. You were lately whipped, sir, as I think.

Clo. O Lord, sir! spare not me.

Count. Do you cry, 'O Lord, sir!' at your whipping, and 'spare not me'? Indeed your 'O Lord, sir!' is very sequent to your whipping: you would answer very well to a whipping, if you were but bound to 't.

Clo. I ne'er had worse luck in my life in my 'O Lord, sir!' I see things may serve long, but not serve ever.   61

Count. I play the noble housewife with the time,
To entertain 't so merrily with a fool.

Clo. O Lord, sir! why, there 't serves well again.

Count. An end, sir; to your business. Give Helen this,
And urge her to a present answer back:
Commend me to my kinsmen and my son:
This is not much.

Clo. Not much commendation to them.   70

Count. Not much employment for you: you understand me?

Clo. Most fruitfully: I am there before my legs.

Count. Haste you again.   [*Exeunt severally.*

SCENE III. *Paris. The* KING'S *palace.*

Enter BERTRAM, LAFEU, *and* PAROLLES.

Laf. They say miracles are past; and we have our philosophical persons, to make modern and familiar, things supernatural and causeless. Hence is it that we make trifles of terrors, ensconcing ourselves into seeming knowledge, when we should submit ourselves to an unknown fear.

Par. Why, 'tis the rarest argument of wonder that hath shot out in our latter times.

Ber. And so 'tis.

Laf. To be relinquished of the artists,—   10

Par. So I say.

Laf. Both of Galen and Paracelsus.

Par. So I say.

Laf. Of all the learned and authentic fellows,—

Par. Right; so I say.

Laf. That gave him out incurable,—

Par. Why, there 'tis; so say I too.

Laf. Not to be helped,—

Par. Right; as 'twere, a man assured of a—

Laf. Uncertain life, and sure death.   20

Par. Just, you say well; so would I have said.

Laf. I may truly say, it is a novelty to the world.

Par. It is, indeed: if you will have it in showing, you shall read it in—what do ye call there?

Laf. A showing of a heavenly effect in an earthly actor.

Par. That's it; I would have said the very same.   30

Laf. Why, your dolphin is not lustier: 'fore me, I speak in respect—

Par. Nay, 'tis strange, 'tis very strange, that is the brief and the tedious of it; and he's of a

most facinerious spirit that will not acknowledge
it to be the—
  Laf. Very hand of heaven.
  Par. Ay, so I say.
  Laf. In a most weak—[*pausing*] and debile
minister, great power, great transcendence: which
should, indeed, give us a further use to be made
than alone the recovery of the king, as to be—
[*pausing*] generally thankful.
  Par. I would have said it; you say well.
Here comes the king.

Enter KING, HELENA, *and* Attendants.
LAFEU *and* PAROLLES *retire.*

  Laf. Lustig, as the Dutchman says: I'll like
a maid the better, whilst I have a tooth in my
head: why, he's able to lead her a coranto.
  Par. Mort du vinaigre! is not this Helen? 50
  Laf. 'Fore God, I think so.
  King. Go, call before me all the lords in court.
Sit, my preserver, by thy patient's side;
And with this healthful hand, whose banish'd sense
Thou hast repeal'd, a second time receive
The confirmation of my promised gift,
Which but attends thy naming.

Enter three or four Lords.

Fair maid, send forth thine eye: this youthful
    parcel
Of noble bachelors stand at my bestowing,
O'er whom both sovereign power and father's
    voice   60
I have to use: thy frank election make;
Thou hast power to choose, and they none to for-
    sake.
  Hel. To each of you one fair and virtuous
    mistress
Fall, when Love please! marry, to each, but
    one!
  Laf. I'ld give bay Curtal and his furniture,
My mouth no more were broken than these boys',
And writ as little beard.
  King.   Peruse them well:
Not one of those but had a noble father.
  Hel. Gentlemen,
Heaven hath through me restored the king to
    health.   70
  All. We understand it, and thank heaven for
    you.
  Hel. I am a simple maid, and therein weal-
    thiest,
That I protest I simply am a maid.
Please it your majesty, I have done already:
The blushes in my cheeks thus whisper me,
'We blush that thou shouldst choose; but, be
    refused,
Let the white death sit on thy cheek for ever;
We'll ne'er come there again.'
  King.   Make choice; and, see,
Who shuns thy love shuns all his love in me.
  Hel. Now, Dian, from thy altar do I fly, 80
And to imperial Love, that god most high,
Do my sighs stream. Sir, will you hear my suit?
  First Lord. And grant it.
  Hel.   Thanks, sir; all the
    rest is mute.
  Laf. I had rather be in this choice than throw
ames-ace for my life.

35 *facinerious.* Wicked.

47 *Lustig.* Frolicsome.

49 *coranto.* A lively dance.

50 *Mort du vinaigre!* A meaningless oath.

65 *bay Curtal and his furniture.* My bay horse with the docked tail and all his trappings.

66 *broken.* Could be either 'lacking teeth' or 'broken in' like a horse.

King: 'Make choice; and, see, Who shuns thy love shuns all his love in me.' Engraving from a painting by Francis Wheatley (1747–1801)

85 *ames-ace.* The lowest throw in a dice game.

105-106 *There's one . . . wine*. There is one off-spring of noble stock still left whose father had strong red blood in his veins.

Helena: 'This is the man'. Engraving by Kenny Meadows from Barry Cornwall's *Works of Shakspere*, 1846

121-128 *She had . . . mighty.* See introduction.

122-123 *Disdain . . . ever.* Let my disdain of her ruin my favour and fortune.

127-128 *yet stand . . . mighty.* You think that your 'blood' is different from hers, because of your status, although physically it is indistinguishable.

142-148 *honours thrive . . . indeed.* See introduction.

Hel. The honour, sir, that flames in your fair eyes,
Before I speak, too threateningly replies:
Love make your fortunes twenty times above
Her that so wishes and her humble love!
   Sec. Lord.   No better, if you please.
   Hel.   My wish receive, 90
Which great Love grant! and so, I take my leave.
   Laf.   Do all they deny her?   An they were sons of mine, I'd have them whipped; or I would send them to the Turk, to make eunuchs of.
   Hel.   Be not afraid that I your hand should take;
I'll never do you wrong for your own sake:
Blessing upon your vows! and in your bed
Find fairer fortune, if you ever wed!
   Laf.   These boys are boys of ice, they'll none have her: sure, they are bastards to the English; the French ne'er got 'em.   101
   Hel.   You are too young, too happy, and too good,
To make yourself a son out of my blood.
   Fourth Lord.   Fair one, I think not so.
 • *Laf.*   There's one grape yet; I am sure thy father drunk wine: but if thou be'st not an ass, I am a youth of fourteen; I have known thee already.
   Hel. [*To Bertram*] I dare not say I take you;
      but I give
Me and my service, ever whilst I live,   110
Into your guiding power.   This is the man.
   King.   Why, then, young Bertram, take her;
      she's thy wife.
   Ber.   My wife, my liege! I shall beseech your highness,
In such a business give me leave to use
The help of mine own eyes.
   King.   Know'st thou not, Bertram,
What she has done for me?
   Ber.   Yes, my good lord;
But never hope to know why I should marry her.
   King.   Thou know'st she has raised me from
      my sickly bed.
   Ber.   But follows it, my lord, to bring me down
Must answer for your raising?   I know her well:
 • She had her breeding at my father's charge. 121
 • A poor physician's daughter my wife!   Disdain
Rather corrupt me ever!

   King.   'Tis only title thou disdain'st in her,
      the which
I can build up.   Strange is it that our bloods,
Of colour, weight, and heat, pour'd all together,
 • Would quite confound distinction, yet stand off
In differences so mighty.   If she be
All that is virtuous, save what thou dislikest,
A poor physician's daughter, thou dislikest. 130
Of virtue for the name: but do not so:
From lowest place when virtuous things proceed,
The place is dignified by the doer's deed:
Where great additions swell's, and virtue none,
It is a dropsied honour.   Good alone
Is good without a name.   Vileness is so:
The property by what it is should go,
Not by the title.   She is young, wise, fair;
In these to nature she's immediate heir,
And these breed honour: that is honour's scorn,
Which challenges itself as honour's born   141
 • And is not like the sire: honours thrive,
When rather from our acts we them derive
Than our foregoers: the mere word's a slave

Debosh'd on every tomb, on every grave
A lying trophy, and as oft is dumb
Where dust and damn'd oblivion is the tomb
Of honour'd bones indeed.   What should be said?
If thou canst like this creature as a maid,
I can create the rest: virtue and she   150
Is her own dower; honour and wealth from me.
 Ber.   I cannot love her, nor will strive to do't.
 King.   Thou wrong'st thyself, if thou shouldst
  strive to choose.
 Hel.   That you are well restored, my lord,
  I'm glad:
Let the rest go.
 King.   My honour's at the stake; which to
  defeat,
I must produce my power.   Here, take her hand,
Proud scornful boy, unworthy this good gift;
That dost in vile misprision shackle up
My love and her desert; that canst not dream,
We, poising us in her defective scale,   161
Shall weigh thee to the beam; that wilt not know,
It is in us to plant thine honour where
We please to have it grow.   Check thy con-
  tempt:
Obey our will, which travails in thy good:
Believe not thy disdain, but presently
Do thine own fortunes that obedient right
Which both thy duty owes and our power claims;
Or I will throw thee from my care for ever
Into the staggers and the careless lapse   170
Of youth and ignorance; both my revenge and
  hate
Loosing upon thee, in the name of justice,
Without all terms of pity.   Speak; thine answer.
 Ber.   Pardon, my gracious lord; for I submit
My fancy to your eyes: when I consider
What great creation and what dole of honour
Flies where you bid it, I find that she, which late
Was in my nobler thoughts most base, is now
The praised of the king; who, so ennobled,
Is as 'twere born so.
 King.   Take her by the hand,   180
And tell her she is thine: to whom I promise
A counterpoise, if not to thy estate
A balance more replete.
 Ber.   I take her hand.
 King.   Good fortune and the favour of the king
Smile upon this contract; whose ceremony
Shall seem expedient on the now-born brief,
And be perform'd to-night: the solemn feast
Shall more attend upon the coming space,
Expecting absent friends.   As thou lovest her,
Thy love's to me religious; else, does err.   190
   [*Exeunt all but Lafeu and Parolles.*

 Laf. [*Advancing*] Do you hear, monsieur? a
word with you.
 Par.   Your pleasure, sir?
 Laf.   Your lord and master did well to make
his recantation.
 Par.   Recantation!   My lord!   my master!
 Laf.   Ay; is it not a language I speak?
 Par.   A most harsh one, and not to be under-
stood without bloody succeeding.   My master!
 Laf.   Are you companion to the Count Rou-
sillon?   201
 Par.   To any count, to all counts, to what is
man.
 Laf.   To what is count's man: count's master
is of another style.

King: 'Here, take her hand'. Engraving from Knight's
Pictorial Edition of the Works of Shakspere, 1839–1843

145 *Debosh'd.* Debauched.

159 *misprision.* Misunderstanding.

161 *poising us.* Adding our royal weight.

170 *staggers.* A disease of horses which made them
giddy; here, therefore, 'irresponsible behaviour'.

186 *Shall . . . brief.* Shall follow swiftly on the now
prepared contract.

203-204 *man . . . man.* Parolles means 'manly' while
Lafeu means 'servant'.

211 *two ordinaries.* Two meal-times.

214 *scarfs.* Military men wore scarfs around the arm or over the shoulder.

237 *pull at ... contrary.* You will have to drink of your own folly first.

247 *as I will by thee.* i.e. as I will pass by thee.

Parolles. Engraving by Kenny Meadows from Barry Cornwall's *Works of Shakspere,* 1846

Par. You are too old, sir; let it satisfy you, you are too old.
Laf. I must tell thee, sirrah, I write man; to which title age cannot bring thee. 209
Par. What I dare too well do, I dare not do.
Laf. I did think thee, for two ordinaries, to be a pretty wise fellow; thou didst make tolerable vent of thy travel; it might pass: yet the scarfs and the bannerets about thee did manifoldly dissuade me from believing thee a vessel of too great a burthen. I have now found thee; when I lose thee again, I care not: yet art thou good for nothing but taking up; and that thou'rt scarce worth.
Par. Hadst thou not the privilege of antiquity upon thee,— 221
Laf. Do not plunge thyself too far in anger, lest thou hasten thy trial; which if—Lord have mercy on thee for a hen! So, my good window of lattice, fare thee well: thy casement I need not open, for I look through thee. Give me thy hand.
Par. My lord, you give me most egregious indignity.
Laf. Ay, with all my heart; and thou art worthy of it. 231
Par. I have not, my lord, deserved it.
Laf. Yes, good faith, every dram of it; and I will not bate thee a scruple.
Par. Well, I shall be wiser.
Laf. Even as soon as thou canst, for thou hast to pull at a smack o' the contrary. If ever thou be'st bound in thy scarf and beaten, thou shalt find what it is to be proud of thy bondage. I have a desire to hold my acquaintance with thee, or rather my knowledge, that I may say in the default, he is a man I know.
Par. My lord, you do me most insupportable vexation.
Laf. I would it were hell-pains for thy sake, and my poor doing eternal: for doing I am past: as I will by thee, in what motion age will give me leave. [*Exit.*
Par. Well, thou hast a son shall take this disgrace off me; scurvy, old, filthy, scurvy lord! Well, I must be patient; there is no fettering of authority. I'll beat him, by my life, if I can meet him with any convenience, an he were double and double a lord. I'll have no more pity of his age than I would have of— I'll beat him, an if I could but meet him again.

Re-enter LAFEU.

Laf. Sirrah, your lord and master's married; there's news for you: you have a new mistress.
Par. I most unfeignedly beseech your lordship to make some reservation of your wrongs: he is my good lord: whom I serve above is my master.
Laf. Who? God?
Par. Ay, sir.
Laf. The devil it is that's thy master. Why dost thou garter up thy arms o' this fashion? dost make hose of thy sleeves? do other servants so? Thou wert best set thy lower part where thy nose stands. By mine honour, if I were but two hours younger, I'ld beat thee: methinks, thou art a general offence, and every man should beat thee: I think thou wast created for men to breathe themselves upon thee.

Par. This is hard and undeserved measure, my lord.

Laf. Go to, sir; you were beaten in Italy for
• picking a kernel out of a pomegranate; you are a
vagabond and no true traveller: you are more
saucy with lords and honourable personages than
the commission of your birth and virtue gives you
heraldry.   You are not worth another word, else
I 'ld call you knave.   I leave you.   [*Exit.* 281

Par. Good, very good; it is so then: good,
very good: let it be concealed awhile.

Re-enter BERTRAM.

Ber. Undone, and forfeited to cares for ever!

Par. What's the matter, sweet-heart?

Ber. Although before the solemn priest I have
    sworn,
I will not bed her.

Par. What, what, sweet-heart?

Ber. O my Parolles, they have married me!
I 'll to the Tuscan wars, and never bed her.   290

Par. France is a dog-hole, and it no more merits
The tread of a man's foot: to the wars!

Ber. There's letters from my mother: what
the import is, I know not yet.

Par. Ay, that would be known.   To the wars,
    my boy, to the wars!
He wears his honour in a box unseen,
That hugs his kicky-wicky here at home,
Spending his manly marrow in her arms,
• Which should sustain the bound and high curvet
Of Mars's fiery steed.   To other regions   300
France is a stable; we that dwell in't jades;
Therefore, to the war!

Ber. It shall be so: I 'll send her to my house,
Acquaint my mother with my hate to her,
And wherefore I am fled; write to the king
That which I durst not speak: his present gift
Shall furnish me to those Italian fields,
Where noble fellows strike: war is no strife
• To the dark house and the detested wife.

Par. Will this capriccio hold in thee? art sure?

Ber. Go with me to my chamber, and advise
    me.   311
I 'll send her straight away: to-morrow
I 'll to the wars, she to her single sorrow.
• *Par.* Why, these balls bound; there's noise
    in it.   'Tis hard:
A young man married is a man that's marr'd:
Therefore away, and leave her bravely; go:
The king has done you wrong: but, hush, 'tis so.
    [*Exeunt.*

SCENE IV.   *Paris.   The* KING'S *palace.*

Enter HELENA *and* CLOWN.

Hel. My mother greets me kindly: is she well?
• *Clo.* She is not well; but yet she has her health:
she's very merry; but yet she is not well: but
thanks be given, she's very well and wants
nothing i' the world; but yet she is not well.

Hel. If she be very well, what does she ail,
that she's not very well?

Clo. Truly, she's very well indeed, but for
two things.

Hel. What two things?   10

Clo. One, that she's not in heaven, whither
God send her quickly! the other, that she's in
earth, from whence God send her quickly!

276 *picking a kernel out of a pomegranate.* For a trivial
offence.

Elizabeth Vernon, Countess of Southampton, whom
Southampton, Shakespeare's noble patron, reluctantly
married in 1598

299 *curvet.* A special kind of leap made by a horse.

309 *dark house.* Madhouse.

314 *these balls bound.* Now you see how the game's
played.

2 *well.* The clown quibbles on the meanings 'well in
health' and the theological 'rid of the body'.

27 *title*. Status or worth.

Maria Macklin, 18th century English actress, as Helena

7 *lark for a bunting*. i.e. I under-estimated him; the bunting is similar to the lark, but has no song.

Enter PAROLLES.

Par. Bless you, my fortunate lady!

Hel. I hope, sir, I have your good will to have mine own good fortunes.

Par. You had my prayers to lead them on; and to keep them on, have them still. O, my knave, how does my old lady?

Clo. So that you had her wrinkles and I her money, I would she did as you say.   21

Par. Why, I say nothing.

Clo. Marry, you are the wiser man; for many a man's tongue shakes out his master's undoing: to say nothing, to do nothing, to know nothing, and to have nothing, is to be a great part of your • title; which is within a very little of nothing.

Par. Away! thou'rt a knave.

Clo. You should have said, sir, before a knave thou'rt a knave; that's, before me thou'rt a knave: this had been truth, sir.   31

Par. Go to, thou art a witty fool; I have found thee.

Clo. Did you find me in yourself, sir? or were you taught to find me? The search, sir, was profitable; and much fool may you find in you, even to the world's pleasure and the increase of laughter.

Par. A good knave, i' faith, and well fed. Madam, my lord will go away to-night;   40 A very serious business calls on him. The great prerogative and rite of love, Which, as your due, time claims, he does ac- knowledge; But puts it off to a compell'd restraint; Whose want, and whose delay, is strew'd with sweets, Which they distil now in the curbed time, To make the coming hour o'erflow with joy And pleasure drown the brim.

Hel.   What's his will else?

Par. That you will take your instant leave o' the king, And make this haste as your own good pro- ceeding,   50 Strengthen'd with what apology you think May make it probable need.

Hel.   What more commands he?

Par. That, having this obtain'd, you presently Attend his further pleasure.

Hel. In every thing I wait upon his will.

Par. I shall report it so.

Hel.   I pray you.   [*Exit Parolles.*] Come, sirrah.   [*Exeunt.*

SCENE V.   *Paris.   The* KING's *palace.*

Enter LAFEU *and* BERTRAM.

Laf. But I hope your lordship thinks not him a soldier.

Ber. Yes, my lord, and of very valiant approof.

Laf. You have it from his own deliverance.

Ber. And by other warranted testimony.

Laf. Then my dial goes not true: I took this • lark for a bunting.

Ber. I do assure you, my lord, he is very great in knowledge and accordingly valiant.

Laf. I have then sinned against his ex- perience and transgressed against his valour; and my state that way is dangerous, since I cannot yet find in my heart to repent.   Here he comes: I pray you, make us friends; I will pursue the amity.

Enter PAROLLES.

Par. [*To Bertram*] These things shall be done, sir.

   Laf. Pray you, sir, who's his tailor?

   Par. Sir?

   Laf. O, I know him well, I, sir; he, sir, 's a good workman, a very good tailor.   21

   Ber. [*Aside to Par.*] Is she gone to the king?

   Par. She is.

   Ber. Will she away to-night?

   Par. As you'll have her.

   Ber. I have writ my letters, casketed my
      treasure,
Given order for our horses; and to-night,
When I should take possession of the bride,
End ere I do begin.   29

   Laf. A good traveller is something at the latter end of a dinner; but one that lies three thirds and uses a known truth to pass a thousand nothings with, should be once heard and thrice beaten.   God save you, captain.

   Ber. Is there any unkindness between my lord and you, monsieur?

   Par. I know not how I have deserved to run into my lord's displeasure.

   Laf. You have made shift to run into 't, boots and spurs and all, like him that leaped into the custard; and out of it you'll run again, rather than suffer question for your residence.

   Ber. It may be you have mistaken him, my lord.

   Laf. And shall do so ever, though I took him at 's prayers.   Fare you well, my lord; and believe this of me, there can be no kernel in this light nut; the soul of this man is his clothes. Trust him not in matter of heavy consequence; I have kept of them tame, and know their natures. Farewell, monsieur: I have spoken better of you †than you have or will to deserve at my hand; but we must do good against evil.   [*Exit.*

   Par. An idle lord, I swear.

   Ber. I think so.

   Par. Why, do you not know him?

   Ber. Yes, I do know him well, and common
      speech
Gives him a worthy pass.   Here comes my clog.

Enter HELENA.

   Hel. I have, sir, as I was commanded from you,
Spoke with the king and have procured his leave
For present parting; only he desires   61
Some private speech with you.

   Ber.   I shall obey his will.
You must not marvel, Helen, at my course,
Which holds not colour with the time, nor does
The ministration and required office
On my particular.   Prepared I was not
For such a business; therefore am I found
So much unsettled: this drives me to entreat you
That presently you take your way for home;
And rather muse than ask why I entreat you,   70
For my respects are better than they seem
And my appointments have in them a need
Greater than shows itself at the first view

40-41 *that leaped into the custard.* At Lord Mayors' Feasts at this time, one of the most common acts was a fool leaping into a giant custard pie.

42 *for your residence.* Why you stay.

HERE COMES MY CLOG   ACT·II·SCENE·V

Bertram and Parolles. Illustration by Byam Shaw, *Chiswick Shakespeare c.* 1900

64 *holds not colour.* Is unsuitable.

80 *homely stars.* Humble origins.

97 *coragio.* Courage.

View of Florence. From John Speed's *A Prospect of the Most Famous Parts of the World,* 1631

10-16 *The reasons . . . guess'd.* I cannot speak about state policy, except as someone outside the council who can only guess by his own imagination what must be happening inside.

To you that know them not.   This to my mother:
[*Giving a letter.*
'Twill be two days ere I shall see you, so
I leave you to your wisdom.
 Hel.   Sir, I can nothing say,
But that I am your most obedient servant.
 Ber. Come, come, no more of that.
 Hel.   And ever shall
With true observance seek to eke out that
Wherein toward me my homely stars have fail'd
To equal my great fortune.
 Ber.   Let that go: 81
My haste is very great: farewell; hie home.
 Hel. Pray, sir, your pardon.
 Ber.   Well, what would you say?
 Hel. I am not worthy of the wealth I owe,
Nor dare I say 'tis mine, and yet it is;
But, like a timorous thief, most fain would steal
What law does vouch mine own.
 Ber.   What would you have?
 Hel. Something; and scarce so much: nothing, indeed.
I would not tell you what I would, my lord:
Faith, yes; 90
Strangers and foes do sunder, and not kiss.
 Ber. I pray you, stay not, but in haste to
  horse.
 Hel. I shall not break your bidding, good my
  lord.
 Ber. Where are my other men, monsieur?
  Farewell.   [*Exit Helena.*
Go thou toward home; where I will never come
Whilst I can shake my sword or hear the drum.
Away, and for our flight.
 Par.   Bravely, coragio!
          [*Exeunt.*

ACT III.

SCENE I. *Florence.* *The* DUKE'S *palace.*

Flourish. Enter the DUKE *of Florence, attended; the two Frenchmen, with a troop of soldiers.*

 Duke. So that from point to point now have
  you heard
The fundamental reasons of this war,
Whose great decision hath much blood let forth
And more thirsts after.
 First Lord.   Holy seems the quarrel
Upon your grace's part; black and fearful
On the opposer.
 Duke. Therefore we marvel much our cousin
  France
Would in so just a business shut his bosom
Against our borrowing prayers.
 Sec. Lord.   Good my lord,
The reasons of our state I cannot yield, 10
But like a common and an outward man,
That the great figure of a council frames
By self-unable motion: therefore dare not
Say what I think of it, since I have found
Myself in my incertain grounds to fail
As often as I guess'd.
 Duke.   Be it his pleasure.
 First Lord. But I am sure the younger of our
  nature,
That surfeit on their ease, will day by day
Come here for physic.
 Duke.   Welcome shall they be;

And all the honours that can fly from us   20
Shall on them settle. You know your places well;
When better fall, for your avails they fell:
To-morrow to the field.   [*Flourish. Exeunt.*

SCENE II. *Rousillon. The* COUNT'S *palace.*

Enter COUNTESS *and* CLOWN.

Count. It hath happened all as I would have
had it, save that he comes not along with her.
Clo. By my troth, I take my young lord to be
a very melancholy man.
Count. By what observance, I pray you?
Clo. Why, he will look upon his boot and
●sing; mend the ruff and sing; ask questions and
●sing; pick his teeth and sing. I know a man
that had this trick of melancholy sold a goodly
manor for a song.   10
Count. Let me see what he writes, and when
he means to come.   [*Opening a letter.*
Clo. I have no mind to Isbel since I was at
●court: our old ling and our Isbels o' the country
are nothing like your old ling and your Isbels o'
the court: the brains of my Cupid's knocked out,
and I begin to love, as an old man loves money,
with no stomach.
Count. What have we here?
Clo. E'en that you have there.   [*Exit.* 20
Count. [*Reads*] I have sent you a daughter-in-
law: she hath recovered the king, and undone
me. I have wedded her, not bedded her; and
sworn to make the 'not' eternal. You shall hear
I am run away: know it before the report come.
If there be breadth enough in the world, I will
hold a long distance. My duty to you.
                    Your unfortunate son,
                              BERTRAM.
This is not well, rash and unbridled boy,   30
To fly the favours of so good a king;
To pluck his indignation on thy head
By the misprising of a maid too virtuous
For the contempt of empire.

Re-enter CLOWN.

Clo. O madam, yonder is heavy news within
between two soldiers and my young lady!
Count. What is the matter?
Clo. Nay, there is some comfort in the news,
some comfort; your son will not be killed so soon
as I thought he would.   40
Count. Why should he be killed?
Clo. So say I, madam, if he run away, as I
hear he does: the danger is in standing to't;
that's the loss of men, though it be the getting of
children. Here they come will tell you more:
for my part, I only hear your son was run away.
                              [*Exit.*

Enter HELENA *and two* Gentlemen.

First Gent. Save you, good madam.
Hel. Madam, my lord is gone, for ever gone.
Sec. Gent. Do not say so.
Count. Think upon patience. Pray you, gen-
     tlemen,   50
I have felt so many quirks of joy and grief,
That the first face of neither, on the start,
Can woman me unto't: where is my son, I pray
     you?

7 *ruff.* For 'ruffle', the flap of a top-boot.

8-10 *I know . . . song.* See introduction.

14 *ling.* Salt cod, with a sexual innuendo.

Edith Evans as the Countess of Rousillon, Stratford-
upon-Avon, 1959

58 *passport.* Beggars were required to carry a licence to wander.

91 *inducement.* At Parolles instigation.

92-93 *The fellow . . . have.* Parolles has too much of the power of 'inducement' which profits him too much with Bertram.

Sec. Gent.   Madam, he's gone to serve the duke of Florence:
We met him thitherward; for thence we came,
And, after some dispatch in hand at court,
Thither we bend again.
● *Hel.*   Look on his letter, madam; here's my passport.
[*Reads*] When thou canst get the ring upon my finger which never shall come off, and show me a child begotten of thy body that I am father to, then call me husband: but in such a 'then' I write a 'never.'
This is a dreadful sentence.
   Count.   Brought you this letter, gentlemen?
   First Gent.   Ay, madam;
And for the contents' sake are sorry for our pains.
   Count.   I prithee, lady, have a better cheer;
If thou engrossest all the griefs are thine,
Thou robb'st me of a moiety: he was my son;
But I do wash his name out of my blood,   70
And thou art all my child.   Towards Florence is he?
   Sec. Gent.   Ay, madam.
   Count.   And to be a soldier?
   Sec. Gent.   Such is his noble purpose; and, believe 't,
The duke will lay upon him all the honour
That good convenience claims.
   Count.   Return you thither?
   First Gent.   Ay, madam, with the swiftest wing of speed.
   Hel. [*Reads*] Till I have no wife, I have nothing in France.
'Tis bitter.
   Count.   Find you that there?
   Hel.   Ay, madam.
   First Gent.   'Tis but the boldness of his hand, haply, which his heart was not consenting to. 80
   Count.   Nothing in France, until he have no wife!
There's nothing here that is too good for him
But only she; and she deserves a lord
That twenty such rude boys might tend upon
And call her hourly mistress.   Who was with him?
   First Gent.   A servant only, and a gentleman
Which I have sometime known.
   Count.   Parolles, was it not?
   First Gent.   Ay, my good lady, he.
   Count.   A very tainted fellow, and full of wickedness.
My son corrupts a well-derived nature   90
● With his inducement.
   First Gent.   Indeed, good lady,
● The fellow has a deal of that too much,
Which holds him much to have.
   Count.   You're welcome, gentlemen.
I will entreat you, when you see my son,
To tell him that his sword can never win
The honour that he loses: more I'll entreat you
Written to bear along.
   Sec. Gent.   We serve you, madam,
In that and all your worthiest affairs.
   Count.   Not so, but as we change our courtesies.   100
Will you draw near?
                     [*Exeunt Countess and Gentlemen.*

   Hel.   'Till I have no wife, I have nothing in France.'

Nothing in France, until he has no wife!
Thou shalt have none, Rousillon, none in France;
Then hast thou all again.   Poor lord! is 't I
That chase thee from thy country and expose
Those tender limbs of thine to the event
Of the none-sparing war? and is it I
That drive thee from the sportive court, where
thou
Wast shot at with fair eyes, to be the mark   110
Of smoky muskets? O you leaden messengers,
That ride upon the violent speed of fire,
●†Fly with false aim; move the still-peering air,
That sings with piercing; do not touch my lord.
Whoever shoots at him, I set him there;
Whoever charges on his forward breast,
●I am the caitiff that do hold him to 't;
And, though I kill him not, I am the cause
His death was so effected: better 'twere
I met the ravin lion when he roar'd   120
With sharp constraint of hunger; better 'twere
That all the miseries which nature owes
Were mine at once. No, come thou home, Rou-
sillon,
●Whence honour but of danger wins a scar,
As oft it loses all: I will be gone;
My being here it is that holds thee hence:
Shall I stay here to do 't? no, no, although
The air of paradise did fan the house
And angels officed all: I will be gone,
That pitiful rumour may report my flight,   130
To consolate thine ear. Come, night; end, day!
For with the dark, poor thief, I'll steal away.
                                         [*Exit.*

SCENE III. *Florence. Before the* DUKE'S *palace.*

Flourish. Enter the DUKE *of Florence,* BER-
TRAM, PAROLLES, Soldiers, Drum, *and* Trumpets.

   Duke. The general of our horse thou art;
      and we,
Great in our hope, lay our best love and credence
Upon thy promising fortune.
   Ber.   Sir, it is
A charge too heavy for my strength, but yet
We'll strive to bear it for your worthy sake
To the extreme edge of hazard.
   Duke.   Then go thou forth;
●And fortune play upon thy prosperous helm,
As thy auspicious mistress!
   Ber.   This very day,
Great Mars, I put myself into thy file:
Make me but like my thoughts, and I shall prove
A lover of thy drum, hater of love. [*Exeunt.* 11

SCENE IV. *Rousillon. The* COUNT'S *palace.*

   Enter COUNTESS *and* Steward.

   Count. Alas! and would you take the letter
      of her?
Might you not know she would do as she has done,
By sending me a letter? Read it again.
   Stew. [*Reads*]
●I am Saint Jaques' pilgrim, thither gone:
   Ambitious love hath so in me offended,
That barefoot plod I the cold ground upon,
   With sainted vow my faults to have amended.
Write, write, that from the bloody course of war
   My dearest master, your dear son, may hie:

113 *still-peering.* Usually emended to *still-piercing.*

117 *caitiff.* Wretch.

124-125 *Whence . . . loses all.* From the field of war, where honour may gain a scar which will signify the danger undergone, or may lose life itself.

Before the Duke's palace, Florence. Engraving from Charles Knight's *Pictorial Edition of Works of Shakspere,* 1839–1843

7 *helm.* Helmet.

Costume design for the Duke of Florence by Tanya Moisewitch, Stratford-upon-Avon, 1958

4 *Saint Jacques.* The shrine of Saint James the Greater at Compostela in Spain

13 *Juno*. Juno's enmity imposed twelve labours on Hercules.

Juno, the wife of Jupiter in classical mythology. From a 19th century engraving

19 *advice*. Judgement.

Florence. Without the walls. Engraving from Charles Knight's *Pictorial Edition of the Works of Shakspere*, 1839–1843

7 *[Tucket]*. A trumpet call.

14 *honesty*. Chastity.

21 *engines*. Devices.

Bless him at home in peace, whilst I from far 10
　His name with zealous fervour sanctify:
His taken labours bid him me forgive;
　I, his despiteful Juno, sent him forth
From courtly friends, with camping foes to live,
　Where death and danger dogs the heels of
　　worth:
He is too good and fair for death and me;
　Whom I myself embrace, to set him free.
　　Count.　Ah, what sharp stings are in her mild-
　　est words!
Rinaldo, you did never lack advice so much,
As letting her pass so: had I spoke with her, 20
I could have well diverted her intents,
Which thus she hath prevented.
　　Stew.　　　　　　Pardon me, madam:
If I had given you this at over-night,
She might have been o'erta'en; and yet she
　writes,
Pursuit would be but vain.
　　Count.　　　　　　What angel shall
Bless this unworthy husband? he cannot thrive,
Unless her prayers, whom heaven delights to hear
And loves to grant, reprieve him from the wrath
Of greatest justice.　Write, write, Rinaldo,
To this unworthy husband of his wife; 30
Let every word weigh heavy of her worth
That he does weigh too light: my greatest grief,
Though little he do feel it, set down sharply.
Dispatch the most convenient messenger:
When haply he shall hear that she is gone,
He will return; and hope I may that she,
Hearing so much, will speed her foot again,
Led hither by pure love: which of them both
Is dearest to me, I have no skill in sense
To make distinction: provide this messenger: 40
My heart is heavy and mine age is weak;
Grief would have tears, and sorrow bids me speak.
　　　　　　　　　　　　　　　[Exeunt.

SCENE V.　*Florence.　Without the walls.　A tucket afar off.*

Enter an old Widow *of Florence,* DIANA, VIO-
LENTA, *and* MARIANA, *with other* Citizens.

　Wid.　Nay, come; for if they do approach the city, we shall lose all the sight.
　Dia.　They say the French count has done most honourable service.
　Wid.　It is reported that he has taken their greatest commander; and that with his own hand he slew the duke's brother. *[Tucket.]* We have lost our labour; they are gone a contrary way: hark! you may know by their trumpets.　9
　Mar.　Come, let's return again, and suffice ourselves with the report of it.　Well, Diana, take heed of this French earl: the honour of a maid is her name; and no legacy is so rich as honesty.
　Wid.　I have told my neighbour how you have been solicited by a gentleman his companion.
　Mar.　I know that knave; hang him! one Parolles: a filthy officer he is in those suggestions for the young earl.　Beware of them, Diana; their promises, enticements, oaths, tokens, and all these engines of lust, are not the things they go under: many a maid hath been seduced by them; and the misery is, example, that so terrible shows in the wreck of maidenhood, cannot

● for all that dissuade succession, but that they are
● limed with the twigs that threaten them. I hope
I need not to advise you further; but I hope your
own grace will keep you where you are, though
there were no further danger known but the
modesty which is so lost. 30
    Dia. You shall not need to fear me.
    Wid. I hope so.

    Enter HELENA, *disguised like a Pilgrim.*

    Look, here comes a pilgrim: I know she will
lie at my house; thither they send one another:
I'll question her. God save you, pilgrim! whi-
ther are you bound?
    Hel. To Saint Jaques le Grand.
● Where do the palmers lodge, I do beseech you?
●   *Wid.* At the Saint Francis here beside the
    port.
    Hel. Is this the way? 40
    Wid. Ay, marry, is't. [*A march afar.*]
    Hark you! they come this way.
If you will tarry, holy pilgrim,
But till the troops come by,
I will conduct you where you shall be lodged;
The rather, for I think I know your hostess
● As ample as myself.
    Hel.   Is it yourself?
    Wid. If you shall please so, pilgrim.
    Hel. I thank you, and will stay upon your
    leisure.
    Wid. You came, I think, from France?
    Hel.   I did so.
    Wid. Here you shall see a countryman of
    yours 50
That has done worthy service.
    Hel.   His name, I pray you.
    Dia. The Count Rousillon: know you such
    a one?
    Hel. But by the ear, that hears most nobly
of him:
His face I know not.
    Dia.   Whatsome'er he is,
He's bravely taken here. He stole from France,
As 'tis reported, for the king had married him
Against his liking: think you it is so?
    Hel. Ay, surely, mere the truth: I know his
    lady.
    Dia. There is a gentleman that serves the
    count
Reports but coarsely of her.
    Hel.   What's his name? 60
    Dia. Monsieur Parolles.
    Hel.   O, I believe with him,
● In argument of praise, or to the worth
Of the great count himself, she is too mean
To have her name repeated: all her deserving
Is a reserved honesty, and that
I have not heard examined.
    Dia.   Alas, poor lady!
'Tis a hard bondage to become the wife
Of a detesting lord.
    Wid. I warrant, good creature, wheresoe'er
    she is,
Her heart weighs sadly: this young maid might
    do her 70
A shrewd turn, if she pleased.
    Hel.   How do you mean?
May be the amorous count solicits her
In the unlawful purpose.

25 *dissuade succession.* Dissuade other girls from following in her footsteps.

26 *limed.* Snared.

38 *palmers.* Pilgrims.

39 *port.* Gate of the city.

46 *ample.* Well.

62 *In argument . . . worth.* In praising her or comparing
her worth.

Helena, disguised as a pilgrim, with the Widow. Engraving by Kenny Meadows from Barry Cornwall's
Works of Shakspere, 1846

74 *brokes*. Bargains.

Helena: 'Which is the Frenchman?' Engraving from a design by H. Gravelot, Theobald's edition, 1773

91 *drum*. The drum carried the colours of the regiment; therefore, its loss was a matter of honour.

95 *ring-carrier*. A go-between or a bawd.

97 *enjoin'd penitents*. Pilgrims bound by oath to perform penance.

4 *hilding*. Worthless fellow.

Wid.   He does indeed;
And brokes with all that can in such a suit
Corrupt the tender honour of a maid:
But she is arm'd for him and keeps her guard
In honestest defence.
   Mar.   The gods forbid else!
   Wid.   So, now they come:

Drum and Colours.

Enter BERTRAM, PAROLLES, *and the whole
       army.*

That is Antonio, the duke's eldest son;
That, Escalus.
   Hel.   Which is the Frenchman?
   Dia.   He; 80
That with the plume: 'tis a most gallant fellow.
I would he loved his wife: if he were honester
He were much goodlier: is't not a handsome
         gentleman?
   Hel.   I like him well.
   Dia.   'Tis pity he is not honest: yond's that
         same knave
That leads him to these places: were I his lady,
I would poison that vile rascal.
   Hel.   Which is he?
   Dia.   That jack-an-apes with scarfs: why is
he melancholy?
   Hel.   Perchance he's hurt i' the battle.   90
   Par.   Lose our drum! well.
   Mar.   He's shrewdly vexed at something:
look, he has spied us.
   Wid.   Marry, hang you!
   Mar.   And your courtesy, for a ring-carrier!
         [*Exeunt Bertram, Parolles, and army.*
   Wid.   The troop is past. Come, pilgrim, I
will bring you
Where you shall host: of enjoin'd penitents
There's four or five, to great Saint Jaques bound,
Already at my house.
   Hel.   I humbly thank you:
Please it this matron and this gentle maid   100
To eat with us to-night, the charge and thanking
Shall be for me; and, to requite you further,
I will bestow some precepts of this virgin
Worthy the note.
   Both.   We'll take your offer kindly.
                                    [*Exeunt.*

SCENE VI.   *Camp before Florence.*

Enter BERTRAM *and the two French* Lords.

   Sec. Lord.   Nay, good my lord, put him to't;
let him have his way.
   First Lord.   If your lordship find him not a
hilding, hold me no more in your respect.
   Sec. Lord.   On my life, my lord, a bubble.
   Ber.   Do you think I am so far deceived in
him?
   Sec. Lord.   Believe it, my lord, in mine own
direct knowledge, without any malice, but to
speak of him as my kinsman, he's a most notable
coward, an infinite and endless liar, an hourly
promise-breaker, the owner of no one good quality
worthy your lordship's entertainment.
   First Lord.   It were fit you knew him; lest,
reposing too far in his virtue, which he hath not,
he might at some great and trusty business in a
main danger fail you.

Ber. I would I knew in what particular action to try him.   19

First Lord. None better than to let him fetch off his drum, which you hear him so confidently undertake to do.

Sec. Lord. I, with a troop of Florentines, will suddenly surprise him; such I will have, whom I am sure he knows not from the enemy: we will ● bind and hoodwink him so, that he shall suppose no other but that he is carried into the leaguer of the adversaries, when we bring him to our own tents. Be but your lordship present at his examination: if he do not, for the promise of his life and in the highest compulsion of base fear, offer to betray you and deliver all the intelligence in his power against you, and that with the divine forfeit of his soul upon oath, never trust my judgement in any thing.

First Lord. O, for the love of laughter, let him fetch his drum; he says he has a stratagem for't: when your lordship sees the bottom of his success in't, and to what metal this counterfeit lump of ore will be melted, if you give him not ● John Drum's entertainment, your inclining cannot be removed. Here he comes.

Enter PAROLLES.

Sec. Lord. [*Aside to Ber.*] O, for the love of laughter, hinder not the honour of his design: let him fetch off his drum in any hand.

Ber. How now, monsieur! this drum sticks sorely in your disposition.

First Lord. A pox on't, let it go; 'tis but a drum.   49

Par. 'But a drum'! is't 'but a drum'? A drum so lost! There was excellent command,—to charge in with our horse upon our own wings, and to rend our own soldiers!

First Lord. That was not to be blamed in the command of the service: it was a disaster of war that Cæsar himself could not have prevented, if he had been there to command.

Ber. Well, we cannot greatly condemn our success: some dishonour we had in the loss of that drum; but it is not to be recovered.   60

Par. It might have been recovered.

Ber. It might; but it is not now.

Par. It is to be recovered: but that the merit of service is seldom attributed to the true and exact performer, I would have that drum or ● another, or 'hic jacet.'

Ber. Why, if you have a stomach, to't, monsieur: if you think your mystery in stratagem can bring this instrument of honour again into his native quarter, be magnanimous in the enterprise and go on; I will grace the attempt for a worthy exploit: if you speed well in it, the duke shall both speak of it, and extend to you what further becomes his greatness, even to the utmost syllable of your worthiness.

Par. By the hand of a soldier, I will undertake it.

Ber. But you must not now slumber in it.

Par. I'll about it this evening: and I will ● presently pen down my dilemmas, encourage my- ● self in my certainty, put myself into my mortal preparation; and by midnight look to hear further from me.

26 *hoodwink.* Blindfold.

41 *John Drum's entertainment.* A beating.

66 *'hic jacet'.* 'Here lies', as in the beginning of an epitaph.

80 *dilemmas.* Alternatives.

81-82 *myself . . . preparation.* Prepare myself for death.

Costume design for Parolles by Tanya Moisewitch, Stratford-upon-Avon, 1958

107 *embossed.* Trapped.

111 *case.* Skin. *smoked.* Found out.

115 *look my twigs.* Get my trap ready.

Mrs Warren as Helena. Engraving from Bell's
Shakespeare, 1773–1778

3 *But I shall . . . upon.* Only by revealing herself to
Bertram, which would ruin her plan.

Ber. May I be bold to acquaint his grace you
are gone about it?
Par. I know not what the success will be, my
lord; but the attempt I vow.
Ber. I know thou'rt valiant; and, to the possi-
bility of thy soldiership, will subscribe for thee.
Farewell.   90
Par. I love not many words.   [*Exit.*
Sec. Lord. No more than a fish loves water.
Is not this a strange fellow, my lord, that so confidently seems to undertake this business, which
he knows is not to be done; damns himself to do
and dares better be damned than to do't?
First Lord. You do not know him, my lord,
as we do: certain it is, that he will steal himself
into a man's favour and for a week escape a great
deal of discoveries; but when you find him out,
you have him ever after.   101
Ber. Why, do you think he will make no deed
at all of this that so seriously he does address
himself unto?
Sec. Lord. None in the world; but return
with an invention and clap upon you two or three
probable lies: but we have almost embossed him;
you shall see his fall to-night; for indeed he is
not for your lordship's respect.   109
First Lord. We'll make you some sport with
the fox ere we case him. He was first smoked
by the old lord Lafeu: when his disguise and he
is parted, tell me what a sprat you shall find him;
which you shall see this very night.
Sec. Lord. I must go look my twigs: he shall
be caught.
Ber. Your brother he shall go along with me.
Sec. Lord. As't please your lordship: I'll
leave you.   [*Exit.*
Ber. Now will I lead you to the house, and
show you
The lass I spoke of.
First Lord.   But you say she's honest.
Ber. That's all the fault: I spoke with her
but once   120
And found her wondrous cold; but I sent to her,
By this same coxcomb that we have i' the wind,
Tokens and letters which she did re-send;
And this is all I have done. She's a fair creature:
Will you go see her?
First Lord.   With all my heart, my lord.
                                                                        [*Exeunt.*

SCENE VII. *Florence.* *The* Widow's *house.*

Enter HELENA *and* Widow.

Hel. If you misdoubt me that I am not she,
I know not how I shall assure you further,
But I shall lose the grounds I work upon.
Wid. Though my estate be fallen, I was well
born,
Nothing acquainted with these businesses;
And would not put my reputation now
In any staining act.
Hel.   Nor would I wish you.
First, give me trust, the count he is my husband,
And what to your sworn counsel I have spoken
Is so from word to word: and then you cannot,
By the good aid that I of you shall borrow,   11
Err in bestowing it.
Wid.   I should believe you;
For you have show'd me that which well approves

You're great in fortune.
Hel.   Take this purse of gold,
And let me buy your friendly help thus far,
Which I will over-pay and pay again
When I have found it. The count he wooes your
    daughter,
Lays down his wanton siege before her beauty,
Resolved to carry her: let her in fine consent,
As we'll direct her how 'tis best to bear it.   20
Now his important blood will nought deny
That she'll demand: a ring the county wears,
That downward hath succeeded in his house
From son to son, some four or five descents
Since the first father wore it: this ring he holds
In most rich choice; yet in his idle fire,
To buy his will, it would not seem too dear,
Howe'er repented after.
   Wid.   Now I see
The bottom of your purpose.   29
   Hel. You see it lawful, then: it is no more,
But that your daughter, ere she seems as won,
Desires this ring; appoints him an encounter;
In fine, delivers me to fill the time,
Herself most chastely absent: after this,
To marry her, I'll add three thousand crowns
To what is past already.
   Wid.   I have yielded:
Instruct my daughter how she shall persever,
That time and place with this deceit so lawful
May prove coherent. Every night he comes
With musics of all sorts and songs composed   40
To her unworthiness: it nothing steads us
To chide him from our eaves; for he persists
As if his life lay on't.
   Hel.   Why then to-night
Let us assay our plot; which, if it speed,
Is wicked meaning in a lawful deed
And lawful meaning in a lawful act,
Where both not sin, and yet a sinful fact:
But let's about it.   [*Exeunt.*

ACT IV.

Scene I. *Without the Florentine camp.*

Enter Second French Lord, *with five or six
other* Soldiers *in ambush.*

   Sec. Lord. He can come no other way but by
this hedge-corner. When you sally upon him,
speak what terrible language you will: though
you understand it not yourselves, no matter; for
we must not seem to understand him, unless some
one among us whom we must produce for an interpreter.
   First Sold. Good captain, let me be the interpreter.
   Sec. Lord. Art not acquainted with him?
knows he not thy voice?   11
   First Sold. No, sir, I warrant you.
   Sec. Lord. But what linsey-woolsey hast thou
to speak to us again?
   First Sold. E'en such as you speak to me.
   Sec. Lord. He must think us some band of
strangers i' the adversary's entertainment. Now
he hath a smack of all neighbouring languages;
therefore we must every one be a man of his own
fancy, not to know what we speak one to another;
so we seem to know, is to know straight our purpose: choughs' language, gabble enough, and good

26 *rich choice.* High esteem.

13 *linsey-woolsey.* A mixture of flax and wool, therefore
a jumble of words.

16-17 *some band . . . entertainment.* A band of foreign
mercenaries in the enemy's pay.

19-22 *we must . . . purpose.* Every man must talk nonsense and nobody will understand the other, but must
pretend to do so.

45 *butter-woman.* Probably because of their chatter.

46 *Bajazet's mule.* Elsewhere Shakespeare associates mules with silence.

54 *baring.* Shaving.

Parolles, ambushed and blindfolded. Engraving from Bell's *Shakespeare*, 1773–1778

enough. As for you, interpreter, you must seem very politic. But couch, ho! here he comes, to beguile two hours in a sleep, and then to return and swear the lies he forges.

Enter PAROLLES.

Par. Ten o'clock: within these three hours 'twill be time enough to go home. What shall I say I have done? It must be a very plausive invention that carries it: they begin to smoke me; and disgraces have of late knocked too often at my door. I find my tongue is too foolhardy; but my heart hath the fear of Mars before it and of his creatures, not daring the reports of my tongue.

Sec. Lord. This is the first truth that e'er thine own tongue was guilty of.

Par. What the devil should move me to undertake the recovery of this drum, being not ignorant of the impossibility, and knowing I had no such purpose? I must give myself some hurts, and say I got them in exploit: yet slight ones will not carry it; they will say, 'Came you off with so little?' and great ones I dare not give. Wherefore, what's the instance? Tongue, I must put you into a butter-woman's mouth and buy myself another of Bajazet's mule, if you prattle me into these perils.

Sec. Lord. Is it possible he should know what he is, and be that he is?   49

Par. I would the cutting of my garments would serve the turn, or the breaking of my Spanish sword.

Sec. Lord. We cannot afford you so.

Par. Or the baring of my beard; and to say it was in stratagem.

Sec. Lord. 'Twould not do.

Par. Or to drown my clothes, and say I was stripped.

Sec. Lord. Hardly serve.

Par. Though I swore I leaped from the window of the citadel—   61

Sec. Lord. How deep?

Par. Thirty fathom.

Sec. Lord. Three great oaths would scarce make that be believed.

Par. I would I had any drum of the enemy's: I would swear I recovered it.

Sec. Lord. You shall hear one anon.

Par. A drum now of the enemy's,—
[*Alarum within.*

Sec. Lord. Throca movousus, cargo, cargo, cargo.   71

All. Cargo, cargo, cargo, villianda par corbo, cargo.

Par. O, ransom, ransom! do not hide mine eyes.
[*They seize and blindfold him.*

First Sold. Boskos thromuldo boskos.

Par. I know you are the Muskos' regiment: And I shall lose my life for want of language: If there be here German, or Dane, low Dutch, Italian, or French, let him speak to me; I'll Discover that which shall undo the Florentine.   80

First Sold. Boskos vauvado: I understand thee, and can speak thy tongue. Kerelybonto, sir, betake thee to thy faith, for seventeen poniards are at thy bosom.

Par. O!

First Sold. O, pray, pray, pray! Manka revania dulche.

Sec. Lord.   Oscorbidulchos volivorco.
First Sold.   The general is content to spare
   thee yet;
And, hoodwink'd as thou art, will lead thee on 90
To gather from thee: haply thou mayst inform
Something to save thy life.
Par.   O, let me live!
And all the secrets of our camp I'll show,
Their force, their purposes; nay, I'll speak that
Which you will wonder at.
First Sold.   But wilt thou faithfully?
Par.   If I do not, damn me.
First Sold.   Acordo linta.
Come on; thou art granted space.
      [*Exit, with Parolles guarded.   A short
                 alarum within.*
Sec. Lord.   Go, tell the Count Rousillon, and
   my brother,
We have caught the woodcock, and will keep him
   muffled   100
Till we do hear from them.
Sec. Sold.   Captain, I will.
Sec. Lord.   A' will betray us all unto ourselves:
Inform on that.
Sec. Sold.   So I will, sir.
Sec. Lord.   Till then I'll keep him dark and
   safely lock'd.   [*Exeunt.*

SCENE II.   *Florence.   The* Widow's *house.*

Enter BERTRAM *and* DIANA.

Ber.   They told me that your name was Fon-
   tibell.
Dia.   No, my good lord, Diana.
Ber.   Titled goddess;
And worth it, with addition! But, fair soul,
In your fine frame hath love no quality?
If the quick fire of youth light not your mind,
● You are no maiden, but a monument:
When you are dead, you should be such a one
As you are now, for you are cold and stern;
And now you should be as your mother was
When your sweet self was got.   10
Dia.   She then was honest.
Ber.   So should you be.
Dia.   No:
My mother did but duty; such, my lord,
As you owe to your wife.
Ber.   No more o' that;
I prithee, do not strive against my vows:
I was compell'd to her; but I love thee
By love's own sweet constraint, and will for ever
Do thee all rights of service.
Dia.   Ay, so you serve us
Till we serve you; but when you have our roses,
You barely leave our thorns to prick ourselves
And mock us with our bareness.
Ber.   How have I sworn! 20
Dia.   'Tis not the many oaths that makes the
   truth,
But the plain single vow that is vow'd true.
What is not holy, that we swear not by,
But take the High'st to witness: then, pray you,
   tell me,
If I should swear by God's great attributes,
I loved you dearly, would you believe my oaths,
● When I did love you ill? This has no holding,
To swear by him whom I protest to love,
That I will work against him: therefore your oaths

30 *poor conditions, but unseal'd.* A poor contract and invalid, because it has no authenticating seal.

38 *I . . . scarre.* A corrupt line with no satisfactory explanation. Perhaps 'scarre' was a misprint for 'snare'.

42-45 *It is an . . . to lose.* See introduction.

65 *though there my hope be done.* After this deed I have no hope of becoming a wife.

73 *braid.* Deceitful.

●Are words and poor conditions, but unseal'd,   30
At least in my opinion.
    Ber.   Change it, change it;
Be not so holy-cruel: love is holy;
And my integrity ne'er knew the crafts
That you do charge men with.   Stand no more off,
But give thyself unto my sick desires,
Who then recover: say thou art mine, and ever
My love as it begins shall so persever.
● *Dia.* †I see that men make ropes in such a scarre
That we'll forsake ourselves.   Give me that ring.
    Ber. I'll lend it thee, my dear; but have no power   40
To give it from me.
    Dia.   Will you not, my lord?
● *Ber.* It is an honour 'longing to our house,
Bequeathed down from many ancestors;
Which were the greatest obloquy i' the world
In me to lose.
    Dia.   Mine honour's such a ring:
My chastity's the jewel of our house,
Bequeathed down from many ancestors;
Which were the greatest obloquy i' the world
In me to lose: thus your own proper wisdom
Brings in the champion Honour on my part,   50
Against your vain assault.
    Ber.   Here, take my ring:
My house, mine honour, yea, my life, be thine,
And I'll be bid by thee.
    Dia. When midnight comes, knock at my chamber-window:
I'll order take my mother shall not hear.
Now will I charge you in the band of truth,
When you have conquer'd my yet maiden bed,
Remain there but an hour, nor speak to me:
My reasons are most strong; and you shall know them
When back again this ring shall be deliver'd: 60
And on your finger in the night I'll put
Another ring, that what in time proceeds
May token to the future our past deeds.
Adieu, till then; then, fail not.   You have won
●A wife of me, though there my hope be done.
    Ber. A heaven on earth I have won by wooing thee.   [*Exit.*
    Dia. For which live long to thank both heaven and me!
You may so in the end.
My mother told me just how he would woo,
As if she sat in 's heart; she says all men   70
Have the like oaths: he had sworn to marry me
When his wife's dead; therefore I'll lie with him
●When I am buried.   Since Frenchmen are so braid,
Marry that will, I live and die a maid:
Only in this disguise I think 't no sin
To cozen him that would unjustly win.   [*Exit.*

SCENE III.   *The Florentine camp.*

Enter the two French Lords *and some two or three* Soldiers.

    First Lord.   You have not given him his mother's letter?
    Sec. Lord.   I have delivered it an hour since: there is something in't that stings his nature; for on the reading it he changed almost into another man.

First Lord. He has much worthy blame laid upon him for shaking off so good a wife and so sweet a lady. 9

Sec. Lord. Especially he hath incurred the everlasting displeasure of the king, who had even tuned his bounty to sing happiness to him. I will tell you a thing, but you shall let it dwell darkly with you.

First Lord. When you have spoken it, 'tis dead, and I am the grave of it.

Sec. Lord. He hath perverted a young gentlewoman here in Florence, of a most chaste renown; and this night he fleshes his will in the spoil of her honour: he hath given her his monumental ring, and thinks himself made in the unchaste composition.

First Lord. Now, God delay our rebellion! as we are ourselves, what things are we!

Sec. Lord. Merely our own traitors. And as in the common course of all treasons, we still see them reveal themselves, till they attain to their abhorred ends, so he that in this action contrives against his own nobility, in his proper stream o'erflows himself. 30

First Lord. Is it not meant damnable in us, to be trumpeters of our unlawful intents? We shall not then have his company to-night?

Sec. Lord. Not till after midnight; for he is dieted to his hour.

First Lord. That approaches apace; I would gladly have him see his company anatomized, that he might take a measure of his own judgements, wherein so curiously he had set this counterfeit. 40

Sec. Lord. We will not meddle with him till he come; for his presence must be the whip of the other.

First Lord. In the mean time, what hear you of these wars?

Sec. Lord. I hear there is an overture of peace.

First Lord. Nay, I assure you, a peace concluded.

Sec. Lord. What will Count Rousillon do then? will he travel higher, or return again into France? 51

First Lord. I perceive, by this demand, you are not altogether of his council.

Sec. Lord. Let it be forbid, sir; so should I be a great deal of his act.

First Lord. Sir, his wife some two months since fled from his house: her pretence is a pilgrimage to Saint Jaques le Grand; which holy undertaking with most austere sanctimony she accomplished; and, there residing, the tenderness of her nature became as a prey to her grief; in fine, made a groan of her last breath, and now she sings in heaven.

Sec. Lord. How is this justified?

First Lord. The stronger part of it by her own letters, which makes her story true, even to the point of her death: her death itself, which could not be her office to say is come, was faithfully confirmed by the rector of the place. 69

Sec. Lord. Hath the count all this intelligence?

First Lord. Ay, and the particular confirmations, point from point, to the full arming of the verity.

Sec. Lord. I am heartily sorry that he'll be glad of this.

19 *fleshes his will.* His lust will be rewarded.

20-21 *monumental.* Memorial.

22 *composition.* Bargain.

24 *as we are ourselves.* In ourselves, unaided by God.

37 *company.* Companion i.e. Parolles.

99 *by an abstract of.* To summarize.

100 *congied with.* Taken leave of.

103 *entertained my convoy.* Engaged my transport.

114 *module.* Image.

Second Lord: '. . . has sat i' the stocks all night'. Engraving from Charles Knight's *Pictorial Edition of the Works of Shakspere, 1839–1843*

134 *muffled.* Blindfold.

135-136 *hush . . . comes.* A cry of warning from blindman's-buff.

First Lord. How mightily sometimes we make us comforts of our losses!

Sec. Lord. And how mightily some other times we drown our gain in tears! The great dignity that his valour hath here acquired for him shall at home be encountered with a shame as ample.

First Lord. The web of our life is of a mingled yarn, good and ill together: our virtues would be proud, if our faults whipped them not; and our crimes would despair, if they were not cherished by our virtues.

Enter a Messenger.

How now! where's your master?

Serv. He met the duke in the street, sir, of whom he hath taken a solemn leave: his lordship will next morning for France. The duke hath offered him letters of commendations to the king.

Sec. Lord. They shall be no more than needful there, if they were more than they can commend.

First Lord. They cannot be too sweet for the king's tartness. Here's his lordship now.

Enter BERTRAM.

How now, my lord! is't not after midnight?

Ber. I have to-night dispatched sixteen businesses, a month's length a-piece, by an abstract of success: I have congied with the duke, done my adieu with his nearest; buried a wife, mourned for her; writ to my lady mother I am returning; entertained my convoy; and between these main parcels of dispatch effected many nicer needs: the last was the greatest, but that I have not ended yet.

Sec. Lord. If the business be of any difficulty, and this morning your departure hence, it requires haste of your lordship.   109

Ber. I mean, the business is not ended, as fearing to hear of it hereafter. But shall we have this dialogue between the fool and the soldier? Come, bring forth this counterfeit module, has deceived me, like a double-meaning prophesier.

Sec. Lord. Bring him forth: has sat i' the stocks all night, poor gallant knave.

Ber. No matter; his heels have deserved it, in usurping his spurs so long. How does he carry himself?   120

Sec. Lord. I have told your lordship already, the stocks carry him. But to answer you as you would be understood; he weeps like a wench that had shed her milk: he hath confessed himself to Morgan, whom he supposes to be a friar, from the time of his remembrance to this very instant disaster of his setting i' the stocks: and what think you he hath confessed?

Ber. Nothing of me, has a'?   129

Sec. Lord. His confession is taken, and it shall be read to his face: if your lordship be in't, as I believe you are, you must have the patience to hear it.

Enter PAROLLES *guarded, and* First Soldier.

Ber. A plague upon him! muffled! he can say nothing of me: hush, hush!

First Lord. Hoodman comes! Portotartarosa.

First Sold. He calls for the tortures: what will you say without 'em?

Par. I will confess what I know without constraint: if ye pinch me like a pasty, I can say no more.   141

First Sold. Bosko chimurcho.

First Lord. Boblibindo chicurmurco.

First Sold. You are a merciful general. Our general bids you answer to what I shall ask you out of a note.

Par. And truly, as I hope to live.

First Sold. [*Reads*] 'First demand of him how many horse the duke is strong.' What say you to that?   150

Par. Five or six thousand; but very weak and unserviceable: the troops are all scattered, and the commanders very poor rogues, upon my reputation and credit and as I hope to live.

First Sold. Shall I set down your answer so?

Par. Do: I'll take the sacrament on't, how and which way you will.

Ber. All's one to him. What a past-saving slave is this!   159

First Lord. You're deceived, my lord: this is Monsieur Parolles, the gallant militarist,—that was his own phrase,—that had the whole theoric of war in the knot of his scarf, and the practice in the chape of his dagger.

Sec. Lord. I will never trust a man again for keeping his sword clean, nor believe he can have every thing in him by wearing his apparel neatly.

First Sold. Well, that's set down.   169

Par. Five or six thousand horse, I said,—I will say true,—or thereabouts, set down, for I'll speak truth.

First Lord. He's very near the truth in this.

Ber. But I con him no thanks for't, in the nature he delivers it.

Par. Poor rogues, I pray you, say.

First Sold. Well, that's set down.

Par. I humbly thank you, sir: a truth's a truth, the rogues are marvellous poor.   179

First Sold. [*Reads*] 'Demand of him, of what strength they are a-foot.' What say you to that?

Par. By my troth, sir, if I were to live this present hour, I will tell true. Let me see: Spurio, a hundred and fifty; Sebastian, so many; Corambus, so many; Jaques, so many; Guiltian, Cosmo, Lodowick, and Gratii, two hundred and fifty each; mine own company, Chitopher, Vaumond, Bentii, two hundred and fifty each: so that the muster-file, rotten and sound, upon my life, amounts not to fifteen thousand poll; half of the which dare not shake the snow from off their cassocks, lest they shake themselves to pieces.

Ber. What shall be done to him?

First Lord. Nothing, but let him have thanks. Demand of him my condition, and what credit I have with the duke.

First Sold. Well, that's set down. [*Reads*] 'You shall demand of him, whether one Captain Dumain be i' the camp, a Frenchman; what his reputation is with the duke; what his valour, honesty, and expertness in wars; or whether he thinks it were not possible, with well-weighing sums of gold, to corrupt him to a revolt.' What say you to this? what do you know of it?

Parolles blindfolded with Bertram and Lords. Illustration by Kenny Meadows from Barry Cornwall's *Works of Shakspere*, 1846

164 *chape.* Metal plate covering the point of a scabbard.

174 *con.* Give.

192 *cassocks.* Military cloaks.

211 *botcher*. A tailor who mends old clothes.

213 *shrieve's fool*. The sheriff's idiot.

216-217 *the next tile*. A metaphor for sudden death.

This is not the Duke's Letter Sir,

———— I pray you Sir put it up again.

Parolles derides Bertram. Engraving from Bell's *Shakespeare*, 1773–1778

254 *Half won . . . make it*. If a bargain is well prepared, it is half won, so ensure the terms are good.

257 *mell*. Mingle.

Par. I beseech you, let me answer to the particular of the inter'gatories: demand them singly.

First Sold. Do you know this Captain Dumain? 210

Par. I know him: a' was a botcher's 'prentice in Paris, from whence he was whipped for getting the shrieve's fool with child,—a dumb innocent, that could not say him nay.

Ber. Nay, by your leave, hold your hands; though I know his brains are forfeit to the next tile that falls.

First Sold. Well, is this captain in the duke of Florence's camp? 219

Par. Upon my knowledge, he is, and lousy.

First Lord. Nay, look not so upon me; we shall hear of your lordship anon.

First Sold. What is his reputation with the duke?

Par. The duke knows him for no other but a poor officer of mine; and writ to me this other day to turn him out o' the band: I think I have his letter in my pocket.

First Sold. Marry, we'll search. 229

Par. In good sadness, I do not know; either it is there, or it is upon a file with the duke's other letters in my tent.

First Sold. Here 'tis; here's a paper: shall I read it to you?

Par. I do not know if it be it or no.

Ber. Our interpreter does it well.

First Lord. Excellently.

First Sold. [*Reads*] 'Dian, the count's a fool, and full of gold,'—

Par. That is not the duke's letter, sir; that is an advertisement to a proper maid in Florence, one Diana, to take heed of the allurement of one Count Rousillon, a foolish idle boy, but for all that very ruttish: I pray you, sir, put it up again.

First Sold. Nay, I'll read it first, by your favour.

Par. My meaning in't, I protest, was very honest in the behalf of the maid; for I knew the young count to be a dangerous and lascivious boy, who is a whale to virginity and devours up all the fry it finds. 250

Ber. Damnable both-sides rogue!

First Sold. [*Reads*] 'When he swears oaths, bid him drop gold, and take it;
After he scores, he never pays the score:
Half won is match well made; match, and well make it;
He ne'er pays after-debts, take it before;
And say a soldier, Dian, told thee this,
Men are to mell with, boys are not to kiss:
For count of this, the count's a fool, I know it,
Who pays before, but not when he does owe it.
Thine, as he vowed to thee in thine ear, 260
PAROLLES.'

Ber. He shall be whipped through the army with this rhyme in's forehead.

Sec. Lord. This is your devoted friend, sir, the manifold linguist and the armipotent soldier.

Ber. I could endure any thing before but a cat, and now he's a cat to me.

First Sold. I perceive, sir, by the general's looks, we shall be fain to hang you. 269

Par. My life, sir, in any case: not that I am afraid to die; but that, my offences being many,

I would repent out the remainder of nature: let me live, sir, in a dungeon, i' the stocks, or any where, so I may live.

First Sold. We'll see what may be done, so you confess freely; therefore, once more to this Captain Dumain: you have answered to his reputation with the duke and to his valour: what is his honesty?   279

• *Par.* He will steal, sir, an egg out of a clois-
• ter: for rapes and ravishments he parallels Nessus: he professes not keeping of oaths; in breaking 'em he is stronger than Hercules: he will lie, sir, with such volubility, that you would think truth were a fool: drunkenness is his best virtue, for he will be swine-drunk; and in his sleep he does little harm, save to his bed-clothes about him; but they know his conditions and lay him in straw. I have but little more to say, sir, of his honesty: he has every thing that an honest man should not have; what an honest man should have, he has nothing.

First Lord. I begin to love him for this.

Ber. For this description of thine honesty? A pox upon him for me, he's more and more a cat.

First Sold. What say you to his expertness in war?

• *Par.* Faith, sir, has led the drum before the English tragedians; to belie him, I will not, and more of his soldiership I know not; except, in that country he had the honour to be the officer
• at a place there called Mile-end, to instruct for
• the doubling of files: I would do the man what honour I can, but of this I am not certain.

First Lord. He hath out-villained villany so far, that the rarity redeems him.

Ber. A pox on him, he's a cat still.

First Sold. His qualities being at this poor price, I need not to ask you if gold will corrupt him to revolt.   310

• *Par.* Sir, for a quart d'écu he will sell the
• fee-simple of his salvation, the inheritance of it;
• and cut the entail from all remainders, and a perpetual succession for it perpetually.

First Sold. What's his brother, the other Captain Dumain?

Sec. Lord. Why does he ask him of me?

First Sold. What's he?

Par. E'en a crow o' the same nest; not altogether so great as the first in goodness, but greater a great deal in evil: he excels his brother for a coward, yet his brother is reputed one of the best that is: in a retreat he outruns any lackey; marry, in coming on he has the cramp.

First Sold. If your life be saved, will you undertake to betray the Florentine?

Par. Ay, and the captain of his horse, Count Rousillon.

First Sold. I'll whisper with the general, and know his pleasure.   330

Par. [*Aside*] I'll no more drumming; a plague of all drums! Only to seem to deserve well, and to beguile the supposition of that lascivious young boy the count, have I run into this danger. Yet who would have suspected an ambush where I was taken?

First Sold. There is no remedy, sir, but you must die: the general says, you that have so traitorously discovered the secrets of your army and made such pestiferous reports of men very

280 *egg.* A synonym for something trivial or valueless.

281-282 *Nessus.* Nessus, a centaur, tried to rape the wife of Hercules; centaurs were a symbol of lust.

298-299 *led the drum . . . tragedians.* Travelling players often had a drummer at their head.

302 *Mile-end.* The drilling ground of the London militia.

303 *doubling of files.* One of the simplest forms of drill.

311 *quart d'écu.* A quarter of a crown.

312 *fee-simple.* Absolute title.

313 *cut the entail.* Break the provision that the estate should pass to his heir.

Parolles: 'Who cannot be crushed with a plot?' Engraving from Bell's *Shakespeare*, 1773–1778

20 *motive*. Instrument.

nobly held, can serve the world for no honest use;
therefore you must die.   Come, headsman, off
with his head.
   Par.   O Lord, sir, let me live, or let me see
my death!
   First Sold.   That shall you, and take your
leave of all your friends   [*Unblinding him.*
So, look about you: know you any here?
   Ber.   Good morrow, noble captain.   349
   Sec. Lord.   God bless you, Captain Parolles.
   First Lord.   God save you, noble captain.
   Sec. Lord.   Captain, what greeting will you
to my Lord Lafeu?   I am for France.
   First Lord.   Good captain, will you give me a
copy of the sonnet you writ to Diana in behalf of
the Count Rousillon? an I were not a very coward,
I'ld compel it of you: but fare you well.
              [*Exeunt Bertram and Lords.*
   First Sold.   You are undone, captain, all but
your scarf; that has a knot on't yet.   359
   Par.   Who cannot be crushed with a plot?
   First Sold.   If you could find out a country
where but women were that had received so much
shame, you might begin an impudent nation.
Fare ye well, sir; I am for France too: we shall
speak of you there.   [*Exit, with Soldiers.*
   Par.   Yet am I thankful: if my heart were great,
'Twould burst at this.   Captain I'll be no more;
But I will eat and drink, and sleep as soft
As captain shall: simply the thing I am
Shall make me live.   Who knows himself a brag-
     gart,   370
Let him fear this, for it will come to pass
That every braggart shall be found an ass.
Rust, sword! cool, blushes! and, Parolles, live
Safest in shame! being fool'd, by foolery thrive!
There's place and means for every man alive.
I'll after them.   [*Exit.*

Scene IV.   *Florence.   The* Widow's *house.*

   Enter Helena, Widow, *and* Diana.

   Hel.   That you may well perceive I have not
     wrong'd you,
One of the greatest in the Christian world
Shall be my surety; 'fore whose throne 'tis needful,
Ere I can perfect mine intents, to kneel:
Time was, I did him a desired office,
Dear almost as his life; which gratitude
Through flinty Tartar's bosom would peep forth,
And answer, thanks: I duly am inform'd
His grace is at Marseilles; to which place
We have convenient convoy.   You must know,
I am supposed dead: the army breaking,   11
My husband hies him home; where, heaven aiding,
And by the leave of my good lord the king,
We'll be before our welcome.
   Wid.   Gentle madam,
You never had a servant to whose trust
Your business was more welcome.
   Hel.   Nor you, mistress,
Ever a friend whose thoughts more truly labour
To recompense your love: doubt not but heaven
Hath brought me up to be your daughter's dower,
As it hath fated her to be my motive   20
And helper to a husband.   But, O strange men!
That can such sweet use make of what they hate,
When saucy trusting of the cozen'd thoughts
Defiles the pitchy night: so lust doth play

With what it loathes for that which is away.
But more of this hereafter.   You, Diana,
Under my poor instructions yet must suffer
Something in my behalf.
  Dia.   Let death and honesty
Go with your impositions, I am yours
Upon your will to suffer.
  Hel.   Yet, I pray you: 30
But with the word the time will bring on sum-
      mer,
When briers shall have leaves as well as thorns,
And be as sweet as sharp.   We must away;
Our waggon is prepared, and time revives us:
●ALL'S WELL THAT ENDS WELL: still the fine's
      the crown;
Whate'er the course, the end is the renown.
                              [*Exeunt.*

SCENE V.   *Rousillon.   The* COUNT'S *palace.*

Enter COUNTESS, LAFEU, *and* CLOWN.

  Laf.   No, no, no, your son was misled with a
●snipt-taffeta fellow there, whose villanous saffron
would have made all the unbaked and doughy
youth of a nation in his colour: your daughter-in-
law had been alive at this hour, and your son here
at home, more advanced by the king than by that
red-tailed humble-bee I speak of.
  Count.   I would I had not known him; it was
the death of the most virtuous gentlewoman that
ever nature had praise for creating.   If she had
partaken of my flesh, and cost me the dearest
groans of a mother, I could not have owed her a
more rooted love.
  Laf.   'Twas a good lady, 'twas a good lady:
we may pick a thousand salads ere we light on
such another herb.
  Clo.   Indeed, sir, she was the sweet-marjoram
●of the salad, or rather, the herb of grace.
  Laf.   They are not herbs, you knave; they are
nose-herbs.   20
● *Clo.*   I am no great Nebuchadnezzar, sir; I
have not much skill in grass.
  Laf.   Whether dost thou profess thyself, a
knave or a fool?
  Clo.   A fool, sir, at a woman's service, and a
knave at a man's.
  Laf.   Your distinction?
  Clo.   I would cozen the man of his wife and do
his service.
  Laf.   So you were a knave at his service,
indeed.   31
  Clo.   And I would give his wife my bauble,
sir, to do her service.
  Laf.   I will subscribe for thee, thou art both
knave and fool.
  Clo.   At your service.
  Laf.   No, no, no.
  Clo.   Why, sir, if I cannot serve you, I can
serve as great a prince as you are.
  Laf.   Who's that? a Frenchman?   40
  Clo.   Faith, sir, a' has an English name; but
●his fisnomy is more hotter in France than there.
  Laf.   What prince is that?
  Clo.   The black prince, sir; alias, the prince
of darkness; alias, the devil.
  Laf.   Hold thee, there's my purse: I give thee

35 *the fine's the crown.* From 'Finis coronat opus', the
end crowns all.

2 *snipt-taffeta.* Slashed silk; a reference to Parolles'
penchant for flashy clothes.

18 *herb of grace.* Rue.

21 *Nebuchadnezzar.* The King of Babylon who went
mad and ate grass.

Nebuchadnezzar. Colour print by William Blake, 1795

---

42 *fisnomy.* Physiognomy. *more hotter.* Because the
prince who warred in France was more in anger there,
and also because he suffered from the 'French disease'
i.e. syphilis.

47 *suggest*. Tempt.

51-52 *prince of the world*. The devil.

53 *narrow gate*. The way to heaven.

57 *broad gate*. Of hell.

66 *unhappy*. Mischievous.

70 *pace*. The gait of a schooled horse.

Lafeu (Anthony Nicholls) and the Countess (Edith Evans), Stratford-upon-Avon, 1959

100 *patch of velvet*. To cover scars and skin eruptions.

103 *two pile and a half*. The thickness of the velvet's pile.

not this to suggest thee from thy master thou talkest of; serve him still.

Clo. I am a woodland fellow, sir, that always loved a great fire; and the master I speak of ever keeps a good fire. But, sure, he is the prince of the world; let his nobility remain in's court. I am for the house with the narrow gate, which I take to be too little for pomp to enter: some that humble themselves may; but the many will be too chill and tender, and they'll be for the flowery way that leads to the broad gate and the great fire.

Laf. Go thy ways, I begin to be aweary of thee; and I tell thee so before, because I would not fall out with thee. Go thy ways: let my horses be well looked to, without any tricks.

Clo. If I put any tricks upon 'em, sir, they shall be jades' tricks; which are their own right by the law of nature.   [*Exit.*

Laf. A shrewd knave and an unhappy.

Count. So he is. My lord that's gone made himself much sport out of him: by his authority he remains here, which he thinks is a patent for his sauciness; and, indeed, he has no pace, but runs where he will.   71

Laf. I like him well; 'tis not amiss. And I was about to tell you, since I heard of the good lady's death and that my lord your son was upon his return home, I moved the king my master to speak in the behalf of my daughter; which, in the minority of them both, his majesty, out of a self-gracious remembrance, did first propose: his highness hath promised me to do it: and, to stop up the displeasure he hath conceived against your son, there is no fitter matter. How does your ladyship like it?

Count. With very much content, my lord; and I wish it happily effected.

Laf. His highness comes post from Marseilles, of as able body as when he numbered thirty: he will be here to-morrow, or I am deceived by him that in such intelligence hath seldom failed.

Count. It rejoices me, that I hope I shall see him ere I die. I have letters that my son will be here to-night: I shall beseech your lordship to remain with me till they meet together.

Laf. Madam, I was thinking with what manners I might safely be admitted.

Count. You need but plead your honourable privilege.

Laf. Lady, of that I have made a bold charter; but I thank my God it holds yet.

Re-enter CLOWN.

Clo. O madam, yonder's my lord your son with a patch of velvet on's face: whether there be a scar under't or no, the velvet knows; but 'tis a goodly patch of velvet: his left cheek is a cheek of two pile and a half, but his right cheek is worn bare.

Laf. A scar nobly got, or a noble scar, is a good livery of honour; so belike is that.

Clo. But it is your carbonadoed face.

Laf. Let us go see your son, I pray you: I long to talk with the young noble soldier.   109

Clo. Faith, there's a dozen of 'em, with delicate fine hats and most courteous feathers which bow the head and nod at every man.   [*Exeunt.*

ACT V.

SCENE I. *Marseilles. A street.*

Enter HELENA, Widow, *and* DIANA, *with two*
Attendants.

● *Hel.* But this exceeding posting day and night
Must wear your spirits low; we cannot help it:
But since you have made the days and nights as one,
To wear your gentle limbs in my affairs,
Be bold you do so grow in my requital
As nothing can unroot you.   In happy time;

Enter a Gentleman.

This man may help me to his majesty's ear,
If he would spend his power.   God save you, sir.
   Gent. And you.
   Hel. Sir, I have seen you in the court of France.
   Gent. I have been sometimes there.   11
   Hel. I do presume, sir, that you are not fallen
From the report that goes upon your goodness;
And therefore, goaded with most sharp occasions,
Which lay nice manners by, I put you to
The use of your own virtues, for the which
I shall continue thankful.
   Gent.   What's your will?
   Hel.   That it will please you
To give this poor petition to the king,
And aid me with that store of power you have 20
To come into his presence.
   Gent. The king's not here.
   Hel.   Not here, sir!
   Gent.   Not, indeed:
He hence removed last night and with more haste
Than is his use.
   Wid.   Lord, how we lose our pains!
   Hel. ALL'S WELL THAT ENDS WELL yet,
Though time seem so adverse and means unfit.
I do beseech you, whither is he gone?
   Gent. Marry, as I take it, to Rousillon;
Whither I am going.
   Hel.   I do beseech you, sir,
Since you are like to see the king before me, 30
Commend the paper to his gracious hand,
Which I presume shall render you no blame
But rather make you thank your pains for it.
I will come after you with what good speed
Our means will make us means.
   Gent.   This I'll do for you.
   Hel. And you shall find yourself to be well
     thank'd,
Whate'er falls more.   We must to horse again.
Go, go, provide.   [*Exeunt.*

SCENE II. *Rousillon. Before the* COUNT'S *palace.*

Enter CLOWN, *and* PAROLLES, *following.*

   Par. Good Monsieur Lavache, give my Lord
Lafeu this letter: I have ere now, sir, been better
known to you, when I have held familiarity with
fresher clothes; but I am now, sir, muddied in
● fortune's mood, and smell somewhat strong of her
strong displeasure.
   Clo. Truly, fortune's displeasure is but sluttish,
if it smell so strongly as thou speakest of: I will
henceforth eat no fish of fortune's buttering.
● Prithee, allow the wind.   10
   Par. Nay, you need not to stop your nose, sir;
I spake but by a metaphor.

The port of Marseilles. Engraving from Knight's
Pictorial Edition of the Works of Shakspere, 1839–1843

---

1 *exceeding posting.* Great speed.

5 *mood.* Anger.

10 *allow the wind.* Go down wind.

20 *purr*. The knave in the card game 'post and pair'.

24 *carp*. A pun on 'the fish reared in ponds' and 'some-one who complains'.

35 *justices*. The justices administered the poor laws.

42-43 *Cox my passion!* God's passion.

Costume design for the Countess of Roussillon by Tanya Moisewitch, Stratford-upon-Avon, 1958–1959

4 *estimation home*. Full value.

Clo. Indeed, sir, if your metaphor stink, I will stop my nose; or against any man's metaphor. Prithee, get thee further.
Par. Pray you, sir, deliver me this paper.
Clo. Foh! prithee, stand away: a paper from fortune's close-stool to give to a nobleman! Look, here he comes himself.   19

Enter LAFEU.

● Here is a purr of fortune's, sir, or of fortune's cat, —but not a musk-cat,—that has fallen into the unclean fishpond of her displeasure, and, as he says, is muddied withal: pray you, sir, use the
● carp as you may; for he looks like a poor, decayed, ingenious, foolish, rascally knave. I do pity his distress in my similes of comfort and leave him to your lordship.   [*Exit.*
Par. My lord, I am a man whom fortune hath cruelly scratched.   29
Laf. And what would you have me to do? 'Tis too late to pare her nails now. Wherein have you played the knave with fortune, that she should scratch you, who of herself is a good lady and would not have knaves thrive long under her?
● There's a quart d'écu for you: let the justices make you and fortune friends: I am for other business.
Par. I beseech your honour to hear me one single word.
Laf. You beg a single penny more: come, you shall ha't; save your word.   40
Par. My name, my good lord, is Parolles.
● *Laf.* You beg more than 'word,' then. Cox my passion! give me your hand. How does your drum?
Par. O my good lord, you were the first that found me!
Laf. Was I, in sooth? and I was the first that lost thee.
Par. It lies in you, my lord, to bring me in some grace, for you did bring me out.   50
Laf. Out upon thee, knave! dost thou put upon me at once both the office of God and the devil? One brings thee in grace and the other brings thee out. [*Trumpets sound.*] The king's coming; I know by his trumpets. Sirrah, inquire further after me; I had talk of you last night: though you are a fool and a knave, you shall eat; go to, follow.
Par. I praise God for you.   [*Exeunt.*

SCENE III. *Rousillon.   The* COUNT'S *palace.*

Flourish.   Enter KING, COUNTESS, LAFEU, *the two* French Lords, *with* Attendants.

King. We lost a jewel of her; and our esteem Was made much poorer by it: but your son, As mad in folly, lack'd the sense to know
● Her estimation home.
Count.   'Tis past, my liege;
And I beseech your majesty to make it Natural rebellion, done i' the blaze of youth; When oil and fire, too strong for reason's force, O'erbears it and burns on.
King.   My honour'd lady, I have forgiven and forgotten all; Though my revenges were high bent upon him, And watch'd the time to shoot.
Laf.   This I must say,   11

But first I beg my pardon, the young lord
Did to his majesty, his mother and his lady
Offence of mighty note; but to himself
The greatest wrong of all.   He lost a wife
Whose beauty did astonish the survey
Of richest eyes, whose words all ears took captive,
Whose dear perfection hearts that scorn'd to serve
Humbly call'd mistress.
  King.   Praising what is lost
Makes the remembrance dear.   Well, call him
    hither;   20
We are reconciled, and the first view shall kill
• All repetition: let him not ask our pardon;
The nature of his great offence is dead,
And deeper than oblivion we do bury
• The incensing relics of it: let him approach,
A stranger, no offender; and inform him
So 'tis our will he should.
  Gent.   I shall, my liege. [*Exit.*
  King.   What says he to your daughter? have
    you spoke?
  Laf.   All that he is hath reference to your
    highness.
  King.   Then shall we have a match.   I have
    letters sent me   30
That set him high in fame.

        Enter BERTRAM.

  Laf.   He looks well on 't.
  King.   I am not a day of season,
For thou mayst see a sunshine and a hail
In me at once: but to the brightest beams
Distracted clouds give way; so stand thou forth;
The time is fair again.
  Ber.   My high-repented blames,
Dear sovereign, pardon to me.
  King.   All is whole;
Not one word more of the consumed time.
• Let's take the instant by the forward top;
For we are old, and on our quick'st decrees   40
The inaudible and noiseless foot of Time
Steals ere we can effect them.   You remember
The daughter of this lord?
  Ber.   Admiringly, my liege, at first
I stuck my choice upon her, ere my heart
Durst make too bold a herald of my tongue:
Where the impression of mine eye infixing,
• Contempt his scornful perspective did lend me,
Which warp'd the line of every other favour;
Scorn'd a fair colour, or express'd it stolen;   50
Extended or contracted all proportions
To a most hideous object: thence it came
That she whom all men praised and whom my-
    self,
Since I have lost, have loved, was in mine eye
The dust that did offend it.
  King.   Well excused:
That thou didst love her, strikes some scores
    away
From the great compt: but love that comes too
    late,
Like a remorseful pardon slowly carried,
To the great sender turns a sour offence,
Crying, 'That's good that's gone.'   Our rash
    faults   60
Make trivial price of serious things we have,
Not knowing them until we know their grave:
Oft our displeasures, to ourselves unjust,
Destroy our friends and after weep their dust:

22 *repetition.* Recollection of the past.

25 *incensing relics.* Memories inciting anger.

39 *forward top.* Fore-lock.

48 *perspective.* An optical glass that distorts.

72 *cesse.* Cease.

74 *digested.* Absorbed.

86 *reave.* Rob.

87 *stead.* Help.

96 *subscribed.* Acknowledged.

100 *heavy satisfaction.* Sadly convinced.

101 *Plutus.* The god of wealth who would know the mystery of turning base metals into gold.

†Our own love waking cries to see what's done,
While shame full late sleeps out the afternoon.
Be this sweet Helen's knell, and now forget her.
Send forth your amorous token for fair Maudlin:
The main consents are had; and here we 'll stay
To see our widower's second marriage-day.   70
　　Count. Which better than the first, O dear
　　　heaven, bless!
● Or, ere they meet, in me, O nature, cesse!
　　Laf. Come on, my son, in whom my house's
　　　name
● Must be digested, give a favour from you
To sparkle in the spirits of my daughter,
That she may quickly come. [*Bertram gives a
　　ring.*] By my old beard,
And every hair that's on 't, Helen, that's dead,
Was a sweet creature: such a ring as this,
The last that e'er I took her leave at court,
I saw upon her finger.
　　Ber.　　　　　　Hers it was not.　　80
　　King. Now, pray you, let me see it; for mine
　　　eye,
While I was speaking, oft was fasten'd to 't.
This ring was mine; and, when I gave it Helen,
I bade her, if her fortunes ever stood
Necessitied to help, that by this token
● I would relieve her. Had you that craft, to
　　reave her
● Of what should stead her most?
　　Ber.　　　　　　My gracious sovereign,
Howe'er it pleases you to take it so,
The ring was never hers.
　　Count.　　　　　Son, on my life,
I have seen her wear it; and she reckon'd it   90
At her life's rate.
　　Laf.　　　　I am sure I saw her wear it.
　　Ber. You are deceived, my lord; she never
　　　saw it:

In Florence was it from a casement thrown me,
Wrapp'd in a paper, which contain'd the name
Of her that threw it: noble she was, and thought
● I stood engaged: but when I had subscribed
To mine own fortune and inform'd her fully
I could not answer in that course of honour
As she had made the overture, she ceased
● In heavy satisfaction and would never   100
● Receive the ring again.
　　King.　　　　　Plutus himself,
That knows the tinct and multiplying medicine,
Hath not in nature's mystery more science
Than I have in this ring: 'twas mine, 'twas
　　Helen's,
Whoever gave it you. Then, if you know
That you are well acquainted with yourself,
Confess 'twas hers, and by what rough enforce-
　　ment
You got it from her: she call'd the saints to
　　surety
That she would never put it from her finger,
Unless she gave it to yourself in bed,   110
Where you have never come, or sent it us
Upon her great disaster.
　　Ber.　　　　　She never saw it.
　　King. Thou speak'st it falsely, as I love mine
　　　honour;
And makest conjectural fears to come into me,
Which I would fain shut out. If it should prove
That thou art so inhuman,—'twill not prove so;—
And yet I know not: thou didst hate her deadly,

And she is dead ; which nothing, but to close
Her eyes myself, could win me to believe,
More than to see this ring.   Take him away. 120
                    [*Guards seize Bertram.*
● My fore-past proofs, howe'er the matter fall,
● Shall tax my fears of little vanity,
Having vainly fear'd too little.   Away with him !
We'll sift this matter further.
    Ber.   If you shall prove
This ring was ever hers, you shall as easy
Prove that I husbanded her bed in Florence,
Where yet she never was.   [*Exit, guarded.*
    King. I am wrapp'd in dismal thinkings.

           Enter a Gentleman.

    Gent.   Gracious sovereign,
Whether I have been to blame or no, I know not :
Here's a petition from a Florentine,   130
● Who hath for four or five removes come short
To tender it herself.   I undertook it,
Vanquish'd thereto by the fair grace and speech
Of the poor suppliant, who by this I know
Is here attending : her business looks in her
With an importing visage ; and she told me,
In a sweet verbal brief, it did concern
Your highness with herself.
    King. [*Reads*] Upon his many protestations to
marry me when his wife was dead, I blush to say
it, he won me.   Now is the Count Rousillon a
widower : his vows are forfeited to me, and my
honour's paid to him.   He stole from Florence,
taking no leave, and I follow him to his country
for justice : grant it me, O king ! in you it best
lies ; otherwise a seducer flourishes, and a poor
maid is undone.   DIANA CAPILET.
    Laf. I will buy me a son-in-law in a fair, and
● toll for this : I'll none of him.
    King. The heavens have thought well on thee,
    Lafeu,   150
To bring forth this discovery.   Seek these suitors :
Go speedily and bring again the count.
I am afeard the life of Helen, lady,
Was foully snatch'd.
    Count.   Now, justice on the doers !

      Re-enter BERTRAM, *guarded.*

    King. I wonder, sir, sith wives are monsters
    to you,
And that you fly them as you swear them lord-
    ship,
Yet you desire to marry.

       Enter Widow *and* DIANA.

                    What woman's that?
    Dia. I am, my lord, a wretched Florentine,
Derived from the ancient Capilet :
My suit, as I do understand, you know,   160
And therefore know how far I may be pitied.
    Wid. I am her mother, sir, whose age and
    honour
Both suffer under this complaint we bring,
● And both shall cease, without your remedy.
    King. Come hither, count ; do you know these
    women?
    Ber. My lord, I neither can nor will deny
But that I know them : do they charge me fur-
    ther?

121 *My fore-past proofs.* The accumulation of proofs.

122 *Shall tax . . . vanity.* Show my fears were not groundless.

131 *removes.* Stopping places on a journey.

149 *toll for this.* In order to sell at a market, one had to register in a 'toll-book'. Lafeu will sell Bertram.

164 *cease.* Die.

Diana (Helen Mirren), Widow (Elizabeth Spriggs), King of France (Sebastian Shaw) and Bertram (Ian Richardson), Stratford-upon-Avon, 1967

170 *this hand*. Bertram's hand.

188 *gamester*. Harlot.

Dia. Why do you look so strange upon your
wife?
Ber. She's none of mine, my lord.
Dia.   If you shall marry,
●You give away this hand, and that is mine;   170
You give away heaven's vows, and those are
mine;
You give away myself, which is known mine;
For I by vow am so embodied yours,
That she which marries you must marry me,
Either both or none.
Laf. Your reputation comes too short for my
daughter; you are no husband for her.
Ber. My lord, this is a fond and desperate
creature,
Whom sometime I have laugh'd with: let your
highness
Lay a more noble thought upon mine honour 180
Than for to think that I would sink it here.
King. Sir, for my thoughts, you have them
ill to friend
Till your deeds gain them: fairer prove your
honour
Than in my thought it lies.
Dia.   Good my lord,
Ask him upon his oath, if he does think
He had not my virginity.
King. What say'st thou to her?
Ber.   She's impudent, my lord,
●And was a common gamester to the camp.
Dia. He does me wrong, my lord; if I were so,
He might have bought me at a common price:
Do not believe him.   O, behold this ring,
Whose high respect and rich validity
Did lack a parallel; yet for all that
He gave it to a commoner o' the camp,
If I be one.
Count. He blushes, and 'tis it:
Of six preceding ancestors, that gem,
Conferr'd by testament to the sequent issue,
Hath it been owed and worn.   This is his wife;
That ring's a thousand proofs.
King.   Methought you said
You saw one here in court could witness it.   200
Dia. I did, my lord, but loath am to produce
So bad an instrument: his name's Parolles.
Laf. I saw the man to-day, if man he be.
King. Find him, and bring him hither.
                         [*Exit an Attendant.*

Ber.   What of him?
He's quoted for a most perfidious slave,
With all the spots o' the world tax'd and de-
bosh'd;
Whose nature sickens but to speak a truth.
Am I or that or this for what he'll utter,
That will speak any thing?
King.   She hath that ring of yours.
Ber. I think she has: certain it is I liked her,
And boarded her i' the wanton way of youth: 211
She knew her distance and did angle for me,
Madding my eagerness with her restraint,
As all impediments in fancy's course
Are motives of more fancy; and, in fine,
Her infinite cunning, with her modern grace,
Subdued me to her rate: she got the ring;
And I had that which any inferior might
At market-price have bought.
Dia.   I must be patient:
You, that have turn'd off a first so noble wife, 220

May justly diet me. I pray you yet;
Since you lack virtue, I will lose a husband;
Send for your ring, I will return it home,
And give me mine again.
 Ber. I have it not.
 King. What ring was yours, I pray you?
 Dia. Sir, much like
The same upon your finger.
 King. Know you this ring? this ring was his
 of late.
 Dia. And this was it I gave him, being abed.
 King. The story then goes false, you threw it
 him
Out of a casement.
 Dia. I have spoke the truth. 230

Enter PAROLLES.

 Ber. My lord, I do confess the ring was hers.
 King. You boggle shrewdly, every feather
 starts you.
Is this the man you speak of?
 Dia. Ay, my lord.
 King. Tell me, sirrah, but tell me true, I
 charge you,
Not fearing the displeasure of your master,
Which on your just proceeding I'll keep off,
By him and by this woman here what know you?
 Par. So please your majesty, my master hath
been an honourable gentleman: tricks he hath
had in him, which gentlemen have. 240
 King. Come, come, to the purpose: did he
love this woman?
 Par. Faith, sir, he did love her; but how?
 King. How, I pray you?
 Par. He did love her, sir, as a gentleman
loves a woman.
 King. How is that?
 Par. He loved her, sir, and loved her not.
 King. As thou art a knave, and no knave.
What an equivocal companion is this! 250
 Par. I am a poor man, and at your majesty's
command.
 Laf. He's a good drum, my lord, but a
naughty orator.
 Dia. Do you know he promised me marriage?
 Par. Faith, I know more than I'll speak.
 King. But wilt thou not speak all thou knowest?
 Par. Yes, so please your majesty. I did go
between them, as I said; but more than that, he
loved her: for indeed he was mad for her, and
talked of Satan and of Limbo and of Furies and
I know not what: yet I was in that credit with
them at that time that I knew of their going to
bed, and of other motions, as promising her marriage, and things which would derive me ill will
to speak of; therefore I will not speak what I
know.
 King. Thou hast spoken all already, unless
thou canst say they are married: but thou art too
fine in thy evidence; therefore stand aside. 270
This ring, you say, was yours?
 Dia. Ay, my good lord.
 King. Where did you buy it? or who gave it
 you?
 Dia. It was not given me, nor I did not
 buy it.
 King. Who lent it you?
 Dia. It was not lent me neither.

221 *diet.* Restrain.

232 *boggle shrewdly.* You take fright.

254 *naughty.* Hopeless.

Costume design for Parolles by Tanya Moisewitch,
Stratford-upon-Avon, 1958

270 *fine.* Subtle.

287 *customer*. Prostitute.

300 *quit*. Acquit.

305 *exorcist*. One that raised as well as laid spirits.

King: 'Is there no exorcist . . .' Entrance of Helena with the Widow. Engraving from painting by Francis Wheatley (1747–1801)

King.   Where did you find it, then?
Dia.   I found it not.
King.   If it were yours by none of all these
   ways,
How could you give it him?
Dia.   I never gave it him.
Laf.   This woman's an easy glove, my lord;
she goes off and on at pleasure.
King.   This ring was mine; I gave it his first
   wife.   289
Dia.   It might be yours or hers, for aught
   I know.
King.   Take her away; I do not like her now;
To prison with her: and away with him.
Unless thou tell'st me where thou hadst this ring,
Thou diest within this hour.
Dia.   I'll never tell you.
King.   Take her away.
Dia.   I'll put in bail, my liege.
● *King.*   I think thee now some common cus-
   tomer.
Dia.   By Jove, if ever I knew man, 'twas you.
King.   Wherefore hast thou accused him all
   this while?   289
Dia.   Because he's guilty, and he is not guilty:
He knows I am no maid, and he'll swear to't;
I'll swear I am a maid, and he knows not.
Great king, I am no strumpet, by my life;
I am either maid, or else this old man's wife.
King.   She does abuse our ears: to prison
   with her.
Dia.   Good mother, fetch my bail. Stay,
   royal sir;   [*Exit Widow.*
The jeweller that owes the ring is sent for,
And he shall surety me.   But for this lord,
Who hath abused me, as he knows himself,
● Though yet he never harm'd me, here I quit him:
He knows himself my bed he hath defiled;   301
And at that time he got his wife with child:
Dead though she be, she feels her young one kick:
So there's my riddle: one that's dead is quick:
And now behold the meaning.

Re-enter Widow, *with* HELENA.

● *King.*   Is there no exorcist
Beguiles the truer office of mine eyes?
Is't real that I see?
Hel.   No, my good lord;
'Tis but the shadow of a wife you see,
The name and not the thing.
Ber.   Both, both.   O, pardon!
Hel.   O my good lord, when I was like this
   maid,   310
I found you wondrous kind.   There is your ring;
And, look you, here's your letter; this it says:
'When from my finger you can get this ring
And are by me with child,' &c.   This is done:
Will you be mine, now you are doubly won?
Ber.   If she, my liege, can make me know
   this clearly,
I'll love her dearly, ever, ever dearly.
Hel.   If it appear not plain and prove untrue,
Deadly divorce step between me and you!
O my dear mother, do I see you living?   320
Laf.   Mine eyes smell onions; I shall weep
   anon:
[*To Parolles*] Good Tom Drum, lend me a hand-
   kercher: so,

I thank thee: wait on me home, I'll make sport
    with thee:
Let thy courtesies alone, they are scurvy ones.
    King. Let us from point to point this story
    know,
● To make the even truth in pleasure flow.
[*To Diana*] If thou be'st yet a fresh uncropped
    flower,
Choose thou thy husband, and I'll pay thy dower;
For I can guess that by thy honest aid
Thou kept'st a wife herself, thyself a maid.   330
Of that and all the progress, more and less,
Resolvedly more leisure shall express:
All yet seems well; and if it end so meet,
The bitter past, more welcome is the sweet.
                         [*Flourish*

EPILOGUE.

    King. The king's a beggar, now the play is
    done:
All is well ended, if this suit be won,
That you express content; which we will pay,
● With strife to please you, day exceeding day:
Ours be your patience then, and yours our parts;
Your gentle hands lend us, and take our hearts.
                       [*Exeunt.* 340

326 *even.* Exact.

ALL·IS·WELL
ENDED   ACT·V·SC·III

The King of France. Illustration by Byam Shaw,
Chiswick Shakespeare c. 1900

338 *strife.* Striving.

689

Measure for Measure

1604

MEASURE FOR MEASURE is an inspired play, where *All's Well* is an excogitated one. With the former coming shortly upon the heels of the latter, *All's Well* gives something of an impression of a trial-run. The situation upon which the plot hangs, the intrigue, is similar. The villain of this piece, Angelo—Count Bertram was not a villain—is caught similarly by the bed-trick, his betrothed substituted for the woman he fancies. The light-weight lying courtier Lucio is shown up and exposed as was the lying and cowardly Parolles. And yet, in spite of similarity of plot and its unravelling, how very different these two plays are which are often thought of as twins!

The ailing King in *All's Well* is totally different from the mysterious Duke—who disguises himself as a Friar, to observe the proceedings of government in his absence. Isabella is a more appealing character than Helena, when all is said; the villainous, tormented Angelo a more powerful creation than the adolescent Count Bertram. Parolles is not rivalled, but the low-life and prison scenes of *Measure for Measure* are more gripping than the army-life around Bertram which, after all, Shakespeare did not know. Moreover, the whole atmosphere is different from that of its predecessor.

It all goes to show the extraordinary variety of his invention, and what little importance he attached to plot, 'sources' and that kind of thing. He took a story he could turn into a play, then let his playwright's expertise and his poetic imagination play upon it. In this case he looked over various versions of the story he had it in mind to dramatise: a closet-drama by George Whitestone and the prose version in his *Heptameron*, but also Cinzio's collection of Italian stories, *Ecatommiti*. With that he set to work, this time both heart and mind were kindled, the play makes a homogeneous integrated impact. We know that the dramatist thought in terms of scenes, and this play provides several of great power.

Government. A main theme is government, the mystery of state, its workings, whether satisfactory or not. We now appreciate, in this century better than before, how much Shakespeare's mind reflected upon the problems of society, of government and order. They were naturally much in mind at this moment of the take-over by James I from Elizabeth, the coming of a new dynasty. The first words of this play are

Of government the properties to unfold . . .

The Duke, withdrawing to observe and test the rule of his Deputy, Angelo, has been too permissive and let slip

> The needful bits and curbs to headstrong weeds . . .
> Sith 'twas my fault to give the people scope,
> 'Twould be my tyranny to strike and gall them
> For what I bid them do: for we bid this be done
> When evil deeds have their permissive pass
> And not the punishment.

The Deputy is a precise, stern, cold-seeming man—when he makes water, his urine is congealed ice, says Lucio—and he puts the law against fornication into effect, thus catching Claudio, who has got his girl with child before marriage. This is pretty harsh; but the detestable Puritans under the Commonwealth brought in the death-penalty against adultery, though it remained a dead letter through the common sense of the country, with which they were never in keeping. The Duke knows well that his Deputy is 'precise, and scarce confesses that his blood flows'. Now

> shall we see,
> If power change purpose, what our seemers be.

Power is apt to corrupt and, now that he has the chance, the Deputy is determined to enforce the death-penalty on the offending Claudio. He is prevented only by himself falling from grace, by arranging an assignation with Claudio's chaste sister, Isabella— as he thinks, but for whom his own betrothed, whom he had deserted for insufficiency of dowry, is substituted. Such is the plot, and it borders all the way along on tragedy, until the Duke reveals himself and puts things right. Shakespeare was also writing *Othello* this year; we may regard *Measure for Measure* as a tragi-comedy.

Various comments of the author by the way illuminate what those in authority have to put up with:

> No might nor greatness in mortality
> Can censure 'scape; back-wounding calumny
> The whitest virtue strikes. What king so strong
> Can tie the gall up in the slanderous tongue?

We see again the contemporary use of rhymed couplets for moral *sententiae*—no point in depreciating such verse, it shows an anachronistic lack of understanding on the part of critics. Again:

> O place and greatness, millions of false eyes
> Are stuck upon thee. Volumes of report
> Run with these false and most contrarious quests
> Upon thy doings, thousand escapes of wit
> Make thee the father of their idle dream,
> And rack thee in their fancies.

This was the kind of thing that Queen Elizabeth, unmarried as she was, had to put up with all her life. There is no end to the nonsense people will say and believe about persons in high place. William Shakespeare was a governmental man; government never had any reason to fear his tongue or pen—he understood too well the mystery of state, the pressures and strains upon those who rule.

The Jacobean Age. James I was now king. A clever, kind, well-educated man, he was more of a don than a monarch; with no sense of dignity and not much of an appearance, he did not care for the public shows in which the great actress, his predecessor, cut such a figure. The Duke is in accord:

> I love the people,
> But do not like to stage me to their eyes;
> Though it do well, I do not relish well
> Their loud applause and aves vehement.

He adds to this a reflection of Essex which Shakespeare noted several times:

> Nor do I think the man of safe discretion
> That does affect it—

i.e. that cultivates popularity as Essex (and Bolingbroke in the plays) had done. James I positively disliked the people thronging around him:

> even so
> The general [i.e. populace], subject to a well-wished king,
> Quit their own part, and in obsequious fondness
> Crowd to his presence, where their untaught love
> Must needs appear offence.

James had been besieged by crowds and sycophants all his way down from the North to take possession of his new kingdom. Unfortunately his first year coincided with a severe outbreak of plague. Mistress Overdone, the bawd—another Mistress Quickly—sums up the times: 'Thus, what with the war, what with the sweat, what with the gallows, and what with poverty, I am custom-shrunk.' The war was not ended till next year, 1604. Meanwhile the gallows claimed some notable exhibits: George Brooke, Lord Cobham's brother, and Father Watson; while Lord Cobham, the great Sir Walter Ralegh and Sir Griffin Markham were condemned to the gallows, but their sentences left suspended over their heads.

It was queasy, uneasy time. We have an unsurpassed picture of contemporary low life, which gave Victorian commentators such embarrassment. It is obvious that William Shakespeare was as well acquainted with this as with the Court—a man of the theatre would be with both. *Measure for Measure* has a full gallery of bawds, pimps, gaolbirds, a provost, a constable, an executioner thrown in—all completely authentic and convincing, a realistic portrayal if to be taken and played comically. The drunken gaolbird, Barnardine, for example, does not care whether his head is chopped off or not. Foreign observers noted that the English cared little for death and took a death-sentence nonchalantly; but they objected to the foreign sentence of breaking on the wheel, leaving men maimed for life.

Elbow, the constable, is another Dogberry, his malapropisms quite as amusing and to the point. Shakespeare is at ease with all this, the bawdy fuller and more flowing than ever—no point in being embarrassed by the facts of life. Even the lofty Deputy, the great Angelo, makes his assignation in a 'garden-house', which was a favourite *locale* for such encounters, as we know from Forman. These creatures' dialogue flows more easily than that of the camp in *All's Well*, except for Parolles with his virtuosity of vituperation. There is a Dickensian inventiveness in the very names of the company in prison:

> 'First, here's young Master Rash. He's in for a commodity of brown paper and old ginger, nine-score and seventeen pounds, of which he made five marks ready money. Marry, then ginger was not much in request, for the old women were all dead. Then there is here one Master Caper, at the suit of Master Threepile the mercer, for some four suits of peach-coloured satin, which now peaches him a beggar. Then have we here young Dizzy, and young Master Deepvow, and Master Copperspur, and Master Starve-lackey, the rapier and dagger man, and young Drop-heir that killed lusty Pudding, and Master Forthright the tilter, and brave Master Shoe-tie the great traveller, and wild Half-Can that stabbed pots, and I think forty more—all great doers in our trade and are now "for the Lord's sake".'

With what gusto Shakespeare wrote that passage! He had recovered his spirits.

Personal. One catches sight of him, for a moment forgetting himself, when he makes the Duke say suddenly in the surroundings of prison: 'Look, th'unfolding star calls up the shepherd'—as if he were out on the Cotswolds once more. (Perhaps he was writing at home in Stratford.)

Many famous passages give us his reflections on life:

> but man, proud man,
> Dressed in a little brief authority,
> Most ignorant of what he's most assured,
> His glassy essence, like an angry ape,
> Plays such fantastic tricks before high heaven
> As makes the angels weep . . .

Man—an angry ape . . . The Duke, in a tremendous formal oration, presents a disenchanted view of life:

> If I do lose thee, I do lose a thing
> That none but fools would keep; a breath thou art,
> Servile to all the skyey influences
> That dost this habitation where thou keep'st
> Hourly afflict.

This is an old man speaking. On the other hand, Claudio, who is young:

> Ay, but to die, and go we know not where,
> To lie in cold obstruction and to rot;
> This sensible warm motion to become
> A kneaded clod; and the delighted spirit
> To bathe in fiery floods, or to reside

> In thrilling region of thick-ribbèd ice,
> To be imprisoned in the viewless winds
> And blown with restless violence round about
> The pendent world—

that was one Elizabethan view of what happened after death.
   There is a revealing reflection from Isabella, the virtuous:

> Women, help heaven! Men their creation mar
> In profiting by them.

Did that speak for William Shakespeare? Isabella has been universally admired, especially perhaps by maiden ladies in universities, for her adamant refusal to sacrifice her chastity to save her brother's life. She would rather die:

> I had rather give my body than my soul.

This moral absolute is less regarded today; a modern audience might well think she attached an exaggerated importance to it. But then, there has supervened the most universal of revolutions—that in the position and status of women. Anyway, without her refusal there would not have been a play.
   More pervasive and more permanent, perhaps, are the themes of justice and of truth against seeming, of what is a man's nature as against what it appears, either to others or even to himself. Angelo's is a convincing progress of discovery of himself: he is not so cold and unimpassioned as he thought himself to be—he is seduced by 'modesty' where he never would be by 'lightness'—and his ignorance of his true self fractures his sense of justice.
   One reflection bespeaks Shakespeare the social man, as always:

> Heaven doth with us as we with torches do,
> Not light them for themselves; for if our virtues
> Did not go forth of us, 'twere all alike
> As if we had them not.

This play has been well-nigh buried under a mountain of moralising—quite superfluously, since all along Shakespeare draws the morals himself:

> That we were all, as some would seem to be,
> Free from our faults, as faults from seeming free . . .
> He who the sword of heaven will bear
> Should be as holy as severe . . . etc.

And by the lips of Isabella Shakespeare pronounces the ultimate moral statement that guided him: forgiveness, charity, mercy:

> Why, all the souls that were were forfeit once,
> And He that might the vantage best have took
> Found out the remedy. How would you be,
> If He, which is the top of judgment, should
> But judge you as you are? O think on that, . . .

English Edwardian actors, Isabella Glyn and S. Hoskins, as Isabella and Lucio

We are already in the atmosphere of the great tragedies.

The Text. First printed in the First Folio, is thought to have been printed from a transcript of an autograph manuscript, prepared by the Company's scribe, Ralph Crane. This triple process of transmission led to a number of confusions and mislineations. For example, the Duke's line quoted above, 'Look, th'unfolding star calls up the shepherd', printed as prose, is obviously a blank verse line. These things are not very important, and do not impede our appreciation of the play.

MEASURE FOR MEASURE.

DRAMATIS PERSONÆ.

VINCENTIO, the Duke.
ANGELO, Deputy.
ESCALUS, an ancient Lord.
CLAUDIO, a young gentleman.
LUCIO, a fantastic.
Two other gentlemen.
PROVOST.
THOMAS, } two friars.
PETER, }
A Justice.
VARRIUS.
ELBOW, a simple constable.
FROTH, a foolish gentleman.

POMPEY, servant to Mistress Overdone.
ABHORSON, an executioner.
BARNARDINE, a dissolute prisoner.

ISABELLA, sister to Claudio.
MARIANA, betrothed to Angelo.
JULIET, beloved of Claudio.
FRANCISCA, a nun.
MISTRESS OVERDONE, a bawd.

Lords, Officers, Citizens, Boy, and Attendants.

SCENE : *Vienna.*

● *A bullet beside a text line indicates an annotation in the opposite column*

ACT I.

SCENE I. *An apartment in the* DUKE'S *palace.*

Enter DUKE, ESCALUS, Lords *and* Attendants.

    Duke. Escalus.
    Escal. My lord.
●   *Duke.* Of government the properties to unfold,
● Would seem in me to affect speech and discourse ;
● Since I am put to know that your own science
● Exceeds, in that, the lists of all advice
    My strength can give you : then no more remains,
● †But that to your sufficiency . . . . .
    . . . . as your worth is able,
    And let them work. The nature of our people,
    Our city's institutions, and the terms   11
● For common justice, you're as pregnant in
    As art and practice hath enriched any
    That we remember. . There is our commission,

The Duke appoints Angelo his deputy. Engraving by Kenny Meadows from Barry Cornwall's *The Works of Shakspere*, 1846

The title refers to the 'Sermon on the Mount'; 'With what measure ye mete, it shall be measured to you again'. (Matthew vii. 2.).

3 *Of government . . . unfold.* To discourse on the qualities necessary to government.

4 *to affect.* To be affected.

5 *put to know.* Must acknowledge.

6 *lists.* Bounds.

8-10 *But that to . . . let them work.* A line is missing here, but one can interpret: 'let your capacity and my authority work together'.

12 *pregnant.* Knowledgeable.

Opposite : Claudio and Isabella. Painting by W. Holman Hunt, 1850

697

18 *special soul*. Special care.

30 *belongings*. Qualities.

31 *thine own so proper*. So completely your own.

31-32 *as to waste . . . they on thee*. His good points should not be only devoted to himself.

The Duke (Alexander Watson), William Poel's production, Royalty Theatre, London, 1893

36 *finely touch'd*. Nobly endowed.

37 *But to fine issues*. Except to produce fine things.

38 *scruple*. The smallest particle.

41 *Both thanks and use*. Both thanks and interest on her loan of gifts.

42 *advertise*. Instruct.

43 *Hold*. Stand firm.

45 *Mortality*. The power to use the sentence of death.

52 *leaven'd*. Carefully considered.

62 *something on*. A part of.

71 *Aves*. Greetings; literally 'hails' from the Latin *Ave*.

From which we would not have you warp.   Call
   hither,
I say, bid come before us Angelo.
                             [Exit an Attendant.
What figure of us think you he will bear?
●For you must know, we have with special soul
Elected him our absence to supply,
Lent him our terror, dress'd him with our love,
And given his deputation all the organs   21
Of our own power: what think you of it?
   Escal.   If any in Vienna be of worth
To undergo such ample grace and honour,
It is Lord Angelo.
   Duke.   Look where he comes.

         Enter ANGELO.

   Ang.   Always obedient to your grace's will,
I come to know your pleasure.
   Duke.   Angelo,
There is a kind of character in thy life,
That to the observer doth thy history
●Fully unfold.   Thyself and thy belongings   30
●Are not thine own so proper as to waste
Thyself upon thy virtues, they on thee.
Heaven doth with us as we with torches do,
Not light them for themselves; for if our virtues
Did not go forth of us, 'twere all alike
●As if we had them not.   Spirits are not finely
   touch'd
●But to fine issues, nor Nature never lends
●The smallest scruple of her excellence
But, like a thrifty goddess, she determines
Herself the glory of a creditor,   40
●Both thanks and use.   But I do bend my speech
●To one that can my part in him advertise;
●Hold therefore, Angelo:—
In our remove be thou at full ourself;
●Mortality and mercy in Vienna
Live in thy tongue and heart: old Escalus,
Though first in question, is thy secondary.
Take thy commission.
   Ang.   Now, good my lord,
Let there be some more test made of my metal,
Before so noble and so great a figure   50
Be stamp'd upon it.
   Duke.   No more evasion:
●We have with a leaven'd and prepared choice
Proceeded to you; therefore take your honours.
Our haste from hence is of so quick condition
That it prefers itself and leaves unquestion'd
Matters of needful value.   We shall write to you,
As time and our concernings shall importune,
How it goes with us, and do look to know
What doth befall you here.   So, fare you well:
To the hopeful execution do I leave you   60
Of your commissions.
   Ang.   Yet give leave, my lord,
●That we may bring you something on the way.
   Duke.   My haste may not admit it;
Nor need you, on mine honour, have to do
With any scruple; your scope is as mine own,
So to enforce or qualify the laws
As to your soul seems good.   Give me your hand:
I'll privily away.   I love the people,
But do not like to stage me to their eyes:
Though it do well, I do not relish well   70
●Their loud applause and Aves vehement;
Nor do I think the man of safe discretion
That does affect it.   Once more, fare you well.

Ang. The heavens give safety to your purposes!

Escal. Lead forth and bring you back in happiness!

Duke. I thank you. Fare you well. [*Exit.*

Escal. I shall desire you, sir, to give me leave
To have free speech with you; and it concerns me
To look into the bottom of my place:
A power I have, but of what strength and nature
I am not yet instructed.   81

Ang. 'Tis so with me. Let us withdraw together,
And we may soon our satisfaction have
Touching that point.

Escal. I'll wait upon your honour. [*Exeunt.*

SCENE II. *A street.*

Enter LUCIO *and two* Gentlemen.

Lucio. If the duke with the other dukes come not to composition with the King of Hungary, why then all the dukes fall upon the king.

First Gent. Heaven grant us its peace, but not the King of Hungary's!

Sec. Gent. Amen.

Lucio. Thou concludest like the sanctimonious pirate, that went to sea with the Ten Commandments, but scraped one out of the table.

Sec. Gent. 'Thou shalt not steal'?   10

Lucio. Ay, that he razed.

First Gent. Why, 'twas a commandment to command the captain and all the rest from their functions: they put forth to steal. There's not a soldier of us all, that, in the thanksgiving before meat, do relish the petition well that prays for peace.

Sec. Gent. I never heard any soldier dislike it.

Lucio. I believe thee; for I think thou never wast where grace was said.   20

Sec. Gent. No? a dozen times at least.

First Gent. What, in metre?

Lucio. In any proportion or in any language.

First Gent. I think, or in any religion.

Lucio. Ay, why not? Grace is grace, despite of all controversy: as, for example, thou thyself art a wicked villain, despite of all grace.

First Gent. Well, there went but a pair of shears between us.

Lucio. I grant; as there may between the lists and the velvet. Thou art the list.   31

First Gent. And thou the velvet: thou art good velvet; thou 'rt a three-piled piece, I warrant thee: I had as lief be a list of an English kersey as be piled, as thou art piled, for a French velvet. Do I speak feelingly now?

Lucio. I think thou dost; and, indeed, with most painful feeling of thy speech: I will, out of thine own confession, learn to begin thy health; but, whilst I live, forget to drink after thee.   40

First Gent. I think I have done myself wrong, have I not?

Sec. Gent. Yes, that thou hast, whether thou art tainted or free.

Lucio. Behold, behold, where Madam Mitigation comes! I have purchased as many diseases under her roof as come to—

Sec. Gent. To what, I pray?

79 *the bottom of my place.* The nature of my duties.

28-29 *there went but a . . . between us.* i.e. we were cut from the same cloth.

31 *lists.* Edges or trimmings.

33 *three-piled.* With pile of triple thickness.

35 *kersey.* Coarse woollen cloth. *piled.* A pun on haemorrhoids, supposed to be a result of venereal disease ('the French disease').

39 *begin thy health.* Propose a toast to thy health.

40 *forget to drink after thee.* Lucio would not drink from the same cup for fear of infection.

Costume design for Lucio, by J. Gower Parks, Stratford-upon-Avon, 1940

50 *dolours.* A pun on 'pains' and 'dollars'.

52 *French crown.* A quibble on 'French coin'; also 'baldness' resulting from the 'French disease'.

84 *the sweat.* The sweating sickness.

91 *Groping for trouts in a peculiar river.* i.e. fishing in private waters (with a sexual innuendo).

103 *put in.* Applied for.

104 *houses of resort.* Brothels.

Brothel. Woodcut from *Holland's Leaguer*, 1632

Lucio.   Judge.
Sec. Gent.   To three thousand dolours a year.
First Gent.   Ay, and more.   51
Lucio.   A French crown more.
First Gent.   Thou art always figuring diseases in me; but thou art full of error; I am sound.
Lucio.   Nay, not as one would say, healthy; but so sound as things that are hollow: thy bones are hollow; impiety has made a feast of thee.

Enter MISTRESS OVERDONE.

First Gent.   How now! which of your hips has the most profound sciatica?
Mrs Ov.   Well, well; there's one yonder arrested and carried to prison was worth five thousand of you all.
Sec. Gent.   Who's that, I pray thee?
Mrs Ov.   Marry, sir, that's Claudio, Signior Claudio.
First Gent.   Claudio to prison? 'tis not so.
Mrs Ov.   Nay, but I know 'tis so: I saw him arrested, saw him carried away; and, which is more, within these three days his head to be chopped off.   70
Lucio.   But, after all this fooling, I would not have it so. Art thou sure of this?
Mrs Ov.   I am too sure of it: and it is for getting Madam Julietta with child.
Lucio.   Believe me, this may be: he promised to meet me two hours since, and he was ever precise in promise-keeping.
Sec. Gent.   Besides, you know, it draws something near to the speech we had to such a purpose.
First Gent.   But, most of all, agreeing with the proclamation.   81
Lucio.   Away! let's go learn the truth of it.
                    [*Exeunt Lucio and Gentlemen.*
Mrs Ov.   Thus, what with the war, what with the sweat, what with the gallows and what with poverty, I am custom-shrunk.

Enter POMPEY.

How now! what's the news with you?
Pom.   Yonder man is carried to prison.
Mrs Ov.   Well; what has he done?
Pom.   A woman.
Mrs Ov.   But what's his offence?   90
Pom.   Groping for trouts in a peculiar river.
Mrs Ov.   What, is there a maid with child by him?
Pom.   No, but there's a woman with maid by him. You have not heard of the proclamation, have you?
Mrs Ov.   What proclamation, man?
Pom.   All houses in the suburbs of Vienna must be plucked down.
Mrs Ov.   And what shall become of those in the city?   101
Pom.   They shall stand for seed: they had gone down too, but that a wise burgher put in for them.
Mrs Ov.   But shall all our houses of resort in the suburbs be pulled down?
Pom.   To the ground, mistress.
Mrs Ov.   Why, here's a change indeed in the commonwealth! What shall become of me?
Pom.   Come; fear not you: good counsellors lack no clients: though you change your place, you need not change your trade; I'll be your tapster still. Courage! there will be pity taken

on you: you that have worn your eyes almost out in the service, you will be considered.

● *Mrs Ov.* What's to do here, Thomas tapster? let's withdraw.

Pom. Here comes Signior Claudio, led by the
● provost to prison; and there's Madam Juliet.

[*Exeunt.*

Enter PROVOST, CLAUDIO, JULIET, *and* Officers.

Claud. Fellow, why dost thou show me thus to the world? 120
Bear me to prison, where I am committed.
  Prov. I do it not in evil disposition,
But from Lord Angelo by special charge.
  Claud. Thus can the demigod Authority
Make us pay down for our offence by weight
The words of heaven; on whom it will, it will;
On whom it will not, so; yet still 'tis just.

Re-enter LUCIO *and two* Gentlemen.

Lucio. Why, how now, Claudio! whence comes this restraint?
  Claud. From too much liberty, my Lucio, liberty:
As surfeit is the father of much fast, 130
● So every scope by the immoderate use
Turns to restraint. Our natures do pursue,
● Like rats that ravin down their proper bane,
A thirsty evil; and when we drink we die.
  Lucio. If I could speak so wisely under an arrest, I would send for certain of my creditors: and yet, to say the truth, I had as lief have the
● foppery of freedom as the morality of imprisonment. What's thy offence, Claudio?
  Claud. What but to speak of would offend again. 140
  Lucio. What, is't murder?
  Claud. No.
  Lucio. Lechery?
  Claud. Call it so.
  Prov. Away, sir! you must go.
  Claud. One word, good friend. Lucio, a word with you.
  Lucio. A hundred, if they'll do you any good.
● Is lechery so look'd after?
● *Claud.* Thus stands it with me: upon a true contract
I got possession of Julietta's bed: 150
You know the lady; she is fast my wife,
● Save that we do the denunciation lack
Of outward order: this we came not to,
● Only for propagation of a dower
Remaining in the coffer of her friends,
From whom we thought it meet to hide our love
● Till time had made them for us. But it chances
The stealth of our most mutual entertainment
With character too gross is writ on Juliet.
  Lucio. With child, perhaps?
  Claud. Unhappily, even so. 160
And the new deputy now for the duke—
Whether it be the fault and glimpse of newness,
Or whether that the body public be
A horse whereon the governor doth ride,
Who, newly in the seat, that it may know
He can command, lets it straight feel the spur;
Whether the tyranny be in his place,
Or in his eminence that fills it up,
● I stagger in:—but this new governor

116 *Thomas tapster.* A generic name for tapsters, who drew liquor from the tap.

119 *provost.* The superintendent of the prison.

131 *scope.* Freedom.

133 *ravin.* Devour ravenously. *proper bane.* Own poison.

138 *foppery.* Folly.

148 *look'd after.* Closely regarded.

149 *true contract.* A betrothal or hand-fasting before witnesses was almost as binding as a marriage ceremony.

152 *denunciation.* Formal announcement.

154 *propagation.* Increase.

157 *made them for us.* i.e. made them friendly toward us.

169 *I stagger in.* I am not sure.

172 *nineteen zodiacs.* Nineteen years.

173 *for a name.* To win a reputation.

177 *tickle.* Insecure.

183 *receive her approbation.* Enter her novitiate.

188 *prone . . . dialect.* Apt language.

196 *tick-tack.* An ancient form of backgammon.

Tick-tack. Woodcut from J. Strutt's *The Sports and Pastimes of the People of England,* 1810

2 *dribbling.* Feeble.

3 *complete.* Mature.

10 *witless bravery.* Foolish finery.

12 *stricture.* Strictness.

15 *strew'd it.* Spread or broadcast it.

28 *Dead to infliction.* Not put into action.

Awakes me all the enrolled penalties   170
Which have, like unscour'd armour, hung by the
          wall
So long that nineteen zodiacs have gone round
And none of them been worn; and, for a name,
Now puts the drowsy and neglected act
Freshly on me: 'tis surely for a name.
     Lucio.   I warrant it is: and thy head stands
so tickle on thy shoulders that a milkmaid, if she
be in love, may sigh it off.   Send after the duke
and appeal to him.
     Claud.   I have done so, but he's not to be
          found.   180
I prithee, Lucio, do me this kind service:
This day my sister should the cloister enter
And there receive her approbation:
Acquaint her with the danger of my state:
Implore her, in my voice, that she make friends
To the strict deputy; bid herself assay him:
I have great hope in that; for in her youth
There is a prone and speechless dialect,
Such as move men; beside, she hath prosperous art
When she will play with reason and discourse,
And well she can persuade.   191
     Lucio.   I pray she may; as well for the en-
couragement of the like, which else would stand
under grievous imposition, as for the enjoying of
thy life, who I would be sorry should be thus
foolishly lost at a game of tick-tack.   I'll to her.
     Claud.   I thank you, good friend Lucio.
     Lucio.   Within two hours.
     Claud.   Come, officer, away!
                                              [*Exeunt.*

SCENE III.   *A monastery.*

Enter Duke *and* FRIAR THOMAS.

     Duke.   No, holy father; throw away that
          thought;
Believe not that the dribbling dart of love
Can pierce a complete bosom.   Why I desire thee
To give me secret harbour, hath a purpose
More grave and wrinkled than the aims and ends
Of burning youth.
     Fri. T.   May your grace speak of it?
     Duke.   My holy sir, none better knows than you
How I have ever loved the life removed
And held in idle price to haunt assemblies
Where youth, and cost, and witless bravery keeps.
I have deliver'd to Lord Angelo,   11
A man of stricture and firm abstinence,
My absolute power and place here in Vienna,
And he supposes me travell'd to Poland;
For so I have strew'd it in the common ear,
And so it is received.   Now, pious sir,
You will demand of me why I do this?
     Fri. T.   Gladly, my lord.
     Duke.   We have strict statutes and most biting
          laws,
The needful bits and curbs to headstrong weeds,
Which for this nineteen years we have let slip; 21
Even like an o'ergrown lion in a cave,
That goes not out to prey.   Now, as fond fathers,
Having bound up the threatening twigs of birch,
Only to stick it in their children's sight
For terror, not to use, in time the rod
Becomes more mock'd than fear'd; so our decrees,
Dead to infliction, to themselves are dead;
And liberty plucks justice by the nose;

● The baby beats the nurse, and quite athwart 30
Goes all decorum.
    Fri. T.   It rested in your grace
To unloose this tied-up justice when you pleased:
And it in you more dreadful would have seem'd
Than in Lord Angelo.
    Duke.   I do fear, too dreadful:
Sith 'twas my fault to give the people scope,
'Twould be my tyranny to strike and gall them
For what I bid them do: for we bid this be done,
When evil deeds have their permissive pass
And not the punishment.   Therefore indeed,
    my father,
I have on Angelo imposed the office; 40
Who may, in the ambush of my name, strike home,
● †And yet my nature never in the fight
To do in slander.   And to behold his sway,
I will, as 'twere a brother of your order,
Visit both prince and people: therefore, I prithee,
Supply me with the habit and instruct me
How I may formally in person bear me
Like a true friar.   Moe reasons for this action
At our more leisure shall I render you;
● Only, this one : Lord Angelo is precise; 50
● Stands at a guard with envy; scarce confesses
That his blood flows, or that his appetite
● Is more to bread than stone: hence shall we see,
If power change purpose, what our seemers be.
                            [*Exeunt.*

Scene IV. *A nunnery.*

Enter ISABELLA *and* FRANCISCA.

    Isab. And have you nuns no farther privileges?
    Fran. Are not these large enough?
    Isab. Yes, truly: I speak not as desiring more;
But rather wishing a more strict restraint
● Upon the sisterhood, the votarists of Saint Clare.
    Lucio. [*Within*] Ho! Peace be in this place!
    Isab.   Who's that which calls?
    Fran. It is a man's voice. Gentle Isabella,
Turn you the key, and know his business of him;
You may, I may not; you are yet unsworn.
When you have vow'd, you must not speak with
    men 10
But in the presence of the prioress:
Then, if you speak, you must not show your face,
Or, if you show your face, you must not speak.
He calls again; I pray you, answer him. [*Exit.*
    Isab. Peace and prosperity! Who is't that
    calls?

Enter LUCIO.

    Lucio. Hail, virgin, if you be, as those cheek-
    roses
● Proclaim you are no less! Can you so stead me
As bring me to the sight of Isabella,
A novice of this place and the fair sister
To her unhappy brother Claudio? 20
    Isab. Why 'her unhappy brother'? let me ask,
The rather for I now must make you know
I am that Isabella and his sister.
    Lucio. Gentle and fair, your brother kindly
    greets you:
Not to be weary with you, he's in prison.
    Isab. Woe me! for what?
    Lucio. For that which, if myself might be his
    judge,
He should receive his punishment in thanks:

30 *athwart.* Awry.

42-43 *And yet my nature . . . slander.* I shall escape
slander.

50 *precise.* Puritanical.

51 *Stands at a guard.* A fencing stance of defence.

53 *Is more.* More inclined.

Ellen Terry as Isabella. Pen and Ink drawing, 1900

5 *votarists of Saint Clare.* Nuns in the order of Saint
Clare, known as the Poor Clares for their 'privilege of
perfect poverty' which forbids ownership even by the
community.

17 *stead.* Help.

30 *story*. Joke.

32 *lapwing*. A bird that had a way of diverting attention from its nest.

39 *Fewness and truth*. Briefly and truly.

42 *seedness*. Sowing.

43 *foison*. Harvest.

Costume design for Isabella by J. Gower Parks, Stratford-upon-Avon, 1940

51-52 *Bore . . . action*. Deluded with the hope.

60 *rebate*. Dull.

62 *use and liberty*. Habitual licence.

63 *run by*. Escaped.

72 *censured*. Sentenced.

83 *would owe*. Possessed.

He hath got his friend with child.

   ● *Isab.*   Sir, make me not your story.
     Lucio.   It is true.   30
I would not—though 'tis my familiar sin
●With maids to seem the lapwing and to jest,
  Tongue far from heart—play with all virgins so:
  I hold you as a thing ensky'd and sainted,
  By your renouncement an immortal spirit,
  And to be talk'd with in sincerity,
  As with a saint.
     Isab.   You do blaspheme the good in mocking me.
   ● *Lucio.*   Do not believe it.   Fewness and truth, 'tis thus:
  Your brother and his lover have embraced :   40
  As those that feed grow full, as blossoming time
●That from the seedness the bare fallow brings
●To teeming foison, even so her plenteous womb
  Expresseth his full tilth and husbandry.
     Isab.   Some one with child by him?   My cousin Juliet?
     Lucio.   Is she your cousin?
     Isab.   Adoptedly; as school-maids change their names
  By vain though apt affection.
     Lucio.   She it is.
     Isab.   O, let him marry her.
     Lucio.   This is the point.

The duke is very strangely gone from hence;   50
●Bore many gentlemen, myself being one,
  In hand and hope of action : but we do learn
  By those that know the very nerves of state,
  His givings-out were of an infinite distance
  From his true-meant design.   Upon his place,
  And with full line of his authority,
  Governs Lord Angelo; a man whose blood
  Is very snow-broth; one who never feels
  The wanton stings and motions of the sense,
●But doth rebate and blunt his natural edge   60
  With profits of the mind, study and fast.
●He—to give fear to use and liberty,
●Which have for long run by the hideous law,
  As mice by lions—hath pick'd out an act,
  Under whose heavy sense your brother's life
  Falls into forfeit : he arrests him on it;
  And follows close the rigour of the statute,
  To make him an example.   All hope is gone,
  Unless you have the grace by your fair prayer
  To soften Angelo : and that's my pith of business
  'Twixt you and your poor brother.   71
   ● *Isab.*   Doth he so seek his life?
     Lucio.   Has censured him
  Already; and, as I hear, the provost hath
  A warrant for his execution.
     Isab.   Alas ! what poor ability's in me
  To do him good?
     Lucio.   Assay the power you have.
     Isab.   My power?   Alas, I doubt—
     Lucio.   Our doubts are traitors
  And make us lose the good we oft might win
  By fearing to attempt.   Go to Lord Angelo,
  And let him learn to know, when maidens sue, 80
  Men give like gods; but when they weep and kneel,
  All their petitions are as freely theirs
●As they themselves would owe them.
     Isab.   I'll see what I can do.
     Lucio.   But speedily.
     Isab.   I will about it straight;

No longer staying but to give the mother
Notice of my affair.   I humbly thank you:
Commend me to my brother: soon at night
I'll send him certain word of my success.
   Lucio.   I take my leave of you.
   Isab.   Good sir, adieu.   90
                          [*Exeunt.*

ACT II.

SCENE I.   *A hall in* ANGELO'S *house.*

Enter ANGELO, ESCALUS, *and a* Justice, Provost,
Officers, *and other* Attendants, *behind.*

   Ang.   We must not make a scarecrow of the
     law,
Setting it up to fear the birds of prey,
And let it keep one shape, till custom make it
Their perch and not their terror.
   Escal.   Ay, but yet
Let us be keen, and rather cut a little,
Than fall, and bruise to death.   Alas, this gentle-
     man,
Whom I would save, had a most noble father!
Let but your honour know,
Whom I believe to be most strait in virtue,
That, in the working of your own affections,   10
Had time cohered with place or place with
     wishing,
Or that the resolute acting of your blood
Could have attain'd the effect of your own pur-
     pose,
Whether you had not sometime in your life
Err'd in this point which now you censure him,
And pull'd the law upon you.
   Ang.   'Tis one thing to be tempted, Escalus,
Another thing to fall.   I not deny,
The jury, passing on the prisoner's life,
May in the sworn twelve have a thief or two   20
Guiltier than him they try.   What's open made
     to justice,
That justice seizes: what know the laws
That thieves do pass on thieves? 'Tis very preg-
     nant,
The jewel that we find, we stoop and take't
Because we see it; but what we do not see
We tread upon, and never think of it.
You may not so extenuate his offence
For I have had such faults; but rather tell me,
When I, that censure him, do so offend,
Let mine own judgement pattern out my death,
And nothing come in partial.   Sir, he must die.
   Escal.   Be it as your wisdom will.
   Ang.   Where is the provost?
   Prov.   Here, if it like your honour.
   Ang.   See that Claudio
Be executed by nine to-morrow morning:
Bring him his confessor, let him be prepared:
For that's the utmost of his pilgrimage.
                      [*Exit Provost.*
   Escal. [*Aside*] Well, heaven forgive him! and
     forgive us all!
Some rise by sin, and some by virtue fall:
†Some run from brakes of ice, and answer none:
And some condemned for a fault alone.   40

Enter ELBOW, *and* Officers *with* FROTH *and*
POMPEY.

   Elb.   Come, bring them away: if these be good
people in a commonweal that do nothing but use

Court-room scene. From a contemporary woodcut

2 *to fear.* To frighten.

10 *affections.* Passions.

19 *passing on.* Passing sentence on.

22-23 *what know . . . thieves.* How can the law know
what sentences thieves are passing on other thieves?
pregnant. Obvious.

28 *For.* Because.

31 *partial.* In my favour.

39 *brakes of ice.* Thickets of vice.

43 *common houses.* Brothels.

Angelo: 'How now, sir!' Engraving from Charles Knight's *Pictorial Edition of the Works of William Shakspere*, 1839–43

54 *precise.* Complete.

57 *comes off well.* Sounds well.

59 *quality.* Occupation.

63 *parcel-bawd.* Part-time bawd.

66 *hot-house.* Bath-house (which was often a brothel).

69 *detest.* Elbow means 'protest'.

81 *cardinally.* He means 'carnally'.

85 *Mistress Overdone's means.* i.e. Pompey, her go-between.

90 *misplaces.* Misuses words.

92-93 *stewed prunes.* A synonym for prostitutes.

94 *distant.* He means 'instant'.

97 *China dishes.* Chinese porcelain was a new luxury item.

their abuses in common houses, I know no law: bring them away.

Ang. How now, sir! What's your name? and what's the matter?

Elb. If it please your honour, I am the poor duke's constable, and my name is Elbow: I do lean upon justice, sir, and do bring in here before your good honour two notorious benefactors. 50

Ang. Benefactors? Well; what benefactors are they? are they not malefactors?

Elb. If it please your honour, I know not well what they are: but precise villains they are, that I am sure of; and void of all profanation in the world that good Christians ought to have.

Escal. This comes off well; here's a wise officer.

Ang. Go to: what quality are they of? Elbow is your name? why dost thou not speak, Elbow?

Pom. He cannot, sir; he's out at elbow. 61

Ang. What are you, sir?

Elb. He, sir! a tapster, sir; parcel-bawd; one that serves a bad woman; whose house, sir, was, as they say, plucked down in the suburbs; and now she professes a hot-house, which, I think, is a very ill house too.

Escal. How know you that?

Elb. My wife, sir, whom I detest before heaven and your honour,— 70

Escal. How? thy wife?

Elb. Ay, sir; whom, I thank heaven, is an honest woman,—

Escal. Dost thou detest her therefore?

Elb. I say, sir, I will detest myself also, as well as she, that this house, if it be not a bawd's house, it is pity of her life, for it is a naughty house.

Escal. How dost thou know that, constable?

Elb. Marry, sir, by my wife; who, if she had been a woman cardinally given, might have been accused in fornication, adultery, and all uncleanliness there.

Escal. By the woman's means?

Elb. Ay, sir, by Mistress Overdone's means: but as she spit in his face, so she defied him.

Pom. Sir, if it please your honour, this is not so.

Elb. Prove it before these varlets here, thou honourable man; prove it.

Escal. Do you hear how he misplaces? 90

Pom. Sir, she came in great with child; and longing, saving your honour's reverence, for stewed prunes; sir, we had but two in the house, which at that very distant time stood, as it were, in a fruit-dish, a dish of some three-pence; your honours have seen such dishes; they are not China dishes, but very good dishes,—

Escal. Go to, go to: no matter for the dish, sir.

Pom. No, indeed, sir, not of a pin; you are therein the right: but to the point. As I say, this Mistress Elbow, being, as I say, with child, and being great-bellied, and longing, as I said, for prunes; and having but two in the dish, as I said, Master Froth here, this very man, having eaten the rest, as I said, and, as I say, paying for them very honestly; for, as you know, Master Froth, I could not give you three-pence again.

Froth. No, indeed.

Pom. Very well; you being then, if you be remembered, cracking the stones of the foresaid prunes,— 111

Froth. Ay, so I did indeed.

Pom. Why, very well; I telling you then, if you be remembered, that such a one and such a one were past cure of the thing you wot of, unless they kept very good diet, as I told you,—

Froth. All this is true.

Pom. Why, very well, then,—

Escal. Come, you are a tedious fool: to the purpose. What was done to Elbow's wife, that he ● hath cause to complain of? Come me to what was done to her.

Pom. Sir, your honour cannot come to that yet.

Escal. No, sir, nor I mean it not.

Pom. Sir, but you shall come to it, by your honour's leave. And, I beseech you, look into Master Froth here, sir; a man of fourscore pound ● a year; whose father died at Hallowmas: was't not at Hallowmas, Master Froth?

● *Froth.* All-hallond eve.   130

Pom. Why, very well; I hope here be truths. He, sir, sitting, as I say, in a lower chair, sir; ● 'twas in the Bunch of Grapes, where indeed you have a delight to sit, have you not?

● *Froth.* I have so; because it is an open room and good for winter.

Pom. Why, very well, then; I hope here be truths.

Ang. This will last out a night in Russia, When nights are longest there: I'll take my leave,   140
And leave you to the hearing of the cause; Hoping you'll find good cause to whip them all.

Escal. I think no less. Good morrow to your lordship.   [*Exit Angelo.*
Now, sir, come on: what was done to Elbow's wife, once more?

Pom. Once, sir? there was nothing done to her once.

Elb. I beseech you, sir, ask him what this man did to my wife.

Pom. I beseech your honour, ask me.   150

Escal. Well, sir; what did this gentleman to her?

Pom. I beseech you, sir, look in this gentleman's face. Good Master Froth, look upon his honour; 'tis for a good purpose. Doth your honour mark his face?

Escal. Ay, sir, very well.

Pom. Nay, I beseech you, mark it well.

Escal. Well, I do so.

Pom. Doth your honour see any harm in his face?   160

Escal. Why, no.

● *Pom.* I'll be supposed upon a book, his face is the worst thing about him. Good, then; if his face be the worst thing about him, how could Master Froth do the constable's wife any harm? I would know that of your honour.

Escal. He's in the right. Constable, what say you to it?

● *Elb.* First, an it like you, the house is a respected house; next, this is a respected fellow; and his mistress is a respected woman.

Pom. By this hand, sir, his wife is a more respected person than any of us all.

Elb. Varlet, thou liest; thou liest, wicked varlet! the time is yet to come that she was ever respected with man, woman, or child.

121 *Come me.* Come.

128 *Hallowmas.* All Saints' Day, November 1.

130 *All-hallond eve.* Hallowe'en, October 31.

133 *Bunch of Grapes.* Rooms of inns were often given names.

135-136 *open room.* A public room and *good for winter*, because it would have a fire burning.

162 *supposed.* He means 'deposed'.

169-170 *an it like you.* If it pleases you. *respected.* He means 'suspected'.

Costume design for Elbow by Alix Stone, Stratford-upon-Avon, 1962

180-181 *Justice or Iniquity?* i.e. Elbow or Pompey. They were two stock characters in the Morality plays.

Elbow: 'O thou caitiff . . .' Engraving from a painting by Robert Smirke (1752–1845)

183 *Hannibal.* He means 'cannibal'.

215 *draw you.* A play on the meanings 'to draw ale for you' and 'to disembowel' as in to 'hang, draw and quarter'.

216 *hang them.* Maybe get them hanged.

228 *bum.* Big padded trunk-hose.

Padded trunk hose. Woodcut from Bulmer's *Pedigree of the English Gallant*, 1653

243 *splay.* Castrate.

Pom. Sir, she was respected with him before he married with her.

●   *Escal.* Which is the wiser here? Justice or Iniquity? Is this true?   181

  Elb. O thou caitiff! O thou varlet! O thou
● wicked Hannibal! I respected with her before I was married to her! If ever I was respected with her, or she with me, let not your worship think me the poor duke's officer. Prove this, thou wicked Hannibal, or I'll have mine action of battery on thee.

  Escal. If he took you a box o' the ear, you might have your action of slander too.   190

  Elb. Marry, I thank your good worship for it. What is't your worship's pleasure I shall do with this wicked caitiff?

  Escal. Truly, officer, because he hath some offences in him that thou wouldst discover if thou couldst, let him continue in his courses till thou knowest what they are.

  Elb. Marry, I thank your worship for it. Thou seest, thou wicked varlet, now, what's come upon thee: thou art to continue now, thou varlet; thou art to continue.   201

  Escal. Where were you born, friend?

  Froth. Here in Vienna, sir.

  Escal. Are you of fourscore pounds a year?

  Froth. Yes, an't please you, sir.

  Escal. So. What trade are you of, sir?

  Pom. A tapster; a poor widow's tapster.

  Escal. Your mistress' name?

  Pom. Mistress Overdone.

  Escal. Hath she had any more than one husband?   211

  Pom. Nine, sir; Overdone by the last.

  Escal. Nine! Come hither to me, Master Froth. Master Froth, I would not have you ac-
● quainted with tapsters: they will draw you,
● Master Froth, and you will hang them. Get you gone, and let me hear no more of you.

  Froth. I thank your worship. For mine own part, I never come into any room in a taphouse, but I am drawn in.   220

  Escal. Well, no more of it, Master Froth: farewell. [*Exit Froth.*] Come you hither to me, Master tapster. What's your name, Master tapster?

  Pom. Pompey.

  Escal. What else?

  Pom. Bum, sir.

● *Escal.* Troth, and your bum is the greatest thing about you; so that in the beastliest sense you are Pompey the Great. Pompey, you are partly a bawd, Pompey, howsoever you colour it in being a tapster, are you not? come, tell me true: it shall be the better for you.

  Pom. Truly, sir, I am a poor fellow that would live.

  Escal. How would you live, Pompey? by being a bawd? What do you think of the trade, Pompey? is it a lawful trade?

  Pom. If the law would allow it, sir.

  Escal. But the law will not allow it, Pompey; nor it shall not be allowed in Vienna.   241

  Pom. Does your worship mean to geld and
● splay all the youth of the city?

  Escal. No, Pompey.

  Pom. Truly, sir, in my poor opinion, they will to't then. If your worship will take order

708

for the drabs and the knaves, you need not to fear the bawds.

Escal.   There are pretty orders beginning, I can tell you: it is but heading and hanging.   250

Pom.   If you head and hang all that offend that way but for ten year together, you'll be glad to give out a commission for more heads: if this law hold in Vienna ten year, I'll rent the fairest house in it after three-pence a bay: if you live to see this come to pass, say Pompey told you so.

Escal.   Thank you, good Pompey; and, in requital of your prophecy, hark you, I advise you, let me not find you before me again upon any complaint whatsoever; no, not for dwelling where you do: if I do, Pompey, I shall beat you to your tent, and prove a shrewd Cæsar to you; in plain dealing, Pompey, I shall have you whipt: so, for this time, Pompey, fare you well.

Pom.   I thank your worship for your good counsel: [*Aside*] but I shall follow it as the flesh and fortune shall better determine.

Whip me? No, no; let carman whip his jade:
The valiant heart's not whipt out of his trade.
                              [*Exit.*   270

Escal.   Come hither to me, Master Elbow; come hither, Master constable. How long have you been in this place of constable?

Elb.   Seven year and a half, sir.

Escal.   I thought, by your readiness in the office, you had continued in it some time. You say, seven years together?

Elb.   And a half, sir.

Escal.   Alas, it hath been great pains to you. They do you wrong to put you so oft upon't: are there not men in your ward sufficient to serve it?

Elb.   Faith, sir, few of any wit in such matters: as they are chosen, they are glad to choose me for them; I do it for some piece of money, and go through with all.

Escal.   Look you bring me in the names of some six or seven, the most sufficient of your parish.

Elb.   To your worship's house, sir?

Escal.   To my house. Fare you well.
                              [*Exit Elbow.*
What's o'clock, think you?   290

Just.   Eleven, sir.

Escal.   I pray you home to dinner with me.

Just.   I humbly thank you.

Escal.   It grieves me for the death of Claudio; But there's no remedy.

Just.   Lord Angelo is severe.

Escal.   It is but needful:
Mercy is not itself, that oft looks so;
Pardon is still the nurse of second woe:
But yet,—poor Claudio! There is no remedy.
Come, sir.   [*Exeunt.*   300

SCENE II.   *Another room in the same.*

Enter PROVOST *and a* Servant.

Serv.   He's hearing of a cause; he will come
          straight:
I'll tell him of you.

Prov.   Pray you, do. [*Exit Servant.*]
                    I'll know
His pleasure; may be he will relent. Alas,
He hath but as offended in a dream!

247 *drabs.* Harlots.

250 *heading and hanging.* Beheading for gentlemen; hanging for commoners.

255 *a bay.* Part of a house that lies under one gable.

263 *shrewd.* Severe.

267-268 *as the flesh and fortune.* As human nature and luck.

269 *carman.* Carter.

298 *Pardon is . . . woe.* Pardon encourages a second offence.

List of punishments. Woodcut from Comenius' *Orbis Sensualium Pictus*, 1689

10 *Under your good correction.* Excuse me for saying so.

12 *doom.* Sentence. *mine.* My concern.

15 *groaning.* i.e. with labour pains.

Angelo: 'Well; what's your suit?' Isabella (Flora Robson), Lucio (Denis Arundel), Provost (Ernest Hare) and Angelo (Charles Laughton), Old Vic Theatre, London, 1933

---

35 *let it be his fault.* i.e. that is condemned.

40 *To fine.* To punish.

All sects, all ages smack of this vice; and he
To die for 't!

Enter ANGELO.

Ang.   Now, what's the matter, provost?
Prov.   Is it your will Claudio shall die to-
   morrow?
Ang.   Did not I tell thee yea? hadst thou not
   order?
Why dost thou ask again?
   Prov.   Lest I might be too rash:
●Under your good correction, I have seen,   10
When, after execution, judgement hath
●Repented o'er his doom.
   Ang.   Go to; let that be mine:
Do you your office, or give up your place,
And you shall well be spared.
   Prov.   I crave your honour's pardon.
●What shall be done, sir, with the groaning Juliet?
She's very near her hour.
   Ang.   Dispose of her
To some more fitter place, and that with speed.

Re-enter Servant.

Serv.   Here is the sister of the man condemn'd
Desires access to you.
   Ang.   Hath he a sister?
Prov.   Ay, my good lord; a very virtuous
   maid,   20
And to be shortly of a sisterhood,
If not already.
   Ang.   Well, let her be admitted.
            [*Exit Servant.*
See you the fornicatress be removed:
Let her have needful, but not lavish, means;
There shall be order for't.

Enter ISABELLA *and* LUCIO.

Prov.   God save your honour!
Ang.   Stay a little while. [*To Isab.*] You're
   welcome: what's your will?
Isab.   I am a woeful suitor to your honour,
Please but your honour hear me.
   Ang.   Well; what's your suit?
Isab.   There is a vice that most I do abhor,
And most desire should meet the blow of justice;
For which I would not plead, but that I must;
For which I must not plead, but that I am
At war 'twixt will and will not.
   Ang.   Well; the matter?
Isab.   I have a brother is condemn'd to die:
●I do beseech you, let it be his fault,
And not my brother.
   Prov.   [*Aside*] Heaven give thee moving
   graces!
Ang.   Condemn the fault, and not the actor
   of it?
Why, every fault's condemn'd ere it be done:
Mine were the very cipher of a function,
●To fine the faults whose fine stands in record, 40
And let go by the actor.
   Isab.   O just but severe law!
I had a brother, then. Heaven keep your honour!
   Lucio. [*Aside to Isab.*] Give't not o'er so: to
   him again, entreat him;
Kneel down before him, hang upon his gown:
You are too cold; if you should need a pin,
You could not with more tame a tongue desire it;

To him, I say!
Isab. Must he needs die?
Ang.   Maiden, no remedy.
Isab. Yes; I do think that you might pardon
  him,
And neither heaven nor man grieve at the mercy.
Ang. I will not do't.
Isab.   But can you, if you would? 51
Ang. Look, what I will not, that I cannot do.
Isab. But might you do't, and do the world
  no wrong,
● If so your heart were touch'd with that remorse
As mine is to him?
Ang.   He's sentenced; 'tis too late.
Lucio. [*Aside to Isab.*] You are too cold.
Isab. Too late? why, no; I, that do speak a
  word,
May call it back again. Well, believe this,
● No ceremony that to great ones 'longs,
Not the king's crown, nor the deputed sword, 60
The marshal's truncheon, nor the judge's robe,
Become them with one half so good a grace
As mercy does.
If he had been as you and you as he,
You would have slipt like him; but he, like you,
Would not have been so stern.
Ang.   Pray you, be gone.
Isab. I would to heaven I had your potency,
And you were Isabel! should it then be thus?
No; I would tell what 'twere to be a judge,
And what a prisoner.
Lucio. [*Aside to Isab.*] Ay, touch him; there's
  the vein.   70
Ang. Your brother is a forfeit of the law,
And you but waste your words.
Isab.   Alas, alas!
Why, all the souls that were were forfeit once;
● And He that might the vantage best have took
Found out the remedy. How would you be,
● If He, which is the top of judgement, should
But judge you as you are? O, think on that;
And mercy then will breathe within your lips,
Like man new made.
Ang.   Be you content, fair maid;
It is the law, not I condemn your brother: 80
Were he my kinsman, brother, or my son,
It should be thus with him: he must die to-
  morrow.
Isab. To-morrow! O, that's sudden! Spare
  him, spare him!
He's not prepared for death. Even for our
  kitchens
We kill the fowl of season: shall we serve heaven
With less respect than we do minister
To our gross selves? Good, good my lord, be-
  think you;
Who is it that hath died for this offence?
There's many have committed it.
Lucio.   [*Aside to Isab.*] Ay, well said.
Ang. The law hath not been dead, though it
  hath slept: 90
Those many had not dared to do that evil,
If the first that did the edict infringe
Had answer'd for his deed: now 'tis awake,
Takes note of what is done; and, like a prophet
● Looks in a glass, that shows what future evils,
Either new, or by remissness new-conceived,
And so in progress to be hatch'd and born,
● Are now to have no successive degrees,

54 *remorse.* Pity.

59 *'longs.* Belongs.

74 *He.* Christ.

76 *top of judgement.* Supreme judge.

Isabella: 'Spare him, spare him.' Engraving from Bell's
edition of the plays of Shakespeare, 1774

95 *glass.* A crystal used for fortune-telling.

98 *degrees.* Stages.

112 *pelting*. Paltry.

119 *Most ignorant . . . assured*. Most certain about what he knows least about. i.e. his own nature.

120 *glassy essence*. Reflection of himself.

122 *spleens*. Traditionally, the spleen was the seat of both grief and laughter.

123 *Would . . . mortal*. Would die of laughter.

132 *avised*. Aware.

136 *That skins the vice o' the top*. That skims off the upper layer of vice.

142 *Such sense, that my sense breeds with it*. Such matter that it arouses my senses.

But, ere they live, to end.
    Isab.   Yet show some pity.
    Ang. I show it most of all when I show
        justice;   100
For then I pity those I do not know,
Which a dismiss'd offence would after gall;
And do him right that, answering one foul wrong,
Lives not to act another. Be satisfied;
Your brother dies to-morrow; be content.
    Isab. So you must be the first that gives this sentence,
And he, that suffers. O, it is excellent
To have a giant's strength; but it is tyrannous
To use it like a giant.
    Lucio. [*Aside to Isab.*] That's well said.
    Isab. Could great men thunder   110
As Jove himself does, Jove would ne'er be quiet,
● For every pelting, petty officer
Would use his heaven for thunder;
Nothing but thunder! Merciful Heaven,
Thou rather with thy sharp and sulphurous bolt
Split'st the unwedgeable and gnarled oak
Than the soft myrtle: but man, proud man,
Drest in a little brief authority,
● Most ignorant of what he's most assured,
● His glassy essence, like an angry ape,   120
Plays such fantastic tricks before high heaven
● As make the angels weep; who, with our spleens,
● Would all themselves laugh mortal.
    Lucio. [*Aside to Isab.*] O, to him, to him, wench! he will relent;
He's coming; I perceive 't.
    Prov.   [*Aside*] Pray heaven she win him!
    Isab. We cannot weigh our brother with ourself:
Great men may jest with saints; 'tis wit in them,
But in the less foul profanation.
    Lucio. Thou'rt i' the right, girl; more o' that.
    Isab. That in the captain's but a choleric word,   130
Which in the soldier is flat blasphemy.
●   *Lucio.* [*Aside to Isab.*] Art avised o' that? more on 't.
    Ang. Why do you put these sayings upon me?
    Isab. Because authority, though it err like others,
Hath yet a kind of medicine in itself,
● That skins the vice o' the top. Go to your bosom;
Knock there, and ask your heart what it doth know
That's like my brother's fault: if it confess
A natural guiltiness such as is his,
Let it not sound a thought upon your tongue 140
Against my brother's life.
    Ang.   [*Aside*] She speaks, and 'tis
● Such sense, that my sense breeds with it. Fare you well.
    Isab. Gentle my lord, turn back.
    Ang. I will bethink me: come again to-morrow.
    Isab. Hark how I'll bribe you: good my lord, turn back.
    Ang. How! bribe me?
    Isab. Ay, with such gifts that heaven shall share with you.
    Lucio. [*Aside to Isab.*] You had marr'd all else.
    Isab. Not with fond shekels of the tested gold,
Or stones whose rates are either rich or poor 150
As fancy values them; but with true prayers
That shall be up at heaven and enter there

●Ere sun-rise, prayers from preserved souls,
From fasting maids whose minds are dedicate
To nothing temporal.
    Ang.   Well; come to me to-morrow.
    Lucio. [*Aside to Isab.*] Go to; 'tis well; away!
    Isab.   Heaven keep your honour safe!
    Ang.   [*Aside*] Amen:
For I am that way going to temptation,
●Where prayers cross.
    Isab.   At what hour to-morrow
Shall I attend your lordship?
    Ang.   At any time 'fore noon. 160
    Isab. 'Save your honour!
            [*Exeunt Isabella, Lucio, and Provost.*
    Ang.   From thee, even from thy virtue!
What's this, what's this? Is this her fault or mine?
The tempter or the tempted, who sins most?
Ha!
Not she; nor doth she tempt: but it is I
●That, lying by the violet in the sun,
Do as the carrion does, not as the flower,
Corrupt with virtuous season. Can it be
That modesty may more betray our sense
Than woman's lightness? Having waste ground
    enough,   170
Shall we desire to raze the sanctuary
And pitch our evils there? O, fie, fie, fie!
What dost thou, or what art thou, Angelo?
Dost thou desire her foully for those things
That make her good? O, let her brother live:
Thieves for their robbery have authority
When judges steal themselves. What, do I love
    her,
That I desire to hear her speak again,
And feast upon her eyes? What is't I dream on?
O cunning enemy, that, to catch a saint, 180
With saints dost bait thy hook! Most dangerous
Is that temptation that doth goad us on
To sin in loving virtue: never could the strumpet,
With all her double vigour, art and nature,
●Once stir my temper; but this virtuous maid
Subdues me quite. Ever till now,
●When men were fond, I smiled and wonder'd
    how.   [*Exit.*

SCENE III. *A room in a prison.*

Enter, severally, DUKE *disguised as a friar,
and* PROVOST.

  Duke. Hail to you, provost! so I think you are.
  Prov. I am the provost. What's your will,
    good friar?
  Duke. Bound by my charity and my blest order,
I come to visit the afflicted spirits
Here in the prison. Do me the common right
To let me see them and to make me know
The nature of their crimes, that I may minister
To them accordingly.
  Prov. I would do more than that, if more
    were needful.

Enter JULIET.

Look, here comes one: a gentlewoman of mine, 10
●Who, falling in the flaws of her own youth,
●Hath blister'd her report: she is with child;
And he that got it, sentenced; a young man
More fit to do another such offence
Than die for this.

153 *preserved souls.* i.e. her fellow nuns.

Angelo: 'Well; come to me to-morrow.' Charles Laughton as Angelo and Flora Robson as Isabella, Old Vic Theatre, London, 1933

159 *cross.* Are at cross purposes.

166-168 *lying by the violet . . . virtuous season.* The summer sun, which warms the violet, kills my coldness.

185 *temper.* Passion.

187 *fond.* Infatuated.

11 *flaws.* Passions.

12 *blister'd her report.* Ruined her reputation.

21 *arraign.* Examine.

23 *hollowly put on.* Insincere.

33 *spare.* Refrain from offending.

38 *instruction.* Religious counsel preparing Claudio for his death.

The Duke (Alexander Watson) disguised as a friar. William Poel's production, Royalty Theatre, London, 1893

39 *Benedicite.* Bless you.

2 *several.* Different.

3 *invention.* Imagination.

11 *boot.* Advantage.

13 *case.* Outer covering.

16-17 *Let's write . . . devil's crest.* Let us cover our ill intent with 'Good Angel'; it is not the devil's motto.

Duke. When must he die?
Prov.   As I do think, to-morrow.
I have provided for you: stay awhile, [*To Juliet.*
And you shall be conducted.
   Duke. Repent you, fair one, of the sin you
      carry?
   Jul. I do; and bear the shame most pa-
      tiently.   20
• *Duke.* I'll teach you how you shall arraign
      your conscience,
And try your penitence, if it be sound,
• Or hollowly put on.
   Jul.   I'll gladly learn.
   Duke. Love you the man that wrong'd you?
   Jul. Yes, as I love the woman that wrong'd
      him.
   Duke. So then it seems your most offenceful
      act
Was mutually committed?
   Jul.   Mutually.
   Duke. Then was your sin of heavier kind
      than his.
   Jul. I do confess it, and repent it, father.
   Duke. 'Tis meet so, daughter: but lest you
      do repent,   30
As that the sin hath brought you to this shame,
Which sorrow is always toward ourselves, not
      heaven,
• Showing we would not spare heaven as we love it,
But as we stand in fear,—
   Jul. I do repent me, as it is an evil,
And take the shame with joy.
   Duke.   There rest.
Your partner, as I hear, must die to-morrow,
• And I am going with instruction to him.
• Grace go with you, Benedicite!   [*Exit.*
   Jul. Must die to-morrow! O injurious love, 40
That respites me a life, whose very comfort
Is still a dying horror!
   Prov.   'Tis pity of him.   [*Exeunt.*

SCENE IV.   *A room in* ANGELO'S *house.*

Enter ANGELO.

   Ang. When I would pray and think, I think
      and pray
• To several subjects.   Heaven hath my empty
      words;
• Whilst my invention, hearing not my tongue,
Anchors on Isabel: Heaven in my mouth,
As if I did but only chew his name;
And in my heart the strong and swelling evil
Of my conception.   The state, whereon I studied,
Is like a good thing, being often read,
Grown fear'd and tedious; yea, my gravity,
Wherein—let no man hear me—I take pride,   10
• Could I with boot change for an idle plume,
Which the air beats for vain.   O place, O form,
• How often dost thou with thy case, thy habit,
Wrench awe from fools and tie the wiser souls
To thy false seeming!   Blood, thou art blood:
• Let's write good angel on the devil's horn;
'Tis not the devil's crest.

Enter a Servant.

                    How now! who's there?
   Serv. One Isabel, a sister, desires access to
you.

Ang. Teach her the way. [*Exit Serv.*] O
    heavens!
Why does my blood thus muster to my heart, 20
Making both it unable for itself,
And dispossessing all my other parts
Of necessary fitness?
So play the foolish throngs with one that swoons;
Come all to help him, and so stop the air
By which he should revive: and even so
The general, subject to a well-wish'd king,
Quit their own part, and in obsequious fondness
Crowd to his presence, where their untaught love
Must needs appear offence.

Enter ISABELLA.

                How now, fair maid?   30
Isab. I am come to know your pleasure.
    Ang. That you might know it, would much
        better please me
Than to demand what 'tis.   Your brother cannot
    live.
    Isab. Even so.   Heaven keep your honour!
    Ang. Yet may he live awhile; and, it may be,
As long as you or I: yet he must die.
    Isab. Under your sentence?
    Ang. Yea.
    Isab. When, I beseech you? that in his re-
        prieve,
Longer or shorter, he may be so fitted   40
That his soul sicken not.
    Ang. Ha! fie, these filthy vices!   It were
        as good
To pardon him that hath from nature stolen
A man already made, as to remit
Their saucy sweetness that do coin heaven's image
In stamps that are forbid: 'tis all as easy
Falsely to take away a life true made
As to put metal in restrained means
To make a false one.
    Isab. 'Tis set down so in heaven, but not in
        earth.   50
    Ang. Say you so? then I shall pose you
        quickly.
Which had you rather, that the most just law
Now took your brother's life; or, to redeem him,
Give up your body to such sweet uncleanness
As she that he hath stain'd?
    Isab.   Sir, believe this,
I had rather give my body than my soul.
    Ang. I talk not of your soul: our compell'd sins
Stand more for number than for accompt.
    Isab.   How say you?
    Ang. Nay, I'll not warrant that; for I can
        speak
Against the thing I say.   Answer to this: 60
I, now the voice of the recorded law,
Pronounce a sentence on your brother's life:
Might there not be a charity in sin
To save this brother's life?
    Isab.   Please you to do't,
I'll take it as a peril to my soul,
It is no sin at all, but charity.
    Ang. Pleased you to do't at peril of your soul,
Were equal poise of sin and charity.
    Isab. That I do beg his life, if it be sin,
Heaven let me bear it! you granting of my suit,
If that be sin, I'll make it my morn prayer   71
To have it added to the faults of mine,
And nothing of your answer.

19 *Teach.* Show.

27-30 *The general . . . appear offence.* See the introduction.

32 *That you might know it.* Angelo takes up *pleasure* and turns it into sexual satisfaction.

40 *fitted.* Prepared for death.

43-44 *from nature . . . already made.* Murdered. *to remit.* To pardon.

45 *saucy sweetness.* Sexual pleasure. *coin heaven's image.* Procreate.

46 *In stamps that are forbid.* Illegitimate.

48 *restrained.* Prohibited.

58 *Stand more . . . accompt.* Are recorded but not weighed against us.

59 *warrant.* Endorse.

66 *It is no sin.* Isabella misunderstands and believes Angelo's 'sin' is pardoning her brother.

68 *equal poise of sin and charity.* The sin would be balanced by the charity.

73 *nothing of your answer.* Nothing for you to answer.

Angelo: 'Nay, but hear me. Your sense pursues not mine.' Engraving from a painting by Robert Smirke (1752–1845)

79 *tax*. Accuse. *black masks*. Nuns' veils.

80 *enshield*. Concealed or hidden.

86 *pain*. Penalty.

90 *But in the loss of question*. Except for argument's sake.

94 *all-building*. Often emended to *all-binding*.

97 *supposed*. Supposed person.

111 *Ignomy*. Ignominy.

112 *houses*. Sorts.

115 *sliding*. Backsliding.

122-123 *feodary*. Confederate. *but only he . . . weakness.* If only he possesses and inherits this weakness.

Ang.   Nay, but hear me.
Your sense pursues not mine: either you are ignorant,
Or seem so craftily; and that's not good.
  Isab.   Let me be ignorant, and in nothing good,
But graciously to know I am no better.
  Ang.   Thus wisdom wishes to appear most bright
● When it doth tax itself; as these black masks
● Proclaim an enshield beauty ten times louder 80
Than beauty could, display'd.   But mark me;
To be received plain, I'll speak more gross:
Your brother is to die.
  Isab.   So.
  Ang.   And his offence is so, as it appears
● Accountant to the law upon that pain.
  Isab.   True.
  Ang.   Admit no other way to save his life,—
As I subscribe not that, nor any other,
● But in the loss of question,—that you, his sister,
Finding yourself desired of such a person,   91
Whose credit with the judge, or own great place,
Could fetch your brother from the manacles
● Of the all-building law; and that there were
No earthly mean to save him, but that either
You must lay down the treasures of your body
● To this supposed, or else to let him suffer;
What would you do?

  Isab.   As much for my poor brother as myself:
That is, were I under the terms of death,   100
The impression of keen whips I 'ld wear as rubies,
And strip myself to death, as to a bed
That longing have been sick for, ere I 'ld yield
My body up to shame.
  Ang.   Then must your brother die.
  Isab.   And 'twere the cheaper way:
Better it were a brother died at once,
Than that a sister, by redeeming him,
Should die for ever.
  Ang.   Were not you then as cruel as the sentence
That you have slander'd so?   110
● *Isab.*   Ignomy in ransom and free pardon
● Are of two houses: lawful mercy
Is nothing kin to foul redemption.
  Ang.   You seem'd of late to make the law a tyrant;
● And rather proved the sliding of your brother
A merriment than a vice.
  Isab.   O, pardon me, my lord; it oft falls out,
To have what we would have, we speak not what we mean:
I something do excuse the thing I hate,
For his advantage that I dearly love.   120
  Ang.   We are all frail.
  Isab.   Else let my brother die,
● If not a feodary, but only he
Owe and succeed thy weakness.
  Ang.   Nay, women are frail too.
  Isab.   Ay, as the glasses where they view themselves;
Which are as easy broke as they make forms.
Women! Help Heaven! men their creation mar
In profiting by them.   Nay, call us ten times frail
For we are soft as our complexions are,
And credulous to false prints.
  Ang.   I think it well: 130
And from this testimony of your own sex,—

Since I suppose we are made to be no stronger
Than faults may shake our frames,—let me be
   bold;
● I do arrest your words.   Be that you are,
That is, a woman; if you be more, you're none;
● If you be one, as you are well express'd
By all external warrants, show it now,
● By putting on the destined livery.
    Isab.   I have no tongue but one: gentle my
     lord,
Let me entreat you speak the former lan-
   guage.   140
    Ang.   Plainly conceive, I love you.
    Isab.   My brother did love Juliet,
And you tell me that he shall die for it.
    Ang.   He shall not, Isabel, if you give me
   love.
●   *Isab.*   I know your virtue hath a license in't,
Which seems a little fouler than it is,
To pluck on others.
    Ang.   Believe me, on mine honour,
My words express my purpose.
    Isab.   Ha! little honour to be much believed,
● And most pernicious purpose! Seeming, seem-
   ing!   150
I will proclaim thee, Angelo; look for't:
Sign me a present pardon for my brother,
Or with an outstretch'd throat I'll tell the world
   aloud
What man thou art.
    Ang.   Who will believe thee, Isabel?
My unsoil'd name, the austereness of my life,
My vouch against you, and my place i' the state,
Will so your accusation overweigh,
That you shall stifle in your own report
And smell of calumny.   I have begun,
● And now I give my sensual race the rein: 160
Fit thy consent to my sharp appetite;
● Lay by all nicety and prolixious blushes,
That banish what they sue for; redeem thy
   brother
By yielding up thy body to my will;
Or else he must not only die the death,
But thy unkindness shall his death draw out
To lingering sufferance.   Answer me to-morrow,
Or, by the affection that now guides me most,
I'll prove a tyrant to him.   As for you,
Say what you can, my false o'erweighs your
   true.   [*Exit.* 170
    Isab.   To whom should I complain?   Did I
     tell this,
Who would believe me?   O perilous mouths,
That bear in them one and the self-same tongue,
Either of condemnation or approof;
Bidding the law make court'sy to their will;
Hooking both right and wrong to the appetite,
To follow as it draws!   I'll to my brother:
● Though he hath fall'n by prompture of the
   blood,
Yet hath he in him such a mind of honour,
That, had he twenty heads to tender down   180
On twenty bloody blocks, he'ld yield them up,
Before his sister should her body stoop
To such abhorr'd pollution.
Then, Isabel, live chaste, and, brother, die:
More than our brother is our chastity.
I'll tell him yet of Angelo's request,
And fit his mind to death, for his soul's rest.
                           [*Exit.*

134 *arrest your words.* Take you at your word.

136 *express'd.* Revealed.

138 *destined livery.* Conduct indicated.

145-147 *I know . . . on others.* Isabella thinks Angelo is trying to trap her by urging her to succumb to his proposals.

150 *Seeming.* Dissembling.

160 *sensual race.* Sensual urge.

162 *prolixious.* Superfluous.

Angelo: '. . . redeem thy brother By yielding up thy body.' Ian Richardson as Angelo and Estelle Kohler as Isabella, Royal Shakespeare Co, 1970

178 *prompture.* Prompting.

5 *absolute.* Resolved.

9 *skyey.* Astrological.

10 *keep'st.* Livest.

Duke: '. . . thou art death's fool'. Woodcut from Stowe's *Survey of London*, 1618

14 *accommodations.* Qualities.

16-17 *fork of a poor worm.* Tongue of a snake.

24-25 *For thy complexion . . . After the moon.* Your disposition changes with the phases of the moon.

29 *bowels.* Offspring.

31 *serpigo.* A skin disease; ringworm.

40 *moe.* More.

41 *makes these odds all even.* Death makes everybody equal.

ACT III.

SCENE I.   *A room in the prison.*

Enter DUKE *disguised as before,* CLAUDIO, *and* PROVOST.

Duke. So then you hope of pardon from Lord Angelo?

Claud. The miserable have no other medicine But only hope:
I've hope to live, and am prepared to die.

Duke. Be absolute for death; either death or life
Shall thereby be the sweeter.   Reason thus with life:
If I do lose thee, I do lose a thing
That none but fools would keep: a breath thou art,
Servile to all the skyey influences,
That dost this habitation, where thou keep'st,   10
Hourly afflict: merely, thou art death's fool;
For him thou labour'st by thy flight to shun
And yet runn'st toward him still.   Thou art not noble;
For all the accommodations that thou bear'st
Are nursed by baseness.   Thou'rt by no means valiant;
For thou dost fear the soft and tender fork
Of a poor worm.   Thy best of rest is sleep,
And that thou oft provokest; yet grossly fear'st
Thy death, which is no more.   Thou art not thyself;
For thou exist'st on many a thousand grains   20
That issue out of dust.   Happy thou art not;
For what thou hast not, still thou strivest to get,
And what thou hast, forget'st.   Thou art not certain;
For thy complexion shifts to strange effects,
After the moon.   If thou art rich, thou'rt poor;
For, like an ass whose back with ingots bows,
Thou bear'st thy heavy riches but a journey,
And death unloads thee.   Friend hast thou none;
For thine own bowels, which do call thee sire,
The mere effusion of thy proper loins,   30
Do curse the gout, serpigo, and the rheum,
For ending thee no sooner.   Thou hast nor youth nor age,
But, as it were, an after-dinner's sleep,
Dreaming on both; for all thy blessed youth
Becomes as aged, and doth beg the alms
Of palsied eld; and when thou art old and rich,
Thou hast neither heat, affection, limb, nor beauty,
To make thy riches pleasant.   What's yet in this
That bears the name of life?   Yet in this life
Lie hid moe thousand deaths: yet death we fear,
That makes these odds all even.   41
Claud.   I humbly thank you.
To sue to live, I find I seek to die;
And, seeking death, find life: let it come on.

Isab. [*Within*] What, ho!   Peace here; grace and good company!

Prov. Who's there? come in: the wish deserves a welcome.

Duke. Dear sir, ere long I'll visit you again.

Claud. Most holy sir, I thank you.

Enter ISABELLA.

Isab. My business is a word or two with Claudio.

Prov. And very welcome.   Look, signior, here's your sister.

Duke. Provost, a word with you.   50

Prov. As many as you please.

Duke. Bring me to hear them speak, where I may be concealed.   [*Exeunt Duke and Provost.*

Claud. Now, sister, what's the comfort?

Isab.   Why,
As all comforts are; most good, most good indeed.
Lord Angelo, having affairs to heaven,
Intends you for his swift ambassador,
● Where you shall be an everlasting leiger:
● Therefore your best appointment make with
  speed;   60
To-morrow you set on.

Claud.   Is there no remedy?

Isab. None, but such remedy as, to save a head,
To cleave a heart in twain.

Claud.   But is there any?

Isab. Yes, brother, you may live:
There is a devilish mercy in the judge,
If you'll implore it, that will free your life,
● But fetter you till death.

Claud.   Perpetual durance?

Isab. Ay, just; perpetual durance, a restraint,
Though all the world's vastidity you had,
● To a determined scope.

Claud.   But in what nature?   70

Isab. In such a one as, you consenting to't,
● Would bark your honour from that trunk you
  bear,
And leave you naked.

Claud.   Let me know the point.

Isab. O, I do fear thee, Claudio; and I quake,
Lest thou a feverous life shouldst entertain,
And six or seven winters more respect
Than a perpetual honour.   Darest thou die?
The sense of death is most in apprehension;
And the poor beetle, that we tread upon,
In corporal sufferance finds a pang as great   80
As when a giant dies.

Claud.   Why give you me this shame?
Think you I can a resolution fetch
From flowery tenderness?   If I must die,
I will encounter darkness as a bride,
And hug it in mine arms.

Isab. There spake my brother; there my
  father's grave
Did utter forth a voice.   Yes, thou must die:
Thou art too noble to conserve a life
● In base appliances.   This outward-sainted deputy,
Whose settled visage and deliberate word   90
● Nips youth i' the head and follies doth emmew
As falcon doth the fowl, is yet a devil;
His filth within being cast, he would appear
● A pond as deep as hell.

Claud.   The prenzie Angelo!

Isab. O, 'tis the cunning livery of hell,
The damned'st body to invest and cover
● In prenzie guards!   Dost thou think, Claudio?
If I would yield him my virginity,
Thou mightst be freed.

Claud.   O heavens! it cannot be.

Isab. Yes, he would give't thee, from this
  rank offence,   100
So to offend him still.   This night's the time
That I should do what I abhor to name,
Or else thou diest to-morrow.

59 *leiger.* Ambassador.

60 *appointment.* Preparation.

67 *durance.* Imprisonment.

70 *determined scope.* Confined limit.

72 *bark.* Strip.

Isabella: 'Darest thou die?' Engraving by H. Fuseli from George Stevens' *The Plays of William Shakspeare*, 1805

89 *appliances.* Means.

91 *emmew.* Drive down into water.

94 *prenzie.* Precise or puritanical.

97 *guards.* Trimmings.

108 *affections.* Passions.

109 *bite the law by the nose.* Resist the law.

114 *trick.* Trifle.

115 *perdurably fined.* Punished perpetually.

119 *obstruction.* Stagnation.

120 *sensible.* Sentient.

123 *thrilling.* Piercingly cold.

124 *viewless.* Invisible.

135 *dispenses with.* Excuses.

141 *shield.* Forbid.

Claud.   Thou shalt not do't.
  Isab. O, were it but my life,
I'ld throw it down for your deliverance
As frankly as a pin.
  Claud.   Thanks, dear Isabel.
  Isab. Be ready, Claudio, for your death to-
    morrow.
  Claud. Yes. Has he affections in him,
That thus can make him bite the law by the nose,
When he would force it? Sure, it is no sin; 110
Or of the deadly seven it is the least.
  Isab. Which is the least?
  Claud. If it were damnable, he being so wise,
Why would he for the momentary trick
Be perdurably fined? O Isabel!
  Isab. What says my brother?
  Claud.   Death is a fearful thing.
  Isab. And shamed life a hateful.
  Claud. Ay, but to die, and go we know not
    where;
To lie in cold obstruction and to rot;
This sensible warm motion to become   120
A kneaded clod; and the delighted spirit
To bathe in fiery floods, or to reside
In thrilling region of thick-ribbed ice;
To be imprison'd in the viewless winds,
And blown with restless violence round about
The pendent world; or to be worse than worst
Of those that lawless and incertain thought
Imagine howling: 'tis too horrible!
The weariest and most loathed worldly life
That age, ache, penury and imprisonment   130
Can lay on nature is a paradise
To what we fear of death.
  Isab. Alas, alas!
  Claud.   Sweet sister, let me live:
What sin you do to save a brother's life,
Nature dispenses with the deed so far
That it becomes a virtue.
  Isab.   O you beast!
O faithless coward! O dishonest wretch!
Wilt thou be made a man out of my vice?
Is't not a kind of incest, to take life
From thine own sister's shame? What should I
    think?   140
Heaven shield my mother play'd my father fair!
For such a warped slip of wilderness
Ne'er issued from his blood. Take my defiance!
Die, perish! Might but my bending down
Reprieve thee from thy fate, it should proceed:
I'll pray a thousand prayers for thy death,
No word to save thee.
  Claud. Nay, hear me, Isabel.
  Isab.   O, fie, fie, fie!
Thy sin's not accidental, but a trade.
Mercy to thee would prove itself a bawd: 150
'Tis best that thou diest quickly.
  Claud.   O hear me, Isabella!

Re-enter DUKE.

  Duke. Vouchsafe a word, young sister, but
    one word.
  Isab. What is your will?
  Duke. Might you dispense with your leisure,
I would by and by have some speech with you:
the satisfaction I would require is likewise your
own benefit.
  Isab. I have no superfluous leisure; my stay

must be stolen out of other affairs; but I will attend you awhile.   [*Walks apart.*

Duke. Son, I have overheard what hath passed between you and your sister. Angelo had never the purpose to corrupt her; only he hath made an assay of her virtue to practise his judgement with the disposition of natures: she, having the truth of honour in her, hath made him that gracious denial which he is most glad to receive. I am confessor to Angelo, and I know this to be true; therefore prepare yourself to death: do not satisfy your resolution with hopes that are fallible: to-morrow you must die; go to your knees and make ready.

Claud. Let me ask my sister pardon. I am so out of love with life that I will sue to be rid of it.

Duke. Hold you there: farewell. [*Exit Claudio.*] Provost, a word with you!

Re-enter PROVOST.

Prov What's your will, father?

Duke. That now you are come, you will be gone. Leave me awhile with the maid: my mind promises with my habit no loss shall touch her by my company.

Prov. In good time.

[*Exit Provost. Isabella comes forward.*

Duke. The hand that hath made you fair hath made you good: the goodness that is cheap in beauty makes beauty brief in goodness; but grace, being the soul of your complexion, shall keep the body of it ever fair. The assault that Angelo hath made to you, fortune hath conveyed to my understanding; and, but that frailty hath examples for his falling, I should wonder at Angelo. How will you do to content this substitute, and to save your brother?

Isab. I am now going to resolve him: I had rather my brother die by the law than my son should be unlawfully born. But, O, how much is the good duke deceived in Angelo! If ever he return and I can speak to him, I will open my lips in vain, or discover his government.

Duke. That shall not be much amiss: yet, as the matter now stands, he will avoid your accusation; he made trial of you only. Therefore fasten your ear on my advisings: to the love I have in doing good a remedy presents itself. I do make myself believe that you may most uprighteously do a poor wronged lady a merited benefit; redeem your brother from the angry law; do no stain to your own gracious person; and much please the absent duke, if peradventure he shall ever return to have hearing of this business.   211

Isab. Let me hear you speak farther. I have spirit to do any thing that appears not foul in the truth of my spirit.

Duke. Virtue is bold, and goodness never fearful. Have you not heard speak of Mariana, the sister of Frederick the great soldier who miscarried at sea?

Isab. I have heard of the lady, and good words went with her name.   220

Duke. She should this Angelo have married; was affianced to her by oath, and the nuptial appointed: between which time of the contract and limit of the solemnity, her brother Frederick

Sarah Siddons as Isabella. Engraving from a design by R. Ramberg

---

164-165 *assay.* Test. *to practise . . . of natures.* To try out his ability to judge people.

170 *satisfy.* Feed.

181 *habit.* Friar's robes.

187 *complexion.* Nature.

192-193 *substitute.* The deputy Angelo.

194 *resolve.* Answer.

199 *discover.* Expose.

224 *limit of the solemnity.* Date appointed for the marriage ceremony.

Costume design for Isabella by J. Gower Parks, Stratford-upon-Avon, 1940

230 *sinew.* Strength.

231 *combinate.* Betrothed.

236-237 *in few.* In few words.

243 *avail.* Benefit.

255 *refer yourself to this advantage.* Insist upon this condition.

260 *stead up.* Keep.

266 *scaled.* Revealed. *frame.* Prepare.

273 *holding up.* Maintaining.

276 *presently.* At once.

4 *brown and white bastard.* A sweet Spanish wine, but also a pun on bastards.

6-7 *two usuries.* Money-lending and whore-mongering, the first of which produces interest, and the second, children.

was wrecked at sea, having in that perished vessel the dowry of his sister. But mark how heavily this befell to the poor gentlewoman: there she lost a noble and renowned brother, in his love toward her ever most kind and natural; with him,
• the portion and sinew of her fortune, her marriage-
• dowry; with both, her combinate husband, this well-seeming Angelo.

Isab. Can this be so? did Angelo so leave her?

Duke. Left her in her tears, and dried not one of them with his comfort; swallowed his vows whole,
• pretending in her discoveries of dishonour: in few, bestowed her on her own lamentation, which she yet wears for his sake; and he, a marble to her tears, is washed with them, but relents not.

Isab. What a merit were it in death to take this poor maid from the world! What corruption in this life, that it will let this man live! But
• how out of this can she avail?

Duke. It is a rupture that you may easily heal: and the cure of it not only saves your brother, but keeps you from dishonour in doing it.

Isab. Show me how, good father.

Duke. This forenamed maid hath yet in her the continuance of her first affection: his unjust unkindness, that in all reason should have quenched her love, hath, like an impediment in the current, made it more violent and unruly. Go you to Angelo; answer his requiring with a plausible obedience; agree with his demands to the point;
• only refer yourself to this advantage, first, that your stay with him may not be long; that the time may have all shadow and silence in it; and the place answer to convenience. This being granted in course,—and now follows all,—we
• shall advise this wronged maid to stead up your appointment, go in your place; if the encounter acknowledge itself hereafter, it may compel him to her recompense: and here, by this, is your brother saved, your honour untainted, the poor Mariana advantaged, and the corrupt deputy
• scaled. The maid will I frame and make fit for his attempt. If you think well to carry this as you may, the doubleness of the benefit defends the deceit from reproof. What think you of it?

Isab. The image of it gives me content already; and I trust it will grow to a most prosperous perfection.

• *Duke.* It lies much in your holding up. Haste you speedily to Angelo. if for this night he entreat you to his bed, give him promise of satis-
• faction. I will presently to Saint Luke's: there, at the moated grange, resides this dejected Mariana. At that place call upon me; and dispatch with Angelo, that it may be quickly.

Isab. I thank you for this comfort. Fare you well, good father.   [*Exeunt severally.* 281

SCENE II. *The street before the prison.*

Enter, on one side, DUKE *disguised as before; on the other,* ELBOW, *and* Officers *with* POMPEY.

Elb. Nay, if there be no remedy for it, but that you will needs buy and sell men and women like beasts, we shall have all the world drink
• brown and white bastard.

Duke. O heavens! what stuff is here?

• *Pom.* 'Twas never merry world since, of two usuries, the merriest was put down, and the worser allowed by order of law a furred gown to keep him warm; and furred with fox and lamb-skins too, to signify, that craft, being richer than innocency, stands for the facing.   11

Elb. Come your way, sir. 'Bless you, good father friar.

Duke. And you, good brother father. What offence hath this man made you, sir?

Elb. Marry, sir, he hath offended the law: and, sir, we take him to be a thief too, sir; for we have found upon him, sir, a strange picklock, which we have sent to the deputy.

Duke. Fie, sirrah! a bawd, a wicked bawd!
The evil that thou causest to be done,   21
That is thy means to live.   Do thou but think
What 'tis to cram a maw or clothe a back
From such a filthy vice: say to thyself,
From their abominable and beastly touches
I drink, I eat, array myself, and live.
Canst thou believe thy living is a life,
So stinkingly depending? Go mend, go mend.

Pom. Indeed, it does stink in some sort, sir; but yet, sir, I would prove—   30

Duke. Nay, if the devil have given thee proofs for sin,
Thou wilt prove his. Take him to prison, officer:
Correction and instruction must both work
Ere this rude beast will profit.

Elb. He must before the deputy, sir: he has given him warning: the deputy cannot abide a whoremaster: if he be a whoremonger, and comes before him, he were as good go a mile on his errand.

Duke. That we were all, as some would seem to be,   40
† From our faults, as faults from seeming, free!

Elb. His neck will come to your waist,—a cord, sir.

Pom. I spy comfort; I cry bail. Here's a gentleman and a friend of mine.

Enter Lucio.

Lucio. How now, noble Pompey! What, at the wheels of Cæsar? art thou led in triumph? What, is there none of Pygmalion's images, newly made woman, to be had now, for putting the hand in the pocket and extracting it clutched? What reply, ha? What sayest thou to this tune, matter and method? Is't not drowned i' the last rain, ha? What sayest thou, Trot? Is the world as it was, man? Which is the way? Is it sad, and few words? or how? The trick of it?

Duke. Still thus, and thus; still worse!

Lucio. How doth my dear morsel, thy mistress? Procures she still, ha?

Pom. Troth, sir, she hath eaten up all her beef, and she is herself in the tub.

Lucio. Why, 'tis good; it is the right of it; it must be so: ever your fresh whore and your powdered bawd: an unshunned consequence; it must be so. Art going to prison, Pompey?

Pom. Yes, faith, sir.

Lucio. Why, 'tis not amiss, Pompey. Farewell: go say I sent thee thither. For debt, Pompey? or how?

Elb. For being a bawd, for being a bawd.

Lucio. Well, then, imprison him: if imprisonment be the due of a bawd, why, 'tis his right: bawd is he doubtless, and of antiquity too; bawd-

---

8 *by order of law a furred gown.* References to usurers in fox-fur occur in Elizabethan literature.

31 *proofs.* Arguments in favour.

38-39 *as good . . . errand.* Proverbial, meaning 'Anything is better than that'.

42 *His neck will come to your waist,—a cord, sir.* As the Duke in his friar's robes wears a cord around his waist, so Pompey's neck will have a hangman's noose around it.

47 *Pygmalion's.* In Greek mythology, Pygmalion was a sculptor who fell in love with the image of a woman he had created.

49 *clutched.* i.e. holding money in it, but with a double meaning.

52 *Trot.* Usually 'old woman'; here perhaps 'fellow'.

54 *The trick of it?* How goes the world?

58 *beef.* A slang word for woman.

59 *the tub.* 1) used in salting beef 2) a sweating treatment used in the cure of venereal disease.

The tub treatment. Woodcut from *Cornelianum Dolium*, 1638

61-62 *powdered.* Preserved. *unshunned.* Inevitable.

73-74 *husband*. Housekeeper.

78 *wear*. The fashion.

80 *mettle*. Spirit but also a pun on 'metal' i.e. the chains.

Lechery. A contemporary woodcut

110 *extirp*. Eliminate.

116 *stock-fishes*. Dried codfish or haddock.

119 *motion generative*. A puppet and therefore incapable of reproduction.

122 *codpiece*. The flap on a pair of breeches that covered the genitals; the rebellion, therefore, means an erection.

130 *detected*. Accused.

135 *clack-dish*. Beggars carried a wooden dish which they clacked. *crotchets*. Whims.

Clack-dish. Wood engraving by W. H. Fairholt from J. O. Halliwell's edition of Shakespeare's works, 1853–65

138 *an inward*. An intimate.

born. Farewell, good Pompey. Commend me to the prison, Pompey: you will turn good husband now, Pompey; you will keep the house.

Pom. I hope, sir, your good worship will be my bail.

Lucio. No, indeed, will I not, Pompey; it is not the wear. I will pray, Pompey, to increase your bondage: if you take it not patiently, why, your mettle is the more. Adieu, trusty Pompey. 'Bless you, friar.   81

Duke. And you.

Lucio. Does Bridget paint still, Pompey, ha?

Elb. Come your ways, sir; come.

Pom. You will not bail me, then, sir?

Lucio. Then, Pompey, nor now. What news abroad, friar? what news?

Elb. Come your ways, sir; come.

Lucio. Go to kennel, Pompey; go. [*Exeunt Elbow, Pompey and Officers.*] What news, friar, of the duke?   91

Duke. I know none. Can you tell me of any?

Lucio. Some say he is with the Emperor of Russia; other some, he is in Rome: but where is he, think you?

Duke. I know not where; but wheresoever, I wish him well.

Lucio. It was a mad fantastical trick of him to steal from the state, and usurp the beggary he was never born to. Lord Angelo dukes it well in his absence; he puts transgression to't.   101

Duke. He does well in't.

Lucio. A little more lenity to lechery would do no harm in him: something too crabbed that way, friar.

Duke. It is too general a vice, and severity must cure it.

Lucio. Yes, in good sooth, the vice is of a great kindred; it is well allied: but it is impossible to extirp it quite, friar, till eating and drinking be put down. They say this Angelo was not made by man and woman after this downright way of creation: is it true, think you?

Duke. How should he be made, then?

Lucio. Some report a sea-maid spawned him; some, that he was begot between two stock-fishes. But it is certain that when he makes water his urine is congealed ice; that I know to be true: † and he is a motion generative; that's infallible.

Duke. You are pleasant, sir, and speak apace.

Lucio. Why, what a ruthless thing is this in him, for the rebellion of a codpiece to take away the life of a man! Would the duke that is absent have done this? Ere he would have hanged a man for the getting a hundred bastards, he would have paid for the nursing a thousand: he had some feeling of the sport; he knew the service, and that instructed him to mercy.

Duke. I never heard the absent duke much detected for women; he was not inclined that way.

Lucio. O, sir, you are deceived.   131

Duke. 'Tis not possible.

Lucio. Who, not the duke? yes, your beggar of fifty; and his use was to put a ducat in her clack-dish: the duke had crotchets in him. He would be drunk too; that let me inform you.

Duke. You do him wrong, surely.

Lucio. Sir, I was an inward of his. A shy fellow was the duke: and I believe I know the cause of his withdrawing.   140

Duke. What, I prithee, might be the cause?

Lucio. No, pardon; 'tis a secret must be locked within the teeth and the lips: but this I
● can let you understand, the greater file of the subject held the duke to be wise.

Duke. Wise! why, no question but he was.

Lucio. A very superficial, ignorant, unweighing fellow.

Duke. Either this is envy in you, folly, or mistaking: the very stream of his life and the
● business he hath helmed must upon a warranted
● need give him a better proclamation. Let him
● be but testimonied in his own bringings-forth, and he shall appear to the envious a scholar, a statesman and a soldier. Therefore you speak unskilfully; or if your knowledge be more it is much darkened in your malice.

Lucio. Sir, I know him, and I love him.

Duke. Love talks with better knowledge, and knowledge with dearer love.   160

Lucio. Come, sir, I know what I know.

Duke. I can hardly believe that, since you know not what you speak. But, if ever the duke return, as our prayers are he may, let me desire you to make your answer before him. If it be honest you have spoke, you have courage to maintain it: I am bound to call upon you; and, I pray you, your name?

Lucio. Sir, my name is Lucio; well known to the duke.   170

Duke. He shall know you better, sir, if I may live to report you.

Lucio. I fear you not.

Duke. O, you hope the duke will return no more; or you imagine me too unhurtful an opposite. But indeed I can do you little harm; you'll forswear this again.

Lucio. I'll be hanged first: thou art deceived in me, friar. But no more of this. Canst thou tell if Claudio die to-morrow or no?   180

Duke. Why should he die, sir?

● *Lucio.* Why? For filling a bottle with a tun-dish. I would the duke we talk of were returned
● again: this ungenitured agent will unpeople the province with continency; sparrows must not build in his house-eaves, because they are lecherous. The duke yet would have dark deeds darkly answered; he would never bring them to light: would he were returned! Marry, this
● Claudio is condemned for untrussing. Farewell, good friar: I prithee, pray for me. The duke,
● I say to thee again, would eat mutton on Fridays. He's not past it yet, and I say to thee, he would mouth with a beggar, though she smelt brown bread and garlic: say that I said so. Farewell.

[*Exit.*

● *Duke.* No might nor greatness in mortality Can censure 'scape; back-wounding calumny The whitest virtue strikes. What king so strong Can tie the gall up in the slanderous tongue? But who comes here?   200

Enter ESCALUS, PROVOST, *and* Officers *with* MISTRESS OVERDONE.

Escal. Go; away with her to prison!

Mrs Ov. Good my lord, be good to me; your honour is accounted a merciful man; good my lord.

Escal. Double and treble admonition, and

The Duke and Lucio. Engraving by Kenny Meadows from Barry Cornwall's *The Works of Shakspere*, 1846

---

144 *the greater file.* The majority.

151 *helmed.* Steered.

152 *proclamation.* Reputation.

153 *bringings-forth.* Achievements.

182-183 *tun-dish.* Funnel, with a sexual innuendo.

184 *ungenitured.* Neutered or impotent.

190 *untrussing.* Undoing his breeches.

192 *mutton.* A play on the use of the word as slang for prostitute.

196 *mortality.* Human life.

206 *forfeit*. Guilty.

214 *Philip and Jacob*. i.e. May 3rd.

222-223 *wrought by*. Acted with.

225 *entertainment*. Acceptance.

232 *See*. The Holy See of Rome.

235-236 *there is so . . . must cure*. There is such pressure on goodness that only its breakdown can cure it.

252 *events*. Affairs.

255 *lent him visitation*. Visited him.

259 *framed to himself*. Made up his mind. *instruction*. Prompting.

266 *shore*. Limit.

● still forfeit in the same kind! This would make mercy swear and play the tyrant.

Prov. A bawd of eleven years' continuance, may it please your honour.

Mrs Ov. My lord, this is one Lucio's information against me. Mistress Kate Keepdown was with child by him in the duke's time; he promised her marriage: his child is a year and a quarter ● old, come Philip and Jacob: I have kept it myself; and see how he goes about to abuse me!

Escal. That fellow is a fellow of much license: let him be called before us. Away with her to prison! Go to; no more words. [*Exeunt Officers with Mistress Ov.*] Provost, my brother Angelo will not be altered; Claudio must die to-morrow: let him be furnished with divines, and have all ● charitable preparation. If my brother wrought by my pity, it should not be so with him.

Prov. So please you, this friar hath been with ● him, and advised him for the entertainment of death.

Escal. Good even, good father.
Duke. Bliss and goodness on you!
Escal. Of whence are you?
Duke. Not of this country, though my chance is now   230
To use it for my time: I am a brother
● Of gracious order, late come from the See
In special business from his holiness.

Escal. What news abroad i' the world?
● *Duke.* None, but that there is so great a fever on goodness, that the dissolution of it must cure it: novelty is only in request; and it is as dangerous to be aged in any kind of course, as it is virtuous to be constant in any undertaking. There is scarce truth enough alive to make societies secure; but security enough to make fellowships accurst: much upon this riddle runs the wisdom of the world. This news is old enough, yet it is every day's news. I pray you, sir, of what disposition was the duke?

Escal. One that, above all other strifes, contended especially to know himself.

Duke. What pleasure was he given to?

Escal. Rather rejoicing to see another merry, than merry at any thing which professed to make him rejoice: a gentleman of all temperance. But ● leave we him to his events, with a prayer they may prove prosperous; and let me desire to know how you find Claudio prepared. I am made to ● understand that you have lent him visitation.

Duke. He professes to have received no sinister measure from his judge, but most willingly humbles himself to the determination of justice: ● yet had he framed to himself, by the instruction of his frailty, many deceiving promises of life; which I by my good leisure have discredited to him, and now is he resolved to die.

Escal. You have paid the heavens your function, and the prisoner the very debt of your calling. I have laboured for the poor gentleman ● to the extremest shore of my modesty: but my brother justice have I found so severe, that he hath forced me to tell him he is indeed Justice.

Duke. If his own life answer the straitness of his proceeding, it shall become him well; wherein if he chance to fail, he hath sentenced himself.

Escal. I am going to visit the prisoner. Fare you well.

Duke. Peace be with you!
[*Exeunt Escalus and Provost.*
● He who the sword of heaven will bear
Should be as holy as severe;
Pattern in himself to know,
† Grace to stand, and virtue go;
More nor less to others paying
Than by self-offences weighing.   280
Shame to him whose cruel striking
Kills for faults of his own liking!
Twice treble shame on Angelo,
To weed my vice and let his grow!
O, what may man within him hide,
Though angel on the outward side!
●† How may likeness made in crimes,
Making practice on the times,
To draw with idle spiders' strings
Most ponderous and substantial things!   290
Craft against vice I must apply:
With Angelo to-night shall lie
His old betrothed but despised;
† So disguise shall, by the disguised,
Pay with falsehood false exacting,
And perform an old contracting.   [*Exit.*

ACT IV.

Scene I. *The moated grange at* St Luke's.

Enter Mariana *and a* Boy.

Boy *sings.*
Take, O, take those lips away,
    That so sweetly were forsworn;
And those eyes, the break of day,
    Lights that do mislead the morn:
But my kisses bring again, bring again;
Seals of love, but seal'd in vain, seal'd in vain.

Mari. Break off thy song, and haste thee
    quick away:
Here comes a man of comfort, whose advice
Hath often still'd my brawling discontent.
                                        [*Exit Boy.*

Enter Duke *disguised as before.*

I cry you mercy, sir; and well could wish   10
You had not found me here so musical:
Let me excuse me, and believe me so,
My mirth it much displeased, but pleased my woe.
    Duke. 'Tis good; though music oft hath such
        a charm
To make bad good, and good provoke to harm.
I pray you, tell me, hath any body inquired for
● me here to-day? much upon this time have I
promised here to meet.
    Mari. You have not been inquired after: I
have sat here all day.   20

Enter Isabella.

● *Duke.* I do constantly believe you. The time
is come even now. I shall crave your forbear-
ance a little: may be I will call upon you anon,
for some advantage to yourself.
    Mari. I am always bound to you.   [*Exit.*
    Duke. Very well met, and well come.
What is the news from this good deputy?
    Isab. He hath a garden circummured with
        brick,
Whose western side is with a vineyard back'd;

275 *sword of heaven.* Sword of authority.

287 *likeness.* This probably means 'suggestion'.

Mariana. William Poel's production, Royalty Theatre,
London, 1893

17 *much upon.* Close to.

21 *constantly.* Certainly.

Isabella (Estelle Kohler), The Duke (Sebastian Shaw), and Mariana (Sara Kestelman) Royal Shakespeare Co, 1970

---

30 *planched*. Made of planks.

40 *In action all of precept*. By describing in words.

42 *concerning her observance*. Her instructions.

44 *possess'd him*. Informed him.

62 *contrarious quests*. Contrary scents.

63 *escapes*. Sallies.

74 *Sith*. Since.

75 *flourish*. Embellish.

76 *tithes*. A tithe was one-tenth of the crops that went to maintain the clergy; but this may be a misprint for 'tilth'.

●And to that vineyard is a planched gate,   30
That makes his opening with this bigger key:
This other doth command a little door
Which from the vineyard to the garden leads;
There have I made my promise
Upon the heavy middle of the night
To call upon him.
   Duke.   But shall you on your knowledge find
    this way?
   Isab.   I have ta'en a due and wary note upon't:
With whispering and most guilty diligence,
●In action all of precept, he did show me   40
The way twice o'er.
   Duke.   Are there no other tokens
●Between you 'greed concerning her observance?
   Isab.   No, none, but only a repair i' the dark;
●And that I have possess'd him my most stay
Can be but brief; for I have made him know
I have a servant comes with me along,
That stays upon me, whose persuasion is
I come about my brother.
   Duke.   'Tis well borne up.
I have not yet made known to Mariana
A word of this. What, ho! within! come forth!

Re-enter MARIANA.

I pray you, be acquainted with this maid;   51
She comes to do you good.
   Isab.   I do desire the like.
   Duke.   Do you persuade yourself that I respect you?
   Mari.   Good friar, I know you do, and have found it.
   Duke.   Take, then, this your companion by the hand,
Who hath a story ready for your ear.
I shall attend your leisure: but make haste;
The vaporous night approaches.
   Mari.   Will't please you walk aside?
             [*Exeunt Mariana and Isabella.*
   Duke.   O place and greatness! millions of false
    eyes   60
Are stuck upon thee: volumes of report
●Run with these false and most contrarious quests
●Upon thy doings: thousand escapes of wit
Make thee the father of their idle dreams
And rack thee in their fancies.

Re-enter MARIANA *and* ISABELLA.

              Welcome, how agreed?
   Isab.   She'll take the enterprise upon her, father,
If you advise it.
   Duke.   It is not my consent,
But my entreaty too.
   Isab.   Little have you to say
When you depart from him, but, soft and low,
'Remember now my brother.'
   Mari.   Fear me not.   70
   Duke.   Nor, gentle daughter, fear you not at all.
He is your husband on a pre-contract:
To bring you thus together, 'tis no sin,
●Sith that the justice of your title to him
●Doth flourish the deceit.   Come, let us go:
●Our corn's to reap, for yet our tithe's to sow.
                     [*Exeunt.*

SCENE II. *A room in the prison.*

Enter PROVOST *and* POMPEY.

Prov. Come hither, sirrah. Can you cut off a man's head?

Pom. If the man be a bachelor, sir, I can; but if he be a married man, he's his wife's head, and I can never cut off a woman's head.

Prov. Come, sir, leave me your snatches, and yield me a direct answer. To-morrow morning are to die Claudio and Barnardine. Here is in our prison a common executioner, who in his office lacks a helper: if you will take it on you to assist him, it shall redeem you from your gyves; if not, you shall have your full time of imprisonment and your deliverance with an un-pitied whipping, for you have been a notorious bawd.

Pom. Sir, I have been an unlawful bawd time out of mind; but yet I will be content to be a lawful hangman. I would be glad to receive some instruction from my fellow partner.

Prov. What, ho! Abhorson! Where's Abhorson, there? 21

Enter ABHORSON.

Abhor. Do you call, sir?

Prov. Sirrah, here's a fellow will help you to-morrow in your execution. If you think it meet, compound with him by the year, and let him abide here with you; if not, use him for the present and dismiss him. He cannot plead his estimation with you; he hath been a bawd.

Abhor. A bawd, sir? fie upon him! he will discredit our mystery. 30

Prov. Go to, sir; you weigh equally; a feather will turn the scale. [*Exit.*

Pom. Pray, sir, by your good favour,—for surely, sir, a good favour you have, but that you have a hanging look,—do you call, sir, your oc-cupation a mystery?

Abhor. Ay, sir; a mystery.

Pom. Painting, sir, I have heard say, is a mystery; and your whores, sir, being members of my occupation, using painting, do prove my occupation a mystery: but what mystery there should be in hanging, if I should be hanged, I cannot imagine.

Abhor. Sir, it is a mystery.

Pom. Proof?

Abhor. Every true man's apparel fits your thief: if it be too little for your thief, your true man thinks it big enough; if it be too big for your thief, your thief thinks it little enough: so every true man's apparel fits your thief. 50

Re-enter PROVOST.

Prov. Are you agreed?

Pom. Sir, I will serve him; for I do find your hangman is a more penitent trade than your bawd; he doth oftener ask forgiveness.

Prov. You, sirrah, provide your block and your axe to-morrow four o'clock.

Abhor. Come on, bawd; I will instruct thee in my trade; follow.

Pom. I do desire to learn, sir: and I hope, if you have occasion to use me for your own turn, you shall find me yare; for truly, sir, for your kindness I owe you a good turn.

4 *he's his wife's head.* The husband was the wife's superior. There is also a quibble on 'maidenheads'.

6 *snatches.* Quips.

9 *common.* Public.

12 *gyves.* Shackles.

Provost: 'What, ho! Abhorson!' Engraving from a painting by Robert Smirke (1752–1845)

30 *mystery.* Trade or profession.

34 *favour.* Face.

46-50 *Every true . . . fits your thief.* Any honest man's clothes will do for a thief.

54 *he doth oftener ask forgiveness.* Before executions the hangman requested the forgiveness of the condemned.

61 *yare.* Ready.

82-83 *his life . . . justice.* Angelo lives his life according to the precepts by which he judges others.

86 *qualify.* Moderate. *meal'd with.* Tainted.

92 *unsisting.* Perhaps 'unresisting' or 'unassisting'. *postern.* Small gate.

101 *siege.* Seat.

103 *Profess'd.* Declared.

Costume design for Claudio by J. Gower Parks, Stratford-upon-Avon, 1940

Prov.   Call hither Barnardine and Claudio :
        [*Exeunt Pompey and Abhorson.*
The one has my pity ; not a jot the other,
Being a murderer, though he were my brother.

Enter CLAUDIO.

Look, here's the warrant, Claudio, for thy death :
'Tis now dead midnight, and by eight to-morrow
Thou must be made immortal.   Where's Bar-
        nardine ?
    Claud.   As fast lock'd up in sleep as guiltless
        labour
When it lies starkly in the traveller's bones :   70
He will not wake.
    Prov.   Who can do good on him ?
Well, go, prepare yourself. [*Knocking within.*]
        But, hark, what noise ?
Heaven give your spirits comfort ! [*Exit Claudio.*]
        By and by.
I hope it is some pardon or reprieve
For the most gentle Claudio.

Enter DUKE *disguised as before.*

                            Welcome, father.
    Duke.   The best and wholesomest spirits of the
        night
Envelope you, good Provost ! Who call'd here of
        late ?
    Prov.   None, since the curfew rung.
    Duke.   Not Isabel ?
    Prov.   No.
    Duke.   They will, then, ere't be long.
    Prov.   What comfort is for Claudio ?   80
    Duke.   There's some in hope.
    Prov.   It is a bitter deputy.
  ● *Duke.*   Not so, not so ; his life is parallel'd
Even with the stroke and line of his great justice :
He doth with holy abstinence subdue
That in himself which he spurs on his power
  ● To qualify in others : were he meal'd with that
Which he corrects, then were he tyrannous ;
But this being so, he's just. [*Knocking within.*
                        Now are they come.
                        [*Exit Provost.*
This is a gentle provost : seldom when
The steeled gaoler is the friend of men.
                        [*Knocking within.*   90
How now ! what noise ?   That spirit's possess'd
        with haste
  ● That wounds the unsisting postern with these
        strokes.

Re-enter PROVOST.

    Prov.   There he must stay until the officer
Arise to let him in : he is call'd up.
    Duke.   Have you no countermand for Claudio
        yet,
But he must die to-morrow ?
    Prov.   None, sir, none.
    Duke.   As near the dawning, provost, as it is,
You shall hear more ere morning.
    Prov.   Happily
You something know ; yet I believe there comes
No countermand ; no such example have we :   100
  ● Besides, upon the very siege of justice
Lord Angelo hath to the public ear
  ● Profess'd the contrary.

Enter a MESSENGER.

This is his lordship's man.

Duke. And here comes Claudio's pardon.

Mes. [*Giving a paper.*] My lord hath sent you this note; and by me this further charge, that you swerve not from the smallest article of it, neither in time, matter, or other circumstance. Good morrow; for, as I take it, it is almost day.

Prov. I shall obey him.   [*Exit Messenger.*

Duke. [*Aside*] This is his pardon, purchased
        by such sin
For which the pardoner himself is in.
● Hence hath offence his quick celerity,
When it is borne in high authority:
● When vice makes mercy, mercy's so extended,
That for the fault's love is the offender friended.
Now, sir, what news?

Prov. I told you. Lord Angelo, belike thinking me remiss in mine office, awakens me with this
● unwonted putting-on; methinks strangely, for he hath not used it before.   121

Duke. Pray you, let's hear.

Prov. [*Reads*]

'Whatsoever you may hear to the contrary, let Claudio be executed by four of the clock; and in the afternoon Barnardine: for my better satisfaction, let me have Claudio's head sent me by five. Let this be duly performed; with a thought that more depends on it than we must yet deliver. Thus fail not to do your office, as you will answer it at your peril.'   130
What say you to this, sir?

Duke. What is that Barnardine who is to be executed in the afternoon?

Prov. A Bohemian born, but here nursed up and bred; one that is a prisoner nine years old.

Duke. How came it that the absent duke had not either delivered him to his liberty or executed him? I have heard it was ever his manner to do so.

● *Prov.* His friends still wrought reprieves for
● him: and, indeed, his fact, till now in the government of Lord Angelo, came not to an undoubtful proof.

Duke. It is now apparent?

Prov. Most manifest, and not denied by himself.

Duke. Hath he borne himself penitently in prison? how seems he to be touched?

Prov. A man that apprehends death no more dreadfully but as a drunken sleep; careless, reckless, and fearless of what's past, present, or to
● come; insensible of mortality, and desperately mortal.

Duke. He wants advice.

Prov. He will hear none: he hath evermore had the liberty of the prison; give him leave to escape hence, he would not: drunk many times a day, if not many days entirely drunk. We have very oft awaked him, as if to carry him to execution, and showed him a seeming warrant for it: it hath not moved him at all.   161

Duke. More of him anon. There is written in your brow, provost, honesty and constancy: if I read it not truly, my ancient skill beguiles me;
● but, in the boldness of my cunning, I will lay my
● self in hazard. Claudio, whom here you have warrant to execute, is no greater forfeit to the law than Angelo who hath sentenced him. To

113-114 *Hence hath . . . authority.* Those in authority can execute their misdeeds with great speed.

115-116 *When vice . . . friended.* If mercy is offered by a vicious man, it is not out of love, but out of sympathy with the vice in the offender.

120 *putting-on.* Insistence.

Duke: 'Pray you, let's hear.' Engraving by Kenny Meadows from Barry Cornwall's *The Works of Shakspere,* 1846

140 *still wrought.* Continued to elicit.

141 *fact.* Crime.

152 *insensible of mortality.* Insensible to death.

165 *cunning.* Knowledge.

166 *in hazard.* At risk.

169 *manifested effect*. Clear demonstration.

171 *present*. Immediate.

176 *limited*. Fixed.

178-179 *to cross . . . smallest*. To deviate from the order in the least.

185 *discover the favour*. Recognize the face.

187 *tie*. Trim.

203 *resemblance*. Probability.

205 *attempt*. Tempt.

207 *hand*. Handwriting.

208 *character*. Handwriting.

216 *tenour*. Sense.

218-219 *unfolding star*. The morning star which indicated to shepherds that it was time to release the sheep from the fold.

223 *shrift*. Confession and absolution.

5 *commodity*. The law forbade interest to be higher than ten per cent. In order to by-pass this statute, money lenders paid out part of the needed sum in kind (commodities) which they usually valued at a price higher than could be obtained for the items. The hapless victim had to sell for cash items like *brown paper* and *old ginger*, and hope to make up the needed sum. Even if he could not, he would still be expected to pay interest on the full sum.

7 *marks*. The mark was worth thirteen shillings and four pence.

make you understand this in a manifested effect, I crave but four days' respite; for the which you are to do me both a present and a dangerous courtesy.

Prov.   Pray, sir, in what?

Duke.   In the delaying death.

Prov.   Alack, how may I do it, having the hour limited, and an express command, under penalty, to deliver his head in the view of Angelo? I may make my case as Claudio's, to cross this in the smallest.

Duke.   By the vow of mine order I warrant you, if my instructions may be your guide. Let this Barnardine be this morning executed, and his head borne to Angelo.

Prov.   Angelo hath seen them both, and will discover the favour.

Duke.   O, death's a great disguiser; and you may add to it. Shave the head, and tie the beard; and say it was the desire of the penitent to be so bared before his death: you know the course is common. If any thing fall to you upon this, more than thanks and good fortune, by the saint whom I profess, I will plead against it with my life.

Prov.   Pardon me, good father; it is against my oath.

Duke.   Were you sworn to the duke, or to the deputy?

Prov.   To him, and to his substitutes.

Duke.   You will think you have made no offence, if the duke avouch the justice of your dealing?   201

Prov.   But what likelihood is in that?

Duke.   Not a resemblance, but a certainty. Yet since I see you fearful, that neither my coat, integrity, nor persuasion can with ease attempt you, I will go further than I meant, to pluck all fears out of you. Look you, sir, here is the hand and seal of the duke: you know the character, I doubt not; and the signet is not strange to you.

Prov.   I know them both.   210

Duke.   The contents of this is the return of the duke: you shall anon over-read it at your pleasure; where you shall find, within these two days he will be here. This is a thing that Angelo knows not; for he this very day receives letters of strange tenour; perchance of the duke's death; perchance entering into some monastery; but, by chance, nothing of what is writ. Look, the unfolding star calls up the shepherd. Put not yourself into amazement how these things should be: all difficulties are but easy when they are known. Call your executioner, and off with Barnardine's head: I will give him a present shrift and advise him for a better place. Yet you are amazed; but this shall absolutely resolve you. Come away; it is almost clear dawn.   [*Exeunt.*

SCENE III.   *Another room in the same.*

Enter POMPEY.

Pom.   I am as well acquainted here as I was in our house of profession: one would think it were Mistress Overdone's own house, for here be many of her old customers. First, here's young Master Rash; he's in for a commodity of brown paper and old ginger, nine-score and seventeen pounds; of which he made five marks, ready

money: marry, then ginger was not much in request, for the old women were all dead. Then is there here one Master Caper, at the suit of Master Three-pile the mercer, for some four suits
• of peach-coloured satin, which now peaches him a beggar. Then have we here young Dizy, and young Master Deep-vow, and Master Copper-spur, and Master Starve-lackey the rapier and dagger man, and young Drop-heir that killed lusty Pudding, and Master Forthlight the tilter, and brave Master Shooty the great traveller, and wild Half-can that stabbed Pots, and, I think, forty more; all great doers in our trade, and are
• now 'for the Lord's sake.'   21

Enter ABHORSON.

Abhor.   Sirrah, bring Barnardine hither.
Pom.   Master Barnardine! you must rise and be hanged, Master Barnardine!
Abhor.   What, ho, Barnardine!
Bar.   [*Within*] A pox o' your throats! Who makes that noise there? What are you?
Pom.   Your friends, sir; the hangman. You must be so good, sir, to rise and be put to death.
Bar.   [*Within*] Away, you rogue, away! I am sleepy.   31
Abhor.   Tell him he must awake, and that quickly too.
Pom.   Pray, Master Barnardine, awake till you are executed, and sleep afterwards.
Abhor.   Go in to him, and fetch him out.
Pom.   He is coming, sir, he is coming; I hear his straw rustle.
Abhor.   Is the axe upon the block, sirrah?
Pom.   Very ready, sir.   40

Enter BARNARDINE.

Bar.   How now, Abhorson? what's the news with you?
Abhor.   Truly, sir, I would desire you to clap into your prayers; for, look you, the warrant's come.
Bar.   You rogue, I have been drinking all night; I am not fitted for 't.
Pom.   O, the better, sir; for he that drinks all night, and is hanged betimes in the morning, may sleep the sounder all the next day.   50
• *Abhor.*   Look you, sir; here comes your ghostly father: do we jest now, think you?

Enter DUKE disguised as before.

Duke.   Sir, induced by my charity, and hearing how hastily you are to depart, I am come to advise you, comfort you and pray with you.
Bar.   Friar, not I: I have been drinking hard all night, and I will have more time to prepare
• me, or they shall beat out my brains with billets: I will not consent to die this day, that's certain.
Duke.   O, sir, you must: and therefore I
      beseech you   60
Look forward on the journey you shall go.
Bar.   I swear I will not die to-day for any man's persuasion.
Duke.   But hear you.
Bar.   Not a word: if you have any thing to
• say to me, come to my ward; for thence will not I to-day.   [*Exit.*

12 *peaches.* Impeaches.

21 *'for the Lord's sake!'* Prisoners begging alms from passers-by used this appeal.

51 *ghostly.* Spiritual.

58 *billets.* Cudgels.

Barnardine: 'I swear I will not die today . . .' Barnardine (Tony Church), the Duke (Tom Fleming), Stratford-upon-Avon, 1962

66 *ward.* Cell.

72 *transport.* Dispatch.

Barnardine in the cells. Engraving by Kenny Meadows
from Barry Cornwall's *The Works of Shakspere,* 1846

91 *holds.* Cells.

92 *journal.* Daily.

93 *under generation.* The people underneath. i.e. on the
other side of the world.

95 *free dependant.* Freely at your service.

104 *cold gradation.* Deliberate slips.

Duke. Unfit to live or die: O gravel heart!
After him, fellows; bring him to the block.
　　　　　　[Exeunt Abhorson and Pompey.

　　　　　　Enter PROVOST.

Prov. Now, sir, how do you find the pri-
　soner?　　　　　　　　　　　　　　70
Duke. A creature unprepared, unmeet for
　death;
● And to transport him in the mind he is
Were damnable.
　Prov.　　　　Here in the prison, father,
There died this morning of a cruel fever
One Ragozine, a most notorious pirate,
A man of Claudio's years; his beard and head
Just of his colour.　What if we do omit
This reprobate till he were well inclined;
And satisfy the deputy with the visage
Of Ragozine, more like to Claudio?　　80
　Duke. O, 'tis an accident that heaven pro-
　vides!
Dispatch it presently; the hour draws on
Prefix'd by Angelo: see this be done,
And sent according to command; whiles I
Persuade this rude wretch willingly to die.
　Prov. This shall be done, good father, pre-
　sently.
But Barnardine must die this afternoon:
And how shall we continue Claudio,
To save me from the danger that might come
If he were known alive?
　Duke.　　　　　Let this be done.　90
● Put them in secret holds, both Barnardine and
　Claudio:
● Ere twice the sun hath made his journal greeting
● To the under generation, you shall find
Your safety manifested.
●　*Prov.* I am your free dependant.
　Duke. Quick, dispatch, and send the head to
　　Angelo.　　　　　　　*[Exit Provost.*
Now will I write letters to Angelo,—
The provost, he shall bear them,—whose contents
Shall witness to him I am near at home,
And that, by great injunctions, I am bound　100
To enter publicly: him I'll desire
To meet me at the consecrated fount
A league below the city; and from thence,
● By cold gradation and well-balanced form,
We shall proceed with Angelo.

　　　　　　Re-enter PROVOST.

Prov. Here is the head; I'll carry it myself.
Duke. Convenient is it.　Make a swift return;
For I would commune with you of such things
That want no ear but yours.
　Prov.　　　　I'll make all speed.　*[Exit.*
Isab. [*Within*] Peace, ho, be here!　　110
Duke. The tongue of Isabel.　She's come to
　know
If yet her brother's pardon be come hither:
But I will keep her ignorant of her good,
To make her heavenly comforts of despair,
When it is least expected.

　　　　　　Enter ISABELLA.

Isab.　　　　　Ho, by your leave!
Duke. Good morning to you, fair and gracious
　daughter.
Isab. The better, given me by so holy a man.

Hath yet the deputy sent my brother's pardon?
    Duke. He hath released him, Isabel, from
    the world:
His head is off and sent to Angelo.   120
    Isab. Nay, but it is not so.
    Duke. It is no other: show your wisdom,
    daughter,
●In your close patience.
    Isab. O, I will to him and pluck out his eyes!
    Duke. You shall not be admitted to his sight.
    Isab. Unhappy Claudio! wretched Isabel!
Injurious world! most damned Angelo!
    Duke. This nor hurts him nor profits you
    a jot;
Forbear it therefore; give your cause to heaven.
Mark what I say, which you shall find   130
By every syllable a faithful verity:
The duke comes home to-morrow; nay, dry
    your eyes;
●One of our covent, and his confessor,
●Gives me this instance: already he hath carried
Notice to Escalus and Angelo,
Who do prepare to meet him at the gates,
There to give up their power. If you can, pace
    your wisdom
In that good path that I would wish it go,
●And you shall have your bosom on this wretch,
Grace of the duke, revenges to your heart,   140
And general honour.
    Isab.   I am directed by you.
    Duke. This letter, then, to Friar Peter give;
'Tis that he sent me of the duke's return:
Say, by this token, I desire his company
At Mariana's house to-night. Her cause and
    yours
●I'll perfect him withal, and he shall bring you
Before the duke, and to the head of Angelo
Accuse him home and home. For my poor self,
●I am combined by a sacred vow
And shall be absent. Wend you with this letter:
Command these fretting waters from your eyes
With a light heart; trust not my holy order,
If I pervert your course. Who's here?

       Enter LUCIO.

    Lucio. Good even. Friar, where's the pro-
vost?
    Duke. Not within, sir.
    Lucio. O pretty Isabella, I am pale at mine
heart to see thine eyes so red: thou must be
patient. I am fain to dine and sup with water
●and bran; I dare not for my head fill my belly;
one fruitful meal would set me to't. But they
say the duke will be here to-morrow. By my
troth, Isabel, I loved thy brother: if the old
fantastical duke of dark corners had been at
home, he had lived.   [*Exit Isabella.*
    Duke. Sir, the duke is marvellous little be-
holding to your reports; but the best is, he lives
not in them.
    Lucio. Friar, thou knowest not the duke so
●well as I do: he's a better woodman than thou
takest him for.   171
    Duke. Well, you'll answer this one day. Fare
ye well.
    Lucio. Nay, tarry; I'll go along with thee: I
can tell thee pretty tales of the duke.
    Duke. You have told me too many of him

123 *close.* Silent.

133 *covent.* Convent.

The Duke (Alexander Watson) and Isabella (Grizelda Hervey), William Poel's production, Royalty Theatre, London, 1893

134 *instance.* Proof.

139 *bosom.* Desire.

146 *perfect.* Inform in full.

149 *combined.* Round.

160 *for my head.* i.e. lest I lose my head.

170 *woodman.* Hunter (here, of women).

184 *medlar*. A fruit that is only edible as it starts to rot ; a slang word for a whore.

1-2 *disvouched*. Contradicted.

19 *of sort and suit*. Of rank and petitioners.

23 *unpregnant*. Stupid.

28 *tongue*. Denounce. *dares her no*. Forbids it.

29 *credent bulk*. Weight of credit.

32 *dangerous sense*. Dangerous passion.

1 *me*. For me.

---

already, sir, if they be true ; if not true, none were enough.

Lucio. I was once before him for getting a wench with child. 180

Duke. Did you such a thing ?

Lucio. Yes, marry, did I : but I was fain to forswear it ; they would else have married me to the rotten medlar.

Duke. Sir, your company is fairer than honest. Rest you well.

Lucio. By my troth, I'll go with thee to the lane's end : if bawdy talk offend you, we'll have very little of it.   Nay, friar, I am a kind of burr ; I shall stick.   [*Exeunt.* 190

SCENE IV. *A room in* ANGELO'S *house.*

Enter ANGELO *and* ESCALUS.

Escal. Every letter he hath writ hath disvouched other.

Ang. In most uneven and distracted manner. His actions show much like to madness : pray heaven his wisdom be not tainted !   And why meet him at the gates, and redeliver our authorities there ?

Escal. I guess not.

Ang. And why should we proclaim it in an hour before his entering, that if any crave redress of injustice, they should exhibit their petitions in the street ?

Escal. He shows his reason for that : to have a dispatch of complaints, and to deliver us from devices hereafter, which shall then have no power to stand against us.

Ang. Well, I beseech you, let it be proclaimed betimes i' the morn ; I'll call you at your house : give notice to such men of sort and suit as are to meet him. 20

Escal. I shall, sir.   Fare you well.

Ang. Good night.   [*Exit Escalus.*

This deed unshapes me quite, makes me unpregnant
And dull to all proceedings.   A deflower'd maid !
And by an eminent body that enforced
The law against it !   But that her tender shame
Will not proclaim against her maiden loss,
How might she tongue me !   Yet reason dares her no ;
For my authority bears of a credent bulk,
That no particular scandal once can touch 30
But it confounds the breather.   He should have lived,
Save that his riotous youth, with dangerous sense,
Might in the times to come have ta'en revenge,
By so receiving a dishonour'd life
With ransom of such shame.   Would yet he had lived !
Alack, when once our grace we have forgot,
Nothing goes right : we would, and we would not.
[*Exit*

SCENE V. *Fields without the town.*

Enter DUKE *in his own habit, and* FRIAR PETER.

Duke.   These letters at fit time deliver me :
[*Giving letters.*
The provost knows our purpose and our plot.
The matter being afoot, keep your instruction,
And hold you ever to our special drift ;

● Though sometimes you do blench from this to that,
As cause doth minister. Go call at Flavius' house,
And tell him where I stay : give the like notice
To Valentinus, Rowland, and to Crassus,
And bid them bring the trumpets to the gate ;
But send me Flavius first.
 Fri. P.   It shall be speeded well. [*Exit.* 10

   Enter VARRIUS.

Duke. I thank thee, Varrius ; thou hast made
  good haste :
Come, we will walk. There's other of our friends
Will greet us here anon, my gentle Varrius.
        [*Exeunt.*

  SCENE VI. *Street near the city gate.*

  Enter ISABELLA *and* MARIANA.

Isab. To speak so indirectly I am loath :
I would say the truth ; but to accuse him so,
That is your part : yet I am advised to do it ;
He says, to veil full purpose.
 Mari.   Be ruled by him.
 Isab. Besides, he tells me that, if peradventure
He speak against me on the adverse side,
I should not think it strange ; for 'tis a physic
That's bitter to sweet end.
 Mari. I would Friar Peter—
 Isab.   O, peace ! the friar is come.

   Enter FRIAR PETER.

 Fri. P. Come, I have found you out a stand
   most fit,   10
● Where you may have such vantage on the duke,
He shall not pass you. Twice have the trumpets
   sounded ;
● The generous and gravest citizens
● Have hent the gates, and very near upon
The duke is entering : therefore, hence, away !
        [*Exeunt.*

    ACT V.

  SCENE I. *The city gate.*

MARIANA *veiled,* ISABELLA, *and* FRIAR PETER,
 at their stand. Enter DUKE, VARRIUS,
 LORDS, ANGELO, ESCALUS, LUCIO, PROVOST,
 OFFICERS, *and* CITIZENS, *at several doors.*

● *Duke.* My very worthy cousin, fairly met !
Our old and faithful friend, we are glad to see you.
 Ang. }
 Escal. } Happy return be to your royal grace !
 Duke. Many and hearty thankings to you both.
We have made inquiry of you ; and we hear
Such goodness of your justice, that our soul
Cannot but yield you forth to public thanks,
● Forerunning more requital.
 Ang.   You make my bonds still greater.
 Duke. O, your desert speaks loud ; and I should
   wrong it,
● To lock it in the wards of covert bosom,   10
When it deserves, with characters of brass,
A forted residence 'gainst the tooth of time
● And razure of oblivion. Give me your hand,
And let the subject see, to make them know
That outward courtesies would fain proclaim
Favours that keep within. Come, Escalus,

Costume design for Mariana by Alix Stone, Stratford-upon-Avon, 1962

---

5 *blench.* Swerve.

11 *vantage on.* A good opportunity to intercept.

13 *generous.* Of good birth.

14 *hent.* Occupied.

1 *cousin.* A term used by a sovereign to noblemen, but not implying kinship.

8 *more requital.* Further rewards. *bonds.* Obligations.

10 *To lock it in the wards of covert bosom.* To keep it locked up in my inmost heart.

13 *razure.* Erasure.

20 *Vail.* Lower.

49 *comfort.* i.e. a future life.

54 *absolute.* Perfect.

56 *dressings.* Robes of office. *characts.* Badges, and insignia.

Costume design for Angelo by J. Gower Parks, Stratford-upon-Avon, 1940

You must walk by us on our other hand;
And good supporters are you.

FRIAR PETER *and* ISABELLA *come forward.*

Fri. P. Now is your time: speak loud and
    kneel before him.

● *Isab.* Justice, O royal duke! Vail your re-
    gard   20
Upon a wrong'd, I would fain have said, a maid!
O worthy prince, dishonour not your eye
By throwing it on any other object
Till you have heard me in my true complaint
And given me justice, justice, justice, justice!

Duke. Relate your wrongs; in what? by
    whom? be brief.
Here is Lord Angelo shall give you justice:
Reveal yourself to him.

Isab.   O worthy duke,
You bid me seek redemption of the devil:
Hear me yourself; for that which I must speak
Must either punish me, not being believed, 31
Or wring redress from you. Hear me, O hear
    me, here!

Ang. My lord, her wits, I fear me, are not
    firm:
She hath been a suitor to me for her brother
Cut off by course of justice,—

Isab.   By course of justice!

Ang. And she will speak most bitterly and
    strange.

Isab. Most strange, but yet most truly, will I
    speak:
That Angelo's forsworn; is it not strange?
That Angelo's a murderer; is't not strange?
That Angelo is an adulterous thief,   40
An hypocrite, a virgin-violator;
Is it not strange and strange?

Duke.   Nay, it is ten times strange.

Isab. It is not truer he is Angelo
Than this is all as true as it is strange:
Nay, it is ten times true; for truth is truth
To the end of reckoning.

Duke.   Away with her! Poor soul,
She speaks this in the infirmity of sense.

Isab. O prince, I conjure thee, as thou be-
    lievest
● There is another comfort than this world,
That thou neglect me not, with that opinion 50
That I am touch'd with madness! Make not im-
    possible
That which but seems unlike: 'tis not impossible
But one, the wicked'st caitiff on the ground,
● May seem as shy, as grave, as just, as absolute
As Angelo; even so may Angelo,
● In all his dressings, characts, titles, forms,
Be an arch-villain; believe it, royal prince:
If he be less, he's nothing; but he's more,
Had I more name for badness.

Duke.   By mine honesty,
If she be mad,—as I believe no other,— 60
Her madness hath the oddest frame of sense,
Such a dependency of thing on thing,
As e'er I heard in madness.

Isab.   O gracious duke,
Harp not on that, nor do not banish reason
For inequality; but let your reason serve
To make the truth appear where it seems hid,
And hide the false seems true.

Duke.   Many that are not mad

Have, sure, more lack of reason. What would
  you say?
   Isab. I am the sister of one Claudio,
Condemn'd upon the act of fornication   70
To lose his head; condemn'd by Angelo:
I, in probation of a sisterhood,
Was sent to by my brother; one Lucio
As then the messenger,—
   Lucio.   That's I, an't like your grace:
I came to her from Claudio, and desired her
To try her gracious fortune with Lord Angelo
For her poor brother's pardon.
   Isab.   That's he indeed.
   Duke. You were not bid to speak.
   Lucio.   No, my good lord;
Nor wish'd to hold my peace.
   Duke.   I wish you now, then;
Pray you, take note of it: and when you have 80
A business for yourself, pray heaven you then
• Be perfect.
•   *Lucio.* I warrant your honour.
•   *Duke.* The warrant's for yourself; take heed
  to't.
   Isab. This gentleman told somewhat of my
  tale,—
   Lucio. Right.
   Duke. It may be right; but you are i' the wrong
To speak before your time. Proceed.
   Isab.   I went
To this pernicious caitiff deputy,—
   Duke. That's somewhat madly spoken.
   Isab.   Pardon it;
The phrase is to the matter.   90
   Duke. Mended again. The matter; proceed.
   Isab. In brief, to set the needless process by,
How I persuaded, how I pray'd, and kneel'd,
• How he refell'd me, and how I replied,—
For this was of much length,—the vile conclusion
I now begin with grief and shame to utter:
He would not, but by gift of my chaste body
To his concupiscible intemperate lust,
Release my brother; and, after much debate-
  ment,
• My sisterly remorse confutes mine honour, 100
And I did yield to him: but the next morn be-
  times,
His purpose surfeiting, he sends a warrant
For my poor brother's head.
   Duke.   This is most likely!
   Isab. O, that it were as like as it is true!
   Duke. By heaven, fond wretch, thou know'st
  not what thou speak'st,
• Or else thou art suborn'd against his honour
• In hateful practice. First, his integrity
• Stands without blemish. Next, it imports no
  reason
That with such vehemency he should pursue
Faults proper to himself: if he had so offended,
He would have weigh'd thy brother by himself
And not have cut him off. Some one hath set
  you on:
Confess the truth, and say by whose advice
Thou camest here to complain.
   Isab.   And is this all?
Then, O you blessed ministers above,
Keep me in patience, and with ripen'd time
Unfold the evil which is here wrapt up
• In countenance! Heaven shield your grace
  from woe,

82 *perfect.* Prepared.

83 *warrant.* Promise.

84 *warrant.* A quibble on an order for arrest.

94 *refell'd.* Refuted.

100 *remorse confutes.* Pity refutes.

106 *suborn'd.* Bribed.

107 *practice.* Plotting.

108 *it imports no reason.* It is senseless.

118 *countenance.* Authority.

128 *lay.* Layman.

130 *swinged.* Thrashed.

Different types of scourges used for public punishment.
From a 16th century woodcut

142 *ungot.* Unbegotten.

145 *temporary.* In temporal matters.

157 *probation.* Proof.

158 *convented.* Summoned.

160 *vulgarly.* Publicly.

As I, thus wrong'd, hence unbelieved go!
 Duke. I know you'ld fain be gone. An
officer!   120
To prison with her! Shall we thus permit
A blasting and a scandalous breath to fall
On him so near us? This needs must be a practice.
Who knew of your intent and coming hither?
 Isab. One that I would were here, Friar
Lodowick.
 Duke. A ghostly father, belike. Who knows
that Lodowick?
 Lucio. My lord, I know him; 'tis a meddling
friar;
●I do not like the man: had he been lay, my lord,
For certain words he spake against your grace
●In your retirement, I had swinged him soundly.
 Duke. Words against me! this is a good friar,
belike!   131
And to set on this wretched woman here
Against our substitute! Let this friar be found.
 Lucio. But yesternight, my lord, she and
that friar,
I saw them at the prison: a saucy friar,
A very scurvy fellow.
 Fri. P. Blessed be your royal grace!
I have stood by, my lord, and I have heard
Your royal ear abused. First, hath this woman
Most wrongfully accused your substitute, 140
Who is as free from touch or soil with her
●As she from one ungot.
 Duke.   We did believe no less.
Know you that Friar Lodowick that she speaks of?
 Fri. P. I know him for a man divine and holy;
●Not scurvy, nor a temporary meddler,
As he's reported by this gentleman;
And, on my trust, a man that never yet
Did, as he vouches, misreport your grace.
 Lucio. My lord, most villanously; believe it.
 Fri. P. Well, he in time may come to clear
himself;   150
But at this instant he is sick, my lord,
Of a strange fever. Upon his mere request,
Being come to knowledge that there was complaint
Intended 'gainst Lord Angelo, came I hither,
To speak, as from his mouth, what he doth know
Is true and false; and what he with his oath
●And all probation will make up full clear,
●Whensoever he's convented. First, for this wo-
man,
To justify this worthy nobleman,
●So vulgarly and personally accused, 160
Her shall you hear disproved to her eyes,
Till she herself confess it.
 Duke.   Good friar, let's hear it.
  [*Isabella is carried off guarded; and
    Mariana comes forward.*
Do you not smile at this, Lord Angelo?
O heaven, the vanity of wretched fools!
Give us some seats. Come, cousin Angelo;
In this I'll be impartial; be you judge
Of your own cause. Is this the witness, friar?
First, let her show her face, and after speak.
 Mari. Pardon, my lord; I will not show my
face
Until my husband bid me.   170
 Duke. What, are you married?
 Mari. No, my lord.
 Duke. Are you a maid?
 Mari. No, my lord.

Duke. A widow, then?
Mari. Neither, my lord.
Duke. Why, you are nothing then: neither maid, widow, nor wife?
● *Lucio.* My lord, she may be a punk; for many of them are neither maid, widow, nor wife.
Duke. Silence that fellow: I would he had
  some cause   181
To prattle for himself.
Lucio. Well, my lord.
Mari. My lord, I do confess I ne'er was married;
And I confess besides I am no maid:
● I have known my husband; yet my husband
Knows not that ever he knew me.
Lucio. He was drunk then my lord: it can be no better.
Duke. For the benefit of silence, would thou wert so too!   191
Lucio. Well, my lord.
Duke. This is no witness for Lord Angelo.
Mari. Now I come to't, my lord:
She that accuses him of fornication,
In self-same manner doth accuse my husband,
And charges him, my lord, with such a time
● When I'll depose I had him in mine arms
With all the effect of love.
Ang. Charges she more than me?
Mari.   Not that I know. 200
Duke. No? you say your husband.
Mari. Why, just, my lord, and that is Angelo,
Who thinks he knows that he ne'er knew my body,
But knows he thinks that he knows Isabel's.
● *Ang.* This is a strange abuse. Let's see thy face.

Mari. My husband bids me; now I will
  unmask.   [*Unveiling.*
This is that face, thou cruel Angelo,
Which once thou sworest was worth the looking on;
This is the hand which, with a vow'd contract,
Was fast belock'd in thine; this is the body 210
That took away the match from Isabel,
And did supply thee at thy garden-house
In her imagined person.
Duke.   Know you this woman?
Lucio. Carnally, she says.
Duke.   Sirrah, no more!
Lucio. Enough, my lord.
Ang. My lord, I must confess I know this
  woman:
And five years since there was some speech of
  marriage
Betwixt myself and her; which was broke off,
● Partly for that her promised proportions
● Came short of composition, but in chief 220
● For that her reputation was disvalued
In levity: since which time of five years
I never spake with her, saw her, nor heard from her,
Upon my faith and honour.
Mari.   Noble prince,
As there comes light from heaven and words from
  breath,
As there is sense in truth and truth in virtue,
I am affianced this man's wife as strongly
As words could make up vows: and, my good lord,
But Tuesday night last gone in's garden-house
He knew me as a wife. As this is true, 230
Let me in safety raise me from my knees;

179 *punk.* Prostitute.

186 *known.* In the biblical sense of 'sexual knowledge'.

198 *depose.* Swear as evidence.

205 *abuse.* Deception.

219 *proportions.* Marriage dowry.

220 *short of composition.* Less than the agreed sum.

221-222 *disvalued in levity.* Cheapened by loose conduct.

Costume design for the Duke by J. Gower Parks, Stratford-upon-Avon, 1940

232 *confixed*. Fixed firmly.

235 *touch'd*. Wounded. i.e. at an end.

236 *informal*. Wild.

242 *Compact*. Confederate.

245 *seal'd in approbation*. Tested and proved.

254 *well-warranted*. Well proved.

263 *'Cucullus . . . monachum'*. The hood does not make the monk.

●Or else for ever be confixed here,
A marble monument!
    Ang.   I did but smile till now:
Now, good my lord, give me the scope of justice;
●My patience here is touch'd. I do perceive
●These poor informal women are no more
  But instruments of some more mightier member
That sets them on: let me have way, my lord,
To find this practice out.
    Duke.   Ay, with my heart;
And punish them to your height of pleasure. 240
Thou foolish friar, and thou pernicious woman,
●Compact with her that's gone, think'st thou thy oaths,
Though they would swear down each particular saint,
Were testimonies against his worth and credit
●That's seal'd in approbation? You, Lord Escalus,
Sit with my cousin; lend him your kind pains
To find out this abuse, whence 'tis derived.
There is another friar that set them on;
Let him be sent for.
    Fri. P. Would he were here, my lord! for he indeed 250
Hath set the women on to this complaint:
Your provost knows the place where he abides
And he may fetch him.
    Duke.   Go do it instantly. [*Exit Provost.*
●And you, my noble and well-warranted cousin,
Whom it concerns to hear this matter forth,
Do with your injuries as seems you best,
In any chastisement: I for a while will leave you;
But stir not you till you have well determined
Upon these slanderers.
    Escal. My lord, we'll do it throughly. 260
                    [*Exit Duke.*
Signior Lucio, did not you say you knew that
Friar Lodowick to be a dishonest person?
● *Lucio.* 'Cucullus non facit monachum:' honest
in nothing but in his clothes; and one that hath
spoke most villanous speeches of the duke.
    Escal. We shall entreat you to abide here till
he come and enforce them against him: we shall
find this friar a notable fellow.
    Lucio. As any in Vienna, on my word.
    Escal. Call that same Isabel here once again:
I would speak with her. [*Exit an Attendant.*]
Pray you, my lord, give me leave to question;
you shall see how I'll handle her.
    Lucio. Not better than he, by her own report.
    Escal. Say you?
    Lucio. Marry, sir, I think, if you handled her
privately, she would sooner confess: perchance,
publicly, she'll be ashamed.
    Escal. I will go darkly to work with her.
    Lucio. That's the way; for women are light
at midnight. 281

Re-enter OFFICERS *with* ISABELLA; *and* PRO-
VOST *with the* DUKE *in his friar's habit.*

    Escal. Come on, mistress: here's a gentle-
woman denies all that you have said.
    Lucio. My lord, here comes the rascal I spoke
of; here with the provost.
    Escal. In very good time: speak not you to
him till we call upon you.
    Lucio. Mum.
    Escal. Come, sir: did you set these women

on to slander Lord Angelo? they have confessed
you did.   291
   Duke. 'Tis false.
   Escal. How! know you where you are?
   Duke. Respect to your great place! and let
     the devil
Be sometime honour'd for his burning throne!
Where is the duke? 'tis he should hear me
     speak.
   Escal. The duke's in us; and we will hear
     you speak:
Look you speak justly.
   Duke. Boldly, at least. But, O, poor souls,
Come you to seek the lamb here of the fox? 300
Good night to your redress! Is the duke gone?
Then is your cause gone too. The duke's unjust
Thus to retort your manifest appeal,
And put your trial in the villain's mouth
Which here you come to accuse.
   Lucio. This is the rascal; this is he I spoke of.
   Escal. Why, thou unreverend and unhallow'd
     friar,
Is't not enough thou hast suborn'd these women
To accuse this worthy man, but, in foul mouth
And in the witness of his proper ear,   310
To call him villain? and then to glance from him
To the duke himself, to tax him with injustice?
Take him hence; to the rack with him! We'll
     touse you
Joint by joint, but we will know his purpose.
What, 'unjust'!
   Duke.   Be not so hot; the duke
Dare no more stretch this finger of mine than he
Dare rack his own: his subject am I not,
Nor here provincial. My business in this state
Made me a looker on here in Vienna,
Where I have seen corruption boil and bubble
Till it o'er-run the stew; laws for all faults, 321
But faults so countenanced, that the strong sta-
     tutes
Stand like the forfeits in a barber's shop,
As much in mock as mark.
   Escal. Slander to the state! Away with him
     to prison!
   Ang. What can you vouch against him, Sig-
     nior Lucio?
Is this the man that you did tell us of?
   Lucio. 'Tis he, my lord. Come hither, good-
man baldpate: do you know me?
   Duke. I remember you, sir, by the sound of
your voice: I met you at the prison, in the absence
of the duke.
   Lucio. O, did you so? And do you remember
what you said of the duke?
   Duke. Most notedly, sir.
   Lucio. Do you so, sir? And was the duke a
fleshmonger, a fool, and a coward, as you then
reported him to be?
   Duke. You must, sir, change persons with me,
ere you make that my report: you, indeed, spoke
so of him; and much more, much worse. 341
   Lucio. O thou damnable fellow! Did not I
pluck thee by the nose for thy speeches?
   Duke. I protest I love the duke as I love
myself.
   Ang. Hark, how the villain would close now,
after his treasonable abuses!
   Escal. Such a fellow is not to be talked withal.
Away with him to prison! Where is the provost?

---

297 *The duke's in us.* The duke's authority is vested in
us.

303 *retort.* Return.

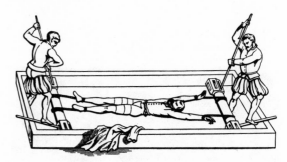

The rack. Woodcut from Foxe's *Ecclesiastical History,*
1576

---

313 *touse.* Tear.

318 *here provincial.* Subject to the laws of that province.

321 *stew.* A cauldron, but also a brothel.

323 *forfeits.* Barber shops hung a comic list of penalties
for bad language, blood-letting, etc.

324 *As much . . . mark.* As much mocked at as heeded.

329 *baldpate.* Referring to the Duke's tonsure.

335 *notedly.* Precisely.

346 *close.* Make terms.

350 *bolts.* Chains.

352 *giglots.* Harlots.

359 *sheep-biting.* Like a cur.

360 *be hanged an hour.* Men were left for an hour after hanging to be sure they were dead.

Duke: 'Lay hold on him.' Painting by Thomas Kirk (1765–1797)

375 *passes.* Actions.

388 *Advertising.* Heedful. *holy.* Wholly, or devoted.

390 *Attorney'd.* Acting in the capacity of a lawyer.

● Away with him to prison! lay bolts enough upon
  him: let him speak no more.   Away with those
● giglots too, and with the other confederate companion!
   Duke.   [*To Provost*] Stay, sir; stay awhile.
   Ang.   What, resists he? Help him, Lucio.
   Lucio.   Come, sir; come, sir; come, sir; foh,
  sir! Why, you bald-pated, lying rascal, you must
  be hooded, must you? Show your knave's visage,
● with a pox to you! show your sheep-biting face,
● and be hanged an hour!   Will't not off?   360
      [*Pulls off the friar's hood, and discovers
                                    the Duke.*

   Duke.   Thou art the first knave that e'er
      madest a duke.
  First, provost, let me bail these gentle three.
  [*To Lucio*] Sneak not away, sir; for the friar and
      you
  Must have a word anon.   Lay hold on him.
   Lucio.   This may prove worse than hanging.
   Duke.   [*To Escalus*] What you have spoke I
      pardon: sit you down:
  We'll borrow place of him.   [*To Angelo*] Sir, by
      your leave.
  Hast thou or word, or wit, or impudence,
  That yet can do thee office? If thou hast,
  Rely upon it till my tale be heard,   370
  And hold no longer out.
   Ang.   O my dread lord,
  I should be guiltier than my guiltiness,
  To think I can be undiscernible,
  When I perceive your grace, like power divine,
● Hath look'd upon my passes. Then, good prince,
  No longer session hold upon my shame,
  But let my trial be mine own confession:
  Immediate sentence then and sequent death
  Is all the grace I beg.
   Duke.   Come hither, Mariana.
  Say, wast thou e'er contracted to this woman? 380
   Ang.   I was, my lord.
   Duke.   Go take her hence, and marry her
      instantly.
  Do you the office, friar; which consummate,
  Return him here again.   Go with him, provost.
      [*Exeunt Angelo, Mariana, Friar Peter
                              and Provost.*
   Escal.   My lord, I am more amazed at his
      dishonour
  Than at the strangeness of it.
   Duke.   Come hither, Isabel.
  Your friar is now your prince: as I was then
● Advertising and holy to your business,
  Not changing heart with habit, I am still
● Attorney'd at your service.
   Isab.   O, give me pardon, 390
  That I, your vassal, have employ'd and pain'd
  Your unknown sovereignty!
   Duke.   You are pardon'd, Isabel:
  And now, dear maid, be you as free to us.
  Your brother's death, I know, sits at your heart;
  And you may marvel why I obscured myself,
  Labouring to save his life, and would not rather
  Make rash remonstrance of my hidden power
  Than let him so be lost.   O most kind maid,
  It was the swift celerity of his death,
  Which I did think with slower foot came on, 400
  That brain'd my purpose.   But, peace be with
      him!
  That life is better life, past fearing death,

Than that which lives to fear: make it your
  comfort,
So happy is your brother.
    Isab.   I do, my lord.

   Re-enter ANGELO, MARIANA, FRIAR PETER,
          and PROVOST.

   Duke. For this new-married man approach-
    ing here,
• Whose salt imagination yet hath wrong'd
Your well defended honour, you must pardon
For Mariana's sake: but as he adjudged your
  brother,—
Being criminal, in double violation
• Of sacred chastity and of promise-breach   410
Thereon dependent, for your brother's life,—
The very mercy of the law cries out
Most audible, even from his proper tongue,
'An Angelo for Claudio, death for death!'
Haste still pays haste, and leisure answers
  leisure;
Like doth quit like, and MEASURE still FOR
  MEASURE.
Then, Angelo, thy fault's thus manifested;
• Which, though thou wouldst deny, denies thee
  vantage.
We do condemn thee to the very block
Where Claudio stoop'd to death, and with like
  haste.   420
Away with him!
   Mari.   O my most gracious lord,
I hope you will not mock me with a husband.
   Duke. It is your husband mock'd you with a
  husband.
Consenting to the safeguard of your honour,
I thought your marriage fit; else imputation,
For that he knew you, might reproach your life
And choke your good to come: for his pos-
  sessions,
Although by confiscation they are ours,
We do instate and widow you withal,
To buy you a better husband.
   Mari.   O my dear lord, 430
I crave no other, nor no better man.
   Duke. Never crave him; we are definitive.
   Mari. Gentle my liege,—   [*Kneeling.*
   Duke.   You do but lose your labour.
Away with him to death! [*To Lucio*] Now, sir,
  to you.
   Mari. O my good lord! Sweet Isabel, take
  my part;
• Lend me your knees, and all my life to come
I'll lend you all my life to do you service.
   Duke. Against all sense you do importune
  her:
Should she kneel down in mercy of this fact,
• Her brother's ghost his paved bed would break,
And take her hence in horror.
   Mari.   Isabel,   441
Sweet Isabel, do yet but kneel by me;
Hold up your hands, say nothing; I'll speak all.
They say, best men are moulded out of faults;
And, for the most, become much more the better
For being a little bad: so may my husband.
O Isabel, will you not lend a knee?
   Duke. He dies for Claudio's death.
   Isab.   Most bounteous sir, [*Kneeling.*
Look, if it please you, on this man condemn'd,
As if my brother lived: I partly think   450

406 *salt.* Lustful.

410 *promise-breach.* i.e. his failure to keep his promise
to pardon Claudio.

Duke: 'and MEASURE still FOR MEASURE . . .' Engraving
by H. Gravelot from Theobald's edition of Shakespeare's
works, 1740

418 *vantage.* Escape.

436 *Lend me your knees.* Plead on your knees for me.

440 *paved bed.* Gravestone.

458 *subjects*. Acts.

469 *advice*. Consideration.

Angelo: '. . . I crave death more willingly than mercy;'
Angelo (Marius Goring), the Duke (Tom Fleming),
Mariana (Yvonne Bonnamy) and Isabella (Judi Dench),
Stratford-upon-Avon, 1962

487 *squarest*. Pattern.

488 *quit*. Acquit.

A due sincerity govern'd his deeds,
Till he did look on me : since it is so,
Let him not die.   My brother had but justice,
In that he did the thing for which he died :
For Angelo,
His act did not o'ertake his bad intent,
And must be buried but as an intent
● That perish'd by the way : thoughts are no
    subjects ;
Intents but merely thoughts.
   Mari.   Merely, my lord.
   Duke. Your suit's unprofitable ; stand up,
    I say.   460
I have bethought me of another fault.
Provost, how came it Claudio was beheaded
At an unusual hour ?
   Prov.   It was commanded so.
   Duke. Had you a special warrant for the
    deed ?
   Prov. No, my good lord ; it was by private
    message.
   Duke. For which I do discharge you of your
    office :
Give up your keys.
   Prov.   Pardon me, noble lord :
I thought it was a fault, but knew it not ;
● Yet did repent me, after more advice :
For testimony whereof, one in the prison, 470
That should by private order else have died,
I have reserved alive.
   Duke.   What's he ?
   Prov.   His name is Barnardine.
   Duke. I would thou hadst done so by Claudio.
Go fetch him hither ; let me look upon him.
                       [*Exit Provost.*
   Escal. I am sorry, one so learned and so
    wise
As you, Lord Angelo, have still appear'd,
Should slip so grossly, both in the heat of blood,
And lack of temper'd judgement afterward.
   Ang. I am sorry that such sorrow I pro-
    cure :
And so deep sticks it in my penitent heart 480
That I crave death more willingly than mercy ;
'Tis my deserving, and I do entreat it.

Re-enter PROVOST, *with* BARNARDINE, CLAUDIO
muffled, and JULIET.

   Duke. Which is that Barnardine ?
   Prov.   This, my lord.
   Duke. There was a friar told me of this man.
Sirrah, thou art said to have a stubborn soul,
That apprehends no further than this world,
● And squarest thy life according.   Thou'rt con-
    demn'd :
● But, for those earthly faults, I quit them all ;
And pray thee take this mercy to provide
For better times to come.   Friar, advise him ; 490
I leave him to your hand.   What muffled fellow's
    that ?
   Prov. This is another prisoner that I saved,
Who should have died when Claudio lost his head ;
As like almost to Claudio as himself.
                    [*Unmuffles Claudio.*
   Duke. [*To Isabella*]   If he be like your
    brother, for his sake
Is he pardon'd ; and, for your lovely sake,
Give me your hand and say you will be mine,

He is my brother too : but fitter time for that.
By this Lord Angelo perceives he's safe ;
Methinks I see a quickening in his eye.   500
● Well, Angelo, your evil quits you well :
Look that you love your wife ; her worth worth
            yours.
● I find an apt remission in myself ;
And yet here's one in place I cannot pardon.
[To Lucio] You, sirrah, that knew me for a fool,
            a coward,
● One all of luxury, an ass, a madman ;
Wherein have I so deserved of you,
That you extol me thus ?
    Lucio. 'Faith, my lord I spoke it but ac-
● cording to the trick. If you will hang me for it,
you may ; but I had rather it would please you I
might be whipt.
    Duke. Whipt first, sir, and hanged after.
Proclaim it, provost, round about the city,
Is any woman wrong'd by this lewd fellow,
As I have heard him swear himself there's
            one
Whom he begot with child, let her appear,
And he shall marry her : the nuptial finish'd,
Let him be whipt and hang'd.
    Lucio. I beseech your highness, do not marry
me to a whore. Your highness said even now, I
made you a duke : good my lord, do not recom-
pense me in making me a cuckold.
    Duke. Upon mine honour, thou shalt marry her.
Thy slanders I forgive ; and therewithal
● Remit thy other forfeits. Take him to prison ;
And see our pleasure herein executed.
    Lucio. Marrying a punk, my lord, is pressing
to death, whipping, and hanging.
    Duke. Slandering a prince deserves it.   530
            [Exeunt Officers with Lucio.
She, Claudio, that you wrong'd, look you restore.
Joy to you, Mariana ! Love her, Angelo :
I have confess'd her and I know her virtue.
Thanks, good friend Escalus, for thy much good
            ness :
● There's more behind that is more gratulate.
Thanks, provost, for thy care and secrecy :
We shall employ thee in a worthier place.
Forgive him, Angelo, that brought you home
The head of Ragozine for Claudio's :
The offence pardons itself. Dear Isabel,   540
● I have a motion much imports your good ;
Whereto if you'll a willing ear incline,
What's mine is yours and what is yours is mine.
So, bring us to our palace ; where we'll show
What's yet behind, that's meet you all should
            know.   [Exeunt.

501 *quits.* Requites.

503 *apt remission.* Readiness to forgive.

506 *luxury.* Lust.

510 *trick.* Custom.

Costume design for the Duke by Alix Stone, Stratford-upon-Avon, 1962

526 *forfeits.* Penalties.

535 *gratulate.* Gratifying.

541 *motion.* Proposition.

Further Reading

The following bibliography has been selected from an enormous literature on the subject, and is intended as a guide for the general reader.

EDITIONS

Recommended editions of Shakespeare in one volume are: The Complete Works edited by Peter Alexander, 1951; the Riverside Shakespeare edited by G. Blakemore Evans; and the Complete Works edited by Charles J. Sisson, 1954. The most useful editions of the plays in separate volumes are the New Arden Shakespeare (general editors, Harold F. Brooks and Harold Jenkins), which cover textual problems and include commentary on the text; the New Penguin Shakespeare (general editor T. J. B. Spencer); and the Pelican Shakespeare (general editor Alfred Harbage). The New Cambridge Shakespeare edited by Arthur Quiller-Couch and John Dover Wilson is stimulating for its introductions and (not always reliable) suggestions. The most detailed textual commentary including stage history up to its date of publication (1888) is in the New Variorum Shakespeare edited by Horace H. Furness. (Paperback edition by Dover Publications, New York.)

GENERAL REFERENCE

Abbott, E. A. *A Shakespeare Grammar*, 1870
Bartlett, John *A New and Complete Concordance . . . to . . . Shakespeare*, 1962
Bullough, Geoffrey *Narrative and Dramatic Sources of Shakespeare*, 1957–73
Greg, W. W. *The Editorial Problem in Shakespeare*, 1942
Greg, W. W. *The Shakespeare First Folio*, 1955
Hinman, Charlton *The Printing and Proof-Reading of the First Folio of Shakespeare*, 1963
Kökeritz, Helge *Shakespeare's Pronunciation*, 1953
Muir, Kenneth *Shakespeare's Sources*, 1961
Munro, J. (ed.) *The Shakespeare Allusion-Book*, 1932
Onions, Charles T. *A Shakespeare Glossary* (revised ed.), 1953
Partridge, Eric *Shakespeare's Bawdy*, 1948
Sisson, C. J. *New Readings in Shakespeare*, 1956
Thomson, J. A. K. *Shakespeare and the Classics*, 1952
Whitaker, V. K. *Shakespeare's Use of Learning*, 1953

SHAKESPEARE'S LIFE

Alexander, Peter *Shakespeare's Life and Art*, 1964
Bentley, G. E. *Shakespeare. A Biographical Handbook*, 1961
Brinkworth, E. R. C. *Shakespeare and the Bawdy Court of Stratford*, 1972
Chambers, E. K. *Shakespeare: A Survey*, 1925
Chambers, E. K. *Sources for a Biography of Shakespeare*, 1946
Chambers, E. K. *William Shakespeare. A Study of Facts and Problems*, 2 vols. 1930
Eccles, Mark *Shakespeare in Warwickshire*, 1961
Fripp, E. I. *Shakespeare, Man and Artist*, 2 vols. 1938
Fripp, E. I. *Shakespeare Studies, Biographical and Literary*, 1930

Fripp, E. I. *Shakespeare's Haunts near Stratford*, 1929
Joseph, Harriet *John Hall, Man and Physician*, 1964
Rowse, A. L. *Shakespeare the Man*, 1973
Rowse, A. L. *Shakespeare's Southampton, Patron of Virginia*, 1965
Rowse, A. L. *Simon Forman. Sex and Society in Shakespeare's Age*, 1974
Rowse, A. L. *William Shakespeare: A Biography*, 1963
Speaight, Robert *Shakespeare. The Man and his Achievement*, 1977

SHAKESPEARE'S CONTEMPORARIES

Aubrey, John *Brief Lives* edited by Andrew Clark, 2 vols. 1898
Bald, R. C. *John Donne: A Life*, 1970
Barker, Richard H. *Thomas Middleton*, 1958
Beaumont, F. and Fletcher, J. *Dramatic Works* edited by Fredson Bowers, 1966–76
Boas, F. S. *Christopher Marlowe: A Biographical and Critical Study*, 1940
Chambers, E. K. *Sir Henry Lee*, 1936
Chapman, George *Plays and Poems* edited by T. Parrott, 1910–1914
Dekker, Thomas *The Dramatic Works* edited by Fredson Bowers, 1953–61
Gerrard, Earnest A. *Elizabethan Drama and Dramatists, 1583–1603*, 1928
Greene, Robert *Life and Complete Works* edited by A. B. Grosart, 1881–86
Harrison, G. B. *The Life and Death of Robert Devereux, Earl of Essex*, 1937
Harvey, Gabriel *Complete Works* edited by A. B. Grosart, 1884
Gabriel Harvey's Marginalia edited by G. C. Moore Smith, 1913
Heywood, John *Works* edited by B. A. Milligan, 1956
Heywood, Thomas *Dramatic Works* edited by R. H.
Horne, David H. *The Life and Minor Works of George Peele*, 1952
Hosking, G. L. *The Life and Times of Edward Alleyn*, 1952
Hunter, G. K. *John Lyly. The Humanist as Courtier*, 1962
Shepherd, 1874
Jenkins, Elizabeth *Elizabeth and Leicester*, 1961
Jones, H. S. V. *A Spenser Handbook*, 1930
Jonson, Ben *Works* edited by C. H. Herford, Percy and Evelyn Simpson, 1925–50
Judson, A. C. *The Life of Edmund Spenser*, 1945
Kyd, Thomas *Works* edited by F. S. Boas, 1901
Leishman, J. B. (ed.) *The Three Parnassus Plays, 1598–1601*, 1949
Lyly, John *Complete Works* edited by R. W. Bond, 1902
Marlowe, Christopher *Complete Works* edited by Fredson Bowers, 2 vols. 1973
Marston, John *Works* edited by H. Harvey Wood, 3 vols. 1934
Maurier, Daphne du *Golden Lads. A Study of Anthony Bacon, Francis and their Friends*, 1975
Middleton, Thomas *Works* edited by A. H. Bullen, 1885–86
Mirror for Magistrates edited by Lily B. Campbell, 1938
Nashe, Thomas *Works* edited by R. B. McKerrow and F. P. Wilson, 1958

Prouty, C. T. *George Gascoigne*, 1942
Rees, Joan *Samuel Daniel : A Critical and Biographical Study*, 1964
Rees, Joan *Fulke Greville, Lord Brooke, 1554–1628*, 1971
Rowse, A. L. *Christopher Marlowe : A Biography*, 1964
Sidney, Sir Philip *Arcadia* edited by Maurice Evans, 1977
Sidney, Sir Philip *The Poems* edited by William A. Ringler, 1962
Sisson, C. J. (ed.) *Thomas Lodge and other Elizabethans*, 1933
Stopes, Charlotte C. *The Life of Henry, Third Earl of Southampton, Shakespeare's Patron*, 1922
Stopes, Charlotte C. *Shakespeare's Warwickshire Contemporaries*, 1907
Strachey, Lytton *Elizabeth and Essex*, 1928
Ward, B. M. *The Seventeenth Earl of Oxford, 1550–1604*, 1928
Webster, John *Complete Works* edited by F. L. Lucas, 1927
Yates, Francis A. *John Florio*, 1934

SHAKESPEARE'S ENGLAND

Black, J. B. *The Reign of Elizabeth, 1558–1603*, 1936
Byrne, M. St Clare *Elizabethan Life in Town and Country* (revised ed.), 1961
Byrne, M. St Clare *The Elizabethan Home*, 1930
Davies, Godfrey *The Early Stuarts, 1603–1660*, 1938
Elton, G. R. *England under the Tudors*, 1956
Harrison, G. B. *England in Shakespeare's Day*, 1928
Harrison, G. B. *The Elizabethan Journals, 1591–1603*, 1938
Harrison, G. B. *A Jacobean Journal, 1603–1606*, 1941
Harrison, G. B. *A Second Jacobean Journal, 1607–1610*, 1958
Jones, Richard F. *Ancients and Moderns*, 1965
Judges, A. V. (ed.) *The Elizabethan Underworld*, 1930
Neale, J. E. *Queen Elizabeth*, 1934
Nicoll, Allardyce *The Elizabethans*, 1957
Rowse, A. L. *The Elizabethans and America*, 1959
Rowse, A. L. *The Elizabethan Renaissance* : vol 1, The Life of the Society, 1971 ; vol 2, The Cultural Achievement, 1972
Rowse, A. L. *The England of Elizabeth*, 1950
Rowse, A. L. *The Expansion of Elizabethan England*, 1955
Shakespeare's England : An Account of the Life and Manners of his Age, 2 vols. 1916–17
Stow's Survey of London edited by C. L. Kingsford, 2 vols. 1908
Strong, Roy *The English Icon : Elizabethan and Jacobean Portraiture*, 1969
Strong, Roy *The Portraits of Queen Elizabeth I*, 1963
Tillyard, E. M. W. *The Elizabethan World Picture*, 1943
Wilson, F. P. *The Plague in Shakespeare's London*, 1927
Wilson, John Dover *Life in Shakespeare's England*, 1911

SHAKESPEARE CRITICISM

Bamborough, J. B. *The Little World of Man*, 1952
Bradby, Anne (ed.) *Shakespearean Criticism, 1919–1935*, 1936
Bush, Douglas *English Literature in the Earlier Seventeenth Century*, 1945
Buxton, John *Elizabethan Taste*, 1965
Clemens, W. H. *The Development of Shakespeare's Imagery*, 1951
Coleridge, S. T. *Notes and Lectures upon Shakespeare*, 1849
Coleridge, S. T. *Shakespearean Criticism* edited by T. M. Raysor, 2 vols. 1930
Eastman, Arthur M. *A Short History of Shakespeare Criticism*, 1968
Eliot, T. S. *Selected Essays*, 1932
Granville-Barker, H. and Harrison, G. B. (eds.) *A Companion to Shakespeare Studies*, 1934

Hazlitt, William *The Characters of Shakespeare's Plays*, 1805
Johnson on Shakespeare edited by Sir Walter Raleigh, 1925
Knights, L. C. *Some Shakespearean Themes*, 1959
Lewis, C. S. *English Literature in the Sixteenth Century*, 1954
Mahood, M. M. *Shakespeare's Wordplay*, 1957
Muir, K. and Schoenbaum, S. *A New Companion to Shakespeare Studies*, 1971
Murry, John Middleton *Shakespeare*, 1936
Ralli, Augustus *A History of Shakespearian Criticism*, 2 vols. 1932
Shakespeare Quarterly edited by J. G. McManaway (periodical)
Shakespeare Survey edited by Kenneth Muir (annual periodical)
Smith, David Nichol (ed.) *Shakespeare Criticism*, 1949
Smith, Gregory *Elizabethan Critical Essays*, 2 vols. 1904
Smith, Logan P. *On Reading Shakespeare*, 1933
Spencer, Theodore *Shakespeare and the Nature of Man*, 1943
Spurgeon, Caroline *Shakespeare's Imagery and What It Tells Us*, 1935
Stewart, J. I. M. *Character and Motive in Shakespeare*, 1951
Wilson, F. P. *Elizabethan and Jacobean*, 1945
Wilson, F. P. *Marlowe and the Early Shakespeare*, 1953

SHAKESPEARE AND THE STAGE

Adams, Joseph Q. *Shakespearean Playhouses*, 1917
Baldwin, T. W. *Organization and Personnel of the Shakespearean Company*, 1927
Banke, C. de *Shakespeare Stage Productions, Then and Now*, 1953
Beckerman, Bernard *Shakespeare at the Globe*, 1962
Bentley, G. E. *The Jacobean and Caroline Stage*, 4 vols. 1941
Bentley, G. E. *The Profession of Dramatist in Shakespeare's Time, 1590–1642*, 1971
Bentley, G. E. *Shakespeare and his Theatre*, 1964
Bethell, S. L. *Shakespeare and the Popular Dramatic Tradition*, 1944
Bradbrook, M. C. *Elizabethan Stage Conditions*, 1932
Bradbrook, M. C. *The Rise of the Common Player*, 1962
Brown, Ivor *Shakespeare and the Actors*, 1970
Chambers, E. K. *The Elizabethan Stage*, 4 vols. 1924
Coghill, Neville *Shakespeare's Professional Skills*, 1964
Gildersleeve, V. C. *Government Regulation of the Elizabethan Drama*, 1908
Greg, W. W. *Henslowe's Papers*, 3 vols. 1904–1908
Greg, W. W. *Dramatic Documents from the Elizabethan Playhouses*, 2 vols. 1931
Harbage, Alfred *As They Liked It*, 1947
Harbage, Alfred *Shakespeare and the Rival Traditions*, 1952
Harbage, Alfred *Shakespeare's Audience*, 1941
Harbage, Alfred *Theatre for Shakespeare*, 1955
Harrison, G. B. *Elizabethan Plays and Players*, 1940
Henslowe's Diary, edited by R. A. Foakes and R. T. Rickert, 1961
Hodges, C. W. *The Globe Restored*, 1953
Holmes, M. *Shakespeare and his Players*, 1973
Holmes, M. *Shakespeare's Public*, 1960
Joseph, Bertram *Acting Shakespeare*, 1960
Knights, L. C. *Drama and Society in the Age of Jonson*, 1937
Lawrence, W. J. *The Physical Conditions of the Elizabethan Public Playhouses*, 1927
Leech, Clifford *The John Fletcher Plays*, 1962
Mehl, Dieter *The Elizabethan Dumb Show*, 1964
Nagler, A. M. *Shakespeare's Stage*, 1958
Poel, William *Shakespeare in the Theatre*, 1913
Purdom, C. B. *Producing Shakespeare*, 1950
Smith, D. Nichol *Shakespeare in the Eighteenth Century*, 1928
Smith, Irwin *Shakespeare's Blackfriars Playhouse*, 1964
Smith, Irwin *Shakespeare's Globe Playhouse*, 1956

INDEX

TO THE READER

An obelisk (†) indicates a probable corruption of the original text for which there is no satisfactory or generally acceptable emendation.

Index

ACKNOWLEDGEMENTS

ACKNOWLEDGEMENTS

With special thanks to:
Ben and John Freeman
Geoff Goode Photographics
Dermot Hayes
Maire Nic Suibhne

Ashmolean Museum, Oxford
William Barnard
Marquis of Bath, Longleat
Birmingham Public Libraries
The Bodleian Library, Oxford
British Film Institute
The British Library
The British Museum
The Duke of Buccleuch and Queensberry
Joe Cocks Studio
A. C. Cooper Ltd.
Corpus Christi College, Cambridge
County Archives, Essex Records Office
Courtauld Institute of Art
Crawford Films Ltd
The Governors of Dulwich College Picture Gallery
Mary Evans Picture Library
John R. Freeman Ltd.

John Napier
Charlotte Parry-Crooke
Marian Pringle and the staff at the Shakespeare Birthplace Trust

The Fine Arts Society Ltd., London
Fitzwilliam Museum, Cambridge
Gilling Castle
Goodwood House
Guildhall Library
Harvard Theatre Collection
William Heinemann Ltd.
Holte Photographics Ltd.
Henry E. Huntingdon Library
By Gracious Permission of Her Majesty the Queen
Alix Jeffry
George E. Joseph
Kunthaus, Zurich
The Museum of London
Liverpool Art Gallery
Magdalene College, Cambridge
Manchester Art Gallery

Sally Rousham
Patrick Rudd
Tantraline Ltd
Robert R. Wark, Huntingdon Library, California

Mander and Mitchenson
Mansell Collection
Mappin Art Gallery
Maudsley Hospital, London
National Galleries of Scotland
National Gallery, London
National Portrait Gallery, London
National Maritime Museum, London
Newport Museum of Art Gallery
National Trust
University College of North Wales
Queen's College, Cambridge
Preston Art Gallery
Duchess of Portland
Earl of Pembroke
Oliver Robinson (Estate of W. Heath Robinson)
Royal Academy of Art

Rita Wuethrich
Sarah Woodcock, Theatre Collection, Victoria and Albert Museum
Beno Zeiner

Royal Holloway College
Royal Shakespeare Theatre
St. Faith's Church, King's Lynn
The Shakespeare Birthplace Trust
Sheffield City Art Galleries
Mr Simon Wingfield Digby, Sherborne Castle
V. Siviter Smith & Co. Ltd.
The Tate Gallery
Arthur Tooth & Sons
United Artists
Victoria and Albert Museum
Wadsworth Atheneum, Hartford
Walker Art Gallery, Liverpool
Warburg Institute, University of London
Weidenfeld and Nicolson
Wolverhampton Art Galleries and Museums